书名题签：韩启德

中华科学技术大词典

— 社会科学卷 —

全国科学技术名词审定委员会　编

名誉总主编　路甬祥
总　主　编　白春礼

2019年·北京

图书在版编目(CIP)数据

中华科学技术大词典.社会科学卷/全国科学技术名词审定委员会编.—北京:商务印书馆,2019
ISBN 978-7-100-17522-7

Ⅰ.①中… Ⅱ.①全… Ⅲ.①科学名词—名词术语—中国—词典②社会科学—科学名词—名词术语—中国—词典 Ⅳ.①H03②C61

中国版本图书馆 CIP 数据核字(2019)第 101227 号

权利保留,侵权必究。

中华科学技术大词典
社会科学卷
全国科学技术名词审定委员会 编

商 务 印 书 馆 出 版
(北京王府井大街36号 邮政编码100710)
商 务 印 书 馆 发 行
北京中科印刷有限公司印刷
ISBN 978-7-100-17522-7

2019年6月第1版　　开本787×1092　1/16
2019年6月北京第1次印刷　　印张36½
定价:120.00元

《中华科学技术大词典》

编辑委员会

名誉总主编：路甬祥

总 主 编：白春礼

副 总 主 编（以姓氏笔画为序）：

孙寿山　李济生　张礼和　张伯礼　张焕乔　陆汝钤
陈运泰　武　寅

常务副总主编：刘　青

编辑委员会委员（以姓氏笔画为序）：

丁一汇　于殿利　才　磊　王　杰　王　璞　王存忠
王英杰　仇伟立　叶大年　代晓明　白春礼　冯　军
曲爱国　朱　星　朱建平　乔格侠　任图生　邬　江
刘　青　刘功臣　刘志荣　刘连安　刘虎威　孙寿山
严加安　严海军　李宇明　李胜利　李济生　余桂林
辛德培　汪朝光　宋　彤　张　晖　张玉森　张礼和
张先恩　张伯礼　张柏春　张晓林　张焕乔　陆汝钤
陈　竺　陈运泰　陈超志　武　寅　周明鑑　周洪波
饶克勤　娄　宇　洪定一　顾红雅　奚大华　高素婷
唐绪军　陶文沂　黄　行　黄群慧　韩布新　程　晓
储成才　温昌斌　谢地坤　路甬祥　裴亚军　潘书祥

《中华科学技术大词典·社会科学卷》

编辑委员会

主　编：唐绪军

副主编：冯　军　黄群慧　张　晖

编辑委员会委员（以姓氏笔画为序）：

才　磊　王　琛　王怡红　王振中　王夏昊　田胜立
代晓明　冯　军　冯士雍　吕　鹏　朱　妍　乔　永
刘　扬　阳　镇　李一军　余　菁　宋小卫　宋姬芳
张　晖　张　维　张　斌　张全海　张学新　张珂莹
陈生明　武　东　赵　云　赵　心　胡家勇　莫纪宏
钱　毅　唐绪军　黄　行　黄长著　黄裕峰　黄群慧
董小麟　董昌娟　蒋　颖　褚　席

《中华科学技术大词典》项目部

主　任：张　晖

副主任：代晓明

成　员：吴　顿　白　杨　王　海

路甬祥序

全国科学技术名词审定委员会(以下简称"全国科技名词委")在其成立30多年来工作的基础上,对科学技术名词审定工作和海峡两岸科技名词对照工作的成果进行系统梳理,编纂出版《中华科学技术大词典》,有利于发挥其规范科学技术名词和加强海峡两岸各领域交流的重要作用。同时,也是全国科技名词委工作成果的重要展示。

科学技术名词作为科学技术概念的语言表达,产生于科技领域,应用于社会各个方面,是科技和经济社会融合发展的结晶。通过科学技术名词的规范表述,促进科技理论、知识和思想的传播交流,这是科学技术名词工作的根本宗旨。科学技术名词也是中华文化宝库的重要组成部分,它凝结着人类智慧和中华民族的创造,映射出科学技术和人类文明进步的轨迹。做好科学技术名词审定、公布、推广等各方面工作,有利于传承弘扬中华优秀科学文化,提高全民族科学文化素养,促进社会文明和谐发展,促进国际经济政治、科技文化的交流与合作。依托全国科技名词委30多年来的工作成果,在会聚数千位科技专家和学术精英的智慧结晶、融合现代科学和中华文化的新理念之基础上,编纂出版《中华科学技术大词典》,必将在普及现代科学技术和传承中华优秀文化中发挥积极作用,也具有宝贵的历史价值。

编纂一部集科技名词规范成果之大成的大型工具书,是当前科技名词规范化工作发展的需要。我国科技名词审定工作从全国科技名词委成立伊始,已经在基础科学、工程技术、农业、医学、人文社会科学等领域审定公布了130多种、40多万条的学科规范名词,出版了近30个学科的海峡两岸科技名词对照本,为我国科技发展和两岸科教文化交流发挥了重要的基础性作用。但是,以往的公布和出版工作都是分学科进行的,其优势是有利于开展审定工作,方便单个学科或行业领域的使用,而不足之处在于次序分散,不利于跨学科,以及综合性、交叉性学科领域的使用,也不利于科技名词的系统认知和社会普及。将这些名词系统分类和编纂集成,有利于学科向综合性、交叉性、系统性方向发展和创新。因而,编纂一部综合性的科学技术名词工具书,既是审定公布工作的深化与延伸,也是响应社会各界规范使用科技名词的基本诉求,必将在促进科技文化交流和实现协同创新方面发挥十分重要的作用。

科学技术名词也是海峡两岸科教文化交流的重要载体。由于历史的原因,海峡两岸分隔近70年,其间正是现代科技大发展时期,新名词术语层出不穷,两岸专家分别定名,形成大量名词术语之间的差异。台湾大学一位气象学教授曾举例说,两岸用同一种语言,但对于同样的气象探测设备,大陆称"无线电探空气球",台湾称"雷保";对于同样的云层气象条件,台湾称"逸入",大陆称"夹卷",造成学术交流的障碍。凡此种种概念相同而称谓不同的情况,约占科技名词术语三分之一以上,严重影响到两岸科技、文化、教育、经贸等各领域的交流和发展。海峡两岸各界对名词术语差异所造成的语言障碍都普遍有相似的经历和深刻的认识。1993年4月,两岸第一次"汪辜会谈"顺乎民意,把探讨"海峡两岸科技名词统一"列入了共同协议之中。随之全国科技名词委制定了《关于开展海峡两岸科学技术名词统一工作的意见》,决定加强与台湾地区学者和有关机构的交流合作,促进两岸科技名词的交流对照与统一工作。此后 20 多年来,两岸科技名词工作成绩斐然,已先后出版了近 30 种分学科的"海峡两岸名词对照本"。本次编纂出版《中华科学技术大词典》,广泛收集审选了各学科名词,成为囊括近百个学科、约 50 万条科技名词的综合性大词典。它的问世,将面向海峡两岸民众,释疑解惑,互动交流,协同科学认知,增进文化认同,为两岸科学文化等各领域的交流合作架起桥梁。它是促进科技创新发展,促进中华文化传承,促进两岸交流与祖国统一的科学文化工程,也是两岸专家学者的共同愿望,意义重大、影响深远。

《中华科学技术大词典》的出版,是两岸专家相互配合、共同努力的结果。双方专家也在这次合作中加深了相互了解,取得了广泛共识。大词典的问世是两岸学术界和专家合作的成果,是海峡所不能阻断的科教文化交流的缩影。我相信在两岸专家共同努力下,两岸科教文化的交流会呈现更加良好的局面。

《中华科学技术大词典》的出版,是我国科学技术名词规范化事业不断发展的重要见证,也是两岸科技文化交流中具有重要意义的盛事。故为序,以示衷心祝贺!

路甬祥

2018 年 8 月 28 日

白春礼序

历经两岸专家学者多年来的共同努力,《中华科学技术大词典》即将问世了,这是两岸科技名词交流对照工作的一件盛事,也是两岸科教文化、经济社会等各个领域交流合作的一项基础工作,我感到由衷的欣慰。

中华文字是历史渊源的载体、民族精神的血脉,是人类文化的瑰丽成果。它不同于西方拼音文字,构成了中国人独有的思维方式和文化传统,使海峡两岸及中华文化圈内所有人民引为自豪。

科学技术名词是中华文化的重要组成部分,许多科学技术名词的定名都折射出中华文化艰辛的发展历程。特别是近代以来,中华民族历经苦难,举步维艰,大批先辈科学家肩负着沉重的历史责任,化解万难,在引进消化西方先进科技概念的基础上,结合中国的文化传统,创制了一大批具有中华文化品位和特点的名词术语,为我国近代科技跟上世界科技的发展创造了条件。

尽管经过了近70年的两岸分隔,但共同的历史传统和语言文化,无时无刻不在提醒着人们,海峡两岸同根同源、同文同宗,都是中华文明的继承者、弘扬者。但是,由于两岸社会长期处于相互隔绝的状态,其间正是全球科学技术飞速发展的历史时期,对于人类社会在相互学习、共同发展中产生的科学技术概念,两岸使用同样的文字却分别定名,其表达科学技术概念的词素词义,悄然发生了不同的演变,给两岸人民带来了交流的障碍,影响了两岸科教文化、经济贸易、人文社会等领域的交流合作。早在30年前恢复交流后不久,就有大陆学者关注到两岸科技名词的不同发展路径,意识到两岸科技名词的差异是造成两岸认知差距的原因之一,因而呼吁从促进计算机信息处理的角度出发,积极研究并推进海峡两岸科技名词的统一,消除语言障碍。

科技名词交流是海峡两岸专家学者的共同呼声。1993年首轮"汪辜会谈"达成的协议中就有探讨两岸科技名词统一的内容。全国科学技术名词审定委员会始终积极、稳妥地推动此项工作,这一举措也逐步得到两岸科技界的广泛认同。多年来两岸合作增加,交往频繁,文化上水乳交融,大陆和台湾地区科技名词交流互鉴,不少过去为一方独有的名词术语,已经逐步从分歧趋于一致。在此形势下,两岸合作编纂一部涵盖科学与技术各领域名词术语的科学技术大词典正逢其时。

2010年7月,两岸科学技术领域专家学者议定,在前期合作的基础上,合编《中华科学技术大词典》等辞书;同时双方协商决定利用信息技术,采用云计算平台开展数据库建设。在两岸专家学者多轮协商并形成共识的基础上,大词典编纂工作得以全面展开。

《中华科学技术大词典》的编纂突出了基础性、通用性、实用性,以广泛收录全球通用的现代科技概念为主,适当收录一些双方各自特有的名词术语,反映两岸科学技术名词差异,以方便两岸科技交流和一般民众使用,并为学习汉语的外国人提供帮助。同时为便于两岸读者使用,对于两岸不同的通用字形采取了分别呈现的形式。这种安排不仅便于双方大众阅读,同时也有助于双方逐步了解对方用字用词的现实情况,以达到化异为同的目的。几年来两岸专家学者实事求是、相互尊重、学风严谨、科学务实,奉献了各自的学识和心智,在两岸文化交流合作中又迈出坚实的一步。我们这次编纂出版《中华科学技术大词典》,既是过去两岸科技名词工作的延续,也为今后在更大的领域开展两岸学术交往,为科技文化、经济社会的进一步交流合作创造了基础条件。多年来的两岸科技名词交流实践充分说明,罔顾历史,无论是对传统文化的否定与切割,还是出于政治私利操控的"去中国化",都经不住历史长河的冲刷,终将因得不到公众的支持而烟消云散。维护两岸和平发展是两岸同胞的民意主流,本次编纂工作一直得到台湾方面有关机构和广大专家学者的协助与支持,编纂成果也将为两岸各界共享,成为促进两岸关系和平发展的一件鲜活的、生动的实例。

《中华科学技术大词典》集科学与技术领域名词术语之大成,汇聚了两岸无数专家学者的智慧,必将发挥传承与弘扬中华文化的历史和现实作用。经过两岸专家学者的不懈努力,《中华科学技术大词典》即将出版,借此机会,我谨向30多年来支持和参与科技名词工作的两岸专家学者致以诚挚的敬意!向参与此次词典编纂工作的所有专家学者,向全国科学技术名词审定委员会事务中心和词典项目部的同仁们,向支持本词典出版的国家出版基金规划管理办公室和投入精干队伍保障出版质量的商务印书馆,表示由衷的感谢!

白春礼
2019 年夏

前　言

2009年7月,以"推进和深化两岸文化教育交流合作"为主题的第五届两岸经贸文化论坛在长沙举行,倡议两岸民间合作编纂中华语文工具书。2010年7月,两岸合编中华语文工具书第二轮会谈决定,两岸合编的工具书由语言文字领域拓展到科学技术领域,以全国科学技术名词审定委员会(以下简称"全国科技名词委")和台湾教育研究院为实施者,组织两岸专家合作编纂《中华科学技术大词典》。2011年3月,两岸专家共同提出编纂出版《中华科学技术大词典》的总体方案。2013年12月,《中华科学技术大词典》正式纳入《2013—2025年国家辞书编纂出版规划》,2016年6月《中华科学技术大词典》获得国家出版基金项目支持。

《中华科学技术大词典》成立编辑委员会,由白春礼院士担任总主编,路甬祥院士为名誉总主编。同时设立词典项目部,负责编纂的日常组织工作。各领域先后共有500多位专家学者参加了本词典的编纂和审定。

《中华科学技术大词典》在全国科技名词委审定公布的130多种学科名词和已出版的近30种海峡两岸科技名词对照本的基础上,参考台湾方面公布的名词数据库资料编纂而成。全书共收录96个学科,约50万条科技名词;并实现大陆名与台湾名,中文名和英文名的对照功能。全书按照学科领域和学科特点,共分为10卷,即数理化卷、地学卷、生物学卷、工程技术卷(上、中、下)、农业卷、医学卷、社会科学卷、人文科学卷。

本词典收录的各学科名词具有以下特点:一是在全国科技名词委公布名词的基础上,参照台湾方面的收词范围扩展而来,基本上反映出海峡两岸科学技术发展现状;二是体现了规范性,充分利用科技名词规范化工作的成果;三是注重科学文化的传承,既收录了当代科学技术领域的科技名词,也适当收录了反映中国近代以来科学和文化发展脉络的科技名词。本词典是两岸专家学者对多年来科技名词领域交流、对照和统一工作成果的一次大规模整理和总结,是两岸合作编写工具书的最新成果,是两岸专家学者的智慧结晶,是两岸共同弘扬中华文化的一次重要实践。

本词典作为两岸专家共同参与编纂的工具书,契合了两岸科学技术发展的现实需求,为两岸在科技、教育、文化、经贸等方面的交流合作提供了必不可少的对照性词汇,可成为两岸各领域交流的参考和依据。同时,可用作全球华语地区科技界人士的参考读物。

本词典编纂期间,编审专家以严肃的科学态度,认真工作,持之以恒,默默奉献。台湾教育研究院及台湾各学科的部分专家学者参与了词目编选,特别是对台湾名、英文名等进行了仔细审读。在此,我们向他们表示衷心的感谢。

《中华科学技术大词典》涉及学科广泛,尤其是进行如此大规模的两岸科技名词梳理、遴选、编纂及全面对照,没有先例,难度巨大,编纂中难免会有疏漏错误之处,欢迎广大专家学者和读者批评指正。

《中华科学技术大词典》编辑委员会

2019 年 3 月 1 日

《中华科学技术大词典·社会科学卷》编纂说明

《中华科学技术大词典·社会科学卷》(以下简称《社会科学卷》)是《中华科学技术大词典》的第9卷,共涉及社会科学领域中的12个分支学科或研究领域,分别为社会学、法学、经济学、经济贸易、管理学、市场学、统计学、会计学、新闻传播学、图书情报与文献学、档案学、编辑出版。共收录词条约39 000条。全部词条按照大陆名音序排序,以便查检。

《社会科学卷》收词以全国科学技术名词审定委员会多年来收集整理的社会科学名词为基础,组织专家进行了编纂加工和审定工作。主要包括三方面:一是对存在的格式、书写、拼写、翻译不准确等问题进行校正;二是对大陆和台湾名词概念不对应,进行了调整、替代;三是增收了部分常用的、特别重要的词条。分卷编辑据此加以校核,形成一审稿。之后由《中华科学技术大词典》项目部进行数据处理,形成二审稿。针对二审稿,第二次组织专家深入细致地审查,解决初审遗留问题,检查处理编辑加工过程中的疏漏,形成三审稿。随后,分卷主编第三次组织专家审查,形成终审稿。终审稿由分卷主编和副主编再次把关,形成报批稿,报送《中华科学技术大词典》编辑委员会审查批准后,交由商务印书馆出版。

各分支学科名词的收集整理来源可靠、工作扎实,为本卷词典的顺利出版打下了坚实的基础。我们邀请了40位相关领域专家学者参加了本卷词典的编纂和审定工作。编审专家学者严谨认真的工作态度和默默奉献的工作精神,保证了本书的高质量出版。台湾同仁对相关学科的两岸名词对照工作给予了很大帮助,体现了两岸专家密切合作的精神风范。

《中华科学技术大词典》项目部和全国科学技术名词审定委员会事务中心各审定室的同志们对词典的编纂出版给予了大力的支持。从组建分卷编辑委员会开始,他们就积极参与,协助联系专家,承担了提供稿件资料、协助组织召开编委会、开展专项检查、誊录与复核编校意见等多项繁杂工作。

值此词典出版之际,我们向所有为词典编纂出版工作做出贡献的专家、学者和同仁们表示衷心的感谢。

由于时间仓促,编者水平有限,难免有各种不足和差错,诚望读者批评指正。

《中华科学技术大词典·社会科学卷》编辑委员会
2019年5月6日

目　录

凡例 …………………………………………………………………	2
词目首字音序索引 ……………………………………………………	4
词目首字笔画索引 ……………………………………………………	10
词典正文 ………………………………………………………………	1—535
附录 ……………………………………………………………………	537
中国历代纪元表 ………………………………………………………	539
国际单位制 ……………………………………………………………	556

词目英文索引
（二维码）

凡　例

1. 词条收录

1.1　本词典所收词条涵盖基础科学、工程技术、农业科学、医学、社会科学、人文及其他领域共计96个学科,例如数学、物理学、化学、天文学、地质学、测绘学、动物学、植物学、航天科学技术、建筑学、机械工程、电子学、材料科学技术、资源科学技术、农学、土壤学、医学、中医药学、经济学、法学、语言学、教育学等。

1.2　本词典收录的词条包括海峡两岸通用的,以及海峡两岸有差异的科学技术名词共约50万条。

1.3　本词典收录的词条按照科学技术相关学科领域归类,共分为10卷。依次为数理化卷、地学卷、生物学卷、工程技术卷(上、中、下)、农业卷、医学卷、社会科学卷、人文科学卷。

2. 词条构成

2.1　本词典所收词条由词目(中文)及其对应的英文构成。

2.2　词目采用两岸名称对照的形式,大陆名列前,台湾名列后,中间以"／"分隔。例如:

电灼式印刷机/放電式列印機

拉克斯-密格拉蒙定理/拉克斯-米爾格雷定理

2.3　词目的字形,分别采用两岸各自通用的字形。例如:

自然循环/自然循環

作业控制中心/作業控制中心

2.4　词目中的大陆名有两条(或以上)同义词时,分别以两条(或以上)词目列出。例如:

背景/背景

本底/背景

2.5　词目中的大陆名对应两条(或以上)台湾同义词时,台湾名在词目中并行排列,中间以逗号隔开。例如:

出口融资/出口融資,籌集出口資金

横节理/橫節理,交錯劈理,Q節理

2.6　词目中的大陆名对应两个(或两个以上)台湾名概念时,对应的台湾名分别以①②……列出。例如:

质量/①質量,②品質

槽轮/①間歇工作輪,星形輪,日內瓦輪,②有槽帶輪

2.7　词目中大陆名和台湾名中"[ ]"内的字为可省略部分。例如:

等离[子]体动力学/電漿動力學

2.8　词目中大陆名和台湾名中"( )"内的汉字、西文字母、阿拉伯数字、罗马数字为该词的特殊标注(如天体名的备注、化合物结构标示、数学概念的符号标识等)。例如:

虹神星(小行星7号)/虹神星(7號小行星)

聚(β-氨基丙酸)/聚(β-胺基丙酸)

广义(g,k)特征标/廣義(g,k)特徵[標]

2.9 本词典收录的词条不单独标出所属学科。

3. 词目排序

3.1 词目按大陆名的首字汉语拼音字母次序排列,首字同音的按笔画排列,笔画少的在前,多的在后;笔画相同的按起笔笔形(横、竖、撇、点、折)的次序排列,起笔笔形相同的按第二起笔笔形的次序排列,以此类推。首字相同的按第二字的汉语拼音字母次序排列,以此类推。

3.2 词目中含有西文字母或阿拉伯数字、罗马数字时,按词目中的汉字汉语拼音排序;词首或词中的西文字母或阿拉伯数字、罗马数字一律不参加排序。

4. 词目对应的英文(或其他外文)

4.1 词目对应的外文主要为英文,也有极少量的其他文种词语或字母。例如拉丁文、法文、德文及希腊字母等。遇有其他外文时,遵从其特殊形式。

4.2 词目对应的英文,在词目之后列出。例如:

计算机辅助设计/電腦輔助設計 computer-aided design

4.3 词义相同的英文并行排列,中间以逗号隔开。例如:

粗钢/粗鋼 crude steel, raw steel

4.4 英文名词一般采用单数形式,必须或习惯采用复数形式的英文名词除外。

4.5 以人名、地名等命名的专有名词,其对应的英文,首字母为大写。

4.6 英文如有英美拼法差异时,一般采用美式拼法。

4.7 英文中出现拉丁文词时,一般遵从各学科领域的格式惯例。例如:

肠产毒性大肠杆菌/腸產毒性大腸桿菌 enterotoxigenic *Escherichia coli*(生物学卷)

南方古猿/南[方古]猿 *Australopithecus*(地学卷)

奥斯特线虫属/牛胃絲蟲屬 *Ostertagia*(农业卷)

尺头/尺頭 caput ulnare(拉)(医学卷)

4.8 英文中出现汉语拼音转写词语时,一般遵从汉语拼音分词习惯。例如:

芎菊上清丸 xiongju shangqing pills

5. 附录

本词典后附有中国历代纪元表、国际单位制。

6. 索引

6.1 本词典列有词目首字音序索引和词目首字笔画索引。

6.2 本词典附有词目英文索引(扫描二维码查取)。

词目首字音序索引

（字右边的号码指词典正文的页码）

A

- a: 阿 1
- ai: 埃 1, 艾 1, 爱 2
- an: 安 2, 鞍 2, 按 2, 案 3, 暗 3
- ang: 肮 3, 昂 3, 盎 3
- ao: 凹 3, 奥 4

B

- ba: 八 5, 巴 5, 扒 5, 把 5, 罢 5, 霸 5, 灞 5
- bai: 白 5, 百 5, 柏 6, 摆 6, 拜 6
- ban: 班 6, 斑 6, 搬 6, 版 6, 办 6, 半 6, 伴 7
- bang: 邦 7, 帮 7, 绑 7, 榜 7
- bao: 包 7, 饱 8, 保 9, 报 11, 鲍 11, 暴 11, 曝 11, 爆 11
- bei: 背 11, 悲 11, 碑 11, 北 11, 贝 11, 备 12, 背 12, 倍 13, 悖 13, 被 13
- ben: 本 13
- beng: 崩 13, 绷 13
- bi: 逼 13, 比 13, 彼 14, 笔 14, 币 14, 必 15, 毕 15, 闭 15, 庇 15, 壁 15, 避 15
- bian: 边 15, 编 16, 贬 17, 扁 17, 变 17, 便 18, 遍 18, 辨 18, 辩 18
- biao: 标 18, 表 20
- bie: 别 20
- bin: 殡 20, 膑 21
- bing: 兵 21, 饼 21, 禀 21, 并 21, 病 21
- bo: 波 21, 玻 21, 剥 21, 播 21, 伯 22, 驳 22, 帛 22, 泊 22, 柏 22, 勃 22, 博 22, 跛 23
- bu: 补 23, 捕 24, 不 24, 布 28, 步 28, 部 28, 簿 29

C

- ca: 擦 30
- cai: 材 30, 财 30, 裁 31, 采 31, 彩 31, 菜 32
- can: 参 32, 残 32, 蚕 33
- cang: 仓 33, 藏 33
- cao: 操 33, 曹 34, 槽 34, 草 34
- ce: 册 34, 侧 34, 测 34, 策 34
- ceng: 层 34
- cha: 叉 35, 差 35, 插 35, 查 35, 察 35
- chai: 拆 35
- chan: 掺 35, 产 35, 铲 37, 颤 37
- chang: 长 38, 尝 38, 常 38, 偿 39, 厂 39, 场 39, 敞 40, 畅 40, 倡 40, 唱 40
- chao: 抄 40, 钞 40, 超 40, 朝 40, 潮 40
- che: 车 41, 彻 41, 撤 41
- chen: 沉 41, 陈 41, 晨 41, 衬 41
- cheng: 称 41, 成 41, 丞 42, 呈 42, 诚 42, 承 42, 城 43, 乘 44, 程 44, 惩 44, 澄 44, 橙 44
- chi: 答 44, 驰 44, 迟 44, 持 44, 尺 45, 赤 45
- chong: 冲 45, 充 45, 虫 45, 重 45, 冲 46
- chou: 抽 46, 筹 47, 臭 47
- chu: 出 47, 初 50, 除 50, 锄 50, 处 50, 储 50, 楚 51, 触 51
- chuan: 穿 51, 传 51, 船 51, 串 52
- chuang: 创 52, 窗 52, 闯 52, 创 52
- chui: 垂 53
- chun: 春 53, 纯 53
- chuo: 辍 53
- ci: 词 53, 辞 54, 慈 54, 磁 54, 次 54, 刺 54

C (cont.)

- cong: 从 54, 丛 55
- cu: 粗 55, 促 55, 猝 55
- cuan: 窜 55
- cui: 催 55, 萃 55
- cun: 村 55, 存 55
- cuo: 挫 56, 措 56, 错 56

D

- da: 搭 57, 达 57, 答 57, 打 57, 大 57
- dai: 呆 58, 代 59, 带 59, 殆 60, 贷 60, 待 60, 怠 60, 戴 60
- dan: 丹 60, 担 60, 单 61, 淡 63
- dang: 当 63, 档 64
- dao: 刀 67, 导 67, 岛 67, 倒 67, 到 67, 倒 67, 盗 68, 道 68, 稻 68
- de: 得 68, 德 68
- deng: 灯 68, 登 68, 等 68, 邓 69, 瞪 69
- di: 低 69, 堤 70, 滴 70, 狄 70, 迪 70, 嫡 70, 抵 70, 底 70, 地 71, 帝 72, 递 72, 第 72, 蒂 74, 棣 74, 缔 74
- dian: 典 74, 点 74, 电 77, 佃 77, 垫 77, 殿 77
- diao: 叼 77

调	77			费	108	gai		gou		胡	168			
掉	77	**E**		刜	109	改	121	勾	137	湖	168	**J**		
	die			fen		盖	121	沟	137	蝴	168			
迭	77	e		分	109	概	121	钩	137	糊	168	ji		
叠	77	阿	92	焚	113	gan		狗	137	互	168	几	181	
蝶	77	讹	92	粉	113	干	122	构	137	户	169	机	181	
ding		额	92	份	113	甘	122	购	137	护	169	奇	182	
丁	77	厄	92	feng		赶	122	媾	138	沪	169	积	182	
钉	77	恶	92	丰	113	感	122	gu		hua		基	182	
顶	77	en		风	114	干	123	估	138	花	169	稽	184	
订	77	恩	92	封	114	gang		孤	138	华	169	激	184	
定	78	er		峰	114	冈	123	古	139	滑	169	羁	184	
dong		儿	92	蜂	114	刚	123	谷	139	化	169	吉	184	
东	79	二	92	冯	114	纲	123	股	139	划	169	级	184	
董	79			奉	114	岗	123	骨	141	画	169	极	184	
动	79	**F**		缝	114	港	123	穀	141	话	169	即	185	
冻	79			fo		杠	123	固	141	huai		急	186	
dou		fa		佛	114	gao		故	142	怀	170	疾	186	
抖	80	发	96	fou		皋	123	顾	143	坏	170	棘	186	
陡	80	罚	97	否	114	高	124	雇	143	hang		集	186	
斗	80	法	97	fu		稿	124	gua		行	162	辑	187	
饾	80	fan		夫	115	告	124	刮	143	航	162	几	187	
du		藩	99	孵	115	ge		寡	143	hao		挤	187	
都	80	翻	99	弗	115	戈	124	挂	143	豪	162	给	187	
督	80	凡	99	伏	115	搁	124	guai		好	162	脊	187	
毒	80	樊	99	服	115	割	124	乖	143	号	162	计	187	
独	80	反	99	俘	115	歌	124	拐	143	耗	162	记	189	
读	81	返	101	浮	115	革	124	guan		he		纪	190	
渎	82	犯	101	符	115	格	124	关	144	合	162	技	190	
牍	82	泛	101	幅	116	隔	125	观	145	和	164	季	193	
笃	82	范	101	辐	116	个	125	官	145	荷	165	剂	193	
堵	82	梵	101	福	116	各	127	馆	145	核	165	济	193	
赌	82	fang		抚	116	gei		管	146	盒	165	既	193	
杜	82	方	101	甫	116	给	127	惯	147	赫	165	继	193	
度	82	坊	102	辅	116	gen		guang		hei		祭	193	
镀	82	防	102	腐	116	根	127	光	148	黑	165	寄	193	
duan		妨	102	父	116	跟	127	广	148	heng		绩	194	
短	82	房	102	付	117	geng		gui		亨	166	jia		
段	83	仿	102	妇	117	更	127	归	150	恒	166	加	194	
断	83	访	103	附	117	耕	127	规	150	横	166	夹	195	
dui		纺	103	复	118	更	127	皈	151	衡	166	家	195	
堆	83	放	103	副	120	gong		硅	151	hong		甲	196	
队	83	fei		赋	120	工	127	轨	151	红	166	假	196	
对	83	飞	103	傅	120	公	131	瓯	151	宏	166	价	196	
兑	85	非	103	富	120	功	135	鬼	151	洪	167	架	198	
dun		菲	108	覆	120	攻	135	柜	151	hou		假	198	
吨	85	扉	108			供	135	gun		侯	167	jian		
敦	85	诽	108	**G**		宫	136	滚	151	后	167	尖	198	
duo		斐	108			龚	136	guo		厚	167	奸	198	
多	86	废	108	ga		共	136	国	151	候	168	坚	198	
夺	91			伽	121	贡	137	过	158	hu		监	198	
堕	91									呼	168			
										孤	168			

兼	198	戒	210	**juan**		**kong**		滥	243	裂	255	论	261	**meng**
缣	198	界	210	捐	224	空	237	**lang**		**lin**		**luo**		蒙	267
拣	198	借	210	涓	224	孔	238	郎	243	邻	255	罗	261	盟	267
检	198	**jin**		卷	224	恐	238	浪	243	林	255	逻	261	猛	267
减	199	巾	210	倦	224	空	238	**lao**		临	255	螺	261	蒙	267
剪	199	金	210	**jue**		控	238	劳	243	**ling**		洛	261	孟	267
简	199	津	212	决	224	**kou**		老	245	灵	256	骆	261	**mi**	
见	200	仅	212	角	225	口	239	**le**		图	256	落	261	弥	267
件	201	紧	212	绝	225	扣	239	乐	245	凌	256			迷	267
间	201	锦	212	**jun**		**ku**		勒	245	零	256	**━━ M ━━**		米	267
建	202	进	212	均	226	苦	239	**lei**		岭	257			秘	267
贱	202	近	215	君	226	库	239	雷	245	领	257	**ma**		密	267
剑	202	晋	215	郡	227	酷	239	累	245	另	257	麻	262	幂	268
健	202	浸	215	竣	227	**kua**		类	246	令	257	马	262	蜜	268
渐	202	禁	215			夸	239	**leng**		**liu**		玛	263	**mian**	
溅	203	**jing**		**━━ K ━━**		跨	239	冷	247	刘	257	码	263	棉	268
鉴	203	茎	216			**kuai**		**li**		浏	257	**mai**		免	268
键	203	京	216	**ka**		会	240	离	247	留	257	埋	263	面	268
箭	203	经	216	卡	228	块	241	礼	248	流	258	买	263	**miao**	
jiang		晶	218	**kai**		快	241	李	248	硫	259	迈	263	描	269
将	203	精	218	开	228	**kuan**		里	248	六	259	麦	263	秒	269
僵	203	景	219	揩	229	宽	241	理	248	**long**		卖	263	**mie**	
讲	203	警	219	凯	229	款	241	力	249	龙	259	脉	264	灭	269
奖	203	净	219	**kan**		**kuang**		历	249	隆	259	**man**		**min**	
降	203	竟	219	刊	229	矿	241	立	249	垄	259	满	264	民	269
jiao		静	221	勘	230	框	241	利	250	**lou**		曼	264	闵	270
交	203	境	221	堪	230	**kui**		例	251	镂	259	漫	264	闽	270
郊	205	镜	221	坎	230	亏	241	隶	251	漏	259	慢	264	敏	270
浇	205	**jiu**		看	230	奎	241	**lian**		**lu**		**mang**		**ming**	
胶	205	纠	221	**kang**		**kun**		连	251	卢	259	芒	264	名	270
焦	205	九	221	康	230	昆	241	联	252	炉	259	忙	264	明	271
角	205	久	222	抗	230	捆	241	廉	254	鲁	259	盲	264	冥	271
矫	206	旧	222	**kao**		**kuo**		恋	254	陆	259	**mao**		铭	271
脚	206	救	222	考	230	扩	241	链	254	录	259	毛	264	命	271
缴	206	厩	222	拷	230			**liang**		路	259	矛	264	**miu**	
校	206	就	222	靠	230	**━━ L ━━**		良	254	露	259	锚	264	谬	271
较	206	**ju**		**ke**				梁	254	**lü**		卯	264	**mo**	
教	206	拘	222	珂	230	**la**		量	254	吕	260	冒	264	摹	271
jie		居	222	柯	230	垃	242	粮	254	旅	260	贸	264	模	271
阶	207	局	222	科	230	拉	242	两	254	履	260	**mei**		摩	272
接	207	矩	223	颗	232	邋	242	亮	254	律	260	没	265	磨	273
揭	207	举	223	可	232	蜡	242	谅	254	绿	260	玫	265	魔	273
街	207	巨	223	渴	236	**lai**		量	255	滤	260	枚	265	末	273
节	207	句	223	克	236	来	242	晾	255	**luan**		梅	266	没	273
劫	208	拒	223	刻	237	莱	242	**liao**		李	260	媒	266	莫	273
杰	208	具	224	客	237	赖	243	辽	255	乱	260	煤	266	墨	273
洁	208	剧	224	课	237	**lan**		聊	255	**lüe**		霉	266	默	273
结	208	据	224	**ken**		兰	243	料	255	掠	260	每	266	**mou**	
截	209	距	224	肯	237	栏	243	**lie**		略	260	美	266	谋	273
姐	210	锯	224	啃	237	蓝	243	列	255	**lun**		魅	267	**mu**	
解	210	聚	224			篮	243	劣	255	伦	260	**men**		模	273
介	210							猎	255	轮	260	门	267	母	273

拇	273	诺	281	匹	287	乞	297	穹	305	熔	317	shan		失	337
木	273			pian		企	298	琼	305	融	317	删	321	师	338
目	273	**O**		偏	287	启	299	qiu		冗	317	扇	321	施	338
牧	274			篇	288	起	299	丘	305	rou		煽	321	湿	338
募	274	ou		片	288	气	299	秋	305	柔	317	闪	321	十	338
睦	274	欧	282	骗	288	弃	299	囚	305	肉	317	扇	321	什	338
穆	274	偶	283	piao		汽	299	求	305	ru		善	321	石	338
		耦	283	剽	288	契	299	球	305	如	317	缮	321	时	338
N				漂	288	砌	299	qu		儒	317	膳	321	识	340
		P		飘	288	qia		区	305	蠕	317	赡	321	实	340
na				漂	288	恰	299	曲	307	乳	317	shang		拾	342
纳	275	pa		票	288	qian		驱	307	入	317	伤	321	食	342
nai		爬	284	pie		千	300	屈	307	ruan		商	321	史	342
奈	275	帕	284	撇	289	迁	300	趋	307	软	317	熵	324	矢	342
耐	275	pai		pin		牵	300	取	307	rui		上	324	使	342
nan		拍	284	拼	289	铅	300	去	307	瑞	318	尚	325	始	342
男	275	排	284	贫	289	谦	300	quan		run		shao		士	342
南	275	牌	285	频	289	签	300	圈	307	润	318	烧	325	氏	342
难	275	派	285	品	289	铃	300	权	307	ruo		少	325	示	342
nei		pan		聘	290	前	300	全	308	弱	318	she		世	342
内	275	攀	285	ping		钱	300	劝	310			奢	325	市	343
neng		盘	285	平	290	钳	300	que		**S**		赊	325	式	345
能	277	判	285	评	293	潜	300	缺	310			蛇	325	事	345
ni		叛	285	苹	294	浅	301	阙	310	sa		舍	325	试	345
尼	277	pang		凭	294	遣	301	确	310	撒	319	设	325	视	346
泥	277	彷	285	屏	294	欠	301	qun		萨	319	社	326	适	346
拟	277	庞	285	瓶	294	嵌	301	裙	311	sai		射	332	室	346
逆	278	旁	285	po		qiang		群	311	塞	319	涉	332	shou	
匿	278	pao		珀	294	强	301			赛	319	赦	333	收	346
nian		抛	285	破	294	抢	302	**R**		san		摄	333	手	347
年	278	跑	285	pou		强	302			三	319	shen		守	348
黏	279	泡	285	剖	294	qiao		ran		散	320	申	333	首	348
ning		pei		pu		敲	302	燃	312	sang		伸	333	寿	349
柠	279	陪	285	普	294	乔	302	染	312	桑	320	身	333	受	349
凝	279	培	285	谱	295	侨	302	rang		丧	320	绅	333	狩	349
niu		赔	286	瀑	295	qie		让	312	sao		深	333	授	349
牛	279	佩	286			切	302	rao		扫	320	神	334	售	350
扭	279	配	286	**Q**		qin		扰	312	se		沈	334	瘦	350
纽	279	pen				侵	302	绕	312	色	320	审	334	shu	
nong		喷	286	qi		亲	302	re		瑟	321	渗	335	书	350
农	280	peng		七	296	秦	303	热	312	sen		慎	335	枢	351
浓	281	朋	286	期	296	qing		ren		森	321	sheng		舒	351
nu		棚	286	欺	297	青	303	人	312	seng		升	335	疏	351
奴	281	膨	286	漆	297	轻	303	仁	315	僧	321	生	335	输	351
努	281	pi		齐	297	倾	303	认	315	sha		声	337	赎	351
nü		批	286	其	297	清	303	任	316	沙	321	省	337	熟	351
女	281	皮	287	奇	297	情	304	ri		砂	321	圣	337	属	352
nüe		毗	287	歧	297	黥	305	日	316	莎	321	胜	337	署	352
虐	281	疲	287	祈	297	请	305	rong		shai		盛	337	蜀	352
nuo		啤	287	骑	297	庆	305	容	316	筛	321	剩	337	术	352
挪	281			旗	297	qiong		溶	317	shai		shi		束	352
						穷	305					尸	337	树	352

竖 352			tie	完 392		枭 421	xuan	yang		
数 352			贴 374	玩 393	X	消 421	宣 441	鞅 447		
shuai	T		帖 374	晚 393		萧 422	悬 441	羊 447		
衰 355			铁 374	万 393	xi	销 422	旋 441	阳 447		
shuang	ta		ting	wang	西 410	小 423	选 442	杨 447		
双 355	他 367		听 374	王 393	吸 410	孝 424	旋 443	养 447		
shui	塔 367		廷 374	网 393	析 410	肖 424	xue	氧 447		
水 357	拓 367		停 374	往 396	牺 410	校 424	削 443	样 448		
税 357	tai		tong	忘 396	息 410	效 424	学 443	yao		
shun	胎 367		通 374	wei	稀 410	xie	雪 443	要 448		
顺 358	太 367		同 375	危 396	嬉 411	楔 424	血 443	腰 449		
瞬 358	态 367		佟 377	威 396	习 411	协 424	xun	邀 449		
shuo	泰 367		铜 377	微 396	洗 411	胁 425	熏 443	谣 449		
说 359	tan		童 377	韦 397	铣 411	挟 425	旬 443	摇 449		
硕 359	贪 367		统 377	违 397	喜 411	斜 425	寻 443	遥 449		
si	摊 367		tou	围 397	系 411	写 425	巡 444	药 449		
司 359	谈 367		偷 378	唯 397	细 412	卸 425	询 444	要 449		
丝 359	弹 367		头 378	维 397	xia	械 425	荀 444	ye		
私 359	探 367		投 378	伪 398	狭 412	谢 425	循 444	耶 449		
思 360	碳 368		透 381	尾 398	瑕 412	xin	训 444	野 449		
斯 360	tang		tu	委 398	辖 412	心 425	讯 444	业 449		
死 361	汤 368		凸 381	卫 398	下 412	芯 426	徇 444	页 450		
四 361	唐 368		突 381	为 399	夏 412	辛 426		夜 450		
似 361	堂 368		图 381	未 399	xian	新 426	Y	液 450		
song	棠 368		途 384	位 399	先 412	薪 428		yi		
松 361	烫 368		涂 384	魏 400	纤 413	信 428	ya	一 450		
讼 361	tao		屠 384	wen	闲 413	xing	压 445	伊 452		
宋 361	逃 368		土 384	温 400	显 413	兴 433	押 445	医 452		
送 361	陶 368		吐 385	文 400	现 414	星 433	鸦 445	依 453		
sou	讨 368		tuan	纹 403	限 415	刑 433	哑 445	仪 453		
搜 361	套 368		团 385	稳 403	线 416	行 434	轧 445	移 453		
su	te		tui	问 404	宪 417	形 437	亚 445	遗 454		
苏 361	特 368		推 385	wo	献 417	型 437	砑 445	已 454		
诉 362	teng		退 385	窝 404	xiang	兴 437	yan	以 455		
素 362	誊 370		tuo	沃 404	乡 417	幸 437	烟 445	义 455		
速 362	ti		托 386	握 404	相 417	性 437	阉 445	艺 455		
塑 362	剔 370		拖 386	斡 404	香 419	姓 438	燕 445	议 455		
suan	梯 370		脱 386	wu	厢 419	xiong	延 446	异 456		
酸 362	提 370		妥 386	乌 404	箱 419	熊 438	严 446	抑 456		
算 362	题 371		椭 386	污 404	详 419	xiu	言 446	佚 456		
sui	体 371		拓 387	巫 405	享 419	休 438	沿 446	译 456		
隋 362	替 372			诬 405	响 419	修 438	研 446	易 456		
随 362	tian		W	无 405	想 419	袖 439	盐 447	益 456		
碎 364	天 372			蜈 408	向 419	xu	筵 447	意 456		
sun	添 372		wa	五 408	项 419	须 439	颜 447	溢 457		
损 364	田 372		挖 388	伍 408	相 420	虚 439	衍 447	劓 457		
suo	填 372		瓦 388	件 408	象 421	需 440	演 447	yin		
缩 365	tiao		wai	侮 408	像 421	许 440	厌 447	因 457		
所 365	挑 372		歪 388	舞 408	橡 421	序 440	验 447	阴 457		
索 365	条 372		外 388	物 408	xiao	叙 441	雁 447	音 457		
锁 366	调 373		wan	误 409	肖 421	绪 441		姻 458		
	跳 374		弯 392			续 441				

殷	458	yu		yue		责	480	诏	483	直	494	猪	505	资	514
银	458	迁	469	约	475	择	480	照	483	值	495	蛛	505	子	517
淫	459	余	469	月	476	泽	480			职	495	竹	505	紫	517
引	459	鱼	470	乐	476			zhe		植	497	逐	505	自	517
隐	459	娱	470	刖	476	zei		折	483	殖	497	主	505	字	523
印	460	渔	470	阅	476	贼	480	哲	484	止	497	助	507		
		逾	470	越	476			谪	484	只	497	住	507	zong	
ying		愉	470			zeng		磔	484	纸	497	贮	507	宗	523
应	460	舆	470	yun		增	480	褶	484	指	497	注	507	综	524
英	461	与	470	云	476	赠	480	浙	484	志	498	驻	508	棕	524
婴	462	宇	470	匀	476					制	498	柱	508	总	524
盈	462	禹	470	允	476	zha		zhen		质	499	著	508	纵	526
营	462	语	470	孕	476	扎	481	贞	484	治	500	铸	508		
赢	463	玉	470	运	476	诈	481	针	484	致	500			zou	
影	463	育	470	晕	477			侦	484	秩	500	zhua		邹	527
应	463	狱	470			zhai		珍	484	掷	500	抓	508	走	527
硬	463	浴	470	——Z——		摘	481	帧	484	智	500			奏	527
		预	470			宅	481	真	484	滞	500	zhuan			
yong		域	473	za		窄	481	甄	484	置	501	专	508	zu	
拥	463	阈	473	杂	478	债	481	诊	484			转	511	租	527
永	464	御	473					阵	484	zhong		传	512	足	527
涌	464	鬻	473	zai		zhan		振	484	中	501			族	527
用	464			灾	478	占	481	赈	484	忠	503	zhuang		阻	527
佣	464	yuan		载	478	詹	481	镇	484	终	503	庄	512	组	527
		元	473	再	478	斩	481			钟	503	装	512	祖	529
you		员	473	在	479	展	481	zheng		种	503	状	513		
优	464	爱	474	载	479	占	482	争	484	中	503			zuan	
尤	465	袁	474			战	482	征	485	仲	503	zhui		钻	529
由	465	原	474	zan				整	485	众	504	追	513		
邮	465	圆	475	暂	479	zhang		正	485	种	504			zui	
犹	466	缘	475	赞	479	张	483	证	487	重	504	zhun		最	529
油	466	源	475			章	483	政	489			准	513	罪	535
游	466	远	475	zao		长	483	挣	490	zhou					
友	466	怨	475	早	479	涨	483			周	504	zhuo		zun	
有	466	院	475	造	479	掌	483	zhi		轴	505	桌	513	尊	535
右	469	愿	475	噪	479	账	483	支	490			卓	513	遵	535
幼	469			躁	479	障	483	芝	491	zhu		酌	513		
诱	469					瘴	483	知	491	朱	505	啄	513	zuo	
				ze				执	493			着	513	左	535
				则	480	zhao								作	535
						招	483					zi		坐	535
						召	483					咨	513	做	535

词目首字笔画索引

(字右边的号码指词典正文的页码)

一画		女	281	水	357	孔	238	旧	222	汇	173	扩	241	同	375
一	450	飞	103	见	200	队	83	归	150	头	378	扫	320	因	457
二画		习	411	牛	279	办	6	目	273	汉	162	地	71	吸	410
二	92	叉	35	手	347	以	455	甲	196	讨	368	场	39	回	173
十	338	马	262	气	299	允	476	申	333	写	425	共	136	则	480
丁	77	乡	417	毛	264	邓	69	电	74	让	312	芒	264	刚	123
厂	39	四画		升	335	劝	310	号	162	礼	248	亚	445	网	393
七	296	丰	113	长	38	双	355	田	372	训	444	芝	491	肉	317
八	5	王	393	仁	483	书	350	由	465	议	455	机	181	年	278
人	312	开	228	什	315	幻	172	只	497	必	15	权	307	朱	505
入	317	天	372	片	338	五画		史	342	讯	444	过	158	先	412
儿	92	夫	115	化	288	玉	470	叨	77	记	189	再	478	廷	374
几	181	元	473	币	169	刊	229	另	257	永	464	协	424	竹	505
	187	无	405	仅	14	未	399	凹	3	司	359	西	410	迁	300
九	221	韦	397	反	212	末	273	囚	305	尼	277	压	445	乔	302
刀	67	云	476	介	99	示	342	四	361	民	269	厌	447	传	51
力	249	专	508	父	210	打	57	生	335	弗	115	在	478		512
三画		扎	481	从	116	正	485	矢	342	出	47	百	5	休	438
三	319	艺	455	分	54	扑	5	失	337	辽	255	有	466	伍	408
干	122	木	273	公	109	功	135	丘	305	奴	281	存	55	伏	115
亏	123	五	408	仓	131	去	307	付	116	召	483	页	450	优	464
工	241	支	490	月	33	甘	122	代	59	加	194	夸	239	延	445
土	127	不	24	氏	476	世	342	仪	453	皮	287	夺	91	仲	503
士	384	太	367	欠	342	艾	1	白	5	边	15	灰	172	件	408
下	342	区	305	风	301	古	139	他	367	孕	476	达	57	任	201
大	412	历	249	丹	113	节	207	丛	55	发	96	列	337	伤	316
与	57	友	466	匀	60	本	13	令	257	圣	337	死	361	价	321
万	470	尤	465	乌	476	术	352	用	464	对	83	成	41	伦	196
上	393	厄	92	勾	404	可	232	印	460	矛	264	夹	195	份	260
小	324	匹	287	六	137	左	535	乐	245	纠	221	轨	151	华	113
口	423	车	40	文	259	石	338	句	476	母	273	划	169	仿	169
巾	239	巨	223	方	400	右	469	册	223	幼	469	迈	263	伙	102
千	210	戈	124	火	101	布	28	卯	34	丝	359	毕	15	伪	177
乞	300	比	13	为	176	龙	259	犯	264	六画		贞	484	自	398
个	297	互	168	斗	399	平	290	外	101	邦	7	师	338	伊	517
久	125	切	302	计	80	灭	269	处	388	式	345	尖	198	血	452
凡	222	瓦	388	订	187	轧	445	包	50	迂	469	劣	255	向	443
广	99	止	497	户	77	东	79	主	7	刑	433	光	148	似	419
门	148	少	325	认	169	卡	228	市	505	动	79	当	63	后	361
义	267	日	316	冗	315	北	11	立	343	吉	184	早	479	行	167
尸	455	中	501	心	425	占	481	冯	249	扣	239	吐	385	全	162
已	337	贝	503	尺	45	凸	482	闪	114	考	230	虫	45	会	434
子	454	冈	11	引	459	卢	381	兰	321	托	386	曲	307		308
卫	517	内	123	巴	5	业	449	半	243	老	245	团	385		174
	398		275						6	执	493	吕	260		240

字	页	字	页	字	页	字	页	字	页	字	页	字	页
合	162	导	67	抗	230	员	473	亨	166	局	222	其	297	呼	168
企	298	异	456	坊	102	听	374	库	239	改	121	耶	449	帖	374
众	504	阵	484	抖	80	别	20	庇	15	张	483	取	307	罗	261
创	52	阳	447	护	169	岗	123	应	460	陆	259	苦	239	帕	284
刖	476	收	346	志	498	财	30		463	阿	1	苹	294	岭	257
杂	478	阶	207	块	241	针	484	冷	247		92	英	461	凯	229
危	396	阴	457	扭	279	钉	77	序	440	陈	41	范	101	账	483
旬	443	防	102	声	337	告	124	辛	426	阻	527	直	494	贬	17
负	117	丞	42	把	5	乱	260	弃	299	附	117	茎	216	购	137
名	270	奸	198	报	9	利	250	忘	396	妨	102	林	255	贮	507
各	127	如	317	拟	277	私	359	闲	413	努	281	枢	351	图	256
多	86	妇	117	劫	208	每	266	间	201	驱	307	柜	151	图	381
争	484	好	162	花	169	兵	21	闵	270	纯	53	枚	265	制	498
色	320	观	145	严	446	估	138	判	285	纲	123	析	410	知	491
冲	45	买	263	芯	426	体	371	兑	85	纳	275	松	361	迭	77
	46	红	166	劳	243	伸	333	沙	321	驳	22	构	137	垂	53
庄	512	纤	413	克	236	佃	77	汽	299	纵	526	杰	208	牧	274
庆	305	约	475	苏	361	佚	456	沃	404	纸	497	丧	320	物	408
刘	257	级	184	杠	123	作	535	泛	101	纹	403	或	177	乖	143
齐	297	纪	190	杜	82	伯	21	没	265	纺	103	画	169	刮	143
交	203	驰	44	材	30	佣	464		273	纽	279	事	345	和	164
次	54	巡	444	村	55	低	69	沟	137			刺	54	季	193
产	35			巫	405	佟	377	沪	169	**八画**		卖	263	委	398
决	224	**七画**		极	184	住	507	沈	334	奉	114	矿	241	供	135
充	45	寿	349	李	248	位	399	沉	41	玩	393	码	263	使	342
闭	15	麦	263	杨	447	伴	7	怀	170	环	170	奈	275	例	251
问	404	玛	263	求	305	身	116	快	241	青	303	奇	182	版	6
闯	52	形	437	甫	127	佛	114	完	392	责	480		297	侦	484
羊	447	进	212	更	352	伽	121	宋	361	现	265	态	367	侧	34
并	21	戒	210	束	254	近	41	宏	166	玫	20	欧	282	凭	294
关	144	远	475	两	452	彻	285	穷	305	表	150	垄	259	侨	302
米	267	违	397	医	114	返	101	灾	478	规	151	转	511	佩	286
灯	68	运	476	否	170	余	469	良	254	瓯	367	斩	481	货	177
污	404	抚	116	还	242	坐	535	证	487	拓	387	轮	260	依	453
汤	368	坏	170	来	251	谷	139	启	299	拣	198	软	317	帛	22
忙	264	扰	312	连	28	妥	386	评	293	担	60	到	67	质	499
兴	433	拒	223	步	198	含	162	补	23	押	445	非	103	征	485
	437	批	286	坚	255	邻	268	初	50	抽	46	歧	297	往	396
宇	470	走	527	肖	421	免	466	社	326	拐	143	肯	237	爬	284
守	348	抄	40		424	犹	70	识	340	拖	386	卓	513	彼	14
宅	481	贡	137	旱	162	狄	70	诈	481	拍	284	尚	325	所	365
字	523	攻	135	呈	42	角	205	诊	484	顶	77	具	224	舍	325
安	2	赤	45	时	338		225	词	53	拆	35	昆	241	金	210
讲	203	折	483	助	507	删	248	诏	483	拥	463	国	151	命	271
许	440	抓	508	里	248	条	321	译	456	抵	70	畅	40	采	31
讥	92	抢	302	呆	58	岛	372	君	226	拘	222	明	271	受	349
论	261	孝	424	围	397	邹	527	灵	256	垃	242	易	456	乳	317
讼	361	坎	230	吨	85	系	411	即	185	拉	242	昂	3	贪	367
农	280	均	226	足	527	言	446	层	34	幸	437	迪	70	贫	289
设	325	抑	456	邮	465	冻	80	尾	398	招	483	典	74	朋	286
访	103	抛	285	男	275	状	513	迟	44	择	480	固	141	股	139
寻	443	投	378	串	52					拇	273	忠	503	肮	3

词目首字笔画索引

字	页	字	页	字	页	字	页	字	页	字	页	字	页	字	页
服	115	祈	297	挤	187	省	337	侯	167	派	285	泰	367	荆	109
胁	425	话	169	拼	289	削	443	追	513	染	312	秦	303	桌	513
周	504	询	444	挖	388	尝	38	待	60	洛	261	班	6	监	198
鱼	470	详	419	按	2	哑	445	徇	444	浏	257	素	362	紧	212
狗	137	建	202	挪	281	显	413	衍	447	济	193	匿	278	剔	370
备	12	录	259	革	124	冒	264	律	260	浓	281	蚕	33	晕	477
枭	421	隶	251	带	59	星	433	须	439	津	212	捕	24	恩	92
饱	7	居	222	草	34	毗	287	叙	441	恒	166	振	484	益	3
变	17	屈	307	荟	175	界	210	剑	202	恢	173	载	478	罢	5
京	216	弧	168	荀	444	思	360	逃	368	恰	299			479	峰	114
享	419	弥	267	荒	172	品	289	爱	474	举	223	赶	122	圆	475
庞	285	承	42	故	142	响	419	食	342	宣	441	起	299	贼	480
夜	450	孟	267	胡	168	哈	160	胜	337	室	346	盐	447	钱	300
底	70	孤	138	南	275	帧	484	脉	264	宫	136	埋	263	钳	300
剂	193	降	203	药	449	罚	97	胎	367	宪	417	捆	241	钻	529
郊	205	函	162	标	18	贱	202	狭	412	突	381	捐	224	铁	374
废	108	限	415	柯	230	贴	374	独	80	穿	51	损	364	铅	300
净	219	姐	210	相	417	骨	141	狩	349	客	237	袁	474	缺	310
盲	264	姓	438	查	421	钞	40	狱	470	诬	405	都	80	氧	447
放	103	始	342	柏	35	钟	503	贸	264	语	470	哲	484	特	368
刻	237	参	32			6	铃	300	怨	475	扁	17	挫	56	牺	410
育	470	线	416			22	钩	137	急	186	祖	529	换	172	造	479
卷	224	组	527	柱	508	卸	425	饼	21	神	334	热	312	乘	44
单	61	绅	333	栏	243	拜	6	弯	392	误	409	恐	238	租	527
炉	259	细	412	柠	279	看	230	孪	260	诱	469	埃	1	积	182
浅	301	终	503	树	352	矩	223	将	203	说	359	莱	242	秩	500
法	97	驻	508	勃	22	选	442	奖	203	郡	227	莫	273	称	41
油	466	经	216	要	448	适	346	亮	254	退	385	荷	165	秘	267
泊	22					449	秒	269	度	82	既	193	晋	215	透	381
沿	446	**九画**		威	396	香	419	咨	513	屏	294	恶	92	笔	14
泡	285	契	299	歪	527	种	503	亲	302	费	108	莎	321	债	481
注	507	奏	527	研	446	音	504	音	457	陡	80	真	484	借	210
泥	277	春	53	厚	167	秋	305	帝	72	孩	160	框	241	值	495
波	21	帮	7	砑	445	科	230	施	338	除	50	档	64	倾	303
泽	480	珂	230	砌	299	重	45	闽	270	院	475	格	124	倒	67
治	500	珀	294	砂	321			差	504	姻	458	校	206	俱	224
性	437	珍	484	面	268	复	118	养	447	架	198			倡	40
学	443	玻	21	耐	275	笃	82	美	266	盈	462	核	165	候	168
宗	523	毒	80	奎	241	段	83	叛	285	急	60	样	448	倍	13
定	78	型	437	牵	300	便	18	送	361	柔	317	根	127	倦	224
审	334	挂	143	残	32	贷	60	类	246	绑	7	索	365	健	202
官	145	封	114	殆	60	顺	358	迷	267	结	208	速	362	臭	47
空	237	持	44	轴	505	修	438	前	300	绕	312	酌	513	射	332
	238	拷	230	轻	303	保	8	首	348	绘	175	配	286	皋	123
穷	305	项	420	鸦	445	促	55	逆	278	给	127	夏	412	息	410
实	340	城	43	背	11	侮	408	总	524			破	294	殷	458
试	345	挟	425	战	12	俘	115	洁	428	骆	261	原	474	航	162
郎	243	政	489	点	482	信	151	洪	167	绝	225	套	368	途	384
房	102	拾	342	虐	74	皈	151	浇	205	统	377	逐	505	爱	2
诚	42	挑	372	临	497	鬼	281	测	34			顾	143	胶	205
衬	41	指	77	竖	255	侵	302	洗	411	**十画**		较	206	留	257
视	346	垫	490	禹	352	侯	470	活	176	耕	127	致	500	凌	256

词目首字笔画索引

字	页	字	页	字	页	字	页	字	页	字	页	字	页
恋	254	袖	439	菲	108	银	458	混	175	斯	360	赎	351	割	124
衰	355	被	13	菜	32	矫	206	淫	459	期	296	赔	286	富	120
高	123	课	237	萃	55	移	453	渔	470	欺	297	黑	165	窜	55
准	513	冥	271	营	462	符	115	液	450	联	252	铸	508	窝	404
病	21	调	77	萧	422	第	72	淡	63	散	320	链	254	窗	52
疾	186		373	萨	319	笞	44	深	333	募	274	销	422	扉	108
疲	287	谅	254	械	425	敏	270	涵	162	董	79	锁	366	遍	18
脊	187	谈	367	梵	101	做	535	梁	254	蒂	74	锄	50	雇	143
效	424	剥	21	梅	265	偿	39	渗	335	落	261	短	82	裙	311
离	247	展	481	检	198	偶	283	情	304	韩	162	智	500	幂	268
唐	368	剧	224	梯	370	偷	378	惯	147	朝	40	犊	82	谢	425
资	514	弱	318	救	222	售	350	寄	193	植	497	剩	337	谣	449
剖	294	陶	368	曹	34	停	374	密	267	森	321	程	44	谦	300
竞	219	陪	285	副	120	偏	287	谋	273	焚	113	稀	410	属	351
部	28	娱	470	票	288	假	196	屠	384	棉	268	税	357	强	301
旁	285	通	374	厢	419		198	弹	367	棚	286	等	68		302
旅	260	能	277	硅	151	得	68	隋	362	棕	524	策	34	疏	351
阅	476	难	275	硕	359	盘	285	堕	91	棣	74	筛	321	隔	125
瓶	294	预	470	奢	325	船	51	随	362	椭	386	筵	447	媒	266
粉	113	桑	320	厩	222	斜	425	隆	259	惠	175	答	57	登	68
料	255	验	447	粪	136	盒	165	隐	459	逼	13	傅	120	缓	172
益	456	继	193	盛	337	彩	31	婚	175	棘	186	牌	285	缔	74
兼	198			雪	443	领	257	绩	194	硬	463	集	186	骗	288
烧	325	十一画		辅	116	脚	206	绪	441	确	310	焦	205	编	16
烟	445	彗	175	虚	439	脱	386	续	441	硫	259	储	50	缘	475
递	72	球	305	堂	368	象	421	骑	297	雁	447	奥	4		
浙	484	理	248	常	38	猪	505	维	397	殖	497	街	207	十三画	
涉	332	堵	82	晨	41	猎	255	绷	13	裂	255	惩	44	瑟	321
消	421	措	56	悬	441	猝	55	综	524	暂	479	御	473	瑞	318
涓	224	描	269	野	449	猛	267	绿	260	辍	53	循	444	瑕	412
海	160	域	473	曼	264	祭	193			斐	108	舒	351	摄	333
涂	384	排	284	晚	393	馆	145	十二画		悲	11	逾	470	填	372
浴	470	掉	77	啄	513	减	199	琼	305	紫	517	鲁	259	摆	6
浮	115	赦	333	距	224	麻	262	斑	6	敞	40	装	512	搬	6
流	258	堆	83	啃	237	康	230	替	372	棠	368	就	222	摇	449
润	318	推	385	略	260	盗	68	款	241	掌	483	敦	85	摊	367
浪	243	授	349	蛇	325	章	321	堪	230	最	529	童	377	聘	290
浸	215	教	206	累	245	商	527	塔	367	量	254	竣	227	蓝	243
涨	483	掠	260	唱	40	族	441	搭	57		255	善	321	蒙	267
烫	368	培	285	患	172	旋	443	揩	229			普	294	献	417
涌	464	接	207	唯	397			越	476	喷	286	尊	535	楔	424
悖	13	掷	500	啤	287	国	473	趋	307	晶	218	道	68	禁	215
宽	241	控	238	逻	261	阉	445	超	40	喊	162	港	123	楚	51
家	195	探	367	崩	13	着	513	堤	70	晾	255	滞	500	想	419
窄	481	据	224	赈	484	盖	121	提	370	景	219	湖	168	概	121
容	316	职	495	婴	462	粗	55	博	22	跑	285	湿	338	赖	243
案	3	基	182	赊	325	断	83	揭	207	跛	23	温	400	剽	288
请	305	勘	230	圈	307	剪	199	喜	411	遗	454	渴	236	甄	484
诺	281	聊	255	铜	377	清	303	插	35	蛛	505	溅	203	感	122
读	81	著	508	铣	411	添	372	裁	31	嵌	301	滑	169	碑	11
扇	321	勒	245	铭	271	渎	82	搁	124	幅	116	游	466	碎	364
诽	108	黄	172	铲	37	渐	202	握	404	赋	120	愉	470	雷	245
										赌	82			零	256

辐	116	催	55	谪	484	需	440	赛	319	稻	68	赠	480	羁	184
辑	187	像	421	谬	271	辖	412	寡	143	稿	124	默	273	赡	321
输	351	微	396	群	311	颗	232	察	35	箱	419	镜	221	黏	279
督	80	徭	449	殿	77	蜡	242	蜜	268	箭	203	赞	479	魏	400
频	289	遥	449	障	483	镀	82	谱	295	篇	288	穆	274	馕	80
鉴	203	腰	449	媾	138	镂	259	嫡	70	僵	203	篮	243	赢	463
睦	274	詹	481	叠	77	舞	408	熊	438	德	68	儒	317	豁	179
盟	267	鲍	11	缝	114	稳	403	缩	365	熟	351	劓	457	十八画	
暗	3	触	51	缣	198	熏	443	十五画		摩	272	邀	449	藩	99
照	483	解	210	十四画		算	362	耦	283	颜	447	衡	166	覆	120
跨	239	禀	21	静	221	管	146	撒	319	糊	168	膨	286	翻	99
跳	374	廉	254	赫	165	舆	470	播	21	遵	535	膳	321	瀑	295
路	259	新	426	截	209	僧	321	撤	41	熵	324	磨	273	邋	242
跟	127	意	456	境	221	魅	267	增	480	潜	300	瘴	483	十九画	
遣	301	阙	310	摘	481	膑	21	鞍	2	潮	40	凝	279	警	219
蜈	408	叁	370	撇	289	孵	115	横	166	澄	44	辨	18	攀	285
蜂	114	粮	254	穀	141	敲	302	槽	34	额	92	辩	18	曝	11
署	352	数	352	聚	224	豪	162	樊	99	履	260	燃	312	簿	29
置	501	塑	362	鞅	447	腐	116	橡	421	嬉	411	激	184	颤	37
罪	535	慈	54	摹	271	瘦	350	飘	288	缮	321	褶	484	爆	11
蜀	352	煤	266	翰	404	旗	297	磔	484	十六画		壁	15	二十画	
错	56	满	264	模	271	精	218	霉	266	操	33	避	15	及以上	
锚	264	源	475	榜	7	熔	317	题	371	燕	445	缴	206	躁	479
锦	212	滤	260	歌	124	煽	321	暴	11	薪	428	十七画		蠕	317
键	203	滥	243	酷	239	漆	297	影	463	翰	162	戴	60	黩	305
锯	224	滚	151	酸	362	漂	288	蝶	77	橙	44	擦	30	魔	273
辞	54	溢	457	碳	368	漫	264	蝴	168	整	485	藏	33	霸	5
筹	47	溶	317	磁	335	滴	70	墨	273	融	317	瞬	358	露	259
签	300	慎	335	愿	475	演	447	镇	484	霍	179	瞪	69	囊	473
简	199	塞	319	殡	20	漏	259	靠	230	噪	479	螺	261	灞	5
毁	173	福	116			慢	264	稽	184						

A

阿贝-海默特判别准则/Abbe-Helmert 準則　Abbe-Helmert criterion
阿布拉兹法/阿布拉茲法　Lex Aebutia
阿达梅茨基和谐图/阿達梅茨基和諧圖　the harmonogram of Karol Adamiecki
阿尔法风险/阿爾發風險　alpha risk, α risk
阿尔法拉比管理者质量论/阿爾法拉比有關管理者品質的論述　Alfarabi on managers' character
阿尔法系数/阿法係數　alpha coefficient
阿尔夫威德森分布/Arfwedson 分布, Arfwedson 分配　Arfwedson distribution
阿尔蒙分布滞后/艾蒙分配落差　Almon distributed lag
阿尔蒙滞后/艾蒙落差　Almon lag
阿弗奇-约翰逊效应/A-J 效果, 艾維克-強生效果　Averch-Johnson effect
阿吉里斯论个性与组织/阿吉里斯論個性與組織　Argyris' view on personality and organization
阿吉里斯心理契约学说/阿吉里斯心理契約學説　psychological contract theory of Argyris
阿吉里斯组织学习理论/阿吉里斯組織學習理論　organizational learning theory of Argyris
阿克莱特工厂制/阿克萊特工廠制　factory system of Arkwright
阿奎利亚法/阿奎利亞法　Lex Aquilia
阿奎那/阿奎那　Thomas Aquinas
阿奎那神学/阿奎納神學　Aquinas' theology
阿拉伯法系/阿拉伯法系　Arab legal family
阿拉伯国家联盟/阿拉伯國家聯盟　League of Arab States, Arab Legal Family
阿拉里克罗马法辑要/阿拉里克羅馬法輯要　Alaric's Breviary
阿莱悖论/亞列士矛盾　Allais paradox
阿勒曼尼法典/阿勒曼尼法典　Alamannic Code
阿罗不可能定理/艾羅不可能定理　Arrow impossibility theorem
阿罗不可能性定理/亞羅不可能定理　Arrow's impossibility theorem
阿罗-德布鲁均衡存在定理/艾羅-德布鲁均衡存在定理　Arrow-Debreu equilibrium existence theorem
阿罗证券/阿羅證券　Arrow securities
阿马尔菲法典/阿馬爾菲法典　Amalphitan Code
阿米代奇约束程序/Armitage 受制程序　Armitage's restricted procedure
阿姆斯特丹股票交易所/阿姆斯特丹股票交易所　Amsterdam Stock Exchange
阿姆斯特丹社会工作学院/阿姆斯特丹社會工作學院　Amsterdam School of Social Work
阿讷西回合/安訥西回合　Annecy Round
阿诺德分布/Arnold 分布, Arnold 分配　Arnold distribution
阿菩莱拉法/阿菩萊拉法　Lex Apuleja
阿奇纳 An 检验/Ajne 的 An 檢定　Ajne's An test
阿特金森成就动机理论/阿特金森成就動機理論　Atkinson's achievement motivation theory
阿提里亚法/阿提里亞法　Lex Atinia
阿提利亚法/阿提利亞法　Lex Atilia
阿佐/阿佐　Azo Portius
埃尔斯伯格悖论/艾司柏格矛盾　Ellsberg paradox
埃利希/埃利希　Eugen Ehrlich
埃伦费斯特模型/Ehrenfest 模型　Ehrenfest model
埃默森参谋本部制/愛默生參謀本部制　Emerson staff-based system
埃默森的十二原则/愛默生的十二原則　efficiency twelve principles of Emerson
埃奇法案/艾奇法案　Edge act
埃奇沃思公式/艾基渥斯公式　Edgeworth formula
埃奇沃思盒/艾吉沃斯箱形圖　Edgeworth box
埃奇沃思近似/Edgeworth 逼近　Edgeworth approximation
埃奇沃思循环/艾吉伍斯循環　Edgeworth cycle
埃奇沃思展开式/艾基渥斯形式展開式　Edgeworth-type expansions
埃奇沃思指数/Edgeworth 指數　Edgeworth index
埃森型逼近/Esseen 型逼近　Esseen-type approximation
埃森引理/Esseen 引理　Esseen's lemma
艾克门达合同/艾克門達合同　accomenda
艾森克个性问卷/艾森克人格問卷　Eysenck personality questionnaire
艾特肯定理/艾特肯定理　Aitken theorem
艾特肯估计[量]/艾特肯估計量, Aitken 估計[量]

Aitken estimator
艾特肯广义最小二乘估计量/艾特肯一般化最小平方法估计量　Aitken GLS estimator
艾辛-史蒂文分布/Ising-Stevens 分布，Ising-Stevens 分配　Ising-Stevens distribution
爱迪生实验研究所/門洛帕克實驗室　Menlo Park Laboratory
爱迪生象限/愛迪生象限　Edison's quadrant
爱尔伯福制/愛爾伯福制　Elberfeld system
爱尔文分布/Elfving 分布，Elfving 分配　Elfving distribution
安德鲁的傅里叶型点图/Andrews 的 Fourier 型描點圖　Andrews' Fourier-type plot
安德森-达林统计量/Anderson-Darling 統計量　Anderson-Darling statistic
安德森分类统计量/Anderson 分類統計量　Anderson's classification statistic
安第斯集团/安第斯　Andean group
安定型创业/安定型創業　entrepreneurial valorization
安东尼模型/安東尼模型　Anthony model
安乐死/安樂死　euthanasia
安诺索夫定理/Anosov 定理　Anosov's theorem
安全/安全［性］　safety, security
安全边际/安全邊際　safety margin, margin of safety
安全边界/安全邊界　margin of safety
安全标准/安全標準　safety standard
安全补贴/安全補貼　safety loading
安全出口管制/安全出口管制　security export control
安全储存/安全儲存　safe storage
安全电子交易协议/安全電子交易協定，保全電子交易協定　secure electronic transaction protocol, SET protocol
安全副本/安全副本　security copy
安全港口/安全船席　safe port, safe berth
安全管理/安全管理　safety management
安全管理对象/安全管理物件　safety management object
安全管理方法/安全管理方法　safety management approach
安全管理责任/安全管理責任，安全管理職責　safety management responsibility
安全管理制度/安全管理系統　safety management system
安全规则/安全管制　safety regulation
安全级别/安全值　security level
安全检查表法/安全檢查表法　safety check list method
安全交易/安全交易　in-house transaction
安全胶片/安全膠片　uninflammable film
安全控制/安全控制　safety control
安全库存量/安全存量　safety stock
安全片基/安全片基　safety base
安全评价/安全評價　safety evaluation
安全全宗/安全全宗　security fonds
安全认证/安全認證　security certification
安全生产/安全生產　safety in production
安全生产法/安全生產法　safety production law
安全事故/安全事故　safety accident
安全套接字层协议/安全通訊端層協定　secure socket layer protocol, SSL protocol
安全提前期/安全前置時間　safety lead time
安全网/安全網　safety net
安全系数/安全係數　safety factor
安全系统工程/安全系統工程　safety system engineering
安全协议/安全協定　security protocol
安全心理学/安全心理學　safety psychology
安全行为/安全行爲　safety behavior
安塞利-布雷得里检验/Ansari-Bradley 離勢檢定　Ansari-Bradley dispersion test
安置/安置就業　placement
安置成本/總搬遷成本　total relocation costs
安装工程定额/安裝工程定額　installation engineering quota
鞍点/鞍點　saddle point
按不变价格计算/按固定價格計算　at constant price
按不变美元价值计算/固定美元價值計算　in constant dollar value
按产品布置/産品式布置　product layout
按当期价格/按當期價格　at current prices
按订单采购/接單採購　procure to order, PTO
按订单加工/接單加工　fabrication to order, FTO
按订单设计/接單設計　engineer to order, ETO
按订单销售/接單銷售　sale to order, STO
按订单研发/接單研發　develop to order, DTO
按订单制造/接單生産　build to order, BTO
按订单装配/接單裝配　assemble to order, ATO
按份共有/按份共有　several co-owenership
按份之债/按份之債　several obligation as contrasted with joint obligation
按跟单信用证所开的汇票/跟單信用狀匯票　bill of exchange drawn under a documentary credit
按功能布置/功能式布置　functional layout, process

按固定价格/按固定價格　at constant prices
按规定日期付款的汇票/按規定日期付款的匯票　bill drawn payable at fixed date
按揭贷款/按揭貸款　mortgage loan
按劳分配/按勞分配　distribution according to work, to each according to his contribution
按历年订阅/按曆年訂閱　subscribe by calendar year
按美元计算/按美元計算　in dollar terms
按钮广告/按鈕廣告　button advertisement
按人头付费/論人計酬　capitation
按日期权/按日選擇權　day-to-day option
按生产要素分配/按生產要素貢獻分配　distribution according to factors of production
按市场价格/按市價　at market prices
按市场价格计算/按市價計算　at market price
按市价发行/按市價發行　issue at market price
按现价计算/按現價計算　in current price
按效果付费/功績報酬　pay for performance
按需采访/按需採訪　acquisition on demand
按需出版/隨選出版, 應需出版　on-demand publishing
按需喷墨/按需噴墨　drop on demand
按需印刷/按需印刷　print on demand
按要素成本[计算]/按要素成本[計算]　at factor cost
按与大小成比例的概率抽选/依單位大小比例機率選取法　selection with probability proportional to size
按语/按語　compiler's comment
按照市场价/現價下單　at the market
按字母顺序/按字典次序　arranged in alphabetical order
案件日程表/案件日程表　case of schedule
案件性质/案件性質　nature of cases
案经/案經　An Jing, the case has been
案据/案據　An Ju, based on document
案卷/案卷　case files
案卷分类方案/歸檔計劃　filing plan
案卷封面/案卷封面　files cover
案卷号/案卷號　files number
案卷级条目著录格式/案卷級條目著錄格式　files level item description format
案卷级整理/案卷級整理　files level arragement
案卷目录/案卷目錄　catalog of files
案卷目录号/案卷目錄號　catalog number of files
案卷排列/案卷排列　files arrangement
案卷题名/案卷標題　title of files
案卷组/案卷組　files series
案卷组管理/案卷組管理　files administration, files management
案卷组区分点/案卷組區分點　files break point
案例/案例, 個案　case
案例表示/案例表示　case representation
案例存储/案例儲存　case storage
案例分析/個案分析　case analysis
案例检索/案例檢索　case retrieval
案例库/案例庫　case base
案例推理/案例推理　case reasoning
案例学习/案例學習　case learning
案例研究培训/個案法訓練　case study training
案情摘要/案情摘要　brief of case
案由/案由　An You, brief of case
案主来源及类型/案主來源及類型　source and type of client
案主中心理论/案主中心理論　client-centered theory
案准/案準　anzhun, quotation from
暗调/暗調　shade, low-key
暗类编排/暗類編排　classified arrangement without formal class heading
暗室/暗房　darkroom
暗退/暗退　fading in dark
暗引/暗引　implicit citation
暗影/暗影　ghost image
肮脏浮动/不純淨的浮動, 骯髒的浮動　dirty floating, dirty float
肮脏浮动汇率制/不純淨的浮動匯率制　dirty floating rate system
昂格尔/昂格爾　R. M. Unger Roberto
盎格鲁和韦里诺法汇编/盎格魯和韋里諾法匯編　Lex Anglorum et Werinorum
盎格鲁-撒克逊法/盎格魯-撒克遜法　Anglo-Saxon law
凹版电子雕刻机/凹版電子雕刻機　electronic engraving machine for gravure cylinder
凹版雕刻机/雕刻機　engraving machine for gravure cylinder
凹版印刷/凹版印刷　recess printing, intaglio printing
凹版纸/凹版紙　plate paper, gravure paper
凹版制作/凹版製作　gravure forme making
凹函数/凹性函數　concave function
凹偏好/凹性偏好　concave preferences
凹室排架法/凹室排架法　Shelving alcove
凹性效用函数/凹型效用函數　concave utility function

凹印设备/凹印設備　gravure equipment
奥地利合理化运动/奧地利合理化運動　rationalization movement of Austria
奥地利学派/奧地利學派　Austrian school
奥恩斯坦-乌伦贝克过程/恩斯坦-歐嫩貝過程，Ornstein-Uhlenbeck 過程　Ornstein-Uhlenbeck process
奥尔森模型/奧爾森模型　Ohlson model
奥古斯丁/奧古斯丁　Aurelius Augustinus
奥古斯丁神学/奧斯定神學　Augustinus' theology
奥肯定律/奧肯法則　Okun's law
奥曼-柏雷定理/奧曼-佩勒斯定理　Aumann-Perles theorem
奥斯陆手册/奧斯陸手冊　Oslo manual

B

八辟/八辟　Ba Bi
八分法/八分法　octave device, eight-section system
八分位数/八分位數　octile
八卦新闻/八卦新聞　gossip journalism, gossips
八千麻袋事件/八千麻袋事件　Eight Thousand Sacks
八议/八議　Ba Yi
八字皱/八字皺　splay crimple
巴伯里-黄-桑托斯模型/Barberis-Huang-Santos 模型,BHS 模型　Barberis-Huang-Santos model, BHS model
巴伯里-史莱佛-维什尼模型/Barberis-Shleffer-Vishny 模型,BSV 模型　Barberis-Shleffer-Vishny model, BSV model
巴尔干化/巴爾幹化　Balkanization
巴伐利亚法/巴伐利亞法　Lex Baiuvariorum
巴伐利亚法典/巴伐利亞法典　Bavarian law
巴盖 Y 统计量/Bagai 的 Y 統計量　Bagai's Y statistic
巴哈德效率/Bahadur 效率　Bahadur efficiency
巴黎[编目]原则/巴黎原則　Paris Principles
巴黎非战公约/巴黎非戰公約　Paris Peace Pact
巴黎俱乐部/巴黎俱樂部,十國集團　Paris Club
巴黎统筹委员会/巴黎統籌委員會　coordinating committee for export control
巴纳德管理理论/巴納德管理理論　management theory of Barnard
巴纳德论领导/巴納德論領導　Barnard's view on leadership
巴切利尔过程/Bachelier 過程　Bachelier process
巴塞尔公约/巴塞爾公約　Basel Convention
巴塞尔协议/巴塞爾協議,巴塞爾協定　Basel Agreement
巴塞尔银行监管委员会/巴塞爾銀行監管委員會　Basel Committee on Banking Supervision
巴塞尔资本协议/巴塞爾資本協定　Basel Capital Accord
巴塞洛缪问题/Bartholomew 問題　Bartholomew's problem
巴思计算尺/巴思計算尺　Barth calculating scale
巴斯德象限/巴斯德象限　Pasteur's quadrant
巴斯模型/Bass 擴散模型　Bass diffusion model
巴苏定律/Basu 定理　Basu's theorem
巴苏模型/巴蘇模型　Basu model
巴塔查利亚距离/Bhattacharyya 距離　Bhattacharyya's distance
巴塔查利亚下界/Bhattacharyya[下]界　Bhattacharyya bounds
巴特利特-戴南德检验/Bartlett-Diananda 檢定　Bartlett and Diananda test
巴特利特检验/巴特力檢定法　Bartlett test
巴泽尔模型/巴洛模型　Barzel's model
扒圆/圓化　rounding
把关人/守門人　gatekeeper
罢工/罷工　strike
罢工权/罷工權　right to strike
罢工险/罷工保險　strike insurance
罢免权/罷免權　right of recall
霸权/霸權　hegemony
霸权国家/霸權國家　hegemony state
灞桥纸/灞橋紙　Baqiao paper
白板规则/白板規則　clean slate rule
白本/白本　old book on white paper
白边/書口,版邊　foredge, margin
白粲/白粲　Bai Can
白盒测试/白箱測試　white box testing
白口/白口　white folding line
白领工人/白領員工,白領勞工,白領工作者　white-collar worker
白领阶层/白領階層　white-collar stratum
白皮书/白皮書　white paper
白旗/白旗　white flag
白文本/無注本　text without annotation
白箱方法/白箱方法　white box approach
白银平价/白銀平價　silver parity
白银券/銀元券　silver certificate
白银市场/白銀市場　silver market
白噪声/白[雜]訊　white noise
百分比条形图/百分比條圖　hundred-percent bar chart
百分点/百分點　percentage point
百分[法]/百分率,百分比　percentage

百分数标准差/百分點標準差，變異係數　percentage standard deviation
百分数分布/百分數分布　percentage distribution
百分数图/百分數圖　percentage diagram
百分数质量控制图/百分數品質管制圖　quality control chart for percentage
百分位数/百分位數　percentile, centile
百分位数秩/百分位數等級　percentile rank
百分误差/百分誤差　percentage error
百货商店/百貨公司　department store
百科词典/百科詞典　encyclopedic dictionary
百科全书/百科全書　encyclopaedia, encyclopedia
百慕大期权/百慕大期權　Bermudan option
百衲本/百衲本　collection of various editions, baina book
百万机会缺陷数/百萬機會缺陷數　defect per million opportunity, DPMO
柏油纸/柏油紙　pitched paper
摆版方式/裝板方式　imposition scheme
拜杜法案/拜杜法案　Bayh-Dole Act
拜伦检验/Beran 檢定　Beran's tests
拜斯-巴洛特表/Buys-Ballot 表　Buys-Ballot table
拜占廷帝国/拜占廷帝國　Byzantine Empire
班级集体借书/班級集體借書　school loan
班级图书室/班級圖書館　classroom library
班轮提单/班輪提單　liner bill of lading
班组/班組　team and group
斑点/斑點，雜色　mottle
搬运生铁和铲铁实验/搬運生鐵和鏟鐵實驗　test of transporting and shoveling pig iron
搬运时间/搬運時間　handling time
版本/版[本]　edition
版本号/版本號　edition number
版本记录页/版本記錄頁　edition recording page
版本鉴定/版本鑒定　textual criticism, edition authentication
版本考订/版本考訂　edition criticism
版本目录/版本目錄　textual bibliography, bibliography of editions
版本说明/版本説明　statement of edition
版本图书馆/版權圖書館　copyright library, legal deposit library
版本项/版本項　edtion item
版本学/版本學　bibliology
版次/版次　edition number
版滚筒制备/版滾筒製備　cylinder preparation
版口/書邊空白，框距　margins
版面/内文版度，版心面積　type area
版面编辑/版面編輯　make-up editor
版面布局结构/布局結構　layout structure
版面空间/版面空間　layout space
版膜/版膜　stencil film
版膜厚度/版膜厚度　stencil film thickness
版式/版式　layout
版式设计/版式設計　layout design
版式文件/版式檔　fixed-layout records
版税/版税，權利金　royalty, copyright royalty
版图/版圖　territory domiciliary and map register
版心/版心　print area, type page
版样/版樣詳圖　comprehensive layout
版子/版子　print plate
办法/辦法　means, measure, regulations
办公自动化/辦公室自動化　office automation, OA
办公自动化系统/辦公室自動化系統　office automation system, OAS
办刊宗旨/辦刊宗旨　editorial philosophy
办理许可证/辦理許可證　presentation of license document
办事机构/辦事機構　administrative body
半/半　semi
半版广告/半版廣告　half page advertisement
半闭合/半閉合　semi-closure
半不变量/半不變量，半不變式　semi-invariant, half-invariant
半不变量母函数/半不變量生成函數　semi-invariant generating function
半参数估计/半母數估計　semiparametric estimation
半参数回归模型/半參數回歸模型　semiparametric regression model
半参数模型/半參數模型　semiparametric model
半成品/半成品　semi-finished product
半程序化决策/半程式化決策　semi-programmed decision
半重复设计/半重複設計　half-replicate design
半独立报酬系统/半獨立報酬系統　semi-independent reward system
半对数尺度/半對數尺度　semi-logarithmic scale
半对数图/半對數圖　semi-logarithmic chart
半对数[坐标]纸/半對數紙　semi-logarithmic paper
半分离均衡/半分離式均衡　semi-separating equilibrium
半分裂法/半分裂法　split half method
半格子方阵/半格子方陣　half-plaid square
半公函/半公函　quasi official letter
半极差/半全距　semi-range
半结构化面试/半結構式面談　semi-structured

interview
半结构化数据/半結構化資料　semi-structured data
半结构化问题/半結構化問題　semi-structured problem
半矩阵/半矩陣　semi-matrix
半距/半寬度　half-width
半开架/半開架　semiopen-shelf
半柯西分布/半柯西分布,半柯西分配　half-Cauchy distribution
半拉丁方/半拉丁方陣　semi-Latin squares
半连续过程/半連續過程　semi-continuous process
半马尔柯夫过程/半馬可夫過程　semi-Markov processes
半年刊/半年刊　semi-annual
半年期保险费/半年期保險費　semi-annual premium
半年期股息/半年期股息　semi-annual dividend
半年息券/半年期息券　semi-annual coupon
半偶族/半屬族　moiety
半偏相关/半偏相關　semipartial correlation
半平均[数]法/半平均數法　semi-average method
半平均数趋势线/半平均數趨勢線　semi-average trend line
半平稳过程/半平穩過程　semi-stationary process
半强有效/半強式效率性　semi-strong-form efficiency
半色调/半色調　halftone
半色调处理/半色調處理　halftoning
半色调图像/半色調影像　halftone image
半熟练工人/半技術工　semi-skilled labor
半衰期/半衰期　half life
半四分位数距/半四分位距,内四分位距　semi-quartile range, interquartile range
半题名/半題名　half title
半通栏广告/半通欄廣告　half banner advertisement
半微微理论/半微微理論　semi-micro-micro theory
半稳定律/半穩定律　semi-stable law
半现行文件/半現行檔　semi-current records
半鞅/半鞅,半平賭過程　semi-martingale
半样本/半樣本　semi-sample
半月刊/半月刊　semi-monthly
半正定矩阵/正半定矩陣　positive semidefinite matrices, positive semidefinite matrix
半正态分布/半常態分配,半常態分布　half-normal distribution, semi-normal distribution
半正态概率纸/半常態機率紙　half-normal probability paper
半正态图/半常態描點圖　half normal plots
半致死[剂]量/中位數致死劑量　median lethal dose

半周期/半週期　half-period
半专门贸易/半專門貿易　semi-special trade
半自动标引/半自動標引　semiautomatic indexing
伴随变差/伴隨變異　concomitant variation
伴随矩阵/伴隨矩陣　adjoint matrix
伴随离差/伴隨離差　concomitant deviation
伴随因子/伴隨因子　concomitant factor
邦弗伦尼不等式/Bonferroni 不等式　Bonferroni inequality
邦联/邦聯制　confederation
邦联条例/邦聯條例　Articles of Confederation
帮派/幫會　secret society
帮派文化/幫派文化　gang culture
帮助侵权/輔助侵害　contributory infringement
帮助文件/求助檔案　help file
绑架罪/綁架罪　crime of kidnapping
榜样学习/榜樣學習　following example
包背装/包背裝　wrapped-back binding
包本/包封面　covering
包边/包邊　overlapping
包工制度/包工制　contractor labor system
包含性检验/包含性檢定　includances tests
包捆扎/紮捆　bundle
包络定理/包絡定理　envelope theorem
包络风险函数/包絡風險函數　envelope risk function
包络幂函数/包絡檢力函數　envelope power function
包络曲线/包絡曲線　envelope curve
包面材料/包面材料　covering material
包签/出貨標籤　shipping label
包容性/包容性,包容度　inclusiveness
包容性法律实证主义/包容性法律實證主義　inclusive legal positivism
包税人/包稅人　tax farmers
包图/包圖　package diagram
包销/包銷,[買斷]承銷　exclusive sales, bought deal, underwrite
包销合同/包銷合約　exclusive sale contract
包销协议/包銷協定　sole sale agreement
包拯/包拯　Bao Zheng
包装/包裝,封裝　package, packaging
包装产品成形/包裝產品成形　forming for packaging
包装成形工艺/包裝成形工藝　forming process for packaging
包装上市/包裝上市　stock listing by packaging
包装消费品/包裝商品　packaged goods
饱和度/飽和度　saturation
饱和模型/飽和模型　saturated model

饱和湿度/飽和濕度 saturated humidity
饱和输出电平/飽和輸出電平 saturated output level
保本基金/保本基金 guaranteed fund
保存本/保存本 reserved material
保存本书库/保存本書庫 reseved books stack
保存期/保存期限 retention period
保存收藏/保存收藏 reserve collection
保存元数据/保存元數據 preservation metadata
保单失效/保單無效,取消保單 avoidance of policy
保兑手续费/保兌手續費 confirmation commission
保兑信用证/保兌信用狀 confirmed credit
保兑银行/保兌銀行 confirming bank
保付商行/保付商行 confirming house
保付书/保付書,確認書 confirming order
保付支票/保付支票 certified check
保辜/保辜 the system of victim protection
保管/保管 storage, retention
保管单位/保管單位 retention unit
保管期限/保管期限 retention period, custodial duration
保管期限分类法/保管期限分類法 retention period classification
保管权转让/移轉 alienation of retention right
保管箱/保管箱 safety deposit box
保护/保護 preservation
保护奥林匹克会徽内罗毕条约/保護奧林匹克會徽奈洛比條約 Nairobi Treaty on the Protection of the Olympic Symbol
保护表演者、录音制品制作者与广播组织罗马公约/保護表演者、錄音製品製作者與廣播組織羅馬公約 Rome Convention for the Protection of Performers, Producers of Phonograms and Broadcasting Organizations
保护成本/保護成本 cost of protection
保护带/保護帶 protection zone
保护的责任/保護的責任 responsibility of protection
保护关税/保護[性]關稅 protective duty, protective tariff
保护国/保護國 protectorate
保护胶/快乾漆 lacquer
保护贸易/保護貿易 protected trade
保护贸易法规/保護貿易法規 protectionist legislation
保护贸易手段/保護貿易手段 protectionist measure
保护贸易政策/保護貿易政策 protectionist policy, protective trade policy
保护贸易制度/保護貿易制度 protective trade system

保护条款/保護條款 safeguard clause
保护性产能/保護性產能 protective capacity
保护性出口税/出口保護性關稅 protective export duty
保护性关税/保護性關稅 safeguarding duty, protective duty, protective tariff
保护性管辖权/保護性管轄權 protective jurisdiction
保护性海运政策/保護性海運政策 protective shipping policy
保护性进口税/進口保護性關稅 protective import duty
保护性缩微摄影/保護性微縮照相 preservation microfilming
保护制度/保護制度 protecting system
保甲制/保甲制 baojia system
保理/保理,應收賬款買賣,應收賬款承購 factoring
保理费/代理收賬手續費 factoring charge
保理业务/代理收賬業務 factoring business
保留工资/保留工資 reservation wage
保留价格/保留價格 reservation price
保留金/保留款 retention money
保留率/保留率 retention rate
保留上下文索引系统/保留內容索引 preserved context indexing system, PRECIS
保留收藏/保留圖書 reserve collection, reserve book collection
保留条款/保留條款 saving clause
保留图书/指定讀物 required reading
保留效用/保留效用 reservation utility
保留意见/保留意見 qualified opinion
保密/保密 secrecy
保密的消息来源/保密的新聞來源 confidential news source
保密资料/保密資料 classified material, confidential material
保全损险/保全損險 insurance against TLO
保释/保釋,取保候審 bail
保释保证金/保釋金 bail bond
保释人/保釋人 bailsman
保守检验/保守檢定 conservative test
保守性偏差/保守性偏誤 conservatism bias
保守置信区间/保守信賴區間 conservative confidence interval
保水渍险/保水漬險 insurance against WPA
保税仓库交货价/保稅倉庫交貨價 in bond price
保税港/保稅港 bonded port
保税工厂/保稅工廠 bonded factory
保税货棚/保稅倉 bond shed

保税货物/保稅貨物　bonded cargo, bonded goods
保税加工/保稅加工　bonded processing
保税加工贸易/保稅加工貿易　bonded processing trade
保税库/保稅商店　bonded store
保税码头/保稅碼頭　legal quay
保税区/保稅區　bonded area, bonded zone
保税制度/保稅制度　bonded system, in bond system
保息股票/保息股票　guaranteed stock
保险/保險　insurance, assurance
保险标/保險標　insurance tender
保险标的物/保險標的物,保險對象　object of insurance
保险承诺书/保險承諾書　insurance binder
保险代理人/保險代理人　insurance agent
保险代位权/保險代位權　insurance subrogation rights
保险单/保險單　insurance policy, assurance policy
保险法/保險法　insurance law
保险费/保險費　insurance premium
保险辅助人/保險輔助人　insurance aider
保险公估人/保險公估人　insurance assessor
保险公司/保險公司　insurance company, insurance corporation, assurance company
保险合同/保險契約　insurance contract
保险给付/保險給付　insurance payment
保险给付种类/保險給付種類　kind of benefit
保险价值/保險價值　insurance value
保险经纪人/保險經紀人　insurance broker, broker for insurance
保险利益/保險利益　insurance interest
保险凭证/保險憑證,保險證書　insurance certificate
保险期间/保險期間　duration of insurance
保险期限/保險期限　period of insurance
保险人/保險人,保險者　insurer
保险商权益/保險商權益　insurer's interest
保险市场/保險市場　insurance market
保险事故/保險事故　insurance accident
保险索赔/保險索賠　insurance claim
保险索赔损失/保險索賠損失　loss on insurance claim
保险条款/保險條款　insurance clause
保险统计/保險統計　insurance statistics
保险危险/保險危險　insurance risk
保险项目表/保險專案表　schedule of insurance
保险信托/保險信託　insurance trust
保险业/保險業　insurance business

保险责任/保險責任　insured liability
保险责任起讫点/保險責任起訖點　commencement and termination of cover
保险诈骗罪/保險詐騙罪　crime of insurance fraud
保险准备金/保險準備金　insurance reserve
保修/保修　warranty
保修费用/保修成本　warranty cost
保修期/保證時期　warranty period
保序回归函数/保序回歸函數,同向回歸函數　isotonic regression function
保养管理/養護管理　maintaining management
保障措施协议/防衛措施協定　agreement on safeguards
保障性住房/保障性住房　government subsidized house
保证/保證　assurance
保证保险/保證保險　guaranty insurance
保证背书/保證背書　endorsement in security
保证储蓄银行/保證儲蓄銀行　guaranty saving bank
保证付款合同/保信契約　del credere contract
保证价格/保證價格　guaranteed price
保证金/保證金,押金　marginal deposit, cash deposit as collateral, margin
保证金存款/保證金存款　margin deposit
保证金额/保證金額　guarantee sum
保证金负债/保證金負債　margin debt
保证金交易/保證金交易　margin trade, margin trading
保证金账户/保證金賬戶　margin account
保证期/保證時期　warranty period
保证人/擔保人　surety
保证条款/保證條款　warranty clause
保证险种/保證險種　guaranteed issue
保证协定/保證協議　guarantee agreement
保证支付/保證支付　guarantee pay
保证资本/保證資本　guaranteed capital
报案/報案　report a case
报表表头/報表表頭　statement heading
报表格式/報表格式　statement form
报酬/報酬　remuneration
报酬率/報酬率　rate of return
报酬率分析/報酬率分析　rate-of-return analysis
报酬率调整/薪資率調整　pay rate adjustment
报酬区间/薪幅　pay range
报酬与波动性比率/收益對風險比率　reward-to-variability ratio
报道性文摘/資訊摘要　informative abstract
报订/報訂　subscription order

报订期／報訂期 subscription order deadline
报费／訂閱費 subscription fee
报复关税／報復關稅 retaliatory tariff
报复陷害罪／報復陷害罪 crime of carrying out retaliation and frame-ups
报复性关税／報復[性]關稅 retaliatory duty, retaliatory tax, retaliatory tariff
报告／報告 report
报告管理／報告管理 reports management
报告绩效／報告績效 performance reporting
报告期／計算期 given period
报关／報關 apply to the customs, declaration at customs
报关程序／報關程式 procedure of customs
报关代理行／報關代理人 customs agency
报关单／報關單，入港申报表 application to pass goods through the customs, bill of entry, customs declaration
报关费／報關費 customs clearing charge, customs clearance fee
报关行／報關行 custom house broker
报关结算代理商／報關行，清算代理 clearing agent
报关退税凭单／報關退税證明書 customs debenture
报夹架／報夾架 newspaper file holder
报价／報價 offer, quote, quotation
报价单／報價單 offering list
报价驱动／報價驅動 quote-driven
报价驱动市场／報價驅動市場 quotation-driven market
报价邀请书／請求報價，報價請求 request for quotation, RFQ
报架／報刊架 newspaper shelving
报刊变动手续费／報刊變動手續費 procedures fee for newspaper and periodical
报刊订单／訂用列表 periodical order, subscription list
报刊订阅费／訂閱費 subscription fee
报刊发行费／報刊發行費 distribution fee for newspaper and periodical
报刊发行费率／報刊發行費率 distribution fee rate for newspaper and periodical
报刊发行起点费／報刊發行起點費 minimal charging of postal circulation
报刊发行站／報刊發行站 distribution station of newspaper and periodical
报刊亭／報攤 kiosk
报刊邮发代号／報刊郵發代號 code of postal newspaper and periodical

报刊转运站／報刊轉運站 transfer station of newspaper and periodical
报亏单／報虧單 deficit order
报眉／報眉 newspaper eyebrow
报盘有效性／報價時效性 validity of offer
报社／報社 newspaper office
[报]实盘／最終報價 firm offer
报送审计／報送審計 documentary audit
报摊／新闻站 newsstand
报童问题／報童問題 newsboy problem, newsvendor problem
报头／報頭 masthead
报网互动／報網互動 newspaper-internet interaction
报销制度／報銷制度 reimbursement system
报眼／報眼 flag
报眼广告／報眼廣告 flag advertisement
报业电子商务／報業電子商務 newspaper e-commerce
[报业]读者俱乐部／[報業]讀者俱樂部 readers club
报业发行系统／報業發行系統 newspaper distribution system
报业广告系统／報業廣告系統 newspaper advertising system, newspaper advertising software
报业集团／報業集團 press group
报业经营管理／報業經營管理 newspaper management
[报业]客户关系管理／顧客關係管理 customer relationship management, CRM
报业新闻技术／報業新聞技術 newspaper news technology
报业转型／報業轉型 the transition of newspaper industry
报溢单／報溢單 overflow report bill
报应刑主义／報應刑主義 penalty for retribution
报账／歸墊 reimbursement
报纸／報紙 newspaper
报纸策划／報紙策劃 newspaper planning
报纸订阅／報紙訂閱 subscription
报纸二维码／報紙二維碼 newspaper two-dimensional code
报纸发行量／報紙發行量 newspaper circulation
报纸风格／報紙風格 newspaper style
报纸广告／報紙廣告 press advertising, newspaper advertising
报纸广告审查／報紙廣告審查 newspaper advertisement censor
报纸零售／報紙零售 newspaper retail
报纸零售连锁店／報紙零售連鎖店 newspaper retail

chain
报纸目录/報紙目錄　newspaper list
报纸配送发行/報紙配送發行　newspaper distribution
报纸投递/報紙投遞　newspaper delivery
报纸印刷/報紙印刷　newspaper printing
报纸专栏/報紙專欄　newspaper column
鲍克斯-詹金斯预测模型/鮑克斯-詹金斯預測模型　Box-Jenkins forecasting model
鲍利方程/Baule 方程式　Baule's equation
鲍利公式/Bowley 公式　Bowley's formula
鲍利偏度系数/Bowley 偏態係數　Bowley's coefficient of skewness
鲍利指数/Bowley 指數　Bowley index
鲍穆尔模型/Baumol 模型　Baumol model
暴力犯罪发生率/暴力犯罪發生率　violent crime rate
暴力取证罪/暴力取證罪　crime of resorting to violence to obtain testimony
暴利/暴利　windfall profits
暴利税/暴利稅　windfall profits tax
曝光时间/曝光時間　exposure time
爆发性过程/發散過程　explosive process
爆发性随机差分方程/發散隨機差分方程式　explosive stochastic difference equation
爆炸罪/爆炸罪　crime of causing explosion
背包问题/背包問題　knapsack problem
悲观估计时间/悲觀時值估計　pessimistic time estimate
悲观准则/悲觀準則　pessimistic criterion
碑帖/碑帖　rubbings from ancient tablets
碑文/碑文　lapidary inscriptions
碑文体/碑文體　lapidary style
北极/北極　Arctic
北监本/北監本　Beijing Imperial Academy edition
北美自由贸易协定/北美自由貿易協定　North American Free Trade Agreement, NAFTA
北欧学派/北歐學派　the North-European school
北齐律/北齊律　Law of the Northern Qi Dynasty
北宋监本/北宋監本　Imperial Academy edition in the Northern Song Dynasty
北魏律/北魏律　Northern Wei Law
北周律/北周律　Law of the Northern Zhou Dynasty
贝茨-奈曼模型/Bates-Neyman 模型　Bates-Neyman model
贝恩假说/班恩假說　Bain's hypothesis
贝恩垄断势力指数/班恩獨占指標　Bain index of monopoly

贝尔-道克萨姆检验/Bell-Doksum 檢定　Bell-Doksum test
贝尔曼方程/貝爾曼方程　Bellman's equation
贝尔曼-哈里斯过程/Bellman-Harris 過程　Bellman-Harris process
贝尔曼最优性原理/貝爾曼最優原則　Bellman principle of optimality
贝尔实验室/貝爾實驗室　Bell Laboratory
贝弗里奇报告/貝佛里奇報告書　Beveridge Report
贝卡利亚/貝卡利亞　Cesare Bonesana Beccaria
贝壳放逐法/貝殼放逐法,陶片放逐法　Ostracism
贝克认知治疗/貝克認知治療　Beck's cognitive therapy
贝律-艾申定理/Berry-Esseen 定理　Berry-Esseen theorem
贝律不等式/Berry 不等式　Berry's inequality
贝伦斯法/Behrens 方法　Behrens method
贝伦斯-费希尔检验/Behrens-Fisher 檢定　Behrens-Fisher test
贝伦斯-费希尔问题/Behrens-Fisher 問題　Behrens-Fisher problem
贝努利试验/伯努利試行　Bernoulli trial
贝齐埃曲线/貝齊爾曲線　Bezier curve
贝塞尔函数/Bessel 函數　Bessel function
贝塞尔校正/Bessel 校正　Bessel's correction
贝塔分布/貝他分布,貝他分配,β 分布　beta distribution
贝塔-伽马分布/貝他-伽瑪分布,貝他-伽瑪分配,β-γ 分布　beta-gamma distribution
贝塔函数/貝他函數,β 函數　beta function
贝塔-惠特尔分布/貝他-Whittle 分布,貝他-Whittle 分配　beta-Whittle distribution
贝塔矩/貝他動差,β 動差　beta moment
贝塔-斯塔西分布/貝他-Stacy 分布,貝他-Stacy 分配,β-Stacy 分布　beta-Stacy distribution
贝塔系数/貝他係數,β 係數　beta coefficient
贝塔先验分布/貝他事前分布,β 事前分布　beta prior distribution
贝叶经/貝葉經　Buddhist sutra written on pattra leaves
贝叶斯博弈/貝氏賽局　Bayesian game
贝叶斯策略/貝氏策略　Bayes strategy
贝叶斯点估计/貝氏點估計　Bayesian point estimates
贝叶斯迭代方法/貝氏演算法　Bayesian Iterative Methods
贝叶斯定理/貝氏定理,貝氏法則　Bayes theorem, Bayesian theorem

贝叶斯法/贝氏[方]法　Bayes approach, Bayes method
贝叶斯法则/贝氏法则,贝氏定律　Bayes law, Bayes rule
贝叶斯方法/贝氏[方]法　Bayes approach
贝叶斯分析[法]/贝氏分析　Bayesian analysis
贝叶斯风险/贝氏風險　Bayes risk
贝叶斯公式/贝氏公式　Bayes formula
贝叶斯估计/贝氏估计　Bayesian estimation, Bayes estimation
贝叶斯估计的相合性/贝氏估计的一致性　consistency of Bayes estimation
贝叶斯估计[量]/贝氏估计[量]　Bayes estimator
贝叶斯估计[量]的渐近效率/贝式估计量漸近效率　asymptotic efficiency of Bayes estimator
贝叶斯估计[量]的容许性/贝氏估计量的可容性　admissibility of Bayes estimator
贝叶斯估计[量]的唯一性/贝氏估计量的唯一性　uniqueness of Bayes estimator
贝叶斯估计[量]的相合性/贝氏估计量的一致性　consistency of Bayes estimator
贝叶斯规则/贝氏规则　Bayes rule
贝叶斯过程/贝氏過程　Bayes process
贝叶斯假设/贝氏假設　Bayes postulate
贝叶斯解/贝氏解　Bayes solution
贝叶斯决策/贝葉斯決策　Bayes decision making
贝叶斯决策法则/贝氏决策法則　Bayes decision rule
贝叶斯均衡/贝氏均衡　Bayesian equilibrium
贝叶斯框架/贝氏理論架構　Bayesian framework
贝叶斯理论/贝氏理論　Bayesian theory
贝叶斯模型/贝氏模型　Bayesian model
贝叶斯区间估计/贝氏區間估計　Bayesian interval estimation
贝叶斯区间估计量/贝氏區間估計量　Bayesian interval estimators
贝叶斯算法/贝氏程式　Bayesian algorithms
贝叶斯统计/贝氏統計學　Bayesian statistics
贝叶斯推断/贝氏推論　Bayesian inference
贝叶斯信息准则/贝氏訊息準則　Bayesian information criteria
贝叶斯序贯抽样/贝氏序列抽樣　Bayesian sequential sampling
贝叶斯学习/贝氏學習　Bayesian learning
贝叶斯因子/贝氏因數　Bayes factor
贝叶斯预测模型/贝氏預測模型　Bayesian forecasting model
贝叶斯置信区间/贝氏信賴區間　Bayesian confidence interval
贝叶斯主观概率分布/贝氏主觀機率分配　Bayesian subjective probability distribution
备案/備案　put on record
备查账户/備查賬戶,備忘賬戶　memorandum account
备抵附加账户/備抵附加賬戶　contra and adjunct account
备抵账户/相對賬戶　contra account
备兑凭单/收款書　covered warrant
备份/備份　backup
备货-订货分离点/顧客訂單分離點,顧客訂單分歧點　customer order decoupling point
备货库/備貨庫　storage, library storage, stockroom
备货型生产/存貨生產,備貨生產　make to stock, MTS
备件/備件　spare part
备考/備考　reference
备忘录/備忘錄　memorandum, memo
备忘录贸易/備忘錄貿易　memorandum trade
备忘账户/備忘賬戶,備查賬戶　memorandum account
备用/備用　standby
备用金/零錢　till money
备用时间/備用時間　standby time
备用系统/備便系統,待機系統　stand-by system
备用信贷/備用信貸　standby credit
备用信用证/備用信用狀　standby letter of credit
备择假设/對立假設　alternative hypothesis
背曝光/背曝光　back exposure
背衬/背托　backing
背对背贷款/背對背貸款　back-to-back loan
背对背担保/相對擔保,對等擔保　counter indemnity
背对背信用证/背對背信用證,對開信用狀,雙邊信用狀　back-to-back letter of credit
背记/背記　commentaries written on the back of the roll
背景/背景　background
背景图/背景圖　context chart
背景音乐/背景音樂　background music, BGM
背靠背排架/背靠背排架　back-to-back shelving
背面抛光/背面抛光　back side polishing
背书/背書　endorsement
背书不符/背書不符,不連續背書　endorsement irregular
背书票据/背書票據,保證票據　backed bill, endorsed bill
背书人/背書者,推薦者　endorser
背书手续费/背書手續費　endorsement commission

背书责任/背書責任　liability for endorsement
背书债券/背書債券，已抵押債券　endorsed bond, backed bond
背书转让/背書轉讓　transfer by endorsement
背信弃义行为/背信棄義行爲　perfidy
倍增过程/繁殖過程　multiplicative process
倍增时间/倍增時間　doubling time
悖论/弔詭，矛盾　paradox
被保险存款/被保險存款　insured deposit
被保险的债券/擔保債券　insured bond
被保险金额/擔保金額　amount secured
被保险人/被保險人　insured
被背书人/被背書人　endorsee
被操纵市场/被操縱市場　rigged market
被担保贷款/被擔保貸款　insured loan
被担保银行/被擔保銀行　insured bank
被盗书/被盜書　stolen book
被动服务/被動服務　passive service
被动贸易/被動貿易　passive trade
被动受托人/被動受託人　passive trustee
被动型客户驱动质量/被動式顧客導向品質模式　reactive customer-driven quality
被动性虚假信息/被動性不實訊息　passive disinformation
被动资料分析/被動資料分析　passive data analysis
被督导者/被督導者　supervisee
被抚养人口/依賴人口　dependent population
被告/被告　defendant
被告人最后陈述/被告人最後陳述　closing statement of defendants
被害人/受害者　victim
被害人陈述/被害人陳述　statements of victims
被寄养儿童/被寄養兒童　children in foster care
被解释变量/被解釋變數　explained variable, response variable
被扰动调和过程/受擾調和過程　disturbed harmonic process
被上诉人/被上訴人　appellee
被申请执行人/被申請執行人　party against whom execution is filed
被选举权/被選舉權　right to be elected
被引频次/被引頻次　cited frequency
被指导人/被指導人　protege
本币外汇买入/買入的本國貨幣外匯，買入本國貨幣匯票　home currency bill bought
本币外汇卖出/賣出的本國貨幣外匯，賣出本國貨幣匯票　home currency bill sold
本埠发行/區域分配　local distribution

本底情报/本底情報　base intelligence
本地贸易/本地貿易　local trade
本地票据/本地票據　local bill
本地数据库/原地資料庫　on-site database
本地支票/本地支票　local check
本公司/本公司　general company
本校法/本校法　collation method according to context, collate according to different parties of the same book
本金/本金　principal
本量利分析/成本-數量-利潤分析　cost-volume-profit analysis
本民族志/本民族志　auto-ethnography
本尼斯组织发展理论/班尼斯群體發展理論　Bennis group development theory
本票/本票，期票　promissory note, term bill
本身利率/本身利率　own rate of interest
本体/本體　ontology
本体构建/本體構建　ontology building
本体学习/本體學習　ontology learning
本体映射/本體映射　ontology mapping
本土化/本地化，在地化　localization
本土社会心理学/本土社會心理學　indigenous social psychology
本位货币/本位貨幣，標準通貨　standard coin
本位金属/本位金屬　standard metal
本位美元/本位美元　standard dollar
本位制/本位制　standard system
本我/本我　id
本我无差异曲线/本我無差異曲線　id-indifference curve
本息剥离/本息剝離　coupon striping
本证/本證　evidence to prove a fact
本质案例研究/内在個案研究　intrinsic case study
本质变异/實質變異　substantial variation
本质可靠性/内涵信度　intrinsic reliability
本质主义/本質論的　essentialist
本族中心主义/種族中心主義，民族中心主義　ethnocentrism
本座/本座　the seat
崩溃/崩盤　crash
绷网机/繃網機　stretching machine
逼近理想解排序法/逼近理想解排序法　technique for sequencing by approximately ideal solution
逼近论/逼近理論　approximation theory
比对试验/比較實驗　comparison experiment
比分检验/計分檢定　score test
比号/比號　sign of ratio

比荷卢国际私法条约/比荷盧國際私法條約 Treaty of Private International Law of Belgium, Holland and Luxemburg
比荷卢经济联盟/荷比盧三國 BeNeLux Economic Union
比价复归/比價復歸 parity recurrence
比较成本/比較成本 comparative cost
比较成本理论/比較成本理論 theory of comparative cost
比较档案学/比較檔案學 compative archival science
比较动态分析/比較動態 comparative dynamics
比较法学/比較法學 science of comparative law
比较公共政策/比較公共政策 comparative public policy
比较管理理论/比較管理理論 comparative management theory
比较国际私法学/比較國際私法學 comparative private international law
比较国际私法学派/比較國際私法學派 Comparative Private International Law School
比较过失/比較過失 comparative negligence
比较环境法/比較環境法 comparative environmental law
比较基线/比較基底 comparison base
比较检验/比較檢驗法 comparison test
比较静态分析/比較静態均衡分析 comparative static analysis
比较静态学/比較静態分析 comparative statics
比较劣势/比較劣勢 comparative disadvantage
比较路径/比較途徑 comparative approach
比较目录学/比較目錄學 comparative bibliography
比较评估法/比較評估法 comparative appraisal method
比较情报学/比較資訊科學 comparative information science
比较试验/比較實驗 comparison experiment
比较死亡率数据/比較死亡率值 comparative mortality figure
比较死亡率指数/比較死亡率指數 comparative mortality index
比较图书馆学/比較圖書館學 comparative librarianship
比较新闻学/比較新聞學 comparative journalism
比较刑法学/比較刑法學 science of comparative criminal law
比较型广告/比較性廣告 comparative advertising
比较研究/比較研究 comparative research
比较优势/比較利益 comparative advantage
比较优势法则/比較利益法則 law of comparative advantage
比较优势论/比較利益理論 theory of comparative advantage
比克-霍奇斯估计[量]/Bickel-Hodges 估計量 Bickel-Hodges estimator
比利时的科学管理/比利時的科學管理 scientific management of Belgium
比例抽样/比例抽樣 proportional sampling
比例代表制/比例代表制 proportional representation
比例分布/比例分布 distribution of proportion
比例风险模型/比例危險模型,比例轉機模型 proportional hazards model
比例符号/比例符號 sign of proportion
比例加权法/比例加權法 proportional weight method
比例均值/比例平均數 proportional mean
比例配置/比例配置 proportional allocation
比例税/比例稅 proportional tax, proportional taxation
比例税率/比例稅率 proportional tax rate
比例死亡率/比例死亡率 proportionate mortality
比例样本/比例樣本 proportional sample
比例原则/比例原則 principle of proportionality
比[率]/比[率] ratio
ρ 比率/ρ 比率 ρ-ratio, rho ratio
t 比[率]分布/t 比率分布 t-ratio distribution
比[率]估计量/比率估計量 ratio estimator
比[率]检验/比例檢定 ratio test
比[率]图/比率圖 ratio diagram, ratio chart
比率延期法/比率延期法 ratio delay method
比奈-西蒙量表/比西[智力]量表 Binet-Simon scale
比特/位元 bit
比欣格分布/Bissinger 分布,Bissinger 分配 Bissinger distribution
彼得斯管理思想/彼得斯管理思想 management thought of Peters
彼得原理/彼得原理 Peter principle
笔记/筆記 notes
笔迹分析法/筆跡分析法 graphology
笔迹考订/筆跡考訂 handwriting criticism
笔录/筆錄 notes, record, transcript
笔名/筆名 pseudonym, pen name
币值稳定/幣值穩定,通貨穩定 stability in value of money, currency stabilization
币值稳定贷款/通貨穩定貸款 currency stabilization loan
币制改革/幣制改革,通貨改革 currency reform,

monetary reform
必备服务/必備服務　mandatory service
必备树/必備樹　prerequisite tree, PRT
必备要素/必備要素　required element
必达要求/必要要求　exclusive requirement
必读书目/必讀書目　standard book catalog
必然事件/必然事件　sure event, certain event
必然性/必然性　certainty
必然性等价/必然性對等　certainty equivalence
必然因果关系/必然因果關係　positive causality
必要的共同诉讼/必要的共同訴訟　necessary co-litigation
必要功能/必要功能　required function
必要共同犯罪/必要共同犯罪　indispensable joint crime
必要劳动/必要勞動　necessary labor
必要劳动时间/必要勞動時間　necessary labor-time
必要条件/必要條件　requirement
必要性/必要性　necessities
必要性原则/必要性原則　principle of necessity
毕业生税/畢業稅　graduate tax
闭包/闭集　closure
闭海或半闭海/閉海或半閉海　enclosed or semi-enclosed seas
闭合式/封閉形式　closed form
闭合式书目/閉合式書目　closed bibliography
闭环控制/封閉循環控制　closed loop control
闭架馆藏/閉架式館藏　closed-access collection
闭架售书/閉架售書　closed-shelf book selling
闭架书库/閉架書庫　closed-shelf stack
闭架图书馆/閉架式圖書館　closed-access library
闭架制/閉架式　closed-shelf system
闭口保险单/封閉型保險單　closed policy
闭锁群体/封閉性人口　closed population
庇古税/皮古稅　Pigou tax, pigouvian tax
庇古效应/皮古效應　Pigou effect
庇护/庇護　asylum
壁式书架排列法/壁式書架排列法　wall shelving
避讳/避諱　taboo tystem
避讳考订/避諱考訂　taboo criticism
避免双重课税协定/避免雙重課稅協定　double taxation avoidance agreement
避免通货膨胀损失的保值措施/避險以對抗通膨　hedge against inflation
避难港/避難港　port of refuge
避税/避稅　avoidance of taxation, tax avoidance
避税公司/避稅公司　tax avoidance corporation
边际报酬递减规律/邊際報酬遞減法則　law of diminishing marginal returns
边际产量/邊際产量　marginal product
边际产量曲线/邊際产量曲線　marginal product curve
边际产品/邊際产量　marginal product
边际产品价值/邊際產值　value of marginal product
边际成本/邊際成本,增支成本　marginal cost, incremental cost
边际成本定价/邊際成本定價　marginal cost pricing
边际出口倾向/邊際出口傾向　marginal propensity to export
边际储蓄倾向/邊際儲蓄傾向　marginal propensity to save
边际定价/邊際定價　marginal pricing
边际分析/邊際分析　marginal analysis
边际革命/邊際革命　marginal revolution, marginalist revolution
边际贡献/邊際貢獻　contribution margin
边际贡献率/邊際貢獻率　contribution margin ratio, CM ratio
边际化/邊際化　marginalization
边际机会成本递增/邊際機會成本遞增　increasing marginal opportunity cost
边际技术替代率/邊際技術替代率　marginal rate of technical substitution
边际技术替代率递减/邊際技術替代率遞減　diminishing marginal rate of technical substitution
边际技术替代率递减规律/邊際替代率遞減法則,邊際技術替代率遞減法則　law of diminishing marginal rate of technical substitution
边际减排成本/邊際防治成本,減少排放之邊際成本　marginal abatement cost, marginal emission reduction cost
边际进口倾向/邊際進口傾向,邊際輸入傾向　marginal propensity to import
边际理性/邊際理性　marginal rationality
边际利率/邊際利率　marginal rate of interest
边际贸易条件/邊際貿易條件　marginal term of trade
边际平衡预算/邊際平衡預算　marginally balanced budget
边际生产力/邊際生產力　marginal productivity
边际生产力递减/邊際生產力遞減　diminishing marginal productivity
边际生产力递减规律/邊際生產遞減律　law of diminishing marginal productivity
边际生产力分配理论/邊際生產力所得分配理論　marginal productivity theory of income distribution

边际生产力工资理论/邊際生產力工資理論　marginal productivity theory of wage
边际生产力理论/邊際生產力理論　marginal productivity theory
边际收益/邊際收益,邊際利得　marginal gain, marginal revenue
边际收益产品/邊際生產收益　marginal revenue product
边际收益递减/邊際報酬遞減　diminishing marginal returns
边际税率/邊際税率　marginal rate of tax, marginal tax rate
边际私人成本/邊際私人成本　marginal private costs
边际私人收益/私人邊際利益　private marginal benefit
边际替代率/邊際替代率　marginal rate of substitution
边际投资倾向/邊際投資傾向　marginal propensity to invest
边际外部成本/邊際外部成本　marginal external cost, marginal externality cost
边际外部效益/邊際外部利益　marginal external benefit
边际消费倾向/邊際消費傾向　marginal propensity to consume
边际效益/邊際效益　marginal benefit
边际效应/邊際影響　marginal effect
边际效用/邊際效用　marginal utility
边际效用递减规律/邊際效用遞減法則　law of diminishing marginal utility
边际效用学派/邊際效用學派　marginal utility school
边际要素成本/邊際要素成本　marginal factor cost
边际支出曲线/邊際支出曲綫　manginal expenditure curve
边际转换率/邊際轉換率　marginal rate of transformation
边疆经济/拓荒經濟　frontier economy
边界/邊界　frontier, boundary
边界生产函数/邊界生產函數　frontier production function
边界条件/邊界條件　boundary condition
边境关税/邊境關税　frontier customs due
边境交货价/邊境交貨價　franco border
边境经济/拓荒經濟　frontier economy
边境贸易/邊境貿易　border trade, frontier trade
边境税收调整/邊境税收調整　border tax adjustment
边境制度/邊境制度　frontier regime
边沁福利函数/邊沁福利函數　Benthamite welfare function
边缘发毛/毛邊　untrimmed
边缘分布/邊際分布,邊際分配　marginal distribution
边缘分类/邊際分類　marginal classification
边缘概率/邊際機率　marginal probability
边缘概率分布/邊際機率分布　marginal probability distribution
边缘概率密度/邊際機率密度　marginal probability density
边缘类别/邊際類別　marginal category
边缘密度/邊際密度　marginal density
边缘密度函数/邊際密度函數　marginal density function
边缘模型/邊緣模型　marginal model
边缘群体/邊緣群體　marginal population
边缘时段/邊緣時段　fringe time
边注/邊注　notes located in the left of a page
PostScript编程语言/PostScript語言　postscript
编档/檔案編排　filing files layout
编发合一/編發合一　integration of editing and distribution
编稿/編稿　compile article
编号/編號,編碼　numbering
编号丛书/編號叢書　numbered series
编后记/編後記　afterword
编辑/編輯　①edit, ②editor
编辑部/編輯部　editorial department
编辑点/剪輯點　edit point
编辑方针/編輯方針　editorial policy
编辑加工/編輯　edit
编辑说明/編輯説明　notes on the use of a compilation
编辑委员会/編輯委員會,編委會　editorial board
编辑学/編輯學　editology
编码/編碼,製碼　encode, coding
编码单位/編碼單位　coded unit
编码单元/編碼單位　coded unit
编码规则/編碼規則　coding rule
编码化策略/編碼化策略　codification tactic
编码手册/編碼簿　codebook
编码值/編碼值　coded value
编码字段/編碼字段　code field
编目/編目　cataloging
编目机构/編目機構　cataloging agency

编目条例／编目规则　cataloging rules
编目员／编目人，编目者　cataloger
编目原则／編目原則　cataloging principles
编年的／編年的　chronological
编年史／編年史　chronicle
编年摘要／編年摘要　chronology abstract
编前会／編前會　the meeting before editing
编审／編審　senior editor
编外人员／編外人員　supernumerary post
编委／編委　editorial board member
编委会／編委會，编辑委員會　editorial board
编写／編寫　compilation and composition
编选／編選　compile and select
编页号／編頁碼　pagination, number the page
编译／編譯　compile and translate
编译委员会／編譯委員會　compilation and translation committee
编造并传播证券、期货交易虚假信息罪／編造并傳播證券、期貨交易虚假資訊罪　crime of fabricating and spreading false information on securities or futures exchange
编造、故意传播虚假恐怖信息罪／編造、故意傳播虚假恐怖資訊罪　crime of fabricating and intently spreading false terrorism information
[编]张号／張號　foliation, folio
编者／編者　editor
编者按／編者按　editor's note
编者按语／編者按語　words of editor
编制／編製　staff quota
编著／編著　authoring, compilation
编著系统／編輯系統　authoring system
编纂／編纂　compile, compilation
编纂大纲／編纂大綱　compilation outline
贬值／折舊　depreciation
贬值率／貶值率，折舊率　ratio of depreciation, rate of depreciation
贬值美元／貶值美元　cheap dollar
扁平化组织／扁平式組織　flat organization
扁平结构／扁平結構　flat structure
扁体字／寬體字　expanded letter
变槽距纹槽／變槽距紋槽　variable groove pitch
变槽深纹槽／變槽深紋槽　variable groove depth
变点模型／轉折點模型　change point model
变动参数模型／變動參數模型　varying parameter model
变动成本／變動成本　variable cost
变动成本法／變動成本法　variable costing
变动成本率／變動成本率　variable expense ratio
变动基期／移位基期　shifting base period
变动价格合同／波動價格合約　fluctuating price contract
变动流程分析／變動流程分析　variation flow analysis
变动率／變動率　rate of change
变革管理／變革管理　change management
变革推动者／變革推動者　change agent
变革型领导者／轉換型領導者　transformational leader
变革型战略实施／改良型策略執行　reform-type strategy implementation
变革阻力／變革阻力　resistance to change
变更／變更　change
变更订单／變更訂單　change order
变更控诉／變更控訴　amendment of charges
变更控制／異動管制　change control
变更控制委员会／變更控制委員會　change control board, CCB
变更判决／變更判決　judgment to change existing legal relationship
变更批准／變更批準　change approval
变更申请／變更請求　change request
变更审核／變更審核　change audit
变更卸货港／變更目的港　change of destination
变更之诉／變更之訴　action to change existing legal relationship
变幻型购买行为／尋求變化的購買行爲　variety-seeking buying behavior
变换／變換，轉換　transformations
z变换／z變換　z-transformation
变换的转移群／變換的遞移群　transitive group of transformations
变换分析／變換分析　transformation analysis
变截距面板数据模型／變截距面板資料模型　variable intercept panel data model
变栏／變欄　changed column
变量／變量，變數　variable
变量变换／變量變換，變數變換　transformation of variables
变量差分法／變量差分法　variate difference method
变量差分相关／變量差分相關　variate difference correlation
变量数列／變量數列　series of variates
变量误差／變量誤差，變數誤差　variable error, errors in variables
变量序列／變量數列　series of variates
变量选择／變數選擇　variable selection

变迁/變遷　change
变式/變式　variant
变态人格/變態人格　abnormal personality
变态心理/變態心理　abnormal psychology
变系数面板数据模型/變係數面板資料模型　variable coefficient panel data model
变现和清偿表/變現和清償表　statement of realization and liquidation
变相贸易壁垒/變相貿易壁壘,隱蔽貿易壁壘　cover trade barrier
变形动画/變形動畫　morph animation
变形球建模/變形球建模　meta modeling
变异/變異,變動　variation
变异曲线/變異曲線　scedastic curve
变异题名/變異題名　variant title
变异稳定化相关法/變異穩定性相關法　variation stabilization correlation method
变异系数/變異係數,差異係數　coefficient of variation, variation coefficient, CV
变异形态/變異型態　pattern of variation
变异性/變異性　variability
便笺/便箋　scratch pad
便利店/便利商店　convenience store
便利品/便利品,便利財　convenience goods, convenience product
便利性/便利性　accessibility and convenience
遍历的/遍歷的　ergodic
遍历定理/遍歷定理　ergodic theorem
遍历理论/遍歷理論　ergodic theory
遍历[性]/遍歷[性]　ergodicity
遍历原理/遍歷原則　ergodic principle
遍历状态/遍歷狀態　ergodic state
辨本/辨本　edition evaluation
辨别效度/辨別效度,區別效度,區辨效度　discriminant validity
辨认/識別　identification
辨伪/辨偽　distinguish the false book
辩护/辯護　defence
辩护词/辯護詞　statements of defence
辩护律师/辯護律師　defense attorney
辩护律师调查取证/辯護律師調查取證　defense counsel's investigation
辩护律师会见通信权/辯護律師會見通信權　defense counsel's right to interview and correspondence
辩护律师阅卷/辯護律師閱卷　defense counsel's access to the case files
辩护权/辯護權　right to defense
辩护人/辯護人　defender
辩护证据/辯護證據　defensive evidence
辩护职能/辯護職能　function of defence
辩护制度/辯護制度　defense system
辩诉交易/辯訴交易,認罪協商　plea bargaining
标称零值/標稱零值　nominal zero
标尺竞争/尺碼競爭　yardstick competition
标底/標底　targeted object
标的/標的　object
标的精密度/標的精度　aimed precision
标的资产/標的物資產　underlying assets
标杆管理/標竿管理　benchmarking
标购/投標採購　buying tender
标记处理/標記處理　method of dealing with marks
标记制度/標記制度　marking system
标价/標價　labeled price
标目/標頭　heading
标盘/標盤　bidding quotation
标签/標簽,標記　label, tagging
标签保险/標簽保險　label insurance
标签抽样/標簽抽樣　ticket sampling
标签理论/標簽理論　labeling theory
标签式题名/標簽式題名　label title
标签云/標簽雲,標記雲　tag cloud
标识/標識　marker
标识变量/標識變數　marker variable
标识符错误检测码/識別符錯誤檢測碼　ID error detection code
标识符号/標識符號　identifier
标识号附注/標識號附注　notes pertaining to identification number
标示因素/標示因素　marking factor
标题/標題　title, headline, caption
标题表/標題表　subject heading scheme
标题词/標題[詞],主題標目　subject heading
标题[词]法/標題法　subject heading method
标引/標引　indexing, indexing
标引词/標引詞　indexing term
标引词专指性/標引詞專一性,索引詞專指性　specificity of index term
标引对象/標引對象　object of indexing
标引方式/標引方式　pattern of indexing
标引服务/索引服務　indexing service
标引规则/標引規則　indexing rule
标引理论/索引理論　indexing theory
标引频率/標引頻率　indexing frequency of terms
标引深度/標引深度　exhaustivity
标引系统/索引系統　indexing system

标引一致性/標引一致性　consistency of indexing
标引语言/索引語言　indexing language
标引原则/索引原則　principles of indexing
标针图/標針圖　pin chart
标注/標記　tagging
标注原则/標注原則　priciple of annotation
标准/標準　standard
标准案卷分类方案/標準檔案分類計劃　standardized filing plan
标准编号及有关记载项/標準編號及有關記載項　standard number and related record item
标准编号与获得方式项/標準編號與獲得方式項　standard number and terms of availability area
标准不合格率/標準不良率　standard fraction defective
标准参照/效標參照　criterion-referenced
标准残差/標準化殘差值　standardized residuals
标准差/標準差　standard deviation
标准差单位/標準差單位　sigma unit
标准成本/標準成本　standard cost
标准成本法/標準成本法　standard costing
标准成色黄金/標準成色黃金　standard gold
标准档案/標準檔案　archival standards
标准动作时间/標準單元時間　standard element time
标准度量/標準量測　standard measure
标准方程/標準方程式　standard equation
标准附录/規範性附錄　normative annex
标准复分/標準複分　standard subdivision
标准杆/平價　par
标准工资率/標準工資率　standard wage rate
标准工作时间/標準工時制　standard hour plan
标准工作条件/標準狀況,標準條件　standard operation condition
标准规范/標準規格　normal specification
标准行业分类法/產業標準分類　standard industrial classification
标准号/標準號　standard number
标准合同/合約範本　model contract
标准化/標準化[程式]　standardization, normalization
标准化变量/標準化變量,標準化變數　standardized variable, standardized variate
标准化残差矩阵/標準化殘差矩陣　standardized residual matrix
标准化出生率/標準化出生率　standardized birth rate
标准化管理/標準化管理　standardization management
标准化合约/標準化契約　standard-form contract
标准[化]回归系数/標準化回歸係數　standardized regression coefficient
标准化结婚率/標準化結婚率　standardized marriage rate
标准化离差/標準化離差　standardized deviate
标准化离婚率/標準化離婚率　standardized divorce rate
标准化-实施-研究-改进模式/標準化-實施-研究-改進模式　standardized-do-study-ameliorate mode, SDSA mode
标准化手册/標準手冊　standards manual
标准化水平/標準化水準　level of standardization
标准化死亡率/標準化死亡率　standardized mortality rate, standardized death rate, standard mortality rate
标准[化]随机变量/標準化隨機變數,正規化隨機變數　standardized random variable
标准化随机样本/標準化隨機樣本　standardized random sample
标准化条例/標準化條例　regulations for standardization
标准化营销组合/標準化行銷組合　standardized marketing mix
标准化原则/標準化原則　standardization principle
标准化值/標準化值　standardized value
标准化指数/標準化指數　standardized index
标准货币/標準貨幣,本位貨幣　standard money
标准货币单位/標準貨幣單位　standard monetary unit
标准货币制度/標準貨幣制度　standard coinage
标准级别/標準級別　level of standard
标准记分/標準計分　standard score
标准绩效/標準績效　standard performance
标准检索/標準檢索　standard retrieval
标准进度/正常步調　normal pace
标准竞争/標準競爭　standard competition
标准会计实务公报/標準會計實務公報　Statement of Standard Accounting Practice
标准拉丁方/標準拉丁方陣　standard Latin square
标准利率/標準利率　standard interest rate
标准率/標準比率　standard fraction
标准贸易模型/標準貿易模型　standard trade model
标准目录/標準目錄　standards catalogue
标准年报/標準年報　annual report of standards
标准评定量表[法]/標準評定量表　standard rating scale

标准普尔/標準普爾　standard and poor
标准普尔股价指数/標準普爾股價指數　Standard and Poor's Stock Price Index
标准普尔综合指数/標準普爾綜合指數　Standard and Poor's Composite Index
标准期/基［準］期　typical period
标准曲线/標準曲線　standard curve
标准容器/標準容器　standard container
标准时间数据/標準時間數據　standard time data
标准式博弈/標準形式賽局　normal-form games
标准书号/標準書號　standard book number, SBN
标准输出/標準輸出,標準產出　standard output
标准水平/標準水準　standard level
标准提单/標準格式提單　standard bill of lading
标准体系/標準系統　standard system
标准条款/標準條款　standard clause
标准通报/標準通報　notification for standards
标准图书馆/標準圖書館　standard library
标准文献/標準文獻　standard document
标准无保留意见/標準意見　standard unmodified opinion
标准误差/標準誤［差］　standard error, standard errors
标准箱/二十呎貨櫃　twenty-feet equivalent unit
标准信用证格式/標準信用證格式　standard credit form
标准样品/標準樣品　standard sample
标准银块/標準銀塊　standard bullion
标准银元/標準銀元　standard silver dollar
标准引用次序/標準引用次序　standard citation order
标准元数据格式/標準元數據格式　standard metadata format
标准战略/標準策略　standard strategy
标准正态变量/標準常態變數　standard normal variables
标准正态分布/標準常態分配,標準常態分布　standard normal distribution
标准正态概率密度函数/標準常態機率密度函數　standard normal probability density function
标准正态离差/標準常態離差　standard normal deviate
标准正态曲线/標準常態曲線　standard normal curve
标准正态随机变量/標準常態隨機變數　standard normal random variables
标准仲裁条款/標準仲裁條款　standard arbitration clause
标准周期市场/標準週期市場　standard-cycle market
标准主题表/標準主題表　subject authority list
标准总体/標準母體　standard population
标准组合/正準組體　canonical ensemble
表达/表達　expression
表达技巧/表達技巧　presentation technique
表达权/表達權　right to express
表达自由/表達自由,表意自由,言論自由　freedom of expression
表格/表格　form
表格管理/表格管理　forms management
表见代理/表見代理　agency by estoppel
表［列］式/表列式　tabular form
表列制度/製表方法　tabulation system
表面磁感应/表面磁感應　surface magnetic induction
表面效度/表面效度　face validity
表面噪声/表面雜音　surface noise
表面整饰/表面整飾　decorative finishing
表面装饰/表面裝飾　surface decoration
表内业务/表內業務　on-balance sheet business
表谱/表譜　table spectrum
表示主义/表示主義　Doctrine of Declaration
表式调查/表式調查　tabular investigation
表态用语/表態用語　statement term
表外业务/表外業務,賬外交易活動　off-balance sheet business
表现蒙太奇/表現蒙太奇　expressive montage
表现主义/表現主義　expressionism
表演/表演　performance
表演合同/表演契約　performance contract
表演理论/表演理論　performance theory
表演权/表演權　right of performance
表演者/表演者　performer
表演者权/表演者權利　performer right
表意性角色/敘情角色　expressive role
表征/表意,意指　signifying
别裁/别裁　analytic cataloging
别除权/别除權　exemption right
别集/别集　collection of one writer's works, individual collection
别辑/别輯　affiliated album
别籍异财/别籍異財　a separate portal, differentiation property
别录/别錄　bielu
别名/别名,假名　alias
别名索引/别名索引　nickname index
殡葬管理服务/殯葬管理服務　funeral management

and service
膑刑/臏刑　Bin punishment
兵役制度/兵役制度　military service
饼图/圓瓣圖　pie diagram
禀赋/資源禀賦　endowment
禀赋效应/禀賦效果　endowment effect
并表监管/合并監管　consolidated supervision
并发检索/并發檢索　simultaneous search
并发用户数/同時上線人數　number of concurrent users
并发指数/并發指數　coincidence index
并购/并購，購并　merger and acquisition, M and A
并购指南/結合指導原則　merger guidelines
并联冗余/并聯複聯　parallel redundancy
并联系统/并聯系統　parallel system
并列版本说明/并列版本說明　parallel edition statement
并列丛书名/并列叢書名　parallel title of series
并列题名/并列題名　parallel title
并列题名项/并列題名項　parallel title item
并列正题名/并列正題名　parallel title proper
并行工程/同步工程　concurrent engineering
并行检索/并行檢索　parallel retrieval, parallel search
并行排架法/并行排架法　parallel arrangement
并行式产品设计方法/同步式產品設計　concurrent product design method
并行与交叉研发组织/并行與交叉研發組織　parallel and intersectant research and development organization
病案档案/病案檔案　medical record archives
病毒式营销/病毒行銷　viral marketing
病假/病假　sick leave
病理性老化/病理性老化　pathological aging
病人角色/病人角色，生病角色　patient role, sick role
波动/波動　fluctuation
波动汇率/波動匯率　fluctuating exchange rate
波动汇率制/波動匯率制　fluctuating exchange rate system
波动率聚类/波動率聚類　volatility clustering
波动率微笑/波動率微笑　volatility smile
波动性/波動[性]，波動率　volatility
波动性风险/波動性風險　volatility risk
波动因子系[统]/波動子系統　system of oscillators
波尔特凯维兹公式/Bortkiewicz 公式　Bortkiewicz formula
波谷/波谷　trough
波拉泽克公式/Pollaczek 公式　Pollaczek's formula
波拉泽克-金特岑公式/Pollaczek-Khintchine 公式　Pollaczek-Khintchine formula
波拉泽克-斯皮策恒等式/Pollaczek-Spitzer 恆等式　Pollaczek-Spitzer identity
波利亚定理/Pólya 定理　Pólya's theorem
波利亚分布/Pólya 分布，Pólya 分配　Pólya distribution
波利兹-西谬斯技术/Politz 和 Simmons 技巧　Politz and Simmons technique
波普尔"三个世界"理论/波普爾"三個世界"理論　Popper's "Three Worlds" Theory
波士顿矩阵/波士頓諮詢集團矩陣　Boston matrix
波特霍夫检验/Potthoff 檢定　Potthoff's test
波特-劳勒期望激励理论/波特-勞勒期望激勵理論　Porter-Lawler's theory of expectancy
波特五力分析/波特五力分析　Porter's Five Forces Analysis
玻尔象限/波爾象限　Bohr's quadrant
玻耳兹曼常数/Boltzman 常數　Boltzman's constant
玻璃动画/玻璃動畫　paint-on-glass animation
玻璃式经营/玻璃式經營　glass type management
玻璃天花板/玻璃天花板，無形障礙　glass ceiling
剥夺/剝奪　deprivation
剥夺勋章、奖章和荣誉称号/剝奪勳章、獎章和榮譽稱號　deprivation of medals, decoration and honorary title
剥夺政治权利/剝奪政治權利　deprivation of political right
剥离/剝離　divestiture
播放器/播放機　player
播音员/播報員　announcer
伯恩鲍姆不等式/Birnbaum 不等式　Birnbaum's inequality
伯恩鲍姆-霍尔检验/Birnbaum-Hall 檢定　Birnbaum-Hall test
伯恩鲍姆-雷蒙德-朱克曼不等式/Birnbaum-Raymond-Zuckerman 不等式　Birnbaum-Raymond-Zuckerman inequality
伯恩鲍姆-索德斯分布/Birnbaum-Saunders 分布，Birnbaum-Saunders 分配　Birnbaum-Saunders distribution
伯恩鲍姆-廷吉分布/Birnbaum-Tingey 分布，BirnbaumTingey 分配　Birnbaum-Tingey distribution
伯恩斯坦不等式/Bernstein 不等式　Bernstein inequality
伯恩斯坦定理/Bernstein 定理　Bernstein theorem

伯尔曼/伯爾曼　Harold J. Berman
伯尔尼同盟/伯恩聯盟　Berne Union
伯克定理/Burke 定理　Burke's theorem
伯克霍尔德逼近/Burkholder 逼近　Burkholder approximation
伯克森线/Berkson 線　Berksonian line
伯力斯引理/Blyth 引理　Blyth's lemma
伯利-米恩斯假说/伯利-米恩斯假説　Berle-Means hypothesis
伯明翰学派/伯明罕學派　Birmingham school
伯努利变异/柏努利變異　Bernoulli variation
伯努利大数定律/柏努利大數法則　Bernoulli law of large numbers
伯努利定理/柏努利定理　Bernoulli theorem
伯努利多项式/柏努利多項式　Bernoulli polynomial
伯努利过程/柏努利過程　Bernoulli process
伯努利级数/柏努利級數　Bernoulli series
伯努利试验/柏努利試驗　Bernoulli trials
伯努利数/柏努利數　Bernoulli numbers
伯奇不等式/Berge 不等式　Berge's inequality
伯特兰德悖论/柏氏矛盾　Bertrand paradox
伯特兰德价格博弈/柏氏價格賽局　Bertrand price game
伯特兰德竞争/柏氏競爭　Bertrand competition
伯特兰德均衡/柏氏均衡　Bertrand equilibrium
伯特兰德模型/伯氏模型　Bertrand model
伯特兰德-纳什均衡/柏氏-奈許均衡　Bertrand-nash equilibrium
伯特兰德行为/柏氏行爲　Bertrand behavior
驳船交货条件/駁船交貨條件　ex lighter terms
驳船上结关/駁船上結關　customs clearance of cargo aboard barge
驳回起诉/駁回起訴　dismiss a suit, dismiss an action
帛书/帛書　silk manuscripts, silk scrolls
泊松变异/卜瓦松變異　Poisson variation
泊松参数/卜瓦松參數　Poisson parameter
泊松大数定律/卜瓦松大數法則　Poisson's law of large numbers
泊松二项分布/卜瓦松二項分布,卜瓦松二項分配　Poisson binomial distribution
泊松分布/卜瓦松分布,卜瓦松分配　Poisson distribution
泊松概率纸/卜瓦松機率紙　Poisson probability paper
泊松过程/卜瓦松過程　Poisson processes
泊松回归/泊松回歸　Poisson regression
泊松截尾正态分布/卜瓦松截略常態分布,卜瓦松截略常態分配　Poisson truncated normal distribution
泊松近似/卜瓦松近似　Poisson's approximation
泊松聚集过程/卜瓦松叢聚過程　Poisson clustering process
泊松-莱克塞斯分布/Poisson-Lexis 分布,Poisson-Lexis 分配　Poisson-Lexis distribution
泊松离散指数/卜瓦松離勢指數　Poisson index of dispersion
泊松-马尔可夫过程/卜瓦松-馬可夫過程　Poisson-Markov process
泊松面板数据回归/卜瓦松經緯資料回歸　poisson panel data regression
泊松模型/泊松模型　Poisson model
泊松-帕斯卡分布/Poisson-Pascal 分布,Poisson-Pascal 分配　Poisson-Pascal distribution
泊松随机样本/卜瓦松隨機變數　poisson random sample
泊松正态变换/卜瓦松常態變換　Poisson normalizing transformation
泊松正态分布/卜瓦松-常態分布,卜瓦松-常態分配　Poisson-normal distribution
泊松指数分布/卜瓦松指數分布,卜瓦松指數分配　Poisson exponential distribution
柏格森-萨缪尔森社会福利函数/柏格森-薩穆森社會福利函數　Berson-Samuelson social welfare function
柏拉图/柏拉圖　Plato
勃艮第罗马法典/勃艮第羅馬法典　Lex Romana Burgundionum
博彩/賭博,投機　gambling
博丹/博丹　Jean Bodin
博登海默/博登海默　Edgar Bodenheimer
博尔韦尔主义/包華主義　Boulwarism
博基斯近似/Borges 逼近　Borges' approximation
博克纳定理/Bochner 定理　Bochner's theorem
博克三分量模型/Bock 三成分模型　Bock's three component model
博克斯检验/Box 檢定　Box's test
博克斯-考克斯变换/博克斯-卡克斯轉換,Box-Cox 變換　Box-Cox transformation
博克斯-考克斯检验/博克斯-卡克斯檢定　Box-Cox test
博克斯-詹金斯方法/卜-金法　Box-Jenkins method
博克斯-詹金斯模型/博克斯-間肯斯模型,Box-Jenkins 模型　Box-Jenkins model
博客/博客,部落格,網誌　blog
博客出版/部落格出版　blog publishing
博雷尔大数定律/Borel 大數法則　Borel law of large

numbers
博雷尔集/博雷爾集合　Borel set
博雷尔-康特立引理/Borel-Cantelli 引理　Borel-Cantelli lemma
博雷尔-坦纳分布/Borel-Tanner 分布,Borel-Tanner 分配　Borel-Tanner distribution
博雷尔域/Borel 域　Borel field
博雷尔族/Borel 族　Borel family
博士学位论文/博士論文　PhD dissertation, doctoral dissertation, Doctor's dissertation
博斯-爱因斯坦分布/Bose-Einstein 分布,Bose-Einstein 分配　Bose-Einstein distribution
博斯-爱因斯坦统计量/Bose-Einstein 統計量　Bose-Einstein statistics
博斯分布/Bose 分布,Bose 分配　Bose distribution
博弈/賽局,對局　game
博弈的扩展形式/博弈的擴展形式　extensive form of game
博弈分析法/博弈分析法　game playing analyse
博弈矩阵/賽局矩陣　game matrix
博弈扩展型/擴展型賽局　extensive form of a game
博弈论/賽局[理]論　game theory, theory of game
博弈树/賽局樹　game tree
博弈值/賽局值　value of a game
博主/部落客　blogger
跛行本位制/跛行本位制　limping standard
跛行婚姻/跛行婚姻　limping marriage
跛行金本位制/跛行金本位制　limping gold standard system
补白/補白　filler
补编/補編,增刊　supplement, the supplementary compilation
补偿/補償　compensation
补偿变量/補償變量　compensation variation
补偿波动/補償波動　compensating fluctuation
补偿策略/補償式策略　compensatory strategy
补偿关税/補償關稅,抵制關稅　compensation duty
补偿交易/補償交易　compensation deal
补偿教育/補救教育　compensatory education
补偿金/補償金　compensation money
补偿贸易/補償貿易,相對貿易　compensation trade, countertrade
补偿贸易合同/補償貿易合約　compensating deal contract
补偿贸易审计/補償貿易審計　audit of compensation trade
补偿赔款/賠補償金　compensation award
补偿曲线/補償曲線　compensation curve
补偿误差/補償誤差　compensating error
补偿性法律/補償性法律　restorative law
补偿性工资差别/補償性工資差異　compensating wage differentials
补偿性进口/補償性進口　compensation import
补偿性倾销/獎勵金傾銷　bounty dumping
补偿性余额/補償性存款,回存餘額　compensating balances
补偿需求/補償性需求　compensated demand
补偿需求函数/受補償需求函數　compensated-demand function
补偿需求曲线/補償性需求曲線　compensated demand curve
补偿原则/補償原則　compensation principle
补偿值/平衡值　equalizing value
补充保障/補充保障　supplemental security
补充标引/補充標引　added indexing
补充定额/補充定額　complementary quota
补充服务/補助性服務　complementary service
补充鉴定/補充鑒定　supplementary expertise
补充目录/補充目錄　supplement catalog
补充判决/補充判決　supplementary judgement
补充平衡/補充平衡　supplemented balance
补充性失业福利/協助失業的津貼,補助性失業福利　supplemental unemployment benefit
补充性特别存款制度/補充性特別存放央行　corset, supplementary special deposits
补充性原则/補充性原則　principle of complementarity
补充养老保险/附加年金,補充退休金　supplementary pension, supplementary pension insurance
补充要素/補充要素　supplementary element
补充侦查/補充偵查　supplementary investigation
补订/補訂　supplement subscription
补概率/餘機率　complementary probability
补货/庫存補充　inventory replenishment
补货提前期/補貨前置期　replenishment lead time
补货周期/補給週期　replenishment period
补间动画/補間動畫　tween
补救/救濟方式　remedy
补救维护/補救性維修　remedial maintenance
补漏白/疊印　trapping
补拟题名/補擬題名　supplied title
补强证据/補強證據　corroborative evidence
补缺采访/回溯性採訪　retrospective acquisition
补缺市场/小眾市場,利基市場　niche market
补色/補色　complementary color

补税/補税　payment of delinquent tax
补税通知/補税通知　notice of deficiency
补贴/補貼　subsidy, subsidization
补贴贷款/補貼貸款　subsidized loan
补贴与反补贴措施协议/補貼及平衡措施協定　agreement on subsidies and countervailing measures
补遗/補遺　addenda, addendum
补余过程/補餘過程　complementary process
捕获/捕獲　capture
捕获法院/捕獲法院　prize court
捕获审判/捕獲審判　prize court adjudication
捕获-释放抽样/捕釋抽樣　capture-release sampling
捕捞努力量/魚獲努力量　fishing effort
捕亡/捕亡　hunt down criminals on the run
不安抗辩权/不安抗辯權　precarious defense, precarious right to defense
不安全投资/不安全投資　insecure investment
不安全行为/不安全行爲　unsafe behavior
不安全状态/不安全狀態　unsafe state
不罢工条款/不罷工條款　no-strike clause
不保兑的不可撤销信用证/無保兑的不可撤銷信用狀　unconfirmed irrevocable letter of credit
不保兑信用证/無保兑信用狀　unconfirmed letter of credit
不变动性/不變性　invariance, non-volatile
不变价格/不變價格,固定價格　constant price
不变检验/不變檢定　invariant test
不变决策问题/不變決策問題　invariant decision problem
不变量/不變量,不變式　invariant
不变美元/不變[價值]美元,定值美元　constant dollar
不变损失函数/不變損失函數　invariant loss function
不变弹性需求曲线/彈性固定的需求曲線　constant-elasticity demand curve
不变先验分布/不變事前分布　invariant prior distribution
不变性法/不變性法　invariance method
不变性检验/不變性檢定　invariance test
不变性原理/不變性原則　principle of invariance
不变因子/不變因子　invariant factor
不变资本/不變資本　constant capital
不成熟-成熟理论/不成熟-成熟理論　theory of immaturity-maturity
不成文宪法/不成文憲法　unwritten constitution
不承认主义/不承認主義　Doctrine of Non-recognition
不充分就业/低度就業　underemployment
不纯正不作为犯/不純正不作爲犯　offense of non-typical omission
不单方接触/不單方接觸　no exparte contact
不当得利/不當得利　unjust advantage, unjust enrichment
不当解雇政策/不公平遣散政策　unjust dismissal policy
不当劳动行为/不公平勞動措施　unfair labor practices
不道德管理/不道德管理　immoral management
不得强迫自证其罪/不得强迫自證其罪　right against self incrimination
不等方差检验/不等變異數檢定　test for unequal variances
不等偏态的/不等偏態的　anomic
不等权数/不等權數　unequal weights
不等式系数/不等式係數　inequality coefficient
不等子类/不等副組　unequal subclasses
不等子组/不等副組　unequal subclasses
不定额保险单/不定額保險單　unvalued policy
不定期出版物/不定期出版物　irregular publication, non-periodical publication
不定期特许/不定期特許　indeterminate franchise
不定期维护/不定期維護　unscheduled maintenance
不定位原则/不定性原則　principle of indeterminacy
不定用途信贷/無限定用途信貸　unrestricted use credit
不定值保险/不定值保險　unvalued insurance
不动产/不動産　real estate
不动产重估价/不動産重估價　reappraisal of real estate
不动产贷款/不動産貸款　real estate loan
不动产登记/不動産登記　registration of real estate
不动产抵押贷款/不動産抵押貸款　real estate mortgage loan
不动产管理/不動産管理　real property management
不动产融资/不動産融資　real estate finance
不动产市场/不動産市場　real estate market
不动产收益/不動産收益　real estate income
不动产投资/不動産投資　real estate investment
不动产信托投资/不動産信託投資　real estate trust investment
不动点/不動點　fixed point
不对称/不對稱　dissymmetry
不对称的/不對稱的　unsymmetrical
不对称时间序列模型/不對稱時間數列模型　asymmetric time series model

不对称析因设计/不對稱析因設計　asymmetrical factorial design
不对称性/不對稱性　asymmetry
不对称性检验/不對稱[性]檢定　asymmetrical test
不对称修整均值/不對稱截尾平均數　asymmetrically trimmed mean
不兑现纸币/不兌現紙幣,名義貨幣　fiat money
不发达国家/低度開發國家　underdeveloped country, less developed country
不发达经济/開發不足經濟　underdeveloped economy
不方便法院/不方便法院　Forum Non Conveniens
不方便法院原则/不方便法院原則　Doctrine of Forum Non Conveniens
不放回/不放回,不歸還　without replacement
不放回抽样/不放回抽樣,不還原抽樣　sampling without replacement
不分类管理法/不分類管理法　no category of management method
不分配约束/不分散式約束　non-distribution constraint
不分皂白的攻击/不分皂白的攻擊　indiscriminate attack
不符合/不符合　non-conformance
不附条件交易/不附條件交易　outright transaction
不告不理/不告不理　nemo judex actore, no trial without complaint
不公开审判/不公開審判　private trial
不公开招股投资公司/封閉型投資公司　closed investment company
不公平竞争方法/不公平競爭方法　unfair methods of competition
不规则背书/不連續背書　irregular endorsement
不规则变动/不規則波動　erratic fluctuation, irregular fluctuation
不规则波动/不規則波動　erratic fluctuation, irregular fluctuation
不规则过程/不規則過程　erratic process
不规则级数/不規則數列　erratic series
不合格/不合格,不良　nonconforming, nonconformaty
不合格产品/不合格産品　non-conforming product
不合格率/不合格率,不良率　unqualified rate
不合格判定数/棄却限,拒收[界]限　rejection limit
不合格品/不合格品,不良品　nonconforming item
不合格品百分率/不良百分率　nonconforming item percentage
不合格品百分数/不良百分數　percent nonconforming items
不合格品分类/不良品分類　nonconforming item classification
不合格品概率分布/不良品機率分布　nonconforming item probability distribution
不合格品率/不良率　percentage nonconforming item, fraction nonconforming item, nonconforming item fraction
不合格品率图/不良率管制圖　fraction nonconforming item chart
不合格品数控制图/不良品數管制圖　nonconforming item chart
不合格品数[目]/不良品數　number of nonconforming items
不合格品预防/不良品預防　nonconforming item prevention
不合格商业票据/不合格商業本票　non-eligible commercial paper
不合格实体控制图/不合格實體控制圖　number of nonconforming items control chart
不婚率/不婚率　never-married rate
不活跃市场/淺碟市場　thin market
不计利息/不計利息,免息　free of interest
不记名提单/不記名提單　unnamed bill of lading, blank bill of lading
不记名委托书/不記名委託書　blank letter of attorney
不记名债券/不記名債券　unregistered bond, blank bond
不结汇进口/不結匯進口　import without foreign exchange settlement
不景气的市场/弱市場　weak market
不可避免原因/不可避免的原因　unavoidable cause
不可撤销保兑信用证/不可撤銷保兑信用狀　irrevocable and confirmed credit, confirmed irrevocable credit
不可撤销的承兑/不可撤銷的承兑　irrevocable acceptance
不可撤销的转让/不可撤銷的轉讓　irrevocable assignment
不可撤销期票/不可撤銷期票　irrevocable promissory note
不可撤销信托/不可撤銷信託　irrevocable trust
不可撤销信用证/不可撤銷信用狀　irrevocable letter of credit
不可重复[字段]/不可重複　nonrepeatable, NR
不可兑换的货币/不可兌換的貨幣　unconvertible currency

不可兑换黄金的美元本位/不可兌換黃金的美元本位　dollar-only standard
不可兑换债券/不可轉換債券　non-convertible bond
不可分割信用证/不可分割信用狀　indivisible letter of credit
不可分割债务/不可分割債務　indivisible obligation
不可分散风险/不可分散的風險　non-diversifiable risk
不可分物/不可分物　indivisible thing
不可否认性/不可否認性　non-repudiation
不可观测误差/不可觀測誤差　nonobservable errors
不可加性/不可加性　nonadditivity
不可解性/不可解性　unsolvability
不可决系数/非判定係數,非決定係數　coefficient of nondetermination
不可抗力/不可抗力　force majesture, force majeure
不可靠度/不可靠度　unreliability
不可靠性/不可靠度　unreliability
不可控系统/不可控系統　uncontrollable system
不可控因素/不可控因子　uncontrolled factor
不可贸易商品/非貿易財　non-trade goods
不可能事件/不可能事件　impossible event
不可逆的/不可撤回性的　irreversible
不可取消订单/不可撤銷訂單　noncancellable, noncancellable order
不可容的/不可容的　inadmissible
不可容性/不可容性　inadmissibility
不可容许估计[量]/不可容估計[量]　inadmissible estimator
不可容许决策/不可容策略　inadmissible strategy
不可容许决策规则/不可容決策規則　inadmissible decision rule
不可容许线性估计[量]/不可容線性估計量　inadmissible linear estimator
不可容许最小充分统计量/不可容最小充分統計量　inadmissible minimal sufficient statistic
不可识别/不可識別　unidentifiable, unidentified, under indentified
不可赎回债券/不可[提前]贖回債券　non-callable bond
不可通约/不可共量　incommensurable
不可退换[图书]/不接受退貨　non-returnable, no returns, NR
不可微优化/不可微最優化　non-differentiable optimization
不可行性/不可行性　infeasibility
不可原谅的拖期/不可原諒的延誤　non-excusable delay
不可约马尔可夫链/不可約馬可夫鏈　irreducible Markov chain
不可转让背书/不可轉讓背書　non-negotiable endorsement
不可转让的单据/不可轉讓的單據,非流通單據　non-negotiable document
不可转让的技术/不可轉讓的技術　untransferable technology
不可转让的票据/不可轉讓的票據　non-negotiable bill
不可转让提单/不可轉讓提單　non-negotiable bill of lading
不可转让信用证/不可轉讓信用狀　non-transferable letter of credit, unassignable letter of credit
不可转让支票/不可轉讓支票　non-negotiable cheque
不利情况/不利情況　unfavorable case
不连接分类/不連接分類　disjunct classification
不连续变量/不連續變量　discontinuous variate
不连续创新/不連續創新　discontinuous innovation
不连续分布/不連續分布,不連續分配　discontinuous distribution
不连续过程/不連續過程　discontinuous process
不连续数据/不連續資料　discontinuous data
不良贷款/呆賬,不良債權　nonperforming loan
不良品浪费/不良品浪費　defective waste
不良债权/不良債權　bad claim
不满意产品/不滿意產品　unsatisfactory product
不睦/不睦　familiar disharmony
不能变现资产/不能變現的資產　irrealizable asset
不能犯/不能犯　unrealized offence
不能犯未遂/不能犯未遂　criminal attempt of unrealized offence
不能接受的发盘/不能接受的報價　offer unacceptable
不能提前赎回的债券/不能提前贖回的債券　bond irredeemable
不能自由兑换的货币/不能自由兌換的貨幣　irredeemable currency
不批准逮捕决定书/不批準逮捕決定書　written decision on disapprovement of an arrest
不平等贸易/不平等貿易　discriminative trade
不平衡报价/不平衡報價　unbalanced quote
不平衡贸易/不平衡貿易　one-sided trade, imbalance trade
不平衡数据/不平衡資料　unbalanced data
不平衡误差/失衡誤差　unbalanced error
不起诉/不起訴　non-prosecution

不起诉决定书/不起訴決定書　written decision on non-prosecution
不确定故意/不確定故意　indeterminate intent
不确定信息/不確定資訊　uncertain information
不确定型决策/不確定狀況下的決策　decision making under uncertainty
不确定性/不確定性,不確定度,未定性　uncertainty, indeterminacy
不确定性分析/不確定性分析　analysis of uncertainty
不确定性概率/不確定性機率　uncertainty probability
不确定性关系/不確定性關係　uncertainty relation
不确定性决策/不明確的判定　uncertainty decision
不确定性下的选择/不確定情況下之選擇　choices under uncertainty
不确定性样本调查/不確定性樣本調查　uncertainty sample survey
不融通物/不融通物　limited merchantable things
不受法律约束的合同/不受法律約束的合約　contract not subject to legal jurisdiction
不同机会理论/不同機會理論　differential opportunity theory
不推回原则/不推回原則　non-refoulement principle
不外借资料/不外借資料　non-loan material
不完美信息博弈/不完美訊息賽局　imperfect information game
不完全贝塔函数/不完全貝他函數　incomplete beta function
不完全多重响应设计/不完全多反應設計　incomplete multiresponse design
不完全分工/不完全專業化　incomplete specialization
不完全伽马函数/不完全伽瑪函數　incomplete gamma function
不完全关税同盟/不完整關稅同盟　incomplete customs union
不完全金融市场/不完全金融市場　incomplete financial market
不完全竞争/不完全競爭　imperfect competition
不完全竞争市场/不完全競爭市場　imperfect competitive market
不完全就业者/未適當就業者　inadequately employed
不完全距/不完全動差　incomplete moment
不完全拉丁方/不完全拉丁方格　incomplete Latin square
不完全名录/不完全名冊　incomplete list
不完全票据/不完整票據　incomplete bill
不完全普查/不完全普查　incomplete census
不完全契约/不完全契約　incomplete contract
不完全契约模型/不完全契約模型　incomplete-contract models
不完全区组/不完全區集　incomplete block
不完全区组设计/不完全區集設計　incomplete block design
不完全市场假说/不完全市場假説　incompleteness market hypothesis
不完全数据/不完全資料　incomplete data
不完全随机化/不完全隨機化　incomplete randomization
不完全信息/不完全訊息,不完全資訊　imperfect information, incomplete information
不完全支付/不完全支付　non-payout
不完全著录/不完全著錄　incomplete description
不完整样本/不完整樣本　fragmentary sample
不稳定分布/不穩定分布　unstable distribution
不稳定性/不穩定性　instability
不显著的/不顯著的　non-significant
不相符/差異　discrepancy
不相关的/不相關的　uncorrelated
不相关随机变量/不相關隨機變數　uncorrelated random variables
不相合估计[量]/不一致估計量　inconsistent estimator
不相合统计量/不一致統計量　inconsistent statistic
不相合性/不一致性　inconsistency
不相隶属关系/不相隸屬關係　non-subjection relation
不相联/不相聯　dissociation
不相容的/互斥的　mutually exclusive
不相容事件/不相容事件,互斥事件　mutually exclusive events
不相容性/不相容　incompatibility
不相容职务/不相容職務　incompatible function
不孝/不孝　unfilial
不协调性/不協和性　discordance
不协调样本/不協和樣本　discordant sample
不雅传播内容/不雅傳播內容　communication indecency
不雅节目/不雅節目,低俗節目　indecent program
不一致估计量/不一致估計量　inconsistent estimator
不义/不義　injustice
不予受理/不予受理　refusal to hear a complaint
不真实过程/不正當過程　dishonest process
不真正连带债务/不真正連帶債務　untrue association debt

不真正义务/不真正義務　obliegenheit
不征税收入/非課稅所得　non-taxable income
不正当竞争/不公平競爭　unfair competition
不正当竞争行为/不正當競爭行爲　behavior of unfair competition
不正当贸易行为/不正當貿易行爲　unfair trade practice
不正当有奖销售/不正當有獎銷售　unfair lottery-attached sale
不知情交易者/不知情交易者　uninformed trader
不指定国别许可证/未指定國別許可證　unspecialized licensing
不足功能/不足功能　insufficient function
不作为/不作爲　omission
布尔不等式/Boole 不等式　Boole's inequality
布尔分布/Burr 分布, Burr 分配　Burr's distribution
布尔检索/布林搜尋　Boolean search, Boolean retrieval
布尔逻辑检索/布林[邏輯]搜尋　Boolean logic searching, Boolean search
布尔什维克/布爾什維克　Bolshevik
布尔算符/布林運算子　Boolean operator
布尔战争/波耳戰爭　Boer War
布告/布告　notice
布告栏系统/電子布告欄系統　bulletin board system, BBS
布景/布景　scenery
布拉德福德定律/布萊德福定律, 布拉福定律　Bradford law
布莱克-德尔曼-托伊模型/BDT 模型　Black-Derman-Toy model, BDT model
布莱克曼线性检验/Blakeman 線性檢定　Blakeman's test for linearity
布莱克曼准则/Blakeman 準則　Blakeman's criterion
布莱克-舒尔斯定价公式/Black-Scholes 定價公式　Black-Scholes pricing formula
布莱克斯顿/布萊克斯頓　William Blackstone
布莱克-斯科尔斯期权定价模型/布雷克-休斯選擇權評價模型　Black-Scholes pricing model for option, Black-Scholes option pricing model
布莱克韦尔定理/Blackwell 定理　Blackwell's theorem
布莱特-斯奈特尔方法/Brandt-Snedecor 法　Brandt-Snedecor method
布兰代斯/布蘭代斯　Louis Dembitz Brandeis
布兰代斯论科学管理/布蘭代斯論科學管理　Brandeis's view on scientific management
布朗方法/Brown 法　Brown's method

布朗管理三阶段论/布朗管理三階段論　three management stages theory of Brown
布朗-穆德过程/Brown-Mood 程序　Brown-Mood procedure
布朗桥/布朗橋　Brownian bridge
布朗运动/布朗運動　Brownian motion
布朗运动过程/布朗運動過程　Brownian motion process
布雷德福分布/Bradford 分布, Bradford 分配　Bradford distribution
布雷德利-特里模型/Bradley-Terry 模型　Bradley-Terry model
布雷迪计划/布雷迪計劃　Brady plan
布雷迪债券/布雷迪債券　Brady bond
布雷顿森林体系/布雷頓森林體系　Bretton Woods system
布雷顿森林协议/布列頓森林協定　Bretton Woods agreement
布雷瓦斯相关系数/Bravais 相關係數　Bravais correlation coefficient
布利斯分类法/布利士分類　Bliss classification, BC, Bliss bibliographic classification
布鲁姆近似/Blum 逼近　Blum approximation
布鲁塞尔关税税则目录/布魯塞爾關稅品目分類表　Brussels' tariff nomenclature
布鲁斯顿方法/Bruceton 法　Bruceton method
布伦克检验/Brunk 檢定　Brunk's test
布洛姆法/Blom 法　Blom's method
布斯塔曼特法典/布斯塔曼特法典　Bustamante Code
布图设计权/布圖設計權　layout design right
布置/布置　layout
布置策略/布置策略　layout strategy
步进移行摄影机/逐步式縮攝機　step-and-repeat camera
部分保险/部分保險　partial insurance
部分变动成本/部分變動成本　partly variable cost
部分承兑/部分承兑　partial acceptance
部分重复/部分重複　fractional replication
部分储备银行制度/部分儲備銀行制度　fractional reserve banking system
部分担保债权人/部分擔保債權人　partly secured creditor
部分放回/部分置換　partial replacement
部分分布表/部分分布表　partial distribution table
部分分数模型/部分得分模式　partial credit model
部分付款/部分付款　payment in part
部分故障/部分故障　partial failure

部分关联/部分相聯　part association
部分混杂/部分混同　partial confounding
部分积累制/部分積累制　partially funded system
部分检验/部分檢驗,局部檢驗　partial test
部分结清/部分結清　partial settlement
部分可交换性/部分可换性　partial exchangeability
部分匹配检索/部分匹配檢索　partial match retrieval
部分平衡不完全区组设计/部分平衡不完全區集設計　partially balanced incomplete block design
部分平衡格[子]方/部分平衡格子方陣　partially balanced lattice square
部分平衡相连区组设计/部分平衡連環區集設計　partially balanced linked block design
部分平衡阵列/部分平衡陣列,部分平衡序列　partially balanced arrays
部分失效/部分故障　partial failure
部分市场战略/部分市場戰略　part market strategy
部分似然/偏概度　partial likelihood
部分题名/部分题名　partial title
部分无响应/部分無回應,部分無反應　partial nonresponse
部分析因设计/部分因子設計　fractional factorial design
部分析因试验/部分因子實驗　fractional factorial experiment
部分现金交易/部分現金交易　partial cash transaction
部分线性模型/部分線性模型　partially linear model
部分相合观测值/部分一致觀測值　partially consistent observation
部分相连区组设计/部分連環區集設計　partially linked block design
部分响应最大似然/部分回應最大似然　partial response and maximum likelihood
部分已付/部分已付　part paid
部分支付/部分支付　partial payment
部分仲裁裁决/部分仲裁判決　partial award
部落/部落　tribe
部门创新体系/部門創新體系　sectoral innovation system
部门档案馆/部門檔案館　departmental archives
部门规章/部門規章　departmental regulation
部门化/部門化　departmentalization
部门间国际分工/部門間國際分工　inter-sectoral specialization among nations
部门目录/部門目錄　branch catalog
部门审核/部門稽核　department audit
部门预算/部門預算　department budget, departmental budget
部门账户/部門賬　sector accounts
部门指数/部門指數　sector index
簿记/簿記　bookkeeping

C

擦金/掃金　bronzing
材料成本差异/材料成本差異　variance of material cost
材料费/材料費　material cost
材料消耗定额/材料消耗定額　material consumption quota
材料预算价格/材料預算價格　material budget price
财产保险/財產保險　property insurance
财产保险公司/財產保險公司　property insurance company
财产清查/實地盤點，實地盤存　physical inventory
财产权/財產權　property right
财产收入/財產所得　property income, income from property
财产税/財產稅，財富稅　property tax, wealth tax
财产刑/財產刑　property-oriented penalties
财阀/財閥　zaibatsu
财富/財富　wealth
财富效应/財富效果　wealth effect
财富状况/財富狀況　endowment position
财力性转移支付/財力性轉移支付　transfer payment for financial ability
财团法人/財團法人　corporate body, incorporated foundation
财务报表/財務報表　financial statement
财务报表分析/財務報表分析　financial statement analysis
财务报表批准日/財務報表批準日　date of approval of the financial statement
财务报表日/財務報表日　date of the financial statement
财务报表审阅/財務報表審查　financial statement review
财务重述/財務重述　financial restatement
财务重组/財務重組　financial restructuring
财务代理人/財務代理人　fiscal agent
财务费用/財務費用　financial expense
财务杠杆/財務槓桿　financial leverage
财务公司/財務公司，融資公司　financial company, finance company
财务公司协会/財務公司協會　association of finance companies
财务管理/財務管理，財務行政　financial administration, financial management
财务计划/財務計劃　financial plan
财务价值/財務價值　fiscal value
财务控制/財務控制，貨幣控制　financial control, monetary control
财务会计/財務會計　financial accounting
财务会计档案室/財務會計檔案室　financial accounting record office
财务会计概念公报/財務會計概念公報　Statement of Financial Accounting Concept
财务会计概念框架/財務會計概念框架　conceptual framework for financial accounting
财务会计准则公报/財務會計準則公報　Statement of Financial Accounting Standards
财务困境/金融困頓，財務危機　financial distress
财务灵活性/財務彈性　financial flexibility
财务评价/財務評估　financial evaluation
财务审计/財務審計　financial audit
财务战略/財務策略　financial strategy
财务账户/財務賬目　financial accounts
财务状况变动表/財務狀況變動表　statement of change in financial position
财务状况表/財務狀況表　statement of financial condition, statement of financial position
财务资本/財務資本　financial capital
财务-资本学派/財務-資本學派　financial-capital school
财务总监/財務總監　chief financial officer, CFO
财务总预算/財務總預算　master financial budget
财政/財政　finance, public finance
财政包干/財政包干制　fiscal responsibility system
财政补贴/財政補貼　fiscal subsidy
财政超收/財政超收　fiscal ultra receives
财政赤字/財政赤字　fiscal deficit
财政刺激/財政刺激，財政獎勵　fiscal incentive
财政措施/財政措施　fiscal measure
财政的/財政的　financial
财政分权/財政分散　fiscal decentralization
财政分权制/財政邦聯主義　fiscal federalism

财政关税/財政關稅　financial duty
财政管理/財政管理　fiscal administration, financial management
财政红利/財政紅利　fiscal dividend
财政汲取能力/財政汲取能力　state fiscal extractive capacity
财政监督/財務監督　fiscal supervision
财政结余/財政結餘　fiscal surplus
财政结转/財政結轉　fiscal carry-over
财政能力/財政能量　fiscal capacity
财政年度/財政年度　fiscal year
财政努力/財政努力　fiscal effort
财政权力/財權　fiscal power
财政审计/財政審計　financial audit, public finance audit
财政失衡/財政失衡　fiscal imbalance
财政收入/財政收入　fiscal revenue
财政收支平衡/財政收支平衡　fiscal balance
财政统计/財政統計　statistics of public finance
财政透支/財政透支　fiscal overdraft
财政拖累/財政拖累　fiscal drag
财政拖累效应/財政拖累效應　fiscal drag effect
财政危机/財政危機　financial crisis
财政增收/財政增收　fiscal revenue increase
财政政策/財政政策,金融政策　fiscal policy, financial policy
财政转移支付/財政轉移支付　fiscal transfer payment
财政资金来源/財政資金來源　revenue source
裁定管辖/裁定管轄　adjudged jurisdiction
裁决/裁決,判決,裁定　ruling, adjudication
裁决员/裁決者　adjudicator
裁量基准/裁量基準　discretion standard
裁切/裁切　cutting, crop
裁切标记/裁切記號　trim mark, cut mark
裁切面装饰/裁切面裝飾　decoration of cutting edges
裁员/裁員,組織縮編　downsizing
采访/採訪　acquisition, purchase
采访部/採訪部　interview department
采访查重/查重　duplicate checking, duplication checking
采访方针/採訪政策　acquisition policy, collection development policy
采访馆员/採訪館員　acquisitions librarian
采访号/採購號　acquisition number, purchasing number, order number
采访计划/採訪計劃　acquisition program
采访模式/採訪模式　acquisition mode

采访目录/採訪目錄　acquisition list
采访权/採訪權　right to gather news
采访系统/採訪系統　acquisition system
采访信息/採購資訊　acquisition purchasing information
采访指南/採訪指南　acquisition guide
采访状态/採訪狀態　acquisition status
采购/採購,購料,購置　purchase, procurement, purchasing
采购订单/採購單,訂購單　purchase order
采购费/採購費　purchase fee
采购管理/採買管理　procurement management
采购管理计划/採購管理計劃　procurement management plan
采购规划/採購規劃　plan purchase and acquisition
采购合同/採購契約　procurement contracts
采购计量单位/採購計量單位　purchasing unit of measure
采购价格/買方價格　purchaser price
采购价格波动/採購價格變異　purchase price variance
采购时间/採購時間　procurement time
采购文件/採購文件　procurement document
采购战略/採購策略　procurement strategy
采购质量函数/取得品質函數　procurement quality function
采购周期/採購週期　procurement cycle
采集经济/採集經濟　gathering economy
采全率/採全率　acquisition comprehensiveness
采写/採訪寫作　interview and writing
采样点/樣本點　sample point
采样方位比/採樣方位比　sampling aspect ratio
采样密度/抽樣密度　sampling density
采用值/採用值　adopted value
采准率/捕獲精度　acquisition accuracy
彩插/彩插　color interpolation
彩虹期权/彩虹期權　rainbow option
彩绘本/彩繪本　color handpainted book
彩排/彩排　camera rehearsal
彩票/彩券　lottery
彩票选择实验/彩券選擇實驗　lottery-choice experiment
彩色复印机/彩色影印機　color copier
彩色广告/彩色廣告　color advertising
彩色胶片/彩色膠片　color film
彩色图像/色彩影像　color image
彩色图像编码/彩色圖像編碼　color image encoding
彩色印刷/全彩印刷　full color printing

菜单式查找/菜單式查找　menu-based search
参/參　associative relationship
参公管理/參公管理　management by referring to civil service law management unit
参见类目/參見類目　see also, reference class
参见索引/帶參見的主題索引　syndetic index
参考磁平/參考磁平　reference magnetic flat
参考价格/參考價格，參考報價　reference price, indicative price
参考价值/參考價值　reference value
参考框架/參考架構　frame of reference
参考链接/參考鏈接　reference linking
参考频率/參考頻率　reference frequency
参考书目/參考書目　bibliography, reference source
参考数据库/參考資料庫　reference database
参考图书馆/參考圖書館　reference library
参考文献/參考文獻　reference, bibliographical reference
参考信息源/參考資源　reference source
参考咨询档案/參考諮詢檔案　reference service archive
参考咨询服务/參考諮詢服務　reference service
参考咨询服务规范/參考諮詢服務規程　reference service regulation
参考咨询馆员/參考館員　reference librarian
参考咨询台/參考檯　reference desk
参考咨询统计/參考諮詢統計　reference statistics
参考资料/參考資料　reference material
参谋职权/幕僚職權　staff authority
参数/參數，母數，量　parameter
参数的可识别性/參數的可識別性　identifiability of parameter
参数点/參數點　parameter point
参数分离/參數分離　parameter separation
参数估计/參數估計　parameter estimation, parametric estimating
参数估算/參數估計　parameter estimation, parametric estimating
参数规划/參數規劃　parametric programming
参数化/參數化　parametrization
参数化线性统计模型/參數化線性統計模型　parameterized linear statistical model
参数假设/參數假設　parametric hypothesis
参数检验/參數檢驗，母數檢定　parametric test
参数矩阵/參數矩陣　parameter matrix
参数空间/參數空間　parameter space
参数模型/參數模型　parametric model
参数偏离/參數漂移　parameter drift
参数偏移/參數移動　parameter shift
参数设计/參數設計　parameter design
参数统计/有母數統計學　parametric statistics
参数统计推断/參數統計推論　parametric statistical inference
参数稳定性/參數穩定性　parameter stability
参数线性规划/參數線性規劃　parametric linear programming
参数向量/參數向量　parameter vector
参议院/參議院　senate
参与/參與，介入感，涉入　engagement, participation, involvement
参与承兑汇票/匯票的參加承兌　intervention for honor
参与观察/參與觀察　participant observation
参与管理/參與式管理　participative management
参与式发展/參與式發展　participatory development
参与式工作日记/參與者工作日志　participant diary
参与式观察/參與式觀察　participatory observation, participant observation
参与式激励计划/參與式激勵計劃　attendance incentive plan
参与式决策/參與式決策　participative policy making
参与式领导/參與式領導　participative leadership
参与式民主/參與式民主　participatory democracy
参与式设计/參與式設計　participative design
参与式行动研究/參與式行動研究　participatory action research, PAR
参与式咨询/參與式諮商　participative counseling
参与约束/參與限制　participation constraint
参与者主张/參與者倡議　participant-advocate
参照/參照　cross reference
参照标准/參考標準　reference standard
参照表/參考表　reference table
参照点/參考點，基準點　reference point
参照法/參照法　reference method
参照集/參考集合　reference set
参照记录/參考記錄　reference record
参照款目/參照款目　reference entry
参照批/參考批　reference lot
参照群体/參考組，參照團體　reference group
参照群体理论/參照群體理論　reference group theory
参照系统/參照系統　syndetic system
参政权/參政權　right of political participation
残本/殘本　shaken copy, imperfect copy, defective copy
残差/殘差，殘餘　residue, residual

残差波动/殘差波動　residual fluctuation
残差处理效应/殘差處理效應　residual treatment effect
残差方差/殘差變異數　residual variance
残差方差准则/差值變異數標準　residual variance criterion
残差方程/殘差方程式　residual equation
残差分析/殘差分析　residual analysis
残差过程/殘差過程　residuation process
残差和/殘差和　sum of residuals
残差均方/殘差均方　residual mean square
残差平方和/殘差平方和　residual sum of squares
残差误差/殘差誤差　residual error
残差效应/殘差效應　residual effects
残差协方差矩阵/殘差共變數矩陣　residual covariance matrix
残差总散点图/殘差全繪圖　overall plot of residuals
残存本/殘存本　superseded issues
残疾人/殘疾人　people with disability
残疾人按比例就业制度/殘疾人按比例就業制度　employing minimum percentage employees with disabilities
残疾人保障法/殘疾人保障法　law on protection of disabled persons
残疾人福利/殘疾人福利　welfare for persons with disabilities
残疾人康复/殘疾人康復　disabled people rehabilitation
残疾人康复机构/殘疾人康復機構　rehabilitation institutions for disabled people
残疾人联合会/殘疾人聯合會　federation of the disabled
残疾人社会工作/殘疾人社會工作　social work for the disabled
残疾人维权/殘疾人維權　disabled people rights protection
残疾社会视角/殘疾社會視角　social perspective of disability
残破书/殘破書　defective book
残缺家庭/殘缺家庭　incomplete family
残损货物检验/破損貨物檢驗　inspection on damaged cargo
残余变动/殘差移動　residual movement
残余风险/殘餘風險　residual risk
残障读者/殘障讀者　handicapped patron, disabled reader
残值/殘值　salvage value
蚕茧纸/蠶繭紙　silk-cocoon fiber paper

蚕食率/競食率　cannibalization rate
仓储费用/倉儲費用,储存成本　warehousing fee, storage cost
仓储合同/倉儲合同　contract of deposit
仓储俱乐部/倉儲俱樂部　warehouse club
仓单/倉單　warehouse receipt
仓库/倉庫　warehouse
仓库管理系统/倉庫管理系統　warehouse management system
仓库货物周转率/倉庫貨物週轉率　warehouse goods turnover rate
仓库交货/倉庫交貨,出倉,出棧　deliver from godown
仓库交货条件/倉庫交貨條件　ex warehouse terms
仓库空间利用率/倉庫空間利用率　warehouse space utilization rate
仓库面积利用率/倉庫面積利用率　warehouse ground area utilization rate
藏书标记/藏書標記　ownership mark
藏书补充参数/藏書補充參數　parameter of collection supplement
藏书补缺/藏書補缺　retrospective collection development
藏书布局/藏書布局　overall arrangement of collection
藏书成分/藏書成分　element of collection
藏书复选/藏書復選　collection reselection
藏书家/藏書家　book collector, bibliophile
藏书建设/館藏發展　collection development
藏书交换目录/藏書交換目錄　stock exchange list
藏书控制/館藏控制　collection control
藏书零增长理论/藏書零增長理論　theory of collection zero-growth
藏书目录/藏書目錄　catalogue of collected books
藏书配置/藏書配置　collection allocation
藏书票/藏書票　bookplate
藏书清点/藏書清點　book counting, inventory
藏书区分/藏書區分　collection division
藏书剔除/圖書剔舊　retirement weeding, negative selection
藏书体系/館藏體系　collection system
藏书选择/圖書選擇　book selection
藏书增长量/藏書增長量　collection growth
藏书章/藏書章　ownership seal
藏书注销/圖書資料注銷　withdrawal
藏书组织/藏書組織　collection organization
操纵/操縱　manipulation
操纵市场/操縱市場,圍標　market rigging

操作化/操作化,運作化　operationalization
操作可靠度/操作可靠度　operation reliability
操作宽放/操作寬放,作業寬放　operation allowance
操作命令/公開市場操作指令　operating directive
操作目标/操作目標　operating target
操作冗余/操作復聯　operation redundancy
操作特性曲线/操作特徵曲線,OC曲線　operating characteristic, OC curve
操作特征函数/操作特徵函數　operating characteristic function
操作条件反射/操作制約,操作條件化學習　operant conditioning
操作系统/作業系統　operating system
操作性情报/作業情報　operational intelligence
操作学习理论/操作學習理論　operation reinforcement theory
操作员表现/作業員績效　operator performance
操作员占优系统/作業員優勢系統　operator dominant system
曹魏律/曹魏律　Cao Wei Law
槽底半径/槽底半徑　bottom radius
槽距不匀/槽距不匀　pitch uneven
草稿/草稿　draft
草稿本/草稿本　scribbling pad
草根/草根　grassroot
草根援助组织/草根支援組織　grassroot support organization, GSO
草根组织/草根組織　grassroot organization, GRO
草筋纸/草筋紙　straw-stalk paper
草签/草簽　initialing
草原法/草原法　grassland law
草纸/草紙　straw paper
册/冊　book
册页装/冊頁裝　album binding
侧推力/側推力,旁壓力　side thrust
测度/測度　measure
测度空间/測度空間　measure space
测度论/測度理論　measure theory
测谎测验/測謊測驗　polygraph test
测绘档案/測繪檔案　cartographic archives
测控条/檢測控制條　control stip
测量/測量　measurement
测量标准误差/測量標準誤[差]　standard error of measurement
测量层次/測量層次　measurement level
测量过程/量測過程　measurement process
测量精密度/量測精確度,測度精確度　precision of measurement
测量可靠性/量測可靠度　reliability of measurement
测量控制体系/測量控制系統　measurement control system
测量理论/測量理論　measurement theory
测量模型/測量模型　measurement model
测量设备/量測設備,量測裝備　measuring equipment
测量误差/測量誤差,量測誤差　measurement error, error of measurement
测量准确度/量測準確度　measurement accuracy
测时/測時　time determination
测试成绩/測驗分數　test score
测试带/測試帶　test tape
测试精密度/試驗精密度　precision of a test
测试数据集/驗證資料　test dataset
测试依赖/測驗依賴　test dependent
测试用样盘/測試用樣盤　template disk for testing
策划编辑/策劃編輯　selected subject editor
策略/策略,戰略　strategy
OPSEC策略/OPSEC策略　operations security tactics, OPSEC tactics
(r,Q)策略/(r,Q)策略　(r, Q) policy
(s,S)策略/(s,S)策略　(s, S) policy
策略捕捉/策略捕捉　policy capturing
策略等价/策略等位　strategic equivalence
策略集合/策略集合　strategy set
策略空间/策略空間　strategy space
策略性投票/策略性投票　strategic voting
策略游戏/策略遊戲　tactful game
策略组合/策略組合　strategy profile
层/層　stratum
层次/調光層次　gradation
层次分类/層次分類　hierarchical classification
层次分析法/分析層級法　analytic hierarchy process
层次分析预测法/分析層次預測法　analytic hierarchy process forecasting method, AHP forecasting method
层次加性加权法/層次加性加權法　weighted method of stratification additivity
层次校正/層次校正　gradation correction
层次可分组设计/層次可分組設計　hierarchical group divisible design
层次模型/層次模型　hierarchical model
层次数据库/階層式資料庫　hierarchical database
层次图/分層圖　strata chart
层次性/層級　hierarchy
层峰结构/科層結構,層級結構　bureaucracy structure

层级效应/效果階層　hierarchy of effect
层级制/層級制　hierarchical system
层架式书库/層架式書庫　tier-shelving bookstack
层间方差/層間變異數　between-stratum variance
层间黏着性/層間黏著性　interlayer adhesion
层累标记制/層累標記制　hierarchical notation
层内方差/層內變異數　stratum variance
层压/層合　lamination
叉车/堆高車　fork lift truck
差别待遇/差別待遇　discriminatory treatment, differential treatment, disparate treatment
差别定价/差別定價　discriminatory pricing
差别关税/差別關稅　differential duty, discriminating tariff, discriminating duty
差别汇率/差別匯率　discriminatory exchange rate
差别计件工资制/差別計件工資制　differentiated rate piece system
差别价格/差別價格　discriminative price
差别贸易/差別貿易　discriminative trade
差别影响/差別性影響　disparate impact
差错方程/誤差方程式　error equation
差额计件工资/差額式按件計酬　differential piece rate
差额预算管理/差額預算管理　budget management by remainder
差额支付/差額補貼　deficiency payments
差分测时法/差分測時法　difference timing
差分法/差分法　method of difference
差分符号检验/差分符號檢定　difference sign test
差分函数/目標函數　fitting function, discrepancy function
差分学/差分學　calculus of finite differences
差分自回归移动平均模型/自我回歸整合移動平均模型　autoregressive integrated moving average model, ARIMA model
差分自回归移动平均预测模型/差分自回歸滑動平均預測模型　autoregressive integrated moving average forecasting model, ARIMA forecasting model
差估计/差量估計　difference estimation
差估计[量]/差量估計[量]　difference estimator
差价/差價　price difference
差价期权/信用價差交換　spread options
差价税/變動關稅　variable levy
差距/差異測量　disparity
差控制图/差量管制圖　difference control chart
X差控制图/X差管制圖　X difference chart
差序格局/差序格局　the pattern of difference sequence
差异的T方法/差異的T方法　T-method for differences
差异度/差異度　difference degree
差异化/差異化　differentiation
差异化营销/差異行銷　differentiated marketing
差异化战略/差異化策略　differentiation strategy
差异集中/差異集中　centralization of difference
差异交往理论/差異交往理論　theory of differential association
差异显著性/差異的顯著性　significance of difference
插播/插播,插補　insert
插播广告/插播廣告　spot advertisement
插补/設算　imputation
插件/插件　plug-in
插入广告/插入式廣告　drop-in commercial
插图/插圖　illustration
插页/插頁　insert, throw-in
插值/插值　interpolation
查办/查辦　check in managing
查表/對照表,速查表　look-up table
查表法/查表　table lookup
查架/查架　reading shelves, shelf checking
查克克-休拉克检验/Chacko-Shorack 檢定法　Chacko-Shorack test
查里尔分布/Charlier 分布, Charlier 分配　Charlier distribution
查纳卡雅·考底利耶论管理/查納卡雅·考底利耶論管理　Kautilya's view on management
查普曼-柯尔莫哥洛夫方程/察普曼-科莫高洛夫方程式　Chapman-Kolmogorov equation
查全率/查全率,回現率　recall ratio
查询/查詢　query
查询扩展/查詢擴展　query expansion
查阅许可/批準查閱　clearance
查准率/查準率　precision ratio
查准评定/查準評定　relevance judgement
察世俗每月统记传/察世俗每月統記傳　Chinese Monthly Magazine
拆借市场/拆借市場,短期資金市場　call market
拆开/拆解　disassemble
掺水股本/掺水股本　watered capital stock
掺水股票/掺水股票　watered stock
产出/產出　output
产出控制/產出控制　output control
产出投资比/產出投資比　output-investment ratio
产地检验证书/產地檢驗證書　inspection certificate of origin

产量定额/產出配額　output quota
产量领导者/產量領導者　quantity leader
产量因子/產量因子　yield factor
产量追随者/產量追隨者　quantity follower
产能管理/產能管理　capacity management
产能竞争/產能競爭　capacity competition
产能清单/產能清單　bill of capacity, bill of resource
产能约束资源/產能受限資源　capacity-constrained resource
产品/產品　product, production
产品保证/產品保證　product assurance
产品标识/產品識別　product identification
产品标准/產品標準　product standard
产品标准化/產品標準化　product standardization, standardization of products
产品部门化/產品部門化　product departmentalization
产品策略/產品策略　product strategy
产品层次结构/產品層次結構　product hierarchy
产品差异化/產品差異化　product differentiation
产品成本差异/產品成本差異　variance of product cost
产品成熟期/產品成熟期　product maturity stage
产品成长期/產品成長期　product growth stage
产品出产计划/主生產日程表,總生產排程表　master production schedule
产品创新/產品創新　product innovation
产品创新平台/產品創新平臺　product innovation platform
产品创造/產品發明　product invention
产品导入期/產品導入期　product introduction stage
产品等级/產品分級　product rating
产品定位/產品定位　product positioning
产品独特性/產品差異　product uniqueness
产品多样化/產品多角化　product diversification
产品发明/產品發明　product invention
产品范围/產品範圍　product scope
产品分析/產品分析　product analysis
产品负荷图/產品負荷圖　product load profile
产品概念/產品概念,產品觀念　product concept
产品工程/產品工程　product engineering
产品观念/產品觀念,產品概念　product concept
产品规格/產品規格　product specification
产品计划/產品布局　product plan
产品间噪声/產品間雜訊　inter-production noise
产品兼容性/產品相容性　product compatibility
产品结构树/產品結構樹　product structure tree
产品结构文件/產品結構檔　product structure file
产品竞争情报/產品競爭情報　product competitive intelligence
产品开发/產品開發　product development
产品开发过程重构/產品開發過程重構　product development process re-engineering
产品开发期/產品開發期　product development stage
产品开发战略/產品開發策略　product-development strategy
产品控制/產品管制　product control
产品捆绑定价/成組產品定價　product bundle pricing
产品-流程矩阵/產品-流程矩陣　product-process matrix
产品流分析/產品流分析　product flow analysis
产品模块化/產品模組化　product modularity
产品耐用性/產品耐久期　durability of products
产品配置器/產品配置器　product configurator
产品品类/產品類別　product category
产品品类量分销率/產品品類量分銷率　product category volume distribution, PCV distribution
产品平台/產品平臺　product platform
产品缺陷/產品缺陷　product defects
产品群/產品群　product group
产品容差/產品允差　product tolerance
产品设计/產品設計　product design
产品审核/產品稽核　product audit
产品生命周期/產品生命週期　product life cycle, PLC
产品生命周期管理/產品生命週期管理　product lifecycle management, PLM
产品市场定义/產品市場定義　product market definition
产品市场竞争/產品市場競爭　product-market competition
产品市场拓展方格/產品市場擴展矩陣　product market expansion grid
产品-市场演变矩阵/產品-市場演變矩陣　product-market evolution matrix
产品适应/產品適應[性]　product adaption
产品数据管理/產品資料管理　product data management, PDM
产品衰退期/產品衰退期　product decline stage
产品线/產品線　product line
产品线长度/產品線長度　product line length
产品线定价/產品線定價　product line pricing
产品线填充/產品線填充　product line filling
产品线延伸/產品線延伸　product line stretching
产品销售队伍结构/產品銷售隊伍結構　product sales force structure
产品形式定价/產品形式差別定價　product-form

pricing
产品性能/產品性能　product performance
产品验收/產品允收　product acceptance
产品有效性/產品有效性　product availability
产品原型/產品原型　product prototype
产品责任/產品責任，商品製作責任　product responsibility, product liability
产品责任法律适用公约/產品責任法律適用公約　Convention on the Law Applicable to Products Liability
产品展示/產品呈現　presentation
产品召回/產品召回　product recall
产品知识/產品知識　product knowledge
产品质量/產品品質　product quality
产品质量变异/產品變異性　product variability
产品质量分级/生產品質分級　grading of product quality
产品质量认证/產品品質認證　production quality authentication
产品质量认证标志/產品品質認證標誌　product quality authentication
产品质量责任/產品品質責任　liability concerning product quality
产品周期/產品週期　product cycle
产品族/產品族　product family
产品组合/產品組合　product mix
产品组合长度/產品組合長度　product mix length
产品组合宽度/產品組合寬度　product mix width
产品组合深度/產品組合深度　product mix depth
产品组合一致性/產品組合一致性　consistency of product mix
产权/財產權　property right
产权规则/財產法則　property rule
产权交易/產權交易　property right deal
产权界定/產權界定　on the boundary of property right
产权理论/財產權分析　approach of property right
产权学派/產權學派　property right school
产权战略联盟/股權式策略聯盟　equity strategic alliance
产权制度改革/產權改革　reform of property rights system
产权转让/業權轉移　transfer of property rights
产销率/產出量　throughput
产学研/產學研　industry-university-institute
产学研合作创新/產學研合作創新　cooperative innovation among industry-college-institute
产学研战略联盟/產學研策略聯盟　strategic alliance of industry-college-institute
产业报纸/產業報紙　trade paper
产业重组法案/產業重組法　industrial reorganization act
产业创新/產業創新　industry innovation
产业创新体系/產業創新系統　industrial innovation system
产业地理集中/產業地理集中　industry geography concentration
产业多样化论/產業多樣化論　diversified industry argument
产业革命/工业革命　industry revolution
产业共性技术/產業共性技術　industrial generic technology
产业关系/勞資和諧　industrial relations
产业环境/產業環境　industry environment
产业基金/產業基金　industry fund
产业集群/產業群聚　industry cluster, industrial cluster
产业技术/產業技術　industrial technology
产业技术轨道/產業技術軌道　industrial technology track, ITT
产业间贸易/產業間貿易　inter-industry trade
产业监管/行業規則　industry regulation
产业结构/產業結構，工業結構　industrial structure, industry structure
产业结构优化/產業結構最優化　optimization of industry structure
产业景框/產業景框　industry scene frame
产业竞争情报/產業競爭情報　industry competitve intelligence
产业聚集/產業集聚　industry agglomeration
产业民主/工業民主　industrial democracy
产业内交易/產業內部貿易　intra-industry trade
产业内贸易理论/產業內貿易理論　intra-industry trade theory
产业内贸易指数/行業內貿易指數　index of intra-industry trade, IIT
产业升级/產業升級　industry upgrading, industrial upgrading
产业政策/產業政策　industrial policy
产业转移/產業轉移　industry transfer
产业资本/產業資本　industrial capital
产业组织/產業組織　industrial organization
产业组织实验/產業組織實驗　industrial organization experiments
铲币/鏟幣　spade money
颤动抽样/跳動抽樣　jittered sampling

长臂管辖/長臂管轄 long-arm jurisdiction
长臂管辖法/長臂管轄法 long-arm jurisdiction statute
长编/長編 chang bian
长焦镜头/望遠鏡頭 telephoto lens
长镜头/長拍鏡頭 long lens
长期/長期關係法則 long run
长期保存政策/長期保存政策 long-term preservation policy
长期边际成本/長期邊際成本 long-run marginal cost
长期病患/長期病患 long-term sickness and incapacity
长期成本/長期成本 long-run cost
长期储蓄/長期儲蓄 permanent saving
长期待摊费用/長期預付費用 long-term prepaid expense
长期订单/長期訂購 standing order, continuation order
长期订户/常年訂閱者 regular subscriber
长期负债/長期負債 long-term liabilities
长期公债/長期公債 long-term public bond
长期供给曲线/長期供給曲線 long run supply curve
长期股权激励/長期持股優 long-term shareholding loyalty incentive
长期股权投资/長期股權投資 long-term equity investment
长期合同/長期合約 long-term contract
长期护理/長期護理 long-term care
长期护理保险/長期護理保險 long-term care insurance
长期汇票/長期匯票,長期票據,遠期票據 long bill, long-term bill
长期货币市场/長期貨幣市場 long-term money market
长期计划/長期計劃[書] long-term plan
长期借款/長期借款 long-term loan
长期借阅/長期借閱 long term loan
长期均衡/長期均衡 long run equilibrium
长期劳动力需求/長期勞動需求 long-run labor demand
长期劳动力需求弹性/長期勞動需求彈性 long-run labor demand elasticities
长期利率/長期利率 long-term interest rate
长期利润/長期利潤 long run profit
长期利润最大化/長期利潤極大化 long run profit maximization
长期贸易/長期貿易 long-term trade
长期平均成本/長期平均成本 long-run average cost
长期平均成本曲线/長期平均成本曲線 long-run average cost curve
长期趋势/長期趨勢 secular trend, long-time trend
长期融资/長期資金融通 long-term financing
长期投资/長期投資 long-term investment
长期外资/長期外資 long-term foreign capital
长期限价证券/長期限價證券 long tap
长期协议/長期協議 standing order
长期信贷/長期信貸 long-term credit, long credit
长期信贷市场/長期信貸市場 long-term credit market
长期信托/長期信託 long-term trust
长期信用证/長期信用狀 long credit
长期[性]失业/長期失業 long-term unemployment, chronic unemployment
长期应付款/長期應付款 long-term payable
长期应收款/長期應收款 long-term receivable
长期预报/長期預測 long-term forecast
长期债权/長期債權 long-term claim
长期债券/長期債券 long-term bond
长期债券收益/長期債券收益 yield of long-term bond
长期债务/長期債務 long-term debt
长期证券/長期證券 long-term security
长期政策规划/長期政策規劃 long-range policy planning
长期资本/長期資本 long capital, long term capital
长期资本流动/長期流動資金 flow of long-term capital
长期资产/長期資產,固定資產 long-term asset
长期资金/長期資金 long-term fund
长期总供给表/長期總供給表 long-run aggregate supply schedule
长期租赁/長期租賃 long lease, long-term lease
长体字/長體字 condensed type
长尾分布/長尾分布 long tail distribution
长尾理论/長尾理論 long tail theory
长销书/長銷書 lasting-selling book
长远价值/長遠價值 long term value
长周期/長週期 long cycles
尝试/試驗,試行 trial
常备目录/常備目錄 ever-prepared book bibliography
常备书/常備書 ever-prepared book
常峰态/常態峰度 mesokurtosis
常规订购方式说明/訂單程式具體規定 order-routine specification

常规科学/常態科學　normal science
常规控制图/Shewhart 管制圖　Shewhart control chart
常规努力/常規努力,正常努力　normal effort
常规算法/慣用演算法　conventional algorithm
常和博弈/常和賽局,定和賽局　constant-sum game, constant sum game
常见问题/常見問題　frequently asked questions, FAQ
常客计划/常客計劃　frequency program
常人/普通人　ordinary people
常人方法论/俗民方法論　ethnomethodology
常任制/常任制　tenure system
常设国际法院/常設國際法院　Permanent Court of International Justice
常设机构/常設機構　standing body
常设仲裁法院/常設仲裁法院　permanent court of arbitration
常设仲裁机构/常設仲裁機構　permanent arbitration agency
常数/常數　constant
常数权重/常數權數,固定權數　constant weight
常态变量之二次式/常態變數之二次式　quadratic form in normal variable
常态单元时间/正常單元時間　normal element time
常系数/常數係數　constant coefficient
常销书/常銷書　often sells book
常业犯/常業犯　professional offender
常用参考书/常用參考書　quick-reference book
常用贷款/常用貸款,長效放款　evergreen loan
常住居民/常住居民　normal residents
常住人口/常住人口　resident population, de jure population
常驻记者/常駐記者,駐地記者　resident correspondent
偿付抵押贷款/償付抵押貸款　lift mortgage
偿付能力/償付能力　solvency
偿付能力约束/清償能力限制　solvency constraint
偿付信用证/償付信用狀　reimbursement credit
偿付[银]行/償付[銀]行　reimbursing bank
偿还信用证/償還信用狀　disposal credit
偿还预付金额的担保/償還預付金額的擔保　guarantee for repayment of advance made on account
偿清贷款/償清貸款　paid-up loan
偿债基金/償債基金,債務基金　sinking fund, debt service fund
偿债基金按期摊付款/償債基金分期付款　sinking fund installment
偿债基金保险/償債基金保險　sinking fund insurance
偿债基金抵押/償債基金抵押　sinking fund mortgage
偿债基金费用/償債基金費用　sinking fund expense
偿债基金累积/償債基金累積　sinking fund accumulation
偿债基金平衡表/償債基金資產負債表　sinking fund balance sheet
偿债基金收益/償債基金收益　sinking fund income
偿债基金投资/償債基金投資　investment of sinking fund, sinking fund investment
偿债基金信托人/償債基金信託人　sinking fund trustee
偿债基金债券/償債基金債券　sinking fund bond
偿债基金证券/償債基金證券　sinking fund security
偿债基金准备金/償債基金準備金　sinking fund reserve
偿债基金资产/償債基金資產　sinking fund asset
偿债能力/償債能力　debt paying ability
偿债收益/償債收益　redemption yield
厂商/廠商　firm
厂商理论/廠商理論　theory of the firm
厂商信用证/廠商信用狀　maker's credit
厂长负责制/廠長負責制　factory director responsibility system
厂中厂/廠中廠　plant within a plant, factory within a factory
场景/場景,布景　scene
场论/場[地]論　field theory
场内交易/場內交易　on-floor translation, transaction on exchange
场内交易人/交易所經紀人　pit trader
场内交易者/場內交易員　floor trader
场内经纪人/場內經紀人　floor broker
场内经纪商/場內經紀人　floor broker
场所支配行为/場所支配行爲　locus regit actum
场外价格水平/場外價格水準　kerb level
场外交易/場外交易　ex pit transaction, kerb transaction, off-the-floor trading
场外交易市场/買賣雙方直接交易市場,場外交易的市場,店頭市場　over-the-counter market, OTC
场外经纪人/場外經紀人　kerb broker, outside broker
场外市场/場外市場　outside market
场外收盘价/場外收盤價　kerb close
场外证券买卖/場外證券買賣　kerb trading

敞口头寸/暴露部位　open position
敞田制/敞田制度　open field system
畅销品/暢銷貨　best seller
畅销书/暢銷書　best seller, bestseller
倡导性广告/宣導廣告　advocacy advertising
倡导者/宣導者　champion
唱片/唱片　phonograph record, gramophone record, record disc
唱片档案/唱片檔案　phonorecord archive
唱片图书馆/唱機圖書館　gramophone library
唱片制作者的权利/唱片製作者的權利　right of producer of recordings
唱针/唱針　reproducing stylus tip
抄本/抄本　antigraph, transcript, hand-copied book
抄件/抄本　antigraph, transcript, hand-copied book
抄送机关/抄送機關　government institution which send duplicate
抄纂/抄纂　copy complication
钞票/紙幣　paper currency, paper money
超饱和设计/超飽和設計　supersaturated designs
超泊松分布/超卜瓦松分布,超卜瓦松分配　super-Poisson distribution, hyper-Poisson distribution
超博弈/超級賽局　supergames
超长文件/超長檔　extra long document
超大文件/超大檔　oversize document
超订/超額訂出,預訂過多　overbooking
超额保险/超額保險　excess coverage
超额储备/超額準備　excess reserves
超额储备金/超額儲備金　excessive reserve
超额担保/超額擔保　over collateralization
超额负担/超額負擔　excess burden
超额供给/超額供給　excess supply
超额利差/超額利差　excess spread
超额利润/超額利潤　excessive profit, excess profit
超额认购/超額認購　oversubscription
超额剩余价值/超額剩餘價值　extra surplus-value
超额系数/超額係數　coefficient of excess
超额需求/超額需求　excess demand
超凡权威/超凡權力　charisma authority
超凡信仰/超凡信仰　paranormal beliefs
超方[格]/超方格　hyper square
超负荷/超載,過載　overload
超高速缓存/快取　cache
超高缩微平片/超微單片　ultrafiche
超过配额/超過配額　above quota
超级股利/超級股利　super dividend
超级股票/超級股票　super share
超级基金/超級基金　superfund

超级可转让支付命令账户/超級可轉讓取款條賬戶　super now
超级市场/超級市場　supermarket
超级数字激光视盘/超級影碟　super video compact disc
超级数字音频光盘/超級音訊光碟　super audio compact disc, SACD
超几何分布/超幾何分布,超幾何分配　hypergeometric distribution
超几何概率/超幾何機率　hypergeometric probability
超几何级数/超幾何數列　hypergeometric series
超Y理论/超Y理論　super theory Y
超立方体/超立方體　hypercube
超链接/超鏈結　hyperlink
超量系数/超量係數　coefficient of excess
超媒体/超媒體　hypermedia, supermedia
超模博弈/超階賽局　supermodular game
超球面正态分布/超球面常態分配,超球面常態分布　hyper-spherical normal distribution
超实时模拟/超即時模擬　super-real-time simulation
超外生/超外生性　super exogenous
超文本/超文本　hypertext
超文本检索/超文字檢索　hypertext information retrieval
超我无差异曲线/超我無差異曲線　superego indifference curve
超希腊-拉丁方/超希臘拉丁方格　hyper-Graeco-Latin square
超现实主义/超現實主義　surrealism
超应力故障/超應力故障　over-stress failure
超应力失效/超應力故障　over-stress failure
超有效性/超有效性　superefficiency
超真实/超真實,過度真實　hyperreality
超正态分布/超常態分配,超常態分布　supernormal distribution, hypernormal distribution
超正态离散/超常態離勢　supernormal dispersion, hypernormal dispersion
超正态性/超常態性　hypernormality
超值分布/超值分布　distribution of exceedance
超值检验/超值檢定　exceedances tests
超值寿命试验/超值壽命試驗　exceedance life test
超指数分布/超指數分布,超指數分配　superexponential distribution
超总体/超母體　superpopulation
朝审/朝審　review of death penalty prisoners
潮湿试验/潮濕試驗　humidity test
车船使用税/車船使用稅　travel tax, vehicle and vessel use tax

车船税/車船税 vehicle and vessel tax
车船运输/車船運輸 trainship
车辆购置税/車輛購置税 vehicles purchase tax
车辆空驶率/空載率,無載率 empty-loaded rate
车体广告/車體廣告張貼物 outside poster
车厢内广告/車廂内廣告 inside card
车厢内交货价[格]/車廂内交貨價[格] free in wagon, free into wagon, FIW
彻底纠正行动/基本校正行動,基本改正行動 basic corrective action
撤回抗诉/撤回抗訴 withdraw a counterappeal
撤回起诉/撤回起訴 withdraw a prosecution
撤回前有效发盘/撤回前有效報價 offer good until withdrawn
撤回上诉/撤回上訴 withdraw an appeal
撤回支票/撤回支票,支票止付 countermand of a check
撤诉/撤訴 withdraw an action
撤销案件/撤銷案件 quash a case
撤销订货/撤銷訂貨 cancellation of order
撤销发盘/撤銷發盤,撤銷報價 cancel offer, cancellation of offer
撤销合同/撤銷合約 cancellation of contract
撤销机关档案/撤銷機關檔案 archive of the revocation office
撤销判决/撤銷判決 abrogation of judgement
撤销外汇合同/撤銷外匯合約 cancellation of exchange contract
撤销委托/撤銷委託 cancel power of attorney
撤销未到期合同/撤銷未到期合約 cancellation of future performance
撤销仲裁裁决/撤銷仲裁裁決 setting aside of arbitral award
沉没成本/沈没成本,沈入成本 sunk cost
沉没成本谬误/沈没成本謬誤 sunk cost fallacy
沉没资本/沈没資產,沈入資產 sunk assets
沉默的螺旋/沈默螺旋 spiral of silence
沉默权/沈默權 right to silence
陈列/陳列 display
陈列柜/陳列櫃 display cabinet
陈律/陳律 Law of Chen Dynasty
陈群/陳群 Chen Qun
陈述/陳述 statement
陈述的听证/陳述的聽證 speech-making hearing
晨报/晨報 morning newspaper, morning paper
衬纸/空白隔紙 interleaf
称谓用语/稱謂用語 appellation term
成本/成本 cost

成本、保险费加空运费价/成本、保險費加空運費價格 cost-insurance-freight by plane
成本补偿法则/成本補償準則 cost-reimbursement rule
成本不变行业/成本不變的產業,成本固定行業 constant cost industry, constant-cost industry
成本差异/成本差異 cost differences
成本导向定价/成本基礎定價法 cost-based pricing
成本导向定价法/成本基礎定價法 cost-based pricing
成本递减行业/成本遞減產業,成本降低產業 decreasing cost industry
成本递增规律/成本遞增法則 law of increasing cost
成本递增行业/成本遞增的產業,遞增成本行業 increasing cost industry
成本动因/成本動因 cost driver
成本分担/成本分擔 cost sharing
成本分析/成本分析 cost analysis
成本-功能矩阵/成本-功能矩陣 cost-function matrix, cost-function worksheet
成本函数/成本函數 cost function
成本集中/成本集中 centralization of cost
成本加成定价/成本加利潤定價 cost-plus pricing
成本加成合同/成本加成契約,成本加成合約 cost-plus contract
成本加酬金合同/成本加酬金合同 cost-plus-fee contract, CPF contract
成本加鼓励酬金合同/成本加鼓勵酬金合同 cost-plus-incentive fee contract, CPIF contract
成本加固定酬金合同/成本加固定酬金合同 cost-plus-fixed fee contract, CPFF contract
成本加提成合同/成本加獎勵費合同 cost-plus-incentive fee contract
成本结构/成本結構 cost structure
成本控制/成本控制 cost control
成本控制政策/控制成本政策 cost containment policies
成本会计/成本會計 cost accounting
成本领先战略/全面成本領導策略 overall cost leadership strategy
成本率方案/成本率方案 cost-ratio plan
成本模型/成本模型 cost model
成本黏性/成本黏性 cost stickiness
成本扭曲/成本扭曲 cost distortions
成本收益分析/成本效益分析 cost-benefit analysis
成本推进型通货膨胀/成本推動型通貨膨脹,成本提高型通貨膨脹 cost push inflation
成本相关产出法/成本相關產出法 cost-related

outcome method
成本效益/成本有效性　cost effectiveness, cost-benefit
成本效益分析/成本效益分析,效益成本分析,成本有效性分析　benefit-cost analysis, cost-benefit analysis, cost-effectiveness analysis
成本效益分析法/成本效益法　cost-benefit approach
成本性态/成本習性　cost behavior
成本中心/成本中心　cost center
成本-主观价值模型/成本-主觀價值模型　cost-worth model
成本转嫁/成本轉嫁　cost passthrough
成本最小化弱公理/弱性成本極小化公設　weak axiom of cost minimization
成本最小原则/[生產的]最低成本法則　least-cost rule of production
成对比较/成對比較　paired comparison
成对变量/成對變量　paired variates
成对抽样/複製抽樣　duplicate sampling
成对数据/成對數據　paired data
成对样本/重抽樣本,複製樣本　duplicate sample, duplicated sample
成分分布/成分分布,成分分配　component distribution
成分分析/成分分析　component analysis
成分品牌化/成分品牌　ingredient branding
成功概率/成功機率　probability of success
成交/成交　closing
成交率/達成率　fill rate
成就测验/成就測驗,學識測驗　achievement test
成名动机/成名動機　motivation for fame
成年礼/成年禮　coming-of-age ceremony, coming-of-age ritual
成批报价/成批報價　block offer
成批到达输入/成批到達輸入　batch arrival input
成批交易/成批交易,整批交易　round lot sale
成批物料清单/材料清單　batch bill of material, batch formula
成批预订/成批預訂　block booking
成品库/成品庫　finished product room
成品库存/成品庫存,成品存貨　finished-good inventory, finished product inventory
成人初显期/成人初顯期,始成年期　emerging adulthood
成熟度/成熟度　readiness
成熟阶段/成熟階段　mature stage
成熟期/成熟期　maturity stage
成套汇票/成套匯票　set bill

成文日期/成文日期　written date
成文宪法/成文憲法　written constitution
成像/成像　imaging
成员馆/成員圖書館　membership library
成员群体/隸屬團體,成員團體　membership group
成长轨迹/成長軌跡　growth trajectory
成长阶段/成長階段　growth stage
成长型基金/成長型基金,增長型基金　growth fund
成长与发展模式/成長與發展模式　growth and development model
成组技术/群組技術　group technology
成组排序/分組排序　scheduling with batching
成组制造单元/成組製造單元　group manufacturing cell
丞相府/丞相府　prime minister house
呈缴本/呈繳本,送存本　deposit copy, copyright deposit
呈缴本登记目录/呈繳書目錄　copyright list
呈缴本制度/呈繳制度　legal deposit system
呈色剂/染色劑　toner
呈同前因/呈同前因　chengtongqianyin
诚实信用原则/誠實信用原則　good faith doctrine
诚信管理体系/信貸管理體制　credit management system
承办/承辦　undertake
承包商违约/承包商違約　default to contractor
承保/承兌,承銷　acceptance, underwriting
承保利润/承保利潤　underwriting profit
承保人/承保人　insurer, underwriter
承保限额/承保限額　underwriting limit
承兑/承兌　acceptance
承兑保证/承兌保證　guarantee of acceptance
承兑费/承兌費用　acceptance fee
承兑函/承兌函　letter of acceptance
承兑汇票/承兌票據,匯票　bill accepted, acceptance draft, acceptance bill
承兑交单/承兌交單　acceptance against document, document against acceptance
承兑交单汇票/承兌交單匯票　document against acceptance bill
承兑交货/承兌交貨　delivery against acceptance
承兑结算/承兌結算　settlement by acceptance
承兑期/承兌期　term of acceptance
承兑人/承兌人　acceptor
承兑商/承兌商　acceptance dealer
承兑手续费/承兌手續費,票據手續費　acceptance commission
承兑提示/承兌提示　presentation for acceptance

承兑通知/承兑通知　acceptance advice
承兑协议/承兌協議,承兌契約　acceptance agreement
承兑信用/承兌信貸　acceptance credit
承兑信用证/承兌信用狀　acceptance credit, acceptance letter of credit
承兑型资金融通/承兌型融資　acceptance type financing
承兑银行/承兌銀行　accepting bank, acceptance bank
承兑佣金/承兌手續費,票據手續費　acceptance commission
承兑责任/承兌責任　liability for acceptance
承购权/購買選擇權　call option
承建单位/承包單位　contractor unit
承揽合同/承攬合同　contract for work
承诺/承諾　acceptance, commitment
承诺不可撤销的拨付额/不可撤銷的支付承諾　irrevocable commitments to disburse
承诺到期收益率/承諾到期收益率　promised yield to maturity
承诺升级/承諾升高　escalation of commitment
承诺支付/承諾支付　acceptance and guarantee
承认规则/承認規則　rule of recognition
承认政治/承認政治,肯認政治　politics of recognition
承认仲裁裁决/承認仲裁裁決　recognition of the award
承袭海/承襲海　patrimonial sea
承销/承銷　consignment inward
承销商/承銷商　underwriter
承销商品预付款/寄售商品預付款　advance consignment-inward
承印物/承印物　substrate, printing stock
承运人/承運人　carrier
承载变量/承載變數　carrier variable
承载能力/容納量　carrying capacity
承转结算/承轉結算　commitment to clearance
城/城　city
城旦春/城旦春　chengdanchong
城建档案/城市建設檔案　urban construction archive
城市/城市,都市　urban, city
城市变迁/城市變遷　urban transformation
城市房地产税/都市房地產稅　urban real estate tax
城市更新/城市更新　urban renewal
城市固体废物/都市固定廢棄物　municipal solid waste
城市管理/都市管理　urban management

城市规划/都市計劃　urban planning
城市规模效应/都市規模效益　urban scale effectiveness
城市化/都市化　urbanization
城市化地区/都市[化地區]　urbanized area
城市化经济/都市化經濟　urbanization economies
城市化驱动机制/城市化驅動力　drive mechanism of urbanization
城市环境保护法/城市環境保護法　Law on Protection of Urban Environment
城市建设档案馆/城市建設檔案館　city construction archives
城市结构规划/都市總體規劃　urban structure planning
城市经济增长/都市經濟成長　urban economic growth
城市竞争力/都市競爭力　urban competitiveness
城市空间/都市地方　urban place
城市空间发展战略/都市成長策略　urban growth strategy
城市空间增长/都市成長　urban growth
城市理论或流派/城市理論或流派　urban theories
城市偏向/都市偏好　urban bias
城市贫困/城市貧困　urban poverty
城市贫困与不平等/城市貧困與不平等　urban poverty and inequality
城市圈经济理论/都市圈經濟理論　economic energy of city theory
城市群/城市群　city cluster
城市人口比重/城市人口比重　urban population as percentage of total population
城市少数族裔聚集/城市少數族裔聚集　urban ethnic enclave
城市社区/都市社區　urban community
城市首位律/城市首位律　law of the primate city
城市舒适度/都市寧適　urban amenities
城市维护建设税/城市維護建設稅　city maintenance and construction tax
城市文化/都市文化　urban culture
城市消费品物价指数/都市消費者物價指數　index of urban consumer prices
城市行政区划/城市行政區劃　urban administrative classification
城市性/都市性[格]　urbanism
城市意象/城市意象　mental map of urban life
城市政策/都市政策　urban policy
城乡二元结构/城鄉二元結構　urban-rural dual structure

城乡二元社会结构/城鄉二元社會結構 urban-rural dual social structure
城乡关系/城鄉關係 urban and rural relations
城乡统筹/城鄉一體化 urban-rural integration
城乡最低生活保障/城鄉最低生活保障 urban and rural minimum living standard scheme
城镇居民基本养老保险制度/城鎮居民基本養老保險制度 basic pension system for urban residents
城镇居民基本医疗保险制度/城鎮居民基本醫療保險制度 basic medical insurance system for urban residents
城镇居民医疗保险/城鎮居民醫療保險 urban residents' medical insurance
城镇廉租房制度/城鎮廉租房制度 low rent housing system in cities and towns
城镇体系/都市體系 urban system
城镇土地使用税/城鎮土地使用税,都市土地使用税 urban and township land use tax
城镇职工医疗保险/城鎮職工醫療保險 employees' medical insurance
城中村/城中村 village in the city
乘法法则/乘法定理 multiplication rule
乘法模型/相乘模型 multiplicative model
乘积测度/乘積測度 product measure
乘积概率函数/乘積機率函數 product probability function
乘积概率空间/乘積機率空間 product probability space
乘积矩/乘積動差 product moment
乘积矩法/乘積動差法 product moment method
乘积矩母函数/乘積動差生成函數 product moment generating function
乘积矩相关/乘積動差相關 product moment correlation
乘积可测空间/乘積可測空間 product measurable space
乘积限分布/乘積極限分布 product limit distribution
乘积限估计[量]/乘積極限估計量 product limit estimator
乘积形式解/乘積形式解 product-form solution
乘幂加速/乘冪加速 acceleration by powering
乘数/乘數 multiplier
乘数-加速原理/乘算加速機械作用 multiplier-accelerator mechanism
乘数效应/乘數效果 multiplier effect
乘数原理/乘數原理 multiplier principle
程式化/例行化,常規化 routinization

程序/程序,程式 program, procedure
程序化的决策技术/程式化的決策技術 programmed decision technique
程序化交易/程式交易 program trading
程序化决策/程式化決策 programmed decision making
程序或结构/程序或結構 procedures or structures
程序偏倚/程序偏誤 procedural bias
程序权利/程式權利 procedural right
程序设计/程式設計 program design
程序图/程序圖 procedure chart
程序违法/程式違法 violation of procedure law
程序文件/程式檔 program document
程序性学习/程式化學習 programmed learning
程序依法院地法/程式依法院地法 procedure is governed by lex fori
程序正义/程式正義 procedural justice
程序主义法范式/程序主義法範式 proceduralist paradigm of law
程序组合法/程式組合法 program combination method
惩罚/處罰 punishment
惩罚函数/懲罰函數 penalty function
惩罚利率/懲罰性貼現率 penalty rate
惩罚性[贷款]利率/滯納金利率 penalty interest rate
惩罚性关税/懲罰性關税 penalty duty
惩罚性赔偿/懲罰性賠償 punitive damages
惩罚性损害赔偿/懲罰性違約金 punitive damage
惩罚制度/違反紀律處理常式 disciplinary procedure
澄清会议/澄清會議 meeting to clarify
橙皮书/橙皮書 orange paper
笞/笞 flogging
驰名商标/馳名商標 well-known trademark
迟延/不可避免延誤 unavoidable delay
持股比率/持股比率 share holding ratio
持久收入/永久性收入,長期收入 permanent income
持久收入假说/恆常所得假設 permanent income hypothesis
持票人/持票人 bill holder, holder of bill
持续创新过程/持續創新過程 process of continuous innovation
持续改进/持續改善 continuous improvement
持续经营假设/繼續經營假設 going concern postulate
持续期缺口/存續期間缺口 duration gap
持续期依赖/持續期間相依性 duration dependence

持续通货膨胀/目前通貨膨脹　ongoing inflation
持续效应/持久性效果　persistence effect
持续性计划/持續性計劃,備用計劃　standing plan
持续性评价/可持續評估　sustainability evaluation
持有期限/持有期間　holding period
持有至到期投资/持有至到期投資　held-to-maturity investment
尺牍/尺牘　chidu
尺度/尺度　scale
尺度变换/尺度變換　change of scale
尺度标记/尺度標記　scale designation
尺度参数/尺度參數　scale parameter, parameter of scale
尺度单位/尺度單位　scale unit
尺度导线/尺度導線　scale guide line
尺度的度量/尺度測度　measure of scale
尺度等变异估计[量]/尺度等變異估計量　scale equivariant estimator
尺度点/尺度點　scale point
尺度数/尺度數　scale number
尺度中断/尺度中斷　scale break
尺度中位数/尺度中位數　scale median
尺度族/尺度族群　scale family
赤池信息量准则/赤池資訊準則,Akaike 資訊準則　Akaike information criterion, AIC
赤池信息准则/艾凱克訊息準則　Akaike information criterion
赤脚医生/赤腳醫生　barefoot doctor
赤字/赤字　deficit
赤字财政/赤字財政,赤字融通　deficit financing, deficit finance
赤字性支出/赤字性支出　deficit spending
冲动性购买/衝動性購買　impulsive purchase
冲动性购买行为/衝動性購買行爲　impluse buying behavior
冲击乘数/衝擊乘數　impact multiplier
冲击-反应模式/衝擊-反應模式　impact-response model
冲击与误差模型/震盪與誤差模型　shock and error model
冲突/衝突　conflict
冲突的传统观点/衝突的傳統觀點　traditional view of conflict
冲突的人际关系观点/衝突的人際關係觀點　human relation view of conflict
冲突的相互作用观点/衝突的相互作用觀點　interactional view of conflict
冲突管理/衝突管理　conflict management

冲突规范/衝突規範　conflict rules
冲突决策/衝突決策　conflict decision
冲突理论/衝突理論　conflict theory
TKI 冲突模型测验/湯瑪士-克里曼衝突二維模式　Thomas-Kilmann conflict mode instrument
冲洗/沖洗　flushing
冲销/沖銷措施　write-off
冲销账户按揭/抵銷賬户不動產擔保　offset account mortgage
充电/充電　charging
充分分割/充分分割　sufficient partition
充分分散的资产组合/多元化投資組合　welldiversified portfolio
充分估计[量]/充分估計量　sufficient estimator
充分就业/充分就業　full employment
充分就业的产出/充分就業下的產值　full-employment output
充分统计量/充分統計量　sufficient statistic
充分统计量的维数/充分統計量的維度　dimensionality of sufficient statistic
充分性/充分性　sufficiency
充军/充軍　punishment of prisoners to remote areas and enrich the military
虫蛀本/蟲蛀本　worm-eaten book
重版书目/重版書目　backlist
重版征订包销/重版徵訂包銷　republication and exclusive sales
重测信度/重測信度,再測信度　test-retest reliability
重抽样方法/重抽樣程序　resampling procedures
重氮胶片/重氮片　diazo film
重叠抽样单元/重複抽樣單位　overlapping sampling unit
重叠设计/重疊設計　overlap design
重叠图法/重疊圖示法　method of overlapping maps
重叠系数/重疊係數　overlapping coefficient
重对数变换/重對數變換　loglog transformation
重对数[定]律/疊對數法則　law of iterated logarithm
重放/重現,重播　playback, replay
重放通道/重放通道　playback channel
重放头/播放頭　playback head
重放系统/重現系統　playback system
重复/重複　repetition, replication
重复保险/重複保險　duplicate insurance, overlapping insurance
重复博弈/重複的賽局　repeated game
重复抽样/重複抽樣　replicated sampling, repeated sampling
重复调查/重複調查　repeated survey

重复对策/重複的賽局　repeated game
重复发盘/重複報價　repeat offer
重复分析/重複分析　replicate analysis
重复购买/重複購買　repeat purchase
重复横断面调查/重複橫斷面調查　repeated cross-sectional survey
重复实验/重複試驗　repeated experiment
重复剔除的占优策略/反覆消除劣勢策略　iterative elimination of dominated strategies
重复投标博弈/反覆出價法　iterative bidding game
重复投资/重複投資　overlapping investment
重复形态/重複型態　repeating pattern
重复性/重複性　repeatability
重复性生产/重複性生産　repetitive production
重复原理/重複原則　principle of replication
重复阅读率/重複閱讀率　duplication rate
重复债务/重複債務　overlapping debt
重复组合/重複組合　combination with repetitions
重构/重新框架　reframing
重购/買回　repurchase
重婚罪/重婚罪　crime of bigamy
重建/理論重構　reconstruction
重刻本/重刻本　reprint edition
重排/重排,重列　re-arrangement
重文/重文　repeated word
重现赛局/重現賽局　recurrence game
重写本/重寫本　rewritten edition
重新编目/重新編目　recataloging
重新测量合同/複測合同　remeasurement contract
重新抽样计划/重新抽樣計劃　resampling schemes
重新定位型新产品/重新定位型新産品　repositioned new product
重新发盘/重新報價　renewed offer
重新分类/重新分類　re-classification
重新估价盈余/盈餘重估　reappraisal surplus
重新鉴定/重新鑒定　renew verifications
重新就业安置/再就業協助,再就業輔導　outplacement
重新框定/重新框架　reframing
重新生成系统/再生系統　regenerative system
重译/重譯　retranslation
重印本/重印本,翻印本　reprint
重影/重影　doubling, ghost image
重影控制块/重影控制塊　doubling patch
重再参数化/重新參數化的程式　reparameterization
重整程序/重整程式　reorganization procedure
重制权/重製權　right of reproduction
重置成本/重置成本　replacement cost

重置成本法/重置成本法　replacement cost method
重置价格/重置價格　replacement price
重置价值/重置價值　replacement value
重装书脊/重裝書脊　rebacked
重组/重組,重整　rehabilitation, restructuring, reorganization
冲孔/衝孔　punching
冲孔机/雞眼機　eyeleting machine
抽查法/抽查法　searching in sampling chronological order, sampling search, sampling checking
抽词标引/摘錄標引　derived indexing, extraction indexing
抽检特性曲线/抽檢特徵曲線　operating characteristic curve
抽奖促销/抽獎式促銷　lottery promotion, sweepstakes
抽逃资金/資金回收　withdrawal of funds
抽屉问题/檔案櫃問題　file drawer problem
抽象/抽象　abstraction
抽象劳动/抽象勞動　abstract labour
抽象社会/抽象社會　abstract society
抽象行政行为/抽象行政行爲　abstract administrative action
抽样/抽樣,取樣　sampling
抽样比/抽樣比,抽出率　sampling fraction, sampling ratio
抽样变异/抽樣變異　sampling variation
抽样变异性/抽樣變異性　sampling variability
抽样标准/抽樣標準　sampling standard
抽样波动/抽樣變動　sampling fluctuation
抽样步长/抽樣長度　sampling length
抽样成本/抽樣成本　cost of sampling
抽样程序/抽樣程序　sampling procedure
抽样单位/抽樣單位　sampling unit
抽样单元/抽樣單位　sampling unit
抽样调查/抽樣調查　sampling survey, survey sampling
抽样调查的标记/抽樣調查的標記　label in survey sampling
抽样方案/抽樣方法,抽樣計劃　sampling scheme, sampling plan
抽样方差/抽樣變異數　sampling variance
抽样方法/抽樣方法　sampling method
抽样分布/抽樣分布,抽樣分配　sampling distribution
抽样分布理论/抽樣分布理論　theory of sampling distribution
抽样后分层/抽樣後分層　stratification after

sampling
抽样计划/抽樣計劃,抽樣方案 sampling scheme
抽样技术/抽樣技術 sampling technique
抽样检验/抽樣檢驗,選擇檢驗 sampling inspection
抽样检验表/抽樣檢驗表 sampling inspection table
抽样检验方案/抽樣檢驗計劃 sampling inspection plan
抽样间隔/抽樣間隔 sampling interval
抽样鉴定法/抽樣鑒定法 sampling appraisal
抽样结构/抽樣結構 sampling structure
抽样精度/抽樣精確度 sampling precision, precision of sampling
抽样矩/抽樣動差 sampling moment
抽样框/抽樣框,抽樣底冊 sampling frame
抽样理论/抽樣理論 sampling theory, theory of sampling
抽样模型/抽樣模型 sampling model
抽样频率/抽樣頻次 sampling frequency
抽样设计/抽樣設計 sampling design
抽样实验/抽樣實驗 sampling experiment
抽样示范教具/抽樣示範教具 sampling demonstrator
抽样说明/抽樣說明 sampling instruction
抽样误差/抽樣誤差 sampling error, errors in sampling
抽样信息期望值/樣本資訊期望值,取樣資訊期望值 expected value of sample information
抽样验证/抽樣驗證 sampling verification
抽样制表/抽樣製表 sampling tabulation
抽样准则/抽樣準則 criteria for sampling
抽印本/抽印本 offprints
筹集贷款/籌集貸款 loan floatation
筹集高额资金/高額籌資 high level of financing
筹资活动/籌資活動 financing activity
臭氧层破坏/臭氧層破壞 destruction of ozone layer
出版/出版 publish, publishing, publication
FTP 出版/FTP 出版 file transfer protocol publishing
UseNet 出版/UseNet 出版 UseNet publishing
Web2.0 出版/Web2.0 出版 Web 2.0 publishing
出版部/出版部 publication department
出版[产]业/出版業 publishing industry
出版产业链/出版產業鏈 publishing industry chain
出版地/出版地 place of publication, location
出版发行附注/出版發行附注 notes pertaining to publication and distribution
出版发行目录/出版發行目錄 list of published books
出版公司/出版公司 publishing company
出版活动/出版活動 publishing activity
出版机构/出版機構 publishing agency
出版权/出版權 publishing right
出版社/出版社 press, publishing house
出版社丛集/出版社叢集 publisher's series
出版社自销/出版社自銷 self-sale by press
出版说明/出版說明 publication explanation
出版体制/出版體制 system of publishing
出版统计/出版統計 publication statistics
出版物/出版物 publication
出版物购销合同/出版物購銷合同 purchase and sale contract
出版物购销形式/出版物購銷形式 purchase and sale form
出版物件标识符/出版物對象標識符 publisher item identifier, PII
出版物流通/出版物流通 publication circulation
出版物市场/出版物市場 publication market
出版物市场调查/出版物市場調查 publication market research
出版物市场定位/出版物市場定位 publication market positioning
出版物市场细分/出版物市場細分 publication market segmentation
出版物市场需求/出版物市場需求 publication market demand
出版物条码/出版物條碼 bar code for publication
出版物营销分类/出版物行銷分類 marketing classification for publication
出版项/出版項 item on publication
出版形式/出版形式 publishing form, form of publications
出版许可/出版許可 imprimatur
出版学/出版學 publishing science
出版载体/出版載體 publishing media
出版者/發行人 publisher
出版者权/出版者權 publisher's rights
出版状态/出版狀態 publishing status
出版自由/出版自由 freedom of the press
出差津贴/出差津貼 mission installation allowance
出厂产品/出廠產品 outgoing product
出厂价/出廠價 price ex-factory
出厂质量/出廠品質 delivery quality
出超/出超 export surplus
出港通知书/出港通知書 clearance notice
出港许可证/出港許可證 clearance permit
出港证/出港證 clearing label

出货分销/出貨分銷　outbound distribution
出货检验/出貨檢驗　outgoing inspection
出价/出價,叫價　bid
出价和要价/買入賣出價　bid and asked price
出借登记/調檔記錄　charge-out
出借登记簿/調檔登記簿　charge-out register
出镜/出鏡　frame-out
出口/出口　export
出口保险/出口保險　export insurance
出口报关手续/出口報關手續　customs clearing procedure for export
出口补贴/出口補貼,輸出獎勵金　export subsidy, export bounty
出口补贴证明/出口補助證明　certificate of export subsidy
出口不足/出口不足　under exporting
出口产业/出口產業　export industry
出口代理人/出口代理人　export commissioner
出口代理商/出口代理商　export agent
出口代理协议/出口代理契約　export agency agreement
出口贷款/出口貸款　export loan, loan for export, loan of export
出口贷款保险/出口貸款保險　export loan insurance
出口单据/出口單據　export document
出口单据押汇透支/出口單據押匯透支　overdraft for export bill
出口导向/出口導向,面向出口　export orientation, export-oriented
出口导向型增长/出口帶動成長　export-led growth
出口导向政策/出口導向政策　export oriented policy
出口订单/出口訂單　export order
出口多样化/出口多樣化　diversification of export
出口额/出口[金]額　value of export, volume of export
出口港/出口港　port of export
出口跟单汇票/出口跟單匯票　outward documentary bill
出口供给曲线/出口供給曲線　export supply curve
出口供给弹性/出口供給彈性　elasticity of export supply
出口鼓励政策/出口擴張政策　export promotion policy
出口关税/出口[關]稅　export tariff, export duty, export tax
出口管制/出口管制,出口控制　export control, export controls
出口合同/出口合約　export contract

出口汇票/出口匯票　export bill, outward bill
出口汇票担保借款利率/出口匯票擔保借款利率　interest rate on loan secured by export trade bill
出口货单/出口貨單,出口艙單　outward manifest, export list
出口货物/出口貨物　outward cargo
出口货物国别价值/以進口國爲基準之出口額　value of export by country of destination
出口技术/出口技術　export technique
出口加工/加工出口　export processing
出口加工贸易/出口加工貿易　processing deal for export
出口加工区/加工出口區　export processing zone
出口价格/出口價格　export price
出口检验/出口檢驗　export inspection
出口检验证[书]/出口檢驗證書　inspection certificate for export
出口奖励/出口獎勵　bounty on export
出口结关/出口結關　outward clearance, customs clearance for export
出口金融公司/出口融資公司　export finance company
出口禁运/出口禁運　export embargo
出口净值/出口淨值　net export value
出口贸易/出口貿易　export trade
出口贸易审计/出口貿易審計　audit of export trade
出口免税证书/出口免税證書　certificate of export duty exemption
出口配额/出口配額　export quota
出口倾向/出口傾向　propensity to export
出口融资/出口融資,籌集出口資金　financing of export, export financing
出口商品/出口商品　export commodity
出口商品的激励政策/出口鼓勵政策　incentive policy of export commodities
出口商品口岸/出口商品口岸　outlet for export product
出口商品目录/出口商品目錄　list of export commodity
出口商品质量证明制度/出口商品質量證明制度　system of quality certificate for export commodity
出口申报单/出口報單　declaration for exportation, declaration for export, export declaration
出口收入弹性/出口收益彈性　income elasticity of export
出口收入稳定/出口收入穩定　stabilization of export receipt
出口收入下降/出口收入下降　shortfall in export

earning
出口收益/出口收益　export earning
出口手续/出口手續　process of export
出口数量管制/出口數量管制　control of export quantum
出口数量指数/出口數量指數　quantum index of export
出口税/出口稅　export tax, export duty
出口税额减免/出口稅額減免　export tax relief
出口提单/出口提單　export bill of lading
出口替代/出口替代　export replacing, export-substitution
出口替代政策/出口替代政策　export substitution policy
出口投资/出口投資　export investment
出口退税/出口退稅,外銷退稅　export tax rebate, export drawback, export rebate
出口托收/出口託收　export collection, outward collection
出口外汇/出口外匯　export exchange
出口外汇保留额/出口外匯保留額　export retention quota
出口外汇分红制/出口外匯分紅制　foreign exchange dividend system
出口外汇支出审计/出口外匯支出審計　audit of foreign exchange payment on export
出口违禁品/出口違禁品　contraband of export
出口物价指数/出口物價指數　price indices of exports
出口限制/出口限制　export restriction, restriction of export, export restrain
出口限制协议/出口限制協定　export restraint agreements
出口销售额/出口銷售額　export sales
出口信贷/出口信貸　export credit
出口信贷保险/出口信貸保險　export credit insurance
出口信贷补贴/輸出信用補助　export credit subsidies
出口信贷担保/出口信貸擔保　export credit guarantee
出口信贷国家担保制/出口信貸[國家]擔保制　export credit guarantee system
出口信贷计划/出口信貸計劃　export credit scheme
出口信贷利率/出口信貸利率　export credit rate
出口信贷账户/出口信貸賬戶　export credit account
出口信用担保/出口信用擔保　guarantee of export credit

出口信用证/出口信用狀　export letter of credit
出口信用状贷款/出口信用狀貸款　export letter-of-credit loans
出口信用状压汇/出口信用狀押匯　export letter-of-credit advance
出口需求弹性/出口需求彈性　elasticity of export demand
出口许可/出口許可,輸出許可　licensing of export
出口许可证/出口許可證,輸出許可證　certificate of export license, export licence, export permit
出口许可证申请书/輸出許可證申請書　application for export licence
出口押汇/出口押匯　bill purchased, outward documentary bill
出口依存度/出口依存度,對出口貿易依存度　degree of dependence on export, dependence degree on export
出口银行信贷/出口銀行信貸　export bank credit
出口预付款/出口預付款　export prepayment
出口账户/出口賬戶　export account
出口招标/出口招標　export tender
出口支出账户/出口支出賬戶　export debit account
出口制造商/出口製造商　exporting manufacturer
出口总额/出口總額　gross export
出库/出庫　warehouse-out
出礼入刑/出禮入刑　penal punishment of behaviors against moral rites
出链/出鏈　outlink
出链数/出鏈數　number of outlinks
出纳/出納　cashier, teller
出票/出票,開票　issue, draw bill, issue warrant
出票后定期付款/出票後定期付款　payable at fixed period after date
出票日期/出票日期　date of draft
出入境管理/出入境管理　exit and entry administration
出入人罪/出入人罪　offence of arbitrarily imposing lighter or heavier sentences than necessary
出生/出生　birth
出生比/出生比　birth ratio
出生地人口/出生地人口　birth-place population
出生地主义/出生地主義　jus soli
出生队列/出生年次　birth cohort
出生率/出生率　natality, birth rate
出生时预期寿命/出生時預期壽命　life expectancy at birth
出生、死亡、迁移过程/生、滅及遷移過程　birth, death and immigration process

出示许可证条款/出示許可證條款　sighting of license clause
出示证据/出示證據　presentation of evidence
出庭律师/出庭律師　barrister
出向存货点/出倉物資儲備站　outbound stock point
出血/出血　bleed off
出血尺寸/出血尺寸　bleed size
出租车营业执照/計程車執照　taxi licenses
出租权/出租權　right of lease
出租人/出租人　lessor
初版/初版　first edition
初版分配试销/初版分配試銷　trial sale of the first edition distribution
初编/初編　the first compilation
初步报关手续/初步報關手續　initial customs house entry
初步范围说明书/初步範圍説明書　preliminary scope statement
初步检验估计量/初步試驗估計量　preliminary-test estimator
初步可行性研究/初步可行性研究　preliminary feasibility study
初步评审/初步評估　preliminary evaluation
初次分配/初次分配　primary distribution
初调查/初步調查,先期調查　preliminary survey
初稿本/初稿　the first draft
初婚率/初婚率　first marriage rate
初级表/初級表　primary table
初级产品/初級產品　primary product
初级产品出口国/初級產品出口國　primary exporting country
初级抽样单元/原始抽樣單位　primary sampling unit
初级单元/主要單位,原始單位　primary unit
初级读本/初級讀本　primer
初级群体/初級團體　primary group
初级商品价格指数/初級商品物價指數　price index of primary commodity
初级市场/初級市場　primary market
初级卫生保健/初級衛生保健　primary health care
初级证券市场/初級證券市場　primary securities market
初审/初審　first refereeing
初始保证金/原始保證金　initial margin
初始化/初始設定　initialization
初始库存/期初存貨　beginning inventory
初始原则/初期理論　incipiency doctrine
初拓本/初拓本　early rubbing

初选/初選　the first selecting stage
初印本/初印本　first edition, original edition, initial print
初诊人数/初診人數　number of first visit
除斥期间/除斥期間　scheduled period
除权判决/除權判決　invalidating judgment
除湿/除濕　dehumidification
除污/除汙　cleaning
除息日/除息日,除權日　ex-dividend date
锄耕文化/鋤耕文化　hoe culture
处断刑/處斷刑　awarding sentence
处断一罪/處斷一罪　awarding single crime
处分权/處分權　right of disposing
处分原则/處分原則　principle of disposition, principle of parties' autonomy in disposition of their legal right
处理/處理　processing, treatment
处理比较/處理比較　treatment comparisons
处理对照/處理對比　treatment contrast
处理均方/處理均方　treatment mean square
处理伦理两难原则/處理倫理兩難原則　principle of managing ethical dilemma
处理误差/處理誤差　processing error
处理效应/處理效應　treatment effect
处理异议/異議處理　handling objection
处理组合/處理組合　treatment combination
处置/處置　disposal
处置日期/處置日期　disposal date
处置文件表/處置檔表　disposal list
处置效应/處分效應　disposition effect
处置性缩微摄影/處置性微縮作業　disposal microfilming
储备货币/準備貨幣　reserve currencies
储备基金/準備[基]金　reserve fund
储备金分析/儲備金分析　reserve analysis
储备净额/儲備淨額　net reserve
储存/儲存　storing, storage
储户/存款人　depositor
储蓄/儲蓄,存款　saving, savings
储蓄保留系数/儲蓄留存係數　saving-retention coefficient
储蓄存单/儲蓄存單　saving deposit certificate
储蓄存款/儲蓄[存款]　savings deposit, saving
储蓄贷款协会/儲貸協會　savings and loans associations
储蓄鼓励/儲蓄鼓勵　thrift encouragement
储蓄国债/儲蓄債券　savings bond
储蓄机构/儲蓄機構,存款貨幣機構　depository

institution, thrift institutions, savings institution
储蓄率/儲蓄率　rate of saving, savings ratio
储蓄倾向/儲蓄傾向　propensity to save
储蓄投资分析/儲蓄投資分析　saving-investment analysis
储蓄投资账户/儲蓄投資賬戶　saving-investment account
储蓄协会保险基金/儲蓄協會保險基金　savings association insurance fund
储蓄银行/儲蓄銀行　savings bank
储蓄账户/儲蓄賬戶　saving account
储蓄资本/儲蓄資本　saving capital
储运网点/儲運網點　storage and transportation outlet
储值卡/儲值卡　store-valued card
楚列斯基分解/Cholesky 分解　Cholesky decomposition
触发策略/扣扳機策略,啟動策略　trigger strategy
触发价格/觸發價格,有連鎖反應的價格　trigger price
触摸屏/觸控螢幕　touch screen
触摸资料/觸摸資料　tactile materials
穿插/分插問題　interspersed
穿孔卡片/打孔卡片　punched card
穿孔卡片目录/穿孔卡片目錄　punch card catalogue
穿孔支票/穿孔支票　perforated check
穿孔纸带/打孔[紙]帶　punched tape
穿行测试/貫穿檢查　walk-through test
传版加密/傳版加密　transmit plate with encryption
传/傳播,擴散　diffusion, communication
传播管理/傳播管理　communication management
传播活动/傳播活動　communication campaign
传播监管制度/通訊傳播監理制度　communications regulatory system
传播教育/傳播教育　communication education
传播科技/傳播科技　communication technology
传播理论/傳播理論　communication theory
传播民族志/傳播民族志　ethnography of communication
传播模式/傳播模式　communication model
传播偏向/傳播偏見,傳播偏倚　bias of communication
传播期刊/傳播期刊　communication journal
传播权/[通訊]傳播權　communications rights
传播失灵/傳播失靈,通訊失敗　communication failure
传播说服矩阵/傳播說服矩陣　communication-persuasion matrix
传播调适论/傳播調節理論,傳播適應理論　communication accommodation theory, CAT
传播效果/擴散效果　spread effect
传播行为/傳播行爲　communication behavior
传播要素/傳播要素　communication element
传播战略/傳播策略　communication strategy
传播政策/傳播政策　communications policy
传播组合/傳播組合　communication mix
传达错误/傳達錯誤　mistake in communication
传递/傳遞,傳送,傳輸　transmission
传递函数模型/轉換函數模型　transfer function model
传来证据/傳聞證據　hearsay evidence
传媒/[傳播]媒體　media, communication media
传媒法/傳媒法　media law
传墨辊/布墨輥,揚墨輥,含墨輥輪　distributor, anilox roller
传票/傳票　process, subpoena
传染效应/傳染效果　contagious effect
传输/傳輸,傳送,傳遞　transmission
传输技术/無線電傳輸技術　transmission technology
传输媒体/傳輸媒介　transmission media
传输性/遞移性　transitivity
传送看板/拉式看板　withdrawal kanban
传统/傳統　tradition
传统出口商品/傳統出口商品　traditional export commodity
传统发明/傳統發明　invention of tradition
传统分销渠道/傳統分銷管道　conventional distribution channel
传统媒体/傳統媒體　traditional media
传统农业/傳統農業　traditional agriculture
传统社会/傳統社會　traditional society
传统图书馆/傳統圖書館　traditional library
传统文化表达/傳統文化表達　expressions of folklore, traditional cultural expressions
传统型权威/傳統威權,傳統權威　traditional authority
传统阅读/傳統閱讀　traditional reading
传统知识/傳統知識　traditional knowledge
传统职业路径/傳統職涯路徑　traditional career path
传闻/傳聞,小道消息,謠傳　grapevine, hearsay
传阅率/傳閱率　pass-along rate
传真/傳真　fax
传真文件/傳真檔　facsimile document
船边交货/船邊交貨[價格]　alongside delivery, free alongside ship

船边交货价/船邊交貨價,[目的港]碼頭交貨價 free on quay, franco quay
船边交货提单/船邊交貨提單 alongside bill of lading
船舶/船,艦 ship
船舶登记/船舶登記 registration of ship
船舶吨税/船舶噸稅 vessel tonnage tax
船舶留置权/船舶留置權 lien of ship, maritime lien
船舶碰撞/船舶碰撞 collision of ships
船舶碰撞准据法/船舶碰撞適用法 applicable law of ship collision
船东保赔协会/防護及補償協會 protection and indemnity club
船货崇拜/船貨崇拜 cargo cult
[船货]抵押契约/[船貨]抵押契約,押船契約 hypothecation agreement
船上交货价/船上交貨價 price free on board
串并联系统/串并聯系統,并串聯系統 series-parallel system, parallel-series system
串行式产品设计方法/序列式產品設計法 serial product design method
串行组织模式/串列組織模式 serial organization model
串联机/串聯機 dedicated machine
串联模型/串鏈模型 series-chain model
串联系统/串聯系統 series system
串墨辊/匀墨輥 distributing roller
串通投标/圍標 bid rigging
创伤记忆/創傷性記憶 traumatic memory
窗口指导/窗口指導 window guidance
窗时排序/窗時排序 window scheduling
闯齐/齊紙 knocking up
创建期资本投资/初期資本投資 initial capital investment
创刊/創刊 start publication
创刊词/創刊詞 creation
创刊号/創刊號 initial issue, start issue
创新/創新 innovation
创新采用群体/創新採用群體 adopter group of innovation
创新簇/創新群聚,創新聚落 innovation cluster
创新动态模型/U-A 模型 U-A model
创新复杂性/革新的複雜性 complexity of innovation
创新环境/創新環境 innovation environment
创新极/創新極 innovation pole
创新集群/創新群聚,創新聚落 innovation cluster
创新兼容性/創新相容性 compatibility of innovation

创新阶段/創新階段 creative phase
创新经济学/創新經濟學 innovation economics
创新可分性/創新可分割性 divisibility of innovation
创新可沟通性/創新的可溝通性 communicability of innovation
创新扩散/創新擴散 innovation diffusion
创新扩散理论/創新傳播理論 diffusion theory of innovation, innovation diffusion theory
创新离群值/創新離差值 innovational outlier
创新流程/創新流程 innovative process
创新能力/創新能力 innovation capability
创新平台/創新平臺 innovation platform
创新网络/創新網路 innovation network
创新系统/創新體系 innovation system
创新相对优势/創新相對優勢 relative advantage of innovation
创新项目小组/創新專案小組 innovation project team
创新型城市/創新城市 innovative city
创新型国家/創新型國家 innovative country
创新型企业/創新型企業 innovative enterprise
创新型人才/創新人才 innovative talent
创新型文化/創新型文化 innovative culture
创新型组织/創新型組織 innovative organization
创新要素/創新元素 innovative element
创新营销/創新行銷 innovative marketing
创新应用过程/創新應用過程 adoption process of innovation
创新源/創新源 innovation source
创新战略/創新策略 innovation strategy
创新者困境/創新者的兩難困境 innovator's dilemma
创新政策/創新政策 innovation policy
创新资源/創新資源 innovation resource
创业板市场/創業板 growth enterprises market
创业成本/開辦費 initial cost
创业的阴暗面/創業過程的負面 dark side of entrepreneurship
创业孵化器/創業育成中心 new-venture incubator
创业革命/創業革命 entrepreneurial revolution
创业管理/創業管理 entrepreneurial management
创业过程/創業過程 creative process
创业机会/創業機會 entrepreneurial opportunity
创业机会学派/創業機會學派 venture opportunity school
创业基金/創業基金 venture fund
创业计划书/事業計劃 business plan
创业绩效/創業績效 entrepreneurial performance

创业阶段/創業階段　start-up stage
创业经济/創業型經濟　entrepreneurial economy
创业精神/創業精神,企業家精神　entrepreneurship
创业评估方法/創業評估方法　entrepreneurial assessment approach
创业前阶段/創業前階段　pre-start-up stage
创业潜能/創業潛能　entrepreneurial perspective
创业团队/創業團隊　entrepreneurial team
创业行为/創業行爲　entrepreneurial behavior
创业型领导/企業型領導　entrepreneurial leadership
创业意向/創業意向　entrepreneurial intention
创业战略/創業戰略　entrepreneurial strategy
创业者战略矩阵/創業者戰略矩陣　entrepreneurial strategy matrix
创意产生/構想　idea generation
创意产业/創意產業　creative industry
创意阶层/創意階級　creative class
创意筛选/創意篩選　idea screening
创造/創造　create
创造力/創造力　creativity
创造型人才/創意人才　creative talents
创造性/創造性　creativeness
创造性的政策构建方法/創新規劃　creative policy formulation
创造性毁灭/創造性毀滅,創造性[的]破壞　creative destruction
创造性张力/創造性張力　creative tension
创造性支出/創造性支出　creative expenditures
创造学/創造學　creatology
创制权/創制權　right of initiative
创作/創作　creation
创作者/創作者　creator
创作自由/創作自由　freedom of creation
垂直差异/垂直性差異　vertical differentiation
垂直磁化/垂直磁化　perpendicular magnetization
垂直非一体化/垂直分解　vertical disintegration
垂直分工/垂直分工　vertical division
垂直供给曲线/垂直之供給曲線　vertical supply curve
垂直管理/垂直管理　vertical administration, line supervision
垂直间隔/垂直間隔　vertical separation
垂直结构/垂直結構　vertical structure
垂直贸易/垂直貿易　vertical trade
垂直市场封锁/垂直市場封殺　vertical market foreclosure
垂直市场划分/垂直市場割分　vertical market division
垂直搜索/垂直搜索　vertical search
垂直搜索引擎/專業搜索引擎　vertical search engine, specialized search engine, professional search engine
垂直调制角/垂直調制角　vertical modulation angle
垂直团体/垂直團體　vertical group
垂直协作/垂直統籌　vertical coordination
垂直型产业内贸易/產業內垂直貿易　vertical intra-industry trade
垂直型国际分工/垂直型國際分工　vertical international division of labor
垂直营销系统/垂直行銷系統　vertical marketing system, VMS
春秋繁露/春秋繁露　Chun Qiu Fan Lu
春秋决狱/春秋決獄　Adjudication of Cases by Chun Qiu
纯策略/單一策略,單純策略　pure strategy
纯粹的出口卡特尔/純粹的出口卡特爾　pure export cartel
纯粹法学派/純粹法學派　Pure Theory School of Law
纯粹竞争/純粹競爭　pure competition
纯粹预期理论/純粹預期理論　pure expectation theory
纯公共品/純粹公共財　pure public goods
纯交换/純交易　pure exchange
纯局势/純局勢　pure situation
纯利率/純利率　pure interest rate
纯利润/純利潤　pure profit
纯利息/純利息　pure interest
纯生过程/純出生過程　pure birth process
纯收入/純收入,淨收入　net revenue
纯随机过程/純隨機過程　pure random process
纯网上零售商/純網路零售商　pure play e-tailor
纯误差/純誤差　pure error
纯现金流匹配专项投资组合/純現金流匹配專項投資組合　pure cash-matched dedicated portfolio
纯易货贸易条件/以物易物淨貿易條件　net barter term of trade
纯正不作为犯/純正不作爲犯　offense of typical omission
辍学率/輟學率　dropout rate
词标引/詞標引　word indexing
词表管理/詞庫管理　thesaurus management
词表管理系统/詞庫管理系統　thesaurus management system
词表控制系统/詞彙控制系統　glossary control system

词表扩充/詞彙擴展　glossary expansion
词表显示/詞表顯示　glossary display
词表映射/詞表映射　glossary mapping
词串索引法/詞串索引法　string indexing system
词典/詞典,辭典　dictionary
词典式策略/詞典戰略　lexicographic strategy
词典式索引/詞典式索引　dictionary index
词对轮排/詞對輪排　paried keyword permution
词对式关键词索引/詞對式關鍵詞索引　paired keyword index
词汇控制/詞彙控制　vocabulary control
词汇索引/詞彙索引　glossarial index
词频/詞頻,字頻　term frequency, word frequency
词义控制/詞義控制　lexical meaning control
词语分析/字詞分析　word analysis
词语计数/詞語計數　words counts
词语考订/詞語考訂　word criticism
词族索引/詞族索引　word tree scheme
词族图/詞族圖　graphic display of concept relations
辞典/辭典,詞典　dictionary
辞书/辭典,詞典　dictionary
辞职/辭職　resignation
慈善捐款/慈善捐款　charitable contribution
慈善募捐/慈善募捐　charitable contribution
慈善事业/慈善事業　charity
慈善组织/慈善組織　charity organization
磁版印本/磁版印本　chinaware sheet printed book
磁层/磁層　magnetic layer
磁层电阻/磁層電阻　magnetosphere resistance
磁成像/磁攝影術,磁性印相法　magnetography
磁带/磁帶　tape, magnetic tape
磁带编辑/磁帶編輯器　tape editor
磁带复制/磁帶拷貝　tape copy
磁带张力/磁帶張力　tape tension
磁粉/磁粉　magnetic powder
磁鼓/磁鼓　drum, magnetic drum
磁迹/磁跡　magnetization trace
磁迹形位/磁跡形位　magnetization trace form
磁介质文件/磁介質檔　magnetic medium for file
磁盘/磁碟　disk, magnetic disk
磁头/磁頭　magnetic head
磁头堵塞/磁頭堵塞　head clogging
磁头缝隙/磁頭間隙　head gap
磁头调整/磁頭調整　head adjustment
磁头消磁器/磁頭消磁器　head for re-demagnetization
磁头芯/磁頭心　head core
磁性版托/磁性版托　magnetic forme base
磁性刻纹头/磁性刻紋頭　magnetic cutter head

磁性印刷/磁性印刷　magnetographic printing
次对角线/次對角線　secondary diagonal
次分面/次分面　subfacet
次级按揭贷款/次級房貸　subprime mortgage loan
次级表/次級表　secondary table
次级调查/次級調查　secondary investigation
次级过程/次級過程　secondary process
次级货币/次級貨幣　secondary money
次级记录/次級記錄　secondary record
次级流动资产/次級流動資產　secondary liquid asset
次级率/次級率　secondary rate
次级生产量/次要產出　secondary production
次级维修/次級維護　secondary maintenance
次级债券/次順位債券　subordinated debenture
次级债务/次位債券　subordinated debt
次级证券/低求償順位債券　junior security
次极小化极大/次大中取小　subminimax
次极小化极大最小充分统计量/次大中取小的最小充分統計量　subminimax minimal sufficient statistic
次生风险/次生風險　secondary risk
次属群体/次級團體　secondary group
次数记录/次數畫記　frequency tally
次序统计量/順序統計量,有序統計量　order statistics
次序统计量的渐近正态性/順序統計量的漸近常態性　asymptotic normality of order statistics
次序统计量的完备性/順序統計量的完備性　completeness of order statistics
次序统计量分布/順序統計量的分布　distribution of order statistics
次序统计量联合密度/順序統計量聯合密度　joint density of order statistics
次要劳动力市场/次要勞動市場　secondary labor markets
次要类目/次要類目　the secondary category
次要因素/次要因子　secondary factor
次优/次佳　second best
次优理论/次佳理論　theory of second best, theory of the second best
刺激-反应模式/刺激-反應模式　stimulus-response model
刺配/刺配　tatto the face of a criminal and send him into exile
从犯/從犯　accessory
从给付义务/從給付義務　secondary obligation of performance
从价罚金/從價罰金　ad valorem penalty

从价法/從價法　ad valorem method
从价关税/從價關稅　ad valorem duty, ad valorem tariff
从价进口关税/從價進口關稅　ad valorem import duty
从价进口税率/從價進口稅率　ad valorem rate of duty
从价税/從價稅　ad valorem tax
从价征税货物/從價徵稅貨物　ad valorem goods
从节点/起始節點　from-node
从量补贴/從量補貼　ad volume subsidy, quantity subsidy
从量关税/從量［關］稅　specific duty, specific tariff
从属关系/從屬關係　subordination
从属机构/從屬機構　subordinate body
从属价值/從屬價值　secondary value
从属市场/從屬市場　subordinate market
从属题名/從屬題名　dependent title
从属题名标识/從屬題名標識　dependent title designation
从属型数据集市/依賴型資料市集　dependent data mart
从属著作/從屬著作　dependent work
从-至表法/起迄表法　from-to table method
从众/從眾　conformity
从众效应/樂隊花車效應　bandwagon effect, herd behavior
丛编附注/集叢附注　notes pertaining to series
丛编规范档/集叢權威檔　series authority file
丛编款目/集叢款目　series entry
丛编题名页/集叢題名頁　series title page
丛编项/集叢項　series item
丛编著者/集叢編著者　series author
丛刊索引/叢刊索引　serial index
丛刻本/叢刻本　edition that is printed as part of a series
丛目/叢目　congmu
丛书/叢書　series
丛书名/叢書名　series title
丛书目录/叢書目錄　bibliography of series
丛书项/叢書項　series statement
丛帖/叢帖　series rubbings
粗比/粗比　crude ratio
粗糙度/粗糙度　raggedness
粗糙集预测模型/粗糙集預測模型　rough set forecasting model
粗产能计划/概略產能規劃　rough-cut capacity planning, RCCP

粗出生率/粗出生率　crude birth rate
粗放型经济增长/粗放型經濟成長　extensive economic growth
粗封面纸板/粗紙版　chipboard
粗离婚率/粗離婚率　crude divorce rate
粗情报/原始情報　raw intelligence
粗人口再生产率/粗繁殖率,粗生殖率　gross reproduction rate, gross reproductive rate
粗死亡率/粗死亡率　crude death rate
粗纹/粗紋　coarse groove
促进贸易的技术援助/促進貿易的技術援助　technical assistance in trade promotion
促销/促銷　promotion
促销定价/促銷訂價［法］　promotional pricing
促销管理/推廣管理　promotion management
促销计划/推廣計劃　promotion plan
促销盈利性/促銷盈利性　profitability of promotion
促销折让/促銷折讓　promotional allowance
促销组合/推廣組合　promotion mix
猝发故意/猝發故意　sudden intention
窜货/轉賣,倒貨　diverting
催办/催辦　remind
催询订单/催詢訂單　chasing order, reminder, claim order
萃智/創新性問題解決理論,萃智［理論］,萃思［理論］　theory of inventive problem solving, TRIZ
村落/村落,村莊　village
村民委员会/村民委員會　village committee
村民自治委员会/村民自治委員會　village selfgovernment committee
村镇环境保护法/村鎮環境保護法　law on environmental protection of town and village
村镇银行/村鎮銀行　village bank
存本/存本　retained copy
存储费用/儲管成本,持有成本　holding cost
存储媒体/儲存媒體　storage medium
存储器/貯存器　memory
存档格式/存檔格式　archive format
存放空间/存放空間　storage space
存活率/存活率　survival rate, survival ratio
存货/存貨,庫存　inventory
存货成本/存貨成本　inventory cost
存货出售/存貨出售　sale of stock
存货单位/庫存計量單位　stock keeping unit, SKU
存货跌价损失/盤損　loss on inventory
存货跌价准备/存貨跌價準備　provision for inventory
存货校准/存貨調節　reconciling inventory

存货模型/存貨模型,庫存模型　inventory model
存货目录/存貨目錄　book inventory bibliography
存货平衡账目/存料餘額記録　balance-of-store record
存货投资加速模型/存貨投資加速模型　accelerator model of inventory investment
存货周期/存貨週期　inventory cycle
存货周转率/存貨週轉率　rate of stock turnover, inventory turnover, inventory turnover ratio
存货周转天数/存貨週轉天數　days inventory outstanding, inventory turnover days
存记/存記　existing record
存款/存款　deposit
存款保护制度/存款保護制度　deposit protection system
存款保险/存款保險　deposit insurance
存款保险制度/存款保險制度　deposit insurance system
存款创造/存款創造　deposit creation
存款抵押贷款/存單質押貸款　loan secured by deposit
存款货币/存款貨幣　deposit money
存款货币流通速度/存款貨幣流通速度　velocity of circulation of deposit money
存款基金/存款基金　deposit fund
存款银行/存款銀行　bank of deposit, deposit bank
存款证明/定期存單　certificate of deposit
存款周转率/存款週轉率　deposit turnover
存款准备金/存款準備金　bank reserve against deposit, deposit reserve
存款准备金率/存款準備金率　deposit reserve rate
存款准备金政策/存款準備政策　policy of reserve requirement
存量/存量　stock
存量破产/存量破產　stock-based insolvency
存量调整/調整庫存量　stock adjustment
存留养亲/存留養親　Cun Liu Yang Qin
存取/存取　access
存托凭证/存託憑證　depository receipt
存在概率/存在機率　existence probability
存在主义法学派/存在主義法學派　Existentialist School of Law
存折储蓄存款/活期儲蓄存款　passbook savings deposit
存址索引/位址索引　location index, location register
存贮介质/介質　media
挫折理论/挫折學説　frustration theory
措施项目/措施專案　measurement item
错报/誤述,不實表達　misstatement
错简/錯簡　wrong compilation
错帖/錯帖　disordered signature
错误组配/錯誤組配　false coordination

D

搭便车/搭便車　free ride, free riding
搭便车动机/搭便車的動機　incentives to free-ride
搭便车问题/搭便車問題　free rider problem
搭便车者/搭便車者　free rider
搭[配销]售/搭售　tie-in sale, tied sale
搭售商品/搭售產品　tying goods
搭售协议/搭售安排　tying arrangement
达到精[密]度/實績精確度　precision attained
达尔文选择/達爾文選擇　Darwinian selection
达莫-库普曼-皮特曼定理/Darmois-Koopman-Pitman 定理　Darmois-Koopman-Pitman theorem
达莫-斯基多维奇定理/Darmois-Skitovich 定理　Darmois-Skitovich theorem
答辩/答辯　answer, pleading
答辩状/答辯狀　answer, pleadings
打包/打包　packing
打包定价/成批定價　bundle pricing
打包期权/打包期權　package option
打工妹/打工妹　rural migrant women
打工仔/打工仔　rural migrant men
打孔机/雞眼機　eyeleting machine
打破铁饭碗/破三鐵　broking "iron chair"
打样/打樣　proofing
打印机/打印機　printer
打印输出/列印　printout
打字稿/打字稿　typescript
打字纸/打字紙　typing paper
大爆炸理论/金融大變革　big bang
大辟/大辟　Da Bi
大标题/大標題　major heading
大不敬/大不敬　great disrespect to one's superior
大部制/大部制　super-ministry system
大传统/大傳統　great tradition
大地产/大地產　latifundium
大都市/大都會　major metropolitan
大都市区/大都會區　metropolitan area
大都市统计区/大都會統計區　metropolitan statistics area
大额存款/大額存款　large deposit
大而不倒政策/尾大不掉政策, 護大政策　too-big-to-fail policy

大而全/大而全　big and all-round
大诰/大誥　the Great Imperial Mandate
大功/大功　Da Gong
大锅饭/大鍋飯　communal pot
大国贸易条件/大國貿易條件　large country terms of trade
大花脸本/大花臉本　illegible edition
大金榜/大金榜　large golden lists
大进化/總體演化　macroevolution
大抗议书/大抗議書　Grand Remonstrance
大科学/大科學　big science
大类广告/一般性廣告　generic advertising, primary advertising
大理论/大理論, 鉅型理論　grand theory
大理寺/大理寺　DaLi Si
大理院/大理院　DaLi Yuan
大量定制生产/大量客製化　mass customization
大量观测/大量觀測　mass observation
大量减税/大量減稅　massive tax cut
大量买进/大量買進　heavy buying
大量抛售/大量拋售　heavy selling
大量生产/大量生產　mass production
大量消费/大量消費　heavy consumption
大量销售/大量銷售　mass sale
大量盈余/大量盈餘　massive surplus
大流水排架法/大流水排架法　large flow discharge frame method
大陆法系/大陸法系　Continental Law System
大陆封锁/大陸制度　continental system
大陆会议/大陸會議　Continental Congress
大陆架/大陸礁層　continental shelf
大面额债券/大面額債券　large bond
大面额纸币/大鈔　large-denomination note
大明律/大明律　Ming Law
大陪审团/大陪審團　grand jury
大批/大批　large lot
大批采购/大量採購　large purchase
大批定货/大訂單　large order
大批交易/巨額交易　extensive transaction
大批量订单/大量訂貨, 大批訂單　bulk order, extensive order

大偏差理论/大離差理論　large deviation theory
大气环境/大氣環境　atmospheric environment
大气环境标准/大氣環境標準　atmosphere environment standard
大气污染/大氣汙染,空氣汙染　air pollution, atmospheric pollution
大气污染防治法/大氣汙染防治法　law on prevention and control of air pollution
大气污染源/大氣汙染源　atmospheric pollution source
大前研一的战略思想/大前研一的戰略思想　strategy thought of Ohmae Kenichi
大清会典/大清會典　the Qing Law
大清律例/大清律例　the Administrative Laws of the Qing Dynasty
大清现行刑律/大清現行刑律　the Existing Criminal Law of the Qing Dynasty
大情报观/大情報觀,宏觀情報觀　macroscopic intelligence idea, macroscopic intelligence
大赦/大赦,特赦　amnesty
大世界悖论/大世界悖論　big world paradox
大事记/大事記,大事年表　event chronicle, chronicle of events, record of important events
大侍君役土地保有/大侍君役土地保有　grand serjeanty
大数定律/大數法則　law of large numbers
大数惯性/大數慣性　inertia of large number
大数据/大數據　big data
大甩卖/賤賣資產　distress sale, fire sale
大同/大同　Great Harmony
大推进理论/大推動論　theory of big push
大推进论/大力推動經濟發展理論　big push theory of development
大卫·李嘉图国际贸易理论/李嘉圖的國際貿易理論　David Ricardo's international trade theory
大五人格模型/大五人格理論　big-five model of personality
大宪章/大憲章　Magna Carta
大萧条/大蕭條,大恐慌　great depression
大小/大小　size
大型多人在线角色扮演游戏/[大型]多人線上角色扮演遊戲　massively multiplayer online role-playing game, MMORPG, massively multiplayer online role play game
大修/大修　overhaul
大选辩论/大選辯論　presidential debate
大学科技园/大學科技園　university science and technology park
大学图书馆/大學圖書館,學術圖書館　university library, academic library
大样/大樣　full-page proof
大样本/大樣本　large sample
大样本理论/大樣本理論　theory of large sample, large sample theory
大样对红/大樣對紅　full-page comparison
大样预校/大樣預校　full-page proof prereading
大业律/大業律　Law of Da Ye of the Sui Dynasty
大营销/巨行銷　megamarketing
大于书芯的封面/出邊封面　overhang cover
大元通制/大元通制　Code of the Yuan Dynasty
大战略矩阵/大戰略矩陣　grand strategy matrix
大中刑律统类/大中刑律統類　Compilation of the Tang Dynasty Criminal Law
大众/大眾　mass
大众传播/大眾傳播　mass communication
大众传播法/大眾傳播法　mass communication law
大众传播教育/大眾傳播教育　mass communication education
大众传媒/大眾媒體　mass media
大众分类法/大眾分類法　folk taxonomy
大众类图书/大眾類圖書　mass market book
大众媒介效果/大眾媒介效果,大眾媒體效果　mass media effect
大众期刊/大眾期刊　popular magazine
大众社会/大眾社會　mass society
大众社会理论/大眾社會理論　mass society theory
大众文化/大眾文化,通俗文化,流行文化　popular culture
大众运输系统/大眾運輸系統　mass transit system
大转型/大轉變,鉅變　great transformation
大转型理论/大轉型理論　theory of great transformation
大庄园/大型農場　latifundio
大咨审团/大諮審團　grand assise
大字本/大字本　enlarged symbol edition, large character edition
大宗采购/大宗採買　bulk buying
大宗订阅/大宗訂閱　bulk subscription
大宗供应优惠税/大宗供應優惠稅　bulk supply tariff
大宗交易/個股大筆交易　block trade
大宗交易商/巨額自營商　block trader
大宗贸易/個股大筆交易　block trade
大宗商品/[大宗]商品,[大宗]物資　commodity
呆账/呆賬　dead account
呆账准备金/呆賬準備　loan loss reserve

呆账准备金制度/呆賬準備金管理規定 regulation on provision for bad debt
呆滞贷款/呆賬,倒賬 dead loan
呆滞损失准备金/呆滯損失準備金 obsolescence reserve
代/代 used for
代表汇率/代表匯率 representative rate of exchange
代表货币/代表貨幣 representative money
代表性/代表性 representativeness
代表性抽样/代表抽樣 representative sampling
代表性偏误/代表性經驗法則 representativeness heuristics
代表性启发法/代表性啟發 representativeness heuristics
代表性消费者/代表性消費者 representative consumer
代表性样本/代表樣本 representative sample
代表作/代表作 magnum opus, representive work
代订/代訂 proxy subscription
代沟/代溝 generation gap
代管存款/託付存款 escrow deposit
代际冲突/代際衝突 intergenerational conflict
代际公平/代際公平 equity between generation, intergenerational equity
代际关系/代際關係 relation between generations
代际交换/代際交換 intergenerational exchange
代际流动/代際流動,代間流動 intergenerational mobility, social mobility
代际平等/代際平等 intergenerational equity
代际转移/代間移轉 intergenerational transfers
代建制/代建制 agent construction
代客买卖业务/代客買賣業務 business of commission
代理/代理 agency, proxy
代理变量/代理變數 proxy variables
代理成本/代理成本 agency cost
代理订阅/代理訂閱 agent subscription
代理法律适用公约/代理法律適用公約 Convention on the Law Applicable to Agency
代理公司/代理公司,代理機構,代理商 nominee company, agency
代理行/業務聯繫銀行 correspondent banking
代理行制度体系/代理銀行體系 agent correspondent banking system
代理合同/代理合同 agency contract
代理机构/代理商 agency
代理经销/代理人分配 agency distribution
代理理论/代理理論 agency theory, agent theory
代理期票/代理行票據 agency bill
代理权/代理權 vicarious authority, power of attorney
代理[权]背书/委任背書 power of attorney endorsement, agency endorsement
代理权争夺/委託書爭奪戰 proxy fights
代理人/代理人 agent
代理商/代理商 commercial agent
代理商贸易/代理商貿易 business through agent
代理收款委托书/代理收款委託書 letter of delegation
代理手续费/代理手續費,代理佣金 agency commission
代理投票权争夺/代理投票權爭奪 proxy contest
代理银行/代理銀行 bank correspondent, agent bank
代理中间商/普通運銷商,仲介,捐客 agent merchant middleman, middleman
代码/代碼,編碼,符碼 code
CODEN 代码/CODEN 代碼 code number for periodicals
代码检索语言/代碼檢索語言 code retrieval language
代码设计/代碼設計 coding design
代码索引/代碼索引 code index
代内公平/代內公平 intra-generational equity
代内流动/代內流動 intra-generation mobility
代签/代簽 procuration endorsement
代收代投/代收代投 commissioned collection and delivery
代收业务/代收業務 business of collection
代书板/代書板 shelf dummy, dummy book
代题名页/代題名頁 title-page substitute
代替本/代用本 surrogate
代天行罚/代天行罰 in the name of god to punish the people
代位继承/代位繼承 succession by subrogation
代销/代銷 sale by proxy, best effort
代销店/代銷店 outlet store, selling agent, consignment bookstore
代谢断裂/代謝斷裂 metabolic rift
代用货币/代用貨幣 substitute money
代执行/代執行 substitutive implementation
带电汇信用证/帶電匯信用狀 letter of credit with telegraphic transfer clause
带基/帶基 tape-based
带宽/頻寬 bandwidth
带盘/帶盤 tape winding

带式排架法/帶式排架法　ribbon arrangement
带速/帶速　tape speed
带薪年休假/帶薪年休假　paid annual leave
带薪休假/帶薪休假　paid leave
带形曲线图/帶形曲線圖　band curve chart
带有漂移项的随机游走/有漂浮項的隨機漫步　random walk with drift
带状分布/帶狀分布,帶狀分配　girdle distribution
带状图/帶形圖　band chart
殆等价/幾乎等價　almost equivariance
贷方对销/貸方對銷　contra credit
贷方风险/貸方風險　lender risk
贷款/貸款,借貸　loan, lending
贷款本金/貸款本金　principal amount of loan
贷款本金偿还额/貸款本金償還額,還本　loan principal repayment
贷款比率/貸款比率　loan ratio
贷款标准/貸款標準　lending criterion
贷款偿还/貸款償還　loan repayment
贷款承诺/貸款承諾,承諾放款契約,放款承諾　loan commitment
贷款出售/放款出售　loan sales
贷款额/貸款金額　volume of credit
贷款额度/貸款額度　loan limit
贷款方案/貸款方案　lending program
贷款方式/貸款方式,貸款類型　pattern of lending
贷款服务/放款售後服務　loan servicing
贷款合同/貸款合約　loan contract
贷款回收/貸款回收　loan recovery
贷款计息/貸款計息　loan pricing
贷款利率/貸款利率,借貸利率　loan rate, loan interest rate, lending rate of interest
贷款利息/貸款利息,借貸利息　lending interest, loan interest
贷款期限/貸款期限　life of loan
贷款人/放款人　lender
贷款申请书/貸款申請書　loan application
贷款投资/貸款投資　loan investment
贷款委员会/貸款委員會,放審會　loan committee
贷款息差/貸款息差　lending margin
贷款限额/貸款限額,放款上限,信用額度　lending limit, loan ceiling, line of credit
贷款限制规则/限制借款規則,限制借款條件　loan restriction
贷款限制条件/限制借款條件,限制借款規則　loan restriction
贷款协议/貸款協議　loan agreement
贷款信托/貸款信託　loan trust

贷款需求/貸款需求　loan demand
贷款业务/貸款業務　lending operation, loan service
贷款银行/貸款銀行　loan bank, lending bank
贷款诈骗罪/貸款詐騙罪　crime of defrauding loans
贷款账户/貸款賬戶　loan account
贷款证券化/貸款證券化　load sercuritization
贷款政策/貸款政策　lending policy
贷款资产/貸款資產　loan asset
贷款资金来源/貸款資金來源　source of fund for loan
贷款总账/貸款總賬　loan ledger
待发货订单/延期訂貨　back order
待发行新股/待發行股票　when-issued stock
待机时间/待機時間　stand-by time
待料时间/待料時間　supply delay time
待签稿库/待簽稿庫　to-be-signed draft library
待摊费用/未攤銷費用　prepaid expense
待续款目/待續款目　open entry
待业/待業　job waiting, waiting for employment
待业保险/待業保險　insurance of waiting for employment
待运提单/待運提單　received for shipment bill of lading
怠工/怠工　labor slowdown, sabotage
戴尔比较法/戴爾比較法　comparative method of Dale
戴罗思-沃森分布/Dimroth-Watson 分布,Dimroth-Watson 分配　Dimroth-Watson's distribution
戴明的质量管理理论/戴明品質管制理論　quality management theory of Deming
戴明环/戴明循環　Deming circle
戴维-巴顿检验/David-Barton 檢定　David-Barton test
戴维空格检验/David 空格檢定　David's empty cell test
戴雪/戴雪　Albert Veen Dicey, A. V. Dicey
戴罪立功/戴罪立功　atonement for offences by doing good deeds
丹德卡校正/Dandekar 校正,Dandekar 修正　Dandekar's correction
丹尼尔-何舍佛-苏布拉马尼亚姆模型/DHS 模型　Daniel-Hirsheifer-Subramanyam model, DHS model
担保/擔保　guarantee
担保成本/擔保成本　bonding expenditure
担保贷款/擔保貸款　loan against collateral, secured loan
担保抵押/擔保抵押　guaranteed mortgage
担保负债/擔保負債　secured liability

担保公司债券/擔保公司債券　guaranteed debenture
担保交易/擔保交易　secured transaction
担保票据/擔保票據　guaranteed bill
担保契约/擔保契約,保證書　deed of security
担保让与/擔保讓與　warranty of alienation
担保书/擔保書　letter of undertaking
担保物权/擔保物權　real rights of security
担保信贷/擔保信貸　secured credit
担保信托公司/擔保信託公司　guaranty trust company
担保信用证/擔保信用狀　guaranteed letter of credit
担保押金/擔保押金　security deposit
担保银行/擔保銀行　guarantor bank
担保责任/擔保債務　liability for guarantee
担保债权人/擔保債權人　secured creditor
担保债券/擔保債券,有擔保的債券　guaranteed bond, secured bond, bond collateral
担保账户/擔保賬戶　secured account
单本位/單本位　single standard
单边冲突规范/單邊衝突規範　unilateral conflict rules
单边出口/單邊出口　unilateral export
单边进口/單邊進口　unilateral import
单边进口限额/單邊進口限額　unilateral import quota
单边贸易/單邊貿易　unilateral trade
单边账户/單邊賬戶　single account
单边支付/單邊支付　unilateral payment
单边指数/單邊指數　unilateral index number
单变量分布/單變量分布　univariate distribution
单变量统计[学]/單變量統計[學]　single variate statistics
单变量预测/單變數預測　single-variable forecasting
单部分资源/單部分資源　monographic resource
单册/單冊　single copy
单侧规范限/單邊規格界限　single specification limit
单侧检验/單邊檢定,單尾檢定　one-sided test, one-tailed test, single tail test
单侧区间估计/單邊區間估計　one-sided interval estimation
单侧容差/單邊允差　unilateral tolerance
单侧统计检验/單尾統計檢定　one-tailed statistical test
单侧置信区间/單邊信賴區間　one-sided confidence region
单层分类编排/單層分類編排　classified arrangement with one level
单层光盘/單層光碟　single layer disk

单纯不连续随机过程/單純不連續隨機過程　purely discontinuous stochastic process
单纯参照/直接參照　direct reference
单纯承兑/單純承兑　absolute acceptance
单纯出口补贴/純粹出口補貼　pure export subsidy
单纯形法/單體法　simplex method
单纯形设计/單體設計　simplex designs
单纯形算法/辛普列斯演算法　simplex algorithm
单纯远期汇率/單純遠期匯率　outright forward rate
单代号网络图/單代號網路圖　activity-on-note network diagram
单点登入/單點登入　single sign on, SSO
单点分布/單點分布　unitary distribution
单点设计/一點設計　one point design
单调递增/單調遞增　monotonically increasing
单调回归/單調回歸　monotone regression
单调结构/單調結構　monotonic structure
单调决策程序/單調決策程式　monotone decision procedure
单调收敛定理/單調收斂定理　monotone convergence theorem
单调似然比/單調概度比　monotone likelihood ratio
单调性公理/單調性公理　monotonicity axiom
单独海损/單獨海損,特别海損　particular average
单独头脑风暴/自我腦力激盪法　solo brainstorming
单独投资/單獨投資　sole investment
单独页面设计/單獨頁面設計　divide page design
单独预测/單獨預測　single forecasting
单方程法/單一方程式法　single-equation method
单方程估计/單一方程式估計　single equation estimation
单方程模型/單方程模式　single-equation model
单方错误/單方錯誤　unilateral mistake
单方寄销/單方寄銷　unilateral consignment
单方面汇兑余额/單方面匯兑餘額　one-sided balance of exchange
单方面转移/片面移轉　unilateral transfers
单方面最惠国条款/單方面最惠國條款　one-sided most favored nation clause
单方行政行为/單方行政行爲　unilateral administrative action
单方优惠关税/單方優惠關稅　one-side preferential duty
单峰/單峰　unimodal
单峰分布/單峰分布,單峰分配　unimodal distribution
单峰偏好/單峰式偏好　single peaked preferences
单峰性/單峰性,單一高峰　unimodality

单个居民/個人住民　resident individual
单供源采购/單供應來源　single sourcing
单轨制/單軌制　one-card system
单环学习/單圈學習　single-loop learning
单级主题索引/單級主題索引　one level subject index
单减量生命表/單減量生命表　single decrement life table
单件生产/單件生產　one-of-a-kind production
单件作业排程/零工式排程　job shop scheduling
单金属本位制/單金屬本位制　monometallism
单据验收/收據驗收　receipt acceptance
单卷式检索工具/單卷式檢索工具　single volume retrieval device
单卡广告牌系统/單卡看板系統　one-card kanban system
单刻本/單刻本　separately published edition
单联结区组设计/單環區集設計　singly linked block design
单面平减/單面平減　single deflation
单面书架/單面書架　single face bookcase, single face bookshelf
单名票据/單名票據　single name paper
单名期票/單名期票　single name promissory note
单目标决策/單目標決策　single-objective decision-making
单亲儿童/單親兒童　single-parent child
单亲家庭/單親家庭　single-parent family
单色本/單色本　unicolor print
单身户/單身戶　one person household
单身家庭/單身家庭　single-person family
单声道唱片/單聲道唱片　monophonodisc
单时估计法/單一時間估計法　single-time estimate
单式记账法/單式簿記　single entry bookkeeping
单式凭证/單式憑證　single account title voucher
单式预算/單一預算　single budget, unitary budget
单帖/單帖　single rubbing
单尾表/單尾表　one tail table
单位/單位　unit
单位产出/單位產出　per unit yield
单位产品/單位產品　unit product
单位成本/單位成本　unit cost
单位成本函数/單位成本函數　unit cost function
单位犯罪/單位犯罪　unit crime
单位方差/單位變異數　unit variance
单位分布/單位分布　unit distribution
单位负责人/單位負責人　person in charge of a unit, principal of a unit

单位根/單根　unit root
单位根检验/單根檢定　unit root test
单位工程/單位工程　unit construction project
单位估价表/單位估價表　unit price table
单位价值指数/單值指數　unit value index
单位矩阵/單位矩陣　identity matrix
单位均匀分布/單位均匀分布,單位均匀分配　unitary uniform distribution
单位利润/單位利潤　unit margin
单位量/單位量　unit quantity
单位缺陷率/每單位缺點數　defect per unit, DPU
单位实体不符合数/單位實體不符合數　nonconformities per item
单位弹性需求/單一彈性之需要　unit elastic demand
单位特征根/單位特性根　unit characteristic roots
单位信托/單位信託　unit trust
单位序贯抽样/單位逐次抽樣　unit sequential sampling
单位样本/單位樣本　unit sample
单位预算/單位預算　unit budget
单位正态分布/單位常態分布,單位常態分配　unit normal distribution
单位正态随机变量/單位常態變量　unit normal variate
单位制/單位制　work unit system
单限区间/單限區間　single limit interval
单线进化论/單線進化論　unilateral evolution
单线式非正式信息沟通/單線式非正式溝通　monoline-mode of informal communication
单相关/簡單相關　simple correlation
单相关系数/簡單相關係數　simple correlation coefficient
单向传播/單向傳播　one-way communication
单向传递/單向傳遞　one-way transmission
单向费率/基本财货费率　commodity rates
单向服务/單向服務　undirectional service
单向贸易/單向貿易　one-way trade
单向配置/單向配置,單因子配置,一元配置　one-way layout
单向通道/只單向通道　unidirectional channel
单向主成分向量集/單向主成分向量集　one-way principle component vector set
单向主成分向量空间/單向主成分向量空間　one-way principle component vector space
单项表/單項表　simple table
单项表式/單項表式　single tabular form
单项价格指数/單項價格指數　individual index of construction cost

单项奖/單項奬　single-item award
单项矩阵/單項矩陣　monomial matrix
单项式/單項式　monomial
单行本/單印本　offprint
单行条例/單行條例　single-line regulation
单行刑法/單行刑法　separate criminal law
单形重心设计/單體重心設計　simplex centroid design
单样本模型/單樣本模型　one-sample model
单样本问题/單樣本問題　one-sample problem
单要素生产率/單要素生產率　single factor productivity
单页印刷品/單頁印刷品　single sheet
单一裁定汇兑/單一裁定匯兌　simple arbitration of exchange
单一产品决策/單個產品決策　individual product decision
单一成本/單一成本　single cost
单一到货价/單一到貨價,統一到貨價　uniform delivered price
单一方程/單一方程式　single equation
单一故障/單一故障　single failure
单一关税/單一[關]稅　single tariff
单一海关单据/單一海關單據　single customs document
单一汇率/單一匯率　single exchange rate, unitary rate
单一货币挂钩/單一貨幣掛鈎　single currency peg
单一加点地图/單一加點地圖　single dotted map
单一交易/單一交易　simple transaction
单一列类法/單因素分類　monothetic classification
单一失效/單一故障　single failure
单一税/單一稅　single tax
单一税率/單一稅率　simple tariff, flat tax rate
单一薪资计划/單一薪資計劃　salary-only plan
单一性检索工具/單一性檢索工具　retrieval device for one kind document
单一银行控股公司/單一銀行控股公司　one-bank holding company
单一银行制度/單一銀行制度　unit bank system, unit banking system
单一预算/單一預算　single budget, unitary budget
单一制/單一制　unitary system
单一制银行/單一制銀行　unit bank
单一资产/單一資產　single asset
单因素方差分析/一因素變異數分析法　one-factor analysis of variance
单因素贸易条件/單因素貿易條件　single factorial terms of trade
单因素期限结构模型/單因素期限結構模型　one-factor term-structure model
单因素实验/單因子實驗　single-factor experiments
单因素试验/單因子實驗　single-factor experiments
单因子方差分析/單因子變異數分析,單向變異數分析　one-way analysis of variance
单因子混杂/單因子混同　mono-confounding
单因子理论/單因子理論　single factor theory
单因子模型/單要素模型　one-factor model
单因子实验设计/單因數實驗設計　single factor experimental design
单语种叙词表/單語詞表　monolingual thesaurus
单元/單元　unit
单元测试/單元測試　unit testing
单元词/單元詞　uniterm
单元词标引/單元詞標引　uniterm indexing
单元词表/單元詞表　uniterm vocabulary
单元词法/單元詞法　uniterm method
单元词卡片/單元詞卡片　uniterm card
单元概念组配标引/單元概念組配標引　unit concept coordinate indexing
单元卡编目法/單元卡編目法　unit card cataloguing, unit entry cataloguing
单元制造/單元製造　cellular manufacturing
单张凹印机/單張凹印機　sheetfed gravure press
单张汇票/單張匯票　sole bill of exchange
单张支票/單張支票　sola cheque
单张纸印刷/張葉印刷　sheet-fed printing
单整过程/整合隨機過程　integrated process
单整自回归条件异方差模型/整合一般自我回歸條件異質變異數模型　integrated generalized autoregressive conditional model
单证/單證　document
单证交换/單證交換　exchange of document
单中心城市/單一中心都市　monocentric cities
淡出/淡出　fade out
淡入/淡入　fade in
当地承兑/當地承兌　local acceptance
当地费用豁免/當地費用豁免　local cost waiver
当地回应/回應在地之需求　local responsiveness
当地货币市场/當地貨幣市場　local money market
当地交货单/當地交貨單　local invoice
当地[交货]价格/當地[交貨]價格　local price
当地交货条件/當地交貨條件　local terms
当地提单/當地提單　local bill of lading
当地营销/地區行銷　local marketing
当地运价/當地運價　local rate

当事人陈述/當事人陳述　parties' statements
当事人更换/當事人更換　replacement of parties
当事人适格/當事人適格　proper party
当事人追加/當事人追加　addition of parties
当庭宣判/當庭宣判　pronouncement of a judgement in court
当选争讼/當選爭訟　election dispute, electoral lawsuit
当期/即期　current issue
当期收益率/當期收益率　current yield ratio
当日汇率/當日匯率　current rate of exchange
档案/檔案　archive
档案保管/檔案保管　files storage, archive keeping
档案保管期限/檔案保管期限　record retention period, custodial duration on archive
档案保管期限表/檔案保管期限表　records retention schedule
档案保护/檔案保護　archive preservation
档案保护技术/檔案保護技術　archive preservation technology
档案编研/檔案編研　arichive compile and research, archival editing and studying
档案标引/檔案標引　archive indexing
档案博物馆/檔案博物館　archive museum
档案材料查找/檔案材料查找　search of archival data
档案材料挑选/檔案材料挑選　selection of archival data
档案参考工具/檔案參考工具　archive reference tool
档案参考资料/檔案參考資料　archival reference material, archive reference
档案残缺/檔案殘缺　deformities
档案出版物/檔案出版物　archival publications
档案词族索引/檔案詞族索引　archive word family indexing
档案存放地点索引/檔案存放地點索引　files storage site index
档案存放位置索引/檔案存放位置索引　files storage place index
档案袋/檔案袋　archive bag
档案登记/檔案登記　archive registration
档案地名索引/檔案地名索引　archive toponym indexing
档案多套制/檔案多套制　archive multiple sets system
档案法规学/檔案法規學　study of archive law
档案法学/檔案法學　studies of archival laws
档案范畴索引/檔案範疇索引　archive scope indexing
档案分类/檔案分類　archival classification
档案分类标引/檔案分類標引　archival classification indexing
档案分类标准/檔案分類標準　principle of archival classification
档案分类方法/檔案分類方法　method of archival classification
档案分类号/檔案分類號　archival classfication number
档案分类检索语言/檔案分類檢索語言　archival classification retrieval language
档案分类目录/檔案分類目錄　archival classification catalogue
档案分类主表/檔案分類主表　archival classification main table
档案分类主题一体化标引/檔案分類主題一體化標引　integrated archival classification subject indexing
档案分面分类法/檔案分面分類法　archive split classification method
档案复分表/檔案複分表　archive compound table
档案复制/檔案複製　archival duplication
档案工作/檔案工作　archive work
档案工作标准/檔案工作標準　archive work standard
档案工作标准化/檔案工作標準化　archive work standardization, archival standardization
档案工作标准体系/檔案工作標準體系　archive work standard system
档案工作管理体制/檔案工作管理體制　archive work management system
档案工作基本原则/檔案工作基本原則　basic principles of archival work
档案工作者/檔案工作者　archive staff
档案公布/檔案公布　archive release
档案关键词/檔案關鍵字　archive keyword
档案馆/檔案館　archive
档案馆管理/檔案館管理　archives administration
档案馆建筑/檔案館建築　archives building
档案馆介绍/檔案館介紹　introduction to archives
档案馆名录/檔案館名錄　archives directories
档案馆网/檔案館網　archives website
档案馆学/檔案館學　science of archives
档案馆指南/檔案館指南　guide to archives
档案管理学/檔案管理學　archival management science, study in archive administration, study of archival management

档案管理自动化/檔案管理自動化　automatization of archive management
档案管辖权/檔案管理權　archival jurisdiction
档案柜/檔案櫃　archive cabinet
档案害虫/檔案害蟲　archival pest
档案害虫熏蒸剂/檔案害蟲蒸薰劑　the archive pests fumigant
档案盒/檔案盒　archive box
档案汇集/檔案匯集　archival collection
档案机读目录/檔案機器可讀目錄　machine-readable catalogue of archive
档案机构/檔案機構　archival institution
档案积累/檔案積累　accumulation of files
档案级光盘/檔案級光碟　archive level CD
档案集中统一管理原则/檔案集中統一管理原則　principle of centralized management of archive, centralize principle of archive
档案纪实节目/檔案類紀錄片節目　archive programme
档案继承权/檔案繼承權　right of archival inheritance
档案寄存/檔案寄存　archive deposit
档案寄存中心/檔案寄存中心　archive deposit center
档案价值/檔案價值　archival value
档案价值鉴定/檔案價值鑒定　archival value appraisal
档案价值扩展率/檔案價值擴展率　expansion ratio of archival value
档案价值时效率/檔案價值時效率　time efficiency of archival value
档案架/檔案架　archive shelf
档案检索/檔案檢索　archive retrieval, archival retrieval
档案检索策略/檔案檢索策略　archive retrieval strategy
档案检索工具/檔案檢索工具　archive retrieval tool
档案检索工具符号/檔案檢索工具符號　archive retrieval tool symbol
档案检索语言/檔案檢索語言　archive retrieval language
档案鉴定/檔案鑒定　archive appraisal
档案鉴定委员会/檔案鑒定委員會　archive appraisal committee
档案鉴定制度/檔案鑒定制度　archive appraisal system
档案降密/檔案降密　archive declassification
档案教育/檔案教育　archival education
档案接收/檔案接收　archive reception

档案解密/檔案解密　archive deciphering
档案局/檔案局　archive bureau
档案捐赠/檔案贈與　archive donation
档案开放/檔案公開　archive open
档案开放原则/檔案公開原則　open archive principles
档案考订/檔案考訂　archival criticism
档案科学技术研究工作/檔案科學與技術研究工作　research work of archival science and technology
档案库藏/檔案庫存　archival inventory
档案库房/檔案庫房　archival storeroom
档案库房防火间距/檔案庫房防火間距　space interval of fire prevention in archival storeroom
档案库房管理/檔案庫房管理　archival store management
档案库房温度控制/檔案庫房溫度控制　temperature control in archival storeroom
档案老化/檔案老化　achival aging
档案利用/檔案利用　utilization of archive
档案利用工具/檔案利用工具　archive utilize tool
档案利用效果登记簿/檔案利用效果登記簿　register of archives utilization effect
档案两步整理论/檔案兩步整理論　theory of two steps on arranging archive
档案霉变/檔案發霉　archive mold
档案密级/檔案密級　archive secrecy level
档案目录中心/檔案目錄中心　archive catalog center
[档案]全宗/全宗[檔案]　archive fonds, archival fonds, fonds
档案人名目录/檔案人名目錄　archive name catalogue
档案人名索引/檔案人名索引　archive name indexing
档案扫描/檔案掃描　archive scanning
档案十进编号法/檔案十進編號法　decimal number method of archive
档案十进分类法/檔案十進分類法　decimal classification of archives
档案实体分类/檔案實體分類　physical archives classification
档案史料学/檔案史料學　science of archival historical materials, study of archival history
档案事务所/檔案事務所　archive office
档案事业/檔案事業　archival undertaking, archive endeavor
档案事业管理/檔案事業管理　administration of archival undertaking
档案事业管理体制/檔案事業管理體制

administrative system of archival and undertaking
档案室/檔案室　record office, archive
档案室立卷制度/檔案室立卷制度　record office filing regulation
档案收集/檔案收集　archive collection, archival collection
档案手册/檔案手冊　manual of archive
档案术语学/檔案術語學　archival terminology, terminology in archival science
档案数字化/檔案數位化　digital archive, archive digitalization
档案缩微化/檔案微縮化　archive micromation
档案索引/檔案索引　archive index
档案特性检索/檔案特性檢索　archive property retrieval
档案提供利用/檔案提供利用　access to archive
档案条形码/檔案條碼　the bar code of archive
档案统计/檔案統計　archive statistics
档案统计学/檔案統計學　study of archive statistics
档案、图书、情报管理一体化/檔案、圖書、資訊管理一體化　the integration of archive, books and intelligence management
档案完整性/檔案完整性　archival integrity
档案网站/檔案網站　archival website
档案文献/檔案文獻　archival
档案文献编排体例/檔案文獻編排體例　compilating style of archival documentation
档案文献编纂/檔案文獻編譯　archival compilation
档案文献编纂学/檔案文獻編纂學　study of archival documentation compilation, science of archival compilation, study of archival document compilation
档案文献标题/檔案文獻標題　title of archival documentation
档案文献标题结构/檔案文獻標題結構　structure of title of archival documentation
档案文献出版物/檔案文獻出版物　publications of archival documentation
档案文献汇编/檔案文獻匯編　collection of archival documentation
档案文献加工/檔案文獻加工　edit of archival documentation
档案文献加工符号/檔案文獻加工符號　editing mark of archival documentation
档案文献校勘/檔案文獻校勘　collation of archival documentation
档案文献刊物/檔案文獻刊物　periodical of archival documentation
档案文献体裁/檔案文獻體裁　form of archival documentation compilation
档案文献遗产/檔案文獻遺產　archival documentary heritage
档案文摘/檔案文摘　abstract of archive
档案污染/檔案汙染　archive contaminated
档案箱/檔案箱，檔案盒　archive kit
档案销毁/檔案銷毀　archives destruction
档案销毁目录/檔案銷毀目錄　archive destruction catalog
档案销毁清册/檔案銷毀清冊　archive destruction list
档案销毁制度/檔案銷毀制度　archive destruction rule
档案信息/檔案資訊　archival information
档案信息分类/檔案資訊分類　archival information classfication
档案信息化/檔案資訊化　archive informatization, informatization of the archive
档案行政管理机构/檔案行政管理機構　archive administration organization
档案行政学/檔案行政學　archival administration science
档案修裱技术/檔案修裱技術　technology of picture mounting on archive
档案修复/檔案修復　archival restoration
档案学/檔案學　archival science, archival science
档案学史/檔案學史　history of archival science
档案赝品/檔案贗品　archive fake
档案移交/檔案移交　archive transfer, transfer archive
档案用耐久纸张/檔案用耐久紙張　permanent paper for archive
档案有机体/檔案有機體　archival organism
档案员/檔案專業人員　archivist
档案阅览室/檔案閱覽室　archive reading room
档案载体/檔案載體　archive media
档案摘要/檔案文摘　abstract of archive
档案展览/檔案展覽　archive exhibition, exhibition on archive
档案征集/檔案徵集　archive acquisition
档案整理/檔案整理，檔案編排　archival arrangement, archive rectification
档案整理编目/檔案整理編目　archive cataloging
档案整理工作方案/檔案整理工作方案　archival arrangement scheme
档案证明/檔案證明　archive certificate
档案职能鉴定理论/檔案職能鑑定理論　theory of file identification function

档案职业道德/檔案職業道德　archival profession ethics
档案制成材料/檔案製成材料　archive materials
档案质量/檔案品質　archival quality
档案中介机构/檔案仲介機構　archive agency
档案主题标引/檔案主題標引　archive subject indexing
档案主题词/檔案主題詞　archive subject words
档案主题词表/檔案主題詞表　archive index thesaurus
档案主题词参照系统/檔案主題詞參照系統　archive subject words reference system
档案主题词法/檔案主題詞法　archive subject words method
档案主题词款目/檔案主題詞款目　archive subject words item
档案主题词字顺表/檔案主題詞字順表　archive subject words alphabetic table
档案主题分析/檔案主題分析　archive subject analysis
档案主题目录/檔案主題目錄　archive subject catalogue
档案著录/檔案著錄，檔案描述　archive description, archival description
档案专题数据库/檔案專題資料庫　archival thematic database
档案专业教育/檔案專業教育　archival profession education
档案专业职务聘任/檔案專業職務聘任　appointment of archival profession post
档案砖/檔案磚　archival brick
档案装具/檔案裝具　archives container, archives harness
档案咨询服务/檔案諮詢服務　archive consulting service
档案资产/檔案資產　archival assets
档案总目录/檔案總目錄　general catalogue of archive
档案组合/檔案組合　archive group, archive combination
档号/檔號　archival code
刀币/刀幣　knife money
刀耕火种/火耕　slash-and-burn agriculture
刀切法/折刀法　jackknife
导出分布/導出分布　derived distribution
导出统计量/導出統計量　derived statistic
导航/導航　navigation
导语/導言　lead

岛屿/島嶼　island
岛屿制度/島嶼制度　regime of islands
倒架/倒架，重新排架　moving books from the bookshelf
到岸价[格]/到岸價格，碼頭交貨價　cost-insurance-freight, CIF, free at dock
到达分布/到達分布，到達分配　arrival distribution
到达港海关区交货条件/海關交貨價　ex customs compound
到达时间间隔/到達時距　interarrival time
到港提单/到港提單　port bill of lading
到馆咨询服务/面對面參考服務　face-to-face reference service
到货合同/目的地契約　arrival contract
到货后销售/到貨後銷售　sale on arrival
到货汇票/到貨匯票　arrival draft, arrival bill
到货通知/到貨通知　arrival notice, advice of arrival
到货通知书/到貨通知書　advice of delivery
到货重量/卸貨地重量　arrival weight
到期负债/到期負債　matured liability
到期后的背书/到期後的背書　endorsement after maturity
到期后付款/到期後付款　payment after due date
到期汇票/到期匯票　due bill
到期票据/到期票據　bill of maturity, matured bill, matured note
到期前的背书/到期前的背書　endorsement before due
到期日缺口模型/到期日缺口　maturity gap
到期收益率/到期收益率，殖利率　yield to maturity
到期条款/到期條款　expiration clause
到期债券/到期債券　matured bond
到期支票/到期支票　matured cheque
到期值/到期值　maturity value
倒查法/逆向搜尋　search in reverse chronological order, backward search, reverse retrieval
倒冲/倒沖　back flush
倒带/倒帶，倒片　rewind
倒金字塔结构/倒金字塔模式　inverted pyramid approach
倒排标目/倒置標目，倒排標題　inverted heading
倒排索引/倒排索引　inverted index
倒排题名/倒排題名　inverted title
倒排文档/逆向檔　inverted file
倒签提单/倒簽提單　anti-dated bill of lading
倒数变换/倒數變換　reciprocal transformation
倒文/倒文　reversed word, inverted words
倒U型理论/倒U型論　inversion of U theory

倒序词典/逆序詞典　reverse dictionary
倒置标题/倒置標題　inverted subject title
盗版/盜印　piracy
盗伐林木罪/盜伐林木罪　crime of poaching lumber
盗窃罪/盜竊罪　larceny, crime of theft
道德/道德　morality
道德发展理论/道德發展理論　moral development theory
道德风险/道德風險,道德危機　moral hazard
道德管理/道德管理　moral management
道德规范/道德規範　moral norm
道德审查/士氣調查　moral survey
道家/道家　Taoism
道奇连续抽样方案/Dodge 連續抽樣計劃　Dodge continuous sampling plan
道奇-罗米格抽样方案/Dodge-Romig 抽樣計劃　Dodge-Romig sampling plan
道奇-罗米格抽样检验表/Dodge-Romig 抽樣檢驗表　Dodge-Romig sampling inspection table
道琼斯工业平均指数/道瓊工業平均指數　Dow Jones Industrial Average, DJIA
道琼斯股价指数/道瓊股價指數　Dow Jones index
道琼斯股票价格指数/道瓊工業指數　Dow Jones Indications of Stock Price
道琼斯威尔希尔全球整体市场指数/道瓊威爾希爾全球整體市場指數　Dow Jones Wilshire global total market index
道威斯计划/道威斯計劃　Dawes plan
道义经济/道義經濟　moral economy
道义经济学/道義經濟學　moral economics
道义劝告/道義說服,道德勸說　jaw control, moral suasion
道义责任论/道義責任論　theory of morality responsibility
稻草人假设/稻草人假設　straw man hypothesis
得分函数/計分函數　score function
得瓦斯-斯帝尔检验/Dwass-Steel 檢定　Dwass-Steel test
德宾多阶方差估计[量]/Durbin 多段變異數估計[量]　Durbin's multistage variance estimator
德宾检验/杜賓檢定,Durbin 檢定　Durbin's test
德宾-沃森检验/杜賓-瓦森檢定,Durbin-Watson 檢定　Durbin-Watson test
德尔菲法/疊慧法,德菲法　Delphi method
德尔塔中性/Delta 中性　delta neutral
德芬涅定理/De Finetti 定理　De Finetti's theorem
德国工作研究/德國工作研究　work study of Germany
德国历史学派/德國歷史學派　German historical school
德国民法典/德國民法典　German Civil Code
德隆-史莱佛-萨默斯-瓦尔德曼模型/DSSW 模型　DeLong-Shleifer-Summers-Waldmann model, DSSW model
德鲁克公司理论/德魯克公司理論　cooperation theory of Drucker
德鲁里报告/德魯里報告　Drury report
德·摩根定理/De Morgan 法則　De Morgan's law
德沃金/德沃金　Ronald M. Dworkin
德沃热茨基随机逼近定理/Dvoretsky 隨機逼近定理　Dvoretsky's stochastic approximation theorem
德意志期货交易所/德意志期貨交易所　Deutsche Terminborse, DTB
德治/德治　rule of virtue
德主刑辅/德主刑輔　Morality Guiding and Penalty Supplementing
灯光示迹图片/燈光示跡圖片　chronocyclegraph
登到记录/點收記錄　check-in record, admission record
登记/登記,記錄　register
登记簿/登記簿　register book
登记目录/登記目錄　registrational bibliography
登记室/登記室　registration
登记室原则/登記室原則　registry principle
登记系统/登記系統　registry system
登临权/登臨權　right of approch
登录号排架法/登錄號排架法　assession order arrangement
登山法/登山法　hill-climbing method
登闻鼓/登聞鼓　drum outside the court for people to beat and file complaints
等产量曲线/等[产]量曲線　isoquant, isoquant curve
等成本曲线/等成本線,等費用線　curve of equal cost, isocost, isocost curve
等待/等待　waiting
等待浪费/等待浪費　waiting waste
等待时间/等待時間　waiting time
等待时间分布/等待時間分布　waiting-time distribution
等待线/等候線　waiting line
等待性失业/等候性失業　wait unemployment
等待制系统/等候系統　waiting system
等额分期付款/等額分期付款　equal installment
等额选举/等額選舉　single-candidate election
等方差/等變異數　equivariance

等分布线/等分配線,均等分布線　line of equidistribution, line of equal distribution
等风险估计[量]/等風險估計[量]　constant risk estimator
等峰分布/等峰分布,等峰分配　equimodal distribution
等峰态/等峰度　isokurtosis
等概率抽选/等機率選取[法]　selection with equal probability, equal-probability-of-selection
等概率抽样/等機率抽樣　sampling with equal probability
等高线图/等高線圖　contour chart
等功效曲线/等檢力曲線　curve of equidetectability
等供应时间订购法/等供應時間訂購法　equal runout method
等候页面广告/等候頁面廣告　waiting-page advertisement
等忽略原则/等忽略原則　principle of equal ignorance
等级/等級　grade
等级关系/等級關係　hierarchical relation
等级价格/等級價格　class price
等级检索/階層式搜尋,分級搜索法　hierarchical search
等级宽度/等級寬度　grade width
等级链/等級鏈,層次鏈　scalar chain
等级列举式分类法/列舉式分類法　enumerative classification
等级评定/評等　rating
等级评定制/等級評定制　class rating system
等级征税/等級徵稅,累進徵稅　class tax
等级制组织/層級組織　hierarchy organization
等剂量/等劑量　equivalent dose
等价变化/對等變量　equivalent variation
等价差异度/等價差異度　equivalence difference measure
等价关系/等價關係　equivalence relation
等价交换/等價交換　exchange at equal value, exchange of equal value
等价类/對等類　equivalence class
等价贸易/等價貿易　trade of equal value
等价偏差/對等偏差　equivalent deviate
等价形式/等價形式　equivalent form of value
等价样本/對等樣本　equivalent samples
等距变换/等度量變換　isometric transformation
等距检验/均等間隔檢定　equal spacings test
等距量表/區間尺度　interval scale
等距图/等度量圖　isometric chart

等可能性准则/等可能性準則　equally liability criterion
等利润曲线/等利潤曲線　isoprofit curve
等量关税/等量關稅,約當關稅　equivalent duty
等幂线/等檢力線　isodynes
等配置/均等配置　equal allocation
等权设计/等權設計　equiweighted design
等权原理/等權數原則　principle of equal weights
等权重指数/等權重指數　equally weighted index
等收益线/等收益線　iso-revenue line
等同标准/一致標準　equivalent standard, identical standard
等同采用/等同採用　equal adoption, adopting by equation
等同关系/等價關係　equivalence relationship
等同原则/等同原則　Doctrine of Equivalents
等尾检验/等尾檢定　equal-tail test
等相关分布/均等相關分布　equally correlated distribution
等正态分布/等常態分布,等常態分配　equi-normal distribution
等值/等化　equating
等值水平/等高水準　contour level
等值线/等值線　isovalue lines, isoline
邓肯检验/Duncan 檢定　Duncan's test
邓析/鄧析　Deng Xi
瞪羚公司/瞪羚公司　gazella company
低保户/低保户　household with minimum living standard insurance
低层码/低層碼　low-level code
低点/低點　low point
低调/暗调,低明调　low-key
低度发展/低度發展　underdevelopment
低风险资本/低風險資本　security capital
低峰度/平[闊]峰　platykurtosis, platykurtic
低估/低估　underestimation
低汇率倾销/低匯率傾銷　low currency dumping
低技能工人/低技術工　less-skilled workers
低价股/跌破面值股票　penny stock
低价揽客/低價攬客　low-balling
低价投标者/較低價投標者　lower bidder
低价有偏估计[量]/低階偏估計[量]　lower order biased estimator
低利贷款/低利貸款　low interest loan
低利率/低利率　low interest rate
低率关税/低率關稅　nuisance tariff
低迷行业/危困產業　distressed industries
低密度住宅/低密度住宅　low-density housing

低能激励/低效能激勵　low-power incentive
低频词/低頻詞彙　low-frequency word
低生育水平/低生育水平　low birthrate
低收入国家/低收入國家　low income country
低水平均衡陷阱理论/低水準均衡陷阱論　theory of low-level equilibrium trap
低俗节目/低俗節目,不雅節目　indecent program
低碳/低碳　low carbon
低碳技术/低碳技術　low carbon technology
低碳经济/低碳經濟　low carbon economy
低息信贷/低息信貸　low cost credit
低效估计量/非有效估計量　inefficient estimator
低效活动/低效活動　low task
X[低]效率/X效率　X-efficiency
低效统计量/非有效統計量　inefficient statistic
低于票面价值/低於票面價值　par below discount
低语境文化/低情境文化　low-context culture
低值易耗品/低值易耗品　low-cost and short-lived consumable item
堤坝式经营/堤壩式經營　dam type management
滴流效应/滴流效應,積極投資效應　trickle-down effect
狄骥/狄驥　Leon Duguit
狄克逊统计量/Dixon 統計量　Dixon's statistic
狄拉克 δ 函数/迪瑞克達爾塔函數　Dirac's delta function
狄利克雷分布/Dirichlet 分布,Dirichlet 分配　Dirichlet distribution
狄利克雷过程/Dirichlet 過程　Dirichlet process
狄利克雷级数分布/Dirichlet 級數分布,Dirichlet 級數分配　Dirichlet-series distribution
狄利克雷条件/帝瑞勒條件　Dirichlet conditions
迪奥西罗法令集/迪奧西羅法令集　Edictum Theodorici
迪尔凯姆/迪爾凱姆　Durkheim
迪基-福勒检验/迪克-福勒檢定　Dickey-Fuller test
迪基-富勒检验/迪克-福勒檢定　Dickey-Fuller test
迪维西亚指数/Divisia 指數　Divisia index
嫡庶/嫡庶　Di Shu, born of wife or concubine
嫡长子继承制/嫡長子繼承制　lineal primogeniture system
抵补利率平价/彌補利息平價　covered interest parity
抵消/抵消　counteract
抵消分录/沖銷分錄,銷除分錄　elimination entry
抵消权/抵銷權　right of offset
抵消信贷/沖消信貸　offset credit
抵押/抵押　hold in pledge, mortgage

抵押保险/抵押保險　mortgage insurance
抵押背书/抵押背書　endorsement in pledge
抵押贷款/抵押貸款,擔保放款　loan on mortgage, mortgage loan
抵押担保证券/不動產抵押證券　mortgage-backed security
抵押服务契约/抵押服務契約　mortgage service contract
抵押负债/抵押負債　mortgage liability
抵押[公司]债券/抵押[公司]債券　mortgage debenture
抵押还款/抵押還款　mortgage repayment
抵押品/抵押物,擔保品　object given as a pledge, collateral
抵押品备忘录/抵押品備忘錄　memorandum of deposit
抵押契约/抵押契據,典契　deed of mortgage
抵押权/抵押權　right of mortgage
抵押权人/抵押權人　holder of mortgage
抵押人/抵押人　mortgager
抵押市场/抵押市場　mortgage market
抵押条款/抵押條款　mortgage clause
抵押透支/抵押透支　overdraft secured
抵押协定/抵押協議　collateral agreement
抵押信贷/抵押信貸　mortgage credit
抵押银行/抵押銀行　mortgage bank
抵押优先权/抵押優先權　priority of mortgage
抵押有价证券/有價證券質押　pledged security
抵押债券/抵押債券　mortgage bond
抵押账户/抵押賬戶　hypothecated account
抵押证券/抵押證券　mortgage-backed security, collateralized security
抵押证书/抵押證書　letter of deposit
抵押支持证券/抵押基礎證券,擔保證券　mortgage-backed securities, MBS
抵押资产/抵押資產　hypothecated asset, mortgage asset, pledged asset
抵押资产价值比/貸款價值比　loan-to-value ratio, LTV ratio
抵押资金/抵押資金　mortgage money
底版/底版　slab
底本/底本　block copy, master edition
底层/底層　subordinate class
底层研究/底層研究,底邊研究　subaltern studies
底色去除/底色去除　under color removal
底色增益/底色增益　under color addition
底图档案目录/底圖檔案目錄　base map archive catalog

底图登记簿/底圖登記簿　base map register
底图柜/底圖櫃　base map cabinet
底图卷放法/底圖捲放法　base map roll release method
底图平放法/底圖平放法　base map flat discharge method
地产图册/地產圖冊　property atlas
地点效用/地域效用　place utility
地点营销/地方行銷　place marketing
地方本级收入/地方本級收入　local level revenue
地方本级支出/地方本級支出　local level expenditure
地方标准/地方標準　local standard
地方财政/地方財政　local financial, local public finance
地方财政标准收入/地方財政標準收入　standard revenue of local finance
地方财政标准支出/地方財政標準支出　standard expenditure of local finance
地方财政收入/地方財政收入　local fiscal revenue
地方财政支出/地方財政支出　local fiscal expenditure
地方档案/地方檔案　local archive
地方档案馆/地方檔案館　local archives
地方法团主义/地方法團主義　local corporatism
地方工会/地方工會　local unions
地方公共产品/地方公共財　local public good
地方化经济/地方化經濟　localization economies
地方环境标准/地方環境標準　local environmental standard
地方基础设施/地方基礎建設　local infrastructure
地方基准点/區域大地基準　local datum
地方立法/地方立法　local legislation
地方上解收入/地方上解收入　local upper-solution income
地方史料收藏/地方史料收藏　local history collection
地方税/地方稅　local taxes
地方税务局/地方稅務局　local tax bureau
地方文献/地方文獻　local collection
地方文献目录/地方文獻目錄　local bibliography
地方文献学/地方文獻學　local document studies
地方新闻/地方新聞　local news
地方信贷/地方信貸　local credit
地方性报纸/地方報　local newspaper
地方性节目/地方自製節目　local origination
地方性知识/局部知識,在地知識,地方知識　local knowledge
地方预算/地方預算　local budget
地方志/地方志　local chronicles, local records
地方志书录/地方志書錄　catalog of local chronicles
地方总工会/地方總工會　local federalion of trade unious
地籍/地籍　cadastre
地价/地價　price of land
地脚/地腳　tail edge, bottom margin, tail margin
地理标志/地理標示　geographical indication
地理不利国/地理不利國　geographically disadvantaged state
地理定价/地理定價　geographical pricing
地理分类法/地理分類法　geography classification
地理级数/地理系列　geographic series
地理景框/地理景框　geography scene frame
地理决定论/地理決定論　geographical determinism
地理联系系数/地理相聯係數　coefficient of geographical association
地理数据模型/地理資料模式　geographic data model
地理细分/地理區隔　geographic segmentation
地理坐标系统/地理坐標系統　geographic coordinate system, GCS
地面推广/地面推廣　ground extension
地名词典/地名辭典　gazetteer, dictionary of place names, geographical dictionary
地名档案/地名檔案　toponymical archive
地名录/地名錄　gazetteer
地名索引/地名索引　geographic index
地名注释/地名注釋　place name annotation
地球村/地球村　global village
地区版杂志/地區版雜志　geographic edition
地区部门化/地區部門化　geographic departmentalization
地区差异指数/區域差異指數　regional difference index, RDI
地区档案馆/地區檔案館　regional archives
地区发行/區域流通　regional distribution
地区发展模式/地方發展模式　locality development model
地区复分/地區複分　place subdivision, geographic subdivision, local subdivision
地区复分表/地區複分表　area subdivisions, geographical subdivisions
地区来源原则/溯源主義　territorial provenance
地区排架法/地區排架法　region arrangement
地区特惠税/區域優惠關稅　regional preferential duty

地区统一价格/地區統一價格　zone uniform price
地区图书馆/區域圖書館　regional library
地区图书馆网/區域圖書館網　regional library network
地区相关原则/屬地主義　territoriality pertinence, territorial pertinence
地区信息中心/地區資訊中心　regional information center
地区性目录/地區性目錄　regional catalog, local bibliography
地区原则/屬地主義　territoriality pertinence, territorial pertinence
地区专业化/區域專業化　regional specialization
地区专业化指数/區域專業化指數　regional specialization index
地区组合法/地區組合法　region combination method
地上权/地上權　right of superficies
地图/地圖　map
地图集/地圖集　atlas
地图目录/地圖書目　cartobibliography
地图图书馆/地圖圖書館　map library
地位/地位,階層　status
地位赋予功能/地位授予功能　status conferral function
地位获得/地位取得　status attainment
地位获得模型/地位獲得模式　status attainment model
地位结晶化/地位結晶化　status crystallization
地位群体/地位團體,身份團體　status group
地下报刊/地下報刊　underground press
地下经济/地下經濟　underground economy, subterranean economy
地役权/地役權　servitude, easement
地域代表制/地域代表制　territorial representation
地域分类法/地域分類法　region classification
地域工资差别/地域差別工資　geographic wage differential
地缘群体/地緣群體　social group sharing native-place ties
IP地址/網際網路協定位址　internet protocol address
地质图书馆/地質圖書館　geological libraries and collections
地租/地租　land rent
帝国主义殖民体系/帝國主義殖民體系　colonial system of imperialism
递标/投標文件的遞交　delivery of tender

递补水准生育率/遞補水準生育率　replacement level fertility
递归系统/遞迴系統　recursive system
递归最小二乘/遞迴最小平方　recursive least squares
递耗式信托/遞延式信託　wasting trust
递耗资产/遞耗資產　depletable assets
递减法/逐步减少法　step down procedure
递减故障率/遞減故障率　decreasing failure rate, DFR
递减平均故障率/平均遞減故障率　decreasing failure rate average, DFRA
递减平均剩余寿命/遞減平均餘命　decreasing mean residual life, DMRL
递减平均失效率/平均遞減故障率　decreasing failure rate average, DFRA
递减失效率/遞減故障率　decreasing failure rate, DFR
递减危险率/遞減危險率　decreasing hazard rate
递阶对策/分級對策　hierarchical game
递升序/遞增次序　ascending order
递修本/遞修本　successively revised edition
递延年金/遞延年金　deferred annuity
递延期限/遞延期限,延期期限　term of deferment
递延收益/遞延收益　deferred income
递延所得税负债/遞延所得稅負債　deferred tax liabilities
递延所得税资产/遞延所得稅資產　deferred tax assets
递延债券/遞延債券　deferred bond
递增法/逐步增加法　step-up procedure
递增故障率/遞增故障率　increasing failure rate, IFR
递增密度/遞增密度　increasing density
递增平均故障率/遞增平均故障率　increasing failure rate average, IFRA
递增平均剩余寿命/遞增平均餘命　increasing mean residual life, IMRL
递增平均失效率/遞增平均故障率　increasing failure rate average, IFRA
递增平均危险率/遞增平均危險率　increasing hazard rate average, IHRA
递增失效率/遞增故障率　increasing failure rate, IFR
递增危险率/遞增危險率　increasing hazard rate, IHR
递增因子/遞增因素　ascending factor
第N代缩微品/第N代微縮品　Nth generation of a microform
第二产业/第二級產業　secondary sector

第二次发行/第二次發行　secondary offering
第二次再投资周期/第二次再投資週期　secondary reinvestment cycle
第二代互联网/第二代互聯網　world wide web 2.0
第二代缩微胶卷/第二代微縮膠卷　second generation microfilm
第二代研发管理/第二代研發管理　second generation of research and development management
第二抵押/第二顺位抵押　second mortgage
第二抵押债券/第二抵押債券　second mortgage bond
第二方审核/第二方審核　second party audit
第二高价拍卖/第二高價拍賣　second-price auction
第二含义/第二含義　second meaning
第二极限定理/第二極限定理　second limit theorem
第二价值/第二價值　second value
第二经济/第二經濟　second economy
第二类错误/型二誤差　type Ⅱ error
第二类截尾/型Ⅱ截斷　type Ⅱ censoring
第二类误差/第二類誤差,第二型誤差　type Ⅱ error, second kind of error, error of the second kind
第二联汇票/第二聯匯票,匯票副本　second bill of exchange
第二受益人/第二受益人　second beneficiary
第二四分位数/第二四分位數　second quartile
第二限制条件/次要限制條件　secondary constraint
第二性/第二性　second sex
第二溢额分保合同/第二溢額再保合約　second surplus reinsurance treaty
第二责任者/第二責任者　secondary author
第二账户/第二賬戶　second account
第二职业/第二職業　secondary job, secondary occupation
第六代研发管理/第六代研發管理　sixth generation of research and development management
第三部门/第三部門　third sector
第三产业/服務業,第三級產業　tertiary sector
第三场所/第三場所　third place
第三代互联网/第三代互聯網　world wide web 3.0
第三代研发管理/第三代研發管理　third generation of research and development management
第三抵押权/第三顺位抵押權　third mortgage
第三方评价/協力廠商評價　third party evaluation
第三方审核/第三方稽核　third party audit
第三方提单/第三者提單　third party bill of lading
第三方物流/協力廠商物流　the third party logistics
第三方物流提供者/協力廠商物流提供者　third-party logistics provider, 3PL provider
第三方信用证/第三者信用狀　third party credit
第三方应用程序/協力廠商應用程式　application, APP
第三方支付/協力廠商支付　third party payment
第三方支票/第三當事人支票　third party check
第三价格拍卖/第三價格拍賣　third-price auctions
第三空间/第三空間　third space
第三类误差/第三類誤差　error of the third kind
第三人效果/第三人效果,第三人效應　third-person effect
第三世界/第三世界　third world
第三条道路/第三條[道]路　the third road, the third way
第三型离散分布/第三型離散分布,第三型離散分配　discrete type Ⅲ distribution
第三者保险/第三者保險　third party insurance
第三者对票据的付款保证/第三者對票據的付款保證　guarantee by avail
第三者条款/第三者條款　third party clause
第三者责任保险/第三人責任保險　third party liability insurance
第四代研发管理/第四代研發管理　fourth generation of research and development management
第四方物流/第四方物流　fourth party logistics
第四市场/第四市場　fourth market
第五代研发管理/第五代研發管理　fifth generation of research and development management
第五媒体/第五媒體　the fifth media
第五项修炼理论/第五項修練　fifth discipline
第一产业/農業,第一級產業　primary sector
第一代互联网/第一代互聯網　world wide web 1.0
第一代研发管理/第一代研發管理　first generation of research and development management
第一抵押/第一顺位抵押　first mortgage
第一抵押债券/第一顺位抵押債券　first mortgage bond
第一方审核/第一方稽核　first party audit
第一价格密封拍卖/封閉最高價式拍賣　first-price sealed-bid auctions
第一价值/第一價值　first value
第一类错误/第一類型錯誤　type Ⅰ error
第一类极值分布/第一型極端值分配　type Ⅰ extreme value distribution
第一类截尾/型Ⅰ截斷　type Ⅰ censoring
第一类误差/第一類誤差　error of the first kind

第一流的工人/一流工人　first class worker
第一期保费/第一期保費　initial call
第一审普通程序/第一審普通程式　ordinary procedure of first instance
第一世界/第一世界　first world
第一受益人/第一受益人　first beneficiary
第一印象/第一印象　first impression
第一责任说明/第一責任說明　first statement of responsibility
第一责任者项/第一責任者項　first liability item
蒂博特假说/蒂柏假說　tiebout hypothesis
蒂德人类本能论/蒂德人類本能論　human instinct theory of Tead
棣莫弗-拉普拉斯定理/棣馬佛-拉卜拉士定理，De Moivre-Laplace 定理　De Moivre-Laplace theorem
缔约国报告制度/締約國報告制度　state party reporting system
缔约过失责任/締約過失責任　contracting fault liability
典簿/典簿　dianbu
典当/典當　pawn broking
典当行/典當行　pawn shop, pawn broker
典当商/典當商　pawn broker
典范矩阵/正準矩陣　canonical matrix
典籍/典籍　dianji, ancient codes and records
典卖/典賣　code sales
典权/典權　right to pawn
典型测度/典型量測　typical measure
典型的回归分析/典型回歸分析　canonical regression analysis
典型调查/典型調查　typical investigation
典型化/典型化　typification
典型季节型态/典型季節型態　typical seasonal pattern
典型事件/典範事件　paradigmatic event
典型随机变量/正準變量　canonical variate
典型特征值/基準特性　typical characteristic
典型相关分析/典型相關分析　canonical correlation analysis
典型相关系数/典型相關係數　canonical correlation coefficient
点差交易/差價交易　spread trading
点抽样/點抽樣　point sampling
点对点技术/點對點技術　peer-to-peer, P2P
点二维分布/點二變量分布，點二變量分配　point bivariate distribution
点二项分布/點二項分布，點二項分配　point binomial distribution

点分系统/計點系統，計點制度　point system
点估计/點估計[值]　point estimate, point estimation
点过程/點過程　point process
点击量/點擊量　click
点击率/點擊率　click-through rate, hit rate, click rate
点校加工/點校加工　collation and punctuation
点密度/點密度　point density
点双列相关/點雙數列相關　point biserial correlation
点弹性/點彈性　point elasticity
点图/點圖　dot diagram
点预测/點預測　point forecasting
点阵字库/位元影像字型　bitmapped font
点-轴开发理论/點軸開發理論　point-axis development theory
电报/電報　telegraph
电报订货/電報訂貨　cable order
电报汇款/電匯　remittance by cable, wire transfer, telegraphic transfer
电报式文摘/電報式文摘　telegraphic abstracts
电报统计/電報統計　telegraph statistics
电报信用证/電報傳遞信用狀，電開信用狀　cable credit
电唱机/電唱機　gramophone, phonograph
电动刻纹头/電動刻紋頭　electrodynamic cutter head
电动拾音头/電動拾音頭　electrodynamic pick-up head
电荷耦合器件/光電偶合器　charge coupled device, CCD
电话采访/電話訪問　telephone interview
电话调查/電話調查　telephone survey
电话访问/[節目中]電訪　telephone coincidental
电话付款/電話付款　pay by phone
电话交谈/叩應　call-in
电话交谈节目/叩應節目　call-in program
电话统计/電話統計　telephone statistics
电话银行/電話銀行　telephone banking
电话营销/電話行銷　telephone marketing
电话征订/電話徵訂　telephone subscription
电话咨询服务/電話諮詢服務　phone-in reference service
电汇/電匯　remittance by cable, wire transfer, telegraphic transfer
电汇汇率/電匯匯率　cable rate, telegraphic transfer rate
电汇汇票/電匯匯票　cable draft, telegraphic money order

电汇买进汇率/電匯買進匯率　telegraphic transfer buying rate
电汇卖出汇率/電匯賣出匯率　telegraphic transfer selling rate
电脑动画/電腦動畫　computer animation
电脑密集再抽样/電腦密集再抽樣　computer intensive resampling
电脑游戏/電腦遊戲　computer game
电气与机械工程合同条件/電氣與機械工程合同條件　condition of contract for electrical and mechanical engineering
电容拾音头/電容拾音頭　capacitance pick-up head
电容式触摸屏/電容式觸控式螢幕　capacitive touch panel
电视暴力/電視暴力　television violence
电视采访/電視訪談　television interview
电视购物/電視購物　television shopping
电视纪录片/電視紀錄片　television documentary
[电视]口播新闻/[電視]乾稿新聞　talking head story
电视迷/電視上癮　television addiction
电视新闻/電視新聞　television news
电视新闻伦理/電視新聞倫理　television news ethics
电视新闻现场直播/現場報導　live news, live report
电视新闻学/電視新聞學　television journalism
电视营销/電視行銷　direct-response television marketing
电视真人秀/電視真人秀　reality television
电视指南/電視指南　television guide
[电视]转播录像/電視轉錄　telerecording
电信统计/電信統計　telecommunication statistics
电影/電影　film
电影广告/電影廣告　cinema advertising
电影合同/電影合同　cinematographic contract
电影胶片/電影膠片　cinefilm, motion picture film
电影权/電影權　motion picture rights
电影作品/電影作品　film work
电铸/電鑄　electroforming galvanic
电子报表/電子報表　electronic report
电子报刊/電子報刊　electronic press
电子报纸/電子報　electronic newspaper, e-newspaper
电子布告栏系统/電子布告欄系統　bulletin board system, BBS
电子采购/電子採購　electronic procurement
电子菜谱/電子菜譜　electronic menu
电子出版/電子出版　electronic publishing
电子出版流程/電子出版流程　electronic publishing process
电子出版物/電子出版品　electronic publication, e-publication
电子出版系统/電子出版系統　electronic publishing system
电子传播/電子傳播　electronic communication
电子词典/電子字典　electronic dictionary
电子辞书/電子辭書　electronic dictionary
电子档案/電子檔[案]　electronic archive, electronic records
电子档案管理/電子檔案管理　electronic files management
电子地图/電子地圖　electronic map
电子雕刻/電子雕刻　electrographic engraving
电子雕刻凹版/電子雕刻凹版　electronic engraving printing
电子雕刻机/電子雕刻機　electronic engraving machine
电子订单/電子訂貨　electronic order
电子订货系统/電子訂貨系統　electronic order system
电子发票/電子發票　e-invoice
电子分色机/電子分色機　color separation scanner
电子服务/電子化服務　e-service
电子付款机支付系统/銷售點支付系統　point-of-sale payments system, POS payments system
电子公告板/電子布告欄系統　bulletin board system, BBS
电子公告系统/電子布告欄系統　bulletin board system, BBS
电子公文/電子公文　electronic administration record, electronic official document
电子广告/電子廣告　electronic advertisement
电子广告牌/電子看板　electronic kanban, e-kanban
电子合同/電子合同　electronic contract
电子货币/電子貨幣，電子錢　electronic currency, electronic money
电子计算机创作作品/電子電腦創作作品　computer-made works
电子交易/電子交易　electronic trading, e-trading
电子交易系统/電子交易系統　electronic trading system
电子教学参考资料/指定數位參考資源　electronic reserves
电子课本/電子課本　electronic textbook
电子录像制品/電子錄影　electronic video recording, EVR
电子媒介/電子媒體　electronic media
电子名片/電子名片　electronic card

电子墨水/電子墨水 electronic ink
电子目录/電子目錄 electronic catalogue
电子期刊/電子期刊 electronic journal, e-journal
电子期刊导航/電子期刊導航 navigation of electronic journal
电子企务/電子化企業,電子化經營 e-business
电子签名/電子簽章 electronic signature
电子钱包/電子錢包,電子錢夾 electronic wallet, e-wallet, e-purse
电子认证/電子認證 electronic authentication
电子商务/電子商務,電子化企業 electronic commerce, e-commerce, e-business
电子商务安全/電子商務安全 e-commerce security
电子商务标准/電子商務標準 e-commerce standard
电子商务产品/電子商務產品 e-commerce product
电子商务管理/電子商務管理 e-commerce management
电子商务过程/電子商務過程 e-commerce process
电子商务环境下的供应链/電子商務供應鏈 e-commerce supply chain, e-business supply chain
电子商务架构/電子商務架構 e-commerce architecture
电子商务交易主体/電子商務交易主體 e-commerce transaction participant
电子商务[经营]模式/電子商務模式 e-commerce model
电子商务谈判/電子商務談判 e-commerce negotiation
电子商务网站/電子商務網站 e-commerce website
电子商务系统/電子商務系統 e-commerce system
电子商务信息安全/電子商務資訊安全 e-commerce information security
电子商务信用/電子商務信用 e-commerce credit
电子市场/電子市場 electronic market
电子书包/電子書包 electronic bag
电子书制作生成器/電子書製作生成器 electronic product generator
电子数据交换/電子資料交換 electronic data interchange, EDI
电子数据交换系统/電子資料交換系統 electronic data interchange system
电子税票/電子稅票 electronic tax receipt
电子通信服务/電子通訊服務 electronic communications service
电子[图]书/電子書 electronic book, e-book
电子图书馆/數位圖書館 digital library
电子图书阅览器/電子書閱讀器 e-book device, e-book reader

电子文本/電子文本 electronic text
电子文档/電子[文]檔 electronic document, eletronic document
电子文件/電子檔[案] eletronic record, electronic file, electronic document
电子文件管理系统/電子檔案管理系統 electronic records management system, ERMS
电子现场制作/外景節目製作 electronic field production, EFP
电子现金/電子現金 e-cash
电子新闻采集/電子新聞採訪 electronic news gathering, ENG
电子信息资源/電子資訊資源 electronic message resource
电子型信息[源]/電子資訊源 electronic information source
电子音乐/電子音樂 electronic music
电子印前处理/電子印前處理 electronic pre-press processing
电子邮件/電子郵件 electronic mail, e-mail, email
电子邮件出版/電子郵件出版 email publishing
电子邮件广告/電子郵件廣告 email advertisement
电子邮件咨询服务/電子郵件諮詢服務 email reference service
电子阅报栏/電子閱報欄 electronic national press, electronic newspaper reading screen
电子阅读/電子閱讀 electronic reading
电子阅读器/電子[書]閱讀器 electronic reader, e-reader
电子杂志/電子雜誌,電子期刊 electronic magazine, e-journal, e-zine
电子证据/電子證據 electronic evidence
电子政务/電子政務 electronic government
电子支付/電子支付 electronic payment
电子支票/電子支票 electronic check
电子纸/電子紙 electronic paper
电子著作权页/電子版權頁 electronic copyright page
电子资金转账/電子資金轉賬 electronic fund transfer
电子资金转账系统/電子資金移轉系統 electronic funds transfer system
电子资源服务成本/電子資源服務成本 cost of electronic service
电子资源管理/電子資源管理 electronic resources management
电子资源管理系统/電子資源管理系統 electronic resource management system, ERMS

电子资源绩效评估/電子資源績效評估　electronic access evaluation
电子资源类型附注/電子資源類型附註　type of electronic resource note
电子资源评估/電子資源評價　electronic resources evaluation
电子资源引进/數位資源引入　introduction of digital resources
电阻式触摸屏/電阻式觸控式螢幕　resistive touch panel, RTP
佃农/佃農　tenant farmer, tenant peasant
垫付费用/預付款,預付費用　advance charge
垫头交易/信用交易　margin trading
殿本/殿本　palace edition
叼纸牙/咬爪　gripper
调拨/分配,配置　allocation
调查/調查　fact-finding, inquiry, survey
调查表/調查資料　survey
调查单元/調查單位　survey unit
调查分析/調查分析　survey analysis
调查回馈/調查回饋　survey feedback
调查结果/調查結果　investigation result
调查设计/調查設計　survey design
调查误差/調查誤差　error in surveys
调查研究/調查研究　sampling survey
调查员查记法/調查員查記法　canvasser method
调查员偏倚/訪問者偏誤　interviewer bias
调度/調度,工作分派,派工　dispatching, expediting
调卷/調卷　check
掉期交易/掉期交易　swap dealing, swap transaction
掉页/掉頁　page pulling off
迭代变量/反覆工具變數　iterative instrumental variables
迭代法/迭代法　iteration method
迭代加权最小二乘法/重複再加權最小平方法　iteratively reweighted least squares
迭代检索/迭代檢索　iterative retrieval
迭代算法/反覆運算演算法　iterative algorithm
迭代优化算法/反覆最適化演算法　iterated optimization algorithms
迭代最小二乘/反覆最小平方　iterative least squares
叠对数定律/疊對數法則　law of iterated logarithm
叠加变异/疊加變異　superposed variation
叠加过程/疊加過程　superposed process
叠加或线性扩散法/疊加或線性擴散法　superposition or linear diffusion method
叠架式书库/疊架式書庫　layer-shelving book stack
蝶式差价期权/蝶狀價差期權　butterfly spread option

蝶形套购/蝶式價差交易　butterfly spread
丁克家庭/丁克家庭　double-income no-kids family, DINK family
钉住汇率/釘住匯率　exchange rate pegging
钉住汇率制度/釘住匯率制度　pegged exchange rate system
钉住价格/釘住價格　pegged price
顶点覆盖问题/頂點覆蓋問題　vertex covering problem
顶级本体/頂層本體　top-level ontology
顶盘/最高行情　highest quotation
订单/訂單,定單　order, order sheet
订单处理提前期/訂單處理提前期　order processing lead time
订单处理周期/訂單處理週期　order cycle time
订单发出/訂單發出　order placement
订单管理/訂單管理　order management
订单号/採購訂單號碼　purchase order number, PO number
订单记录/訂單的記錄　order record
订单间隔期/訂單間隔期　order interval
订单控制/訂單控制　order control
订单满足能力/訂單滿足能力　order-fulfillment ability
订单切入点/訂單拉動點　order penetration point
订单请求/訂單之請求　order request
订单驱动/委託單驅動　order-driven
订单驱动式生产/訂單驅動式生產　order-driven production
订单确认书/訂單確認書　confirmation of order
订单输入/訂單輸入　order entry
订单统计/訂單統計　orders-received statistics
订单赢得要素/訂單贏得要素　order winner
订单资格要素/訂單合格要件　order qualifier
订到率/訂到率　order fulfill rate
订货/訂貨　ordering
订货策略/訂貨政策,訂購政策　order policy
订货点系统/訂購點系統　order point system
订货费用/訂購成本　ordering cost
订货会/訂貨會　order-placing meeting
订货量/訂購量　order quantity
订货满足率/訂貨滿足率　fulfillment rate
订货日期/訂貨日期　date of order
订货审核/訂貨審核　ordering verification
订货型生产/接單生產,訂單生產　make to order, MTO
订货周期/訂貨週期　lead time
订口/訂口　binding edge

订口空白/訂口空白　binding margin
订口留白/訂口留白　back margin
订口余白/訂口餘白　backedge area
订书推荐卡/訂書推薦卡　recommendation card, requisition card, suggestion card
订数/已訂數量　quantity of order
订销局/訂銷局　subscription office
订阅/訂閱　subscribe, subscription
订阅代理/訂閱代理　subscription agent
定比尺度/比例尺度，等比尺度　ratio scale
定标/定標　scaling
定底式期权/下跨式交易策略　bottom straddle
定顶式期权/上跨式交易策略　top straddle
定额/配額　quota
定额保险/定額保險　fixed sum insurance
定额储蓄/定額儲蓄　fixed amount saving
定额分保/定額分保　quota share reinsurance
定额计价/定額計價　fixed rate pricing
定额流动资金/定額流動資金　normed current fund
定额税率/定額稅率　fixed tax rate
定额原理/定額原理　fixed amount principle
定额租金/配額租　quota rent
定稿/定稿　final text, version final
定稿本/定稿本　difinitive edition
定格动画/定格動畫　stop-motion animation
定购单/訂購單　buying order
定基指数/定基指數　fixed-base index
定价/定價，價格　price, pricing
定价操作数/定價運算元　pricing operator
定价方法/定價法　pricing method
定价效率/價格效率　pricing efficiency
定价政策/定價政策　pricing policy
定价制度/定價制度　pricing system
定金/定金，保證金　money paid on account, deposit
定理/定理　theorem
定量/量化　quantify
定量变量/屬量變數　quantitative variable
定量测量/計量測定值　variable measurement
定量的/屬量的，計量的　quantitative
定量分类/屬量分類　quantitative classification
定量分析/量化分析，數量分析　quantitative analysis
定量风险分析/定量風險分析　quantitative risk analysis
定量假设/離散增量假設　quantum hypothesis
定量决策/定量決策　quantitative decision making
定量模拟/定量模擬　quantitative simulation
定量模型/定量模型　quantitative model
定量设计变量/屬量設計變數　quantitative design variable
定量数据/量化資料，定量資料，屬量資料　variable data, quantitative data
定量数据分析/量化資料分析　quantitative data analysis
定量数列/屬量數列　quantitative series
定量研究/量化研究　quantitative research
定量预测/屬量預測，數量預測　quantitative forecasting
定量战略计划矩阵/數量策略規劃矩陣　quantitative strategic planning matrix
定率税/定率稅　rated tax
定锚与调整/錨定與調整　anchoring and adjustment
定牌生产/原廠委託製造，製造代工　original equipment manufacturing, OEM
定期补货/定期補貨　periodic replenishment
定期出版书目/定期出版書目　serial biliography
定期存款/定期存款　time deposit
定期贷款/定期貸款　term loan, time loan
定期抵押/定期抵押　term mortgage
定期抵押担保贷款/定期抵押擔保貸款　secured time loan
定期付款/定期付款　payment on term, scheduled payment, payable at fixed date
定期回购/定期再買回　term repo
定期汇票/定期匯票　time draft, period bill, fixed term bill of exchange
定期交货/定期交貨　delivery on term
定期交易/定期交易　time bargain
定期票据/定期票據　time bill, term bill, fixed bill
定期维护/定期維護　scheduled maintenance
定期系统/定期系統　periodic system
定期信贷/定期信貸　term credit
定期信托/定期信託　limited trust
定期信用证/定期循環信用狀　periodic credit
定期宣判/定期宣判　judgement pronounced on appointed day
定期债券/定期債券　term bond, bond term
定期支付票据/定期支付票據　bill payable on fixed date
定期租赁/定期租賃　term lease
定时截尾试验方案/定時中止試驗計劃　fixed time test plan
定式合同/附合契約　contracts of adhesion
定数截尾试验方案/定數中止試驗計劃　fixed number test plan
定题服务/定題服務，專題選粹服務　selective dissemination of information, SDI

定题服务检索系统/定題服務檢索系統　SDI service retrieval system
定题情报服务/專題選粹服務　selective dissemination of information
定位策略/定位策略　positional strategies
定位陈述/定位宣言　positioning statement
定位存储/定位儲存　fixed-location storage
定位精度/選擇性定址　addressability
定位学派/定位學派　positioning school
定息股票/定息股票　fixed interest stock
定息债券/定息債券　fixed interest bearing bond
定向服务/定向服務　directional transfer
定向搜索/定向搜索　beam search
定向投资/投資目標　target investment
定向政策矩阵/定向政策矩陣　directional policy matrix
定性变量/屬性變數　qualitative variable
定性分类/屬性分類　qualitative classification
定性分析/質化分析,質性分析　qualitative analysis
定性风险分析/定性風險分析　qualitative risk analysis
定性决策/定性決策　qualitative decision-making
定性模拟/定性模擬　qualitative simulation
定性模型/定性模型　qualitative model
定性推理/定性推理　qualitative reasoning
定性选择/屬質性選擇　qualitative choice
定性研究/定性研究,質化研究　qualitative research
定性因变量/屬質應變數　qualitative dependent variable
定性与限值因变量模型/屬質與受限相依變數模型　qualitative and limited dependent variable models
定性预测/定性預測,屬性預測　qualitative forecasting
定性预测法/屬質性預測方法　qualitative forecasting methods
定性资料/定性資料　qualitative data
定性资料分析/質性資料分析　qualitative data analysis
定序尺度/順序尺度,次序尺度　ordinal scale
定义-度量-分析-改进-控制模式/DMAIC 模式　define-measure-analyze-improve-control mode, DMAIC mode
定义对照/定義對比　defining contrast
定义关系/定義關係　defining relation
定影/定影過程　fixing
定值保险/定值保險　valued insurance
定值美元/幣值穩定的美元　stable dollar
定制/客製化　customization
定制出版/定制出版　customized publishing
定制物流/定制物流　customized logistics
定组研究/小規模重訪法,固定樣本連續調查法　panel study
东方主义/東方主義　orientalism
东非共同体/東非共同體　East African Community
东京证券交易所股价指数/東京東證股票指數　Tokyo Topix stock index
东西洋考每月统记传/東西洋考每月統記傳　Eastern Western Monthly Magazine
东亚奇迹/東亞奇跡　East-Asia miracle
董事/董事　director
董事会/董事會　board of directors
董事长/董事長　chairman of the board
董仲舒/董仲舒　Dong Zhongshu
动差矩阵/動差矩陣　moment matrix
动产/動產　personal estate
动产抵押/動產質押　pledge of movable
动产随人/動產隨人　mobilia personam sequuntur
动产信贷银行/動產信貸銀行　credit mobilier
动产质押债券/動產質押債券,質押信託債券　bond collateral trust
动磁拾音头/動磁拾音頭　magnetodynamic pick-up head
动画/動畫　animation
Flash 动画/Flash 動畫　Flash animation
动画新闻/動[畫]新聞　animation news
动画原画/動畫原畫　original animation
动机/動機　motivation
动机测试/動機測試　motive test
动机性生产率水平/激勵生產力水準　motivated productivity level, MPL
动静模型/移動者-滯留者模型　mover-stayer model
动量效应/動量效應　momentum effect
动漫/動漫畫　anime
动漫产业/動漫產業　animation industry
动漫出版/動漫出版　animation publishing
动素分解图/動素分解圖　therblig chart
动素分析/動素分析　therblig analysis
动素符号/動素符號　therblig symbol
动态保值/動態對沖,動態避險　dynamic hedging, dynamic hedge
动态乘数/動態乘數　dynamic multiplier
动态 X[低]效率/動態 X 效率　dynamic X-efficiency
动态定价/動態定價　dynamic pricing
动态对策/動態對策　dynamic game
动态对冲/動態對沖,動態避險　dynamic hedging, dynamic hedge

动态分析／動態分析　dynamic analysis
动态跟踪系统／動態追蹤系統　dynamic tracking system
动态规划／動態規劃　dynamic programming
动态规划嵌入原理／動態規劃嵌入原理　dynamic programming embedding principle
动态结算／動態結算　dynamic settlement
动态决策／動態決策　dynamic decision-making
动态联立方程模型／動態聯立方程式模型　dynamic simultaneous equations models
动态贸易模型／動態貿易模型　dynamic trade model
动态模型／動態模型　dynamic model, dynamical model
动态能力／動態能力　dynamic capability
动态排法／動態策略　dynamic policy
动态批量规划／動態批量規劃　dynamic lot sizing
动态瓶颈／動態瓶頸　wandering bottle neck
动态情报研究／動力情報分析　dynamic intelligence analysis
动态失真／動態失真　dynamic distortion
动态数据／動態資料　dynamic data
动态数据系统／動態資料系統　dynamic data system, DDS
动态随机过程／動態隨機過程　dynamic stochastic process
动态统计／動態統計　dynamic statistics
动态投入产出分析／動態投入產出分析　dynamic input-output analysis
动态投入产出模型／動態投入產出模型　dynamic input-output model
动态投资／動態投資　dynamic investment
动态系统／動態系統　dynamic system
动态效率／動態效率　dynamic efficiency
动态信息[源]／動態資訊源　dynamic information source
动态性／動態性　dynamicity
动态页面／動態頁　dynamic page
动态预测／動態預測　dynamic forecasting
动物福利法／動物福利法　animal welfare law
动物胶／動物膠　animal glue
动物精神／動物本能　animal spirits
动员／動員　mobilization
动员预付款／動員預付款　advanced payment of mobilization
动轴／移軸　moving axis
动作／動作　motion
动作分界点／動作分界點　breakpoint
动作基本要素／動作基本要素　action basic factor, therblig
动作经济性／動作經濟　motion economy
动作经济原则／動作經濟原則　economic principle of motion
动作浪费／動作浪費　motion waste
动作研究／行動研究　action research
动作要素分析法／動作要素分析法　ready-work factor, RWF
动作游戏／動作遊戲　action game
动作与时间研究／工時學　motion-time study
冻结期／凍結期　freeze window
抖动图像处理／不連續色調混色　dithering
抖晃率／抖動　jitter
陡度分布／突出分布，突出分配　abrupt distribution
斗鸡博弈／懦夫賽局　chicken game
斗牛士债券／鬥牛士債券　matador bond
斗杀／鬥殺　kill in a fight
斗伤／鬥傷　injury in a fight
斗讼／鬥訟　lawsuit
馄版／餛版　multiple blocks
都柏林核心集／都柏林核心集　Dublin Core, DC
都柏林核心元数据／都柏林核心集　Dublin Core, DC
都柏林核心元数据集／都柏林核心元資料集　Dublin Core Metadata Element Set, DCMES
都察院／都察院　the Court of Censors
都市报／都市報　metropolis newspaper
督促程序／督促程式　proceedings for supervising and urging the clearance of debt
督导功能／督導功能　function of supervision
督导资格／督導資格　supervisory qualification
毒品合法化／毒品合法化　legalization of drugs
毒丸术／毒藥政策　poison pill
独白／獨白　monologue
独裁型风格／獨裁式風格　autocratic style
独裁者博弈／獨裁者賽局　dictator game
独创性／原創性　originality
独家代理／獨家代理，專屬代理制度　exclusive agency, sole agent
独家分销／獨家配銷　exclusive distribution
独家经营／獨家經營　exclusive dealing, sole trade
独家经营许可证／獨家經營許可證　exclusive licence
独家授权／獨家授權　exclusive authorization
独家新闻／獨家[新聞]　exclusive
独家许可证／獨家許可證，排他許可證　sole license
独家专利权／獨家專利權　exclusive patent right
独居老人／獨居老人　elderly people living alone
独立保存／獨立保存　independent preservation

独立报酬系统／獨立報酬系統　independent reward system
独立标引／獨立標引　standalone indexing
独立成本／獨立成本　separate cost
独立[的]／獨立[的]　independent
独立的犯罪构成／獨立的犯罪構成　independent constitution of a crime
独立董事／獨立董事　independent director
独立二项分布／獨立二項分布　independent binomial distribution
独立二项试验／獨立二項試驗　independent binomial experiment
独立访客／獨立訪客　unique visitor
独立检验证明书／獨立檢驗證明書　independent inspection certificate
独立媒介／獨立媒體　independent media
独立模型／獨立模型　independence model
独立品／獨立物品　independent goods
独立权／獨立權　right of independence
独立删失／獨立設限　independent censoring
独立实验／獨立實驗　independent experiment
独立式书架／獨立式書架，自支式書架　free-standing shelving
独立事件／獨立事件　independent event
独立书店／獨立書店　independent bookstore
独立随机变量／獨立隨機變數　independent random variable
独立随机抽样／彼此獨立的隨機抽樣法　independent random sampling
独立随机样本／獨立隨機樣本　independent random sample
独立同分布随机变量／獨立且相同分布隨機變數　independent and identically distributed random variables, IID random variables
独立投资项目／獨立投資專案　independent project
独立行动／獨立行動　independent action
独立型数据集市／獨立型資料市集　independent data mart
独立性／獨立性　independence
独立性检验／獨立性檢定　independence test, test for independence
独立需求／獨立需求　independent demand
独立需求库存／獨立需求庫存　independent demand inventory
独立宣言／獨立宣言　Declaration of Independence
独立样本／獨立樣本　independent sample
独立因子／獨立因素　independent factor
独立优惠价零售店／獨立優惠價零售店　independent offprice retailer
独立增量过程／獨立增量過程　independent increments process, process with independent increments
独生子女／獨生子女　single child
独有的协同效应／獨有的協同效應　private synergy
独占区域／排他性地域限制　exclusive territories
独占许可／專屬授權　exclusive license
独资企业／獨資企業　single proprietorship
独尊儒术／獨尊儒術　Confucianism monopoly
读出面／讀出面　read-out surface
读功率／讀功率　read power
读校法／讀校法　proofreading technique of reading out loudly
读鞫／讀鞫　read judgement
读律佩觽／讀律佩觽　Du Lyu Pei Xi
读书会／讀書會　study circle
读者／讀者　reader
读者参与／讀者涉入度　reader involvement
读者到馆量／讀者到館量　number of library visitors
读者到馆率／讀者到館率　rate of library visitors
读者登记／讀者註冊　reader registration
读者登记档／讀者登記檔　reader file
读者调查／讀者調查　reader survey
读者分类目录／讀者分類目錄　reader's classified catalog
读者服务／讀者服務　reader service
读者服务部／閱覽組　reader service department
读者工作／讀者工作　reader work
读者记录／讀者記錄　reader record
读者教育／讀者教育　reader education
读者结构／讀者結構　reader structure
读者借阅记录／讀者借閱記錄　patron borrowing record, patron record
读者借阅率／讀者借閱率　readership, lending rate
读者借阅请求／用戶請求　reader's request, patron's request, user's request
读者俱乐部／讀者俱樂部　readers' club
读者来信／讀者投書　letters to the editor
读者来信专栏／通訊專欄　correspondence column
读者类型／讀者類型　user type, patron type
读者论坛／讀者論壇　readers' forum
读者满意度／讀者滿意度　reader satisfaction
读者目录／讀者目錄　reader's catalog
读者区／讀者區　reader area
读者权益／讀者權利　reader rights
读者群／讀者群，閱讀群體　reader group, reader groups

读者题名目录/讀者書名目録　reader's title catalog
读者统计/讀者人次統計　reader statistics
读者投诉/讀者投訴　complaints from readers
读者心理/讀者心理　reader's mind, reader psychology
读者心理学/讀者心理學　reader psychology
读者兴趣/讀者興趣　reader's interests
读者须知/讀者須知　information for readers, notice to readers
读者需求/讀者需求　reader's demand, reader requirement, user need
读者学/讀者學　reader studies
读者意见/讀者意見　reader's suggestions
读者意见表/讀者意見表　reader's opinionaire
读者意见调查/讀者意見調查　opinion survey of reader, audience survey
读者阅览卡/讀者閱覽卡　reader's card
读者阅览证/讀者閱覽證　reader's ticket
读者账号/使用者賬戶　user's account
读者指南/讀者指南　reader guide
读者忠诚度/讀者忠誠度　reader loyalty
读者著者目录/讀者作者目録　reader's author catalog
读者咨询记录/讀者諮詢記録　reader's advisory record
渎职罪/瀆職罪　crime of malfeasance
犊皮纸/犢皮紙　vellum
笃疾/篤疾　fatal illness
堵墨/積墨　backing away
堵头布/頂帶　headband
赌博市场/賭博市場　wagering market
赌徒谬误/賭徒謬誤　gambler's fallacy
赌徒破产/賭者破産　gambler's ruin
杜邦分析体系/杜邦分析體系　DuPont system
杜比数字/數位杜比　Dolby digital
杜宾-沃森检验/杜賓-瓦森檢定　Durbin-Watson test
杜宾-沃森统计量/杜賓-瓦森統計量　Durbin-Watson statistics
杜列特尔方法/Doolittle 技巧　Doolittle technique
杜威十进分类法/杜威十進分類法　Dewey Decimal Classification, DDC
杜预/杜預　Du Yu
度牒/度牒　dudie, monks' certificate
360 度绩效评价/360 度績效評估　360-degree performance appraisal
度量传递性/度量遞移性　metric transitivity
镀基铜/鍍基銅　basic coppering

镀制版铜/鍍製版銅　skin coppering
短边规则/短邊規則　short-side rule
短工/短工,零工　journeyman, short-time workers
短量索赔/由於重量不足而索賠　claim for short weight
短路带磁通/短路帶磁通　short-circuit flux
短评/短評　editorial note
短期/短期　short-run
短期保存文件/短期保存檔　ephemera
短期保险/短期保險　short-term insurance
短期边际成本/短期邊際成本　short-run marginal cost
短期变动/短期變動　short time change
短期波动/短期波動　short term fluctuation, short time fluctuation
短期成本/短期成本　short-run cost
短期成本函数/短期成本函數　short run cost function
短期贷款/短期貸款　short-term loan
短期订阅/短期訂閱　short-term subscription
短期放款/短期放款　money at call
短期费用/短期費用　short period cost
短期负债/短期負債　short-term liability
短期公债/短期公債　short-term bond
短期供给曲线/短期供給曲綫　short-run supply curve
短期合同/短期合約　short-term contract
短期汇兑/短期匯兑　short exchange
短期汇票/短期匯票　short bill, short-term bill
短期货币市场/短期貨幣市場　short-term currency market, short-term money market
短期计划/短期計劃　short-term plan
短期价格/短期價格　short period price
短期价值/短期價值　short period value
短期交易/短期交易　short-dated business
短期借款/短期借款　short loan, short-term borrowing
短期均匀性/短期均匀性　short-term uniformity
短期可交割证券/短期可交割證券　securities realizable at short notice
短期利率/短期利率　short-term interest rate
短期利润/短期利潤　short-run profit
短期平均成本/短期平均成本　short-run average cost
短期倾销/短期傾銷　short period dumping
短期趋势/短期趨勢　short time trend
短期生产/短期生産　short-run production
短期生产计划/短期生産計劃　short-term production

planning
短期收益率/短期收益率　short-term yield
短期私人资本流动/短期私人資本流動　private short-term capital movement
短期调整模型/短期調整模型　short-run adjustment model
短期投资/短期投資　current investment, temporary investment, short-term investment
短期外借藏书/短期外借藏書　short loan collection, SLC
短期外资/短期外資　short-term foreign capital
短期息票/短期息票　short coupon
短期信贷/短期信貸　short-term credit
短期信贷市场/短期信貸市場　short-term credit market
短期有价证券/短期有價證券　short-term security
短期债权/短期債權　short-term claim
短期债券/短期債券　short bond, near-term bond
短期债务/短期債務　short-term debt, current debt, quick liability
短期证券/短期證券　short-dated security
短期支票/短期支票　short check
短期资本/短期資本　short-term capital
短期资本交易/短期資本交易　short-term capital transaction
短期资本利得/短期資本利得　short-term capital gain
短期资本流动/短期資本流動,短期資金流動　flow of short-term capital, short-term capital movement
短期资本市场/短期資本市場　short-term capital market
短期资本损益/短期資本損益　short-term capital gain and loss
短期资产/短期資產　short lived asset, short-term asset
短期资金融通/短期資金融通　short-term financing
短期租赁/短期租賃　short lease
短缺/短缺　shortage
短缺索赔/短缺索賠　claim for shortage
短线交易者/短線搶帽客　scalper, short-term trader
短线买卖/即買即賣　in-and-out
短信服务/短訊息服務　short message service
短语标题/短語標題　phrase subject heading
短语检索/短語檢索　phrase retrieval, phrase search
段落检索/段落檢索　passage search, passage retrieval
段落式著录格式/段落式著錄格式　paragraphy format
段落注/段落注　notes after a paragraph
断尾回归模型/受限回歸模型,截斷回歸模型　censored regression mode, truncated regression model
断续分布/斷續分布,干擾分布　interrupted distribution
堆码/層積　stacking
堆墨/堆墨　ink piling
队列条令/隊列條令　Mandatory Regulation on Formation
对版不准/未套準　out of register
对比/對比　contrast
对比蒙太奇/對比蒙太奇　comparative montage
对比误差/比較誤差　comparison error
对策/賽局,對局　game
对策鞍点/對策鞍點　saddle point of game
对策现象/對策現象　game phenomenon
对策值/對策值　game value
对称不等区组排列/對稱不等區集排列　symmetrical unequal block arrangement
对称抽样/對稱抽樣　symmetric sampling
对称分布/對稱分布　symmetric distribution
对称估计法/對稱估計法　symmetric estimation method
对称函数/對稱函數　symmetric function
对称行列式/對稱行列式　symmetric determinant
对称化/對稱化　symmetrization
对称矩阵/對稱矩陣　symmetric matrix
对称均衡/對稱均衡　symmetric equilibrium
对称密度/對稱密度　symmetric density
对称设计/對稱設計　symmetric design
对称稳定律/對稱穩定律　symmetric stable law
对称误差/對稱誤差　symmetric error
对称析因设计/對稱因子設計　symmetric factorial design
对称信息/對稱資訊　symmetrical information
对称[性]/對稱[性]　symmetry
对称性检验/對稱性檢定　test for symmetry, symmetric test
对称压缩/對稱壓縮　symmetrical compression
对称圆形分布/對稱圓形分布,對稱圓形分配　symmetric circular distribution
对称正定矩阵/正定對稱矩陣　positive definite symmetric matrix
对称中心/對稱中心　center of symmetry
对称子式/對稱子式　symmetric minor
对冲/避險　hedge, hedging
对冲基金/對沖基金,避險基金　hedge fund

对冲交易/套頭交易業務,平衡交易業務　hedging operation
对冲交易合同/套頭交易合約,平衡交易合約　hedging contract
对冲率/避險比率　hedging ratio
对等基金/對等基金　counterpart fund
对等原则/對等原則　parity principle
对服务对象的伦理责任/對服務對象的倫理責任　ethical responsibility for client
对服务机构的伦理责任/對服務機構的倫理責任　ethical responsibility for service agency
对付款地点有限制的承兑/限制付款地之附條件承兑　acceptance qualified as to place
对付款时间有限制的承兑/限制付款時間之附條件承兑　acceptance qualified as to time
对附属公司投资/對附屬公司投資　investment in affiliated company
对公众的伦理责任/對公眾的倫理責任　ethical responsibility for the public
对话/對話,對白　dialogue
对话场/對話場　interacting Ba
对话管理/對話管理　dialogue management
对话式阅读/對話閱讀　dialogic reading
对环境问题的应对和行动/對環境問題的應對和行動　response to environmental problem
对己汇票/對己匯票　draft to order
对角分布/對角分布,對角分配　diagonal distribution
对角化/對角轉換　diagonalized
对角回归/對角回歸　diagonal regression
对角线化/對角轉換　diagonalized
对校法/對校法　collate with different editions of the same book
对开信用证/對開信用狀,背對背信用狀　counter letter of credit, reciprocal letter of credit, back-to-back letter of credit
对开信用证贸易/對開信用狀貿易,互惠易貨貿易　reciprocal barter
对抗关税/相對關稅　counter tariff
对抗平衡/對抗平衡　counterbalancing
对抗式程序/當事人對等的訴訟程式　adversarial process
对口标引/對口標引　alternative indexing
对立事件/餘事件　complementary event
对偶/對偶　dual
对偶变换/對立變換　antithetic transforms
对偶变量/對立變量　antithetic variates
对偶规划/對偶規劃　dual programming
对偶过程/對偶過程　dual process

对偶可行解/對偶可行解　dual feasible solution
对偶问题/對偶問題　dual problem
对偶原理/對偶原理,對偶原則　principle of duality, duality principle
对偶制家庭/對偶制家庭　pairing family
对偶最优解/對偶最佳解　dual optimal solution
对平均数的平均[离]差/對平均數的平均離差　mean deviation about the mean, average deviation about the mean
对人权/對人權　right in personam
对人知觉/個人知覺　person perception
对任意原点的矩/對任意原點的動差　moment about arbitrary origin
对世权/對世權　right in rem
对世义务/對世義務　obligations erga omnes
对数/對數　logit
对数凹分布/對數凹分布,對數凹分配　log concave distribution
对数变换/對數變換　logarithmic transformation
对数查准率/對數查準率　log precision
对数尺度/對數尺度　logarithmic scale
对数分布/對數分布,對數分配　logarithmic distribution
对数伽马分布/對數伽瑪分布,對數伽瑪分配　log-gamma distribution
对数概率纸/對數機率紙　logarithmic probability paper
对数级数分布/對數數列分布,對數數列分配　logarithmic series distribution
对数检索法/對數搜尋法　logarithmic search
对数卡方分布/對數卡方分布,對數卡方分配　log-chi squared distribution
对数罗吉斯特分布/對數成長分布,對數成長分配　log-logistic distribution
对数模型/對數模型　logit model
对数似然比统计量/對數概似比統計量　log-likelihood ratio statistic
对数似然函数/對數概似函數,對數可能性函數　log-likelihood function, log-likelihood
对数透视原理/學科對數原理　logarithmic perspective principle
对数凸分布/對數凸分布,對數凸分配　log convex distribution
对数凸容忍限/對數凸容許界限　log convex tolerance limit
对数图/對數圖　logarithmic chart
对数线性模型/對數線性模型　log-linear model
对数线性形式/線性對數形式　log-linear form

对数优[势]比/對數優劣比　lods
对数正态/對數常態　log-normal
对数正态分布/對數常態分配,對數常態分布　log-normal distribution
对数正态概率分布/對數機率分配　log-normal probability distribution
对数秩检验/對數等級檢定　log-rank tests
对条约的保留/對條約的保留　reservation to treaties
对外偿付能力/對外償付能力　external solvency
对外承包工程/對外承包工程　external contracted projects
对外出口/對外出口　export abroad
对外储备/對外儲備　external reserve
对外贷款/對外貸款　overseas lending
对外短期负债/對外短期負債　external short-term liability
对外负债/對外負債　external liability
对外公共债务/對外公共債務　external public debt
对外汇款单/對外匯款單　foreign money order
对外开放/對外開放　open to the outside
对外空物体的管辖权/對外空物體的管轄權　jurisdiction over space objects
对外劳务合作/對外勞務合作　foreign labor service cooperation
对外贸易/對外貿易　foreign trade, external trade
对外贸易不平衡/對外貿易不均衡　unbalance in foreign trade
对外贸易乘数原理/對外貿易乘數原則　principle of foreign trade multiplier
对外贸易代理/對外貿易代理　foreign trade agency
对外贸易额/對外貿易額　value of foreign trade
对外贸易方向/對外貿易方向　direction of foreign trade
对外贸易管制/對外貿易管制　foreign trade control
对外贸易价格指数/對外貿易價格指數　index number of price of foreign trade
对外贸易结构/對外貿易商品結構　foreign trade structure
对外贸易经营者/對外貿易經營者　foreign trade operator
对外贸易扩张/擴大對外貿易　expansion of foreign trade
对外贸易逆差/對外貿易逆差　foreign trade deficit
对外贸易区/對外貿易區　foreign trade zone
对外贸易顺差/對外貿易順差　favorable balance in foreign trade, foreign trade surplus
对外贸易依存度/對外貿易依存度　degree of dependence on foreign trade
对外贸易指数/對外貿易指數　foreign trade index number
对外贸易仲裁/對外貿易仲裁　foreign trade arbitration
对外贸易资金融通/對外貿易資金融通　foreign trade financing
对外清偿能力/對外清償能力　external liquidity
对外投资/對外投資　investment abroad
对外投资区位选择说/對外投資區位理論　the location theory of foreign direct investment
对外账户/對外賬戶　outward account
对外证券投资/對外證券投資　outward portfolio investment
对外支付/對外支付　external payment, foreign payment
对外资金援助/對外資金援助　external financial assistance
对席裁判/對席裁判　try and judge with adversary parties
对象/對象,目標　object
对象错误/物件錯誤　mistake of target
对象化/客體化　objectification
对象图/對象圖,目標圖　object diagram
对象专业化原则/物件專門化原則　product focused
对销贸易/相對貿易　counter trade
对应分析/對應分析　correspondence analysis
对账/對賬　reconciling
对照/對比　contrast
对照分析/對比分析　contrast analysis
对照索引/對照索引,對照表　concordance
对折页/對折頁　folio
对中位数的平均[离]差/對中位數的平均離差　mean deviation about the median
对重平衡/對抗平衡　counterbalancing
对自然资源的永久主权/對自然資源的永久主權　permanent sovereignty over natural resources
兑换价格/兌換價格　conversion price
兑换平价/平價兌換　conversion at parity, conversion at par, conversion at par
兑换期票/兌換期票　bill for term
兑换现金/兌換現金　exchange for cash
兑换佣金/匯兌佣金　exchange commission
兑换制度/兌換制度　convertibility system
兑现信贷/兌現信貸　encashment credit
吨公里/延噸公里　ton-kms
敦煌藏经洞/敦煌藏經洞　Dunhuang library cave
敦煌汉简/敦煌漢簡　Han Dynasty wooden clips from Dunhuang

敦煌遗书/敦煌文書　Dunhuang documents, Dunhuang manuscripts
多胞形/多胞形　polytope
多边发展银行/多邊發展銀行　multilateral development bank
多边关税协定/多邊關稅協定　multilateral tariff treaty
多边技术援助/多邊技術援助　multilateral technical assistance
多边结算/多邊結算　multilateral settlement
多边结算协定/多邊清算協定　multilateral clearing agreement
多边恋/多邊戀　multilateral love
多边贸易/多邊貿易　multilateral trade
多边贸易保护/多邊貿易保護　multinational safeguard
多边贸易承诺制度/多邊貿易承諾制度　system of multilateral trade commitment
多边贸易谈判/多邊貿易談判　multilateral trade negotiation, MTN
多边贸易协定/多邊貿易協定　multilateral trade agreement
多边清算/多邊清算　multilateral clearing
多边外汇支付协定/多邊外匯支付協定　multilateral exchange payments agreement
多边无差别贸易/多邊無差別貿易　multilateral and non-discriminatory world trade
多边协定/多邊協定　multilateral agreement
多边协调标准/多邊調和標準　multilaterally harmonized standard
多边形建模/多邊形建模　polygon
多边援助/多邊援助　multilateral aid
多边援助机构/多邊援助機構　multilateral assistance agency
多边支付/多邊支付　multilateral payment
多变量分布/多變量分布,多變量分配　multivariate distribution
多变量分析/多變量分析　multivariate analysis
多变量过程/多變量過程　multivariate processes
多变量回归/多變量回歸,多元回歸　multiple regression
多变量矩/多變量動差　multivariate moment
多变量马尔可夫过程/多重馬可夫過程　multiple Markov process
多变量切比雪夫不等式/多變量Chebyshev不等式　multivariate Chebyshev inequality
多变量统计/多變量統計　multivariate statistics
多变量线性回归/多變量線性回歸,多元線性回歸　multiple linear regression, multivariate linear regression
多变量协方差不等式/多變量互變異數不等式　multivariate covariance inequality
多变量协方差分析/多變量互變異數分析　multivariate analysis of covariance
多变量因子分析/多因子分析　multiple factor analysis
多变量预测/多變數預測　multi-variable forecasting
多变量质量控制/多變量品質管制　multivariate quality control
多变量中心极限定理/多變量中央極限定理　multivariate central limit theorem
多变生涯/多變職涯　protean career
多步对策/多步對策　multi-step game
多步预测/多期預測　multi-step forecast
多部分单行资源/多部單色資源　multi-part monographic resource
多部分资源/多部資源　multi-part resource
多层次理论/多層次理論　multi-level theory
多层次团队决策理论/多層次團隊決策理論　multilevel theory of team decision making
多层次著录/多層次著錄　multi-level description
多层分类编排/多層分類編排　classified arrangement with several levels
多层用处表/多階用途表　multi-level where-used
多尺度预测方法/多尺度預測方法　multi-scale forecasting method
多重比较/多重比較　multiple comparisons
多重比较的S法/多重比較的S法　S-method of multiple comparisons
多重比较的T方法/多重比較的T方法　T-method of multiple comparisons
多重比较检验/多重比較檢定　multiple comparison test
多重捕捉调查/多次捕釋調查　multiple recapture census
多重插补/多重插補法　multiple imputation
多重持牌/多重掛牌,多處交易所掛牌　multiple listing
多重[的]/多重的　multiple
多重二项检验/多元二項檢定　multi-binomial test
多重费希尔K统计量/多重費雪K統計量　polykays
多重分布/多元分布　manifold distribution
多重分层/多重分層　multiple stratification
多重分类/多重分類　multiple classification
多重共线/多元共線性　multi-collinearity

多重共线性/線型重合,多元共線性,複共線性　multi-collinearity
多重故障模型/多重故障模型　multiple failure model
多重回归方程/多元回歸方程式　multiple regression equation
多重汇率/複匯率　multiple exchange rate
多重汇率制/複匯率制　multiple exchange rate system
多重积分/多重積分　multiple integral
多重极差检验/多重全距檢定　multiple range test
多重决策方法/多重決策法　multiple decision method
多重决策问题/多重決策問題　multi-decision problem, multiple decision problem
多重均衡/多元均衡　multiple equilibrium
多重均衡博弈/多元均衡賽局　games with multiple equilibria
多重列类法/多特性分類法　polythetic classification
多重列联表/複列聯　multiple contingency
多重判定系数/多元判定係數　multiple coefficient of determination
多重曲线相关/複曲線相關　multiple curvilinear correlation
多重认同/多重認同,多重身份　multiple identities
多重筛选法/多重篩選法　multiple hurdle model
多重上市/多重掛牌,多處交易所掛牌　multiple listing
多重特征/多重特性　multiple characteristics
多重替代法/多重插補法　multiple imputation
多重条形图/多元長條圖　multiple bar chart
多重线性过程/多重線性過程　multilinear process
多重线性回归/多重線性回歸　multilinear regression
多重线性相关/複線性相關　multiple linear correlation
多重相关系数/複相關係數　coefficient of multiple correlation
多重项目/多元計分項目　polytomous item
多重协方差/複互變異數　multiple covariance
多重正态相关/複常態相關　multiple normal correlation
多重指标/多元指標　multiple indicators
多重指数平滑法/多重平滑法　multiple smoothing method
多次重复/多次重複　multiple replication
多次抽样/多次抽樣,多重抽樣　multiple sampling
多次抽样检验方案/多重抽樣檢驗計劃　multiple sampling inspection plan

多代产品扩散/多代產品擴散　product diffusion of generations
多代理仿真/多代理模擬　multi-agent simulation
多代理系统/多元決策者系統　multi-agent sysetm
多党制/多黨制　interactive multi-party system
多点竞争/多點競爭　multipoint competition
多点市场竞争/多點市場競爭　multimarket competition
多方案报价/多方案報價　multi-program quote
多方程模型/複方程模型　multi-equational model
多方法的设计/多重方法設計,混合方法設計　multiple method design
多方账户/多方賬戶　multiple party account
多峰[的]/多峰的　multimodal
多峰分布/多峰分布　multimodal distribution
多峰偏好/多峰型態偏好　mutiple peaked preferences
多峰性/多峰性　multimodality
多个随机起点/多個隨機開始　multiple random starts
多供源采购/多重供應[來]源　multiple sourcing
多国贸易/多國貿易　multicountry trade
多哈回合/杜哈回合　Doha round
多核心模式/多核心模式　multi-nuclei model
多货贸易/多貨貿易　multicommodity trade
多级标引/多級標引　multi-level indexing
多级记分项目/多元計分項目　polytomous item
多级检索/多級檢索　multi-level retrieval
多级决策/多級決策　multi-level decision making
多级库存系统/多層庫存系統　multi-echelon inventory system
多级模糊综合评价/多級模糊綜合評價　multi-stage fuzzy comprehensive appraisal
多级主题索引/多級主題索引　multi-level subject index
多角套汇/重複套匯　compound arbitrage
多阶段博弈/多[階]段賽局　multi-stage game
多阶[段]抽样/多段抽樣　multi-stage sampling
多阶[段]分析/多段分析　multi-stage analysis
多阶[段]估计/多段估計　multi-stage estimation
多阶段决策/多階段決策　multi-stage decision making
多阶[段]决策过程/多[階]段決策過程　multi-stage decision process
多阶[段]决策问题/多段決策問題　multiple-stage decision problem
多阶段销售税/多階段銷售稅　multiple-stage sales tax

多卷册标识/多卷冊標識　multi-volume code
多卷集出版物/多卷集出版物　multi-volume publication
多卷书/多卷書　multi-volume book
多款目著录/多入口著錄　multiple entry description
多栏关税［制］/多欄式關稅　multiple column tariff
多类［列联］表/多類［列聯］表　polytomic table
多媒体/多媒體　multimedia
多媒体编辑工具/多媒體編輯工具　multimedia creative software tool
多媒体出版物/多媒體出版物　multimedia publication
多媒体电子出版物/多媒體電子出版物　multimedia electronic publication
多媒体稿库/多媒體稿庫　multimedia draft library
多媒体家用平台/家用多媒體平臺　multimedia home platform
多媒体检测/多媒體檢測　multimedia detection
多媒体检索/多媒體檢索　multimedia retrieval
多媒体脚本/多媒體腳本　multimedia script
多媒体内容校对/多媒體內容校對　multimedia content check
多媒体培训/多媒體培訓　multimedia training
多媒体配套文献/多媒體組件　multimedia kit
多媒体设计/多媒體設計　multimedia design
多媒体数据库/多媒體資料庫　multimedia database
多媒体素材/多媒體素材　multimedia source material
多媒体随选视讯/多媒體隨選　multimedia on demand, MOD
多媒体通信/多媒體通訊　multimedia communication
多媒体消息服务/多媒體訊息服務　multimedia messaging service, MMS
多媒体延伸/多媒體延伸　multimedia extension, matrix math extension, MMX
多媒体整合/多媒體整合　multimedia integration
多媒体著作工具/多媒體著作工具　multimedia authoring tool
多媒体资料/多媒體資料　multimedia material
多媒体作品/互动多媒體作品　interactive multimedia works
多面书架/多面書架　multi-faced bookstack
多面向模式/多相模式　facets model
多面性/關係的多面性　multiplexity
多目标规划/多目標規劃　multi-objective programming
多目标决策/多目標決策　multi-objective decision, multiple objective decision making
多目标控制系统/多目標控制系統　multi-objective control system
多目标排序/多目標排序　multicriteria scheduling
多目标效用函数/多目標效用函數　multi-objective utility function
多偶制/多偶婚制，一夫多妻制　polygamy, polygyny
多频谱/多頻譜　polyspectra
多品牌策略/多品牌策略　multibrand strategy
多期分析/多期分析　multiperiod analysis
多渠道发行/多管道發行　multi-channel distribution, multi-channel release
多渠道分销系统/多管道分銷系統　multi-channel distribution system
多渠道商店/實體與網路兼營商店　bricks and clicks, clicks-and-mortar
多人对策/多人對局　multi-person game
多式联运/多式聯運　multimodal transport
多属性决策/多屬性決策　multiple attribute decision making, multi-attribute decision making
多数代表制/多數代表制　majority representation
多数决策规则/多數決策規則　majority rule for policy making
多数权益/多數權益　majority interest
多数人之债/多數人之債　obligation with several creditors or several debtors
多数同意/多數決　majority voting
多水平分析/多水平分析　multilevel analysis
多水平连续抽样方案/多水準連續抽樣計劃　multi-level continuous sampling plans
多态/多型　polymorphism
多特征多方法矩阵/多特質-多方法矩陣　multi-trait multi-method matrix
多特征决策/多屬性決策　multiple attribute decision making, multiattribute decision making
多头/作多　long position
多头合同/多頭合約　long contract
多头交易/多頭交易　bull transaction
多头-空头/多頭-空頭　bull bear
多维贝塔分布/多變量貝他分布，多變量貝他分配，多變量β分布　multivariate beta distribution
多维标引/多維標引　multi-dimensional indexing
多维伯尔分布/多變量 Burr 分布，多變量 Burr 分配　multivariate Burr's distribution
多维泊松分布/多變量卜瓦松分布，多變量卜瓦松分配　multivariate Poisson distribution
多维超几何分布/多變量超幾何分布，多變量超幾何分配　multivariate hypergeometric distribution
多维尺度/多維尺度　multi-dimensional scaling

多维单调失效率分布/多變量單調故障率分布　multivariate monotone failure rate distribution

多维递减失效率分布/多變量遞減故障率分布　multivariate decreasing failure rate distribution, MDFR distribution

多维递增失效率分布/多變量遞增故障率分布　multivariate increasing failure rate distribution, MIFR distribution

多维动态模型/多維動態模型　multi-temporal model

多维度方法/多維度方法,多構面方法　multi-dimensional approach

多维多项分布/多變量多項分布　multivariate multinomial distribution

多维二项分布/多變量二項分布,多變量二項分配　multivariate binomial distribution

多维分布/多變量分布,多變量分配　multivariate distribution

多维F分布/多變量F分布,多變量F分配　multivariate F-distribution

多维分析/多維分析　multi-dimensional analysis

多维负超几何分布/多變量負超幾何分布,多變量負超幾何分配　multivariate negative hypergeometric distribution

多维负二项分布/多變量負二項分布,多變量負二項分配　multivariate negative binomial distribution

多维列联表/多維列聯表　multi-dimensional contingency table

多维逆超几何分布/多變量反超幾何分布,多變量反超幾何分配　multivariate inverse hypergeometric distribution

多维帕累托分布/多變量Pareto分布,多變量Pareto分配　multivariate Pareto distribution

多维帕斯卡分布/多變量Pascal分布,多變量Pascal分配　multivariate Pascal distribution

多维数据模型/多維資料模型　multi-dimensional data model

多维随机变量/多元隨機變數　multivariate random variable

多维性/多向度　multi-dimensionality

多维正态分布/多維常態分布,多維常態分配,多變量常態分布　multi-dimensional normal distribution, multivariate normal distribution

多维指数/多維指數　multi-dimensional index

多维指数分布/多變量指數分布,多變量指數分配　multivariate exponential distribution

多维组织/多構面組織,多維度組織　multi-dimensional organization

多文组合标题法/多文組合標題法　menthod of combinating several archives headlined titles

多物品批量模型/多物品批量模型　multiple-item lotsizing model

多析因设计/複因子設計　multi-factorial design

多纤维协定/多邊纖維協定　multifibre arrangement

多向参照/多向參照　scatter reference

多向服务/多向服務　multi-directional services

多向沟通模式/多樣溝通模態　multiple communication pattern

多项分布/多項分布,多項分配　multinomial distribution

多项分类/多元分類　manifold classification

多项概率单位模型/多項式常態機率模型　multinomial probit model

多项概率函数/多項機率函數　multinomial probability function

多项罗吉特/多項勝算對數模型　multinomial logit

多项式分布滞后/多項分配落遲　polynomial distributed lag

多项式概率/多項機率單元模型　multinomial probit, MNP

多项式回归/多項式回歸　polynomial regression

多项式趋势/多項式趨勢　polynomial trend

多项式时间算法/多項式時間演算法　polynomial-time algorithm

多项式危险函数模型/多項式危險函數模型　polynomial hazard function model

多项式滞后/多項落遲　polynomial lags

多项试验/多項試驗　multinomial trial

多项选择模型/多項式選擇模型　multinomial choice model

多项准则/多重準則　multiple criteria

多项总体/多項母體　multinomial population

多相抽样/多相抽樣　multi-phase sampling

多相过程/多相過程　multiple phase process

多选问题/多選問題　multiple choice question

多样化经营/多樣化經營　diversified business

多样化投资/多角化投資　diversified investment

多样性管理/多元管理　diversity management

多样性培训/員工多元化訓練　diversity training

多样性指数/多樣化指數　index of multiplicity

多因素模型/多因素模型　multi-factor model

多因子模型/多要素模型　multi-factor model

多用途数字光盘/數位多功光碟　digital versatile disc

多余参数/多餘參數,擾嚷參數,擾亂參數　nuisance parameter

多语言信息检索/多語資訊檢索　multilingual

information retrieval
多语种参考咨询系统/多語參考諮詢系統 multilingual reference system
多语种对照词典/多語種對照詞典 multilingual dictionary, polyglot dictionary
多语种题名/多語種題名 multilingual title
多语种信息检索/多語種資訊檢索 multiple language information search
多语种叙词表/多語詞表 multilingual thesaurus
多元贝塔分布/多變量貝他分布,多變量貝他分配,多變量 β 分布 multivariate beta distribution
多元变量/多元變量 multivariable variants
多元波利亚分布/多變量 Pólya 分布,多變量 Pólya 分配 multivariate Pólya distribution
多元伯尔分布/多變量 Burr 分布,多變量 Burr 分配 multivariate Burr's distribution
多元泊松分布/多變量卜瓦松分布,多變量卜瓦松分配 multivariate Poisson distribution
多元泊松过程/多元卜瓦松過程 multiple Poisson process
多元测量/多元量測 multiple measurements
多元超几何分布/多變量超幾何分布,多變量超幾何分配 multivariate hypergeometric distribution
多元抽样分布/多元變量抽樣分配 multivariate sampling distribution
多元单调失效率分布/多變量單調故障率分布 multivariate monotone failure rate distribution
多元递减失效率分布/多變量遞減故障率分布 multivariate decreasing failure rate distribution, MDFR distribution
多元递增失效率分布/多變量遞增故障率分布 multivariate increasing failure rate distribution, MIFR distribution
多元动态模型/多維動態模型 multi-temporal model
多元多项分布/多變量多項分布 multivariate multinomial distribution
多元二项分布/多變量二項分布,多變量二項分配 multivariate binomial distribution
多元法/多重研究法 multi-method
多元方差分析/多變量變異數分析 multivariate analysis of variance, MANOVA
多元分布/多變量分布,多變量分配 multivariate distribution
多元 F 分布/多變量 F 分布,多變量 F 分配 multivariate F-distribution
多元 t 分布/多元 t 分配 multivariate t-distribution
多元分层/多元分層 multi-dimension stratification
多元分析/多變量分析 multivariate analysis

多元符号秩检验/多變量符號秩檢定 multivariate signed rank test
多元负超几何分布/多變量負超幾何分布,多變量負超幾何分配 multivariate negative hypergeometric distribution
多元负二项分布/多變量負二項分布,多變量負二項分配 multivariate negative binomial distribution
多元概率模型/多元常態機率模型 multivariate probit model
多元过程/多變量過程 multivariate processes
多元化/多元化,多角化 pluralism, diversification
多元化战略/多角化策略 diversification strategy
多元回归/多元回歸,多變量回歸 multiple regression
多元回归分析/多元回歸分析 multiple regression analysis
多元回归模型/多元回歸模型 multiple regression model
多元回归系数/複回歸係數 coefficient of multiple regression
多元检索/多方面檢索 multi-aspect retrieval, polynomial search
多元矩/多變量動差 multivariate moment
多元控制图/複式管制圖 multiple control chart
多元马尔可夫过程/多重馬可夫過程 multiple Markov process
多元逆超几何分布/多變量反超幾何分布,多變量反超幾何分配 multivariate inverse hypergeometric distribution
多元帕累托分布/多變量 Pareto 分布,多變量 Pareto 分配 multivariate Pareto distribution
多元帕斯卡分布/多變量 Pascal 分布,多變量 Pascal 分配 multivariate Pascal distribution
多元嵌套 Logit 模型/多變數巢式羅吉特機率模型 multivariate nested logit model
多元切比雪夫不等式/多變量 Chebyshev 不等式 multivariate Chebyshev inequality
多元时间序列/多元時間序列 multivariate time series
多元市场/多元市場 multiple market
多元统计/多變量統計 multivariate statistics
多元文化论/多元文化論 multiculturalism
多元线性/線性多元變數 linear multivariate
多元线性回归/多元線性回歸,多變量線性回歸 multiple linear regression, multivariate linear regression
多元线性回归模型/多元線性回歸模型 multiple linear regression model

多元线性判别分析/線性多元鑒別分析　linear multiple discriminant analysis
多元相关/多項相關　polychoric correlation
多元协方差不等式/多變量互變異數不等式　multivariate covariance inequality
多元协方差分析/多變量互變異數分析　multivariate analysis of covariance
多元性/相異性,異樣性,多樣性　diversity
多元选择模型/多元選擇模型　multiple choice model
多元一体/多元一體　pluralistic integration
多元因子分析/多因子分析　multiple factor analysis
多元正态分布/多元常態分配,多變量常態分布　multivariate normal distribution
多元正态回归/多維常態回歸　multi-dimensional normal regression
多元指数分布/多變量指數分布,多變量指數分配　multivariate exponential distribution
多元质量控制/多變量品質管制　multivariate quality control
多元中心极限定理/多變量中央極限定理　multivariate central limit theorem
多元主义/多元主義,多元論　pluralism
多元资本主义/多元資本主義　varieties of capitalism
多元自回归/多變量自[身]回歸　multivariate autoregression
多元自回归移动平均/多元自我回歸移動平均　multivariate arma
多章节文献/多章節文獻　multipart item
多值决策/複值決策　multi-valued decision
多中心城市/多中心城市　polycentric cities
多种保险业务/多種保險業務　multiple line insurance
多种货币本位制度/多種貨幣本位制度　multiple currency standard
多种货币贷款/多種貨幣貸款　multi-currency loan
多种货币干预/多種貨幣干預　multi-currency intervention
多种货币经营/多種貨幣經營　multi-currency operation
多著者著作/多作者著作　multi-author work
多专业服务/多專業服務　multi-disciplinary service
多准则决策/多準則決策　multi-criteria decision making
夺文/奪文　duowen, lost word
堕落天使/堕落的天使　fallen angel
堕胎权/堕胎權　right of abortion

E

阿党/阿黨　be subservient to the ruler and gang up for private interests
讹文/訛文　wrong word
额定保证金/額定保證金　margin requirement
额定输出电平/額定輸出電平　rated output level
额外变量/額外的變數　extraneous variable
额外补贴/特殊津貼　perquisite
额外回报/超額報酬　excess returns
额外利润/額外利潤　premium return
额外期间交叉设计/額外期間交叉設計　extra period change over design
厄威克管理原则/厄威克管理原則　management principles of Urwick
恶臭防治法/惡臭防治法　law on prevention and control of malodor pollution
恶臭控制/惡臭控制　malodor control
恶逆/惡逆　beating or murdering one's senior elders
恶性通货膨胀/惡性通貨膨脹,急劇性通貨膨脹　hyperinflation, galloping inflation, wheelbarrow inflation
恶意串通/惡意串通　malicious collusion
恶意收购/惡意收購,敵意并購　hostile takeover
恶意占有/惡意占有　dishonest possession
恩赐制/恩賜制　bestowal system
恩格尔法则/恩格爾法則　Engel's law
恩格尔-格兰杰两步法/恩格爾-葛蘭哲兩步驟法則　Engel-Granger two steps procedure
恩格尔曲线/恩格爾曲線　Engel curve
恩格尔系数/恩格爾係數　Engel coefficient
恩格塞特分布/Engset 分布,Engset 分配　Engset distribution
儿童/兒童　children
儿童保护法/兒童保護法　child protection act
儿童创伤/兒童創傷　children trauma
儿童电视节目/兒童電視節目　children's television program
儿童读物/兒童書　readings for children
儿童福利/兒童福利　child welfare
儿童福利院/兒童福利院　child welfare institute
儿童福利政策/兒童福利政策　child welfare policy
儿童个案工作/兒童個案工作　casework for children
儿童社会工作/兒童社會工作　social work for children
儿童社区工作/兒童社區工作　community work for children
[儿童]收养/[兒童]收養　adoption
儿童收养中心/兒童收養中心　center for adoption and guardianship
儿童受众/兒童閱聽眾　child audience
儿童团体工作/兒童團體工作　group work for children
二版/二版　metal positive
二变量截面/二變量截略　bivariate truncation
二重指数回归/雙指數回歸　double exponential regression
二次抽样/雙重選樣　double sampling
二次抽样检验/二重抽樣檢驗　double sampling inspection
二次创新/二次創新　secondary innovation
二次档案文献/二次檔案文獻　secondary archival documentations
二次对照/二次對比　quadratic contrast
二次分量/二次成分　quadratic component
二次分析/二手資料分析,次級資料分析　secondary analysis
二次估计[量]/二次估計[量],二次式估計量　quadratic estimator
二次故障/二次故障　secondary failure
二次规划/二次[型]規劃　quadratic programming
二次检索/二次存取　secondary access
二次均方收敛/二次均方收斂　convergence in quadratic mean
二次均值/二次平均值　quadratic mean
二次内插/二次内插　quadratic interpolation
二次平均收敛/二次平均收斂　quadratic mean convergence
二次趋向/二次趨勢　quadratic trend
二次售卖/再次發行　secondary distribution
二次损失函数/二次損失函數　quadratic loss function
二次统计量/二次統計量　quadratic statistic
二次文献/二次文獻　secondary document

二次污染物/二次汙染物　secondary pollutant
二次响应/二次反應　quadratic response
二次项/二次項　quadratic term
二次型/二次形［式］　quadratic forms
二次正态分布/二次常態分布，二次常態分配　quadri-normal distribution
二等票据/二等票據　second class paper
二分变量/二分變數　dichotomous variable
二分法/二分法，對分法　bisection method, dichotomy
二分搜索法/二分搜尋　dichotomous search
二分项目/二元試題　dichotomous item
二级标准/次級標準　secondary standard
二级单元/次級單位　secondary unit
二级抵押市场/二級抵押市場　secondary mortgage market
二级反致/二級反致　renovi au second degre
二级价格歧视/二級差別訂價　second-degree price discrimination
二级批发/二級批發　secondary wholesale
二级识别/二級識別　secondary characterization
二级市场/二級市場，次級市場　secondary market, second market
二级下标/二次下標　secondary subscript
二级现金储备/二級現金儲備　secondary cash reserve
二级样本/次級樣本　secondary sample
二级银行/二級銀行　secondary bank
二级债券市场/二級債券市場　secondary bond market
二级准备金/二級準備金　secondary reserve
二级资本/二級資本　second tier capital
二阶抽样/二段抽樣　two-stage sampling
二阶抽样单元/次級抽樣單位，二段抽樣單位　secondary sampling unit, two-stage sampling unit
二阶单调随机占优/二階單調隨機占優　second degree stochastic monotonic dominance
二阶单整/二階單整　integrated of order two
二阶段最小二乘估计量/二階最小平方法估計量　two-stage least squares estimator
二阶极小化极大［性］/二階大中取小［性］　second order minimaxity
二阶模型/二階模型　second order model
二阶频谱/二階頻譜　second-order spectrum
二阶平稳过程/二階平穩過程　second order stationary process
二阶随机抽样/二段隨機抽樣　two-stage random sampling

二阶随机占优/二階隨機占優　second order stochastic dominance
二进制记数法/二進位記數　binary notation
二轮多数选举制/二輪多數選舉制　the two-round majority voting system
二人沟通/二人間傳播　dyadic communication
二手品/二手貨　second-hand goods
二手数据/次級資料　secondary data
二手营销数据/二次行銷資料　secondary marketing data
二维贝塔分布/二變量貝他分布，二變量貝他分配，二變量β分布　bivariate beta distributions
二维泊松分布/二變量卜瓦松分布，二變量卜瓦松分配　bivariate Poisson distribution
二维超几何分布/二變量超幾何分布，二變量超幾何分配　bivariate hypergeometric distribution
二维［的］/二變量的　bivariate
二维动画/二維動畫　two-dimensional animation, 2D animation
二维对数分布/二變量對數分布，二變量對數分配　bivariate logarithmic distribution
二维多项分布/二向量多項分布，二向量多項分配，二變量多項式分布　bivector multinomial distribution, bivariate multinomial distribution
二维二项分布/二變量二項分布，二變量二項分配　bivariate binomial distribution
二维非参数族/二變量無母數族群　bivariate nonparametric family
二维F分布/二變量F分布，二變量F分配　bivariate F-distribution
二维分区组/二維區集劃分　two-dimensional blocking
二维伽马分布/二變量伽瑪分布，二變量伽瑪分配，二變量γ分布　bivariate gamma distribution
二维格［子］方/二變量格子　two-dimensional lattice
二维格［子］设计/二維格子設計　two-dimensional lattice design
二维码/二維［條］碼　two-dimensional bar code
二维威布尔分布/二變量韋伯分布，二變量韋伯分配，二變量Weibull分布　bivariate Weibull distribution
二维线性回归/二變數線性回歸　two variable linear regression
二维虚拟演播室/二維虛擬演播室　two-dimensional virtual studio
二维指数分布/二元指數分配，二變量指數分配，二變量指數分布　bivariate exponential distribution
二线书库/二線書庫　second-tier stack

二向分层/二因子分層　two-way stratification
二向排列/雙向配置,雙因子配置　two-way layout
二项变异/二項變異　binomial variation
二项抽样/二項抽樣　binomial sampling
二项等待时间分布/二項等待時間分布,二項等待時間分配　binomial waiting time distribution
二项定理/二項式定理　binomial theorem
二项分布/二項分布,二項分配　binomial distribution
二项分布的正态近似/二項分布的常態逼近,二項分配的常態逼近　normal approximation to binomial distribution
二项分布检验/二項式檢定　binomial test
二项分类/二項分類　binomial classification
二项概率分布/二項機率分布,二項機率分配　binomial probability distribution
二项概率函数/二項機率函數　binomial probability function
二项概率纸/二項機率紙　binomial probability paper
二项级数/二項級數　binomial series
二项矩/二項動差　binomial moment
二项离散指数/二項離勢指數　binomial index of dispersion
二项曲线/二項式曲線　binomial curve
二项实验/二項實驗　binomial experiment
二项[式]/二項式　binomial
二项[式]模型/二項[式]模型　binomial model
二项随机变量/二項隨機變數　binomial random variable
二项系数/二項式係數　binomial coefficient
二项展开/二項展開　binomial expansion
二项展开式/二項展式　binomial expansion
二项总体/二項母體　binomial population
二型计数模型/第二型計數器模型　type two counter model, counter model type II
二样本检验/二樣本檢定　two-sample test
二样本t检验/雙樣本t檢定　two sample t-test
二样本实验/二樣本實驗　two-sample experiments
二样本位置族/二樣本位置族群　two-sample location family
二样本问题/二樣本問題　two-sample problem
二乙基锌去酸法/二乙基鋅去酸法　diethylzinc deacidification
二义组配/歧義協調　ambiguity coordination
二因子分析/二因子分析　two-factor analysis
二因子交互作用/二因子交互作用　two-factor interaction
二元/二元,二變量　bivariate
二元贝塔分布/二變量貝他分布,二變量貝他分配,二變量β分布　bivariate beta distributions
二元泊松分布/二變量卜瓦松分布,二變量卜瓦松分配　bivariate Poisson distribution
二元对数分布/二變量對數分布,二變量對數分配　bivariate logarithmic distribution
二元多项分布/二向量多項分布,二向量多項分配,二變量多項式分布　bivector multinomial distribution, bivariate multinomial distribution
二元二项分布/二變量二項分布,二變量二項分配　bivariate binomial distribution
二元非参数族/二變量無母數族群　bivariate nonparametric family
二元分布/二變量分布　bivariate distribution
二元F分布/二變量F分布,二變量F分配　bivariate F-distribution
二元t分布/二變量Student分布,二變量Student分配　bivariate 'Student' distribution
二元符号检验/二變量符號檢定　bivariate sign test
二元伽马分布/二變量伽瑪分布,二變量伽瑪分配,二變量γ分布　bivariate gamma distribution
二元概率单位模型/二元常態機率模型　bivariate probit model
二元经济/雙元經濟　dual economy
二元经济结构/雙元經濟體制,雙元經濟結構　dual economic structure, economic dualism
二元均匀分布/二變量均匀分布,二變量均匀分配　bivariate uniform distribution
二元柯西分布/二變量柯西分布,二變量柯西分配　bivariate Cauchy distribution
二元模型/二變量模型　bivariate model
二元帕累托分布/二變量Pareto分布,二變量Pareto分配　bivariate Pareto distribution
二元帕斯卡分布/二變量Pascal分布,二變量Pascal分配　bivariate Pascal distribution
二元式中央银行制度/二元式中央銀行制度　dual central bank system
二元随机变量/二元隨機變數　bivariate random variable
二元统计序列/二變量統計數列　bivariate statistical series
二元威布尔分布/二變量韋伯分布,二變量韋伯分配,二變量Weibull分布　bivariate Weibull distribution
二元信息/二進制資訊　binary information
二元性组织/二元性組織　ambidextrous organization
二元选择模型/二元選擇模型　binary choice model
二元正态分布/二元常態分配,二變量常態分布,二

变量常态分配　bivariate normal distribution
二元正态随机分布/二元常態隨機變數　bivariate normal random variable
二元指数分布/二變量指數分布,二變量指數分配　bivariate exponential distribution, BVE
二元中心极限定理/二變量中央極限定理　bivariate central limit theorem
二元主义/雙重性,二元性　dualism

二值变量/二分變數,雙類別變數　binary variable
二值概率单位模型/二分常態機率模型　binary probit model
二值试验/二元試驗　binary experiment
二值图像/二進制影像　binary image
二值序列/二元序列　binary sequence
二值选择模型/二分選擇模型,間斷式選擇模型　dichotomous choice model

F

发包规划/發包規劃　plan contracting
发表偏倚/出版偏向　publication bias
发表权/公開發表權,出版權　right of publication
发病率/患病率,疾病發生率,疾病侵襲率　morbidity rate, incidence rate, attack rate
发病率统计/疾病統計　morbidity statistics
发布/發布　release
发达国家/先進國家,已開發國家　advanced country, developed country, developed world
发稿/發稿　dispatching, send manuscript to the press
发稿计划/發稿計劃　dispatch plan
发函/發函　out-letter
发货/發貨　delivery
发货单/發貨單　publication dispatch advice document
发货地点/發貨地點　point of departure
发货港/發貨港　port of dispatch
发货清单/配送清冊　dispatch list
发货区/集貨區　shipping area
发货人背书/發貨人背書　shipper endorsement
发明/發明　invention
发明人/發明人　inventor
发明专利/發明專利　patent for invention
发排/發排　send to typeset
发盘和接盘/報價與承諾　offer and acceptance
发盘价/報價　offered price
发盘确认书/報價確認書　confirmation of offer
发起人/發起人,發起者,主辦者　initiator, sponsor
发起设立/發起設立　incorporation by promotion
发生数/發生數　case reported
发文/發文　outward outgoing document
发文处理/發文處理　disposition of sending an official doucment
发文汇集/發文匯集　collection of outward
发文机关标志/發文機關標誌　the symbol of issuing documents' office
发文压印留底簿/發文壓印留底簿　letterpress copybook
发现权/發現權　right of discovery
发现型人才/發現型人才　discovery talent
发现性控制/偵測性控制　detective control
发现者情结/發現者情結　discoverer's complex
发行/發行　distribution
发行部/發行部　distribution department
发行钞票准备金/發行鈔票準備金　reserve against note
发行成本/發行成本　flotation cost
发行代理商/發行代理商　distribution agency
发行单位/發行單位　distribution unit
发行定位/發行定位　distribution positioning
发行对象/發行對象　object of distribution
发行范围/銷售區域　territory of distribution, sales territory
发行方式/發行方式　mode of distribution
发行工作者/發行工作者　distribution staff
发行公司/發行公司　distribution company
发行公债/發行公債　issue of government bond
发行股票/發行股票　issue stock
发行号/發行號　issue, publish
发行集团/發行集團　distribution group
发行量/發行量　circulation
发行量审计/發行量稽核　circulation audit
发行企业/發行企業　distribution corporation
发行渠道/配銷通路　channel of distribution
发行权/配銷權,經銷權,發布權　right of distribution
发行时效/發行時效　publication aging
发行损耗比率/發行損耗比率　distribution loss ratio
发行网/發行網路　distribution network
发行网点/發行網點　distribution outlet
发行系统/發行系統　distribution system
发行效益/發行效應　distribution effect
发行协会/發行協會　distribution association
发行信息/發行資訊　distribution information
发行银行/發行銀行,開狀銀行　bank of emission, issuing bank
发行佣金/發行佣金　distribution commission
发行债券/發行債券　issue bond
发行站/發行點　distribution station
发行折扣/折扣　discount
发行纸币/發行紙幣　issue paper money

发言人/發言人　spokesperson
发样征订/發樣徵訂　sample copy for subscription
发运/調度,配送　dispatch
发运点/起運點　shipping point
发运方式/傳送模式　transportation mode
发运周期/配送週期　shipment cycle
发展/發展　development
发展的质量/發展品質　development quality
发展极/發展極　poles of development
发展计划/發展計劃　development plan
发展经济学/發展經濟學　development economics
发展路径/發展取徑　developmental approach
发展权/發展權　right to development
发展新闻学/發展新聞學　development journalism
发展型社会福利/發展型社會福利　developmental social welfare
发展性社会工作/發展性社會工作　developmental social work
发展援助/發展援助　development assistance
发展政策/發展政策　development policy
发展中国家/發展中國家,開發中國家　developing country
发展中国家边缘化/發展中國家邊緣化　marginalization of developing countries
发展中国家城市/發展中國家城市　city in developing country
发展主义/發展主義,開發主義　developmentalism
罚函数法/罰函數法　penalty function method
罚金/罰金,罰款　fine
罚款/罰款,罰金　fine
法案/法案　draft law
法不阿贵/法不阿貴　law applies equally to those in power
法的本质/法的本質　nature of law
法的创制/法的創制　law-making
法的分类/法的分類　divisions of law
法的功能/法的功能　functions of law
法的价值/法的價值　value of law
法的历史类型/法的歷史類型　historical type of law
法的起源/法的起源　origin of law
法的实施/法律施行　enforcement of law
法的适用/適用法律　application of law
法典/法典　code
法典编纂/法規編纂　codification
法定比率/法定比率　legal ratio
法定呈缴/法定呈繳　legal deposit
法定存款准备金/法定準備金　reserve requirements
法定存款准备金率/法定存款準備率　legal reserve ratio
法定代理/法定代理　legal agency
法定代理人/法定代理人　legal representative
法定抵押/法定抵押　legal mortgage, statutory mortgage
法定服务机构/法定服務機構　statutory service agency
法定福利/強制性福利　mandated benefit
法定股本/核定股本　authorized stock
法定关税税率/法定關稅稅率　statutory tariff
法定管辖/法律管轄權,法律管轄區　legal jurisdiction
法定汇兑平价/法定匯兑平價　official par of exchange
法定汇价制/法定匯價制　official rate system
法定货币/法定貨幣,法令貨幣　legal currency, fiat money
法定计量单位/法定計量單位　legal measuring unit
法定监护/法定監護　legal custody
法定缴存图书馆/呈繳圖書館　legal deposit library
法定利率/法定利率　legal interest rate
法定平价/法定平價　official parity price, mint parity
法定清算/法定清算　legal liquidation
法定情节/法定情節　legal circumstances
法定权力/正當權,合理權　legitimate power
法定权利/法定權利　legal right
法定权威性/法定權威性　statutory authority
法定诉讼代理人/法定訴訟代理人　statutory representative
法定外币储备/法定外匯儲備　official foreign currency reserve
法定信托/法定信託　statutory trust
法定刑/法定刑　statutory sentence
法定义务/法定義務　legal duty
法定盈余/法定盈餘　revenue requirement
法定盈余公积/法定準備　statutory reserves
法定营业公积金/法定盈餘公積準備金　legal earned surplus reserve
法定预算/法定預算　legal budget
法定债权人/法定債權人　legal creditor
法定债券/法定債券　legal bond
法定债务限额/法定債務限額　legal debt limit
法定仲裁/法定仲裁　statutory arbitration
法定转让/法定轉讓　legal assignment
法定准备金/法定公積,法定準備　legal reserve
法定准备金率/存款準備率　legal reserve ratio, required reserve ratio

法定资本/法定資本　statutory capital, legal capital
法定资产/法定資產　legal asset
法定最低准备金/法定最低準備金　legal minimum reserve
法定最高利率/法定最高利率　legal maximum of interest rate
法定最高限额/法定最高限額　statutory ceiling
法定作者/法定作者　legal author
法都引理/Fatou 引理　Fatou's lemma
法范式/法範式　paradigms of law
法官/法官　judge
法官立法/法官立法　making law by judges
法官造法/司法性立法　judicial legislation
法规汇编/法規匯編　compilation of laws
法规清理/法規清理　sorting out laws and regulations
法国民法典/法國民法典　French Civil Code
法家/法家　legalism
法经/法經　Canon of Laws
法兰克福特/法蘭克福特　Felix Frankfurter
法兰克福学派/法蘭克福學派　Frankfurt School
法兰克福指数/法蘭克福指數　DAX index
法兰克人法/法蘭克人法　Lex Francorum
法理/法理　de jure
法理型权威/法定權威　legal authority
法理学/法理學　jurisprudence
法令/法令, 條例　decree ordinance
法律/法律　law
法律案例报告/判案匯編　law report
法律保留/法律保留　legal reservation, legal retainment
法律部门/法律部門　legal department
法律承认/法律承認　de jure recognition
法律程序/法律程序　legal procedure
法律冲突/法律衝突　conflict of laws
法律的功利主义方法/法律的功利主義方法　utilitarianism method of law
法律的量/法律的量　quantity of law
法律多元主义/法律多元主義　legal pluralism
法律符号学方法/法律符號學方法　method of legal semeiology
法律公布/法律公布　promulgation of law
法律功利主义/法律功利主義　legal utilitarianism
法律顾问/法律顧問　corporate lawyer
法律关系/法律關係　jural relation
法律关系客体/法律關係客體　object of legal relation
法律关系内容/法律關係內容　content of legal relation
法律关系运作/法律關係運作　operation of legal relation
法律关系主体/法律關係主體　subject of legal relation
法律规避/法律規避　evasion of law
法律规范/法律規範　legal norm
法律规则/法律規則　legal rule
法律机制/法律機制　legal mechanism
法律继承/法律繼承　succession of law
法律家长主义/法律家長主義　legal paternalism
法律价值/法律價值　legal value
法律监督/法律監督　legal supervision
法律解释/法規解釋　legal interpretation
法律解释方法/法律解釋方法　method of legal interpretation
法律经济分析/法律經濟分析　economical analysis on law
法律经济学/法律經濟學　economics of law
法律救济/法律上的救濟　legal relief
法律局限/法律局限　legal limitation
法律科学/法律科學　legal science
法律类推/法律類推　legal analogy
法律理性/法律理性　legal rationality
法律历史学方法/法律歷史學方法　historical approaches to law
法律漏洞/法律漏洞　gaps in law
法律面前人人平等/法律面前人人平等　everybody is equal before the law
法律目的/法律目的　purpose of law
法律评论/法律評論　law review
法律权威/法律權威　legally constituted authority
法律确信/法律確信　opinio juris
法律人类学/法律人類學　anthropology of law
法律认识错误/法律認識錯誤　mistake of legal comprehending
法律儒家化/法律儒家化　Confucianization of law
法律失效/法律失效　invalidity of law
法律事实/法律事實　legal fact, legal matter, juristic fact
法律思想/法律思想　legal thought
法律溯及力/法律溯及力　retroactivity of law
法律体系/法律體系, 法制　legal system
法律条文/法律規定　letter of the law, legal provision
法律调整/法律調整　legal adjustment
法律图书馆/法律圖書館　law library
法律推理/法律推理　legal reasoning

法律文本/法律文本　legal text
法律文化/法律文化　legal culture
法律系统工程/法律系統工程　system engineering of law
法律现实主义/法律現實主義　legal realism
法律效力/法律效力　validity of law
法律心理/法律心理　legal psychology
法律行为/法律行爲　legal act, legal behavior
法律行为无效/法律行爲無效　voidance of legal act
法律形态/法律形態　mode of law
法律修改/法律修改　modification of law
法律选择/法律選擇　choice of law
法律选择规则/法律選擇規則　choice of law rules
法律移植/法律移植　transplantation of law
法律意识/法律意識　legal consciousness
法律优位/法律優位　primacy of law
法律语言/法律語言　legal language
法律御准/法律御準　Approbation des Loix
法律渊源/法律淵源　sources of law
法律原理/法律原理　legal doctrine
法律原则/法律原則　legal principle
法律援助/法律扶助　legal aid
法律责任/法律責任　legal liability
法律知识/法律知識　legal knowledge
法律执行/法律執行　legal enforcement
法律职业/法律專業　legal profession
法律制裁/法律制裁　legal sanction
法律秩序/法律秩序　legal order
法律仲裁/法律仲裁　legal arbitration
法律咨询/法律諮詢　legal advice
法权/法權　right by law
法人/法人　legal person, corporate juridical person, judicial person
法人犯罪/法人犯罪　corporate crime
法人股/法人股　corporate shares, legal corporate equity securities
法人行动者/法人行動者　corporate actor
法人作品/法人作品　works of legal person
法社会学/法律社會學　sociology of law
法条竞合/法條競合　overlap of articals of law
法团主义/統合主義,組合主義　corporatism
法托引理/Fatou 引理　Fatou's lemma
法务会计/法務會計　forensic accounting
法系/法系　genealogy of law
法修辞学/法修辭學　legal rhetoric
法学概论/法學概論　outline of the science of law
法学阶梯/法學階梯　Institutes of Justinian
法学体系/法學體系　the system of the science of law
法学研究方法/法學研究方法　methodology of law
法益/法益　legal interest
法意解释/法意解釋　interpretation in accordance with the intention of legislator
法与道德/法與道德　law and morality
法与经济/法與經濟　law and economy
法与正义/法與正義　law and justice
法与政策/法與政策　law and policy
法与政治/法與政治　law and politics
法与宗教/法與宗教　law and religion
法域/法域　legal district, territorial legal unit
法院/法庭　court
法院地法主义/法院地法主義　Lex Fori Doctrine
法院仲裁/法院仲裁　judicial arbitration
法院主管/法院主管　scope of case-accepting
法约尔理论/法約爾理論　Fayol's theory
法约尔十四原则/法約爾十四原則　14 principles of management of Fayol
法约尔五要素/法約爾五要素　five factors of management
法则/法則,定律　law
法哲学/法哲學　philosophy of law
法正林/法正林　normal forest
法正蓄积量/法正蓄積　normal growing stock
法制/法制,法律體系　legal system
法治/法治　rule of law
藩刻本/藩刻本　Vassal King edition under the patronage of princes and marquises
翻刻本/翻刻本　reprint edition
翻口广告/翻口廣告　flanging advertising
翻墙/翻牆　crosse the internet blockade
翻译/翻譯　translation
翻译出版/翻譯出版　publishing in translation
翻译模式/詮釋基模　interpretive scheme
翻译强制许可证/翻譯強制許可證　compulsory license of translation
翻译权/翻譯權　right of translation
翻译题名/翻譯題名　translated title
翻译优化/翻譯優化　translation enhancement
凡例/注記　explanatory note
樊山批判/樊山批判　Fanshan Critique
反本质主义/反本質論　anti-essentialism
反补贴/反補貼　anti-subsidy
反补贴税/反補貼關稅,抵銷關稅,平衡税　countervailing duty
反不正当竞争法/反不正當競爭法案　law against unfair competition

反差/反差　contrast
反差系数/反差係數　contrast coefficient
反查/需求追蹤　pegging
反盗版技术/反盜版技術　anti-pirate technology
反对称性/反對稱性　antisymmetry
反复测时法/反覆測時法　repetitive timing
反供给函数/逆供給函數　inverse supply function
反供给曲线/逆供給曲線　inverse supply curve
反谷物法法案/反穀物法案提案　anti-corn law bill
反合并法/反結合法案　anti-combination laws
反击广告/反制廣告　counteradvertising
反级数/反數列　antiseries
反价值/反價值　anti-values
反竞争滥用/反競爭濫用　anticompetitive abuse
反竞争情报/反情報工作　counter-intelligence, defensive competitive intelligence
反竞争效应/反競爭效果　anticompetition effect
反竞争行为/反競爭行爲　anticompetitive practices
反科学运动/反科學運動　anti-science movement
反馈/回饋　feedback
反馈回路/回饋環路　feedback loop
反馈系统/回饋系統　feedback system
反馈循环/回饋循環　feedback cycle
反例/反例　counterexample, anomalies
反垄断豁免/反托拉斯例外　antitrust exemptions
反垄断市场/反托拉斯市場　antitrust market
反垄断委员会/反壟斷委員會　anti-monopoly committee
反垄断政策/反托拉斯政策　antitrust policy
反垄断执法机构/反壟斷執法機構　anti-monopoly law enforcement agency
反歧视/反向歧视　reverse discrimination
反倾销/反傾銷　anti-dumping
反倾销补贴/反補貼關稅津貼,平衡稅津貼　countervailing subsidy
反倾销法/反傾銷法　anti-dumping law
反倾销[关]税/反傾銷[關]稅　anti-dumping duty
反倾销关税税则/反傾銷關稅稅則　anti-dumping tariff
反倾销协议/反傾銷實務　anti-dumping agreement
反求法/反求法　method of counter invention
反全球化/反全球化　anti-globalization
反全球化运动/反全球化運動　anti-globalization movement
反社会化/反社會化　antisocialization
反射壁/反射界限　reflecting barrier
反射利益/反射利益　reflective interest
反身性/反身性,反思性,自反性　reflexivity
反生产行为/反生產行爲　counter-productive behavior
反实证主义方法论/反實證主義方法論　anti-positivist methodology
反事实和因果推理/反事實因果理論　counterfactuals and causal inference
反事实推理/反事實推理　counter-factual reasoning
反思理性法/自反律　reflexive law
反诉/反訴　counterclaim
反调和平均值/逆調和平均數　contra-harmonic mean
反通货膨胀/平抑通貨膨脹　disinflation
反通胀政策/反通貨膨脹政策　anti-inflation policy
反托拉斯/反托拉斯　antitrust
反托拉斯惩处与救济/反托拉斯懲處與救濟　antitrust penalties and remedies
反托拉斯法/反托拉斯法,反獨占法　antitrust law
反文化/反文化　anti-culture
反洗钱/反洗錢　anti-money laundering
反向拆细/反向分割　reverse split
反向回购协议/附賣回協定　matched sale-purchase transaction, reverse repurchase agreements
反向技术转让/反向技術轉讓　reverse transfer of technology
反向假冒/反向假冒　reverse passing off
反向交易/反向交易　reverse trade
反向优惠/反向優惠　reverse preference
反向运动/反制運動　counter-movements
反序排列/反序排列　contragraduation
反演/反演,反轉　inversion
反演指数/互換指數　index of reversion
反意标引/反意標引　antisense indexing
反营销/逆行銷,反行銷　demarketing
反应/反應　reaction
反应变量/被解釋變數　explained variable, response variable
反应不足/反應不足　under reaction
反应函数/反應函數　reaction function
反应曲线/反應曲線　reaction curve
反应型式/回答模式　response style
反应型营销/被動式行銷　reactive marketing
反应性指标/反映性指標　reflective indicators
反应者/反應者　reactor
反映指标/反映性指標　reflective indicators
反永续规则/禁止權利長期不確定法則　rule against perpetuities
反正切变换/反正切變換　inverse tangent transformation, arc-tangent transformation

反正弦变换/反正弦變換　inverse sine transformation, arc sine transformation
反正弦分布/反正弦分布,反正弦分配　arc sine distribution
反证/反證　evidence to disprove a fact
反致/反致　renvoi
反秩/反秩　anti-rank
反众数/反眾數　antimode
反周期政策/反循環政策　counter-cyclical policy
反转胶片/反轉片　reversal film
反坐/反坐　sentence the accuser to the punishment facing the person he falsely accused
返工/重做　rework
返还模式/返回模式　return mode
返回测试/回溯測試　backtesting
返回时间/回歸時間　return time
返回周期/回歸期　return period
返回状态/回歸狀態　return state
返客/返客　cashback
返派/返任　repatriation
返修/返修　repair
犯罪/犯罪　commit a crime
犯罪地/犯罪地　locality of a crime
犯罪动机/犯罪動機　criminal motive
犯罪对象/犯罪對象　target of crime
犯罪构成/犯罪構成　constitution of a crime
犯罪故意/犯罪意圖　criminal intent
犯罪既遂/犯罪既遂　completion of a crime
犯罪客观方面/犯罪客觀方面　objective elements of a crime
犯罪客体/犯罪客體　criminal object
犯罪率/犯罪率　crime rate
犯罪目的/犯罪意圖　criminal intent
犯罪统计/犯罪統計,刑事統計　crime statistics
犯罪未遂/犯罪未遂　attempt of crime
犯罪嫌疑人/嫌疑犯　suspect
犯罪嫌疑人、被告人供述和辩解/犯罪嫌疑人、被告人供述和辯解　confession and defense of the accused
犯罪新闻/犯罪新聞　crime news
犯罪形态/犯罪形態　criminal pattern
犯罪预备/犯罪預備　crime in preparation
犯罪中止/犯罪中止　discontinuance of crime
犯罪主观方面/犯罪主觀方面　subject elements of crime
犯罪主体/犯罪主體　subject of crime
泛函中心极限定理/泛函中央極限定理　functional central limit theorem
泛化/一般化　generalization
泛灵论/泛靈信仰　animism
泛媒体/泛媒體　pan-media
泛媒体时代/泛媒體時代　pan-media age
泛美开发银行/泛美開發銀行,美洲［國家］開發銀行　Inter-American Development Bank
泛网络出版/泛網路出版　pan-network publishing
泛在图书馆/泛在圖書館　ubiquitous library
泛在知识环境/泛在知識環境　ubiquitous knowledge environment
范畴/範疇　category
范畴表/類目表　category
范畴号/範疇號　notation
范畴数据分析/類別資料分析　categorical data analysis
范·德尔·瓦尔登检验/Van Der Waerden檢定　Van Der Waerden's test
范例/範例　example
范式/典範　paradigm
范围/範圍,全距　range, scope
范围变更/範圍變更　scope change
范围定义/範圍定義　scope definition
范围分解/範圍分解　scope breakdown
范围管理/範圍管理　scope management
范围核实/範圍確認　scope verification
范围基准/範圍基準　scope baseline
范围检查/範圍檢查　scope inspection
范围检索/距離搜尋　range search, range retrieval
范围经济/範圍經濟,範疇經濟　economies of scope, economics of scope
范围说明书/範圍說明書　scope statement
范围验收/範圍驗收　scope acceptance
范围注释/範圍注解　scope note
梵夹装/梵夾裝　Buddhist binding
R方/R方　R-squared
方案策划/專案規劃　project planning
方案、规划与预算制［度］/設計計劃預算制度　planning-programming-budgeting system, PPBS
方案偏好/方案偏好　alternative preference
方案优选/方案最佳化　configuration optimization
方案征集/方案徵集　proposal solicitation
方便抽样/方便抽樣法,便利抽樣　convenient sampling, convenience sampling
方便旗/方便旗　flag of convenience
方差/變異數　variance
方差比/變異數比［率］　variance ratio, ratio of variances
方差比分布/變異數比分布　variance ratio

distribution
方差比检验/變異數比檢定 variance ratio test
方差的稳定化/變異數的穩定化 stabilization of variance
方差分量/變異數成分 component of variance, variance component
方差分量的贝叶斯估计/變異數成分的貝氏估計 Bayes estimation of variance components
方差分量模型/變異數成分模型 variance component model
方差分析/變異數分析 analysis of variance, ANOVA
方差分析表/變異數分析表 analysis of variance table, ANOVA table
方差分析模型/變異數分析模型 analysis of variance model
方差估计量/變異數的估計量 estimator of variance
方差函数/變異數函數 variance function
方差均值比/變異數對平均數比 variance-to-mean ratio
方差膨胀因子/變異數膨脹因數 variance inflation factor
方差齐性/變異數齊一性,變異數的均齊性 homogeneity of variance
方差图/序列變異圖 variogram
方差稳定变换/變異數穩定變換 variance stabilizing transformation
方差稳定化变换/變異數穩定轉換 variance stabilizing transformations
方差稳定化相关法/變異數穩定相關法 variance-stabilization correlation method
方差-协方差矩阵/變異數-共變異數矩陣,變異數-互變異數矩陣 variance-covariance matrix
方差最大法/變異數最大法 varimax method
方程/方程式 equation
Bootstrap方法/自助重抽法 bootstrap method
Q方法/Q型技術,Q型技巧 Q-technique
R方法/R型技術,R型技巧 R-technique
方法本体/方法本體 method ontology
方法标准/方法標準 method standard
方法发明/方法發明 process invention
方法矩阵/多特質-多方法矩陣 multitrait-multimethod matrix
方法库/方法庫 method base
方法库管理系统/方法庫管理系統 method base management system
方法库系统/方法庫系統 method base system
方法论/方法論,方法學 methodology

Q方法论/Q方法論 Q methodology
方法论之争/關於方法論的討論 methodenstreit
方法时间衡量/方法時間衡量 methods time measurement, MTM
方格/方格 square lattice
方略馆/方略館 fanglue academy
方位角调整/方位調整 azimuth adjustment
方向数据/方向資料 directional data
方向性计划/方向性計劃 directional plan
方向预测/方向預測 direction forecasting
方阵/方陣,方格 square, square array
方正模式/方正模式 founder mode
方志/方志 local chronicle, chorography
坊刻本/坊刻本 bookshop edition
防尘护套/防塵套,護封 dust jacket
防错法/防錯法 fool-proof method, error-proofing method
防护林/保安林 protection forest
防混淆/抗混淆 anti-aliasing
防火门/防火門 fire-resistant door
防卫过当/防衛過當 unjustifiable self-defense
防卫挑拨/防衛挑撥 instigation of defense
防消片/防消片 film for frevent degaussing
防御商标/防禦商標 defense trademark
防御型推理/防禦性推理 defensive reasoning
防御性公开市场操作/防衛性公開市場操作 defensive open market operation
防御性医疗/防禦性醫療 defensive medicine
防御者/防衛者 defender
防粘脏喷雾/防粘噴粉器 anti-setoff spray
妨害对公司、企业的管理秩序罪/妨害對公司、企業的管理秩序罪 crime of disrupting the managerial order of companies and enterprises
妨害公务罪/妨害公務罪 crime of disrupting public service
妨害民事诉讼行为/妨害民事訴訟行爲 obstruction of civil procedure
妨害社会管理秩序罪/妨害社會管理秩序罪 crime of disrupting the order of social administration
妨害文物管理罪/妨害文物管理罪 crime of impairing the control of cultural relics
房地产/不動財,不動產 real estate, real property
房地产经纪人/房地產經紀人 house agent
房地产投资/房地產投資 investment in real estate
房屋投资保证/住宅投資保證 housing investment guaranty
仿分/仿分 subdivision by analogy, divide like
仿古纸/仿古紙 antique paper

仿生制造/仿生製造　bionic manufacturing
仿真/仿真　emulation
仿真本/仿真本　imitative book
仿真技术/模擬技術　simulation technology
仿制战略/模仿策略　imitation strategy
访谈/訪談，面談　interview
访谈实验/訪談實驗　interview test
访谈者/訪談者　interviewer
访谈资料/訪談資料　interview data
访问/訪問　access
访问级编目/訪問級編目　access level cataloging
访问拒绝数/存取遭拒數　number of access denied
访问控制/存取控制　access control
访问量/訪問次數　number of visits
访问限制/接近限制　restriction on access
访问许可/存取允許，存取許可　access permission
纺织/紡織　spinning and weaving
纺织工业/紡織工業　textile industry
放大倍率/放大倍率　magnification
放大件/放大件　enlargement
放大效应/擴張效果　magnification effect
放大资料/非縮微媒體　macroform
放高利贷者/高利貸金主　loan shark
放回/放還，重置　replacement
放回抽样/放回抽樣，歸還抽樣　sampling with replacement
放火罪/放火罪　crime of arson
放开/斷開，脱開　release load
放宽非关税壁垒/放寬非關稅壁壘　liberalization of non-tariff barrier
放宽检验/簡縮檢驗　reduced inspection
放宽进口限制/放寬進口限制　liberalization of import restriction
放款机构/放款機構　lending institution
放款人/放債者　moneylenders
放款业务/放款業務　advance business
放弃期权/放棄期權　abandon option
放权让利/放權讓利　decentralization of power and transfer of profits
放任型风格/放任式風格　laissez-faire style
放射性污染/輻射汙染　radioactive contamination
放射性污染防治法/放射性汙染防治法　Law on Prevention and Control of Radioactive Pollution
放射性物质/放射性物質　radioactive material
放松管制/自由化，解除管制　deregulation
放松信贷/放寬信貸　ease of credit
放松银根政策/放寬銀根政策　easy money policy
放行/釋放　release

放映权/放映權　right of showing
放映式图书/放映式圖書　projected book
放债人/放債者　moneylenders
飞地经济/內圈經濟，隔絕經濟　enclave economies
飞机场交货价格/飛機場交換價格　FOA, FOB airport
飞托/飛托　fly mounting
非保留印刷品/非保留印刷品　disposable material
非本地发明/非本地發明　not invented here, NIH
非本馆读者/非本館讀者　unaffiliated user, external user
非必要动作浪费/非必要動作浪費　unnecessary motion waste
非标准拉丁方/非標準拉丁方陣　non-standard Latin square
非标准意见/非標準意見　non-standard opinion
非补偿策略/非補償式策略　non-compensatory strategy
非参数的/非參數的，參數無關的　nonparametric
非参数方法/非參數方法，無母數方法　nonparametric method
非参数分析/無母數分析　nonparametric analysis
非参数假设/非參數假設　nonparametric hypothesis
非参数检验/無母數檢定，非參數檢定　nonparametric testing, nonparametric test
非参数模型/非參數模型　nonparametric model
非参数统计学/非參數統計學，無母數統計學　nonparametric statistics
非参数族/非參數族　nonparametric family
非参与观察/非參與觀察　non-participatory observation
非操作时间/非操作時間　non-operating time
非产权战略联盟/非股權式策略聯盟　nonequity strategic alliance
非常规拍摄/隱藏式攝影，偷拍　candid camera, use of hidden recording devices
非程序化决策/非程式化決策　nonprogrammed decision making
非程序化决策技术/非程式化決策技術　nonprogrammed decision technique
非道德管理/非道德管理　amoral management
非等级关系/非等級關係　non-hierarchical relationship
非缔约方/非締約方　non-contracting party
非点源污染/非點源汙染　nonpoint source pollution
非店铺零售/無店面零售　nonstore retailing
非定和博弈/非常數和賽局　nonconstant-sum game
非独占性许可证/非獨占性許可證　non-exclusive

license
非对称分布/不對稱分配　asymmetrical distribution
非对称数字用户线路/非對稱用戶回路　asynchronous digital subscriber loop, ADSL
非对称性/不對稱性　asymmetry
非对称[性]分布/不對稱分布　asymmetrical distribution
非对称性检验/不對稱[性]檢定　asymmetrical test
非对称压缩/非對稱壓縮　asymmetric compression
非法保险单/非法保險單，地下保單　illegal policy
非法报酬/非法報酬　illegal consideration
非法出版物/非法出版物　illegal publication
非法电台/地下廣播，地下電臺　pirate broadcasting
非法合同/非法合約，違法合約　illegal contract
非法合营/非法合夥　illegal partnership
非法获益/非法獲利　illicit gain
非法价格歧视/非法差別取價　unlawful price discrimination
非法经营/非法經營　illegal operation
非法利润/非法利潤　illegal profit
非法贸易/非法貿易　illegal trade
非法人团体/非法人團體　non-corporated body
非法收入/非法所得　illegal income
非法狩猎/非法狩獵　crime of illegally hunting
非法现金需求/非法現金需求　illegal demand for currency
非法移民/非法移民　illegal immigration
非返还模式/非返還模式　non return mode
非峰荷期/離峰期　off-peak period
非概率抽样/非機率抽樣，非隨機抽樣　non-probability sampling
非公共部门/非公共部門　non-public sector of the economy
非公募基金会/私募基金會　private foundation
非公室告/非公室告　cases forbidden to bring to court in the Qin Dynasty
非共同提取退休金计划/非提撥年金計劃　noncontributory pension plan
非固定奖金/非固定獎金　discretionary bonus
非固定进口税/非固定進口稅　variable import levy
非顾客研究/非客戶研究　noncustomer research
非关联失效/非關聯故障　non-relevant failure
非关税壁垒/非關稅[貿易]障礙　non-tariff barrier
非关税壁垒商品清单/非關稅壁壘清單　inventory of non-tariff barrier
非关税措施/非關稅措施　non-tariff measure
非关税干扰/非關稅干擾　non-tariff distortion of composition
非关税减让/非關稅減讓　non-tariff concession
非关税贸易壁垒/非關稅貿易障礙　non-tariff trade barriers
非关税贸易干扰措施/非關稅貿易干擾措施，非關稅貿易干擾手段　non-tariff trade distortive device
非关税贸易干扰手段/非關稅貿易干擾手段，非關稅貿易干擾措施　non-tariff trade distortive device
非官方汇率/非官方匯率　unofficial rate of exchange
非官方经济/非官方經濟　unoffical economy
非归零反转转换/非歸零反轉轉換　NRZI conversion
非合作博弈/非合作賽局　noncooperative games
非合作对策/非合作對策　non-cooperative game
非合作均衡/非合作賽局均衡　non-cooperative equilibrium
非合作瓦尔拉斯均衡/非合作瓦拉斯均衡　non cooperative Walras equilibrium
非合作性均衡/非合作均衡　noncooperative equilibrium
非互惠非歧视性普遍优惠制/非互惠非歧視性普遍優惠制　generalized non-reciprocal and non-discriminatory system of preference
非互惠性优惠待遇/非互惠性優惠待遇　non-reciprocal preferential treatment
非互惠原则/非互惠原則　principle of non-reciprocity
非会员银行/非會員銀行　nonmember bank
非婚生育率/非婚生育率　illegitimacy fertility rate
非货币成本/非貨幣成本　non-money cost
非货币利息/非貨幣利息　non-money interest
非货币收入/非貨幣收入　non-monetary income, non-money income
非货币性财富/非貨幣性財富　non-monetary wealth
非货币性负债/非貨幣性負債　non-monetary liabilities
非货币性黄金/非貨幣性黃金　non-monetary gold
非货币性投资/非貨幣性投資　non-monetary investment
非货币性资产/非貨幣性資產　non-monetary assets
非货币性资产交换/非貨幣性資產交換　exchange of non-monetary assets
非货币支出/非貨幣支出　non-money expenditure
非货币资本/非貨幣資本　non-money capital
非基本史料题目/非基本史料題目　topics of non-base historical data
非基变数/無基變數　non-base variable
非计划投资/非計劃投資　unplanned investment
非价格竞争/非價格競爭　non-price competition
非简约设计/非簡約設計　unreduced design
非结构化决策/非結構化決策　unstructured

decision-making
非结构化面试/非結構式面談　unstructured interview
非结构化数据/無結構資料　unstructured data
非结构化问题/非結構化問題　ill-structured problem, unstructured problem
非结晶区/非結晶區　noncrystalline region
非金融部门/非金融部門　non-financial sector
非金融交易/非金融交易　non-financial transaction
非金融净资产/非金融淨資產　net non-financial asset
非金融企业/非金融企業　non-financial enterprise
非金融市场/非金融市場　non-financial market
非金融资产/非金融資產　non-financial asset
非经常性损益/非經常損益　non-recurring gain or loss
非经济活动人口/非經濟活動人口　economically inactive population
非经济因素/非經濟因素　non-economic factors
非竞争性/非抗對性,非敵對性　non-rival, non-rivalness
非竞争性歧视模型/歧視的非競爭模型　noncompetitive models of discrimination
非竞争性招标/非競爭性招標　non-competitive bidding
非居民纳税人/非居民納稅人　non-resident taxpayer
非居民企业/非居民企業　non-resident enterprise
非均衡/失衡　disequilibrium
非均衡发展理论/不均衡發展理論　unbalanced development theory
非均衡模型/失衡模型　disequilibrium models
非均衡增长/不均衡成長　unbalanced growth
非均衡增长模型/不平衡成長理論　unbalanced growth model
非可操控性应计项目/非可操控性應計項目　nondiscretionary accrual
非渴求品/非渴求產品　unsought product
非课税品/非課稅品　tax-free article
非控时间/非控時間　run-out time
非控制检索点/非受控檢索點,非受控存取點　uncontrolled access point
非控制语言/無控制語言　uncontrolled language
非控主题词/非控主題詞　uncontrolled subject term
非劳动力人口/非勞動力人口　non-labor force population
非劳动收入/非勞動所得　unearned income
非累积信用证/非累積信用狀　non-cumulative credit
非劣解/非劣解　non-inferior solution

非零和博弈/非零和賽局　non-zero-sum game
非零和博弈政策/非零和賽局型政策　non-zero-sum game policy
非流动负债/非流動負債　non-current liabilities
非流动资产/非流動資產　non-current assets
非流通单据/非流通單據,不可轉讓的單據　non-negotiable document
非流通股的流动性/非流通股的流動性　liquidity of non-tradable share
非流通资料/非流通資料　non-circulating, not for circulation
非逻辑思维/非邏輯思考　non-logic thinking
非贸易壁垒/非貿易壁壘　non-trade barrier
非贸易货币/非貿易貨幣　non-trade currency
非贸易货物/非貿易貨物　non-trade commodity
非贸易区/非貿易區　non-trade area
非贸易收入/非貿易收入　non-trade receipt
非贸易性发行/非貿易性發行　non-trade distribution
非贸易账户/非貿易賬戶　non-commercial account
非耐用品/非耐久財　nondurable goods
非内容检索/非内容檢索　noncontent search, noncontent retrieval
非排他/無法排他　nonexclusive
非排他性/非排他性　non-excludability
非匹配期望/非匹配期望　disconfirmed expectation
非偏好样本/非偏好樣本　nonpreferred sample
非平稳时间序列/非平穩時間序列,非平穩時間數列　non-stationary time series
非平稳随机过程抽样/非穩定隨機過程抽樣　sampling from nonstationary stochastic process
非平稳性/非平穩性,非恆定性　non-stationarity
非平稳性高斯过程/非平穩高斯過程　non-stationary Gaussian process
非平稳性过程/非平穩過程　non-stationary process
非破坏性试验/非破壞性試驗　non-destructive testing, NDT
非期刊类连续出版物/非期刊類連續出版物　non-periodical serials
非齐性[的]/非均齊的　non-homogeneous
非齐性转移概率/非均齊遞移機率　non-homogeneous transition probability
非奇异分布/非奇異分布　non-singular distribution
非奇异线性最小二乘/非奇異線性最小平方　non-singular linear least squares
非歧视性待遇/非歧視性待遇　non-discriminatory treatment
非歧视性贸易/非歧視性貿易　non-discriminatory trade

非歧视性原则/非歧視性原則　rule of non-discrimination
非企业法人/非企業法人　non-business corporation
非契约成本/非契約成本　non-contractual cost
非契约收入/非契約收入　non-contractual income
非强制性政策工具/非強制性政策工具　noncompulsory policy instrument
非倾销证明书/非傾銷證明書　non-dumping certificate
非全日制用工/非全日制用工　part-time employment
非人称化权威/非個人性權威　impersonal authority
非人力资本/非人力資本　non-human capital
非人员沟通渠道/非人員溝通管道　non-personal communication channel
非冗余关系/非冗餘關係　non-redundant tie
非商品贸易/非商品貿易　non-merchandise trade
非商业广告/非商業性廣告　non-commercial advertising
非商业交易/非商業交易　non-commercial transaction
非上市公司/未上市公司　unlisted company
非上市股票/非上市股票　outside share
非生产性劳动/低生產力員工　unproductive labor
非生产性物料/非生產物料　nonproduction material
非实物货币/非實物貨幣　non-physical money
非市场产品/非市場財　non-market goods
非市场价值/非市場評價　non-market valuation
非受限工作/非限制性工作　unrestricted job
非书资料/非書資料　non-book material, NBM
非熟练劳动/非技術勞工　unskilled labor, unskilled workers
非数字容差/非數字允差　non-numerical tolerance
非似然比/非概度比　unlikelihood ratio
非讼程序/非訟程式　non-litigation procedure
非随机化决策规则/非隨機化決策規則　non-randomized decision rule
非随机解释变量/非隨機性解釋變數　nonstochastic explanatory variables
非随机缺失/非隨機缺失　not missing at random
非随机样本/非隨機樣本　non-random sample
非同一控制下的企业合并/非同一控制下的企業合并　business combination not involving enterprises under common control
非同质分布的分解/異質分布的解析　dissection of heterogeneous distribution
非统计控制状态/非統計控制狀態　state out of statistical control
非凸性损失函数/非凸性損失函數　non-convex loss function
非完全多重共线性/不完全多重共線性　no perfect multicollinearity
非文本资料/非文本資料　non-textual material
非文件材料/非檔材料　non-record material
非文献信息源/非文獻資訊源　non-documentary information sources
非稳定性投机/動盪投資　destabilizing speculation
非无保留意见/非無保留意見　modified opinion
非物质文化/非物質文化　intangible culture, non-material culture
非物质文化遗产/無形文化遺產　intangible cultural heritage
非吸收状态/非吸收狀態　non-absorbing state
非系列题目/非系列題目　non-series of topics
非系统性风险/非系統風險　unsystematic risk, diversifiable risk
非现期资料/非現期資料　non-current material
非现行文件/非現行檔　non-current records
非限制抽样/不限制抽樣　unrestricted sampling
非线性/非線性　non-linear
非线性编辑/非線性編輯，非線性剪輯　non-linear editing
非线性变换/非線性變換　non-linear transformation
非线性参数化/非線性參數化　non-linear parametrization
非线性定价/非線性定價　non-linear pricing
非线性更新理论/非線性更新理論　non-linear renewal theory
非线性规划/非線性規劃　non-linear programming
非线性回归/非線性回歸　non-linear regression
非线性回归模型/非線性回歸模型　non-linear regression model
非线性回归预测模型/非線性回歸預測模型　non-linear regression forecasting model
非线性假设检验/非線性假設檢定　non-linear hypothesis testing
非线性模型/非線性模型　non-linear model
非线性趋势/非線性趨勢　non-linear trend
非线性投入产出模型/非線性投入產出模型　non-linear input-output model
非线性相关/非線性相關　non-linear correlation
非线性预测/非線性預測　non-linear forecasting
非线性自回归模型/非線性自我回歸　non-linear autoregressive model
非线性最小二乘法/非線性最小平方法　non-linear least squares method

非线性最小二乘估计/非線性最小平方估計　non-linear least squares estimation
非相关多元化/非相關多角化　unrelated diversification
非相关文献发现法/不相交文獻發現法　disjoint literature discovery
X 非效率/X 無效率　X-inefficiency
非序贯实验设计/非逐次實驗設計　non-sequential experimental design
非叙词/非敘詞　non-descriptor
非循环统计量/非循環統計量　non-circular statistic
非循环网络/非循環網路　acyclic network
非循环信用证/非循環信用狀　non-revolving credit
非循环元素/非循環元素　non-cyclic element
非言语/非語文　nonverbal
非言语传播/非語文傳播　nonverbal communication
非言语沟通/非語言溝通　nonverbal communication
非言语互动/非語文互動　nonverbal interaction
非研发创新/非研發創新　non-research and development innovation, non-R and D innovation
非意愿生育/意外生育　unwanted fertility
非音乐性录音资料/非音樂性錄音資料　non-musical sound recording
非银行的银行/非銀行銀行,不完全銀行　nonbank bank
非银行金融机构/非銀行金融機構　non-bank financial organ, nonbank financial institution
非银盐胶片档案/非銀鹽膠片檔案　non-silver film archive
非印刷载体/北印媒體　non-print media
非印刷资料/北印資料　non-print material
非营利公司/非營利公司　non-profit corporation
非营利性医疗机构/非營利性醫院　not-for-profit hospital
非营利组织/非營利組織　non-profit organization, NPO
非营利组织国际分类标准/非營利組織國際分類法　international standard classification of non-profit organization
非营利组织会计制度/非營利組織會計制度　accounting system for non-profit organization
非营业性发行/非營業性發行　non-operating distribution
非营业盈余/不勞而穫　unearned surplus
非邮发报刊/非郵發報刊　non-post distributed newspaper and periodical
非语言沟通/非語言溝通　nonverbal communication
非原假设/非虛無假設　non-null hypothesis
非原始资料/非原始文件　non-source document

非再生资源/非再生[性]資源,不可更新的资源　nonrenewable resources
非增值作业/非增值作業　non-value-added activity
非正常汇率/異常匯率　abnormal exchange rate
非正常先验分布/非正常先驗分布,非正常事前分布　improper prior distribution
非正规部门/非正式部門　informal sector
非正规就业/非正式雇傭　informal employment
非正规武装部队/非正規武裝部隊　irregular armed force
非正交数据/非正交數據　non-orthogonal data
非正式出版物/非正式出版物　informal publication
非正式创新网络/非正式創新網路　informal innovation network
非正式法律/非官方法　unofficial law
非正式访谈/非正式訪談　informal interview
非正式沟通/非正式溝通　informal communication
非正式规则/非正式的規則　informal rules
非正式交流/非正式溝通　informal communication
非正式金融部门/非正式金融部門　indigenous financial sector, informal financial sector
非正式经济/非正式經濟　informal economy
非正式群体/非正式群體,非正式團體　informal group
非正式社会控制/非正式社會控制　informal social control
非正式信贷市场/非正式信貸市場　informal credit market
非正式制度/非正式制度　informal institutions
非正式组织/非正式組織　informal organization
非正态分布/非常態分布　non-normal distribution
非正态曲线/非常態曲線　abnormal curve
非正态性/非常態性　abnormality, disnormality
非正态总体/非常態母體　non-normal population
非正则估计/非正規估計　non-regular estimator
非正则化设计/非正規化設計　non-normalized design
非指导式咨询/非指導式諮商　non-directive counseling
非指导性面试/非指導式面試,非定向面試　non-directive interview
非中介化/去中介　disintermediation
非中介模式/非中介模式　non-intermediary model
非中心贝塔分布/非中心貝他分布,非中心貝他分配,非中心β分布　non-central beta distribution
非中心参数/非中心參數　non-centrality parameter
非中心多元贝塔分布/非中心多變量貝他分布,非中心多變量貝他分配,非中心多變量β分布　non-

central multivariate beta distribution
非中心多元 F 分布/非中心多變量 F 分布,非中心多變量 F 分配　non-central multivariate F-distribution
非中心 F 分布/非中心 F 分布,非中心 F 分配　non-central F-distribution
非中心 t 分布/非中心 t 分布,非中心 t 分配　non-central t-distribution
非中心复合设计/非中央合成設計　non-central composite design
非中心卡方分布/非中心卡方分布,非中心卡方分配　non-central chi-square, χ^2 distribution
非中心威沙特分布/非中心 Wishart 分布,非中心 Wishart 分配　non-central Wishart distribution
非中心置信区间/非中心信賴區間　non-central confidence interval
非周期态/非週期狀態　aperiodic state
非洲开发银行/非洲開發銀行　African Development Bank
非洲联盟/非洲聯盟　African Union
非主流经济学/異端經濟學　heterodox economics
非主题标引/非主題標引　non-subject indexing
非住宿式服务机构/非住宿式服務機構　non-residential care agency
非注册股票/非註冊股票　letter stock
非自然形态/非自然型態　unnatural pattern
非自相关/非自我相關　nonautocorrelation
非自由兑换证券/不能兌換的證券　inconvertible securities
非自由兑换纸币/非自由兌換紙幣　inconvertible paper currency
非自愿失业/非自願失業　involuntarily unemployed
菲利浦曲线/菲利普曲線　Phillips curve
菲尼斯/菲尼斯　John Finnis
扉页/書名頁　title page, fly page
诽谤/誹謗　defamation
诽谤罪/誹謗罪　crime of defamation
斐波那契算法/斐波那契法　Fibonacci algorithm
废除关税壁垒/廢止關稅障礙　abolition of customs barrier
废除进口关税/廢止進口關稅　abolition of import tariff
废料/殘料　scrap
废料分析/廢料分析　scrap analysis
废弃损失/廢棄損失　obsolescence losses
废物管理/廢棄物管理　waste management
废物回收利用/廢物回收利用　recycling and reuse of waste
费德勒权变模型/費德勒權變模型,費德勒權變模式　Fiedler contingency model
费率差别区别对待/差別費率　rate discrimination
费率基准/費率基準　rate base
费率结构/費率結構　rate structure
费率削减/費率削減　rate cutting
费米-迪拉克统计量/Fermi-Dirac 統計量　Fermi-Dirac statistic
费舍曼-琼斯-豪瑟假设/費舍曼-瓊斯-豪瑟假設　Featherman-Jones-Hauser hypothesis
费氏职位分析/弗氏工作分析　Fleishman job analysis
费希尔-贝伦斯检验/費雪-貝倫檢定,費雪-拜潤檢定　Fisher-Behrens test
费希尔 z 变换/費雪 z 變換　Fisher's z-transformation
费希尔方程/費雪方程式　Fisher equation
费希尔分布/費雪分布,費雪分配　Fisher's distribution
费希尔 B 分布/費雪 B 分布,費雪 B 分配　Fisher's B-distribution
费希尔 z 分布/費雪 z 分布　Fisher's z-distribution
费希尔公式/費雪公式　Fisher formula
费希尔检验/費雪檢定　Fisher's test
费希尔 z 检验/費雪 z 檢定　Fisher's z-test
费希尔精确概率检验/費雪精確機率檢定　Fisher exact probability test
费希尔理想方程/費雪理想公式　Fisher's ideal formula
费希尔模型/費雪模型　Fisher model
费希尔-奈曼定理/費雪-尼曼定理　Fisher-Neyman theorem
费希尔-欧文检验/費雪-歐文檢定　Fisher-Irwin test
费希尔球面正态分布/費雪球面常態分布,費雪球面常態分配　Fisher's spherical normal distribution
费希尔确切概率/費雪精確機率　Fisher exact probability
费希尔相合估计量/費雪一致估計量　Fisher's consistent estimator
费希尔效应/費雪效果　Fisher effect
费希尔信息/費雪訊息　Fisher's information
费希尔信息矩阵/費雪訊息矩陣　Fisher's information matrix
费希尔-许-罗伊分布/費雪-許-羅伊分布,費雪-許-羅伊分配　Fisher-Hsu-Roy distribution
费希尔-耶茨系数/費雪-葉慈檢定　Fisher-Yates test
费用/費用,成本　cost, expense
费用付讫/費用付訖　charge paid
费用估算/成本估計　cost estimating

费用管理/成本管理　cost management
费用管理计划/成本管理計劃　cost management plan
费用函数/成本函數　cost function
费用汇总/成本匯總　cost summary
费用基准/成本基準　cost baseline
费用绩效指数/成本績效指標　cost performance index, CPI
费用决算/費用決算　cost audit
费用控制/成本控制　cost control
费用清单/費用清單　statement of expense
费用实报实销合同/費用實報實銷合同　cost reimbursable contract
费用索赔/費用索賠　fee claim
费用预付/費用預付　charge prepaid
费用预算/成本預算　cost budgeting
费用中心/費用中心　expense center
刖/刖　amputating criminal's feet as penalty in ancient China
分版校对/分版校對　sub-version proofreading
分保/再保[險]　reinsurance
分辨力/解析能力　resolution power
分辨率/解析度　resolution
分别比率估计量/分離比估計量　separate ratio estimator
分布/分布　distribution
F 分布/F 分布, F 分配　F-distribution
G 分布/G 分布, G 分配　G-distribution
S 分布/S 分布, S 分配　S-distribution
t 分布/t 分布, t 分配　t-distribution
z 分布/z 分布, z 分配　z-distribution
λ 分布/λ 分布, λ 分配　lambda distribution
分布的混合/分布的混合　mixture of distributions
分布的近似变换/分布的近似變換　transformation approximation to distribution
分布的无记忆性/分布的無記憶性　memoryless property of distribution
分布的最小吸引域/分布的最小引域　minimum domain of attraction of a distribution
分布分析/分布分析, 分配分析　distribution analysis
分布函数/分布函數, 分配函數　distribution function
分布曲线/分布曲線, 分配曲線　distribution curve
分布式保管模式/分散式保管模式　distributed retention pattern
分布式服务/分散式業務　distributed service
分布式检索/分散式搜尋　distributed search, distributed retrieval
分布式决策/分散式決策　distributed decision making

分布式决策支持系统/分散式決策支援系統　distributed decision support system
分布式数据库/分散式資料庫　distributed database
分布式谈判/分配式談判　distributive bargaining
分布图/分布圖, 分配圖　distribution diagram
分布误差/分布誤差　distribution error
分布型/分布型　types of distributions
分布滞后/分布時差　distributed lag
分布滞后模型/遞延分配落差模型　distributed lag model
分布自由法/分布不拘法, 分布無關法　distribution-free methods
分布自由检验/分布不拘檢定, 分布無關檢定　distribution-free tests
分步查询/分步查詢　querying step by step
分步成本法/分步成本法　process costing
分部报告/分部報告　segment reporting
分部分类账/分部分類賬　sectional ledger
分部工程/分部工程　part project
分部结平/分部結平　sectional balancing
分部试算/分部試算　sectional balancing
分册卷/分冊　sub-series
分层标准/分層標準　criteria of classification
分层抽样/分層抽樣　stratified sampling
分层叠架式书库/分層疊架式書庫　tier-layer shelving bookstack
分层定价/雙層定價　two tiered pricing
分层多阶抽样/分層多段抽樣　stratified multiple stage sampling, stratified multi-stage sampling
分层法/分層法　strata method
分层目的抽样/分層立意抽樣　stratified purposive sampling
分层目的样本/分層立意樣本　stratified purposive sample
分层签发/分層簽發　layered sign and issue
分层随机抽样/分層隨機抽樣　stratified random sampling
分层随机样本/分層隨機樣本　stratified random sample
分层体系/分層體系　stratification system
分层网络/層次化網路　layered networks
分层线性模型/階層線性模式　hierarchical linear model, HLM
分层序列法/分層序列法　lexicographic method
分层样本/分層樣本　stratified sample
分层样品/分層樣本　stratified sample
分层原则/分層原則　principle of stratification
分层整群抽样/分層群聚抽樣　stratified cluster

sampling
分层准则/分層準則　criteria for stratification
分拆上市/權益分割　equity carve-out
分次交货/分次交貨　split delivery
分丛编说明/分叢編説明　sub-series statement
分担责任者/分擔責任者　shared responsibility, shared authorship
分地区定价/分地區定價　zone pricing
分段回归/分段回歸　segmented regression
分段检索法/分段檢索法　search stage by stage, segment retrieval
分段胶片/分段膠片　unitised film
分段条形图/分段長條圖　section bar diagram
分段线性回归模型/逐段回歸模型　piecewise regression model
分段组合标记制/分段組合標記制　faceted notation
分对数变换/羅吉特機率轉換　logit transformation
分发/分發　distributing, distribution
分封制/分封制　enfeoffment system
分封制度/分封制度　system of enfeoffment
分割市场/分散型市場　fragmented market
分格法/分格法　cell method
分工负责、互相配合、互相制约/分工負責、互相配合、互相制約　division of responsibilities, work in coordination and mutual restraint
分公司/分公司　branch company, branch corporation
分公司制度/分公司制度　brand office system
分股/股票分割　stock split
分股投资公司/分享投資公司　split investment company
分户目录/分户目錄　ledger catalogue
分化/分化　differentiation
分级法/分級法,排序法　ranking method
分级管理/分級管理　level-to-level administration
分级数据/分級數據　ranked data
分级阅读/分級閲讀　grade level reading
分辑/分輯　section
分辑题名/分輯題名　section title
分家/分家　divide up family property and live apart
分拣/歸類,分類　sorting
分拣架/分揀架　preshelving shelf
分拣输送系统/分揀系統　sorting and picking system
分解/分解　decomposition
分解技术/分解技術　breakdown technology
分解与协调原则/分解與協調原則　principle of decomposition and coordination
分解原理/分解原則　decomposition principle

分界值/分界值　dividing value
分镜/分鏡腳本,故事板　storyboard
分卷题名/分卷題名　divisional title
分库/分署庫房　branch repository
分块对角矩阵/集區對角矩陣　block diagonal matrix
分类/分類,歸類,範疇化　classification, sorting, categorizing
ABC 分类/ABC 分類法　ABC classification
分类变数/類別變項　categorical variable
分类标目/分類標目　classification heading
分类标引/分類標引　classification indexing
分类标准/分類標準　standard of classification
分类表/分類表,分類系統　classification scheme, classification table, classification schedule
分类表补编/分類表補編　supplement to the manual of classification
分类参照/分類參照　classification reference
分类测度/類別測度　categorical measure
分类法/分類法　classification
分类法电子版/分類系統電子版　electronic version of classification system
分类法网路版/分類系統網路版　web version of classification system
分类分析款目/分類分析款目　classification analytic entry
分类附加款目/分類附加款目　classification added entry
分类广告/分類廣告　classified advertising
分类号/分類號　classification number, classification code, class notation
分类计数/分類計數　classified counting
分类检索/分類檢索　classification retrieval
分类检验/分類檢驗,歸類檢驗　sorting inspection
分类款目/分類款目　classification entry
分类流水排架法/分類流水排架法　classification flow frame method
分类模型/類別模型　categorical model
分类目录/分類目録　classified catalog
分类排架法/分類排架法　classification and arrangement method
分类频数/分類次數　classification frequency
分类频数序列/分類次數數列　classified frequency series
分类器/分類器　classifier
分类商品价格/商品目録價格　catalogue price
分类商品目录/分類商品目録　classified catalogue
分类书目/分類書目　systematic bibliography
分类数据/類別資料　categorical data

分类随机变量/類別的隨機變數　categorical random variable
分类索引/分類索引　classified index
分类体系/分類系統　classification system
分类序列/類別序列　categorical series
分类学/分類學,分類法　taxonomy
分类与判别/分類及判別　classification and discrimination
分类原则/分類原則　principle of classification
分类账簿/分類賬簿　ledger
分类账式借书登记法/分類賬式借書登記法　ledger charging system
分类账余额/分類賬餘額　ledger balance
分类指数/分類指數　classification index
分类主题词表/分類主題詞表　classified thesaurus
分类主题目录/分類主題目錄　classified subject catalog
分类主题一体化/分類主題一體化　integration of classification and thesauri
分类主要款目/分類主要款目　classification main entry
分类组织/分類組織　classification organizing information
分类组织法/分類組織法　classification organization method
分类作业/分類作業,歸類作業　sorting operation
分离变化/分隔變化　isolated change
分离点/分離點,區分點　separation point, breakdown point
分离定理/分離定理　separation theorem
分离法则/分離法則　law of segregation
分离均衡/分離式均衡　separating equilibrium
分离型商业银行/分離型商業銀行　divisional commercial bank
分立/衍生企業,衍生事業　spin-off
分立式目录/區分式目錄　divided catalog, split catalog
分量/分量　component
分量条形图/成分長條圖　component bar chart
分裂检验法/分裂測驗法　split test method
分流/分流　shunt
分面/分面　facet, array
分面标记制/標記系統　facet marking system
分面分析/分面分析　facet analysis
分面公式/分面公式　facet formula
分面叙词表/分面敘詞表　facet thesaurus, thesauro facet
分面组配/分面協調　facet coordination

分面组配分类法/分面組配分類法　faceted coordination classification
分年龄活动参与率/年齡別活動率　age-specific activity rate
分年龄生育率/年齡別生育率　age-specific fertility rate
分年龄死亡率/年齡別死亡率　age-specific death rate
分配策略/分配型策略　distributional strategy
分配额度/分配額度　distribution quota
分配公平/分配之公平,分配公正　distributional equality, distributive equity
分配寄销/分配寄銷　distribution sales
分配理论/分配理論　distribution theory
分配配额/分配配額　allocated quota
分配效应/分配效果　distributional effect
分配性政策/分配政策　distributive policy
分配正义/分配正義　distributive justice
分批成本法/分批成本法　job order costing
分期偿还/攤還　amortization
分期偿还抵押贷款/分期償還的抵押貸款　installment mortgage
分期储蓄/分期儲蓄,零存整付　installment savings
分期分批出售/分期分批出售　sale by installment
分期分批交货/分期分批交貨　installment delivery
分期付款/分期付款　payment by installment, installment, amortizing
分期付款购买/分期付款購買　hire-purchase
分期付款期权/權利金遞延支付選擇權,分期付款式選擇權　deferred premium option, installment option
分期付款信贷/分期付款信貸　installment credit
分期缴费保险/分期保費保險　installment insurance
分期收款销售商品/分期付款銷貨　installment sale
分期支付的保险费/分期支付的保險費　installment premium
分歧点/談判破裂點　disagreement point
分切/縱剪,剪條,開縫　slitting
分区/分區　zoning
分区规划制/區域規劃系統　zoning systems
分区组/區集劃分　blocking
分区组效率/區劃效率　blocking efficiency
分权化/分權化,去中心化　decentralization
分全宗/分組合　sub-fond
分散标引/分散標引　decentralized indexing
分散化/多角化　diversification
分散库存控制/分散庫存控制　decentralized inventory control

分散模型/非集權制　decentralized model
分散统计制度/分散式統計制度　decentralized statistical system
分散投资/分散投資,资产组合多样化　decentralized investment, portfolio diversification
分散型研发组织/分散型研發組織　decentralized research and development organization
分色/分色　color separation
分色打样/逐色樣張,單色樣張　progressive proof
分数求积自回归移动平均模型/部份整合型自我回歸移動平均模型　autoregressive fractionally integrated moving average model
分税制/分税制　separate tax system, tax-sharing system
分税制财政体制/分税制財政體制　revenue sharing system
分死因死亡比/原因別死亡比　cause-specific death ratio
分死因死亡率/原因別死亡率　cause-specific death rate
分位数/分位數　quantile
分位数回归/分位數回歸　quantile regression
分位数检验/分位數檢定　quantile test
分位数图形分析/分位數圖形分析　fractile graphical analysis
PEST 分析/PEST 分析　political-economical-social-technological analysis, PEST
STEEPLE 分析/STEEPLE 分析　sociocultural-technological-economical-environmental-political-legal and ethical analysis, STEEPLE
SWOT 分析/SWOT 分析,本身優劣勢及外在環境分析　strength-weakness-opportunity-threat analysis, SWOT analysis
分析标引/分析標引　analytical indexing
分析表/分析表　analytical table
5M1E 分析法/5M1E 分析法　man-machine-material-method-measurement and environment analysis
SMART 分析法/SMART 分析　SMART analysis
分析法学派/分析法學派　Analytic School of Law
分析款目/分析款目　analytical entry
分析目录/分析目錄　analytical bibliography
分析趋势/分析趨勢　analytic trend
分析图/分析圖　analysis chart
分析误差/分析誤差　analytical error
分析型风格/分析型風格　analytic style
分析性程序/分析程式　analytical procedure
分析者/分析者　analyzer
分析著录/分析著錄　analytical description

分析著录格式/分析著錄格式　analytical description format
分项工程/分項工程　item project
分页设计/分頁設計　separate page design
分载并联系统/分載並聯系統　shared load parallel system
分整/分數差分　fractional differencing
分整 EGARCH 模型/分數差分 EGARCH 模型　fractionally integrated EGARCH model, FIEGARCH model
分整 GARCH 模型/分數差分 GARCH 模型　fractionally integrated GARCH model, FIGARCH model
分整自回归移动平均模型/分整自回歸移動平均模型　autoregressive fractionally integrated moving average model, ARFIMA model
分支泊松过程/分支卜瓦松過程　branching Poisson process
分支点/分支點　branch point
分支定界法/分支定界法,分支限界法　branch and bound method
分支更新过程/分支更新過程　branching renewal process
分支过程/分支過程,分枝過程　branching process
分支机构/分支機構　branch organization
分支马尔可夫过程/分支馬可夫過程　branching Markov process
分支世系制度/分支世系制度　segmental lineage system
分支有界算法/分支有界演算法　branch-and-bound algorithm
分众/分眾　demassified
分众分类法/大眾分類　folksonomy
分子式索引/分子式索引　formula index
分组/分組,歸類,分類　grouping
分组标引/分組標引　group indexing
分组泊松分布/分組卜瓦松分布,分組卜瓦松分配　grouped Poisson distribution
分组格/分組格,分類格　grouping lattice
分组观测值/分組觀察值　grouped observations
分组合/分組　sub-group
分组校正/分組校正　correction for grouping
分组频数分布/分組次數分配　grouped frequency distribution
分组平均校正/分組平均校正　average correction for grouping
分组筛选方法/群篩選法　group screening method
分组数据/分組數據　grouped data

分组统计/分类統計　classification statistic
分组图/分類圖　classification chart
分组问题/分類問題　classification problem
分组序贯抽样方案/分組逐次抽樣計劃　group sequential sampling plan
分组序贯概率比检验/分組逐次機率比檢定　grouped sequential probability ratio test
分组因子/組因子,區集因子　group factor, block factor
分组原理/分組原理,分類原理　classification principle
分组原则/分類原則　principle of classification
焚化/焚化　incineration
粉碎式销毁/碎紙機銷毀　shredding
份额分布/份額分布　share distribution
丰裕中的贫困/豐裕中的貧困　poverty in the midst of opulence
风险/風險　risk
风险爱好者/風險愛好者　risk lover
风险标/風險標　risk tender
风险传播/風險傳播　risk communication
风险代理费用/依訴訟結果所定之費用　contingency fee
风险的市场价格/風險的市場價格　market price of risk
风险登记册/風險清單　risk register
风险点/風險點　risk point
风险度量/風險評估　calculated risk taking
风险防范体系/風險防範體系　risk prevention system
风险防范原则/風險防範原則　risk precautionary principle
风险分担/風險分擔　risk sharing
风险分解结构/風險因素分解結構　risk breakdown structure, RBS
风险分摊/分散風險　risk spreading
风险分析/風險分析,安全度分析　risk analysis
风险工资/風險薪資　at-risk pay
风险共担原则/風險分擔原則　risk-sharing principle
风险沟通/風險溝通　risk communication
风险管理/風險管理　risk management
风险管理规划/風險管理規劃　risk management planning
风险管理计划/風險管理計劃　risk management plan
风险规避/風險規避,風險祛避　risk avoidance, risk averse, risk aversion
风险规避支出法/規避風險支出法　averting expenditure method
风险函数/風險函數　risk function
风险核查/保險物件的檢查　inspection of risk
风险回避/風險規避,風險祛避　risk avoidance, risk averse, risk aversion
风险基础审计/風險基礎審計　risk-based audit
风险基金/創業基金　venture fund
风险集/風險集合　risk set
风险计量模型/風險矩陣模型　risk metrics model
风险记录/風險記錄　risk record
风险监控/風險監控　risk monitoring and control
风险减轻/風險沖抵　risk mitigation
风险接受/風險驗收　risk acceptance
风险矩阵/風險矩陣　risk matrix
风险决策/風險性決策　risk decision
风险控制/風險管控　risk control
风险类别/風險類別,風險等級　class of risk, risk category
风险利益分析/風險效益分析　risk-benefit analysis
风险率/涉險率　hazard rate
风险模型/危險率模型,轉機率模型　hazard model
风险偏好/風險偏好　risk preference
风险评估程序/風險評估程式　risk assessment procedure
风险评审技术/風險評審技術　venture evaluation and review technique, VERT
风险认知/風險知覺　risk perception
风险社会/風險社會　risk society
风险识别/風險確認　risk identification
风险事件/風險事件　risk event
风险数据库/風險資料庫　risk database
风险态度/風險態度　risk attitude
风险套利/風險套利　risk arbitrage
风险调整回报率/風險調整報酬率　risk adjusted return rate
风险调整贴现率/風險調整折現率　risk adjusted discount rate, required rate of return
风险投资/風險投資,創業投資　risk investment, venture capital
风险投资机构/創業投資機構　venture capital institution
风险投资基金/創業投資基金　venture capital fund
风险无偏性/風險不偏性　risk unbiasedness
风险系数/風險係數　coefficient of risk
β风险系数/貝塔風險係數　beta risk coefficient, β risk coefficient
风险型决策/風險狀況下的決策　decision making under risk

风险性资产/具風險資產　risky asset
风险选择/風險選擇　risk selection
风险厌恶/風險袪避,風險規避　risk avoidance, risk averse, risk aversion
风险厌恶者/風險厭惡者　risk averter
风险溢价/風險溢價　risk premium
风险因素/風險因素　risk element
风险因子/風險因子　risk factor
风险应对/風險應對　risk response
风险应对规划/風險應對規劃　risk response planning
风险应对开发/風險應對開發　risk response development
风险知觉/風險知覺　risk perception
风险中性/風險中立　risk indifferent, risk neutral
风险中性的纳什均衡/風險中立之納許均衡　risk neutral nash equilibrium
风险中性者/風險中立者　risk neutral parties
风险转换/風險轉換　risk transformation
风险转嫁/調升風險　risk shifting
风险转移/風險轉移　passing of risk, risk transference
风险转移效应/風險移轉　risk shift effect
风险转移型创新/風險移轉創新　risk-transferring innovation
风险资本家/禿鷹資本家　vulture capitalist
风险资本主义/冒險資本主義　venture capitalism
风险资产比率/風險資產比率　risk asset ratio
封/封　envelop
封闭二项抽样规则/封閉二項抽樣規則　closed binomial sampling rule
封闭格式/封閉格式　closed format
封闭经济/閉鎖經濟　closed economy
封闭人口/封閉性人口　closed population
封闭社会/封閉社會　closed society
封闭式抵押/封閉式抵押,限額抵押　closed mortgage
封闭式共同基金/封閉型共同基金　closed-end mutual fund
封闭式基金之谜/封閉型基金之謎　close-end fund puzzle
封闭式拍卖/封閉式拍賣　sealed-bid auctions
封闭式投资基金/封閉式[投資]基金　close-end investment fund
封闭式问题/封閉式問題　closed-ended question
封闭文件全宗/封閉檔全宗　closed record fonds
封闭系统/封閉式系統,封閉式制度　closed system
封闭小组/封閉式團體　closed group
封闭型市场/不公開市場　closed market
封闭性公司/封閉性公司　close corporation
封闭序贯计划/封閉逐次方案　closed sequential scheme
封闭序贯t检验/封閉逐次t檢定　closed sequential t-test
封闭因子/區段因子　blocking factors
封底/封底　back cover
封顶保底期权/封頂保底期貨,利率上下限選擇權　corridors, collars
封顶保底证券/利率上下限證券　collared issue
封二/封二　inside front cover
封建社会/封建社會　feudal society
封面/封面　cover
封面报道/封面報導　cover story
封面题名/封面題名　cover title
封面文字/封面文字　cover line
封面要目/封面要目　side title
封签/封簽　publishing label
封三/封三　inside back cover
封四/封底　back cover
封一/封面　front cover
封装的/封裝的　EPS, Encapsulated PostScript
封装[法]/封裝[法]　encapsulation
峰/尖峰　peak
峰度/峰度,峰態　kurtosis
峰度的测度/峰度的測定數　measures of kurtosis, measures of peakness
峰度检验/峰度檢定　test for kurtosis
峰度系数/峰度係數,峰態係數　coefficient of kurtosis
蜂巢排架法/蜂巢排架法　honeycombing
蜂鸣营销/話題行銷　buzz marketing
冯·米泽斯分布/馮米賽斯分布,馮米賽斯分配　von Mises distribution
冯·诺伊曼比/馮紐曼比　von Neumann's ratio
冯·诺依曼-摩根斯坦效用函数/馮紐曼-摩根斯坦效用函數　von Neumann-Morgenstern utility function
冯特实验心理学/馮特實驗心理學　experimental psychology of Wundt
冯·耶林/馮·耶林　Rudolf von Ihering
奉献策略/奉獻策略　dedication strategy
缝隙长度/間隙長度　gap length
缝隙宽度/隙寬　gap width
缝隙深度/間隙深度　gap depth
佛罗伦萨银行管理/佛羅倫斯銀行管理　Florence bank management
否定意见/否定意見　adverse opinion

夫妇式家庭/夫妻家庭,配偶家庭　conjugal family
夫琅和费模式/弗勞恩霍夫爾模式　Fraunhofer model
夫妻财产制/夫妻財產制　marital property regime
夫妻财产制法律适用公约/夫妻財產制法律適用公約　Convention on the Law Applicable to Matrimonial Property Regimes
夫妻共同财产/夫妻共同財產　community property of spouses
夫妻家庭/夫妻家庭　husband and wife family
夫妻平权/夫妻平權　equal rights between wife and husband
夫妻特有财产/夫妻特有財產　peculiar property of spouses
孵化器/企业育成中心　business incubator
弗吉尼亚权利法案/佛吉尼亞權利法案　Virginia Bill of Rights
弗拉斯卡蒂手册/法城手冊　Frascati manual
弗莱堡学派/弗賴堡學派　Freiburg school
弗里德曼秩检验/傅里德曼等級檢定　Friedman rank test
弗里曼-图基变换/弗里曼-塔基變換　Freeman-Tukey transformation
伏尔泰/伏爾泰　Voltaire
服从/服從　obedience
服务/服務,勞務　service
服务安全性/服務安全性　service security
服务包/服務包　service package
服务报酬/服務報酬　service remuneration
服务补救/服務補救　service recovery
服务补救悖论/服務補救悖論　service recovery paradox
服务不可分性/服務的不可分割性　service inseparability
服务部门/服務部門　service sector
服务差异化/服務差異化　services differentiation
服务成本定价法/服務成本定價法　cost-of-service pricing
服务创新/服務創新　service innovation
服务对象价值/服務對象價值　client's value
服务管理/服務管理　service management
服务计划/服務計劃　service plan
服务价格/服務價格　price of service
服务价值/服務價值　service value
服务阶级/服務階級　service class
服务可靠性/服務可靠性　service reliability
服务蓝图/服務藍圖　service blueprint
服务-利润链/服務-利潤鏈　service-profit chain

服务贸易/服務貿易,勞務貿易　service trade
服务贸易总协定/服務業一般貿易協定　general agreement on trade in services
服务期/服務期間　service period
服务缺口/服務缺口　service gap
服务商标/服務商標　service trademark
服务审计/服務審計　service audit
服务生产模型/服務生產模型　servuction model
服务失误/服務失誤　service failure
服务台/服務檯　service counter
服务提供模式/服務提供模式　service provision model
服务提供商/服務提供者　service provider
服务外包/服務外包　service outsourcing, outsourcing of service
服务无形性/服務無形性　service intangibility
服务性租赁/服務性租賃　service lease, wet lease
服务业/服務業　service industry
服务易变性/服務易變性　service variability
服务易逝性/服務易逝性　service perishability
服务元数据/服務性詮釋資料　service metadata
服务支持性/服務支持性　service support performance
服务质量/服務品質　service quality, SERVQUAL
服刑人员/服刑人員　prisoner
服刑人员子女/服刑人員子女　children of prisoners
服制/服制　inslitution of mourning apparel
俘获理论/捕捉理論　capture theory
浮动担保/浮動擔保　floating security
浮动订货点/浮動訂貨點　floating order point
浮动工资/變動薪資　variable pay
浮动股利优先股/可調整股利特別股　adjustable rate preferred stock
浮动关税/浮動關稅　sliding tariff
浮动汇率/浮動匯率　floating exchange rate
浮动汇率制度/浮動匯率制度　floating exchange rate system
浮动利率/浮動利率　floating interest rate
浮动条款/波動條款　fluctuating clause
浮凸字体图书/浮凸字體書籍　embossed book
浮息票据/浮動利率票據　floating rate note
浮游资金/游資　floating fund
符号/符號,記號　sign, symbol
符号变动/符號變異　variation of sign
符号代号标准/符號代號標準　code symbol standard
符号分析/符號學分析　semiotic analysis
符号规则/符號規則　rule of sign
符号互动/符號互動　symbolic interaction

符号互动理论/符號互動理論　symbolic interaction theory
符号货币/代幣　token money
符号检验/符號檢定　sign test
符号模型/符號模型　symbolic model
符号消费/符號消費　symbolic consumption
符号学/符號學　semiology, semiotics
符号秩检验/符號秩檢定　signed rank test
符合性/符合性，一致性　conformance
幅比/幅比　amplitude ratio
幅度/幅度　amplitude
幅面/格式　format
幅面尺寸/幅面尺寸　format size
辐射式书库/輻射式書庫　radiating book stack
福费廷/福費廷　forfaiting
福果案/福果案　Forge's Case
福柯/傅科　Michel Foucault
福莱特协作四原则/福萊特協作四原則　four cooperation principles of Follet
福利/福利　welfare, well-being
福利标准/福利標準　welfare criterion
福利第一基本定理/福利第一基本定理　first fundamental theorem of welfare
福利定理/福利理論　welfare theorem
福利多元主义/福利多元主義　welfare pluralism
福利国家/福利國家　welfare state
福利函数/福利函數　welfare function
福利计划/福利計劃　welfare program
福利经济学/福利經濟學　welfare economics
福利经济学第二定理/福利經濟學第二福利定理　the second theorem of welfare economics, second welfare theorem
福利经济学第一定理/福利經濟學第一福利定理　the first theorem of welfare economics
福利秘书制度/福利秘書制度　welfare secretary system
福利损失/福利損失　welfare loss
福利危机/福利危機　welfare crisis
福利效应/福利效果　welfare effect
福利债券/福利債券　bond bonus
福利最大化/福利極大化　welfare maximization
福斯特准则/佛斯特準則　Foster's criteria
福特制/福特制　Ford system
福特主义/福特主義　Fordism
福祉管理/福利管理　welfare management
抚养比/扶養比，依賴人口比率　dependency ratio
抚养儿童义务判决的承认和执行公约/撫養兒童義務判決的承認和執行公約　Convention concerning the Recognition and Enforcement of Decisions relating to Maintenance Obligations towards Children
抚养权/監護權　custody
抚养制度/撫養制度　child-rearing system
甫刑/甫刑　Penal Law named after Marquis of Fu
辅币/輔幣　subsidiary coin, auxiliary coin
辅文/輔文　reference material written by compiler
辅助/輔助　ancillarity
辅助材料/輔助材料　auxiliary materials
辅助工资/輔助工資　auxiliary wages
辅助功能/次要功能，次要機能　secondary function
辅助估计量/輔助估計量　ancillary estimator
辅助活动/支持活動　support activity
辅助加工时间/輔助加工時間，輔助程序時間　auxiliary process time
辅助矩/輔助動差　auxiliary moment
辅助款目/輔助款目　secondary entry
辅助书库/輔助書庫　auxiliary stack room
辅助索引/輔助索引　auxiliary index
辅助统计量/輔助統計量　auxiliary statistic, ancillary statistic
辅助信息/輔助訊息，輔助資訊　auxiliary information, supplementary information, ancillory information
辅助性贸易/輔助性貿易　complementary trade
辅助叙词表/輔助敘詞表　supplemental thesaurus
辅助因子/輔助因子　subsidiary factor
腐蚀凹版/凹板印花　gravure printing
腐刑/腐刑　penalty of castration
父系社会/父系社會　patriarchal society
父项/上層物料項目　parent item
付酬因素/計酬因數　compensable factor
付费博客/付費博客　paid blog
付费式服务体系/付費式服務體系，服務使用者付費制度　fee-for-service system
付费受众/付費受眾　paying audience
付汇/付匯　foreign exchange payment
付款保证/付款保證　payment guarantee
付款不足/付款不足　payment insufficient
付款方式/付款方式　type of payment
付款跟单汇票/跟單付款匯票　documentary payment bill
付款行/付款銀行　paying bank
付款交单/付款交單，提示交單　document against payment, document against presentation
付款交单汇票/付款交單匯票　document against payment bill

付款交货/付款交貨　delivery against payment, delivery on payment
付款凭证/付款憑證,付款憑單　payment statement, paying certificate
付款手续费/付款手續費　payment commission
付款通知/付款通知書,支付委託書　advice of payment, payment order
付款最后期限/最終付款期限　final date for payment
付讫保险/付訖保險　paid-up insurance
付讫支票/付訖支票　paid-up cheque, paid cheque
付息/付息　payment of interest
付息债券/債券息票　coupon bond
付现/付現　pay cash
付现价格/付現價格,現金價格　cash price
付现交单/付現交單　document against cash
付现交易/現金交易　for cash
付印/付印　for press, send to press
付印样/付印樣　pattern before printing
负超几何分布/負超幾何分布,負超幾何分配　negative hypergeometric distribution
负储蓄/負儲蓄　dissaving
负担行为/負擔行爲　art of credit
负多项分布/負多項式分布,負多項式分配　negative multinomial distribution
负二项分布/負二項分布,負二項分配　negative binomial distribution
负二项模型/負二項式模型　negative binomial model
负二项式模型/負二項式模型　negative binomial model
负反馈/負回饋　negative feedback
负方差分量估计值/變異數成分的負估計值　negative estimate of variance component
负荷报告/負荷報告　load report
负荷图/負荷圖　load chart
负矩/負動差　negative moment
负均衡利率/負均衡利率　negative equilibrium rate of interest
负理想解/負理想解,反理想解　negative ideal solution
负利率/負利率　negative interest rate, negative rate of interest
负利息/負利息　negative interest
负面报道/負面報導　negative reporting
负面功能/負面功能　unwanted function
负面要求/負面要求　negative appeal
负偏度/負偏度　negative skewness
负片/負片　negative film

负税人/負稅人　tax bearer
负所得税/負所得稅　negative income tax
负投资/負投資,投資縮減　negative investment
负外部性/負外部性　negative externality
负现金流量/負現金流量　negative cash flow
负相关/負相關,負相聯　negative correlation
负像/負像　negative image
负像母片/負像母片　master negative
负信用/負信用　negative credit
负选择假说/負向選擇假說　negative selection hypothesis
负因子多项分布/負因子多項分布,負因子多項分配　negative factorial multinomial distribution
负载均衡/負載均衡　load balance
负债/負債,債務　liability, debt
负债比率/負債比率　total debt ratio
负债表/資產負債表　balance sheet
负债管理/負債管理　liability management
负债管理理论/負債管理理論　liability management theory
负债权益比率/負債股本比率　debt-equity ratio
负债业务/負債業務　liability business
负债账户/負債賬戶　liability account
负指数分布/負指數分布,負指數分配　negative exponential distribution
妇联/婦聯　women's federation
妇女参与发展/婦女參與發展　women's participation in development
妇女地位/婦女地位　women's status
妇女福利/婦女福利　welfare for women
妇女赋权/婦女賦權　women's empowerment
妇女回家论/婦女回家論　women going back home
妇女解放/婦女解放　women's liberation
妇女经验/婦女經驗　women's experiences
妇女期刊/婦女期刊　women's periodical
妇女权益保障法/婦女權益保障法　law on the protection of women's rights and interests
妇女社会工作/婦女社會工作　women social work
妇女问题/婦女問題　female problem
妇女无偿劳动/婦女無償勞動　women's unpaid work
妇幼比/婦幼比　child-woman ratio
附带民事诉讼/附帶民事訴訟　incidental civil action
附加产品/擴增產品　augmented product
附加费用/附加費用,額外費用　additional charge
附加福利/額外津貼　fringe benefits
附加功能/附加功能　additional feature
附加股息/附加股息,增發股息　supplementary

dividend
附加关税/追徵關稅,額外關稅 extra duty, additional duty
附加合同/附約 accessory contract
附加价值定价/附加價值訂價 value-added pricing
附加款目/附加款目 added entry
附加款目格式/附加款目格式 added entry format
附加税/附加税 surtax
附加条件/附加條件 additional condition
附加条款/附加條款 add-on clause, additional clause
附加险/附加險 accessory risk
附加刑/附加刑 accessory punishment
附加议定书/附加議定書 additional protocol
附加预期的菲利浦斯曲线/附加預期的菲利浦曲線 expectations-augmented Phillips curve
附加账户/附加賬户 adjunct account
附加值的/附加價值的 value-added
附件/附件 annexe, annexed matter, accompanying material
附件登记簿/附件登記簿 annex register
附件目录/附件目録 annex catalogue
附件说明/附件説明 instructions of annex
附录/附録 appendix
附录式检索工具/附録式檢索工具 appendix-retrieval system
附期限的法律行为/附期限的法律行爲 juristic act subject to stipulation of time limited
附认购权证债券/附認股權證債券 warrants bond
附属产品定价/專屬品訂價 captive-product pricing
附属出口公司/附屬出口公司 subsidiary export company
附属丛编题名/附屬叢編題名 subseries title
附属档案馆/附屬檔案館 annex archives
附属文件中心/附屬檔中心 annex center of files
附属协议/附屬協議 ancillary agreement
附属刑法/附屬刑法 accessory criminal law
附属资本/補充資本 supplementary capital
附说明书的发盘/附説明書的報價 offer by description
附条件背书/附條件背書 qualified endorsement, conditional endorsement
附条件财政补助金/附條件財政補助金 conditional grant
附条件承兑票据/附條件承兑票據 qualified acceptance of bill
附条件发盘/附條件報價 conditional offer
附条件法律行为/附條件法律行爲 juristic act subject to conditions
附条件合同/附條件合約,搭售契約 conditional contract, tying contract
附条件交付契约/附條件交付契約 escrow agreement
附条件融资/附條件融資 conditional financing
附条件销售/附條件銷售 conditional sale
附条件销售单/附條件銷售單 conditional bill of sale
附条件债券/附條件債券 conditional bond
附条件最惠国待遇/附條件最惠國待遇 conditional most favored nation treatment
附条款保险单/附條款保險單 claused insurance policy
附条款票据/附條款票據 claused bill
附条款提货单/附條款提單 claused bill of lading
附条款信用证/附條款信用狀 claused letter of credit
附息汇票/附息匯票 interest bill of exchange
附息票据/附息票據 interest bill
附样报盘/附樣報價 sample offer
附有凭证的发票/跟單商業發票 invoice with document attached
附有认股权证的公司债券/附有認股權證的公司債券 warrant bond
附则/附則 supplementary provisions
附注/附注 note appended
附注项/附注項 note appended item, note area
复保险/複保險 double insurance
复本/複本 added copy, duplicate, extra copy
复本交换/複本交换 publication exchange
复本交换目录/複本交换目録 list of duplicates for exchange
复本量/複本量 duplicate of the volume
复本位/複本位 bimetallic standard
复本位货币制度/雙元金屬貨幣制度 bimetallic monetary system
复本信度/複本信度 alternate form reliability
复比率估计量/雙比率估計量 double-ratio estimator
复非正态曲线/複合非常態曲線 complex abnormal curve
复分/複分 subdivision
复分表/複分表 subdivisions
复分号/複分號 subdivision number
复关联/複相聯 multiple association
复合比率估计值/複合比率估計值 compound ratio estimate
复合表/多重分類表 complex table
复合泊松分布/複合卜瓦松分布,複合卜瓦松分配

compound Poisson distribution, composed Poisson distribution

复合泊松过程/複合卜瓦松過程　compound Poisson process

复合超几何分布/複合超幾何分布,複合超幾何分配　compound hypergeometric distribution

复合抽样计划/複合抽樣方案　composite sampling scheme

复合出版/複合出版　composite publishing, hybrid publishing model

复合传播/複合傳播　composite transmission

复合单元/複合單位　complex unit

复合费用/複合費用　compound expense

复合分布/複合分布,複合分配　compound distribution

复合负多项分布/複合負多項分布,複合負多項分配　compound negative multinomial distribution

复合概率/重组机率,複合機率　recombination probability, compound probability

复合高斯分布/複合高斯分布,複合高斯分配　complex Gaussian distribution

复合估计值/複合估計值　composite estimate

复合故障/複合故障,組合故障　combined failure

复合关税/複合關稅,多欄式關稅　multiple tariff, compound duty, compound tariff

复合关税税率/複合關稅稅率　compound tariff

复合关税制/多欄式關稅制　multiple tariff system

复合汇率/複匯率　multiple exchange rate

复合汇率制/複匯率制　multiple exchange rate system

复合假设/複合假設　composite hypotheses

复合频率分布/混合次數分布　compound frequency distribution

复合期权/複合期權　compound option

复合设计/複合設計　composite design

复合失效/組合故障　combined failure

复合实验/複合實驗　compound experiments

复合事件/複合事件　compound event

复合收益率/複利獲益率　compound yield

复合数字对象/複合數字物件　hybrid digital object

复合税率/複合稅率　complex tariff

复合套汇/重複套匯　compound arbitrage

复合题名/複合題名　compound title

复合图书馆/複合圖書館,混合型圖書館　hybrid library

复合威沙特分布/複合威夏分布,複合威夏分配　complex Wishart distribution

复合文件/複合檔案　compound records

复合系统/複合制　composite system

复合银行业务制度/複合銀行業務制度　multiple banking system

复合中央银行制度/複合中央銀行制度　compound central bank system

复合主题标目/複合主題標目　compound sbject heading

复合资产/複合資產　multiple asset

复核/複核　cross validation

复解调/複合解調　complex demodulation

复决权/複決權　referendum

复刊/復刊　reopened

复利利率/複利利率　compound interest rate

复利率/複利率　compound rate

复利贴现/複利貼現　compound discount

复频数表/多元次數表　multiple frequency table

复曲线相关/複曲線相關　multiple curvilinear correlation

复审/復審　secondary review

复式记账法/複式簿記　double entry bookkeeping

复式裂区设计/雙重裂區設計　split-split plot design

复式凭证/複式憑證　multiple account titles voucher

复式税则/複式稅則,複式關稅　complex tariff

复式图/複式圖　multiple chart

复式预算/複式預算　multiple budget, dual-budget

复税制/複稅制　multiple taxation

复位/歸架　reintegration

复相关/複相關　multiple correlation

复相关比/複相關比　multiple correlation ratio

复相关系数/複相關係數,多元相關係數　multiple correlation coefficient, coefficient of multiple correlation

复向通道/多方向性通道　multidirectional channel

复写副本/複寫副本　carbon copy

复型分支过程/複型分支過程,多型分支過程　multi-type branching process, multitype branching process

复选/複選　the second selecting stage

复印比/複印比　copy ratio

复印磁平/複印磁平　copy magnetic flat

复印件/影印件　photocopy

复印效应/複印效應　copy effect

复杂产品/複雜產品　complex product

复杂产品创新/複雜產品創新　complex product innovation

复杂产品系统/複雜產品系統　complex product system

复杂技术/複雜技術　complex technology

复杂人假设/複雜人假設 complex man hypothesis
复杂社会/複雜社會 complex societies
复杂适应系统/複雜調適系統 complex adaptive system
复杂系统/複雜系統 complex system
复杂型购买行为/複雜型購買決策 complex buying behavior
复杂性/複雜度 complexity
复杂罪过/複雜罪過 complicated culpability
复指数/複合指數 complex exponentials
复制/複製,拷贝 copy, replication, duplication
复制保护技术/防拷貝軟體 copy protection
复制技术/複製技術 reprographics, reprography
复制件/影印件,拷贝 copy
复制品/複製品 reproduction, duplication, replica
复制权/複製權 right of reproduction, reproduction right
复制生产线/複製生產線 replicating production line
复制委托书/複製委託書 replication certification of authority, reproduction certification of entrustment
复制型创业/複製型創業 entrepreneurial reproduction
复制用样盘/複製用樣盤 template disk for reproduction
复转换设计/雙重變換設計 double change-over design
副本/副本 duplicate
副本库/副本庫 archives of the grand secretariat

副本未兑付/第二聯匯票未兌付 second unpaid
副标目/副標頭 subheading
副标题/副標題 subtitle, subhead, side-head
副产品/副產品 by-product
副产品定价/副產品定價 by-product pricing
副刊/增刊,別冊 supplement
副题名/副題名,副標題 subtitle, subtitle
副研究馆员/副研究館員 associate research librarian
副主编/副主編 associate managing editor, associate editor
赋词标引/賦詞標引 assigned term indexing
赋税原理/課稅原則 principle of taxation
傅里过程/富利過程 Furry process
傅里叶变换/傅立葉轉換,傅立葉變換 Fourier transformation
傅里叶分析/傅立葉分析 Fourier analysis
傅里叶级数/傅立葉級數 Fourier series
傅里叶逆变换/逆傅立葉轉換 inverse Fourier transform
富比尼定理/Fubini 定理 Fubini theorem
富勒/富勒 Lon Luvois Fuller
富媒体/富媒體 rich media
富媒体广告/富媒體廣告 rich media advertisement
覆盖律模型/法則統攝模型 the covering law model
覆盖率/涵蓋率 coverage rate
覆膜/覆膜 film laminating
覆膜机/覆膜機 film laminating machine

G

伽马分布/伽瑪分布　gamma distribution
伽马分布时滞/伽瑪分配落差　gamma distributed lags
伽马风险/伽瑪風險　gamma risk
伽马函数/伽瑪函數　gamma function
伽马密度/伽瑪密度,γ密度　gamma density
伽马系数/伽瑪係數　gamma coefficient
伽马值/伽瑪值　gamma value
改编/改編　adaptation
改编权/改編權　right of adaptation
改进二项概率纸/改良二項機率紙　improved binomial probability paper
改进时间/修正時間　modification time
改进型产品/改良型產品　improvement product
改刊/改刊　change journal
改组债券/改組債券　reorganization bond
盖亚假说/蓋亞假說　Gaia hypothesis
盖印/蓋章　stamping
盖尤斯/蓋尤斯　Gaius
概差/可能誤差　probable error
概化理论/概化理論　generalizability theory
概化他人/概化他人　generalized others
概化效度/類推性,通則性　generalizability
概括/普同化　generalizing
概率/機率　probability
概率比检验/機率比檢定　probability ratio test
概率比例抽样/機率比例抽樣　probability proportional sampling
概率测度/機率測度　probability measure
概率测度理论/機率測度理論　measure theory of probability
概率场/機率域　probability field
概率乘法定理/機率乘法定律,機率乘法定理　multiplication law of probability, multiplication theorem of probability
概率抽样/機率抽樣　probability sampling
概率传递/機率傳輸　probability transmission
概率单位/機率單位　probit
概率单位变换/機率單位變換　probit transformation
概率单位分析/機率單位分析　probit analysis
概率单位回归/機率單位回歸　probit regression
概率单位回归线/機率單位回歸線　probit regression line
概率单位模型/常態機率模型,波比模式　probit model
概率的频率理论/機率次數理論　frequency theory of probability
概率分布/機率分配,機率分布　probability distribution
概率分布表/機率分配表　probability distribution table
概率分布函数/機率分配函數　probability distribution function
概率公理/機率公設　axioms of probability
概率函数/機率函數　probability function
概率和影响矩阵/概率和影響矩陣　probability and impact matrix
概率积分变换/機率積分變換　probability integral transformation
概率极限/機率極限,機率界限　probability limit
概率集/機率集合　probability set
概率加法法则/機率加法法則　additive law of probability, addition rule of probability
概率检索/機率檢索　probabilistic retrieval
概率矩/機率動差　probability moment
概率空间/機率空間　probability space
概率律/機率定律,機率法則　probability law
概率论/機率論　probability theory
概率密度/機率密度　probability density
概率密度估计/機率密度估計　estimation of probability density
概率密度函数/機率密度函數　probability density function, pdf
概率模型/機率模型　probabilistic model, probability model
概率母函数/機率生成函數,機率母函數　probability generating function
概率评估/機率估測　probability assessment
概率区间/機率區間　probability interval
概率曲面/機率曲面　probability surface
概率曲线/機率曲線　probability curve
概率生成函数/機率生成函數,機率母函數

probability generating function
概率事件/機率事件 probability event
概率思想/機率思考 probability thinking
概率图/機率繪圖 probability plot
概率推断原理/概率推斷原理 principle of probability extrapolation
概率向量/機率向量 probability vector
概率信息处理/機率資訊處理 probabilistic information processing
概率样本/機率樣本 probability sample
概率意义独立性/機率意義的獨立性 independence in probability sense
概率有界的/機率有界的 bounded in probability
概率元/機率元素 probability element
概率运算/機率運算 probability calculus
概率直方图/機率直方圖 probability histogram
概率值分析/機率單位分析 probit analysis
概率纸/機率[繪圖]紙 probability paper
概率质量函数/機率質量函數 probability mass function, pmf
概念/概念 concept
概念标引/概念標引 concept indexing
概念测试/觀念測試 concept testing
概念地图/概念地圖 concept map
概念法学/概念法學 jurisprudence of conceptions
概念分解/概念分解 concept decomposition
概念化/概念化 conceptualization
概念技能/觀念性能力 conceptual skill
概念检索/概念檢索 concept retrieval, conceptual retrieval
概念聚类阵/概念聚類陣 conceptually clustered matrix
概念空间/概念空間 concept space
概念模型/概念模型 conceptual model
概念设计/概念設計 conceptual design
概念生成/概念生成 concept generation
概念实在论/概念實在論 conceptual realism
概念史/概念史 conceptual history
概念图/概念地圖 concept map
概念唯名论/概念唯名論 conceptual nominalism
概念系统/概念系統 conceptual system
概念限定组配/概念限定組配 concept limit collocation
概念相交组配/概念相交組配 concept intersection collocation
概念型风格/概念型風格 conceptual style
概念选择/概念選擇 concept selection
概念转换/概念轉換 concept translation

概念组配/觀念協調 concept coordination
概念组配索引/觀念協調索引 concept coordinate index
概述要素/概述要素 preliminary element
概算定额/概算定額 budget estimate quota
概算造价/經費概算 budgetary estimation
概算指标/概算指標 budget estimate index
概则/概則 general rules
干胶印/乾膠印 letterset printing
干名犯义/干名犯義 Gan Ming Fan Yi
干扰/干擾 disturbance, interfering, jamming
干扰变量/干擾變數 intervening variable
干扰宽放/干擾寬放 interference allowance
干扰容限/干擾寬放 interference allowance
干扰误差/干擾誤差 errors of disturbances
干扰系数/干擾係數，擾亂係數 coefficient of disturbancy, coefficient of distrubancy
干扰效应/史楚普干擾效應 Stroop interference effect
干涉主义/干預主義 interventionism
干托/乾裱 dry mounting
干银法/乾銀處理法 dry silver process
干预分析/干預分析 intervention analysis
干预价格/干預價格 intervention price
干预行政/干預行政 administrative intervention
甘特奖励工资制/甘特獎勵工資制 Gantt premium system
甘特进度图/甘特進度圖 Gantt progress chart
甘特图/甘特圖 Gantt chart
赶工/趕工 crashing
感官品质/感官品質 sensory quality
感官试验/感官試驗 sensory test
感官特性/感官特性 sensory characteristic
感光测定曲线/感光測定曲線 sensitomeristic curve
感光层/感光層 photosensitive layer
感光度/感光度 sensitivity
感光胶/照相乳膠 photo emulsion
感光介质文件/感光介質檔 photo-responsive medium for files
感光膜片/感光膜片 indirect photosensitive film
感光特性曲线/感光特性曲線 photosensitive properties curve
感色性/感色性 color sensitivity
感性诉求/感性訴求 emotional appeal
感召权力/參照權 referent power
感知风险/知覺風險 perceived risk
感知公正/感知公正 perceived justice
感知控制视角/感知控制視角 perceived-control

perspective
感知品质／知覺品質　perceived quality
感知属性／感知屬性　sensory attribute
感知图／知覺圖　perceptual map
干中学／邊做邊學　learning by doing
冈贝尔不等式／Gumbel 不等式　Gumbel's inequality
冈贝尔分布／Gumbel 分布，Gumbel 分配　Gumbel distribution
刚性规范／剛性規範　rigid norm
刚性宪法／剛性憲法　rigid constitution
纲目分类法／綱目分類法　categorical classification of archives
岗位工资／職位工資　post wage
岗位工资制／崗位工資制　post wage system
岗位津贴／職位津貼　post allowance
岗位配置分析／崗位配置分析　position arrangement analysis
岗位聘任制／崗位聘用制　post employment system
岗线／波峰線　crest line
港口费／港口費　port charge
港口附加费／港口附加費　port surcharge
港口结关／港口結關　port clearance
港口险／港口險　harbor risk
港务费／港務費，入港稅　harbor due
杠杆货币合同／槓桿貨幣合約　leveraged currency contract
杠杆收购／融資購并，融資買斷　leveraged buyout, LBO
杠杆租赁／融資租賃　leveraged lease
杠杆作用／槓桿作用　leverage
皋司／皋司　Gao Si
高保真彩色／高保真彩色　Hi-Fi Color
高参与工作系统／高涉入工作系統　high-involvement work system
高层管理／高層管理　top management
高层管理者／高階管理者　top manager
高承诺工作系统／高承諾工作系統　high-commitment work system
高-低定价／高低訂價法　high-low pricing
高低界图／高低圖　high-low graph
高调／高調，明調　high key
高度相关／高度相關　high correlation
高尔顿个体差异问题／高爾頓個別差異問題　Galton's individual difference problem
高尔顿卵形线／高爾頓肩形曲線　Galton ogive
高尔顿-麦卡利斯特分布／高爾頓-麥克亞利斯特分布，高爾頓-麥克亞利斯特分配　Galton-McAlister distribution
高尔顿梅花阵／高爾頓梅花陣　Galton's quincunx
高尔顿图／高爾頓圖　Galton graph
高风险藏书／高風險藏書　high-risk collection
高峰／高峰　hump
高峰负荷定价／尖峰定價法　peak-load pricing
高峰期／尖峰期　peak period
高杠杆点／高度槓桿點　high leverage point
高估／高估　overestimation
高关税／高關稅　high duty
高管发展计划／高階主管發展計劃　executive development program
高管薪酬水平／高級職員薪酬，經理人員報酬　executive compensation
高光曝光／無網屏曝光　highlight exposure
高汇价／高匯率　high exchange
高级检索／高級檢索，高級搜索　advanced search
高级内容访问系统／高級內容訪問系統　advanced access content system, AACS
高级书写纸／高級印書紙　bank paper
高级文化／高級文化，高尚文化，上層文化　high culture
高技术／高科技　high technology
高技术产业／高科技產業　high-technology industry
高技术产业集群／高科技產業群聚　high-technology industrial cluster
高绩效工作系统／高績效工作系統　high performance work system
高阶混杂／高階混同　higher order confounding
高阶滞后结构／高階滯後結構　higher order lag structures
高阶转移矩阵／高階遞移矩陣　higher transition matrix
高阶自回归／高階自身回歸　higher order autoregressive
高科技创业／高科技創業　high technology venture
高科技企业／高科技企業　high technology enterprise
高科技园区／科技園區　high technology park
高丽纸／高麗紙　Korean white paper
高利贷／高利貸　usury
高利贷法／高利貸取締法　usury law
高利率／高利率　high interest rate
高利润／高毛利　high margin
高利息／高利息　high interest
高龄老人／高齡老人　ripe old age elderly
高密度激光唱盘／高密度雷射唱盤　digital versatile disc-audio, DVD-A
高密度激光视盘／高密度影音光碟　digital versatile disc-video, DVD-V

高密度只读光盘/高密度唯讀光碟　digital versatile disc-read only memory, DVD-ROM
高密度住宅/高密集住宅　high density housing
高能货币/強力貨幣　high powered money
高能激励/高效能激勵　high power incentive
高频词/高頻詞　high frequency word
高清拍摄/高清拍攝　high definition filming
高清晰电视/高畫質電視　high definition television, HDTV
高清晰度电视/高解析度電視　high definition television, enhanced definition television, EDTV
高情景文化/高情境文化　high context culture
高山细缝战略/高山細縫戰略　mountain gap strategy
高收益债券/高報酬債券　high yield bond
高斯-泊松分布/高斯-卜瓦松分布,高斯-卜瓦松分配　Gauss-Poisson distribution
高斯-杜立特法/高斯-杜立德法　Gauss-Doolittle method
高斯分布/高斯分布,高斯分配　Gauss distribution, Gaussian distribution
高斯分布函数/高斯分布函數　Gaussian distribution function
高斯过程/高斯過程　Gauss process, Gaussian process
高斯-马尔可夫定理/高氏-馬可夫定理　Gauss-Markov theorem
高斯求积/高斯數值積分　Gaussian quadrature
高斯曲线/高斯曲線　Gaussian curve
高斯-塞德尔法/高斯-賽德法　Gauss-Seidel method
高斯时间序列/高斯時間數列　Gaussian time series
高斯-温克莱不等式/高斯-文克勒不等式　Gauss-Winckler inequality
高斯线性过程/高斯線性過程　Gaussian linear process
高斯噪声/高斯干擾　Gaussian noise
高速复制/高速率複製　high-speed duplication
高速缓冲存储器/快取記憶體　cache memory
高息率证券/高配息證券　high coupon
高校图书办站/高校圖書代辦站　college book agency
高效活动/高效活動　high task
高新技术/高新技術　high and new technology
高新技术开发区/高新技術開發區　high technology industrial development zone
高薪酬战略/高薪策略　high wage strategy
高于票面价值/高於票面價值　par above premium
高增长企业/高增長企業　high-growth venture

稿酬/稿酬,稿費　remuneration
稿费/稿費,稿酬　remuneration
稿件/稿件　manuscript
稿件布局结构/稿件布局結構　manuscript layout
稿源/稿源　contribution source
告示牌/告示牌,看板招牌　billboard
告诉才处理/告訴才處理　a legal principle of acceptance at complaint only
告诉才处理的案件/告訴才處理的案件　case accepted at complaint only
戈德菲尔德-匡特检验/高德裴爾德-匡特檢定　Goldfeld-Quandt test
戈德索普阶级分类法/戈德索普階級分類　Goldthorpe class scheme
戈登法/戈登法　Gordon technique
戈登增长模型/Gordon成長模型　Gordon growth model
搁版/架　shelf
割礼/割禮　circumcision ceremony
割平面［算］法/割平面法　cutting plane algorithm
割让/割讓　cession
割体/殘割　mutilation
割线法/橫切法　secant method
歌谱/聲樂總譜　vocal score
革命/革命　revolution
格斗游戏/格鬥遊戲　fighting game
格界/格界　cell boundary
格距/格距　cell interval
格均值/格平均值　cell mean
格拉布斯估计/Grubbs估計　Grubbs' estimator
格拉布斯规则/Grubbs規則　Grubbs' rule
格拉姆-查里尔A型数列/Gram-Charlier A型級數　Gram-Charlier series type A
格拉姆-查里尔B型数列/Gram-Charlier B型級數　Gram-Charlier series type B
格拉姆-查里尔C型数列/Gram-Charlier C型級數　Gram-Charlier series type C
格拉姆准则/Gram準則　Gram's criterion
格拉提安/格拉提安　G. F. Gvatian
格拉提安教令集/格拉提安教令集　Decretum Gratiani
格拉西尔调查/格拉西爾調查　Glacier investigation
格兰杰表述定理/葛蘭哲展開定理　Granger representation theorem
格兰杰非因果性/葛蘭哲非因果關係　Granger non-causality
格兰杰因果关系/葛蘭哲因果關係　Granger causality

格兰杰因果检验/葛蘭哲因果關係檢定　Granger causality test
格兰维尔/格蘭維爾　Ranulph de Glanville
格劳秀斯/格勞秀斯　Hugo Grotius
格雷调查/格雷調查　Goehre survey
格雷钦定律/葛萊興法則　Gresham's law
格离差/格離差　cell deviation
格里奇检验/葛瑞瑟檢定　Glejser's test
格列高利法典/格列高利法典　Codex Gregorianus
格列文科定理/格列文科定理　Glivenko's theorem
格列文科-坎特里引理/格列文科-康泰利引理　Glivenko-Cantelli lemma
格鲁斯下垂/格魯斯下垂　Groos droop
格伦南德不确定原则/葛蘭得不確定性原則　Grenander's uncertainty principle
格罗夫斯-克拉克税/格駱夫-克拉克賦稅　Groves-Clarke tax
格罗夫斯-莱迪亚德机制/格駱夫-勒雅機制　Groves-Ledyard mechanism
格耐登科定理/Gnedenko 定理　Gnedenko's theorem
格耐登科-科罗留科定理/Gnedenko-Koroljuk 定理　Gnedenko-Koroljuk theorem
格耐登科-科罗留科分布/Gnedenko-Koroljuk 分布，Gnedenko-Koroljuk 分配　Gnedenko-Koroljuk distribution
格频数/格次數　cell frequency
M 格设计/M 格子設計　M-lattice design
格氏职业生涯发展阶段理论/葛氏職涯發展階段理論　Greenhouse's career development stage theory
格式/格式　format
ASF 格式/進階串流格式　advanced streaming format
AVI 格式/聲訊-視訊號交插檔　audio video interleaved
MOV 格式/MOV 檔案格式　MOV format
MPEG 格式/視訊壓縮規格　moving picture experts group format
RM 格式/RM 格式　realmedia format
RMVB 格式/RMVB 格式　realmedia variable bit
WAV 格式/WAV 格式　waveform audio format
WMA 格式/視窗媒體聲頻　windows media audio
WMV 格式/WMV 格式　windows media video
格式存改/格式存改　method of dealing with forms
格式合同/格式合同　format contract
格式化/格式化　formatting
格式化文本/格式化本文　formatted text
格式加密/格式加密　format encryption
格式条款/格式條款　format clause, form clause

格式要素/格式要素　format elements
格式转换/格式轉換　format conversion
格限/格限　cell limit
格扎里管理者质量论/格扎里有關管理者品質的論述　Ghazali on managers' character
格值/格值　cell value
格子/格子　lattice
格子抽样/格子抽樣，網格抽樣　grid sampling, lattice sampling
格子方/格子方陣　lattice square, plaid square
格子分布/格子分布　lattice distribution
格子设计/格子設計　lattice design
格子随机变量/格子隨機變數　lattice random variable
隔代家庭/隔代家庭　grandparent family
隔段排架法/隔段排架法　bay shelving
隔离经济/孤立經濟體　insular economy
隔离危机/危機隔離　crisis insulation
隔离效应/隔離效應　isolation effect
隔日交易/隔日交易，夕賣朝買交易　bed-and-breakfast deal
隔夜拆借/隔夜拆借　overnight loan
隔夜逆回购协定/隔夜附買回協定　overnight rps
个案法/個案法　case method
个案工作/個案工作　case work
个案管理/個案管理　case management
个案控制研究/個案控制研究　case-control studies
个案研究/個案研究　case study
个案研究法/個案研究法　case study method
个别登记/個人登記　individual accession, individual registration
个别登记号/個別登記號　individual accession number
个别督导/個別督導　individual supervision
个别化/個體化　individuation
个别化取向/個案取向　idiographic individual-oriented approach
个别计价法/個別認定法　specific identification
个别劳动时间/個體勞動時間　individual labor-time
个别劳动争议/個別勞動爭議　individual labor dispute
个别内差/個體內差異　intraindividual difference
个别元素/個別元素　specific metadata
个人保险/個人保險，私人保險　private insurance
个人成长/個體成長　individual growth
个人持股公司/私有股權公司　personal holding company
个人担保贷款/個人擔保貸款　loan on personal

guarantee
个人的具体变量/個人專屬變項　individual specific variable
个人抵押贷款/個人抵押貸款　loan on personal security
个人电视收视率/個人電視收視率　individual-using-television rating
个人对个人/消費者對消費者　consumer to consumer, C2C
个人广播收听率/個人廣播收聽率　individual-using-radio rating
个人广告/個人廣告　personal advertising
个人价值/個人價值　personal value
个人建构理论/個人建構理論　personal construct theory
个人决策/個人決策　personal decision making, individual decision making
个人可支配的实际收入/實際個人可支配所得　real personal disposable income
个人可支配收入/個人可支配所得　personal disposable income
个人宽放/私事寬放　personal allowance
个人来文审查机制/個人來文審查機制　a legal institution of human rights relief under the International Human Rights Law
个人老化/個人老化　individual aging
个人理性约束/個別理性限制,個人理性限制式　individual rationality constraint, individual-rationality constraint
个人利益服从整体利益/個人利益服從整體利益　subordination of individual interest to the general interest
个人努力均衡理论/個人努力均衡理論　balance theory of individual effort
个人偏好/個人偏好　personal preference
个人剖析/個人剖析　individual profiling
个人契约/個人契約　personal contract
个人认同/個人認同,個人身份　personal identity
个人收入/個人所得　personal income
个人收益原则/個體性原則　principle of individuality
个人书信文件/書信　personal letter
个人数字图书馆/個人數位圖書館　personal digital library
个人所得税/個人所得稅　individual income tax, personal income tax
个人投资/個人投資　personal investment
个人退休账户/個人退休[金]賬户　individual recruitment account, IRA

个人网/個人網　personal network
个人文件/個人文件　personal papers
个人信贷/個人信用　personal credit
个人信贷机构/個人信貸機構　personal credit institution
个人信贷市场/個人信貸市場　personal credit market
个人信息源/個人資訊來源　personal information source
个人选择/個人選擇　individual choice
个人营销/人物行銷　person marketing
个人知识/個人知識　personal knowledge
个人知识管理/個人知識管理　personal knowledge management
个人职责/個人責任　personal responsibility
个人主义/個人主義　individualism
个人著者/個人著者　personal author
个人著作/個人著作　personal authorship
个人著作目录/個人著作目錄　personal bibliography, individual bibliography
个体差异/個別差異　individual difference
个体工商户/個體户　self-employment people
个体化的不平等/個體化的不平等　individualized inequality, inequality individualization
个体经济/個體經濟　individual economy
个体理性/個人理性　individual rationality
个体论谬误/個體論謬誤　individualistic fallacy
个体偏好/個人偏愛　individual preference
个体生长/個體成長　individual growth
个体书店/個體書店　individual bookstore
个体性/個體性　individuality
个体学习/個體學習　individual learning
个体营销/個人行銷　individual marketing
个体知识/個人知識　personal knowledge
个体宗教性/個體宗教性　individual religiosity
个性测验/人格測驗　personality test
个性层次模型/個性層次模型,性格階層模型　personality hierarchical model
个性工作匹配理论/個性工作適配理論,性格工作適配理論,人格工作適配理論　personality-job fit theory
个性化策略/個性化戰略　personalization tactics
个性化服务/個性化服務,個人化服務,客製化服務　individualized service, personalized service
个性化检索/個性化檢索　personalized information retrieval
个性化图书馆/個性化圖書館　MyLibrary
个性化推荐/個性化推薦　personalized

recommendation
个性化消费/個性化消費　individual consumption
12个月移动平均/十二個月移動平均　moving average by 12 months
各取所需/各取所需　to each according to his needs
各向同性/各向同性,等向性,均向性　isotropy
各向同性分布/各向同性分布,均向同性分布　isotropic distribution
给定价格/計算期價格　given price
根本法/基本法　basic law
根本违约/根本違約　fundamental breach of contract
根本性创新/根本性創新　fundamental innovation
根本性逆差/根本性逆差　fundamental deficit
根本原因分析/根本原因分析　root cause analysis
根查/追尋　tracing
根据提单而产生的债权/根據提單條款索賠　claim based on bill of lading
跟单承兑/跟單承兌　documentary acceptance
跟单承兑汇票/跟單承兌匯票,押匯承兌匯票　documentary acceptance bill
跟单承兑信用证/跟單承兌信用狀　documentary acceptance letter of credit
跟单发票/跟單商業發票　invoice with document attached
跟单光票/跟單光票,無跟單匯票　documentary clean bill
跟单汇兑/跟單匯兌　documentary remittance
跟单汇票/跟單匯票　documentary bill of exchange
跟单期票/跟單期票,跟單本票　documentary promissory note
跟单托收/跟單託收　documentary collection
跟单信用证/跟單信用狀　documentary letter of credit
跟进/跟催　follow-up
跟进者/跟進者　second mover
跟随战略/跟隨戰略　following strategy
跟踪摄影/追蹤攝影,跟鏡　follow shot
更换保险/更換保險　replacement insurance
更替水平/替代水準,遞補水準　replacement level
更替水平生育率/遞補水準生育率　replacement level fertility
更替型合同模式/更替型合同模式　novation contract model
更新/更新　renewal
更新定理/更新定理　renewal theorem
更新方程/更新方程式　renewal equation
更新分布/更新分布　renewal distribution
更新过程/更新過程,再生過程　renewal process

更新函数/更新函數　renewal function
更新价格/重置價格　replacement price
更新价值/重置價值　replacement value
更新理论/更新理論　renewal theory
更新随机变量/更新隨機變數　renewal random variable
更新投资/更新投資　replacement investment
更正广告/更正廣告　corrective advertising
耕地保护/耕地保護　farmland protection
耕地非农化/農地變更　farmland conversion
耕地占用税/耕地占用稅　farmland occupancy tax
更好新产品战略/更好新產品戰略　better widget strategy
工厂法/工廠法案　factory acts
工厂管理委员会/工廠管理委員會　factory management committee
工厂委员会/工廠委員會　factory commission
工厂直销店/暢貨中心　factory outlet
工程/工程　engineering
211工程/211工程　Project 211
985工程/985工程　Project 985
工程保险费/工程保險費　engineering project insurance
工程变更/工程變更　engineering change
工程承包费/工程承包費用　engineering contract fee
工程单价/工程單價　engineering unit price
工程范围变更索赔/工程範圍變更索賠　scope variation claim
工程服务/工程服務　engineering service
工程更新与改造/工程更新與改造　engineering renewal and transformation
工程管理/工程管理　engineering management
工程基础定额/工程基礎定額　basic quota of engineering
工程计量/工程量測　engineering measure
工程技术/工程技術　engineering technology
工程价款结算/工程款結算　construction cost settlement
工程价款收入/工程款收入　engineering income
工程监理/工程監理　engineering surveillance
工程决策/工程決策　engineering decision
工程科学/工程科學　engineering science
工程例会/工程例會　engineering regular meeting
工程量列表/工程量清單　bill of engineering quantity
工程量列表计价/工程量清單計價　engineering quantity list valuation
工程评估/工程評估　engineering evaluation
工程设计/工程設計　engineering design

工程统计/工程統計　engineering statistics
工程拖期索赔/工程延誤索賠　delay claim
工程项目分类法/工程項目分類法　engineering project classification
工程项目管理模式/專案管理方式　project management mode
工程修复管理/工程修復管理　engineering repairing management
工程研究中心/工程研究中心　engineering research center
工程预算/工程預算　construction budget
工程预算定额/工程預算定額　budget quota of engineering
工程再造/再造工程,組織再造　reengineering
工程再造小组/工程再造小組　reengineering team
工程再造指挥/工程再造指揮　reengineering czar
工程造价/工程費　engineering cost
工程造价数据/工程造價資料　reference material of construction cost
工程造价指数/造價指數,施工費用指數　index of construction cost
工程哲学/工程哲學　philosophy of engineering
工会/工會　labor union
工会法/工會法　trade union law
工会会员/工會會員　union membership
工会经费/工會經費　trade union funds
工会垄断模型/獨占工會模型　monopoly-union model
工会图书馆/工會圖書館　trade union library
工会运动/工會運動　trade union movement, union movement
工会组织/工會組織　union organization, network of alliances
工会组织者/工會組織者　union organizer
工件/工件　job
工件顺序/分批工作通知單　job order
工件特征/工件特徵　job characteristic
工匠/工匠　artisan
工具变量/工具變數　instrument variable
工具变量估计/工具變數估計法　instrumental variable estimation
工具变量估计法/工具變數法　instrumental variable method
工具变量估计量/工具變數估計式　instrumental variable estimator
工具变量模型/工具變數模型　instrumental variable model
工具理性/工具理性　instrumental rationality

工具论/工具論　instrumentalist
工具书/參考書　reference book
工具书架/參考書架　reference book shelf
工具书台/參考書檯　reference book stand
工具书特藏/工具書特藏　reference collection
工具性/工具性　instrumentality
工具性角色/工具角色　instrumental role
工料合同/工料合同　labor and material contract
工龄工资制/年資敘薪制,年功薪資制　seniority wage system
工票/工作命令　work order
工期/工期　project duration
工期定额/工期定額　duration quota
工期固定-资源均衡/工期固定-資源平準　resource leveling with fixed completion time
工期索赔/工期索賠　construction period claim
工期优化/工期優化　optimization of time
工人/工人　worker
工人代表/員工代表　worker's representation
工人技术能力评估/工人技術評估　assessments of worker technical competence
工人教育协会/勞工教育協會　workers' educational association
工人阶级/工人階級,勞工階級　working class
工人考核条例/工人評估條例　ordinances of worker assessment
工人自治/員工自治　workers' autonomy
工伤/工傷　work-related injury
工伤保险/工傷保險,職業傷害保險　work-related injury insurance, insurance against injury, employment injury insurance
工伤认定/工傷認定　ascertainment of work-related injuries
工商登记管理档案/工商登記管理檔案　file administration of business registration
工商行政管理/工商管理　industrial and commercial administration
工时/工時,人工小時　man-hour, labor hour
工时测定/工時評估　work time evaluation
工时利用率/工時利用率　utilization rate of work-hour
工时清单/工時清單　bill of labor
工时研究/工時研究　work time research
工时与动作研究/時動研究,時間與動作研究　time and motion study
工效学/人體工學,人因工程學　ergonomics
工薪阶层/工資勞動者,薪勞　wage earner
工序/工序　operation

工序分类法/工序分類法　working procedure classification
工序检验/工序檢驗　procedure detection
工序组合法/工序組合法　working procedure combination method
工业/工業　industry
工业保护论/工業保護說　industry protection argument
工业产品/工業品　industrial product
工业产品价格/工業產品價格　price of industrial product
工业产权/工業產權　industrial property right
工业城市/工業都市　industrial city
工业谍报/產業間諜　industrial espionage
工业动力学/產業動力學　industrial dynamics
工业动力学六步骤/工業動力學六步驟　six steps of industrial dynamics
工业法庭/勞工法庭　industrial court
工业革命/工業革命,產業革命　industrial revolution
工业革命前/工業革命以前　pre-industrial
工业关系/勞資和諧　industrial relations
工业化/工業化　industrialization
工业品出口/工業品出口　industrial export
工业普查/工業普查　industrial census
工业起飞/工業起飛　industrial take-off
工业区位/產業區位　industrial location
工业区位论/產業區位理論　industrial location theory
工业设计/工業設計　industrial design
工业设施管理/工業設施管理　industrial facility management
工业社会/工業社會　industrial society
工业社会工作/工業社會工作　industrial social work
工业生产指数/工業生產指數　industrial production index
工业统计/工業統計　industrial statistics
工业用地/工業土地使用　industrial land use
工业用户广告/產業廣告　industrial advertising
工业增长/工業成長　industrial growth
工业自由贸易区/工業自由貿易區　industrial free trade area
工业综合经济效益指数/工業綜合經濟實效指標　industry composite economic performance index
工艺创新/製程創新　process innovation
工艺计量学/工藝計量學　technometry
工艺流程分析/工藝流程分析　operating process analysis
工艺流程图/作業流程圖　operation process chart
工艺流分析/流程分析,製程流分析　process flow analysis
工艺路线/工藝路線　routing, bill of operation
工艺路线柔性/途程彈性　routing flexibility
工艺专业化原则/工藝專門化原則　process focused
工资/工資,薪酬,薪資　salary, wage
工资差别/工資差異　wage differentials
工资差距/工資幅度　wage range spread
工资带/工資帶　wage band
工资单/工資額　wage bill
工资单位/工資單位　wage unit
工资等级/工資標準　wage scale
工资等级重叠率/工資幅度重疊　wage range overlap
工资分级制度/工資分級制度　wage-rate system
工资分析/工資分析　payroll analysis, wage analysis
工资刚性/工資剛性　wage rigidity
工资管理系统/工資管理系統　payroll system
工资核算/工資記賬,薪金計算　wage accounting
工资混合制/混合式薪資制　pay mix system
工资基金/工資基金　payroll fund, wage fund
工资基金理论/工資基金論　wage fund theory
工资基金说/工資基金說　wage fund doctrine
工资-价格螺旋/工資-物價螺旋　wage-price spirals
工资-价格螺旋上升/工資物價螺旋膨脹　wage-price spiral inflation
工资结构/工資結構,薪資結構　salary structure, wage structure
工资结构调查/工資結構調查　wage structure survey
工资结算/工資結算　pay card
工资决定/工資決定　wage determination
工资控制/工資控制　wage control
工资率/工資率　wage rate
工资率差异/工資率差異　wage rate variance
工资膨胀率/工資通貨膨脹　wage inflation
工资品/工資品　wage good
工资歧视/工資歧視　wage discrimination
工资曲线/工資曲線　wage curve
工资审计/工資審計　wage audit
工资收入/工資所得　wage income
工资所得税/薪資稅　payroll tax
工资谈判能力理论/工資議價學說　bargain theory of wages
工资弹性/工資彈性　wage flexibility
工资铁律/工資鐵律　iron law of wages
工资统计/工資統計　wage statistics
工资推进通货膨胀/工資推動性膨脹　wage-push inflation

工资形式/工资形式　payroll form, wage form
工资压缩/薪資壓縮　pay compression
工资政策/工资政策　wage policy
工资政策线/工資政策線　pay policy line
工资支票/薪資支票　pay cheque
工资指标/工資標竿　wage guidepost
工资指数/工資指數　wage index
工资指数化/工資指數化,薪資指數比　wage indexation
工资制度/工资制度　wage system
工资租金比率/工資租金比率　wage-rental ratio
工作/工作　work
工作安排/工作安排　work arrangement
工作班组/工作群體　work group
工作包/工作包　work package
工作不安全感/工作無保障　job insecurity
工作场所创伤/職場創傷　workplace trauma
工作场所性骚扰/工作場所性騷擾　sexual harassment in working place
工作场所学习/工作場所學習　workplace learning
工作沉迷/沈迷於工作　immersion in business
工作持续时间/持續時間　duration
工作抽样/工作抽樣　work sampling, activity sampling
工作的时间成本/工作的時間成本　time costs of working
工作地/工作站,工作中心　work center
工作定义/工作定義　activity definition
工作分工/工作分工　work division
工作分解结构/工作細分結構　work breakdown structure, WBS
工作分解结构报告/工作分解結構報告　work breakdown structure report
工作分解结构编码/工作細分結構代碼　work breakdown structure code
工作分解结构层次结构/工作細分結構層次結構　work breakdown structure level
工作分享/工作分擔　job sharing
工作分享制/員工參與工作制　work sharing system
工作丰富化/工作豐富化　job enrichment
工作负荷/工作負荷　workload
工作概率单位/作業機率單位　working probit
工作岗位/工作崗位　working post
工作规范/工作規範　job specification
工作环境/工作環境　environment for working, working environment
工作计划/工作計劃　job plan
工作记忆广度/工作記憶廣度　working memory span
工作技能测验/工作技能測驗　job skill test
工作绩效/工作績效　work performance
工作-家庭平衡/職-家平衡　work-family balance
工作假设/作業假設　working hypothesis
工作简单化/工作簡單化　job simplification
工作进度表/工作時序　work schedule
工作救助计划/以工代賑計劃　welfare to work, work relief program
工作卷入/工作投入　job involvement
工作扩大化/工作擴大化　job enlargement
工作理事会/工作理事會　job council
工作量法/工作時數折舊法　depreciation working hours method
工作伦理/工作倫理　work ethics
工作轮换/工作輪調　job rotation
工作满意度/工作滿意度,工作滿足　job satisfaction
工作满意度调查/工作滿意度問卷　job satisfaction survey
工作评价/工作評鑒　job evaluation
工作评价计划/工作評鑒制　job evaluation plans
工作强化/工作加強　job intensification
工作清单/工作清單　activity list
工作权利法/工作權法　right-to-work laws
工作任期/工作年資,在職期間　job tenure
工作任职要求/工作技能清單　job specification
工作生活平衡计划/工作生活平衡計劃　work life balance plan
工作时间/工作時間,工作時數,工時　working hours, hours of work
工作士气/工作士氣　job morale
工作说明书/工作敘述　statement of work
工作态度/工作態度　job attitude
工作特征模型/工作特性模型　job characteristics model
工作条件/工作條件　working condition
工作条件和工资标准化/工作條件和工資標準化　work condition and wage standardization
工作团队/工作團隊　work team
工作文件/工作檔　working papers
工作效率/工作效率　work efficiency
工作压力/工作壓力　work stress
工作样本测验/工作樣本測驗　work sample test
工作要素法/工作要素法　working factor, WF
工作责任制/工作責任制　job responsibility system
工作知觉/工作知覺　job perception
工作指导培训/工作指導培訓　job instruction training

工作质量/工作品質　work quality
工作专业化/工作專門化　work specialization
公报/公報,官報　communique
公比问题/共同比率問題　common ratio problem
公差范围/容許全距　tolerance range
公差分析/允差分析　analysis of tolerance
公牍纸/公牘紙　public document paper
公法/公法　public law
公法财团/公法財團　Stiftungen des oeffentlichen Rechts
公法人/公法人　legal person of public law
公法社团/公法社團　koerperschaft oeffentlichen Rechts
公费医疗/健保　socialized medicine, reimbursed medical service
公费医疗制度/健保計劃　public medical care
公告/公告　proclamation, announcement
公告送达/公告送達　service by publication
公共/公共　public
公共安全事件/公共安全事件　public safety incident
公共部门/公部門　public sector
公共部门战略管理/公部門策略管理　strategic management in public sector
公共部门战略规划/公部門策略規劃　strategic planning in public sector
公共部门资源管理/公部門資源管理　resource management in public sector
公共财政/公共財政　public finance
公共仓库/公共倉庫　public warehouse
公共产品/公共財　public goods
公共传播/公共傳播　public communication
公共档案/公共檔案　public archive
公共档案馆/公共檔案館　public archives
公共对象请求代理体系结构规范/公共物件請求代理體系結構規範　common object request broker architecture criterion, CORBA
公共方差/共同變異數　common variance
公共风险管理/公共風險管理　public risk management
公共服务/公共服務　public service
公共服务定价/公部門定價法　public sector pricing
公共工程/公共工程　public work
公共供给/公家提供　public provision
公共关系/公共關係　public relationship, public relation
公共关系从业人员/公關業務人員　public relations practitioner
公共关系广告/公關廣告　public relations advertising
公共关系计划/公關計劃　public relations plan
公共关系战略/公關策略　public relation strategy
公共管理/公共管理　public management
公共管理过程/公共管理過程　public management process
公共管理环境/公共管理環境　public management environment
公共管理客体/公共管理客體　objects of public management
公共管理模式/公共管理範式　public management model
公共管理职能/公共管理職能　public management function
公共管理主体/公共管理主體　subjects of public management
公共管制/公共管制　public regulation
公共广播电视台/公共電視臺　public broadcasting service
公共机构市场/機構市場　institutional market
公共教育/公眾教育　public education
公共接入点/公用接入點　public access points
公共借阅权/公共出借權　public lending right, PLR
公共近用广播/公共近用廣播　public access broadcasting
公共距离/公眾距離　public distance
公共决策/公共決策　public decisions
公共科技管理/公共科技管理　public science and technology management
公共科研机构/公共科研機構　public scientific research institute
公共空间/公用空間　public space
公共利益/公共利益,公眾利益,公益　public interest
公共利益理论/公共利益理論　public interest theory
公共领域/公共領域　public sphere, public arena
公共伦理/公共倫理　public ethics
公共论坛/公共論壇　public forum
公共媒体/公共媒體　public media
公共品博弈/公共財賽局　public goods game
公共品实验/公共財實驗　public goods experiments
公共契约/公共契約　public contract
公共区域/公共區域　public area
公共权利/公共權利　public rights
公共设施/公共設施　public facility, public utilities
公共社会服务机构/公共社會服務機構　public social service agency
公共生产/公家生產　public production
公共市场/公共市場　public market
公共事务/公共事務　public affairs

公共收入/公共收入　public revenue
公共私营合作制/公私夥伴關係　public private partnership, PPP
公共投资/公共投資　public investment
公共投资部门/公共投資部門　public investment sector
公共投资支出/公共投資支出　public investment expenditure
公共图书馆/公共圖書館　public library
公共图书馆法案/公共圖書館法案　public libraries act
公共图书馆服务体系/公共圖書館服務體系　public library service system
公共图书馆宣言/公共圖書館宣言　Public Library Manifesto
公共危机/公共危機　public crisis
公共危机管理/公共危機管理　public crisis management
公共卫生事件/突發公共衛生事件　public health emergency
公共卫生统计/公共衛生統計　public health statistics
公共文件/公共檔　public records, public archive
公共消费/公共消費　public consumption
公共消费品/公共消費財　public consumption goods
公共新闻学/公共新聞學　citizen journalism
公共信贷/公共信貸　public credit
公共信托/公共信託　public trust
公共信息/公共資訊　common information, public information
公共信息资源/公共資訊資源　public information resources
公共信息资源管理/公共資訊資源管理　public information resources management
公共行政/公共行政　public administration
公共需求/大眾需求　public demand
公共选择/公共選擇　public choice
公共选择理论/公共選擇理論　public choice theory
公共选择学派/公共選擇學派　public choice school
公共域信息/公用域資訊，公用域消息　public domain information
公共政策/公共政策　public policy
公共政策途径/公共政策途徑　public policy approach
公共政策问题/公共政策問題　public policy issue
公共支出/公共支出　public expenditures
公共知识/大眾知識　public knowledge
公共秩序/公共秩序　public order

公共秩序保留/公共秩序保留　reservation of public order legal system
公共住房/公共住宅　public housing
公共资金/公共基金　public fund
公共资源/共同資源　common resource
公共组织/公共組織　public organization
公关活动/公關活動　public relations activity
公关喂新闻/公關餵新聞　news feeds
公海/公海　the high seas
公海自由/公海自由　the legal principle of freedom of the high seas
公害/公害　public nuisance
公害法/公害法　the law of anti-pollution
公害事件/公害事件　pollution event
公积金/公積金　provident fund
公鉴/公鑒　gongjian
公开定价/公開定價　open pricing
公开发行/公開發行，公共發行　public release, public offering
公开个别许可证/無限制個別許可　open individual license
公开喊价/公開喊價競價　open-outcry auction
公开价格/公開價格　open price
公开审判/公開審判　open trial
公开市场/公開市場　market overt
公开市场操作/公開市場操作　open market operation
公开市场回购/公開市場買回　open-market purchase
公开市场交易/公開市場操作　open market operation
公开市场业务/公開市場操作　open market operation
公开投标/公開投標，競標　public tender, open tender, competitive bid
公开文件/公文書　public document
公开销售制度/公開銷售制度　open selling system
公开效应/宣示效果　announcement effect
公开性专有信息/公開專有資料　open proprietary information
公开许可证制度/無限制許可制度　open license system
公开一般许可证/無限制一般許可　open general license
公开招标/公開招標　open tenderring, public bidding
公立学校/公立學校　public school
公民/公民　citizen
公民参与/公民參與　citizen participation, public

participation
公民登记册/户籍名册　civil registers
公民基本义务/公民基本義務　basic obligations of citizens
公民记者/公民記者　citizen journalist, citizen reporter
公民精神/公民精神　civism
公民利益群体/公民利益團體　citizen interest groups
公民权/公民權　civil right
公民社会/公民社會,市民社會　civil society
公民社会指数/公民社會指數　civil society index
公募/公募　public placement
公募基金/公募基金　public placement fund
公募基金会/公募基金會　public foundation, public raising foundation
公平/公平　equity, justice
公平博弈/公平賭局,公平賽局　fair game
公平工资目标/公平工資目標　equity pay objective
公平获取/公平獲取　equitable access
公平价格/合理的價格　just price
公平交易法/公平交易法　fair trade law
公平交易惯例/公平交易慣例　fair trade practice
公平交易价格/公平交易價格　fair trade price
公平就业/公平就業　fair employment
公平就业机会/公平就業機會　equal employment opportunity
公平就业机会法/平等就業法　equal employment opportunity act
公平理论/公平理論　equity theory
公平贸易/公平貿易　fair trade
公平贸易理论/公平貿易理論　theory of just trade
公平租金/公平租金　fair rent
公仆型领导/僕人領導　servant leadership
公权/公權　public right
公权法律关系/公權法律關係　legal relation of public right
公权力/公權力　public power
公然犯/公然犯　ovent crime
公认的国际惯例/公認的國際慣例　established international practice
公社性/共同性　communality
公示催告/公示催告　public disclosure dunning
公示催告程序/公示催告程式　procedure of public disclosure dunning
公司/公司　company, corporation
公司标准/公司標準　company standard
公司财务/公司理财　corporate finance
公司财务会计报告/公司財務會計報告　financial accounting report of the company
公司层的合作战略/公司級戰略聯盟　corporate-level cooperative strategy
公司层战略/總體策略　corporate-level strategy
公司重组/公司重組,公司重整　corporate reconstruction
公司创业/公司創業　corporate entrepreneurship
公司法/公司法　company law, act of company, law of company
公司法人格否认/公司法人格否認　disregard of corporate personality
公司分立/公司分立　division of company
公司风险投资/企業風險投資　corporate venture capital
公司广告/企業廣告　corporate advertising
公司规模/廠商規模　firm size
公司合并/公司合并,廠商合并　company merger, corporate merger, firm merger
公司解散/公司解散　dissolution of company
公司刊/公司刊　company magazine
公司控制权市场/公司控制權市場　market for corporate control
公司名称/行號名稱　name of company
公司内部汇票/公司內部匯票　house bill
公司清算/公司清算　liquidation of company
公司情报/公司情報　corporate intelligence
公司设立/公司設立　establishment of company
公司式垂直营销系统/公司式垂直行銷通路系統　corporate vertical marketing system, corporate VMS
公司所在地/公司所在地　the location of company
公司网站/企業網站　corporate website
公司行为/公司行為　corporate behavior
公司型投资基金/公司型投資基金　corporate type investment fund
公司债券/公司債　debenture, corporate bond
公司债券溢价/公司債券溢價　premium on corporate bond
公司章程/公司章程　articles of company
公司治理/公司治理,公司統理　corporate governance
公司治理结构/公司治理結構　corporate governance structure
公诉/公訴　public prosecution
公诉案件/公訴案件　public prosecution case
公诉程序/公訴程式　procedure of indictment
公诉权/公訴權　right of public prosecution
公诉人/公訴人　public prosecutor

公诉书/公訴書　bill of indictment
公网传版/公網傳版　internet transmission of layout
公文/公文　official document
公文版记/公文版記　note version of official doucments
公文版头/公文版頭　the first edition of official doucments
公文标题/公文標題　title of official doucments
公文表达方式/公文表達方式　expression way of official doucments
公文表达要素/公文表達要素　expression elements of official documents
公文材料/公文材料　material of official documents
公文处理程序/公文處理常式　processing program of official document
公文处理流程再造/公文處理流程再造　document processing process reengineering
公文袋/公文袋　document envelope
公文份号/公文份號　copy number of official doucments
公文稿本/公文稿本　official script
公文格式/公文格式　format of official documents
公文管理/公文管理　document management
公文结构/公文結構　structure of official documents
公文筐测验/公文籃測驗　in-basket test
公文文体/公文文體　literary style of official doucment
公文写作/公文寫作　the writing of official documents
公文修辞/公文修辭　rhetoric of official documents
公文正文/公文正文　the text of official documents
公文纸/公文紙　paper of public documents reused for printing
公文主题/公文主題　subject of official documents
公文主体/公文主體　main body of official doucments
公文专用词语/公文專用詞語　special words of official documents
公务案卷/公務檔　office files
公务卡/公務卡　civil service card
公务联系作用/公務聯繫作用　the fuction of official business contact
公务目录/公務目錄　staff catalog, official catalogue
公务员/公務員,文官　civil servant
公务员辞退/公務員解雇　civil servant expulsion
公务员辞职/公務員辭職　civil servant resignation
公务员法/公務員法　civil servant act
公务员岗位津贴/公務員補助,公務員補貼　stipend for civil servant

公务员回避/公務員迴避　avoidance of civil servant
公务员回避制度/公務員迴避制度　system of avoiding conflict of interest
公务员考核/公務人員考績　assessment of civil servant
公务员考核制度/公務員評估系統　civil servant evaluation system
公务员控告/公務員控告　civil servant accusation
公务员录用/公務員録用　civil servant recruitment
公务员免职/公務員免職,公務員撤職　civil servant dismissal
公务员培训/公務員訓練　civil servant training
公务员任职/公務員任用　civil servant appointment
公务员申诉/公務員申訴,公務員上訴　civil servant appeal
公务员退休制度/公務員退休制度　retirement system of civil servant
公务员行为规范/公務員行爲規範　code of conduct of civil servant
公务员职位轮换/公務員輪崗制度　shift posts of civil servant
公务员制度/公務員制度　civil servant system
公物/公物　public property
公序良俗/公序良俗　public order and good custom
公序良俗原则/公序良俗原則　the principle of public order and good social customs
公益产权/公有產權　public property right
公益创投/公益創投　venture philanthropy
公益服务/公益性服務　public welfare service
公益腐败/公益腐敗　corruption in charitable sector
公益广告/公益廣告,公共服務宣導,宣導廣告　public service advertising, public service announcement, social advertising
公益基金/公益基金　non-profit fund
公益捐赠/公益捐贈　charity donation
公益信托/公益信託　charitable trust
公益营销/公益行銷　non-profit marketing
公益组织/公益組織　public interest organization, commonwealth organization
公意/總意志,普遍意志　general will
公因子/公因子　common factor
公因子方差/公因子變異數　common factor variance, communality
公因子分析法/共因數分析　common factor analysis
公因子空间/公因子空間　common factor space
公营公司/公營公司　public corporation
公营造物/公營造物　anstalten a legal institution, establishment in public law

公用企业/公用企業　public unility
公用事业/公用事業　public utility
公用事业基金/公用事業基金　utility fund
公用事业融资/公用事業融資　public utility finance
公用事业债券/公用事業債券　utility bond
公有产权/公共財產權　common property rights
公有领域/公有領域　public domain
公有制/公共所有權　public ownership
公有制经济/公經濟　public economy
公有制形式/公有制形式　form of public ownership
公钥/公開金鑰　public key
公允价值/公允價值,公平價值　fair value
公允价值变动损益/公允價值變動損益　gains or losses from change in fair value
公债管理/債務管理　debt management
公债回收/公債贖回　retirement of public debt
公债基金/公債基金,債券基金　bond fund
公章/公章　official seal
公正世界信念/公正世界信念,公平世界信念　belief in a just world
公证档案/公證檔案　notarial archives
公制纸张规格/公制紙張規格　metric paper size
公众/公眾　public
公众参与/公眾參與　public participation, civic participation
公众传播/公眾傳播　public communication
公众股/公眾股　public share
功绩晋升制/根據成績提級　merit promotion system
功绩制/功績制　merit system
功利主义/功利主義　utilitarianism
功利主义社会福利函数/功利社會福利函數　utilitarian social welfare function
功率谱/功率譜,冪次譜相　power spectrum
功率曲线/檢力曲線　power curve
功能/功能　function
功能不良冲突/反功能性衝突,破壞性衝突　dysfunctional conflict
功能财政/職能財政　functional finance
功能测试/外功能測試　function testing
功能词/功能詞　function word
功能定义/功能定義　function definition
功能分类/功能分類　function categorizing
功能分析系统技术/功能分析系統技術　function analysis system technology, FAST
功能观/功能觀　functional perspective
功能互换/功能的替換性　functional interchangablility
功能计量/功能計量　function measurement
功能价值/功能價值　functional value

功能阶段/功能階段　function phase
功能评价/功能評價　function evaluation
功能性/官能性　functionality
功能性冲突/功能性衝突　functional conflict
功能性收入分配/功能性所得分配,收入的功能分配　function distribution of income, functional distribution of income
功能性元数据/功能性詮釋資料　functional metadata
功能折扣/功能折扣　functional discount
功能整理/功能整理　function reorganization
功能主义/功能論　functionalism
功能主义分层理论/功能主義分層理論　functional theory of stratification
功能组织/功能組織　functional organization
功效函数/檢力函數　power function
功效曲线/檢力曲線　power curve
功效效率/檢力有效性　power efficiency
攻击/攻擊,侵犯　aggression
供带盘/供帶盤　pop-up box
供方/供應商,賣主　vendor, supplier
供货商参与创新/供應商參與創新　supplier involvement in technological innovation
供货商发票/供應商發票　supplier invoice
供货商关系/供應商關係　supplier partnership
供货商管理/供應商管理　supplier management
供货商管理库存/供應商管理庫存　vendor-managed inventory
供货商绩效评价/供應商績效評估　supplier performance review
供货商融资/賣方融資　vendor financing
供货商搜索/供應商搜索　supplier search
供货商选择/供應商選擇　supplier selection
供货商选择和评价/供應商選擇和評估　supplier selection and evaluation
供货商议价能力/供應商的議價能力　bargaining power of supplier
供给/供給　supply
供给变动/供給變動　change in supply, supply change
供给表/供給表　supply schedule
供给法则/供給法則　law of supply
供给方/供給面　supply side
供给函数/供給函數　supply function
供给价格/供給價格　supply price
供给价格弹性/供給的價格彈性　price elasticity of supply
供给理论/供給理論　theory of supply

供给量变动/供給量的變動 changes in the quantity supplied
供给曲线/供給曲線 supply curve
供给弹性/供給彈性 elasticity of supply
供给学派经济学/供給經濟學 supply-side economics
供款计划/相對提撥制 contributory plan
供求机制/供求機制 mechanism of supply and demand
供求均衡/供需均衡 supply-demand equilibrium
供选方案/替選方案,備[選方]案 alternative
供应管理/供應管理 supply management
供应链/供應鏈 supply chain
供应链风险管理/供應鏈風險管理 supply chain risk management
供应链管理/供應鏈管理 supply chain management
供应链管理系统/供應鏈管理系統 supply chain management system
供应链契约/供應鏈契約 supply chain contract
供应链协调/供應鏈協調 supply chain coordination
供应链整合/供應鏈整合 integration of the supply chain
供应商/供應商,供應者 supplier
供应商关系管理/供應商關係管理 supplier relationship management
供应商检验/供應商檢驗 vendor inspection
供应商控制/供給者控制 supplier control
供应商信贷/供應商信貸 supplier's credit
供应商质量/供應商品質 vendor quality
供应条件曲线/提供曲線 offer curves
供用电、水、气、热力合同/供用電、水、氣、熱力合同 contracts for electricity, water, gas and power supply
宫廷化/宮廷化 courtization
龚柏兹法则/Gompertz 法則 Gompertz's law
龚柏兹曲线/Gompertz 曲線 Gompertz curve
共出链/共出鏈 co-linking
共出链强度/共出鏈強度 co-linking strength
共词分析/共字分析 co-word analysis
共词强度/共字強度 co-word strength
共等级/同序排列 cograduation
共轭标准方/共軛標準方格 conjugate standard square
共轭分级/共軛分級 conjugate ranking
共轭过程/共軛過程 conjugate process
共轭拉丁方/共軛拉丁方格 conjugate Latin squares
共轭梯度算法/共軛斜度演算法 conjugate gradient algorithm
共轭先验分布/共軛事前分布,共軛事前分配 conjugate prior distribution
共轭转置/共軛轉換 conjugate transpose
共轭族/共軛族 conjugate family
共犯从属性/共犯從屬性 the theory of subordinateness of accomplices
共犯独立性/共犯獨立性 the theory of independence of accomplices
共决/共同决定 codetermination
共链分析/共鏈分析 co-link analysis
共谋/共謀,勾結 conspiracy, collusion
共入链/共入鏈 co-linked
共入链强度/共入鏈強度 co-linked strength
共生/共生 symbiosis
共时/共時,同步 synchronic
共识/共識 consensus
共同保险/共同保險,共保,互助保险 co-insurance, participating insurance
共同辩护/共同辯護 joint defense
共同财产/共同財產 common property
共同财产资源/公共財產資源 common property resources
共同成本/共同成本 common costs
共同承保人/共同承保人 co-assurer
共同承兑人/共同承兑人 joint acceptor, co-acceptor
共同出资/聯合出資 joint contribution
共同代理/共同代理 joint agency
共同贷款/聯貸 participating loan
共同担保人/共同擔保人 co-guarantor
共同但有区别的责任/共同但有區別的責任 common but differentiated responsibilities
共同抵押/共同抵押,聯合抵押 joint mortgage
共同对外关税/共同對外關稅,非會員關稅 common external tariff
共同发明/共同發明 joint invention
共同犯罪/共同犯罪 fellowship in crime
共同方法变异偏差/共同方法變異 common method variance
共同付费/部份負擔金額 copayment
共同共有/共同共有 joint ownership
共同关税/共同關稅 common customs tariff, common tariff
共同过错/共同過錯 joint fault
共同过失/造成意外的疏忽 contributory negligence
共同海损/共同海損 general average
共同海损保证金/共同海損保證金 average deposit
共同海损担保/共同海損擔保 general average guarantee

共同海损理算/共同海損理算　general average adjustment
共同海损理算书/共同海損理算書　statement of general average
共同海损清算/共同海損清算　general average settlement
共同海损索赔/共同海損索賠　claim for general average
共同海损条款/共同海損條款　general average clause
共同海损准据法/共同海損準據法　Applicable Law of General Average
共同合同/共同合約　joint contract
共同基金/共同基金,互助基金　mutual fund
共同结果效应/共同結果效應　common consequence effect
共同决策制/勞資共同決定　codetermination system
共同决定/共同決定　codetermination
共同目标/共同目標　common purpose
共同农业政策/共同農業政策　common agriculture policy
共同配额/共同配額　common quota
共同侵权行为/共同侵權行爲　joint act of tort
共同市场/共同市場　common market
共同诉讼/共同訴訟　co-litigation
共同诉讼人/共同訴訟人　co-litigant
共同随机趋势/共同隨機趨勢　common stochastic trend
共同所有权/共同所有權　ownership in common
共同题名/共同題名　common title
共同体/共同體　gemeinschaft
共同体与社会/共同體與社會　gemeinschaft and gesellschaft
共同条令/共同條令　common mandatory regulations
共同投资基金/共同投資基金　mutual investment fund
共同危险行为/共同危險行爲　joint dangerous action
共同协议/聯合協定　joint agreement
共同性分析/共同性分析　commonality analysis
共同原因机制/共同變因機制　common cause mechanism
共同原因模型/共同原因模型　common-cause model
共现分析/共現分析　co-occurrence analysis
共线/共線的　collinear
共线性/共線性　collinearity
共享领导/分享式領導　shared leadership
共享心理模型/共享心智模型,共享心智模式　shared mental model
共享性/共用性　shareability
共享阅读/分享閱讀　shared-book reading
共引/共被引　co-citation
共引分析/共被引分析　co-citation analysis
共引强度/共被引強度　co-citation strength
共有/共有　co-ownership
共有产权/共有産權,公共財產權　common property right
共有档案/共有檔案　joint archives
共有价值拍卖实验/共同價格拍賣實驗　common value auction experiments
共有媒体/共有媒體　total media
共有遗产/共有遺産　joint heritage
共有资料/共有資料　shared ownership of material
共有租赁/共同租賃　tenancy in common
共轴性/共軸性　coaxality
共轴圆/共軸圓　coaxial circles
贡献率/貢獻率　contribution rate, degree of contribution
勾结机会/勾結機會　collusion opportunities
沟通/溝通　communication
沟通管理/溝通管理　communication management
沟通管理计划/溝通管理計劃　communication management plan
沟通规划/溝通規劃　communication planning
沟通过程/溝通過程　communication process
沟通理论/溝通理論　communication theory
沟通目标/溝通目標　communication goal
沟通能力/溝通能力,傳播能力　communication competence, communicative ability
沟通渠道/溝通渠道,溝通管道　communication channel
沟通适应/溝通適應　communication adaptation
沟通网络/溝通網路　communication network
沟通行为/溝通行動,傳播行動　communicative action
钩校法/鉤記制度　tick system
狗仔/狗仔隊　paparazzi
构成比/成分比　component ratio
构成要件该当性/構成要件該當性　deservedness of constitutional elements
构思/構念　construct
构形/形相　configuration
构造变量/結構變數　structural variables
构造学派/構造學派　configurational school
购并/購買合并　consolidation by purchase
购并递盘/收購投標　take-over bid
购方企业/主并公司　acquiring enterprise

购后行为/購後行爲　postpurchase behavior
购货代理契约/購貨代理契約　buying agency agreement
购货单/購貨單　purchase slip
购货发票/購貨發票　purchase invoice
购货费用/購貨費用　buying expense
购货合同/購貨合約　buying contract, purchase contract
购货净额/購貨淨額　net purchase
购货确认书/購貨確認書　purchase confirmation
购货税/購貨稅　purchase tax
购货佣金/購貨佣金　buying commission, purchase commission
购货账/進貨賬戶,進貨清單　account of goods purchased
购买出口汇票/購買出口匯票　purchase of export bill
购买订金/購貨訂金　purchase deposit
购买动机调查/動機研究　motivation research
购买法/購買法　purchase method
购买服务/服務購買　purchase of public service
购买决策/購買決策　purchase decision
购买力/購買力　purchasing power
购买力风险/購買力風險　purchasing power risk
购买力平价/購買力平價　purchasing power parity, PPP
购买力平价汇率/購買力平價匯率　purchasing power parity of exchange rate
购买力平价理论/購買力平價理論,購買力平價説　theory of purchasing power parity
购买力债券/購買力債券　purchasing power bond
购买力证券/購買力證券　purchasing power security
购买频率/購買頻率　purchase frequency
购买外汇申请书/購買外匯申請書　purchase application for foreign exchange
购买限额/購買限額　buying quota
购买性支出/購置支出　purchase expenditure
购买要约/購貨報價　buying offer
购买者黑箱模型/購買行爲黑箱模型　black box model of buyer behavior
购买者决策过程/購買者決策過程　buyer decision process
购买者认知失调/購買者認知失調　buyer cognitive dissonance
购买者信息来源/購買者資訊來源　buyer source of information
购买者准备阶段/購買者準備階段　buyer-readiness stage

购买中心/購買中心,採購中心　buying center
购买资金融通/購買資金融通　finance purchase
购物代理/購物代理　comparison shopping agent
购物点/購物點,採購點　point-of-purchase, POP
购物中心/購物中心　shopping center
购销形式/購銷形式　mode of purchase and sale
购置成本/取得成本　acquisition cost
购置价格/取得價格　acquisition price
购置能力/購置能力　purchasing capacity
媾和/媾和　making peace
估定关税/估定關稅　duty assessment
估计/估計　estimation
估计标准误差/估計標準誤差　estimate standard error
估计参数/估計參數　estimated parameter
估计的无偏性/估計的不偏性　unbiasedness in estimation
估计方程/估計方程式　estimating equation
估计接近度/估計接近度　closeness in estimation
估计空间/估計空間　estimation space
估计理论/估計理論　theory of estimation
估计量/估計量,估計式　estimator
估计量的标准误差/估計量標準誤差　standard error of estimator
估计量的方差/估計量的變異數　variance of estimator
估计量的绝对有效性/估計量的絕對有效性　absolute efficiency of estimator
估计量精度/估計量精確度　precision of estimator
估计量准则/估計量準則　criteria for estimator
估计时间/估計時間　estimated time
估计死亡率/估計死亡率　estimated death rate
估计误差/估計誤差　estimate error, error of estimation
估计值/估計值　estimate
估计值准则/估計值準則　criteria for estimate
估计准确度/估計準確度　accuracy of estimation
估计准则/估計準則　criteria for estimation
估价单/估價單　bill of estimate
估算利息/設算利息　imputed interest
估算租金/設算租金　imputed rent
估损人/估損人　claim assessor
估值/估價　valuation
孤本/孤本　the only copy extant, unique copy
孤独/孤獨　loneliness
孤儿/孤兒　orphan
孤立批/孤立批,分隔批　isolated lot
孤立性/絕緣,隔離　isolation

古版书/搖籃本　incunabulum
古币学/錢幣學　numismatics
古代城市/古代城市　ancient city
古代法/古代法　archaic law
古代社会/古代社會　ancient society
古德哈特定律/葛哈德法則　Goodhart's law
古德曼-克鲁斯卡尔 τ/古德曼-克拉斯卡的 τ　Goodman-Kruskal tau
古典二分法/古典二分法　classical dichotomy
古典货币理论/古典貨幣理論　classical theory of money
古典假设/傳統假設檢定　classical hypothesis
古典假设检验法/古典的假設檢定方法　classical method of hypothesis testing
古典价值理论/古典價值理論　classical theory of value
古典经济社会学/古典經濟社會學　classical economic sociology
古典经济学/古典經濟學　classical economics
古典卡特尔模型/古典卡特爾模型　classical cartel model
古典理论和相关思想/古典理論和相關思想　classical theories and relevant thought
古典契约/古典契約　classical contract
古典统计学/古典統計量　classical statistics
古典线性回归模型/古典線性回歸模型　classical linear regression model, CLRM
古典行政组织理论/古典行政組織理論　classical administrative organization theory
古典学派/古典學派　classical school
古典政治经济学/經典的政治經濟學　classical political economics
古典自然法学派/古典自然法學派　Classical Natural Law School
古典自由主义/古典的自由主義　classical liberalism
古惯例/古慣例　the ancient custom
古籍/古籍　ancient book
古籍保护/古籍保護　ancient books protection
古籍数字化/古籍數位化　digitization of ancient books
古籍修复/古籍修補　mending and repairing of ancient books
古籍整理/古籍整理　collation of ancient books
古旧书/古籍書　antiquarian book
古旧书店/古舊書店　antiquarian bookstore
古旧资料/古舊資料　antiquarian material
古卷/古代卷軸　ancient scroll
古立克部门化原则/古立克部門化原則　departmentalization principle of Gulik
古立克管理七职能/古立克管理七職能　seven management functions theory of Gulik
古诺竞争/古諾競爭　Cournot competition
古诺均衡/庫諾均衡　Cournot equilibrium
古诺模型/庫諾模型　Cournot model
古诺行为假定/古諾行爲假設　cournot's behavioral assumption
古普塔对称性检验/古普塔對稱性檢定　Gupta's symmetry test
古普塔子集选择法/古普塔子集選擇法　Gupta's subset selection method
古钱学/錢幣學　numismatics
古特利常数/Goutereau 常數　Goutereau's constant
古文书学/古文書學　diplomatic, paleography
古文献学/古文獻學　classic philology
古文字学/古文字學　palaeography
谷物法/穀物法　corn law
谷物法案的废止/穀物法案的廢止　repeal of corn laws
H 股/H 股　H-share
股本/股本, 資本存量　stock of capital, capital stock
股本回报率/權益報酬率　return on equity, return of equity
股本认购/認繳股款　capital subscription
股本衍生工具/股本衍生工具　equity derivative
股本溢价/股本溢價, 股票升水　capital stock premium, premium on capital stock
股本溢价之谜/股本溢價之謎　equity premium puzzle
股东/股東　stockholder, equity holder, shareholder
股东表决权/股東投票權　shareholder voting rights
股东表决权排除制度/股東表決權排除制度　the system of exclusion of shareholders' voting rights
股东财富最大化/股東財富最大化　shareholder wealth maximization
股东大会/股東大會　general meeting of shareholder, meeting of stockholder
股东代表诉讼/股東代表訴訟　shareholders representative litigation
股东名册/股東名冊　list of shareholders
股东权/股東權　shareholders' right
股东权益/股東權益　stockholders equity
股东权益净值/股東權益淨值　stockholders net equity
股东权益与资产比率/股東權益與資產比率　equity to asset ratio
股东委托书/投票委託書　proxy statement

股份/股份　stock, share
股份保险/股份保險　joint stock insurance
股份分配/股份分配　share allocation
股份公司/合股公司　joint stock company
股份合作制/股份合作制　joint stock cooperative system
股份回购/股份回購　shares repurchase
股份汇票/股份匯票　share draft
股份交换/股份交換　shared exchange
股份交易/股份交易　share exchange
股份交易并购/股票交易并購　stock trade-off merger
股份联合有限公司/股份聯合有限公司　joint stock limited partnership
股份赎回/股份贖回　stock redemption
股份信托证券/股份信託證券　stock trust certificate
股份有限公司/股份有限公司　joint stock limited company, company limited by share
股份制/股份制,合股制　joint stock system
股份制书店/股份制書店　joint-stock bookstore
股份制银行/合股銀行　joint-stock bank
股份转让/股份轉讓　transfer of shares
股份资本/股份資本　share capital
股份资本变更/變更股份資本　alteration of share capital
股金提款单账户/股權提款賬戶　share draft account, SDA
股金账户/股金賬戶　share account
股利/股利　share dividend, dividend
股利收益率/股利收益率　dividend yield ratio
股利所得/股利收益　dividend income
股利贴现模型/股利貼現模型　dividend discount model, DDM
股利无关论/股利無關論　dividend irrelevance
股利宣布日/宣告日　announcement date
股利政策/股利政策　dividend policy
股利支付率/股利支付率,股利發放率　dividend payout ratio
股票/股票　stock, capital stock certificate
股票拆细/股票分割　stock split
股票偿还盈余/股票贖回公積　surplus from stock redemption
股票贷款/股票貸款　stock loan
股票抵押贷款/股票抵押貸款　stock collateral loan
股票发行溢价/股票發行溢價　share premium
股票分割/股票分割　stock split
股票红利/股票紅利　share bonus
股票回购/股票回購　stock repurchase
股票回购协议/股票附買回合約　stock repurchase agreement
股票汇票/股票匯票　stock draft
股票基金/股票基金　stock fund
股票价格/股票價格　stock price
股票价格指数/股票價格指數　market index of stock price, stock price index, share index
股票价值/股價　stock value
股票交易/股票交易　stock deal
股票交易所/股票交易所　stock broking firm, stock exchange
股票交易指数/股票交易指數　stock exchange index
股票经纪人/證券經紀人　stockbroker
股票留置权/股票留置權　lien on share
股票流通量/流通在外股　outstanding share
股票内在价值法/内在價值法　intrinsic value method
股票牌价/股票牌價　share quotation
股票期权/股票選擇權　stock option
股票升水/股票升水,股本溢價　capital stock premium, premium on capital stock
股票升值收益/股票升值收益　stock appreciation right, SAR
股票市场/股票市場　stock market
股票市场泡沫/股票市場泡沫　stock market bubble
股票市场信用/股票市場信用　stock market credit
股票套利/股票套利　stock arbitrage
股票投资/股票投資　investment in stock, share investment, stock investment
股票投资信托/股票投資信託　stock investment trust
股票退股/股票注銷　retirement of stock
股票销售/股票銷售　stock sale
股票溢价/股本溢價　premium on capital stock
股票指数/股票指數　stock index
股票指数期货/股票指數期貨　stock index future
股票指数套利/股票指數套利　stock index arbitrage
股票转让/股票轉讓　stock transfer, transfer of stock
股票转让税/股票轉讓稅　stock transfer tax
股权/股權　ownership of stock
股权比例规定/股權比例規定　stipulation of equity ratio
股权登记日/股權登記日　record date
股权分置/股權分度　equity division
股权互换/權益交換契約　equity swap
股权激励/股權激勵　equity incentive
股权类金融产品/股權類金融產品　equity class

financial products
股权凭证/股權憑證　equity security
股权收益率/股本收益率　rate of return on equity
股权投资/股權投資　equity investment
股权稀释/稀釋股本　dilution
股权溢价/股權溢價　equity premium
股权-引致型创新/股權增加式創新　equity generating innovation
股权再融资/股票增資　seasoned equity offering, SEO
股权置换/權益交換契約　equity swap
股息率/股息率　dividend rate
股指期货/股指期貨　stock index futures
股指套利/股票指數套利　stock index arbitrage
骨亲/骨親　guqin
縠纸/縠紙　mulberry paper
固定比例的强化/定比強化,定比增強　fixed ratio reinforcement
固定比率/固定率　fixed rate
固定边际总数卡方检验/卡方固定邊際總數檢定　chi-square test with fixed marginal totals
固定变量/固定變量　fixed variate
固定参数/固定參數　fixed parameter
固定产能/固定產能　fixed capacity
固定成本/固定成本　fixed cost
固定贷款/固定貸款　fixed loan
固定订货点模型/固定訂貨點模型　fixed-quantity reorder point model
固定订货量模型/固定訂貨量模型　fixed reorder quantity inventory model
固定费用/固定費用　fixed charge
固定负债/固定負債,長期負債　permanent liability, fixed liability
固定工资/固定工資,基本工資　regular wage
固定股利政策/固定股利政策　cyclical dividend policy
固定关税/固定關稅　fixed duty
固定汇兑/固定匯兌　fixed exchange
固定汇兑平价/固定平價匯兌　absolute par of exchange
固定汇率/固定匯率　fixed exchange rate, fixed rate of exchange
固定汇率制/固定匯率制　fixed exchange rate system, fixed rate system
固定机会/固定機會　chance of fixation
固定基期指数/定基指數　fixed base index
固定计划订单/固定計劃訂單　fixed planned order
固定价格/固定價格　fixed price, constant price

固定价格合同/固定價格合約,固定價格契約　fixed price contract, price fixing agreement
固定价格销售/固定價格銷售　fixed price offer for sale
固定价格协议/固定價格協議　fixed price agreement
固定价位招标/固定價格招標　fixed price tender offer
固定间隔的强化/定期增強,週期增強　fixed interval reinforcement
固定间隔期模型/固定再訂購週期模式　fixed reorder cycle inventory model
固定检验/固定檢驗　fixed inspection
固定缴款计划/確定提撥制　defined contribution plan
固定利率贷款/固定利率貸款　fixed rate loan
固定利率抵押/固定利率抵押　fixed rate mortgage
固定利息/固定利息　fixed interest
固定利息投资/固定利息投資　fixed interest investment
固定利息证券/固定利息證券　fixed interest bearing security, fixed interest security
固定年金/固定年金　fixed annuity
固定排架法/固定排架法　fixed shelving, absolute location
固定平价/固定平價　fixed parity
固定期限合同/定期合同　fixed term contract
固定期限劳动合同/固定期限勞動合同　fixed term labor contract
固定权数/固定權數　fixed weight
固定权数量指数/固定權數量指數　quantum index with fixed weights
固定式书架/固定式書架　fixed shelving
固定式网框/固定式網框　fixed screen frame
固定试验次数法/固定試驗次數法　method of fix experiment number
固定收入/固定收入　fixed income
固定收益计划/確定給付制　defined benefit plan
固定收益证券/固定收入證券　fixed income security
固定税率/固定稅率　fixed general tariff
固定税率制/固定稅率制　fixed general tariff system
固定提存计划/確定提撥制　defined contribution plan
固定投入/固定投入　fixed inputs
固定投资/固定投資　fixed investment
固定投资信托/固定投資信託　fixed investment trust
固定投资总额/固定投資總額　gross fixed investment

固定位置布置/固定位置布置　fixed position layout
固定系数模型/固定係數模型　fixed coefficient model
固定效应/固定效果　fixed effect
固定效应模型/固定效應模型，固定效果模式　fixed effect model
固定性投资信托/非歧視性信託　non-discretionary trust
固定样本/固定樣本，設定樣本　fixed sample, panel
固定样本量抽样设计/固定樣本大小抽樣設計　fixed sample-size sampling design
固定样本量试验/固定樣本大小試驗　fixed sample-size experiment
固定样本组调查/追蹤調查，同樣本調查　panel survey
固定因子平方和/固定因子平方和　sum of squares for fixed factors
固定影响变截距模型/固定效應變截距模型　variable intercept panel data model with fixed effect
固定影响变系数模型/固定效應變係數模型　varying coefficient panel data model with fixed effect
固定债券/固定債券　fixed debenture
固定债务/固定債務　fixed debt
固定资本/固定資本　fixed capital
固定资本积累总额/固定資本形成毛額　gross fixed capital formation
固定资本投资/固定資本投資　fixed capital investment
固定资本系数/固定資本係數　fixed capital coefficient
固定资本消耗准备/固定資本消耗準備　provisions for the consumption of fixed capital
固定资本形成/固定資本形成，固定資本組成　fixed capital formation
固定资产/固定資產　fixed asset
固定资产对公司净值比率/固定資產對淨值之比率　fixed asset to net worth ratio
固定资产对权益资本比率/固定資產對股東權益之比率　fixed asset to equity capital ratio
固定资产净值/固定資產淨值　net value of fixed asset
固定资产清理/處分固定資產　disposal of fixed asset
固定资产投资方向调节税/固定資產投資方向調節稅　fixed assets investment orientation regulation tax
固定资产再估价/固定資產重估價　reappraisal of fixed asset
固定资产折旧/固定資產折舊　depreciation of fixed asset
固定字段/固定欄　fixed field
固定总价合同/固定價格契約　fixed price or lumpsum contract
固定总价加奖励酬金合同/固定總價加獎勵契約　fixed price incentive fee contract, FPIF contract
固体废物污染/固體廢物汙染　pollution of solid waste
固体废物综合利用/固體廢物綜合利用　comprehensive utilization of solid wastes
固有法/固有法　indigenous law
固有风险/固有風險　inherent risk
固有故障/固有故障　inherent failure
固有可靠性/固有可靠度　inherent reliability
固有可用性/固有可用度　inherent availability
固有偏倚/固有偏誤　inherent bias
固有失效/固有故障　inherent failure
固有延迟/固有延遲，固有延誤　inherent delay
固有准确度/內在準確度　intrinsic accuracy
故事语法/故事法則　story grammar
故意杀人罪/故意殺人罪　crime of intentional homicide
故意伤害罪/故意傷害罪　crime of malicious injury
故障/故障，失效　failure
故障分布/故障分布，故障分配　failure distribution
故障分析/故障分析　failure analysis
故障概率/故障機率　probability of failure
故障过程/故障過程　failure process
故障间隔时间/故障間隔時間　time between failures, TBF
故障率/故障率，失效率　failure rate
故障率水平/故障率水準　failure rate level
故障密度函数/故障密度函數　failure density function
故障模式/故障模式　failure mode
故障排除者/故障處理者　disturbance handler
故障频率/故障次數　failure frequency
故障频率分布/故障次數分布　failure frequency distribution
故障时间/故障時間　failure time
故障时间分布/故障時間分布，故障時間分配　failure time distribution
故障树分析/故障樹分析　fault tree analysis, FTA
故障数据/故障數據　failure data
故障图/故障圖　hazard plots
故障形态/故障型態　failure pattern
故障修理/故障維修　breakdown maintenance

故障诊断时间/故障診斷時間　access time
顾客/顧客,客户　customer
顾客保留/顧客留住,顧客維繫　customer retention
顾客部门化/顧客部門化　customer departmentalization
顾客导向公司/顧客導向公司　customer centered company
顾客导向营销/顧客導向行銷　consumer oriented marketing
顾客订单/顧客訂單　customer order
顾客订单确认/顧客訂單確認,顧客訂單承諾　customer order promising
顾客订货服务系统/顧客訂貨服務系統　customer order servicing system
顾客对顾客电子商务/消費者對消費者　consumer to consumer, C2C
顾客对顾客在线营销/消費者對消費者線上行銷　consumer to consumer online marketing, C2C online marketing
顾客对企业电子商务/顧客對企業電子商務　consumer to business, C2B
顾客对企业在线营销/消費者對企業線上行銷　consumer to business online marketing, C2B online marketing
顾客份额/顧客份額　share of customer
顾客服务/顧客服務　customer service
顾客服务水平/顧客服務水準　customer service level
顾客感知价值/顧客感知價值　customer perceived value
顾客关系管理/顧客關係管理　customer relationship management, CRM
顾客价值分析/顧客價值分析　customer value analysis
顾客价值营销/顧客價值行銷　customer value marketing
顾客满意度/顧客滿意　customer satisfaction
顾客期望/客戶期望,顧客要求　customer expectation
顾客数据库/客戶資料庫　customer database
顾客细分定价/顧客差別定價　customer segment pricing
顾客销售队伍结构/顧客銷售隊伍結構　customer sales force structure
顾客需求/客戶需求　customer demands
顾客需要/顧客欲求　customer needs
顾客盈利性/顧客利益性　customer profitability
顾客盈利性分析/顧客利潤率分析　customer profitability analysis
顾客欲望/客戶需要　customer wants
顾客忠诚/顧客忠誠性　customer loyalty
顾客终身价值/顧客終身價值　customer lifetime value
顾客资产/顧客資產　customer equity
雇工/雇傭勞動　employing labor, wage labor
雇佣成本/雇傭成本　hiring costs
雇佣关系/雇傭關係,勞資關係　employment relationship
雇佣率/雇傭率　hiring rate
雇佣年龄歧视法案/年齡歧視　age discrimination in employment act
雇佣作品/雇傭作品　works created by an employee during the employment period
雇员报酬/受雇人員報酬　compensation of employees
雇员歧视/員工歧視　employee discrimination
雇主/雇主　employer
雇主人员/雇主人員　employer's personnel
雇主设备/雇主設備　employer's equipment
雇主要求/雇主要求　employer's requirement
雇主与咨询工程师标准服务协议书/雇主與諮詢工程師標準服務協議書　condition of the client-consultant model service agreement
雇主责任/雇主責任　employer's liability
刮墨刀/刮墨刀　doctor blade, squeegee
刮墨刀线/刮墨刀線　doctor blade streak
刮墨胶条/刮墨膠條　squeegee blade
刮墨角度/刮墨角度　squeegee angle
刮墨面/刮墨面　squeegee side
刮墨区/刮墨區　squeegee area
刮墨压力/刮墨壓力　squeegee pressure
寡头垄断/寡占　oligopoly
寡头垄断定价/寡占定價　oligopoly pricing
寡头垄断市场/寡占市場,獨占市場　oligopoly monopoly market
寡占售价/寡占售價　oligopsony price
寡占行为/寡占者行為　oligopolistic behavior
挂接主题索引/掛接主題索引　articulated subject index
挂靠机构/掛靠機構　attached organization
挂名首脑/虛位領導人,形式領導人　figurehead
挂图/掛圖　wall map
乖离率/偏置量　bias
拐点/反折點　inflection point
拐点预测/拐點預測　turning point forecasting
拐卖妇女、儿童罪/拐賣婦女、兒童罪　crime of abducting and trafficking women and children

拐折需求曲线/拗折的需求曲线　kinked demand curve
关防/關防　guanfang
关键/關鍵　key
关键比/關鍵比　critical ratio
关键成功因素/關鍵成功因素　key success factor, KSF
关键成功因素分析/關鍵成功因素分析　key success factor analysis
关键词/關鍵字　keyword
关键词表/關鍵詞表　go-list
关键词法/關鍵字法　keyword method
关键词检索/關鍵詞檢索　keyword search, keyword retrieval
关键词轮排索引/輪排主題索引　permuterm index
关键词索引/關鍵詞索引　catchword index, keyword index
关键词与上下文索引/關鍵詞和上下文索引　keyword and context index, KWAC
关键工作/關鍵工作　key job
关键共性技术/關鍵共性技術　key common technology
关键故障/嚴重故障　critical failure
关键货币/關鍵通貨　key currency
关键技术/關鍵技術　key technology
关键绩效指标/關鍵績效指標　key performance index, KPI
关键里程碑事件时间表/里程碑進度計劃　milestone schedule
关键路径/要徑　critical path
关键路径法/要徑法　critical path method, CPM
关键情报课题/關鍵智慧主題　key intelligence topic
关键事件法/關鍵事件法,關鍵事例法　critical incident technique
关键特性/關鍵特性　key characteristic
关键通货原理/關鍵貨幣原理　key currency principle
关键通货制度/關鍵貨幣制度　key currency system
关键线路/要徑　critical path
关键线路法/要徑法　critical path method, CPM
关键帧/關鍵幀　key frame
关键帧动画/關鍵幀動畫　key frame animation
关键知情人/關鍵情報導人　key informant
关键字段/關鍵欄,主要欄位　key field
关联/相聯　association
关联变量/相聯變量　associated variate
关联表/相聯表　association table
关联词组标引系统/關聯短語標引系統　linked phrase indexing system, LIPHIS
关联度/相聯度　degree of association
关联方交易/關係人交易　related party transaction
关联分析/相聯分析　association analysis
关联符号/關聯符號　relation marks
关联矩阵/關聯矩陣　incidence matrix
关联贸易/關聯交易　related trade
关联模型/關聯模型　association model
关联强度/關聯強度　strength of association
关联设计矩阵/設計的關聯矩陣　incidence matrix of design
关联失效/有關故障　relevant failure
关联图/關聯圖　interrelationship diagram
关联系数/相聯係數,關聯程度係數　association coefficient, coefficient of association, interdependence coefficient
关联效应/關聯效應　linkage effects
关联性/相關性　relevance, association
关门点/關門點　shut down point
关税/關稅　customs tax, tariff, customs duty
关税保护/關稅保護　tariff protection
关税报复/關稅報復　tariff retaliation
关税壁垒/關稅壁壘　tariff barrier, customs barrier, tariff wall
关税法/關稅法　tariff act
关税费用/海關稅費　customs fee and charge
关税负担者/關稅負擔者　incidence of duty
关税和货物税税率调节措施/關稅和貨物稅稅率調節措施　customs and excise regulator
关税豁免/關稅豁免　exemption of duty
关税减让/關稅減讓　concession of tariff, tariff diminution
关税减让表/關稅減讓表　schedule of concession
关税结构/關稅結構　tariff structure
关税联盟/關稅聯盟　tariff alliance
关税率/關稅率　tariff rate
关税配额/關稅配額　customs quota, tariff quota
关税水平/關稅水平　tariff level
关税税率/關稅稅率　rate of duty, tariff
关税税则/關稅稅則　customs tariff
关税特定减免/關稅特定減免　specific reduction of customs duty
关税同盟/關稅同盟　customs union
关税同盟论/關稅同盟理論　theory of customs union
关税退税/關稅退稅　duty drawback
关税效应/關稅效應,關稅影響　tariff effect
关税协定/關稅協定　tariff agreement
关税战/關稅戰爭　tariff war

关税征收审计/關稅徵收審計　audit of collection and payment on customs duty
关税政策/關稅政策　tariff policy
关税转嫁/關稅轉嫁　shifting of tariff
关税自主权/關稅自主權　tariff autonomy
关系/關係　connection
关系冲突/關係衝突　relationship conflict
关系合同理论/關係合同理論　relational contract theory
关系建立/關係建立　relationship building
关系矩阵/社會矩陣,社交矩陣　sociomatrix
关系类型/關係類型　type of relationship
关系模型/關聯式模型　relational model
关系纽带/關係紐帶　ties
关系契约/關係契約　relational contract
关系强度/關係強度　strength of ties
关系强度理论/關係強度理論　strength of ties theory
关系数据库/關聯式資料庫　relational database
关系网/關係網　relationship network
关系营销/關係行銷　relationship marketing
关于播送人造卫星传输节目信号公约/關於播送人造衛星傳輸節目信號公約　Convention Relating to the Distribution of Programme Carrying Signals Transmitted by Satellite
关于对收养的管辖权、准据法及判决的承认的公约/關於對收養的管轄權、準據法及判決的承認的公約　Applicable Law and recognition of Decrees Relating to Adoptions
关于扶养义务准据法公约/關於扶養義務準據法公約　Convention on the Law Applicable to Maintenance Obligations
关于合同义务法律适用的公约/關於合同義務法律適用的公約　Convention on the Law Applicable to Contractual Obligations
关于婚姻效力的公约/關於婚姻效力的公約　Convention of relating to Conflicts of Laws with regard to the Effects of Marriage on the Rights and Duties of the Spouses in their Personal Relationship and with regard to their Estates
关于信托的法律适用及其承认的公约/關於信託的法律適用及其承認的公約　Convention on Applicable Law in Trusts and their Recognition
关栈存货价格/貨棧價格　price in bond
观测点/觀測點　observational point
观测方程/觀察值方程式　observation equation
观测频数/觀察次數　observed frequency
观测误差/觀測誤差　error of observation
观测研究/觀測研究　observational studies
观测营销研究/觀測行銷研究　observational marketing research
观测值/觀測值　observation, observed value
观测值组合/觀察值組合　combination of observations
观察/觀察,觀測　observation
观察变项/觀察變項　observed variables
观察法/觀察法　observation method
观念统计/觀念統計　ideological statistics
官本位/官本位　bureaucrat-oriented
官产学研联盟/官產學研聯盟　government-industry-university-institute alliance
官当/官當　Guan Dang
官方储备/官方儲備　official reserve
官方储备交易/官方準備交易　official reserve transaction
官方单一汇率/官方單一匯率　official unitary exchange rate
官方法/官方法　official law
官方汇价/官方匯價　official quotation of exchange
官方汇率/官方匯率,法定匯率　official exchange rate, official rate of exchange
官方简讯/官方簡訊　official newsletter
官方结算差额/官方清算平衡　official settlement balance
官方美元储备/官方美元儲備　official dollar reserve
官方税率/官方稅率　official tariff rate
官方统计/官方統計　official statistics
官方外汇市场/官方外匯市場　official foreign exchange market
官方外汇资产/官方外匯資產　official foreign exchange asset
官方文件/正式記錄,官方檔　official record
官房学/重商主義的經濟或財政　cameralism
官刻本/官刻本　official block printed edition
官僚法/官僚法　bureaucratic law
官僚化/官僚化,科層化　bureaucratization
官僚制/官僚制,科層制　bureaucracy
官僚制理论/官僚理論　bureaucracy theory
官僚组织理论/官僚理論　bureaucracy theory
官员财产申报/官員財產申報　official property declaration system
馆编件号/館編件號　archival code, collection code
馆藏/館藏　holding, collection, holdings
馆藏发展政策/館藏發展政策　collection development policy
馆藏分析/館藏分析　collection analysis

馆藏管理/館藏管理　collection management
馆藏积累/館藏成長　accumulation of holding
馆藏记录/館藏記錄　holdings record
馆藏结构/館藏結構　collection structure
馆藏空间/館藏空間,典藏空間　collection space
馆藏宽度/館藏寬度　collection breadth
馆藏利用/館藏利用　collection utilization
馆藏量/藏書量　holdings, book capacity
馆藏目录/館藏目錄　holdings inventory
馆藏目录室/館藏目錄室　holdings inventory room
馆藏评估/館藏評鑒　collection assessment, collection evaluation
馆藏深度/館藏深度　collection depth
馆藏特色/館藏特色　collection strength
馆藏维护/館藏維護　collection maintenance
馆藏新度/館藏新度　collection currency
馆藏要览/館藏清冊　summary of records
馆藏重点/館藏重點　collection emphasis
馆藏注释/館藏注釋　holdings note
馆藏资料展览/文獻展覽　library materials exhibition, library materials display
馆际互借/館際互借　inter library loan, ILL
馆际互借规则/館際互借規則　inter library loan code
馆际借出/館際借閱　interlibrary lending
馆际借入/館際借入　interlibrary borrowing
馆际协议/館際互惠協定　interlibrary reciprocal agreement
馆内阅览/館內閱覽　reading in the library
馆配/館配　library supply
馆配商/館配商　library supplier, vendor
馆外服务点/推廣機構　extension agencies
馆外服务工作/圖書館推廣活動　extension work
馆外流动服务工作/館外流動服務工作　extension library service
馆外流通/圖書館推廣服務　circulation out of library, library outreach, library extension
馆外用户/館外用戶　outside user
馆员/館員　librarian
馆员工作守则/館員工作守則　staff handbook, staff introduction book
馆员手册/館員工作手冊　procedure manual, work manual
管道层次/管道層次　channel level
管道差异化/管道差異　channel differentiation
管道长度/銷售通路長度　channel length
管道成员/銷售通路成員　channel member
管道冲突/銷售通路衝突　channel conflict

管道沟通/管道溝通　channel communication
管道管理/通路管理　channel management
管道库存/管道存貨　pipeline inventory
管道宽度/通路寬度　channel width
管道领袖/銷售通路領導者　channel captain
管道权力/銷售管道權力　channel power
管理/管理　management
管理变量/管理變數　management variable
管理标准/管理標準,管理規範　management standard
管理部分/管理部分　management segment
管理层次/管理層次　management level
管理层干预/管理層干預　management intervention
管理层激励计划/管理激勵計劃　management incentive plan
管理层凌驾/管理階層逾越　management override
管理层认定/管理階層聲明　management assertion
管理层声明书/管理層聲明書　management statement, management representation
管理层收购/管理階層收購　management buyout, MBO
管理成本/管理成本,行政成本　managed cost, administrative cost
管理程序论/管理程式論　theory of management program
管理创新/管理創新　management innovation
管理费用/管理費用　administration expense
管理革命/管理革命　managerial revolution
管理革命理论/管理革命理論　theory of managerial revolution
管理工程/管理工程　management engineering
管理固定成本/管理固定成本　managed fixed cost
管理过程/管理程式,管理程序　management process
管理过程学派/管理程式學派,管理程序學派　management process school
管理汇率/管理匯率　managed exchange rate
管理技能/管理技能　managerial skill
管理继承/管理繼承　management succession
管理价值模式/管理價值模式,管理價值模型　management value model
管理建议书/管理建議書　management recommendation, management letter
管理金本位制/管理金本位制　managed gold standard
管理经济学/管理經濟學　managerial economics
管理开发/管理發展　management development
管理科学/管理科學　management science, administration science

管理客体/管理客體　management object
管理控制/管理控制　managing control
管理跨度/控制幅度　span of control
管理会计/管理會計學　management accounting, managerial accounting
管理理论的丛林/管理理論的叢林　management theory jungle
管理绿色化/管理綠色化，綠色管理　greening of management
管理伦理/管理倫理　management ethics
管理贸易/管理貿易　managed trade
管理模式/管理模式　management mode, management model
管理目标/管理目標　managerial goal, management objective
管理培训/管理訓練　management training
管理评审/管理評估　management review
管理情报研究/管理智慧分析　management intelligence anlysis
管理人员股票期权/管理人員股票選擇權　executive stock option
管理式垂直营销系统/管理式垂直行銷通路系統　administered vertical marketing system, administered VMS
管理式医疗/管理式照護　managed care
管理事务流程图/管理事務流程圖　management affair flow chart
管理事务流分析/管理事務流程分析　management affair process analysis
管理松懈/管理上的鬆弛　managerial slack
管理通货制度/管理通貨制度　managed currency system
管理统计学/管理統計學　managerial statistics
管理系统/管理系統　management system
管理系统分析/管理系統分析　management system analysis
管理系统工程/管理系統工程　management system engineering
管理效果/管理效果，管理效能　management effectiveness
管理效率/管理效率　management efficiency
管理心理学/管理心理學　management psychology
管理信息/管理資訊　management information
管理信息系统/管理資訊系統　management information system, MIS
管理型负债/管理性負債　managed liabilities
管理型继任人/管理型繼任人　managerial successor
管理性缩微摄影/行政管理用的微縮品　administrative microfilming
管理循环方法/管理循環方法　management circle method
管理研究团体/管理研究團體　management research group
管理游戏/管理競賽　management game
管理元数据/行政性詮釋資料　administrative metadata
管理哲学/管理哲學　management philosophy
管理者/管理者　manager
管理者角色/管理者角色　manager role
管理者与所有者/經理人對所有權人　managers vs. owners
管理之神/管理之神　management god
管理支持/管理支援　management support
管理职能/管理功能　management function
管理职位描述问卷/管理崗位描述問卷，職位分析問卷調查　management position description questionnaire
管理中心地说/管理中心地說　theory of management center place
管理主体/管理主體　management subject
管理咨询/管理顧問　management consulting
管理子系统/管理子系統　managerial subsystem
管理自主权模型/管理自主權模型　model of managerial discretion
管理坐标理论/管理方格理論　managerial grid theory
管辖/管轄　jurisdiction
管辖冲突/管轄衝突　conflicts of jurisdiction
管辖根据/管轄根據　jurisdiction basis
管辖恒定原则/管轄恆定原則　principle of constant jurisdiction
管辖权异议/管轄權異議　jurisdiction objection
管辖权转移/轉移管轄　transfer of jurisdiction
管辖协议/管轄協議　jurisdiction agreement
管制/管制　regulation
管制浮动汇率/管制浮動匯率　managed floating exchange rate
管制汇价/管制匯價　administered exchange rate
管制货币/管制貨幣　managed currency
管制价格/管制價格　controlled price, managed price
管制利率/管制利率　regulated interest rate
管制贸易/貿易管制　controlled trade
管制外汇制度/管制外匯制度　controlled exchange system
管制性政策/管制政策　regulative policy
惯犯/慣犯　habitual criminal

惯例/例規　routine
惯例价格/習慣價格　customary price
惯性/慣力　inertia
惯性努力区域/慣性努力區域　inert effort area
光船租赁合同/光船租賃合同　bareboat charter party
光带宽度法/光帶寬度法　light band width
光导体/光導體　photoconductor
光滑函数/平滑型函數　smooth function
光滑频率曲线/平滑次數曲線　smooth frequency curve
光滑频数曲线/平滑次數曲線　smooth frequency curve
光聚合柔性版/光聚合柔性版　flexographic forme
光聚合树脂版/光聚合樹脂版　photopolymer forme
光刻胶/光刻膠　photoresist
光亮镀铜/光亮鍍銅　glazed skin coppering
光敏印版/光敏印版　photosensitive plate
光盘/光碟　compact disk, compact disc, optical disc
光盘出版物/光碟出版物　CD-base publication
光盘档案/光碟檔案　record of optical disk
光盘读写速度/光碟讀寫速度　read and write speed of CD
光盘复制/光碟複製　CD replication
光盘基准面/光碟基準面　disk reference plane
光盘检索/唯讀式光碟檢索　CD-ROM retrieval, CD-ROM search
光盘刻录机/光碟燒錄機　optical disc recorder
光盘数据库/CD 資料庫　CD database
光盘注塑机/噴射成型機　injection molding machine
光票/光票　straight bill, clean bill
光票和跟单汇票/光票和跟單匯票　clean bill and documentary bill
光票信用证/光票信用狀　clean letter of credit
光圈/光圈　aperture
光通量/光通量　luminous flux
光纤/光纖　fiber
光学参数/光學參數　optical parameter
光学密度/光學密度　optical density, optics density
光学字符识别/光學識別　optical character recognition, optical character reader
广播/廣播　radio, broadcast
广播电视从业人员/廣播電視從業人員　broadcaster
广播电视节目/廣播電視節目　radio and television program
广播访谈/廣播訪談　radio interview
广播节目主持人/廣播節目主持人　disc jockey, DJ
广播开机率/廣播開機率　persons using radio, PUR

广播权/廣播權　right of broadcasting
广播谈话节目/廣播談話節目，談話廣播　talk radio
广播卫星/廣播衛星　broadcasting satellite, BS
广播新闻/廣播新聞　radio news
广播组织权/廣播組織權　right of broadcasting organization
广电媒体/廣電媒體　broadcast media
广电新闻/廣電新聞　broadcast news
广范围投资/擴大投資範圍　wider range investment
广告/廣告　advertisement, advertising
POP 广告/POP 廣告，賣場廣告　point of purchase advertising, POP advertising
广告版面/廣告版面　advertising space
广告标题/廣告標題　advertising title
广告部/廣告部門　advertising department
广告策划/廣告策劃，廣告計劃　advertising plan
广告策略/廣告策略　advertising strategy
广告代理公司/廣告媒體代理公司　representative firm, advertising agency
广告代理人/廣告代理人　advertising agent
广告代理商/廣告代理　advertising agency
广告发布者/廣告發布者　publisher of advertisement
广告法/廣告法　advertising law
广告费率/廣告費率　advertising rate
广告干扰度/廣告干擾度　advertising interference ratio
广告歌曲/廣告曲　jingle
广告规避/廣告規避　advertising avoidance
广告规格/廣告規格　advertising size
广告合同/廣告合同　advertising contract
广告节目化/廣告節目化，節目式廣告　program length advertising
广告津贴/廣告津貼，廣告折讓　advertising allowance
广告经理/廣告經理　advertising manager
广告经营者/廣告經營者　advertising manager
广告礼品/廣告贈品　advertising specialty
广告媒体/廣告媒體　advertising media, advertising medium
广告每千人成本/廣告每千人成本　cost-per-mill thousand, CPM
广告目标/廣告目標　advertising objective
广告牌/看板　kanban
广告牌控制系统/看板控制系統　kanban control system
广告商/廣告主　advertiser
广告商标/廣告商標　advertising marks
广告涉入/廣告涉入　advertising involvement

广告时间/廣告時間　advertising time
广告投资回报/廣告投資回報,廣告投資收益　return on advertising investment
广告研究/廣告研究　advertising research
广告音乐/廣告音樂　advertising music
广告印象/廣告印象　advertising impressions
广告语/廣告語　advertising slogan
广告预算/廣告預算　advertising budget
广告运动/廣告活動　advertising campaign
广告占版率/廣告占版率　occupancy rate
广告正文/廣告正文　advertising body
广告主/廣告主,贊助商　advertiser, sponsor
广告准则/廣告準則　guideline of advertisement
广义贝叶斯决策规则/廣義貝氏決策規則　generalized Bayes' decision rule, extended Bayes decision rule
广义超几何分布/廣義超幾何分布,廣義超幾何分配　extended hypergeometric distribution
广义传染分布/廣義散播分布　generalized contagious distribution
广义对数伽马分布/廣義對數伽瑪分布,廣義對數伽瑪分配,廣義對數 γ 分布　generalized log-gamma distribution
广义对数伽马回归模型/廣義對數伽瑪回歸模型,廣義對數 γ 回歸模型　generalized log-gamma regression model
广义多重的费希尔 K 统计量/廣義多重的費雪 K 統計量　generalized polykays
广义多项分布/廣義多項分布　generalized multinomial distribution
广义多元线性回归分析/一般的多元直線型回歸分析　general multiple linear regression analysis
广义二变量指数分布/廣義二變量指數分布,廣義二變量指數分配　generalized bivariate exponential distribution
广义二项分布/廣義二項分布,廣義二項分配　generalized binomial distribution
广义方差/廣義變異數　generalized variance
广义分布/廣義分布　generalized distribution
广义 STER 分布/廣義 STER 分布,廣義 STER 分配　generalized STER distribution
广义伽马分布/廣義伽瑪分布,廣義伽瑪分配,廣義 γ 分布　generalized gamma distribution
广义格兰杰因果关系/廣義格蘭傑因果檢驗　generalized Granger causality
广义工具变量估计/一般化工具變數法　generalized instrumental variable estimate
广义货币供应/廣義貨幣供給　broad money supply

广义极大似然估计量/廣義最大概度估計量　generalized maximum likelihood estimator
广义极值分布/一般化極值分配　generalized extreme value distribution
广义极值模型/一般極端值模型　generalized extreme value models
广义经典线性估计/一般化傳統一次式估計法　generalized classical linear estimation
广义经典线性估计量/廣義古典線性估計量　generalized classical linear estimator
广义矩估计/廣義矩方法　generalized method of moment, GMM
广义均方误差/一般均方差　generalized mean squared error
广义可分组设计/廣義可分組設計　extended group divisible design
广义离散/廣義離勢　generalized dispersion
广义岭回归估计量/一般脊回歸估計式　generalized ridge regression estimator
广义幂级数分布/廣義冪級數分布　generalized power series distribution
广义逆矩阵/廣義逆矩陣　generalized inverse matrix
广义偏最小二乘/偏一般最小平方法　partial generalized least squares
广义平稳定律/廣義穩定法則　generalized stable law
广义平稳时间序列/廣義平穩時間數列　wide-sense stationary time series
广义平稳性/廣義平穩性　wide-sense stationary
广义似然比/廣義概度比　generalized likelihood ratio
广义似然比检验/廣義概度比檢定　generalized likelihood ratio tests
广义线性估计/一般線性估計式　generalized linear estimator
广义线性估计值/廣義線性估計值　generalized linear estimate
广义线性模型/廣義線性模型　generalized linear models, GLM
广义线性统计模型/一般線性統計模型　general linear statistical model
广义线性自回归预测模型/廣義線性自回歸滑動平均模型　generalized linear auto regressive forecasting model
广义序贯概率比检验/廣義逐次機率比檢定　generalized sequential probability ratio tests
广义正态分布/廣義常態分布,廣義常態分配　generalized normal distribution
广义直角设计/廣義直角設計　generalized right angular designs

广义自回归条件异方差均值模型/一般自我回歸條件異質變異均數模型 generalized autoregressire conditional heteroskedasticity in mean model, GARCH-M model
广义最小二乘法/廣義最小二乘法 generalized least squares, GLS
广义最小二乘估计量/廣義最小平方估計量 generalized least squares estimators
广州体系/廣州貿易制度 canton system
归档/歸檔,存卷 filing, place on file
归档范围/歸檔範圍 filing range
归档时间/歸檔時間 filing time
归档文件/歸檔檔案 archived files
归档文件编号/歸檔檔案編號 archived files numbering
归档文件编目/歸檔檔案編目 archived files cataloguing
归档文件分类/歸檔檔案分類 archived files classifying
归档文件分类方案/歸檔檔案分類方案 classification scheme of archived files
归档文件分类方法/歸檔檔案分類方法 classification method of archived files
归档文件目录/歸檔檔案目錄 catalog of files, archived files catalog
归档文件排列/歸檔檔案排列 archived files arraying
归档文件整理/歸檔檔案整理 arrangement of archived files
归档文件装订/歸檔檔案裝訂 archived files binding
归档文件装盒/歸檔檔案裝盒 archived files boxing
归档要求/歸檔要求 filing requirement
归档章/歸檔章 filing seal
归化/歸化 naturalization
归还/歸還 replevin
归还登记/歸還登記 check-in
归还日期/歸還日期,到期日 date of return
归架/歸架,上架 reintegration, reshelving
归类/歸類,分类 sorting
归类检验/歸類檢驗,分類檢驗 sorting inspection
归类限/歸類界限,分类界限 sorting limit
归零测时法/歸零測時法 return to zero timing
归纳/普同化 generalizing
归纳方法/歸納法 inductive method
归纳统计学/歸納統計學 inductive statistics
归纳推断/歸納推論 inductive inference
归纳行为/歸納行爲 inductive behavior
归纳学习/歸納式學習 inductive learning

归属/隸屬 affiliation
归因/歸因,出處 attribution
归因理论/歸因理論 attribution theory
归因偏差/歸因偏差,歸因偏誤 attribution bias
归因误差/歸因謬誤,歸因錯誤 attribution error
规定到期日/固定到期日 fixed maturity date
规定发货日期/確定交貨日期 definite date for delivery
规定容差/規定允差 mandatory tolerance
规定信息源/規定資訊源 prescribed source of information
规范/規範,规格 specification
规范标目/規範標目 authorized heading
规范标准/規格標準 specification standard
规范档/規範文件 normative document
规范分析/規範分析 normative analysis
规范格式/記錄格式 authority format
规范工作/規範工作 authority work
规范化规则/標準化規則 normalization rule
规范记录/權限記錄 authority record
规范记录的功能需求/規範記錄的功能需求 functional requirements for authority records, FRAR
规范记录号/權限記錄號 authority record number
规范检验/量規檢驗 gage inspection
规范经济学/規範經濟學 normative economics
规范控制/權威控制 authority control
规范款目/規範款目 authority entry
规范类文件/規範類檔案 class specific document
规范区域/規格區域 specification band
规范容差/規格允差 specification tolerance
规范文档/權威檔,權限檔案 authority file
规范系统/規範系統 authority system
规范宪法/規範憲法 normative constitution
规范形式/規範形式 authorized form
规范性/規範性 normative
规范性决策理论/規範性決策理論 normative decision theory
规范性宪法学/規範性憲法學 normative constitutional theory
规范性要素/規範性要素 normative element
规范责任论/規範責任論 theory of normative liability
A规格/A版 A size
规格上限/規格上限 upper specification limit
规格下限/規格下限 lower specification limit
规划包/計劃包 planning package
规划过程/規劃程序 planning process

规划区域/規劃區域　planning region
规划设计时间/規劃設計階段　planning and design phase
规划收益/規劃收益　planning gain
规模报酬/規模報酬　return to scale
规模报酬不变技术/固定規模報酬技術　constant return to scale technologies
规模报酬递减/規模報酬遞減,規模不經濟　decreasing returns to scale
规模报酬递增/規模報酬遞增,規模經濟　increasing return to scale, scale increasing returns
规模不经济/規模不經濟　diseconomies of scale
规模经济/規模經濟　scale economy
规模恰当/規模恰當　appropriate module size
规模收入分配/所得大小之分配　size distribution of income
规模收益不变/固定規模報酬　constant returns to scale
规训/規訓,紀律　discipline
规则/規則　regulation
3σ规则/三標準差規則　three-sigma rule
规制改革/管制革新　regulatory reform
规制影响分析/管制影響評估　regulatory impact analysis
皈依/改宗　conversion
硅谷/矽谷　Silicon Valley
轨道间距/軌矩　track pitch
匦函/匦函　A casket in which the imperial court receives letters from the subjects of a feudal ruler
鬼薪/鬼薪　Gui Xin
柜台交易/櫃檯交易　over-the-counter trading
滚动计划法/滾動式規劃法　roll planning method
滚动结算/滾動結算　rolling settlement
滚动式规划/滾動[式]規劃　rolling wave planning, rolling planning
滚动套期保值/滾動套期保值　rolling hedging
滚动通过产出率/滾動通過產出率　rolled throughput yield, RTY
滚动预测/滾動預測　rolling forecasting
滚动预算/滾動預算　rolling budget
滚筒/滾筒　drum, cylinder
滚筒包衬/滾筒襯墊　cylinder packing
滚筒车磨/滾筒車磨　cylinder griding
滚筒镀铬/滾筒鍍鉻　cylinder chrome-plating
滚筒腐蚀/滾筒腐蝕　cylinder etching
滚筒抛光/滾筒拋光　cylinder polishing
滚筒型扫描仪/鼓掃描器　drum scanner
滚雪球抽样/[滾]雪球抽樣　snowball sampling

滚压/滾壓　rolling
滚枕/滾枕　cylinder bearer
国富论/國富論　Wealth of Nations
国际保障制度/國際保障制度　international safeguard system
国际比价/國際比價　international parity
国际比较项目/國際比較計劃　international comparison project
国际避税/國際避稅　international tax evasion
国际编目原则声明/國際編目原則聲明　Statement of International Cataloguing Principles
国际标准/國際標準　international standard
国际标准分类/國際標準分類　international standard classification
国际标准行业分类/國際標準行業分類　international standard industrial classification
国际标准化组织/國際標準化組織　International Standards Organization, ISO
国际标准技术报告号/國際標準技術報告號　International Standard Technical Report Number, ISRN
国际标准连续出版物号/國際標準期刊號　International Standard Serial Numbering, ISSN
国际标准书号/國際標準書號　International Standard Book Number, ISBN
国际标准书目著录/國際書目著錄標準　International Standard Bibliographic Description, ISBD
国际标准文本代码/國際標準文本編碼　International Standard Text Code, ISTC
国际标准音像制品编码/國際標準錄音錄影資料代碼　International Standard Recording Code, ISRC
国际标准乐谱号/國際標準樂譜號　International Standard Music Number, ISMN
国际标准指数/國際標準指數　International Standard Index
国际标准组织/國際標準組織　International Standard Organization
国际博览会/國際博覽會　international fair
国际不等价交换/國際不等價交換　international unequivalent exchange
国际不法行为/國際不法行爲　international tort
国际财团/國際財團　international consortium
国际财团银行/國際銀行財團　consortium bank
国际财务报告准则/國際財務報告標準,國際會計準則　International Financial Reporting Standards, IFRS
国际测量标准/國際測量標準　international

measuring standard
国际长期资本/國際長期資本　international long-term capital
国际长期资本流动/國際長期資本流動,長期資金的國際流動　international long-term capital movement
国际出版物交换/出版品國際交換　international publication exchange
国际储备/國際儲備,國際準備　international reserve
国际储备对进口的比率/國際儲備對進口的比率　rate of international reserve to import
国际储备过剩/國際儲備過剩　international reserve ease
国际储备货币/國際儲備貨幣　international reserve currency
国际储备资产/國際儲備資產　international reserve asset
国际储存安排/國際儲存安排　international stocking arrangement
国际传播机制/國際傳播機制　international transmission mechanism
国际贷款/國際貸款　international loan
国际贷款市场/國際放款市場　international loan market
国际担保/國際擔保　international guarantee
国际单位/國際單位　international unit
国际定价/國際定價　international pricing
国际短期资本/國際短期資本　international short term capital
国际短期资本流动/國際短期資本流動　international short term capital movement
国际多边贷款/國際多邊貸款　international multilateral loans
国际多元化战略/國際市場多元化戰略　international diversification
国际法/國際法　international law
国际法编纂/國際法編纂　codification of international law
国际法的渊源/國際法的淵源　source of international law
国际法基本原则/國際法基本原則　fundamental principle of international law
国际法客体/國際法客體　object of international law
国际法院/國際法院　International Court of Justice
国际法中的承认/國際法中的承認　recognition in international law
国际法主体/國際法主體　subject of international law

国际犯罪/國際犯罪　international crime
国际分包/國際分包　international sub-contracting
国际分工/國際分工　international division of labor
国际付款支付书/國際付款支付書　international payment order
国际负债/國際負債　international indebtedness
国际复兴开发银行/國際重建興開發銀行,世界銀行　International Bank of Reconstruction and Development, IBRD
国际更正权/國際更正權　international right of correction
国际公法/國際公法　international public law
国际公司/國際公司　international corporation
国际公司法/國際公司法　international corporation law
国际股票/國際股票　international stock
国际股票市场/國際股票市場　international stock market
国际股票投资/國際股權投資　international equity investment
国际管理货币制度/國際管理通貨制度　international managed currency system
国际惯例/國際慣例　international practice, international usage
国际海底区域/國際海底區域　international sea-bed area
国际海事法/國際海事法,海商法　International Maritime Law
国际海事仲裁规则/國際海事仲裁規則　Rule of International Maritime Arbitration
国际海洋法/國際海洋法　international law of the sea
国际海洋法法庭/國際海洋法法庭　International Tribunal for The law of the Sea
国际航空法/國際航空法　international air law
国际航行海峡/國際航行海峽　straits used for international navigation
国际合作/國際合作　international cooperation
国际合作总署/國際合作總署　International Cooperation Administration
国际河流/國際河川　international river
国际互联网信息中心/國際互聯網資訊中心　Internet Information Center
国际化战略/國際化策略　international strategy
国际划拨价格/國際間移轉定價　international transfer price
国际环境法/國際環境法　international environmental law

国际汇兑/國際匯兑　international exchange
国际汇兑清算/國際匯兑清算　foreign exchange clearance
国际汇票/國際匯票　international money order, international bill of exchange, foreign bill of exchange
国际货币/國際貨幣　international money, international currency
国际货币储备/國際貨幣儲備　international currency reserve
国际货币改革/國際貨幣改革　international monetary reform
国际货币管理/國際貨幣管理　international money management
国际货币合作/國際貨幣合作　international monetary cooperation
国际货币会议/國際貨幣會議　International Monetary Conference
国际货币机构/國際貨幣機構　international monetary institution
国际货币基金份额/國際貨幣基金份額　quotas of IMF
国际货币基金净提款额/國際貨幣基金淨提款額　net drawing
国际货币基金平价/國際貨幣基金平價　IMF par value
国际货币基金协定/國際貨幣基金協定　International Monetary Fund Agreement
国际货币基金信贷/國際貨幣基金信貸　IMF credit
国际货币基金组织/國際貨幣基金組織　International Monetary Fund, IMF
[国际货币基金组织]备用信贷协定/[國際貨幣基金組織]備用信貸協定　standby credit arrangement
[国际货币基金组织]标准货币篮子方式/[國際貨幣基金組織]標準貨幣籃子方式　standard currency basket system
[国际货币基金组织的]特别提款权/特別提款權　special drawing right, SDR
[国际货币基金组织]第一档信贷/[國際貨幣基金組織]第一檔信用貸款　first credit tranche
[国际货币基金组织]第一档信用贷款/[國際貨幣基金組織]第一檔信用貸款　first credit tranche
[国际货币基金组织]特种信托基金/[國際貨幣基金組織]特種信託基金　special trust fund
[国际货币基金组织]提款权/[國際貨幣基金組織]提款權　drawing rights of International Monetary Funds
国际货币流通/國際貨幣流通　international movement of money
国际货币市场/國際金融市場　international monetary market
国际货币体系/國際貨幣制度　international monetary system
国际货币危机/國際貨幣危機　international monetary crisis
国际货币协定/國際貨幣協定　international monetary arrangement
国际货币政策/國際貨幣政策　international monetary policy
国际货币秩序/國際貨幣秩序　international monetary order
国际货物买卖法/國際貨物買賣法　law of international sale of goods
国际技术转让/國際技術轉讓　international technology transfer
国际技术转让的法律适用/國際技術轉讓的法律適用　application of law in international technology transfer
国际技术转让交易/國際技術貿易　international technology transfer transactions
国际技术转让行动守则/國際技術轉讓行動守則　International Code of Conduct for the Transfer of Technology
国际技术转让周期/國際技術轉讓週期　international technology transfer cycle
国际价格水准/國際價格水準　international price level
国际价值/國際價值　international value
国际价值规律/國際價值規律　law of international value
国际间的债权/國際間的債權　international claim
国际间货物买卖/國際間貨物買賣　international sale of goods
国际间交易的结算/國際間交易的結算　settlement of international transaction
国际间收支调整/國際間收支調整　inter-country balance-of-payments adjustment
国际间易货贸易/國際間以貨易貨貿易　international barter
国际交易/國際交易　international transaction
国际结算/國際清算　international settlement
国际结算单位/國際結算單位　international liquidity unit
国际结算货币/國際清算貨幣　international settlement currency
国际借贷/國際借貸　international borrowing and

lending
国际借贷论/國際借貸理論 theory of international loan, theory of international indebtedness
国际借款/國際借款 international borrowing
国际金本位制/國際黃金本位 international gold standard
国际金融/國際金融 international finance
国际金融公司/國際金融公司 international finance corporation
国际金融机构/國際金融機構 international financial institution
国际金融理论/國際金融理論 theory of international finance
国际金融市场/國際金融市場 international financial market, world banking market
国际金融体系/國際金融制度 international financial system
国际金融危机/國際金融危機 international financial crisis
国际金融稳定性/國際金融穩定性 international financial stability
国际金融协定/國際金融協定 international finance agreement
国际金融中心/國際金融中心 international financial center
国际金银复本位制/國際金銀複本位制 international bimetallism
国际经纪人/國際經紀人 international broker
国际经济/國際經濟 international economy
国际经济合作/國際經濟合作 international economic co-operation
国际经济合作会议/國際經濟合作會議 International Economic Co-operation Conference
国际经济合作银行/國際經濟合作銀行 International Bank for Economic Co-operation, IBEC
国际经济交流/國際經濟交流 international economic interflow
国际经济新秩序/國際經濟新秩序 new order of international economy
国际经济学/國際經濟學 international economics
国际经济秩序/國際經濟秩序 international economic order
国际经济综合体/國際經濟綜合體 international economic complex
国际竞争/國際競爭 international competition
国际竞争能力/國際競爭能力 international competitive ability

国际竞争性招标/國際公開招標 international competitive bidding
国际纠纷/國際糾紛 international discord
国际居间贸易/國際居間貿易,國際仲介貿易,國際轉口貿易 international intermediary trade
国际卡特尔/國際卡特爾,國際同盟產銷 international cartel
国际会计/國際會計 international accounting
国际会计准则公报/國際會計準則公報 Statement of International Accounting Standards
国际会计准则理事会/國際會計準則理事會 International Accounting Standards Board, IASB
国际劳工准则/國際勞工標準 international labor standard
国际劳工组织/國際勞工組織 International Labor Organization
国际礼让/國際禮讓 Comitas Gentium
国际礼让说/國際禮讓説 doctrine of Comitas Gentium
国际利率/國際利率 world interest rate
国际利息战/國際利息戰 world interest war
国际联合保护知识产权局/國際聯合保護智慧財產權局 United International Bureau for the Protection of Intellectual Property Right
国际联盟/國聯 the League of Nations
国际卖主寡头垄断/國際寡占 international oligopoly
国际贸易/國際貿易 international trade
国际贸易白皮书/國際貿易白皮書 white paper on international trade
国际贸易标准分类/國際貿易標準分類 standard international trade classification
国际贸易差额/國際貿易差額 balance of international trade
国际贸易纯粹理论/國際貿易純粹理論 pure theory of international trade
国际贸易地区分布/國際貿易地區分布 international trade by region
国际贸易额/國際貿易額 value of international trade
国际贸易发展协会/國際貿易發展協會 International Trade Development Association
国际贸易港口/國際貿易港口 international trade port
国际贸易供给分析/國際貿易供給分析 supply analysis of international trade
国际贸易供给曲线/國際貿易供給曲線 international trade offer curve

国际贸易关系/國際貿易關係　international trade relation
国际贸易惯例/國際貿易慣例　customary practice in international trade, international trade custom
国际贸易伙伴/國際貿易夥伴　international trading partner
国际贸易交易会/國際貿易交易會　international trade fair
国际贸易局部均衡/國際貿易部分均衡　partial equilibrium of international trade
国际贸易理论/國際貿易理論　theory of international trade
国际贸易量/國際貿易量　quantum of international trade
国际贸易逆差/國際貿易逆差　adverse balance of international trade
国际贸易融资/國際貿易融資　international trade financing
国际贸易商品结构/國際貿易商品結構　international trade by commodity
国际贸易术语解释通则/國際貿易術語解釋通則　International Rules for the Interpretation of Trade Terms
国际贸易术语通则/國際貿易術語通則　International Code of Trade Terms
国际贸易统计/國際貿易統計　international trade statistics
国际贸易宪章/國際貿易憲章　International Trade Charter
国际贸易一般均衡/國際貿易一般均衡　general equilibrium of international trade
国际贸易证书/國際貿易證書，廠商進出口卡　international trading certificate, ITC
国际贸易中心/國際貿易中心　international trade center
国际贸易仲裁制度/國際貿易仲裁制度　international trade arbitration system
国际贸易自由化/國際貿易自由化　liberalization of international trade
国际民事管辖权/國際民事管轄權　international civil jurisdiction
国际民事诉讼程序法/國際民事訴訟程式法　international civil procedure law
国际民事诉讼费用担保/國際民事訴訟費用擔保　guarantee of the pre-litigation preservation of property in the international civil litigation
国际民事诉讼中的送达/國際民事訴訟中的送達　service of legal instrument in international civil litigation
国际拍卖/國際拍賣　international auction
国际赔偿基金/國際賠償基金　International Compensation Fund, ICF
国际赔偿责任/國際賠償責任　international compensation liability
国际批发贸易中心/國際批發貿易中心　International Centre for Wholesale Trade
国际票据法/國際票據法　law of international bill
国际贫困标准/國際貧困標準　international poverty line standard
国际贫困线/國際貧窮線　international poverty line
国际平衡/國際平衡　international equilibrium
国际期货市场/國際期貨市場　international futures market
国际企业/國際企業　international enterprise
国际倾销/國際傾銷　international dumping
国际清偿能力/國際清償能力　international liquidity
国际清算/國際清算　international clearing
国际清算联盟/國際清算聯盟　International Clearing Union
国际清算银行/國際清算銀行　Bank for International Settlement
国际人道主义法/國際人道主義法　internatioal humanitarian law
国际人力资源管理/國際人力資源管理　international human resource management
国际人权法/國際人權法　international human rights law
国际人权宪章/國際人權憲章　international bill of rights
国际商标注册/國際商標註冊　international registration of trademark
国际商法/國際商法　international trade law, law of international trade
国际商会/國際商會　International Chamber of Commerce
国际商会仲裁庭调解与仲裁规则/國際商會仲裁庭調解與仲裁規則　Rule of Conciliation and Arbitration of the International Chamber of Commerce
国际商会仲裁院/國際商會仲裁院　International Court of Arbitration of International Chamber of Commerce
国际商品/國際商品　international commodity, international goods, international merchandise
国际商品存储/國際商品儲存　international commodity stock

国际商品交易清算所/國際商品交易清算所 International Commodity Clearing House

国际商品交易委员会/國際商品貿易委員會 Commission on International Commodity Trade

国际商品统一分类/國際商品統一分類 Harmonized Commodity Description and Coding System

国际商品协议/國際商品協定 international commodity agreement

国际商事仲裁/國際商事仲裁 international commercial arbitration

国际商业/國際商業 international commerce

国际商业惯例/國際商業慣例，國際商業習慣 international commercial practice

国际审计与鉴证准则委员会/國際審計與鑒證準則理事會 International Auditing and Assurance Standards Board, IAASB

国际生产一体化/國際生產過程一體化 international production integration

国际生产折中论/國際生產折衷論 eclectic theory of international production

国际十进分类法/國際十進分類法 universal decimal classification, UDC

国际石油卡特尔/國際石油卡特爾 international petroleum cartel

国际石油资本/國際石油資本 international petroleum capital

国际市场/國際市場 international market

国际市场价格/國際市場價格 international market price

国际市场营销/國際行銷 international marketing

国际市场证券/國際市場證券 intercourse security

国际事务支出/國際事務支出 international affair expenditure

国际收支/國際收支餘額 balance of payments

国际收支不平衡/國際收支不平衡 disequilibrium of balance of payment, imbalance in world payment, payments disequilibrium

国际收支差额/國際收支差額 balance of international payment

国际收支赤字/國際收支赤字 payments deficit

国际收支官方结算/國際收支官方結算 official settlement

国际收支货币分析法/國際收支貨幣分析法 monetary approach to balance of payment

国际收支结构/國際收支結構 balance of payment structure

国际收支经常账户顺差/國際收支經常賬户順差 surplus of the nation on current account

国际收支逆差/國際收支逆差 international payment deficit, adverse balance of payment

国际收支平衡/國際收支平衡 payment equilibrium, equilibrium of balance of payment, balance of payment equilibrium

国际收支平衡表/國際收支平衡表 international balance of payment, balance of international payments

国际收支顺差/國際收支順差 favorable balance of payment, international payment surplus

国际收支弹性分析方法/國際收支彈性分析方法 elasticity approach to balance of payment

国际收支调整机制/國際收支調整機制 adjustment mechanism of balance of payment, mechanism of adjustment of balance of payment

国际收支调整理论/國際收支調整理論 theory of balance of payment adjustment

国际收支危机/國際收支危機 balance of payments crises

国际收支吸收分析法/國際收支平衡吸收分析法，國際收支平衡歸納分析法 absorption approach to balance of payment

国际收支依赖性经济模型/國際收支依賴性經濟模型 dependent economy model of balance of payment

国际收支盈余/國際收支盈餘 payments surplus, balance of payment surplus

国际收支状况/國際收支狀況 balance of payment position

国际收支总差额/國際收支總差額 overall balance of international payment

国际书目控制/國際書目控制 universal bibliographic control, UBC

国际双重课税/國際雙重課稅 international double taxation

国际水道/國際水道 international wartercourses

国际水法/國際水法 law of international watercourses

国际税收/國際稅收 international tax

国际税收协定/國際稅收協定 international tax agreements

国际司法解决/國際司法解決 international judicial settlement

国际司法协助/國際司法協助 international judicial assistance

国际私法/國際私法 private international law, international private law

国际私法的国际立法/國際私法的國際立法 international legislation of international private law

国际私法的渊源/國際私法的淵源 sources of international private law

国际私法二元论/國際私法二元論 Dualism of International Private Law

国际私法中的管辖权/國際私法中的管轄權 jurisdiction in international private law

国际谈判/國際協商 international negotiation

国际逃税/國際逃稅,國際偷稅,國際避稅 international tax evasion

国际套利/國際套利 international interest arbitrage

国际条约/國際條約 international treaty

国际通货/國際通貨 universal currency

国际通货平准基金/國際通貨平準基金 international buffer stock

国际同业拆放市场/國際銀行同業拆放市場 international interbank market

国际偷税/國際偷稅,國際逃稅,國際避稅 international tax evasion

国际投资/國際投資 international investment

国际投资贷款/國際投資貸款 international investment loan

国际投资的相对优势说/國際投資的相對優勢說 theory of relative superiority of international investment

国际投资结构/國際投資結構 international investment structure

国际投资净额/國際投資淨額 net international investment

国际投资纠纷仲裁/國際投資糾紛仲裁 arbitration of international investment dispute

国际投资区位理论/國際投資區位理論 international investment location theory

国际投资市场/國際投資市場 international investment market

国际投资信托/國際投資信託 international investment trust

国际投资银行/國際投資銀行 international investment bank

国际图书博览会/國際書展 international book fair

国际外包/國際委外代工 international outsourcing

国际外汇市场/國際外匯市場 international exchange market

国际外汇危机/國際外匯危機 international exchange crisis

国际物价指数/國際物價指數 international price index

国际项目管理专业人员资质认证/國際專案管理專業資質認證 international project management professional, IPMP

国际协议/國際協定 international agreement

国际信贷/國際信貸 world credit

国际信托投资公司/國際信託投資公司 international trust and investment company

国际信息交流/國際資訊交流 international communication of information

国际刑法/國際刑法 international criminal law

国际刑法学/國際刑法學 science of international criminal law

国际刑事法院/國際刑事法院 international criminal court

国际刑事责任/國際刑事責任 international criminal liability

国际性垄断/國際性壟斷 international monopoly

国际许可证交易制度/國際許可證交易制度 international licensing arrangements

国际一揽子投资/國際一籃子投資 package of international investment

国际移民/國際移民 international migration

国际银行设施/國際金融設施 international banking facilities

国际银行同业间拆放利率/國際銀行同業間拆放利率 international interbank call rate

国际银行业务理论/國際銀行業務理論 theory of international bank business

国际银行业务区/國際銀行業務區 international banking zone

国际银行业务设施/國際銀行業務設施 international banking facility

国际银团/國際銀團 international consortium of bank

国际营销/國際行銷 international marketing

国际硬通货/國際硬通貨 international hard currency

国际援助/國際援助 international aid

国际债务/國際債務 international bond, international debt

国际展览会/國際展覽會 international exhibition

国际账户/國際賬戶 international account

国际招标/國際招標 international bidding

国际招聘/國際招募 international recruitment

国际争端/國際爭端 international dispute

国际争端的司法解决/國際爭端的司法解決 judicial settlement of international disputes

国际证券/國際證券 international security

国际证券存单／國際證券收據　international depositary receipt
国际政策协调理论／國際政策協調　international policy coordination
国际支付／國際支付　international payment
国际支付危机／國際支付危機　international payment crisis
国际支付制度／國際支付制度　international payments system
国际支票／國際支票　international cheque
国际制裁／國際制裁　international sanction
国际中介贸易／國際居間貿易，國際仲介貿易，國際轉口貿易　international intermediary trade
国际仲裁／國際仲裁　international arbitration
国际仲裁法庭／國際仲裁法庭　International Court of Arbitration
国际仲裁会议／國際仲裁會議　international arbitration congress
国际专利／國際性專利　international patent
国际专业化／國際專業化　international specialization
国际准则／國際標準　international standard
国际资本／國際資本　international capital
国际资本流动／國際資本流動　international capital flow, international capital movement
国际资本市场／國際資本市場　international capital market
国际资本市场一体化／國際資本市場一體化　international capital market integration
国际租赁／國際租賃　international lease
国际组织／國際組織　international organization
国际组织的继承／國際組織的繼承　succession between international organizations
国际组织的责任／國際組織的責任　responsibility of international organizations
国际组织法／國際組織法　law of international organizations
国家／國家　state
国家标准／國家標準　national standard
国家代码／國家代碼　country code
国家档案馆／國家檔案館　national archives
国家地役／國家地役　state servitude
国家豁免／國家豁免　state immunity
国家继承／國家繼承　state succession
国家监督／國家監督　national supervision
国家行为／國家行爲　act of state
国家元首／國家元首　heads of state
国家责任／國家責任　state responsibility
国家主权／國家主權　national sovereignty

国库／國庫　state treasury
国库存款／國庫存款　treasury deposit
国民储蓄／國民儲蓄　national savings
国民储蓄率／國民儲蓄率　national saving rate
国民待遇／國民待遇　national treatment
国民生产净值／國民生產淨額　net national product, NNP
国民生产总值／國民生產毛額　gross national product, GNP
国民收入／國民所得　national income
国民消费／國民消費　national consumption
国内法／國內法　domestic law
国内生产总值／國內生產毛額　gross domestic product, GDP
国内市场／國內市場　domestic market
国外发行代号／國外發行代號　code of foreign distribution
国外投资／國外投資，外人投資　external investment, foreign investment
国外资产／國外資產，海外資產　external asset, overseas asset
国有资产／國有財產　state-owned assets
国债／國債，公債　government bond, public debt, treasury bond
国债发行／國債發行　circulation of government bonds
过版／過版　transfer
过程／過程，流程　process
过程变量／製程變數　process variable
过程变异分析／製程變異分析　process variation analysis
过程变异性／製程變異性　process variability
过程标准差／製程標準離差　process standard deviation
过程部门化／流程部門化　process departmentalization
过程冲突／過程衝突　process conflict
过程抽样／製程抽樣　process sampling
过程反应曲线／製程反應曲線　process reaction curve
过程方法／流程途徑　process approach
过程分布／製程分布　process distribution
过程分析／製程分析　process analysis
过程固有限／自然製程界限　natural process limit
过程极差／製程全距　process range
过程监控／製程追查　process surveillance
过程检验／製程檢驗　process inspection
过程接收／製程允收　process acceptance

过程决策程序图/過程決策程式圖　process decision program chart, PDPC
过程控制图/製程管制圖　process control chart
过程描述/進程描述　process description
过程模型/程序模式　process model
过程能力/製程能力　process capability
过程能力图/製程能力管制圖　process capability chart
过程能力指数/製程能力指標　process capability index
过程平均不合格率/過程平均不合格率　process averaging unqualified rate
过程平均不合格品率/製程平均不良品率　process average fraction nonconforming item
过程平均质量/製程平均品質　process average quality
过程评价/過程評估,程序評估　process evaluation
过程容差/製程允差　process tolerance
过程柔性/流程彈性,製程彈性　process flexibility
过程设计/流程設計,製程設計　process design
过程审核/流程稽核　process audit
过程实施/過程實施　process execution
过程数据/製程資料　process data
过程水平/製程水準　process level
过程特性/製程特性　process characteristic
过程维护/過程維護　process maintenance
过程西格玛/流程標準差　process sigma
过程型激励理论/程式型動機理論,程式型激勵理論　procedural motivation theory
过程型组织/過程型組織　process-oriented organization
过程诊断/過程診斷　process diagnosis
过程质量控制/製程品質管制　in-process quality control, IPQC
过程中检验/製程檢驗　in-process inspection, process inspection
过程咨询/程序諮詢　process consultation
过程组/過程群組　process group
过错/過錯　liability for fault
过错推定/過錯推定　presumption of fault
过错责任原则/過錯責任原則　fault principle
过度标引/過度標引　excessive indexing, excess indexing
过度波动/超額波動　excess volatility
过度城市化/過度城市化,過度都市化　overurbanization
过度反应/過度反應,反應過度　over reaction

过度离散/過度離勢　overdispersion
过度拟合/過度配適,過度適配　overfitting
过度识别/過度識別,過度認定　overidentified, over-identification
过度投资/過度投資　overinvestment
过度专业化/過度專業化　over-professionalization
过度自信/過度自信　over confidence
过渡内阁/過渡内閣　transitional cabinet
过渡性贷款/過渡性貸款　stop-gap loan
过渡银行/過渡性銀行　bridge bank
过渡用语/過渡用語　transition term
过境/過境　transit
过境关税/過境關稅　transit tariff
过境货物/過境貨物　floating goods
过境加工贸易/過境加工貿易　transit improvement trade
过境贸易/轉口貿易　transit trade
过境税/過境稅,通行稅　transit tax, transit toll, transit duty
过刊/過刊,过期雜志　back number, back issue, back periodical file
过刊登记/過刊登記　registration of back issues
过量生产浪费/過量生產浪費　overproduction waste
过录本/過錄本　book with previous annotate and comments
过滤/過濾　filtering
过期订单/過期訂單　past due order
过期汇票/過期匯票　stale bill of exchange
过期刊物/過期刊物　back issue
过期票据/過期票據　overdue bill, past due note
过期提单/過期提單　stale bill of lading
过期未付款项/過期未付款項　overdue payment
过期未还图书/過期未還圖書　overdue book
过期应收票据/過期應收票據　note receivable past due
过期账款/過期賬款　past due account
过期支票/過期支票　out of date cheque, stale cheque, overdue cheque
过剩产能/過剩產能,超額產能　excess production capacity
过剩功能/過剩功能　surplus function
过剩库存/過剩存貨　excess inventory
过失/過失　liability of negligence
过失相抵规则/過失相抵規則　principle of negligence offset
过账/過賬　posting

H

哈代公式/哈代公式　Hardy's formula
哈代求和法/哈代總和法　Hardy summation method
哈尔西奖金制/哈氏獎勵工資制　Halsey's premium system
哈里斯大纸草/哈里斯大紙草　Great Harris Papyrus
哈里逊法/哈里森法　Harrison's method
哈里游动/哈里斯漫步　Harris walk
哈利逼近/Harley 逼近　Harley approximation
哈林顿/哈林頓　James Harrington
哈罗德-多马模型/哈羅德-杜馬模型　Harrod-Domar model
哈罗德-多马增长模型/哈羅德-杜馬成長模型　Harrod-Domar growth model
哈罗德中性/哈羅德中性成長　Harrod-neutral growth
哈奇扬算法/哈奇揚演算法　Khachiyan algorithm
哈特/哈特　Herbert Lionel Adolphus Hart
哈特利检验/哈特里檢定　Hartley's test
哈特利-拉奥方案/Hartley-Rao 方案　Hartley-Rao scheme
哈特内斯人性论/哈特内斯人性論　human nature theory of Hartness
哈特-斯科特-罗迪诺反垄断改进法案/哈特-史高特-羅帝諾法　Hart-Scott-Rodino Act
哈耶克/哈耶克　F. A. Hayek
哈耶克新自由主义/哈耶克新自由主義　Hayek neo-liberalism
孩子的成本-效用/孩子的成本-效用　cost-utility of child
海报/海報, 布告, 公告　poster
海盗版/海盜版　piratical edition
海盗罪/海盜罪　crime of piracy
海德归因理论/海德歸因理論　Heider's attribution theory
海关/海關　customs house
海关程序/海關手續　customs procedures
海关的出库许可证/海關的出庫許可證　permit for withdrawing
海关担保制度/海關擔保制度　customs guarantee system, system of customs guarantee
海关档案/海關檔案　customs archive

海关发票/海關發票　customs invoice
海关估价/海關估價　customs valuation
海关关税法/海關關稅法　customs tariff law
海关过境保证/海關過境保證　transshipment bond
海关监管货物/海關監管货物　goods under customs supervision
海关检查/驗關　customs inspection
海关检查人员/海關檢查人員　land waiter
海关检疫条例/海關檢疫條例　sanitary custom-house regulation
海关进口税则/海關進口稅則　customs import tariff
海关扣押货物/海關扣押货物　seized goods
海关免税仓库/海關免稅倉庫　customs free depot
海关免税货单/海關免稅貨單, 自由貨單　free list
海关的入库许可证/海關的入庫許可證　permit for warehousing
海关申报单/申報單　declaration form
海关提供的特惠措施/海關特惠區　special customs-privileged facility
海关统计/通關統計　customs statistics
海关退税/海關退稅　customs drawback
海关退税货物/海關退稅貨物　drawback cargo
海关退税申报/海關退稅申報　drawback entry
海关许可证/海關許可證　customs permit
海关的转运许可证/海關的轉運許可證　permit for transshipment
海关装载许可证/海關裝載許可證　loading permit
海量数据/大量資料　massive data, mass data
海林格距离/Hellinger 距離　Hellinger distance
海难救助/海難救助　marine salvage
海难统计/海難統計　statistics of damaged vessels
海瑞/海瑞　Hai Rui
海萨尼转换/Harsanyi 轉換　Harsanyi transformation
海商法/海商法　maritime law
海商法中的船舶抵押/海商法中的船舶抵押　marine mortgage
海上保险/海上保險　marine insurance
海上保险商/海上保險人　marine insurer
海上抵押/海上抵押　maritime mortgage
海上贸易/海上貿易　sea commerce, floating trade, marine trade
海上碰撞国际规则/海上避碰國際規則　the national

rules of collision at sea

海上侵权的法律适用/海上侵權的法律適用 application of law of the torts on the sea

海上优先受偿权/海上優先受償權 marine lien

海氏价值评价法/海氏價值評價法 Hay guide-chart profile

海事国际私法/海事國際私法 private international maritime laws

海事仲裁/海事仲裁 maritime arbitration

海事仲裁委员会/海事仲裁委員會 Maritime Arbitration Commission

海损/海損 marine loss, sea damage

海损理赔代理人/海損理賠代理人 average agent

海损理算/海損理算,海損精算 average adjustment

海损理算人/海損理算人,海損精算人 average stater

海损理算书/海損理算書,海損精算書 average statement

海损理算员/海損理算員,海損精算員 averager

海损条款/海損條款 sea damage terms

海损协议书/海損合約 average agreement

海外负债/海外負債 overseas liability

海外合资企业/海外合資企業 overseas joint venture

海外津贴/海外津貼 overseas premium

海外经济合作/海外經濟合作 overseas economic cooperation

海外控股公司/海外控股公司 overseas holding company

海外利率/海外利率 overseas interest rate

海外贸易/海外貿易 overseas trade

海外情报单位/海外情報單位 intelligence overseas unit

海外私人投资/海外私人投資 overseas private investment

海外私人投资公司/海外私人投資公司 overseas private investment corporation, OPIC

海外提单/海外提單 overseas bill of lading

海外投资/海外投資 overseas investment

海外投资保险/海外投資保險 overseas investment insurance

海外投资保证/海外投資保證 guarantee of overseas investment

海外投资利润保险/海外投資利潤保險 overseas investment profit insurance

海外需求/海外需求 overseas demand

海外业务经营/海外業務 foreign operation

海外业务融资/海外業務融資 financing of overseas business

海湾/海灣 bays

海峡/海峽 strait

海牙法/海牙法 Hague Law

海牙规则/海牙規則 Hague Rules

海牙国际私法公约/海牙國際私法公約 Hague Conventions on Private International Law

海牙国际私法会议/海牙國際私法會議 Hague Conference on Private International Law

海牙国际私法会议章程/海牙國際私法會議章程 Statute of the Hague Conference on Private International Law

海牙婚姻公约/海牙婚姻公約 Convention relating to the Settlement of the Conflict of the Laws Concerning Marriage

海牙离婚与别居公约/海牙離婚與別居公約 Convention on the Recognition of Divorces and Legal Separations

海洋法/海洋法 law of the sea

海洋环境保护法/海洋環境保護法 law on protection of marine environment

海洋环境污染/海洋環境汙染 marine pollution

海洋科学研究/海洋科學研究 marine scientific research

海洋运输保险/海上運輸保險 marine transportation insurance

海因里希法则/海因里希法則 Heinrich rule

海运保险代理人/海上保險代理人 marine insurance agent

海运保险单/海上保險單 marine insurance policy

海运保险法/海上保險法 marine insurance law

海运保险费/海上保險費 marine insurance premium

海运保险公司/海上保險公司 marine insurance company

海运保险合同/海上保險合約 marine insurance contract

海运保险条款/海上保險條款 marine insurance clause

海运保险辛迪加/海上保險辛迪卡,海上保險聯保 marine syndicate

海运保险中的船舶双重估值/雙重船舶估值 dual valuation

海运法/海運法 merchant marine act

海运货物保险/海上貨物保險 marine cargo insurance

海运货物成数分保合同/海上貨物成數分保條約 marine cargo quota share reinsurance treaty

海运提单/海運提單 marine bill of lading

海战法/海戰法 law of naval warfare

含湿量/含濕量，比較濕度　specific humidity
含佣金价格/含佣金價格　price including commission
函授教育/函授教育　correspondence education
p 函数/p 函數　p-function
函数逼近法/函數逼近法　function approaching method
函数关系模型/函數關係模型　functional relationship model
函数生产指数/函數生產指數　functional production index
函数指数/函數指數　functional index number
函套装/函套裝　case binding
涵化/涵化，納入　acculturation, inclusion, cultivation
涵化理论/涵化理論　cultivation theory
涵化研究/涵化研究　cultivation study
韩非法制思想/韓非法制思想　legal system thought of Hanfei
韩国综合股价指数/韓國綜合股價指數　Korea composite stock price index
喊价调整/喊價調整　bidding adjustment
汉堡规则/漢堡規則　Hamburg rules
汉堡制/漢堡制　Hamburg system
汉迪管理哲学/漢迪管理哲學　management philosophy of Charles Handy
汉律/漢律　Han Code
汉谟拉比法典/漢摩拉比法典　Code of Hammurabi
汉萨同盟/漢撒聯盟　Hanseatic league
汉语主题词表/漢語主題詞表　Chinese Thesaurus
旱滩坡纸/旱灘坡紙　Hantanpo paper
翰林待诏/翰林待詔　Hanlin Daizhao, academician awaiting orders
翰林院/翰林院　Hanlin Academy
行长/欄寬　line length
行话/行話　jargon
行会/行會　gild, guild
行纪合同/行紀合同　contract of commission agency
行间/行間　interlinear
行间方差/列間變異［數］　between-row variation, between-row variance
行列设计/行列設計　row and column design
行平方和/列平方和　row sum of squares
行尾分词/分音節　hyphenation
行业/行業　industries
行业标准/工業標準，產業標準　industry standard
行业标准分类/行業標準分類　standard classification of industries
行业分类/行業分類　classification of industries
行业分类体系/行業分類制度　industry classification system
行业工会/職業工會　craft union
行业供给曲线/產業供給曲線　industry supply curve
行业名录/產業目錄　industry directory
行业内合作/同行間合作　intra-group cooperation
行业内交易/同行間交易　intra-group transaction
行业剖析/行業剖析　industry profiling
行业期刊/行業期刊　industry journal
行业统一定额/行業統一定額　unified industry quota
行业协会/同業公會　trade association, business association
行业性集体合同/行業性集體合同　industrial collective contracts
行业自律/業界自律　industry self-regulation
航海条例/航海法案　navigation acts
航空管制取消法案/航空解除管制法　airline deregulation act
航空器/航空器　aircraft
航空运输险/航空運輸險　aviation insurance
航空照片/空照圖　aerial photograph
航空自由/航空自由　freedom of aerial navigation
航图/航圖　chart
豪华本/豪華版　deluxe edition
豪华装/豪華裝　costly binding
好莱坞/好萊塢　Hollywood
号码索引/號碼索引　numerical index
号外/號外　hot news extra edition, extra of a newspaper
耗竭性资源/耗竭性資源　depletable resources
耗散结构理论/耗散結構理論，消散結構理論　dissipative structure theory
耗损时期/耗損時期　wear-out period
合版/合版　co-edition
合编者/合編者　joint editor
合并/合并　merger, combination
合并报价单/合并報價單　combined quotation
合并财务报表/合并財務報表　consolidated financial statement
合并订单/合并訂貨單　combined order
合并发盘/聯合報價　combined offer
合并方差/綜合變異數　pooled variance
合并数据/合并資料　pooled data
合并损益计算书/合并損益表　combined profit and loss statement
合并样本方差/綜合樣本變異數　pooled sample variance
合并资产负债表/合并資產負債表　combined

balance sheet, consolidated balance sheet
合成肥料/化学肥料　synthetic fertilizers
合成画面/蒙太奇,鏡頭組接　montage
合成谬误/合成謬誤　fallacy of composition
合成评比法/合成評比法　synthetic leveling
合成期权/合成式選擇權契約　synthetic options
合成时间标准/合成時間標準　synthetic time standard
合成数据/合成數據　synthetic data
合成纤维/合成纖維　synthetic fibers
合成证券/合成式證券　synthetic securities
合订本/合訂本　bound volume, composite volume
合订本期刊/期刊合訂本　bound periodical
合法的举债幅度/合法的舉債幅度　legal debt margin
合法化/合法性　legitimation
合法经营/合法經營　legitimate operation
合法律性/合法律性　legality
合法贸易/合法貿易　lawful trade
合法票据/合法票據　just bill, eligible bill
合法契约/合法契約　legal contract
合法权威/合法權威　legitimate authority
合法收入/合法收入　legitimate income
合法投资/合法投資　legal investment
合法性/合法性,正当性　legitimacy
合法性机制/合法性機制　mechanism of legitimacy
合法性危机/合法性危機,正當性危機　legitimation crisis
合法用户/合法用戶　legitimate user
合法证券/合法證券　legal security
合格/合格　conformity
合格工人/合格工人　qualified worker
合格监督/符合性監督　conformity surveillance
合格判定数/允收界限　acceptance limit
合格票据/合格票據　eligible paper
合格品/良品　non-defective unit
合格认证/合格認證　conformity certification
合股/合股　joint stock
合股银行/合股銀行　joint-stock bank
合规性稽核/合規性稽核　compliance-based audit
合伙/合夥　partnership
合伙企业/合夥企業　partnership enterprise
合伙契约/合夥契約　partnership agreement
合伙人/合夥人,工作夥伴　partner
合伙协议/合夥契約　partnership agreement
合伙债务/合夥債務　debt of partnership
合集/合集　collection
合计/合計,總數,總量　total

合刊/合刊　combined issue
合理保证/合理確信　reasonable assurance
合理成本估算/合理成本估算　should-cost estimate
合理化运动/合理化運動　rationalization movement
合理价值/合理價值　reasonable value
合理利润/合理利潤　reasonable profit
合理使用/合理使用　fair use
合理使用条款/合理使用原則　fair-use doctrine
合理索赔/合理索賠　legitimate claim
合理性规范/合理性規範　rationality norm
合理演绎法/合理演繹法　reasonable deduction
合理原则/合理原則　rule of reason
合谋/共謀　collusion
合群立会/合群立會　social community
合署办公/聯合辦事　joint office
合同/合約,契約　contract
合同保证金/合約保證金　contract deposit
合同变更/合約變更　modification of contract
合同筹资/合約融資　contract financing
合同到期/合約到期　expiration of contract
合同缔结地法/從簽約地法　Lex Loci Contractus
合同法律关系/合約法律關係　legal relationship in contract
合同法律关系客体/合約法律關係客體　subject of legal relationship in contract
合同法律关系主体/合約法律關係主體　object of legal relationship in contract
合同范本/合約範本　model contract
合同附带的保证/合約附帶的保證　guarantee incidental to contract
合同工/合約制工人　worker of contract system
合同工作分解结构/合約工程分類結構　contract work breakdown structure, CWBS
合同工作说明书/合約工作聲明　contract statement of work
合同公证/合約公證　notarization of a contract
合同管理/合約管理　contract administration
合同管理计划/合約管理計劃　contract management plan
合同规定价格/合約約定價格　contract stipulated price
合同货币/合約貨幣　contract currency
合同集/合約集　contract set
合同价/合約價格　contract price
合同鉴证/合約鑒證　identification of contract
合同解除/合約解除,取消合約　rescission of a contract, discharge of contract
合同金额/合約金額　contract amount

合同履行/履行合同　fulfill contract
合同期限/合約期限　term of contract
合同权利/契約權利　contractual right
合同生效/合約生效　execution of contract
合同示范文本/合約示範文本　demonstration version of contract
合同收尾/合約收尾　contract closure
合同授权/簽訂授權合約　contract authority
合同条件/契約條件　condition of contract
合同条款/合約條款,契約條款　contract clause, contractual provision
合同通用条件/合約通用條款　general condition of contract
合同文件/契約文件,契約書,契約檔　contract document
合同协定优惠待遇/條約優惠待遇　treaty benefit
合同协议书/合約協議書　contract agreement
合同义务/契約義務　contractual obligation
合同有效期/合約有效期　life of contract, period of contract
合同诈骗罪/合約詐騙罪　crime of contractual fraud
合同终止/合約終止　termination of contract
合同专用条件/特別契約條款　special condition of contract
合同转让/合約轉讓　assignment of contract
合宪性解释/合憲性解釋　interpretation according to the constitution
合样/合樣　edited sample combination
合宜批/合宜批　convenience lot
合议庭/合議庭　collegial bench
合议庭评议/合議庭評議　deliberations of collegial bench
合议制/合議制　collegial system
合意管辖/合意管轄　consensual jurisdiction
合意增长率/有保證的成長率　warranted rate of growth
合营企业验资/合營企業驗資　verification of capital of joint venture
合约/合約,契約　contract
合约储蓄机构/契約儲蓄機構　contractual savings institution
合约基础/契約基數　contract base
合约谈判能力理论/契約協商理論　bargain theory of contract
合著/合著　joint publication, joint work
合著者/合著者　joint author, co-author
合资/合資　joint capital
合资经营期满/中止共同投資　termination of joint venture
合资扩散模式/合資企業擴散模式　joint venture diffusion model
合资企业/合資企業,合資公司　joint venture
合作/合作　cooperation
合作保存/合作保存　collaborative preservation
合作编目/合作編目　cooperative cataloguing
合作博弈/合作賽局　cooperative game
合作博弈理论/合作的賽局理論　cooperative game theory
合作采访/合作採訪　cooperative acquisition
合作参考咨询/合作參考諮詢　cooperative reference
合作出版/合作出版　cooperative publishing
合作创新/合作創新　cooperative innovation
合作对策/合作賽局　cooperative game
合作馆藏发展/合作發展館藏　cooperative collection development
合作化/合作化　cooperativization
合作化运动/合作運動　cooperative movement
合作伙伴网络/合作夥伴網路　partner network
合作经济/經濟合作　economic cooperation
合作竞争/合作性競爭　cooperative competition
合作开发/合作開發　cooperative development
合作商务/協同商務　collaborative commerce
合作剩余/合作剩餘　cooperative surplus
合作式图书馆服务/合作式圖書館服務　cooperative library service
合作型战略实施/合作型策略執行　cooperation-type strategy implementation
合作性均衡/合作均衡　cooperative equilibrium
合作研发/合作研發　research and development cooperation, research and development collaboration
合作医疗/合作醫療　cooperative health services
合作议价模型/談判合作模型　bargaining cooperative models
合作银行/合作銀行　bank for cooperative
合作战略/合作策略　cooperative strategy
合作组织/合作組織　cooperation organization
合作作品/合作作品　joint work
和而不同/和而不同　harmony in diversity
和解/和解　conciliation
和解程序/和解程式　conciliation proceedings
和解员/斡旋者　conciliator
和离/和離　ancient Chinese legal institution of two sides agreement to divorce
和平共处五项原则/和平共處五項原則　Five Principles of Peaceful Coexistence
和平解决国际争端/和平解決國際爭端　peaceful

settlement of international disputes
和平利用外层空间委员会/和平利用外太空委員會　Committee on Peaceful Uses of Outer Space
荷兰式拍卖/荷式拍賣　Dutch auction
荷兰式拍卖招标/荷蘭式競標　Dutch auction tender offer
核定产能/實證產能　demonstrated capacity
核定税款/核定稅款　tax demand
核对表/檢核表　check list
核对法/核對法　check in work
核稿/核稿　examine manuscript
核估计/核估計　kernel estimation
核红/核紅　cross validation
核回归估计/核回歸估計　kernel regression estimation
核近似/核逼近　kernel approximation
核密度估计/核密度估計　kernel density estimation
核判别分析/核判別分析　kernel discriminant analysis
核签/核簽　check and issue
核实/驗證　verification
核心产品/核心產品　core product
核心存款/核心存款　core deposit
核心读者/核心讀者　core reader
核心馆藏/核心館藏　core collection
核心级编目/核心級編目　core level cataloging
核心技术/核心技術　core technology
核心加选择计划/核心加選擇計劃　core plus option plan
核心家庭/核心家庭　nuclear family
核心价值观/核心價值　core value
核心竞争力/核心能耐,核心專長　core competence
核心竞争力分析/核心競爭能力分析　core competence analysis
核心劳动标准/核心勞動標準　core labor standard
核心领导者/核心領導者　core leader
核心媒体体系/核心媒體體系　core media system
核心期刊/核心期刊　core journal
核心期刊目录/核心期刊目錄　core list
核心区/集節區域　nodal region
核心受众/核心受眾　core audience
核心通货膨胀/核心通貨膨脹　core inflation
核心网站/核心網站　core website
核心用户/核心用戶　core user
核心元数据/核心元資料　core metadata
核心元素/核心單元　core element
核心员工/核心員工　core employee
核心知识/核心知識　core knowledge

核心资本/核心資本　core capital
核心作者/核心作者　core author
核准/核準　authorization
盒式磁带/卡式磁帶　cassette tape, cartridge tape
盒式光盘/卡式光碟　optical disc cartridge
盒式音带/卡式錄音帶　recorded audio cassette
盒须图/盒鬚圖　box-and-whisker plot
赫尔馆/胡爾館　Hull House
赫尔米希的标准化/赫爾米希的標準化　Hellmisch's standardization
赫尔默特变换/赫爾默特變換　Helmert transformation
赫尔默特分布/赫爾默特分布,赫爾默特分配　Helmert distribution
赫尔默特准则/赫爾默特準則　Helmert criterion
赫芬达尔指数/赫芬德指數　Herfindahl index
赫福德工厂布局/赫福德工廠布局　plant layout of Herford
赫格洛兹定理/海格勒斯定理　Herglotz's theorem
赫克歇尔-俄林的国际贸易理论/漢克夏-歐林的國際貿易理論　Heckscher-Ohlin theory of international trade
赫克歇尔-俄林定理/漢克夏-歐林定理　Heckscher-Ohlin theorem
赫克歇尔-俄林要素禀赋理论/漢克夏-歐林的要素稟賦理論　factor endowment theory of Heckscher-Ohlin
赫里格尔-斯洛克姆权变论/赫里格爾-斯洛克姆權變論　contingency theory of Hellriegel-Slocum
赫利-布雷定理/Helly-Bray 定理　Helly-Bray theorem
赫利第一定理/海里第一定理　Helly's first theorem
赫灵竞争情报循环模型/赫林模型　Herring model
赫斯-加罗-莫顿模型/HJM 模型　Heath-Jarrow-Morton model, HJM model
赫希曼基准/赫希曼準則　Hirschman criteria
赫兹/赫茲　Hertz, Hz
黑白广告/黑白廣告　black and white advertise
黑白胶片/黑白片　black and white film
黑带/黑帶　black belt, BB
黑带大师/黑帶大師,大黑帶　master black belt, MBB
黑海战略/黑海戰略　black ocean strategy
黑盒测试/黑箱測試　black box testing
黑口/黑口　black folding line
黑塞矩阵/漢森矩陣,赫士矩陣　Hessian matrix
黑社会/幫派,秘密社會　gang, secret society
黑市/黑市　black market

黑市汇兑/黑市匯兑 black market exchange
黑市价格/黑市價格 black market price, off-the-book quotation
黑市交易/黑市交易 black market bargain
黑市外汇汇率/黑市外匯匯率 black market exchange rate
黑市物价调查/黑市物價調查 black market price survey
黑体字法/黑體字法 black-letter law
黑箱/黑箱,黑盒子 black box
黑箱方法/黑箱法 black box approach
黑箱系统/黑箱系統 black box systems
亨特-斯坦定理/Hunt-Stein 定理 Hunt-Stein theorem
恒等误差/相同分布误差 identical errors
恒定故障率/常数故障率 constant failure rate
恒定故障期/常数故障週期 constant failure period
恒定失效率/常数故障率 constant failure rate
恒定失效期/常数故障週期 constant failure period
恒定误差/常数误差 constant error
恒定相对风险厌恶/固定相對風險趨避 constant relative risk averse
恒定相对风险厌恶效用函数/固定相對風險趨避效用函數 constant relative risk averse utility function
恒幅录音/恆幅錄音 constant amplitude recording
恒久状态/恆久狀態 persistent state
恒生指数/恆生指數 Hang Seng Index
恒速录音/恆速錄音 constant velocity recording
横断面分析/横斷分析 cross section analysis
横幅广告/横幅廣告 banner advertisement
横挂式/横掛式 horizontal hanging type
横截面数据/横斷面資料 cross-sectional data
横排/横向排法 horizontal format, landscape
横剖面分析/横斷面資料分析 cross-section analysis
横切面研究/横斷面研究 cross-sectional study
横丝绺/横絲流 across the grain
横条图/横條圖 horizontal bar chart
横向并购/水平并購,水平購并 horizontal acquisition
横向磁化/横向磁化 transverse magnetization
横向公平/横向公平 horizontal equity
横向沟通/横向溝通,平行溝通 lateral communication
横向国际专业化/水平國際專業化 horizontal international specialization
横向兼并/水平并購 horizontal merger
横向录音/横向錄音 lateral recording
横向贸易/水平貿易 horizontal trade
横向平等与纵向平等/横向平等與縱向平等 horizontal equity vs. vertical equity
横向市场划分/水平市場分割 horizontal market division
横向限制竞争行为/水平限制行為 horizontal restrictive practices
横向研究/横斷面研究 cross-sectional study
横向一体化/水平整合 horizontal integration
横向职业生涯路径/跨域職涯路徑 transverse career path
横轴/横軸 axis of abscissa
横坐标/横尺度 horizontal scale
衡量性原则/衡量性原則 principle of balancing
衡平法/衡平法 equity
衡平法理学/衡平法理學 equity jurisprudence
衡平法上的权利/衡平法上的權利 equitable right
衡平谦抑原则/衡平謙抑原則 equitable restraint principle
红本/紅本 Hongben
红本处/紅本處 Hongben Division
红海战略/紅海戰略 red ocean strategy
红利计划/分紅 bonus plan
红利率/紅利率 bonus rate
红利之谜/股利之謎 dividend puzzle
红利自动转投计划/股利自動再投資 automatic dividend reinvestment plan
红皮书/紅皮書 red paper, red book
红狮与日标志/紅獅與日標志 Red Lion and Sun Emblem
红十字标志/紅十字標志 Red Cross Emblem
红十字国际委员会/紅十字國際委員會 International Committee of the Red Cross
红水晶标志/紅水晶標志 Red Crystal Emblem
红条款信用证/紅邊條款信用狀 letter of credit with red clause
红外线触摸屏/紅外線觸控式螢幕 infrared touch screen
红新月标志/紅新月標志 Red Crescent Emblem
红珠实验/紅珠實驗 red bead experiment
宏观过程/總體過程 macro process
宏观环境/宏觀環境,總體環境 macroenvironment
宏观计量模型/總體計量模型 macro econometric models
宏观鉴定论/宏觀鑒定論 macro-appraisal theory
宏观鉴定战略/宏觀鑒定戰略 macro-appraisal strategy
宏观经济调控/宏觀經濟調控 macroeconomic

regulation
宏观经济统计学/總體經濟統計學　macroeconomic statistics
宏观经济稳定/總體經濟穩定　macroeconomic stabilization
宏观经济学/總體經濟學　macroeconomics
宏观社会学/宏觀社會學　macro-sociology
宏观调控/宏觀調控　macro-regulation
宏观调控手段/宏觀控制手段　macro-control means
洪-斯坦模型/Hong-Stein 模型, HS 模型　Hong-Stein model, HS model
侯-李模型/Ho-Lee 模型　Ho-Lee model
后保管模式/後保管模式　post-storage mode
后到先办/後到先服務　last come first served
后到先服务规则/後到先服務規則　last come first served, LCFS
后电影开发/後電影開發　post-film development
后端生产线/下游生產線　downstream
后发优势/後發優勢　advantage of backwardness
后方一致检索/後方一致檢索　end match retrieval
后工业城市/後工業都市　post-industrial city
后工业社会/後工業社會　post-industrial society
后合同义务/後合同義務　obligation of subsequent contract
后悔理论/遺憾理論　regret theory
后悔值准则/後悔值準則　regret value criterion
后记/後記, 跋　afterword
后继背书人/連續背書人　subsequent endorser
后继标识系统/後繼標識系統　successive designations for serials
后进市场/後進市場　follow market
后进先出/後進先出[原則]　last-in-first-out
后进先出法/後進先出法　last in first out, LIFO
后凯恩斯经济学/後凱因斯主義　post-Keynesian economics
后凯恩斯主流经济学/後凱因斯主流經濟學　post-Keynesian mainstream economics
后控词表/後控制詞彙　post-controlled vocabulary
后期物业管理/後期物業管理　later-stage property management
后期行动者/後進者　late mover
后期制作/音訊後製　post-production
后社会史/後社會史　post-social history
后塑文化/後塑文化　post-figurative culture
后弯曲线/後彎曲線　backward-bending curves
后魏律/後魏律　Laws of Houwei Dynasty
后物质主义价值取向/後物質主義價值取向　post-material value orientation

后现代分层理论/後現代分層理論　post-modernity stratification theory
后现代女性主义/後現代女性主義　postmodern feminism
后现代社会/後現代社會　post-modern society
后现代性/後現代性　post-modernity
后向差分/向後差分　backward difference
后向差分函数/倒差分函數　backward difference function
后向差分运算子/向後差分算子　backward difference operator
后向方程/向後方程式　backward equation
后向关联/向後關聯　backward linkage
后向过程/向後過程　backward process
后向消元法/向後消去程序　backward elimination procedure
后向纵向一体化/向後垂直整合　backward vertical integration
后续背书/連續背書　successive endorsement
后续跟进安排/後續跟進安排　follow-up plan
后续工作/後續工作　succeeding activity
后续款目/後續款目　succeeding entry
后续问题/續問　following-up questions
后学院科学/後學院科學　post-academic science
后验法/後驗法　a posteriori method
后验分布/事後分布, 事後分配　posterior distribution
后验风险/事後風險　posterior risk
后验概率/後驗機率, 事後機率, 原因機率　probability of cause, posterior probability
后验密度函数/事後密度函數　posterior density function
后移算子/後移算子　backward shift operator
后印本/後印本　postprint
后援参考咨询服务/後備參考諮詢　backup reference service
后殖民理论/後殖民理論　postcolonial theory
后殖民主义/後殖民主義　post colonialism
后转/後轉　backward shifting
后组词/後組詞　post-coordinated term
后组式标引/後組式標引, 後組式索引　postcoordinate indexing
后组式检索语言/後組式檢索語言　post-coordination retrieval language
后组式索引/後組式索引　post-coordinate index
后组式语言/後組式語言　post-coordinate index language
厚描/厚描法, 深描法, 深厚描述　thick description

候选人形象/候選人形象　candidate image
候选人资格/候選人資格　candidacy eligibility
呼叫期权/呼叫期權　shout option
呼叫中心/客服中心　call center
弧弹性/弧彈性　arc elasticity
胡贝尔损失函数/胡伯損失函數　Huber loss function
胡佛–费希尔的区域经济发展阶段理论/胡佛–費雪區域經濟發展階段論　Hoover-Fisher's theory of stages of regional economic development
湖北革命实录馆/湖北革命實錄館　Hubei Revolutionary Records Museum
蝴蝶效应/蝴蝶效應　butterfly effect
蝴蝶装/蝴蝶裝　butterfly binding, butterfly folding
糊版/糊版　filling in
糊壳机/糊盒機　pasting box machine
互补型战略联盟/互補性策略聯盟　complementary strategic alliance
互补性商品/互補品　complementary goods, complements
互补性资产/互補性資產　complementary assets
互操作性/可交互運作性，交互作用　interoperability
互差/互離差　mutual deviation
互偿/互償，抵换　trade-off
互斥及周延事件/互斥及周延事件　exclusive and exhaustive event
互斥性/互斥性　mutual exclusivity
互动/互動　interaction
互动传播/互動傳播　interactive communication
互动电视/互動電視　interactive television
互动公平/互動公平　interactional justice
互动媒体/互動媒體　interactive media
互动模式/互動模式，交互作用模型　interaction model
互动网络/互動網路　interaction network
互动仪式/互動儀式　interaction ritual
互动营销/互動行銷　interactive marketing
互动游戏广告/互動遊戲廣告　interactive game advertisement
互换合约/互換合約　swap contract
互换货币协定/互換貨幣協議　reciprocal currency arrangement
互换货币协议/互換貨幣協定　swap agreement
互换检验/互換測驗　reversal tests
互换交易/互換交易　swap trade
互换期权/交換選擇權　swaption
互换市场/互換市場，外匯調期市場　swap market
互换外汇限额/互換外匯限額　swap line

互惠/互惠　reciprocity
互惠保险基金/互惠保險基金　unitized insurance fund
互惠待遇/互惠待遇　reciprocal favorable treatment
互惠待遇原则/待遇互惠原則　principle of reciprocal treatment
互惠分保/互惠分保　reciprocal reinsurance
互惠关税/互惠關稅，相互優惠關稅　reciprocal duty, mutual preferential duty, reciprocal tariff
互惠关税条约/互惠關稅條約　reciprocal tariff treaty
互惠合同/互惠合約　reciprocal contract
互惠基金/互惠基金，共同基金　swap fund, mutual fund
互惠交易/互惠交易　reciprocal dealing
互惠借阅/互惠借閱　reciprocal borrowing
互惠贸易/互惠貿易　commercial reciprocity, reciprocal trade
互惠贸易协议/互惠貿易協定　reciprocal trade agreement
互惠市场/互惠市場　reciprocal market
互惠条约/互惠條約　reciprocal treaty
互惠通商政策/互惠通商政策　bargaining policy
互惠外汇头寸/互惠外匯頭寸　swap position
互惠协定/互惠協定　reciprocal arrangement
互惠协定关税/互惠協定關稅　bargaining tariff
互惠信贷/互惠信貸　swap credit
互惠原则/互惠原則　principle of reciprocity, reciprocity
互借协定/相互互借協定　inter-lending agreement
互联网/網際網路　internet
互联网产业/互聯網產業　internet industry
互联网出版/互聯網出版　online publishing
互联网出版物/互聯網出版物　internet publication
互联网出版者/互聯網出版者　online publisher
互联网大众出版物/互聯網大眾出版物　the internet public publication
互联网地图/互聯網地圖　internet map
互联网地址分配机构/互聯網地址分配機構　Internet Assigned Numbers Authority
互联网电视/網路電視　internet television, web television, internet protocol television, IPTV
互联网技术商/互聯網技術商　internet technology business
互联网教育出版物/互聯網教育出版物　internet education publication
互联网期刊/互聯網期刊　online journal
互联网审查/互聯網審查　internet censorship
互联网条约/互聯網條約　internet treaties

互联网图书/互聯網圖書　internet book
互联网文学出版物/網路文學出版物　internet literary publication
互联网学术出版物/網路學術出版物　internet scholarly publication
互联网音像出版物/網路音像出版物　internet audio and video publication
互联网游戏出版物/網路遊戲出版物　internet gaming publication
互联网运营商/網路運營商　network operator
互联网杂志/網路雜誌　online magazine
互联网专业出版物/網路專業出版物　the internet professional publication
互链/互惠鏈接　reciprocal links
互逆相关性/互逆相關性　reversible relevance
互谱/交叉譜[相]　cross-spectrum, cross spectrum
互谱密度/交叉譜相密度　cross-spectral density
互投赞成票/選票互助　logrolling
互为话语性/交互話語性,互語性,交互論述　interdiscursivity
互文性/互文性　intertextuality
互相关函数/交叉相關函數　cross-correlation function
互相关图/交叉相關圖　cross-correlogram
互相关系数/交叉相關係數　cross-correlation coefficients
互相收受汇票/互相收受匯票　keep open account
互象征文化/互象徵文化　cofigurative culture
互协方差函数/交叉共變數函數　cross-covariance function
互协方差母函数/交叉共變數母函數　cross-covariance generating function
互益组织/互益組織　mutually-beneficial organization, mutually-supportive society
互助保险/互助保險,共同保險　mutual insurance, participating insurance
互助储蓄/相互儲蓄　mutual saving
互助储蓄银行/互助儲蓄銀行　mutual saving bank
互助会/民間標會　rotating saving and credit association
互助基金/互助基金,共同基金　mutual fund
互助条约/互助條約　treaty of mutual assistance
互助银行/互助銀行　mutual bank
户籍/户籍　huji, household register, residential registration
户籍人口/户籍人口　residentially registered population
户口登记/户籍登記　household registration
户口管理制度/户籍管理制度　Hukou system
户量/户量　volume of household
户外广告/户外廣告　outdoor advertising
户外媒介/户外媒體　out-of-home media
户外显示屏/户外顯示幕　outdoor screen
护封/護封　book jacket
护理院/養護中心　nursing home
护身符/護身符　amulet
护条/書鏈　joint
沪深300指数/滬深300指數　Shanghai Shenzhen 300 index
花絮/花絮,漫談　talk-about
花园城市/花園城市　garden city
华格纳法则/華格納法則　Wagner's law
华沙公约/華沙協定　Warsaw Convention
滑动板书架/滑動書架　sliding shelves
滑动钉住汇率/機動釘住匯率　sliding peg exchange rate
滑动关税/機動關稅　sliding duty, sliding scale tariff
滑动价格/機動價格　sliding scale price
滑动检验/滑動檢定　slippage test
滑动平价/機動平價,可調整平價　sliding parity
滑准税/準浮動關稅　quasi-sliding tariff
化学品安全评价/化學品安全評價　safety assessment for chemical substances
化学武器的禁用/化學武器的禁用　prohibition on the use of chemical weapons
化学物质风险评价/化學物質風險評價　risk assessment of chemical substances
化学性污染/化學汙染　chemical pollution
化妆品/化妝品　cosmetic products, cosmetics
化妆品标识/化妝品標識　cosmetics identification
划变/掃換,轉場　wipe
划定保管期限/訂定保存期限　scheduling
划分/分割　compartmentalization, partition
划汇转账/劃撥轉賬　giro transfer
划线/格線　ruling
划线支票/劃線支票　crossed cheque, cross check
画册/畫集　album
画幅/影幅　frame
画刊/畫刊　illustrated magazine, pictorial
画面比例/畫面比例,寬高比,縱橫比　aspect ratio
画外音/畫外音　offscreen voice
画像/畫像　portrait
话语/話語,論述,論域　discourse
话语分析/話語分析,論述分析　discourse analysis
话语共同体/論述社群　discourse community
话语间性/交互話語性,互語性,交互論述

interdiscursivity
话语社区/論述社群　discourse community
话语心理学/話語心理學,論述心理學　discursive psychology
怀特检验/懷特檢定　White test
坏账/壞賬　bad account, bad debt
坏账损失/壞賬損失　loss on bad debt
坏账准备/壞賬準備　provision for bad debt
坏账准备规则/壞賬備付管制　regulation on provisions for bad debt
还本付息/還本付息　loan and interest payment
还本付息比率/負債比率　debt service ratio
还款保证/還款保證　repayment guarantee
还盘/還價,議價　counter offer
还实盘/確認議價　counter offer firm
还书/還書　book return, return a book
还书处/還書櫃檯　book drop, return desk
还书箱/還書箱　book drop
环保法庭/環境保護法庭　environmental protection court
环保统计/環境保護統計　environmental protection statistics
环保验收/環境保護驗收　environment acceptance
环保意识/環境意識　environmental awareness
环比/環比,鏈比　chain relative, link relatives
环比法/環比法　method of link relatives
环比指数/環比指數,鏈指數　chain index, link index
环衬/襯頁紙　lining paper
环境/環境　environment
环境保护/環境保護　environmental protection
环境保护法/環境保護法　environmental protection law
环境保护规划/環境保護規劃　environmental protection planning
环境保护基本法/環境保護基本法　basic law on environmental protection
环境保护目标责任制/環境保護目標責任制　target responsibility system for environmental protection
环境保护协议/環境保護協定　agreement on environmental protection
环境保护许可/環境保護許可　permission on environmental protection
环境保护政策/環境保護政策　policy of environmental protection
环境保护主义/環境保護主義　environmentalism
环境变量/環境變數　environment variable
环境标准/環境標準　environmental standard
环境不确定性/環境不確定性　environmental uncertainty
环境产权/環境產權　environmental property right
环境超系统/環境超系統　environmental super system
环境成本/環境成本　environmental costs
环境调查/環境調查　environmental survey
环境法/環境法　environmental law
环境法的基本原则/環境法的基本原則　basic principle of environmental law
环境法的基本制度/環境法的基本制度　basic institutions on environmental law
环境法的体系/環境法的體系　system of environmental law
环境法的渊源/環境法的淵源　sources of environmental law
环境法典/環境法典　environmental code
环境法律关系/環境法律關係　legal relation of environment
环境法律规范/環境法律規範　environmental legal norm
环境法律权利/環境法律權利　environmental legal right
环境法律义务/環境法律義務　environmental legal obligation
环境法律意识/環境法律意識　legal consciousness of environment
环境法律责任/環境法律責任　environmental legal liability
环境法制/環境法制　environmental legal instituions
环境法治/環境法治　environmental rule of law
环境方针/環境政策　environmental policy
环境分析/環境分析　environmental analysis
环境风险/環境風險　environmental risk
环境风险分析/環境風險分析　environmental risk analysis
环境复杂性/環境複雜性　environmental complexity
环境公平/環境公平　environmental fairness
环境公益诉讼/環境公益訴訟　environmental public interest lawsuit
环境管理/環境管理　environmental management
环境管理会计/環境管理會計　environmental management accounting
环境管理体系/環境管理系統　environmental management system
环境管理体系认证/環境管理制度認證　environmental management system certification
环境话语/環境話語　environmental discourse
环境绩效/環境效益　environment performance

环境监测/環境監測　environmental monitoring
环境监督/環境監督　environmental supervision
环境健康/環境衛生　environmental health
环境纠纷/環境糾紛　environmental disputes
环境纠纷处理/環境糾紛處理　disposal of environmental disputes
环境决策/環境決策　environmental decision making
环境可持续性/環境可持續性　environmental sustainability
环境可行性/環境可行性　environmental feasibility
环境立法/環境立法　environmental legislation
环境流/環境流　environmental flow
环境民事诉讼/環境民事訴訟　environmental civil lawsuits
环境民事责任/環境民事責任　environmental civil liability
环境目标/環境目標　environmental objective
环境难民/環境難民　environment refugees
环境评估/環境評估　environmental assessing
环境破坏/環境破壞,環境損害　environmental destruction, environmental damage
环境侵权行为/環境侵權行爲　environmental torts
环境权/環境權　environmental rights
环境扫描/環境掃描,環境偵測　environment scanning
环境社会学/環境社會學　environmental sociology
环境审核/環境稽核　environmental audit
环境试验/環境試驗　environmental test
环境税费制度/環境稅費制度　environmental tax and fee institution
环境司法/環境司法　environmental judicature
环境思想学派/環境思想學派　environment school of thought
环境诉讼/環境訴訟　environmental suit
环境损害/環境損害　environmental damage
环境条约/環境條約　environmental treaty
环境统计/環境統計　environmental statistics
环境危害/環境危害　environmental hazard
环境维权/環境維權　environmental rights protection
环境稳定性/環境穩定性　environmental stability
环境问题/環境問題　environmental problem
环境污染/環境汙染　environmental pollution
环境污染事故/環境汙染事故　pollution accident
环境污染损害赔偿/環境汙染損害賠償　compensation for environmental pollution damage
环境污染物/環境汙染物　environmental pollutant
环境污染责任保险/環境汙染責任保險　insurance for environmental damage caused by pollution
环境牺牲/環境犧牲　environmental victimization
环境信访/環境信訪　environmental letters and visits
环境信息/環境資料　environmental information
环境刑事诉讼/環境刑事訴訟　environmental criminal ligitation
环境刑事责任/環境刑事責任　environmental criminal liability
环境行政处罚/環境行政處罰　environmental administrative sanction
环境行政代执行/環境行政代執行　environmental administrative fungible execution
环境行政罚款/環境行政罰鍰　environmental administrative fine
环境行政复议/環境行政覆議　environmental administrative reconsideration
环境行政诉讼/環境行政訴訟　environmental administrative lawsuit
环境行政责任/環境行政責任　environmental administrative liability
环境学派/環境學派　environmental school
环境因果结构/環境因果結構　causal structure of environment
环境因素/環境因素　environmental factor
环境影响/環境影響　environmental impact
环境影响报告表/環境影響報告表　environmental impact list
环境影响报告书/環境影響評估報告　environmental impact statement
环境影响登记表/環境影響登記表　environmental impact registrative form
环境影响评估/環境影響評估　environmental impact assessment
环境影响评价/環境影響評估　environmental impact assessment
环境影响评价制度/環境影響評價制度　institution of environmental effect assessment
环境应力/環境壓力　environmental stress
环境预测/環境預測　environmental forecasting
环境运动/環境運動　environmental movement
环境正义范式/環境正義範式　environmental justice paradigm, EJP
环境政策/環境政策　environmental policy
环境执法/環保法令執行　environmental law enforcement
环境指标/環境指標　environmental indicator
环境质量/環境品質　environmental quality
环境质量标准/環境品質標準　environmental quality

standard
环境仲裁/環境仲裁　environmental arbitration
环境主义/環境保護主義　environmentalism
环路计划/回路計劃, 循環計劃　loop plan
环球债券/環球債券　global bond
环绕分布/包裝分布　wrapped distributions
环绕柯西分布/包裝柯西分布, 包裝柯西分配　wrapped Cauchy distribution
环绕正态分布/包裝常態分布, 包裝常態分配　wrapped normal distribution
环式信息交流网络/環式資訊交流網路　network of cycle-mode communication
环系索引/環系索引　ring system index
环形极差/環形全距　circular range
环状白斑/墨皮斑　hickies
缓冲/緩衝　buffer
缓冲带/緩衝帶　buffer zone
缓冲分析/環域分析　buffer analysis
缓冲库存/緩衝存貨　inventory buffer
缓冲区分析/環域分析　buffer analysis
缓交订单/緩交訂單, 未交貨訂單　order backlog
缓刑/緩刑　suspend execution of a sentence
幻灯片/幻燈片　slide
幻方设计/魔術方塊設計　magic square design
幻影会面/幻影會面　phantom interview
换订/換訂　changing subscription
换汇汇率/換匯匯率　swap rate
换汇套利/換匯套利　swap arbitrage
换基检验/換基檢定　base reversal test
换片器/換片器　record changer
换算表/換算表　commutation table
患病率/傷病率, 疾病盛行率　morbidity rate, prevalence rate
患病行为/生病行爲　illness behavior
荒诞新闻学/狂論新聞學, 怪論新聞學　gonzo journalism
黄金保值条款/黃金償付條款　gold clause
黄金比效果/黃金比效果　gold scale effect
黄金尺度/黃金尺度　golden yardstick
黄金储备/黃金儲備, 黃金準備, 黃金庫存　gold reserve, gold stock
黄金储备率/黃金儲備率　gold reserve ratio
黄金储存/黃金儲存　gold holding
黄金担保借款/黃金擔保借款　gold collateral loan
黄金钉住货币/黃金釘住貨幣　gold pegged currency
黄金非货币化/黃金非貨幣化　gold demonetization
黄金分割法/黃金分割演算法　golden cut algorithm, golden section method
黄金份额/黃金額度　gold tranche
黄金股票/黃金存量　gold stock
黄金规则/黃金法則　golden rule
黄金及美元储备/黃金及美元儲備　gold and dollar reserve
黄金及外汇储备/黃金及外匯儲備　gold and foreign exchange reserve
黄金价值/黃金價值　gold value
黄金交易服务/黃金交易服務　gold transaction service
黄金禁运/黃金禁運　gold embargo
黄金利润/黃金利潤　gold profit
黄金流入/黃金流入　inflow of gold
黄金率资本存量/黃金率資本存量　golden-rule capital stock
黄金偏好/黃金偏好　preference for gold
黄金平价/黃金平價　gold parity
黄金期货/黃金期貨　gold futures
黄金期货市场/黃金期貨市場　gold futures market
黄金升水/黃金升水　gold premium
黄金时间/黃金時段　prime time
黄金市场/黃金市場　gold market
黄金输出/黃金輸出　gold export
黄金输出点/黃金輸出點　export gold point, outgoing gold point, gold export point
黄金输出入点/黃金輸出入點, 黃金輸送點　gold point
黄金输入/黃金輸入　gold import
黄金输入点/黃金輸入點　gold import point
黄金双重价格/黃金雙重價格　dual gold price
黄金双轨制/黃金雙軌制, 黃金兩價制　two-tier gold price system
黄金套利/黃金套利　gold arbitrage
黄金外流/黃金外流, 黃金枯竭　flight of gold, gold outflow, gold drain
黄金危机/黃金危機　gold crisis
黄金债券/黃金債券　gold bond, bond gold, gold debenture
黄金账户/黃金賬戶　gold account
黄金证券/黃金證券　gold certificate
黄金准备金/黃金準備金　gold cover
黄金资产/黃金資産　gold asset
黄老之术/黃老之術　rule of Huang and Lao
黄皮书/黃皮書　yellow book
黄犬契约/黃狗契約　yellow dog contracts
黄色新闻/黃色新聞　yellow journalism
黄页/黃頁　yellow page
灰暗区贸易限制措施/灰色地帶貿易限制措施　grey

area trade restriction
灰度图像/灰度影像　grayscale image
灰平衡/灰色平衡　gray balance
灰色成分替代/灰色成分替代　gray component replacement
灰色文献/灰色文獻　gray literature
灰色系统理论/灰色系統理論　grey system theory
灰色系统模型/灰色模型　grey system model
灰色系统预测模型/灰色系統預測模型　grey system forecasting model
灰梯尺/灰色級數表　gray scale
灰箱方法/灰箱法　grey box approach
恢复订阅/恢復訂閱　resuming subscription
恢复时间/恢復時間　recovery time
恢复原顺序/還原順序　restoration of original order
恢复原状/恢復原狀　reconversion
回避/迴避　challenge system
回答误差/反應誤差　response error
回荡效应/回沖效應　backwash effect
回访/再度查訪　callback
回复零状态/零回歸狀態　null recurrent state
回购/回購　buy back
回购合同/回購協議　buy-back agreement
回购契约/回購契約　buy-back contract
回购协议/附賣回協定,附賣回交易　repurchase agreement, reverse repurchase agreement
回顾抽样/回顧抽樣　retrospective sampling
回顾性研究/回顧研究　retrospective studies
回归/回歸　regression
回归标记制/回歸標記制　back tracking marking system
回归参数/回歸參數　regression parameter
回归插补/回歸插補法　regression imputation
回归方差分析/回歸式變異數分析　analysis of variance in regression
回归方程/回歸方程式　regression equation
回归分析/回歸分析　regression analysis
回归估计量/回歸估計量　regression estimator
回归估计值/回歸估計值　regression estimate
回归函数/回歸函數　regression function
回归教育/回歸教育　regression education
回归理论/回歸理論　theory of regression
回归模型/回歸模型　regression model
回归平方和/回歸平方和　regression sum of squares, explained sum of squares, ESS
回归平面/回歸平面　regression plane
回归曲面/回歸曲面　regression surface
回归曲线/回歸曲線　regression curve
回归设计/回歸設計　regression design
回归填补法/回歸插補法　regression imputation
回归误差/回歸誤差　regression error
回归系数/回歸係數　regression coefficient
回归系数的标准误/回歸係數標準誤　standard error of regression coefficient
回归线/回歸線　regression line
回归相依性/回歸相依性　regression dependence
回归因变量/回歸應變數　regressand
回归值/回歸值　regression value
回归自变量/回歸自變數　independent variables in regression
回扣/回扣　kickback
回扣促销/折扣推廣　rebate promotion
回扣式付款/回扣,擔保佣金　accommodation payment
回馈控制/回饋控制　feed back control, post action control
回墨/回墨　flooding
回墨板/回墨板　ink flooding blade
回声室效应/回聲室效應　echo chamber effect
回收期法则/還本期限法則　payback period rule
回溯编目/回溯編目　retrospective cataloging
回溯标记制/回溯標記制　retrospective notation
回溯创新/回溯創新　reverse innovation
回溯数据库/回溯建庫　retrospective database
回溯性检索/回溯檢索　retrospective retrieval
回溯性书目/回溯性書目　retrospective bibliography
回头背书/回頭背書　back endorsement
回望期权/回顧式選擇權　lookback option
回忆录/傳記,實錄　memoir
回译/回譯　retranslation
回应型法/回應型法　responsive law
回应性/回應性　responsiveness
回应因子/感應因子,響應因子　response factor
回转/回轉　switch-back
回转设计/回轉設計　switch-back design
毁约/毁約　breach of promise
汇编/匯編　omnibus volume, collection and compilation
汇编作品/匯編作品　compilation work
汇拨支付/匯撥支付　payment by remittance
汇兑/匯兑　remittance
汇兑差额/匯兑餘額　balance of exchange
汇兑极限/匯兑限額　limit of exchange
汇兑平价/匯兑平價,匯兑牌價　par of exchange, parity of exchange
汇兑容量/匯兑容量　exchange capacity

汇兑顺差/匯兑順差,順匯　favorable exchange
汇兑损失/匯兑損失　exchange loss
汇兑损失准备/匯兑損失準備　reserve for exchange loss
汇兑条款/匯兑條款　currency exchange clause
汇兑银行/匯兑銀行,外匯指定銀行　bank of exchange, exchange bank
汇兑自由化/匯兑自由化　liberalization of exchange
汇兑最低限度/匯兑最低限度　inferior limit of exchange
汇费/匯費　remittance charge
汇合分析/匯合分析　confluence analysis
汇合关系/匯合關係　confluent relation
汇划/外匯轉移　foreign exchange transfer
汇划银行/劃撥銀行,直接轉賬銀行　giro bank
汇集/匯集　collective
汇集全宗/匯集全宗　collected fonds
汇价/匯率報價　exchange quotation
汇价变动/匯價變動　exchange movement
汇价波动/匯價波動　exchange fluctuation
汇款单/匯票　remittance bill
汇款结算/匯款結算　remittance settlement
汇款金额/匯款金額　amount of remittance, remitting amount
汇款书/匯款書　letter of remittance
汇款通知书/匯款通知書　remittance advice
汇款银行/匯款銀行　remittance bank
汇款支票/匯款支票　remittance cheque, remittance check
汇率/匯率　foreign exchange rate, rate of exchange, exchange rate
汇率贬值/匯率貶值　devaluation of exchange rate
汇率波动/匯率浮動　exchange rate fluctuations
汇率差价/匯率差價　exchange rate differential
汇率超调/調整過度　overshooting
汇率传递/匯率轉嫁　exchange rate pass-through
汇率低估/匯率低估　exchange rate undervalued
汇率动态学/匯率動態　exchange-rate dynamics
汇率格局/匯率格局　pattern of exchange rate
汇率更改/更改匯率　exchange alteration
汇率过头/匯率調整過度　exchange rate overshooting
汇率机制/匯率機制,匯率制度　exchange rate mechanism, exchange rate regime
汇率间接标价法/匯率間接標價法　indirect quotation of exchange rate
汇率决定理论/匯率決定理論　theory of exchange rate determination
汇率上浮/匯率上升　float upward of exchange rate
汇率伸缩性/匯率伸縮性,彈性匯率　flexibility of exchange rate, exchange rate flexibility
汇率调整/匯率調整　exchange rate adjustment
汇率稳定/匯率穩定　stabilization of exchange rate
汇率下跌/匯率下跌　exchange rate depreciation
汇率下浮/匯率下滑　float downward of exchange rate
汇率直接标价法/匯率直接標價法　direct quotation of exchange rate
汇率制度/匯率制度　exchange rate system
汇率自动平衡条例/匯率自動平衡條例　self-balancing act of exchange rate
汇票/匯票,匯款單　bill of exchange, money order
汇票背书日期/匯票背書日期　date of endorsement
汇票承兑人/匯票承兑人,匯票付款人　acceptor of bill
汇票副本/匯票副本,第二聯匯票　second bill of exchange
汇票和支票法/匯票和支票法　law of bill of exchange and cheque
汇票汇款/匯票匯款　remittance by draft
汇票金额/匯票金額　amount of draft
汇票通知书/匯票通知書　advice of bill
汇票托收/匯票託收　collection of bill
汇票样本/匯票樣本　specimen of draft
汇票债务人/匯票債務人　party liable on bill of exchange
汇票执票人/匯票持有人　holder of bill of exchange
汇市/外匯市場　foreign exchange market
汇险贴水/匯險貼水　exchange risk premium
汇总表/摘要表　summary table
汇总经济数据/總合經濟資料　aggregate economic data
汇总误差/匯總誤差　tabulating error
汇总账户/匯總賬户　summary account
会典/會典　huidian
会后文献/會後文獻　post-meeting publication, post-conference literature
会聚技术/會聚技術　nano-bio-info-cogno, NBIC
会刊/會刊　proceedings of a conference, journal of a society or association
会签/會簽　sign jointly
会前文献/會前出版物　premeeting publication, pre-conference literature
会商/會商　consultation
会谈记录/會談記錄　record of session
会议管理/會議管理　conference management

会议简介/會議簡介　brief introduction of meeting, brief introduction to the conference
会议录/會議記錄　proceedings
会议论文/研討會論文　conference paper
会议售书服务/會議售書服務　sales on meeting
会议文件/會議檔　conference documents
会议文献/會議文獻　assembly documents, conference literature
会员公司/會員公司　member corporation
会员私人价值拍卖/會員私人價值拍賣　affiliated private value auctions
会员图书馆/會員圖書館　subscription library
会员银行/會員銀行　member bank
会展情报/會議和商展情報　trade show intelligence, exhibition competitive intelligence
会中文献/會中文獻　mid-meeting publication, mid-conference literature
荟萃分析/後設分析,統合分析　meta-analysis
绘本/圖畫書　picture book, picture storybook
彗星条纹/彗星條紋　comet streak
惠塔克周期图/維特克週期圖　Whittaker periodogram
惠特尔分布/Whittle 分布,Whittle 分配　Whittle distribution
惠特尼管理制/惠特尼管理制　Whitney management system
婚内强奸/婚內強姦　inner-marriage rape
婚前性活动/婚前性活動　premarital sex
婚外恋/婚外戀　extra-marriage affair
婚外性活动/婚外性活動　extra-marital sex
婚姻登记/婚姻登記,結婚登記　registration of marriage
婚姻缔结地法/婚姻締結地法　Lex Loci Celebrationis
婚姻挤压/婚姻擠壓　marriage squeeze
婚姻市场理论/婚姻市場理論　marriage market theory
婚姻调适/婚姻調適　marriage adaptation
婚姻制度/婚姻制度　marriage system
婚姻住所/婚姻住所　matrimonial domicile
混巢/混巢　cluttered nest
混沌变异/混亂變異　chaotic variation
混合本位制/混合本位制　hybrid standard
混合比率/混合比率　hybrid ratio
混合标引/混合標引　mixed indexing, composite indexing
混合并购/多角化購并　conglomerate acquisition
混合策略/混合策略　mixed strategy

混合策略单纯形/混合策略單純形　simplex of mixed strategy
混合策略均衡/混合策略均衡　mixed-strategy equilibrium
混合成本/混合成本　mixed cost
混合抽样/混合抽樣　mixed sampling
混合出版/混合出版　mixed publishing
混合存货/混合存貨　mixed inventory
混合代表制/混合代表制　mixed representation system
混合贷款/混合貸款　mixed loan
混合抵押品/混合質押品　mixed collateral
混合订单/混合訂單　blend order
混合方法/質量并用法　mixed method
混合分布/混合分布　mixed distribution
混合分类/混合分類　mixed classification
混合福利经济/混合福利經濟　mixed economy of welfare
混合关税/混合關稅　mixed tariff, mixed duties
混合观测值/混合觀測值　mixed-up observations
混合过错/混合過錯　mixed fault
混合海上保险单/混合海上保險單　mixed marine insurance policy
混合横截面时间序列样本/混合橫斷面與時間數列樣本　pooled cross-section time series sample
混合货币/混合貨幣　mixed currency
混合兼并/混合兼并　mixed mergence, conglomerate mergence
混合兼并案例/多角化結合個案　conglomerate merger cases
混合经济/混合式經濟,混合經濟體系　mixed economy
混合局势/混合局勢　mixed situation
混合矩/混合動差　mixed moment
混合控股公司/混合控股公司　mixed holding company
混合利润最大化/混合利潤最大化　mixed profit maximization
混合联合公司/混合整合企業　mixed integrated enterprise
混合马尔科夫过程/混合馬可夫過程　mixed Markov process
混合模型/混合模型　mixed model
混合 Logit 模型/混合勝算對數模型　mixed logit
混合模型的研究/混合模型研究　mixed model research
混合配额/混合配額　mixed quota
混合谱/混合頻譜　mixed spectrum

混合设计/混合設計　mixed design
混合施工队/混合施工隊　mixed team
混合实验/混合實驗　experiment with mixture
混合式分类法/混合式分類法　mixed classification system
混合收入/混合收入,混合所得　mixed income, compound income
混合所有制/混合所有制,混合所有權　mixed ownership
混合所有制经济/混合所有制經濟　diversified ownership economy
混合析因试验/混合因子試驗　mixed factorial experiment
混合系数/混合係數　mixed coefficient
混合系统/混合制　hybrid system
混合销售/組合出售　combination sale
混合效果模型/混合效果模式,混合效應模型　mixed-effect model
混合效力处理/混合效力處理　the administrative decision to the same counterpart with the mixed effects of interests and burdens at the same time
混合协议/混合協議　mixed agreement
混合型加网/混合型加網　hybrid screening
混合型兼并/聯合企業合并　conglomerate merger
混合型债券/混合型債券　combination bond
混合型证券/混合式證券　hybrid securities
混合性档案文献/混合性檔案文獻　mixed archival documentations
混合学习预测方法/混合學習預測方法　hybrid learning forecasting model
混合延伸/混合延伸　mixed extension
混合研究/質量并用法　mixed method
混合样本比例/混合的樣本比例　pooled sample proportion
混合预测/混合預測　hybrid forecasting
混合责任者/混合責任者　joint author
混合账户/混合賬戶　mixed account
混合整数规划/混合整數規劃　mixed integer programming
混合指数响应法则/混合指數反應定律　mixed exponential response law
混合制系统/混合系統　mixed system
混合仲裁/混合仲裁　mixed arbitration
混合资金融通/混合資金融通　mixed financing
混合自回归-回归系统/混合自身回歸及回歸系統　mixed autoregressive-regressive system
混合自回归移动平均过程/混合自身回歸移動平均過程　mixed autoregressive-moving average process, ARMA process
混流排程/混流排程　mixed-model scheduling
混流生产/混線生產,混合模式生產　mixed-model production
混流装配线/混流裝配線　mixed-model assembly line
混录/混錄　mixed record
混凝土制度/混凝土制度　concrete system
混同均衡/混和均衡　pooling equilibrium
混淆/混淆　confusion
混淆变量/混淆變項　confounding variable
混业经营/混合經營　mixed operation
混杂/混同,交絡　confounding
混杂析因试验/混同因子實驗　confounding factorial experiment
混杂因子/混淆變項　confounding variable
混杂原理/混同原則　principle of confounding
混杂子组/混同小組　sub-group confounded
活动/活動　action
活动费用估算/活動成本估算　activity cost estimating
活动分析/活動分析　activity analysis
活动记录/活動記錄　activity record
活动理论/活動理論　activity theory
活动书架/活動書架　adjustable shelving, movable shelf
活动图/活動圖　activity diagram
活动债券/活動債券　active bond
活法/活法　living law
活校/活校　correct the word errors in collation
活期存款/活期存款　urrent deposit, demand deposit
活期贷款/活期貸款　call loan, demand loan
活期贷款市场/短期放款市場　call money market
活期账户资产负债表/經常項目資產負債表　current account balance sheet
活页补充材料/活頁材料　loose-leaf material
活页出版物/活頁出版物　loose-leaf publication
活页技术资料/技術資料表單,技術產品說明單　technical data sheets
活页式目录/活頁目錄　loose-leaf catalog
活页塑料夹装订/塑膠圈裝　plastic comb binding
活页装/活頁裝訂　loose-leaf binding
活字泥版印本/活字泥版印本　movable clay sheet printed book
活字印本/活字印本　movable type edition
火车上交货价/火車上交貨價　free on board train
火车头理论/火車頭理論　locomotive theory
火警探测系统/火警警報系統　fire detection system

火灾和意外保险公司/火災和意外保險公司　fire and casualty insurance company
火灾统计/火災統計　fire statistics
伙伴关系/合夥　partnership
伙伴关系管理/夥伴關係管理　partner relationship management
伙伴合同模式/夥伴模式　partnering model
或引渡或起诉/或引渡或起訴　aut dedere aut judicare
或有负债/或有負債　contingent liabilities
或有利润/或有利潤　contingency profit
或有免疫/應急免疫　contingent immunization
或有期权/或有期權　contingent option
或有商品/應機性商品　contingent commodity
或有事项/或有事項　contingency
或有收费/或有公費　contingent fee
或有损失/或有損失　loss contingency
或有消费/條件式消費　contingent consumption
或有要求权/或有求償權　contingent claim
或有证券/或有證券　contingent securities
或有资产/或有資產　contingent asset
货币/貨幣　currency, money
货币本位制/貨幣本位制　monetary standard
货币比价调整/貨幣比價調整　monetary realignment
货币边际效用/貨幣的邊際效用　marginal utility of money
货币贬值/貨幣貶值　downward revaluation, currency depreciation, currency devaluation
货币贬值率/通貨貶值率　rate of depreciation currency
货币标准/貨幣標準　currency standard
货币标准重量/貨幣標準重量　mint weight
货币补偿额/貨幣補償額　monetary compensatory amount
货币不能自由兑换性/貨幣不能自由兌換性　inconvertibility of currency
货币不稳定/貨幣不穩定　monetary instability
货币超中性/貨幣超級中立性　superneutrality of money
货币成本/貨幣成本　money cost
货币成本总额/貨幣成本總額　total money cost
货币乘数/貨幣乘數　monetary multiplier, money multiplier
货币乘数效应/貨幣乘數效果　money multiplier effect
货币冲击/貨幣性衝擊,貨幣性干擾　monetary shock, monetary disturbance
货币传导机制/貨幣傳導機制,貨幣傳遞機能　monetary transmission mechanism, conduction mechanism of mongetary
货币存款/貨幣存款　currency holding
货币存量/貨幣存量　money stock
货币单位/貨幣單位　monetary unit
货币等价物/貨幣等價物　money equivalent
货币钉住黄金/貨幣釘住黃金　peg currency to gold
货币兑换/貨幣兌換　exchange of money, money exchange
货币兑换商/外幣兌換者　moneychanger
货币发行/發行貨幣　issuance of currency, currency issue
货币发行制度/貨幣發行制度　currency issuing system
货币分析/貨幣分析　monetary analysis
货币风险/通貨風險　currency risk
货币负债/通貨負債　currency liability
货币功能/貨幣功能　monetary function
货币供给/貨幣供給　money supply
货币供给内生性/貨幣供給內生性　endogeneity of money supply
货币供给外生性/貨幣供給外生性　exogeneity of money supply
货币供应量/貨幣供應量,貨幣供給額　currency supply volume
货币供应量可控性/貨幣供給可控制性　money supply controllability
货币购买力/貨幣購買力　purchasing power of money
货币购买力指数/貨幣購買力指數　index of purchasing power of money
货币规则/貨幣法則　monetary rule
货币互换/通貨交換　currency swap
货币幻觉/貨幣幻覺　monetary crank, money illusion
货币黄金/貨幣黃金　monetary gold
货币汇率/貨幣匯率　monetary exchange rate
货币机制/貨幣機制　monetary mechanism
货币集团/貨幣集團　monetary bloc, currency bloc
货币计量假设/貨幣計量假設　money measurement postulate
货币价格/貨幣價格　money price
货币价值/貨幣價值　monetary value, value of money
货币间接本位制/貨幣間接本位制　indirect standard
货币间接证券/貨幣間接證券　monetary indirect security
货币交换/貨幣交換　pecuniary exchange

货币金融危机／貨幣金融危機　monetary and financial crisis
货币紧缩／貨幣緊縮　monetary squeeze, monetary deflation
货币经纪公司／貨幣經紀公司　money brokerage firm
货币经纪人／貨幣經紀人　money broker
货币经济／貨幣經濟　monetary economy, money economy
货币经济学／貨幣經濟學　monetary economics
货币经理人／貨幣經理人　money manager
货币竞争性贬值／貨幣競爭性貶值　competitive depreciation
货币均衡／貨幣均衡　money equilibrium
货币可兑换性／通貨可轉換性，通貨自由兌換性　currency convertibility
货币扩张／貨幣擴張　monetary expansion
货币利率／貨幣利率　money interest rate, money rate of interest
货币利率交叉互换／交叉貨幣利率交換契約　cross-currency interest rate swap
货币利息／貨幣利息　monetary interest
货币联盟／貨幣同盟　monetary union
货币流动分析／貨幣流動分析　money flow analysis
货币流动账户／貨幣流動賬戶　money flow account
货币流量／貨幣流量　money flow
货币流入／貨幣流入　money inflow
货币流通／貨幣流通　money circulation
货币流通规律／貨幣流通規律　law of current of money, law of money circulation
货币流通渠道／貨幣流通管道　channel of money circulation
货币流通速度／貨幣流通速度　velocity of money circulationm, transactions velocity of money
货币论／貨幣學派　monetary approach
货币面纱／貨幣面紗　monetary veil
货币赔偿／貨幣賠償　monetary indemnity
货币批发市场／批發貨幣市場　wholesale money market
货币平衡／貨幣平衡　monetary equilibrium
货币平价／貨幣平價　currency parity, monetary parity
货币期货／貨幣期貨　currency futures
货币期权／通貨選擇權　currency option
货币强制储蓄／貨幣強制儲蓄　monetary forced saving
货币区／通貨區域　currency areas
货币渠道／貨幣傳遞管道　money channel
货币商品／貨幣商品　currency commodity, money commodity
货币蛇形运动／貨幣蛇形運動，蛇形貨幣　currency snake
货币社会学／貨幣社會學　sociology of money
货币社会意义／貨幣社會意義　social meaning of money
货币升值／貨幣升值　currency appreciation, appreciation of currency
货币时间价值／貨幣時間價值　time value of money
货币市场／貨幣市場　money market, monetary market
货币市场操作／貨幣市場操作　money market operation
货币市场存款帐户／貨幣市場現金賬戶　money market deposit account
货币市场互助基金／貨幣市場互助基金　money market mutual fund
货币市场基金／貨幣市場基金　money market fund
货币市场均衡／貨幣市場均衡　money market equilibrium
货币市场利率／貨幣市場利率　money market rate
货币市场证券／貨幣市場證券　money market security
货币收入／貨幣收入，貨幣所得　monetary income, money income
货币数量理论／貨幣數量說　quantity theory of money
货币数量论／貨幣數量學說　theory of money amount
货币弹性／貨幣彈性　money flexibility
货币套利／貨幣套利　money arbitrage
货币体系／貨幣體系　monetary system
货币替代／通貨替代　currency substitution
货币投机／貨幣投機　currency speculation
货币投资过剩理论／貨幣投資過剩理論　monetary over-investment theory
货币外流／貨幣外流　money outflow
货币危机／貨幣危機　monetary crisis
货币效用／貨幣效用　utility of money
货币协定／貨幣協定　monetary agreement, monetary arrangement
货币信托／貨幣信託　money trust
货币形态／貨幣形態　money form
货币性／貨幣性　moneyness
货币性金融资产／貨幣性金融資産　monetary financial asset
货币性流动资产／貨幣性流動資産　monetary

current asset
货币性流动资金/貨幣性營運資金　monetary working capital
货币性流动资金调整/貨幣性營運資金調整　monetary working capital adjustment
货币性项目/貨幣性項目　monetary item
货币性资产/貨幣性資產　monetary asset
货币需求/貨幣需求　money demand
货币学派/通貨學派　currency school
货币一体化/貨幣一體化　monetary integration
货币债权/貨幣債權　money claim
货币债券/貨幣債券　currency bond
货币债务/貨幣債務　currency indebtedness, monetary debt
货币账户/貨幣賬戶　monetary account
货币证券/貨幣證券　currency securities
货币政策/貨幣政策　currency policy, monetary policy
货币政策乘数/貨幣政策乘數　monetary policy multiplier
货币政策传导机制/貨幣傳遞機能　monetary transmission mechanism
货币政策工具/貨幣政策工具　monetary policy tool, monetary policy instrument
货币政策目标/貨幣政策目標　monetary policy target, goal of monetary policy, monetary policy objective
货币职能/貨幣職能　functions of money
货币制度/貨幣制度　currency system, monetary institution
货币中心银行/貨幣中心銀行　money center bank
货币中性/貨幣中立性　neutrality of money
货币周转/貨幣週轉　money turnover
货币周转账户/貨幣週轉賬戶　money circuit account
货币主义/重貨幣論　monetarism
货币主义者/主貨幣學派　monetarist
货币准备金/貨幣準備金　monetary reserve
货币资本/貨幣資本　money capital
货币总量/貨幣總計數　monetary aggregates
货币总需求/總和貨幣需求　aggregate money demand
货车上交货价/貨車上交貨價　free on wagon
货船上结关/貨船上結關　custom clearance of cargo aboard ship
货到付款/貨到付款　pay arrival, payment against arrival, cash on delivery
货到付款价格/貨到付款價格　cash on delivery price, COD price

货到付款手续费/貨到付款手續費　cash on delivery commission, COD commission
货到付款销售/貨到付款銷售　cash on delivery sale, COD sale
货到付款账单/貨到付款賬單　cash on delivery bill, COD bill
货到付款证/貨到付款證明　cash on delivery certificate, COD certificate
货垛/貨垛　goods stack
货架/貨架　rack
货架份额/貨架占有率　share of shelf
货损率/貨損率　cargo damage rate
货物报关单/貨物報關單　goods declaration
货物到达/貨物到達　arrival of the goods, AOG
货物抵押贷款/貨物抵押貸款　goods credit
货物跟踪系统/貨物跟蹤系統　goods tracked system
货物价值和原产地综合证书/貨物價值和原產地綜合證書　combined certificate of value and origin
货物价值证明书/貨價證明書　certificate of value
货物结关/貨物結關　clearance of goods
货物清单/貨物清單　bill of goods
货物收据/貨物收據　receipt for goods
货物损失索赔/貨物破損索賠　claim for cargo damage
货物瑕疵索赔/貨物瑕疵索賠　claim arising from defect of goods
豁免区/豁免區　exempt zone
豁免员工/豁免員工　exempt employee
豁免证券/豁免證券　exempted securities
霍尔顿差异测度/霍爾丹差異測度　Haldane's discrepancy measure
霍尔特法/霍爾特法　Holt's method
霍夫丁不等式/Hoeffding 不等式　Hoeffding's inequality
霍夫丁独立性检验/Hoeffding 獨立性檢定　Hoeffding's independence test
霍夫曼定理/霍夫曼定律　Hoffman law, Hoffman theorem
霍克西调查/霍克西調查　Hoxie investigation
霍兰德二元对称检验/霍蘭德爾二變量對稱性檢定　Hollander's bivariate symmetry test
霍兰德平行性检验/霍蘭德爾平行性檢定　Hollander's parallelism test
霍奇斯-阿杰恩检验/Hodges-Ajne 檢定　Hodges-Ajne's test
霍奇斯-莱曼单样本估计量/Hodges-Lehmann 單樣本估計量　Hodges-Lehmann one-sample estimator
霍奇斯-莱曼样本估计量/Hodges-Lehmann 估計量

Hodges-Lehmann estimator
霍奇斯-莱曼样本估计值/Hodges-Lehmann 估計值　Hodges-Lehmann estimate
霍奇斯双变量符号检验/Hodges 二變量符號檢定　Hodges bivariate sign test
霍桑实验/霍桑試驗　Hawthorne test study
霍桑效应/霍桑效應　Hawthorne effect
霍氏跨文化模型/霍氏跨文化模式　Hofstede crosscultural model
霍特林分布/郝得霖分布, 郝得霖分配　Hotelling distribution
霍特林检验/郝得霖檢定　Hotelling's test
霍特林模型/郝得霖模型　Hotelling model
霍特林 T 统计量/郝得霖 T 統計量　Hotelling's T statistic
霍特林 T^2 统计量/郝得霖 T^2 統計量　Hotelling's T^2 statistic
霍维茨-汤普森估计量/霍維茨-湯普遜估計量　Horvitz-Thompson estimator
霍维兹/霍維茲　Morton J. Horwitz

J

几乎必然收敛/幾乎必然收斂　convergence almost surely
几乎处处收敛/幾乎到處收斂　convergence almost everywhere
几乎容许判决函数/幾乎可容決策函數　almost admissible decision function
机场交货价/機場交貨價　ex aerodrome
机动车第三者责任保险/機動車第三者責任保險　third party liability insurance of motor vehicle
机读档案/機器可讀資料　machine-readable archive
机读目录/機讀目錄,機器可讀編目　machine readable catalog, MARC
机读目录格式/機讀編目格式　machine readable catalog format
机读目录记录/機讀編目格式記錄　machine readable catalog record
机读文件/機讀檔案,機器可讀紀錄　machine readable records, machine readable archives
机读叙词表/機器可讀詞表　machine readable thesaurus
机构/機構　institution
机构督导/機構督導　agency supervisor
机构人员/機構人員　institutional personnel
机构索引/機構索引　corporate index
机构投资者/機構投資者　institutional investor
机构为本的实习模式/機構爲本的實習模式　institution-based internship model
机构养老服务/機構養老服務　institution-based elderly care
机构与学院的伙伴关系/機構與學院的夥伴關係　institution-college partnership
机构照顾/院內照護　institution-based care
机构知识库/機構典藏　institutional repository, IR
机关报/機關報　official newspaper
机关报刊/機構刊物　house organ
机关管理/辦公室管理　office management
机关刊物/機關刊物　official organ
机关文件中心/機關文件中心　agency records center
机会/機會　opportunity
机会成本/機會成本　opportunity cost
机会抽样/機遇抽樣　chance sampling

机会窗口/機會窗口　opportunity window
机会分析/機會分析,機會研究　opportunity analysis
机会管理方法/機會管理方法　opportunity management approach
机会结点/機會點,隨機點　chance node
机会开发/機會開發　opportunity exploitation
机会缺陷率/機會缺陷數　defect per opportunity, DPO
机会识别/機會識別　opportunity identify
机会研究/機會研究　opportunity study
机会因子/機遇因素　chance factor
机会约束/機遇限制　chance constraint
机会约束规划/可能性受限之規劃　chance constrained programming
机会主义/機會主義　opportunism
机会主义行为/機會主義行爲　opportunistic behavior
机密案卷/機密案卷　secret file
机密文件/機密檔案　confidential document
机密性/機密性　confidentiality
机密证书/機密證書　letterclose
机器/機器　machine
机器翻译/機器翻譯　machine translation
机器辅助时间/機器輔助時間　machine attention time
机器环境/機環境　machine environment
机器空闲能力分析/機器空閒能力分析　machine idle capability analysis
机器排序/機器排程　machine scheduling
机器运转时间/機器運轉時間　machine hour
机器掌控时间/機器控制時間　machine controlled time
机上交货价/機上交貨價　ex plane
机械表演/機械表演　performance by equipment
机械参数/物理參數　physical parameter
机械录音/機械錄音　mechanical recording
机械设备管理/機械設備管理　mechanical equipment management
机械设备台账/機械設備臺賬　detail of facility
机械式组织/機械式組織　mechanistic organization
机械台班单价/機械臺班單價　machine working unit

price
机械图纸/機械製圖　mechanical drawing
机械消耗定额/機械消耗定額　machine consumption quota
机械型职位设计法/機械型職位設計法　mechanistic job design method
机要工作/機要工作　confidential work
机要邮递/機要郵遞　confidential mail
机制设计/機制設計　mechanism design
机制纸/機質紙　machine-made paper
机制转换模型/體制轉換模型　regime-switching model
机助标引/機助標引　machine-aided indexing
奇偶性/奇偶性　parity
积层架/積層架　multilayer frame
积分谱/整合頻譜　integrated spectrum
积分营销/積分行銷　integral marketing
积极管理/積極管理　active management
积极抗辩/確認的抗辯　affirmative defense
积极老龄化/積極老齡化,活力老化　active aging
积极倾听/主動傾聽　active listening
积极时效/積極時效　positive prescription
积极式函证/積極式函證　positive confirmation
积极受众/主動閱聽人　active audience
积极修辞/積極修辭　positive rhetoric
积极约束/有效限制　active constraint
积极债券管理/積極債券管理　active bond management
积极主义者/行動[實踐]主義者　activist
积极资产组合/積極投資組合　active portfolio
积累蒙太奇/積累蒙太奇　accumulation montage
积木分析法/積木分析法　building block analysis
积性异方差性/乘法性非均齊變異性　multiplicative heteroscedasticity
积压/積壓　overstock, backlog
基/基準,基本　base
基本部类/基本部類　main divisional titles
基本大类/基本類別　basic class, main class
基本单位/基本單位　elementary unit
基本的犯罪构成/基本的犯罪構成　basic constitution of a crime
基本动作分解/基本動作分解　element breakdown
基本动作时间/基本動作時間　element time
基本动作时间研究法/基本動作時間研究法　basic motion study, BMS
基本对照/基本對比　elementary contrast
基本法/基本法　basic law
基本范畴/基礎性範疇　fundamental category

基本非可行解/基本非可行解　basic non-feasible solution
基本概率集/基本機率集合　fundamental probability set
基本概念/基本概念　basic concept
基本更新方程/基本更新方程式　fundamental renewal equation
基本工资/基本工資　basic wage
基本工资政策/基本薪資政策　base pay policy
基本功能/基本功能　basic function
基本故障率/基本故障率　basic failure rate
基本归因错误/基本歸因謬誤　fundamental attribution error
基本规范/基本規範　basic norm
基本汇率/基本匯率　basic rate of exchange
基本活动/主要活動　primary activity
基本级编目/基本級編目　basic level cataloging
基本价格/基本價格　basic price
基本检索/基本搜尋　basic search
基本建设投资/基本建設投資　capital construction investment
基本建设支出/基本建設支出　capital construction expenditure
基本解/基本解　fundamental solution
基本经济规律/基本經濟規律　basic economic law
基本经济制度/基本經濟制度　basic economic institutions
基本均衡汇率/基本平衡匯率　fundamental equilibrium exchange rate, FEER
基本可行解/基本可行解　basic feasible solution
基本库存量/基本庫存量　base inventory level, basic stock
基本款目/基本條目　basic entry
基本利率/基本利率　basic rate of interest
基本每股收益/基本每股盈餘　basic earnings per share
基本目录/基本目錄　principle catalog
基本农田保护制度/基本農田保護制度　system of protecting the basic farmland
基本频数/基本次數　fundamental frequency
基本权利/基本權利　fundamental rights
基本人权/基本人權　fundamental human rights
基本失效率/基本故障率　basic failure rate
基本史料题目/基本史料題目　topics of foundational historical data
基本事件/基本事件　elementary event
基本收藏/基本收藏　basic collection, basic level collection

基本收支差额/基本收支差額　basic balance of payment
基本随机过程/基本隨機過程　fundamental random process
基本完全类/本質完備類　essentially complete class
基本维度/基本維數　basic dimension
基本薪酬/基本薪酬　base compensation
基本型营销/基礎行銷　basic marketing
基本需要/基本需要　basic needs
基本义务/基本義務　fundamental duties of citizens
基本元/基本元素　fundamental element
基本元数据/基本元資料　basic metadata
基本政策/基本政策　major policy
基本著录/基本著錄　basic description
基本专利/基本專利　basic patent
基变量/基本[變]量　basic variable
基藏书库/基藏書庫　main collection, main stock, basic book storehouse
基层管理者/第一線管理者　first-line manager
基层图书馆/基層圖書館　basic level library
基层信息中心/基層資訊中心　primary information center
基层医疗/基礎醫療　primary care
基差/基差　basis
基差风险/基差風險　basis risk
基础标准/基本標準　basic standard
基础波动性/基礎波動性　fundamental volatility
基础工业/基礎工業　basic industry
基础货币/基礎貨幣　base money
基础技术/基礎技術　basic technology
基础科学/基礎科學　basic science
基础科学研究/基礎科學研究　basic scientific research
基础库存系统/基礎庫存系統　base stock system
基础利率/基礎利率　base interest rate
基础趋势/基礎趨勢　underlying trend
基础设施/基礎建設　infrastructure
基础数字汇集/基礎數字匯集　collection of essential data
基础研究/基礎研究　basic research
基点/基本點　basis point
基点定价/基點定價　basing point pricing
基点制/基點體系　basing point system
基弗不等式/Kiefer 不等式　Kiefer inequality
基弗-沃尔弗威茨过程/Kiefer-Wolfowitz 過程　Kiefer-Wolfowitz process
基格/基格　basic cell
基解/基解　basic solution

基金拆分/基金拆分　fund split
基金单位/基金單位　fund unit
基金的一揽子成本/基金的一籃子成本,基金的全部成本　all-in cost of fund
基金公司/基金公司　fund company
基金会/基金會　foundation
基金余额/基金餘額　fund balance
基金账户/基金賬戶　fund account
基金中的基金/組合基金　fund of fund, FOF
基金资产/基金資產　fund asset
基尼集中率/吉尼集中度　Gini concentration ratio
基尼集中系数/吉尼集中係數　Gini's coefficient of concentration
基尼假设/吉尼假設　Gini's hypothesis
基尼系数/吉尼係數　Gini coefficient
基尼指数/吉尼指數　Gini's index
基欧计划/自雇者退休金計劃　Keogh plan
基期/參考期間　base period, reference period
基期变动/基的變換　change of basis
基期加权指数/基期加權指數　base-period weight index
基期权重/基期權數　base weight
基数/基數　radix
基数效用/基數效用　cardinal utility
基数效用论/基數效用論　theory of cardinal utility
基线/基線,底線　baseline
基线风险/基線危險率,基線轉機率　baseline hazard
基线生存函数/基線存活函數　baseline survivor function
基向量/基向量　base vector
基因频率/基因次數　gene frequency
基因频率分析/基因次數分析　gene frequency analysis
基于案例推理/案例爲本的推理,案例本位推理　case based reasoning, CBR
基于合同的诉讼/以合約爲基礎的訴訟　action founded in contract
基于技术的创新/技術基礎的創新　technology based innovation
基于价值的管理/價值管理　value based management
基于科学的创新/基於科學的創新　science-based innovation
基于内容的多媒体信息检索/内容爲基的多媒體資訊檢索　content based multimedia information retrieval, CBR
基于设施的服务/設施地提供服務　facilities based service

基于胜任力的训练/能力本位訓練 competency based training
基于时间的竞争/基於時間的競爭 time based competition
基于事实的决策方法/基於事實的決策方法 factual approach to decision making
基于位置的服务/行動定位服務 location based service
基于现场的服务/現場提供服務 field based service
基于遗传算法的预测模型/遺傳演算法的預測模型 genetic algorithm based forecasting model
基于智慧个体的预测方法/基於智慧個體預測方法 intelligent agent based forecasting method
基于主体的计算金融学/基於主體的計算金融學 agent based computational finance, ACF
基于主体的计算经济学/基於主體的計算經濟學 agent based computational economics, ACE
基于主体建模/基於主體建模 agent based modeling, ABM
基于状态维护/設備狀態基準維修 condition based maintenance
基准带/基準帶 benchmark tape
基准风险/基差風險 basis risk
基准工作/基準工作 benchmark job
基准开始日期/基準開始日期 baseline start date
基准利率/基準利率 base interest rates
基准偏磁/基準偏磁 baseline magnetic bias
基准趋势法/基準趨勢法 benchtrending
基准日期/基準日期 base date
基准投资组合/基準投資組合 benchmark portfolio
基准完成日期/基準完成日期 baseline finish date
基准线/零基線 zero line
基准销售量/基線銷售 baseline sale
基准职位/關鍵職位 key job
稽核发行量/稽核發行量 audited circulation
激光/雷射 laser
激光成像/雷射成像 laser imaging
激光雕刻机/雷射雕刻機 laser engraver
激光母盘刻录机/雷射母盤燒錄機 laser beam recorder
激光烧蚀掩膜/雷射燒蝕掩膜 laser ablation mask
激光视盘/雷射影碟 laser disc
激光照排机/雷射排版機 laser imagesetter
激光致盲武器的禁用/雷射致盲武器的禁用 prohibition on the use of laser blinding weapon
激活情报/激活情報 activate information
激进经济学派/極端政治經濟學派 radical economics, radical political economics school
激进女性主义/激進女性主義 radical feminism
激进人文主义理论/激進人文主義理論 radical humanist theory
激进型融资策略/激進型投資策略 aggressive financing strategy
激励/激勵 motivating
激励代理/激勵代理 incentive agency
激励工资/激勵性薪資 incentive pay
激励机制/誘因機制 incentive mechanism
激励理论/激勵理論,動機理論 motivational theory
激励契约/誘因契約 incentive contract
激励潜能分数/激勵潛能分數,動機潛能分數 motivating potential score
激励问题/誘因問題 incentive problem
激励相容/誘因相符性 incentive compatibility
激励相容机制/與誘因相符的機制 incentive-compatible mechanisms
激励相容约束/誘因相容限制 incentive compatibility constraint
激励型职位设计法/激勵型職位設計法 motivational job design method
激励性规制/誘因管制 incentive regulation
激励性契约/誘因契約 incentive contract
激励性薪酬/誘因式報酬 incentive based pay
激励约束/誘因限制 incentive constraint
羁押/羈押 custody
吉布拉特定律/吉爾布瑞特法則 Gibrat's law
吉布拉特分布/吉爾布瑞特分布,吉爾布瑞特分配 Gibrat's distribution
吉布斯采样技术/吉布斯抽樣技術 Gibbs sampling techniques
吉布斯取样器/吉布斯抽樣量 Gibbs sampler
吉尔里联结率/吉利鄰近比 Geary's contiguity ratio
吉芬反论/季芬反論 Giffen's paradox
吉芬商品/季芬財 Giffen goods
吉亨检验/Gehan 檢定 Gehan test
吉瑞纳序贯过程/Jirina 逐次程序 Jirina sequential procedures
级别管辖/級別管轄 grade jurisdiction
级差地租/差額地租 differential rent
A级股票/A級股票 class A share
级式过程/爆花過程 cascade process
级数/級數 series
极差/全距 range
极差表/全距表 table for range
极差分析法/距離分析 range analysis
极差控制图/全距管制圖,範圍控制圖 range control chart, r-control chart

极差平方比检验/全距平方比檢定　range square ratio test
极差曲线图/全距曲線圖　range curve chart
极差图/全距圖　range chart
极大化极大准则/大中取大準則　maximax criterion
极大化极小策略/小中取大策略　maximin strategy
极大化极小原则/小中取大原則　maximin principle
极大化极小准则/小中取大準則　maximin criterion
极大似然/最大概似　maximum likelihood
极大似然法/最大概似法,最大概度法　maximum likelihood method
极大似然方程/最大概度方程式　maximum likelihood equation
极大似然估计量/最大概度估计量　maximum likelihood estimator, MLE
极端过程/極端過程　extreme process
极端强度/極端強度　extreme intensity
极高光/極高光　catch light
极化效应/極化效應　polarization effect
极均值/极值平均　extreme mean
极限定理/極限定理　limit theorem
极限方差/極限變異數　limiting variance
极限分布/極限分布,極限分配　limit distribution
极限风险无效性/極限風險無效性　limiting risk deficiency, LRD
极限风险有效性/極限風險有效性　limiting risk efficiency, LRE
极限过程/極限過程　limiting process, limit process
极限可用性/有限可用度　limiting availability
极限类目/極限類目　ultimate class
极限设计/極限設計　limiting design
极限值/極限值　limit value
极限质量/界限品質　limiting quality, LQ
极线楔形图/楔形圖　polar-wedge diagram
极小化极大不变估计/大中取小不變估計值　minimax invariant estimation
极小化极大策略/大中取小策略　minimax strategy
极小化极大法则/大中取小規則　minimax rule
极小化极大风险/大中取小風險　minimax risk
极小化极大估计/大中取小估計值　minimax estimation
极小化极大估计量/大中取小估計量　minimax estimator
极小化极大检验/大中取小檢定　minimax test
极小化极大设计/大中取小設計　minimax design
极小化极大损失函数/大中取小損失函數　minimax loss function
极小化极大稳健估计/大中取小穩健估計　minimax robust estimation
极小化极大稳健估计量/大中取小穩健估計量　minimax robust estimator
极小化极大原理/大中取小原則　minimax principle
极小化极大准则/大中取小準則　minimax criterion
极性/極性　polarity
极值分布/極值分布,極值分配　extreme value distribution
极值过程/極值過程　extremal process
极值回归模型/極值回歸模型　extreme value regression model
极值理论/極值理論　extreme value theory
极值模型/極值模型　extreme model
极值强度/極值強度　extremal intensity
极值商/兩極商　extremal quotient
极值统计量/極端統計量　extremal statistic
极值秩和检验/極秩和檢定　extreme rank sum test
极锥/極錐　polar cone
即成犯/即成犯　discontinuing offense
即发侵权/即發侵權　imminent infringement
即付交易/即付交易,當場交易　bargain on spot
即付票据/[來取]即付票據　bill payable on demand
即年指标/即時引用指數　immediacy index
即期本票/即期本票　demand promissory note
即期承兑/即期承兌　immediate acceptance
即期存款/即期存款　deposit at sight
即期贷款/即期貸款　lending at sight
即期付款交单/即期付款交單　document against payment at sight
即期付现/即期付現　immediate cash payment, prompt cash payment
即期汇兑/即期匯兑　sight exchange
即期汇率/即期匯率　sight rate, spot exchange rate
即期汇票/即期匯票,見票即付票據　sight bill, sight draft
即期汇票买入价/即期匯票買入價　buying rate for sight bill
即期汇票卖出价/即期匯票賣價　selling rate for sight bill
即期交易/即期交易　bargain on term
即期利率/即期利率　spot interest rate
即期年金/即期年金　immediate annuity
即期条款/即期條款　sight clause
即期外汇/即期外匯,現匯　spot exchange
即期外汇交易/即期外匯交易　spot exchange transactions
即期外汇市场/即期外匯市場,現匯市場　spot exchange market

即期现金报酬/即期現金報酬　immediate cash consideration
即期现金交易/即期現金交易　spot cash transaction
即期信用额度/即期信用額度　demand line credit
即期信用证/即期信用狀　sight letter of credit, sight credit, letter of credit at sight
即期债务/即期債務　demand obligation
即期支票/即期支票　demand check
即期资金/即期資金　immediate fund
即时采访/即時採訪　just-in-time acquisition
即时参考资料/即時參考資料，快速參考資料，便捷參考書　ready reference material
即时开放/即時開放存取　immediate open access model
即时强制/即時強制　instant compulsion
即时清算/即時清算　speedy clearance
即时通信/即時通訊，實時通訊　real-time communication, instant messaging
即时习惯国际法/即時習慣國際法　instant international customary law
即时消息/即時消息　instant message
即时战略游戏/即時戰略遊戲　real-time strategy game
急件/急件　urgent document
疾病/疾病　disease, illness, sickness
疾病保险/疾病保險　sickness insurance
疾病的文化解释/疾病的文化解釋　cultural context of illness
疾病调查/疾病調查　sickness survey
疾病二次侵袭率/疾病二次侵襲率　secondary attack rate
疾病基金/疾病基金　sickness funds
疾病谱/疾病譜　spectrum of disease
棘轮/棘輪　ratchet
棘轮理性/棘輪理性　ratchet rationality
棘轮期权/棘輪期權　ratchet option
棘轮效应/棘輪效應　ratchet effect
集/集　collection
集成并行模型/整合平行模式　integrated-parallel model
集成产品开发团队/整合式產品小組　integrated product team, IPT
集成产品模型/整合式產品模型　integrated product model, IPM
集成创新/整合式創新　integrated innovation
集成词表/整合式詞表　integrated thesaurus
集成电路布图设计/積體電路布圖設計　integrated circuit's layout design
集成电路卡/積體電路卡　integrated circuit card, IC-card
集成管理/綜合管理　integrated management
集成信息服务/整合資訊服務　integrated information service, IIS
集成性/整合　integration
集成性资源/整合性資源　integrating resources
集成学习预测方法/整合學習預測方法　ensemble learning forecasting method
集对分析/集對分析　set pair analysis
集函数/集合函數　set function
集合竞价/集合競價　call auction
集会/集會　congregation
集会自由/集會自由　freedom of assembly
集货/集貨　publication consolidation
集计模型/總和模型　aggregate model
集结法/集結法　aggregation method
集聚/群聚　agglomeration
集聚效应/群聚效應　effect of agglomeration
集刊/論文集　collected papers
集群创新/群聚創新　cluster innovation
集群创新系统/群聚創新系統　cluster innovation system
集群方法/叢集法，群集法，聚類法　cluster method
集束式非正式信息沟通/集束式非正式溝通　concentration of beam-mode informal communication
集体/集體　collectivity
集体创业/集體創業　collective entrepreneurship
集体合同/集體合同，集體契約　collective contract
集体化/集體化　collectivization
集体记忆/集體記憶　collective memory
集体决策/群體決策　group decision making
集体劳动争议/集體勞動爭議　collective labor disputes
集体企业/集體企業　collective enterprise
集体认同/集體認同　collective identity
集体商标/集體商標　collective trademark
集体书店/集體書店　collective bookstore
集体诉讼/集體訴訟　class action suits
集体所有权/集體所有權　collective ownership
集体所有制/集體所有制　collective ownership
集体谈判/集體協商　collective bargaining
集体消费/集體消費　collective consumption
集体协商/集體協商　collective bargaining
集体行动/集體行動　collective action
集体行动理论/集體行動理論　collective action theory
集体行动逻辑/集體行動的邏輯　logic of collective

集体行为/集體行爲 collective behavior
集体性/共同性 communality
集体选择/集體選擇 collective choice
集体选择理性/集體理性 collective rationality
集体主义/集體主義 collectivism
集体著作/集體著作,合著 composite work
集体传记研究/集體傳記研究 prosopography
集体自卫/集體自衛 collective self-defence
集体作者/集體作者 collective author
集团采购/集團採購 consortia acquisition, group procurement, group purchasing
集拓/集拓 variety of rubbings
集约化作物/密集作物 intensive crop
集约农业/密集農作 intensive farming
集约型经济增长/密集經濟成長 intensive economic growth
集约型信息源/集約型資訊源 quaternary source
集中比率/集中率 concentration ratio
集中编目/集中編目,集中著錄 centralized cataloging
集中采购/集中採購 central purchasing, centralized acquisition
集中参数/集中参数 concentration parameter
集中度/集中度 degree of concentration
集中度指数/集中指標 concentration indices
集中方差检验/成塊變異數檢定 lumped variance test
集中管理的案卷/集中管理的案卷 central files
集中化检验/集中檢驗 centralized inspection
集中化统计制度/集中化統計制度 centralized statistical system
集中化议价/集中協議 centralized bargaining
集中化营销/集中行銷 concentrated marketing
集中进口制度/集中進口制度 centralized importation system
集中库存控制/集中庫存控制 centralized inventory control
集中量数/中心位置测量数 central location measure
集中模式/集權制 centralized model
集中派工/集中派工 centralized dispatching
集中曲线/集中曲線 curve of concentration
集中趋势/集中趨勢,中央趨勢 central tendency
集中趋势测度/集中趨勢測度 measure of central tendency
集中趋势的测度/集中趨勢測量數 measures of central tendency
集中式版面/集中式版面 edition with focusing theme
集中式保管模式/集中的保管模式 central retention pattern
集中式实习/集中式實習 focused fieldwork
集中似然函数/集中的概似函數 concentrated likelihood function
集中销售/集中銷售 central selling
集中型研发组织/集中型研發組織 centralized research and development organization
集中性/集中性 concentration, centrality
集中战略/集中策略 concentricity strategy
集中征订/集中徵訂 centralization subscription
集中指数/集中指數 index of concentration
集装单元/集裝單元 assembly unit
集装化/集裝化 containerization
集资诈骗罪/集資詐騙罪 crime of fraud in financing
辑/專輯 special issue
辑录方式/輯錄方式 style of edition
辑录体/輯錄體 compiling style
辑佚/輯佚 gathering of scattered writings
几何分布/幾何分布,幾何分配 geometric distribution
几何分布滞后模型/幾何分布滯後模型 geometric distributed lag model
几何概率/幾何機率 geometrical probability
几何规划/幾何規劃 geometric programming
几何极差/幾何全距 geometric range
几何模型/幾何模型 geometry model
几何平均数/幾何平均數 geometric mean
几何移动平均控制图/幾何移動平均數管制圖 geometric moving average control chart
挤出效应/排擠效果 crowding-out effect
给付之诉/給付之訴 action for performance
给惠国/給惠國 preference giving country
给予特许权/給予特許權,授予特許權 grant of franchise
脊线/脊線 ridge lines
计点值/計點值 point value
计划/計劃,方案 scheme, plan
计划成本法/計劃成本法 plan cost method
计划到货量/計劃到貨量 planned order receipt
计划订单/計劃訂單 planned order
计划发出订货量/計劃發出訂貨量 planned order released
计划发行/計劃發行 systematic distribution, systematic circulation
计划负荷/計劃負荷 planned load
计划活动/規劃 planning

计划交易额/計劃交易額 planned volume of transaction
计划经济/計劃經濟 planned economy
计划期/計劃時距 planning horizon
计划生育/生育控制,家庭計劃 birth control, family planning
计划生育政策/計劃生育政策 family planning policy, policy of family planning
计划、实施、研究、改进模式/計劃、實施、研究、改善模式 plan-do-study-ameliorate mode, PDSA mode
计划调节/計劃調節 planned adjustment
计划停工期/計劃停工期 scheduled downtime
计划投资/計劃投資 planned investment
计划外投资/計劃外投資 investment outside the plan
计划文件/計劃檔案,計劃書 program records
计划协调技术/計劃評核術 program evaluation and review technique, PERT
计划型变革/規劃性變革 planned change
计划学派/計劃學派 planning school
计划值/計劃值 planned value, PV
计划制定的权变论/計劃制定的權變論 contingency theory of planning
计价物/計價商品 numeraire
计件工资/計件工資 piece rate wage
计件工资制/計件工資制 piece rate wage system
计件值/計件值 piece value
计量比对/計量比對 metrological comparison
计量标准/計量標準 metrological standard
计量抽样/計量抽樣,屬量抽樣,變量抽樣 variable sampling, sampling by variable
计量抽样方案/計量抽樣計劃 variable sampling plan
计量抽样检验/屬量抽樣檢驗 sampling inspection by variables
计量法律学/計量法律學,法律統計學 jurimetry
计量分类表/屬量分類表 quantitative classified table
计量环境学/計量環境學 environmetry
计量基准/計量基準 metrological benchmark
计量检定/計量檢定 metrological verification
计量检验/計量檢驗,屬量檢驗 inspection by variable, variable inspection, econometric test
计量经济学/計量經濟學,經濟計量學 econometrics
计量精度/屬量精確度 quantitative precision
计量控制限/計量管制界限 variable control limit
计量模型/計量經濟模型 econometric model
计量器具/測量儀器 measuring instruments
计量确认/計量確認 metrological confirmation
计量认证/計量認證 measurement authentication
计量生物统计学/計量生物學 biometrics
计量特性/計量特徵 metrological characteristic
计量统计/屬量統計 statistics of variables, quantitative statistics
计量响应/有無計數反應,屬量響應 quantal response, quantitative response
计量心理学/計量心理學 psychometry
计量验收抽样/屬量允收抽樣,計量值允收抽樣 acceptance sampling by variable
计量遥测学/計量遙測學 telemetry
计量值/計量值 variable value
计量值控制图/計量值管制圖 control chart by variable
计量职能/計量職能 metrological function
计量准则/屬量準則 quantitative criterion
计日工报价/計日工報價 daily quote
计日工作/計時制,日工制 day work
计时工资/計時工資,時薪 hourly wage
计时工作/計時工作 time work
计数变数/計數變數 count variable
计数测度/計數測度 counting measure
计数抽样/屬性抽樣,計數值抽樣 sampling by attribute
计数抽样检验/屬性抽樣檢驗 sampling inspection by attributes
计数分布/計數分布,計數分配 counting distribution
计数过程/計數過程 counting process
计数检验/計數檢驗,屬性檢驗,屬性檢定 inspection by attribute, attribute inspection, counting inspection
计数模型/計數器模型,統計模型 counter model, count model
计数器/計數器 gate counter
计数数列/屬性數列 qualitative series
计数验收抽样/屬性允收抽樣,計數值允收抽樣 acceptance sampling by attributes
计数值/計數值 attribute value
计数值控制图/計數值管制圖 control chart by attribute
计算机/電腦 computer
计算机编目/電腦編目 computer cataloging, computerized cataloging
计算机编目系统/電腦編目系統 computerized cataloging system
计算机程序法律保护指令/電腦程式法律保護指令 directive on the legal protection of computer programs

计算机打样/電腦打樣　CTProof
计算机动画/電腦動畫　computer animation
计算机犯罪/電腦犯罪　computer crime
计算机仿真/電腦模擬　computer simulation
计算机辅助报道/電腦輔助報導　computer assisted reporting
计算机辅助标引/電腦輔助索引　computer assisted indexing
计算机辅助参考咨询/電腦輔助參考服務，電算機輔助參考服務　computer assisted reference service
计算机辅助访谈/電腦輔助面訪　computer assisted personal interview
计算机辅助工程/電腦輔助工程　computer aided engineering, CAE
计算机辅助工艺规划/電腦輔助製程規劃　computer aided process planning, CAPP
计算机辅助工装设计/電腦輔助工裝設計　computer aided frock design, CAFD
计算机辅助培训/電腦輔助培訓　computer aided training
计算机辅助软件工程/電腦輔助軟體工程　computer aided software engineering, CASE
计算机辅助设计/電腦輔助設計　computer aided design, CAD
计算机辅助设施布置技术/電腦輔助設施配置技術　computerized relative allocation of facility technique, CRAFT
计算机辅助制造/電腦輔助製造　computer aided manufacturing, CAM
计算机绘谱/電腦繪譜　computer drawing spectrum
计算机集成制造系统/電腦整合製造系統　computer-integrated manufacturing system, CIMS
计算机胶片输出/電腦膠片輸出　CTFilm
计算机软件/電腦軟體　computer software
计算机软件保护条约草案/電腦軟體保護條約草案　Treaty for the Protection of Computer Software
计算机输出缩微胶片/電腦輸出微縮片　computer output microfilm, computer output microform
计算机输出缩微系统/電腦輸出微縮系統　computer output microfilm system, COM
计算机输入缩微胶片/電腦輸入微縮片　computer input microfilm, computer input microform
计算机输入缩微系统/電腦輸入微縮系統　computer input microfilm system, CIM
计算机图像处理/電腦繪圖　computer image processing
计算机图形学/電腦圖形學　computer graphic, CG
计算机网络/電腦網路　computer network

计算机文档类型附注/電腦文檔類型附注　type of computer file note
计算机文件/電腦檔案　computer file
计算机文献检索/電腦為本的文件檢索　computer based document retrieval
计算机信息检索/電腦本位資訊檢索　computer based information retrieval
计算机音乐/電腦音樂　computer music
计算机印刷/電腦印刷　computer print, CTPrint
计算机硬件/電腦硬體　computer hardware
计算机游戏/電腦遊戲　computer game
计算机在机制版/電腦在機製版　computer press, CTPress
计算机支持协同工作/電腦支援協同工作　computer supported cooperative work, CSCW
计算机直接制版/電腦直接製版　computer to plate
计算机直接制网版/電腦直接製網版　computer to screen
计算机中介传播/電腦中介傳播　computer mediated communication, CMC
计算机自动抽词/電腦自動抽詞　computer-automatic word extraction
计算机字/電腦用字　computer word
计算价/計算期價格　given price
计算金融学/計算金融學　computational finance
计算经济学/計算經濟學，經濟計量學　computational economics
计算年/計算年　given year
计算期/計算期　given period
计算期加权指数/本期加權指數　current weight index
计算期权数/本期權數　current weight
计算误差/計算誤差　calculation error
计帐/計賬　jizhang
记分/計分　score
t记分/t記分　t-score
z记分/z計分　z-score
记分板/計分板　score board
记分标准化/計分標準化　normalization of scores
记分单/計分單　score sheet
记分法/計分法　scoring method
记分统计量/計分統計量　score statistic
记录/記錄　recording, record
记录层/記錄層　recorded layer
记录分辨力/記錄分辨力，記錄解析力　recording resolving power
记录分辨率/記錄解析度　recording ratio
记录检验/記錄檢定　records test

记录通道/記錄通道　record channel
记录头/記錄頭,錄音頭　recording head
记录头标区/記錄頭標區　leader
记录系统/記錄系統　recording system
记名保单/記名保單　order policy
记名背书/記名背書,全名背書,完全背書　endorsement in full, full endorsement
记名付款/記名付款　payable to order
记名股票/記名股票　inscribed stock
记名票据/記名票據　order bill, note to order, order instrument
记名提单/記名提單　named bill of lading, order bill of lading, straight bill of lading
记名债券/記名債券　non-bearer bond, bond registered
记名证券/記名證券　inscribed security
记名支票/記名支票　check payable to order, specific cheque
记事簿/記事簿　commonplace book
记数点/記數點　count point
记数信用证/記數信用狀　notation credit
记叙方式/記敘方式　narrative way
记忆/記憶　memory
记账/記賬　keep account
记账本位币/功能性貨幣　functional currency
记账单位/記賬單位　unit of account
记账公债/無實體公債　book entry government bond
记账货币/記賬貨幣　currency of account, money of account
记账交易/記賬交易　for the account
记账凭证/記賬憑單　underlying voucher
记账易货贸易/託付易貨貿易　escrow barter trade
记者/記者　journalist, reporter
记者俱乐部/記者俱樂部　press club
记者站/記者站　reporter station
记者招待会/新聞記者會　news conference
纪检档案/紀檢檔案　discipline inspection records
纪律/紀律,規訓　discipline
纪律条令/紀律條令　mandatory regulation on discipline
纪念集/紀念集　memorial book
纪念图书馆/紀念圖書館　memorial library
纪事考订/紀事考訂　event criticism
纪要/紀要　summary, outline, minute
技科学/技科學　technoscience
技能工资/技能基礎薪資制　skilled-based pay
技能类别/技術類別　skill categories
技能培训/技能訓練　skill training

技能知识/技術訣竅　know-how
技术/技術　technique, technology
技术编辑/技術編輯　technical editor
技术变革/技術變革　technology change
技术变迁/技術變遷,技術演化　technological change, technology evolution
技术变迁模型/有技術變動的模型　models with technological change
技术标准/技術標準　technical standard
技术标准化/技術標準化　technological standardization
技术标准联盟/技術標準聯盟　technological standard alliance
技术标准目录/技術標準目錄　list of technical standard
技术并购/技術并購　technology based merger and acquisition, technology based M and A
技术差距/技術差距　technology gap
技术成熟度/技術成熟度　technology maturity
技术承包/技術合約　technological contract
技术冲击/科技衝擊　technological shock
技术出口/技術出口　technology export
技术创新/技術創新,技術革新　technological innovation, technical innovation
技术创新测度/技術創新測度　measure of technological innovation
技术创新的动态模型/技術創新的動態模型　A-U model
技术创新风险/技術創新風險　technological innovation risk
技术创新管理/技術創新管理　technological innovation management
技术创新绩效/技術創新績效　technological innovation performance
技术创新联盟/技術創新聯盟　technological innovation alliance
技术创新能力/技術創新能力　technological innovative capability
技术创新审计/技術創新審計　technological innovation audit
技术创新体系/技術創新體系　technological innovation system
技术创新网络/技術創新網路　technological innovation network
技术创新效率/技術創新效率　technological innovation efficiency
技术创新战略/技術創新策略　technological innovation strategy

技术措施/技術措施　technical measure
技术单元模型/技術單元模型,技術單元模式　skill blocks model
技术导向性竞争情报/技術導向性競爭情報　technology oriented competitive intelligence
技术多样化/技術多樣化,技術多角化　technology diversification
技术发明/技術發明　technical invention
技术法规/技術法規　technical regulation
技术范式/技術範式　technology paradigm
技术方程式/技術方程式　technical equation
技术费用/技術費用　technical fee
技术风险/技術風險　technology risk
技术服务/技術服務　technical service, technological service
技术改造/技術改造,技術改進　technical betterment, technological transformation
技术赶超/技術趕超　technology catching-up
技术革命/技術革命　technology revolution, technological revolution
技术公报/技術通報　technical circular, technical bulletin
技术共同体/技術共同體　technological community
技术管理/技術管理　technology management
技术管理体系/技術管理體系　technology management system
技术规范/技術規範　technical specification
技术轨迹/技術軌跡　technology trajectory
技术合理化战略/技術合理化戰略　technology rationalization strategy
技术合同/技術合同　contract of technology trade
技术合作/技術合作　technical cooperation, technological collaboration
技术合作投入/技術合作投入　technical cooperation input
技术核心能力/技術核心能力　technological core competence
技术环境/技術環境　technical environment, technological environment
技术环境因素/技術環境因素　technological segment
技术获取/技術獲取　technology acquisition
技术机会/技術機會　technology opportunity
技术积累/技術積累　technology accumulation
技术基础结构/技術基礎結構　technological infrastructure
技术集成/技術整合　technology integration
技术集群/技術群聚,技術聚落　technology cluster
技术技能/技術能力　technical skill, technological competence
技术监测/技術監測　technology monitoring
技术监测能力/技術監測能力　technological supervised capability
技术鉴定/技術鑒定　technical appraisal
技术交底/技術交底　technical disclosure
技术交换/技術交換　technical exchange
技术交易/技術交易　technology trading
技术教育/技術教育　technical education
技术接受行为/技術接受行爲　technology acceptance behavior
技术结构/技術結構　technical structure, technology structure
技术进步/技術進步　technical progress, technological progress
技术进步率/技術進步率　rate of technical progress
技术景观/技術景觀　technology landscape
技术竞争情报/技術競爭情報　competitive technical intelligence
技术决定论/技術決定論　technological determinism
技术诀窍/技術專門知識　technological know-how
技术开发/技術開發　technical development, technological development
技术科学/技術科學　science of technology
技术可行性/技術可行性　technical feasibility
技术跨越/技術跨越　technology leapfrogging
技术困境/技術困境　technical dilemma
技术扩散/技術擴散　technology diffusion
技术理性/技術理性　technical rationality
技术联盟/技術聯盟　technology alliance
技术链/技術鏈　technology chain
技术领先/技術領先　technology leadership
技术领先战略/技術領導者策略　technology leader strategy
技术垄断优势/技術壟斷優勢　technology monopoly advantage
技术路径图/技術路徑圖,技術路線圖　technology road map
技术贸易/技術貿易　technology trade, trade in technology
技术贸易发展趋势/技術貿易發展趨勢　trend of technology trade
技术贸易结算/技術貿易結算　settlement of technology trade
技术贸易同盟/技術貿易同盟　technology trading union
技术秘密/技術秘密　technological secret
技术密集型/技術密集型　technology intensive

技术密集型产品/技術密集型產品　technology intensive product
技术密集型产业/技術密集型產業　technology intensive industry
技术密集型企业/技術密集型企業　technology intensive enterprise
技术密集型投资/技術密集型投資　technology intensive investment
技术模仿/技術模仿　technology imitator
技术内化/技術内化　technology internalization
技术能力/技術能力　technical skill, technological competence
技术培训/技術培訓　technical training
技术评估/技術評估,科技評量　technology assessment
技术评价/技術評估,技術評等　technology evaluation
技术期刊/科技雜誌,科技刊物　technical journal
技术签证/技術簽證　technical visa
技术桥梁人物/技術橋梁人物　technology gatekeeper
技术情报矩阵/技術情報矩陣　technical intelligence matrix
技术趋同/技術趨同　similarity of technology
技术融合/技術融合　technology fusion
技术设计/技術設計　technical design
技术审计/技術稽核　technology audit
技术生命周期/技術生命週期　technology lifecycle
技术市场/技術市場　technology market
技术手册/技術手册　technical manual
技术数据/技術檔案　technical archive
技术数据报告/技術數據報告　technical data report
技术梯度/技術梯度　technological gradient
技术替代率/技術替代率　technical rate of substitution, TRS
技术同化能力/技術同化能力　technological assimilation capacity
技术统治论/技術官僚制　technocracy
技术投资/技術投資　technology investment
技术图纸/技術圖紙,工程圖　technical drawing
技术推进说/技術驅動理論　technology driving theory
技术外溢/技術外溢　technological spillovers
技术完好状态/操作妥善度　operational readiness
技术文献/技術文獻　technical literature
技术误差/技術誤差　technical error
技术系数/技術係數　technological coefficient, technical coefficient

技术系数矩阵/技術係數矩陣　technical coefficients matrix
技术系统/技術系統　technology system
技术细节附注/技術細節附注　technical details note
技术相互依存论/技術互依觀點　technology interdependence view
技术效率/技術效率　technical efficiency
技术信息/技術資訊　technical information
技术性贸易壁垒/技術性貿易壁壘　technical barriers to trade, TBT
技术性贸易壁垒协议/技術性貿易障礙協定　agreement on technical barriers to trade
技术性失业/技術性失業　technological unemployment
技术性支出/技術性支出　technical expense
技术性仲裁/技術性仲裁　technical arbitration
技术许可/技術授權　technology licensing
技术选择/技術選擇　technological choice, technology choice
技术学习/技術學習　technology learning
技术要素/技術要素　technical element
技术依存度/技術依存度　external technology dependency
技术移植/技術移植　technology transplantation
技术异化/技術異化　technological alienation
技术溢出/技術溢出　technology spillover
技术引进/技術引進,技術輸入,技術進口　acquisition of technology, technology acquisition, technology import
技术引进和发展/技術引進和發展　technology acquisition and development
技术引进能力/技術引進能力　technological imported capability
技术营销/技術行銷　technology marketing
技术优势/技術優勢　technological superiority
技术预测/技術預測　technological forecasting
技术预见/技術預見　technology foresight, technological foresight
技术元数据/技術詮釋資料　technical metadata
技术援助/技術援助　technical assistance
技术援助基金/技術援助基金　technical assistance fund
技术援助契约/技術援助合約　technical assistance contract
技术约束/生產技術之限制　technological constraints
技术跃迁/技術躍遷　technology leap
技术战略/技術策略　technology strategy
技术哲学/技術哲學　philosophy of technology

技术整理/技術整理　technical arrangement
技术政策/技術政策　technology policy
技术质量鉴定/技術質量鑒定　technical qualitative evaluation
技术中心/技術中心　technology center
技术专家/技術專家　technical expert
技术专利/技術專利　technical patent
技术转换曲线/技術轉換曲線　technical transformation curve
技术转让/技術轉讓　technology transfer
技术转让的支付方式/技術轉讓的支付方式　payment of technology transfer
技术转让协议/技術轉讓協議　technology transfer agreement
技术转让专利权/技術轉讓專利權　technology transfer patent
技术转移/技術移轉　technology transfer
技术状态审核/組態稽核　configuration audit
技术追赶/技術追趕　technological catching-up
技术追随/技術追隨　technology follow
技术咨询/技術諮詢　technological consultancy, technical consultation
技术资产/技術資產　technical asset
技术子系统/技術子系統　technical subsystem
技术组合分析/技術組合分析　technology portfolio analysis
季节变动指数/季節變動指數　indexes of seasonal variation
季节波动/季節波動　seasonal fluctuation
季节工/季節工　seasonal worker
季节基数/季節基數　seasonal base
季节调整/季節調整　seasonal adjustment
季节性/季節性　seasonality
季节性波动/季節變動　seasonal fluctuations
季节性贷款/季節性貸款　seasonal loan
季节性单位根/季節性單根　seasonal unit root
季节性关税/季節性關稅　seasonal duty, seasonal tariff
季节性库存/季節性存貨　seasonal inventory
季节性贸易/季節性貿易　seasonal trade
季节性模型/季節模型　seasonal model
季节性失业/季節性失業　seasonal unemployment
季节性时间序列/季節性時間序列　seasonal time series
季节性调整/季節性調整　seasonal adjustment, seasonally adjusted
季节性协整/季節性共整合　seasonal cointegration
季节性自回归移动平均模型/季節性自我相關整合移動平均模型　seasonal arima models
季节虚拟变量/季節虛擬變數　seasonal dummy
季节因素/季節因數　seasonal factor
季节折扣/季節折扣　seasonal discount
季节指数/季節指數　seasonal index
季刊/季刊　quarterly
剂量变换值/劑量變換值　dose metameter
剂量-反应/劑量-反應　dosage-response
剂量死亡曲线/劑量死亡率曲線　dosage mortality curve
济贫法/濟貧法　poor law
既得权说/既得權說　doctrine of vested rights
既判力/既判力　res judicata
继承/繼承　succession, inheritance
继承权/繼承權　right of succession
继承依被继承人属人法/繼承依被繼承人屬人法　succession governed by lex personalis of the decedent
继承依遗产所在地法/繼承依遺產所在地法　succession governed by lex personalis of the place of the estate
继承制度/繼承制度　succession system, inheritance system
继电器第二装配组实验/繼電器第二裝配組實驗　second relay assemblage experiment
继电器装配检验室实验/繼電器裝配檢驗室實驗　relay assemblage inspection room experiment
继任计划/接班規劃　succession planning
继受取得/繼受取得　derivative acquisition
继嗣/繼嗣　descent
继续犯/繼續犯　continuous crime
继续教育/進修教育，擴充教育　further education
继续性合同/繼續性合同　continuous contract
祭司档案/祭司檔案　pontifical archives
寄存/寄存，委託保管　deposit
寄存文件/寄存檔　deposit file
寄售合同/寄售合約　consignment sale contract
寄售货物/寄售貨物，寄售存貨　consignment stock
寄售库存/寄售存貨　consignment inventory, consigned stock
寄售利润/寄售利潤　consignment profit
寄售商品/寄售商品　consignment merchandise
寄售损益/寄售損益　consignment profit and loss
寄售业/寄售業　consignment business
寄销/寄銷，寄售　sale on consignment
寄销品账户/寄售商品賬戶　consignment out account
寄样订货/寄樣訂貨　feedback subscription

绩效/績效 performance
绩效报告/績效報告 performance report
绩效测量基准/績效測量基準 performance measurement baseline
绩效工资制度/績效基礎薪資制度,績效基礎薪資系統 performance-based pay system
绩效管理/績效管理 performance management
绩效管理体系/績效管理系統,績效管理制度 performance management system
绩效衡量/績效衡量 performance measures
绩效回馈/績效回饋 performance feedback
绩效监测/績效偵測 performance monitoring
绩效奖金/績效獎金 performance bonus
绩效考核/業績評定 assessment of performance
绩效评定因子/績效評定因素 performance rating factor
绩效评估/績效評估,效益評估 performance appraisal
绩效评估面谈/績效評估面談 performance appraisal interview
绩效评估原则/績效評估原則 performance appraisal principle
绩效评价/績效評估 performance evaluation
绩效取样/績效抽樣 performance sampling
绩效审计/績效審計 performance audit
绩效预算/績效預算 performance budget
绩效指标/績效指標 performance indicator
绩优报酬/功績薪給制 merit pay
加班费/加班費 overtime pay
加班工作和轮班工作/加班和輪班工作 work extra hours and shifts
加伯利埃尔检验/Gabriel檢定 Gabriel's test
加伯利埃尔-森统计量/Gabriel-Sen 統計量 Gabriel-Sen statistic
加成定价/加成定價法 markup pricing
加法定理/加法定理 additive theorem
加法运算/加法運算 additive operation
加菲尔德文献集中定律/加爾非文獻集中定律 Garfield's law of concentration
加负担处理/加負擔處理 administrative decision imposing burden
加工/加工 processing
加工成本/加工成本 machining cost
加工废料/加工廢料 processing waste
加工过程模拟/加工過程模擬 machining process simulation, MPS
加工和补偿贸易/加工和補償貿易 processing and compensation trade

加工贸易/加工貿易 improvement trade, processing deal, processing trade
加工贸易合同/加工貿易合約 processing deal contract
加工时间/加工時間 processing time
加工顺序/加工順序 processing sequence
加工周期/排程總製造時間 makespan
加工装配式生产/加工裝配式生產 fabrication-assembly production
加急订单/緊急訂單 rush order
加价/加價,漲價,增高標價 markup
加零规则/零規則 rule of zero
加盟店/加盟店 franchiser, franchise chain
加密/加密,暗碼化 encryption
加密技术/加密技術 encryption technique
加权/加權 weighting
加权标引/加權標引 weight indexing
加权抽样/加權抽樣 weighting sampling
加权点方案/加權評分法 weighted-point plan
加权法/加權法 weighting method, weight method
加权复合相对指数/加權複合相對指數 weighted composite relative index number
加权观测值/加權觀測值 weighted observations
加权函数/加權函數 weighting function
加权几何均值/加權幾何平均數 weighted geometric mean
加权检索/加權檢索 weighted retrieval, weighted search
加权均值/加權平均數 weighted mean
加权平方和/加權平方和 weighted sum of squares
加权平方误差损失函数/加權平方誤差損失函數 weighted squared error loss function
加权平均/加權平均 weighted average
加权平均资本成本/加權平均資金成本 weighted average cost of capital, WACC
加权平均总市值/加權平均總市值 weighted average total market value
加权算术平均/加權算術平均 weighted arithmetic mean
加权误差/加權誤差 weight error
加权系数/加權係數 weighting coefficient
加权线性回归/加權線性回歸 weighted linear regression
加权移动平均/加權移動平均數 weighted moving average
加权移动平均法/加權移動平均法 method of weighted moving averages
加权因子/加權因子 weighting factor

加权指数/加權指數　weighted index number
加权指数移动均值控制图/指數加權移動平均數管制圖　control chart of exponential weighted moving average, EWMA
加权综合数量指数/加權總合物量指數　weighted aggregates quantity index
加权综合物价指数/加權總合物價指數　weighted aggregates price index
加权综合指数/加權總合指數　weighted aggregate index number
加权最小二乘/加權最小平方　weighted least squares
加权最小二乘法/加權最小平方法　weighted least square method, WLS
加权最小二乘估计量/加權最小平方估計量　weighted least square estimator
加时/超時　overtime
加速老化/加速老化　accelerated aging
加速失效时间模型/加速失敗時間模型　accelerated failure time model
加速试验/加速試驗　accelerated test
加速寿命试验/加速壽命試驗　accelerated life test
加速随机逼近/加速隨機逼近　accelerated stochastic approximation
加速因子/加速因子　accelerated factor
加速原理/加速原理　acceleration principle, accelerator principle
加速折旧/加速折舊　accelerated depreciation
加速主义假说/加速膨脹假說　accelerationist hypothesis
加特检验/Gart 檢定　Gart's test
加网/加網　screening
加网线数/加網線數　screening ruling, screen frequency
加伍德分布/Garwood 分布，Garwood 分配　Garwood distribution
加性函数/加法函數　additive function
加性价值函数/可加值函數　additive value function
加性一致性/相加性一致性　additive consistency
加压/加壓　apply pressure
加严检验/加嚴檢驗　tightened inspection
加印/加印　additional printing
加总偏差/匯總偏誤　aggregation bias
夹板/夾板　splint
夹层贷款证券化/夾層貸款證券化　mezzanine loan securitization
夹层融资/夾層融資　mezzanine financing
夹批/夾批　annotate and comments in the context

夹签/夾簽　Jiaqian
夹在中间/夾在中間　stuck in the middle
夹注/夾注　let-in note, cut-in note
家计调查/家計調查　family budget investigation
家刻本/家刻本　family edition
家庭/家庭　family, household
家庭暴力/家庭暴力　domestic violence
家庭财产调查/家庭財產調查　family property survey
家庭策略/家庭策略　family strategy
家庭冲突理论/家庭衝突理論　family conflict theory
家庭档案/家庭檔案　family archive
家庭功能/家庭功能　family function
家庭沟通理论/家庭溝通理論　family communication theory
家庭关系/家庭關係　family relationship
家庭规模/家庭人數　family size
家庭和产业档案/家庭和產業檔案　family and estate archive
家庭和社会风险/家庭和社會風險　family and social risk
家庭户/共同生活戶　family household
家庭寄养/家庭寄養　family foster care
家庭结构/家庭結構　family structure
家庭解体/家庭解體　family disintegration
家庭金融公司/家庭金融公司　household finance corporation
家庭角色/家庭角色　family role
家庭劳务价格指数/家庭勞務價格指數　family service price index
家庭联产承包责任制/家庭聯產承包責任制　household contract responsibility system
家庭伦理/家庭倫理　family ethic
家庭平均户规模/家庭平均戶規模　average household size
家庭全宗/家庭全宗　family archival fonds
家庭社会工作/家庭社會工作　family social work
家庭社会学/家庭社會學　sociology of family
家庭生产/家戶生產　household production
家庭生产函数/家庭生產函數　household production function
家庭生活教育指导/家庭生活教育指導　family life education and guidance
家庭生命周期/家庭生命週期　family life cycle
家庭史/家庭史　history of family
家庭手工业/家庭工業，傳統農村工業　cottage industry
家庭养老/家庭養老　family-based elderly care

家庭照顾/家庭照顾　family care
家庭治疗/家庭治療,家族治療　family therapy
家庭综合保险单/綜合保險單　household policy
家务/家務　household work
家园沟通/家庭溝通　family communication
家长式领导/家長式領導　paternalistic leadership
家长式权威/父系權威　patriarchal authority
家长制/家長制　patriarchy
家长作风/家長式主義　paternalism
家支/家支　lineage
家中购物/家中購物　in-home shopping
家族/氏族　clan
家族包装/家族包裝　family packaging
家族档案/家族檔案　family clan archives
家族合伙/家庭合夥　family partnership
家族和产业档案馆/家族和產業檔案館　family and estate archives
家族品牌/家族品牌　family branding
家族企业/家族企業　family enterprise, family business
家族全宗/家族全宗　family clan fonds
家族主义/家族主義,家庭主義　familism
甲骨档案/甲骨檔案　archive on tortoise shells or bones
甲骨档案汇编/甲骨檔案編譯　compilation of oracle-bone script
甲骨文/甲骨文　oracle bone inscription
甲骨资源/甲骨資源　oracle resource
假币/偽鈔　counterfeit money
假定/假定,假設　assumption
假定均值/暫定平均數　arbitrary mean
假定利息/假定利息　hypothetical interest
假定平价/假定平價　hypothetical par
假定平均数/假定平均數,參考均數,假想均數　assumed mean, assumed average
假定原点/假定原點,暫定原點　assumed origin, arbitrary origin
假关联/假相聯　illusory association
假冒/仿冒品　counterfeiting
假冒注册商标/假冒註冊商標　counterfeit registered trademark
假冒注册商标罪/假冒註冊商標罪　crime of counterfeiting registered trademarks
假冒专利/假冒專利　counterfeit patent
假名作品/假名作品　pseudonymous work
假设/假設,擬說　hypothesis
假设检验/假設檢驗,假設檢定　hypothesis testing, test of hypotheses

假设检验理论/假設檢定理論　theory of hypotheses testing
假设模型/假設模型　hypothesize model
假设总体/假設母體　hypothetical population
假释/假釋　parole
假托/託詞　pretexting
假相关/假相關　illusory correlation
假想防卫/假想防衛　imaginative defense
价比/價比　price-relative
价差交易/價差交易　spread transaction
价差套利/價差套利　spread arbitrage
价格/價格　price
价格保护计划/價格保護計劃　price protection plans
价格变动/價格變動　price change
价格变动保证金/價格變動保證金　variation margin
价格波动/波動的價格　fluctuation in price
价格波动准备/價格波動準備　reserve for price fluctuation
价格博弈/價格賽局　price game
价格补偿性变动/價格補償性變動　price compensating variation
价格补偿指数/物價補償指數　price compensation index
价格补贴/價格補貼,價格支持　price subsidy, price support
价格操纵/操縱價格　manipulation of price
价格差异/價格差異　price differential
价格承诺/價格具結　price undertaking
价格点/價格點數　price point
价格冻结政策/價格凍結政策　price stop policy
价格发现/價格發現　price discovery
价格反应系数/價格反應係數　coefficient of price reaction
价格反转/價格反轉　price reversal
价格刚性/價格僵固　price rigidity
价格杠杆/價格槓桿　price leverage
价格革命/價格革命　price revolution
价格公开制/價格公開制　open price system
价格管理/價格管理　price administration
价格管理制度/價格管理制度　price management system
价格管制/價格管制　price control
价格划线/價格底限　price lining
价格机制/價格機制,價格制度　price mechanism, price system
价格挤压/價格壓榨　price squeeze
价格剪刀差/價格剪　price scissors
价格接受者/價格接受者　price taker

价格结构/價格結構　price structure
价格竞争/價格競爭　price competition
价格理论/價格理論　price theory
价格联盟/價格聯盟　price association
价格领导/價格領導,價格導向　price leadership
价格领导者/吸引價格　price leader
价格垄断/價格壟斷,限價,統一定價　price-fixing, monopoly pricing
价格敏感度指数/價格敏感度指數　price sensitivity index
价格黏性/價格黏性　price stickiness
价格歧视/價格歧視,差別定價　price discrimination
价格契约/價格契約　price contract
价格上限/價格上限　price ceilings
价格上限管制/價格上限管制　price cap regulation
价格双轨制/元價格制度　double track prices system, dual price system
价格弹性/價格彈性　price elasticity
价格体系/價格制度　price system
价格条件/價格條件　terms of price
价格条款/價格條款　price clause
价格调节机制/價格調整機構　price adjustment mechanism
价格调整/價格調整　price adjustment
价格调整策略/價格調整策略　price adjustment strategy
价格听证会/價格聽證會　public hearing over price
价格维持协定/價格維持協議　price maintenance agreement
价格维持政策/價格維持政策　price maintenance policy
价格系数/價格係數　price coefficient
价格下限/價格下限,最低統一訂價　minimum price fixing, price floor
价格限定/價格固定　price fixing
价格线/價格線　price line
价格消费曲线/價格消費曲線　price consumption curve
价格效应/價格效應　price effect
价格协定/價格協議　price agreement
价格信号/價格信號　price signal
价格战/價格戰　price war
价格折扣/價格折扣　price discount
价格折让/價格折讓　price allowance
价格政策/價格政策　price policy
价格指数/價格指數,物價指數　price index, price indices
价格注水率/價格注水率　price waterfall

价格自动调整功能/價格自動調整功能　function of automatic adjustment
价格总水平/價格總水準　general price level
价值/價值　value
价值悖论/價值的矛盾　paradox of value
价值标准/價值標準　standard of value
价值冲突/價值衝突　value conflict
价值储藏/價值儲藏　store of value
价值传递网络/價值傳遞網路,價值傳送網路　value-delivery network
价值单位/價值單位　unit of value
价值导向定价/價值基礎訂價法　value-based pricing
价值分析/價值分析　value analysis
价值附加型促销/增值促銷　value-added promotion
价值工程/價值工程　value engineering
价值工程对象/價值工程物件　value engineering subject
价值工程实施计划/價值工程實施階段　value engineering implementation plan
价值观/價值觀　value
价值观与生活方式分类/價值觀與生活方式分類　value and life style typology, VALS typology
价值管理专家/價值管理專家　value specialist
价值规律/價值規律　law of value
价值函数/價值函數　value function
价值衡量测度/價值衡量測度　value metrics
价值交换系统/價值交換系統　value-exchange system
价值矩阵/價值矩陣　value matrix
价值理论/價值說　value theory
价值理性/價值理性　value rationality
价值链/價值鏈　value chain
价值链分析法/價值鏈分析　value chain analysis
价值量/價值量　quantity of value
价值配置/價值構形　value configuration
价值手段/價值尺度　measure of values
价值团队/價值團隊　value team
价值相关性/價值相關性　value relevance
价值形式/價值形態　form of value
价值型投入产出模型/價值型投入產出模型　value input-output model
价值增加型促销/價值增加型促銷　value-increasing promotion
价值增值/價值增值　self-expansion of value
价值证券/價值證券　value securities
价值指数/價值指數　value index, value index number
价值中立/價值中立　value free

价值主张/價值主張　value proposition
价值状态/貨幣性　moneyness
架构创新/架構創新　architectural innovation
假期工资/休假報酬　vacation pay
假日效应/假日效果　holiday effect
尖峰度/尖峰度　leptokurtosis
尖峰曲线/尖峰曲線　leptokurtic curve
奸非/奸非　adultery of the criminal law in the feudal China
坚挺货币/強勢貨幣　strong currency
监本/監本　imperial academy edition
监测/監控　monitoring
监测抽样检验/監測抽樣檢驗　monitoring sampling inspection
监督/監督,督導　supervision
监候/監候　Jian Hou
监护/監護　guardianship
监控/監控,監視,監督　surveillance
监控过程/監控過程　monitoring and controlling process
监理/監視,監督　surveillance
监理报告/監理報告　surveillance report
监理单位/監查單位　surveillance unit
监理工程师/監理工程師　surveillance engineer
监理规划/監理規劃　surveillance plan
监理机构/監理機構　surveillance organization
监理例会/監理例會　surveillance regular meeting
监理细则/監理細則　surveillance regulation
监理意见/監理意見　surveillance suggestion
监事/監事　supervisor
监事会/監事會　board of supervisors
监守自盗/監守自盜　embezzlement
监听/監聽　monitoring
监狱图书馆/監獄圖書館　prison library, correctional library
兼爱/兼愛　universal love
兼并/合并　merger
兼并方/主并者　acquirer
兼并和收购会计/并購會計　acquisition and purchase accounting
兼并套利/兼并套利　merger arbitrage
兼容性/相容性,契合度　compatibility
兼祧/兼祧　Jiantiao, be heir to both one's father's and uncle's property
兼业农户/兼業農戶　part-time farmer
兼营业务的控股公司/兼營業務的控股公司　holding operating company
兼职/兼任,兼差　concurrent post, moonlighting

缣帛档案/縑帛檔案　silken archive
拣除/揀除　pick out
拣货/揀貨,訂單分揀　order picking, order selection
拣选/撿料　picking and sorting
拣选区/揀選區　sorting area
检查/檢查,檢驗　inspect
检查表/檢查表　check sheet
检查风险/偵測風險,偵查風險　detection risk
检查权/檢查權　inspection right
检查水平/檢驗水準,抽檢百分比　inspection level
检察监督原则/檢察監督原則　principle of supervision by the prosecutor
检出质量曲线/出廠品質曲線　outgoing quality curve
检错码/錯誤偵測碼　error detection code, EDC
检索/檢索　retrieval
检索标识/檢索標識　search pattern of a document, search designation
检索策略/檢索策略　retrieval strategy, search strategy
检索成本效益比/檢索成本獲利比,檢索本益比　search cost-benefit ratio
检索词/檢索詞　search term
检索词扩展/詞目擴檢　term expansion
检索次数/檢索次數　retrieval times
检索点/檢索點,存取點　point of access, access point
检索范围/檢索範圍　search field limits
检索方便性/檢索方便性　retrieval convenience
检索费用/檢索費用　search cost, retrieval cost
检索服务/檢索服務　retrieval service
检索工具/檢索工具　retrieval tools, retrieval device
检索功能/檢索功能　retrieval function
检索过程/搜尋程序　search procedure, search process, search session
检索技巧/檢索技巧　search skill
检索技术/檢索技術　retrieval technique
检索结果/搜尋結果　search result
检索界面/檢索界面　search interface, retrieval surface
检索历史/搜尋紀錄　search history, search session
检索命令/檢索命令　search command
检索年限/檢索年限　search year interval
检索设备/檢索裝置　retrieval device
检索时间/搜尋時間　search time
检索式/檢索式　search formulation, search request formulation
检索速度/搜尋速度　search speed

检索算法/檢索演算法　search algorithm, retrieval algorithm
检索提问单/檢索提問單　search profile, search request form
检索途径/檢索途徑　retrieval approach, retrieval channels
检索系统/檢索系統　retrieval system
检索系统评价/檢索系統評價　retrieval system evaluation
检索限定/佇列查尋限制,佇列查找限制,佇列搜尋限制　search limit
检索效果评价/檢索效果評價　search effectiveness evaluation, retrieval effectiveness evaluation
检索效率/檢索效率　retrieval efficiency
检索协议/檢索協議　retrieval protocol
检索性刊物/檢索期刊　retrieval periodicals
检索要求/檢索要求　search request, search demands
检索一致性/檢索一致性　retrieval consistency
检索语法/檢索語法　grammar of search expression
检索语言/檢索語言　retrieval language, search language
检索指南/搜索指南　search guide
检索周期/搜尋週期　search cycle
检索字段/檢索欄位　search field
检验/檢驗,檢定,檢查　test, inspection
F 检验/F 檢定　F-test
t 检验/t 檢定　t-test
u 检验/u 檢定　u-test
z 检验/z 檢定　z-test
检验报告/檢驗報告　inspection report
检验悖论/檢驗詭論　inspection paradox
检验表/檢驗表,檢查表　inspection table
检验成本/檢驗成本　inspection cost
检验程序/檢定程序　test procedure
检验的随机比较/檢定的隨機比較　stochastic comparison of tests
检验的稳健性/檢定的穩健性　robustness of test
检验度/檢驗度　degree of inspection
检验法/檢驗方法　inspection method
检验方案/檢驗計劃　inspection plan
检验功效/檢[定]力　power of test
检验机构认可/檢驗機構認可　inspection authority accreditation
检验假设/檢定假設　testing hypothesis
检验量/檢驗量　amount of inspection
检验批/檢驗批　inspection lot
检验水平/檢定水準　level of a test

检验统计量/檢定統計量　test statistic
检验图/檢驗圖　inspection diagram
检验误差/檢驗誤差　inspection error
检验系数/檢驗係數　test coefficient
检验准确度/檢驗準確度　test accuracy
检疫费/檢疫費　sanitary fee
检疫港口/檢疫港口　quarantine harbor
检疫规定/檢疫規定　inspection and quarantine regulation
检疫证书/檢疫證書　quarantine certificate
减法/減法　subtraction
减价/減價　reduce price
减税/減稅　tax reduction, tax abatement, tax break
减税债券/減稅債券　tax relief bond
减速措施/減速丘　speed bump
减刑/減刑　commutation
减意标引/減意標引　broader concept indexing
减员增效/減員增效　reducing personnel and increasing efficiency
减值/重估減值　write-down
剪报/剪報　newspaper clipping, press cutting
剪刀运动/剪刀移動　scissors movement
剪辑/剪輯,剪接,編輯　cutting
剪辑师/剪輯師　editor
剪纸动画/剪紙動畫　cutout animation
简报/簡報　brief report
简编/簡編,簡略編目　minimal cataloging
简编目录/簡編目錄　finding list
简策/簡策　Jiance, slip documents
简策装/簡策裝　ordinary binding
简单对象访问协议/簡單物件訪問協定　simple object access protocol, SOAP
简单多数/簡單多數決　simple majority
简单多数选举制/簡單多數選舉制　simple majority system of election
简单二项抽样方案/簡單二項抽樣計劃　simple binomial sampling plan
简单非线性相关/簡單非線性相關　simple non-linear correlation
简单非正态曲线/簡單非常態曲線　simple abnormal curve
简单格[子]设计/簡單格子設計　simple lattice design
简单过失/單純過失　simple negligence
简单函数/簡單函數　simple function
简单回归/簡單回歸　simple regression
简单回归分析/簡單回歸分析　simple regression analysis

简单加性加权法/簡單加性加權法　weighted method of simple additivity
简单假设/簡單假設　simple hypothesis
简单检索/簡單查找　simple search
简单交互效应/簡單交互作用　simple interaction
简单结构/簡單結構　simple structure
简单马尔可夫过程/簡單馬可夫過程　simple Markov process
简单排序法/簡單排序法　simple ranking method
简单平均价格指数/簡單平均物價指數　simple average price index
简单区组设计/簡單區集設計　simple block design
简单商品经济的基本矛盾/簡單商品經濟的基本矛盾　basic contradiction of simple commodity economy
简单生灭过程/簡單生滅過程　simple birth and death process
简单事件/簡單事件　simple event
简单随机抽样/簡單隨機抽樣　simple random sampling
简单随机样本/簡單隨機樣本　simple random sample
简单条形图/簡單長條圖　simple bar chart
简单系统/簡單系統　simple system
简单线性的技术推动模型/簡單線性的技術推動型　simple linear technology-push model
简单线性回归分析/簡單直線型回歸分析　simple linear regression analysis
简单线性回归模型/簡單線性回歸模型　simple linear regression model
简单线性相关/簡單線性相關　simple linear correlation
简单线性最小二乘法/簡單線性最小平方法　simple linear least squares method
简单相对指数/簡單相對指數　simple relative index
简单相合性/簡單一致性　simple consistency
简单信托/簡單信託,普通信託　simple trust
简单性/簡單性　simplicity
简单样本/簡單樣本　simple sample
简单再生产/簡單再生產　simple reproduction
简单债券/簡單債券　simple bond
简单整群抽样/簡單群聚抽樣,簡單叢聚抽樣　simple cluster sampling
简单知识组织系统/簡單知識組織系統　simple knowledge organization system, SKOS
简单指数/簡單指數　simple index
简单综合法/簡單綜合法　simple aggregate method
简单综合物价指数/簡單綜合物價指數　simple aggregated price index, simple aggregative price index
简单综合指数/簡單綜合指數　simple aggregate index
简单罪状/簡單罪狀　simple count of a crime
简牍/簡牘　bamboo and wooden slips
简牍档案汇编/簡牘檔案編譯　compilation of documents written on bamboo and wood
简化/簡化　simplification
简化编目/簡化編目　simplified cataloging
简化变量/簡約變量　reduced variate
简化抽样方案/簡縮抽樣計劃　reduced sampling plan
简化二重抽样/簡縮雙重抽樣　reduced double sampling
简化方程/簡縮方程式　reduced equation
简化设计/簡約設計　reduced design
简化式方程/縮減式方程式　reduced form equation
简化式模型/簡化模型　reduced form model
简化形式法/簡縮形式法　reduced form method
简化样本/簡縮樣本　reduced sample
简捷法/簡捷法　short cut method
简历/簡歷　resume
简令/簡令　briefing
简略分类/簡略分類　broad classification
简略寿命表/簡易生命表　abridged life table
简明词典/簡明字典　concise dictionary
简明合同格式/簡明合同格式　short form of contract
简明题名/簡明題名　short title
简算值/簡算值　remission value
简讯/簡訊,快訊　brief, news flash, news brief
简要法/簡要法,輪廓法　skeleton method
简要书目记录/簡要書目記錄　brief record
简要著录/簡要著錄　simplified description
简易程序/簡易程序　summary proceeding
简易判决/即決判審,無訟争性之裁判　summary judgment
简易寿命表/簡易生命表　abridged life table
简易信息聚合/簡易聚合　really simple syndication, RSS
简约/簡約,精簡　parsimony
见票付款期票/見票付款票據　note after sight
见票后付款的汇票/見票後付款的匯票　bill payable after sight
见票后若干日付款的汇票/見票後若干日付款的匯票　bill drawn payable at certain time after sight
见票即付/見票即付　payment at sight

见票即付汇票/見票即付匯票　bill at sight, bill payable at sight, bill drawn payable at sight
见票即付款的票据/見票即付款的票據　instrument payable on demand
见票即付票据/見票即付票據　note on demand, note at sight
见票即付支票/見票即付支票　check payable at sight
见习计划/見習指派　understudy assignment
见证式新闻/見證式新聞　eyewitness news
件/件　piece
件号/件號　file number
间谍/間諜　spy
间谍活动/間諜活動　spying
间断测量/間斷測時　discontinuous timing
间隔/間隔　spacings
间隔层/隔片,間隔件　spacer
间接凹版印刷/間接凹版印刷　indirect gravure printing
间接标引/間接標引　indirect indexing
间接材料/間接材料　indirect materials
间接成本/間接成本　indirect cost
间接抽样/間接抽樣　indirect sampling
间接出口/間接出口　indirect export
间接出口奖励金/間接出口獎勵金　indirect export bounty
间接处罚/間接處罰　indirect penalties
间接档案类别/間接檔案類別　indirect archival category
间接档案全宗/間接檔案全宗　indirect fonds
间接抵押贷款/間接抵押貸款　second mortgage lending
间接抵制/次級杯葛　secondary boycott
间接发行/間接發行　indirect issuing
间接法制版/間接法製版　indirect screen making
间接反致/間接反致　indirect remission
间接费/間接成本　indirect cost
间接服务/間接服務　indirect service
间接故意/間接故意　indirect intention
间接规制/間接管制　indirect regulation
间接国家税/間接國家稅　indirect national tax
间接汇兑/間接匯兌　indirect exchange
间接汇价/間接匯價,間接報價　indirect quotation
间接汇率/間接匯率　indirect rate
间接汇票/間接匯票,外埠付款票據,付款地匯票　indirect bill, domicile bill, indirect exchange bill
间接机制/間接機制　indirect mechanism
间接检索/間接檢索　indirect retrieval

间接交付/間接交付　indirect payment
间接进口/間接進口　indirect import
间接进口附加关税/間接進口附加關稅　surtax on indirect import
间接劳动/間接勞工　indirect labor
间接劳动标准/間接勞工標準　indirect labor standard
间接买卖/間接買賣　indirect business
间接贸易/間接貿易　roundabout trade, indirect trade
间接民主/間接民主　indirect democracy
间接平版印刷/間接平版印刷　indirect planographic printing
间接平价/間接平價　indirect parity
间接歧视/間接歧視　indirect discrimination
间接侵权/間接侵害　indirect infringement
间接情报源/第二手資料,次級資料來源　secondary source
间接渠道/間接管道　indirect channel
间接融资/間接融資,間接金融　indirect finance, indirect financing
间接时间研究/間接時間研究　indirect time study
间接使用价值/間接使用價值　indirect user value
间接收益/次級效益　secondary benefit
间接税/間接稅　indirect tax
间接套利/間接套利　indirect arbitrage
间接统计/間接統計　secondary statistics
间接投资/間接投資　indirect investment
间接凸版印刷/間接凸版印刷　inderect relief letterset printing
间接效应/間接影響　indirect effect
间接效用函数/間接效用函數　indirect utility function
间接薪酬/間接薪酬　indirect compensation
间接选举/間接選舉　indirect election
间接印刷/間接印刷　indirect printing
间接营销渠道/間接行銷管道　indirect marketing channel
间接应用国际标准/間接應用國際標準　indirect application of an international standard
间接占有/間接占有　indirect possession
间接正犯/間接正犯　Mittelbare Taterschaft
间接证据/間接證據　indirect evidence
间接最小二乘法/間接最小平方法　indirect least square method, ILS method
间接最小二乘估计/間接最小平方估計式　indirect least squares estimator
间色/次要色　secondary color

间隙估计值/間隙估計值　gap estimate
间隙检验/間隙檢定　gap test
间歇失效/間歇故障,間斷故障　intermittent failure
建仓/建倉　take a position
建构效度/建構效度,構念效度　construct validity
建构性叙述/建構性敘述　constructed narrative
建立世界知识产权组织公约/建立世界智慧財產權組織公約　Convention Establishing the World Intellectual Property Organization
建设工程合同/建設工程合約　construction project contract
建设项目/建設工程　construction program, construction project
建设性财政/建設型財政　constructive finance
建设性冲突/建設性衝突　constructional conflict
建设-移交模式/BT 模式　build-transfer model, BT model
建设-拥有-运行-移交模式/BOOT 模式　build-own-operate-transfer model, BOOT model
建设-拥有-运营模式/BOO 模式　build-own-operate model, BOO model
建设-运行-培训-移交模式/BOTT 模式　build-operate-train-transfer model, BOTT model
建设-运营-转让模式/BOT 模式　build-operate-transfer model, BOT model
建设-租赁-移交模式/BLT 模式　build-lease-transfer model, BLT model
建议书/要保書　proposal
建议性仲裁/建議性仲裁　advisory arbitration
建议邀请书/建議邀請書　request for proposal, RFP
建议制度/建議制度,提案制度　suggestion system
建制教派/建制教派　established sect
建筑工程流程再造/建築工程流程再造　construction process reengineering, CPR
建筑管理模式/建築管理模式　construction management model
建筑图书馆/建築圖書館　architecture library
建筑物区分所有权/建築物區分所有權　building differentiation owership
建筑物灾害统计/建築物災害統計　building damage statistics
建筑业/營造業　construction
建筑业统计/營造統計　construction statistics
建筑作品/建築作品　works of architecture
贱民宗教/賤民宗教　pariah religion
剑桥现金余额方程式/劍橋現金餘額方程式　cambridge cash balance equation
剑桥学派/劍橋學派　Cambridge school
剑桥之争/劍橋之爭　Cambridge controversies
剑桥资本争论/劍橋資本爭論　Cambridge capital argument
健康/健康　health
健康、安全和环境管理/健康、安全與環境管理　health, safety and environment management
健康保险/健康保險　health insurance
健康传播/健康傳播　health communication
健康促进/健康促進　health promotion
健康服务的消费主义/健康服務的消費主義　consumerism of health care service
健康老龄化/健康老齡化　healthy aging
健康权/健康權　right of health
健康生产函数/健康生產函數　health production function
健康医疗范式/健康醫療範式　healthy model of health care
健康预期寿命/健康預期壽命　active life expectancy
健康知识/健康知識　health knowledge
健康职业/健康職業　health occupation
健康状况/健康狀態　health status
健康资本/健康資本　health capital
健全货币/健全貨幣　sound money
渐进等价检验/漸近等價檢定　asymptotically equivalent test
渐进决策途径/漸進決策途徑　incremental decision-making approach
渐进式变革/漸進式改變　incremental change
渐进无偏估计量/漸近不偏估計量　asymptotically unbiased estimator
渐进型创新/增量創新　increment innovation
渐进性创新/漸進式創新　incremental innovation
渐近贝叶斯方法/漸近貝氏程序　asymptotic Bayes procedure
渐近标准误差/漸近標準誤差　asymptotic standard error
渐近次大化最小/漸近次大中取小　asymptotically subminimax
渐近方差/漸近變異數　asymptotic variance
渐近方差-协方差矩阵/漸近變異數-共變數矩陣　asymptotic variance-covariance matrix
渐近分布/漸近分布,漸近分配　asymptotic distribution
渐近功效/漸近檢力　asymptotic power
渐近极大化极小性质/漸近大中取小性質　asymptotic minimax property
渐近检验/漸近檢定　asymptotic test
渐近局部最优设计/漸近局部最適設計

asymptotically locally optimal design
渐近均值/漸近平均值　asymptotic mean
渐近理论/漸近理論　asymptotic theory
渐近偏误/漸近偏誤　asymptotic bias
渐近偏倚/漸近偏誤　asymptotic bias
渐近平稳/漸近平穩　asymptotically stationary
渐近期望/漸近期望值　asymptotic expectation
渐近弱辅助/漸近弱輔助　asymptotically weakly ancillary
渐近推断/漸近推論　asymptotic inference
渐近无偏性/漸近不偏誤性　asymptotic unbiasedness
渐近无偏最优功效检验/漸近不偏最強力檢定　asymptotically unbiased most powerful test
渐近线/漸近線　asymptote
渐近相对效率/漸近相對效率　asymptotic relative efficiency
渐近相对有效性/漸近相對有效性　asymptotic relative efficiency
渐近协方差矩阵/漸近互變異收矩陣　asymptotic covariance matrix
渐近性质/漸近特性　asymptotic property
渐近有效估计[量]/漸近有效估計量　asymptotically efficient estimator
渐近有效性/漸近有效性,漸近效率　asymptotic efficiency
渐近展开/漸近展開式　asymptotic expansion
渐近正态分布/漸近常態分配　asymptotic normal distribution
渐近正态[性]/漸近常態[性]　asymptotic normality
渐近最大功效检验/漸近最強力檢定　asymptotically most powerful test
渐近最短无偏置信区间/漸近最短不偏信賴區間　asymptotically shortest unbiased confidence interval
溅镀/濺鍍　sputtering
溅镀靶材/濺鍍靶材　sputtering target
溅镀机/濺鍍機　sputtering station
鉴定/評鑒,辨識　appraisal, identification
鉴定成本/鑒定成本　appraisal cost
鉴定过程/鑒定過程　qualification process
鉴定结论/鑒定結論　expert conclusion
鉴定人/鑒定人　appraiser
鉴定小组/評鑒小組　appraisal group
鉴定意见/專家證詞　expert testimony, expertise
鉴证业务/鑒證業務　assurance engagement
键阅率/命中率　hit rate
箭线图/箭頭圖　arrow diagram
将到期负债/將到期負債　maturing liability
僵化汇率/僵化匯率　rigid exchange rate

僵化价格/僵化價格　rigid price
僵化利率/僵化利率　rigid interest rate
讲稿/講稿　lecture notes
讲演/講演　oration
奖金/獎金,紅利　bonus
奖金池/紅利基金　bonus pool
奖金制/獎金制　premium plan
奖励出口制/獎勵出口制　incentive export system
奖励工资/工資獎勵　wage-incentive
奖励关税/獎勵租稅　favour tax
奖励计划/誘因計劃　incentive scheme, incentive plan
奖励体系/獎酬系統,獎酬制度,獎賞系統　reward system
奖励性减税/獎勵性減稅　incentive reduction
奖励制度/獎勵制度　award system
奖赏权力/獎酬權,獎賞權　reward power
奖学金/獎學金　scholarships
降低成本型新产品/降低成本型新產品　new cost-cutting product
降低贷款利息/降低貸款利息　reduce loan interest
降低利率贷款/降低利率貸款　marking-down loan
降级/降級　degrade
降阶自回归模型/降階自我回歸模型　reduced rank AR model
降密/降低機密等級　downgrade
降水日数/降水日數　number of days with precipitation
交表婚/交表婚　cross-cousin marriage
交并原理/聯集交集原則　union intersection principle
交叉补贴/交叉補貼　cross-subsidy
交叉发盘/交叉報價　cross offer
交叉分类/交叉分類　crossed classification
交叉分析/交叉分析　intersectional analysis
交叉幅频谱/交叉幅頻譜　cross amplitude spectrum
交叉关系/交叉關係　intersection relations
交叉汇率/交叉匯率　cross rate of exchange
交叉货币基差互换/交叉貨幣基差交換契約　cross-currency basis swap
交叉货仓/交叉貨倉　cross-dock
交叉加权指数/交叉權數指數　crossed weight index
交叉列表/交叉表列　cross-tabulation
交叉蒙太奇/交叉蒙太奇　cross montage
交叉强度函数/交叉強度函數　cross intensity function
交叉设计/交叉設計　cross-over design
交叉试验/交叉試行　change-over trial
交叉弹性/交叉彈性　cross elasticity

交叉套期保值/交叉避險　cross hedging
交叉相关/交叉相關　cross-correlation
交叉销售/交叉銷售　cross-selling
交叉协方差/交叉變異數　cross-covariance
交叉选择/保證匯率選擇權　quanta option
交叉学科/跨學科,跨領域　interdisciplinary
交叉验证/交叉驗證　cross-validation
交叉验证准则/交叉確認準則　cross-validation criterion
交叉样本/貫穿樣本　interpenetrating samples
交叉因子/交叉因子　crossed factors
交叉引用/交叉引用　cross-reference
交叉影响法/交叉影響法　cross-effect analysis approach
交叉职能培训/跨功能培訓　cross-functional training
交叉指数/交叉指數　crossed index number
交叉子样本/貫穿子樣本　interpenetrating subsamples
交叉组配/相交協調,交集協調　intersection coordination
交错抽样/鋸齒形抽樣,曲形抽樣　zigzag sampling
交单/標單　tender document
交迭容差/重複允差　overlapping tolerance
交付/交付　delivery
交付缺口/交付缺口　delivery gap
交付提单/交付提單,提示提單　surrender of bill of lading
交付外币/結售外幣　surrender foreign currency
交付周期/交貨週期　delivery cycle
交感巫术/交感巫術　sympathetic magic
交割/交割　delivery
交割价格/交割價格　delivery price
交割延期费/交割延期費　backwardation
交互记忆系统/交換記憶系統　transactive memory system
交互设计/交互設計　interaction design
交互式创新/互動式創新　interactive innovation
交互式电视点播系统/互動隨選視訊　video on demand
交互式多媒体/互動式多媒體　interactive multimedia
交互式光盘/互動式光碟　compact disc interactive, CD-I
交互式广告/互動式廣告　interactive advertisement
交互式检索/交互式檢索　interactive search
交互式信息服务/交互型資訊服務　interactive information services
交互图/相互作用圖　interaction diagram

交互小说/交互小説　interactive novel
交互效应分量/交互作用成分　interaction component
交互效应均方/交互作用均方　interaction mean square
交互效应平方和/交互作用平方和　interaction sum of squares
交换/交換　exchange
交换馆员/圖書交換員　exchange librarian
交换广告/交換廣告　exchange advertising
交换价格/匯價　exchange price
交换价值/交換價值　value in exchange, exchange value
交换经济/交換經濟　exchange economy
交换媒介/交易媒介　medium of exchange
交换市场/交換市場　exchange market
交换条件/等值交換　quid pro quo
交换效应/交互作用　interaction effect
交货安排/交貨日程表　delivery schedule
交货不足索赔/短交索賠,數量不足索賠　claim for short delivery
交货地点/交貨地點　place of delivery, point of delivery
交货定价/送貨到家訂價　delivered pricing
交货方式/交貨方式　mode of delivery
交货付款/交貨後付款　payment on delivery, payable on delivery, payment after delivery
交货港/交貨港　delivery port, port of delivery
交货价格/交貨價格,送達價格　delivered price, delivery price
交货[日]期/交貨日期,到期日　date of delivery, due date
交货受阻通知书/中止交貨通知書　advice of circumstance preventing delivery
交货数量/交貨數量,送達數量　delivered quantity
交货条件/交貨條件　delivery term
交货通知/交貨通知　delivery advice
交流声电平/哼聲位準　hum level
交融/交融　fusion
交谈/交談　conversation
交替更新过程/交替更新過程　alternating renewal process
交替类目/替代類　alternative class, alternative location
交替排序法/交替排序法　alternation ranking method
交替题名/別題名　alternative title
交通强度/交通擁擠度　traffic intensity

交通事故统计/交通事故統計　statistics of traffic accidents
交通事故责任强制保险/交通事故責任強制保險　compulsory insurance of traffic accident liability
交通统计/交通統計　transportation and communication statistics
交通拥堵/交通擁擠　traffic congestion
交通拥堵税/壅塞税，擁擠税　congestion tax
交通运输行政管理/運輸管理　transportation administration
交通肇事罪/交通肇事罪　crime of causing traffic casualties
交钥匙方式出口/整廠輸出　turnkey export
交钥匙工程/整廠營運計劃　turnkey project
交钥匙工程合同/整廠營運工程合約　turnkey contract
交钥匙合同方式出口/以統包合約方式出口　export by turnkey contract
交钥匙模式/交鑰匙模式　turnkey model
交钥匙投资/整廠營運投資　turnkey investment
交易/交易　exchange, trading, transaction
交易标准指数/交易標準指數　transaction standard index
交易差额/交易差額　transaction balance
交易成本/交易成本　transaction cost
交易成本经济学/交易成本經濟學　transaction-cost economics
交易磋商/議價交易，洽談業務　negotiation of business
交易动机/交易動機　transactions motive
交易额/交易額　volume of transaction, trading volume
交易方程式/交易方程式　equation of exchange
交易方式/交易方式　mode of dealing
交易费用/交易成本　transaction cost
交易风险/交易風險　transaction risk
交易惯例/交易習慣，商業習慣　course of dealing
交易合同/交易合約　business contract
交易货币/交易貨幣　transaction currency
交易机制/交易機制　mechanism of exchange, trading mechanism
交易价格/交易價格　transaction price
交易量/交易量　trading volume
交易平衡/交易平衡　balance of transaction
交易税/交易稅　transaction tax
交易所/交易所　exchange
交易所会员管理制度/交易所會員管理制度　membership regulatory system of stock exchange

交易所交易/交易所交易　transaction on exchange
交易所交易基金/指數股票型基金　exchange traded fund, ETF
［交易所］较低收盘价/較低收盤價　lower closing quotation
交易维度/交易維度，交易構面　transaction dimension
交易系统/交易系統　trading system
交易限额/交易限額　trading limit
交易效率/交易效率　trading efficiency
交易信用/商業信用　trade credit
交易型领导/交易型領導　transactional leadership
交易性金融资产/交易性金融資產　held for trading financial assets
交易需求/交易需求　transaction demands
交易佣金/交易回扣　trading commissions
交易暂停/交易停滯　trading halt
交易账户/交易賬戶　transaction account
交战规则/交戰規則　rules of combat
交战资格/交戰資格　belligerent qualification
交织/交插　interleaving
郊区化/郊區化　suburbanization
浇制封印/模印　seal casting, seal moulding
胶订/膠裝　adhesive binding
胶卷/膠卷　film
胶卷正片/正像本　positive copy
胶盘/膠盤　lacquer disk
胶盘刻纹/膠盤刻紋　cutting on disk
胶盘原版/膠盤原版　lacquer original
胶片绘制动画/膠片繪製動畫　drawn on film animation
胶片酶解/膠片酶解　film deterioration by enzyme
胶印/膠印　offset printing
胶印故障/膠印故障　offset printing trouble
胶印机/膠印機　offset press
胶粘装订/膠裝　adhesive binding
焦点编码/聚焦編碼　focused coding
焦点变量/焦點變項　focus variables
焦点访谈/焦點訪談　focused interview
焦点互动/焦點互動　focused interaction
焦点均衡/焦點均衡　focal equilibrium
焦点［小］组/焦點團體　focus group
焦点小组访谈/焦點團體訪談　focus group interview
焦土政策/焦土政策　scorched-earth policy
焦尾本/焦尾本　book of which a part was damaged by fire
角变换/角變換　angular transformation
角变量/角變數　angular variable

角点解/角解　corner solution
角谷静夫不动点定理/卡苦達尼定理　Kakutani theorem
矫诏/矯詔　Jiao Zhao
矫正教育/矯正教育　social rehabilitation education
矫正社会工作/矯正社會工作　social work for rehabilitation
矫正性税收/矯正稅　corrective tax
矫制/矯制　Jiao Zhi
脚注/注腳　footnote, foot note
缴费率/繳費率　contribution rate
缴款通知/繳款通知　payment notice
缴入盈余/盈餘公積　paid-in surplus
校本/校本　corrected edition
校雠/校讎　textual criticism, collate the text
校次/校次　correction time
校点本/校點本　collated and punctuated text
校对/校對　proofreading, proofread
校对符号/校對符號　proofreader's mark
校法四例/校法四例　four collation methods
校勘/校勘　textual criticism
校勘古本/校勘古本　restoration of ancient text
校勘记/校勘記　narration of collation
校勘学/校勘學　biblio-textual criticism
校色/改色,色彩校正　color correction
校色表/校正標　calibration target
校验误差/校誤　check error
校样/校樣　proof
校正/校正,更正　correction
校正本/校正本　fair copy
校正分类/校正分類　corrective sorting
校正概率单位/校正機率單位　corrected probit
校正功效函数/校正檢力函數　power function revised
校正矩/校正動差　corrected moment
校正时间序列/校正時間數列　corrected time series
校正因子/校正因子　correction factor
校准/校準　calibration
校准带/校準帶　calibration tape
较佳选择权/較佳選擇權　better-of-two option
较优同阶有偏估计量/較佳同階偏誤估計量　better same order biased estimator
教材/教材　teaching material
教材征订目录/教材徵訂目錄　subscription bibliography for teaching publication
教化/教化　cultivation
教皇教令集/教皇教令集　Dictatus Papae
教会/教會　church

教会档案/教會檔案　church archive
教会档案馆/教會檔案館　church archives
教会法/教律　canon law
教科书/教科書　textbook
教练计划/教導法　coaching
教区记事录/教區記事錄　parish register
教权制/教權制　hierarchism
教师用书/教師用書　teacher's guide book
教师资格培训/師資訓練,教師培訓　qualified teacher training
教士宗教-先知宗教/教士宗教-先知宗教　priest-prophet religion
教唆犯/教唆犯　instigator
教堂/教堂　church
教学档案/教學檔案　teaching archives
教学设计/教學設計　instructional design
教养方式/教養方式　parenting pattern
教育/教育　education
教育产业/教育產業　education industry
教育冲突论/教育衝突論　conflict theory of education
教育电视/教育電視　educational television, ETV
教育服务/教育服務　educational service
教育功能/教育功能　educational function
教育功能论/教育功能論　functionalism of education
教育管理/教育管理　education administration
教育规划/教育規劃　educational planning
教育机会/教育機會　educational opportunity
教育机会均等/教育機會均等　equality of educational opportunity
教育经济学/教育經濟學　economics of education
教育救助/教育救助　educational aid
教育类图书/教育類圖書　educational book
教育媒介/教育媒介　educational media
教育券/教育憑證　educational voucher
教育社会化/教育社會化　socialization of education
教育社会学/教育社會學　sociology of education
教育深化/教育深化　educational deepening
教育生产函数/教育生產函數　educational production functions
教育收益率/教育收益率　education earning rate
教育统计/教育統計　educational statistics
教育心理测试/教育心理測驗　educational psychometry
教育心理学/教育心理學　psychology of education
教育学/教育學　pedagogy
教育优先区/教育優先區　educational priority areas
教育与心理统计学/教育及心理統計學　educational

and psychological statistics
教育政策/教育政策 education policy
教育支出/教育支出 educational expenditures
阶层分化/階層化 stratification
阶乘/階乘 factorial
阶乘函数/階乘函數 factorial function
阶乘和/階乘和 factorial sum
阶乘矩/階乘動差 factorial moment
阶乘矩法/階乘動差法 method of factorial moments
阶乘矩母函数/階乘動差生成函數 factorial moment generating function
阶乘累积量/階乘累積 factorial cumulant
阶乘累积量母函数/階乘累積生成函數 factorial cumulant generating function
d阶单整/d階單整 integrated of order d
阶调/階調 tone gradation
阶调校正/自動音調校正 tone correction
阶调值/階調值 tone value
阶调值总和/階調值總和 tone value sum
阶段/階段 stage, phase
阶段博弈/階段賽局 stage game
阶段性就业/階段性就業 periodic employment
阶段组合法/階段組合法 stage combination method
p阶分位数/p階分位數 quantile of order p
阶级/階級 class
阶级分析/階級分析 class analysis
阶级结构化/階級結構化 class structuration
阶级利益/階級利益 class interest
阶级认同/階級認同, 階級身份 class identity
阶级位置/階級位置 class position
阶级文化/階級文化 class culture
阶级消亡/階級消亡 death of class
阶级意识/階級意識 class consciousness
阶距/階距 step interval
阶-门模型/階段-閘門模型 stage-gate model
阶梯变量/階梯變數 ladder variable
阶梯法/階梯法 staircase method
阶梯分布/階梯分布 staircase distribution
阶梯函数/階梯式函數 step function
阶梯设计/階梯設計 staircase design
阶梯式经济发展理论/梯狀經濟發展理論 ladder-shaped economic development theory
阶梯图/階梯圖 staircase chart
阶梯指数/階梯指標 ladder indices
阶条件/階條件 order condition
q阶移动平均过程/q階移動平均過程, q階移動平均數過程 moving average process of order q
p阶自回归过程/p階自身回歸過程 autoregressive process of order p
接触拷贝/接觸拷貝, 接觸性複製 contact copy
接管/接管 takeover
接口/介面 interface
接口标准/介面標準 interface standard
接口层次决策模型/介面層級決策模式, 介面層級決策模型 interface hierarchy decision-making model
接口管理/介面管理 interface management
接口设计/使用者介面設計 user interface design
接纳/接納, 接受 acceptance
接排式索引/接排式索引 run-on style
接片/接片 splicing
接入技术/接入技術 access technology
接收报告/接收報告 receiving report
接收错误/允收錯誤 acceptance error
接收的抽样风险/允收抽樣風險 sampling risk of acceptance
接收风险/允收風險 risk of acceptance
接收概率/允收機率 probability of acceptance
接收界限/接受界限, 允收界線 acceptance boundary
接收区域/接受區域, 允收區域 acceptance zone
接收数/允收數 acceptance number
接收系数/允收係數 acceptance coefficient
接收限/允收界限 acceptance limit
接收域/允收域 region of acceptance
接收证书/工程驗收證書 taking-over certificate
接收值/允收值 acceptance value
接收准则/接受準則, 允收準則 acceptance criterion
接受报价/承諾報價 acceptance of offer
接受存款的机构/領有執照的存款機構 licensed deposit-taker
接受订单/確認訂單 acknowledgement of order
接受分析/接收分析 reception analysis
接受分析研究/接收分析, 接收研究 reception study
接受理论/接收理論 reception theory
接受域/接受域 acceptance region
接头/接頭 connector
接续犯/接續犯 creep offense
接准/接準 jiezhun
揭帖/揭帖 Jietie
街道办事处/街道辦事處 street office, sub-district office
街角社会/街角社會 Street Corner Society
街居制/街居制 residence-based administration
节本/節本 abbreviated version, abridged edition
节本词典/節略版詞典 abridged dictionary
节点/節點 node
节假日工资/假日支薪 holiday pay

节录/節錄, 摘录, 節縮[本] abridgement, extract, integration-chapter
节略文献/節縮本 abridgement
节目/節目 programme
节目式广告/節目式廣告, 廣告節目化 program-length advertising, PLA
节能减排/節能減排 energy saving, emission reducing
节拍/循環時間 cycle time
节译/節譯 abridged translation
节欲论/忍欲說 abstinence theory
节约法令/禁奢法律 sumptuary laws
劫持航空器罪/劫持航空器罪 crime of hijacking aircraft
杰克逊闭网络/傑克遜閉網路 Jackson closed network
杰克逊开网络/傑克遜開網路 Jackson open network
杰文斯动作研究/傑文茲動作研究 motion study of Jevans
洁本/潔本 expurgated version
洁净室/無塵室 clean room
结案/結案 case closed, termination
结案条件/結案條件 condition for termination
结办案卷/關閉案卷 closed file
结构/結構, 構造 structure
结构变数/結構變數 structural variables
结构参数/結構參數 structural parameter
结构等价/關係模式結構同位 structure equivalence
结构等同性/結構等價, 結構等效 configural equivalence
结构洞/結構洞 structural hole
结构方程/結構方程式 structural equation
结构方程模型/結構方程式模型, 結構方程式模式 structural equation model, structural equation modeling
结构分解分析/結構分解分析 structural decomposition analysis, SDA
结构改变/結構性改變 structural change
结构改革/結構重整 structure reform
结构功能分析/結構功能分析 structural-functional analysis
结构功能主义/結構功能論 structural functionalism
结构惯性/結構慣性 structural inertia
结构函数/結構函數 structure function
结构化/結構化 structuration, structuring
结构化查询语言/結構化查詢語言 structured query language, SQL
结构化程序设计/結構化程式設計 structured programming
结构化方法/結構化方法 structured method
结构化分析/結構化分析 structured analysis
结构化检索/結構化檢索, 結構化查詢 structured retrieval
结构化金融产品/結構化金融產品 structured financial products
结构化决策/結構化決策 structured decisionmaking
结构化面试/結構化面談 structured interview
结构化设计/結構化設計 structured design
结构化数据/結構化資料 structured data
结构化问题/結構化問題 well-structured problem, structured problem
结构化学习模式/結構化學習模式 structured learning model
结构化组/結構性團體 structured group
结构空洞/結構洞 structural hole
结构轮排/結構輪排 structured permutation
结构失衡/結構失衡 structure unbalance
结构史/結構史 histoire structurale
结构式观察/結構式觀察法 structured observation
结构式家庭治疗/結構家庭治療, 結構家族治療 structural family therapy
结构式模型/結構模型 structural model
结构式索引/結構索引 structured index
结构属性/結構屬性 structural attribute
结构调整/結構調整 structural adjustment
结构调整贷款/結構調整貸款 structural adjustment loans
结构突变/結構性變遷 structural break
结构型通货膨胀/結構型通脹 structural inflation
结构型问卷/結構式問卷 structured questionnaire
结构性失业/結構性失業 structural unemployment
结构性数据/結構性資料 structural data
结构性元数据/結構性詮釋資料 structural metadata
结构性债券/結構性證券 structured note
结构主义/結構主義 structuralism
结构转型/結構變遷 structural transformation
结构子系统/結構子系統 structural subsystem
结构自回归条件异方差模型/結構性自我回歸條件異質變異模型 structural arch model
结构组合法/結構組合法 structure combination method
结关单/結關單, 出港申報表, 離港證明 bill of clearance, clearance certificate
结关手续费/結關手續費, 出港手續費 clearance fee
结果/結果 outcome

结果变量／結果變項　outcome variable
结果犯／結果犯　consequential offense
结果公平／結果公正　outcome fairness
结果加重犯／結果加重犯　offense aggravated by consequence
结果评估／結果評估，成果評估　outcome evaluation
结合犯／結合犯　combinative crime
结合方案／相聯方案　association scheme
结合分析／聯合分析　conjoint analysis
结合审核／合并稽核　combined audit
结汇／結匯　foreign exchange settlement, settlement of exchange
结汇进口许可证／結匯進口許可證　license to import with exchange
结汇统计／結匯統計　foreign exchange settlements statistics
结汇银行／結匯銀行　handling bank
结婚率／結婚率　marriage rate
结晶区／結晶區　crystal region
结块／結塊　blocking
结清余额／結清餘額　settlement of balance
结社／結社　association
结社权／結社權　right of association
结社自由／結社自由　freedom of association
结绳／結繩　keep records by tying knots, knotted rope
结束符／結束符　dingbat
结束阶段／結束階段　concluding phase
结算／結算，清算　settlement, settle account
结算单／結算單　document of settlement
结算方式／結算方式，交割方式　method of settlement
结算货币／結算貨幣　currency of settlement, settlement currency
结算价／結算價　settlement price, make-up price
结算金额／結算金額　amount of settlement
结算日／結算日，結賬日　date closing, account day, make-up day
结算书／結算書　statement of settlement
结算通知书／結算通知書　advice of settlement
结算银行／清算銀行　clearing bank
结算逾期／逾期結算　delay in settlement
结算资金／結算資金　settlement fund
结尾用语／結尾用語　ending term
结账／結賬　closing the account, closing
结账价格／結賬價格，補償價格　made-up price
截词符／截詞符　truncation operator
截词检索／截詞檢索，切截字查詢　truncation retrieval, truncation search
截点／截點　cutoff point
截断／截斷　truncation
截断点／截斷點　truncation point
截断回归模型／截斷回歸模型　truncated regression model
截断数据／截略資料　truncated data
截断误差／截斷誤差　truncation error
截稿期限／截稿期限，截稿時間　dead-line
截集／割集　cut set
截面图／截面圖　sectional view
截面研究途径／橫斷研究法　cross-sectional approach
截取回归模型／受限回歸模型，截斷回歸模型　censored regression mode, truncated regression model
截取数据／受限資料　censored data
截取因变量／受限相依變數　censored dependent variable
截删／刪除　censoring
截塔分布／zeta 分布，zeta 分配　zeta distribution
截尾／截尾　truncation
截尾泊松分布／截略卜瓦松分布，截略卜瓦松分配　truncated Poisson distribution
截尾抽样／截略抽樣　curtailed sampling
截尾抽样检验／截略抽樣檢驗　curtailed sampling inspection
截尾点／截略點　point of truncation
截尾二重抽样／截略雙重抽樣　truncated double sampling
截尾二项抽样／截略二項抽樣　curtailed binomial sampling
截尾分布／截斷分配，截略分布　truncated distribution
截尾检验／截略檢驗　curtailed inspection
截尾均值／截斷的平均數　truncated mean
截尾 D 判别准则／截略 D 型判別準則　truncated D-criteria
截尾寿命试验／截略壽命試驗　truncated life test
截尾数据／截略資料　truncated data
截尾序贯程序／截略逐次程序　truncated sequential procedures
截尾序贯对策／截略逐次賽局　truncated sequential games
截尾序贯概率比检验／截略逐次機率比檢定　truncated SPRT
截尾样本量序贯分析／截略樣本大小逐次分析　truncated sample size sequential analysis
截尾正态分布／截略常態分布，截略常態分配

truncated normal distribution
截尾正态均值/截略常態平均數　truncated normal mean
截尾最优 D 设计/截略 D 型最適設計　truncated D-optimal design
截形校正/截形校正　corrections for abruptness
姐妹情谊/姐妹情誼,姊妹情誼　sisterhood
解除出口禁令/解除出口禁令　removal of export ban
解除外汇管制/解除外匯管制　decontrol of foreign exchange
解雇/解雇,遣退　dismissal, layoff
解雇率/解雇率　layoff rate
解雇赔偿金/解雇賠償金　damages in unlawful dismissal
解码/解碼　decoding, decode
解码器/解碼器　decoder
解密/解密　declassification
解密文档/解密檔案　declassified documents, declassified files
解耦库存/中介性安全存貨　decoupling inventory
解聘/解聘,裁員　layoff
解释变量/解釋變數　explanatory variable
解释结构主义/詮釋結構主義　interpretive structuralism
解释人类学/解釋人類學　hemeneutic anthropology
解释性报道/解釋性報導　interpretative report
解释性新闻/解釋性新聞　interpretative news
解释性研究/解釋性研究　explanatory research
解释性传记/解釋性傳記　interpretive biography
解释学/詮釋學　hermeneutics
解说词/旁白,畫外音　offscreen sound, OS
解题目录/解題目錄　annotated catalog
解调/解調　demodulation
解析调查/解析調查　analytic survey
解析回归/解析回歸,分析回歸　analytic regression
解析机/解析機　analytic engine
解像力/解像力　resolution ratio
解约/解約　break of engagement
解约金/解約金　cancellation money
介入/介入,干涉　intervention
介入方案/介入方案　intervention plan, intervention scheme
介绍性题名/介紹性題名　introduction title
介质/媒體　medium
戒牒/戒牒　Buddhist certificate
界/界　bound
界河/界河　boundary river

界线/界線　boundary line
借代/借代　metonymy
借贷股票/借貸股票　loan stock
借贷规则/借貸規則　rule of debit and credit
借贷互利说/借貸互利說　theory of reciprocity in debt and credit
借贷记账法/借貸簿記　debit-credit bookkeeping
借贷价值比率/抵借價值比率　loan-value ratio
借贷市场/貸款市場　loan market
借贷套利/借貸套利　round-tripping
借贷资本/借貸資本,借款資本　loan capital
借方对销/借方對銷　contra debit
借记卡/轉賬卡　debit card
借鉴/借鑒　duplication
借壳上市/借殼上市　back door listing
借款偿还保证/借款償還保證　guarantee of repayment
借款单据/貸款單據,借貸票據　loan note
借款能力/借款能力　ability to borrow
借款人/借債人　borrower
借款支票/借款支票　purchase money note
借入资金/借入資金　borrowed fund
借书处/借書處　circulation counter, circulation desk
借书记录/借書記錄　circulation record
借书站/借書站　book delivery station, book-lending station
借项通知单/借項通知單　debit advice
借阅单/借閱單　production ticket
借阅期限/借書期限　circulation period, loan period
借阅权限/借閱權　borrowing privileges
借阅限制/借閱限制　circulation restriction
借阅政策/借閱政策　lending policy
借阅状态/項目狀態　item status
巾箱本/巾箱本　pocket edition
金本位/金本位　gold standard
金本位集团/金本位集團　gold bloc
金本位制/金本位制　gold standard system
金币汇兑/金幣匯兌　gold exchange
金边债券/金邊債券,優良債券　bond gilt-edged, gilt-edged bond
金法郎/黃金法郎　gold francs
金汇兑本位制/金匯兌本位制　gold exchange standard
金汇兑制/金匯兌制　gold exchange system
金价上升/金價升值,金價上漲　increase in price of gold
金匠银行/金匠兼銀行家　goldsmith-bankers
金刻本/金刻本　Jin Dynasty edition

金块本位制/金塊本位制　gold bullion standard
金块论战/金銀本位主義論争　bullion controversy
金马奖/金馬獎　Golden Horse Awards
金牛业务/金牛事業　cash cow business
金券/金券　gold note
金融/金融　finance
金融安全网/金融安全網　financial safety net
金融不稳定/金融不穩定　financial unrest
金融产品/金融產品　financial product
金融产品创新/金融產品創新　innovation in financial product
金融超市/金融超市　financial supermarket
金融传染/金融傳染　financial contagion
金融创新/金融創新　financial innovation
金融脆弱性/金融脆弱性　financial fragility
金融二元性/金融體制雙元性　financial dualism
金融分析/財務分析　financial analysis
金融风险/金融風險　financial risk
金融风险管理/金融風險監管　financial risk regulation
金融服务/金融服務　financial service
金融服务贸易/金融服務貿易　trade in financial service
金融服务业/金融服務業　financial service industry
金融改革/金融改革　financial reform
金融工程/財務工程　financial engineering
金融工具/金融工具　financial instrument
金融公司/金融公司　finance corporation
金融寡头/金融寡頭,金融寡占　financial oligarch, financial oligopoly
金融管制/財務控制　financial control
金融货币危机/金融貨幣危機　financial and monetary crisis
金融机构/金融機構　financial institution
金融机制/金融機制　financial mechanism
金融集团/金融集團　financial conglomerate
金融计量经济学/財務計量經濟學　financial econometrics
金融监管/金融監管　financial regulation
金融监管体系/金融監管體系　financial regulatory system, financial supervisory system
金融监管体制/金融監管體制　financial regulatory system
金融交易/金融貿易　financial trade
金融结构/金融結構　financial structure
金融经济学/金融經濟學　financial economics
金融恐慌/金融恐慌　financial panic
金融控股公司/金融控股公司　financial holding company
金融流通/金融流通　financial circulation
金融垄断/金融壟斷　financial monopoly
金融票据/融通票據,票券　financial bill
金融票据市场/金融票據市場　financial bill market
金融期货/金融期貨　financial future
金融期货合约/金融期貨合約　financial futures contract
金融期货市场/金融期貨市場　financial futures market
金融期权市场/金融期權市場　financial option market
金融浅化/金融淺化　financial shallowing
金融全球化/金融全球化　financial globalization
金融深化/金融深化　financial deepening
金融深化理论/金融深化理論　theory of financial deepening
金融市场/金融市場　finance market, financial market
金融市场压力/金融市場壓力　pressure on the money market
金融市场自由化/金融市場自由化　liberalization of financial market
金融数学/數理金融　mathematical finance
金融体系/金融體系,金融體制　financial system
金融体制改革/金融體制改革　financial system reform
金融统计/金融統計　financial statistics
金融投资/財務投資　financial investment
金融投资贷款/金融投資貸款　loan for financial investment
金融危机/金融危機,金融風暴　financial crisis
金融稳定/金融穩定　finance stability
金融相关率/金融相關率　financial interrelations ratio
金融协定/金融協議　financial agreement
金融信托投资公司/金融信託投資公司　financial trust and investment company
金融信用/財政信用　financial credit
金融信用制度/財政信用系統　financial credit system
金融性资本净流出/金融性資本淨流出　net financial capital outflow
金融压制/金融壓制　financial repression
金融衍生品/衍生性金融商品　financial derivatives, derived class financial product
金融一体化/金融整合　financial integration
金融诈骗罪/金融詐騙罪　crime of financial fraud

金融债权/金融債權　financial claim
金融债券/金融債券　bank debenture, financial bond
金融中介/金融中介機構　financial intermediary, financial intermediation
金融中介机构/金融仲介機構　financial intermediary
金融中介机构理论/金融仲介機構理論　finance intermediary organs theory
金融中介理论/金融仲介理論　theory of financial medium
金融中介率/金融仲介比率　financial intermediation ratio
金融资本/金融資本　finance capital, financial capital
金融资产/金融資產　financial asset
金融资产管理公司/金融資產管理公司　financial asset management corporation, financial asset management company
金融自由化/金融自由化，金融鬆綁　financial deregulation, financial liberalization
金融租赁公司/金融租賃公司　financial leasing companies
金伞降落/黃金降落傘　golden parachute
金石档案汇编/金石檔案編譯　compilation of bronze inscription
金石拓片/金石拓片　rubbings from bronzeware or stone tablets
金石文献/金石文獻　bronze and stone inscriptions
金氏职业生涯发展阶段理论/Ginzberg 職涯發展階段理論　Ginzberg's theory of career development stage
金属本位/金屬本位　metallic standard
金属本位货币/金屬本位貨幣　metallic standard money
金属本位制/金屬本位制　metallic standard system
金属带/金屬帶　metal tape
金属化/金屬化　metallization
金属货币/金屬貨幣　metallic money
金属货币价值/金屬貨幣價值　metallic monetary value
金属货币论/貨幣金屬論　metallism
金属货币制度/金屬貨幣制度　metallic monetary system
金属期货/金屬期貨　metal futures
金属切削实验/金屬切削實驗　metal cutting test
金属印刷/金屬印刷　metal decoration
金属铸币/金屬鑄幣　metallic coin
金税工程/金税工程　golden tax project
金文档案/金文檔案　inscription archives
金镶玉/金鑲玉　white lining on yellow paper

金银混合本位制/金銀混合本位制　symmetallism
金钟奖/金鐘獎　Golden Bell Awards
金铸币本位制/金幣本位制　gold coin standard
津贴/津貼　allowance
仅限馆内使用/僅在圖書館內閱讀，限館內閱覽　library use only
紧后工作/後續工序　successor activity
紧急避险/緊急避險　urgent act of rescue
紧急程度/緊急程度　urgency level
紧急贷款/緊急貸款　emergency loan
紧急订单/緊急訂單　rush order
紧急关税/緊急關稅　emergency tariff
紧急广播服务/緊急廣播服務　special emergency radio service
紧急信贷/緊急信貸　emergency credit
紧急准备金/緊急準備金　emergency reserve
紧密插值/接觸内插　osculatory interpolation
紧密中心性/鄰近居中　closeness centrality
紧前工作/緊前工序　predecessor activity
紧俏劳动力市场/緊俏的勞動市場　tight labor markets
紧随领先者战略/緊隨領先者戰略　technology follower strategy
紧缩信用政策/緊縮信用政策　tight money policy
紧缩性财政政策/緊縮性財政政策　tight fiscal policy
紧缩性货币政策/緊縮貨幣政策，高利率政策　dear money policy, tight money policy
紧缩[性]政策/緊縮政策　contractionary policy, deflationary policy
紧要文件管理/重要檔案管理　vital records management
紧张理论/緊張論　strain theory
紧追权/緊追權　right of hot pursuit
锦标赛理论/競賽理論　tournament theory
锦标赛选择/對決篩選　tournament selection
锦衣卫/錦衣衛　imperial security police
进步/進步　progress
进呈本/進呈本　presentation edition, submitted edition
[进出口差额]补偿制度/[進出口差額]補償制度　compensation system
进出口单位价格指数/進出口單位價格指數　index number of unit value, import or export
进出口公司/進出口公司　import and export corporation
进出口合同/進出口合約　import-export contract
进出口货物/進出口貨物　cargo imported and

exported
进出口货物保险/進出口貨物保險　insurance of import and export goods
进出口价格弹性/進出口價格彈性　price elasticity of import and export
进出口连锁[制]/進出口連鎖[制]　import-export link system
进出口贸易/進出口貿易　export and import trade
进出口贸易额/進出口貿易額　value of import and export
进出口贸易结构/進出口貿易結構　export and import structures
[进出口]配额制度/[進出口]配額制度　quota system
进出口商品分类统计表/進出口貿易商品分類統計　commodity classification for foreign trade statistics
进出口商品价格对比指数/進出口商品價格對比指數　index number of price-ratio of import and export product
进出口商品结构/進出口商品結構,進出口商品組合　commodity composition of import and export, composition of import and export commodity
进出口弹性/進出口彈性　elasticity of export and import
进出口限制/進出口限制　restraint on export and import
进出口许可证/輸出入許可證　import-export license
进出口银行/進出口銀行　import and export bank
进出口指数/進出口指數　index number of import and export
进出口总水平/進出口總水準　level of total import and export
进出口组合贸易/進出口組合貿易　combination deal trade
进度/進度,排程　schedule
进度报告/進度報告　schedule report
进度变更控制系统/進度變更控制系統　schedule change control system
进度变更申请/進度變更申請　schedule change application
进度管理计划/進度管理計劃　schedule management plan
进度计划/進度計劃　schedule plan
进度控制/進度控制　schedule control
进度偏差/進度偏差　schedule variance
进度偏差分析/進度偏差分析　schedule variance analysis
进度图/進度圖　progress chart

[进港]结关证/輸入檢查證　inward clearing bill
进攻型新闻手法/侵入式新聞手法　aggressive journalism
进关栈报单/進倉申報單　declaration for warehouse
进化/進化,演化　evolution
进化论功能主义/進化論功能主義　evolutionary functionalism
进化稳定均衡/穩定進化均衡　evolutionarily stable equilibrium
进货贷款/購貨貸款　purchase loan
进货分销/進貨分銷　inbound distribution
进货合同/進貨合約　contract of purchase
进货检验/進貨檢驗　receiving inspection, incoming inspection
进谏行为/進諫行爲　voice behavior
进口/進口　import
进口保证金/進口保證金,進口押金　import deposit
进口报[关]单/進口報[關]單　import entry, import declaration, home use entry
进口报关单证/進口報關單證　inward clearance certificate
进口壁垒/進口壁壘,進口障礙　import barrier
进口补贴/進口補貼　import subsidy
进口成本/進口成本　import cost
进口承诺/進口承諾　import commitment
进口程序/進口程式　import procedure
进口代办行/進口代辦行　indent house
进口代理商/進口代理商　import commission agent, import agent
进口订单统计/進口訂單統計　import order statistics
进口订货单/進口訂貨單　import order
进口额/進口額　value of import, volume of import
进口发票/進口發票　import invoice
进口费用/進口費用　import charge
进口附加税/進口附加稅　import surtax
进口港/進口港　port import
进口供给/進口供應　import supply
进口关税/進口[關]稅　import duty, import tariff
进口关税险/進口關稅險　import duty risk
进口管制/進口管制　import control, import restriction
进口合同/進口合約　import contract
进口汇票/進口匯票　inward bill, import bill of exchange
进口货单/進口艙單　inward manifest
进口货物/進口貨物　inward cargo
进口货物国别价值/以出口國爲基準之進口額

value of import by country of origin
进口货源/進口貨源　source of import
进口技术/進口技術　imported technology
进口价格/進口價格　import price
进口检验/進口檢驗　import inspection
进口奖励/進口獎勵　bounty on import
进口奖励金/進口獎勵金　import bounty
进口结构/進口結構　import structure
进口结关/進口結關　clearance inward
进口结汇/進口結匯　import exchange settlement
进口结汇保证金/進口結匯保證金　pre-settlement requirement for import
进口结算/進口結算　import settlement
进口经纪人/進口經紀人　import broker
进口竞争货物/進口競爭貨物　import competing goods
进口量/進口量　import volume, import quantum
进口垄断/進口專營,進口獨占　import monopoly
进口贸易/進口貿易　import trade
进口贸易票据/進口貿易票據　import trade bill
进口能力指数/進口能力指數　capacity to import index
进口拍卖/進口拍賣　import auction
进口配额/進口配額　import quota
进口配额制/進口配額制,進口限額制度　import quota system
进口偏向型增长/偏向進口部門的成長　import-biased growth
进口倾向/進口傾向,輸入傾向　propensity to import
进口权/進口權　right of import
进口商行/進口商行　import house
进口商品/進口商品　import commodity
进口申报单/進口報單　declaration for import, import declaration
进口申请[书]/進口申報書,進口報單　application for import
进口收入弹性/進口收益彈性,進口所得彈性　income elasticity of import, import income elasticity
进口手续/進口手續　process of import
进口手续费/進口手續費　import commission
进口数量指数/進口數量指數　quantum index of import
进口税/進口[附加]税　import tax, import duty
进口税减免/進口税減免　relief from duty
进口税收/進口税收　import levy
进口缩减/進口減縮,縮減進口　import curtailment
进口提单/進口提單　inward bill of lading, import bill of lading

进口替代/進口替代　import substitution, import replacing
进口替代和出口导向型增长/進口替代與出口導向型增長　import substitution and export-led growth
进口替代战略/進口替代戰略　import substitution strategy
进口替代政策/進口替代政策　import substitution policy
进口停止/停止進口　suspension of import
进口通知/進口通知　import announcement
进口外汇/進口外匯　import exchange
进口违禁品/進口違禁品　contraband of import
进口物价指数/進口物價指數　price indices of imports
进口限额/進口限額　import limit, quantitative regulation of import
进口限制/進口限制　import ban, import restraint, restriction of import
进口信用证/進口信用狀　import credit, import letter of credit
进口需求/進口需求　import demand
进口需求曲线/進口需求曲線　import demand curve
进口需求弹性/進口需求彈性　elasticity of import demand
进口许可/進口許可,輸入許可　licensing of import
进口许可程序/進口許可程式　import licensing procedure
进口许可证/進口許可證,輸入許可證　import licence, certificate of import license, import permit
进口许可证及交货检验制度/進口許可證及交貨檢驗制度　import certificate and delivery verification system, ICDV
进口许可证制/進口許可證制　import license system
进口押金/進口押金,進口保證金　import deposit
进口押金制/進口押金制　import deposit scheme
进口依存度/進口依存度,對進口貿易依存度　degree of dependence on import, dependence degree on import
进口用汇审计/進口用外匯審計　audit of exchange used for import
进口佣金/進口手續費　import commission
进口优先权/進口優先權　import priority
进口预付款/進口預付款　import prepayment
进口远期汇票/進口遠期匯票　import usance bill
进口账户/進口賬戶　import account
进口证明书/進口證明書　import certificate
进口值/進口值　import value
进口资金融通/進口資金融通　import financing

进口自由化/進口自由化　import liberalization, liberalization of import
进口总额/進口總額　gross import
进口总值/進口總值　gross import value
进口最低限价制/進口最低限價制　import floor price system
进料控制/進料管制　incoming material control
进料评等级计划/進料評等級計劃　incoming material rating plan
进入壁垒/進入障礙　barrier to entry, entry barrier
进入扼制价格/進入扼制價格　enter to containing price
进入威胁/進入威脅　threat of new entry
进入障碍/進入障礙，参進障礙　barrier to entry, entry barrier
进向存货点/進倉物資儲備站　inbound stock point
进销差价/進銷差價　difference between purchase
近代宪法/近代憲法　pre-modern constitution
近海贸易/近海貿易　short sea trade
近交系数/近親係數　inbreeding coefficient
近邻估计/近鄰估計　near-neighbor estimation
近邻归集/近鄰插補法　nearest neighbor imputation
近期市场行情/近期市場行情　near-time market trend
近期文献报道服务/近期文件請求報導服務　recent current literature report service
近亲系数/近親係數　inbreeding coefficient
近视策略/近視政策　myopic policy
近似/近似,逼近　approximation
近似不相关回归/似無關回歸　seemingly unrelated regression, SUR
近似定理/近似度定理　proximity theorem
近似方差/近似變異數　approximate variance
近似F分布/近似F分布,近似F分配　approximate F-distribution
近似分析/近似度分析　proximity analysis
近似平衡设计/幾乎平衡設計　nearly balanced designs
近似商标/近似商標　similar trademark
近似算法/近似演算法　approximate algorithm
近似F统计量/似F統計量,F狀統計量　F-like statistic
近似t统计量/似t統計量　t-like statistic
近似误差/近似誤差　approximate error
近似正态性/近似常態性　approximate normality
近似最佳线性估计量/近似最佳線性估計量　nearly best linear estimator
近因/近因　immediate cause

近因误差/近因誤差　recency error
近因效应/近因效應　regency effect
晋律/晉律　Law of Jin Dynasty
晋升/升遷　promotion
浸解/浸解　maceration
禁飞区/禁飛區　no-fly zone
禁毁日期/禁毀日期　barrier date
禁毁书目/禁毀書目　list of banned books
禁忌/禁忌　taboo
禁忌搜索算法/禁忌搜索演算法　taboo search algorithm
禁书/禁書　forbidden book, prohibited book, banned book
禁用改变环境技术/禁用改變環境技術　environmental modification
禁欲主义/制欲主義　asceticism
禁止背信弃义/禁止背信棄義　prohibition of perfidy
禁止不当联结原则/禁止不當聯結原則　principle of prohibition of undue linkage
禁止不分皂白攻击/禁止不分皂白攻擊　prohibition of indiscrimination attacks
禁止出版/禁止出版　publishing prohibited
禁止出口/禁止出口　ban on export
禁止出口货物/禁止出口貨物　prohibited article for exportation
禁止出口协议/禁止出口協議　non-exportation agreement
禁止登载/禁止登載　journaling prohibited
禁止发售/禁止發售　sale prohibited
禁止发行/禁止發行　distribution prohibited
禁止反悔原则/禁止反悔原則　doctrine of estoppel
禁止反言/禁反言　estoppel
禁止概率/禁止機率　taboo probability
禁止进口/禁止進口　ban on import
禁止进口货物/禁止進口貨物　prohibited article for importation
禁止开放期/禁止期　embargo period
禁止使用武力/禁止使用武力　prohibition of use of force
禁止双重危险/禁止雙重危險　prohibition against double jeopardy
禁止性关税/禁止性關稅,寓禁關稅　prohibitive duty, prohibitive tariff
禁止性规范/禁止性規範　prohibitive norm
禁止性进口关税/禁止性進口關稅　prohibitive import duty
禁止赠礼法/禁止贈禮法　Lex Cincia
禁止状态/禁止狀態　taboo state

禁止恣意原則/禁止恣意原則　principle of prohibition of arbitrariness
禁治产人/禁治產人　interdicted person
茎叶分析/莖葉分析　stem and leaf analysis
茎叶图/莖葉圖　stem and leaf display
京控/京控　Jing Kong
经办用语/經辦用語　handling term
经常读者/經常讀者　frequent reader
经常国际贸易/經常國際交易　current international transaction
经常项目/經常項目,經常賬,經常專案　current items, current account
经常项目余额/經常賬餘額　current balance
经常[性]支出/經常[性]支出　current payment, current expenditure, recurrent expenditure
经常性转移/經常性移轉　current transfers
经常账户/經常賬　current account
经常账户赤字/經常項目逆差　current account deficit
经常账户顺差/經常項目順差　current account surplus
经典测量模型/經典測量模型　classical measurement model
经典测验理论/古典測驗理論　classical test theory
经典模型/古典模型　classical model
经典排序/經典排序　classical scheduling
经典条件反射/古典制約　classical conditioning
经典统计力学/古典統計力學　classical statistical mechanics
经典推断/古典推論　classical inference
经纪存款/經紀轉存款　brokered deposit
经纪费用/經紀費用　brokerage expense
经纪人/經紀人,中介商,掮客　broker, broker agent
经纪人手续费/經紀人手續費,經紀人佣金　brokerage fee, brokerage commission
经纪人佣金/經紀人佣金,經紀人手續費　brokerage fee, brokerage commission
经济/經濟　economy
经济崩溃/經濟崩解　economic disintegration
经济变量/經濟變數　economic variable
经济表/經濟表　tableau economique
经济补偿金/經濟補償金　economic compensation
经济差距/經濟差距　economic gap
经济成本/經濟成本　economic cost
经济承包责任制/經濟承包責任制　economic responsibility contract system
经济订货量/經濟訂購量　economic order quantity, EOQ
经济发展/經濟發展　economic development
经济发展与环保的冲突/經濟發展與環保的衝突　conflict between environment and economic development
经济法/經濟法　economic law
经济法规/經濟法規　economic laws and regulations
经济法律关系/經濟法律關係　economic legal relations
经济法律事实/經濟法律事實　economic legal facts
经济法律责任/經濟法律責任　economic legal responsibilities
经济法体系/經濟法體系　economic law system
经济法学/經濟法學　science of economic law
经济犯罪/經濟犯罪　economic crime
经济范畴/經濟範疇　economic category
经济封锁/經濟封鎖　economic blockade
经济共同体/經濟共同體　economic community
经济惯习/經濟慣習　economic habitus
经济规律/經濟規律　law of economy
经济合作白皮书/經濟合作白皮書　white paper on economic cooperation
经济合作条约/經濟合作條約　treaty of economic cooperation
经济合作与发展组织/經濟合作與發展組織　Organization for Economic Cooperation and Development, OECD
经济和技术交流/經濟和技術交流　economic and technical interchange
经济互助委员会/經濟互助委員會,經濟互助理事會　Council for Mutual Economic Aid, CMEA
经济环境/經濟環境　economic environment
经济活动的空间分布/經濟活動的區域分布　regional distribution of economics activity
经济活动人口/經濟活動人口　economically active population
经济货币化/經濟貨幣化　monetization of the economy
经济基础/經濟基礎　economic base
经济集团/經濟集團　economic group
经济集中/經濟集中　economic concentration
经济计量分析/計量分析　econometric analysis
经济技术开发区/經濟技術開發區　economic and technical development zone
经济间谍/經濟間諜　economic espionage, commercial spy, business espionage
经济竞争/經濟競爭　economic rivalry
经济控制论/經濟控制論　economic cybernetics
经济浪漫主义/經濟浪漫主義　economic

romanticism
经济理性／經濟理性　economic rationality
经济立法／經濟立法　legislation on economic law
经济利润／經濟利潤　economic profit
经济伦理／經濟倫理　economic ethics
经济民主／經濟民主　economic democracy
经济模型／經濟模型　economic model
经济评价／經濟評估　economic evaluation
经济起飞／經濟起飛　economic takeoff
经济区域化／經濟區劃　economic regionalization
经济全球化／經濟全球化　economic globalization, economy globalization
经济人／經濟人　economic man
经济人假设／經濟人假設　economic person assumption
经济社会学／經濟社會學　economic sociology
经济生产批量／經濟生產批量　economic production lot, EPL
经济时间序列／經濟時間數列　economic time-series
经济适用房／經濟型量入爲出住宅　economically affordable housing
经济数据／經濟統計資料　economic data
经济衰退／不景氣　recession
经济司法／經濟司法　economic judicature
经济特区／經濟特區　special economic zone, SEZ
经济体制／經濟體制,經濟制度　economic system
经济体制改革／經濟體制改革　economic system reform
经济同盟／經濟同盟　economic union
经济统计［学］／經濟統計［學］　economic statistics
经济危机／經濟危機　economic crisis
经济稳定性损失／經濟穩定所致損失　economic stability loss
经济物品／經濟財　economic goods
经济宪法／經濟憲法　economic constitution
经济相互依存度／經濟相互依存度　economic interdependency
经济效率／經濟效率　economic efficiency
经济效益／經濟效益　economic effect of distribution, economic benefit
经济信息／經濟情報　economic information, economic intelligence
经济信息化／經濟資訊化　economic informatization
经济信息论／經濟資訊論　economic information theory
经济刑法学／經濟刑法學　economic criminology
经济行动／經濟行動　economic action
经济行政法／經濟行政法　economic administrative law
经济性裁员／經濟性裁員　redundancy
经济性规制／經濟調整　economic regulation
经济学／經濟學　economics
经济亚系统／經濟亞系統　economic subsystem
经济一体化／經濟一體化,經濟整合　economic integration, integration of economy
经济一体化理论／經濟一體化理論　theory of international economic integration
经济依赖度／經濟依存度　economic dependency ratio
经济移民／經濟移民　economic immigrants
经济影响评价／經濟影響評估　economic impact assessment
经济与货币联盟／經濟貨幣同盟　economic and monetary union
经济预测／經濟預測　economic forecasting
经济预测方法／經濟預測方法　economic forecasting methods
经济阈值／經濟門檻　economic threshold
经济援助／經濟援助　economic aid
经济责任审计／經濟責任審計　accountability audit
经济责任制／經濟責任制　economic responsibility system
经济增加值／經濟附加價值　economic value added, EVA
经济增长／經濟成長　economic growth
经济增长方式／經濟增長方式　mode of economic growth
经济增长理论／經濟成長論　theory of economic growth
经济增长率／經濟成長率　economic growth rate
经济执法／經濟執法　enforcement of economic law
经济职权／經濟職權　economic functions
经济职责／經濟職責　economic responsibility
经济指标／經濟指標　economic barometer
经济指数／經濟指數　economic index number
经济制裁／經濟制裁　economic sanction
经济制度／經濟制度　economic institutions
经济制度的社会建构／經濟制度的社會建構　social construction of economic institution
经济中心／經濟中心　economic center
经济周期／經濟循環　economic cycle
经济周期理论／景氣循環論　business cycle theory
经济转型／經濟轉型,經濟變遷　economic transition
经济资源／經濟資源　economic resource
经济租金／經濟租　economic rent
经济最优人口／經濟最適人口數　economic optimum for population

经济作物/經濟作物　cash crop
经理/經理　manager
经理角色学派/經理角色學派　managerial role school
经理逻辑/經理邏輯　manager logic
经理三职能/經理三職能　three functions of executive
经理信息系统/主管資訊系統　executive information system
经理型企业模型/經理型企業模型　model of managerial enterprise
经理支持系统/主管支援系統　executive support system
经理资本主义/管理資本主義　managerial capitalism
经世文编/經世文編　Jingshi Wenbian
经销/經銷　dealing, distributing
经销合同/經銷合同　agreement to sell
经销商/經銷商, 代理商, 自營商　dealer, distributor
经许可转让的技术/經許可轉讓的技術　licensed technology
经验贝叶斯方法/經驗貝氏程序　empirical Bayes procedure
经验贝叶斯估计/經驗貝氏估計, 貝氏估計法　empirical Bayes estimation
经验贝叶斯估计量/經驗貝氏估計量　empirical Bayes estimator
经验贝叶斯推断/經驗貝氏推論　empirical Bayes inference
经验费率/經驗費率　experience rating
经验分布/實證分配　empirical distribution
经验分布函数/經驗分布函數, 經驗分配函數　empirical distribution function
经验分析/經驗分析　empirical analysis
经验概率/經驗機率　empirical probability
经验概率单位/經驗機率單位　empirical probit
经验决策/經驗決策　experiential decision making
经验曲线/經驗曲線　experience curve
经验曲线理论/經驗曲線理論　experience curved shape theory
经验生存函数/經驗存活函數　empirical survival function
经验图书馆学/經驗圖書館學　empirical library science
经验学派/經驗學派　empirical school
经验知识/經驗知識　experiential knowledge
经验主义/經驗主義　empiricism
经营成本/營運成本　working cost
经营档案/經營檔案　managing archives

经营范围/公開市場操作目標值域　operating range
经营费用/營運費用　working expense
经营风险/經營風險　business risk
经营风险基础审计/風險導向審計方法　business risk-based audit
经营杠杆/營業槓桿　operating leverage
经营管理自主权/經營管理自主權　management autonomy
经营合伙人/營運合夥人　working partner
经营活动/經營活動　operating activity
经营交钥匙工程项目/整廠營運　turnkey operation
经营领域/經營範圍　scope of operation
经营秘密/經營秘密　business secret
经营情况表/營業概況表　statement of operation
经营外汇业务/經營外匯業務　operation of foreign exchange
经营性亏损/經營虧損　operation losses
经营性租赁/營業租賃　operating lease
经营者/營業人　business operator
经营者持大股/經營者持大股　management as the biggest shareholder
经营者集中/經營者集中　merger of enterprises
经营者义务/經營者義務　business operators' obligations
经营周期/營業週期　operating cycle
经营资本/經營資本　management capital
经院经济思想/經院經濟思想　scholastic economic thought
经院哲学/士林學派　scholasticism
经折装/經摺裝　sutra binding
晶体刻纹头/晶體刻紋頭　crystal cutter head
晶体拾音头/晶體拾音頭　crystal pick-up head
精耕细作/密集耕作　intensive cultivation
精减系统模型/精簡系統模型　model of the coherent system
精简结构/精簡結構　coherent structure
精简系统/精簡系統　coherent system
精简原则/精簡原則　principle of parsimony
精刻本/精刻本　fine woodblock edition
精炼贝叶斯均衡/完全貝氏均衡　perfect Bayesian equilibrium
精[密]度/精確度　precision
精品书/精品書　fine book
精情报/精情報　finished intelligence, refined intelligence, deep-processed intelligence
精确抽样理论/精準抽樣理論　exact sampling theory
精确检索/精確檢索　accurate search, precise search

精确卡方检检/精準卡方檢定　exact chi-square test
精确识别/精確識別　exact identification
精确统计检验/精準統計檢定　exact statistical test
精确线搜索/精確線搜索　exact line search
精确性/精確性　accuracy
精确置信区间/精確的信任區間　exact confidence interval
精神病人/精神病人　mental patient
精神障碍/精神障礙,精神病　mental disorder
精算公平保费/精算費率　actuarially fair premium
精算师/保險精算師　actuary
精细生产/精實生產,精簡生產　lean production, lean manufacturing
精细套印/精細套印　close register
精益研发/精益研發　lean research and development
精英/精英,菁英　elite
精英教育/精英教育　elite education
精英理论/菁英理論　elite theory
精英文化/菁英文化　elite culture
精英循环/精英循環　elite circulation
精英再生产/精英再生產　elite reproduction
精英政治/精英政治　meritocracy
精装/精裝　hardcover binding
精装本/精裝本　hardcover edition
精装联动线/精裝聯動線　hardcover binding line
精准设计/精準設計　exact design
景象室/景象室　ops room
警备条令/警備條令　mandatory regulation on garrison
警告/警告　disciplinary warning
警戒控制限/警戒管制界限　warning control limits
净超额准备/淨超額準備　net excess reserves
净出口/淨出口　net export
净贷款/貸出淨額　net lending
净繁殖率/淨繁殖率,淨增殖率　net reproduction rate, net reproductive rate
净改变系统/淨改變系統　net-change system
净国外投资/外人投資淨額　net foreign investment
净回归系数/淨回歸係數　coefficient of net regression
净价/淨價,實價　net price
净进口/淨進口　net import
净进口值/淨進口值　net import value
净利差/淨利差　net interest margin
净利润/純利潤,淨利　pure profit, net profit
净迁移率/淨遷徙率　net-migrants rate, net migration rate
净实际收入/淨實際收入　net real income

净收入/淨收入,純收益,淨所入　net revenue, net income
净损失/絕對損失　deadweight loss
净投资/淨投資　net investment
净现金流量/淨現金流量　net cash flow
净现值/淨現值　net present value, NPV
净相关/淨相關　net correlation
净相关系数/淨相關係數　coefficient of net correlation
净销售额/銷貨淨額,銷售淨額　net sale
净效益现值/淨效益的現值　present value of net benefits
净需要量/淨需求　net requirement
净移出/淨遷出　net out-migration
净移入/淨遷入　net in-migrant
净营运资本/淨營運資本　net working capital
净再生产率/淨生殖率　net reproduction rate
净值/淨值　net worth
净值获利率/淨值獲利率　net worth earning ratio
净资本支出/淨資本支出　net capital expenditure
净资产负债率/負債淨值比率　debt-to-net worth ratio
净资产收益率/權益報酬率,股本回收率,股權回報率　return on equity, ROE
净租金/淨租金　net rental
净租赁/租賃淨額　net lease
净作业时间/淨作業時間　net operation time
竞标/競標　competitive bid
竞标规则/喊價法則　bidding rules
竞价/互相競價　bid against each other
竞价承销/競價承銷　competitive bidding underwriting
竞赛促销/競賽式促銷　contest promotion
竞选传播研究/競選傳播研究,宣傳研究　campaign study
竞选广告/競選廣告,宣傳廣告　campaign advertising
竞业限制/競業限制　limitation of competition
竞争/競爭　competition
竞争策略情报/競爭策略情報　competitive strategy intelligence
竞争导向公司/競爭導向公司　competitor-centered company
竞争地位/競爭定位　competitive position
竞争对等法/競爭對等法　competitive-parity method
竞争对手/競爭者　competitor
竞争对手跟踪/競爭對手追蹤　competitor tracking
竞争对手监视/競爭對手監視,競爭對手監聽

competitor monitoring
竞争对手剖析/競爭對手剖析　competitor profiling
竞争对手情报/競爭對手情報　competitor intelligence
竞争对手识别/競爭對手識別　competitor identifying
竞争法/競爭法　competition act
竞争法则/競爭法則　law of competition
竞争分析/競爭分析　competitive analysis
竞争风险/競爭風險,互競風險　competing risk
竞争规制/競爭規制　competition regulation
竞争过程/競爭過程　competition process
竞争环境/競爭環境　competitive environment
竞争环境分析/競爭環境分析　competitive environment analysis
竞争环境情报/競爭環境情報　intelligence of competitive environment
竞争机制/競爭機制　mechanism of competition
竞争监视/競爭監測　competitive monitoring, competition environment monitoring
竞争均衡/競爭性均衡　competitive equilibrium
竞争均衡范式/競爭均衡典範　competitive-equilibrium paradigm
竞争理论/競爭理論　competition theory
竞争模拟/競爭模擬　competition simulation
竞争能力/競爭能力　competitive power
竞争企业供给曲线/競爭廠商之供給曲線　competitive firm supply curve
竞争前技术/競爭前技術　pre-competitive technology
竞争情报/競爭情報　competitive intelligence
竞争情报保护/競爭情報保護　protection of competitive intelligence
竞争情报部门/競爭情報部門　competitive intelligence unit
竞争情报产品/競爭情報產品　competitive intelligence product
竞争情报分析/競爭情報分析　competitive intelligence analysis
竞争情报分析师/競爭情報分析員　competitive intelligence analyst
竞争情报风险/競爭情報風險　competitive intelligence risk
竞争情报顾问/競爭情報顧問　competitive intelligence consultant
竞争情报价值/競爭情報價值　competitive intelligence value
竞争情报价值链/競爭情報價值鏈　competitive intelligence value chain
竞争情报力/競爭情報能力　competitive intelligence competence
竞争情报流程/競爭情報流程　competitive intelligence process
竞争情报盲点分析/競爭情報盲點分析　blind spots in competitive intelligence analysis, blind spots in CI analysis
竞争情报模拟系统/競爭情報模擬系統　competitive intelligence simulation system
竞争情报培训/競爭情報訓練　competitive intelligence training
竞争情报评估/競爭情報評估　competitive intelligence assessment
竞争情报人际网络/人際情報網路　human intelligence network
竞争情报人员/競爭情報人員　competitive intelligence practitioners, competitive intelligence personnel
竞争情报软件/競爭情報軟體　competitive intelligence software
竞争情报审计/資訊稽核　competitive intelligence audit
竞争情报四分卫法/競爭情報四分衛　competitive intelligence quarterbacking
竞争情报搜集/競爭情報收集　competitive intelligence collection, competitive intelligence gathering
竞争情报团队/競爭情報團隊　competitive intelligence teams
竞争情报推动者/競爭情報催化者　competitive intelligence facilitator
竞争情报系统/競爭情報系統　competitive intelligence system
竞争情报需求/競爭情報需求　competitive intelligence needs
竞争情报循环/競爭情報週期　competitive intelligence cycle
竞争情报战略/競爭情報戰略　competitive intelligence strategy
竞争情报战争游戏/競爭情報戰略遊戲,競爭情報策略遊戲　war game, war gaming
竞争情报职业道德/競爭情報倫理學　competitive intelligence ethics, competitive intelligence moral
竞争上岗/競爭上崗　taking up a post through competition
竞争态势分析/競爭形勢分析　competitive situation analysis
竞争态势矩阵/競爭態勢矩陣　competitive profile matrix

竞争信息系统/競爭資訊系統　competitive information system, CIS
竞争性报价/競爭性報價,具競爭力的報價　competitive offer
竞争性反抗/競爭性對抗　competitive rivalry
竞争性关税/競爭性關稅,優惠關稅　competitive tariff
竞争性货币/競爭性貨幣　competing currency
竞争性假设分析/競爭條件分析　analysis of competitive hypothesis, ACH
竞争性流动/競賽流動　contest mobility
竞争性拍卖/競爭拍賣　competitive auction
竞争性商品/競爭性商品　rival commodity
竞争性市场/可競爭市場　contestable market
竞争性市场结构/競爭之市場結構　competitive market structure
竞争性市场理论/可競爭市場理論　contestable market theory, theory of contestable market
竞争[性]行为/競爭行爲　competitive behavior
竞争性需求/競爭性需求　competitive demand
竞争性营销战略/競爭性行銷策略　competitive marketing strategy
竞争性招标/競爭性招標　competitive bidding
竞争优势/競爭優勢　competitive advantage
竞争战略/競爭策略　competitive strategy
竞争战略分析/競爭策略分析　competitive strategy analysis
竞争战略风险/競爭策略風險　competitive strategic risk
竞争者分析/競爭者分析　competitor analysis
竞争政策/競爭政策　competition policy
竞争资本/競爭資本　competitive capital
静电成像/電子照像術　electrostatic imaging, electrophotography
静电辅助/靜電輔助器　electrostatic assist
静电复印法/靜電複印法　electrostatic xerography
静电喷墨/靜電噴墨　electrostatic inkjet
静电网版印刷/靜電絲網印刷　electrostatic screen printing
静电印刷/靜電印刷　electrostatic printing
静态X[低]效率/靜態X效率　static X-efficiency
静态对策/靜態對策　static game
静态分析/靜態分析　static analysis
静态决策/靜態決策　static decision-making
静态均衡/靜態平衡　static equilibrium
静态列昂惕夫模型/靜態Leontief模型　static Leontief model
静态模型/靜態模型,單時模型　unitemporal model
静态排法/靜態調度　static scheduling
静态人口统计/靜態人口統計　static demography
静态数据/靜態資料　static data
静态统计/靜態統計　static statistics
静态投入产出分析/靜態投入產出分析　static input-output analysis
静态投入产出模型/靜態投入產出模型　static input-output model
静态投资/靜態投資　static investment
静态系统/靜態系統　static system
静态信息源/靜態資訊源　static information source
静态页面/靜態頁面　static page
静态预测/靜態預測　static forecasting
静态预算/靜態預算　static budget
静态资本结构理论/靜態資本結構理論　static theory of capital structure
静坐罢工/霸占罷工　sit-down strike
境内个人/境內個人　domestic individual
境内机构/境內機構　domestic institutions
境内所得/境內所得　domestic income
境外采购/境外採購　offshore purchase
境外货币市场/境外貨幣市場　offshore currency market
境外加工/境外組裝　offshore assembly
境外市场/境外市場　external market
境外所得/境外所得　overseas income
境外投资中心/境外投資中心　offshore investment center
境外银行中心/境外金融業務中心　offshore banking center
境外债券市场/境外債券市場　offshore bond market
境外账户/境外賬戶　external account
境外资金/境外資金　offshore fund
镜面/鏡面　mirror
镜头角度/鏡頭角度　camera angle
镜像/鏡像　mirror image
镜像自我/鏡[中自]我　looking-glass self
纠错块/糾錯塊　error checking and correcting block
纠错码/改錯碼　error correction code
纠正/校正,改正　correct
纠正措施/矯正措施　corrective action
九朝律考/九朝律考　Compilation of Information Law of Nine Dynasties
九卿会审/九卿會審　Jiuqing Huishen, joint inquisition of time ministers
九刑/九刑　general title of written criminal books in the western Zhou Dynasty
九章律/九章律　Law of Han Dynasty

久期/持續時間　duration
久期模型/持續期間模型　duration model
旧标目/舊標目　earlier heading
旧刊本/舊刊本　old printing edition
旧书/舊書　secondhand book, used book
旧书目录/舊書目錄　secondhand catalog
救赎/買回，回饋　redemption
救助/貸款救援　bail out
救助报酬/救助報酬　salvage remuneration
厩律/廄律　the Chinese ancient law of regard to livestock
就地审计/就地審計　on-site audit
就绪时间/就緒時間　ready time
就业/就業　employment
就业保护法/就業保障法　employment protection act
就业保障/就業安全　job security
就业补贴/雇傭補貼　employment subsidies
就业不足/低度就業　underemployment
就业促进/就業促進　employment promotion
就业促进法/就業促進法　employment promotion law
就业服务/雇傭服務　employment services
就业服务公司/雇傭服務公司　employment service company
就业机会/就業機會　opportunities of employment
就业结构/就業體制　employment structure
就业理论/就業理論　theory of employment
就业能力/就業能力　employment ability
就业培训/就業培訓　employment training
就业培训中心/就業培訓中心　employment training center
就业歧视/就業歧視　employment discrimination
就业人员/就業者，就業人口　employed persons
就业水平/就業水準　employment level
就业条件/雇用條件　conditions of employment
就业统计/就業統計　employment statistics
就业团/工作營　job corps
就业协议/雇傭契約　employment contracts
就业援助/就業援助　employment aid
就业增长率/進用率　accession rate
就业政策/就業政策　employment policy
就业制度/雇傭制度　employment system
拘留/拘留　detention
居家养老服务/居家養老服務　home-based elderly care
居间合同/居間合同　brokerage contract
居间贸易/居間貿易，轉口貿易，中介貿易　intermediary commerce

居民储蓄/居民儲蓄　household savings
居民纳税人/居民納稅人　resident taxpayer
居民企业/居民企業　resident enterprise
居民委员会/居民委員會　committee of neighborhood, residents committee
居民自治委员会/居民自治委員會　residents self-government committee
居延汉简/居延漢簡　Juyan Hanjian
居中优势/居中優勢　interim dominance
居住支出/居住支出　resident expenditure
局/局　play
局本/局本　local official press edition
局部表/局部表列　local tabulation
局部独立/局部獨立性　local independence
局部渐近可容许性/局部漸近可容許性　local asymptotic admissibility
局部渐近有效性/局部漸近有效性　local asymptotic efficiency
局部渐近最大功效检验/局部漸近最強力檢定　locally asymptotically most powerful test
局部渐近最强无偏检验/局部漸近最強不偏檢定　asymptotically locally most powerful unbiased tests
局部渐近最严格检验/局部漸近最逼近強力檢定　locally asymptotically most stringent test
局部截尾分布/部分截略分布　partial truncated distributions
局部解/局部解　local solution
局部均衡/部分均衡　partial equilibrium
局部均衡分析/部分均衡分析　partial equilibrium analysis
局部控制/局部控制　local control
局部清点/局部查記　partial enumeration
局部色彩变化/局部色彩變化　partial color change
局部生产率指数/部分生產力指數　partial productivity index
局部搜寻/區域尋找　local search
局部调整模型/部分調整模型　partial adjustment model
局部统计量/局部統計量　local statistic
局部相关系数/偏相關係數　coefficient of partial correlation, partial correlation coefficient, partial coefficient of correlation
局部预期理论/局部預期理論　local expectation theory
局部最大功效检验/局部最強力檢定　locally most powerful test
局部最大功效秩序检验/局部最強力等級順序檢定　locally most powerful rank order test

局部最小方差无偏估计量/局部最小變異不偏估計量　locally minimum variance unbiased estimator
局部最小值/區域最小　local minimum
局部 D 最优设计/局部 D 型最適設計　locally D-optimal design
局内人-局外人假设/同仁-外人假說　insider-outsider hypothesis
局内人-局外人模型/局内人與局外人模型　insider-outsider model
局内人信条/局内人信條　insider doctrine
局势/形勢，局面　situation
局外人信条/局外人信條　outsider doctrine
局中人/對局者，賽者　player
矩/動差　moment
矩比/動差比率　moment ratio
矩的渐近展开式/動差漸近展開式　asymptotic expansion of moment
矩法/動差法　method of moments
矩分布/動差分布　moment distribution
矩估计/動差估計　moment estimation
矩估计法/動差估計法　moment estimation method
矩估计量/動差估計量　moment estimator
矩函数/動差函數　moment function
矩空间/矩陣空間　matrix space
矩量法/動差法　method of moments
矩量矩阵/動差矩陣　moment matrix
矩[量]母函数/動差母函數，動差生成函數　moment generating function
矩匹配方法/動差配適法　moment matching method
矩系数/動差係數　moment coefficient
矩心/矩心　centorid
矩形比/方性比　squareness ratio
矩形分布/矩形分布，矩形分配　rectangular distribution
矩形格[子]设计/矩形格子設計　rectangular lattice design
矩形结合方案/矩形相聯方案　rectangular association scheme
矩形直方图/矩形直方圖　rectangular histogram
矩阵/矩陣　matrix
ADL 矩阵/ADL 矩陣　ADL matrix
V 矩阵/V 矩陣　V-matrix
矩阵博弈/矩陣賽局　matrix game
矩阵抽样/矩陣抽樣　matrix sampling
矩阵对策/矩陣對局　matrix game
矩阵对策的数学模型/矩陣對策的數學模型　mathematical model of matrix game
矩阵结构/矩陣式結構　matrix structure

矩阵式[项目管理]组织/矩陣式專案管理組織　matrix type organization of project management
矩阵图/矩陣圖　matrix diagram
矩阵资料分析法/矩陣資料分析法　matrix data analysis method
矩阵组织/矩陣[式]組織　matrix organization
举债能力/舉債能力　debt capacity
举证时限制度/舉證時限制度　the system of time limit for evidence
举证责任/舉證責任　burden of proof
举证责任倒置/舉證責任倒置　burden of proof by defendant
举证责任分配/舉證責任分配　distribution of the burden of proof
举证责任转换/舉證責任轉換　shift of burden of proof
举止/舉止　manner
巨额非常性交易/巨額非常性交易　large special non-recurring transaction
巨额贸易逆差/巨額貿易逆差　large trade deficit
巨额贸易顺差/巨額貿易順差　large trade surplus
巨额票据/巨額票據　large bill
巨额资本股份/巨額股本　large capital stock
巨系统/巨系統　giant system
巨灾保险公司/巨災保險公司　catastrophe insurance company
句法分析法/語法分析方法　syntax analysis method
句法关系/語法關係　syntactic relations
句法控制/句法控制　grammar control
拒访率/拒查率　refusal rate
拒付/拒付　effect a protest
拒付费/拒付費　protest fee
拒付汇票/拒付匯票　bill dishonored, dishonored draft
拒付汇票证书/拒付匯票證書　protest for dishonor
拒付票据/拒付票據　dishonoured note, rejected bill
拒付通知书/拒付通知書　protest note
拒付应收票据/拒付應收票據　note receivable dishonored
拒付支票/拒付支票　rejected check, protest check, dishonored cheque
拒借/拒絕　refuse
拒借率/拒借率　loan refused rate
拒绝承兑/拒絕承兌　non-acceptance
拒绝错误/棄却錯誤　rejection error
拒绝的抽样风险/棄却的抽樣風險　sampling risk of rejection
拒绝风险/棄却風險　risk of rejection

拒绝概率/棄却機率　probability of rejection
拒绝交易/拒絕交易　refusal to deal
拒绝界/棄却界　rejection boundary
拒绝履行/拒絕履行　refusal of performance
拒绝线/棄却線　rejection line
拒绝域/臨界域　critical region, rejection region
拒绝质量水平/拒收品質水準　reject quality level
拒赔/拒賠　claims rejected
拒鲨条款/驅鯊劑　shark repellent
拒收/拒收　rejection
拒收产品/拒收產品　rejected product
拒收批/拒收批　reject lot
具体的发展/個別性發展　idiographic development
具体的技术进步/包含性技術進步　embodied technological progress
具体计划/具體計劃　specific plan
具体劳动/具體勞動　concrete labor
具体权利/特定權利　specific right
具体行政行为/具體行政行爲　concrete administrative action, concrete administrative act
具体政策/具體政策　specific policy
俱乐部/俱樂部　club
俱乐部商品/俱樂部財　club goods
剧本/劇本　screenplay
据呈前情/據呈前情　jucheng qianqing
距的阶/動差階數　order of moments
距离分布/距離分布　distance distribution
距离衰减规律/距離衰減原理　principle of distance decay
距离综合评价法/距離綜合評判方法　distance integrated evaluation method
锯齿边缘/鋸齒狀　aliasing
锯齿效应/鋸齒效應　saw-tooth effect
锯齿形抽样/鋸齒形抽樣,曲形抽樣　zigzag sampling
锯形/鋸齒形,折形　zigzag form
聚点均衡/焦點均衡　focal equilibrium
聚合/聚合　aggregation
聚合度/聚合度　degree of polymerization
聚合效度/聚斂效度,幅合效度　convergent validity
聚集分析/集群分析　cluster analysis
聚集函数/加總函數　aggregation function
聚集经济/聚集經濟　economies of agglomeration
聚焦检索/聚焦檢索　focused retrieval
聚类/叢聚,群聚　cluster
聚类点/叢聚點　cluster point
聚类点过程/叢聚點過程　cluster point process
聚类方法/叢集法,群集法,聚類法　cluster method
聚类分析/叢聚分析,群聚分析　cluster analysis, clustering analysis
聚类检索/聚類檢索　clustering retrieval
聚类群体/聚類群體　cluster group
聚束图分析/束圖分析　bunch-map analysis
聚碳酸酯料/聚碳酸酯　polycarbonate
聚碳酸酯料真空干燥机/聚碳酸酯真空乾燥機　polycarbonate vacuum dryer
聚珍本/聚珍本　collected gems edition
聚酯片基/聚酯片基　polyester
捐赠/捐贈　donation
捐赠人/捐贈人　donor
捐赠图书/贈書　donated book, gift book
涓滴效应/涓滴效應　trickling-down effects
卷积/褶合式,褶積　convolution
卷式缩微品/捲式微縮品　roll type microfilm
卷筒凹印机/捲筒凹印機　roll paper gravure press
卷筒纸印刷/捲筒紙印刷　roll paper printing
卷/卷　volume
卷端题名/卷端題名　caption title
卷号/卷次號　volume number
卷夹/檔夾　folder
卷内备考表/卷內備考表　file note, file memo, preliminary examination table of records
卷内文件目录/卷內檔目錄　innerfile item catalog, document catalog of records
卷首语/序言　preface
卷轴本/卷軸本　scroll-style binding
卷轴式/卷軸式　scroll type
卷轴装/卷軸裝　scroll binding
卷宗/卷宗　folder
倦怠/工作倦怠　burnout
决标/決標　award of contract
决策/決策　①decision making, ②decision
决策变量/決策變數　decision variable
决策标准/決策準則　decision making criteria
决策不确定性/決策不確定性　decision making uncertainty
决策程序/決策程序,決策程式　decision procedure
决策的防范分析/決策的防範分析　prevention analysis of decision
决策的经济社会模型/決策之社會經濟模式,決策之社會經濟模型　socioeconomic model of decision making
决策分工/決策分工　division of labor in policy making
决策分析/決策分析　decision analysis
决策风格/決策風格　decision making style
决策个体/決策者　decision maker

决策规则/決策規則,決策法則　decision rule
决策函数/決策函數　decision function
决策函数空间/決策函數空間　decision function space
决策环境/決策環境　decision environment
决策活动/決策活動　decision activity
决策集权/決策集權　policy centralization
决策阶段/決策階段　decision phase
决策竞争情报/決策競爭情報　competitive decision intelligence, competitive intelligence for decision
决策矩阵/決策矩陣　decision matrix
决策角色/決策角色　decisional role
决策科学/決策科學　decision science
决策空间/決策空間　decision space
决策框架/決策框架　decision framing
决策[理]论/決策理論　decision making theory
决策[理论]学派/決策理論學派　decision making school
决策论方法/決策理論法　decision theoretic approach
决策模型/決策模型　decision model, decision-making model
决策目标/決策目標　decision object
决策能力/決策能力　policy-making competence
决策情报研究/決策情報分析　decision-making intelligence analysis
决策时滞/決策落後　decision lags
决策树/決策樹　decision tree
决策树法/決策樹法　decision tree method
决策问题/決策問題　decision making problem, decision problem
决策系统/決策系統　decision making system
决策线/決策線　decision line
决策心理机制/決策心理機制　mental mechanism of decision
决策者/政策制定者　policy maker
决策支持系统/決策支援系統　decision support system, DSS
决策支持系统工具/決策支援系統工具　decision support system tool
决策支持系统生成器/決策支援系統產生器　decision support system generator
决策支援/決策支援　decision support
决定/決定　decision
决事比/決事比　a typical case in the Han Dynasty
决水罪/決水罪　crime of breaching dikes
决算/決算　final account
决算草案/決算草案　draft for final accounts
决议/決議　resolution

角色/角色　role
角色扮演/角色扮演　role play
角色表现/角色表現　role performance
角色超载/角色過荷,角色負荷過重　role overload
角色冲突/角色衝突　role conflict
角色丛/角色組　role-set
角色分离/角色分離　nonrole
角色规范/角色規範　role norm
角色紧张/角色緊張　role strain
角色距离/角色距離　role distance
角色模糊/角色模糊　role ambiguity
角色扭曲/角色扭曲　role distortion
角色期待/角色期待　role expectation
角色认同/角色認同,角色認定　role identity
角色失败/角色失敗　role failure
角色序列阵/角色序列陣　role-ordered matrix
角色主张/角色主張　role assertion
绝版/絕版　out of print
绝版书/絕版書　out of print edition, exhausted edition, last edition
绝对变异/絕對變異　absolute variation
绝对剥夺/絕對剝奪　absolute deprivation
绝对测度/絕對測度　absolute measure
绝对层/絕對層　absolute layer
绝对多数选举制/絕對多數選舉制　absolute majority system of election
绝对份额/絕對份額　absolute share
绝对风险厌恶/絕對風險規避　absolute risk aversion
绝对购买力平价/絕對購買力平價　absolute purchasing power parity
绝对豁免说/絕對豁免說　doctrine of absolute immunity
绝对豁免主义/絕對豁免主義　absolute immunity doctrine
绝对价格/絕對價格　absolute price
绝对进口供应额/絕對進口供應額　absolute availability of import
绝对矩/絕對動差　absolute moment
绝对[离]差/絕對離差　absolute deviation
绝对离散/絕對離勢　absolute dispersion
绝对连续[性]/絕對連續[性]　absolute continuity
绝对配额/絕對配額　absolute quota
绝对贫困/絕對貧窮　absolute poverty
绝对频率法/絕對頻率法　absolute frequency method
绝对平价/絕對平價　absolute par
绝对权力/絕對權力　absolute power
绝对剩余价值/絕對剩餘價值　absolute surplus-value

绝对无偏估计[量]/絕對不偏估計[量]　absolutely unbiased estimator
绝对误差/絕對誤差　absolute error
绝对效率/絕對有效性　absolute efficiency
绝对性修改/絕對性修改　absolute change
绝对义务/絕對義務　absolute duty
绝对优势/絕對利益　absolute advantage
绝对优先权/絕對優先權　first priority
绝对优先原则/絕對優先規則　absolute priority rule
绝对有效性/絕對有效性　absolute efficiency
绝对阈限/絕對臨界　absolute threshold
绝对正态记分检验/絕對常態計分檢定　absolute normal score test
绝对值罚函数/絕對值懲罰函數　absolute value penalty function
绝对主义/絕對論　absolutism
绝密文件/絕對機密檔案　top secret document, top secret papers
均等风险决策规则/均險決策規則　equalizer decision rule
均等牺牲/同等犧牲　equal sacrifice
均方/均方　mean square
均方差/平均差方　mean square deviation
均方根误差/均方根誤差　root mean square error
均方连续波动估计[量]/均方連續波動估計量　mean square consecutive fluctuation estimator
均方连续差/均方接續差　mean square successive difference
均方列联/均方列聯　mean square contingency
均方收敛/均方收斂　mean square convergence
均方[误]差/均方[誤]差　mean square error, MSE
均方误差的期望值/均方誤差的期望值　expected value of mean square error
均方误差准则/均方差準則　mean square error criteria
均分原则/等分原則　principle of equipartition
均衡/均衡　equilibrium
均衡的作业计划/均衡的作業計劃　level schedule
均衡点/均衡點　equilibrium point
均衡发展理论/均衡發展論　balanced development theory
均衡分布/均衡分布　equilibrium distribution
均衡分析/均衡分析　equilibrium analysis
均衡工资/均衡工資　equilibrium wage
均衡汇率/均衡匯率　equilibrium rate of exchange
均衡价格/均衡價格　equilibrium price
均衡交易量/平衡交易量　equilibrium volume of transaction
均衡利率/均衡利率　equilibrium rate of interest
均衡路径/均衡路徑　equilibrium path
均衡贸易条件/均衡貿易條件　equilibrium term of trade
均衡频数/均衡次數　balance frequency
均衡生产法/均衡生產法　level production method
均衡数量/均衡數量　equilibrium quantity
均衡条件/均衡條件　equilibrium condition
均衡运动模式/均衡運動模式　balanced motion pattern
均价期权/平均價格選擇權　average rate option
均匀分布/均勻分布,均勻分配　uniform distribution
均匀化/均勻化,一致化　uniformization
均匀记分检验/均勻計分檢定　uniform score test
均匀离散分布/均勻離散分布,均勻離散分配　uniform discrete distribution
均匀密度/均等密度　uniform densities
均匀拟合度/均勻適合度　uniform goodness of fit
均匀谱/均勻頻譜　uniform spectrum
均匀寿命表/均勻生命表　uniform life table
均匀随机变量/均齊隨機變數　uniform random variable
均匀随机数/均勻隨機數　uniform random numbers
均匀随机向量/均等隨機向量　uniform random vector
均匀先验分布/均勻事前分布,均勻事前分配　uniform prior distribution
均匀性试验/均勻性試驗,一致性試驗　uniformity trials
均值/均值,平均數　mean, average
均值-方差分析/平均數-變異數分析,平均報酬與風險為抵換分析法　mean-variance analysis
均值-方差准则/平均數-變異數準則　mean-variance criterion
均值分析/平均數分析　analysis of means
均值回归/平均數復歸　mean reversion
均值及极差控制图/平均數及全距管制圖　mean and range chart
均值校正/平均數校正　correction for mean
均值可加性/平均數可加性　additivity of means
均值控制图/平均數管制圖　control chart for mean, x-control chart
均值替换法/均值插補法　mean imputation
均值质量控制图/平均數品質管制圖　quality control chart for means
均质区域/均向區　homogeneous region
君权/君權　monarchical power
君主立宪/君主立憲　constitutional monarchy

君主制/君主政體　monarchy
君主专制政体/專制君主政體，絕對王權　absolute monarchy
君子/君子　gentleman
郡县制/郡縣制　prefectures and counties system
郡斋本/郡齋本　local government edition

竣工后试验/完工後測試　test after completion
竣工结算/竣工結算　completion settlement
竣工决算/竣工決算　final account of completed project
竣工时间/完工時間　time for completion
竣工试验/竣工試驗　test on completion
竣工验收/竣工驗收　final acceptance

K

卡波坦变换/Kapteyn 變換　Kapteyn's transformation
卡波坦分布/Kapteyn 分布,Kapteyn 分配　Kapteyn's distribution
卡车交货价/卡車上交貨價　free on truck
卡迪司法/卡迪司法　Kadi jurisprudence
卡尔多程式化事实/卡爾曼特徵事實　Kaldor stylized facts
卡尔曼滤波/卡爾曼過濾器　Kalman filter
卡尔曼滤波模型/卡爾曼過濾器模型　Kalman filter models
卡尔曼增益/卡爾曼獲益　Kalman gain
卡尔沃主义/卡爾沃主義　Calvo doctrine
卡方/卡方　chi-square, χ^2
卡方独立性检验/卡方獨立性檢定　chi-square test for independence
卡方分布/卡方分布,卡方分配　chi-square distribution, χ^2 distribution
卡方划分/卡方分割　partition of chi-squared
卡方检验/卡方檢定　chi-square test, test of chi-square
卡方近似/卡方逼近　chi-square approximation, χ^2 approximation
卡方统计量/卡方統計量　chi-squared statistic
卡根-林尼克-拉奥定理/Kangan-Linnik-Rao 定理　Kagan-Linnik-Rao theorem
卡里曼准则/Carleman 準則　Carleman's criterion
卡里斯玛型/卡理斯瑪,魅力　Charisma
卡里指数/Carli 指數　Carli's index
卡马卡算法/卡瑪卡演算法　Karmarkar algorithm
卡内基钢铁产业一体化/卡內基鋼鐵產業一體化　Carnegie steel industry integration
卡内基基金制/卡內基基金制　Carnegie fund system
卡内基学派/卡內基學派　Carnegie school
卡彭检验/Capon 檢定　Capon test
卡片式检索工具/卡片式檢索工具　card type retrieval tool, card retieval system
卡片式目录/卡片式目錄　card catalog
卡片式著录格式/卡片描述格式　card description format
卡片索引/卡片索引,目錄卡　card index
卡片游戏/卡片遊戲　card game

卡普兰-迈耶估计[量]/Kaplan-Meier 估計[量]　Kaplan-Meier estimator
卡斯特组织变革论/卡斯特的組織變革論　Kast's organization change theory
卡特尔/卡特爾　cartel
卡特尔稳定性/卡特爾穩定性　cartel stability
卡特债券/卡特債券　bond Carter
卡通/卡通片　cartoon
卡文迪什实验室/卡文迪許實驗室　Cavendish laboratory
开办成本/開動成本　start-up cost
开标/開標　bid opening, tender opening
开出汇票/開匯票　issue of bill of exchange
开出提单/發放提單　issuance of bill of lading
开出信用证/開發信用狀　issuance of letter of credit
开窗卡片/孔卡　aperture card
开发成本/開發成本　development cost
开发公司/開發公司　development corporation
开发阶段/開發階段　development phase
开发区/開發區　development zone
开发税/開發稅　development tax
开发信贷/開發信貸　development credit
开发信贷报表/開發信貸報表　statement of development credit
开发性金融机构/開發融資機構　development finance institution
开发许可证/開發許可證　development certificate
开发银行/開發銀行　development bank
开发债券/開發債券　development bond
开发者界面/開發者介面　developer interface
开发资金融通/開發資金融通　development financing
开放车间/開放廠　open shop
开放存档/開放存檔　open archive
开放存取/公開取用　open access
开放存取出版/開放存取出版,開放獲取出版,公開取用出版　open access publishing
开放存取期刊/公開取用期刊　open access journal, OAJ
开放档案/開放檔案,公開檔案　open archive, liberalization of access to archive

开放档案目录/公開檔案目錄　open archival directory
开放登记机制/開放登記機制　open registry mechanism
开放抵押/開放抵押　open mortgage
开放订单/已開立訂單　open order
开放度/開放程度　degree of openness
开放格式/開放格式　open format
开放获取/公開取用　open access
开放获取期刊/公開取用期刊　open access journal, OAJ
开放结构/開放結構　open texture
开放经济/開放經濟　open economy
开放链接/開放式定位址　open URL
开放描述/開放描述　open description
开放平台/開放平臺　open platform
开放日期/開放日期　access date
开放社会/開放社會　open society
开放时间/開館時間　library hours
开放式编码/開放式編碼　open coding
开放式创新/開放式創新　open innovation
开放式词表/開放式詞表　open-ended thesaurus
开放式共同基金/開放式共同基金,開放型相互基金　open-end mutual fund
开放式基金/開放式基金　open-end fund
开放式投资基金/開放式投資基金,開放型投資基金　open-end investment fund
开放式问题/開放式問題　open-ended question
开放式印前处理接口/開放式印前介面　open prepress interface, OPI
开放式印前界面/開放式印前介面　open prepress interface, OPI
开放式装具/開放式裝具　open enclosure
开放条件下内生经济增长模型/開放經濟內生成長模型　endogenous growth model to open economy
开放文件组合/開放檔案組合　open record group
开放系统/開放性系統　open system
开放小组/開放式團體　open group
开放信息系统参考模型/開放檔案信息系統參考模型,OAIS参考模型　reference model for an open archival information system, OAIS reference model
开放型系统互连/開放式系統連結　open system inter-connection, OSI
开放性/開放性　openness
开放性案卷/公開檔案　open files
开放序贯计划/開放逐次方案　open sequential scheme
开工日期/動工日期　commencement date

开馆时间/圖書館開放時間　opening hour
开航权/開航權　right of sailing
开皇律/開皇律　First Code of Sui Dynasty
开架馆藏/開架式館藏　open-shelf collection, open-stack collection
开架目录/開架目錄　open-shelf catalogue
开架售书/開架售書　open-shelf book selling
开架书库/開架書庫　open-shelf stock
开架图书馆/開架制圖書館　open-shelf library, open-stacks library
开架制/開架借閱　open-shelf system
开口组/開端組　open-ended classes
开立信用证/開立信用狀　establishment of credit
开明绅士/開明紳士　liberal gentry
开明营销/開明行銷　enlightened marketing
开盘委托/開盤指令　at-the-opening order, opening only order
开始到开始关系/開始到開始關係　start to start
开始到完成关系/開始到完成關係　start to finish
开始年份/始年　origin year
开源信息/公開源資訊　open source information
开证行/開狀行　issuing bank
开证申请人/開證申請人　applicant for the credit
开证押金/信用狀保證金　marginal deposit
揩金/揩金　bronzing
凯恩斯/凱因斯　Keynes
凯恩斯革命/凱因斯經革命　Keynesian revolution
凯恩斯国际贸易理论/凱因斯經外貿論　Keynesian theory of foreign trade
凯恩斯计划/凱因斯計劃　Keynes plan
凯恩斯经济学/凱因斯經濟學　Keynesian economics
凯恩斯融资动机/凱因斯融資動機　Keynes' finance motive
凯恩斯体系/凱因斯體系　Keynesian system
凯恩斯消费规律/凱因斯消費規律　Keynes law of consumption
凯恩斯效应/凱因斯效應,凱因斯效果　Keynes effect
凯利归因理论/凱利歸因理論　Kelley's attribution theory
凯姆-麦迪尔不等式/Camp-Mediell不等式　Camp-Mediell inequality
凯姆-泡尔森近似/Camp-Paulson逼近　Camp-Paulson approximation
凯珀统计量/Kuiper統計量　Kuiper statistic
凯斯顿过程/Kesten過程　Kesten's process
刊号/刊號　publication number
刊名/刊名　journal name

刊头/刊頭　masthead
刊头广告/刊頭廣告　headline advertisement
勘误表/勘誤表　erratum, corrigendum
勘验笔录/勘驗筆錄　record of on-site investigation
勘验、检查笔录/勘驗、檢查筆錄　record of investigation of crime scene and inspection
堪培拉手册/坎培拉手冊　Canberra manual
坎贝尔定理/Campbell 定理　Campbell's theorem
坎曼特检验/Kamat 檢定　Kamat's test
坎普-保尔森近似/Camp-Paulson 逼近　Camp-Paulson approximation
坎特利不等式/Cantelli 不等式　Cantelli's inequality
坎托罗维奇定理/坎特羅維區定理　Kantorovitch theorem
坎托型分布/Cantor 型　Cantor-type
看不见的手/看不見的手　invisible hand
看不见的学院/無形學院　invisible college
看跌/看跌　bearish
看跌期权/看跌期權,賣[出選擇]權　put option
看涨买进/看漲買進,投機買進　speculative buying
看涨期权/看漲期權　call option
康德拉季耶夫周期/康迪耶夫經濟循環週期　Kondratieff cycle
康托诺维奇定理/Kantorowitch 定理　Kantorowitch's theorem
康亚斯条件/Konyus 條件　Konyus conditions
康亚斯指数/Konyus 指數　Konyus index number
抗辩决策过程/抗辯式訴訟過程　adversary process
抗辩权/抗辯權　right to defence
抗衡力量/抗衡力量,反制力量　countervailing power
抗拒理论/抗拒理論　reactance theory
抗税/抗税,租税反抗　refusal to pay tax, tax revolt
抗诉/抗訴　protest
考核者偏差/評估者偏差　rater bias
考绩制度/考績制度　merit rating system
考克斯定理/Cox 定理　Cox's theorem
考克斯回归模型/Cox 回歸模型　Cox's regression model
考克斯检验/卡克斯檢定　Cox's test
考克斯局部极大似然估计量/卡克斯部分最大概似估計量　Cox's partial maximum likelihood estimator
考克斯-斯图尔特检验/Cox-Stuart 檢定　Cox-Stuart's test
考勤/出勤　attendance
考任制/考任制　civil service examination
考试晋升制/考試晉升制　examination-based promotion system

拷贝/①拷貝,複印,複製,②複製品　①copy, ② replica
拷贝片/拷貝片　duplicating film
靠岸条款/靠岸條款　shore clause
靠词标引/靠詞標引　homoionym indexing
珂罗版印本/珂羅版印刷品　Collotype
珂罗版印刷/珂羅版印刷,科羅版印刷　Collotype printing
柯尔莫哥罗夫表达式/Kolmogorov 表式　Kolmogorov representation
柯尔莫哥罗夫不等式/Kolmogorov 不等式　Kolmogorov's inequality
柯尔莫哥罗夫定理/Kolmogorov 定理　Kolmogorov's theorem
柯尔莫哥罗夫方程/Kolmogorov 方程式　Kolmogorov equations
柯尔莫哥罗夫公理/Kolmogorov 公設　Kolmogorov axioms
柯尔莫哥罗夫拟合优度检验/Kolmogorov 適合度檢定　Kolmogorov test for goodness of fit
柯尔莫哥罗夫-斯米尔诺夫分布/Kolmogorov-Smirnov 分布　Kolmogorov-Smirnov distribution
柯尔莫哥罗夫-斯米尔诺夫检验/Kolmogorov-Smirnov 檢定　Kolmogorov-Smirnov test
柯尔莫哥罗夫-斯米尔诺夫统计量/Kolmogorov-Smirnov 統計量　Kolmogorov-Smirnov statistics
柯赫伦-奥科特变换/柯克蘭-歐克特轉換　Cochrane-Orcutt transformation
柯赫伦定理/柯克蘭定理　Cochran theorem
柯里/柯里　Brainerd Currie
柯西法/柯西法　Cauchy method
柯西分布/柯西分布,柯西分配　Cauchy distribution
柯西-施瓦兹不等式/柯西-施瓦茨不等式　Cauchy-Schwarz inequality
柯西准则/柯西準則　Cauchy criterion
科布-道格拉斯生产函数/柯布-道格拉斯生產函數　Cobb-Douglas production function
科布-道格拉斯效用函数/柯布-道格拉斯效用函數　Cobb-Douglas utility function
科层化/科層化,官僚化　bureaucratization
科层制/科層制,官僚制　bureaucracy
科层组织/科層組織,官僚組織　bureaucracy, ideal administrative organization system
科技报告/科技報告　scientific and technical report
科技查新/科技查新　novelty search service
科技产业集聚/科技產業群聚　science and technology industrial cluster
科技成果/科技成果　scientific and technological

achievement
科技出版物/科技出版物　scientific publication
科技档案/科技檔案　archive of science and technology, scientific and technical archive
科技档案保管单位/科技檔案保管單位　science and technology archive storage unit
科技档案编研/科技檔案編譯　compilation and research of technological archive
科技档案参考资料/科技檔案參考資料　reference material of scientific and technical archive
科技档案复用/科技檔案複用　science and technology archive multiplexing
科技档案汇编/科技檔案匯編　science and technology archives collect and edit
科技档案简介/科技檔案簡介　brief introduction of science and technology archives
科技档案室/科技檔案室　science and technology records office
科技档案套用/科技檔案套用　science and technology archive apply mechanically
科技档案文摘/科技檔案文摘　abstract of scientific and technical archive, science and technology archive digest
科技档案效益/科技檔案效益　science and technology archive benefit
科技档案摘要/科技檔案文摘　abstract of scientific and technical archive, science and technology archive digest
科技服务业/科技服務業　science and technology service industry
科技管理/科技管理　science and technology management, S and T management
科技管理学/科技管理學　management of science and technology
科技活动年鉴/科技活動年鑑　annal of scientific and technical activities
科技进步法/科技進步法　law of science and technology progress
科技论文/科學論文　scientific paper
科技期刊/學術雜志　scientific journal
科技情报学/科技資訊科學　scientific and technical information science
科技人力资源/科技人力資源　human resource of science and technology
科技统计/科技統計　science and technology statistics
科技文件成套性/科技檔案成套性　complete set of scientific and technological documents
科技文献/科學文獻　scientific literature
科技信息/科技資訊　scientific and technical information
科技用户/科學技術使用者　science and technology information user
科技政策/科技政策　science and technology policy
科技支撑计划/科技支撐計劃　science and technology support program
科技中介/科技［仲介］服務機構　science and technology service agency
科举社会/科舉社會　society of imperial examination
科举制［度］/科舉制度　imperial examination, imperial examination system
科克法学总论/科克法學總論　Coke's institutes
科克伦-奥克特估计/科克倫-奧克特估計　Cochrane-Orcutt estimation
科克伦定理/Cochran 定理　Cochran's theorem
科克伦检验/Cochran 檢定法　Cochran's test
科克伦 Q 检验/Cochran 的 Q 檢定　Cochran's Q-test
科克斯-英格索尔-罗斯模型/CIR 模型　Cox-Ingersoll-Ross model, CIR model
科罗济克定理/Koroljuk 定理　Koroljuk's theorem
科目汇总表/分類賬目摘要　categorized accounts summary
科尼什-费希尔展开式/柯尼希-費雪展式,Cornish-Fisher 展開式　Cornish-Fisher expansion
科普期刊/科普期刊　popular science periodical
科氏培训效能评价模型/科式訓練成效評估模式,科式訓練成效評估模型　Kirk Patrick's four-level model of evaluation
科斯/科斯　Ronald Harry Coase
科斯猜想/寇斯猜測　Coase conjecture
科斯第二定理/寇斯第二定理　Coase theorem II
科斯第一定理/寇斯第一定理　Coase theorem I
科斯定理/寇斯定理　Coase theorem
科特变革理论/科特變革理論　change theory of Kotter
科特变革模型/科特改變模型　Kotter change model
科特根合理化运动/科特根合理化運動　rationalization movement of Kottgen
科特领导理论/科特領導理論　leadership theory of Kotter
科学/科學　science
科学传播/科學傳播　science communication
科学的规范结构/科學的規範結構　normative structure of science
科学的精神气质/科學的精神氣質　ethos of science
科学的社会病状/科學的社會病狀　social pathology

of science
科学的社会研究/科學的社會研究　social study of science
科学的世俗化/科學的世俗化　secularization of science
科学的适应/科學的適應　accommodation of science
科学的效用/科學的效用　utility of science
科学的制度规范/科學的制度規範　institutional norm of science
科学的制度化/科學的制度化　institutionalization of science
科学的自主性/科學的自主性　autonomy of science
科学发现的优先权/科學發現的優先權　priority in scientific discovery
科学发现国际登记日内瓦条约/科學發現國際登記日內瓦條約　Geneva Treaty on the International Recording of Scientific Discoveries
科学发展观/科學發展觀　the Scientific Outlook on Development
科学范式/科學範式　scientific paradigm
科学革命/科學革命　scientific revolution, revolution in science
科学共识/科學共識　consensus in science
科学共同体/科學社群,科學界,科學團體　scientific community
科学贡献的知名度/科學貢獻的知名度　visibility of scientific contribution
科学管理理论/科學管理理論　scientific management theory
科学基金/科學基金會　science foundation
科学基金制/科學基金制　institution of science foundation
科学激励/科學激勵　scientific inspiration
科学计量学/科學計量學　scientometrics
科学技术档案/科技檔案　archive of science and technology, scientific and technical archive
科学技术档案馆/科學技術檔案館　science and technology archive
科学家共同体/科學社群,科學界　community of scientists, scientific community
科学家矛盾心理/科學家矛盾心理　ambivalence of scientist
科学家社会角色/科學家社會角色　social roles of scientist
科学交流/科學溝通　scientific communication
科学交流学派/科學交流學派　science communication school
科学决策/科學決策　scientific decision making

科学伦理学/科學倫理學　ethics of science
科学评价/科學評價　scientific evaluation
科学社会学/科學社會學　sociology of science
科学生产率/科學生產率　scientific productivity
科学史/科學史　history of science
科学数据/科學資料　scientific data
科学数据共享/科學資料共享　scientific data sharing
科学网络数据库/科學網路資料庫　web of science database
科学文化/科學文化　culture of science
科学学/科學學　scienology, science of science
科学研究纲领/科學研究綱領　scientific research program
科学研究信息化/網路化科研平臺　e-Science
科学引文索引/科學引文索引　science citation index, SCI
科学哲学/科學哲學　philosophy of science
科学争论/科學爭論　scientific debate
科学政策/科學政策　science policy
科学知识/科學知識　scientific knowledge
科学知识的积累/科學知識的積累　accumulation of scientific knowledge
科学知识的体系化/科學知識的體系化　synthesization of scientific knowledge
科学知识社会学/科學知識社會學　sociology of scientific knowledge
科学知识社会学的强纲领/科學知識社會學的強綱領　strong program in the sociology of scientific knowledge
科学知识图谱/知識領域圖譜　mapping knowledge domain
科学中的不连续性/科學中的不連續性　discontinuity in science
科学中的公有制/科學中的公有制　shared ownership in science
科学中的马太效应/科學中的馬太效應　Matthew effect in science
科学中的越轨行为/科學中的越軌行爲　deviant behavior in science
科学中的直觉/科學中的直覺　intuition in science
科学主义/科學[萬能]主義　scientism
科学资源配置/科學資源配置　allocation of resources in science
科研管理/科研管理　research management
颗粒/顆粒　grain
颗粒度/粒度　graininess
可背书支票/可背書支票　endorsable check
可比价值/同值同酬　comparable worth

可比较标准/可比較標準　comparable standard
可比性/可比性　comparability
可避免质量成本/可避免的品質成本　avoidable quality cost
可变比例/變動比例　variable proportion
可变比例的强化/變率增強,變率強化　variable-ratio reinforcement
可变成本/變動成本　variable cost
可变磁阻拾音头/可變磁阻拾音頭　magnetic variable reluctance pick-up head
可变概率/可變機率　variable probability
可变更合同/可變更合同　vocable contract
可变间隔的强化/變時增強,變時強化　variable-interval reinforcement
可变劳动力成本/變動勞動成本　variable labor costs
可变利率/變動利率　variable interest rate, variable rate
可变利率债券/變動利率債券　variable rate bond
可变批量抽样方案/可變批大小抽樣計劃　variable lot size sampling plan
可变权数/可變權數　variable weight
可变数据印刷/可變資料列印　variable data printing
可变投入品/變動投入　variable inputs
可变投入品价格/可變投入價格　variable input price
可变投资税/變動投資稅　variable investment tax
可变现价值/可變現價值　realizable value
可变现净值/可變現淨值,淨變現價值　net realizable value
可变现资产/可變現資產　realizable asset
可变薪酬/變動薪酬　variable compensation
可变形模型/可變形模型　deformable model
可变因子/可變動生產要素　variable factor
可变资本/可變動資本　variable capital
可辩驳性/可辯駁性　defeasibility
可擦光盘/可消除光碟　compact disc-erasable, CD-E
可擦写多用途数字光盘/可[重複]讀寫多用途數位光碟　digital versatile disc-rewritable
可擦写光盘/可重寫光碟　compact disc-rewritable
可参与优先股/參加特別股　participating preferred stock
可操控性应计项目/裁決性應計數　discretionary accrual
可测变换/可測變換　measurable transformation
可测函数/可測函數　measurable function
可测集/可測集合　measurable set
可测量性/可測度性,可衡量性　measurable
可查明变异/可尋變異　assignable variation
可查明原因/可尋原因　assignable cause

可撤销的报价/可撤銷的報價　revocable offer
可撤销的财产转让/可撤銷的財產轉讓　revocable transfer of property
可撤销的法律行为/可撤銷的法律行爲　rescissible civil act
可撤销合同/可撤銷合同,可撤銷合約　contract voidable, voidable contract
可撤销信用证/可撤銷信用狀　revocable credit
可持续创新/可持續創新　sustainable innovation
可持续发展/可持續性發展,永續發展　sustainable development
可持续农业/永續農業　sustainable agriculture
可持续生计/可持續生計　sustainable livelihood
可持续性/可維持性,永續性　sustainability
可持续增长率/可持續增長率　sustainable growth rate
可重构/可重構性　reconfigurability
可重记录型 DVD/可重寫 DVD,可再寫入 DVD　versatile disc-rewritable, DVD-RW, DVD＋RW
可重写光盘/可重複讀寫光碟　compact disc-rewritable, CD-RW
可重用性/可再用性　reusability
可出口量/可出口量　export availability
可达边界点/可達界限點　accessible boundary point
可达点/可達點　accessible point
可达性/接近性　accessibility
可贷资本/可貸資本　lendable capital
可贷资金/可貸資金　loanable fund
可贷资金理论/可貸資金説　loanable fund theory
可贷资金需求曲线/可貸資金的需求曲線　demand curve of loanable funds
可得信用/可動用信用額度　available credit
可抵扣暂时性差异/可減除暫時性差異　deductible temporary difference
可读性/可讀性　readability
可兑换货币/可交換的通貨,可兑性通貨　convertible currency, redeemable currency
可兑换性/可兑性　convertibility
可兑换债券/可換股債券　convertible bond
可兑换纸币/可兑換紙幣　redeemable paper money
可反驳的法律推定/可反駁的法律推定　rebuttable presumption of law
可反驳的事实推定/可反駁的事實推定　rebuttable presumption of fact
可防御状态/可防禦狀態　defensible position
可访问出版/可訪問出版　accessible publishing
α可分解性/α可分解性　α-resolvability
可分离规划/可分規劃　separable programming

可分离过程/可分離過程　separable process
可分平衡不完全区组设计/可分平衡不完全區集設計　resolvable balanced incomplete block design
可分散风险/可分化風險　diversifiable risk
可分设计/可分設計　resolvable design
可分之债/可分之債　divisible liability
可分组不完全区组设计/可分組不完全區集設計　group divisible incomplete block design
可分组设计/可分組設計　group divisible design
可分组旋转设计/可分組旋轉設計　group divisible rotatable design
可服务度/可服務度　serviceability
可更新活页出版物/可更新活頁出版物　updating loose-leaf publication
可公度性/單位共通性　commensurability
可供出售金融资产/可供出售金融資產　financial assets available for sale
可供交换目录/可供交換目錄　catalogue for exchange
可供目录/可供目錄　in-print bibliography
可估[的]/可估計的　estimable
可估函数/可估計函數　estimable function
U可估计的/U可估計的　U-estimable
可观测变量/可觀測變數　observable variable
可耗竭资源/耗竭性資源　exhaustible resources
可互换件/可互換零件　interchangeable part
可回收成本/可回收成本　recoverable cost
可回收金额/可回收金額　recoverable amount
可回收资源/可回收資源　recyclable resource
可获得的最优价格/可購買的最優價格　best price obtainable
可计算一般均衡模型/可計算一般均衡模型　computable general equilibrium model, CGE model
σ可加/σ可加[的]　sigma-additive, σ-additive
可加模型/加法模型　additive model
可加随机游动过程/可加隨機漫步過程　additive random walk process
可加性/可加性　additivity
可加性检验/可加性檢定　additivity test
可交付成果/可交付項　deliverable item
可交换的/可交換的　exchangeable
可交换随机变量/可互換隨機變數　interchangeable random variable
可交换性/可互換性　interchangeability
可交易票据/可交易票據　tradable instrument
可交易证券/可交易證券　tradable security
可接收过程水平/允收製程水準　acceptable process level
可接收可靠性水平/允收可靠度水準　acceptable reliability level, ARL
可接收质量水平/允收品質水準　acceptable quality level, AQL
可接受工序水平/允收製程水準　acceptable process level
可解性/可解性　solvability
可竞争性/可競爭性　contestability
可拒收过程水平/拒收製程水準　rejectable process level
可靠度指标/信度指標　index of reliability
可靠数据/可靠數據　reliable data
可靠性/可靠性，信度　reliability
可靠性保证/可靠度保證　reliability assurance
可靠性参数/可靠度參數　reliability parameter
可靠性抽样方案/可靠度抽樣計劃　reliability sampling plan
可靠性分配/可靠度配置　allocation of reliability, reliability allocation
可靠性分析/可靠度分析　reliability analysis
可靠性改进/可靠度改進　reliability improvement
可靠性工程/可靠度工程　reliability engineering
可靠性工程师/可靠度工程師　reliability engineer
可靠性管理/可靠度管理　reliability management
可靠性函数/可靠度函數　reliability function
可靠性计划/可靠度方案　reliability program
可靠性框图/可靠度區集圖　reliability block diagram
可靠性理论/可靠度理論　theory of reliability
可靠性评估/可靠度評估，可靠度評量　reliability evaluation
可靠性评价/可靠度評鑒　reliability assessment
可靠性设计/可靠度設計　reliability design
可靠性试验/可靠度試驗　reliability test
可靠性数据系统/可靠度數據系統　reliability data system
可靠性系数/可靠度係數　reliability coefficient
可靠性验证/可靠度驗證　reliability demonstration
可靠性验证试验/可靠度驗證試驗　reliability demonstration test, reliability compliance test
可靠性预测/可靠度預測　reliability prediction
可靠性增长/可靠度成長　reliability growth
可靠性指数/可靠度指數　reliability index
可靠性组织/可靠度組織　reliability organization
可控成本/可控制成本　controllable cost
可控排序/可控排序　controllable scheduling
可控系统/可控系統　controllable system
可控因素/可控因子　controlled factor
可扩展性/延伸性　extensibility

可累计优先股/累積特別股　cumulative preferred stock
可利用资源总量/可利用資源總額　total available resources
可列可加性/可數可加性　countable additivity
可录多用途数字光盘/可錄多用途數位光碟　digital versatile disc-recordable
可录光盘/可燒錄光碟　compact disc-recordable
可贸易商品和不可贸易商品/可貿易商品和不可貿易商品　tradable and non-tradable commodity
可能界限/可能界限　probable boundary
可能性/可能性　possibility
可逆边界/可逆邊界　invertibility boundary
可逆变换/可逆變換　reversible transformation
可逆关系/可逆關係　reversible relation
可逆设计/可逆設計　reversal design
可逆性/可逆性,可反性　invertibility, reversibility
可逆性条件/可逆條件　invertibility condition
可逆自回归滑动平均模型/可逆自回歸滑動平均模型　invertible autoregressive moving average model, invertible ARMA model
可取消租赁/可取消租約　cancelable lease
可容许风险/容許風險　tolerable risk
可容许性/可容性　admissibility
可伸缩性/可擴縮性,延展性　scalability
可识别参数/可識別参數　identifiable parameter
可识别单元/可識別單位　identifiable unit
可识别性/可識別性　identifiability
可实现的收入/可實現的收入　realizable income
可视分析/目视分析　visual analysis
可视管理/目视管理　visual management
可视化分析/視覺化分析　visualization analysis
可视化工具/軟體集　visual studio
可视化检索/可視化查詢　visualization search
可视密码技术/可視密碼技術　visual password technology
可收回价值/可收回價值　recoverable value
可收回损失/可收回損失　recoverable loss
可赎回股票/可贖回股票　redeemable stock
可赎回债券/可贖回債券　callable bond, redeemable bond, bond callable
可数概率空间/可數機率空間　countable probability space
可数性/可數性　enumerability
可调节钉住/可調整釘住　adjustable peg
可调整产能/可調整產能　adjustable capacity
可调整钉住汇率/可調整的釘住匯率　adjustable peg rate of exchange
可调整钉住汇率制/可調整釘住匯率體制　system of adjustable peg
可调整利率抵押贷款/浮動利率房貸　adjustable rate mortgage
可贴现票据/可貼現票據　bankable bill, discountable note
可维护性/可維修性　maintainability
可维修件/可維修件　repairable part
可相伴设计/可相聯設計　associable design
可信度/可信度　degree of belief
可信性/可信度,可靠性　credibility, dependability
可行广义最小二乘法/可行的一般化最小平方法　feasible generalized least squares, FGLS
可行广义最小二乘估计量/可行的一般化最小平方估計　feasible generalized least squares estimator
可行基/可行基　feasible base
可行性/可行性　feasibility
可行性标准方法/可行性標準方法　feasibility criteria approach
可行性分析/可行性分析　feasibility analysis
可行性研究/可行性研究　feasibility study
可行性研究报告/可行性研究報告　feasibility study report
可行域/可行域　feasible domain
可修复系统/可修複系統　repairable system
可选产品定价/可選產品定價　optional-product pricing
可选要素/可選要素　optional element
可选择的争端解决方法/另类的争端解决方式　alternative dispute resolution
可选择方案评价/複案評估　alternative evaluation
可移植文件格式/可攜式檔格式　portable document format, PDF
可疑文件/可疑檔案　questioned documents
可疑域/可疑域　region of doubt
可用产能/可用產能　available capacity
可用库存/可用存貨　available inventory
可用特性/可用特性　available characteristic
可用性/可用性　usability
可预测性/可預測性　predictability
可原谅并给予补偿的拖期/可原諒可補償的工期延誤　excusable and compensable delay
可原谅但不给予补偿的拖期/可原諒但不予補償的工期延誤　excusable but not compensable delay
可原谅的拖期/可原諒的工期延誤　excusable delay
可约过程/簡化過程　reduction process
可约马尔科夫链/可簡化馬可夫鏈　reducible Markov chains

可再生能源/可再生能源　reproducible energy, renewable energy
可再生自然资源/再生自然資源　renewable natural resources
可再贴现商业票据/可再貼現商業票據　commercial bill eligible for rediscount
可展期信用证/可展期信用狀　renewable credit
可支配收入/可支配所得　disposable income
可支配资力总额/可處分資源總額　total disposable means
可支取的资金/可支取的資金　drawable fund
可直接入库库存/直接入庫存貨,免驗入庫存貨　dock-to-stock inventory
可制造性/可製造性　manufacturability
可制造性设计/可製造性設計　design for manufacturability, DFM
可转换保险/可轉換保險　convertible insurance
可转换股票/可轉換股票　convertible stock
可转换性理论/可轉換性理論　convertibility theory
可转换优先股/可轉換優先股　convertible preferred stock
可转换债券/可轉換債券,可轉換公司債,可換股債券　convertible bond, bond convertible
可转换证券/可轉換證券　convertible security
可转让存款单/可轉讓存單　negotiable certificate of deposit
可转让单证/可轉讓單證　negotiable document
可转让定期存款/可轉讓定期存款　negotiable time deposit
可转让库单/可轉讓倉單,倉庫收據　negotiable warehouse receipt
可转让票据/可轉讓票據,流通票據,可過戶證券　negotiable bill, assignable instrument, negotiable instrument
可转让期票/可轉讓期票　negotiable promissory note
可转让提单/可轉讓提單　negotiable bill of lading
可转让提款单/可轉讓提款單　negotiable order of withdraw, NOW
可转让信用票据/可轉讓信用票據　negotiable credit instrument
可转让信用证/可轉讓信用狀　assignable credit, negotiable letter of credit, transferable letter of credit
可转让性/可轉移性　transferability
可转让许可证/可轉讓排放許可證　transferable permits
可转让债券/可轉讓債券,流通債券　transferable bond, negotiable bond
可转让账户/可轉讓賬戶　transferable account
可转让支付命令账户/可轉讓取款條賬戶,可轉讓提款指令賬戶　negotiable order of withdrawal account, NOW account
可转让支票/可轉讓支票,流通支票　negotiable cheque
可转让资产/可轉讓資產　transferable asset
可转移效用/具轉移性之效用　transferable utility
可追加记录型光盘/可錄寫一次光碟,光碟燒錄片　compact disc-recordable, CD-R
可追溯固定成本/可追溯固定成本　traceable fixed cost
可追溯性/追溯性　traceability
可自由兑换通货/可自由兌換貨幣　convertible currency
可自由支配开支/權衡性花費　discretionary spending
渴求产品/渴求產品　desirable product
克格茨检验/Klotz 檢定　Klotz's test
克拉克-格罗夫斯机制/克拉克-葛羅夫機制　Clark-Grove mechanism
克拉克税/克拉克賦稅　Clarke tax
克拉伦登宪章/克拉倫登憲章　Constitutions of Clarendon
克莱顿[反托拉斯]法/克萊頓反托拉斯法　Clayton antitrust act
克莱姆法则/克拉馬法則　Cramer's rule
克莱姆-冯·米塞斯拟合优度检验/克拉馬-洪密斜斯適合度檢定　Cramer-Von Mises goodness of fit test
克莱姆-拉奥不等式/克拉馬-羅不等式　Cramer-Rao inequality
克莱姆-拉奥下界/克拉馬-羅下限　Cramer-Rao lower bound
克莱姆-拉奥有效性/克拉馬-羅有效係數,克拉馬-羅有效度　Cramer-Rao efficiency
克雷格定理/Craig 定理　Craig's theorem
克雷格效应/Craig 效果　Craig effect
克利福-奥荷德检验/Cliff-Ord 檢定　Cliff-Ord test
克鲁斯凯统计量/Kruskal 統計量　Kruskal statistic
克鲁斯凯-沃利斯检验/Kruskal-Wallis 檢定　Kruskal-Wallis test
克罗内克矩阵积/Kronecker 矩陣乘積　Kronecker product of matrices
克罗内克设计积/Kronecker 設計乘積　Kronecker product of designs
克努特-维克方/Knut-Vik 方陣　Knut-Vik square
克托莱体重指数/Quetelet 體重指數　Quetelet's

body mass index
刻板印象/刻板印象　stereotype
刻板印象威胁/刻板印象威脅　stereotype threat
刻本/刻本　blockprinted edition, wood-block edition
客观法/客觀法　objective law
客观概率/客觀機率　objective probability
客观化/客觀化　objectification
客观评定法/客觀評定法　objective rating
客观性/客觀性　objectivity
客观证据/客觀證據　objective evidence
客观指标/客觀指數　objective index
客观主义/客觀主義　objectivism
客观主义学派/客觀主義學派　school of objectivism
客户/客户　client
客户承兑［汇票］/客户承兑［匯票］　customer acceptance
客户的可获得性/客户的可獲得性　customer availability
客户端/客户端,用户端　client
客户关系/客户關係,顧客關係　customer relationship
客户关系管理/客户關係管理,顧客關係管理　customer relationship management, CRM
客户关系管理系统/客户關係管理系統,顧客關係管理系統　customer relationship management system
客户结单/客户賬單　customer's statement
客户情报/客户情報　customer intelligence, prospect intelligence
客户驱动质量/客户驅動品質,顧客驅動品質　customer-driven quality
客户议价能力/購買商的議價能力　bargaining power of buyer
客户知识/客户知識　customer knowledge
客户追随者效应/客户效果,顧客效果　clientele effect
客体我/客我　me-self
客位/客位　etic
课税标准/課税標準,課税税基　tax criterion, tax basis
课税对象/課税客體　object of taxation
课税公平/課税公平　tax equity
课税主体/課税主體　subject of taxation
课题分类法/課題分類法　subject classification
课予义务诉讼/課予義務訴訟　demanding performance of liabilites lawsuit
肯道尔 τ/Kendall 的 τ,Kendall 等級相關係數　Kendall's tau, kendau's τ
肯德尔的 S 记分/Kendall 的 S 計分　Kendall's S-score
肯德尔偏相关系数/肯得偏相關係數,Kendall 偏相關係數　Kendall's partial correlation coefficient
啃老族/啃老族　youths living on the elder
空巢/空巢　empty nest
空巢家庭/空巢家庭　empty nest family
空巢老人/空巢老人　empty nester
空巢综合征/空巢症候群　emptiness syndrome, empty nest syndrome
空间不可能定理/空間不可能定律　spatial impossibility theorem
空间成本分析法/空間成本分析法　spatial cost analysis method
空间的生产/空間的生產　production of space
空间点过程/空間點過程　spatial point processes
空间非均匀性/空間非均勻性　spatial non-uniformity
空间非线性定价/空間非線性定價　spatial nonlinear pricing
空间分布/空間分布　spacial distribution
空间分类/空間分類　spatial classification
空间分析/空間分析　spatial analysis
空间格局/空間型態　spatial pattern
空间估计量/空間估計量　spatial estimator
空间寡头垄断/空間寡占　spatial oligopoly
空间管理/空間管理　space management
空间缓冲/空間緩衝　space buffer
空间回归模型/空間自我回歸模型　spatial autoregressive model
空间价格均衡/空間價格均衡　spatial price equilibrium
空间经济计量学/空間計量經濟學　spatial econometrics
空间竞争/空間競爭　spatial competition
空间竞争理论/空間競爭理論,霍德林理論　spatial competition theory
空间均衡分析/空間均衡分析　spatial equilibrium analysis
空间垄断/空間獨占　spatial monopoly
空间模型/空間模型　spatial model
空间频率/空間頻率　spatial frequency
空间频率响应/空間頻率回應　spatial frequency response
空间生产/空間生產　production in space
空间失配理论/空間不對稱理論　spatial mismatch theory
空间数据模型/空間資料模式　spatial data model
空间投票理论/空間投票理論　spatial theory of voting

空间系统样本/空間系統樣本　spatial systematic sample
空间相互作用/空間互動　spatial interaction
空间相互作用模型/空間互動模型　spatial interaction model
空间序列/空間數列　spatial series
空间自相关/空間自我相關　spatial autocorrelation
空距理论/空間理論　spatial theory
空卡运输/空陸聯運　airtruck
空气污染指标/空氣汙染指標　measures of air pollution
空气质量/空氣品質　air quality
空事件/空事件,零事件　null event
空手/空手　transport empty, transport unloaded
空头/空頭,短部位,作空　short interest, short position
空头股票/空頭股票　kiting stock
空头票据/空頭票據　kite bill
空头套期保值/賣出避險,空頭避險　short hedge
空头头寸/短部位,作空　short position
空头支票/空頭支票,拒付支票　accommodation kite, kiting cheque, dishonoured cheque
空心点/空心點　hickie
空心字/外框字,描邊字　outline font
空运进口提单/空運進口提單　import airway bill
空战法/空戰法　laws of aerial warfare
空张控制器/空張檢測器　no-sheet detector
空中劫持/空中劫持　aerial hijacking
孔版印刷/孔版印刷　permeographic printing
孔茨五职能说/孔茨五職能說　five management functions theory of Koontz
孔径/光圈　aperture
孔隙广告/孔隙廣告　interstitial advertisement
孔子礼治思想/孔子禮論　Li governance of Confucius
恐怖主义/恐怖主義　terrorism
恐慌汇率/恐慌匯率,下跌匯率　panic rate
恐慌价格/恐慌價格,下跌價格　panic price
恐惧要求/恐懼要求　fear appeal
空白背书/空白背書　blank endorsement, open endorsement, endorsement in blank
空白背书汇票/空白背書匯票　bill endorsed in blank
空白部分起脏/版面汙染　catch-up
空白承兑/空白承兑　acceptance in blank
空白犯罪构成/空白犯罪構成　blank constitution of a crime
空白票据/空白票據　blank bill
空白信用证/空白信用狀　blank credit
空白支票/空白支票　blank cheque
空白转让书/空白轉讓書,空白過戶憑證　blank transfer
空白罪状/空白罪狀　blank facts about a crime
空格检验/空格檢定　empty cell test
空闲能力分析/空閒能力分析　idle capability analysis
空闲时间/閒置時間　idle time
控告式诉讼/控告式訴訟　accusatory proceedings
控股公司/控股公司　controlling company, holding company
控股股东/控股股東　majority shareholder
控股投资/控股投資　investment holding
控股银行制度/控股銀行制度　share holding banking system
控诉证据/控訴證據　accusation evidence
控制变量/控制變數　control variable
控制变量技术/控制變數技術　control variate technique
控制变异/控制異變數　control variance
控制测量/管制規測　control gaging
控制测试/控制測試　test of control
控制处理/管制處理　control treatment
控制点/管制點　point of control, control point
控制风险/控制風險　control risk
控制环境/控制環境　control environment
控制[活动]/控制　control, controlling
控制计划/管制計劃　control plan
控制块/控制塊　control patch
控制论/控制[理]論　control theory, cybernetics
控制频率/控制頻率　control frequency
控制上限/管制上限　upper control limit, UCL
控制失灵/控制失靈　dysfunction of control
控制收敛定理/受制收斂定理　dominated convergence theorem
控制数/管制數　control number
控制数据/控制資料　control data
控制水平/管制水準　level of control, control level
控制图/控制圖,管制圖　control chart
D控制图/D管制圖　D-chart
s控制图/s管制圖　s-chart
控制图表/管制用紙　control sheet
控制图模式/管制圖型　control chart pattern
控制图因子/管制圖因子,管制圖因素　control chart factor
控制系统/控制系統,管制系統,操縱系統　control system
控制下限/管制下限　lower control limit, LCL

控制限/管制界限　control limit
控制限系数/管制界限係數　control limit factor
控制线/管制線　control line
控制因子/管制因子　control factor
控制源/控制點　locus of control
控制账目/統制賬戶　control account
控制账目计划/統制賬戶計劃　control account plan, CAP
口岸查验/口岸查驗　check and examination at ports
口岸检查机关/口岸檢查機關　inspection office at port
口碑/口碑　word of mouth, WOM
口碑营销/口碑行銷　word-of-mouth marketing
口承文化/口承文化　oral culture
口述调查/口述調查　oral survey
口述历史/口述歷史　oral history
口述作品/口述作品　oral works
口头报盘/口頭報價　verbal offer
口头传承/口述傳統,口說傳統　oral tradition
口头拍卖/口頭拍賣　oral auction
口头起诉/口頭起訴　oral complaint
口头情报/口頭情報　oral information
口头协定/口頭協定　oral agreement
口语/口語　verbal
扣缴/扣繳　withholding
扣缴义务人/扣繳義務人　withholding agent
扣押/扣押　seizure
扣押财产/扣押財產　seizure of property
苦役踏车/苦役踏車　treadmill of production
库存/庫存,存貨　inventory
库存变动/存貨變動　inventory change, change in stocks
库存策略/存貨政策　inventory policy
库存成本/存貨成本　inventory cost
库存出版物资金/庫存出版物資金　commodity stock capital
库存订货系统/庫存訂貨系統　inventory ordering system
库存费用/存貨成本　inventory cost
库存股/庫藏股　treasury stock
库存管理/存貨管理　inventory management
库存计划/存貨計劃　inventory planning
库存记录文件/盤存記錄檔　inventory record file
库存旧书目录/庫存舊書目錄　stock list
库存控制/存貨控制　inventory control
库存浪费/庫存浪費　inventory waste
库存量/存貨存量　inventory stock
库存模型/庫存模型,存貨模型　inventory model
库存商品/庫存商品　commodity stock
库存收据/庫存收據　inventory receipt
库存书/庫存書,存貨簿　stock book
库存损耗/庫存損耗　inventory deterioration
库存缩水/存貨縮減　inventory shrinkage
库存提成差价/庫存提成差價　stock price difference
库存投资/存貨投資　inventory investment
库存现金/庫存現金,庫存貨幣　cash in hand, vault cash
库存增长/存貨增加　increase in stocks
库存周期/庫存週期　inventory cycle time, stock cycle time
库存周转次数/存貨週轉次數　inventory turnover time
库存周转天数/存貨週轉天數　days inventory outstanding, inventory turnover days
库德-理查森公式/Kuder-Richardson 公式　Kuder-Richardson formula
库德职业兴趣量表/Kuder 職業興趣量表　Kuder occupational interest survey
库尔贝克-莱伯尔距离函数/Kullback-Leibler 距離函數　Kullback-Leibler distance function
库尔贝克-莱伯尔信息/Kullback-Leibler 訊息　Kullback-Leibler information
库房编号/庫房編號　warehouse number
库房排架/庫房排架　warehouse shelf
库房平面图/庫房平面圖　stack plan, storage plan
库克公共管理/庫克公共管理　Cook public administration
库克旅游计划法/庫克旅遊計劃法　Cook travelling plan method
库拉圈/庫拉圈　Kula ring
库尼亚斯不等式/Kounias 不等式　Kounias' inequality
库氏生涯决定社会学论/庫氏生涯決定社會學論　Krumboltz sociological theory of career
库位管理/庫位管理　stock management
库兹涅茨倒 U 型曲线/庫斯奈倒 U 型線　Kuznets inverted u-shaped curve
库兹涅茨假说/庫斯奈倒 U 型理論　Kuznets hypothesis
酷儿/酷兒　queer
夸富宴/誇富宴　potlatch
跨部门治理/跨部門治理　cross-sectoral governance
跨层次研究/跨層次研究　cross-level study
跨国并购/跨國并購　cross-border merger
跨国公司/跨國公司,國際公司　international corporation, multinational corporation,

multinational enterprise
跨国公司管理体制/跨國公司管理體制　management system of transnational corporation
跨国集团/跨國集團　multinational group
跨国界损害/跨國界損害　transboundary damages
跨国联合制/跨國聯合制　transnational combination system
跨国企业/跨國企業　multinational enterprise
跨国人力资源系统/跨國人力資源管理系統　transnational human resource system
跨国银行/跨國銀行　multinational bank, supernational bank, transnational bank
跨国战略/跨國策略　transnational strategy
跨国战略联盟/跨國策略聯盟　cross-border strategic alliance
跨国中央银行制度/跨國中央銀行制度　multinational central bank system
跨国主义/跨國主義　transnationalism
跨库检索/跨庫檢索　cross-search, cross-database search, integrated search
跨库检索系统/整合檢索系統　cross-database retrieval system, federated retrieval system, integerated retrieval system
跨媒体/跨媒體　cross-media
跨媒体出版技术/跨媒體出版技術　cross-media publishing technology
跨媒体传播/跨媒體傳播　cross-media dissemination
跨期贸易/跨代貿易　intertemporal trade
跨期模型/時際模型　intertemporal model
跨期套利/跨期套利　inter-period arbitrage
跨期预算约束/跨代預算模型　intertemporal budget constraint
跨区域流动/區域間移民　interregional migration
跨市套利/跨市套利,市場間套利　inter-market arbitrage
跨文化/跨文化　cross-cultural
跨文化比较/跨文化比較　cross-cultural comparison
跨文化冲突/跨文化衝突　cross-cultural conflict, cultural conflict
跨文化传播/跨文化傳播　cross-cultural communication
跨文化沟通/跨文化交流　cross-cultural communication
跨文化认同/跨文化認同　intercultural identity
跨文化社会心理学/跨文化社會心理學　cross-cultural social psychology
跨文化研究/跨文化研究,異文化研究　cross-cultural studies

跨文化意识/跨文化意識　cross-cultural awareness
跨学科流动/跨學科流動　inter disciplinary transfer
跨学科研究/跨領域研究　inter disciplinary research
跨页广告/跨頁廣告　double spread advertisement, double-page spread
跨语言[信息]检索/跨語言[資訊]檢索　cross language information retrieval
跨语种检索/跨語種檢索　cross language retrieval
跨越式发展/跨越式發展　great-leap-forward development
跨职能团队/跨部門合作團隊　cross-function team
跨专业服务/跨專業服務　cross-disciplinary service
会计/會計　accountant, accounting
会计报表附注/會計報表附注　financial statement footnote
会计差错/會計差錯　accounting error
会计成本/會計成本　accounting cost
会计档案/會計檔案　accounting files
会计等式/會計方程式,會計恆等式　accounting equation
会计分录/會計分錄　accounting entry
会计估计变更/會計估計變更　change in accounting estimate
会计关系/會計關係　accounting relationship
会计国际化/會計國際化　internationalization of accounting
会计核算/會計估計　accounting calculation
会计机构/會計機構　accounting agencies
会计基本假设/會計假定　accounting postulate, accounting assumption
会计计量/會計衡量　accounting measurement
会计记录/會計記賬　accounting recording
会计监督/會計監督　accounting supervision
会计科目/會計科目,賬目名稱　account title
会计控制/會計控制　accounting control
会计利润/會計利潤　accounting profits
会计年度/會計年度　fiscal year
会计凭证/會計憑證　accounting voucher
会计期间假设/會計期間假設　accounting period postulate
会计确认/會計確認　accounting recognition
会计人员/會計人員　accountant, accounting personnel
会计事项/會計事項　accounting event
会计透明度/會計透明度　accounting transparency
会计稳健性/會計穩健性　accounting conservatism
会计系统/會計系統,會計制度　accounting system
会计信息/會計情報,會計資料　accounting

information
会计信息含量/會計資訊內涵　accounting information content
会计信息失真/會計資訊失真　accounting information distortion
会计信息系统/會計情報制度,會計資料系統　accounting information system
会计学/會計學　accounting
会计循环/會計循環　accounting cycle
会计要素/會計要素　accounting element
会计责任/會計責任　accounting responsibility
会计账簿/會計簿籍　accounting book
会计政策/會計政策　accounting policy
会计政策变更/會計政策變更　change in accounting policy
会计主体假设/會計主體假設　accounting entity postulate
会计准则/會計標準　accounting standard
块抽样/塊狀抽樣　chunk sampling
块对角/區塊對角化　block-diagonal
块效应/集區影響　block effect
块状图/區集圖　block diagram
块状需求/塊狀需求　lumpy demand
快报/時事通訊,業務通訊　newsletter
快速换模法/分鐘內更換模具法　single minute exchange of die procedure, SMED procedure
快速消费品/快速消費品　fast-moving consumer goods, FMCGs
快速仲裁/簡易仲裁　expedited arbitration
快周期市场/快週期市場　fast-cycle market
宽大误差/仁慈誤差,寬容評價誤差　leniency error
宽带网络/寬頻網路　broadband network
宽带薪资结构/扁平寬幅薪資結構　broadbanding pay structure
宽度/寬度　width
宽放率/寬放率　time ratio
宽放时间/時間寬放　allowance, time allowance
宽高比/寬高比,縱橫比　aspect ratio
宽跨式期权/跨騎買賣權　straddle
宽猛相济/寬猛相濟　use a proper mixture of severity and gentleness
宽频带/寬頻　broad band
宽容/政策寬容　forbearance
宽松货币政策/寬鬆貨幣政策,低利率政策　cheap money policy, easy money policy
宽松型劳动力市场/鬆散的勞動市場　loose labor markets
款目/款目,項,分錄　item, entry
款目词/款目字　entry word
矿产资源法/礦產資源法　mineral resources law
矿业统计/礦業統計　statistics of mineral industry, mining statistics
框架分析/框架分析　frame analysis
框架论/框架理論　framing theory
框架效应/框架效應　framing effect
亏本出口/流血輸出　bleeding export
亏本出售/虧本出售　sacrifice sale
亏舱费/虧艙費　dead freight
亏量/失效度,虧數　deficiency
亏损标/赤字標　deficit tender
亏损表/虧損表　statement of deficit
奎里蒂法/奎里蒂法　jus Quiritium
昆努依尔检验/Quenouille檢定　Quenouille's test
捆绑商品/被搭售產品　tied goods
捆绑销售/捆綁銷售　bundling
扩大基期/擴大基期　broadened base
扩大量/擴大量　extensive magnitude
扩大再生产/擴大再生產　reproduction on an extended scale
扩检/擴展搜索　search expansion
扩散/擴散　diffusion
扩散过程/擴散過程　diffusion process
扩散性/擴散性　diffusibility
扩散指数/擴散指數　diffusion index
扩印/放大曬印　enlarging print
扩展保险范围/增列保險責任範圍　extended coverage
扩展的色域/擴展的色域　extended gamut
扩展服务项目/推廣服務　outreach programme
扩展个案法/擴展個案法　extended case study
扩展结构只读式光盘/延展唯讀光碟　compact-read only memory-extended architecture, CD-ROM-XA
扩展性期望效用函数理论/一般化預期效用理論　generalized expected utility theory
扩张紧缩期权/擴張緊縮選擇權　expanded or contracted option
扩张路径/擴張路徑　expansion path
扩张政策/擴張政策　expansionary policy

L

垃圾处理/垃圾處理　refuse disposal
垃圾桶决策模式/垃圾筒模型　garbage can policy-making model
垃圾邮件/垃圾郵件　spam
垃圾债券/垃圾債券　junk bond
拉奥-布莱克威尔定理/Rao-Blackwell 定理　Rao-Blackwell theorem
拉奥记分检验/Rao 計分檢定　Rao's scoring test
拉奥-库珀模型/Rao-Kupper 模型　Rao-Kupper model
拉德布鲁赫/拉德布魯赫　Gustav Radbruch
拉丁方/拉丁方陣　Latin square
拉丁方变换集/拉丁方陣的變換集合　transformation set of Latin squares
拉丁方分层/拉丁方陣分層　Latin square stratification
拉丁方设计/拉丁方陣設計　Latin square design
拉丁方种类/拉丁方陣類　species of Latin squares
拉丁矩形/拉丁矩形　Latin rectangle
拉丁立方/拉丁立方體　Latin cube
拉丁美洲共同市场/拉丁美洲共同市場　Latin American common market
拉丁美洲经济体系/拉丁美洲經濟體系　Latin American Economic System
拉丁美洲自由贸易市场/拉丁美洲自由貿易市場　Latin American Free Trade Market
拉丁美洲自由贸易协会/拉丁美洲自由貿易協會　Latin American Free Trade Association
拉东-尼科迪姆导数/Radon-Nikodym 導數　Radon-Nikodym derivative
拉东-尼科迪姆定理/Radon-Nikodym 定理　Radon-Nikodym theorem
拉动式供应链/拉動式供應鏈　pull supply chain
拉断强度/張力強度　tensile strength
拉弗曲线/拉法爾曲線　Laffer curve
拉格朗日乘数法/拉格朗日乘數法　Lagrange multiplier method
拉格朗日乘数检验/拉格朗日乘數檢定　Lagrange multiplier test
拉格朗日乘数统计量/拉格朗日乘數統計量　Lagrange multiplier statistic
拉格朗日函数/拉格朗日函數　Lagrange function
拉格瑞多项式/Laguerre 多項式　Laguerre polynomials
拉克斯-密格拉蒙定理/拉克斯-米爾格雷定理　Lax-Milgram theorem
拉美模式/拉美模式　Latin American model
拉姆达图/λ 圖　lambda gram, λ gram
拉姆达准则/λ 準則　lambda criterion, λ criterion
拉姆齐法则/倫賽法則　Remsey rule
拉普拉斯变换/Laplace 變換　Laplace transform
拉普拉斯定理/Laplace 定理　Laplace's theorem
拉普拉斯分布/Laplace 分布, Laplace 分配　Laplace distribution
拉普拉斯连贯定理/Laplace 接續法則　Laplace's law of succession
拉瑟瑙管理思想/拉瑟瑙管理思想　management thought of Rathenau
拉氏价格指数/拉氏物價指數　Laspeyres price index
拉式策略/拉式策略　pull strategy
拉式系统/拉式[生產]系統　pull system
拉斯贝尔指数/拉氏指數　Laspeyres' index
拉斯基/拉斯基　Harold Joseph Laski
拉页测试/書頁拉力測試　pull test
拉页广告/雜誌扉頁廣告　gatefold
拉兹/拉茲　Joseph Raz
邋遢本/邋遢本　corrupted edition, sloppy edition
蜡盘/蠟　wax
来料加工/來料加工　processing of imported materials
来料加工贸易/委託加工　trade of processing with customer's material
来源表/來源表　source table
来源分析/來源分析　stream analysis
来源检验/來源檢驗　source inspection
来源联系/來源聯繫　source relation
来源识别码/來源識別碼　source identified code, SID
来源原则/來源原則　principle of provenance
莱昂法典/萊昂法典　Fuero de Espanoles
莱比锡实验室/萊比錫實驗室　Leipzig lab
莱根德多项式/Legendre 多項式　Legendre

polynomials
莱克塞斯分布/Lexian 分布, Lexian 分配　Lexian distributions
莱曼检验/Lehmann 檢定　Lehmann's test
莱曼选择/Lehmann 選擇　Lehmann alternatives
莱斯利检验/Leslie 檢定　Leslie's test
赖斯伯利斯公式/拉氏公式　Laspeyres' formula
赖特阶级分析法/賴特階級分類　Wright class scheme
兰格模型/蘭格模式　Lange mode
兰开斯特卡方划分/Lancaster 卡方分割　Lancaster's partition of chi-squares
兰台/蘭臺　Lantai
栏目/欄目, 專欄　column
蓝筹股/績優股　blue chip
蓝海战略/藍海戰略　blue ocean strategy
蓝领工人/藍領工人　blue-collar worker
蓝皮书/藍本書　blue book
蓝牙/藍牙　bluetooth
蓝印本/藍印本　blue print
篮中训练/籃中訓練　in-basket training
滥用支配地位/優勢地位的濫用　abuse of dominant position
滥用职权罪/濫用職權罪　crime of abusing the office
郎吏社会/郎吏社會　court officials category
郎特里管理思想/郎特里管理思想　management thought of Rowntree
浪费/浪費　waste
劳埃德法/Lloyd 法　Lloyd's method
劳动/勞動　labor
劳动安全法规/勞動安全規範　occupational safety regulation
劳动安全基准/勞動安全基準　Labor Safety Standards
劳动保护/勞動保護　labor protection
劳动保护法/勞工保護法　protective labor laws
劳动保护管理制度/勞動保護管理體制　administrative system of labor protection
劳动保险/勞工保險　labor insurance
劳动报酬/勞動報酬　employment payment
劳动边际产量/勞動邊際產量　marginal product of labor
劳动参与率/勞動參與率　labor force participation rate
劳动成本指数/單位勞動成本指數　unit labor cost index
劳动的性别分工/勞動的性別分工　gender division of labor

劳动地域分工/勞動的地區分工　regional division of labor
劳动定额/勞動定額, 勞動配額　labor quota
劳动定员/勞動定員　manpower quota
劳动对象/勞動對象　labor object
劳动二重性/勞動二重性　two fold character of labour
劳动法/勞動法, 勞工法　labor law
劳动分工/勞動分工　division of labor
劳动服务贸易/勞務貿易　labour service trade
劳动供给/勞動供給　labor supply, supply of labor
劳动供给曲线/勞動供給曲線　labor supply curve
劳动供给弹性/勞動供給彈性　elasticity of labor supply
劳动关系/勞動關係, 勞工關係, 勞資關係　labor relation, labor relationship
劳动关系顾问/勞動關係顧問　labor relation consultant
劳动管理/勞工管理　labor management
劳动规章制度/勞動規章制度　labor rules and regulations
劳动过程/勞動過程　labor process
劳动合成谬误/勞動合成謬誤　lump-of-labor fallacy
劳动合同/勞動合同, 勞動契約　labor contract
劳动合同的变更/勞動合同的變更　modification of labor contract
劳动合同的解除/勞動合同的解除　discharge of labor contract
劳动合同的终止/勞動合同的終止　termination of labor contract
劳动合同法/勞動合同法　labor contract law
劳动合同制/勞動合同制　labor contract system
劳动基准/勞動標準　labor standards
劳动纪律/勞動紀律　labor discipline
劳动价值论/勞動價值說　labor theory of value
劳动监察/勞動監察　labor monitoring
劳动监察员/勞動監察員　labor supervisor
劳动监督检查/勞動監督檢查　labor supervision and inspection
劳动交换/勞動交換　employment agencies, labor exchange
劳动节约型/節省勞動型　labor-saving
劳动节约型技术/節省勞動型技術　labor-saving technology
劳动节约型技术进步/節省勞動或多用資本的技術進步　labor-saving or capital-using technology progress
劳动解构/勞動解構　decomposition of labor

劳动经济学/勞動經濟學 labor economics
劳动纠纷/勞資爭議 labor dispute
劳动就业权/就業權 employment right
劳动空间分工/空間勞動分工 spatial division of labor
劳动力/勞動力,勞工 labor force, laborer
劳动力边际成本/勞動邊際成本 marginal cost of labor
劳动力变动统计/勞動力異動統計 labor turnover statistics
劳动力成本/勞動力成本 labor cost
劳动力调查/勞動力調查 labor force survey
劳动力计划管理/勞動力計劃管理 manpower planning management
劳动力价格/勞動力價格 price of labor
劳动力价值/勞動力價值 value of labor force
劳动力流动/勞動力流動性,勞工移動 labor mobility, labor movement, mobility of labor
劳动力流动率/員工進退率 labor turnover rate
劳动力人口/勞動力人口 labor force population
劳动力商品/勞動力商品 labour-power as a commodity
劳动力市场/勞動市場 labor market
劳动力市场存量流量模型/勞動市場存量流量模型 stock-flow model of labor market
劳动力市场分割理论/勞動力市場分割理論 labor market segmentation theory
劳动力市场歧视/勞動市場歧視 labor market discrimination
劳动力统计/勞動力統計 labor force statistics
劳动力无限供给/勞動力無限供給 unlimited supplies of labor
劳动力无限供应/無限勞動力供給 boundless supply of labor
劳动力需求/勞動力需求 labor demand
劳动力指数/勞動力指數 index of labor
劳动密集程度/勞力投入密集度 labor intensity
劳动密集型/勞動密集 labor intensive
劳动密集型产品/勞力密集產品 labor intensive product
劳动密集型产业/勞力密集產業 labor intensive industry
劳动密集型技术/勞力密集技術 labor intensive techniques
劳动密集型企业/勞力密集企業 labor intensive enterprise
劳动能力鉴定/勞動能力鑑定 labor capacity appraisal

劳动年龄/勞動年齡 working age
劳动年龄人口/工作年齡人口 working age population
劳动歧视/勞動歧視 labor discrimination
劳动强度/勞動強度 intensity of labour
劳动权/勞動權 labor rights
劳动生产率/勞動生產率,勞動生產力 labor productivity, productivity of labor
劳动生产率指数/勞動生產率指數 labor productivity index
劳动使用型技术/多用勞動的技術 labor-using technology
劳动市场歧视/勞動市場歧視 labor market discrimination
劳动收入/勞動所得 labor income
劳动手段/勞動資料 means of labor
劳动统计/勞工統計 labor statistics
劳动卫生法规/職業衛生法規 occupational health regulation
劳动卫生基准/勞動衛生基準 labor health standards
劳动消耗定额/勞動定額 labor consumption quota
劳动-休闲权衡/勞動休閒取捨 labor-leisure tradeoff
劳动需求的工资弹性/勞動需求的工資彈性 wage elasticity of labor demand
劳动需求弹性/勞動需求彈性 elasticity of labor demand, labor demand elasticities
劳动与休闲的替代效应/勞動和閒暇之間的替代效應 substitution effect between labor and leisure
劳动责任/勞動責任 work duty
劳动增强型/加強勞動型 labor-augmenting
劳动增强型技术进步/加強勞動型技術進步 labor-augmenting techincal progress
劳动者利益/勞動者利益 interest of laborer
劳动争议/勞工糾紛,勞資糾紛 labor disputes
劳动争议案件/勞資糾紛事件 events of labor dispute
劳动争议处理机构/勞動紛爭仲裁機構 disposing agencies of labor dispute
劳动争议诉讼/勞動爭議訴訟 labor dispute litigation
劳动争议调解/勞動爭議調解,勞動糾紛調解 mediation of labor dispute
劳动争议调解仲裁法/勞動爭議調解仲裁法 mediation and arbitration of labor disputes law
劳动争议仲裁/勞動爭議仲裁,勞資爭議仲裁 arbitration of labor disputes

劳动争议仲裁委员会/勞動爭議仲裁委員會 labor dispute arbitration committee
劳动专业化/勞工專業化 specialization of labor
劳动资料/勞動資料 means of labor
劳动总产量/勞動總產出 total product of labor
劳动组织优化/勞動組織優化 optimization of labor organization
劳工联合会/勞工聯盟 labor federation
劳工赔偿法/工人補償立法 workmen's compensation act
劳工输入国/勞工輸入國 labor importing country
劳伦斯-洛希权变论/勞倫斯-洛希權變論 contingency theory of Lawrence-Lorsch
劳氏海损契约/勞氏海損契約 Lloyd's average bond
劳务分包/勞務分包 labor subcontract
劳务合同/勞務合同 contract for labour service
劳务进口/勞務進口 service import
劳务派遣/勞務派遣 labor dispatch
劳务派遣服务/勞務派遣服務 dispatch service
劳务派遣协议/勞務派遣協議 labor dispatch agreement
劳资关系/勞資關係 labor-capital relation, management-union relation
老龄工作/老齡工作 work concerning the aging
老龄化/老化 aging
老龄化进程/老化過程 aging process
老龄化社会/老人社會,高齡化社會 aging society
老龄化指数/老化指數,老年幼年比 aging index, aged-child ratio
老龄问题/老齡問題,老年問題 aging problem
老龄协会/老齡協會 elderly association
老年/老年 senility
老年传播/老人傳播 aging communication
老年公寓/老年公寓 elderly apartment
老年忽视/老年忽視 neglect of the elderly
老年活动中心/老人活動中心 activity centre for the elderly
老年教育学/老年教育學 pedagogy of the elderly
老年经济学/老年經濟學 economics of the elderly
老年期/老年期 old age
老年歧视/老年歧視,年齡歧視 age discrimination
老年人/老年人 elderly people
老年人福利/老年人福利 welfare for the old
老年人口学/老年人口學 demography of the elderly
老年人权益保障法/老年人權益保障法 law on protection of rights and interests of the elderly
老年社会保障/老年社會保障 social security for the elderly
老年社会服务/老年社會服務 social service for the elderly
老年社会工作/老年社會工作 social work for the elderly
老年社会学/老年社會學 sociology of aging
老年团体/老年團體 elderly group
老年问题/老年問題,老齡問題 aging problem
老年系数/老年係數 old population coefficient, proportion of old population
老年心理学/老年心理學 psychology of aging
老年型人口/老年型人口 old population
老年学/老人學 gerontology
老年亚文化群理论/老年亞文化群理論 elderly subculture theory
老年医学/老人醫學 geriatrics
老人传播/老人傳播 aging communication
老人福利院/老人福利院 elderly home
老少残疾/老少殘疾 young and old or disabled
老中产阶级/舊中產階級,舊中等階級 old middle class
老子辩证思想/老子人學思想 dialectic thought of Lao-tzu
老字号/老字號 an old and famous shop or enterprise
乐观估计时间/樂觀時間估計 optimistic time estimate
乐观准则/樂觀準則 optimistic criterion
勒贝格测度/Lebesgue 测度 Lebesgue measure
勒口/勒口 flap
勒纳对称定理/婁納對稱性定理 lerner symmetry theorem
勒纳垄断力指数/獨占力的婁納指標 lerner index of monopoly power
勒纳指数/婁納指數 lerner index
勒夏特列的法国组织协会/勒夏特列的法國組織協會 French Organization Association of Le Chatelier
雷定三因素领导效率模式/雷定三因素領導效率模式 three dimensional leadership efficiency model of Reddin
雷可夫定理/Raikov 定理 Raikov's theorem
累犯/累犯 repeat offender
累积发病率/累積發生率 cumulative incidence rate
累积分布/累積分布,累積分配 cumulative distribution
累积分布函数/累積分布函數,累加分配函數 cumulative distribution function, CDF
累积概率分布/累積機率分布,累積機率分配

cumulative probability distribution
累积概率函数/累加機率函數　cumulative probability function
累积过程/累積過程　cumulative process, accumulated process
累积和分布/累積和分布　cumulative sum distribution
累积和控制图/累積和管制圖　cumulative sum control chart
累积和图/累積和圖　cumulative sum chart
累积[离]差/累積離差　accumulated deviation
累积联合概率函数/累加聯合機率函數　cumulative joint probability function
累积量/累積量　cumulant
累积量表/古特曼量表　Guttman scale
累积量母函数/累積量生成函數　cumulant generating function
累积频率/累積次數　cumulative frequency, accumulated frequency
累积频率表/累積次數表　cumulative frequency table
累积频率多边形/累積次數多邊形　cumulative frequency polygon
累积频率分布/累積次數分布　cumulative frequency distribution
累积频率曲线/累積次數曲線　cumulative frequency curve
累积频数/累積次數　cumulative frequency, accumulated frequency
累积频数表/累積次數表　cumulative frequency table
累积频数曲线/累積次數曲線　cumulative frequency curve
累积平方和/累加均方　cumulative sum of squares
累积平均图/累積平均數圖　cumulative average chart
累积曲线/累積曲線,肩形曲線,累積次數圖　cumulative curve, ogive
累积寿命期/累積壽命期　addition of life length
累积死亡率/累積死亡率　cumulative mortality rate
累积损坏/累積損壞　cumulative damage
累积索引/累積索引　cumulative index
累积投票制度/累積投票制　cumulative voting
累积危险函数/累積危險函數　cumulative hazard function
累积误差/累積誤差　cumulative error
累积相对频率/累加相對次數　cumulative relation frequency
累积相对频率分布/累加相對次數分配　cumulative relative frequency distribution

累积相对频率曲线/累加相對次數曲線　cumulative relative frequency curve
累积正态分布/累積常態分布,累積常態分配　cumulative normal distribution
累计测时法/累計測時法　cumulative timing
累计额/累進總和　progressive total
累计方差贡献率/累計方差貢獻率　cumulative variance contribution rate
累计和控制图/累計和管制圖　cumulative sum control chart
累计净收益计算书/累計淨收益計算書　statement of accumulated net income
累计频率分布/累積次數分布表　cumulative frequency distribution
累计频率曲线图/累積次數曲線圖　cumulative frequency curve chart
累计频率直方图/累積次數多邊形　cumulative frequency polygon
累计频数曲线图/累積次數曲線圖　cumulative frequency curve chart
累计受众/累計受眾　cumulative audience
累计提前期/累計前置時間　cumulative lead time, aggregate lead time
累加平均数/累進平均數　progressive average
累进税/累進稅　progressive tax
累进税率/累進稅率　progressive tax rate
累退税/累退稅　regressive tax, regressive taxation
累退税率/遞減累進稅率　degressive tax rate
类/類　class
类比式政策构建方法/類比規劃　analogous formulation
类别/類別　category
类别化/分類　classification
类分布/類別分布　categorical distribution
k类估计量/k類估計量　k-class estimator
类合并/類合併　pooling of classes
类户分类法/類戶分類法　category and name classification
类列/陣列　array
类名/類名　class term, class name
γ类模型/γ模型　γ model
δ类模型/δ模型　δ model
类目/類目　class
类目参照/類目參照　class reference
类目仿分/類目仿分　subdivision by analogy
类目设置/類別設定　class setting, set-up of classes
类似服务/類似服務　similar services
类似商品/類似商品　similar goods

类图/類圖　class diagram
类推性原理/同型原理　principle of analogy
类型/類型　genres
类罪名/類罪名　category charge
冷冻干燥/冷凍乾燥法　freeze drying
冷媒介/冷媒介,涼媒介　cool medium, cool meida
冷门债券/登记交易债券　cabinet bond
离岸价[格]/離岸價格,發貨地價格　free on board, FOB
离岸银行业务/境外金融　offshore banking
离别情绪/離別情緒　separation mood
离差/離差,偏差　deviation
离差平方和/離差平方和　sum of squares of deviations
离婚/離婚　divorce
离婚率/離婚率　divorce rate
离婚准据法/離婚準據法　applicable law of divorce
离群值/離群[觀測]值,奇異值　outlier
离群值倾向分布/離群值傾向的分布　outlier prone distribution
离散/離勢　dispersion
离散变量/離散變數　discrete variable
离散测度/離勢測度　measures of dispersion
离散的/離散的　discrete
离散订货量/離散訂貨量　discrete order quantity
离散度/分割離度　spread of separation
离散对数正态分布/離散對數常態分布,離散對數常態分配　discrete lognormal distribution
离散范围/離勢全距　range of dispersion
离散分布/離散分布,離散分配　discrete distribution
离散分布原理/離散分布原理　discrete distribution principle
离散分析/離勢分析　analysis of dispersion
离散概率法则/離散機率法則　discrete probability law
离散概率分布/離散型機率分布,離散型機率分配　discrete probability distribution
离散过程/離散過程　discrete process
离散拣货/個別訂單揀貨　discrete order picking
离散矩形分布/離散矩形分布,離散矩形分配　discrete rectangular distribution
离散矩阵/離勢矩陣　dispersion matrix
离散均匀分布/離散單一分配　discrete uniform distribution
离散空间/離散空間　discrete space
离散幂级数分布/離散冪級數分布,離散冪級數分配　discrete power series distribution
离散敏感度/離勢敏感度　sensitivity of dispersion

离散牛顿法/離散型牛頓法　discrete Newton method
离散帕累托分布/離散 Pareto 分布,離散 Pareto 分配　discrete Pareto distribution
离散频率函数/離散次數函數　discrete frequency function
离散频谱/離散質譜　discrete spectrum
离散频数函数/離散次數函數　discrete frequency function
离散趋势/離勢趨勢　dispersion tendency
离散设计/離散設計　discrete design
离散时间决策过程/離散時間決策過程　discrete time decision process
离散时间马尔可夫链/離散時間馬可夫鏈　discrete-time Markov chain
离散数据/離散資料　discrete data
离散随机变量/離散隨機變數　discrete random variable
离散随机过程/離散隨機過程　discrete stochastic process
离散位置族/離散位置族　discrete location family
离散系数/離散係數,散布係數　coefficient of divergence, coefficient of dispersion
离散型动态投入产出模型/離散型動態投入產出模型　dynamic input-output model in discrete form
离散型生产/離散型生產,離散式生產　discrete production
离散选择模型/離散選擇模型　discrete choice model
离散指数/離勢指數　dispersion index
离散指数族/離散指數族　discrete exponential family
离散最优设计/離散最適設計　discrete optimal design
离散最优线性设计/離散型最適線性設計　discrete linear-optimal design
离土不离乡/離土不離鄉　leave the farmland but not one's hometown
离线/離線　off line
离线观看/離線觀看　off line viewing
离线归档/離線歸檔,線外歸檔　off line filing
离线检测/離線檢測　off line inspection
离线浏览/離線流覽　off line browse
离线模式/離線模式　off line mode
离线下载/離線下載　off line download
离线载体/離線載體　off line carrier
离校年龄/離校年齡　school-leaving age
离休/離休　leave position to rest
离职/離職　turnover
离职率/離職率,辭職率　quit rate, separation rate
离职者/離職者　job leavers

离子成像/離子成像　ionography
礼不下庶人,刑不上大夫/禮不下庶人,刑不上大夫　criminal law not applying to the senior officials and the etiquette not applying to the common people
礼法合一/禮法合一　combine with the law and etiquette
礼教/禮教　feudal ethical and rites
礼品订阅/禮品訂閱　gift subscription
礼物/禮品　gift
礼物交换/禮物交換　gift exchange
礼仪/禮節　etiquette
礼治/禮治　rule by rites, rule of courtesy
礼治秩序/禮治秩序　rule of rite
李嘉图等价定理/李嘉圖等值定理,李嘉圖對等　Ricardian equivalence, Ricardian equivalence theorem
李嘉图经济/李嘉圖經濟　Ricardian economy
李嘉图贸易模型/李嘉圖貿易模型　Ricardian trade model
李嘉图模型/李嘉圖模型　Ricardian model
李嘉图派社会主义者/李嘉圖派社會主義者　Ricardian socialist
李嘉图群氓假设/李嘉圖群氓假設　Rabble hypothesis of Ricardo
李嘉图学派/李嘉圖學派　Ricardian school
李克特[态度]量表/李克特式[態度]量表　Likert-type attitude scale, Likert-type scale
李斯特的经济发展阶段理论/李斯特經濟發展階段論　List's theory of stages regional economic growth
李特尔公式/立特公式　Little formula
李雅普诺夫定理/李昂普諾夫定理　Lyapunov theorem
李约瑟命题/李約瑟命題　Needham thesis
里阿波夫不等式/Liapounov 不等式　Liapounov's inequality
里阿波夫定理/Liapounov 定理　Liapounov's theorem
里阿波夫条件/Liapounov 條件　Liapounov's condition
里昂惕夫悖论/李昂鐵夫矛盾　Leontief paradox
里昂惕夫表/李昂鐵夫表,投入產出表　Leontief table
里程碑计划法/里程碑計劃法　milestone planning approach
里程碑事件/里程碑事件　milestone event
里程碑图/里程碑圖　milestone diagram
里坊制/里坊制　fang
里斯-费希尔定理/黎氏-費雪理論　Riesz-Fischer theorem
理舱费在内的船上交货价/理艙費在內的船上交貨價　free on board stowed
理查森区域经济增长模式/理查森區域經濟成長模型　Richardson regional economic growth model
理藩院/理藩院　Lifan Yuan
理合/理合　lihe
理化检验/理化檢驗　physical and chemical test
理货/理貨　tally
理校法/理校法　collation method according to general studies, collate without any books and materials
BI 理论/映像原理　brand image theory, image theory
X 理论/X 理論　X theory
Y 理论/Y 理論　Y theory
Z 理论/Z 理論　Z theory
理论编码/理論編碼　theoretical coding
理论变量/理論變數　theoretical variable
理论抽样/理論抽樣,理論性取樣　theoretical sampling
理论档案学/理論檔案學　theoretical archival science, study of archival theory
理论分布/理論分布　theoretical distribution
理论概率/理論機率　theoretical probability
理论检验/理論驗證　theory testing
理论建构/理論建構　theory construction, theory building
理论矩/理論動差　theoretical moment
理论均值/理論平均數　theoretical mean
理论框架/理論架構　theoretical framework
X 理论-Y 理论/X 理論-Y 理論　X theory-Y theory
理论频数/理論次數　theoretical frequencie
理论情报学/理論資訊科學　theoretical information science
理论统计学/理論統計學　theoretical statistics
理论图书馆学/理論圖書館學　theoretical library science
理论误差/理論誤差　theoretical error
理论性编码/理論編碼　theoretical coding
理论油墨容积/理論油墨容積　theoretical ink volume
理论预测/理論預測　theoretical forecasting
理论知识/理論知識　theoretical knowledge
理论众数/理論眾數　theoretical mode
理赔/理賠　payment of claim, claim settlement
理赔代理人/理賠代理人　claim settling agent
理赔费/理賠費　claim settling fee

理赔数据/醫療[保險]給付資料　claim data
理想点/理想點　ideal point
理想公式/理想公式　ideal formula
理想解/理想解　ideal solution
理想社会理论/理想社會學說　ideal society theory
理想指数/理想指數　ideal index number
理想质量/理想品質　ideal quality
理想主义/理想主義　idealism
理性/理性　reason
理性的铁笼/理性的鐵籠　iron cage of rationality
理性犯罪/理性犯罪　rational crime
理性决策/理性決策　rational decision making
理性决策模型/理性決策模型,理性決策模式　rational decision model
理性蒙太奇/理性蒙太奇　rational montage
理性情绪疗法/理情治療法　rational emotive therapy
理性傻瓜/理性的傻子　rational fools
理性行为公理/理性行爲公理　rational behavior axiom
理性选择/理性選擇　rational choice
理性选择理论/理性選擇理論　rational choice theory
理性预期/理性預期　rational expectations
理性预期宏观经济学/理性預期宏觀經濟學　rational expectations macroeconomics
理性预期假说/理性預期假說　rational expectations hypothesis
理性预期均衡/理性預期均衡　rational expectations equilibrium
理性预期模型/理性預期模型　rational expectation model
理性预期学派/理性預期學派　rational expectations school
理性资本主义/理性資本主義　rational capitalism
力场分析/力場分析法　force field analysis
历期分析/貫時分析,長期資料分析　longitudinal analysis
历时效应/階段效果　period effect
历时性/歷時[的]　diachronic
历史成本/歷史成本　historical cost
历史成本会计/歷史成本會計　historical cost accounting
历史档案/歷史檔案　historical archive
历史档案馆/歷史檔案館　historical archives
历史地理学/歷史地理學　historical geography
历史多元论/歷史多元論　historical pluralism
历史法学派/歷史法學派　historical school of law
历史汇率/歷史匯率　historical rate
历史价值/歷史價值　historical value

历史解释/歷史解釋　historical interpreatation
历史联系/歷史聯繫　historical relation
历史模拟法/歷史模擬法　historical simulation method
历史人口学/歷史人口學　historical demography
历史人类学/歷史人類學　historical anthropology
历史社会学/歷史社會學　historical sociology
历史时间/歷史時間　historical time
历史事件简介/歷史事件簡介　brief introduction of historical events
历史文献/歷史檔案文件　historical document
历史信息/歷史資訊　historical information
历史性海湾/歷史性海灣　historic bays
历史性权利/歷史性權利　historical right, historical title
历史学派/歷史學派　historical school
立案/立案　filing a case
立案管辖/立案管轄　jurisdiction over placing cases on file
立案监督/立案監督　supervision over filing a case
立场论/立場理論,立足點理論　standpoint theory
立档单位/立檔單位　fonds constituting unit
立档单位与全宗历史考证/立檔單位與全宗歷史考證　archive unit and historical textual criticism of fonds
立地指数/地位指數　site index
立法/立法　legislation
立法程序/立法程式　legislative process
立法的基本原则/立法的基本原則　the basic principles of legislative
立法规划/立法規劃　legislative plan
立法机关/立法機構　legislature
立法技术/立法技術　legislative technology
立法监督/立法監督　legislative oversight
立法解释/立法解釋　legislative interpretation
立法权/立法權　legislative power
立法提案权/立法提案權　legislative proposal power
立法体系/立法體系　legislative system
立法学/立法學　science of legislation
立法预测/立法預測　legislative prediction
立法职能/立法職能　legislative function
立功/立功　meritorious service
立即付款/立即付款　prompt payment
立即付现/立即付現　immediate cash
立即交货/立即交貨　immediate delivery
立即支付/立即支付　immediate payment
立卷特征/立卷特徵　filing features
立体地图/立體地圖　solid map

立体电影/立體電影 anaglyph, stereoscopic film, three-dimensional film
立体格[子]方/立方格子 cubic lattice
立体格[子]设计/立方格子設計 cubic lattice design
立体交叉布局/立體交叉布局 vertical and crisscross layout
立体商标/立體商標 three-dimensional trademark
立体声/身歷聲 dimensional sound
立体声唱片/身歷聲唱片 stereophonic record
立体声拾音技术/身歷聲拾音技術 stereophonic pickup technology
立体图/立體圖,軸測圖 stereogram, solid diagram, axonometric chart
立体照片/立體照片 stereographics
立项/立項 project launching
利差/利率差距 interest rate spread
利改税/利改税 substitution of tax payment for profit delivery
利基受众/利基閱聽眾 niche audience
利基战略/利基市場策略 niche market strategy
利己主义/利己主義 egoism
利克特量表/李克特量表,李克特量尺 Likert scale
利克特领导方式理论/李克特領導風格理論 leadership style theory of Likert
利莱福斯检验/Lilliefors 檢定 Lilliefors test
利率/利率 interest rate, rate of interest
利率差幅/利率差幅 split margin
利率差距/利率差距,利差 interest rate differential
利率对冲/利率對沖 interest rate hedge
利率风险/利率風險 interest rate risk
利率风险定价/利率風險定價 interest rate risk pricing
利率风险结构/利率的風險結構 risk structure of interest rate
利率管制/利率管制 control of interest rate
利率互换/利率互換,利率交換 interest rate swap
利率结构/利率結構 structure of interest rate
利率平价/利率平價 interest rate parity
利率平价理论/利率平價理論 interest rate parity theory, interest rate parity theorem
利率平价论/利率平價論 interest rate parity theory
利率平价说/利率平價説 theory of interest rate parity
利率平价条件/利率平價條件 interest-parity condition
利率期货/利率期貨 interest rate futures
利率期货市场/利率期貨市場 interest futures market
利率期权/利率選擇權 interest rate option
利率期限结构/利率期限結構 term structure of interest rate
利率上升/利率上升 rising of interest rate
利率上限/利率上限 interest rate ceiling, interest rate cap
利率体系/利率體系 system of interest rate
利率下限/利率下限 interest rate floor
利率预测互换/利率預測交換 interest rate anticipation swap
利率政策/利率政策 interest rate policy
利马国际私法条约/利馬國際私法條約 Treaty to Establish Uniform Rules on Private International Law
利普希茨函数/李普西兹函數 Lipschitz function
利普希茨条件/李普西兹條件 Lipschitz condition
利润/利潤 profit, profitability
利润表/損益表 income statement
利润分配/利潤分配 profit appropriation
利润分享计划/利潤分享計劃,利潤分享制 profit-sharing plan
利润分享与管理分担/利潤分享與管理分擔 profit share and management allocation
利润理论/利潤説 profit theory
利润率/利潤率 rate of profit
利润率下降/利潤率下降 falling rate of profit
利润平滑/盈餘平穩化,損益平穩化 income smoothing
利润税/利潤税 profit tax
利润损失保险/利潤損失保險 loss-of-profit insurance
利润损失保险单/利潤損失保險單 loss-of-profit policy
利润图/利潤圖 profit chart
利润增减分析表/利潤差異分析表 statement of variation in profit
利润中心/利潤中心 profit center
利润总额/總利潤 total profit, aggregate profit
利润最大化/利潤極大化,追求利潤最大 profit maximization
利润最大化弱公理/弱性利潤極大化公設 weak axiom of profit maximization
利税分流/利税分流 separating profits and taxes
利他主义/利他主義 altruism
利特尔法则/利特爾法則 Little's law
利维指数/Livi 指數 Livi's index
利息/利息 interest
利息保障倍数/盈利對利息的倍數 interest coverage

ratio
利息兑换券/利息兌換券　limited coupon
利息[理]论/利息理論　interest theory, theory of interest
利息平衡税/利息平衡稅　interest equalization tax
利息平价/利息平價　interest parity
利息税/利息稅　interest tax
利息税盾/利息稅盾　interest tax shield
利益冲突/利益衝突　conflict of interest
利益法学派/利益法學派　interest school of law
利益共享/利益共用　pool of interest
利益汇集/利益匯聚　aggregation of interest
利益集团/利益團體　interest group
利益集团模型/利益團體模型　interest group model
利益结合原则/利益結合原則　interest integration principle
利益均等原则/利益均等原則　principle of equal advantage
利益细分/利益區隔　benefit segmentation
利益相关者/利益關係者,利害關係人　stakeholder
利益相关者管理/利益相關者管理　stakeholder management
利用决定论/利用決定論　theory of use determination, utilize determinism
利用限制/利用限制　restricted access
例外费率/例外[費]率　exception rate
例外管理/例外管理　management by exception
例外条款/例外條款,免責條款,除外條款　exception clause, escape clause
例外原则/例外原則　exception principle
例行保养/例行維修　routine maintenance
例行的政策构建方法/例行規劃　routine policy formulation
例行化/例行化,常規化　routinization
隶属关系/隸屬關係　relationship of administrative subordination
隶属函数/隸屬函數　membership function
连带/連帶　tie
连带保证/連帶保證　joint and several guarantee
连带契约/共同合約　joint contract
连带责任/連帶責任,共同責任　joint and several liability
连带之债/連帶之債　joint and several debt
连贯性原理/連續性原理　principle of continuousness
连环关系/環比　link relative
连环画/連環畫　comic book
连接分类/連接分類　conjunct classification
连接函数/連結函數　link function
连接区域/連接區域　connection area
连接区组/連環區集　linked blocks
连锁博弈/連鎖店賽局　chain-store game
连锁超市/超市連鎖店　supermarket chain
连锁店/連鎖商店　chain store
连锁店悖论/連鎖店矛盾　chain store paradox
连锁董事/連結董事　interlocking directorates
连锁经营总部/連鎖經營總部　chain bookstore headquarter
连锁贸易/連鎖貿易　linked trade
连锁融资/連鎖融資　link financing
连锁书店/連鎖書店　chain bookstore
连锁银行制度/連鎖銀行體系　chains banking system
连通设计/連接設計　connected design
连通性/連接　connectivity
连续报道/連續報導　follow-up
连续变量/連續變項,連續變數　continuous variables
连续补货/連續補貨　continuous replenishment
连续测时法/連續測時法　continuous timing
连续抽样/連續抽樣　continuous sampling
连续出版物/連續出版物　serial
连续出版物编目/連續性刊物編目　serial cataloging
连续出版物采访/連續出版物採訪　serial acquisition
连续出版物记录/期刊記錄　serial record
连续调/連續色調　continuous tone
连续调查/接續調查　successive survey
连续调值/連續調值　continuous tone value
连续对策/連續對局　continuous game
连续犯/連續犯　continuing crime
连续分布/連續分布,連續分配　continuous distribution
连续复利/連續複利　continuous compounding
连续概率分布/連續機率分布,連續機率分配　continuous probability distribution
连续过程/連續過程　continuous process
连续校正/連續性校正　continuity correction
连续竞价/連續雙向競價　continuous double auction
连续剧/連續劇　soap opera, television series
连续均匀分布/連續單一分配,矩形分配　continuous uniform distribution
连续马尔科夫过程/連續馬可夫過程　continuous Markov process
连续蒙太奇/連續蒙太奇　continuous montage
连续喷墨/連續噴墨　continuous inkjet
连续色调/連續色調　continuous tone
连续时间决策过程/連續時間決策過程　continuous time decision process
连续时间马尔科夫链/連續時間馬可夫鏈

continuous time Markov chain
连续时间盘点/連續時間盤點 continuous time review
连续时间序列/連續時間序列 continuous time series
连续数据/連續數據,連續資料 continuous data
连续随机变量/連續隨機變數 continuous random variable
连续随机过程/連續隨機過程,連續機率過程 continuous stochastic process
连续型动态投入产出模型/連續式動態投入產出模型 dynamic input-output model in continuous form
连续型生产/連續生產 continuous production
连续性理论/連續理論 continuity theory
连续性强化/連續性增強 continuous reinforcement
连续性资源/連續性資源 continuing resource
连续正规化设计/連續正規化設計 continuous normalized design
连续正规化线性最优设计/連續正規化線性最適設計 continuous normalized linear optimal design
连续总体/連續母體 continuous population
连载/連載 serial
连坐/連坐 implicated in the crime
联邦制/聯邦制 federalism
联邦制组织/聯邦制組織 federation organization of Handy
联播/聯播 affiliate, simultaneous broadcasting
联产品/聯[合]產品 joint product
联单/整套匯票 set of exchange
联动线/聯動線 binding line
联发/聯發 connect and development
联行/往來銀行,通匯銀行 correspondent bank
联行往来利息/聯行往來利息 interest on inter-branches account
联号/連接符 connective
联合背书/共同背書 joint endorsement
联合编目/聯合編目 union cataloging
联合补货系统/聯合補貨系統 joint replenishment system
联合操作程序图/多項活動作業程序圖 multiple activity operation chart
联合成本/聯合成本 joint cost
联合充分统计量/聯合充分統計量 jointly sufficient statistic
联合充分性/聯合充分性 joint sufficiency
联合出票人/共同出票人 co-maker
联合促销/聯合推廣 joint promotion
联合贷款/聯合貸款 syndicated loan

联合担保债券/聯合保證公司債 bond joint and several
联合档案室/聯合檔案室 union record office
联合抵押公司债券/聯合抵押公司債券 bond consolidated mortgage
联合抵制/杯葛 boycott
联合抵制交易/一致的拒絕交易 concerted refusal to deal
联合订货/聯合訂貨 joint order
联合方差比检验/聯立變異數比檢定 simultaneous variance ratio test
联合分保/聯合分保 pool reinsurance
联合分布/聯合分布,聯合分配 joint distribution
联合分类法/聯合分類法 collective classification
联合浮动汇率/聯合浮動匯率 joint floating exchange rate
联合概率/聯合機率 joint probability
联合概率分布函数/聯合機率分布函數 joint probability distribution function
联合概率函数/聯合機率函數 joint probability function
联合概率密度/聯合機率密度 joint probability density
联合概率密度函数/聯合機率密度函數 joint probability density function
联合杠杆/總槓桿 total leverage
联合工作/合并工作 combined work
联合估计/聯立估計 simultaneous estimation
联合国/聯合國 United Nations
联合国安理会常任理事国/聯合國安理會常任理事國 Permanent Members of the United Nations Security Council
联合国安全理事会/聯合國安全理事會 United Nations Security Council
联合国大会/聯合國大會 United Nations General Assembly
联合国经济及社会理事会/聯合國經濟暨社會理事會 United Nations Economic and Social Council
联合国秘书处和秘书长/聯合國秘書處和秘書長 secretariat and secretary general of the United Nations
联合国气候变化框架公约/聯合國氣候變化框架公約 United Nations Framework Convention on Climate Change
联合国托管理事会/聯合國託管理事會 Trusteeship Council of United Nations
联合国维持和平部队/聯合國維持和平部隊 United Nations Peacekeeping Force

联合国宪章/聯合國憲章　Charter of the United Nations
联合国专门机构/聯合國專門機構　specialized agencies of the United Nations
联合回归/聯合回歸　joint regression
联合家庭/聯合家庭　joint family
联合检验/聯合測驗　joint test
联合交易/聯合交易　combination deal
联合经营/聯合經營　joint adventure
联合矩/聯合動差　joint moment
联合矩母函数/聯合動差生成函數　joint moment generating function
联合决定变量/共同決定變數　jointly determined variables
联合垄断化/聯合壟斷　joint monopolization
联合目录/聯合目錄　union catalog
联合判别区间/聯立判別區間　simultaneous discrimination intervals
联合配额/聯合配額　combination quota
联合票据/聯合票據　joint note
联合品牌/共同品牌　co-branding
联合区间估计/聯合區間估計　joint interval estimator
联合全宗/聯合全宗　collective fonds
联合容忍区间/聯立允差區間　simultaneous tolerance intervals
联合商标/聯合商標　united brand
联合审核/聯合稽核　joint audit
联合生产/複合性生產　joint production
联合式多种经营/聯合企業的多角化經營　conglomerate diversification
联合数字参考咨询/協作數位參考諮詢　collaborative digital reference
联合投标/聯合投標　syndicated tender
联合投资/聯合投資　joint investment
联合图像专家组/聯合照相專家群　joint photographic expert group, JPEG
联合文件全宗/聯合檔案全宗　collective record fonds
联合文件组合/聯合檔案組合　collective record group
联合相关/聯合相關　joint correlation
联合效率/聯合效率　joint efficiency
联合行文/聯合行文　joint send official doucment
联合营销/共同運銷　joint marketing
联合有效估计[值]/聯合有效估計[值]　joint efficient estimate
联合预测区间/聯合預測區間　joint prediction intervals
联合运输/聯合運輸,複合運輸　joint transport, intermodal transportation
联合账户/聯合賬戶,共同賬戶,聯名賬戶　joint account
联合招标/聯合招標　joint invitation to tender
联合执行委员会/聯合董事會　joint executive committee
联合置信区间/聯立信賴區間　simultaneous confidence intervals
联合置信[区]域/聯合信賴區域　joint confidence region
联合仲裁条款/聯合仲裁條款　joint arbitral clause
联合子公司/聯合子公司　joint subsidiary
联合租赁/聯合租賃　joint tenancy
联合作业分析/多項活動作業分析　multiple activity operation analysis
联机的/聯機的　on-line
联机分析处理/線上分析處理,線上解析處理　online analytical processing, OLAP
联机公共检索目录/線上公用目錄　online public access catalog, OPAC
联机检索/連線檢索,網上搜索　online retrieval, online search
联机检索系统/連線檢索系統　online searching system
联机联合编目/線上聯機編目　online union cataloging
联机目录/線上目錄　online catalog
联机事务处理/線上交易處理　online transaction processing, OLTP
联机游戏/線上遊戲　online game
联结管理/共同管理　joint management
联结因素/聯結因素　connectingfactor
联结组配/聯結協調　connection coordination
联立方程/聯立方程式　simultaneous equations
联立方程式的标准化/聯立方程式的標準化　normalization in simultaneous equations
联立方程预测模型/聯立方程式預測模型　simultaneous equation forecasting model
联立方程[组]模型/聯立方程式模型,多元方程式模型　simultaneous equations model
联络馆员/聯絡館員　liaison librarian
联络者/聯絡者　liaison
联盟/聯盟,結盟　coalition
联盟的标准条款/工會標準條款　union standards clause
联盟谈判/聯合協議　coalition bargaining

联系/聯鎖 linkages
联想/聯想 association
联谊会/聯誼會 fellowship society
联姻理论/聯姻理論 alliance theory
联营出口公司/聯營出口公司 allied export selling company
联营投资基金/聯營投資基金 pooled investment fund
廉价出售/廉價出售 distress selling
廉租房/廉租房 low-rent housing
廉租房制度/廉租房制度 public rental housing
恋物/戀物,物神 fetish
链/鏈,连锁,串 chain, run
链比/鏈比 chain relative
链比的修正/鏈比的修正 adjustment of chain relatives
链长/[連]串长 run length
链带公司科学管理/鏈帶公司科學管理 scientific management of Blet Company
链法/連鎖法 chain method
链基/鏈基 chain base
链接/鏈結,連結 link, hyperlink
链接变量/連結變數 linked variable
链接分析/鏈結分析 link analysis, hyperlink analysis
链接函数/連結函數 link function
链接机制/連結機制 linking mechanism
链可靠性/鏈可靠度 chain reliability
链模型/鏈模型 chain model
链区组设计/鏈區集設計 chain block design
链式抽样方案/鏈抽樣計劃 chain sampling plan
链式迁移/連鎖遷徙 chain migration
链式索引/連鎖指數,鏈指數 chain index
链式信息交流网络/鏈式資訊交流網路 network of zip-mode communication
链形二项模型/鏈二項模型 chain binomial model
链状短语标引系统/鏈狀短語標引系統 linked phrase indexing system
良好投资环境/良好投資環境 favorable investment climate
良好性状偏好/规则型偏好 well-behaved preferences
良好性状无差异曲线/规则型無異曲線 well-behaved indifference curves
良心/良識 conscience
良心自由/良心自由 freedom of conscience
梁律/梁律 the Laws of Liang Dynasty
量表/量表 scale

量规/量規 gage
粮食安全/糧食安全 food security
粮食流通体制/糧食流通體制 grain distribution system
粮食收购/糧食收購 grain collection
粮食援助公约/糧食援助協定 Food Aid Convention
两倍标准差限/二標準差界限 two-sigma limits
两步最小二乘/二段最小平方 two-stage least squares
两部模型/兩部模型 two-part model
两部收费/兩部定價法 two-part tariff
两党制/兩黨制 two-party system
两点分布/二點分布,二點分配 two-point distribution
两点套利/兩地套利 two-point arbitrage
两分问题/兩分問題 dichotomous question
两合公司体制/兩合公司體制 commandite system
两基金的货币分离/兩基金的貨幣分離 two fund monetary separation
两级传播理论/兩級傳播理論 two-step flow theory, two-step flow theory of communication
两阶段股利贴现模型/兩階段股利折現模型 two-stage dividend discount model
两阶段评标法/兩階段評價模型 two-stage evaluation method
两阶段最小二乘法/二階段最小平方 two-stage least squares, 2SLS
两阶段最小二乘估计方法/二階段最小平方法 method of two-stage least square estimation
两截法/兩截法 two-segment method
两两相互独立/成對獨立性 pairwise independence
两期/兩期 two-period
两期模型/兩期模型 two period model
两权分离/二權分離 separation of two rights
两缺口模式/兩缺口模式 two-gap model
两人对策/兩人對局 two-person game
两人零和对策/二人零和賽局 two-person zero-sum game
两人无限零和对策/兩人無限零和對策 two-person infinite zero-sum game
两项分类/二元分類 dichotomous classification
两院制/兩院制 bicameral constitution
两值期权/兩值期權 binary option
两种方式分组/雙向分類,雙因子分類 two-way classification
亮调/亮調 highlight
谅解备忘录/諒解備忘錄 memorandum of understanding

量/數量　quantity
量比/量比　quantity relative
量贩式网络推广/量販式網路推廣　discount-style network promotion
量化精度/量化精度　quantization precision
量化预测法/數量性預測方法　quantitative forecasting methods
量力而行法/量入爲出法　affordable method
量刑/量刑　weigh sentences
量刑情节/量刑情節　circumstances for the discretionary action of sentencing
量子统计力学/量子統計力學　quantum statistical mechanics
晾纸/調濕　airing paper
辽刻本/遼刻本　Liao Dynasty edition
聊天室/聊天室,討論室　chat room
聊天室广告/聊天室廣告　advertisement in chat room
料筒/料筒　stacking tube, feed tank
列/[縱]行　column
列昂惕夫逆矩阵/李昂鐵夫逆轉,李昂鐵夫逆矩陣　Leontief inverse, Leontief inverse matrix
列表/列表,表列　list, tabulation
列表表示/列表陳示　tabular presentation
列表排法/策略列表　list policy
列间方差/行間變異數　between-column variance
列举/列舉　enumeration
列举抵扣项目/列舉扣除　itemized deduction
列举目录/列舉目錄　enumerative bibliography
列联/列聯　contingency
列联表/列聯表　contingency table
2×2列联表的费希尔精确检验/2×2列聯表的費雪精準檢定　Fisher's exact test for the 2 × 2 contingency table
列联表检验/列聯表的檢定　contingency table test
列联定理/列聯定理　contingency theorem
列联系数/列聯係數　contingency coefficient
列平方和/行平方和　column sum of squares
列线图/列線圖　alignment chart
列向量/行向量　column vector
列值/行值　column value
列总计/行總和　column total
劣等品/劣等物品　inferior goods
劣势策略/劣式策略　dominated strategy
猎头公司/獵人者　head-hunter
裂变分支/裂變分支　segment
裂区法/分裂區集法　split plot method
裂区混杂/分裂區集混同　split plot confounding

裂区排列/分裂區集排列　split plot arrangement
裂区设计/分裂區集設計　split-block design, split plot design
邻避现象/鄰避效應　not-in-my-backyard phenomenon
邻接/鄰近性　adjacency
邻接权/鄰接權　neighboring right
邻近检索/鄰近檢索　proximity search
邻里/鄰里　neighborhood
林达尔机制/林達機制,林道機制　Lindahl mechanism
林达尔均衡/林達均衡,林道均衡　Lindahl equilibrium
林达尔税收/林達稅,林道稅　Lindahl taxes
林德伯格-费勒定理/Lindeberg-Feller 定理　Lindeberg-Feller theorem
林德伯格条件/Lindeberg 條件　Lindeberg's condition
林德利定理/Lindley 定理　Lindley's theorem
林德利积分方程/Lindley 積分方程式　Lindley's integral equation
林肯计划/林肯計劃　Lincoln plan
林特纳模型/林特納模型　Lintner model
林业统计/林業統計　forestry statistics
临床试验/臨床試驗　clinical trials
临床研究/臨床研究　clinical research
临检/臨檢　visit and search
临界比/臨界比　critical ratio
临界参数/臨界參數　threshold parameter
临界点/臨界點　critical point
临界函数/臨界函數　critical function
临界水平/臨界水準　critical level
临界值/臨界值　critical value
临界最小努力理论/臨界最小努力理論　theory of critical minimum effort
临时保险/臨時保險　facultative insurance, provisional insurance
临时报关/臨時報關　sight entry
临时报关单/臨時報關單　bill of sight
临时波动性/短暫波動度　transitory volatility
临时出口/暫時出口　temporary export
临时贷款/暫時貸款　temporary loan
临时读者/臨時讀者　temporary reader
临时兑换券/臨時兌換券　emergency note
临时发票/臨時發票　provisional invoice
临时分类/暫時分類　temporal classification
临时工/臨時工　temporary worker
临时工程/臨時工程　temporary work
临时关税/臨時關稅　provisional tariff

临时合同/臨時合約　provisional contract
临时汇率/臨時匯率　provisional rate
临时进口/暫時進口　temporary import
临时禁令/臨時禁令　interlocutory injunction
临时批准免税进口/暫時免稅進口　temporary admission
临时融通/暫時融資　temporary accommodation
临时适用议定书/臨時性適用議定書　protocol of provisional application
临时投资/流動投資,短期投資　liquid investment
临时透支/臨時透支　occasional overdraft
临时许可证/臨時許可證　provisional licence
临时延期批准/臨時延遲批準　temporary delay approval
临时用工/臨時性勞動力　contingent work force
临时债券/臨時債券　bond interim
临时账户/臨時賬戶　provisional account
临修/臨時修理,小修　temporary repair
临终关怀/臨終照護,安寧照護　end-of-life care
临终者角色/臨終者角色　death role
灵魂/靈魂　soul
灵活福利计划/自助式福利計劃　cafeteria plan
灵活期权/靈活期權　flex option
灵敏度/敏感度　sensitivity
灵敏度分析/敏感性分析　sensitivity analysis
灵敏度曲线/敏感度曲線　sensitivity curve
灵敏度数据/敏感度數據　sensitivity data
灵性/靈性　spirituality
灵性视角/靈性視角　spiritual perspective
囹圄/囹圄　prison
凌刻本/凌刻本　Ling family edition
零[部]件检验/零件檢驗　parts inspection
零成本期权/區間遠匯　range forward, zero-cost option
零次文献/零次文獻　pre-primary literature, zero-level document
零存整取/零存整付儲蓄　installment saving
零担货物/零擔貨物　less-than-carload cargo
零担运输/卡車零擔運輸　less-than-truckload
零工/臨時工作　odd jobs
零和博弈/零和賽局　zero-sum game
零和权力/零和權力　zero-sum power
零和问题/零和問題　zero-sum problem
零基预算/零基預算　zero-based budget
零假设/虛無假設,稻草人假設,原始假設　null zero hypothesis, straw man hypothesis, null hypothesis
零件/零件　part
零件编码和分类/零件編碼和分類　part coding and classification
零件标准化/零件標準化　part standardization
零件代码/零件代碼　part number
零件通用化/零件通用化　part commonality
零件族/零件族　part family
零件族采购合同/零件族採購合同　family contract
零结果/零結果　zero result
零库存技术/零庫存技術　zero-inventory technology
零利率/零利率　zero interest rate
零利润/零利潤　zero profit
零利润点/零利潤點　zero profit point
零利润均衡/零利潤均衡　zero profit equilibrium
零利润条件/零利潤條件　zero profit condition
零偏度/零偏度　zero skewness
零频数/零次數　zero frequency
零缺陷/無瑕疵　zero defect, ZD
零缺陷管理/零缺點管理　zero defect management
零售/零售　retail, retailing
零售估值[评价]法/零售估價法　retail valuation method
零售广告/零售商廣告　retail advertising
零售价格维持/零售價管制　retail price maintenance
零售竞争/零售競爭　retail competition
零售目录/零售目錄　catalog
零售商/零售商　retailer
零售商合作组织/零售商合作組織　retailer cooperative
零售税/零售稅　retail sales tax
零售网点/零售網點　retail outlet
零售物价指数/零售物價指數　retail price index
零售业/零售業　retail trade
零售银行/零售銀行　retail bank
零售银行业务/零售銀行業務　retail banking
零售银行业务创新/零售銀行業務創新　innovation in retail banking
零售折扣/零售折扣　retail discount
零售之轮观念/零售之輪理論,零售輪轉假設　wheel-of-retailing concept
零投资供给/零投資供給　zero-investment supply
零投资资产组合/零投資組合　zero-investment portfolio
零息债券/零息債券,無息債券　zero coupon bond
零相关/零相關　zero corrlation
零星订购/零星訂購　sporadic subscription
零星工作项目费/零星工作專案費　charge for sporadic work
零一规划/0-1規劃　zero-one programming
零一律/零壹律　law of zero or unity
零余额账户/零餘額賬戶　zero-balance account

岭回归/脊回歸　ridge regression
岭迹/脊軌跡　ridge trace
领班质量控制/領班品質管制　foremen quality control, FQC
领导层次/領導層次　leadership hierarchy
领导-成员交换理论/領導-成員交換理論　leadership-member exchange
领导方法/領導方法　leadership method
领导方式双因素理论/領導方式雙因素理論　two dimension theory
领导风格/領導風格　leader style, leadership style
领导风格理论/領導型態理論　leadership style theory
领导关系/領導關係　relationship-oriented leadership
领导归因理论/領導歸因理論　attribution theory of leadership
领导环境/領導環境　leadership environment
领导活动/領導活動　leading
领导绩效/領導績效　leadership performance
领导决策/領導決策　decision making of leader
领导角色/領導角色　leadership role
领导客体/領導客體　objects of leadership
领导力/領導力,領導才能　leadership
领导连续统一体理论/領導行爲連續論　leadership continuum theory
领导权变理论/權變領導[理]論　contingency theory of leadership
领导[权]力/領導力　leadership power
领导群体结构/領導群體結構　leadership group structure
领导授权/領導授權　leadership empowerment, leadership delegation
领导素质/領導素質　leader quality
领导特质理论/領導的特質理論　particularity theory of leadership, trait theory of leadership
领导体制/領導體制　leadership system
领导文化/領導文化　leadership culture
领导行为理论/領導的行爲學派理論　behavioral theory of leadership
领导行为评价/領導行爲評鑒　leader behavior assessment
领导学/領導學　leadership science
领导艺术/領導藝術　art of leadership
领导原则/領導原則　principle of leadership
领导战略/領導策略　leadership strategy
领导者/領導者　leader
领导者-参与模型/領導者-參與模型　leader-participation model
领导者管理/領導者管理　leader management
领导者匹配训练/領導者匹配訓練　leader attach training
领导主体/領導主體　subject of leadership
领海/領海　territorial sea
领海基线/領海基線　baselines of the territorial sea
领海宽度/領海寬度　breadth of the territorial sea
领空/領空　territorial airspace
领料单/領料單,揀料單,撿料單　picking list
领陆/領陸　territorial land
领事裁判权/領事裁判權　consular jurisdiction
领事婚姻/領事婚姻　consular marriage
领水/領水　territorial waters
领土/領土　territory
领土的取得和变更/領土的取得和變更　acquisition and changes of territory
领土主权/領土主權　territorial sovereignty
领先工资水平政策/領先工資水準政策　lead pay level policy
领先市场/領先市場　lead market
领先用户/先驅使用者　lead user
领先指针法/主導指標法　leading indicators method
领域本体/領域本體　domain ontology
领域分析/領域分析　domain analysis
领域-任务本体/領域-任務本體　domain-task ontology
领域知识/領域知識　domain knowledge
领子期权/上下限選擇權　collar option
另类媒介/非主流媒體,替代性媒體　alternative media
另类新闻学/另類新聞學　alternative journalism
令/令　order
刘易斯-费-拉尼斯模型/劉易斯與費景漢-拉尼斯模型　Lewis-Fei-Ranis model
刘易斯管理理论/路易斯管理理論　factory management of Lewis
浏览器/瀏覽器　browser
留存比率/留存比率,盈餘保留率　retention ratio
留存利润/保留利潤　retained profit
留存收益/保留盈餘,未分配盈餘　retained earning
留存溢利/淨利潤　retained profits
留存盈余表/留存盈餘表　statement of returned earning
留守儿童/留守兒童　left-behind children
留守妇女/留守婦女　left-behind wives
留置/留置　lien
留置权/留置權　lien
留置权证[书]/留置權證[書]　letter of lien, lien

letter
留置送达/留置送達 service by leaving rejected legal instrument at the place of abode
流程/節目表,流程表 rundown
流程创新/製程創新 process innovation
流程分析/製程分析 process analysis
流程改进/流程改善,製程改善 process improvement
流程控制/製程控制 process control
流程路径/流程路徑 flow path
流程时间/流程時間 flow time
流程图/流程圖 flow diagram, flow chart
流程系统/程序系統 process system
流程型组织/流程型組織 processing organization
流程再造理论/流程再造理論 process reengineering theory
流动比率/流動比率 liquidity rate
流动表/流動表 mobility table
流动抵押/流動抵押 floating mortgage
流动儿童/流動兒童 migrant children
流动负债/流動負債 circulating liability, floating liability, liquid liability
流动公司债券/流動公司債券 floating debenture
流动公债/流動公債 floating bond
流动检验/流動檢驗 flowing inspection
流动偏好理论/流動性偏好理論 theory of liquidity preference
流动人口/流動人口 moving population
流动书贩/流動書商 mobile bookseller
流动头寸/流動頭寸 liquidity position
流动外汇/浮動外匯 floating exchange
流动销售/流動銷售 mobile sale
流动性/流動性 liquidity, mobility
流动性比率/流動性比率 liquidity ratio
流动性风险/流動性風險 liquidity risk
流动性过剩/流動性過剩 liquidity surplus
流动性监管/流動性監管 supervision on liquidity
流动性交易者/流動性交易者 liquidity trader
流动性偏好理论/流動偏好説 liquidity preference theory
流动性升水/流動性升水 liquidity premium
流动性陷阱/流動性陷阱 liquidity trap
流动性约束/流動性限制 liquidity constraints
流动性-增强型创新/流動性-增強型創新 liquidity-enhancing innovation
流动银行/流動銀行 mobile bank
流动债务/流動債務 floating debt
流动准备金/流動準備金 liquid reserve

流动资本/流動資本 circulating capital, current capital, floating capital
流动资本变动表/流動資本變動表 statement of change in working capital
流动资产/流動資產 circular asset, floating asset, liquid asset
流技术/流技術 stream technology
流浪儿童/流浪兒童,街頭遊童 street children, waif
流浪儿童救助保护中心/流浪兒童救助保護中心 rescue and protection centre for street children
流浪乞讨人员救助管理/流浪乞討人員救助管理 assistance and management of vagrants and beggars
流量/流量 traffic, flow
流量破产/流量資不抵債 flow-based insolvency
流量与存量/流量與存量 flow vs. stock
流媒体/串流媒體 streaming media
流媒体电视/流媒體電視 streaming television
流媒体技术/流媒體技術 streaming media technology
流水生产/一貫作業 flow production
流水线/流水線,流程線 flow line
流水作业排程/流程式排程 flow-shop scheduling
流通本/流通本 service copy
流通费用/流通費用 circulation cost
流通分析/流通分析 circulation analysis
流通馆藏/流通館藏 circulating collection
流通环节/流通環節 circulation link
流通货币/流通中通貨 currency in circulation
流通货币的担保/流通貨幣的擔保 currency backing
流通记录/流通記錄 circulation record
流通加工/流通加工 distribution processing
流通量/流通量 circulation
流通票据/流通票據,可轉讓票據 negotiable instrument, negotiable bill
流通手段/流通手段 medium of circulation
流通物/流通物 merchantable thing
流通债券/流通債券,可轉讓債券 negotiable bond
流通支票/流通支票,可轉讓支票 negotiable cheque
流行病统计/流行病統計 epidemiological statistics
流行病学/流行病學 epidemiology
流行文化/流行文化,大眾文化 pop culture, popular culture
流行音乐产业/流行音樂產業 pop music industry
流言/閒話,八卦 gossip
流言式非正式信息沟通/流言式非正式溝通 gossip-mode of informal communication
流转库/暫存器,寄存器 temporary storage
流转税/流轉稅,銷售稅,營業[額]稅 turnover tax,

business tax, sales tax
硫税/含硫税 sulfur tax
硫酸盐污染/硫酸鹽汙染 sulfate pollution
六法全书/六法全書 Liufa Quanshu
六分法/六分法 six-fold bibliographical classification system
六个特征立卷法/六個特徵立卷法 six characteristics filing method
六科/六科 Liuke, six ke
六礼/六禮 Liuli, six li
六西格玛品质/六西格瑪品質 six sigma quality
六西格玛设计/六西格瑪設計 design for six sigma, DFSS
龙鳞式/龍鱗式 dragon scales binding
隆礼重法/隆禮重法 Xun's idea of equal emphasis on etiquette and law
垄断/獨占 monopoly
垄断的无谓损失/獨占的無謂損失 deadweight loss of monopoly
垄断关税/壟斷關稅 monopoly tariff
垄断和兼并委员会/獨占與結合委員會 monopoly and merger commission
垄断货物/壟斷貨物 monopoly goods
垄断价格/壟斷價格 monopolistic price
垄断价格法则/壟斷價格法則 law of monopoly price
垄断竞争理论/獨占競爭理論 the theory of monopolistic competition
垄断竞争市场/壟斷競爭市場 monopolistic competition market
垄断力量/壟斷力,獨占力 monopoly power
垄断倾销/壟斷傾銷 monopoly dumping
垄断市场/壟斷市場 monopolistic market, captive market
垄断收入/公賣利益 monopoly revenue
垄断协议/壟斷協議 monopoly agreement
垄断行为/獨占行爲實驗,實施獨占 monopoly behaviors, monopolization
垄断[性]竞争/壟斷性競爭,獨占性競爭 monopolistic competition
垄断者/獨占者,獨賣者 monopolist
垄断资本主义/獨占資本主義 monopoly capitalism
垄断租金/獨占地租 monopoly rent
镂空版印刷/模版印刷 stencil printing
漏订/漏訂 absence of subscribing
漏斗实验/漏斗實驗 funnel experiment
漏检/漏報 miss, omissions
漏检率/漏檢率 missing retrieval ratio, miss ratio, undetected rate
漏损保险/滲漏保險 leakage insurance
漏损保险单/滲漏保險單 leakage policy
卢德主义/破壞機械運動 luddism
卢因变革模型/勒溫變革模型,勒溫變革模式 Lewin's change model
卢因领导风格理论/勒溫領導風格理論 leadership style theory of Lewin
卢因组织变革论/勒溫三階段變革過程模型 Lewin's organization change theory
炉边谈话/爐邊談話 Fireside Chats
鲁棒性/穩健性 robustness
鲁宾逊·克鲁索经济/魯賓遜式經濟 Robinson Crusoe economy
陆源污染/陸源汙染 land-based pollution
录放头/錄放頭 recordback head
录囚/錄囚 Luqiu
录像/錄影 image transcription, video recording
录像带/錄影帶 video tape, videotape, video cassette
录像档案/影像檔案 video archive
录像师/錄影師 videographer
录像资料/視訊資料,視頻資料 video material
录音/錄音 audio recording, sound recording
录音材料/錄音材料 sound recording material
录音磁带/錄音帶 phonotape
录音带/錄音帶,數位卡帶 audio tape, AT
录音档案/錄音檔案 recording archive, sound archive
录音工程师/錄音工程師 recording engineer
录音资料/錄音資料 sound recordings
录制/錄製 recording
录制者权/錄製者權 rights for phonogram producers
路径/路徑 path
路径动画/路徑動畫 path animation
路径分析/[路]徑分析 path analysis
路径-目标理论/路徑-目標理論 path-goal theory
路径系数法/路徑係數法 path coefficients method
路径依赖/路徑依賴,路徑相依 path dependence
路径依赖式决策/路徑依賴決策 path dependency in policy making
路径依赖型期权/路徑相依選擇權 path-dependent option
路线抽样/路線抽樣 route sampling
路线图模型/路線圖模型 road map model
路演/法人說明會 road show
露边式索引/露邊式索引 visible edge card index
露点温度/露點溫度 dew point temperature

吕刑/吕刑　Lyu Code
旅行售货员问题/旅行推銷員問題　traveling salesman problem
旅游统计/觀光統計　tourism statistics
旅游文化/旅遊文化　tourist culture
旅游业/旅遊業　tourism
履历/履歷　resume
履行不能/履行不能　impossibility of performance
履行迟延/履行遲延　delay of performance
履行地法/履行地法　lex loci solutions
履行判决/履行判決　carry out legally effective judgments
履行义务保证/履行義務保證　guarantee of performance
履行意愿/履行意願　willingness to perform
履约保证/履約保證　bond performance
履约保证金/履約保證金　contract bond
履约担保/履約擔保　performance security
履约证书/履約證書, 履約證明　performance certificate
律/律　Chinese ancient law
律例馆/律例館　Lyuli Guan
律令格式/律令格式　Lyuling agency
绿带/綠帶　green belt
绿皮书/綠皮書　green book, green paper
绿色GDP/綠色GDP　green GDP
绿色壁垒/綠色壁壘　green barrier
绿色采购/綠色採購　green stocking
绿色创新/綠色創新　green innovation
绿色犯罪学/綠色犯罪學　green criminology
绿色革命/綠色革命　green revolution
绿色货币/綠色貨幣　green currency
绿色技术创新/綠色技術創新　green technological innovation
绿色物流/綠色物流　green logistics
绿色消费/綠色消費　green consumption
绿色信贷/綠色信貸　green credit
绿色印刷/綠色印刷　green printing
绿色营销/綠色行銷　green marketing
绿色政治家/綠色政治家　green politician
绿色制造/綠色製造　green manufacturing
绿条款信用证/綠色條款信用狀　green clause credit
绿箱政策/綠色措施　green box policies
绿鞋期权/綠鞋期權　green shoes option
滤波[器]/過濾器, 篩選器　filter
孪生分布/孿生分布　twinned distributions
乱伦/亂倫, 近親交媾　commit incest
乱码/亂碼　messy code

掠夺性定价/掠奪性定價　predatory pricing
掠夺性定价政策/掠奪性定價政策　predatory pricing policy
掠夺性价格/掠奪性價格　predatory price
掠夺性倾销/掠奪性傾銷　predatory dumping
略式承兑/略式承兑　non-formal acceptance
伦敦股票交易所/倫敦股票交易所, 倫敦證券交易所　London Stock Exchange
伦敦国际仲裁院/倫敦國際仲裁院　London Court of International Arbitration
伦敦金融时报指数/倫敦金融時報指數　London Financial Times stock exchange index
伦敦同业拆放利率/倫敦銀行同業拆放利率　London interbank offered rate
伦敦学派/倫敦學派　London school
伦理/倫理　ethics
伦理本位社会/倫理本位社會　ethic-centered society
伦理的公正观/倫理的正義觀　justice view of ethics
伦理的功利观/倫理的功利觀, 倫理的效用觀　utilitarian view of ethics
伦理的权力观/倫理的權力觀　right view of ethics
伦理氛围/倫理氣候　ethical climate
伦理决策/倫理決策　ethical decision-making
伦理困境/倫理困境　ethical dilemma
伦理两难/倫理兩難　ethical dilemma
伦理两难情境下抉择的次序/倫理兩難情境下抉擇的次序　scenarios of making choice from ethical dilemmas
伦理问题/倫理議題　ethical issues
伦理行为/合倫理的行爲　ethical behavior
伦理型领导/倫理領導　ethical leadership
伦理性宗教/倫理性宗教　ethical religion
伦理议题/倫理議題　ethical issues
伦理原则/倫理守則　ethical guideline
伦理准则/倫理準則　ethical principle
轮岗培训/輪調培訓　rotation training
轮换抽样/輪換抽樣　rotation sampling
轮廓剪影动画/輪廓剪影動畫　profile silhouette animation
轮廓字/外框字, 描邊字　outline font
轮流出价讨价还价/輪流提案之談判　alternating-offer bargaining
轮排标引/輪排標引　rotational indexing
轮排法/輪排法　rotation, permutation
轮排索引/輪排索引　rotated index, permuted index
轮排显示/輪排顯示　rotated display
轮盘赌选择/輪盤篩選　roulettee wheel selection
轮式信息交流网络/輪式資訊交流網路　network of

wheel-mode communication
轮转式摄影机/輪轉式拍攝機　rotary camera
轮作/輪作　convertible husbandry, swidden
论辩/論辯　argument
论题/論題　talking point
论文标识号/論文標識號　article identifier
论文集/論文集　collected papers
论文选编/研究論文選集　selected papers
论心定罪/論心定罪　criminal judged according to one's motive and thought
论证理论/論證理論　theory of legal argumentation
罗宾逊-帕特曼法/羅賓遜-派得曼法案　Robinson-Patman act
罗伯津斯基线/芮萌斯基線　Rybzynski line
罗德岛法/羅德島法　Lex Rhodia
罗尔斯/羅爾斯　John Rawls
罗尔斯标准/羅斯標準　Rawls criterion
罗尔斯社会福利函数/勞斯[社會]福利函數　Rawlsian welfare function, Rawlsian social welfare function
罗尔斯正义/勞斯正義　Rawlsian justice
罗吉斯蒂过程/成長過程　logistic process
罗吉斯蒂寿命表/成長生命表　logistic life table
罗克奇价值观调查/Rokeach 價值調查, 羅克奇價值調查　Rokeach values survey
罗勒氏指数/Rohrer 指数　Rohrer's index
罗列式版本目录/羅列式版本目錄　textual bibliography of list style
罗马法/羅馬法　Roman law
罗马公约/羅馬公約　Rome Convention
罗马国际统一私法协会/羅馬國際統一私法協會　International Institute for the Unification of Private Law
罗马-日耳曼法系/羅馬-日爾曼法系　Romano-Germanic family
罗马条约/羅馬條約　Treaty of Rome
罗姆方格/Room 方格　Room's squares
罗纳德·德沃金/羅奈爾得·德沃金　Ronald Myles Dworkin
罗森鲍姆检验/Rosenbaum 檢定　Rosenbaum's test
罗斯托基准/羅斯托準則　Rostow criteria
罗斯托经济增长阶段论/羅斯托階段成長論　Rostow's theory of stages regional economic growth
罗特利斯贝格尔人际关系学说/羅特利斯貝格爾人際關係學說　human relation theory of Roethlisberger
罗纹纸/羅紋紙　white paper with silk stripes
罗夏墨迹测验/羅夏克墨漬測驗, 羅夏克墨漬投射測驗　Rorschach inkblot test
罗兹分布/Rhodes 分布, Rhodes 分配　Rhodes' distribution
逻辑差/邏輯非　logical negation
逻辑关系/邏輯關係　logical relation
逻辑归档/邏輯歸檔　logical filing
逻辑规则/邏輯法則　rules of logic
逻辑和/邏輯和　logical disjunction, logical sum
逻辑回归/勝算比回歸模式　logistics regression
逻辑积/邏輯積　logical product, logical multiplication
逻辑卷/邏輯卷　logical file
逻辑框架法/邏輯框架法　logical framework approach
逻辑模型/邏輯模型　logic model
逻辑思维/邏輯思維, 邏輯思考　logical thinking
逻辑斯谛分布/羅吉斯分布　logistic distribution
逻辑斯谛回归/邏輯斯諦回歸　logistic regression
逻辑斯谛曲线/羅吉斯曲線, 推理曲線　logistic curve
逻辑斯谛人口增长/邏輯斯諦人口增長　logistic population growth
逻辑要求/邏輯要求　logical appeal
逻辑运算/邏輯運算　logical operation
螺旋沟通模式/螺旋溝通模式, 螺旋溝通模型　helical model of communication
螺旋装/螺旋裝　spiral binding
洛克斐勒定理/洛克斐勒定理　Rockafellar theorem
洛伦兹曲线/羅倫斯曲線, Lorenz 曲線　Lorenz curve
洛伦兹曲线法/Lorenz 曲線法　Lorenz curve method
洛马克斯分布/Lomax 分布, Lomax 分配　Lomax distribution
洛桑学派/洛桑學派　Lausanne school
洛杉矶学派/洛杉磯學派　Los Angeles school
洛特卡定律/洛特卡定律　Lotka's law
洛指数/Lowe 指数　Lowe index
骆驼评级制度/駱駝評等制度　camel rating system
落后/低度發展　underdevelopment

M

麻沙本/麻沙本　Masha edition
麻沙纸/麻沙紙　Masha paper
麻醉功能/麻醉功能　anesthesia function
马伯里诉麦迪逊案/馬伯里訴麥迪森案　Marbury v. Madison
马丁德尔论管理评价标准/馬丁德爾論管理評價標準　Martindell's view on management evaluation standard
马多-莱普尼克分布/Madow-Leipnik 分配　Madow-Leipnik distribution
马尔顿斯条约/瑪爾頓斯條款　Martens Clause
马尔科姆·波多里奇国家质量奖/瑪律科姆·波多里奇國家品質獎　Malcolm Baldrige National Quality Award, MBNQA
马尔可夫不等式/馬可夫不等式　Markov inequality
马尔可夫反应函数/馬可夫反應函數　Markov reaction functions
马尔可夫更新过程/馬可夫更新過程,馬可夫再生程式　Markov renewal process
马尔可夫估计[值]/馬可夫估計值　Markov estimate
马尔可夫过程/馬可夫過程,馬可夫程式　Markov process
马尔可夫[机制]转换模型/馬可夫轉換模型　Markov switching model
马尔可夫决策法/馬可夫模型　Markov decision making method
马尔可夫决策过程/馬可夫決策過程　Markov decision processes
马尔可夫链/馬可夫鏈　Markov chain
马尔可夫时间/馬可夫時間　Markov time
马尔可夫完美均衡/馬可夫完全均衡　Markov perfect equilibrium
马尔可夫性/馬可夫性質　Markov property
马尔可夫预测法/馬可夫模型預測法　Markov forecasting approach
马尔可夫预测模型/馬可夫預測模型,馬可夫預測模式　Markov prediction model
马尔萨斯人口理论/馬爾薩斯人口論　Malthus population theory
马尔萨斯主义/馬爾薩斯思想,馬爾薩斯學派　Malthusianism

马尔辛克维齐定理/Marcinkiewicz 定理　Marcinkiewicz's theorem
马哈拉诺比斯广义距离/Mahalanobis 一般化距離　Mahalanobis' generalized distance
马哈拉诺比斯距离/Mahalanobis 距離　Mahalanobis distance
马基雅维利主义/馬基維利主義,權謀霸術主義　Machiavellianism
马克思/馬克思　Karl Marx
马克思阶级理论/馬克思階級理論　Marxism class theory
马克思主义/馬克思主義　Marxism
马克思主义法学/馬克思主義法學　Marxist Jurisprudence
马克思主义法学方法/馬克思主義法學方法　methodology of jurisprudential study of Marxism
马克思主义话语/馬克思主義話語,馬克思主義論述　Marxist discourse
马克思主义架构/馬克思主義架構　Marxist framework
马克思主义理论/馬克思主義[理論]　Marxist theory
马克思主义批判理论/馬克思主義批判理論　Marxist critical theory
马克思主义人权观/馬克思主義人權觀　Marxist Doctrine of Human Rights
马克斯韦尔-博尔茨曼统计/Maxwell-Boltzmann 統計量　Maxwell-Boltzmann statistic
马克斯韦尔分布/Maxwell 分布,Maxwell 分配　Maxwell distribution
马来西亚吉隆坡指数/馬來西亞吉隆坡指數　Kuala Lumpur stock index
马斯洛需要层次论/馬斯洛需要理論,馬斯洛需求理論　need theory of Maslow, Maslow's theory of hierarchy of need
马斯特里赫特条约/馬斯垂克條款　Maastrict treaty
马太效应/馬修效應,錦上添花效應　Matthew effect
马锡五审判方式/馬錫五審判方式　Ma Xiwu trial
马歇尔-埃奇沃思-鲍利指数/Marshall-Edgeworth-Bowley 指數　Marshall-Edgeworth-Bowley index
马歇尔-奥尔金分布/Marshall-Olkin 分布,Marshall-

Olkin 分配　Marshall-Olkin distribution
马歇尔国际贸易理论/馬歇爾國際貿易理論　Marshell's theory on international trade
马歇尔计划/馬歇爾計劃　Marshall plan
马歇尔-勒纳条件/馬歇爾-勒納條件,馬歇爾-婁納條件　Marshall-Lerner condition
马歇尔消费者剩余/馬歇爾消費者剩餘　Marshallian consumer surplus
玛丽·里士满/瑪麗·里士滿　Mary Richmond
码/碼　code
CODEN 码/期刊碼　coden
码价核算制/碼價核算制　code price accounting system
码头交货价/碼頭交貨價　ex pier
码头交货条件/碼頭交貨條件　ex quay terms
码洋/總定價　total price, total price volume
埋伏式营销/伏擊行銷　ambush marketing
买断/買斷　buyout, outright purchase
买方/買方,買主　buyer
买方报价/買方出價　bid price
买方仓库交货价/買方倉庫交貨價　ex buyer's godown
[买方]递实盘/最終出價　firm bid
买方发盘/購貨報價　buying offer
买方寡头垄断/寡頭聯買　oligopsony
买方垄断/獨買　monopsony
买方垄断的无谓损失/買方壟斷的無謂損失　deadweight loss of monopsony
买方市场/買方市場,購買者市場　buyer's market
买方套购保值/買方套購保值,买入對沖　buyer's hedging
买方信贷/買方信貸,買方信用　buyer's credit
买方行为/買方行爲　act of buyer
买方远期信用证/買方遠期信用狀　buyer's usance credit
买进本国货币的套汇/買進本國貨幣的套匯　inward arbitrage
买进对冲/買期保值　hedge buying
买进远期外汇/預購遠期外匯　forward exchange bought
买空/買空　going long, buy short
买空-卖空/買空-賣空　bull bear
买卖合同/買賣合同　sales contract
买卖婚姻/買賣婚姻　mercenary marriage
买卖活跃的市场/活絡的市場,自由市場　active market
买卖价差/買賣價差　bid-ask spread, quote spread
买卖清单/買賣清單　bought and sold note

买期保值/買期保值　hedge buying
买入-出售价差/買賣權平價說　put-call parity
买入电汇/買入電匯　telegraphic transfer bought
买入汇率/買入匯率　exchange buying rate
买入价/買價　buying price
买入认股权证/認購權證　call warrant
买入外币汇票/買入外幣匯票　foreign currency bill bought
买入外国汇票/買入外國匯票　foreign bill bought
迈尔斯-布里格斯个性类型测量表/麥布二氏類型量表,麥布二式人格類型量表　Myers-Briggs type indicator
迈尔斯的工业心理学/邁爾斯的工業心理學　industrial psychology of Myers
麦卡勒姆改革/麥卡勒姆改革　McCallum reform
麦考利公式/Macaulay 公式　Macaulay's formula
麦克杜格尔模式/麥克杜格爾模式　MacDougall model
麦克翰法则/Makeham 定律　Makeham's law
麦克利兰成就动机理论/麥克萊蘭成就動機理論　McClelland's theory of achievement motivation
麦克利兰需要理论/麥克利蘭需求理論　McClelland's need theory
麦克尼马尔检验/McNemar 檢定　McNemar's test
麦肯锡 7S 体系/麥肯錫 7S 模型　7S system of Mckinsey
卖场/賣場　store
卖场促销/賣場促銷　store promotion
卖场导购/獨立購物指南　shopping guide
卖场咨询/賣場諮詢　shopping consultation
卖出对冲/賣期保值　hedge selling
卖出外币汇票/賣出外幣匯票　foreign currency bill sold
卖出外汇/賣出外匯　foreign exchange sold
卖方/賣方　seller
卖方仓库交货价/賣方倉庫交貨價　ex seller's godown
卖方发货人/賣方發貨人　seller-consignor
卖方负担风险/賣方負擔風險　seller's risk
卖方汇价/賣方匯價　selling exchange rate
卖方加倍权/雙倍的賣方選擇權　seller's option to double, SOD
卖方留置权/賣方留置權　seller's lien
卖方市场/賣方市場,销售者市場　seller's market
卖方双倍选择权/賣方雙倍選擇權　seller's option to double
卖方信贷/賣方信貸,賣方信用　seller's credit
卖方行为/賣方行爲　act of seller

卖方选择/賣方選擇 seller's selection
卖方选择权/賣方選擇權 seller's option
卖回条款/賣回條款 put provision
卖空/賣空,融券 sell short, going short
卖空外币/賣空外幣 short selling foreign currency
卖期保值/賣期保值 hedge selling
卖契/買賣契約 deed of bargain and sale
卖淫/賣淫 prostitution
卖主盈余/賣方盈餘 seller's surplus
脉冲函数/脈衝函數 pulse function
脉冲响应函数/脈衝反應函數,衝擊反應函數 impulse response function, IRF
脉冲噪声/脈衝雜訊,散粒雜音 shot noise
满意度/滿意度 satisfaction degree
满意决策模型/滿意式決策模型,滿意式決策模式 satisficing decision model
满意理论/滿意論 satisficing theory
满意型决策/滿意型決策 satisfaction type decision
满秩线性模型/全秩線性模型 full rank linear model
满秩指数族/全秩指數族 exponential family of full rank
曼彻斯特学派/曼徹斯特學派 Manchester school
曼哈顿计划/曼哈頓計劃 Manhattan project
曼-惠特尼检验/Mann-Whitney 檢定 Mann-Whitney test
曼-惠特尼 U 统计量/曼-懷特尼 U 統計量 Mann-Whitney U statistic
曼-肯德尔检验/Mann-Kendall 檢定 Mann-Kendall test
曼特尔-亨塞尔检验/Mantel-Haenzel 檢定 Mantel-Haenzel test
漫画/漫畫 cartoon, comic
慢收敛/遲收斂 slow convergence
慢速摄影分析/慢速攝影動作研究 memomotion study
慢周期市场/慢週期市場 slow-cycle market
芒斯特伯格的工业心理学/芒斯特伯格的工業心理學 industrial psychology of Munsterberg
忙期/忙期 busy period
盲人读物/點字書 readings for the blind
盲人图书馆/盲人圖書館 library for the blind
盲文出版物/盲文出版物 braille publication
毛边纸/毛邊紙 rough-edged paper
毛抄本/毛抄本 handwritten editions by Maojin in the Ming dynasty
毛收入/毛所得 gross income
毛装/毛裝 full-dressed
矛盾性阶级位置/矛盾階級位置 contradictory class location
锚定效应/定錨效應 anchoring effect
卯簿/卯簿 maobu
冒充注册商标/冒充註冊商標 falsely marked as registered trademark
冒充专利/冒充專利 falsely marked as patent
冒号分类法/冒號式分類法 colon classification, CC
冒名著作/冒名著作 pseudepigraph
冒险投资/冒險投資 risky investment
冒险型创业/風險型創業 entrepreneurial venture
冒险游戏/冒險遊戲 adventure game
贸易/貿易 trade
贸易保护法/貿易保護法 trade protective legislation
贸易保护主义/貿易保護主義 trade protectionism
贸易保护主义理论/貿易保護主義理論 theory of trade protectionism
贸易保护主义者/貿易保護主義者 trade protectionist
贸易壁垒/貿易壁壘,貿易障礙 trade wall, barrier to trade, trade barrier
贸易波动/貿易波動 fluctuation in trade
贸易补贴/貿易補貼 trade subsidy
贸易差额/貿易差額 trade gap, balance of trade
贸易城市/貿易城市 trading cities
贸易促进/貿易促進 trade promotion
贸易代理合同/佣金代理合約 commission contract
贸易额/貿易金額 volume of trade
贸易风险/貿易風險 trade hazard, trade risk
贸易格局/貿易格局,貿易結構 pattern of trade
贸易公司/貿易公司 trading corporation
贸易构成/貿易構成,貿易組合 composition of trade
贸易管制/貿易管制,貿易限制 trade control, restriction on trade
贸易惯例/貿易慣例,商業習慣 trade practice, trace usage, trade custom
贸易合同/貿易合約 trade contract
[贸易合同中的]付款条件/付款條件 payment terms
贸易合作组织/貿易合作組織 organization for trade cooperation
贸易恢复/貿易恢復 recovery of trade
贸易汇票额/貿易匯票金額 volume of trade bill
贸易伙伴/貿易夥伴 trade partner
贸易伙伴国/貿易夥伴國 trading partner country
贸易货币/貿易貨幣 trade currency, trading currency
贸易机构/貿易機構 trading mechanics
贸易集中/貿易集中 concentration of trade

贸易结合/商業聯合　trade combination
贸易禁运/貿易禁運　trade embargo
贸易净差额/貿易淨差額　net balance of trade
贸易竞争对手/貿易競爭對手　trade competitor, trade rival
贸易纠纷索赔/貿易糾紛索賠　claim for trade dispute
贸易利得/貿易利益　trade gains
贸易利益/貿易獲利　gains from trade
贸易量/貿易量　trade quantity, trade volume
贸易流量/貿易流量　flow of trade, trade flow
贸易模式/貿易型態　trade pattern
贸易摩擦/貿易摩擦　trade conflict, trade friction
贸易逆差/貿易逆差　trade deficit, passive balance of trade, unfavourable balance of trade
贸易年度/貿易年度　trade year
贸易扭曲/貿易扭曲　trade distortions
贸易平衡/貿易平衡　trade balance
贸易歧视/貿易歧視　trade discrimination
贸易渠道/貿易管道　trade channel
贸易收入/貿易收入　trade receipt
贸易收入条件/所得貿易條件　income terms of trade
贸易收益/貿易收益　gain from trade
贸易收支账户/貿易賬餘額　balance of trade account
贸易数量配额/貿易數量配額　quantitative trade quota
贸易数量限额/貿易數量限額　quantitative restriction of trade
[贸易]顺差/[貿易]順差　active trade balance, favorable balance of trade, trade surplus
贸易谈判/貿易談判　trade negotiation
贸易条件/貿易條件　trade term, term of trade
贸易条件恶化理论/貿易條件惡化論　theory of the terms of trade worsening, trade terms vicious theory
贸易条件理论/貿易條件論　theory of terms of trade
贸易条件效应/貿易條件效果　terms-of-trade effect
贸易条件指数/貿易條件指數　index of terms-of-trade, terms-of-trade index
贸易条款/貿易條款　trade clause
贸易条例/貿易條例　trade regulation
贸易同盟/貿易同盟　trade bloc
贸易统计/貿易統計　statistics of trade
贸易投资/貿易投資　trade investment
贸易外收入/貿易外收入,無形收入　invisible receipt
贸易外收支项目/貿易外收支項目,無形貿易項目　invisible item of trade
贸易外支付/貿易外支付,無形支付　invisible payment
贸易协定/貿易協定　trade agreement
贸易协定书/貿易協定書　trade protocol
贸易信息/貿易資訊,商業情報　trade information
贸易性发行/貿易性發行　trade distribution
贸易询价/貿易詢價　trade inquiry
贸易盈余/貿易盈餘　trade surplus
贸易优先权/貿易優先權　trade preference
贸易与环境决定/貿易與環境決議　decision on trade and environment
贸易战/貿易戰　trade war
贸易站/商站　trading post
贸易折扣/貿易折扣　trade discount
贸易争端/貿易糾紛　trade dispute
贸易政策/貿易政策　trade policy
贸易支付协定/貿易支付協定　trade and payment agreement
贸易支票/貿易支票　trading cheque
贸易值/貿易值　trade value
贸易值指数/貿易值指數　trade value index
贸易制裁/貿易制裁　trade sanction
贸易转向/貿易轉換　trade diversion
贸易转移效果/貿易轉移效果　trade diversion effect
贸易状况/貿易狀況　trading condition
贸易资本/貿易資本　capital for trading purpose, capital in trade
贸易自由/貿易自由　liberty of trading
贸易自由化/貿易自由化　liberalization of trade, trade liberalization
贸易总差额/貿易總差額　general balance of trade
贸易总额/貿易總額　total trade, total volume of trade
贸易总收益/貿易總收益　total gain from trade
贸易总收益指数/貿易總收益指數　total gain from trade index
贸易总条件/貿易總條件　gross terms of trade
没有法定汇率的货币/無法定匯率的貨幣　currency without legal rate
没有约定的发盘/不受約束力的報價　offer without engagement
玫瑰图/玫瑰圖　rose diagram
枚举数据/點計數據,點計資料　enumeration data
梅奥学说/梅奧理論　Mayo theory
梅茨勒悖论/梅滋樂矛盾　Metzler paradox
梅花型/梅花陣式　quincunx
梅林变换/Mellin 變換　Mellin transform
梅林顿-皮尔逊逼近/Merrington-Pearson 逼近

Merrington-Pearson approximation
梅隆银行/梅隆銀行　Mellon Bank
梅特卡夫卡片制/梅特卡夫卡片制　card system of Metcalfe
梅因/梅因　Henry James Sumner Maine
媒介/媒介,媒體　medium, media
媒介策划/媒體企畫　media planning
媒介策略/媒體策略　media strategy
媒介产业/媒體產業　media industry
媒介倡导/媒體倡導,媒體倡議　media advocacy
媒介代理费制/媒體佣金　media commission
媒介帝国主义/媒介帝國主義　media imperialism
媒介购买/媒體購買　media-buying
媒介购买者/媒體購買者　media buyer
媒介监测/媒體觀察,媒體監督　media watch
媒介接近使用权/媒體近用權,媒體進用權　right of access to the media
媒介近用/媒介近用,媒介進用　media access
媒介景观/媒介景觀　mediascape
媒介可信度/媒介可信度　media credibility
媒介框架/媒介框架,媒體框架　media frame
媒介伦理准则/媒體倫理準則　media ethic code
媒介全球化/媒介全球化　media globalization
媒介融合/媒介融合　media integration, media convergence
媒介生产/新聞產製　news production
媒介使用/媒介使用　media use
媒介事件/媒介事件,媒體事件　media event
媒介素养/媒體素養,媒體識讀　media literacy
媒介所有权/媒體所有權　media ownership
媒介所有制/媒體所有權　media ownership
媒介效果/媒介效果,媒介影響　media effect
媒介效果模式/媒介效果模式　media effect model
媒介效果研究/媒介效果研究,媒體效果研究　media effects research
媒介选择/媒介選擇　media choice
媒介研究/媒體研究　media research
媒介依附论/媒介依賴理論　media dependency theory
媒介再现/媒體再現　media representation
媒体/媒體,媒介　media
媒体报道/媒體報導　media coverage
媒体曝光/媒體曝光　media exposure
媒体分类/媒體分類　media classes
媒体功能/媒體功能　media function
媒体关系/媒體關係　media relationship
媒体关系营销/媒體關係行銷　media relationship marketing
媒体规范/媒體規範　media specification
媒体框架/媒體框架,媒介框架　media frame
媒体民族志/媒體民族志　media ethnography
媒体频度折扣/媒體頻度折扣　frequency discount of media
媒体审判/媒體審判　media trial
媒体事件/媒體事件,媒介事件　media event
媒体资产管理/媒體資產管理　media asset management
媒体组合/媒體組合　media mix
煤矿开采/採煤　coal mining
煤炭工业/煤炭工業　coal industry
霉斑书页/霉斑書頁　foxed page
每百单位产品不合格数/每百單位產品不良數　nonconforming per hundred items
每百单位缺陷数/每百單位缺點數　defects per hundred units
每个特别提款权单位/每單位特別提款權　per SDR
每股收益/每股收益　earnings per share, EPS
每日价格波动限额/每日價格波動限額　daily price movement limit
每日平价/每日平價,每日等價　daily parity
每月劳动调查/每月勞工調查　monthly labor survey
美国联邦储备系统/美國聯邦準備系統　Federal Reserve System
美国千禧年数字著作权法案/美國數位千禧年著作權法　Digital Millennium Copyright Act
[美]联邦准备金/[美]聯邦準備金　Federal Reserve
[美]联邦准备率/[美]聯邦準備比率　Federal Reserve Ratio
[美]联邦资金市场/[美]聯邦資金市場　Federal Fund Market
美术编辑/美術編輯　art editor
美术设计/藝術設計　art design
美术作品/美術作品　works of art
美学性/美感　aesthetics
美元本位/美元本位　dollar standard
美元贬值/美元貶值　dollar depreciation
美元承兑汇票/美元承兌匯票　dollar exchange acceptance
美元储备/美元儲備　dollar reserve
美元存单/美元存單　Yankee dollar certificate of deposit, Yankee $ CD
美元贷款/美元貸款　dollar loan
美元兑换率/美元兌換率　dollar rate
美元购买力/美元購買力　dollar's buying power
美元过剩/美元過剩　dollar glut
美元荒/美元短缺　dollar shortage

美元黄金本位/美元黃金本位　dollar-gold standard
美元汇兑本位制/美元匯兑本位制　dollar exchange standard system
美元汇票/美元匯票　dollar bill of exchange
美元平价/美元平價　dollar parity
美元缺口/美元差距　dollar gap
美元升值/美元升值　dollar upvaluation
美元信用证/美元信用狀　dollar credit
美元溢价/美元溢價,美元升水　dollar premium
美元债券/美元債券　bond dollar
美元资产/美元資產　dollar asset
美洲出口贸易促进委员会/美洲出口貿易促進中心　Inter-American Export Promotion Council
美洲储蓄和贷款银行/美洲儲蓄和貸款銀行　Inter-American Savings and Loans Bank
美洲国家商务仲裁委员会/美洲國家商務仲裁委員會　Inter-American Commercial Arbitration Commission
美洲国家组织/美洲國家組織　Organization of American States
魅力型领导/魅力型領導　charismatic leadership
门单/門單　Men Dan
门户网站/入口網站　web portal
门禁社区/門禁社區　gated community
门槛价格/臨界價格　threshold price
门槛人口/臨界人口　threshold population
门市销售/門市銷售　bookshop sales
门限广义回归条件异方差模型/門檻一般化自我回歸條件異質變異模型　threshold GARCH model, TGARCH model
门限自回归模型/門檻自[我]回歸模型　threshold autoregressive model, TAR model
门诊量/門診人次數　number of clinical visits
蒙版工艺/遮光法,蒙罩法　masking
蒙代尔-弗莱明模型/蒙代爾-弗萊明模型　Mundell-Fleming Model
蒙代尔模式/蒙代爾模式　Mundell Model
蒙片/掩色片,遮光片　mask
蒙赛尔色系/孟色耳色系　Munsell color
蒙太奇/蒙太奇,鏡頭組接　montage
蒙特卡罗法/蒙特卡羅法　Monte-Carlo method
蒙特卡罗模拟/蒙地卡羅模擬分析　Monte-Carlo simulation
蒙特利尔协议/蒙特婁協定　Montreal agreement
盟府/盟府　Mengfu, documents custody
盟书/盟書　Mengshu, treaty of alliance
猛犬债券/公牛債券,外國債券　bulldog bond
蒙古房/蒙古房　Mongolian copying office

孟子仁政思想/孟子仁義思想　Ren thought of Mencius
弥散/分散　dispersion
弥散性宗教/普化宗教,擴散式宗教　diffused religion
迷思/迷思　myth
米彻尔利希方程/Mitscherlich 方程式　Mitscherlich equation
米尔斯比率/米勒比例,Mills 比率　Mills' ratio
米兰达规则/米蘭達規則　Miranda rule
米兰银行/米蘭銀行　Midland Bank, Ltd.
米勒-奥尔模型/Miller-Orr 模型　Miller-Orr model
米勒分布/Miller 分布,Miller 分配　Miller distribution
米勒-莫迪利安尼定理/MM 定理　Miller-Modigliani proposition
米其林公司的科学管理/米其林公司的科學管理　scientific management of Michelin Company
秘档目录/秘檔目錄　secret archives catalogue
秘阁/秘閣　imperial library
秘阁本/秘閣本　palace library edition
秘密贸易/秘密貿易　clandestine trade
秘密投票/秘密投票　secret ballot
秘密文件/秘密檔　secret papers
秘密信托/秘密信託　secret trust
秘密削减价格/秘密減價　secret price cuts
秘密侦查/秘密偵查　covert investigation
秘密准备金/秘密準備金　hidden reserve, secret reserve
密闭式装具/密閉式裝具　airtight enclosure
密度/密度　density
密度范围/濃度域　density range
密度估计/密度估計　estimation of density
密度函数/密度函數　density function
密度梯度/密集梯度　density gradients
密封发盘/密封報價　offer under seal
密封式装具/密封式裝具　hemetically sealed fitting airpfoof enclosure
密封通价投标/密封投標　sealed tender
密封投标/封閉式喊價　sealed-bid
密级/密級　securtity classification
密级和保密期限/密級和保密期限　degree of security, duration of confidentiality
密级与保管期限项/密級與保管期限項　degree of security and duration of storage item
密集抽样/密集抽樣　intensive sampling
密集架/密集[排]架　compact shelf, dense shelf
密集量/密集量　intensive magnitudes

密集排架/密集排架　compact shelving
密集排架法/密集排架法　compact shelving
密集书架/緊緻[的]書架　compact bookshelf
密集型分销/密集配銷,密集分配　intensive distribution
密件/密件　confidential letter
密码/密碼　code, cipher
密纹唱片/長放唱片　long-play record, LP
密西西比泡沫事件/密西西比泡沫事件　Mississippi bubble
密歇根领导理论/密西根式領導理論　Michigan leadership theory
密钥/金鑰　key, secret key
密钥管理/金鑰管理　key management
幂/乘冪　power
幂和/同次和,同冪和　power sum
幂集/冪集　power set
幂矩/乘冪動差　power moment
幂均值/乘冪平均　power mean
幂律模型/乘冪律模型　power law model
蜜月效应/蜜月效果　honeymoon effect
棉花恐慌/棉花荒歉　cotton famine
棉连纸/棉連紙　mianlian paper
棉纸/棉紙　cotton paper
免费报纸/免費報紙　free newspaper
免费广告/免費廣告　free advertising
免费礼品促销/贈品促銷　free gift promotion
免费媒体/免費媒體,無償媒體　free media
免费品/自由財　free goods
免费网游/免費網遊　free online game
免费资源/自由資源　free resource
免付利息/免付利息　waiving interest
免关税/免關稅　free of duty
免赔额/自行負擔額,扣除額,扣除費用　deductible
免税/免稅　tax exemption, exempt from taxation, duty-free
免税报单/免稅報單　free entry
免税出口/免稅出口,自由輸出　free export
免税出口货物/免稅出口貨物　tax-free export
免税单/免稅單　bill of sufferance
免税工业园区/免稅工業園區　customs free industrial zone
免税货物/免稅貨物,無稅貨物　duty-free goods, non-dutiable goods
免税货物进口报单/免稅貨物進口報單　entry for free goods, entry of free goods
免税交易/免稅交易　tax-free transaction
免税进口/免稅進口,自由進口　free import
免税进口货物/免稅進口貨物　tax-free import, imported tax-free goods
免税贸易区/免稅貿易區　tax-free trade zone
免税品/免稅品　free article
免税品报关/免稅品報單　free of duty entry
免税品[转运]进口报关单/免稅品[轉運]進口報關單　transshipment free entry
免税期/租稅假期　tax holiday
免税期限/免稅期限　limitation of period for tax exemption
免税区/免稅區,自由貿易區,免稅地帶　free zone, free perimeter
免税商品/免稅商品　duty-free goods
免税收入/免稅收入　income exempt from taxation
免税投资/免稅投資　tax-free investment
免税信贷/免稅信貸　tax sparing credit
免税债券/免稅債券　tax-exempt bond
免税证明/免稅證明　tax-free certificate
免税制度/免稅制度　tax exemption system
免税组织/免稅組織　tax-exempt organization
免息/免息,不計利息　free of interest
免疫策略/免疫策略　immunization strategy
免疫[假设]/免疫[假設]　immunization hypothesis
免责条款/免責條款,除外條款　escape clause, exemption clause
免债公债/免稅公債　tax-free bond
免征出口关税/免徵出口稅　exempt from export tariff
免征关税/免徵關稅　duty exemption, exempt from customs duty
免征所得税/免徵所得稅　free of income tax
面/[界]面　face
面板/面板　panel
面板数据/面板資料　panel data
面板数据分析/面板資料分析　panel data analysis
面板数据模型/面板資料模型　panel data model
面对面沟通/面對面溝通　face-to-face communication
面对面谈判/面對面談判　face-to-face bargaining
面积条形图/地區長條圖　area bar chart
面截距/面截距　intercept of a plane
面具/面罩　mask
面试/訪問調查,面談　personal interview, interview
面向拆卸设计/易拆解設計　design for disassembly, DFD
面向成本的设计/面向成本設計　design for cost, DFC
面向对象的/物件導向　object-oriented
面向对象方法/物件導向方法　object-oriented

method
面向对象分析/物件導向分析　object-oriented analysis, OOA
面向对象设计/物件導向設計　object-oriented design
面向服务的设计/服務導向的設計　design for service
面向环保设计/環境化設計　design for environment, DFE
面向检测的设计/可測性設計　design for testing, DFT
面向实体标引/面向實體標引　entity-oriented indexing
面向提问标引/面向提問標引　questioning-oriented indexing
面向用户原则/面向用戶原則　user-oriented principle
面向再循环设计/再生設計　design for recycling, DFR
面向制造与装配设计/易製造與裝配之設計　design for manufacture and assembly, DFMA
面向质量的设计/品質導向的設計　design for quality
面向主题/主題導向　subject-oriention
面向装配设计/易組裝設計　design for assembly, DFA
面源/面源　area source
面源污染/面源汙染　area-source pollution
面值/面值　face value, par value
面值股票/面值股票　stock with par value
面子/面子　face, mianzi
描点/描點　plot
描述功能/描述功能　descriptive function
描述控制/描述控制　descriptive control
描述式写作/描述式寫作　descriptive writing
描述统计学/敘述統計學　descriptive statistics
描述性编目/記述編目　descriptive cataloging
描述性调查/敘述調查　descriptive survey
描述性决策理论/描述性決策理論　descriptive decision theory
描述性理论/描述性理論　descriptive theory
描述性目录/描述性目錄　descriptive list
描述性条款/描述性條款　descriptive provision
描述性统计/描述性統計　descriptive statistics
描述性问题/描述性問題　descriptive question
描述性宪法学/描述性憲法學　descriptive constitutional theory
描述性研究/描述性研究　descriptive research, descriptive study
描述性营销研究/描述性行銷研究　descriptive marketing research
描述性元数据/描述性詮釋資料　descriptive metadata
秒表时间研究/馬表時間研究　stopwatch time study
灭绝种族罪/滅絕種族罪　crime of genocide
民办非企业单位/民辦非企業單位　private nonenterprise unit, non-governmental non-enterprise unit
民办社工服务机构/民辦社工服務機構　non-governmental social work service agency
民变/民變　mass uprising
民法/民法　civil law
民法典/民法典　civil code
民间黄金市场/民間黃金市場　private gold market
民间文学表达形式保护条约/民間文學表達形式保護條約　Treaty for the Protection of Expressions of Folklore
民间文学艺术/民間文學藝術　expressions of folklore
民间信仰/民間信仰　folk belief
民间组织/民間組織　civil organization, mass organization
民间组织管理/民間組織管理　management of nongovernmental organization
民权/市民權，公民權　civil rights
民权法/民權法　Civil Rights Act
民生科技/民生科技　science and technology relating to the people's livelihood
民事法律关系/民事法律關係　civil legal relation
民事法律事实/民事法律事實　civil fact of law
民事判决/民事判決　civil judgement
民事权利/民事權利　civil right
民事权利能力/民事權利能力　capacity for civil rights
民事上诉状/民事上訴狀　appeal petition
民事司法统计/民事統計　civil justice statistics
民事诉讼/民事訴訟　civil action
民事诉讼案件的合议庭/民事訴訟案件的合議庭　collegiate bench of civil cases
民事诉讼程序/民事訴訟程序，民事訴訟程式　civil procedure
民事诉讼当事人权利平等/民事訴訟當事人權利平等　litigant's equity of rights in litigation
民事诉讼的诚信原则/民事訴訟的誠信原則　principle of bona fides in the civil lawsuit
民事诉讼第三人/民事訴訟第三人　third-party in civil lawsuit

民事诉讼法律关系/民事訴訟法律關係　legal relationships in civil action
民事诉讼法律关系客体/民事訴訟法律關係客體　object of legal relationships in civil action
民事诉讼法律关系内容/民事訴訟法律關係內容　matter of legal relationships in civil action
民事诉讼法律关系主体/民事訴訟法律關係主體　subject of legal relationships in civil action
民事行为能力/民事行爲能力　civil capacity
民事义务/公民義務　civil obligation
民事责任/民事責任　civil liability
民事责任能力/民事責任能力　capacity for civil responsibility
民事证据/民事證據　evidence in civil procedure
民事执行/民事執行　civil law's execution
民事主体/民事主體　subject of civil legal relation
民俗宗教/民間宗教　folk religion
民意测验/民意測驗,民意調查　public opinion polling
民意测验与问卷调查方法/民意測驗與問卷調查方法　polling and survey techniques
民意调查/民意調查,民意測驗　public opinion polling, opinion survey
民营化/民營化　privatization
民营图书馆/民營圖書館　non-state-run libraries
民用航空法/民航管理法　civil aeronautics act
民用物体/民用物體　civilian assets
民政/民政　civil administration
民政部门/民政機構　civil affairs department
民众大会/民眾大會　comitia
民主/民主　democracy
民主管理/民主管理　democratic management
民主化/民主化　democratization
民主化创新/民主化創新　democratizing innovation
民主集中制/民主集中制　democratic centralism
民主权利/民主權利　democratic rights
民主社会/民主社會　democratic society
民主型风格/民主式風格　democratic style
民主政治/民主政治　democratic politics
民族/民族　nation
民族科学/民族科學　ethno-science
民族平等/民族平等　national equality
民族文化/民族文化　ethnic culture
民族音乐/民族音樂　ethnic music
民族志/民族志　ethnography
民族志访谈法/民族志訪談法　ethnographic interview
民族志影片/民族志電影　ethnographic film
民族主义/民族主義　nationalism
民族资产阶级/民族資產階級　nationalist bourgeoisie
闵科夫斯基不等式/Minkowski 不等式　Minkowski's inequality
闽刻本/閩刻本　Min-family edition
闽本/閩本　Fujian edition
敏感性检验/敏感檢定　sensitive test
敏感性训练/敏感度訓練　sensitivity training
敏捷性/敏捷性,機敏性　agility
敏捷制造/敏捷製造　agile manufacturing
名册/名冊　roll
名称标目/名稱標目　name heading
名称标引/名稱標引　name indexing
名称参照/名稱參照　name reference
名称规范档案/標準名稱檔案　name authority file, NAF
名称规范记录/標準名稱記錄　name authority record, NAR
名称款目/名稱款目　name entry
名称索引/名稱索引　name index
名称-题名参照/名稱-題名參照　name-title reference
名称-题名附加款目/名稱-題名附加款目　name-title added entry
名称-题名款目/名稱-題名款目　name-title entry
名称-题名索引/名稱-題名索引　name-title index
名称组合法/名稱組合法　name combination method
名词索引/名詞索引　word index
名刺/名刺　Mingci, calling card
名公书判清明集/名公書判清明集　Minggongshupan-Ching Ming Ji
名录/名錄,目錄　name catalogue, directory
名目利率/名目利率　nominal interest rates
名人档案/名人檔案　personage archive
名人广告效应/名人廣告效應　celebrity advertising effect
名实分离/名實分離　inconsistency between nominal terms and actual practice
名义保护率/名目保護率　nominal rate of protection
名义本金额/象徵性本金　notional principal
名义尺度/名目尺度　nominal scale
名义定义/名目定義　nominal definition
名义工资/名目工資　nominal wages
名义工资指数/名目工資指數　nominal wage index
名义关税/名義關稅　nominal tariff
名义规范/名目規格　nominal specification
名义汇率/名義匯率,掛牌匯率,名目匯率　nominal

名义汇率/名義匯率 nominal exchange rate, nominal rate of exchange
名义汇票/名義匯票,名义上的交易 nominal exchange
名义货币/名義貨幣 nominal money
名义货币持有额/名義貨幣持有額 nominal money holdings
名义货币供给/表面資金供應 nominal money supply
名义货币余额/名義貨幣餘額 nominal money balance
名义价格/名目價格 nominal price
名义交易/名義交易 nominal transaction
名义利率/名義利率,掛牌利率,名目利率 nominal rate of interest, normal interest rate
名义利息/名義利息 nominal interest
名义群体法/名目群體技術 nominal group technique
名义收入/名目所得 nominal income
名义收益率/名義收益率,名目收益率,掛牌收益率 nominal yield ratio
名义数据/名目資料 nominal data
名义税率/名義稅率 nominal tax rate
名义小组/類別團體 nominal group
名义账户/名義賬戶,虛賬戶 nominal account
名义值/名目值 nominal value
名义资本/名義資本,額度股本,票面股本 nominal capital
名义资产/名義資產 nominal asset
名义组织/類別團體 nominal group
名誉权/名譽權 right of fame
明补/價格明補 clear-sighted subsidies
明抄本/明抄本 Ming handwritten edition
明大诰/明大誥 Ming Dagao
明德慎罚/明德慎罰 promotion of ethical and prudent penalty
明发谕旨/明發諭旨 open-channel imperial edicts
明会典/明會典 Code of Ming Dynasty
明见式索引/明見式索引 visible index
明刻本/明刻本 Ming dynasty edition
明尼苏达多相个性问卷/明尼蘇達人格測驗試題 Minnesota multiphasic personality inventory
明清档案/明清檔案 archive of Ming dynasty and Qing dynasty
明示/明示 clearly indicate
明示承认/明示承認 express recognition
明退/明退 fading in light
明晰产权/產權釐清 clarification of property rights
明细分类账/明細分類賬 subsidiary ledger

明星业务/明星業務 star business
冥婚/冥婚 ghost marriage
铭文/銘文,碑銘 inscription
命令/命令 command, order
命令文件/命令檔 programming record
命令型风格/指令式風格 directive style
命名/命名 denominate
命中点/命中點 hitting point
谬误/錯誤 fallacies
谬误回归/假性回歸 spurious regressions
谬相关/無意義相關 nonsense correlation
摹本/摹本 reproduction copy
摹刻本/摹刻本 reengraved edition
摹写本/摹寫本 facsimile
模仿/模仿 imitation
模仿产品/模仿產品 me-too product
模仿创新/模仿創新 imitative innovation
模仿创新模型/模仿創新模型 imitative innovation model
模仿反应/模仿反應 me-too response
模仿机制/模仿機制 imitative mechanism
模仿理论/模仿理論 copy-cat theory
模仿型创业/模仿型創業 entrepreneurial imitation
模糊/模糊[的],乏晰[的] fuzzy
模糊等价关系/模糊等價關係 fuzzy equivalent relation, fuzzy equivalence relation
模糊等价矩阵/模糊等價矩陣 fuzzy equivalent matrix, fuzzy equivalence matrix
模糊度/模糊度 fuzzy, ambiguity
模糊分类/模糊分類 fuzzy classification, fuzzy classify
模糊关系/模糊關係 fuzzy relation
模糊规划/模糊規劃 fuzzy programming
模糊集合/模糊集 fuzzy set
模糊集理论/模糊集合理論 fuzzy set theory
模糊检索/模糊檢索 fuzzy search
模糊矩阵/模糊矩陣 fuzzy matrix
模糊聚类/模糊聚類 fuzzy clustering, fuzzy cluster
模糊决策/模糊決策 fuzzy decision, fuzzy decision making
模糊控制块/模糊控制塊 fuzzy control patch
模糊理论/模糊理論 fuzzy theory
模糊联盟/模糊聯盟 fuzzy coalitions
模糊逻辑/模糊邏輯 fuzzy logic
模糊幂集/模糊冪集 fuzzy power set
模糊排序/模糊排序 fuzzy scheduling
模糊匹配/模糊匹配 fuzzy match
模糊前端/模糊前端 fuzzy front end

模糊数学/模糊數學 fuzzy mathematics
模糊先验分布/乏資訊事前分布 vague prior distribution
模糊先验概率/模糊事前機率 vague prior probability
模糊相似关系/模糊相似關係 fuzzy similarity relation, fuzzy similar relation, fuzzy resembling relation
模糊相似矩阵/模糊相似矩陣 fuzzy similar matrix
模糊信息/模糊資訊,乏晰資訊 fuzzy information
模糊预测模型/模糊預測模型 fuzzy forecasting model
模糊综合评价/模糊綜合評判 fuzzy comprehensive evaluation, fuzzy synthetic evaluation
模块/模組 module
模块创新/模組創新 modularity innovation
模块独立/模組獨立 module independence
模块化方法/模組化途徑 modular approach
模块设计/模組設計 modular design
模块式文摘/模塊式文摘 modular abstract
模块物料列表/模組物料清單 modular bill of material
模拟/模擬,類比 simulation, analogy
模拟测量/模擬量測 simulated measurement
模拟处理技术/模擬處理技術 analog technology
模拟打样/模擬打樣 analog proofing
模拟方法/模擬法 simulation method
模拟封印/模印 seal casting, seal moulding
模拟估算/模擬估算 analogous estimating
模拟化声音/類比錄音 analog sound
模拟计算机/類比計算機 analogue computer
模拟模型/模擬模型 simulation model
模拟倾销/類比傾銷 spurious dumping
模拟商店/虛擬商店 virtual store
模拟视频/類比視訊 analog video
模拟退火/模擬控溫 simulated annealing
模拟退火算法/模擬退火演算法 simulated annealing algorithm
模拟现实游戏/模擬現實遊戲 simulate reality game
模拟印刷/模擬印刷 analog printing
模拟预测模型/類比預測模型 simulation forecasting model
模拟装置/模擬器 simulator
iPad 模式/iPad 模式 iPad mode
Kindle 模式/Kindle 模式 Kindle mode
模式变项/模式變項 pattern variable
模式抽样/型態抽樣 patterned sampling
模式函数/型態函數 pattern function
模式识别/圖形識別 pattern recognition
模数混合模型/模數混合模型 modulus mixed model
模塑/造模,模製 moulding
模态/模態,形式 modality
模特法/模組法 model method, modular arrangement of predetermined time standard
模特排时法/模特排時法 modular arrangement of predetermined time standard
模温控制器/模溫控制器 mould heater
模型/模型 model
BS 模型/Brennan-Schwartz 模型 Brennan-Schwartz model
GREP 模型/GREP 模型 GREP model
IS-LM 模型/IS-LM 模型 IS-LM model
LHR 模型/LHR 模型 LHR model
Probit 模型/常態機率模型,機率單元模型 probit model, probit
Tobit 模型/杜賓模型 Tobit model
模型比较/模型比較 model comparison
模型辨识/模型辨識 model identification
模型的估计/模型估計 model estimation
模型的评价/模型適合度評估 model evaluation
模型的修正/模型修正 model modification
模型动画/模型動畫 model animation
模型对象/模型物件 model object
模型方法/模型法 model method
模型库/模型庫 model base
模型库管理系统/模型庫管理系統 model base management system
模型库系统/模型庫系統 model base system
模型模拟试验/模型模擬試驗 model simulation test
模型群/模型群 model group
模型设定/模型設定 model specification, specification of model
模型生成/模型生成 model generation
模型生命表/模型生命表 model life table
模型实验/模型實驗 model experiment
模型误导/模型不正確的設定 model misspecification
模型选择问题/模型選擇問題 model selection problem
模型诊断/模型診斷 model diagnostic checking
摩擦性失业/摩擦性失業 frictional unemployment
摩尔第二定律/第二摩爾定律 Moore's second law
摩尔定律/摩爾定律 Moore's law
摩根财团/摩根財團 House of Morgan
摩根斯特恩分布/Morgenstern 分布,Morgenstern 分配 Morgenstern distribution

摩兰检验统计量/Moran 檢定統計量　Moran's test statistic
摩西检验/Moses 檢定　Moses test
摩西控制跨度/摩西控制跨度,摩西控制範圍　span of control by Moses
磨损页/磨損頁　torn page
魔弹论/魔彈理論,子彈理論　bullet theory, magic bullet theory
魔术师/魔術師　magician
末端校正/末端校正　end correction
没收财产/没收財產　confiscation of property
莫蒂估计[量]/Murthy 估計[量]　Murthy's estimator
莫尔条纹/莫氏圖案　Moire fringe
莫尔纹/莫氏花紋　Moire pattern
莫斯泰勒 k 样本滑动量检验/Mosteller 的 k 樣本滑動檢定　Mosteller's k-sample slippage test
莫塔拉公式/Mortara 公式　Mortara formula
墨滴尺寸调制/墨滴尺寸調制　drop size modulate
墨滴速度/墨滴速度　drop velocity
墨菲法则/墨菲定律　Murphy's law
墨家/墨家　Mohism
墨印本/墨印本　black print
墨子社会思想/墨子社會思想　social thought of Mo-tzu
默认/預設　default
默认契约/隱含性契約　implicit contract
默示/默示　imply
默示承认/默示承認　implied recognition, tacit recognition
默许/默許　acquiescence
默许租赁/默許租賃　tenancy at sufferance
谋大逆/謀大逆　Mou Dani
谋反/謀反　rebel
谋叛/謀叛　insurgence
模板/模板　template
模版/模版,列印墊板　platen
模版印刷/模版印刷　stencil printing
模具/字模　mould
模切/模切削　die cutting
模切机/模切機　die-cutting machine
母本/母本　master, master matrics
母公司/母公司　parent company
母函数/母函數,生成函數　generating function
母盘玻璃清洗/母盤玻璃清洗　glass master cleaning
母盘前期制作/母帶前期製作　pre-mastering
母盘制作系统/母盤製作系統　mastering system
母片/母片　master

母权制/母權制　matriarchy
母体回归参数/母體回歸參數　population regression parameters
母体回归平面/母體回歸平面　population regression plane
母体文献/母體文獻　master literature
母系社会/母系社會　matrilineal society
母系制/母系制　matrilineal system
母性/母性　motherhood
拇指规则/直覺原則　rule of thumb
木记/木記　rectangular or oval figure occurring after a preface, table of contents or chapter, marking the end
木简/木牘　wooden slips
木偶动画/木偶動畫　puppet animation
目标/目標　goal
目标成本/目標成本　target cost
目标成本定价/目標成本法　target costing
目标导向性竞争情报/目標導向性競爭情報　target-oriented competitive intelligence
目标服务对象/目標服務物件　target service object
目标公司/目標公司,標的公司　target company, target firm
目标管理/目標管理　management by objective, MBO
目标规划法/目標規劃方法　goal programming approach
目标函数/目標函數,目標方程式　objective function
目标价格/目標價格　target price
目标精[密]度/目標精確度　precision aimed
目标库存量/目標存貨量　target inventory level
目标利润定价/目標利潤定價　target profit pricing
目标平均数/目標平均數　objective average
目标评价/目標評估　objective evaluation
目标区/目標區　target zones
目标群体指数/目標群體指數　target group index
目标任务法/目標任務法　objective-and-task method
目标设定理论/目標設定理論　goal-setting theory
目标设置理论/目標設定理論　goal-setting theory
目标市场/目標市場　target market
目标市场选择/目標市場選擇　market targeting
目标-手段分析法/目標-手段分析法　means-ends analysis method, objective-method analysis
目标受众/目標閱聽者,目標閱聽人,目標對象　target audience
目标叙词表/目標敘詞表　target thesaurus
目标因子/目標因素　target factor
目标营销/目標行銷　target marketing

目标用户/目標用戶　target user
目标与价值观子系统/目標與價值觀子系統　goal and value subsystem
目标总体/目標母體　target population
目次项/目次項　contents note
目的地交货价/目的地交貨價　franco domicile
目的地买方指定地点交货价/目的地買方指定地點交貨價　franco rendu
目的港/目的港　port of destination
目的港驳船交货价/目的港駁船交貨價　free overside price
[目的港]船上交货/[目的港]船上交貨　ex ship
[目的港]码头交货价/[目的港]碼頭交貨價　ex dock, ex quay, ex wharf
目的解释/目的解釋　teleological Interpretation
目的税/指定用途税　earmarked tax
目的刑罚/目的刑罰　offense to intent
目的行为主义/目的行爲主義，目標行爲論　purposive behaviorism
目的性/目的性　purposefulness
目的样本/立意樣本　purposive sample
目检/目視檢驗　visual inspection
目录/目錄，清單　catalogue, list, directory
目录抽样/表冊抽樣　list sampling
目录购买者/目錄購買者　catalog buyer
目录柜/卡片櫃　card cabinet, catalog cabinet
目录盒/目錄盒　catalog cabine
目录盒标签/目錄盒標籤　tray label

目录价格/目錄價格　list price
目录卡片/目錄卡片　catalog card
目录式检索工具/目錄式檢索工具　catalog type retrieval tool
目录销售商/目錄銷售商　catalog house
目录学/目錄學　bibliography
目录学家/目錄學家　bibliographer
目录营销/目錄行銷　catalog marketing
目录征订/目錄徵訂　mailing booklist for subscription
目录专题/目錄專題　catalogue
目视控制/目視控制　visual control
牧业税/牧業税　animal husbandry tax
募集设立/募集設立　incorporation by stock floatation
睦邻组织运动/睦鄰組織運動　social settlement movement
穆德-布朗估计/Mood-Brown 估計　Mood-Brown estimation
穆德-布朗中位数检验/Mood-Brown 中位數檢定　Mood-Brown median test
穆德 W 检验/Mood 的 W 檢定　Mood's W-test
穆迪综合股票指数/穆迪綜合股票指數　Moody's composite stock index
穆尔乌托邦思想/莫爾烏托邦思想　Utopia thought of More
穆尼管理理论/穆尼管理理論　management theory of Mooney

N

纳什定理/奈許定理　Nash theorem
纳什均衡/奈許均衡　Nash equilibrium
纳什均衡存在性定理/奈許均衡存在定理　Nash equilibrium existence theorem
纳什谈判解/奈許談判解　Nash bargaining solution
纳什讨价还价理论/奈許理論　Nash bargaining theory
纳税/納税　pay duty
纳税保证/納税保證　warranty for tax payment
纳税保证金/納税保證金　security of tax payment
纳税储蓄债券/納税儲蓄債券　tax saving note
纳税担保/納税擔保　guaranty for tax payment
纳税单位/課税單位　taxpaying unit
纳税抵押/納税抵押　mortgage for tax payment
纳税检查/税務檢查　tax inspection
纳税均等/納税均等,税捐均等　equality of taxation
纳税年度/課税年度　taxable year
纳税期限/納税期限,交税最後期限　tax deadline
纳税人/納税[義務]人　taxpayer
纳税申报/申報納税　tax declaration
纳税申报单/納税申報單　tax returns
纳税通知书/納税通知書　tax paper
纳税质押/納税質押　pledge for tax payment
纳税遵从/守法納税　tax compliance
纳斯达克指数/納斯達克指數　NASDAQ index
奈曼 ψ^2 检验/Neyman ψ^2 檢定　Neyman's ψ^2 test
奈曼模型/Neyman 模型　Neyman model
奈曼配置/Neyman 配置　Neyman allocation
奈曼-皮尔逊定理/Neyman-Pearson 理論　Neyman-Pearson theory
奈曼-皮尔逊[基本]引理/Neyman-Pearson[基本]引理　Neyman-Pearson fundamental lemma
奈曼-皮尔逊检验的渐近功效/尼曼-皮遜檢定的漸近檢力　asymptotic power of Neyman-Pearson
奈曼-斯科特模型/Neyman-Scott 模型　Neyman-Scott model
奈曼因子分解定理/Neyman 分解定理　Neyman's factorization theorem
奈曼最短无偏置信区间/Neyman 最短不偏信賴區間　Neyman's shortest unbiased confidence interval
耐火极限/耐火極限　duration of fire resistance
耐久性/耐久性,耐用度　durability
耐久性试验/耐久度試驗　endurance test
耐磨性/抗磨損力　wear resistance, abrasion resistance
耐用品/耐久財　durable goods
耐用纸/耐用紙　permanent paper
男同性恋/男同性戀者,男同志　gay
男性霸权/男性宰制,男性主控　male-dominated
男性凝视/男性凝視　male gaze
男性气质/男性特質,陽剛特質　masculinity
男性中心主义/男性中心主義　androcentrism
男主外女主内/男主外女主内　husband is breadwinner and wife is homemaker
南北对话/南北對話　north-south talks
南北贸易/南北貿易　south-north trade
南北模型/南北模型　north-south models
南海泡沫/南海泡沫　South sea bubble
南极/南極　Antarctica
南监本/南監本　Nanjing Imperial Academy edition
南南合作/南南合作　south-south cooperation
南南贸易/南南貿易　south-south trade
南宋监本/南宋監本　imperial academy edition in the Southern Song Dynasty
NP 难问题/NP 難題　NP-hard problem
难民/難民　refugee
内爆/内爆　implosion
内部案例/内部案例　within-case
内部半价差/内部半價差　inside half-spread
内部储备/内部儲備　inner reserve
内部创新/内部創新　internal innovation
内部创业/内部創業　intrapreneuring
内部创业评价工具/内部創業評價量表　intrapreneurship assessment instrument
内部发行/内部發行　published interior
内部方差/内部變異數　internal variance
内部公共关系/内部公共關係　internal public relation
内部公平/内部公平　internal equity
内部惯性区域/内部慣性區域　internal inert area
内部规模经济/内部規模經濟　economy of inside scale, internal economics of scale

内部化理论/内部化[理]論　internalization theory
内部货币与外部货币/内部貨幣與外部貨幣　inside and outside money
内部价[格]/内部價格　internal prices
内部交易/内部交易　internal transaction
内部均衡/内部均衡　internal balance
内部开发中心/内部發展中心　in-house development center
内部考订/内部考訂　internal criticism
内部可控/内控點　internal locus of control
内部控制/内部控制　internal control
内部控制程序/内部管制程序　internal-control procedure
内部控制评价/内部控制評價　evaluation of internal control
内部控制缺陷/内部控制缺陷　deficiency in internal control
内部控制审计/内部控制查核　audit of internal control
内部控制制度/内部控制制度　internal control system
内部扩散模式/内部擴散模式　internal diffusion model
内部劳动力市场/内部勞動市場,内部人力市場　internal labor market
内部期刊/内部期刊　restricted periodical, internally distributed periodical
内部牵制/内部牽制　internal check
内部情报员/内部情報員　internal sources
内部人/局内人　insiders
内部审计/内部審計　internal audit
内部审计准则公报/内部審計準則公報　Statement of Internal Auditing Standards
内部失效成本/内部失效成本　internal failure cost
内部时间/内部時間　internal time
内部收益率/内在報酬率　internal rate of return
内部调整准备时间/内部整備時間　internal setup time
内部-外部矩阵/内部-外部矩陣　internal-external matrix
内部文件/内部檔　internal restricted document
内部消息/内線消息　inside information
内部效度/内部效度,内在效度　internal validity
内部效率/内部效率　internal efficiency
内部信息[源]/内部資訊源　internal information source
内部行政关系/内部管理體制　internal administrative relationship
内部需求/國内需求　domestic demand
内部研究资料/未出版的科研資料　unpublished research materials
内部一致信度/内部一致性信度　internal consistency reliability
内部因素评价矩阵/内部因素評估矩陣　internal factor evaluation matrix
内部引文/内部引文　internal citation
内部营销/内部行銷　internal marketing
内部营销数据库/内部行銷資料庫　internal marketing database
内部增长率/内部成長率　internal growth rate
内部招聘/内部招募　internal recruitment
内部资料性出版物/内部資料性出版物　internally ciculated publication
内部最小二乘/内部最小平方　internal least squares
内插/内插[法]　interpolation
内地海关/内地海關　inland customs house
内地贸易税/内地貿易稅,内陸關稅　inland duty
内点方法/内在點法　interior-point method
内罚函数法/内部懲罰函數法　interior penalty function method
内府本/内府本　imperial court edition
内府抄本/内府抄本　imperial court handwritten edition
内府写本/内府抄本　imperial court handwritten edition
内阁/内閣　cabinet
内阁制/内閣制　cabinet system
内滚筒型设备/内滾筒型設備　internal drum device
内含报酬率/内部報酬率　internal rate of return, IRR
内含利息/内含利息　implicit interest
内行/專業,職業　expert
内化/内[在]化　internalization
内回归/内部回歸　internal regression
内婚制/内婚制　endogamy
内聚/内聚,凝聚　cohesion
内卷/内卷　involution
内控质量标准/内控品質標準　inner quality standard
内陆国/内陸國　land-locked states
内曼-凯尔斯检验/Newman-Keuls 檢定　Newman-Keuls test
内幕交易/内幕交易,内線交易　insider dealing
内幕交易、泄露内幕信息罪/内幕交易、洩露内幕資訊罪　crime of insider trading or divulge inside information
内幕人员/内幕人員　inside person in the securities

market
内幕新闻/内幕新聞　inside edition
内幕信息/局内人資訊　insider information
内企业家/内部創業者　intrapreneur
内驱力/驅力　drive
内群体/内團體　inner group
内容/内容　content
内容把关/内容控制　content control
内容分发网络/内容分發網路　content delivery network, CDN
内容分析/内容分析　content analysis
内容分析法/内容分析　content analysis
内容服务/内容服務　content service
内容附注/内容附注　content notes
内容格式/内容格式　content format
内容管理系统/内容管理系統　content management system
内容加密/内容加密　content encryption
内容检索/内容檢索　content search, content retrieval, content-based retrieval
内容鉴定/内容鑒定　content appraisal
内容联系/内容聯繫　content relation
内容排架法/内容排架法　content arrangement
内容索引/内容索引　content index
内容提要/内容提要　summary, headline
内容效度/内容效度　content validity
内容型激励理论/内容型激勵理論　substantial motivation theory
内容元数据/内容詮釋資料　content metadata
内容制作/内容製作　content fabrication
内设机构/内設機構　internal agency
内设计/内設計　interior design
内生变量/内生變量,内生變數　endogenous variable
内生变迁/内生變遷　endogenous transition
内生式发展/内生式發展　endogenous development
内生型现代化/内生型現代化　endogenous modernization
内生性技术突破/内生性技術突破　endophytism of technology breakthrough
内生增长/内生成長　endogenous growth
内生增长理论/内生成長理論　endogenous growth theory
内生增长模型/内生成長模型　endogenous growth models
内水/内水　internal waters
内务管理文件/内務管理檔　housekeeping records
内务条令/内務條令　mandatory regulation on routine service

内向型/内向型　inward-looking
内向型经济/内向型經濟　inward-oriented economy
内页广告/内頁廣告　inside page
内隐领导理论/内隱領導理論　implicit leadership theory
内源融资/内部融通　internal financing
内源性/内生　endogenous
内在变异/内在變異　inward variation
内在付现成本/隱含付現成本　implied cash cost
内在个案研究/内在個案研究　intrinsic case study
内在观点/内在觀點　internal point of view
内在怀疑论/内在懷疑論　internal scepticism
内在货币/内在貨幣　inside money
内在价值/内在價值　intrinsic value
内在奖励/内在報酬　intrinsic reward
内在精[密]度/内在精確度　intrinsic precision
内在可用性/内在可用度　intrinsic availability
内在社会控制/内在社會控制　internal social control
内在稳定器/内在穩定器　built-in stabilizers
内在效度/内在效度,内部效度　internal validity
内噪声/内干擾　interior noise
能级对应原理/能級對應原理　competence theory
能力/能力,能耐　capability
能力比/能力比　capability ratio
能力需求计划/產能需求規劃　capacity requirement planning, CRP
能源法/能源法　law on energy
能源规划/能源規劃　energy planning
能源政策/能源政策　energy policy
能指/能指,符號具,符徵　signifier
尼尔斯检验/Daniels 檢定　Daniels test
尼奎斯特－香农定理/Nyquist-Shannon 定理　Nyquist-Shannon theorem
泥板档案/泥板檔案　clay tablet archives
泥版文书/泥板檔案　clay tablet
泥印/泥印　mud seal
泥足法庭/泥足法庭　pie-powder court
拟办/擬辦　propose
拟遍历假设/準遍歷假設　quasi-ergodic hypothesis
拟独立[性]/準獨立性　quasi-independence
拟分析修匀/擬分析修勻　pseudo-analytical graduation
拟稿/擬稿　make a draft
拟合/配適　fitting
拟合不足/缺適性　lack of fit
拟合函数/目標函數　fitting function, discrepancy function
拟合优度/擬合優度,適合度　goodness of fit,

goodness of fitting
拟合优度度量/擬合優度度量,配適度測度 goodness-of-fit measure
拟合优度检验/配適性檢定,適合度檢定 goodness-of-fit test, test for goodness-of-fit
拟合优度卡方检验/卡方適合度檢定 chi-square test for goodness-of-fit
拟合值/配適值 fitted value
拟极差/準全距 quasi-range
拟极大似然估计/準最大概似估計 quasi-maximum likelihood
拟极大似然估计量/準最大概度估計量 quasi-maximum likelihood estimator
拟加性形式/擬加性形式 quasi-additivity form
拟拉丁方/準拉丁方陣 quasi-Latin square
拟马尔夫链/準馬可夫鏈 quasi-Markov chain
拟牛顿法/準牛頓法 quasi-Newton method
拟似然/準概度 quasi-likelihood
拟随机抽样/準隨機抽樣 quasi-random sampling
拟态/擬態,模仿 mimesis
拟凸函数/擬凸函數 quasi-convex function
拟析因设计/準因子設計 quasi-factorial design
拟线性估计量/準線性估計量 quasilinear estimator
拟线性偏好/準線型偏好 quasilinear preferences
拟线性效用函数/準線型效用 quasilinear utility
拟因子/準因子 quasi-factor
拟正规方程/準正規方程式 quasi-normal equations
拟制学说/擬制學說 fiction theory
拟制血亲/擬制血親 fictional blood kinship
逆/逆,反 inverse
逆贝塔分布/反轉貝他分布,反轉貝他分配,反轉β分布 inverted beta distribution
逆变换/逆變換 inverse transformation
逆差/逆差 deficit balance, adverse balance
逆插值/反插值 inverse interpolation
逆超几何分布/逆超幾何分布,逆超幾何分配 inverse hypergeometric distribution
逆城市化/逆都市化 counter urbanization
逆抽样/逆抽樣 inverse sampling
逆狄利克雷分布/反轉 Dirichlet 分布,反轉 Dirichlet 分配 inverted Dirichlet distribution
逆多项抽样/逆多項抽樣 inverse multinomial sampling
逆多项式/逆多項式 inverse polynomial
逆二项抽样/逆二項抽樣 inverse binomial sampling
逆反/心理抗拒 psychological inversion
逆分布/逆分布 inverse distribution
逆伽马分布/逆迦瑪分配 inverted gamma distribution
逆伽马密度/逆迦瑪密度 inverted gamma density
逆伽马密度函数/逆迦瑪密度函數 inverted gamma density function
逆概率/逆機率 inverse probability
逆高斯分布/逆高斯分布,逆高斯分配,逆 Gauss 分布 inverse Gaussian distribution
逆阶乘级数分布/逆階乘級數分布,逆階乘級數分配 inverse factorial series distribution
逆矩/逆動差 inverse moment
逆累积分布函数/逆累積分布函數 inverse cumulative distribution function
逆弹性法则/逆彈性準則 inverse elasticity rule
逆相关/反相關 inverse correlation
逆向分销/逆向配銷 reverse distribution
逆向工程/逆向工程,反向工程 reverse engineering
逆向竞拍/反向拍賣 reverse auction
逆向排程/逆向排程 backward scheduling
逆向倾销/逆向傾銷 reverse dumping
逆向物流/逆向物流 reverse logistics
逆向选择/逆向選擇 adverse selection
逆向移动平均过程/可逆移動平均過程 invertible ma process
逆向营销/逆向行銷 reverse marketing
逆需求/逆需求 inverse demand
逆序回归函数/逆序回歸函數,反向回歸函數 antitonic regression function
逆序列相关/逆序列相關 inverse serial correlation
逆序文献频率法/逆序文獻頻率法 inverse document frequency weight
逆元素/逆元素,反元素 inverse element
逆正态记分检验/逆常態計分檢定 inverse normal scores test
逆指数平均/反指數平均 inverse exponential average
逆转试验/互換實驗 reversal experiment
匿名产品/匿名產品 anonymous product
匿名经典/佚名經典著作 anonymous classic
匿名性/匿名性 anonymity
匿名作品/匿名作品,不具名作品 anonymous work
年表/年表,大事記 chronology, chronological table
年代排架法/年代排架法 chronological order
年代学/年代學,編年學 chronology
年度报告/年報 annual report
年度分类法/年度分類法 time classification, annual classification
年度合同/年度合約 annualized contract
年度计划/年度計劃 yearly plan

年度目标/年度目標　annual objective
年度实际利率/年度實際利率　yearly effective rate of interest, YER
年度收入与支出/歲入與歲出　annual receipts arid outlays
年度索引/年度索引　annual index
年度-问题分类法/年度-問題分類法　year-question classification
年度综述/年度評論　annual review
年度-组织机构分类/年度-組織機構分類法　year-organisation classification
年画/年畫　new year picture, the Spring Festival picture
年减量/年減量　annual decrement
年鉴/年鑒　yearbook, almanac, annal
年金/年金　annuity
年刊/年刊　annual
年利率/年利率　annual rate
年龄别生育率/年齡別生育率　age-specific fertility rate
年龄别死亡率/年齡別死亡率　age-specific death rate
年龄分布/年齡分布　age distribution
年龄分层理论/年齡分層理論　age stratification theory
年龄构成/年齡構成　age composition
年龄鉴定论/年齡鑒定論　age appraisal theory
年龄-教育-收入剖面图/年齡-教育-薪資剖面　age-education-earnings profiles
年龄-收入剖面图/年齡-薪資剖面　age-earnings profile
年龄相依分支过程/年齡相依分支過程　age-dependent branching process
年龄相依生灭过程/年齡相依生死過程　age-dependent birth and death process
年龄性别结构/年齡性別結構　age-gender structure, age-sex structure
年龄-性别死亡率/年齡性別死亡率　age-sex specific death rate
年龄中位数/年齡中位數　median age
年龄组/年齡組　age group
年平均每日交通量/年平均每日交通量　average annual daily traffic
年谱/年譜　biographical chronicle, chronicle, chronological life
年轻人口/年輕人口　young population
年数总和法/年數加總折舊法　depreciation sum-of-the-years-digits method

年薪制/年薪制　annual pay system
年增量/年增量　annual increment
年中人口/年中人口　mid-year population
年终股息/年終股息　year-end dividend
年总增加率/年總增加率　annual rate of total increase
黏合/結合，束縛　bonding
黏接层/接著層　adhesive layer
黏接强度/黏結強度　adhesion strength
黏土动画/黏土動畫　clay animation
黏性交易/黏性交易　sticky deal
黏蝇纸效应/蒼蠅紙效果　flypaper effect
柠檬市场/劣貨市場　lemons market
柠檬问题/劣貨問題　lemons problem
凝聚性/凝聚性，結合性　coherency
凝视/凝視　gaze
牛鞭效应/牛鞭效應　bullwhip effect
牛顿迭代法扩展/牛頓迭代法擴充　Newton iteration extension
牛顿法/牛頓法　Newton method
牛皮纸/牛皮紙　kraft paper
牛市/買超市場，市場看漲　bull market
牛市或熊市差价期权/牛熊市價差期權　bull or bear spread option
牛仔经济/牛仔經濟　cowboy economy
扭曲操作/長短期互換操作　operation nudge, operation twist
扭曲效应/扭曲效果　distorting effect
扭送/扭送　seize and deliver to authorities concerned
纽带频率/連結頻率　the frequency of ties
纽伦堡国际军事法庭/紐倫堡國際軍事法庭　Nuremberg international military tribunal
纽伦堡审判/紐倫堡審判　Nuremberg Trials
纽伦堡原则/紐倫堡原則　Nuremberg Principles
纽曼五职能说/紐曼五職能說　five management functions theory of Newman
纽约承兑信用证/紐約承兑信用狀　New York acceptance credit
纽约慈善学院/紐約慈善學院　New York School of Philanthropy
纽约期货交易所/紐約期貨交易所　New York Futures Exchange
纽约商品交易所/紐約商品交易所　Commodity Exchange of New York, New York Mercantile Exchange
纽约时报诉萨利文案/紐約時報訴薩利文案　New York Times v. Sullivan
纽约投资市场/紐約投資市場　New York

investment market
纽约银行同业拆放利率/紐約銀行同業拆放利率 New York interbank offered rate
纽约证券交易所综合指数/紐約證券交易所綜合指數 New York stock exchange composite index
农产品/農産品 agricultural products
农产品产地价格/農産品産地價格 agricultural prices at farm gate
农产品价格支持与补贴政策/農産品價格支持計劃與補貼政策 agricultural price support and subsidies
农产品贸易平衡/農産品貿易平衡 agricultural trade balance
农产品期货/農産品期貨 farm product futures
农产品期权/農業選擇權 agricultural options
农产品质量安全/農産品品質安全 quality safety of agricultural products
农村部门/農村部門 rural sector
农村地区/農村地區 rural areas
农村调查/農村調查 rural survey
农村发展/農村發展 rural development
农村发展战略/鄉村發展策略 rural development strategies
农村合作医疗/農村合作醫療 rural cooperative medical service
农村经济/鄉村經濟 rural economy
农村劳动力转移/農村勞動力轉移 rural labor force transfer
农村社区/農村社區,鄉村社區,田園社區 rural community
农村剩余劳动力/農村剩餘勞動力 rural surplus labor
农村双层经营体制/農村雙作業系統 rural dual operation system
农村消费者物价指数/鄉村消費者物價指數 rural consumer price index, index of rural consumer prices
农村新型合作医疗制度/農村新型合作醫療制度 new cooperative medical insurance system in countryside
农村养老社会保险/農村養老社會保險 social old-age insurance in countryside
农村支持体系/農村支持制度 rural support system
农村自治/農村自治 rural autonomy
农村综合发展/整合式農村發展 integrated rural development
农家书屋/農家書屋 rural reading room
农民专业合作社/農民專業合作社 farmer professional cooperative
农奴/農奴 serf
农奴制/農奴身份,農奴制度 serfdom
农药安全使用制度/農藥安全使用制度 institution of safety application of pesticides
农药污染/農藥汙染 pesticides pollution
农业/農業 agriculture
农业补偿政策/農業補償政策 agricultural compensation policy
农业部门的外汇贡献/農業部門的外匯貢獻 foreign exchange contribution of agricultural sector
农业部门的资本贡献/農業部門的資本貢獻 capital contribution of agricultural sector
农业部门市场贡献/農業部門市場貢獻 market contribution of agricultural sector
农业产业化/農業工業化 agricultural industrialization
农业的女性化/農業的女性化 feminization of agriculture
农业环境保护/農業環境保護 agricultural environmental protection
农业金融/農業金融 agricultural finance
农业劳动生产力指数/農業勞動生產力指數 agricultural labor productivity index
农业贸易/農業貿易 agricultural trade
农业普查/農業普查 agriculture census
农业区位论/農業選地理論 agricultural location theory
农业人口/農業人口 agriculture population
农业生产统计/農業生產統計 agriculture production statistics
农业生产指数/農業生產指數 agricultural production indices
农业剩余/農産品剩餘 agriculture surplus
农业税/農業稅 agricultural tax
农业特产税/農業特産稅 special agricultural product tax
农业图书馆/農業圖書館 agricultural library
农业土地生产力指数/農業土地生產力指數 agricultural land productivity index
农业推广/農業推廣 agricultural extension
农业协定/農業協定 agreement on agriculture
农业信用合作社/農業信用合作社 agricultural credit cooperative
农业学会/農業學會,農民團體 agricultural society
农业银行/農業銀行 agricultural bank
农业灾害统计/農業災害統計 agricultural damage statistics

农业制度/農業制度　agrarian system
农业资本/農業資本　agricultural capital
农作物保险/作物保險　crop insurance
农作制度/耕作制度　farming system
浓度控制/濃度控制　concentration control
奴隶社会/奴隸社會　slave society
奴隶制/奴隸制度　slavery
努力/努力　effort
努力博弈理论/努力博弈理論　game theory of effort
努力点/努力點　effort point
女权运动/女權運動　women's right movement
女权主义/女權主義　feminism
女权主义法学/女權主義法學　feminist legal theory
女权主义方法论/女權主義方法論　feminist methodology
女权主义论/女權主義論　feminist theory
女同性恋/女同性戀［者］　lesbian
女性气质/女性特質,陰柔特質　femininity
女性文化/女性文化　female culture
女性学/女性學　women studies
女性主义/女性主義　feminism
女性主义的社会学/女性主義的社會學　feminist sociology
女性主义方法论/女性主義方法論　feminist methodology
女职工特殊保护/女職工特殊保護　labor protection for female workers
虐待部属罪/虐待部屬罪　crime of maltreating subordinates
虐待老年人/虐待老年人　elderly abuse
虐恋/虐戀　sadomasochism
挪用/挪用　appropriation
挪用公款罪/挪用公款罪　crime of misappropriating public funds
挪用资金罪/挪用資金罪　crime of misappropriating capital
诺贝尔奖/諾貝爾獎　Nobel prize
诺成合同/諾成合同　consensual contract
诺里斯-拉瓜迪亚法/諾利斯-拉瓜蒂亞法案　Norris-Laguardia act
诺模图/諾模圖　Nomogram
诺模图法/諾模圖法　Nomography
诺斯悖论/諾思悖論　North paradox
诺特循环趋势检验/循環趨勢的 Noether 檢定　Noether's test for cyclical trend

O

欧拉常数/Euler 常数　Euler's constant
欧拉方/Euler 方阵　Eulerian square
欧朗分布/Erlang 分布,Erlang 分配　Erlang distribution
欧朗公式/Erlang 公式　Erlang's formula
欧盟/歐洲聯盟,歐盟　European Union, EU
欧盟 1996 年关于数据库法律保护的指令/歐盟 1996 年關於資料庫法律保護的指令　EU Directive on the Legal Protection of Databases
欧盟委员会/歐洲經濟組織　European Commission
欧姆斯迪得-图基关联性检验/Olmstead-Tukey 相聯檢定　Olmstead-Tukey test of association
欧式距离/歐式距離　Euclidean distance
欧式期权/歐式選擇權　European option
欧特周期图/歐特週期圖　Alter periodiagram
欧文分布/Irwin 分布,Irwin 分配　Irwin distribution
欧文管理思想/歐文管理思想　management thought of Owen
欧文主义/歐文主義　Owenism
欧元/歐元　Euro
欧元交易/歐元交易　Euro-based transaction, Euro trading
欧元利率/歐元利率　Euro interest rate
欧元面额/歐元面額　Euro denomination
欧元面额贷款/歐元面額貸款　Euro-denominated loan
欧元面额支票/歐元面額支票　Euro-denominated cheque
欧元市场/歐元市場　Euro market
欧元收入/歐元收入　Euro earnings
欧元债券/歐市外幣債券　eurobond
欧元账户/歐元賬戶　Euro account
欧元资产市场/歐元資產市場　Euro-asset market
欧洲百货公司管理/歐洲百貨公司管理　department store management of Europe
欧洲大陆收据存单/歐洲大陸定存單　continental depositary receipt
欧洲大陆通货/歐洲大陸通貨　continental currency
欧洲发展基金/歐洲發展基金　European Development Fund
欧洲复兴和发展银行/歐洲復興發展銀行　European Bank for Reconstruction and Development
欧洲共同体单一市场法/歐洲共同體單一市場法　Single Market Act of the European Community
欧洲国际军事法庭/歐洲國際軍事法庭　International Military Tribunal at Nuremberg
欧洲货币/歐洲貨幣,歐洲通貨　Eurocurrency
欧洲货币单位/歐洲貨幣單位,歐洲通貨單位　European currency unit
欧洲货币浮动幅度/歐洲貨幣浮動幅度,歐洲通貨波帶　European currency band
欧洲货币市场/歐洲貨幣市場,歐元市場　Eurocurrency market
欧洲货币体系/歐洲貨幣體系,歐洲貨幣制度　European monetary system
欧洲货币辛迪加贷款利息/歐洲貨幣辛迪加貸款利息　interest on Syndicated Eurocurrency credit
欧洲货币信贷/歐洲貨幣信貸　Eurocurrency credit
欧洲结算/歐洲清算制度　European clear
欧洲金融期货交易所/歐洲金融期貨交易所　European Financial Future Exchange
欧洲金融市场放松管制/歐洲金融市場放鬆管制,歐洲金融市場自由化　deregulation of European financial market
欧洲经济合作委员会/歐洲經濟合作委員會　Committee for European Economic Cooperation
欧洲经济与货币联盟/歐洲經濟與貨幣聯盟　Economic and Monetary Union of the European Community, European Economic and Monetary Union
欧洲联盟/歐洲聯盟,歐盟　European Union, EU
欧洲美元/歐洲美元　Eurodollar
欧洲美元贷款/歐洲美元貸款　Eurodollar loan
欧洲美元利率/歐洲美元利率　Eurodollar rate
欧洲美元期货合约/歐洲美元期貨契約　Eurodollar futures contract
欧洲美元市场/歐洲美元市場　Eurodollar market
欧洲美元债券/歐洲美元債券　bond Eurodollar, Eurodollar bond
欧洲期权交易所/歐洲選擇權交易所　European Options Exchange

欧洲商业票据/歐洲商業票據　Eurocommercial paper
欧洲投资银行/歐洲投資銀行　European Investment Bank, EIB
欧洲信用卡/歐洲信用卡　Euro-card
欧洲债券/歐洲債券　Euro-bond
欧洲债券市场/歐洲債券市場　Euro-bond market
欧洲支票/歐洲支票　Euro-check
欧洲质量管理基金会/歐洲品質管理基金會　European Foundation for Quality Management, EFQM
欧洲质量组织/歐洲品質組織　European Organization for Quality, EOQ
欧洲中央银行/歐洲中央銀行　European Central Bank
欧洲专利条约/歐洲專利協定　European Patent Convention
欧洲综合货币单位/歐洲綜合貨幣單位　Euro-composite unit
偶发参数/偶發參數　incidental parameter
偶发宽放/偶發寬放　incidental allowance
偶发缺陷/偶發缺點　incidental defect
偶发性创新/偶發性創新　serendipitous innovation
偶发性倾销/偶發性傾銷　occasional dumping, sporadic dumping
偶函数/偶函數　even function
偶然/機遇　chance
偶然变异/偶然變異　accidental variation
偶然波动/偶然波動　accidental fluctuation
偶然故障/機遇故障　chance failure
偶然失效/機遇故障　chance failure
偶然式非正式信息沟通/偶爾式非正式溝通　incidentally-mode of informal communication
偶然误差/偶然誤差,機遇誤差　error by chance, chance error
偶然因果关系/偶然因果關係　contingent causation
偶然原因/機遇原因　chance cause
偶然运动/偶然移動　accidental movement
偶数/偶數　even number
偶数项和/偶總和　even summation
偶像崇拜/偶像崇拜　idolatry
偶遇抽样/偶遇抽樣　accidental sampling
耦合/耦合　coupling
耦合分析/耦合分析　coupling analysis
耦合强度/耦合強度　coupling strength

P

爬山法/登山法 hill-climbing method
帕金森法则/帕金森定律 Parkinson's law
帕兰德的区位理论/帕蘭德區位理論 Palander location theory
帕累托标准/柏拉圖判準 Pareto criterion
帕累托分布/柏拉圖分配, Pareto 分布, Pareto 分配 pareto distribution
帕累托分析法/柏拉圖分析法 Pareto analysis method
帕累托改进/柏拉圖改善 Pareto improvement, Pareto improving
帕累托潜在改进/潛在柏拉圖改善 potential Pareto improvement
帕累托曲线/柏拉圖曲線 Pareto curve
帕累托图/柏拉圖圖 Pareto chart, Pareto diagram
帕累托效率/柏拉圖效率 Pareto efficiency
帕累托型分布/柏拉圖型分布, 柏拉圖型分配 Pareto-type distribution
帕累托指数/柏拉圖指數 Pareto index
帕累托最优/柏拉圖最適[性] Pareto optimality, Pareto optimum
帕累托最优公理/柏拉圖-最適公理 Pareto-optimality axiom
帕姆函数/Palm 函數 Palm function
帕舍指数/裴氏指數 Paasche index
帕氏价格指数/裴氏物價指數 Paasche price index
帕斯卡分布/巴斯卡分布, 巴斯卡分配 Pascal distribution
帕斯卡滞后分布/巴斯卡落遲分配 Pascal lagged distribution
帕维特分类/帕維特分類 Pavitt's category
帕西奥利簿记法/帕西奧利簿記法 Paccioli's bookkeeping
拍复印电平/拍複印電平 film copy level
拍卖/[競價]拍賣 auction, sale by auction, bid auction
拍卖竞标/拍賣出價 auction bidding
拍卖利率优先股/競價股利特別股 auction rate preferred stock
拍卖师/拍賣人, 喊價者 auctioneer
[拍卖时的]最后叫价/[拍賣時的]最後叫價 closing bid
拍卖市场/喊價市場 auction market
拍卖市场环境/拍賣市場環境 auction market settings
拍卖投标人/拍賣出價者 auction bidders
拍片比/拍攝比例 shooting ratio
排/行 row
排版/排版 type setting, composition
排版规则/排版規則 typesetting rule
排程/排程 scheduling
排斥/排斥 exclusion
排除妨害请求权/排除妨害請求權 disruption removal claim
排队/排隊 queuing
排队长度/隊長 queuing length
排队过程/排隊過程, 等候過程 queuing process
排队论/等候理論 queuing theory
排队问题/排隊問題 queuing problem
排放/排放物[量] emission
排放标准/排放標準 emission standard
排放交易/排放交易 emission trading
排放控制受益者/排放管制之受益者 beneficiaries of emissions control
排架/排架 shelving
排架法/排架法 stack arrangement
排架分类法/排架分類法 shelf classification
排架管理/排架管理 shelflisting
排架目录/排架目錄 shelf list
排架顺序/排架順序 shelf order, shelving sequence
排检规则/歸檔規則 filing rule
排检款目格式/排檢款目格式 rotated entry format
排检项/排檢項 access points area
排检与编号项/排檢與編號項 retrieval and number item
排列/排列 arrangement, permutation
排列分布/排列分布 permutation distribution
排列规则/等待規則 queuing discipline
排列检验/排列檢定 permutation test
Alexa 排名/Alexa 排名 Alexa rank
排刷/排刷 broad scrub
排他成本/排他成本 exclusion cost

排他权/排他權　exclusive right
排他性/排他性,互斥性　principle of exclusiveness
排他性法律实证主义/排他性法律實證主義　exclusive legal positivism
排他性供给契约/排他性供給契約　exclusive supply contract
排他性交易/排他性交易　exclusive dealing
排他性交易合同/排他性交易契約　exclusive dealing contract
排他性限制/排他限制　exclusion restriction
排他性行为/排他性行爲　exclusionary practice
排他许可证/排他許可證,獨家許可證　sole license
排污费/排汙費　effluent fee
排污申报登记制度/排汙申報登記制度　institution of report and registration of discharge
排污收费制度/排汙收費制度　institution of charge for discharging pollutants
排序/定序　arrange in order, parallelism, sequencing
排序投票制/偏好順序投票　rank-order voting
排印本/排印本　font-changed text
牌记/牌記　publication notice, Paiji
牌价/牌價,市場行情　market quotation
派版校对/派版校對　dispatched proofreading
派出机构/派出機構　dispatched administrative institution, dispatched office
派工/派工　dispatching
派生标引/派生標引　derivative indexing
派生存款/派生存款,引申存款　derivative deposit, derived deposit
派生的犯罪构成/派生的犯罪構成　derivative constitution of a crime
派生诉讼/代表訴訟　derivative suit
派生文献/派生文獻　derivative document
派息日/配息日　date of payment
攀比效应/湊熱鬧效果　bandwagon effect
盘/片盤　reel
盘标/盤標　disc mark
盘存/存量證明　inventory verification
盘存表/盤存表　inventory sheet
盘点/盤點　stocktaking
盘购方/主并者　acquirer
盘基/基體　substrate
盘亏/盤虧　inventory loss
盘片描述协议/碟片描述協定　disc description protocol, DDP
盘式磁带/盤式磁帶　disc tape
盘塔/碟塔　disc tower
盘盈/盤存盈餘　inventory profit

盘账/審計賬目　examine the account
判别/判別　discrimination
判别比/判別比　discrimination ratio
判别分析/判別分析,區別分析　discrimination analysis, discriminant analysis
判别函数/判別函數　discriminant function
判别力/判別力　discrimination power
判定树法/決策樹法　decision tree method
判定树预测方法/決策樹預測方法　decision tree forecasting method
判定系数/決定係數　coefficient of determination
判断抽样/判斷抽樣,立意抽樣　judgment sampling
判断矩阵/判斷矩陣　judgment matrix
判断样本/判斷樣本,立意樣本　judgment sample
判例/判例,預斷裁決,預審　pre-judication
判例集/判例集　casebook
叛乱团体/叛亂團體　insurgent group
叛逃罪/叛逃罪　crime of defection
彷徨变异试验/波動檢定　fluctuation test
庞氏骗局/老鼠會,金字塔騙局　Ponzi scheme, pyramid scheme
旁白/旁白,畫外音　off-screen sound, OS
旁观者效应/旁觀者效應　bystander effect
旁系血亲/旁系血親　collateral relative by blood
旁站/預備,待命　stand by
旁证/情境證據　circumstantial evidence
旁注/旁注　marginalia
抛补利率平价/已抛補利率平價　covered interest rate parity
抛光涂料纸/鏡面銅版紙,玻璃銅版紙　cast-coated paper
抛售货币/抛售貨幣　flight from currency
抛物线回归/抛物線回歸　parabollic regression
跑片/跑片　bicycling
泡沫/泡沫　bubbles
泡沫法案/泡沫法案　bubble act
泡沫经济/泡沫經濟　bubble economy
泡泡政策/泡泡政策　bubble policy
陪审制度/陪審制度　jury system
培根分类法/培根分類法　Baconian Classification
培训/訓練　training
培训班/訓練班　training class
培训计划/培訓計劃,訓練計劃　training plan
CIRO 培训评估方法/背景評鑒　context evaluation, input evaluation, reaction evaluation and output evaluation method
培训评估模式/培訓評估模型　training evaluation mode

培训迁移/培訓遷移，訓練遷移　training transfer
培训师/訓練師　trainer
培训需求分析/培訓需求分析，培訓需要分析　training need analysis
培训中心/培訓中心，訓練中心　training center
培训专员/訓練管理員　training specialist
赔偿/賠款，補償，擔保賠償　indemnification, indemnity
赔偿方法/賠償辦法　measure of indemnity
赔偿条约/賠償條約　reparation treaty
赔款委员会/賠款委員會　reparations commission
佩卡姆法则/派克漢法則　Peckham rule
佩特罗尼乌斯法/佩特羅尼烏斯法　Lex Petronia
配比基金/相對基金　matching fund
配补本/配補本　complement edition
配第-克拉克定理/貝第-克拉克定律　Petty-Clark law
配对比较法/配對比較法　paired-comparison method
配对实验/配對實驗　matched pair experiment
配额/配額　quota
配额抽样/配額抽樣　quota sampling
配额权利/配額權利　quota right
配额限制/配額限制　quota restriction
配额样本/配額樣本　quota sample
配发/配發　configure
配股/現金增資　rights offering
配给/配給　rationing
配给交易/配給交易　rationing transaction
配给令状/配給令狀　Allocatione Facienda
配给证/配給證　rationing coupon
配偶权/配偶權　conjugal rights
配送/配送　distribution
配送库存/配送庫存　distribution inventory
配送时间/配送時間　distribution time
配送需求计划/配送需求規劃　distribution requirement planning, DRP
配送中心/配銷中心　distribution center
配帖/配帖　association
配页/集頁，搜頁　gathering, gathering leaves of a book
配页机/資料收集機　gathering machine
配置/配置　allocation
配置管理/配置管理　configuration management
配置图/配置圖　deployment diagram
配置效率/配置效率，分配效率　allocative efficiency
喷笔/噴筆，噴槍　air brush
喷墨成像/噴墨成像　inkjet imaging
喷墨印刷/噴墨印刷　inkjet printing

喷墨印刷机/噴墨印刷機　inkjet printing press
喷水消防系统/噴水式消防系統　sprinkler system
朋党/朋黨　clique, faction
朋友/朋友　friend
棚户区/棚戶區　shantytown, squatter settlement
膨胀分布/膨脹分布　inflated distribution
膨胀因子/膨脹因子　inflation factor
批/批　lot, batch
批办/批辦　approval in managing, approval in operating
批办意见/批辦意見　opinion of approve in managing, opinion of approval in operating
批本/批本　annotated edition
批变异/批變異　batch variation
批不合格率/批不合格率　batch unqualified rate
批查找/批查找　batch search, differed search
批处理/批處理　batch processing
批次号/批次號　lot number, batch number
批发/批發　wholesale, wholesaling
批发价格/批發價格　wholesale price
批发价格指数/批發價格指數，躉售物價指數，批發物價指數　wholesale price index
批发商/批發商　wholesaler, merchant wholesaler
批发网点/批發網點　wholesale outlet
批发业/批發業　wholesale trade
批发业统计/批發業統計　wholesale statistics
批发银行/批發銀行　wholesale bank
批发折扣/批發折扣　wholesale discount
批复/批復　official reply
批号/批號　lot number
批间波动/批間波動　between-lot variation
批接收准则/批允收準則　lot acceptance criterion
批量/批量，批大小　lot size, batch size
批量保护/批量保護　mass conservation
批量订货/批量定貨　batch order
批量复制/批量複製　bulk copy
批量拣货/批量揀貨　batch picking
批量卡/批量卡　batch card
批量生产/批量生產　batch production
批量外借/批量外借　bulk lending
批量折扣/量販折扣　bulk discount
批量折扣模型/批量折扣模型　quantity discount model
批买零卖/整買零賣　buy wholesale and sell retail
批判法律研究/批判法律研究　critical legal studies
批判法学/批判法學　critical jurisprudence
批判话语分析/批判話語分析，批判論述分析　critical discourse analysis

批判理论/批判理論　critical theory
批判实务/批判實務　critical practice
批判主义方法论/批判主義方法論　critical methodology
批评语言学分析/批判語言學分析　critical linguistic analysis
批容差/批允差　lot tolerance
批容许不合格率/批不良百分率容差,批允差不良率　lot tolerance percent defective, lot tolerance fraction defective, LTFD
批容许故障率/批允差故障率　lot tolerance failure rate, LTFR
批容许失效率/批允差故障率　lot tolerance failure rate, LTFR
批销/成批銷售　wholesale
批语去留/批語去留　method of dealing with remarks
批允许不合格率/批容許不良率　lot tolerance percent defective, LTPD
批质量/批品質　quality of a lot
批质量保护/批品質保護,批品質保障　lot quality protection
批质量水平/批品質水準　lot quality level
批准/認可,核準　approval
批准发行证券/證券發行核準制　approval for issue of securities
批准进口/批準進口,進口許可　approval of import
皮尔-里德曲线/Pearl-Read 曲線　Pearl-Read curve
皮尔逊-德宾比/Pearson-Durbin 比　Pearson-Durbin ratio
皮尔逊检验/Pearson 檢定　Pearson test
皮尔逊卡方分布/Pearson 卡方分布,Pearson 卡方分配　Pearson's chi-squared distribution
皮尔逊卡方检验/Pearson 卡方檢定　Pearson's chi-squared test
皮尔逊列联系数/Pearson 列聯係數　Pearson's contingency coefficient
皮尔逊偏度系数/Pearson 偏[態量]度係數　Pearson measure of skewness
皮尔逊曲线/Pearson 曲線　Pearson curve
皮尔逊相关系数/Pearson 相關係數　Pearson's correlation coefficient
皮尔逊准则/Pearson 準則　Pearson criterion
皮克不等式/Peek 不等式　Peek's inequality
皮特曼估计[量]/Pitman 估計[量]　Pitman estimator
皮特曼检验/Pitman 檢定　Pitman's test
皮特曼-摩根检验/Pitman-Morgan 檢定　Pitman-Morgan test

皮特曼效率/Pitman 效率　Pitman efficiency
皮下注射理论/皮下注射理論　hypodermic needle theory
皮下注射模式/皮下注射模式　hypodermic needle model
皮尤-希克森权变论/皮尤-希克森權變論　contingency theory of Pugh-Hickson
毗连区/鄰接區　contiguous zone
毗邻区间/毗鄰區間　intervals abutting one another
疲劳/疲乏　fatigue
疲劳故障/疲乏故障　fatigue failure
疲劳宽放/疲勞寬放　fatigue allowance
疲劳模型/疲乏模型　fatigue model
疲劳寿命/疲乏壽命　fatigue life
疲劳研究/疲勞研究　fatigue study
啤酒游戏/啤酒遊戲　beer game
匹配/配對　matching
匹配方法/配對法　matching method
匹配分布/配對分布　matching distribution
匹配概率/機率撮合　probability matching
匹配系数/配對係數　matching coefficient
匹配型融资策略/匹配型融資策略　matching financing strategy
匹配样本/配對樣本　matched samples
匹配原则/配對原則　matching principle
匹兹堡调查/匹茲堡調查　Pittsburgh survey
偏差/偏差,離差量數　bias, deviance
偏差度/偏差度　preference-deviation measure
偏差范围/變異範圍　range of variation
偏差分析/變異分析　variance analysis
偏磁比/偏磁比　magnetic bias ratio
偏磁噪声磁平/偏磁雜訊磁平　partial magnetic noise magnetic flat
偏磁噪声电平/偏磁雜訊電平　partial magnetic noise level
偏度/偏度,偏態　skewness
偏度的四分位度量/四分位偏態量測　quartile measure of skewness
偏度系数/偏度係數,偏態係數　coefficient of skewness
偏关联/偏相聯　partial association
偏关联系数/偏相聯係數　partial association coefficient
偏好/偏好　preference
偏好表/偏好表　preference table
偏好反转/偏好逆轉,嗜好逆轉　preference reversal
偏好关系/偏好關係　preference relation
偏好函数/偏好函數　preference function

偏好结构/偏好結構　preference structure
偏好排序/偏好順序　preference ranking
偏好试验/偏好試驗　preferred test
偏好信息/偏好資訊　preference information
偏好样本/偏好樣本　preferred sample
偏回归/偏回歸　partial regression
偏回归系数/偏回歸係數　partial regression coefficient
偏F检验/偏F檢定　partial F-test
偏见/偏見　prejudice
偏离-份额分析法/偏離-分配分析　shift-share analysis
偏离许可/偏離許可　deviation permit
偏列联/偏列聯　partial contingency
偏态/偏態　skewness
偏态的测度/偏態的測定數　measures of skewness
偏态分布/偏分配　skewed distributions
偏态检验/偏態檢定　test for skewness
偏态系数/偏態係數,偏度係數　coefficient of skewness
偏相关/偏相關　partial correlation
偏相关比/偏相關比　partial correlation ratio
偏相关系数/偏相關係數,部分相關係數　partial correlation coefficient
偏向输入的技术进步/偏向輸入的技術進步　import biased technical progress
偏向型增长/偏頗成長　biased growth
偏斜分布/偏斜分布　skew distribution
偏斜回归/偏斜回歸　skew regression
偏斜控制限/偏斜管制界限　sloping control limit
偏斜频数分布/偏斜次數分布　skewed frequency distribution
偏斜相关/偏斜相關　skew correlation
偏斜总体/偏斜母體　skewed population
偏倚/偏倚,偏誤　bias
偏倚交叉/偏誤交叉　crossing of biases
偏振/偏振,極化　polarization
偏秩相关/偏等級相關　partial rank correlation
偏自回归矩阵/偏自[我]回歸矩陣　partial autoregressive matrix
偏自相关/偏自[我]相關　partial autocorrelation
偏自相关函数/偏自[我]相關函數　partial autocorrelation function
偏自相关系数/偏自[我]相關係數　partial autocorrelation coefficient
偏最小二乘法/偏最小平方　partial least squares
篇后注/篇後注　end note
篇名关键词索引/篇名關鍵詞標引　title keyword index
篇章页/輯頁,中扉頁,隔頁　middle title page
片段情报分析/片段情報分析　clip intelligence analysis
片盘/片盤　reel
片式缩微品/片式縮微品　chip-type microform
片头动画/片頭動畫　title animation
骗税/騙稅　tax fraud
剽窃/剽竊　plagiarize
漂移故障/漸變故障　drift failure
飘口/飄口　overhang cover edges
漂绿/漂綠　greenwash
票据/票據　bill, note
票据保证/票據保證　guarantee of bill
票据变造/票據變造　alternation of bill
[票据]承兑付款/[票據]承兑付款　payment by acceptance
票据承兑行/期票承兑銀行　acceptance house
[票据]承兑合同/[票據]承兑合同　acceptance contract
票据承兑率/票據貼現率,匯票承兑匯率　acceptance rate
票据承兑市场/票據承兑市場　bill acceptance market
票据承兑通知/票據承兑通知　advice of bill accepted
票据承兑业/票據承兑業　acceptance business
票据承兑账户/[票據]承兑賬户　acceptance account
票据代理/票據代理　agency for bill
票据当事人/票據當事人　party of bill, party to instrument
[票据]到期日/到期日　maturity date
[票据的]部分背书/[票據]部分背書　partial endorsement
[票据的]合法持有人/[票據]合法持有人　lawful holder
[票据的]票面/[票據]票面　face of instrument
票据抵押贷款/票據質押貸款　loan on bill, loan on note
[票据]恶意出票人/[票據]惡意出票人　mala fide drawer
票据发行/票據發行　note issue
票据法/票據法,票券金融管理法　law of bill, law of negotiable instrument
票据付款通知/票據付款通知　advice of bill paid
票据关系/票據關係　bill relation
票据交换所/票據交換所　clearing house
票据金额/票據金額　amount of instrument
票据经纪人/票據經紀人　bill broker

[票据]拒付声明/[票據]拒付聲明,[票據]拒絕承兌聲明 statement of dishonor
[票据]拒绝承兑声明/[票據]拒絕承兌聲明,[票據]拒付聲明 statement of dishonor
票据抗辩/票據抗辯 bill defense
票据面额/票據面額 face of note
票据能力/票據能力 capacity of bill
票据期限/票據期限 term of bill
票据清算/票據清算 bill clearing
票据市场/票據市場 bill market
票据收款通知/票據收款通知 advice of bill collected
票据贴现/票據貼現 discount of bill, note discount
票据贴现市场/票據貼現市場 bill discount market
票据投资/票據投資 investment bill
票据涂销/票據塗銷 cancellation of bill, obliteration of negotiable instrument
票据托收/票據託收 bill collection
票据伪造/票據偽造 forgery of bill
票据信贷/票據信貸 bill credit
票据行为/票據行爲 act of bill
票据预约/票據預約 bill pre-engagement
票据原因关系/票據原因關係 cause of issuing or transferring bill
票据责任/票據責任 bill liability
[票据]直接关系人/[票據]直接關係人 immediate party
票据资金关系/票據資金關係 cause of bill payment
票面价格/票面價格 par price
票面价值/票面價值,面值,面额 par value, face value
票面利率/票面收益率,名目利率 coupon rate, nominal rate
票拟/票擬 draft proposed
票外承兑/票外承兑 extrinsic acceptance
撇脂定价/撇脂定價 skimming pricing
拼版/拼貼版 paste-up
拼大版/拼大版 imposition
拼箱/未滿載貨櫃 less than container load
贫乏型管理/不作爲管理 impoverished management
贫困/貧窮 poverty
贫困测度/貧窮測度 poverty measurement
贫困代际转移/貧困代際轉移 intergenerational transmission of poverty
贫困恶性循环理论/貧困惡性循環論 theory of vicious circle of poverty
贫困化增长/貧困化增長 immiserizing growth
贫困救助/貧困救助 poverty relief
贫困距/貧窮缺口 poverty gap
贫困线/貧窮線,貧窮水準 poverty level, poverty line
贫民窟/貧民窟,貧民區 slum
贫穷文化/貧窮文化 poverty culture
频道/頻道 channel
频道经营者/頻道經營者 channel operator
频率/頻率,相對次數 relative frequency
频率表/次數表 frequency table, table of frequency distribution
频率尺度/相對次數尺度 relative frequency scale
频率分布/[相對]次數分布 relative frequency distribution, frequency distribution
频率分布函数/次數分布函數 frequency distribution function
频率函数/次數函數 frequency function
频率函数正态化/次數函數常態化 normalization of frequency function
频率曲线/次數曲線 frequency curve
频率图/次數分配圖 frequency chart
频率响应函数/次數反應函數 frequency response function
频率直方图/次數直方圖 frequency histogram
频谱带回归/帶狀譜相回歸 band spectrum regression
频谱分布函数/頻譜分布函數 spectral distribution function
频谱分析/頻譜分析 spectral analysis
频谱函数/頻譜函數 spectral function
频谱加权函数/頻譜加權函數 spectral weight function
频谱密度/頻譜密度 spectral density
频谱平均数/頻譜平均數 spectral average
频谱视窗/頻譜視窗 spectral window
频数/[絕對]次數 absolute frequency
频数多边形/次數多邊形[圖] frequency polygon
频数分布/次數分布 frequency distribution
频数分布表/次數分布表 frequency distribution table
频数分布函数/次數分布函數 frequency distribution function
频数函数/次數函數 frequency function
频数密度/[相對]次數密度 relative frequency density
频数曲线/次數曲線 frequency curve
频数直方图/次數直方圖 frequency histogram
频域/頻率領域 frequency domain
品红/洋紅 magenta
品类发展指数/品類發展指數 category development

index, CDI
品类杀手／類別殺手　category killer
品牌／品牌　brand
品牌产品线延伸／品牌產品線延伸　brand line extension
品牌承诺／品牌允諾　brand promise
品牌定位／品牌定位　brand positioning
品牌发展指数／品牌發展指標　brand development index, BDI
品牌个性／品牌人格　brand personality
品牌估价／品牌鑒價　brand valuation
品牌化／品牌化　branding
品牌间竞争／品牌間競爭　interbrand competition
品牌接触／品牌接觸　brand contact
品牌经理／品牌經理　brand manager
品牌扩散／品牌增殖　brand proliferation
品牌联想／品牌聯想　brand association
品牌命名／品牌命名　brand naming
品牌内竞争／品牌內競爭　intrabrand competition
品牌认知／品牌知曉，品牌知名　brand awareness
品牌审计／品牌審計　brand auditing
品牌渗透率／品牌滲透率　brand penetration ratio
品牌稀释／品牌稀釋　brand dilution
品牌形象／品牌形象，品牌影像　brand image
品牌延伸／品牌延伸　brand extension
品牌战略／品牌策略　brand strategy
品牌知识／品牌知識　brand knowledge
品牌忠诚／品牌忠誠　brand loyalty
品牌转换者／品牌轉換者　brand switcher
品牌资产／品牌權益　brand equity
品牌组合／品牌組合　brand portfolio
品位分类／品位分類　rank classification
品味／品味　taste
品味公众／品味公眾　public with taste
品味理论／品味理論　taste theory
品味文化／品味文化　tasting the culture
品质／品質　quality
品质波动／品質變異　quality variation
品质方针／品質政策　quality policy
品质环／品質環　quality loop
品质检验证书／品質檢驗證書　inspection certificate of quality
品质圈／品管圈　quality circle
品质认证／品質認證　quality certification
品质审核／品質稽核　quality audit
品质手册／品質手冊　quality handbook
品质维度／品質構面　quality dimension
品质屋／品質屋　house of quality

品质职能／品質功能　quality function
聘任制／聘任制，聘用合同制　contract system of employment
平安险／平安險　free from particular average
平板电脑／平板電腦　tablet computer
平版印刷／平版印刷　planographic printing
平仓／平倉　closed position, closing out a position
平等／平等　equality
平等服务／平等服務　equal service
平等互利原则／平等互利原則　principle of equality and mutual
平等机会政策／平等機會政策　equal-opportunity policy
平等权／平等權利　equal rights
平等选举／平等選舉　equal election
平等原则／平等原則　principle of equality
平等主义者／平等主義者　egalitarian
平调／平調　flat key
平叠帖书芯／平疊帖書芯　multi-layer block
平顶假设／平頂假設　flat-top hypothesis
平凡解／明顯解　trivial solution
平方变异／平方變異　variation of squares
平方根变换／平方根變換　square root transformation
平方根估计[量]／平方根估計量　root estimator
平方和／平方和　sum of squares
平方误差渐进有效性／平方誤差漸近有效性　square error asymptotic efficiency
平方误差损失／平方誤差損失　squared error loss
平方误差损失函数／平方誤差損失函數　squared error loss function
平方误差相合性／平方誤差一致性　squared error consistency
平方相干函数／平方一致性函數　squared coherency function
平放／平放　flat-filing
平放排架法／平放排架法　flat shelving
平衡／平衡　balance
平衡报道／平衡報導　balanced report
平衡[表]账目审计／結餘賬戶審計　audit for balance account
平衡不完全区组设计／平衡不完全區集設計　balanced incomplete block design, BIBD
平衡不完全型／平衡不完全型　balanced incomplete type
平衡差／平衡差　balanced difference
平衡度／平衡度　balance degree
平衡方程／平衡方程　balance equation
平衡格[子]设计／平衡方格設計　balanced lattice

design
平衡关税/平衡關稅　parity duty, balance tariff
平衡混杂/平衡混同　balanced confounding
平衡混杂设计/平衡混同設計　balanced confounding design
平衡基金/平衡基金　balance fund
平衡计分卡/平衡計分卡　balanced scorecard
平衡理论/平衡理論,均衡理論　balance theory
平衡模型/平衡模型　balanced model
平衡设计/平衡設計　balanced design
平衡试验/平衡實驗　balanced experiment
平衡图/平衡圖　balance chart
平衡完全型/平衡完全型　balanced complete type
平衡误差/平衡誤差　balanced error
平衡析因试验设计/平衡因子實驗設計　balanced factorial experimental design
平衡线路/平衡線路　balanced line
平衡序列/平衡序列　balanced sequence
平衡延误/平衡線遲延　balancing delay
平衡样本/平衡樣本　balanced sample
平衡预算/平衡預算　balanced budget
平衡预算乘数/平衡預算乘數　balanced budget multiplier
平衡预算归宿/平衡預算歸宿　balanced budget incidence
平衡预算规则/預算平衡準則　balanced budget rule
平衡增长/均衡成長　balanced growth
平滑/平滑　smoothing
平滑功效/平滑檢力　smoothing power
平滑过程/平滑過程　smoothing process
平滑回归分析/平滑回歸分析　smooth regression analysis
平滑检验/平滑檢定　smooth test
平滑系数/平滑係數　smoothing coefficient
平滑性检验/平滑度檢定　test of smoothness
平滑转换回归/平滑傳遞回歸　smooth transition regression
平滑转换自回归过程/平滑傳遞自我回歸過程　smooth transition autoregressive process
平滑自助法/平滑自助法　smoothed bootstrap
平价/平價,等價　parity price, at par
平价比[率]/平價比率,對等比率　parity rate, parity ratio
平价兑换/平匯　exchange at par
平价发行/平價發行　par issue
平价购买力/平價購買力　purchasing power of parity
平价行情/平價報價　parity quotation
平价汇率/平價匯率　par exchange rate

平价交换/平價交換　par clearance
平价期权/平價期權　at the money, at-the-money option
平价债券/平價債券　par bond
平价指数/平價指數,對等指數　parity index
平减价格指数/平減價格指數　deflating price indices
平减指数/平減指數　deflator
GNP 平减指数/國民生產毛額平減指數　GNP deflator
平件/平件　normal document
平均保险费/平均保險費　average premium, level premium
平均遍历定理/平均遍歷定理　mean ergodic theorem
平均不合格率/平均不良率　mean fraction nonconforming
平均不准确度/平均不準確度　average inaccuracy
平均操作时间/平均操作時間　mean operating time
平均差/平均[離]差,均差　mean deviation, mean difference, average deviation
平均查全率/平均查全率　recall level average
平均产量/平均產量　average product
平均产量曲线/平均生產曲線　average product curve
平均成本/平均成本　average cost
平均成本定价法/平均成本定價法　average cost pricing
平均抽检数/平均抽檢數　average sampling number, ASN
平均储蓄倾向/平均儲蓄傾向　average propensity to save
平均发散度/平均發散度　average divergence
平均风险/平均風險　average risk
平均服务率/平均服務率　mean service rate
平均概率单位差/平均機率單位差　mean probit difference
平均固定成本/平均固定成本　average fixed cost
平均故障间隔时间/平均故障間隔時間　mean time between failures, MTBF
平均[顾客]保留成本/平均保留成本　average retention cost
平均[顾客]获取成本/平均購置成本　average acquisition cost
平均极差/平均全距　mean range, average range
平均检出水平/平均出廠水準　average outgoing level
平均检出质量/平均出廠品質　average outgoing quality, AOQ
平均检出质量界/平均出廠品質界限　average

outgoing quality limit, AOQL

平均检出质量上限/平均出廠品質界限　average outgoing quality limit, AOQL

平均检出质量水平/平均出廠品質水準　average outgoing quality level

平均检验量/平均檢驗量　average amount of inspection

平均绝对离差/平均絕對離差　average absolute deviation, mean absolute deviation, MAD

平均绝对[误]差/平均絕對誤差　mean absolute error

平均可变成本/平均變動成本　average variable cost

平均可靠度水平/平均可靠度水準　mean reliability level, MRL

平均可用度/平均可用度　average availability

平均库存/平均存貨　average inventory

平均会计收益率/平均會計利潤率　average accounting return, AAR

平均劳动成本/勞動平均成本　average cost of labor

平均利润/平均利潤　average profit

平均利润率/平均利潤率　average rate of profit

平均连接/平均連接　average linkage

平均链长/平均連串長度　average run length, ARL

平均临界值法/平均臨界值法　average critical value method

平均旅行成本/平均通勤成本　average travel cost

平均毛收入统计/平均所得毛額統計　gross average earning statistics

平均模型/平均模型　average model

平均年龄/平均年齡　mean age

平均缺陷数/平均不良數　average number of defects

平均人口/平均人口　average population, mean population

平均三角差/平均三角離差　mean trigonometric deviation

平均剩余寿命/平均餘命時間　mean residual lifetime

平均失效时间/故障前平均時間　mean time to failure, MTTF

平均收敛/平均數收斂　mean convergence

平均收益/平均收益　average revenue

平均首次故障时间/首次故障前平均時間　mean time to first failure

平均寿命/平均壽命　mean life

平均受教育年数/平均教育年數　average years for formal education

平均数/平均數, 均值　mean, average

平均数法/平均數法　method of average

平均数法则/平均數定律　law of average

平均数分布/平均數分布　distribution of average

平均数上侧链/平均數以上連串　runs above average

平均数下侧链/平均數以下連串　runs below average

平均税率/平均稅率　average rate of tax, average tax rate

平均停机时间/平均停機時間　mean down time

平均维修工作时间/平均維護工作時間　mean time of maintenance actions

平均无故障时间/故障前平均時間　mean time to failure, MTTF

平均误差/平均誤差　mean error, average error

平均线性连续差/平均線性接續差　mean linear successive difference

平均消费倾向/平均消費傾向　average propensity to consume

平均斜率/平均斜率　average slope

平均新优于旧的/平均新比舊佳的　new-better-than-used in expectation, NBUE

平均修复时间/平均修復時間　mean time to repair, MTTR

平均样本量/平均樣本數　average sample number, ASN

平均样本量函数/平均樣本數函數　average sample number function

平均样本量曲线/平均樣本數曲線　average sample number curve

平均要素成本/平均要素成本　average cost of factor

平均正常时间/平均可操作時間　mean up time

平均值/平均值　mean value, average value

[平]均值差估计/平均值差估計　estimation of difference of means

平均质量水平/平均品質水準　average quality level

平均质量水平线/平均品質水準線　average quality level line

平均质量线/平均品質線　average quality line

平均秩/平均秩　mean rank

平均主义/平等主義　equalitarism

平均准备金/平均準備金　mean reserve

平均准则/平均準則　average criterion

平均总成本/平均總成本　average total cost

平均总检验量/平均總檢驗量　average total inspected

平均总检验数/平均總檢驗數　average total inspection, ATI

平均总检验数曲线/平均總檢驗數曲線　average total inspection curve

平均组间相关/平均組間相關　average intercorrelation

平均组内相关/平均組內相關　average intracorrelation
平面媒体/平面媒體　print media
平面图/平面圖　plan chart, surface diagram
平面网印机/平面網印機　flat surface screen printing machine
平面文献/平面文獻　flat document
平面型扫描仪/平板掃描器　flat-bed scanner
平面型设备/平面型設備　flat-bed device
平民院/平民院　civilian parliament
平权行动/平權行動,平權運動,平權措施　affirmative action
平时宪法/平時憲法　peacetime constitution
平水本/平水本　Pingshui edition
平台式摄影机/平床式拍攝機　planetary camera
平网印刷机/平網印刷機　flat screen printing machine
平稳等待线/平穩等待線　stationary queue
平稳分布/平穩分布　stationary distribution
平稳高斯过程/平穩高斯過程　stationary Gaussian process
平稳更新过程/平穩更新過程　stationary renewal process
平稳过程/平穩過程　stationary process
平稳时间序列/平穩時間序列,平穩時間數列,恆定時間序列　stationary time series
平稳随机过程/平穩隨機過程　stationary stochastic process
平稳随机过程抽样/穩定隨機過程抽樣　sampling from stationary stochastic process
平稳随机过程的遍历性/平穩隨機過程的遍歷性　ergodicity of stationary stochastic process
平稳性/平穩性　stationarity
平稳性的阶/穩定性階數　order of stationarity
平稳性假定/平穩性假設　stationarity assumption
平行本位制度/平行本位制度　parallel standard
平行表婚/平行表婚　parallel cousin marriage
平行波动/平行波動　parallel fluctuation
平行承发包模式/平行承發包模式　parallel contract
平行传播/水平溝通　horizontal communication
平行贷款/平行貸款　parallel loan
平行工作/并行工序　concurrent activity
平行关系/平行關係　parallel relation
平行汇率/平行匯率　parallel rate of exchange
平行货币/平行貨幣,平行通貨　parallel currency
平行货币市场/平行貨幣市場　parallel money market
平行机/并連機　parallel machine
平行检验/平行檢驗　parallel examine

平行进口/平行進口,平行輸入　parallel import
平行贸易/平行貿易　parallel trading
平行蒙太奇/平行蒙太奇　parallel montage
平行融资/平行融資　parallel financing
平行市场/平行市場　parallel market
平行顺序移动/平行順序移動　parallel-serial movement
平行堂婚/平行堂婚　parallel cousin marriage
平行文/平行文　parallel file
平行移动/平行運動　parallel movement
平压印刷/平壓印刷　platen printing
平移不变[的]/平移不變[的]　translation invariant
平移参数/平移參數　translation parameter
平整/修平　flattening
平装/平裝　paper-cover binding, soft-cover binding
平装本/平裝本　paperback
平装优先/平裝優先　paper preferred
平准化法/平準化法　leveling
平准基金/平準基金　buffer fund, equalization fund, stabilization fund
评标/評標,標書評審　bidding evaluation, tender evaluation
评标委员会/評標委員會　committee for bidding evaluation, tender evaluation committee
评定工人技术等级/考工評定　assessing workers and fixing their technical grades
评定量表模式/評等量尺　rating scale model
评定量尺模式/評等量尺　rating scale model
评估/評估,評鑒　assessment, evaluation
OPSEC评估/OPSEC評估　operation security assessment, OPSEC assessment, OA
评估比率/評估比率　appraisal ratio
评估成本/評估成本　appraisal cost
评估方法/評估方法　evaluation method
评估阶段/評估階段　evaluation phase
评估可靠性/評估可靠度　assessed reliability
评估研究/評估研究　evaluation research
评估值/評估值　assessed value
评价/評價　evaluation, assessment
评价方案/評價方案　evaluation scheme
评价函数/評估函數　evaluation function
评价客体/評估客體　evaluation object
评价体系/評估制度　appraisal system
评价者信度/評分者信度　interrater reliability
评价指标/評價指標　evaluation indicator
评价中心/評鑒中心,評量中心,評估中心　assessment center
评价主体/評價主體　evaluation subject

评论/評論　comment
评论性文摘/評估性摘要　evaluative abstract
评论员/評論員　pundit, commentator
评审/評定　evaluation
评述性书目/評述性書目　pure bibliography
评注本/評注本　annotated text
苹果数字多媒体机/蘋果數位多媒體機　Apple TV
凭单付款/交單付款　payment against document
凭单付款信用证/交單付款信用狀　payment against document credit
凭单付现/交單付現　cash against document
凭单交货/憑單交貨　deliver goods against surrender of the document
凭单据出售货物/憑單據出售貨物　sale by document
凭发票付款/憑發票付款　payment on invoice
凭国际标准销售/憑國際標準銷售　sale by international standard
凭汇票付款/憑匯票付款　payment by bill, payment by draft
凭汇票付款信用证/憑匯票付款信用狀　payment against draft credit
凭交货收据付款/憑交貨收據付款　payment on receipt of goods
凭据/憑據　voucher, credential
凭票即付汇票/憑票即付匯票　money order payable to bearer
凭商标销售/憑商標銷售　sale by trademark
凭收据付款信用证/憑收據付款信用狀　payment on receipt credit
凭信托收据交单/憑信託收據交單　document against trust receipt
凭信用销售/憑信用銷售　sale on credit
凭样品销售/憑樣品銷售　sale by sample
凭运单付款/憑運輸單證付款　payment against presentation of shipping document
凭账单付款/憑賬單付款　payment on statement
凭证/憑證　voucher
凭证价值/憑證價值　certificate value
凭证式国债/憑證式國債　certificate treasury bond
凭证依据作用/憑證依據作用　certificate function
屏幕分辨率/螢幕解析度　screen resolution
屏幕设计/介面設計　interface design
瓶颈/瓶頸　bottleneck
珀森论科学管理目标/珀森論科學管理目標　Person's thirteen aims of scientific management
破产/破產　bankruptcy
破产财产/破產財產　bankrupt estate
破产撤销权/破產撤銷權　rescission right in bankruptcy
破产成本/破產成本　bankruptcy cost
破产程序/破產程式　bankruptcy procedure
破产抵销权/破產抵銷權　right of offset in bankruptcy
破产法/破產法[案]　bankruptcy law, bankruptcy act
破产法院/破產法庭　bankruptcy court
破产管理人/破產管理人　bankruptcy administrator
破产管辖权/破產管轄權　bankruptcy jurisdiction
破产临界期间/破產臨界期間　critical period of bankruptcy
破产免责/破產免責　bankrupt exemption from liability
破产能力/破產能力　bankruptcy capacity
破产清算书/破產清算書　statement of liquidation
破产人/破產人　the bankrupt
破产申请/破產申請　bankruptcy petition
破产申请人/破產申請人　applicant for bankruptcy
破产属地主义/破產屬地主義　doctrine of territory in bankruptcy
破产溯及主义/破產溯及主義　doctrine of retrospective of bankruptcy
破产宣告/破產宣告　adjudication of bankruptcy
破产原因/破產原因　cause of bankruptcy
破产债权/破產債權　credit of bankrupt
破产终止/破產終止　termination of bankruptcy
破订/破訂　untermed subscription
破坏广播电视设施、公用电信设施罪/破壞廣播電視設施、公用電信設施罪　crime of sabotaging radio and television facilities or public telecommunication facilities
破坏交通工具罪/破壞交通工具罪　crime of sabotaging means of transportation
破坏金融管理秩序罪/破壞金融管理秩序罪　crime against the control of financial order
破坏性创新/破壞性創新　distruptive innovation
破坏性检验/損壞性的測試　destructive testing
破坏性竞争/破壞性競爭　destructive competition
破坏性试验/破壞性試驗　destructive test
破裂图/破裂圖　rupture diagram
破损图书/破損圖書　damaged book
剖面分析/縱斷面分析　profile analysis
剖面曲线/縱斷面曲線　profile curve
剖面图/剖面圖，縱斷面圖　profile cartography, profile graph
普遍定期审查制度/普遍定期審查制度　universal periodic review

普遍获取/通用存取 universal access
普遍进化/普遍進化 general evolution
普遍利用/普遍利用 general use
普遍税率/普遍税率,一般税率 general tariff
普遍性/普遍性 universality
普遍性管辖权/普遍性管轄權 universal jurisdiction
普遍优惠关税/普遍優惠關稅 general preferential duty
普遍优惠关税制度/普遍優惠關稅制度 general preferential duty system
普遍优惠征税制/普遍優惠徵稅制 generalized system of preference tariff treatment
普遍优惠制/普遍優惠制 generalized system of preference
普遍主义/普遍主義 universalism
普遍主义规范/普遍主義規範 universalist norm
普遍主义-国际主义学派/普遍主義-國際主義學派 universalism-internationalism school
普查/普查 census
普查年/普查年 census year
普查日/普查日 census day
普尔三原则/普爾三原則 three management principle of Poor
普惠制/優惠關稅制度,通用優選系統 generalized system of preferences
普及版图书/普通版圖書,普及版本 trade book
普及读物/普及讀物 popular book, popular reading matter
普莱克特均匀分布/Plackett 均匀分布,Plackett 均匀分配 Plackett's uniform distribution
普赖斯定律/普賴斯定律 Price's law
普赖斯曲线/普賴斯曲線 Price curve
普赖斯指数/普賴斯指數 Price's indicator
普雷维什-辛格命题/普雷維什-辛格命題 Prebisch-Singer Thesis
普利策新闻奖/普利茲獎 Pulitzer Prizes
普鲁士邦法/普魯士邦法 Civil Code of the Prussian Federation
普鲁士民法典/普魯士民法典 Prussian Civil Code
普罗文化/普羅文化,大眾文化 mass culture
普那路亚家庭/普那路亞家庭 Punaluan family
普苏-肯经营方式/普蘇-肯經營方式 business operation type of Pūsu-Kēn
普通承兑/普通承兑,不帶保留條件的承兌 general acceptance
普通带/普通帶 ordinary tape
普通贷款/普通貸款 simple loan
普通抵押/普通抵押 puisne mortgage

普通法/普通法,判例法,習慣法 common law
普通法程序法/普通法程序法 common law procedure act
普通法法系/普通法法系 common law family
普通法婚姻/習慣法婚姻 common law marriage
普通共同诉讼/普通共同訴訟 general colitigation
普通股/普通股 common stock, ordinary stock
普通关税/普通關稅 ordinary customs duty
普通合伙/普通合夥 general partnership
普通交易/普通交易 regular transaction
普通金融机构/普通金融機構 ordinary financial institution
普通利息/普通利息 ordinary interest
普通目录学/普通目錄學 general bibliography science
普通年金/普通年金 ordinary annuity
普通票据/普通票據 ordinary bill
普通期权/普通選擇權 vanilla options
普通提款权/一般提款權 reserve position, ordinary drawing right
普通图书/普通版圖書 trade book, trade edition
普通图书馆学/普通圖書館學 general librarianship
普通信用证/普通信用狀 general credit, ordinary credit
普通刑法/普通刑法 ordinary criminal law
普通需求函数/一般需求函數 ordinary-demand function
普通许可证/普通許可證,一般許可證 general licence
普通银行/普通銀行 ordinary bank
普通支票/普通支票 ordinary check
普通最小二乘/普通最小平方,一般最小平方 ordinary least square
普通最小二乘法/普通最小平方法,一般最小平方法 generalized least square method, ordinary least square method, ordinary least square
谱/頻譜,譜相 spectrum
谱牒档案/譜牒檔案 genealogy archive
谱方法/譜相方法 spectral method
谱估计/譜相估計 spectral estimation
谱密度函数/譜相密度函數 spectral density function
谱系表/系譜表 genealogical table
谱系生灭过程/層次生滅過程 hierarchical birth and death process
谱系树/譜系樹,親緣樹 genealogical tree
谱系学路径/譜系學路徑 genealogical approach
瀑布模型/瀑布模型 waterfall model

Q

七出/七出　Qichu
七分法/七分法　seven-fold bibliographical classification system
七国集团/七國集團，七大工業國　Group of Seven, Group of 7
七十七国集团/七十七國集團　Group of Seventy-Seven, Group of 77
七章法典/七章法典　Las Partidas
期/①期，②期刊號　number
期待可能性/期待可能性　probability of anticipation
期待利益/期待利益　interest in expectancy
期待权/期待權　right of expectancy
期号/發行號數　issue number
期后事项/期後事項　subsequent event
期汇合约升水/遠期外匯合約溢價　forward exchange contract premium
期汇合约损益/遠期外匯合約損益　forward exchange contract gain or loss
期汇合约贴水/遠期外匯合約折價　forward exchange contract discount
期货/遠期期货　forward goods
期货合同的交割结构/期貨合約的交割結構　delivery structure of futures contract
期货合约/期貨契約　futures contract
期货基金/期貨基金　futures fund
期货价格/期貨價格　future price
期货交割/期貨交割　future delivery
期货交货合同/期貨交貨合約　contract for future delivery
期货交易/期貨交易　future goods transaction, dealing in future, future business
期货买卖/期貨買賣，買賣選擇權　option trading, forward bargain
期货贸易/期貨貿易　forward trade
期货期权/期貨選擇權[契約]　future option, option on future
期货清算所/期貨清算所　future clearing house
期货市场/期貨市場　forward market, future market
期货市场的信息功能/期貨市場的資訊功能　information role of future market
期货市场清算所/期貨市場交換所　clearing house in future market
期货损失/期貨損失　loss forwarded
期货头寸/期貨部位　forward position
期货外汇/期貨外匯　future exchange
期货销售[额]/期貨銷售[額]　forward sale
期货转现货/期貨轉現貨交易　exchange for physical
期间费用/期間費用　period expense
期刊/期刊　periodical, journal
期刊出版规律/期刊出版規律　periodical publishing regularity
期刊出版周期/期刊出版週期　journal publishing cycle
期刊登记/期刊登記　periodical record, periodical registration
期刊订户/期刊訂戶　periodical subscriber
期刊架/書報雜誌架　magazine rack, magazine stack, periodical stand
期刊精华本/期刊精選本　carefully selected edition of periodicals
期刊联合目录/期刊聯合目錄　union list of periodicals
期刊论文/期刊論文　journal article
期刊名称/期刊刊名　journal title
期刊目录/期刊目錄　periodical bibliography, serial bibliography
期刊评价/期刊評鑒　journal evaluation
期刊社/期刊社　periodical agency
期刊式检索工具/期刊式檢索工具　periodical-retrieval tools
期刊索引/期刊索引　periodical index
期刊文献/期刊文獻　journal literature
期刊验收/期刊驗收　periodical check-in
期刊预订/期刊訂購　periodical subscription
期刊增补目录/期刊增補目錄　supplement list of journals
期刊主题索引/期刊主題索引　periodical subject index
期末库存/期末存貨　ending inventory
期末账项调整/期末賬項調整　final adjustment of accounts
期票/期票，本票　promissory note, term bill

期票出票人/期票出票人　maker of promissory note
期票买入价/期票買入價　buying rate for time bill
期请用语/期請用語　language for request, language for petition
期权/選擇權[契約]　option
期权定价理论/選擇權定價理論　option pricing theory
期权费/選擇權權利金　option premium
期权交易/選擇權交易　option dealing
期权交易合同/選擇權合同　option contract
期权交易所/選擇權交易所　option exchange
期权市场/選擇權市場　option market
期日/期日　legal date
期望报酬率/預期報酬率　expected rate of return, expected return
期望边际收益/預期邊際收益　expected marginal profit
期望抽样比/期望抽出率　expected sampling fraction
期望风险/期望風險　expected risk
期望概率/期望機率　expected probability
期望概率单位/期望機率單位　expected probit
期望工作持续时间/期望工作持續時間　expected activity time
期望理论/期望理論　expectancy theory
期望频次/期望頻數　expected frequency
期望寿命/期望壽命　expecting life
期望损害赔偿/預期性損害賠償　expectation damages
期望损失/期望損失　expected loss
期望效用/預期效用　expected utility
期望效用函数/預期效用函數　expected utility function
期望效用理论/預期效用理論　expected utility theory
期望影响因子/期望影響因子　expectancy impact factor
期望值/期望值　expected value
期限/期間　term
期限错配/存放期限不合　maturity mismatch
期限匹配策略/到期策略　maturity strategy
期限升水/期限貼水　term premium
欺骗性定价/欺騙性定價　deceptive pricing
欺骗性广告/欺騙式廣告　deceptive advertising
欺诈/欺騙　cheat
漆书/漆書　text written in lacquer, lacque calligraphy
齐次方程/齊次方程式　homogeneous equation
齐次过程/均齊過程　homogeneous process
齐次转移概率/均齊遞移機率　homogeneous transition probability
齐列式版面/齊列式版面　manuscript with uniform layout
齐普夫定律/齊普夫定律,Zipf 法則　Zipf's law
齐性/均齊性,同質性　homogeneity
齐性的/同質的,齊次的　homogeneous
齐性检验/均齊性檢定　test of homogeneity
其他材料/其他材料　other material
其他国外公债/其他公共外債　other external public debts
其他诉讼参与人/其他訴訟參與人　participant to court proceedings
其他题名信息/其他题名信息　other title information
其他业务成本/其他業務成本　other operating cost
其他业务收入/其他業務收入　other operating revenue
其他应付款/其他應付款　other payable
其他应收款/其他應收款　other receivable
其他责任说明/其他責任說明　other statement of responsibility
其他责任者项/其他責任者項　other liability items
奇异分布/奇異分布　singular distribution
奇异加权设计/奇異加權設計　singular weighting design
奇异矩阵/奇異矩陣　singular matrix
奇异期权/變型選擇權　exotic option
奇异线性最小二乘法/奇異線性最小平方法　singular linear least squares method
歧视/歧視　discrimination
歧视性壁垒/歧視性壁壘　discriminatory barrier
歧视性定价/歧視性定價　discriminatory pricing
歧视性关税/歧視性關稅,差別關稅　discriminating duty, discriminating tariff, differential tariff
歧视性拍卖/歧視性的拍賣　discriminative auction
歧视与不平等/歧視與不平等　discrimination and inequality
祈雨/祈雨　pray for rain
骑缝证书/騎縫證書　indenture
骑马订/騎馬訂　saddle stitch
骑马订装/騎馬訂裝　saddle stitching
骑马装订联动生产线/騎馬裝訂聯動生產線　saddle stitching line
旗帜广告/旗幟廣告　banner advertisement
乞鞫/乞鞫　Qiju, Qiju system, request for re-examination

企图独占/企圖獨占　attempted to monopolize
企业/企業　enterprise
企业办学/企業辦學　enterprise-run education
企业标准/企業標準　enterprise standard
企业成长/企業成長　firm growth
企业成长阶段/企業成長階段　firm growth stage
企业成长理论/公司成長理論　corporate growth theory
企业创新体系/企業創新體系　corporate innovation system
企业创新网络/企業創新網路　enterprise innovation networks
企业促销/企業推廣　business promotion
企业单位/企業單位　enterprise
企业档案/企業檔案　business archive
企业档案馆/企業檔案館　business archive
企业的激励与约束机制/企業激勵與約束機制　motivative and restraint mechanisms of enterprise
企业定额/企業定額　enterprise quota
企业对顾客[电子商务]/企業對消費者[電子商務]　business to consumer, B2C, B to C
企业对顾客在线营销/企業對消費者線上行銷　business to consumer online marketing, B2C online marketing, B to C online marketing
企业对企业/企業對企業　business to business, B2B, B to B
企业对企业在线营销/企業對企業線上行銷　business to business online marketing, B2B online marketing, B to B online marketing
企业法人/企業法人　business legal body
[企业]方针/政策　policy
企业公共关系/企業公共關係　corporate public relations
企业公民/企業公民　corporate citizen
企业购买过程/企業購買程序,企業購買流程　business buying process
企业购买者行为/組織市場購買行爲分析　business buyer behavior
企业管理途径/企業管理途徑　business approach
企业合并/企業并購　merge of enterprises
企业集团/企業集團,事業集團,系列企業　enterprise group, business group
企业家/企業家　entrepreneur
企业家精神/企業家精神,創業精神　entrepreneurship
企业家素质学派/創業特質學派　entrepreneurial trait school
企业家型继任人/企業家型繼承人　entrepreneurial successor
企业家学派/企業家學派　entrepreneurial school
企业结构/廠商結構　firm structure
企业经营再造/企業管理流程再造　enterprise management reengineering
企业竞争情报/企業競爭情報　enterprise competitive intelligence
企业流程再造/企業流程再造　enterprise process reengineering, business process reengineering, BPR
企业描述/業務描述　business description
企业民主管理/企業民主管理　democratic management of enterprises
企业内部[组织]电子商务/企業內部[組織]電子商務　intrabusiness organizational e-commerce
企业内分工/企業內部勞動分工　division of labor within enterprise
企业年金/企業年金　enterprise annuity
企业努力均衡理论/企業努力均衡理論　balance theory of firm effort
企业培训/企業內培訓　training in the enterprise
企业迁移/企業遷移　firm migration
企业清算/企業清算　enterprise liquidation
企业融资/企業融資　corporate financing
企业社会责任/企業社會責任　corporate social responsibility
企业数字著作权管理/企業數字版權管理　enterprise digital rights management, E-DRM, ERM
企业所得税/企業所得稅,營利事業所得稅　enterprise income tax, business income tax, corporate income tax
企业投入产出模型/企業投入產出模型　enterprise input-output model
企业投资/公司投資　corporate investment
企业图书馆/工商圖書館　corporate library, enterprise library
企业文化/企業文化,組織文化　corporate culture, organizational culture
企业信息/企業資訊　enterprise information
企业信息化/企業資訊化　enterprise informatization
企业形象识别系统/企業識別系統　corporate identity system, CIS
企业型政府/企業型政府　entrepreneurial government
企业运行机制/企業經營機制　enterprise operating mechanism
企业运营六活动/企業運營六活動　six activities of enterprise operation

企业责任/雇用人責任　enterprise liability
企业职工基本养老保险/企業職工基本養老保險　basic old-age insurance for the employees in the enterprises
企业质量体系认证/企業品質體系認證　quality system certification
[企业]资信证明/財務狀況證明書　certificate of financial standing
企业资源计划/企業資源計劃,企業資源規劃　enterprise resource planning, ERP
企业字号/企業字號,商號　enterprise code, corporate name
启动贷款/首次貸款　start-up loan
启动过程/啟動過程　initiating process
启动阶段/創業階段　start-up stage
启动问题/啟動問題　start-up problem
启动知识/啟動知識　knowledge activation
启发式/啟發,捷思法　heuristic
启发式检索/試探式搜尋　heuristic search
启发式算法/啟發性演算法,探試演算法　heuristic algorithm
启事/啟事　announcement
启运港/啟運港　port of departure
启运港船边交货/啟運港船邊交貨　free in steamer
[启运港]船边交货价/[啟運港]船邊交貨價　free alongside ship
启运港码头交货价/啟運港碼頭交貨價　free on board quay
启运机场交货价/啟運機場交貨價　free on board airport
起脊/起脊　backing
起居注/起居注　Imperial Diary
起毛/起毛　fluff
起膜/起膜　delamination
起泡/起泡　bubble
起讫标记制/起訖標記制　commencement and termination marking system
起始实验/初步實驗　preliminary experiment
起首用语/起首用語　first term
起诉/起訴　sue
起诉便宜主义/起訴便宜主義　doctrine of prosecuting discretion
起诉法定主义/起訴法定主義　doctrine of commencement of action by law
起诉状一本主义/起訴狀一本主義　exclusiveness of the bill of prosecution
起源场/起源場　originating Ba
起脏/起髒　scumming
起重机械/吊重機械　hoisting machinery
起作用约束/有效限制　active constraint
气垫式衬版/氣墊式襯版　air backcushion
气候变化/氣候變化　climatic change
气球型期权/氣球型期權　balloon option
气溶胶/氣溶膠　aerosol
气刷/氣刷　air brush
气调杀虫/氣調殺蟲　the gas adjustment insecticidal method
气味商标/氣味商標　olfactory trademark
气相去酸法/氣相去酸法　vapour-phase deacidification
气象统计/氣象統計　meteorological statistics
弃权/棄權,迴避　abstention
弃市/棄市　execute the death penalty in the crowd in Qin Dynasty
汽车第三者责任保险/汽車第三者責任保險　third party liability insurance of automobile
汽车尾气排放标准/汽車廢氣排放標準　auto emission standards
汽油配给/汽油配給　gasoline rationing
汽油税/汽油稅　gasoline tax
契/契　Qi, deed
契合法/求同法　method of agreement
契据/契約　deed
契据登记簿/契約登記簿　register of deeds
契据抵押贷款/契據質押貸款　loan on deed
契勘/契勘　Qikan
契税/契稅　contract tax, deed tax
契约/契約　contract
契约抵押/契約質押　pledge of obligation
契约经济理论/契約的經濟理論　economic theory of contract
契约奴/契約勞工　indentured servant
契约曲线/契約[曲]線　contract curve
契约失灵/契約失靈　contract failure
契约式垂直营销系统/契約式垂直行銷系統　contractual vertical marketing system, contractual VMS
契约外包/契約外包　contracting out
契约相互保证金/契約相互保證金　mutual deposit on a contract
契约效力/契約有效期　validity of contract
契约型投资基金/契約型投資基金　contractual type investment fund
契约性条约/契約性條約　contractual treaty
砌砖制度/砌磚制度　brickwork system
恰好辨识模型/恰好識別模型　just identified model

恰好识别/恰好識別,恰好認定　just identified
千人成本/每千次曝光成本　cost per thousand impressions
千文架阁法/千文架閣法　a method of file storage in Song Dynasty
千禧年运动/千禧年運動　millennium movement
迁出比例/遷出率　emigrants rate
迁出率/人口移出率　emigration rate
迁出人口/遷出人口　emigrants
迁入比例/遷入率　immigrants rate
迁入率/人口移入率　immigration rate
迁移/遷移,遷徙,移轉　migration, transfer
牵连犯/牽連犯　implicated offense
牵连管辖/牽連管轄　connected jurisdiction
牵头保险公司/主辦保險公司　lead insurance company
牵头银行/主辦銀行　lead bank
铅印/鉛印　letterpress printing
铅印本/鉛印本　letterpress, stereotype edition
谦敬用语/謙敬用語　modest term
签发/簽發　sign and issue
签发大样/簽發大樣　large sample issue
签发人/簽發人　issuer
签发小样/簽發小樣　sample issue
签认/簽認　signature and approval
签售/簽售　signature sale
签署/簽署　sign
签约转包/簽約外包　contract out
签账卡/簽賬卡　charge card
签证银行/[指定]簽證銀行　licensing bank, appointed licensing bank
钤记/鈐記　Qianji, lower official seal
钤印本/鈐印本　seal book
前背书人/前手背書人　preceding endorser
前端控制/前端控制　front control, headend control
前方一致检索/前方一致檢索　front match retrieval
前后比较/前後比較　pre-post comparison
前进色/前進色　advancing color
前科/前科　criminal record
前口/前口　fore edge
前馈控制/前饋控制　feedforward control, preliminary control
前馈系统/前饋系統　feedforward system
前期物业管理/前期物業管理　early-stage property management
前期制作/前製作業　pre-production
前切口/書口,餘白　fore-edge margin
前切口排架法/前切口排架法　fore-edge shelving

前摄干扰/順向干擾　proactive interference
前生殖期性游戏/前生殖期性遊戲　pre-reproductive period sex games
前塑文化/前塑文化　prefigurative culture
前现代高度文明的法/前現代高度文明的法　the law of pre-modern high cultures
前线团体/先導團體　front group
前向差分/前向差分　forward difference
前向方程/前向方程式　forward equation
前向联系/向前關聯　forward linkage
前向纵向一体化/向前垂直整合　forward vertical integration
前象征文化/前塑文化　prefigurative culture
前言/前言　foreword
前瞻性调查/未來性研究　prospective studies
前缀/前綴,前標　prefix
钱德勒企业史理论/錢德勒企業史理論　enterprise history theory of Chandler
钱珀努恩分布/Champernowne 分布,Champernowne 分配　Champernowne distribution
钳口命令/箝口令　gag order in ancient China
潜变量/潛在變數,隱性變數　latent variable
潜变量模型/潛變量模型　latent variable model
潜伏期/潛伏期　incubation period
潜科学/潛科學　potential science
潜类分析/潛在組群分析　latent class analysis
潜马尔可夫模型/潛馬可夫模型　latent Markov model
潜特质模型/潛特質模型　latent trait models
潜隐记忆/潛隱記憶　cryptomnesia
潜影/潛影　latent image
潜预算分析/潛預算分析　latent budget analysis
潜在变量/潛在變項,潛在因子　latent variable, latent factor
潜在产出/潛在產出　potential output
潜在出口限额作用律/貿易作用遞減論　law of sinking export quota
潜在的出口市场/潛在的出口市場　potential export market
潜在读者/潛在讀者,隱含讀者　potential reader
潜在货币/潛在貨幣　latent currency
潜在结构/潛在結構　latent structure
潜在结构分析/潛在結構分析　latent structure analysis
潜在竞争/潛在競爭　potential competition
潜在类别分析/潛在類別分析　latent class analysis, LCA
潜在利润/潛在的利潤　potential profit

潜在[票据]拒付/潜在[票據]拒付　latent dishonor
潜在缺陷/潜在缺陷　potential defect
潜在市场/潜在市場　potential market
潜在受众/潜在受眾　potential audience
潜在特质/潜在特質　latent trait
潜在投资/潜在投資　potential investment
潜在需求/潜在需求　potential requirement
潜在因子/潜在因子型　latent factor
潜在用户/潜在用戶　potential user
潜在语义标引/潜在語義標引　latent semantic indexing, LSI
浅标引/淺標引　shallow indexing
浅层生态学/淺層生態學　shallow ecology
浅阅读/淺閱讀　shallow reading
遣散费/遣散費　severance pay
欠发达/低度發展　underdevelopment
欠发达的发展/欠發達的發展　the development of underdevelopment
欠发达国家/低度開發國家　underdeveloped country, less developed country
嵌入过程/嵌入過程　imbedded process
嵌入式的客观性/鑲嵌的客觀　embedded objectivity
嵌入性/鑲嵌　embeddedness
嵌套抽样/套層抽樣　nested sampling
嵌套短语标引系统/巢套詞組索引系統　nested phrase indexing system, NEPHIS
嵌套对数单位模型/巢式羅吉特機率模型　nested logit model
嵌套分类/套層分類　nested classification
嵌套行列设计/套疊列行設計　nested row-column design
嵌套假设/套疊假設　nested hypotheses
嵌套检索/嵌套檢索　nesting retrieval
嵌套模型/套層模型　nested model
嵌套平衡不完全区组设计/套疊不完全平衡區集設計　nested balanced incomplete block design
嵌套设计/套層設計　nested design
嵌套实验/嵌套實驗,巢式實驗,鑲嵌實驗　nested experiment
嵌套随机因子/套層隨機因子　nested random factor
嵌套因子/套層因子　nested factor
强大数定律/强大數法則　strong law of large number, strong law of large numbers
强单峰的/强單峰的　strongly unimodal
强度/强度量　intensity
强度分布/强度分布　strength distribution
强度函数/强度函數　intensity function
强度率/强度率　intensity rate

强分布自由的/强分布不拘的　strongly distribution free
强关系/强連結　strong tie
强化理论/强化理論,增強理論　reinforcement theory
强化效应/强化效應,增強效應　reinforcement effect
强化学习/强化性學習　reinforcement learning
强化学习预测法/强化學習預測法　reinforce learning forecasting model
强奸罪/强姦罪　crime of rape
强截集/强截集　strong cut set
强拟凸函数/强擬凸函數　strongly quasi-convex function
强平稳随机过程/强平穩隨機過程　strong stationary stochastic process
强外生性/强外生性　strong exogeneity, strongly exogenous
强完备性/强完備性　strong completeness
强相合估计量/强一致估計量　strongly consistent estimator
强行法/强行法　jus cogens
强一致性/强一致性　strong consistency
强有效/强效率性　strong-form efficiency
强制保险/强制保險　compulsory insurance, enforced insurance
强制保养/强制保養　obliged maintenance
强制辩护/强制辯護　compulsory defense
强制出口管理/强制出口管理　mandatory restriction on export
强制储蓄/强制儲蓄　compulsory saving, forced saving
强制储蓄策略/强制儲蓄策略　forced-savings strategy
强制措施/强制措施　compulsory measure
强制代扣款/强制代扣款　compulsory check-off clause
强制缔约/强制締約　forced contracting
强制清算/强制清算　compulsory liquidation
强制权力/强制力　coercive power
强制审计/强制審計　compulsory audit
强制收购/强制收購　compulsory takeover
强制消费/强制消費　forced consumption
强制销售/强制銷售　forced sale
强制信托/强制信託　involuntary trust
强制性标准/强制性標準　mandatory standard
强制性清算/强制性清算　enforced liquidation
强制性认证/强制性認證　compulsory certification
强制性许可证制度/强制性許可證制度　mandatory

licensing system
强制性政策工具/強制性政策工具 compulsory policy instrument
强制性制度变迁/強制性制度變遷 forced institutional change
强制许可/強制授權 compulsory licensing
强制仲裁/強制仲裁 mandatory arbitration, obligation arbitration, compulsory arbitration
强制准备金/強制準備金 compulsory reserve
抢夺罪/搶奪罪 crime of forcible seizure
抢劫罪/搶劫罪 crime of robbery
抢救性保护/搶救性保護 salvage preservation
抢注域名/搶注域名 cyber squatting
强迫分配法/強制分配法 forced distribution method
强迫机制/強迫機制 coercive mechanism
强迫选择法/強制選擇法 forced-choice scale
敲出期权/觸及失效選擇權 knock-out option
敲定价格/履約價格 exercise price, striking price
敲门发行/敲門發行 knock at the door to distribute
敲入期权/觸及生效選擇權 knock-in option
敲诈勒索罪/敲詐勒索罪 crime of extortion
敲竹杠/敲竹槓 hold-up
乔维纳特准则/Chauvenets 準則 Chauvenets criterion
侨汇/僑匯 overseas Chinese remittance
切比雪夫-埃尔米特多项式/Chebyshev-Hermite 多項式 Chebyshev-Hermite polynomials
切比雪夫不等式/Chebyshev 不等式 Chebyshev inequality, Chebyshev's inequality
切尔诺夫效率/Chernoff 有效係數 Chernoff efficiency
切孔胶粘订/破脊膠裝 notch binding
切口/刃口 cutting edge
切口留白/切口外白邊 foredge
切口装饰/切口裝飾 decoration of cutting edge
切片分析/切片分析 slice analysis technique
切普曼-罗宾思不等式/Chapman-Robbins 不等式 Chapman-Robbins inequality
切普曼-罗宾思下界/Chapman-Robbins 下界 Chapman-Robbins lower bound
切齐/裁邊 cropping
切尾平均数/截尾平均數 trimmed mean
切尾最小二乘估计量/修剪的最小平方估計式 trimmed least square estimator
切纸尺寸/紙張裁切尺寸 cut size paper
切纸机/切紙機 paper-cutting machine
侵犯财产罪/侵犯財產罪 crime against property
侵犯公民人身权利-民主权利罪/侵犯公民人身權利-民主權利罪 crime of infringement upon citizen's rights and democratic rights of the person
侵犯邻接权/侵犯鄰接權 infringement of neighboring rights
侵犯商标权/侵犯商標權 infringement of trademark right
侵犯商业秘密/侵犯商業秘密 infringement of business secrets
侵犯商业秘密罪/侵犯商業秘密罪 crime of infringing on business secrets
侵犯通信自由罪/侵犯通信自由罪 crime of infringing on freedom of correspondence
侵犯隐私/隱私侵犯 invasion of privacy
侵犯知识产权罪/侵犯智慧財產權罪 crime of infringement upon intellectual property rights
侵犯著作权/違反著作權 infringement of copyright
侵犯专利权/侵犯專利權 infringement of patent rights
侵略/侵略 aggression
侵略罪/侵略罪 crime of aggression
侵权/侵權 tort
侵权法/過失責任法規 tort law
侵权行为/侵權行爲 act of tort
侵权行为地/侵權行爲地 place of tort
侵权行为地法/侵權行爲地法 Lex Loci Delicti
侵权预算/侵權預算 infringement budget
侵占他人作品/侵占他人作品 infringement of the work of others
侵占罪/侵占罪 crime of misappropriation
亲笔文件/手稿 holograph
亲和图/親和圖 affinity diagram
亲密关系/親密關係 intimacy
亲民/親民 endear oneself to the people
亲亲得相首匿/親親得相首匿 an ancient Chinese legal principle of allowing the relatives to mutually conceal their offences
亲亲尊尊/親親尊尊 being harmonious and respectful to one deserved to be close to or respected
亲权/親權 parental right
亲善市场论/模擬自由市場論 simulated free market theory
亲社会行为/利社會[性]行爲 prosaically behavior, prosocial behavior
亲属/親屬 kinsfolk, kinship
亲属称谓/親屬稱謂 kinship terminology
亲属法/親屬法 law of descent
亲属制度/親屬體系 kinship system

亲水性/親水性　hydrophilic
亲验式学习/體驗性學習　experiential learning
亲缘/姻親　affinity
亲子关系/親子關係　parent-child relationship
亲子阅读/親子閱讀　parent-child reading
亲子制度/親子制度　institutions for parenthood
秦律/秦律　Law of the Qin Dynasty
秦墓竹简/秦墓竹簡　Qinmu Zhujian
秦始律/秦始律　First Law of Qin Dynasty
青版/青版，藍版　cyan plate
青册/青冊　qing ce
青春期/青春期，青少年期　adolescence, puberty
青春期性教育/青春期性教育　sex education for adolescence
青年/青年　youth
青年参与/青年參與　youth participation
青年赋权/青年賦權　youth empowerment
青年话语/青年話語　discourse on youth
青年群体组织/青年社團組織　youth group and organization
青年社会问题/青年社會問題　social problems of youths
青年社会学/青年社會學　sociology of youth
青年学/青年學　study of youth
青年[亚]文化/青年[亞]文化　youth subculture
青年研究/青年研究　youth studies
青年运动/青年運動　youth movement
青年志愿者/青年志工　youth volunteer
青年志愿者活动/青年志願者活動　youth volunteer activity
青色/青色　cyan
青少年/青少年　adolescence, teenagers
青少年读物/青少年讀物　adolescence literature, juvenile literature, young adult book
青少年读者服务/青少年讀者服務　juvenile reader service
青少年犯罪/青少年犯罪，青少年非行　juvenile delinquency
青少年福利/青少年福利　youth welfare
青少年宫/青少年宮　youth palace
青少年权益/青少年權益　youths' rights
青少年社会工作/青少年社會工作　social work for teenagers
青少年越轨/青少年越軌　juvenile deviance
青铜器铭文/青銅器銘文　bronze inscriptions
轻博客/輕博客　light blog, tumblelog, lofter
轻度读者/輕度讀者　casual reader
轻微不合格/次要不良　minor defective

轻微故障/次要故障　minor failure
轻微缺陷/次要缺點　minor defect
轻尾分布/輕尾分布　light-tailed distribution
倾力推销/傾力推銷　high pressure selling
倾向分布/傾向分配　propensity distribution
倾向指数/傾向分數　propensity score
倾销/傾銷　dumping
倾销差价/傾銷差價　dumping margin
倾销法案/傾銷法案　dumping code
倾销关税/傾銷關稅　dumping duty
倾销价格/傾銷價格　dumping price
倾销市场/傾銷市場　dumping field
倾销政策/傾銷政策　dumping policy
倾斜控制限/傾斜管制界限　slanting control limit
倾斜控制线/傾斜管制界限線　slanting control limit line
清偿/清償，清算　clear out, liquidation
清偿单位/清償單位　liquidity unit
清偿基础/清償基礎　liquidity basis
清偿能力高/高清償能力　high level of liquidity
清偿危机/清償危機，週轉危機　liquidity crisis
清偿债务备忘录/清償債務備忘錄　memorandum of satisfaction
清抄本/清抄本　Qing Dynasty handwritten edition
清单/清單　checklist
清单矩阵/清單矩陣　checklist matrix
清稿本/清稿本　clean original draft
清会典/清會典　Qing Dynasty Code
清洁浮动/乾淨浮動　clean float
清洁空气法/空氣淨化法　clean air act
清洁能源/清潔能源　clean energy
清洁生产/清潔生產　clean production, cleaner production
清洁收据/清潔收據，清潔收貨單　clean receipt
清洁提单/清潔提單　clean bill of lading
清洁债券/結清債券　bond clean
清刻本/清刻本　Qing Dynasty edition
清理/清除　cleaning
清理程序中优先清偿的债务/優先清償債務　liquidation preferential debt
清末礼法之争/清末禮法之爭　dispute on etiquette and law of the late Qing
清算/清算　liquidation, settlement
清算报告/清算報告　liquidation report
清算表/清算表　liquidation statement
清算程序/清算程式　liquidation procedure
清算分配/清算分配　liquidating distribution
清算公司/清算公司　liquidation company

清算股利/清算股利　liquidating dividend
清算价格/清算價格，結算價格，補償價格　clearing price, make-up price
清算价值/清算價值　liquidation value, salvage value
清算日/結算日　make-up day
清算式资产负债表/清算式資產負債表　statement of affair
清算收益/清算收益　liquidation income
清算损益/清算損益　liquidation profit and loss
清算所/票據交換所　clearing house
清算协定/清算協定　clearing agreement
清算账户/結算賬戶　clearing account
清算制度/清算制度　clearing system
清算资产负债表/清算資產負債表　liquidation balance sheet
清晰度/清晰度　sharpness, resolution, clarity
清晰度增强/清晰度增強　sharpness enhancement
清样/清樣　clean proof, modified paper pattern
情报/情報，資訊，信息　information, intelligence
情报编译/情報編譯　information translating and editing
情报层级/情報層級　intelligence level
情报传递模式/資訊通訊模式　information communication model
情报对象/情報目標　intelligence target
情报分析人员/情報分析人員　intelligence analysis personnel
情报分析与研究/情報分析研究　information analysis and research
情报服务/資訊服務　information service
情报跟踪研究/情報跟蹤分析　intelligence tracking analysis
情报工作/資訊工作　information work
情报过程/情報過程　intelligence-related process
情报过程管理/情報過程管理　intelligence process management
情报活动/情報業務，資訊活動　information activity
情报机构/情報機構　intelligence institution
情报基本要素/情報必要元素　essential elements of intelligence, EEI
情报技巧/間諜情報技術　trade craft
情报价值/資訊價值　informational value, information value
情报检索[系统]/資訊檢索[系統]　information retrieval system
情报简报/情報簡報　intelligence briefing
情报交换小组/情報資料交流小組　information exchange group
情报交流/資訊通訊　information communication
情报接近/情報接近　intelligence approach
情报经纪人/情報經紀人　intelligence broker
情报控制/資訊控制　information control
情报框架/情報框架　intelligence framework
情报链/情報鏈　intelligence chain
情报流通/資訊流通　information circulation
情报人员/情報人員　intelligence expert, intelligence agent
情报社会学/資訊社會學　information sociology
情报失察/情報漏洞　intelligence failure
情报室/情況室　situation room
情报搜集过程/資訊收集過程　information collection process
情报文化/資訊文化　information culture
情报现象/資訊現象　information phenomenon
情报心理学/資訊心理學　information psychology
情报行动/情報行動　intelligence operation
情报行为/資訊行爲　information behavior
情报需求分析/情報需求分析　intelligence need analysis
情报学/資訊科學　information science
情报学方法论/資訊科學方法論　methodology of information science
情报学会/資訊科學學會　society for information science
情报学家/資訊科學家　information scientist
情报学教育/資訊科學教育　information science education
情报学史/情報學史　history of information science
情报学研究范式/資訊科學研究典範　information science research paradigm
情报研究支持系统/情報分析支援系統　intelligence analysis support system, support system for intelligence analysis
情报研究质量控制/情報分析品質控制　quality control in intelligence analysis
情报诱导/情報誘出　intelligence elicitation
情报语言学/資訊語言學　information linguistics
情报员/情報員　intelligence agent, intelligencer
情报源/資訊[資]源　information source
情报战/情報戰　intelligence war
情报支持/情報保障　intelligence support
情报资产/情報資產　intelligence assets
情报资产构建/情報資產建設　intelligence asset building
情感/情感　emotion
情节编织/情節賦予，情節設計，情節安排

emplotment
情景分析/情景分析　scenario analysis
情景规划/情境規劃　scenario planning, foresight planning, informed flexibility
情景面试/情境式面談　situational interview
情景模拟培训/模擬訓練　simulation training
情景式危机沟通理论/情境式危機溝通理論　situational crisis communication theory, SCCT
情景喜剧/情境喜劇　sitcom
情景主义/情境主義　situationalism
情境管理/情境管理　situation management
情境规律/情境律　law of situation
情境化/情境化　contextualize
情境领导理论/情境領導理論　situational leadership theory
情境嵌入研究/情境嵌入研究　context-embedded research
情境效应/情境效應　contextual effect
情境行为/情境行爲　contextual behavior
情境依存效应/情境依存效應　context dependent effect
情境因素/情境因素　contextual factor
情商测验/情緒商數測試　emotional quotient test
情势变更/情勢變更　change of circumstance
情势变更原则/情勢變更原則　Doctrine of Rebus sic principle of change of circumstance
情绪/情緒　emotion
情绪胜任力/情緒能力　emotional competency
情绪宣泄/情感宣洩　emotional catharsis
情绪智力/情緒智力　emotional intelligence, EI
黥刑/黥刑　Qing Penalty
请购单/請購單　purchase requisition
请即汇付/請即匯付　kindly remit
请求捐赠/請求捐贈　solicited gift
请求卖方回应/請求賣方回應　request for seller's response
请求权/請求權　right of claim
请示/請示　asking for instruction
请愿书/請願書　petition
庆元条法事类/慶元條法事類　Qingyuan Tiaofa Shilei
穷尽抽样/徹底抽樣　exhaustive sampling
穷尽调查/徹底調查　exhaustive survey
穷举搜索/徹查，竭盡式搜尋　exhaustive search
穹形函数/肩形函數　ogive function
穹形曲线/肩形曲線　ogive curve
琼克霍尔k样本检验/Jonckheere的k樣本檢定　Jonckheere's k-sample test

琼斯模型/Jones模型　Jones model
丘奇-奥尔福德管理原则/丘奇-奧爾福德管理原則　management principle of Church and Alford
丘奇论管理职能/丘奇論管理職能　Church's view on management function
秋审/秋審　Qiushen, autumn trial
囚徒困境/囚徒困境，囚犯兩難　prisoner's dilemma
囚徒困境博弈/囚犯兩難賽局　prisoner's dilemma game
求实原则/求實原則　pricinple of seeking truth
求真精神/實存論取向　realistic approach
求职/工作搜尋　job search
求职面试/員工面試　employment interview
求职性失业/搜尋性失業　search unemployment
球面对称分布/球面對稱分布，球面對稱分配　spherically symmetric distribution
球面方差/球面變異數　spherical variance
球面方差函数/球面變異數函數　spherical variance function
球面分布/球面分布，球面分配　spherical distribution
球面均值方向/球面均值方向　spherical mean direction
球面正态分布/球面常態分布，球面常態分配　spherical normal distribution
区分/金融分工化　compartmentalization
区分全宗/區分全宗　separate fonds
区分原则/區分原則　principle of distinction
区际冲突法/區際衝突法　interregional conflicts law
区际法律冲突/區際法律衝突　interregional conflict of laws
区际司法互助/區際司法互助　interregional judicial assistance
区间分布/區間分布　interval distribution
区间估计/區間估計　interval estimation
区间估计[值]/區間估計[值]　interval estimate
区间预测/區間預測　interval forecasting
区位经济/區域經濟　location economic
区位决策/區位選擇　location decision
区位理论/區位理論　location theory
区位商/區位商數　location quotient
区位因素/區位因數　location factors
区位优势/區位優勢　superiority of location
区域/區域　region
区域比较因子/地區比較因子　area comparability factor
区域标准/區域標準　regional standard
区域产业结构政策/區域產業結構政策　regional

industry structure policy
区域产业竞争力/區域產業競爭力　regional industry competitiveness
区域产业政策/區域產業政策　regional industry policy
区域城市系统/區域城市系統　regional system of cities
区域乘数/區域乘數　local multiplier, regional multiplier
区域抽样/區域抽樣,地區抽樣　area sampling
区域创新/區域創新　regional innovation
区域创新环境/區域創新環境　regional innovation environment
区域创新能力/區域創新能力　regional innovation capability
区域创新体系/區域創新體系　regional innovation system, RIS
区域创新网络/區域創新網路　regional innovation network
区域创新系统/區域創新系統　regional innovation system
区域大小/區域大小　size of a region
区域定价政策/空間定價政策　spatial pricing policy
区域多项式/區域多項式　zonal polynomial
区域发展/地區發展　regional development
区域发展战略/區域經濟發展策略　regional development strategy
区域公共品/空間公共財　spatial public good
区域股票市场/區域股票市場　regional stock market
区域规划/區域計劃　regional planning
区域合作/區間合作　region cooperation
区域环境/區域環境　regional environment
区域环境法/區域環境法　regional environmental law
区域价格/區域價格　zone price
区域间合作/區域間合作　inter-regional co-operation
区域间投入产出表/區域投入產出表　interregional input-output table
区域间投入产出模型/域間投入產出模型　interregional input-output model
区域拣货/區域揀貨　zone picking
区域经济发展/區域經濟發展　regional economy development
区域经济合作/區域經濟合作　regional economic cooperation
区域经济集团/區域性經濟團體　regional economic grouping
区域经济学/區域經濟學　regional economic, regional economy
区域经济一体化/區域性經濟一體化　regional economic integration
区域经济增长/區域經濟增長　regional economy growth
区域经济增长模型/區域性經濟增長模型　regional economic growth model
区域竞争/區間競爭　region competition
区域竞争力/地區競爭力　regional competitiveness
区域可持续发展/區域永續發展　regional sustained development
区域联合目录/區域聯合目錄　regional union catalog
区域贸易/區域貿易　inter-regional trade
区域贸易商品/區域貿易商品　inter-regional goods
区域内贸易/區域間貿易　inner-regional trade, intra-regional trade
区域曲线/區域曲線　zone curve
区域曲线图/區域曲線圖　zone curve chart
区域软实力/區域軟實力　regional soft power
区域市场/區域市場　regional market
区域收敛/區間趨同　region convergence
区域投入产出模型/區域投入產出模型　regional input-output model
区域图/區域圖,地區圖　area chart, zone chart, area graph
区域物流中心/區域物流中心　regional logistics center
区域限批/區域限批　regional license restriction
区域销售队伍结构/區域式銷售隊伍結構,地區型銷售隊伍結構　territorial sales force structure
区域形象/區域形象　regional image
区域形象设计/區域形象設計　project of regional image
区域性广告/區域性廣告,地方廣告,在地廣告　local advertising, regional advertising
区域性国际组织/區域性國際組織　regional international organization
区域性集体合同/區域性集體合同　regional collective contract
区域性贸易/區域性貿易　regional trade
区域样本/區域樣本　area sample
区域政策/區域政策　regional policy
区域治理/區間治理　region governance
区域组织租金/區域組織租金　regional organization rent
区组/區組,區集　block
区组间/區集間的　interblock
区组间比较/區集間比較　interblock comparison

区组间估计／區集間估計　interblock estimation
区组内／區集内　intrablock
区组内差／區集内差　intrablock difference
区组内估计[值]／區集内估計[值]　intrablock estimate
区组内子群／區集内子群　intrablock subgroup
区组设计／區集設計　block design
区组替代／區集替代　block replacement
曲棍球杆图／曲棍球杆圖　hockey stick graph
曲面网印机／曲面網印機　curved surface screen printing machine
曲面印刷／曲面印刷　curved surface screen printing
J 曲线／J 型曲線　J-curve
OC 曲线／OC 曲線　OC-curve
S 曲线／S 曲線　S-curve
曲线估计／曲線估計　curve estimation
曲线回归／曲線回歸　curvilinear regression
曲线拟合／曲線配適　curve fitting
曲线弹性／彈性曲線　curve of flexibility
曲线相关／曲線相關　curvilinear correlation
曲线运动／曲線運動　ballistic movement
曲指数族／曲線指數族　curved exponential family
驱逐出境／驅逐出境　banish
屈服力／屈服力　yield force
趋势／趨勢　trend
趋势比率法／趨勢比例法　ratio to trend method
趋势分析／趨勢分析　trend analysis
趋势过程／趨勢過程　trending process
趋势拟合／趨勢配適　trend fitting
趋势平稳过程／趨勢平穩過程　trend-stationary process
趋势情报研究／趨勢情報分析　trend intelligence analysis
趋势曲线／趨勢線　trend curve
趋势图／趨勢圖　trend chart
趋势推延法／趨勢推延法　trend projection
趋势外推法／趨勢外推法　trend extrapolation
趋势循环曲线的季节调整／趨勢循環曲線的季節調整　trend-cycle curve seasonal adjustment
趋势与随机游走／趨勢與隨機漫步　trends and random walks
趋势值／趨勢值　trend value
趋势周期／趨勢循環　trend-cycle
趋向线分析预测法／趨向線分析預測法　trend line analysis forecasting approach
取保候审／取保候審,保釋　bail
取保候审决定书／取保候審決定書　written dicision on bail
取得时效／取得時效　prescriptive acquisition
取货单／提單　carrier's note
4E 取向／4E 取向　4E orientation
取消／消去[法]　elimination
取消订单／取消訂單　order canceled, OC, canceled order
取消订单费用／取消訂單費用　cancellation charge
取消订阅／取消訂閱　cancel a subscription, unsubscribe, subscription cancelling
取消价格控制／取消價格控制　price decontrol
取消特别提款权／取消特別提款權　cancellation of special drawing right, cancellation of SDR
取效行为／成事行爲　perlocutionary act
取样偏差／抽樣偏差,抽樣偏誤　sampling bias
取证／取證　collection of evidences
取之不尽资源／取之不盡資源　widow's cruse
去个人化／去個人化　depersonalization
去技能化／去技術化　deskilling
去加重／解强　de-emphasis
去偶合／去偶合,解耦　decoupling
去湿／除濕　dehumidification
去酸／去酸,脱酸　deacidification
去医学化／去醫學化　demedicalization
去语境化／去語境化　decontextualization
去政治化／去政治化　de-politicization
去中心化／去中心化　decentralization
圈地法案／圈地法案　act of enclosure, enclosure act
圈占荒地权／圈占荒地權　enclosure of wasteland right
权变估值法／假設性市場評價法,條件評估法　contingent valuation method
权变管理／權變管理　contingency management
权变决策理论／權變決策理論　contingency policy-making theory
权变理论／權變理論　contingency theory
权变理论学派／權變理論學派　contingency theory school
权变领导理论／權變領導理論　contingency leadership theory
权函数／權數函數　weight function
权衡理论／抵換理論　trade-off theory
权基／權數基　weight base
权交叉／權數交叉　weight crossing
权矩阵／加權矩陣　weight matrix
权力／權力　power
权力发行／權力發行　authority distribution
权力分立／權力分立,分權　separation of powers
权力和责任／權力和責任　authority and

responsibility
权力精英/權力精英 power elite
权利/權利 right
权利法案/權利法案 Bill of Rights
权利管理电子信息/權利管理電子信息 electronic rights management information
权利滥用/權利濫用 abuse of right
权利能力/權利能力 capacity of rights
权利请愿书/權利請願書 petition of right
权利瑕疵担保/權利瑕疵擔保 security for defects of right
权利宣言书/權利宣言書 claim of rights
权利义务对等原则/權利義務對等原則 reciprocity principle of rights and obligations
权利质权/權利質權 pledge of rights
权利转让证书/權利轉讓證書 letter of transfer
权能分治/權能分治 separation of sovereignty and governance
权偏倚/權數偏誤 weight bias
权威/權威 authority
权威接受论/權威接受論 acceptance theory of authority
权威论证/權威式論證 authoritative argument
权威人格/權威人格 authoritarian personality
权威型管理/權威型管理 authority management
权益/權益 equity
权益乘数/權益乘數 equity multiplier
权益工具/債券工具 equity instrument
权益结合法/權益結合法 pooling-of-interest method
权益资本/權益資本 equity capital
权益资本成本/權益資金成本 cost of equity capital
权责发生制/應計基礎[會計] accrual basis of accounting
ψ权重/ψ權數 psi-weight
全不相联/完全不相聯 complete dissociation
全部数据/全部數據 overall data
全程管理/全程管理 whole course management
全动作动画/全動作動畫 full animation
全额包销/全額包銷 exclusive sale underwriting
全额付款/全額付款 payment in full
全额累进税/全額累進所得稅 full progressive income tax
全额预算管理/全額預算管理 whole-budget management
全概率/全概率,總機率 total probability
全归储蓄者的存单/儲蓄券 all-savers certificate
全国经济普查/全國經濟普查 national economic census

全过程质量管理/全過程品質管制 whole process quality management
全集/全集 collected edition, complete works
全检/全數檢驗 one hundred-percent inspection
全交互式电视/全互動式電視 full interactive television
全角/全形 full size
全局误差/全域誤差 global error
全局最大值/全域最大值 global maximum
全局最小值/全域最小值 global minimum
全录/全錄 integration-all
全媒体/全媒體 all media, omnimedia
全媒体出版/全媒體出版 federated media publishing
全媒体记者/全媒體記者 omnimedia journalist
全面标引/全面標引 comprehensive indexing
全面查点/全部列舉 complete enumeration
全面成本管理/全面成本管理 total cost management
全面创新管理/全面創新管理 total innovation management, TIM
全面规划、合理布局原则/全面規劃、合理布局原則 principle of overall planning and rational layout
全面降低关税/全面調降關稅 across-the-board tariff reduction
全面教育/綜合教育 comprehensive education
全面库存法/全部存貨 wall-to-wall inventory
全面生产维护/全面生產維護 total productive maintenance, TPM
全面收藏/全面收藏 comprehensive collection
全面调整关税税率/全面調整關稅 across-the-board tariff change
全面性政策规划/全面性政策規劃 comprehensive policy planning
全面预算/總預算,整體預算 master budget
全面整合营销/整合行銷 total integrated marketing
全面质量管理/全面品質管制 total quality management, company wide management
全面质量环境管理/全面環境品質管理 total quality environment management
全面最惠国条款/全面最惠國條款 comprehensive most-favoured nation clause
全民读书月/全民讀書月 National Reading Month
全民健康保险/全民健康保險 national health insurance
全民医保/全民醫保 universal medical coverage
全民阅读/全民閱讀 nation-wide reading, national reading
全名背书/全名背書,記名背書,特別背書

endorsement in full
全能银行/全方位業務銀行,綜合銀行　full service bank, universal bank
全屏广告/全屏廣告　full screen advertisement
全球变暖/全球暖化　global warming
全球采购/全球採購　global sourcing
全球产业/全球化產業　global industry
全球传播/全球傳播　global communication
全球创新体系/全球創新體系　global innovation system
全球电子交易系统/全球化交易系統　globex
全球定位系统/全球定位系統　global positioning system
全球供应链/全球供應鏈　global supply chain
全球广告/全球廣告　global advertising
全球化/全球化　globalization
全球化环境/全球化環境　global segment
全球化人力资源管理/全球人力資源管理　global human resource management
全球化与城市发展/全球化與城市發展　globalization and urban development
全球环境变化/全球環境變遷　global environmental change
全球环境问题/全球環境問題　global environmental problems
全球结社革命/全球結社革命　global associational revolution
全球金融市场/全球金融市場　global financial market
全球经济/全球經濟　global economy
全球气候变化/全球氣候變遷　global climate change
全球信息网络/全球資訊網路　international information network, IIN
全球性补偿贸易/全球性補償貿易　global compensation trade
全球性城市/全球城市,全球都市　global city
全球性储备/全球性儲備　global reserve
全球性进口配额/全球性進口配額　global import quota
全球性贸易战略/全球性貿易策略　universal trade strategy
全球性贸易政策/全球性貿易政策　universal trade policy
全球性配额/全球性配額　global quota
全球性社会/全球社會　global society
全球虚拟团队/全球虛擬團隊　global virtual team
全球移动通信系统/全球行動通訊系統　global system for mobile communications

全球营销/全球行銷　global marketing
全球战略/全球策略　global strategy
全球整合/全球整合　global integration
全权委托偏好原理/全權委託偏好原理　carte-blanche preference principle
全时空创新/全時空創新　all time and space innovation
全式提单/詳式提單　long form bill of lading
全数检验/全數檢驗,總檢驗　total inspection
全数字动画/全數字動畫　full-digital animation
全体一致决策规则/全體一致決策規則　unanimity rule for policy making
全文标引/全文標引　full-text indexing
全文检索/全文檢索　full-text retrieval, full-text search
全文检索系统/全文檢索系統　full-text retrieval system
全文浏览器/全文瀏覽器　China academic journals, CAJ
全文数据库/全文資料庫　full-text database
全文数字化文献/全文數位文獻　digital full-text literature
全文索引/全文索引　full-text index
全文下载/全文下載　full-text download
全息电影/全息電影　holographic movie
全息照相/雷射全像術　holography
全息制品/立體圖像　hologram
全衔背书/全銜背書,記名背書　indorsement in full
全险/全險　all risks insurance
全相关/完全相關,總相關　total correlation, complete correlation
全相关矩阵/完全相關矩陣　complete correlation matrix
全新产品/全新產品　entirely new product
全新购买/全新採購　new-task buying
全薪劳动力/全薪勞動力　all-salaried workforce
全信道式信息交流网络/全通道式資訊交流網路　network of channel-mode communication
全信息/完全訊息　complete information, comprehensive information
全形拓/全形拓　composite rubbing
全序/全序　total order
全要素创新/全要素創新　all elements innovation
全要素生产率/總要素生產力　total factor productivity
全译/全譯　cover to cover translation
全因子实验/全因子實驗　full factorial design, FFD
全引目录/全引目錄　full cited catalog

全域/全域　universe
全员参与/全員參與　involvement of people
全员创新/全員創新　highly involvement innovation
全员质量管理/全員品質管制　company-wide quality control, CWQC, all stuff quality management
全职妻子/全職妻子　housewife
全宗/全宗　fonds
全宗单/全宗單　fonds list
全宗号/全宗號　number of archival fonds, number of fonds
全宗介绍/全宗介紹　guide to an archival fonds
全宗卷/全宗卷　fonds descriptive file
全宗卡片/全宗卡片　fonds card
全宗名册/全宗名冊　fonds roster
全宗名称/全宗名稱　name of fonds
全宗群/全宗群　fonds complex
全宗原则/全宗原則　fonds principle
全宗指南/全宗指南　fonds guide
劝服论/說服理論　persuasion theory
劝说性广告/說服性廣告　persuasive advertising
缺藏/缺藏　gap in the collection, lacuna
缺册/缺冊　missing volume
缺点/缺點　demerit
缺点控制图/缺點數管制圖　demerit control chart
缺点图/缺點數圖　demerit chart
缺乏弹性/無彈性的　inelastic
缺货/缺貨　stockout, out of stock
缺货登记/缺貨登記　shortage registration
缺货订单/缺貨訂單　backorder
缺货费用/缺貨成本　shortage cost
缺货率/缺貨率　stock-out rate
缺货损失/銷貨成本, 短缺成本　stock-out cost
GDP 缺口/GDP 缺口　GDP gap
缺期/期刊缺期　missing issue
缺勤/曠工　absenteeism
缺失观测值/遺漏觀測值　missing observation
缺失模式功能/缺失機率函數　missing pattern function
缺失数据/遺漏資料, 遺漏數據　missing data
缺失值/遺漏值　missing value
缺席判决/缺席判決　default judgment
缺陷/缺陷, 瑕疵　defect
缺陷产品/缺陷產品　deficient product
缺陷分类/缺點分類　defect classification, classification of defects
缺陷机会数/缺陷機會數　defect opportunity
缺陷数/缺點數　number of defect
缺陷数控制图/缺陷數控製圖　count chart for number of defects
缺陷通知期限/缺陷通知期限　defect notification period
缺陷图/缺點圖　defect chart
缺陷维修/缺陷維修　defect preserve
缺陷预防/缺點預防　defect prevention
缺陷责任期/缺陷責任期　defect liability period
缺陷责任证书/缺陷責任證書　defect liability certificate
缺页/缺頁　page missing
阙补/闕補　fill in the missing pages or chapters in bibliographic descriptions
阙佚书目/闕佚書目　desiderata list, waiting list
阙字/闕字　misunderstanding due to missing characters
确定保险/確定保險　definite insurance
确定的订单/最終訂單　firm order
确定的固定总价合同/確定的固定總價合同　firm-fixed-price contract, FFP contract
确定供款型养老金计划/確定型退休金提撥制　defined-contribution plan
确定故意/確定故意　determinate intention
确定价格/確定價格　definite price
确定目标/確定目標　determine objective
确定判决/確定判決　effective judgment
确定日期交货/確定日期交貨　definite time delivery
确定使用货币/確定使用貨幣　definitive money
确定误差/確定誤差　ascertainment error
确定先验概率的方法/確定先驗概率的方法　method of determination prior probability
确定销售/最終銷售　firm sale
确定型决策/確定狀況下的決策　decision making under certainty
确定性过程/確定性過程　deterministic process
确定性决策/確定決策　certainty decision
确定性模型/確定性模型　deterministic model
确定性排序/確定性調度　deterministic scheduling
确定性趋势/確定趨勢　deterministic trend
确定性效应/確定性效果　certainty effect
确定性需求/確定性需求　deterministic demand
确定询价/確定詢價, 最終詢價　definite inquiry, firm inquiry
确切订单/確定訂單　definite order
确认/確認　validation
确认判决/確認判決　declaratory judgment
确认诉讼/確認訴訟　action of declaration, confirmation lawsuit
确认议付信用证/確認讓購信用狀　confirmed

negotiation letter of credit
确认之诉/確認之訴　declaratory action
裙带资本主义/裙帶資本主義　crony capitalism
群/群[落],群[體]　cluster, group
群岛国/群島國　archipelagic state
群岛基线/群島基線　archipelagic baseline
群岛水域/群島水域　archipelagic waters
群分析/集群分析　cluster analysis
群婚/群婚　group marriage
群间变异/叢聚間變異　intercluster variation
群间方差/叢聚間變異數　variance between clusters
群聊/群聊　group chat
群内变异/叢聚內變異　intracluster variation
群内方差/叢聚內變異數,組內變異數　variance within clusters, within-group variance
群书目录/群書目錄　books catalog
群体/團體　group
群体传播/團體傳播　group communication
群体传递/群體傳輸　group transmission
群体动力理论/團體動力學理論　group dynamics theory
群体动力学/團體動力學　group dynamics
群体归因误差/群體歸因誤差　group attribution error
群体规范/群體規範,團體規範　group norm
群体规模/群體大小　group size
群体互动/團體互動　group interaction
群体极化/團體極化　group polarization
群体计件制/群體計件制　group piece work
群体结构/群體結構,團體結構　group structure
群[体]决策支持系统/群體決策支援系統,團體決策支援系統　group decision support system, GDSS
群体力学/人口動力學　population dynamics
群体盲思/群體迷思　groupthink
群体凝聚力/團體凝聚力　group cohesiveness
群体努力均衡理论/群體努力均衡理論　balance theory of group effort
群体判断过程模型/群體判斷過程模型　group judgment process model
群体偏好映射/群體偏好映射　group preference mapping
群体认同/群體認同,團體認同　group identity, group identification
群体实验/分組試驗　group experiment
群体事件/群體事件　group event
群体思维/團體思維　group thinking, group mentality
群体文化/群體文化　group culture
群体效能感/集體效能　collective efficacy
群体行为/團體行爲　group behavior
群体行为学派/群體行爲學派　group behavior school
群体压力/團體壓力　group pressure
群体意识/團體意識　group consciousness
群体运行过程/團體運行結構　group operation process
群体支持系统/團體支持系統　group support system
群体知识/集體知識　collective knowledge
群体自尊/群體自尊　collective esteem
群效用函数/群體效用函數　group utility function
群学习预测方法/群學習預測方法　group learning forecasting method
群众评议法/群眾評議法　mass appraisal method

R

燃烧武器的法律规定/燃燒武器的法律規定　law provisions on incendiary weapons
染料/染料　dye
染料聚酯/燃料聚酯　dye polymer
染色丝网/染色絲網　dyed mesh
让步/讓步　concession
让步式谈判/讓步協議　concession bargaining
扰动振荡/受擾振盪　disturbed oscillation
扰乱公共秩序罪/擾亂公共秩序罪　crime of disrupting public order
扰乱市场秩序罪/擾亂市場秩序罪　crime of disrupting market order
扰乱无线电通讯管理秩序罪/擾亂無線電通訊管理秩序罪　crime of disrupting wireless communication order
绕线室实验/繞線室實驗　winding room test
热点/熱點　hotspot
热点新闻/熱門新聞　hot news
热货条款/熱貨條款　hot cargo clause
热键/熱鍵　hot key
热媒介/熱媒介　hot media
热门股票/熱門股票　hot issue
热敏复制法/熱感應複製法　thermography
热敏印版/熱敏印版　thermal plate
热敏印刷/感熱式列印　thermal printing
热喷墨/熱噴墨　thermal inkjet
热钱/熱錢,游资　hot money
EVA 热熔胶/EVA 熱熔膠　ethylene vinyl acetate
PUR 热熔胶/PUR 熱熔膠　polyurethane reactive
热熔印刷/熱敏複製法　thermography
热审/熱審　hot-trial
热升华印刷/熱升華印刷　thermal dye transfer printing
热塑加膜/熱塑加膜　thermoplastic lamination
热污染/熱汙染　thermal pollution
热转移/熱轉移　thermal transfer
热转移印刷/熱轉移印刷　thermal transfer printing
热转印/熱轉印,熱轉寫　heat transfer
热字/熱字　hot word
人本主义/人本主義　humanism
人本主义理论/人本主義理論　humanistic theory

人才/人才　talent
人才交流/人員交流　personnel exchange
人才交流中心/人員交流中心　personnel exchange center
人才流失/人才外流　internal brain drain
人才培养/人才教育　talent education
人才识别/人才辨別　human talent distinguishing
人才市场/人才市場　personnel market
人才选拔/人才選拔　qualified personnel selecting
人才最佳创造年龄/人才最佳創造年齡期　optimum creative age periods of human talents
人道主义/人道主義　humanism
人道主义干涉/人道干涉　humanitarian intervention
人的潜能/人力潛能　human potential ability
人的现代化/人的現代化　individual modernization
人格/人格　personality
人格责任论/人格責任論　theory of personality liability
人格尊严/人格尊嚴　personal dignity
人工标引/人工標引　manual indexing
人工标引语言/人工標引語言　artificial indexing language
人工标准/人工標準　labor standard
人工分类/人爲分類　artificial classification
人工更新/人工更新　artificial regeneration
人工工日单价/人工工日單價　unit price of workday
人工股票市场/人工股市　artificial stock market
人工环境/人爲環境　artificial environment
人工金融市场/人工金融市場　artificial financial market
人工空闲能力/人工空閒能力　man idle capability
人工免疫系统预测模型/人體免疫系統預測模型　artificial immune system based forecasting model
人工情报/人工情報　human intelligence
人工神经网络/類神經網路分析　artificial neural networks
人工语言/人造語言　artificial language
人工制表/人工製表　manual tabulation
人工智能/人工智慧　artificial intelligence, AI
人机对话系统/人機對話系統　human-computer dialog system

人机交互/人機互動　human-computer interaction
人机交互技术/人機交互技術　human-computer interaction technique
人机界面/人機界面,人機介面　human-computer interface, human-machine interface
人机系统/人機系統　man-machine system
人-机作业分析/人-機作業分析　man-machine operation analysis
人-机作业图/人-機[作業]圖　man-machine chart
人际法律冲突/人際法律衝突　interpersonal conflict of laws
人际服务/人際關係服務　interpersonal service
人际沟通/人際溝通,人際傳播　interpersonal communication
人际关系/人際關係　interpersonal relationship
人际关系角色/人際角色　interpersonal role
人际关系学派/人際關係學派　human relationship school
人际关系学说/人際關係理論　human relations theory
人际技能/人際技巧　interpersonal skill
人际竞争情报/人際競爭情報　interpersonal competitive intelligence
人际距离/人際距離　interpersonal distance
人际私法/人際私法　private interpesonal law
人际吸引/人際吸引　interpersonal attraction
人际信任/人際信賴　interpersonal trust
人际需求/人際需求　interpersonal need
人际影响/人際影響　interpersonal influence
人均收入/平均每人所得　income per capita
人口/人口　population
人口爆炸/人口爆炸　population explosion
人口爆炸论/人口爆炸論　theory on population explosion
人口变动/人口變動　population change, population movement
人口承载力/人口負載能力　population carrying capacity
人口城市化/人口都市化　population urbanization
人口登记/人口登記　population register
人口分布/人口分布　population distribution
人口构成/人口組成　composition of population
人口估计/人口推估　population estimation
人口惯性/人口慣力　population momentum
人口规划/人口預測　population projection
人口红利/人口紅利　population dividend
人口环境/人口環境　demographic environment
人口机械变动/人口機械變動　mechanical change of population
人口金字塔/人口金字塔　population pyramid
人口经济年龄金字塔/人口經濟年齡金字塔　age pyramid of demographic-economy
人口老龄化/人口老齡化　aging population
人口老龄化指数/人口老齡化指數　aging population index
人口零增长/人口零成長,零人口成長　zero population growth
人口流动/人口流動　population flow
人口论/人口論　essay on the principle of population
人口密度/人口密度　density of population, population density
人口逆淘汰/人口反淘汰　population adverse selection
人口年轻化/人口年輕化　rejuvenation of population
人口普查/人口普查　demographic census, population census, census
人口普查档案/人口普查檔案　census archive
人口迁移/人口遷移　population migration
人口迁移的推力拉力因素/人口遷移的拉力與推力因素　pull and push factors of migration
人口容量/人口容量　population capacity
人口特征变量/人口特徵變量　population characteristic variable
人口统计/人口統計　demographic statistics
人口统计表/人口統計表　census return, census schedule
人口统计[学]/人口[統計]學,人口統計　demography, demographic statistics
人口推力/人口推力　population push
人口细分/人口統計區隔化　demographic segmentation
人口压力/人口壓力　population pressure, pressure of population
人口原理/人口論　essay on the principle of population
人口再生产/人口再生產　human reproduction, population reproduction
人口再生产类型/人口再生產類型　pattern of population reproduction
人口增长/人口增長,人口成長　population growth, population increase
人口增长率/人口成長率　population growth rate
人口政策/人口政策　population policy
人口质量/人口品質　quality of population
人口转变/人口轉型　demographic transition
人口自然变动/人口自然變動　natural change of

人类发展指数/人力發展指數　population
人类发展指数/人力發展指數　human development index
人类共同遗产/人類共同遺產　common heritage of mankind
人类关系区域档案/人類關係區域檔案　human relations area files
人类基因组计划/人類基因體計劃　human genome project
人类例外范式/人類例外範式　human exceptionalism paradigm
人类史/人類史　human history
人类行为学派/人類行爲學派　human behavior school
人类行为与社会环境/人類行爲與社會環境　human behavior and social environment
人类需要/人類需求　human need
人类学/人類學　anthropology
人类学研究/人誌學研究　ethnographic research
人类中心说/人類中心主義　anthropocentrism
人类-自然二元论/人類-自然二元論　human-nature dualism
人力/人力　manpower
人力网络/人力網路　human network
人力知识/人力知識　know-who
人力资本/人力資本　human capital
人力资本贸易理论/人力資本貿易說　human capital theory of trade
人力资本投资/人力資本投資　human capital investments, investment in human capital
人力资源/人力資源　human resource
人力资源本地化/人力資源在地化　human resource localization
人力资源成本/人力資源成本　human resource cost
人力资源法律体系/人力資源法律系統　human resources legal system
人力资源供给/人力資源供給　human resource supply
人力资源管理/人力資源管理　human resource management
人力资源管理外包/人力資源管理外包,人力資源管理委外　human resource management outsourcing
人力资源管理现代化/人力資源管理現代化　modernization of the human resource management
人力资源管理研究/人力資源管理研究　human resource management study
人力资源规划/人力資源規劃　program of the human resource, human resource planning
人力资源结构/人力資源結構　structure of the human resource, human resource structure
人力资源开发/人力資源發展　development of human resource, human resource development
人力资源会计/人力資源會計　human resource accounting
人力资源类型/人力資源型態　types of the human resources
人力资源内部环境/人力資源内部環境　internal environment of human resource
人力资源盘点法/人力資源盤存法　human resource inventory method
人力资源配置/人力資源配置　allocation of the human resources
人力资源实践/人力資源實踐　human resource practice
人力资源外部环境/人力資源外部環境　human resource external environment
人力资源信息系统/人力資源資訊系統　information system of human resource, human resource information system
人力资源预测/人力資源預測　human resource forecasting
人力资源战略/人力資源策略　strategy of the human resource, human resource strategy
人力资源政策/人力資源政策　policy of the human resources
人力资源职能/人力資源職能　human resource function
人力资源专员/人力資源專員　human resource specialist
人民/人民　the people
人民币/人民幣　renminbi
人民团体/人民團體　mass organization
人民主权/人民主權　people's sovereignty, the people's sovereignty
人名标目/人名標目　personal name heading
人名录/人名録　who's who
人名注释/人名注釋　name annotation
人情/人情　favor, social communication
人权/人權　human rights
人权与人权理论/人權與人權理論　human rights and human rights theory
人身保护法/人身保護法　Habeas Corpus Act
人身保险/人身保險,人壽保險　personal insurance, life insurance
人身检查/人身檢查　personal scrutiny

人身权/人身權利　personal right
人身特别保护权/人身特別保護權　personal right of special protection for NPC member
人身自由/人身自由　personal freedom
人事测评/人事評量　personnel assessment
人事测验/人事測驗　personnel test
人事档案/人事檔案,人事資料　personnel file, personnel archive
人事档案管理/人事檔案管理　management of personnel files
人事档案室/人事檔案室　personnel record office
人事调动/人事調轉　personnel transfer
人事管理/人事管理　personnel administration, personnel management
人事接替图/人事接替圖　personnel replacement chart
人事制度改革/人事制度改革　reform of personnel system
人事专员制度/人事專員制度　personnel commissioner system
人寿保险/人壽保險,人身保險　personal insurance, life insurance
人寿保险公司/人壽保險公司　life insurance company
人数不确定的代表人诉讼/人數不確定的代表人訴訟　representative litigation of an uncertain number of participants
人数确定的代表人诉讼/人數確定的代表人訴訟　representative litigation of certain number of participants
人头税/人頭稅　head tax, poll tax
人为贸易壁垒/人爲的貿易障礙　artificial trade barrier
人为误差/人爲誤差　human error
人文教育/人文主義教育　liberal arts education
人文区位学/人文生態學,人類生態學　human ecology
人文主义/人文主義　humanism
人我关系/人己關係　self-other relation
人物简介/人物簡介　profile
人物评述注释/人物評述注釋　comment on historic figures
人物全宗/人物全宗　personage fonds
人物全宗指南/人物全宗指南　person fonds guide
人物传记/傳記　biography
人性假设/人性假設　human nature assumption
人役权/人役權　personal servitude
人因分析/人因分析　human factor analysis

人员差异化/人員差異化　people differentiation
人员的稳定/人員的稳定　stability of tenure of personnel
人员分析/人員分析　person analysis
人员沟通管道/人員溝通管道　personal communication channel
人员零基预测/人員零基預測　zero-based forecast
人员流分析/人員流分析　personnel flow analysis
人员配备要求/人員安置條件　staffing requirements
人员推销/人員銷售　personal selling
人员选拔/人員甄選　personnel selection
人造变量/人爲變數　artificial variable
人造林/人造林　artificial forest
人造系统/人造系統,人工系統　man-made system
人-职位匹配/人-職位適配,個人-工作適配　person-job fit
人-职位-组织匹配/個人-工作-組織適配　person-job-organization fit
人治/人治　rule by man
人种/種族　race
人-组织匹配/人-組織適配,個人-組織適配　person-organization fit
仁政/仁政　benevolent governance
认购股份/認購股份　subscription of share
认购价格/認購價格　subscription price
认股/認股　subscription for shares
认股价格/認購價格　subscription price
认股权/認股權　subscription right
认股权证/認股[權]證　warrant
认缴份额/認購額度　subscription quota
认缴股金/認繳股金　subscription to capital stock
认识论/認識論,知識論　epistemology
认识时滞/認知時差　recognition lag
认售权证/認售權證　put warrant
认同/認同　identity, identification
认同危机/認同危機　identity crisis
认证/認證　authenticate, attestation, authentication
CCC认证/CCC認證　CCC authentication
认证撤销/認證撤銷　certification revocation
认证机构/認證機構　certification authority, certificate authority, CA
认证机构认可/認證機構認可　certification authority accreditation
认证技术/認證技術　authentication technology
认证证书/合格證書　mark of conformity
认证制度/認證制度　certification system
认证注销/認證注銷　certification cancellation
认知/認知　cognition

认知不协调/認知失調,認知失諧 cognitive dissonance
认知的/認知的 cognitive
认知负荷/認知負荷 cognitive load
认知过程模型/認知過程模型 cognitive process model
认知技能/認知技術 cognitive skill
认知理论/認知理論 cognitive theory
认知能力/認知能力 cognitive ability
认知能力测验/認知能力測驗 cognitive ability test
认知偏差/認知偏誤 cognitive bias
认知偏向/認知偏見 cognitive bias
认知评价理论/認知評價理論 cognitive evaluation theory
认知-情感个性系统/認知-情感個性系統,認知-情感性格系統 cognitive-affective personality system
认知人类学/認知人類學 cognitive anthropology
认知失调/認知失調,認知失諧 cognitive dissonance
认知失调论/認知失諧理論 theory of cognitive dissonance
认知图/認知圖 cognitive map
认知习惯/認知習慣 cognitive custom
认知-兴趣-愿望-行动模型/知曉-興趣-欲望-行動模式 awareness-interest-desire-action model, AIDA model
认知学派/認知學派 cognitive school, school of cognitive
认知一致/認知一致 cognitive conformity
认知一致性/認知一致性 cognitive consistency
任期制/任期制 termed system
任人唯亲作风/族閥主義 nepotism
任务本体/任務本體 task ontology
任务冲突/任務衝突 task conflict
任务分析/任務分析 task analysis
任务环境/任務環境 task environment
任务绩效/任務績效 task performance
任务加奖金制/任務獎金制度 task and bonus system
任务可用性/任務可用度 mission availability
任务时间/任務時間 mission time
任务中心模式/任務中心模式 task-centered model
任选港交易/任意卸貨港交貨 optional delivery
任选股权/任選股權 share option
任选目的港/選擇目的港 optional destination
任选要求/選擇性要求 optional requirement
任意背书/任意背書,授權背書 facultative endorsement
任意词检索/任意詞檢索 any word search, any word retrieval
任意法/任意法 jus dispositivum
任意分布/任意分配 arbitrary distribution
任意港货物/選擇卸貨港貨物 optional cargo
任意一致检索/任意一致檢索 any part match retrieval
日报/日報 daily, daily newspaper
日本东京股票交易所/日本東京股票交易所 Japan Tokyo Stock Exchange
日常交易支付/日常交易支付 payment for current transaction
日常生活史/日常生活史 history of everyday life
日程表/時程表 schedule
日记账/日記賬 journal, daybook
日经指数/日經[股價]指数 Nikkei index
日历/日曆 calendar
日历差价期权/跨期價差期權 calendar spread option
日历效应/日曆效果 calendar effect
日美元汇率/日美元匯率 yen-dollar rate
日内瓦回合/日内瓦回合 Geneva Round
日元/日元,日幣 Japanese yen
日元汇兑/日元匯兌 yen exchange
日元汇率/日元匯率 yen exchange rate
日元汇票/日元匯票,日元債券 yen bill, yen bond
日元辛迪加贷款/日元聯合貸款 yen syndicated loan
日元信贷/日元信貸 yen credit
日元信用证/日元信用狀 yen letter of credit
容差/容差 tolerance
容差设计/容差設計 tolerance design
容具符号/容具符號 containing symbol
容量/容量 capacity
容量限制/容量限制 capacity constraint
容忍不确定性/容忍不確定性 tolerance for ambiguity
容忍区间/容許區間 tolerance interval
容忍失败/容忍失敗 tolerance for failure
容忍限/容許界限 tolerance limit
容许策略/可容策略 admissible strategy
容许估计[量]/可容估計[量] admissible estimator
容许估计量的唯一性/可容估計量的唯一性 uniqueness of admissible estimator
容许假设/可容假設 admissible hypothesis
容许检验/可容檢定 admissible test
容许决策规则/可容決策規則 admissible decision rule
容许决策函数/可容決策函數 admissible decision function

容许[区]域/可容區域　admissible region
容许缺陷/可允許缺點　allowable defect
容许设计/可容設計　admissible design
容许数/可容數　admissible number
容许性/可容性　admissibility
容许因子/容許因子　tolerance factor
溶变/溶變　dissolve off
熔断机制/熔斷機制　circuit breaker
融合/融合　convergence
融合发展/融合發展　fusion development
融媒体/融媒體　convergence media
融通背书/融通背書　accommodation endorsement
融通票据/融通票據　accommodation note, accommodation bill, accommodation bill
融通提单/融通提單　accommodation bill of lading
融通支票/融通支票　accommodation cheque
融资/融資　financing
融资安排/融資安排　financing arrangement
融资贷款人/融資貸款人　financing lender
融资方式/融資方式　mode of financing, financing method
融资公司/融資公司　funding corporation
融资交易/融資交易　financing transaction
融资融券/融資證券　securities financing
融资性租赁/融資性租賃　financing lease
融资主办人/融資主辦人　financing sponsor
融资主体/融資主體　financing subject
融资租赁/融資租賃　finance lease, financial lease, financial leasing
冗余/冗餘, 多餘　redundancy
冗余标引/冗餘標引　redundant indexing
冗余系统/複聯系統　redundant system
冗余证券/冗餘證券　redundant securities
冗员分析/冗員分析　excessive employee analysis
柔版激光制版/柔版雷射製版　laser flexographic forme-making
柔版印刷工艺/柔版印刷工藝　flexographic printing technology
柔性/彈性　flexibility
柔性按揭/彈性不動產擔保　flexible mortgage
柔性版/彈性凸版　flexography
柔性版印刷/柔版印刷　flexographic printing
柔性版印刷机/柔性版印刷機　flexographic press
柔性宪法/柔性憲法　flexible constitution
柔性制造系统/靈活加工系統, 可調加工系統　flexible manufacture system
柔印设备/柔印設備　flexographic printing equipment
肉刑存废之争/肉刑存廢之爭　Chinese history of dispute over the retention or abolition of corporal punishment
如有变化无须另补通知的发盘/以修正不另行通知爲條件的報價　offer subject to change without notice
儒家/儒學　Confucianism
儒家德治思想/儒家德治思想　De government thought of Confucianism
蠕动钉住汇率/蠕動釘住匯率　crawling peg
乳剂/乳劑　emulsion
入藏/登錄　accessioning
入藏登记/造冊，登錄記錄　register, accession register, accession record
入藏登记表/登錄簿　accession register
入藏目录/造冊清單　accession list
入藏顺序/登錄順序　accession order
入藏文献/入藏文獻　accessioned document
入藏物/入藏物　accession of material
入藏新书/登錄新書　accession
入超/入超　import surplus, import excess, excess of import over export
入度/内度　in-degree
入港税/入港稅，港務費　harbor due
入伙/入夥　join the partnership enterprise
入境许可/入境許可　entry permit
入口词表/入口詞表　lead-in vocabulary
入库/進倉　warehouse entry
入库保税品/入庫保稅品　warehouse bond
入链/入鏈　inlink
入链数/入鏈數　number of inlinks
入职培训/職前訓練　orientation training
入住/居住　occupancy
软币区/弱勢貨幣地區　soft currency area
软磁盘/軟碟　floppy disk
软打样/軟式打樣　soft proofing
软贷款/弱勢貨幣貸款，弱勢通貨貸款　soft loan
软调/平調，大版底片　flat
软广告/軟廣告　soft advertising
软技术/軟技術，不成熟技術　soft technology
软件/軟體　software
软件可靠性/軟體可靠度　software reliability
软件能力成熟度模型/軟體能力成熟度模型　capability maturity model for software
软科学/軟科學　soft science
软实力/軟實力　soft power
软通货/弱勢通貨　soft currency, soft money
软文/軟文　text ads, advertorial
软新闻/軟性新聞　soft news

软信息/軟訊息,不可驗證訊息　soft information
软预算约束/軟性預算約束　soft budget constraint
软债权结构/軟債權結構　soft bullet structure
软质封面/軟質封面　soft bound, soft cover
软着陆/軟著陸　soft landing
瑞典斯德哥尔摩商会仲裁院/瑞典斯德哥爾摩商會仲裁院　the Arbitration Institute of the Stockholm Chamber of Commerce
瑞典学派/瑞典學派　Swedish school
瑞利分布/Rayleigh 分配,Rayleigh 分布　Rayleigh distribution
瑞利检验/Rayleigh 檢定　Rayleigh test
瑞士联合银行/瑞士聯合銀行　United Bank of Switzerland
瑞士民法典/瑞士民法典　Swiss Civil Code
瑞士苏黎士商会仲裁院/瑞士蘇黎士商會仲裁院　Court of Arbitration of The Zurich Chamber of Commerce
瑞文标准推理测验/瑞文氏標準圖形推理測驗　Raven standard progressive matrices
润版/潤版　dampening
润湿过度著墨不良/油墨著墨不良　blinding
润湿液/水槽溶液　fountain solution
润湿装置/潤濕裝置　damping unit

弱大数定律/弱大數法則　weak law of large numbers
弱关系/弱關係　weak tie
弱广义逆矩阵/弱廣義逆矩陣　weak generalized inverse matrix
弱假设/弱勢假設　weak assumption
弱可持续发展/弱永續發展　weak sustainable development
弱连接强度/弱連帶優勢　strength of weak tie
弱偏好/弱偏好　weak preference
弱偏好集/弱偏好點集合　weakly preferred set
弱平稳过程/弱平穩過程　weakly stationary process
弱平稳性/弱平穩性,弱恆定性　weak stationarity
弱势货币/弱勢貨幣　weak currency
弱势群体/弱勢團體　disadvantaged group
弱势群体利益最大化原则/弱勢群體利益最大化原則　maximum principle in favor of disadvantaged groups
弱收敛/弱收斂　weak convergence
弱外生性/弱外生性　weak exogenous
弱信号/弱信號　weak signal
弱序/弱順序　weak-ordering relation
弱一致性/弱一致性　weak consistency
弱有效/弱式效率性　weak-form efficiency

S

撒克逊法/撒克遜法 Lex Saxonum
撒克逊法律汇编/撒克遜法律匯編 Archaionomia
撒切尔主义/柴契爾主義 Thatcherism
萨柏工作价值观问卷/薩柏工作價值觀量表 Super's work values inventory
萨尔特曼隐喻诱引技术/薩爾特曼隱喻抽取技術 Zaltman metaphor elicitation technique
萨利克法典/薩利克法典 Lex Salica
萨满教/薩滿教 Shamanism
萨氏职业生涯发展阶段理论/Super 職涯發展階段理論 Super's stage of career development theory
萨维尼/薩維尼 Savigny Friedrich Karlvon
塞勒-凯弗维尔法案/希勒-基佛渥法案 Celler-Kefauver act
塞瓦尔-赖特效应/Sewall-Wright 效應 Sewall-Wright effect
赛博空间/網路空間，網際空間 cyberspace
三包责任/三包責任 guarantees responsibility of repair, replacement and return
三倍赔偿/三倍損害賠償 treble damages
三边贸易/三邊貿易，三角貿易 trilateral trade, triangular trade
三变量/三元 trivariate
三不出/三不出 a Chinese ancient divorce rules about a wife's three objections against being cast off and sent to her parent
三步成长模式/三步成長模式 3-P growth model
三朝本/三朝本 Song wood-block edition survived and was emended during the Yuan and Ming Dynasties
三重比较/三重比較 triple comparisons
三重表/三重表 triple table
三重伽马函数/三重伽瑪函數 trigamma function
三重格[子]/三重格子 triple lattice
三重格[子]设计/三重格子設計 triple lattice design
三重税则/三重稅則 treble tariff
三次档案文献/三次檔案文獻 teritary archival documentations
三次设计/三次設計 triplication design
三次文献/三次文獻 tertiary document
三次样条函数/三次弧狀函數 cubic spline function

三从四德/三從四德 three obediences and four virtues for women
三等商业票据/三等商業本票 third class commercial paper
三点分析/三點試驗 three point assay
三定方案/三定方案 Sanding scheme
三法司/三法司 Sanfa Si, three interdependent judicial departments
三方关系/三角關係 triad
三分法/三分法 trichotomy
三纲五常/三綱五常 Sangang Wuchang, the three cardinal guides and five constant virtues
三轨制/三軌制 three-card system
三级价格歧视/三級價格歧視 third-degree price discrimination
三级数定理/三級數定理 three series theorem
三检制/三級檢查制度 three inspection system
三角测量/三角測量 triangulation
三角分布/三角分布，三角分配 triangular distribution
三角汇兑/三角匯兑 three cornered exchange, triangular exchange
三角检验/三角檢定 triangle test
三角贸易/三角貿易，三邊貿易 trilateral trade, triangular trade
三角套汇/三角套匯 three point arbitrage, triangular arbitrage
三角套利/三角套利 triangular arbitrage
三角[形]多连接区组设计/三角多重環區集設計 triangular multiply linked block design
三角[形]结合方案/三角相聯方案 triangular association scheme
三角[形]连接区组/三角聯環區集 triangular linked block
三角[形]设计/三角設計 triangular design
三角易货贸易/三角以物易物貿易 triangular barter trade
三阶段最小二乘法/三階段最小平方法 three stage least squares, 3SLS
三阶交互效应/三重交互作用 triple interaction
三阶整群抽样/三段叢聚抽樣 three-stage cluster

sampling

三阶最小二乘[法]／三階段最小平方法，三段最小平方[法]　three stage least squares, three stage least squares method

三阶最小二乘估计量／三段最小平方法估計式　three-stage least squares estimator

三库／三庫　Sanku

三面切／三面切　three-knife trimming

三面切书机／三面切書機　three-knife trimmer

三民主义／三民主義　Three Principles of the People

三农问题／三農問題　agriculture, countryside and farmer issues

三圈理论／三環理論　theory of three circles

三赦／三赦　San She, sanshe system

三审制／三審制　triditing system

三时估计法／三時間估計　three-time estimate

三世说／三世說　the theory of three phases of historical development

三同时制度／三同時制度　three simultaneity system

三网融合／三網融合　triple networks convergence, triple-play

三维电影／三維顯示　three-dimensional movie

三维动画／三維動畫　three-dimensional animation

三维格[子]方／三維格子　three-dimensional lattice

三维投影图／三維投影圖　three-dimensional projection chart

三维虚拟演播室／三維虛擬演播室　three-dimensional virtual studio

三维音效／三維音效　3d sound effect

三无人员／三無人員　people without identification documents

三线典藏制／三線典藏制　triple book reservation system

三线书库／三線書庫　third-tier stack

三线图／三重線性圖　trilinear chart

三向配置／三向配置，三因子配置　three-way layout

三项式分布／三項分布，三項分配　trinomial distribution

三叶草组织／三葉草組織　shamrock organization, clover organization

三宥／三宥　Sanyou, sanyou system

三元回归／三元回歸　trivariate regression

三章之法／三章之法　Sanzhang Zhi Fa, sanzhang method

三种方式分组／三向分類　three-way classification

三资企业／三資企業　three-capital enterprise, foreign direct invested enterprise

三I组织／三I組織　the triple I organization

散点图／散布圖　scatter diagram, scatter plot

散工制／散作制度　putting-out system

散料抽样／散料抽樣　bulk sampling

散页印刷品／散頁印刷品　leaflet

散装出口／組合式輸出　knock-down export

散装[化]／散裝[化]　in bulk

散播分布／散播分布　contagious distribution

散播过程／散播過程　contagious process

散播极限定理／散播極限定理　contagious limit theorem

散布／散布　scatter

散失档案／散失檔案　removed archives

桑代克图／Thorndike 圖　Thorndike chart

桑托斯依附理论／桑托斯的依附理論　Santos dependence theory

丧亲／傷慟　bereavement

丧失抵押品赎回权／抵押品贖取權的喪失　foreclosure

扫描／掃描　scanning

扫描分辨力／掃描分辨力　scanning resolution

扫描仪／掃描器　scanner

色标／色標　color mark

色补偿／色彩改正　color calibration

色彩管理／色彩管理　color management

色彩校正／色彩校正　color correction

色彩空间／色彩空間　color space

色彩深度／色彩濃度　color depth

色彩特性／色彩特性　color profile

ICC色彩特性文件／ICC色彩特文檔　ICC profile, ICC specific document

色导表／校正標　calibration target

色的并列／并列色　juxtaposition of color

色调／色調　color tone

色空间／色空間　color space

CIE-LAB色空间／CIE-LAB色空間　CIE LAB color space

CIE-LUV色空间／CIE-LUV色空間　CIE LUV color space

色空间编码／色空間編碼　color space encoding

色令／色令　color ream

色诺芬论劳动分工／色諾芬論勞動分工　Xenophon's view on labor division

色情／色情，情色　eroticism

色情电话／色情電話　dial-a-porn

色情片／色情片　porno film

色情频道／鎖碼頻道　encoded channel

色情书刊／色情出版品　pornography

色情渲染论／色情渲染論　theory of playing up

pornography
色温/色温 color temperature
色相/色相 hue
色域/色域 color gamut
色域映射/色域映射 gamut mapping
瑟斯顿测度/瑟斯顿測度 Thurstone scaling
森林法/森林法 forest law
森林砍伐/森林砍伐 deforestation
森林资源/森林資源 forest resources
僧伽/僧伽 sangha
僧院制度/僧院制度 monasticism
沙动画/沙動畫 sand animation
沙赫双样本检验/Schach 雙樣本檢定 Schach's two-sample test
沙普利-福克曼定理/夏普力-福克曼定理 Shapley-Folkman theorem
沙因组织变革论/沙恩的組織變革論 Schein's organization change theory
砂目/砂目 grain
莎氏准则/Shah 準則 Shah's criterion
筛选过程/篩選過程 screening process
筛选检验/篩選檢驗 screening inspection
筛选设计/篩選設計 screening design
筛选实验/篩選實驗 screening experiment
筛选问题/過濾問題 filter question
删失/設限 censor, censoring
删失抽样/設限抽樣 censored sampling
删失观测值/設限觀察值 censored observation
删失检验/設限檢定 censored test
删失数据/受限資料 censored data
删失样本/設限樣本 censored sample
扇出/扇出 fan-out
扇入/扇入 fan-in
煽情新闻/煽色腥新聞 sensational journalism
闪告/閃告 flash-screen advertisement
闪光曝光/閃光曝光 flash exposure
扇区/扇區 sector
扇形假说/扇形假說 sector hypothesis
扇形理论/扇形理論 sector theory
扇形图/扇形圖 sector diagram, sector chart
善本/善本書 rare book, book rarity
善本书馆藏/善本書館藏 rare book collection
善本书库/善本書庫 rare book stack
善本书图书馆/善本書圖書館 rare book library
善意/善意 good faith
善意购买人/善意收買人 bona fide purchaser
善意歧视/良性歧視 benign discrimination
善意取得/善意取得 Innocent Purchase

善意原则/誠信原則 good faith principle
善意占有/善意占有 bona fide possession
善治/善治 good governance
缮印/繕印 transcription
膳宿/膳宿 accommodation
赡徇制/贍徇制,恩寵制 patronage system
赡养/贍養 support for the elderly
赡养费/贍養費 alimony
赡养协议/贍養協議 elderly support agreement
赡养制度/贍養制度 elderly support system
伤残保险/傷殘保險,失能保險 disability insurance
伤残抚恤/傷殘撫恤 disability pension
伤害分析/損害分析 damage analysis
商标/商標 trademark, identification mark, merchandise mark
商标保护制度/商標保護制度 trademark protection system
商标变更/商標變更 change of registered matter
商标标识/商標標識 mark of registered trademark
商标撤销/商標撤銷 revocation of registered trademarks
商标淡化/商標淡化 trademark dilution
商标档案/商標檔案 trade mark archive
商标的正当使用/商標的正當使用 fair use of trademark
商标法/商標法 trademark law, merchandise mark
商标管理/商標管理 trademark management
商标国际注册/商標國際註冊 international registration of trade marks
商标国际注册马德里协定/商標國際註冊馬德里協定 Madrid Agreement concerning the International Registration of Marks
商标合法性/商標合法性 legitimacy of trademark
商标评审委员会/商標評審委員會 trademark review and adjudication board
商标侵权/商標侵權 trademark infringement
商标权/商標權 trademark right, ownership of trademark, right of trademark
商标权限制/商標權限制 limitations on trademark right
商标使用费/商標使用費 brand royalty
商标使用要求/商標使用要求 requirements for the use of trademarks
商标使用在先原则/商標使用在先原則 principle of prior trademark use
商标条款/商標條款 brand clause, trademark clause
商标无效/商標無效 invalid of the trademark
商标许可/商標許可 licensing of trademark

商标续展/商標續展　renewal of registration
商标异议/商標異議　trademark apposition
商标争议/商標争議　trademark dispute
商标主管机关/商標主管機關　administrative department of trademark affairs
商标注册/商標註冊　trademark registration
商标注册商品和服务分类尼斯协定/商標註冊商品和服務分類尼斯協定　The Nice Agreement concerning the International Classification of Goods and Services for the Purposes of the Registration of Marks
商标注册在先原则/商標註冊在先原則　principle of prior trademark registration
商标专用权/商標專用權　exclusive right to use trademark
商标转让/商標轉讓　transfer of trademark
商定保险值/約定保險額　agreed insured value
商定程序/協議程式　agreed upon procedure
商法/商[業]法　commercial law, mercantile law, law merchant
商法人/商法人　commercial legal person
商港/商港，通商口岸　commercial port
商号/商號　trade name
商回归/商回歸　quotient regression
商会/商會　chamber of commerce
商流/商流　commodity circulation
商贸公司/商業公司，貿易公司　commercial company
商品/商品　commodity, goods
商品拜物教/商品拜物教　commodity fetishism
商品绑售/商品綁售　commodity bundling
商品包装装潢/商品包裝裝潢　packages and decorations of commodity
商品保险/商品保險　commodity insurance
商品本位/商品本位　commodity standard
商品标准分类/商品標準分類　standard classification of commodities
商品出口/商品出口　merchandise export
商品[抵押]贷款/商品[抵押]貸款　loan on goods, loan secured by commodity, commodity loan
商品二因素/商品二因素　two characteristics of a commodity
商品广告/產品廣告　product advertising
商品化/商品化　commodification
商品化形象权/商品化形象權　right of merchandization
商品黄金/商品黄金　commodity gold
商品货币/商品貨幣　merchandise money, commodity currency, commodity money
商品货币理论/商品貨幣理論　commodity theory of money
商品及劳务输出/商品及勞務輸出　export of goods and service
商品价格/商品價格　price of merchandise, commodity price
商品价格指数/商品價格指數　commodity price index
商品检验/商品檢驗　commodity inspection
商品检验合格证书/商品檢驗合格證書　certificate of inspection
商品检验证/商品檢驗證書　inspection and testing certificate
商品交换/商品交換　exchange of commodity
商品交易/商品交易　commodity transaction
商品交易差额/商品交易差額　merchandise balance
商品交易会/商品交易會　commodity fair
商品交易期货合同/商品期货交易合約　commodity exchange futures contract
商品交易所/商品交易所　board of trade, commodity exchange
商品进口/商品進口　merchandise import
商品经纪人/商品經紀人　commodity broker
商品经济/商品經濟　commodity economy
商品经营资本/商品交易資本　commodity dealing capital
商品劳务法/商品勞務法　commodity-service method
商品利率/商品利率　commodity rate of interest
商品流通/商品流通　commodity circulation, circulation of commodity
商品流通分析/商品流通分析　commodity-flow analysis
商品流通渠道/商品流通通路　commodity circulation channel
商品贸易/商品貿易　merchandise trade
商品贸易顺差/商品貿易順差　visible trade surplus
商品贸易条件/商品貿易條件，商品交易條件　commodity terms of trade
商品名称/商品名稱　name of commodity
商品票据/商品票據　commodity paper
商品期货/商品期貨　commodity futures
商品期货交易/商品期貨交易　commodity futures trading
商品期货交易所/商品期貨交易所　commodity futures exchange
商品期货市场/商品期貨市場　commodity futures market

商品期票/商品期票　merchandise note
商品商标/商品商標　commodity trademark
商品市场/商品市場　commodity markets
商品税/商品租税　commodity taxation
商品套利/商品套利　commodity arbitrage
商品完好率/商品完好率　rate of the goods in good condition
商品销售利润/商品銷售利潤　sale profit of commodity
商品销售账/商品銷售賬　merchandise book
商品协议/商品協議　commodity agreement
商品询价/對商品詢價　inquiry for merchandise
商品账户/商品賬戶　merchandise account
商品证券/商品證券　commodity securities
商品住房/商品住房　commercial housing
商品准备货币/商品準備貨幣　commodity reserve currency
商品自由流通原则/商品自由流通原則　principle of free movement of goods
商洽用语/商洽用語　discussion term
商情晴雨表/商情晴雨表,商情行情表　business barometer
商人/商人　merchant
商人法/商人法　law of merchant
商人信用证/商人信用狀　merchant's letter of credit
商人银行/商人銀行　merchant bank
商事登记/商業登記　commercial registration
商事行为/商事行爲　commercial act
商事仲裁/商務仲裁　commercial arbitration
商事主体/商事主體　commercial entity
商书/商書　document of Shang Dynasty
商务广告/企業對企業廣告　business-to-business advertising
商务社交网络/商務社交網路　business social networking service, BSNS
商务条约/商務條約　commercial treaty
商务智慧技术/商業智慧技術　business intelligence technique
商务智能/商業智慧　business intelligence
商鞅变法/商鞅變法　Shangyang Reform
商业/商業　merchandising business, commerce
商业按揭支持证券/商業不動產擔保證券　commercial mortgage-backed securities, CMBS
商业保险/商業保險　commercial insurance
商业本票/商業本票　commercial paper
商业承兑信用证/商業承兑信用狀　trade acceptance credit
商业贷款/商業貸款　business loan, commercial loan

商业单据/商業單據　commercial document
商业道德/商業道德　business ethics
商业电影/商業電影　commercial film, CF
商业发票/商業發票　commercial invoice
商业方法专利/商業方法專利　business method patent
商业诽谤/商業誹謗　trade libel
商业费用/商業費用　commercial cost
商业分析/商情分析　business analysis
商业风险/商業風險　commercial risk
商业惯例/商業慣例,商業習慣　usage of trade, commercial custom
商业汇兑/商業匯兑　commercial exchange
商业汇票/商業匯票　commercial bill of exchange
商业贿赂/商業賄賂　commercial bribery
商业伙伴情报/商業夥伴情報　partner intelligence
商业货币/商業貨幣　commercial money
商业价值/商業價值　commercial value
商业交易/商業交易　business transaction
商业金融工具/商業金融工具　commercial instrument
商业金融公司/商業金融公司　commercial finance company
商业经纪人/商業經紀人　merchandise broker
商业开发贷款/企業拓展貸款　business development loan
商业利润/商業利潤　commercial gain, commercial profit
商业联合体/商業聯合體　merchandising conglomerates
商业垄断/商業獨占　commercial monopoly
商业伦理/企業倫理　business ethics
商业秘密/商業秘密,營業秘密,業務秘密　trade secret, business secret
商业秘密的保护/商業秘密的保護　protection of trade secret
商业秘密的保护范围/商業秘密的保護範圍　scope of business secret protection
商业秘密的保密性/商業秘密的保密性　confidentiality of business secret
商业秘密的实用性/商業秘密的實用性　practical applicability of business secret
商业秘密构成要件/商業秘密構成要件　essential elements of business secret
商业免税区/商業免税區　commercial free zone
商业名称/商業名稱　commercial name
商业模式/商業模式,經營模式　business model
商业模式创新/商業模式創新　business model

innovation
商业判断原则/商業判斷法則　business judgment rule
商业票据/商業票據　mercantile paper, commercial draft, commercial paper
商业票据经纪行/商業票據經紀商　commercial paper house
商业票据利率/商業票據利率　commercial paper rate
商业票据市场/商業票據市場　commercial paper market
商业票据账户/商業票據賬戶　commercial bill account
商业评级网站/商業評級網站　commercial rating website
商业普查/商業普查　commercial census
商业欺骗分析/商業欺詐分析　commercial fraud analysis
商业情报/商業情報　business intelligence
商业融资/商業融資　commercial financing
商业数据库/商用資料庫　commercial database
商业所得税/營利事業所得稅　business income tax
商业统计/商業統計,商情統計　commercial statistics, business statistics
商业图表/商業圖表　business graphic
商业外观/商業外觀　trade dress
商业习惯法/商業習慣法　law merchant
商业信贷/商業信貸,商業信用　mercantile credit, merchandise credit, commercial credit
商业信贷保险/商業信用保險　commercial credit insurance
商业信贷公司/商業信用公司,銷售金融公司　commercial credit company
商业信息/工商資訊,商業資訊　business information
商业信用/交易信用,貿易信用　commercial credit, trade credit
商业信用证/商業信用證　commercial letter of credit
商业信誉/商業信譽　commercial prestige
商业性标识/商業性標識　mark for business
商业性工联主义/務實工會主義　business unionism
商业性文件中心/商業性檔中心　commercial record center
商业银行/商業銀行　commercial bank, merchant bank
商业银行贷款/商業銀行貸款　commercial bank loan
商业银行风险管理/商業銀行風險管理　risk management of commercial bank
商业银行负债业务/商業銀行負債業務　liability business of commercial bank
商业银行信贷/商業銀行信貸　commercial bank credit
商业银行业务/商業銀行業務　commercial banking
商业银行资产负债管理/商業銀行資產負債管理　management of assets and liabilities of commercial bank
商业用地/商業土地使用　commercial land use
商业预测/商業預測,商情預測,景氣預測　business forecasting
商业圆桌会议/企業協進會　business roundtable
商业杂志/商業雜誌　business magazine
商业账簿/商業賬簿　commercial account
商业折扣/商業折扣　commercial discount
商业政策/商業政策　commercial policy
商业指标/景氣指標　business indicator
商业周期/商情循環,景氣循環　business cycle
商业周期指标/商情循環指標　business cycle indicator
商业资本/商業資本,商人資本　merchant capital, capital for trading purpose, commercial capital
商业资本主义/商業資本主義　commercial capitalism
商誉/商譽　goodwill
熵/熵　entropy
上标/上標　superscript
上不封顶/上不封頂　setting no ceiling limit
上层阶级/上層階級　upper class
上层阶级文化/上層階級文化　upper-class culture
上传/上傳　upload
上访/上訪　launch complaints to higher authorities
上光/上光　coating, varnishing
上架凳/梯凳　step stool
上架时间/上架時間　shelving time
上交叉/上交叉　up-cross
上缴朱批奏折制度/上繳朱批奏摺制度　returned vermilion rescript archives system
上解中央支出/上解中央支出　expenditures on upper solution to the central government
上界/上［邊］界　upper boundary, upper bound
上决策线/上決策線　upper decision line, UDL
上开口组/開放組　open-ended class
上门服务/及門服務　door-to-door service
上门推销/逐戶銷售　house-to-house selling
上升流动/向上流動　upward mobility
上市/上市　listing
上市标准/上市標準　listing standard
上市公告书/上市公告書　listed company statement

上市公司/上市公司　listed company
上市条件/上市標準　listing standard
上市暂停/上市暫停　listing suspension
上市证券/上市證券　listed securities
上市终止/上市終止　listing termination
上四分位数/上四分位數　upper quartile
上诉不加刑/上訴不加刑　no appeal resulting in additional punishment
上诉法院/上訴法院　appellate court
上诉期限/上訴期限　time limit for appeal
上诉权/上訴權　right of appeal
上诉人/上訴人　appellant
上诉审/上訴審　trial on appeal
上网本/隨身型易網機,輕省筆電　netbook
上位标引/上位標引　broader concept indexing, generic indexing
上位词/上位詞　hypernym, superordinate
上位概念/上位概念　upper concept
上位功能/上位功能　higher order function
上位类/上位類　superordinate class
上位主题/上位主題　superordinate subject
上下[估计]法/上下[估計]法　up and down method
上下链/上下連串　runs up and down
上下位词/上下位詞　generic word
上下文/上下文　context
上下文检索/上下文檢索　context search, context retrieval
上下文敏感/上下文有關　context-aware, context-sensitive
上下文无关语言/上下文無關語言　context-free language
上下文相关/上下文相關　context dependent
上限/上限　upper limit
上行沟通/向上溝通　upward communication
上行文/上行文　uplink file
上演权/上演權　performing right
上游垄断企业/上游獨占廠商　upstream monopoist
上谕/上諭　imperial order
上谕档/上諭檔　imperial order archives
上涨/價格利得　price gain
上证综合指数/上證綜合指數　Shanghai composite index
上置信区间/上信賴區間　upper confidence interval
尚同/尚同　identification with the superior
尚贤/尚賢　esteem of virtuousness
烧埋银/燒埋銀　silver buried burning
烧钱/焚錢,燒鈔票　burning money
少数民族/少數民族　ethnic minority
少数民族档案/少數民族檔案　archives of minority nationality
少数民族语言文字出版物/少數民族語言文字出版物　ethnolinguistics publication
少儿期刊/少兒期刊　children's periodical
少年儿童馆藏/少年兒童館藏　juvenile collection
少年儿童图书馆/少年兒童圖書館　children's library
奢侈品/奢侈品　luxury goods
奢侈品关税/奢侈品關稅　luxury tariff, luxury duty, luxury tax
赊购/賒購　purchase on credit
赊购发票/賒購發票,賒銷發票　charge ticket
赊销/賒銷　sale on account, sale on credit, charge sale
赊销发票/賒購發票　charge ticket
赊账/賒賬　give credit
赊账订阅/賒賬訂閱　gracing
赊账公司/賒銷合約　charge company
赊账购货/賒賬進貨　account purchase
赊账交易/賒賬交易　transaction on credit
赊账支付/賒賬支付　payment on account
蛇形浮动/蛇行浮動　snake
"蛇形浮动"货币/"蛇形浮動"貨幣　snake currency
舍入/捨入　rounding
舍入误差/捨入誤差,零頭誤差　roundoff error, rounding error
设备保养/設備保養　facility maintenance
设备冲突/設備干擾,機具干擾　machine interference
设备分配/設備分配,機具分配　machine assignment
设备负荷/設備負荷,機具負荷　machine load
设备监造/設備監造　equipment survey
设备可用性/設備可用度　equipment availability
设备利用率/設備利用率　utilization rate of equipments
设备停歇时间/機器閒置時間　machine idle time
设备无关/裝置無關　device independence
设备无关颜色/設備無關顏色　device independent color
设备相关/裝置相依　device dependence
设备相关颜色/設備相關顏色　device dependent color
设备运转率/開工率　operation rate
设备主导排程/設備主導排程　processor-dominated scheduling
设备综合工程学/設備綜合科技　terotechnology
设定/預設　default
设定错误/設定錯誤　miss-pecification
设定误差/設定誤差　specification error

设计/設計 design
设计变更通知/設計變更通知 design change notice
设计变量/設計變數 design variable
设计标准/設計標準 design standard
设计采购施工与交钥匙工程合同条件/設計採購施工與交鑰匙工程合同條件 condition of contract for engineering procurement construction and turnkey project
设计-采购-施工总承包模式/工程-採購-安裝模式，EPC 模式 engineering-procurement-construction, EPC model
设计产能/設計產能 designed capacity
设计抽样/設計抽樣 sampling by design
设计的正交性/設計的正交性 orthogonality of designs
设计的最优性/設計的最適性 optimality of design
设计方程/設計方程 design equation
设计概算/設計概算 budgetary estimation of design
设计功能/設計功能 design function
设计-管理模式/DM 模式 design-manage model, DM model
设计和开发/設計開發 design and development
设计-建造与交钥匙工程合同条件/設計-建造與交鑰匙工程合同條件 condition of contract for design-build and turnkey
设计矩阵/設計矩陣 design matrix
设计驱动的创新/設計驅動的創新 design-driven innovation
设计缺陷/設計缺陷 design defect
设计-施工/設計-施工 design-build, DB
设计-施工-融资-运行模式/DBFO 模式 design-build-finance-operate model, DBFO model
设计效应/設計效應 design effect
设计学派/設計學派 design school
设计因子/設計因子 design factor
设计-招标-建造/設計-招標-建造 design-bid-build, DBB
设计周期/設計週期 design cycle
设权证券/設權證券 empowering securities
设施/設施 facility
设施处置/設施處置 facility disposal
设施管理/設施管理 facility management
设施规划/設施規劃 facility strategic planning
设施选址/設施位址，店址選擇 facility location
设施租赁/設施出租 facility renting
社店联合寄销/社店聯合寄銷 united distribution
社会/社會 society
社会安全税/社會安全稅 social security tax
社会安全体系/社會安全體系 social security system
社会包容/社會包容，社會納入 social inclusion
社会保护/社會保護 social protection
社会保险/社會保險 social insurance
社会保险法/社會保險法 social insurance law
社会保险费/社會保險費 social insurance fee
社会保险基金筹集方式/社會保險基金籌集方式 social insurance fundraising method
社会保险基金筹集模式/社會保險基金籌集模式 social insurance fundraising model
社会保险税/社會保險稅 social insurance tax
社会保险统计/社會保險統計 social insurance statistics
社会保险账户/社會保險賬戶 social insurance account
社会保险资格/社會保險資格 qualification for social insurance
社会保障/社會保障 social security
社会保障法/社會保障法 social security law
社会保障管理/社會保障管理 social security management
社会保障基金/社會保險基金 social security fund
社会保障计划/社會保障方案 social protection program
社会本能/社會本能 social instinct
社会比较/社會性的比較 social comparison
社会比较理论/社會比較理論 social comparison theory
社会必要劳动时间/社會必要勞動時間 labor-time socially necessary
社会边际效益/社會邊際效益，邊際社會收益 marginal social benefit, social marginal benefit
社会表征/社會表徵 social representation
社会病理学/社會病理學 social pathology
社会病态/社會病態 social pathological phenomena
社会剥夺/社會剝奪 social deprivation
社会不平等/社會不平等 social inequality
社会潮流/社會潮流，社會趨勢 social trend
社会称许性/社會期許，社會讚許 social desirability
社会成本/社會成本 social cost
社会承认/社會承認 social recognition
社会冲击理论/社會衝擊理論 social impact theory
社会冲突/社會衝突 social conflict
社会冲突中的认知论题/社會衝突中的認知論題 cognitive issue in social conflict
社会重建/社會重建 social reconstruction
社会传染/社會傳染 social contagion
社会传统/社會傳統 social tradition

社会存在/社會存在　social fact
社会达尔文主义/社會達爾文主義　social Darwinism
社会单元/社會單元　social unit
社会地位/社會地位　social status
社会调查/社會調查　social survey
社会调查法/社會調查法　social survey method
社会动机/社會動機　social motivation
社会动员/社會動員　social mobilization
社会对抗/社會對抗　social opposition
社会惰化/社會閒散,社會撈混,社會偷懶　social loafing
社会惰性/社會惰性　social inertia
社会发展/社會發展　social development
社会法/社會法則　social law
社会法学派/社會法制學派　social legality school
社会分层/社會階層[化]　social stratification
社会分割/社會分割　social segmentation
社会分工/社會分工　social division of labor
社会分化/社會分化　social differentiation
社会分裂/社會分裂　social dissociation, social cleavage
社会分析与职能鉴定论/社會分析與職能鑒定論　social analysis and functional appraisal
社会风气/社會風氣　social morale
社会封闭/社會封閉　social closure
社会服务/社會服務　social service
社会服务机构/社會服務機構　social service agency
社会服务类事业单位/社會服務類事業單位　public organizations which provide social services
社会服务项目/社會服務項目　social service program, social service project
社会福利/社會福利,社會福祉　social welfare
社会福利[国家]实质法范式/社會福利[國家]實質法範式　social-welfare substantive law
社会福利函数/社會福利函數　social welfare function
社会福利设施/社會福利設施　social welfare facilities
社会福利社会化/社會福利社會化　socialization of social welfare
社会福利损失/社會福利損失　social welfare loss
社会福利统计/社會福利統計　social welfare statistics
社会福利院/社會福利院　social welfare institute
社会福音论/社會福音理論　social gospel theory
社会抚恤/社會撫恤　pensions for servicemen
社会改革/社會改革,社會革新　social reform
社会干预/社會干預　social intervention

社会感染/社會傳染　social contagion
社会革命/社會革命　social revolution
社会隔绝/社會隔離　social isolation
社会个案工作/社會個案工作　social casework
社会工程/社會工程,社交工程　social engineering
社会工作/社會工作　social work
社会工作本土化/社會工作本土化　indengenisation of social work, the localization of social work
社会工作的理论/社會工作的理論　theories of social work
社会工作的理论基础/社會工作的理論基礎　theoretical foundation of social work
社会工作的实施理论/社會工作的實施理論　social work practice theory
社会工作督导/社會工作督導,社工督導　social work supervision
社会工作方法/社會工作方法　methods of social work
社会工作服务/社工服務　social work service
社会工作服务对象/社會工作服務對象　client of social work
社会工作服务组织/社會工作服務組織　social work service organization
社会工作功能/社會工作功能　the function of social work
社会工作过程/社會工作過程　social work process
社会工作技巧/社會工作技巧　social work skill
社会工作价值观/社會工作價值觀　values of social work
社会工作价值内核/社會工作價值內核　core values of social work
社会工作间接服务/社會工作間接服務　indirect social work service
社会工作教育/社會工作教育　social work education
社会工作课程/社會工作課程　social work curriculum
社会工作理论/社會工作理論　social work theory, theories for social work
社会工作伦理/社會工作倫理　ethics of social work
社会工作伦理守则/社會工作倫理守則　ethical codes for social work
社会工作模式/社會工作模式　models of social work
社会工作培训/社會工作培訓　social work training
社会工作人才/社會工作人才　talented personnel in social work
社会工作师/社會工作師　professional in social work
社会工作实务/社會工作實務　social work practice
社会工作实务领域/社會工作實務領域　area of

social work practice
社会工作实习/社會工作實習 social work fieldwork, social work internship
社会工作实习督导/社會工作實習督導 supervision on social work internship
社会工作实习机构/社會工作實習機構 social work internship institutions
社会工作实习模式/社會工作實習模式 model of social work internship
社会工作实习生/社會工作實習生 social work intern
社会工作使命/社會工作使命 mission of social work
社会工作相近专业/社會工作相近專業 social work-related profession
社会工作行政/社會工作行政 social work administration
社会工作研究/社會工作研究 social work research
社会工作研究的方法论/社會工作研究的方法論 methodology for social work research
社会工作研究伦理/社會工作研究倫理 ethics for social work research
社会工作者/社會工作員,社會服務員,社工員 social worker
社会工作者角色/社會工作者角色 social worker's roles
社会工作直接服务/社會工作直接服務 direct social work service
社会工作职业/社會工作職業 social work profession
社会工作专业/社會工作專業 social work major
社会工作专业博士/社會工作專業博士 Doctor of Social Work
社会工作专业服务关系/社會工作專業服務關係 professional relationship of social work service
社会工作专业化/社會工作專業化 the professionalization of social work
社会工作专业教育/社會工作專業教育 professional social work education
社会工作专业人才/社會工作專業人才 professional social work personnel
社会工作专业人才队伍建设/社會工作專業人才隊伍建設 enhance professionalism of social work personnel
社会工作专业硕士/社會工作專業碩士 Master of Social Work
社会工作专业学士/社會工作專業學士 Bachelor of Social Work

社会公德/社會公德 social morality
社会功能/社會功能 social function
社会功能运作/社會功能運作 social functioning
社会共同体/社會共同體 social community
社会构成/社會構成 social constitution
社会关系/社會關係 social relationship
[社会]关系论/社會關係說,關係理論 social relationship theory, relations theory
社会管理/社會管理 social management
社会规范/社會規範,社會管制 social norm, social regulation
社会规范机制/社會規範機制 social normative mechanism
社会规划/社會計劃 social planning
社会过程/社會過程,社會歷程 social process
社会合作/社會合作 social cooperation
社会核算矩阵/社會核算矩陣,社會會計矩陣 social accounting matrix, SAM
社会互动/社會互動 social interaction
社会化/社會化 socialization
社会化标签/社會性標記 social tagging
社会化大生产/社會化大生產 socialized production
社会化服务/社會服務 social service
社会化媒体/社群媒體,社交媒體 social media
社会化搜索/社會化搜索 social search
社会划分/社會劃分 social division
社会环境/社會環境,社會氛圍 societal environment, social environment
社会活动/社會活動 social activity
社会机会成本/社會機會成本 social opportunity cost
社会机制/社會機制 social mechanism
社会基础/社會基礎 social base
社会集合/社會集團 social aggregation
社会集体/社會集體 social collective
社会计划模式/社會計劃模式,社會規劃模式 social planning model
社会计量学/社會計量學 sociometry
社会技术系统矩阵/社會技術系統矩陣 matrix structure of socio-technical system
社会技术系统理论/社會科技系統論 socio-technical system theory
社会技术系统内部结构/社會技術系統内部結構 internal structure of socio-technical system
社会技术系统外部结构/社會技術系統外部結構 external structure of socio-technical system
社会技术系统学派/社會技術系統學派 socio-technical system school

社会继替/社會繼替　social inherit and supersede
社会价值/社會價值　social value
社会价值观/社會價值體系　social value system
社会建构/社會建構　social construction
社会建构论/社會建構論　social constructionism
社会建构主义/社會建構主義　social constructivism
社会建设/社會建構　social construction
社会交换理论/社會交換理論　social exchange theory
社会交往/社會溝通，社交溝通　social communication
社会阶层/社會階層　social class
社会结构/社會結構　social structure
社会解体/社會解體　social disintegration
社会解体理论/社會解體理論　social disorganization theory
社会津贴/社會津貼　social allowance
社会进步/社會進步　social progress
社会进化论/社會演化論　social evolutionism
社会经济地位指数/社經地位指標　socioeconomic index
社会经济福利指标/社會經濟福利指標　community economic well-being indicator
社会经济形态/社會經濟形態　social economic form
社会竞争/社會競爭　social competition
社会救助/社會救助　social assistance, social relief, social relief and aid
社会救助统计/社會救助統計　social assistance statistics
社会距离/社會距離　social distance
社会决策图式/社會決策基模　social decision schema
社会决定论/社會決定論　social determinism
社会角色/社會角色　social role
社会均等指标/社會均等指標　social equality indicator
社会均衡/社會均衡　social equilibrium
社会科学/社會科學　social science
社会科学情报学/社會科學資訊學　social scientific information science, social science-related information studies
社会科学信息/社會科學資料　social science information
社会科学研究信息化/社會科學研究信息化　e-social science
社会科学引文索引/社會科學引文索引　social science citation index, SSCI
社会刻板印象/社會刻板印象　social stereotype

社会控制/社會控制　social control
社会劳动/社會勞動　social labor
社会老年学/社會老年學　social gerontology
社会类别化/社會類別化，社會分類　social categorization
社会理论/社會理論　social theory
社会理性/社會理性　social rationality
社会力量/社會力　social force
社会连带主义法学派/社會連帶主義法學派　Social Solidarist School of Law
社会流动/社會流動　social mobility
社会矛盾/社會矛盾　social contradiction
社会民主主义/社會民主主義　social democracy
社会模式/社會模式，社會模型　social model, social pattern
社会母体/社會母體　social matrix
社会目标模式/社會目標模式　social target pattern
社会凝聚/社會凝聚　social cohesion
社会纽带/社會紐帶　social bond, social tie
社会排斥/社會排除　social exclusion
社会偏好/社會偏好　social preference
社会平均劳动强度/社會平均勞力投入密集度　social average labor intensity
社会评价/社會評價　social evaluation
社会歧视/社會歧視　social discrimination
社会企业/社會型企業　social enterprise
社会气氛/社會氣氛，社會氛圍　social climate
社会契约/社會契約　social contract
社会契约论/社會契約論　social contract theory
社会契约整合理论/綜合社會契約論　integrative social contract theory
社会强制/社會強制　social coercion
社会侵蚀/社會侵蝕　social erosion
社会倾销/社會傾銷　social dumping
社会圈/社會圈　social circle
社会权力/社會權力　social power
社会权利/社會權　social right
社会权威/社會權威　social authority
社会群体/社會群體　social group
社会人/社會人　social man
社会人假设/社會人假設　social person assumption
社会人类学/社會人類學　social anthropology
社会人类学基本概念/社會人類學基本概念　basic concepts of social anthropology
社会认识论/社會認識論　social epistemology
社会认同/社會認同　social identity
社会认同理论/社會認同理論，社會認定理論　social identity theory

社会认知结构/社會結構認知　social cognitive structure
社会融合/社會整合　social integration
社会上层建筑/社會超結構　social superstructure
社会设计/社會設計　social projection
社会审计/社會稽核　social audit
社会渗透理论/社會滲透理論　social penetration theory
社会生活/社會生活　social life
社会生活噪声/社會生活雜訊　noise of social activities
社会生态学/社會流行病學　social ecology
社会生物学/社會生物學　social biology, sociology of biology
社会失调/社會失調　social dissonance, social disharmony, social maladjustment
社会时间/社會時間　social time
社会实在/社會實在,社會實體　social reality
社会史/社會史　social history
社会世界/社會世界　social world
社会市场经济/社會市場經濟　social market economy
社会事件/社會事件　social event
社会事务/社會事務　social affair
社会适应/社會適應　social adjustment
社会书签/社會書簽　social bookmark
社会思想/社會思想　social thought
社会态度/社會態度　social attitude
社会淘汰/社會淘汰　social selection
社会体/社會體　Gesellschaft
社会体系/社會體系　social system
社会调适/社會適應　social adjustment
社会贴现率/社會貼現率　social discount rate, social rate of discount
社会同化/社會同化　social assimilation
社会统计[学]/社會統計　social statistics
社会投资/社會投資　social investment
社会图/社會圖,社網圖　sociogram
社会团结/社會團結,社會連帶　social solidarity
社会团体/社會團體　social group, social association
社会团体监督/社會團體監督,社會群體監督　supervision by social group
社会脱节/社會脫節　social dislocation
社会网络/社會網路　social network
社会网络分析法/社會網路分析　social network analysis
社会危害性/社會危害性　social harmfulness
社会危机/社會危機　social crisis

社会唯名论/社會唯名論　social nominalism
社会唯实论/社會唯實論　social realism
社会文化模式/社會文化模式　sociocultural model
社会文化因素/社會文化因素　sociocultural segment
社会稳定/社會穩定　social stability
社会问题/社會問題　social issue, social problem
社会物质条件/社會物質條件　social material condition
社会系统/社會系統,社會體系　social system
社会闲散效应/社會閒散效應,社會撈混效應,社會偷懶效應　social loafing effect
社会现象/社會現象　social phenomenon
社会相符行为/社會相符行爲　socially conforming behavior
社会效益/社會效益　social effect
社会协作系统学派/社會協作系統學派　socio-collaborative system school
社会-心理模式/社會-心理模式　socio-psychological pattern
社会心理子系统/心理社會子系統,心理社會次系統　psychosocial subsystem
社会心态/社會心態　social mentality
社会新闻/市政新聞　city news, social news
社会信贷/社會信貸　social credit
社会信任理论/社會信任理論　social trust theory
社会信息/社會訊息　social information
社会信息化/社會資訊化　social informatization
社会行动/社會行動,社會行爲　social action
社会行动模式/社會行動模式　social action model
社会行政/社會行政　social administration
社会形式/社會形式　social form
社会形态/社會形構,社會形成　social formation
社会形态学/社會形態學　social morphology
社会性/社會性,社交性　sociability
社会性别/社會性別　social gender
社会性别分析/社會性別分析　social gender analysis
社会性别化/社會性別化　social gendered
社会性别理论/社會性別理論　social gender theory
社会性别与发展/社會性別發展　social gender and development
社会性别主流化/社會性別主流化　social gender mainstreaming
社会性软件/社會性軟體　social software
社会需要/社會需要,社會需求,社交需要　social need
社会选择/社會選擇　social choice, social selection
社会选择函数/社會選擇函數　social choice function
社会选择理论/社會選擇理論　social selection theory

社会学/社會學　sociology
社会学本土化/社會學本土化　the localization of sociology
社会学解释/社會學解釋　sociological interpretation
社会学习/社會學習　social learning
社会学习理论/社會學習[理]論　social learning theory
社会学有限论/社會學有限論　sociological finitism
社会学主义/唯社會學主義　sociologism
社会循环论/社會循環論　social cyclical theory
社会压力/社會壓力　social pressure
社会演化/社會演化,社會進化　social evolution
社会养老保险制度/社會養老保險制度　social pension system
社会医疗保险/社會醫療保險　medical social insurance
社会医学/社會醫學　social medicine
社会遗传/社會遺傳　social gene
社会意识/社會意識　social consciousness
社会意识形态/社會意識形態　social ideology
社会营销/社會行銷　social marketing
社会营销观念/社會行銷觀念　societal marketing concept
社会影响评价/社會影響評估　social impact evaluation
社会优待/社會優待　socially preferential treatment
社会优抚/社會優撫　social special care and treatment
社会舆论监督/民意監督　supervision by public opinion
社会预警/社會預警　social alarming
社会原子化/社會原子化　social atomization
社会原子论/社會原子論　social atomism
社会阅读/社會閱讀　social reading
社会越轨/社會越軌　social deviance
社会运动/社會運動　social movement
社会再生产/社會再生產,社會再製　social reproduction
社会责任/社會責任　social responsibility
社会责任[理]论/社會責任論　social responsibility theory
社会哲学/社會哲學　social philosophy
社会诊断/社會診斷　social diagnosis
社会整合/社會整合　social integration
社会正义/社會正義　social justice
社会政策/社會政策　social policy
社会支持网/社會支持網　social support network
社会支出/社會支出　social expenditure
社会支配性取向/社會優勢取向　social dominance orientation
社会知觉/社會知覺　social perception
社会知识/社會知識　social knowledge
社会指标统计/社會指標統計　social index statistics
社会制裁/社會制裁　social sanction
社会制度/社會制度,社會系統　social system, social institution
社会制约/社會制約,社會強制　social conditioning, social constraint
社会质量/社會質量　social quality
社会治理/社會治理　social governance
社会秩序/社會秩序　social order
社会中介组织/社會中介組織　social intermediary organization
社会主义/社會主義　socialism
社会主义法治/社會主義法治　socialist rule of law
社会主义公有制/社會主義公有制　socialist public ownership
社会主义经济学/社會主義經濟學　socialist economics
社会主义市场经济/社會主義市場經濟　socialist market economy
社会助长/社會助長,社會促進　social facilitation
社会转型/社會轉型　social transition
社会资本/社會資本　social capital
社会资源理论/社會資源理論　social resources theory
社会自然/社會自然　socionature
社会自治原则/社會自治原則　principle of autonomy to society
社会总福利/社會總福利　social total welfare
社会总效益/社會總利得　total social benefit
社会组织/社會組織　social organization
社会组织备案制/社會組織備案制　social organization registration system
社会组织发展指数/社會組織指數　development index of social organization
社会组织分类管理/社會組織分類管理　categorized management of social organizations
社会组织能力建设/社會組織能力建設　capacity building in social organization
社会组织年检/社會組織年度檢查　annual inspection of social organizations
社会最优状态/社會最適　social optimum
社交传播/社交傳播　phatic communication
社交媒体/社交媒體,社群媒體　social media
社交网络服务/社交網路服務,社會網路服務,社群

網路服務　social networking service, SNS, social network service
社交支持/社會支持　social support
社论/社論　editorial
社区/社區　community
社区报[纸]/社區報　community newspaper
社区动员/社區動員　community mobilization
社区发展/社區發展　community development
社区服务/社區服務　community service
社区服务机构/社區服務機構　community service agency
社区服务站/社區服務站　community service station
社区服务中心/社區服務中心　community service ccnter
社区工作/社區工作　community work
社区共同天线系统/社區共同天線系統　community antenna television system
社区广播/社區廣播　community broadcast
社区建设/社區營造　community building
社区矫正/社區矯正　community rehabilitation
社区接入点/社區接入點　community access point
社区解放论/社區解放論　community liberated
社区居委会/社區居委會　neighbourhood council
社区媒介/社群媒介　community media
社区失落论/社區失落論　community lost
社区书店/社區書店　community bookstore
社区图书馆/社區圖書館　community library
社区新闻学/社區新聞學　community journalism
社区信息服务/社區資訊服務　community information service
社区续存论/社區續存論　community saved
社区学校/社區學校　community school
社区研究/社區研究　community studies
社区养老服务/社區養老服務　community-based elderly care
社区意识/社區意識　sense of community
社区营销/社區行銷　community marketing
社区照顾/社區照顧　community-based caregiving
社区志愿者/社區志願者　community volunteer
社区自治/社區自治　community autonomy, community self-governance
社区组织/社區組織　community organization
社群信息学/社群資訊學　community informatics
社群云/社區雲端　community cloud
社群主义/社群主義　communitarianism
社团法人/社團法人　mass organization as legal person
社团图书馆/學會圖書館，社會團體圖書館　society library
射击游戏/射擊遊戲　shooting game
射频识别/射頻識別　radio frequency identification
射频识别技术/無線射頻識別　radio frequency identification, RFID
射频识别系统/無線射頻識別系統　radio frequency identification system
涉农产业/農企業　agribusiness
涉他合同/涉他合同　contract concerning third party
涉外不当得利/涉外不當得利　unjust enrichment involving foreign elements
涉外不动产/涉外不動產　real estate involving foreign elements
涉外财产保全/涉外財產保全　property preservation involving foreign elements
涉外动产/涉外動產　personal property involving foreign elements
涉外法定继承/涉外法定繼承　intestate succession involving foreign elements
涉外夫妻财产/涉外夫妻財產　matrimonial property involving foreign elements
涉外公证/涉外公證　notarization involving foreign elements
涉外合同/涉外合同　contract involving foreign elements
涉外婚姻/涉外婚姻　marriage involving foreign elements
涉外继承/涉外繼承　succession involving foreign elements
涉外监护/涉外監護　custody involving foreign elements
涉外结婚/涉外結婚　marriage concerning foreign affairs
涉外离婚/涉外離婚　divorce concerning foreign affairs
涉外流通票据/涉外流通票據　negotiable instruments involving foreign elements
涉外民事案件/涉外民事案件　civil cases involving foreign affairs
涉外民事法律关系/涉外民事法律關係　civil legal relationship involving foreign elements
涉外民事关系/涉外民事關係　civil relationship involving foreign elements
涉外民事诉讼/涉外民事訴訟　civil litigation involving foreign elements, foreign-related civil lawsuit
涉外民事诉讼程序/涉外民事訴訟程序　civil procedure for cases involving foreign

涉外民事诉讼管辖/涉外民事訴訟管轄　civil jurisdiction involving foreign elements
涉外民事诉讼期间/涉外民事訴訟期間　time limit in foreign-related civil lawsuit
涉外期间/涉外期間　period involving foreign elements
涉外侵权/涉外侵權　tort involving foreign elements
涉外认证/涉外認證　certification involving foreign elements
涉外收养/涉外收養　adoption involving foreign elements
涉外收养关系/涉外收養關係　adoption relationship involving foreign elements
涉外死亡宣告/涉外死亡宣告　declaration of death involving foreign elements
涉外送达/涉外送達　foreign-related service
涉外诉讼竞合/涉外訴訟競合　parallel proceedings involving foreign elements
涉外特殊地域管辖/涉外特殊地域管轄　special teriterrial jurisdciton involving foreign elements
涉外无人继承财产/涉外無人繼承財產　foreign-related bona vacantia
涉外协议管辖/涉外協議管轄　agreement to jurisdiction involving foreign elements
涉外因素/外來單元　foreign elements
涉外仲裁/涉外仲裁　arbitration involving foreign elements
涉外仲裁裁决/涉外仲裁裁決　arbitration award involving foreign elements
涉外仲裁裁决的效力/涉外仲裁裁決的效力　the effect of arbitration award involving foreign elements
涉外仲裁费用/涉外仲裁費用　costs of arbitration involving foreign elements
涉外仲裁协议/涉外仲裁協議　arbitration agreement involving foreign elements
涉外仲裁中的保全措施/涉外仲裁中的保全措施　preserving measures in arbitration involving foreign elements
涉外仲裁中的调解/涉外仲裁中的調解　mediation in arbitration involving foreign elements
涉外专属管辖/涉外專屬管轄　exclusive jurisdiction involving foreign elements
赦免/赦免　pardon
摄影冲洗两用机/拍攝沖洗機　camera-processor
摄影构图/攝影構圖　composition of a picture
摄影光盘/相片光碟　photo CD
摄影机/攝影機　camera
摄影记者/攝影師　cameraman, photographer
摄影镜头/攝影鏡頭　photographic len
摄影师/攝影師,攝影機操作員　camera operator
摄影作品/攝影作品　photographic works
摄制权/攝製權　production right
申报价格/申報價格　reported price
申不害/申不害　Shen Buhai
申明亭/申明亭　Shenming Ting, Shenming Pavilion
申请单/空白申請單　application form
申请废除合同的诉讼/申請廢止合約的訴訟　action for annulment of contract
申请付款/申請付款　pay on application
申请回避/申請迴避　for withdrawal
申请检校/申請檢校　apply calibration
申请执行/申請執行　application for execution
申请执行人/申請執行人　applicant of enforcement
申请仲裁/申請仲裁　filling of award
申诉/申訴,上訴　petition, appeal
伸缩汇率制度/彈性匯率制度　flexible exchange rate system
身处其中的局外人/身處其中的局外人　outsider within
身份/身份　status, identity
身份权/身份權　right based on legal status
身份人格/身份人格　status personality
身份认证/身份鑒別　identity authentication
身份社会/身份社會　status society
身份识别/身份識別　identity recognition
身份问题/定名問項　identity question
身份制/身份制　status system
身体/身體　body
身体辅助动作/身體輔助動作　body assist motion
身体研究/身體研究　body studies
身体语言/肢體語言　body language
绅士教育/紳士教育　gentrification education
深层结构/深層結構　deep structure
深层生态学/深層生態學,深度生態學　deep ecology
深度/深度　depth
深度报道/深度報導　in-depth reporting
深度标引/深度索引[法]　depth indexing
深度访谈/深度訪談　in-depth interview
深度分层/深度分層　deep stratification
深度描述/深厚描述,厚描法,深描法　thick description
深喉/深喉嚨　deep throat
深描/深描,厚描　deep description, thick description
深阅读/深閱讀　deep reading
深圳成分指数/深圳成分指數　Shenzhen stock

exchange component index
神话／神話　myth
神经网络／神經網路分析　neural networks
神经网络模型／[類]神經網路模型　neural network model
神经网络算法／神經網路演算法　neural network algorithm
神经网络预测模型／神經網路預測模型　neural network forecasting model
神经元／神經元　neuron
神秘顾客购物／神秘購物　mystery shopping
神秘主义／神秘主義　mysticism
神庙档案馆／神廟檔案館　temple archive
神判／神判　ordeal
神圣-凡俗／神聖-凡俗　sacred-profane
神职人员权利法／神職人員權利法　Articuli Cleri
沈命法／沈命法　Shenming Fa
审查／检查制度　censorship
审查和批准预算／預算審查和批準　review and approval of budget
审查起诉／審查起訴　review and determination of prosecution
审读／審讀　reading for examination
审稿／審稿　read and evaluate
审核报告／評價報告　appraisal report
审核发现／審核發現　audit finding
审核范围／稽核範圍　audit scope
审核方案／稽核方案　audit programme
审核机构认可／審核機構認可　auditing authority accreditation
审核结论／稽核結論　audit conclusion
审核委托方／稽核委託方　audit client
审核员资格认可／稽核員資格認可　auditor qualification recognition
审核原则／審核原則　examining principle
审核准则／稽核準則　audit criteria
审核组／稽核組　audit team
审计／審計,稽核,查核　audit, auditing
审计报告／審計報告,審核報告,查核報告　audit report
审计报告日／審計報告日　date of the auditor's report
审计成本／審計成本　audit cost
审计程序公报／審計程序公報　Statement of Auditing Procedure
审计抽样／審計抽樣,查核抽樣　audit sampling
审计档案／審計檔案,查核檔案　audit file
审计定价／審計定價　audit pricing

审计法／審計法　law of audit
审计费用／審計公費　audit fee
审计风险／審計風險　audit risk
审计风险模型／審計風險模型　audit risk model
审计跟踪／審計存底,審計追蹤,審計軌跡　audit trail
审计工作底稿／審計工作底稿　audit working paper, audit workpaper, audit documentation
审计函证／審計函證　audit confirmation
审计监督／審計監督,稽核監督　audit intendance, supervision by audit, audit supervision
审计检验／稽核檢驗　audit inspection
审计金融机构／核釋金融機構　auditing financial institution
审计轮换制／會計師輪調會計,事務所輪調會計　auditor rotation system
审计品质／審計品質　audit quality
审计期望差距／審計期望差距　audit expectation gap
审计失败／審計失敗　audit failure
审计师／審計官　auditor
审计师变更／審計師變更　auditor change, auditor switching
审计师独立性／審計獨立性　auditor independence
审计师任期／稽核員任期　auditor tenure, audit-firm tenure
审计诉讼／審計訴訟　audit litigation
审计委员会／審計委員會　audit committee
审计学／審計學　auditing
审计意见／審計意見,查核意見　audit opinion
审计意见购买／審計意見購買　audit opinion shopping
审计责任／審計責任　auditing responsibility
审计证据／查核證據　audit evidence
审计职业怀疑／審計職業懷疑　audit professional skepticism
审计职业判断／審計專業判斷　audit professional judgment
审计准则／審計準則　auditing standard
审计准则公报／審計準則公報　Statement of Auditing Standard
审美功能／美學功能　aesthetic function
审美文化／審美文化　aesthetic culture
审判监督程序／審判監督程式　trial supervision procedure
审判权／審判權　jurisdiction authority
审批／審批　examination and approval
审慎经营规则／審慎經營規則　rules of prudential management

渗透定价/渗透訂價　penetration pricing
渗透份额/渗透份額　penetration share
渗透过程/渗透過程　percolation process
慎改原则/慎改原則　pricinple of discreetly changing
升级/升級　upgrading
升降台/升降檯　lift table
升水货币/升水貨幣　premium currency
升水率/升水率,期货溢價率　rate of premium, contango rate
升值/升值　appreciation
生产/生產　production
生产报告和状态控制/生產報告和狀態控制　production reporting and status control
生产成本/生產成本　cost of production
生产调度/生產調度　production dispatching
生产方成本调查/生產者成本調查　producer's costs survey
生产费用/產品收費　product charge
生产工具/生產工具　instrument of production
生产关系/生產關係　productive relations
生产观念/生產觀念　production concept
生产管理/生產管理　production management
生产广告牌/生產卡片　production card
生产国际化/生產國際化,生產全球化　production internationalization, internationalization of production
生产过剩/生產過剩　overproduction
生产函数/生產函數　production function
生产计划/生產計劃　production planning, production plan
生产计划与控制策略/生產規劃與控制策略　production planning and control strategy
生产价格/生產[者]價格　price of production, producer prices
生产间隔期/生產間隔期　production interval
生产经济区/生產的經濟區域　economic region of production
生产救助/生產救助　production assistance
生产均衡化/生產平滑化　production smoothing
生产可能集/產品可能組合　product-possibility set
生产可能性曲线/生產可能線　production possibility curve, PPC
生产控制/生產管制　production control
生产理论/生產理論　production theory
生产力/生產力　productivity
生产力弹性/生產效率彈性　elasticity of productivity
生产力统计/生產力統計　productivity statistics
生产链/生產鏈　production chain

生产率/生產力　productivity
生产率运动/生產力運動　productivity movement
生产模式/生產方式　mode of production
生产能力/生產能力,可生產性,產能　production capacity, producibility
生产批/生產批　production lot
生产驱动型哲学/生產驅動哲學　production-driven philosophy
生产缺陷/生產缺陷　production defect
生产三要素论/生產三要素論　three factor of production
生产商标/生產商標　trademark of manufacture
生产设备和设计施工合同条件/生產設備和設計施工合同條件　condition of contract for plant and designbuild
生产收入/生產所得　produced income
生产速率/生產[速]率　production rate, production level
生产弹性/生產彈性　elasticity of production
生产统计/生產統計　production statistics
生产维护/生產維護　productive maintenance
生产物价指数/生產者物價指數　producer price index
生产物流/生產物流　production logistics
生产限/生產界限　production limit
生产线/生產線　production line
生产效率/生產效率　production efficiency, productive efficiency
生产信息与控制系统/生產資訊與控制系統　production information and control system, PICS
生产性互补品/生產上的互補品　complements in production
生产性投资/生產性投資　productive investment
生产性物料/生產物料　production material
生产要素/生產要素,生產因素　factor of production
生产要素禀赋/富饒的生產要素　productive factor endowment
生产要素管理/生產要素管理　productive factor management
生产要素国际移动/生產要素國際移動　international transfer of productive factor
生产要素利用型投资/生產要素投資導向　factor oriented investment
生产要素市场/生產要素市场　market for factors of production
生产要素需求/要素需求線　demand for factors of production
生产运营战略/生產及作業策略　production and

operation strategy
生产账户/生產賬 production account
生产者/生產者 producers
生产者风险/生產者風險 producer risk, PR
生产者服务/生產者服務 producer service
生产者合作社/生產者合作社 producers' cooperative
生产者均衡/生產者均衡 producer equilibrium
生产者驱动型价值链/生產者主導型價值鏈 producer-driven value chain
生产者剩余/生產者剩餘 producer surplus
生产支付/生產支付 production payment
生产指令/生產指令 production order, manufacturing order
生产指数/生產指數 production index
生产周期/生產週期 period of production
生产主义/生產主義 productivism
生产资料/生產資料,生產財 means of production, producer goods
生产资料所有制/生產資料所有制 ownership of the means of production
生产作业计划/生產作業排程表 production operation schedule
生成函数/生成函數,母函數 generating function
生存分析/存活分析 survival analysis
生存概率/存活機率 survival probability
生存工资/維生工資 subsistence wage
生存-关系-成长理论/生存-關係-成長需要理論,生存-關係-成長需求理論, ERG 理論 existencerelatedness-growth theory, ERG theory
生存函数/存活函數,殘存函數 survival function
生存率/存活率 survival rate, survival ratio
生存模型/存活模型 survival model
生存权/生存權 right to live
生存时间/存活時間 survival time
生存特性曲线/存活特徵曲線 survival characteristic curve
生存线/維生水準 subsistence level
生化需氧量/生化需氧量 biochemical oxygen demand
生活成本/生活費 cost of living
生活成本调整条款/生活成本調整條款 cost-of-living adjustments clause
生活方式/生活方式 lifestyle
生活方式型企业/生活方式型企業 lifestyle venture
生活费用/生活成本 living cost
生活费用调整/生活費用調整 cost-of-living adjustment

生活费用指数/生活費指數 cost of living index number, CLIN
生活机会/生活機會 life-chance
生活救助/生活救助 living assistance
生活史/生活史,生命史 life history
生活史研究/生命史研究 life history research
生活世界的殖民化/生活世界的殖民化 life-world colonization
生活水平/生活程度 living standard
生活特性问卷/生活特性問卷 life characteristic questionnaire
生活条件/生活條件 living condition
生活质量/生活品質 quality of life
生计/生計,生活資料 means of livelihood, livelihood
生境/棲息地 habitat
生理统计/生理統計 physiology statistics
生理性老化/生理性老化 physiological aging
生灭过程/生滅過程 birth-and-death process
生命表/生命表 life table
生命竞赛/生命競賽 competition of life
生命历程/生命歷程 the life course
生命权/生命權 right of life
生命统计/生命統計 vital statistics
生命指数/生命指數 vital index
生命周期/生命週期,壽命週期 life cycle
生命周期成本/生命週期成本 life cycle cost, LCC
生命周期法/生命週期法 life cycle approach
生命周期分析/生命週期分析 life cycle analysis
生命周期管理/生命週期管理 life cycle management
生命周期假说/生命週期假說 life cycle hypothesis
生态补偿机制/生態補償機制 mechanism of ecological compensation
生态创新/生態創新 eco-innovation
生态非理性/生態非理性 ecological irrationality
生态风险/生態風險 ecological risks
生态环境/生態環境 eco-environment
生态经济学/生態經濟學 ecological economics
生态理性/生態理性 ecological rationality
生态女性主义信仰/生態女性主義信仰 eco-feminist theology
生态文明/生態文明 eco-civilization
生态系统/生態系統 ecosystem
生态系统理论/生態系統理論 eco-systemic theory
生态现代化/生態現代化 ecological modernization
生态消费者/生態消費者 eco-consumer
生态效度/生態效度 ecological validity

生态效率/生態效益　eco-efficiency
生态[学]谬误/生態謬誤　ecological fallacy
生物安全/生物安全　bio-safety
生物多样性/生物多樣性　biodiversity
生物多样性公约/生物多樣性公約　Convention on Biological Diversity
生物决定论/生物決定論　biological determinism
生物科技进步/生物技術進步　biological technology advancement
生物量/生質能　biomass
生物统计[学]/生物統計[學]　biostatistics
生物污染/生物性汙染　biological pollution
生物武器的禁用/生化武器的禁用　prohibition on the use of biological weapons
生物型职位设计法/生物型職位設計法　biological job design method
生物中心说/生物中心説　biocentric
生物资产/生物資產　biological assets
生物资源/生物資源　biological resources
生效的专利/生效的專利　patent in force
生育保险/生育保險　maternity insurance
生育代价及补偿/生育代價及補償　bearing cost and compensating
生育率/生育率　fertility rate
生育率革命/生育率革命　fertility revolution
生育水平/生育水準　fertility level
生育梯度/生育梯度　fertility gradient
生育制度/生育制度　fertility system
生育转变/生育轉型　fertility transition
生长发育/生長發育　growth and development
生长曲线模型/成長曲線模型　growth curve model
声画对位/聲畫對位　counterpoint of sound and picture
声卡/聲頻卡　audio card
声望/聲望　prestige
声望定价/聲望定價　prestige pricing
声望分层/聲望分層　prestige stratification
声像/聲像　acoustic image
声像文件/視聽記錄　audio-visual record
声音淡出/聲音淡出　sound fade out
声音淡入/聲音淡入　sound fade in
声音导演/聲音導演　sound director
声音份额/聲占率　share of voice
声音切变/聲音切變　sound cut off
声音艺术/聲音藝術　sound art
声誉效应/聲譽效果　reputation effect
省管县改革/省管縣改革　reform on direct management of counties by provinces
省图书馆/省級圖書館　provincial library
圣本笃规程/聖本篤規程，聖伯納條理　the Rule of Saint Benedict
圣地/聖地　holy land
圣吉的学习型组织/聖吉的學習型組織　learning organization theory of Senge
圣事/聖事　sacramentales
胜任力/能力　competency
胜任特征/勝任力　competence
胜者全得博弈/贏家全得博弈　winner-take-all game
盛衰周期/超漲超跌循環　boom-bust cycle
剩余/剩餘　surplus
剩余产品出口理论/剩餘產品出路説　vent-for-surplus theory
剩余等待时间/剩餘等待時間　residual waiting time
剩余工序松弛时间规则/剩餘工序寬裕時間規劃　slack time per remaining operation
剩余股利模型/剩餘股利模式　residual dividend approach
剩余股利政策/剩餘股利政策　residual dividend policy
剩余价值/剩餘價值　surplus value
剩余价值[理]论/剩餘價值[理]論　theory of surplus value
剩余价值率/剩餘價值率　rate of surplus-value
剩余控制权/剩餘控制權　residual rights of control
剩余劳动力/剩餘勞動力　surplus labor
剩余劳动时间/剩餘勞動時間　surplus labor-time
剩余权利/剩餘權利　residual right
剩余伸长/殘餘伸度　residual elongation
剩余收益/剩餘收益,殘餘收益　residual income
剩余损失/殘餘損耗　residual loss
剩余索取权/剩餘請求權　residual claimancy
剩余误差/殘差誤差　residual error
剩余型福利/剩餘型福利　residual welfare
剩余需求/剩餘需求　residual demand
剩余需求曲线/剩餘需要曲線　residual demand curve
剩余资金/剩餘資金　excess fund
尸体检查/剖檢　postmortem examination
失败预测模型/失敗預測模型　failure prediction model
失地农民/失地農民　landless peasants
失范/脱序,迷亂　anomie
失火罪/失火罪　crime of negligently causing a fire
失控状态/超出管制狀態　out of control state
失落/失落　lose
失能/失能　disability

失望理论/失望理論 disappointment theory
失效/失效,故障 failure
失效保险单/失效保險單 lapsed a policy
失效成本/失效成本 failure cost
失效分布/故障分布,故障分配 failure distribution
失效分析/故障分析 failure analysis
失效概率/故障機率 probability of failure
失效股票/失效股票 lapsed share
失效过程/故障過程 failure process
失效间隔时间/故障間隔時間 time between failures, TBF
失效率/失效率,故障率 failure rate
失效率水平/故障率水準 failure rate level
失效密度函数/故障密度函數 failure density function
失效模式与影响分析/故障模式與影響分析 failure mode and effect analysis, FMEA
失效频率/故障次數 failure frequency
失效频率分布/故障次數分布 failure frequency distribution
失效频数/故障次數 failure frequency
失效前平均时间/故障前平均壽命 mean time to failure
失效时间/故障時間,至失效時間 time to failure, failure time
失效时间分布/故障時間分布,故障時間分配 failure time distribution
失效数据/故障數據 failure data
失效专利/失效專利 ineffective patent
失业/失業 unemployment
失业保险/失業保險 unemployment insurance
失业保险基金/失業保險基金 unemployment fund
失业补偿/失業補償 unemployment compensation
失业补偿金/失業補償,失業救助 unemployment benefit, unemployment compensation
失业补助金/失業補償,失業救助 unemployment benefit, unemployment compensation
失业救济/失業救助 unemployment relief
失业率/失業率 unemployment rate
失业统计/失業統計 unemployment statistics
失业者/失業者,失職者,喪失工作者 unemployment, job loser, unemployed person
失真/失真,畸變,扭曲 distortion
失真机理/曲解機制 distorter mechanism
师生比/師生比 teacher-student ratio
师徒传承/徒弟制度 apprenticeship
师爷/師爺 shiye, adviser
施工定额/施工定額 construction quota

施工合同条件/施工合同條件 condition of contract for construction
施工任务单/工程任務單 job assignment notice
施工图预算/施工圖預算 working drawing budget
施工现场承包责任制/施工現場承包責任制 spot responsibility contract system
施工现场条件变化索赔/施工現場條件變化索賠 claim for site-condition change
施皮策恒等式/Spitzer 等式 Spitzer's identity
施塔克尔贝格模型/史塔克堡模型 Stackelberg model
施瓦兹不等式/Schwarz 不等式 Schwarz inequality
湿地/濕地 wetland
湿度计/濕度計 hygrometer
湿压湿印刷/濕對濕印花 wet-on-wet printing
湿租赁/濕租賃,服務性租賃 wet lease
十恶/十惡 Shi E
十分位数/十分位數 decile
十分位数距/十分位數距 interdecile range
十进分类法/十進分類法 decimal classification
十三部分类法/十三部分類法 thirteen-part classification
十小时工作日法案/工作十小時提案 ten hours bill
什一税/十一稅 tithing
石刻/石刻 stone carving
石刻档案/石刻檔案 marble archive, lithic record
石门心学/石門心學 Sekimon Shingaku
石渠阁/石渠閣 Shiqu Court
石室金匮/石室金匱 Shishi Jinkui
石印/石印 stone lithography
石印本/石印本 lithograph
石油冲击/石油危機 oil shock
石油美元/石油美元 oil dollar, petrodollar
石油输出国组织/石油輸出國家組織 Organization of the Petroleum Exporting Countries, OPEC
石油探勘/石油探勘 oil drilling
石油通货/石油通貨 petrocurrency
时变参数/依時變動參數 time-varying parameter
时变协变量/依時變動共變數 time-varying covariate
时变性/時變 time-variant
时差/時差 float
时代复分/時代複分 period subdivision, historical subdivision, chronological subdivision
时代复分表/時代複分表 historical subdivision
时段/時段,時距 time bucket
时段订货点法/時段訂購點法 time-phased order point

时段法/時段法　time phasing
时段排程/區段排程　block scheduling
时机细分/時機細分　occasion segmentation
时际私法/時際私法　Private Law Intertemporal
时价/時價,现行價格　prevailing price
时间比较因子/時間比較因子　time comparability factor
时间标准/時間標準　standard time, time standard
时间波动/時間波動　time fluctuation
时间参数/時間參數　time parameter
时间常数/時間常數　time constant
时间成本优化/工期-費用優化　time-cost optimization
时间定额/時間配額　time quota
时间定价/時間定價　time pricing
时间对偶/時間對偶　time antithesis
时间分布/時間分布　time distribution
时间分类法/時間分類法　time classification
时间分配理论/時間分配理論　theory of time allocation
时间管理/時間管理　time management
时间衡量单位/時間衡量單位　time measurement unit, TMU
时间互换试验/時間互換測驗　time reversal test
时间缓冲/時間緩衝　time buffer
时间加权回报率/時間加權回報率　time-weighted rate of return
时间价值/時間價值　time value
时间间隔/時間區間　time interval
时间考订/時間考訂　time criticism
时间连续过程/依時連續過程　temporally continuous process
时间联系/時間聯繫　time relation
时间码/時碼　time code
时间偏好/時間偏好　time preference
时间属性/時間屬性　temporal attribute
时间相连/時間相聯　associated in time
时间相依故障/時間相依故障　time-dependent failure
时间相依协变量/時間相依共變量　time-dependent covariate
时间项/時間項　time item
时间性/時間性　temporality
时间序列/時間序列,時間數列,時序數列　time series, chronological series
时间序列的随机干扰/時間數列的隨機激震　random shock form of time series
时间序列分解法/時間數列分解　time-series decomposition
时间序列分析/時間序列分析,時間數列分析　time series analysis
时间序列季节性调整/時間序列季節性調整　seasonal adjustment of time series
时间序列交叉分析/時間數列交叉面分析　time series cross-section analysis
时间序列模型/時間序列模型,時間數列模型　time series model
时间序列数据/時間序列資料　time series data
时间序列数据和横断面数据/時間數列與橫斷面資料　time-series and crosssection data
时间序列图/時間數列圖　time series chart
时间序列相关/時間數列相關　correlation of time series
时间序列研究/時間序列研究　time series study
时间序列预测/時間數列預測　time series prediction
时间序列预测模型/時序預測模型　time series forecasting model
时间序列阵/時間序列陣　time-ordered matrix
时间研究/時間研究　time study
时间研究观测表/時間研究觀測表　time study observation sheet
时间依赖性/依時相依性　time dependence
时间因子/時間因子　time factor
时间用语/時間用語　time term
时间优惠率/時間偏好率　rate of time preference
时间折现系数/時間折現係數　time-discount coefficient
时间转换/時間平移　translation of time
时间组合法/時間組合法　time combination method
时界/時界　time fence
时距曲线/時距曲線　time-distance curve
时空伸延/時空伸延　time-space distanciation
时空压缩/時空壓縮　time-space compression
时期分类法/時期分類法　period classification
时齐过程/時齊過程　temporally homogeneous process
时事版/時事版　current event version
时效/時效　prescription
时效性/時效性　timeliness
时序案卷/時序案卷　chronological file
时序馆藏目录/時序館藏目錄　chronological inventory, chronological list
时序图/時序圖,順序圖　time chart, chronological chart, sequence diagram
时域/時間區域　time domain
时域估计/時間領域估計式　time domain estimation

时政期刊/時政期刊　political journal
时滞/時間落差　time lag
识别/風險特徵描述，識別，鑒定　characterization, identification
识别标题/識別標題　identification caption
识别不足/識別不足，不足認定　under-identification, underidentification
识别的阶条件/階數認定條件式　order condition for identification
识别的秩条件/認定的秩條件　rank condition for identification
识别题名/識別題名　key-title
识别性/識別性　distinctiveness
识字调查/識字調查　literacy survey
识字率/識字率　literacy rate
识字图书/識字圖書　alphabet book
实地/實地　field, on-site
实地调查/實地訪查　field survey
实地观察/實地觀察　field observation
实地盘存制/實地盤存制，實地盤點制　periodic inventory system
实际贬值/實質貶值　real depreciation
实际产品/實質產品　actual product
实际成本法/實際成本法　actual cost method
实际成本贸易条件/實際成本貿易條件　real cost term of trade
实际尺寸/實際大小　actual size
实际对外贸易量/實際對外貿易量　physical volume of foreign trade
实际费用/實際成本　actual cost, AC, real cost
实际负债/實際負債　real liability
实际个人收入/實際個人收入　real personal income
实际工资/實際工資，實質工資　actual wage, real wage
实际工资指数/實質工資指數　real wage index, indices of real wages
实际购买力/實際購買力　real purchasing power
实际国际汇兑比率/實際國際匯兌比率　real ratio of international exchange
实际回报率/實質報酬率　real rate of return
实际汇兑平价/實際匯兌平價　real par of exchange
实际汇率/實際匯率　real rate, effective exchange rate, actual rate of exchange
实际货币/實際貨幣　real money
实际价格/［交易］實際價格，實現價格　actual price, realized price, true price
实际交货/實際交貨　actual delivery
实际交易/實際交易　real transaction

实际交易价格/實際交易價格　price of actual transaction
实际金融资产/實際金融資產　real financial asset
实际开价/實際報價，實盤　actual quotation
实际利率/實際利率，實質利率　actual interest rate, effective interest rate, real interest rate
实际利率平价条件/實質利率平價條件　real interest parity condition
实际利润/實際利潤　actual profit
实际利息/實際利息　real interest, true interest
实际利用/實際利用　practical use
实际履行/實際履行　actual performance
实际年利率/實際年利率，有效年利率　effective annual interest rate
实际人口/现在人口　effective population, population de facto
实际商业周期/實際商業循環　real business cycle
实际升值/實質升值　real appreciation
实际时间/實際時間　actual time, observed time
实际收入/實際收入，實質所得　real income
实际收益/實際收益　effective yield, real earning
实际数/實際數　actual number
实际税率/實際稅率　effective tax rate
实际投资/實際投資　physical investment, real investment, true investment
实际销售额/實際銷售額　effective sale
实际信贷成本/實際信貸成本　true cost of credit
实际修理时间/實際修理時間　passive repair time
实际余额效应/實質餘額效果　real balance effect
实际增长率/實際成長率　real growth rate
实际支出/實際支出　real expenditure
实际支付条款/實際支付條款　effective payment clause
实际值/實際值　actual value
实际资本收益率/實際資本收益　yield of real capital
实价/實價，最終價格　net price, firm price
实践场/實踐場　exercising Ba
实践合同/實踐合同　real contract
实践理论/實踐理論　practice theory
实践逻辑/實作邏輯　logic of practice
实践社群/演練小組，實務社群　community of practice, CoP
实践智力/實用智力　practical intelligence
实缴资本/實收資本　paid-in capital
实例查询/實例查詢　query by example, QBE
实录/實錄　Shilu, memoir
实盘交易/最終成交價　firm bargain
实平均/真平均數　true mean

实施成本/執行成本　enforcement cost
实施过程/實施過程　executing process
实施阶段/實施階段　execution phase
实施时滞/行政時差　administration lag
实时到达/暫態到貨　instantaneous arrival
实时顾客化定制生产/即時顧客化訂製生產　instant customerization
实时检索系统/即時檢索系統　real time retrieval system
实时奖金/即時獎金　spot bonus
实时流媒体协议/即時流媒體協議　real-time streaming protocol, RTSP
实时模拟/即時模擬　real-time simulation
实时性/即時性　immediacy
实收资本/實收資本,投入股本　paid-up capital, paid-in capital
实体/實體　entity
实体材料隔热屋顶/實體材料隔熱屋頂　entity material insulating roof
实体档案/實體檔案　archival entity
实体动画/實體動畫　pixilation
实体法/實體法　substative law
实体符号/實體符號　entity symbol
实体关系模型/實體關係模型　entity-relationship model
实体馆藏/實體館藏　physical collection
实体经济/實質經濟　real economy, substantive economy
实体书店/實體書店　physical bookstore
实体系统/實體系統　physical system
实物补贴/實物補助　in-kind transfer
实物分类法/實物分類法　real object classification
实物福利/實物福利,非現金收益　benefit in kind
实物价格/現貨價格　physical price
实物库存/實地盤點,實地盤存　physical inventory
实物期权/實物期權　real option, managerial option
实物情报/實物情報　information in kind
实物收入/實物所得,非貨幣所得　income in kind
实物投入/實物投入　input in kind
实物投资/實物投資　investment in kind
实物信贷/實物信貸　loan on real credit
实物信息[源]/物質資訊源　physical information source
实物型投入产出模型/實物型投入產出模型　physical input-output model
实物证据/實物證據　object evidence
实物支付/實物支付　payment in kind
实物资本/實物資本　physical capital, real capital
实物资产/實物資產,有形資產　asset in kind, physical asset, real asset
实习/實習　internship
实习馆员/實習館員　library intern, resident librarian
实习生/實習生　apprentice
实现/實現,具體化　realization
实现价差/實現價差　realized spread
实现价格/實現價格,實際價格　realized price
实现模型/可兌現模型　realizable model
实销实结/實銷實結　clearance according real selling
实行犯/實行犯　executor of crime
实行终了的未遂/實行終了的未遂　criminal behavior finished without a result
实行终了中止/實行終了中止　offense suspended after commission
实验/實驗　experiment
实验报告/實驗室報告　laboratory report
实验变量/實驗變數　experimental variable
实验单元/實驗單位　experimental unit
实验法/實驗法　experimentation
实验分析/實驗分析　experiment analysis
实验观察/實驗觀察法　experimental observation
实验环境/實驗環境　experimental environment
实验计划/實驗計劃　planning of experiment
实验经济学/實驗經濟學　experimental economics
实验控制/實境控制　experimental control
实验民族志/實驗民族志　experimental ethnography
实验设计/實驗設計　experimental design
实验社会心理学/實驗社會心理學　experimental social psychology
实验室观察/實驗室觀察　laboratory observation
实验室认可/實驗室認證　laboratory accreditation
实验室手册/實驗室手冊　laboratory manual
实验数据手册/實驗數據手冊　laboratory data manual
实验条件/實驗情境　experimental condition
实验效度/實驗效度　experimental validity
实验心理学/實驗心理學　experimental psychology
实验性治疗/實境處理　experimental treatment
实验研究/實驗研究　experimental study, experimental research
实验研究法/實驗研究法　experimental research method
实验营销研究/實驗行銷研究　experimental marketing research
实验证据/實驗證據　experimental evidence
实验主义/實驗主義　experimentalism

实验主义方法论／實驗主義方法論　experimentalist methodology
实洋／實際價格　discounted price, actual price
实用归纳法／實用歸納法　practical induction
实用新型／實用新型　utility model
实用性／實用性　practical applicability
实用性社会性别需求／實用性社會性別需求　practical gender need
实用艺术作品／實用藝術作品　work of applied art
实在道德／實在道德　real morality
实在规则／實在規則　real rule
实证分析／實證分析　positive analysis
实证经济学／實證經濟學　positive economics
实证图书馆学／實證圖書館學　evidence-based librarianship
实证主义／實證主義, 實證論　positivism
实证主义方法论／實證主義方法論　positivist methodology
实值／實質價值　real value
实值期权／價内發行　in-the-money option
实质独立／實質獨立　independence in essence
实质非理性法／實質非理性法　substantively unrational law
实质非线性／實質非線性　intrinsically nonlinear
实质货币需求／實質貨幣需求　real money demand
实质理性法／實質理性法　substantively rational law
实质利率平价／實質利率平價　real interest rate parity
实质显著／實質的顯著性　substantive significance
实质线性／實質線性　intrinsically linear
实质性／實質　substantive
实质性程序／證實程式, 證實程序　substantive procedure
拾音头／拾音頭　pick-up head
食品安全／食品安全　food security, food safety
食品补贴／食物補貼　food subsidy
食人俗／食人[習]俗　anthropophagi, cannibalism
史蒂文斯-克雷茨分布／Stevens-Craig分布, Stevens-Craig分配　Stevens-Craig distribution
史籍／歷史記載, 歷史檔案　historical record
史料编辑／史料編輯　historical editing
史密森币值调整／史密森幣值調整　Smithsonian currency realignment
史密森汇率幅度／史密森匯率幅度　Smithsonian band
史密森货币制度／史密森貨幣制度　Smithsonian monetary system
史密斯法／史密斯法　Smith Act

史志／史志　history book of China
史志目录／史志目錄　historical bibliography
矢积检索／向量積檢索　vector product retrieval
矢量图／向量圖　vector diagram
矢量图像／向量影像　vector image
使命陈述／使命宣言, 使命聲明　mission statement
使命感营销／使命感行銷　sense-of-mission marketing
使能工具／啟動工具　enable tool
使用／使用　use
使用参照／使用參照　use reference
使用功能／使用功能　use function
使用价值／使用[者]價值　use value, user value
使用可用性／操作可用度　operational availability
使用片／使用片　using chip
使用权转让／使用權轉讓　transfer of right to use
使用寿命／使用壽命, 操作壽命　working life, service life
使用与满足理论／使用與滿足理論　uses-and-gratification theory
使用者／使用者　user
使用者成本／使用者成本　user cost
使用者付费／使用者付費　user charge
始成年期／始成年期, 成人初顯期　emerging adulthood
士大夫／士大夫　the mandarin
士绅／仕紳　gentry
士绅化／仕紳化, 縉紳化　gentrification
氏族／氏族　clan
示范效应／示例效果　demonstration effect
世界储备额／世界儲備金　world reserve
世界观／世界觀　world view
世界货币／世界貨幣　universal money, world money, world currency
世界货币市场／世界貨幣市場　world monetary market
世界货币制度／世界貨幣制度　world monetary system
世界金融市场／世界金融市場　world financial market
世界经济／世界經濟　world economy
世界经济白皮书／世界經濟白皮書　white paper on world economy
世界贸易／世界貿易　world trade
世界贸易量／世界貿易量, 全球貿易金額　volume of world trade, quantum of world trade
世界贸易中心联合会／世界貿易中心聯合會　World Trade Centers Association, WTCA

世界贸易组织/世界貿易組織　World Trade Organization, WTO
世界农产品贸易/世界農產品貿易　world agricultural trade
世界企业/全球化企業　world enterprise
世界清算手段/世界清償能力　world liquidity
世界市场/世界市場　world market
世界输出量/全球出口金額　volume of world export
世界体系/世界體系　world-system
世界体系理论/世界體系理論　world-system theory
世界通行信用证/世界通行信用狀　worldwide letter of credit
世界图书与著作权日/世界書香日　World Book and Copyright Day, World Reading Day
世界卫生组织/世界衛生組織　World Health Organization
世界银行/世界銀行,國際復暨開發銀行　International Bank of Reconstruction and Development, IBRD, World Bank
世界银行集团/世界銀行集團　World Bank Group
世界债券市场/世界債券市場　world bond market
世界知识产权组织/世界智慧財產權組織　World Intellectual Property Organization, WIPO
世界知识产权组织表演与录音制品条约/世界智慧財產權組織表演及錄音物條約　WIPO Performances and Phonograms Treaty
世界知识产权组织仲裁与调解中心/世界智慧財產權組織仲裁與調解中心　Arbitration and Mediation Centre of WIPO
世界知识产权组织著作权条约/世界智慧財產權組織著作權條約　World Intellectual Property Organization Copyright Treaty
世俗化/世俗化　secularization
世俗化命题/世俗化命題　secularization thesis
世系/族譜,系譜　genealogy, descent group
市场/市場　market
市场壁垒/市場障礙　market barrier
市场波动/市場波動　market fluctuation
市场博弈/市場賽局　market game
市场补缺者/市場利基者　market nicher
市场补缺者战略/市場利基者策略　market nicher strategy
市场操作/市場經營　market operation
市场测试/行銷測試,試銷　test marketing
市场超额需求/市場超額需求　market excess demand
市场出清/市場出清,市場結算　clearing market, market clearing
市场创新/市場創新　market innovation
市场刺激/市場刺激　market incentive
市场导向公司/市場導向公司　market-centered company
市场导向型企业/市場導向廠商　market-oriented firm
市场导向型投资/市場導向型投資　market-oriented investment
市场调查/市場調查,商情調查　market survey
市场定位/市場定位　market positioning
市场防御战/市場防禦戰　defensive warfare
市场分割理论/市場區隔理論　market segmentation theory
市场分析/市場分析　market analysis
市场分析报告/市場分析報告　market analysis report
市场份额/市場份額,市場占有率　market pie, share of market, market share
市场风险/市場風險　market risk
市场供给曲线/市場供給曲線　market supply curve
市场供给物/市場提供物　market offering
市场共性/市場通用性　market commonality
市场规模/市場大小　market size
市场机会分析/市場機會分析　market opportunity analysis, MOA
市场机制/市場機能　market mechanism
市场集中度/市場集中度　market concentration ratio
市场纪律/市場紀律　market discipline
市场绩效/市場績效　market performance
市场价差/市場價差　market difference
市场价差互换/市場間價差交換　intermarket spread swap
市场价格/市場價格　market price
市场间利率价差/市場間利差　intermarket sector spread
市场结构/市場結構　market structure
市场进攻战/市場進攻戰　offensive warfare
市场进入/進入市場　market entry
市场进入阻挠/阻却進入　entry deterrence
市场经济/市場經濟　market economy
市场均衡/市場均衡　market equilibrium
市场开发/市場開發　market development
市场开发战略/市場發展策略　market-development strategy
市场控制/市場控制　market control
市场篮子/一籃子市場,市場籃　market basket
市场累加法/市場累加法　market build-up
市场力量/市場力量　market force, market

strength, market power
市场利率/市場利率　market rate of interest, market interest rate
市场领导者/市場領導者　market leader
市场领导者战略/市場領導者策略　market leader strategy
市场流动性/市場流動性　market liquidity
市场模型/市場模型　market model
市场模型的分类/市場模型分類　classification of market models
市场内利率价差/市場內利差　intramarket sector spread
市场配额/市場配額　market quota
市场撇脂定价/市場吸脂訂價法　market-skimming pricing
市场歧视/市場歧視　market discrimination
市场区位理论/市場區位論　market location theory
市场缺陷论/市場失靈論　market failure view
市场容量/市場胃納　market capacity
市场社会学/市場社會學　sociology of market
市场社会主义/市場社會主義　market socialism
市场深度/市場深度　market depth
市场渗透/市場滲透　market penetration
市场渗透定价/市場滲透訂價法　market penetration pricing
市场渗透率/市場滲透率　market penetration ratio
市场渗透战略/市場滲透策略　market penetration strategy
市场剩余/市場剩餘　market surplus
市场失灵/市場失靈　market failure
市场收益率/市場收益率,市場報酬率　market rate of return, market yield
市场水平分析/市場水準分析　market level analysis
市场税/市場稅　market due
市场索赔/市場索賠　market claim
市场弹性/彈性強度　resiliency
市场体系/市場制度,市場系統　market system
市场调节价/市場調節價　market-regulated price
市场挑战者/市場挑戰者　market challenger
市场挑战者战略/市場挑戰者策略　market challenger strategy
市场贴现率/市場貼現率　market discount rate
市场投资组合/市場資產組合　market portfolio
市场退出/市場退出　market withdrawal
市场微观结构/市場微結構　market microstructure
市场吸引力/市場吸引力　market attractiveness
市场细分/市場細分化　market segmentation
市场协调博弈/市場整合賽局　market coordination game
市场信号分析/市場信號分析　market signal analysis
市场信息/市場資訊　market information
市场银根松动/市場銀根鬆動　easiness of money market
市场营销/行銷　marketing
市场营销对策/行銷策略　marketing game
市场营销观念/行銷概念,行銷觀念　marketing concept
市场营销情报/行銷偵查　marketing intelligence
市场影响成本/市場影響成本　market impact cost
市场有效性/市場效率性　market efficiency
市场与销售预测/銷售額預測　market and sale forecasting
市场预测/市場預測　market forecasting, market forecast
市场增加值/市場增值　market value added, MVA
市场增进论/市場增進論　market-enhancing view
市场增长率/市場增長率　market growth rate
市场占有率/市場占有率,市占率　market share, share-of-market
市场占有率理论/市場占有率理論　market share theory
市场支配地位/市場支配地位,市場優勢地位　market dominant position, market dominant status
市场指数/市場指數　market index
市场中性/中性市場　market neutral
市场转型/市場轉型　market transition
市场转型理论/市場轉型理論　market transition theory
市场转型研究/市場轉型研究　market transition research
市场状态/市場狀態　market situation
市场追随者/市場跟隨者　market follower
市场追随者战略/市場跟隨者策略　market follower strategy
市场准入/市場進入　market access
市场组合/市場資產組合　market portfolio
市价标准/市價基礎　market value basis
市价基础/市價基礎　market value basis
市价收入比率模型/本益比模型　price earnings ratio model
市价委托/市價委託　market order
市价下跌/市價下跌　fall in market price
市净率/市淨率,股價與賬面價值比率　price-to-book ratio
市净率估值法/市淨率估值法　price per book value

市式事试 345

valuation method
市面价值/市價　market value
市民社会/市民社會,公民社會　civil society
市区/都市[化]地區　urban area, urbanized area
市图书馆/市立圖書館　municipal library, city library
市盈率/市盈率,本益比　price-to-earning ratio
市盈率估值法/市盈率估值法　price-earnings ratio valuation method
市政管理/市政管理　municipal management, urban management
市政债券/地方政府公債　municipal bond
B-B式胶印/B-B式膠印　blanket-to-blanket offset
Y式信息交流网络/Y式資訊交流網路　network of Y-mode communication
事故/事故　accident
事故倾向/事故傾向　accident proneness
事故树分析法/事故樹分析法　accident tree analysis
事故统计/事故統計　accident statistics
事故预防/事故預防　accident prevention
事后/事後　post-hoc
事后复查/事後調查　post-enumeration survey
事后投资/事後投資　ex post investment
事后整群抽样/事後叢聚抽樣　post cluster sampling
事后诸葛偏差/事後之見的偏誤　hindsight bias
事件/事件　event, incident
事件空间/事件空間　event space
事件列表/事件列表　event listing
事件流网络/事件流網路　event flow network
事件史/事件史　history of the event
事件史分析/事件史分析　event history analysis
事件研究/事件研究[法]　event study
事件营销/事件行銷　event marketing
事件状态网络/事件狀態網路　event-state network
事前政策分析/事前政策分析　ex-ante policy analysis, prospective policy analysis
事实/事實　fact
事实表/事實表　fact table
事实承认/事實承認　de facto recognition
事实婚姻/事實婚姻　de facto marriage
事实检索/事實檢索　fact retrieval
事实检索系统/事實檢索系統　fact retieval system
事实认识错误/事實認識錯誤　factual mistake
事实行为/事實行為　factual behavior
事实[型]数据库/事實資料庫　factual database
事实性/事實性　facticity
事实知识/技術知識　know-what
事务/交易　transaction

事务处理系统/交易處理系統　transaction processing system, TPS
事务分析/交易分析,異動分析　transaction analysis
事务型领导者/交易型領導者　transactional leader
事物分类体系/事物分類體系　classification system of things
事业编制/事業編製　business establishment
事业单位/事業單位　public service unit, state-owned public service organization
事业单位法人/事業單位法人　public institution as legal person
事业委员会/公用事業管理委員會　utility commission
事由/事由　pertinence
事由卷/個案檔,專案檔　case paper, case file
试产订单/試產訂單　pilot order
试错法/嘗試錯誤　trial-and-error
试调查/試[探調]查　pilot survey
试法/試誤法　trial and error method
试婚/試婚　trial marriage
试刊/試刊　trial issue
试片/預覽　preview
试生产/先導試驗　trial production
试算平衡/試算表　trial balance
试探检索法/試探檢索法　exploratory search
试位法/試位法　regula falsi method
试销期/試銷期　trial sale period
试行本/試行本　trial text
试验/試驗　test, experiment
试验发展/試驗發展　experiment and development
试验方法/試驗法,實驗方法　test method, experimental method
试验工厂/試驗工廠,先導工廠　pilot plant
试验规范/試驗規格　test specification
试验设计模型/實驗設計模型　experimental design model
试验数据/試驗數據,實驗資料　experimental data
试验条件的齐性/實驗條件的均齊性　homogeneity of experimental condition
试验误差/實驗誤差　experimental error
试验小组/試驗小組　test panel
试验性提问/試驗性提問　test question
试验因子/實驗因子　experimental factor
试验证据/試驗證據　trial evidence
试验中技术/試驗中技術　technology in test
试用标准/試用標準　tentative standard
试用控制限/試驗管制界限　trial control limit
试用劳动制度/勞動試用制　probationary labor

system
试用率/試用率　trial rate
试用期/試用期　probationary period
视窗/視窗　window
视角/視角　field of view
视觉资料/視覺材料　visual material
视频/視訊　video
视频编辑/視訊編輯　video editing
视频采集/視訊擷取　video capture
视频采集卡/視訊擷取卡　video capture card
视频处理/數位視訊處理　video processing
视频点播/隨選視訊　video on demand, VOD
视频多用途数字光盘/視頻多用途數位光碟　digital versatile disc-video
视频服务器/視訊伺服器　video server
视频广告/視頻廣告,影音廣告　video advertisement, video advertising
视频技术/視頻技術　video technology
视频剪辑软件/視訊短片軟體　video editing software
视频剪辑师/視訊短片師　video editor
视频流/視訊串流　video streaming
视频码流/碼化視訊位元流　video bitstream
视频设计师/視頻設計師　motion designer
视频师/視頻師　video division
视频输出/視訊輸出級,信號輸出級　video output
视频网站/視頻網站　video website
视频文件/視頻檔案　video record
视频制作师/視頻製作者　video producer
视听传播/視聽傳播　audiovisual communication
视听教学/視聽教學　audiovisual teaching
视听设备/視聽器材　audiovisual equipment
视听语言/視聽語言　audiovisual language
视听资料/視聽資料　audiovisual material
视听资料目录/視聽資料目錄　list of audiovisual materials
视听作品国际登记条约/視聽作品國際登記條約　Treaty on the International Registration of Audiovisual Works
视障用户/視障使用者　visually disabled user, visually impaired user
适当的自私/適當的自私　proper selfishness
适度标引/適度標引　moderate indexing
适度服务/適當服務　adequate service
适度偏态/溫和偏度　moderate skewness
适度人口/最適人口　optimum population, optimum population size
适航/適航　seaworthiness
适合性原则/適合性原則　principle of suitability

适销性/適銷性　marketability
适销证券/適銷證券　marketable security
适应/適應　adaptation
适应策略/適應策略　adaptive strategy
适应的M估计[量]/適應的M型估計[量]　adaptive M-estimator
适应的修削均值/適應的截尾平均數　adaptively trimmed mean
适应性/適應性　adaptability
适应性绩效/適應性績效　adaptive performance
适应性决策/可適應性決策　adaptive decision making
适应性营销组合/調適的行銷組合　adapted marketing mix
适应性预期/適應性預期　adaptive expectation
适应值/適應值　adaptive value
适用技术/適當技術　appropriate technology
适用信息/有用訊息　useful information
适用刑法人人平等原则/適用刑法人人平等原則　principle of being equal of all people in criminal law
适用性/適用性　fitness for use
适用性担保/就物之效用爲擔保　warranty of fitness
室编件号/室編件號　file code
收到支付金额/付款收據　receipt of payment
收费服务/論量計酬　fee-for-service
收费凭单/收費單　charge ticket
收费清单/收費清單　list of charge
收费网游/收費網遊　charge online game
收付实现制/現金基礎　cash basis of accounting
收割战略/收割策略　harvest strategy
收购/購并　acquisition
收购-出售协议/收購-出售協議　buy-sell agreement
收购价/收購價　purchase price
收购收购者/收購收購者　pac-man
收购溢价/收購溢價　acquisition premium
收回/收回　withdraw from sale
收回权/收回權　right of retraction
收货点/收貨點　receiving point
收货检验/進料檢驗　material receipt inspection
收货区/收貨區,接收場地　receiving space, receiving area
收货人指示提单/收貨人指示提單　consignee's order bill of lading
收货通知单/收貨單　receiving advice document, mate's receipt
收集/收集　collect
收紧银根/銀根緊俏　tight money
收款回执/簽收　acknowledgement of receipt

收款凭证/收款憑證,收入傳票　receipt voucher, receiving voucher
收敛/收斂　convergence
收敛[区]域/收斂域　region of convergence
收敛速度/收斂速度,收斂率　convergence rate, speed of convergence
收敛系数/收斂係數　coefficient of convergence
收敛原则/收斂原則　convergence principle
收敛准则/收斂準則　convergence criterion
收盘汇率/收盤匯率　closing rate
收盘价/收盤價格　closing price
收入/收入,收益,歲入　earning, income, revenue
收入保障法/所得安全法　income security act
收入补偿的需求曲线/收入補償的需求曲線　income-compensated demand curve
收入不均/薪資不均,所得不均[度]　earning inequality
收入不平等/所得不均　income inequality
收入费用观/收入費用觀　revenue-expense view
收入分布/所得分布　income distribution
收入分配/所得分配　income distribution
收入分配差距/所得差距　income gap
收入分配理论/所得分配[理]論,收入分配論　income distribution theory, theory of income distribution
收入货币流通速度/貨幣的所得流通速度　income velocity of money
收入均衡指数/所得對等指數　income parity index
收入模型/收入模型　revenue model
收入市场份额/市場收入份額　revenue market share
收入受益人/收益受益人　income beneficiary
收入税/收入稅　revenue tax
收入弹性/所得彈性　income elasticity
收入替代方案/所得替代方案　income replacement program
收入为本的社会政策/收入爲本的社會政策　means-tested social policy
收入维持/所得支撐　income maintenance
收入细分/收入細分　income segmentation
收入消费曲线/所得消費曲線,消費-收入比　income consumption curve
收入效应/所得效果　income effect
收入再分配/所得重分配　income redistribution, redistribution of income
收入账户/現金收入賬户　account of receipt
收入转移/所得移轉　income transfer, transfer of income
收视率/觀眾市占率　audience share rate
收缩估计/縮小估計式　shrinkage estimator
收缩业务/組織縮編,裁員　downsizing
收缩战略/緊縮策略　retrenchment strategy
收尾过程/關閉過程　closing process
收尾阶段/收尾階段　follow-up phase
收文/收文　inward document, incoming correspondence, in-letter
收文处理/收文處理　process of received file
收文登记/收文登記　register of received file
收文审核/收文審核　examine and verify of received file
收养制度/收養制度　adoption system
收益/收益,利得,報酬　gain, yield, return
收益递减/報酬遞減　diminishing return
收益递减规律/報酬遞減法則　law of diminishing return
收益法/收入法　income method
收益分享/收益分享[計劃]　gainsharing
收益分享计划/利潤共用制,收益分享制　gain-sharing plan, revenue sharing plan
收益共享契约/收入分成合同　revenue sharing contract
收益管理/進項管理　revenue management, yield management
收益函数/獲益函數　gain function
收益及保留盈余表/收益及保留盈餘表　statement of income and retained earning
收益留存率/盈餘保留率　earning retention ratio
收益率/收益率　earning rate
收益率分析/投資報酬率分析　rate-of-return analysis
收益率规制/投資報酬率管制法　rate-of-return regulation
收益率模型/殖利率模型　yield ratio model
收益能力/收益能力　earning capacity
收益曲线/收益曲線　yield curve
收益曲线追踪/駕馭殖利率曲線　riding the yield curve
收益申报/公布收益　declaration of income
收益性支出/收益支出　revenue expenditure
收支对照表/收支對照表　statement of revenue and expenditure, statement of income and expenditure
收支两条线[管理]/收支兩條線[管理]　separating management of revenue and expenditure, separated management of income and expense
收支顺差/國際收支順差　active balance of payment
手本/手本　script
手册/手冊　handbook, manual, enchiridion

手持终端/手持終端　handheld terminal, HHT
手风琴式对折法/手風琴式對折法　accordion type folding method
手稿本/手稿本　author's handwriting manuscript
手稿部/手稿部　manuscript department
手稿管理员/手稿管理員　manuscriptcurator
手稿汇集/手稿匯集　manuscript collection
手稿寄存/手稿寄存　manuscript depositing
手稿库/手稿庫　manuscript repository
手稿全宗/手稿全宗　manuscript group
手稿组合/手稿全宗, 手稿檔　manuscript combination
手工雕刻凹版/手工雕刻凹版　hand engraving intaglio plate
手工加膜/手工加膜　hand lamination
手工检索/人工檢索　manual retrieval
手工检索系统/手工檢索系統　manual retrieval system
手工生产/手工生產　craft production
手工叙词标引法/調處索引法, 操縱索引, 後组式索引　manipulative indexing
手工业制度/手工業制度　handicraft system
手工纸/手工紙　handmade paper
手机/手機, 行動電話　cell phone, cellular telephone, mobile phone
手机办公/手機辦公　mobile office
手机报/手機報　mobile newspaper
手机报刊/手機報刊　mobile newspaper and periodical
手机博客/手機博客　m-blog
手机操作系统/手機作業系統　mobile phone operating system
手机出版/手機出版　m-publishing
手机出版服务/手機出版服務　m-service
手机出版物/手機出版物　m-publication
手机电视/移動式電視　mobile TV
手机动漫/手機動漫　m-anime
手机二维码技术/手機二維碼技術　mobile two-dimensional code technology
手机广播/手機廣播　m-broadcast
手机广告/手機廣告　mobile advertisement
手机媒体/手機媒體　m-media
手机上网/手機上網　internet access on mobile phone
手机视频/手機視頻, 手機視訊, 手機影像　cell phone video
手机书/手機書　m-book
手机图书馆/手機圖書館　mobile phone library
手机图书行销/手機圖書行銷　mobile book marketing
手机网页广告/手機網頁廣告　mobile web advertisement
手机网游/手機網遊　m-online game
手机文学/手機文學　m-literature
手机下载/手機下載　mobile download
手机小说/手機小說　m-novel
手机银行/行動銀行　mobile banking
手机营销/手機行銷　m-marketing
手机游戏/手機遊戲　m-game
手机阅读/手機閱讀　m-reading
手机阅读模式/手機閱讀模式　mobile reading mode
手机杂志/手機雜誌　m-magazine
手机证券/手機證券　m-bond
手机支付/手機支付　mobile payment
手机终端/行動通訊終端機　mobile terminal
手校本/手校本, 手批本　marginalia and proofread edition
手控时间/手控時間　manual time
手控元素/手控元素　manual element
手批本/手批本, 手校本　marginalia and proofread edition
手实/手實　Shou Shi
手书/手書　holograph, handwriting
守法/守法　abide by law
守时性/時效性　timeliness
首版时间/首版時間　first edition date
首播/[電視]首播, [電影]首輪　first run
首播节目/首播節目, 新播節目　first-run show
首创精神/首創精神　initiative
首次订阅/首次訂閱　new business
首次返回时间/首次返回時間　first return time
首次公开发行/首次公開發行, 初次公開募集　initial public offering, IPO
首次公开发行溢价/首次公開發行溢價, 初次公開募集溢價　initial public offering premium
首次公开募股/初次公開發行　initial public offering, IPO
首次通过时间/首次通過時間　first passage time, first entrance time
首都/首都　capital
首发式/首發式　first publication ceremony
首脑机关/領導機關　leading organ
首属群体/初級團體　primary group
首席创新官/首席創新官　chief innovation officer
首席技术官/技術長　chief technology officer, CTO
首席社论员/總主筆　chief editorial writer

首席知识官/知識長　chief knowledge officer, CKO
首席执行官/執行長　chief executive officer, CEO
首要分子/首要分子　ringleader
寿命/壽命　lifetime
寿命表/生命表　life table
寿命分布/壽命分布　life distribution
寿命试验/壽命試驗　life test, life testing
受艾滋病影响儿童/受艾滋病影響兒童　AIDS-affected children
受保护的产业/受保護的產業　protected industry
受保护贸易/受保護貿易　sheltered trade
受偿意愿/接受意願,願意接受金額　willingness to accept
受访者/受訪者　interviewee
受供养人口年龄比率/年齡撫養比率　age dependency
受雇人/受雇人　employee
受贿罪/受賄罪　crime of accepting bribe
受惠国/受惠國　beneficiary country, preference receiving country
受教育机会/受教育機會　opportunity of education
受控变量/受控變數　controlled variable
受控变异性/受控變異性　controlled variability
受控标引/受控標引　controlled indexing
受控词/受控詞　controlled term, controlled vocabulary
受控词表/受控詞彙　controlled vocabulary
受控访问/受控存取　controlled access
受控过程/受控製程　controlled process
受控检索点/受控檢索點,受控存取點　controlled access point
受控实验/受控實驗　controlled experiment
受控语言/受控語言,受控詞彙　controlled language, controlled vocabulary
受控状态/管制狀態　in control state
受控状态下/管制狀態下　under control
受领迟延/受領遲延　delay in receipt
受留置权保障的债权/受留置權保障的債權　claim protected by lien
受人口流动影响的儿童/受人口流動影響的兒童　migration-affected children
受审核方/受稽核方　auditee
受托储蓄银行/信託儲蓄銀行　trustee saving bank
受托代销商品/代銷品　goods-in on consignment
受托管理人证券/信託管理人證券　trustee security
受托人/受託[管理]人,被信託者　trustee
受托人投资/受託人投資　trustee investment
受托人债券/受託人債券　trustee bond

受委付人/受領廢棄財產者　abandonee
受委托人/受委託人　devolved party
受限变量/受限變數　limited variable
受限工作/受限工作　restricted work
受限因变量/受限應變數　limited dependent variable
受限因变量模型/受限應變數模型　limited dependent variable model
受限制的投资公司/受限制的投資公司　regulated investment company
受限制浮动/不純淨的浮動　dirty floating
受限最小平方法/受限最小平方法　restricted least square
受信买方/受信買方,開狀申請人　accredited buyer
受信投资人/有資信的投資者　accredited investor
受益原则/受益[課稅]原則　benefit principle
受众/受眾,閱聽人　audience
受众参与/閱聽人參與　audience engagement
受众分层/受眾分層,閱聽眾區隔,閱聽人分眾化　audience fragmentation, audience segmentation
受众极化/閱聽人兩極化　audience polarization
受众接受/閱聽人接收　audience reception
受众接受分析/閱聽人接收分析　audience reception analysis
受众结构/閱聽眾組成　audience composition
受众流动理论/閱聽眾流動理論　audience flow theory
受众目标/閱聽眾目標　audience objective
受众商品/閱聽眾商品　audience commodity
受众态度/閱聽眾態度　audience attitude
受众细分/閱聽眾零碎化,閱聽人分眾化,閱聽人分層化　audience fragmentation
受众效果/閱聽人效果　audience effect
受众研究/受眾研究,閱聽人研究　audience study, audience research
受众占有率/觀眾市占率　audience share rate
狩猎/狩獵　hunting
狩猎-采集社会/狩獵採集社會　hunting and gathering society
狩猎采集文化/狩獵採集文化　culture of gatherer-hunter
授权/授權,賦權　delegation of authority, empowerment
授权背书/授權背書,任意背書　facultative endorsement
授权分保/授權分保　facultative insurance
授权付款/授權付款　authority to pay
授权付款通知书/授權付款通知書　advice of authority to pay

授权股份/核定股本　authorized stock
授权申请书/授權申請書　application for delegation of authority
授权书/授權書　letter of authority
授权投资/授權投資　authorized investment
授权行为/授權行爲　act of authorization
授权用户/經授權的使用者　authorized user
授权资本制/授權資本制　authorized capital system
授信/給予信貸，授予信貸　grant of credit
授益处理/授益處理　administrative decision awarding interest
售出者[保值]套购/賣方避險　seller's hedging
售后租回/售後租回　sale and leaseback, sale-leaseback
售后租回合约/售後租回合約　sell and leaseback agreement
售汇/售匯　exchange surrendering
售缺/售缺　sellout
瘦狗业务/瘦狗業務　dog business
书报摊/書報攤　book and newspaper stand
书背/書背　book back
书本上的法/書本上的法　written law
书本式活页目录/書本書活頁目錄　sheaf catalog
书本式检索工具/書本式檢索工具　book type retrieval tool, book retrieval device
书本式目录/書本式目錄　book catalog
书本式著录格式/書目描述格式　book description format
书标/標簽　label
书车/圖書載重車　book truck, book cart
书橱/書櫃　bookcase
书次号/書號　book number
书袋卡/書後卡　book card
书单/書單　booklist
书挡/書夾　bookend
书店/書店　bookshop, bookstore
书耳/書耳　book ear
书稿档案/書稿檔案　manuscript archive
书格高度/書格高度　height between two panels
书后注/書後注　note after the text
书脊/書脊　spine
书脊槽/書鏈　joint
书脊题名/書脊題名　spine title
书记/書記　clerk
书记官/書記官　chief secretary
书架/書架　bookstack, bookshelve
书架标签/書架標簽　shelf guide
书架标签插座/書架標簽托架　shelf label holder

书架侧护板/書架側護板　stack end panel
书架方便区/書架方便區　convenience zone
书架容量/書庫容量　stack capacity
书肩/書肩　book shoulder
书脚/書尾　book tail
书卡袋/書後袋　book pocket
书刊交换协议/圖書交換協議　book exchange agreement
书刊流通记录单/書刊流通程序單　book routing slip
书刊破损检查/書刊破損檢查　wear and damage inspection of book
书壳/書殼　book case
书壳翘曲/書殼翹曲　book-case warping
书口/書口　centerfold of a leaf
书库/書庫　book stack
书库管理/書庫管理　stack maintenance
书库空间/書庫空間　shelving space
书吏/書吏　Shuli
书眉/頂端邊際　top margin
书面订购/書面訂單　written order
书面合同/書面合約，正式合約　letter contract, written contract
书面契约/書面協議　written agreement
书面信托/書面委託　express trust
书面许可证/書面許可證　written permission
书名页/書名頁　title page, fly page
书目/書目　bibliography, booklist, catalog
书目编纂者/書目編纂者　bibliographer
书目单元/書目單元　bibliographical unit
书目格式/書目格式　bibliographic format
书目工作管理/書目工作管理　management of bibliographical service
书目记录/書目紀錄　bibliographic record
书目记录的功能需求/書目紀錄功能需求　functional requirements for bibliographic records, FRBR
书目检索/書目檢索　bibliographical retrieval
书目检索工具/目錄工具書　bibliographic tool
书目检索系统/文獻目錄檢索系統　bibliographic retrieval system
书目控制/書目控制　bibliographic control
书目控制论/書目性控制理論　bibliographical control theory
书目评论/書目評論　bibliographic essay
书目数据/書目數據　bibliographic data
书目数据库/書目資料庫，文獻查目資料庫　bibliographical database, bibliography database
书目索引/書目索引　bibliographical index

书目题解／書目題解　bibliography
书目信息／書目信息　bibliographic information
书目之书目／書目之書目　bibliography of bibliographies
书目中心／書目中心　bibliographic center
书目著录／著錄　description
书帕本／書帕本　gift edition
书棚本／書棚本　bookstore edition
书评／書評　book review, book report, book appraisal
书签／書簽　title label on the cover of an ancient chinese book, bookmark
书签带／書簽帶　bookmark tape
书签丝带／書簽絲帶　bookmark ribbon
书商服务／供書商服務　vendor service, supplier service
书市／書市　book bazaar, book fair
书帖／書帖　signature
书头／書頭　bookhead
书托／書托　reading easel
书芯／書芯　bookblock
书芯断裂／書芯斷裂　bookblock breakaway
书信备查簿／書信備查簿　letter book
书信协议／書信協議　letter agreement
书型排架法／書型排架法　grouping by size
书讯／書訊　book trade newsletter
书业电子商务／書業電子商務　e-commerce
书业通讯／書業通訊　book trade newsletter, book trade journal
书衣／書衣　covering case
书院本／書院本　academy edition
书札／書札　letters
书札集／書札集　book of letters
书佐／書佐　Shuzuo
枢密院／樞密院　Privy Council
枢轴量／基準量　pivotal quantity
舒适性／舒適性　comfort
舒斯特周期图／Schuster 週期圖　Schuster's periodogram
疏离指标／疏離指標，餘相關指標　indicators of alienation
疏水性／疏水的　hydrophobic
输出额／出口金額　amount of export
输出过程／輸出過程　output process
输出基础理论／出口基礎理論　export base theory
输出节点／輸出節點　output node
输出倾销／輸出傾銷　export dumping
输出设计／輸出設計　output design

输出为先的对开信用证／輸出爲先的對開信用狀　back-to-back credit export first
输墨装置／油墨單位　inking unit
输入额／進口金額　amount of import
输入过程／輸入過程，輸入處理　input process
输入节点／輸入節點　input node
输入设计／輸入設計　input design
输入-输出／輸入-輸出　input-output
输入-输出控制／輸入輸出控制，入出管制　input-output control
输入-输出图／輸入-輸出圖　input-output chart
输入为先的对开信用证／輸入爲先的對開信用狀　back-to-back credit import first
输入型通货膨胀／進口型通貨膨脹　imported inflation
输纸装置／輸紙裝置　infeed unit
赎回基金／償贖基金　redemption fund
赎回价格／贖回價格　satisfaction price
赎回条款／贖回條款，買回條款　call provision
赎刑／贖刑　redemption penalty
熟练工人／技術［勞］工　skilled labor, skilled worker
熟练劳动说／熟練勞動說　labor skill theory of trade
熟练性无能／專精的無能　skilled incompetence
属／屬　broader term
属地法／屬地法　territorial law
属地管辖权／屬地管轄權　territorial jurisdiction
属地原则／屬地原則　territoriality principle
属概念／屬概念　genus, generic concept
属类／屬類　sub-series
属类著录／類屬描述　generic description
属人法／屬人法　lex personalis
属人管辖权／屬人管轄權　personal jurisdiction
属人主义／屬人主義　system of personal law
属性／屬性　attribute
属性测量／屬性量測值　attribute measurement
属性关联／屬性相聯　association of attribute
属性设计变量／屬性設計變數　qualitative design variable
属性数据／屬性資料　attribute data
属性数据分析／屬性資料分析，計數資料分析　analysis of attribute data
属性数据模型／屬性資料模式　attribute data model
属性特征／屬性特徵　qualitative characteristic
属性统计／屬性統計　statistics of attribute, qualitative statistics, attribute statistics
属性相关／屬性相關　correlation of attributes
属性相互偏好独立／屬性相互偏好獨立　attribute preference independent

属性值/屬性值　attribute value
属种关系/語源關係　generic relationship
署名/署名　signature
署名权/署名權　right of authorship
署名文章/署名文章　byline
蜀本/蜀本　Sichuan edition
术语标准/術語標準　terminology standard
术语服务/術語服務　terminology service
APQT束/APQT束　APQT bundle
束联系数/束聯係數　coefficient of colligation
树形图/樹形圖　tree diagram
树枝状图/樹枝形結構聯繫圖　dendogram
竖挂装/豎掛裝　vertical hanging binding
竖排/垂直格式　vertical format
数据/數據,資料　data
数据安全/資料安全　data security
数据包/分封,封包　packet
数据备份/資料備份　data replica
数据编辑/資料編輯　data edit
数据标识数据/資料標識資料　data identification data
数据表/資料表　data table
数据采集/數據擷取　data acquisition
数据仓库/資料倉儲　data warehouse, DW
数据仓库系统/資料倉儲系統　data warehousing system
数据操纵/數據操作　data manipulation
数据池/混合資料　pooling data
数据处理/資料處理　data processing
数据传递/資料傳送　data transfer
数据传递速率/資料傳輸率　data transfer rate
数据存储结构/資料儲存結構　data storage structure
数据存储设计/資料儲存設計　data storage design
数据档案馆/資料檔案館　data archive
数据导出区/數據匯出區　data lead-out area
数据导入区/數據導入區　data lead-in area
数据独立性/數據獨立性　data independence
数据段/資料區段　data segment
数据分析/資料分析　data analysis
数据工程/資料工程　data engineering
数据工程再造/資料重建　data reengineering
数据共享/資料共用　data sharing
数据管理/資料管理　data management
数据广播/資料廣播　data broadcasting
数据恢复/資料恢復　data recovery
数据集市/資料超市　data mart
数据检查/資料檢視　data scrutiny
数据简化/數據簡化　reduction of data
数据建模/資料模型化　data modeling
数据结/數據結,數據同分值　ties in data
数据结构/資料結構　data structure
数据聚类/集群分析　cluster analysis
数据库安全/資料庫安全性　database security
数据库出版/資料庫出版　database publishing
数据库法律保护指令/資料庫法律保護指令　directive on the legal protection of database
数据库管理系统/資料庫管理系統　database management system, DBMS
数据库管理员/資料庫管理者　database administrator, DBA
数据库集成商/資料庫整合者　database integrator
数据库技术/資料庫技術　database technology
数据库检索/資料庫檢索　database search
数据库商/資料庫經銷商　data provider, database vendor
数据库使用权/資料庫使用權　database access right, access right of database
数据库使用统计/使用統計　usage statistics
数据库试用/資料庫試用,資料庫試轉　database trial
数据库系统/資料庫系統　database system, DBS
数据库新闻/資料庫新聞　database journalism
数据库营销/資料庫行銷　database marketing
数据来源/資料來源　source of data
数据列表/數據的表列　tabulation of data
数据流/資料流程　data flow
数据流程图/資料流程圖　data flow diagram, DFD
数据录入/資料登錄　data input
数据模型/資料模型　data model
数据拟合/資料配適　data fitting
数据清洗/資料清理　data cleaning
数据驱动/資料驅使　data-driven
数据生成过程/資料衍生過程　data generating process
数据收集/資料搜集,資料收集　data collection
数据探测法/資料偵伺　data snooping
数据通信/資料通訊　data communication
数据挖掘/資料探勘,資料挖掘　data mining
数据文件/資料檔,資料記錄　data file, data record
数据误差/數據誤差,資料誤差　error in data
数据语义/資料語意學　data semantic
数据预处理/資料預處理　data preprocessing
数据元素/資料單元　data element
数据源/資料源　data source
数据整合/資料整合　data consolidation
数据整理/資料分類,資料縮減　data sorting, data reduction

数据字典/資料字典　data dictionary
数理经济学/數理經濟學　mathematical economics
数理统计学/數理統計學　mathematical statistics
数理学派/數理學派　mathematical school
数量变异法/數量變異法　quantity variation method
数量检验/數量檢驗　inspection of quantity
数量检验证书/數量檢驗證書　inspection certificate of quantity
数量经济学/數量經濟學　quantitative economics
数量竞争/數量競爭　quantity competition
数量能力/數量能力　quantitative ability
数量特性/數量特性, 屬量特性　quantity characteristic, quantitative characteristic
数量限制/數量限制　quantitative restriction
数量验收/數量驗收　quantity acceptance
数量折扣/數量折扣　quantity discount
数量指标/物量指數　quantity index
数量指数/［物］量指數　volume index, quantum index, quantity index number
数列表/數列表　series table
数码激光视盘/數碼影音光碟　compact disc-digital video, VCD
数码印刷/數位印刷　digital printing
数学模拟/數學模擬　mathematical simulation
数学模型/數學模式　mathematical model
数学期望/數學期望　mathematical expectation
数学学派/數學學派　quantitative school, mathematical school
数值检索/資料檢索　data retrieval
数值数据库/數據資料庫　numeric database
数值型数据/數值資料, 數字資料　numeric data
数值预测/數值預測　numerical prediction
数字/數字　figure
数字保存/數位保存　digital preservation
数字保存系统/數位保存系統　digital preservation system
数字报/數位報　digital newspaper
数字报刊/數位報刊　digital press
数字标牌/數位標牌　digital signage
数字博物馆/數位博物館　digital museum
数字彩色胶印机/彩色數位平印機　digital offset color press, DOCP
数字参考咨询/數位參考諮詢　digital reference service
数字成像/影像數位化　digital imaging
数字城市/數位城市　digital city
数字尺度/數字尺度　number scale
数字出版/數位出版　digital publishing
数字出版基地/數位出版基地　digital publishing base
数字出版流程/數位出版流程　digital publishing process
数字出版平台/數位出版平臺　digital publishing platform
数字出版物/數位出版物　digital publication
数字处理技术/數位文書處理技術　digital technology
数字传播/數位傳播　digital communication
数字传输/數位傳輸　digital transmission
数字打样/數位打樣　digital proofing
数字档案/數位檔案　digital archive
数字档案长期保存/數位檔案長期保存　long-term preservation for archive
数字档案馆/數位檔案館　digital archive
数字电视/數位電視　digital television, DTV
数字电影/數位電影　digital film
数字对象/數位物件　digital object
数字对象标识符/數位物件識別符　digital object identifier, DOI
数字多功能磁盘/數位多用途光碟　digital versatile disc, DVD
数字多媒体广播/地面數位多媒體廣播　digital multimedia broadcasting
数字放映机/數位放映機　digital player
数字分销/數位發行　digital distribution
数字复合出版/數位複合出版　digital composite publishing
数字馆藏/數位典藏　digital collection
数字馆藏发展政策/數位典藏政策　digital collection policy
数字合成技术/數位合成技術　digital synthesis technology
数字鸿沟/數位落差　digital divide, digital gap
数字互动媒介/數位互動媒體　digital interactive media
数字化/數位化　digitized, digitization
数字化产品模型/數位化產品模型　digital product model
数字化对象/數位化對象　digitized object
数字化工作流程/數位化工作流程　digital workflow
数字化技术/數字化技術　digitization technology
数字化声音/數位化聲音　digitized sound
数字化图书/數位化圖書　digital book, e-book
数字化图书馆信息服务/數位化圖書館資訊服務　digital library information service platform
数字化文献/數位文獻　digital literature

数字化信息[源]/數位資訊源　digital information source
数字化资料/數位資料　digital data
数字化资源/數位化資源　digital resource
数字激光视盘/數字影音光碟　compact disc-digital video
数字技术/數位技術　digital technology
数字录音/博碼調變,脈衝調變　pulse code modulation
数字贸易/數位貿易　digital trade
数字媒介/數位媒介　digital medium
数字媒体/數位媒體　digital media
数字媒体设计/數位媒體設計　digital media design
数字媒体艺术/數位媒體藝術　digital media art
数字模拟转换/數位類比轉換　digital-analog conversion
数字内容/數位内容　digital content
数字内容产业/數位内容產業　digital content industry
数字内容管理/數位内容管理　digital content management, DCM
数字迁移/數位遷移　digital migration
数字签名/數位簽章　digital signature
数字前端系统/數位前端系統　digital front end system
数字权益/數位著作權　digital rights
数字商品/數字商品　e-commerce commodity
数字社区/數位社群　digital community
数字摄像机/數位攝影機　digital camera
数字摄影/數位照相術　digital photography
数字声音/數位聲音　digital sound
数字时间戳/數字時間戳記　digital time stamp
数字视频/數位視訊　digital video
数字视频编辑/數位視訊編輯　digital video editing
数字视频光盘/數位影音光碟,數位視訊光碟　digital video disc, DVD
数字输出值/數位輸出值　digital output level
数字水印/數位浮水印　digital watermark
数字通信/數位通訊　digital communication
数字图书馆/數位圖書館　digital library
数字图书馆技术/數位圖書館技術　digital library technology
数字图书馆联盟/數位圖書館聯盟　digital library consortia
数字图书馆门户网站/數位化圖書館網站　digital library website
数字图像/數位影像　digital image
数字图像处理/數位影像處理　digital image processing
数字图形处理/數位圖形處理　digital graphic processing
数字网络媒体/數位網路媒體　digital network media
数字文档/數位文件　digital document
数字文件/數位資料　digital record
数字文献/數位文件　digital document
数字现金/電子鈔票　digital cash
数字线性磁带/數位線性磁帶　digital linear tape
数字新闻学/數位新聞學　digital journalism
数字信封/數位包封　digital envelope
数字信息/數位訊息,數位資訊　digital information
数字信息环境/數位資訊環境　digital information environment
数字学术出版/數位學術出版　digital scholarly publishing
数字样张/數位校樣　digital proof
数字遗产/數位遺產　digital heritage
数字音频/數位聲訊　digital audio
数字音频编辑/數位音訊剪接　digital audio editing
数字音频工作站/數位音訊工作站　digital audio workstation
数字音频光盘/光碟-數位聲訊　compact disc-digital audio, CD-DA
数字音频广播/數位音訊廣播　digital audio broadcasting
数字音频设备/數位音訊設備　digital audio device
数字音像/數位聲訊　digital audio
数字音像制品/數位音像製品　digital audio-visual publication
数字音乐/數位音樂　digital music
数字印前技术/數位印前技術　digital prepress technology
数字印前系统/數位印前系統　digital prepress system
数字印刷/數位印刷　digital printing
数字印刷机/數位印刷機　digital printer
数字影像/數位影像　digital image
数字影院系统/數位影院系統　digital theater system, DTS
数字油画/數位油畫　digital painting
数字有声书/數位有聲書　digital talking book
数字摘要/數位摘要　digital digest
数字照相机/數位相機　digital camera
数字证书/數位憑證　digital certificate
数字指纹/數位指紋　digital fingerprinting
数字著作权/數位版權　digital copyright, digital right

数字著作权管理/數位版權管理,數位著作權管理　digital rights management, DRM

数字资产/數位資產　digital asset

数字资产管理/數位資產管理　digital asset management, DAM

数字资产管理系统/數位資產管理系統　digital asset management system, DAMS

数字资源/數位資源　digital resource

数字资源长期保存/數位資源長期保存　long-term preservation of digital resource

数字资源存档/數位資源存檔　digital resource archieving

数字资源导航/數位資源導航　navigation of digital resource

数字资源访问控制/數位資源存取控制　access control of digital resource

数字资源管理政策/數位資源管理政策　digital resource management policy

数字资源建设/數位資源發展　digital resource development

数字资源生命周期/數位資源生命週期　life cycle of digital resource

数字资源许可协议/數位資源授權協議　digital resource license agreement

数字资源整合/數位資源整合　integration of digital resource

数罪并罚/數罪并罰　joinder of punishment for plural crimes

衰变/衰變　decay

衰减/衰減,減弱　attenuation

衰减函数/關係衰減函數　decay function

衰减校正/衰減校正　correction for attenuation

衰减器/衰減器　attenuator

衰退产业/沒落產業　declining industry

衰退期/衰退期　decline stage

双倍赔偿条款/雙倍賠償條款　double indemnity clause

双倍余额递减法/倍數餘額遞減法折舊　double declining balance depreciation method

双边保护条款/雙邊防衛條款　bilateral safeguard clause

双边不对称信息/雙邊訊息不對稱　bilateral asymmetric information

双边冲突规范/雙邊衝突規範　all-sided conflict rules, bilateral conflict rules

双边的/雙邊的　bilateral

双边寡占/雙邊寡占　bilateral oligopoly

双边合伙人/雙邊合作　bilateral partner

双边合同/雙邊合約,雙邊契約　bilateral contract

双边荷式拍卖/雙邊荷式拍賣　double dutch auction

双边价格/雙邊價格　bilateral price

双边检验/兩端檢定　two-sided test

双边交易/雙邊交易　bilateral transaction

双边进口配额/雙邊進口配額　bilateral import quota

双边垄断/雙邊獨占　bilateral monopoly

双边贸易/雙邊貿易　bilateral trade

双边贸易协定/雙邊貿易協定　bilateral trade agreement

双边清算/雙邊清算　bilateral clearing

双边税率/雙邊稅率　bilateral tariff

双边税收协定/雙邊稅收協定　bilateral tax agreement

双边谈判/雙邊談判　bilateral negotiation

双边套利/雙邊套利　bilateral arbitrage

双边条约/雙邊條約　bilateral treaty

双边协定/雙邊協定　bilateral convention

双边协商/雙邊協商　bilateral consultation

双边协调标准/雙邊協調標準　bilateral harmonized standard

双边协议配额/雙邊配額　bilateral quota

双边信贷互惠协定/雙邊互惠協定　bilateral swap agreement

双边援助/雙邊援助　bilateral assistance

双边支付/雙邊支付　bilateral payment

双变量分布/二元分配　bivariate distribution

双仓库存系统/兩堆存貨系統,兩箱存儲系統　two-bin inventory system

双侧规范/雙邊規格　two-sided specification

双侧规范限/雙邊規格界限　double specification limit

双侧检验/雙尾檢定,雙邊檢定　two-sided test, two-tailed test

双侧截尾/雙邊截略　two-sided truncation

双侧指数分布/雙邊指數分布,雙邊指數分配,雙尾指數分配　two-tailed exponential distribution, bilateral exponential distribution

双层可录光盘/雙層可錄光碟　dual-layer recordable disc

双层盘/雙層盤　dual-layer disk

双超几何分布/雙超幾何分布,雙超幾何分配　double hypergeometric distribution

双城市假设/雙城市假設　dual-city hypothesis

双赤字/雙赤字　twin deficits

双重背书/雙重背書　double endorsement

双重标引/雙變址　double indexing

双重标准/雙重標準　double standard

双重泊松分布/雙卜瓦松分布,雙卜瓦松分配 double Poisson distribution
双重测度/雙重測度 dual scaling
双重二分法/雙重二分法 double dichotomy
双重法定汇率制度/雙重法定匯率制度 dual official rate system
双重反致/雙重反致 double renvoi
双重非中心F分布/雙重非中心F分布,雙重非中心F分配 doubly noncentral F distribution
双重分销/雙重配銷 dual distribution
双重负担/雙重負擔 double burden
双重工资标准/雙層薪資計劃 two-tier pay plan
双重关键词索引/雙重關鍵字和上下文索引 double KWIC index
双重关税/雙重關稅 dual duty, double tariff
双重关税税率/雙重關稅稅率 double line tariff
双重管理体制/雙重管理體制 dual management system
双重汇率/雙重匯率,雙元匯率 dual exchange rate, two-tier foreign exchange rate, two-tier exchange rate
双重汇率制/雙重匯率制 dual exchange rate system, two-tier exchange rate system
双重混杂/雙重混同 double confounding
双重或多重国籍/雙重或多重國籍 dual or multiple nationality
双重货币记录/雙重貨幣紀錄 dual currency record
双重价额条款/雙重船舶估值條款 dual valuation clause
双重鉴定/雙重評鑒 dual appraisal
双重截尾正态分布/雙截略常態分布,雙截略常態分配 doubly truncated normal distribution
双重可诉原则/雙重可訴原則 doctrine of double actionability
双重课税/雙重課稅,重複課稅 double taxation
双重课税协议/雙重課稅協定 double taxation agreement
双重税制/雙重稅制 two-tier tax system
双重随机泊松过程/雙隨機卜瓦松過程 doubly stochastic Poisson process
双重外汇市场/雙重外匯市場 dual exchange market, two-tier foreign exchange market
双重运动/雙重運動,雙向運動 double movement
双重自助法/雙靴環法 double bootstrap
双代号网络图/雙代號網路圖 activity-on-arrow network diagram
双对数尺度/雙對數尺度 double logarithmic scale
双对数模型/雙對數的母體回歸模型 log-log model

双对数图/雙對數圖 double logarithmic chart
双二项分布/雙二項分布,雙二項分配 double binomial distribution
双方错误/共同錯誤 mutual mistake
双方代理/雙方代理 bilateral agency
双方行政行为/雙方行政行爲 bilateral administrative action
双峰分布/雙峰分布,雙峰分配 bimodal distribution
双峰曲线/雙峰曲線 bimodal curve
双峰性/雙峰性 bimodality
双伽马函数/雙伽瑪函數 digamma function
双寡头博弈/雙占賽局 duopoly game
双寡头市场/雙占市場 duopoly market
双管式问题/雙管的問題 double-barreled question
双轨教育/雙軌教育 double-track education
双轨贸易/雙軌貿易 two-way trade
双轨银行业务/雙軌銀行業務 dual banking
双轨制/雙[重]軌制 dual-track approach, two-card system, dual-track system
双轨制银行体系/雙軌制銀行體系 dual banking system
"双轨制"运转/"雙軌制"作業 operation of two-tier system, operation of double-track system
双行排架法/雙行排架法 double row frame method
双环学习/雙環學習 double-loop learning
双极量表/二極量表 bipolar scale
双极因子/二極因子 bipolar factor
双记名票据/雙記名票據 two named paper
双矩阵博弈/雙矩陣賽局 bimatrix game
双卡广告牌系统/雙卡看板系統 two-card kanban system, dual-card kanban system
双可逆设计/雙互換設計 double reversal design
双栏本/雙欄本 double column
双联本印刷/左右輪轉 half-sheet work
双列相关/雙數列相關 biserial correlation
双面排架法/雙面排架法 back-to-back shelving
双面书架/雙面書架 double face bookcase, double face bookshelf
双面印刷/雙面印刷 perfecting, perfect printing
双名汇票/雙名匯票 two party draft
双年刊/二年刊 biennial
双频谱/雙頻譜 bispectrum
双频谱分析/雙頻譜分析 bispectral analysis
双曲正割分布/雙曲正割分布,雙曲正割分配 hyperbolic secant distribution
双人沟通/二人間傳播 dyadic communication
双色版/雙色調,雙套色 duotone
双手作业程序图/左右手作業程序圖 right-and-left-

hand chart
双手作业分析/雙手作業分析　right-and-left-hand operation analysis
双数列的/雙數列的　biserial
双数列相关比/雙數列相關比　biserial ratio of correlation
双缩法/雙面平減法　double deflation method
双套制/雙套制　dual-filing system
双调和函数/雙調和函數　biharmonic function
双头垄断/雙占　duopoly
双位法/雙位法　two-site method
双系亲属关系/雙系親屬關係　bilateral kinship
双限制概率模型/雙重限制常態機率模型　two-limit probit model
双限制 Tobit 模型/雙重限制杜彬模型　two-limit Tobit model
双线性/雙線性　bilinearity
双线性方法/雙線性方法　bilinear method
双线性规划问题/雙線性規劃問題　bilinear programming problem
双线性过程/雙線性過程　bilinear process
双线性时间序列/雙線性時間數列　bilinear time series
双向传播/雙向溝通　two-way communication
双向倒转出版物/雙向倒轉出版物　tete-beche publication
双向方差分析/雙向方差分析　two-way ANOVA
双向公开竞价/雙邊拍賣　double auction
双向贸易/雙向貿易　two-way trade
双向拍卖实验/雙拍賣實驗　double auction experiment
双向容差/雙邊允差　bilateral tolerance
双向适应/雙向適應　dual adaptation
双向[性]/雙邊性　bilateral
双向选择/雙向選擇　two-way choice
双项频数表/雙項次數表　double frequency table
双性恋/雙性戀　bisexual
双样本/複式抽樣　double sample
双因素方差分析/二因素變異數分析法,雙因素變異數分析　two-factor analysis of variance, two-way analysis of variance
双因素理论/激勵-保健理論　motivation-hygiene theory
双因素贸易条件/雙因素貿易條件　double factorial terms of trade
双因素贸易条件指数/雙因素貿易條件指數　double factorial terms of trade index
双因子理论/二因子理論　two-factor theory

双因子模型/雙因子模型　bifactor model
双因子实验设计/雙因數實驗設計　two factors experimental design
双语词典/雙語對照字典　bilingual dictionary
双月刊/雙月刊　double monthly, bimonthly
双指数分布/雙指數分布,雙指數分配　double exponential distribution
双周刊/雙週刊　biweekly
水产养殖/養殖漁業　aquaculture
水产养殖统计/水產養殖統計　aquaculture statistics
水处理/水處理　water treatment
水辊/水輥　dampener roller
水基胶/水基膠　water-based adhesive
水解纤维素/水解纖維素　hydrocellulose
水井战略/水井戰略　water well strategy
水利法/水利法　water law
水利社会/水利社會,水力社會　hydraulic society
水墨平衡/水墨平衡　ink-water balance
水能/水力　water power
水平/水準　level
水平多元化/水平多角化　horizontal diversification
水平分工/水平分工　horizontal division of labor
水平分析/水平分析　horizon analysis
水平供给曲线/水平之供給曲線　horizontal supply curve
水平扫描/水平掃描　horizontal scanning
水平市场/水平市場　horizontal market
水平型国际分工/水平型國際分工　horizontal international division of labor
水平营销系统/水平式行銷系統　horizontal marketing system
水平预测/水準預測　level forecasting
水权/水權　water right
水市场/水市場　water market
水土保持法/水土保持法　law on water and soil preservation
水污染/水汙染　water pollution
水污染防治法/水汙染防治法　water pollution prevention and control law
水印标记/浮水印　watermark
水质立法/水質立法　water quality legislation
水质量标准/水質標準　water quality standard
水资源/水資源　water resources
水渍险/水漬險　with particular average, WPA
税盾/稅盾　tax shield
税法/稅法　tax law
税费改革/稅費改革　tax-for-fee reform
税负率/稅負率　tax bearing rate

税负能力/稅負能力　tax bearing capacity
税负转嫁/租税轉嫁　tax shifting
税赋平衡计划/稅賦平衡計劃　tax equalization plan
税后利润/稅後利潤　profit after tax
税基/稅基　tax base
税款滞纳金/稅款滯納金　penalty tax
税率/稅率　tax rate, rate of taxation
税率表/稅率表　schedule of tax
税目/稅目　taxable item
税契/稅契　Shuiqi
税前利润/稅前利潤　pre-tax profit
税前收入/稅前收入　pre-tax income
税前损失/稅前損失　pre-tax loss
税前账面收益/稅前賬面收益　pre-tax accounting income
税收/稅收,租税,賦税　tax, taxation, tax revenue
税收保全/稅收保全　tax revenue preserve
税收的无谓损失/賦税之絕對損失　deadweight loss of tax
税收抵免/稅款抵免,稅款減除,稅額抵減　tax credit
税收法定原则/稅收法定原則　doctrine of statutory taxation
税收返还/稅收返還,退税　tax return, tax rebate
税收负担/租税負擔　tax bearing, tax burden
税收负担转嫁/稅負轉嫁　shift the tax burden
税收管辖权/稅收管轄權　jurisdiction of taxation
税收规避/稅負規避　tax dodge
税收互换/稅收互換　tax swap
税收豁免/租税豁免　tax exclusion
税收减免/租税減免　tax exemption, tax reduction
税收减免证券/租税減免證券　tax exempt security
税收结构/租税結構　tax structure
税收努力/課税努力　tax effort
税收起征点/[税的]起徵點　tax threshold
税收收入/租税收入　tax revenue
税收统计/賦税統計　tax statistics
税收协定/稅收協定,租税協定　tax convention, tax treaty
税收协调/租税調和　tax coordination
税收优惠/稅收優惠,租税優惠　preferential tax treatment, tax preference
税收优先权/稅收優先權　tax priority right
税收征收/徵税　tax collection
税收政策/賦税政策　tax policy
税收支出/税式支出　tax expenditure
税收滞纳金/稅收滯納金　tax surcharge
税收中性/稅收中性,中性税收　neutral taxation, tax neutrality
税收种类/税種　type of tax
税务代理/賦税代理　tax agency
税务档案/稅務檔案　taxation archive
税务登记/稅務登記　tax registration
税务行政原则/稅務行政法則　principle of tax administration
税则目录/稅則目錄,稅則品名　tariff nomenclature
税制/稅制　tax system
税制改革/租税改革　tax reform
税制设计/租税設計　tax design
顺差/順差　favourable variance, active balance, black figure
顺差国家/順差國家　surplus country
顺查法/順查法　search in chronological order
顺排文档/順排文檔　sequential file
顺位/順位　sequence
顺向排程/順向排程,正向排程,前往後排程　forward scheduling
顺序标记制/序數記號　non-hierachical notation, ordinal notation
顺序-层累混合标记制/順序-層累混合標記制　semi-hierachical notation
顺序词典/順序詞典　proper order dictionary
顺序平衡序列/串聯平衡序列　serially balanced sequence
顺序搜索/序列搜尋　sequential search
顺序统计量/順序統計量,次序統計量　order statistic
顺序统计量的渐近正态性/順序統計量的漸近常態性　asymptotic normality of order statistics
顺序统计量的完备性/順序統計量的完備性　completeness of order statistics
顺序统计量分布/順序統計量的分布　distribution of order statistics
顺序移动/序列移動　serial movement
瞬间抽样/瞬間抽樣　snap sampling
瞬时/瞬間　wink
瞬时动作分析/暫態動作分析　instantaneous action analysis
瞬时格兰杰因果关系/暫態格蘭傑因果關係　instantaneous Granger causality
瞬时故障率/瞬時故障率　instantaneous failure rate
瞬时失效率/瞬時故障率　instantaneous failure rate
瞬时死亡率/瞬時死亡率　instantaneous death rate
瞬时响应/暫時反應　transient response
瞬时转移概率/瞬時遞移機率　instantaneous transition probability
瞬态/瞬時狀態　transient state, instantaneous state

说服/說服　persuasion
说服策略/說服策略　persuasion strategy
说服效应/勸服效果　persuasion effect
说服型广告/說服性廣告　persuasive advertising
说服责任/說服責任　burden of persuasion
说明方式/說明方式　description way
说明记录/說明記錄　general explanatory record
说明款目/說明款目　general explanatory entry
说明体广告/描述性廣告　descriptive advertising
硕士学位论文/碩士論文　Master's thesis, MA thesis
司法/司法　administration of justice
司法案卷/法律案卷　legal file
司法部/司法部　department of justice
司法监督/司法監督　judicial supervision
司法矫正/司法矯正　judicial correction
司法解释/司法解釋　judicial interpretation
司法统计/司法統計　judicial statistics
司寇/司寇　Sikou
司隶校尉/司隸校尉　Sili Xiaowei
丝纶簿/絲綸簿　Imperial Utterances
丝网/絲網　screen mesh, silking
丝网厚度/絲網厚度　thickness of mesh
丝网膜版/網板　screen stencil
丝网目数/絲網目數　mesh count
丝网通孔率/絲網通孔率　open mesh area percentage
丝网延伸率/絲網延伸率　relative mesh elongation
丝网张力/絲網張力　mesh tension
私法/私法　private law
私法人/私法人　private legal person
私法自治/私法自治　autonomy of private law
私家藏书目录/私家藏書目錄　bibliomaniac's bibliography
私刻本/私刻本　private edition
私募基金/私募股權基金　private equity fund
私权/私權　private right
私人/私人　private
私人保险/私人保險,個人保險　private insurance
私人边际成本/私人邊際成本　private marginal cost
私人部门/私部門　private sector
私人藏书/私人藏書　private collection
私人成本/私人成本　private cost
私人储蓄/私人儲蓄,個人儲蓄　personal saving, private saving
私人存款/私人存款　private deposit
私人贷款/私人貸款　private loan
私人档案/私人檔案　private archive

私人对外投资/私人對外投資　private external investment
私人对外直接投资/私人對外直接投資　private direct foreign investment
私人非金融机构/私人非金融機構　private non-financial institute
私人非金融媒介机构/私人非金融媒介機構　private non-financial intermediary
私人服务机构/私人服務機構　private service agency
私人国外投资/私人國外投資　private foreign investment
私人化支票/私人化支票　personalized cheque
私人价值拍卖/私人價值拍賣　private value auction
私人价值拍卖模型/私人價值拍賣模型　private value auction model
私人金融机构/私人金融機構,私人財務公司　private financial institution
私人金融媒介机构/私人金融媒介機構　private financial intermediary
私人空间/私人空間,個人空間　personal space
私人劳动/私人勞動　private labour
私人贸易/私人貿易　private trade
私人票据/私人票據　private bill, private note
私人权益资本/私募股本　private equity, PE
私人融资的基础设施项目/私人融資的基礎設施項目　privately financed infrastructure project
私人投资/私人投資　private investment
私人投资支出/私人投資支出　private investment expenditure
私人图书馆/私立圖書館　private library
私人外国资本/私人外國資本　private foreign capital
私人文件/私人文件,私人檔案　private record, personal paper, personal document
私人物品/私有財　private goods
私人信贷/私人信貸　private credit
私人信息/私有訊息,私有資訊　private information
私人银行/私人銀行,個人服務銀行業　private bank, private banking
私人债务/私人債務　private debt
私人支票/私人支票　personal cheque
私人主动融资模式/私人主動融資模式,民間主動融資模式　private finance initiative model, PFI model
私人资本/私人資本　personal capital, private capital
私塾/私塾　Chinese old-style private school
私下和解/私下和解　private workout
私营公司/私營公司,私營企業　private company, private corporation

私营企业主/私營企業主　private entrepreneur
私有财产/私有財產　private property
私有产权/私有產權　private property right
私有化/私有化, 民營化　personalization, privatization
私有经济/私有經濟, 私人經濟　private economy
私有品牌/私有品牌　private brand
私有制/私人所有權　private ownership
私钥/私密金鑰　private key
思乡病/思鄉病, 懷鄉病　nostalgia
思想-表达二分法/思想-表達二分法　idea-expression dichotomy
思想犯罪/思想犯罪　ideological offense
思想史/思想史　intellectual history
思想自由/思想自由　freedom of thought
斯波纳引理/斯波那輔理　Sperner lemma
斯达汉诺夫运动/斯達漢諾夫運動　Stakhanovism Movement
斯德哥尔摩学派/斯德哥爾摩經濟學派　the Stockholm school
斯蒂芬迭代过程/Stephan 迭代過程　Stephan's iterative process
斯卡夫定理/史卡夫定理　Scarf theorem
斯堪的那维亚法律现实主义/斯堪的那維亞法律現實主義　Scandinavian legal realism
斯堪的纳维亚法学派/斯堪的那維亞學派　Scandinavian school
斯坎伦计划/史甘隆計劃　Scanlon plan
斯科特心理测验/斯科特心理測驗　psychology test of Scott
斯克托维切-达模斯定理/Skitovich-Darmois 定理　Skitovich-Darmois theorem
斯拉法经济学/斯拉法經濟學　Sraffian economics
斯勒茨基定理/史拉斯基定理　Slutsky theorem
斯勒茨基方程/史拉斯基等式　Slutsky equation
斯勒茨基恒等式/史拉斯恆等式　Slutsky identity
斯勒茨基收入效应/史拉斯所得效果　Slutsky income effect
斯勒茨基替代效应/史拉斯替代效果　Slutsky substitution effect
斯勒茨基条件/史拉斯基條件式　Slutsky condition
斯勒茨基需求函数/史拉斯需要函數　Slutsky demand function
斯鲁茨基定理/Slutzky 定理　Slutzky's theorem
斯鲁茨基方程/Slutzky 方程式　Slutzky's equation
斯鲁茨基过程/Slutzky 過程　Slutzky process
斯鲁茨基-尤尔效应/Slutzky-Yule 效應　Slutzky-Yule effect

斯米尔诺夫-伯恩鲍姆-廷及分布/Smirnov-Birnbaum-Tingey 分布, Smirnov-Birnbaum-Tingey 分配　Smirnov-Birnbaum-Tingey distribution
斯米尔诺夫分布/Smirnov 分布, Smirnov 分配　Smirnov's distribution
斯米尔诺夫检验/Smirnov 檢定　Smirnov test
斯密分工论/斯密分工論　Smith's view on labor division
斯内德克 F 分布/Snedecor 的 F 分布, Snedecor 的 F 分配　Snedecor's F-distribution
斯彭塞公式/Spencer 公式　Spencer formula
斯皮尔曼-布朗公式/Spearman-Brown 公式　Spearman-Brown formula
斯皮尔曼二因子定理/Spearman 二因子定理　Spearman two-factor theorem
斯皮尔曼估计量/Spearman 估計量　Spearman estimator
斯皮尔曼相关检验/Spearman 相關檢定　Spearman test for correlation
斯皮尔曼相关系数/Spearman 相關係數　Spearman's correlation coefficient, Spearman correlation coefficient
斯皮尔曼秩相关系数/Spearman 秩相關係數, Spearman 等級相關係數　Spearman's population rank correlation coefficient, Spearman's coefficient of rank correlation
斯塔克尔伯格产量领导者模型/史塔克堡數量領導模型　Stackelberg quantity leader model
斯塔克尔伯格价格领导者模型/史塔克堡價格領導模型　Stackelberg price leadership model
斯塔克尔伯格均衡/史塔克堡均衡　Stackelberg equilibrium
斯塔克尔伯格领导者/史塔克堡模型之領導者　Stackelberg leader
斯塔克尔伯格之追随者/史塔克堡模型之追隨者　Stackelberg follower
斯塔西分布/Stacy 分布, Stacy 分配　Stacy's distribution
斯坦二阶置信方法/Stein 二段信賴程序　Stein two-stage confidence procedure
斯坦福-比奈量表/史丹佛-比奈量表　Stanford-Binet scale
斯坦三重系统/Steiner 三重系統　Steiner's triple system
斯特朗-坎贝尔兴趣问卷/斯特朗-坎貝爾興趣問卷　Strong-Campbell interest inventory
斯特林分布/Stirling 分布, Stirling 分配　Stirling distribution

斯特林公式／Stirling 公式　Stirling's formula
斯特林近似／Stirling 近似　Stirling's approximation
斯特奇斯规则／Sturges 规则　Sturges' rule
斯托尔帕-萨缪尔森定理／史托普-薩彌爾遜定理　Stopler-Samuelson theorem
死产率／死產率　still-birth rate
死校／死校　collate the word similarities and differences
死亡／死亡　death
死亡表／死亡表　mortality table
死亡抚恤／死亡撫恤　death compensation
死亡概率／死亡機率　probability of death, mortality probability
死亡过程／死亡過程　death process
死亡率／死亡率　death rate, mortality rate
死亡权利／死亡權利　right to die
死亡统计／死亡統計　mortality statistics
死亡仪式／死亡儀式　death ritual
死刑／死刑　capital punishment
死刑复核／死刑複核　review of death sentence
死刑复核程序／死刑複核程式　death sentence review procedure
死刑复奏／死刑複奏　cautious to death
死刑缓期执行／死刑緩期執行　death sentence with a two-year reprieve
死循环物料需求计划系统／閉環物料需求規劃系統　closed-loop material requirement planning system
死因／死因　cause of death
死因统计／死因統計　cause-of-death statistics
死账／呆賬　dead account
四步情报周期法／四步情報週期　four-step intelligence cycle
四部分类法／四部分類法　four-fold bibliographical classification system
四分法／四分法　four-section system
四分位距／四分位距　quartile range
四分位离散系数／四分位離勢係數　quartile coefficient of dispersion
四分位数／四分位數　quartile
四分位数变异／四分位變異　quartile variation
四分位数差／四分位離差　quartile deviation
四分位数系数／四分位數係數　quartile coefficient
四格表／四元表　fourfold table
四角分析／四角分析　four corners analysis
四角号码检字法／四角號碼檢字法　filing rules by four corners
四维电影／四維電影　four dimensional film
四元相关／四元相關　fourfold correlation

似不相关回归／似不相關回歸　seemingly unrelated regression
似不相关回归模型／似不相關聯的回歸方程式　seemingly unrelated regression model, SUR model
似然／概度　likelihood
似然比／概度比,概似比　likelihood ratio
似然比的渐近分布／概度比率的漸近分布,概度比率的漸近分配　asymptotic distribution of likelihood ratio
似然比法／概度比法　likelihood ratio method
似然比检验／概度比檢定,概似比檢定　likelihood ratio test
似然比统计量／概度比統計量　likelihood ratio statistic
似然比相依性／概度比相依性　likelihood ratio dependence
似然比原理／概似比原則　likelihood ratio principle
似然比指数／概似比指標　likelihood ratio index
似然比置信区域／概度比的信賴區域　likelihood ratio confidence region
似然方程／概度方程式　likelihood equation
似然函数／概似函數,概度函數　likelihood function
似然原理／概似原則　likelihood principle
似我误差／似我誤差　similar-to-me error
松弛变量／鬆弛的變數　slack variable
松弛变数／鬆弛變量,附加變數　slack variable
松散耦合／鬆散連結　loose coupling
讼师／訟師　Song Shi
宋抄本／宋抄本　Song handwritten edition
宋刻本／宋刻本　Song dynasty edition
宋刑统／宋刑統　Main Code of the Song Dynasty
送达回证／送達回證　proof of service of a legal instrument
搜查／搜尋　search
搜查证／搜查令狀　search warrant
搜索网站／搜索網站　search site
搜索引擎／搜尋引擎　search engine
搜索引擎广告／搜尋引擎廣告　search engine advertisement
搜寻商品／搜尋財　search goods
搜寻意愿／搜尋意願　willingness to search
苏伯拉曼尼姆广义散播分布／Subrahmaniam 廣義散播分布,Subrahmaniam 廣義散播分配　Subrahmaniam's generalized contagious distribution
苏俄泰勒制／蘇俄泰勒制　Taylor system of Soviet Russia
苏格拉底论管理／蘇格拉底論管理　Socrates' view on management

苏格兰法/蘇格蘭法　Scots law
苏卡特梅检验/Sukhatme 檢定　Sukhatme's test
苏卡特梅 d 统计量/Sukhatme 的 d 統計量　Sukhatme d-statistic
苏黎世黄金总库/蘇黎世黄金聯營　Zurich Gold Pool
苏美尔庙宇公司/蘇美爾廟宇公司　Sumer Temple Company
苏南模式/蘇南模式　Sunan model
诉的变更/訴的變更　alternation of action
诉的分离/訴的分離　separation of action
诉的合并/訴的合并　joinder of actions
诉的要素/訴的要素　elements of action
诉的追加/訴的追加　addition of action
诉前财产保全/訴前財產保全　attachment of property before the institution of an action
诉前证据保全/訴前證據保全　evidence preserve before litigation
诉权/訴權　right of action
诉权消灭主义/訴權消滅主義　theory of elimination of the right of action
诉讼/訴訟　action
诉讼保全质权/訴訟保全質權　preserve pledge
诉讼标的/訴訟標的　subject matter of a litigation
诉讼财产保全/訴訟財產保全　attachment of property in litigation
诉讼参加人/訴訟參加人　party in a litigation
诉讼代表人/訴訟代表人　litigation representative
诉讼代理人/訴訟代理人　agent ad litem, attorney, representative in civil procedure
诉讼代理人送达/訴訟代理人送達　service of legal instrument by litigation agent
诉讼档案/訴訟檔案　lawsuit archive
诉讼费用/訴訟費用,訴訟成本　litigation cost, legal expense
诉讼和解/訴訟和解　lawsuit conciliation
诉讼理由/訴訟事由　cause of action
诉讼目的/訴訟目的　purpose of action
诉讼契约/訴訟契約　contract of action
诉讼请求的变更/訴訟請求的變更　changing of claim
诉讼请求的放弃/訴訟請求的放棄　abandon of claim
诉讼请求的追加/訴訟請求的追加　addition of claim
诉讼权利能力/訴訟權利能力　capacity of litigious right
诉讼权利义务的承担/訴訟權利義務的承擔　burden of right and obligation of action
诉讼时效/訴訟時效　limitation of action, statute of limitation
诉讼时效期间/訴訟時效期間　prescribed period for litigation
诉讼时效期间的延长/訴訟時效期間的延長　extension of the limitation of action
诉讼时效期间中断/訴訟時效期間中斷　interruption of the limitation of action
诉讼时效期间中止/訴訟時效期間中止　suspension of the limitation of action
诉讼调解/訴訟調解　mediation in litigation
诉讼系属/訴訟系屬　action dependence
诉讼行为能力/訴訟行爲能力　capacity for litigation
诉讼中止/訴訟中止　suspension of litigation
诉讼终结/訴訟終結　termination of litigation
诉讼主体/訴訟主體　subject of litigation
诉状/訴狀　Suzhuang
素质教育/素質教育　quality-oriented education
速动比率/速動比率　quick ratio
速动资产/速動資產　quick asset
速度评定/速度評定　speed rating
速遣费/速遣費　dispatch money
塑料线烫订/塑膠線燙訂　plastic thread sealing
酸性有害气体/酸性有害氣體　acid harmful gas
算法/演算法　algorithm
算术尺度/算術尺度　arithmetic scale
算术-几何平均不等式/算數幾何平均不等式　arithmetic-geometric mean inequality
算术平均/算術平均　arithmetic mean
算术平均数/算術平均數　arithmetic mean, arithmetic average
算术图/算術圖　arithmetic graph
算子/[運]算子　operator
隋律/隋律　Laws of the Sui Dynasty
随访/複查,追蹤　follow-up
随机/隨機,概率　stochastic, random
随机逼近方法/隨機逼近程序　stochastic approximation procedure
随机比较/隨機比較　stochastic comparison
随机变量/隨機變數　random variable, variate
随机变量的期望值/隨機變數的期望值　expected value of a random variable
随机变量的收敛性/隨機變數之收斂　convergence of random variable
随机变量序列/隨機變數序列　sequence of random variable, series of random variable
随机变异/隨機變異,機遇變異　random variation
随机标签/隨機標記　random label

随机波动/機遇波動,隨機變動　random fluctuation
随机波动率模型/隨機波動模型　stochastic volatility model
随机博弈/隨機賽局,機遇性賽局　stochastic game
随机抽取/隨機抽取　draw at random
随机抽选/機遇選擇,隨機選取　selection by chance, random selection
随机抽样/隨機抽樣　random sampling
随机抽样误差/隨機抽樣誤差　random sampling error
随机传递性/隨機遞移性　stochastic transitivity
随机存储器/隨機存取記憶體　random access memory, RAM
随机到达/隨機到達　random arrival
随机递减/隨機遞減　stochastically decreasing
随机递增/隨機遞增　stochastically increasing
随机定律/機遇法則　law of chance, chance law
随机独立/隨機獨立　stochastic independence
随机法/隨機法　stochastic approach
随机泛函方程/隨機泛函方程式　stochastic functional equation
随机分布/隨機分布　random distribution
随机分量/隨機成分　random component
随机分配/隨機分派　random assignment
随机分歧/隨機分歧　random bifurcation
随机故障/隨機故障　random failure
随机故障期/隨機故障期　random failure period
随机观测/隨機觀測　random observation
随机规划/隨機規劃　stochastic programming
随机过程/隨機過程　stochastic process, random process
随机函数/隨機函數　random function
随机核/隨機核　stochastic kernel
随机恒定的/隨機恆定的　stochastic definite
随机化/隨機化　randomization, randomize
随机化部分析因设计/隨機化部分因子設計　randomized fractional factorial design
随机化策略/隨機化策略　randomized strategy
随机化的/隨機化的　randomized, stochasticized
随机化检验/隨機化檢定　randomized test
随机化决策函数/隨機化決策函數　randomized decision function
随机化模型/隨機化模型　randomized model
随机化区组/隨機化區集　randomized block
随机化区组设计/隨機化區集設計　randomized block design
随机化试验/隨機化實驗　randomized experiment
随机化算法/隨機演算法　randomized algorithm
随机化完全区组设计/隨機化完全區集設計　randomized complete block design
随机化原则/隨機化原則　principle of randomization
随机化最小充分统计量/隨機化最小充分統計量　randomized minimal sufficient statistic
随机回归元/隨機性回歸因數　stochastic regressor
随机机制/機遇機制　chance mechanism
随机积分/隨機積分　stochastic integral, random integration
随机级数/隨機數列　random series
随机假设/隨機性假設　stochastic assumption
随机检索/隨機檢索　random retrieval, stochastic retrieval
随机截距和斜坡模型/隨機常數項斜率模式　random intercept and slopes model
随机截距模型/隨機常數項模型　random intercept model
随机矩阵/隨機矩陣　stochastic matrix
随机可积性/隨機可積分性　stochastic integrability
随机可微性/隨機可微分性　stochastic differentiability
随机连续性/隨機連續性　stochastic continuity
随机路径/隨機路線　random path
随机脉冲过程/隨機脈衝過程　random impulse process
随机漫步/隨機漫步　random walk
随机漫步理论/隨機漫步理論　random walk theory
随机漫步模型/隨機漫步模型　random walk model
随机模拟/隨機模擬　stochastic simulation
随机模型/隨機模型　stochastic model, random model
随机排列/隨機排列　random permutation
随机排序/隨機排序　stochastic scheduling
随机配置设计/隨機配置設計　random allocation design
随机平衡设计/隨機平衡設計　random balance design
随机起点/隨機起點　random start
随机区间/隨機區間　random interval
随机区组试验/集區隨機試驗　block randomized experiment
随机趋势/隨機趨勢　stochastic trend
随机缺失/隨機缺失　missing at random, MAR
随机扰动/隨機擾動,隨機干擾　stochastic disturbance, random perturbation
随机扰动项/隨機干擾項　stochastic disturbance term
随机失效/隨機故障　random failure

随机试验/隨機實驗　random experiment
随机收敛/隨機收斂　stochastic convergence
随机数/隨機數,亂數　random number
随机数表/隨機數表,亂數表　random number table
随机数字/隨機數字　random digit
随机数字表/隨機數字表　random digit table
随机顺序/隨機順序　random order
随机凸性域分割/隨機凸形切割　random tessellation
随机无偏样本/隨機不偏樣本　random unbiased sample
随机误差/隨機誤差　random error
随机系数/隨機係數　random coefficient
随机系数模型/隨機係數模型　random coefficient model
随机现象/隨機現象　random phenomena
随机线图/隨機線圖　random linear graph
随机线性方程/隨機線性方程式　random linear equation, stochastic linear equation
随机线性约束/隨機線性限制　stochastic linear restriction
随机相依性/隨機相依性　stochastic dependence
随机响应/隨機反應　randomized response
随机向量/隨機向量　random vector
随机向量变换/隨機向量變換　transformation of random vector
随机向量的正交变换/隨機向量的正交變換　orthogonal transformations of random vector
随机项/隨機項　stochastic term
随机效应/隨機效果　random effect
随机效应模型/隨機效應模型　random-effect model
随机性/隨機性　randomness
随机性检验/隨機[性]檢定　randomization test, testing for randomness
随机需求/隨機需求　stochastic demand
随机序贯概率比检验/隨機逐次機率比檢定　randomized sequential probability ratio test
随机选择/隨機選取,隨機抽樣　random selection, sampling
随机样本/隨機樣本　random sample
随机移动/隨機移動　random movement
随机因素/隨機因子　random factor
随机因子平方和/隨機因子平方和　sum of squares for random factor
随机影响变截距模型/隨機影響變截距模型　variable intercept panel data model with random effect
随机影响变系数模型/隨機影響變係數模型　varying coefficient panel data model with random effect
随机优势决策/隨機優勢決策　stochastic dominance decision
随机游动/隨機漫步　random walk
随机游走/隨機漫步　random walk
随机原因/隨機原因　random cause
随机增长法则/成長隨機法則　stochastic law of growth
随机正交变换/隨機正交變換　random orthogonal transformation
随机正态记分检验/隨機常態計分檢定　random normal score test
随机装配/隨機裝配　random assembly
随机自变量/獨立隨機變數　independent random variable
随机组合设计/隨機組合設計　randomly combined design
随机组设计/隨機組設計　random group design
随手登记档/隨手登記檔　the Grand Council's digest of memorials and edicts
随手画法/隨手畫法　free hand method
随书光盘/隨書光盤　CD attached with a book
碎股/零頭股票　odd lot
碎片化/破碎化,片段化　fragmentation
损害发生地法/損害發生地法　law of place of damage
损害函数法/損害函數法　damage function method
损害赔偿的诉讼/損害賠償的訴訟　action for damage
损害赔偿通知条款/索賠通知條款　claim notice clause
损害赔偿责任/損害賠償責任　liability for damage
损害预防原则/損害預防原則　principle of damage prevention
损耗曲线/損耗曲線　damage curve
损毁信用/損毀信用　injury to credit
损失/虧損　loss
损失补偿/損失補償　loss compensation
损失分摊/損失分攤　loss apportionment
损失估算/損失估算　loss assessment
损失函数/損失函數　loss function
损失矩阵/損失矩陣　loss matrix
损失评估/損害評估　damage evaluation
损失时间/損失時間　lost time
损失厌恶/損失厭惡　loss aversion
损失制系统/損失系統　loss system
损益/損益,盈虧　loss and gain
损益单/損益單　lose and overflow report bill
损益平衡图/損益平衡圖　break-even-chart

损益相抵规则／損益相抵規則　break-even rule of profit and loss
缩版量／縮版量　distorted compensation value
缩编谱／縮編譜　short score
缩放／縮放　scaling
缩混／混音　mixing
缩检／精煉檢索　narrow search
缩微保存／縮微保存　microfilming preservation
缩微出版物／縮微出版物,微縮出版品　microform publication, microfilm publication
缩微档案／微縮檔案　microfile
缩微负片／微縮負片　negative microfilm
缩微复制件／微縮複製件　microcopy
缩微检索工具／縮微檢索工具　microform retrieval device
缩微胶卷／顯微膠片,縮影卷片　microfilm
缩微胶卷阅读机／縮影卷片閱讀機　microfilm reader
缩微[胶卷]正片／縮微[膠卷]正片　positive microfilm
缩微胶片／縮影膠片,超微膠片　microfilm, superfiche, ultrafiche
缩微胶片条／條狀微縮片　microfilm strip
缩微卡片／微縮卡片,縮影卡片　microcard
缩微率／縮小倍率　reduction ratio
缩微目录／微縮目錄　mirco catalogue retrieval tool, micro bibliography
缩微品／微縮品　microform
缩微品档案／微縮品檔案　microform archive
缩微品还原机／縮微閱讀複印器　micro reader-printer
缩微平片／微縮膠片,微縮單片,縮影單片　microfiche
缩微平片阅读机／微縮膠片閱讀機　microfiche reader
缩微摄影机／微縮攝影機　microform camera
缩微摄影技术／微縮技術　microphoto graphy, micrographics
缩微收藏物／微縮品的徵集　acquisition microfilming
缩微型信息[源]／縮微型資訊[源]　micro information source
缩微影像／微[縮]影像,微縮圖像　microimage
缩微阅读器／微縮閱讀機　microform reader
缩微纸带／縮影紙帶　microtape
缩小贸易差额／縮小貿易逆差　reduce trade deficit
缩写／縮寫　abbreviation
缩印本／縮印本　miniprint
缩印本词典／縮印本詞典　compact dictionary

所得税／所得税　income tax
所得税率／所得税率　rate of income tax
所得税退税／所得税退税　rebate on income tax
所得系数／所得係數　income coefficient
所见即所得／所見即所得　what you see is what you get
所有权／所有權　ownership
所有权保留／所有權保留　retention of ownership
所有权凭证／權狀　document of title
所有权与经营权分离／所有權與控制權分離　separation of ownership and control
所有权转让／所有權轉讓　ownership transfer
所有商品量分销率／所有商品量分銷率　all commodity volume distribution, ACV distribution
所有者权益／所有者權益,業主權益　owner's equity
所有者权益变动表／權益變動結算表　statement of change in owners' equity
所有制／所有制　proprietorship
所有制结构／所有制結構　ownership structure
所指／所指,符號義,符旨　signified
索霍工厂管理体系／索霍工廠管理體系　management system of Soho plant
索款即付／索款即付　payable on demand
索利尔的应用心理学／索利爾的應用心理學　application psychology of Sollier
索洛模型／梭羅模型　Solow model
索洛余项／梭羅殘差　Solow residual
索洛增长模型／梭羅成長模型　Solow growth model
索赔／索赔,理賠,求償　claim
索赔报告／索賠報告　statement of claim
索赔代理人／索賠代理人　claim agent
索赔单证／索賠單證　claim document
索赔金额／索賠金額　claim amount
索赔清单／索賠清單　claim note
索赔书／索賠函　claim letter
索赔条款／索賠條款　claim clause
索赔通知／索賠通知　notice of claim, claim notice
索赔资产／索賠資產　claim asset
索取号／參考碼,檢索碼　reference number
索书号／索書號碼　call number
索书条／索書單　call slip
索引／索引　index
索引编制法／索引編製法　indexing
索引词／索引詞　index term
索引地图／索引圖　index map
索引法／索引法　indexing method
索引号／索引號碼　index number

索引款目／索引款目　index entry
索引数据库／索引資料庫　index database
索引文档／索引文檔　index file
锁槽／鎖槽　locked groove, concentric groove
锁定效应／鎖定效果　lock-in effect
锁线订／鎖線訂　thread sewing
锁线机／鎖線機　book-sewing machine
锁眼式投资／鎖眼式投資　keyhole investment

T

他校法/他校法　collation method of using other materials, collate according to other books and materials
他人影响/他人影響　influence from others
他物权/他物權　Jura in Re Aliana
他益信托/他益信託　benefit-to-others trust
他引/他引　other-citation
他者/他者,他人　others
他主占有/他主占有　adverse possession
塔式垂直布局/塔式垂直布局　tower-type vertical layout
塔式书库/塔式書庫　tower-type book stack
塔维斯托克研究所/塔維斯托克研究所　Tavistock Institute
拓本/拓本,膳本　rubbing edition
拓片/拓片　rubbings
胎儿死亡比/胎兒死亡比　fetal death ratio
胎儿死亡率/胎兒死亡率　fetal mortality, fetal death rate
太空船地球/太空船地球　spaceship earth
太平刑律/太平刑律　Taiping Criminal Law
太平洋经济共同体/太平洋經濟共同體　Pacific Economic Community
太史寮/太史寮　Taishi Liao
太阳能/太陽能　solar energy
态度/態度　attitude
态度测量/態度測量　attitude measurement
态度调查/態度調查　attitude survey
态度改变/態度改變,態度變遷　attitude change
态度量表/態度量表　attitude scale
态度形成/態度形成　attitude formation
态度指标/態度指標　attitude index
泰伯公司科学管理/泰伯公司科學管理　scientific management of Tabor Factory
泰勒定理/Taylor 定理　Taylor's theorem
泰勒制/泰勒制　Taylor system
贪婪社会/貪求社會　greedy society
贪婪算法/貪婪算法　greedy algorithm
贪污贿赂罪/貪汙賄賂罪　crime of embezzlement and bribery
贪污罪/貪汙罪　crime of embezzlement

摊销/攤銷　amortization
谈话分析/交談分析,會談分析,會話分析　conversation analysis
谈话广播/談話廣播,廣播談話節目　talk radio
谈话节目/談話節目,脱口秀　talk show
谈判/談判,協商　negotiation, bargain
谈判代理人/協議代表　bargaining agent
谈判能力/議價力量　bargaining power
谈判实验/談判實驗　bargaining experiment
谈判协议/談判協議　bargaining agreement
谈判者/談判者,協商者　negotiator
谈判者的利他主义/談判者的利他主義　altruism of bargainer
谈判支持系统/協商支援系統　negotiation support system
弹出式广告/快顯廣告,立體造型廣告,網路彈跳式廣告　pop-up advertisement
弹性/彈性,伸縮性　elasticity, flexibility
弹性分析法/彈性學派　elasticity approach
弹性分析预测法/彈性分析預測法　elastic analysis forecasting method
弹性工资计划/彈性工資計劃　elastic wage plan
弹性工作时间/彈性工作時間　elastic working time
弹性工作制/彈性工時制　flextime, flexible work schedule
弹性关税/彈性關稅　elastic tariff, flexible tariff
弹性汇率/彈性匯率,伸縮匯率,浮動匯率　flexible exchange rate
弹性系数/彈性係數　coefficient of elasticity
弹性薪酬/彈性薪酬　flexible compensation
弹性信用发行制度/彈性信用發行制度　elastic fiduciary issue system
弹性预算/彈性預算　flexible budget
弹性制度/有彈性的制度　flexible institution
探查技术/導出技術　elicitation technique
探试性研究/先導研究,試探研究　pilot study
探索性调查/探索調查　exploratory survey
探索性数据分析/探索性資料分析　exploratory data analysis, EDA
探索性学习/探索性學習　explorative learning
探索性因子分析/探索性因素分析　exploratory

factor analysis, EFA
探索性营销研究/探索性行銷研究　exploratory marketing research
探索者/探索者　prospector
探险学习法/探險學習法　adventure learning
探针/探針　probe
碳税/碳稅　carbon tax
汤姆森条件/湯姆森條件　Thomsen condition
汤普森规则/Thompson 規則　Thompson's rule
汤刑/湯刑　Criminal Laws of Shang Dynasty
汤因比馆/湯恩比館　Toynbee Hall
唐刻本/唐刻本　Tang dynasty edition
唐六典/唐六典　Six Code in Tang Dynasty
唐律疏议/唐律疏議　Code and Its Notes of Tang Dynasty
唐明律合编/唐明律合編　Tang Ming Law
唐纳利领导模式/唐納利領導模式　leadership model of Donnelly
唐纳利组织变革论/唐納利的組織變革論　Donnelly's organization change theory
唐斯克定理/Donsker 定理　Donsker's theorem
堂帖/堂帖　Tangtie
棠阴比事/棠陰比事　Tangyin Typical Cases
烫金/燙金　blocking
烫印/熱箔戳記,燙金印刷　hot foil-stamping
烫印机/燙印機　hot foil-stamping machine
逃避关税/逃避關稅　evade payment of duty
逃汇/逃避外匯管制　evade foreign exchange control
逃税/逃稅　tax evasion
陶瓷拾音头/陶瓷拾音頭　ceramic pick-up head
讨价还价博弈/談判賽局　bargaining game
讨价还价模型/談判模型　bargaining model
讨厌变量/多餘變數,擾亂變數　nuisance variable
套购保值/避險保值　hedge
套购套售交易/套購套售交易　cross trade
套购选择权/套購選擇權,等價買賣選擇權　straddle option
套合/上書殼　casing in
套汇/套匯　exchange arbitrage, arbitrage of exchange
套汇汇率/套匯匯率　arbitrage rate, cross rate of exchange
套汇交易/套匯交易,套利交易　arbitrage transaction
套汇业务/套匯業務　swap facility
套利/套利　arbitrage
套利定价理论/套利定價理論　arbitrage pricing theory
套利交易/套利交易　covered interest arbitrage
套利者/套利者　arbitrageur
套录编目/套錄編目,拷貝編目　copy cataloging, derived cataloging
套期保值/套期保值,避險保值　hedging, hedge
套期保值率/避險比率　hedging ratio
套色打样/逐色樣張,單色樣張　progressive proof
套帖书芯/套帖書芯　single-layer block
套筒式凹版/套筒式凹版　sleeve-type forme
套筒式印版滚筒/套筒式印版滾筒　sleeve forme cylinder
套筒印版/套筒印版　sleeve forme
套头交易/套頭交易業務,平衡交易業務　hedging operation
套头交易合同/套頭交易合約,平衡交易合約　hedging contract
套印本/套印本　chromatic print
套印不准/套印不準,未套準　mis-register, out of register
套准/套準　register
套准标记/套準記號,定位記號　register mark
特别报价/特別報價,廉售報價　special offer
特别背书/特別背書,記名背書　special endorsement
特别程序/特別程式　special procedure
特别代理/特別代理　special agency
特别订单/特殊訂單　special order
特别附加险/特別附加險　special additional risk
特别关税率/特別關稅率　special customs rate
特别货币安排/特別貨幣安排　special monetary arrangement
特别减税债券/特別減稅債券　special tax reduction bond
特别进口/特別進口　special import
特别纳税调整/特別納稅調整　special tax payment adjustment
特别权力关系/特別權力關係　special power relationship
特别融资/特別融資　special finance
特别税捐公债/特別稅捐公債　special assessment bond
特别税捐基金/特別稅捐基金　special assessment fund
特别提款权/特別提款權　special drawing right, SDR
特别提款权本位/特別提款權本位　SDR standard
特别提款权的逐日汇率/特別提款權的逐日匯率　daily special drawing right rate, daily SDR rate
特别提款权估值/特別提款權估值　valuation of special drawing right, valuation of SDR

特别提款权平价/特别提款權平價　SDR parity
特别通知信用证/特别通知信用狀　specially advised credit
特别投资/特别投資　special investment
特别信贷/特别信貸，特别信用狀　special credit
特别信贷基金/特别信貸基金　special credit fund
特别信用证/特别信用狀　special letter of credit
特别刑法/特别刑法　special criminal law
特别许可证/特别許可證　special license
特别优惠/特别優惠　special favor
特别优惠待遇/特别優惠待遇　special preferential treatment
特别账户/特别賬户　special account
特别准备基金/特别準備基金　special reserve fund
特别准备金/特别準備金　special reserve
特别资本/特别資本　special capital
特藏/特藏　special collection
特藏本/特藏本　special edition
特藏符号/特藏符號　special collection symbol
特藏目录/特藏目錄　special collection catalog
特产出口商/特産出口商，專門出口商　special exporter
特大城市/巨型都會，巨大都市　megacity, megalopolis
特定保险/特定保險　specific insurance
特定常规武器禁止或限制使用/禁止或限制使用某些可被認爲具有過份傷害力或濫傷作用的常規武器　prohibition or restriction of the use of certain conventional weapon
特定出生率/特殊出生率　specific birth rate
特定多数/二分之一以上多數決　qualified majority
特定放宽检验程序/特種減數檢驗程序　special reduced inspection procedure
特定机会研究/特定機會研究　special opportunity study
特定检索/特定檢索　specific retrieval, specific search
特定减免税/特定減免税，強制性税捐減免　mandatory duty reduction or exemption
特定留置权/特定留置權，個別留置權　particular lien
特定率/特定率　specific rate
特定年/計算年　given year
特定生育率/特殊生育率　specific fertility rate
特定文献类型标识/文獻類型標識　specific material designation, SMD
特定物/特定物　individually defined thing
特定性/特定性　specificity

特定许可证/特定許可證　specific license
特定要素/特定要素　specific factor
特定要素模型/特定要素模型　specific factor model
特发报刊/特發報刊　special distributed newspaper and periodical
特惠/特别優惠　special favor
特惠标准/特惠標準　test for preference
特惠关税/特惠税率　reduced tariff
特惠汇率/優惠匯率　preferential exchange rate
特惠进口/特許進口　privileged import
特惠路线/優先安排　preferential routing
特惠贸易/優惠貿易　preferential trade
特惠贸易协定/優惠貿易協定　preferential trading agreement
特惠区域/優惠地區　preferential area
特惠税率/減税税率　reduced tax rate
特惠条款/優惠條款　preferential clause
特惠制/特惠制　preferential system
特急件/特急件　extra urgent document
特价品/特價品　bargain
特价品搜寻者/特價品搜尋者　bargain hunter
特价书/特價書　discount book
特刊/特刊　special issue, special number
特雷诺测度/Treynor 式衡量　Treynor measure
特里芬两难/特里芬兩難　Triffin dilemma
特里-霍弗丁检验/Terry-Hoeffding 檢定　Terry-Hoeffding test
特里检验/Terry 檢定　Terry's test
特里四职能说/特里四職能說　four management functions theory of Terry
特派记者/特派記者　accredited journalist
特区专用口岸/特區專用口岸　open port for special use by special zone
特色数据库/特色資料庫　characteristic database, special database
特色资源/特色資源　special resource
特赦/特赦　special pardon, special amnesty
特殊保单/特殊保單，單獨保險單　specific policy
特殊承兑/特殊承兑，有條件承兑　special acceptance
特殊处境儿童/特殊處境兒童　children in special situation
特殊地域管辖/特殊地域管轄　jurisdiction on the basis of special factors
特殊风险/特殊風險　specific risk
特殊绩效认可计划/特殊績效認可計劃　special performance recognizing plan
特殊品/特殊品　specialty product
特殊侵权行为/特殊侵權行爲　special tort

特殊情况说明/特殊情況説明 special case description
特殊区域环境保护法/特殊區域環境保護法 Law on Protection of Environment in Special Areas
特殊权利/特殊權利 sui generis right
特殊群体就业/特殊群體就業 employment of disadvantage group
特殊性交易/不合常规交易 unusual transaction
特殊因子/特定因子 specific factor
特殊诱因/特殊誘因 special inducement
特殊装/特殊裝 special binding
特效/特效,特殊效果 special effect
特写/特寫[版] feature
特性/特性 characteristic
特性检索/專用檢索,全結構檢索 specific search, specific retrieval
特性文件链接空间/特性檔連結空間 profile connection space
特需文献/專題文獻 special literature
特许出口/特許出口 special permission export
特许独占/特許獨占 franchise monopoly
特许公司/特許公司 chartered company, chartered corporation
特许经销商/授權經銷商 authorized dealer
特许经营/特許經營 franchise, franchising
特许经营权/加盟事業,[經營]特許權 franchise
特许经营商/特許經營商 franchise dealer
特许经营许可/授權經營特許權 franchise licensing
特许经营组织/特許專營組織 franchise organization
特许贸易公司/特許貿易公司 chartered trading company
特许期/特許期 concession period
特许权/特許權 franchise right, chartered right
特许权使用费/經銷費 franchise fee
特许权所有人/特許權所有人 concessionaire
特许税/特許税 franchise tax
特许投标/特許的招標 franchise biding
特许协议/特許協議 franchise agreement
特许银行/特許銀行 chartered bank
特许原因/特許原因 franchise factor
特许债券/特許債券 bond privileged
特许证/特許證 charter of concession
特许证书/特許證書 letter patent
特许资源/特許資源 licensed resource
特选撮要每月纪传/特選撮要每月紀傳 A Monthly Record of Important Selections
特约编辑/特約編輯 invited editor
特约经销店/特約經銷店 authorized bookstore
特约撰稿人/特約撰稿人 invited author
特征/特徵 characteristic
特征多项式/特徵多項式 characteristic polynomial
特征方程/特徵方程 characteristic equation
特征根/特徵根 characteristic root
特征根分布/特徵根分布 latent root distribution
特征函数/特徵函數 characteristic function
特征行列式/特徵行列式 characteristic determinant
特征化/特徵化 characterisation
特征价格法/特徵價格法 hedonic price method
特征模型/特徵模型 character model
特征评价法/屬性評量法 attribute approach
特征曲线/特徵曲線 characteristic curve
特征寿命/特徵壽命 characteristic life
特征图/特徵圖 characteristic diagram
特征向量/特徵向量,固有向量 eigenvector, characteristic vector
特征因子/特徵因子 eigenfactor
特征值/特徵值,固有值 eigenvalue, characteristic value
特质风险/特質風險 idiosyncratic risk
特质考评指标体系/特質量表 trait scale
特种保险单/特種保險單,特殊格式保險單 special policy
特种出版物/特種出版物 user-oriented edition, special publication
特种关税减让/特種關稅減讓 special tariff concession
特种基金存款/特種基金存款 special fund deposit
特种贸易/特種貿易 special commerce
特种收入基金/特種收入基金 special revenue fund
特种文献/特種文獻 specific document
特种信托/特種信託 special trust
特种字体或符号/特別字元 pi-character
誊录簿/謄錄簿 transcribed book
誊写本/手抄本 scribal copy
剔除/撤架 weeding
剔除登记/剔除登記 deaccession register, discards register
剔换检验/補正檢驗 rectifying inspection
剔旧图书出售/淘汰圖書銷售 weeded book sale
梯难度/梯難度 step difficulty
梯形索引/梯形索引 cut-in index, step index
提词器/提詞機,讀稿機 teleprompter
提存/提存 debtor's submission of the subject matte of an obligation to competent authorities
提存准备金/提存準備金 covered reserve
提单/提貨單 bill of loading, bill of lading

提单背书/提單背書　endorsement of bill of lading
提单持有人/提單持有人　holder of bill of lading
提单抵押/提單質押　pledge of bill of lading
提单副本/提單副本　sub-bill of lading
[提单]正面条款/[提單]正面條款　face clause
提点刑狱司/提點刑獄司　Tidian Xingyusi
提高利率贷款/提高利率貸款　marking-up loan
提供外汇的既定配额/外匯分配的固定額度　fixed quota for allotment of exchange
提供者/醫療服務提供者　provider
提货报关代理人/提貨報關代理人　delivery and customs agent
提货担保书/提貨擔保書　letter of guarantee for production of bill of lading
提货单副本/提貨單副本　memorandum bill of lading
提货单据/提貨單據　delivery of document
提货单正本/正本提單　original bill of lading
提货通知/提貨通知　cargo delivery notice
提款货单/提款憑單　withdrawal instruction
提款通知/提款通知　drawing advice
提款通知书/提款通知書　advice of drawing
提款银行/提款銀行　drawing bank
提洛同盟/提洛聯盟　Delian league
提前偿付率/提前償付率　prepayment rate
提前交货/提前交貨　advance delivery
提前进入战略/早期進入策略　early entry strategy
提前期/前置時間　lead time
提前期补偿/前置期沖銷　lead-time offset
提前期内库存/前置期存貨　lead-time inventory
提前期内需求/提前期內需求　demand during lead time
提前赎回承诺收益率/約定贖回收益率　promised yield to call
提前退休方案/提前退休方案　early retirement program
提前支付条款/加速條款　acceleration clause
提请批准逮捕书/提請批準逮捕書　application for approval of arrest
提请仲裁/提請仲裁　submit to arbitration
提取方差/萃取變異　extracted variance
提审/提審　bring the case up for trial
提升福利/福利改善　welfare improving
提示附录/提示性附錄　informative annex
提示汇票/提示匯票　presentation of bill
提示银行/提示銀行　presenting bank
提问法/提問法　quiz method
提醒型广告/提醒性廣告　reminder advertising

提要/匯總　summary
提要附注/提要附注　note pertaining to abstract
提要期刊/梗要刊物,文摘雜志　synoptic journal
提要式版本目录/提要式版本目錄　textual bibliography of summary style
提要项/提要項　epitome item
提要用语/提要用語　wording of summary
提喻法/提喻法　synthetic technique
题本/題本　memorial
题解/題解　instruction comment on archival material
题录/目錄,型錄　catalog
题名/題名　title
题名变更/題名變更　title change
题名标目/書名標目　title heading
题名参照/書名參照　title reference
题名分析款目/題名分析款目　title analytic entry
题名附加款目/題名附加款目　title added entry
题名检索/題名檢索　title search, title retrieval
题名款目/書名款目　title entry
题名录/題名錄　passing names list
题名目录/書名目錄　title catalog
题名前页/題名前頁　label title page
题名索引/題名索引　title index
题名项/題名項　title item, title area
题名页/題名頁　title page
题名页题名/題名頁題名　title page title
题名与责任说明附注/題名與責任說明附注　note pertaining to title and statement of responsibility
题名与责任者说明项/題名與責任者說明項　title and statement of responsibility
题名帧/題名幀　title frame
题名主要款目/題名主要款目　title main entry
题目/題目　topic
题目价值/題目價值　value of topic
题目研究/題目研究　research on topic
题内关键词索引/關鍵字和上下文索引　keyword-in-context index, KWIC
题上信息/題上信息　avant-title
题署珍藏本/題署珍藏本　association copy
题外关键词索引/上下文外關鍵字索引　keyword-out-of-context index, KWOC
体积图/體積圖　volume chart
体力劳动/操作工,體力工　manual labor
体例手册/體例手冊　style manual
体态语言/肢體語言　body language
体系分类法/體系分類法,列舉式分類法　hierachical classification, enumerative classification
体系解释/體系解釋　systematic interpretation

体系理论/系統理論　system theory
体验广告/體驗廣告　experiential advertising
体验式营销/體驗行銷　experiential marketing
体育新闻/體育新聞, 運動新聞　sports journalism, sports news
体育游戏/體育遊戲　sport game
体制创新/體制創新　institutional innovation
体重指数/肥胖指數　body mass index, BMI
替代/替代[方案]　alternative, substitution
替代F比/替代F比　substitute F-ratio
替代t比/替代t比　substitute t-ratio
替代标准/替代標準　alternate standard, alternative standard
替代担保/替代擔保　substitute security
替代方案/替代方案　scheme of alternative
替代公债/替代公債　substitution obligation
替代互换/替代交換　substitution swap
替代模型/替代模式　model of substitution
替代品/替代品　substitute, substitute goods
替代弹性/[價格]替代彈性　elasticity of substitution, price elasticity of substitution
替代威胁/替代威脅　threat of substitutes
替代效应/重置效果, 替代效果　replacement effect, substitution effect
替代性纠纷解决方式/另類的爭端解決方式　alternative dispute resolution
替代性媒介/替代性媒體, 非主流媒體　alternative media
替代样本/替代樣本　substitute sample
替代医疗/替代醫療　alternative medical treatment
替代责任/代負責任　vicarious liability
替代账户/貨幣替代賬戶　substitution account
天朝田亩制度/天朝田畝制度　Tianchao Tianmu System
天府/天府　Tianfu
天赋人权说/天賦人權說　jus nafural
天命/天命　mandate of heaven
天人感应/天人感應　Tianren Ganying
天使基金/天使基金　angel fund
天使投资人/天使投資人　angel investor
天体运动/天體運動　nudist movement
天天低价/每日低價　everyday low pricing, EDLP
天头/天頭　head margin
天文统计/天文統計　astronomical statistics
天下/天下　land under heaven
天线/天線　antenna
添订/添訂　added ordering
添附/添附　accretion

田口方法/田口法　Taguchi method
田纳西河流域综合开发工程/田納西河流域的綜合開發與治理　Tennesse valley comprehensive development and management
田野笔记/田野筆記, 田野札記　field note
田野调查/田野調查, 實地研究, 田野研究　field research, field study
田野实验/田野實驗　field experiment
填充/填充　filling
填充料/填充料　filler
挑选型抽样/挑選型抽樣　rectifying sampling
条法事类/條法事類　Tiaofa Shilei
条杠/條帶效應　banding
条痕/條痕, 條紋　streak
条记/條記　Tiaoji
条件定向法/條件定向法　conditional directive method
条件独立[性]/條件獨立[性]　conditional independence
条件对数单位模型/條件羅吉特機率模型　conditional logit model
条件方差/條件變異數　conditional variance
条件方程/條件方程式　condition equation
条件分布/條件分布, 條件分配　conditional distribution
条件分布函数/條件分布函數, 條件分配函數　conditional distribution function
条件符号检验/條件符號檢定　conditional sign test
条件概率/條件機率　conditional probability
条件概率函数/條件機率函數　conditional probability function
条件概率密度/條件機率密度　conditional probability density
条件故障率/條件故障率　conditional failure rate
条件回归/條件回歸　conditional regression
条件极大似然估计量/條件最大概似估計量　conditional maximum likelihood estimator
条件价值法/假設性市場評價法, 條件評估法　contingent valuation method
条件检验/條件檢定　conditional test
条件矩检验/條件動差檢定　conditional moment test
条件均方和函数/條件均方和函數　conditional sum of squares function
条件均值/條件平均數　conditional mean
条件可靠性/條件可靠度　conditional reliability
条件密度函数/條件密度函數　conditional density function
条件幂函数/條件乘方函數　conditional power

function
条件期望/條件期望　conditional expectation
条件期望值/條件期望值　conditional expected value
条件生存概率/條件存活機率　conditional survival probability
条件生存函数/條件存活函數　conditional survival function
条件失效率/條件故障率　conditional failure rate
条件收益/條件性報酬　conditional payoff
条件数/條件數目　condition number
条件说/條件說　condition theory
条件损失/條件損失　conditional loss
条件替换定理/條件替換定理　conditional substitution theorem
条件统计量/條件統計量　conditional statistic
条件稳定性/條件穩定性　conditional stability
条件无偏估计量/條件不偏估計量　conditional unbiased estimator
条件限制/條件　conditionality
条件选择模型/條件選擇模型　conditional choice model
条件要素需求/條件性要素需求　conditional factor demand
条件异方差自回归移动平均模型/CHARMA 模型　conditional heteroscedastic ARMA model, CHARMA model
条件在险价值/條件風險值　conditional value-at-risk, conditional VaR
条件置信区间/條件信賴區間　conditional confidence interval
条例/條例　regulation, statute
D 条例/條例 D　regulation D
条令/條令　doctrine ordinance
条码系统/條碼系統　bar code system
条码自动识别技术/條碼自動識別技術　bar code automatic identification technology
条目/條目　entry
条式索引/條片式索引　strip index
条条与块块/條條與塊塊　Tiao-Kuai
条形码/條碼　bar code
条形图/長條圖　bar chart, bar diagram
条约/條約　treaty
条约不溯及既往/條約不溯及既往　non-retroactivity of treaty
条约草案/條約草案,草約　protocol
条约缔结/條約締結　conclusion of treaty
条约对第三方无损益/條約不使第三者負擔義務　pacta tertiis nec nocent nec prosunt
条约继承/條約繼承　succession to treaty
条约法/條約法　law of treaty
条约加入/條約加入　accession to treaty
条约解释/條約解釋　treaty interpretation
条约批准/條約批準　ratification of treaty
条约签署/條約簽署　signature of treaty
条约生效/條約生效　entry into force of treaty
条约索引/條約索引　treaty index
条约修正与修改/條約修正與修改　amendment and modification of treaty
条约以外事项的继承/條約以外事項的繼承　succession with respect to matters other than treaties
条约作准文本/條約作準文本　authentic texts of treaty
条奏/條奏　Tiaozou
调版/調版　adjusted version
调幅/調幅　amptitude modulation, AM
调幅加网/調幅加網　amplitude modulated screening
调幅网点/調幅網點　amplitude modulated, AM
调稿/調稿　adjust draft
调和分布/調和分布,調和分配　harmonic distribution
调和分析/調和分析　harmonic analysis
调和过程/調和過程　harmonic process
调和平均数/調和平均數　harmonic mean, harmonic average
调剂/調整　adjustment
调剂目录/調劑目錄　adjusting bibliography
调架/調架　stack adjustment
调节变量/調節變量　moderating variable
调节聚焦理论/調節聚焦理論,調節焦點理論　regulatory-focus theory
调节性政策/寬鬆政策　accommodative policy
调节指数/修正指數　deflating index
调解/調解　mediation
调墨油/調墨油,康版油　compound
调频广播/調頻[廣播]　frequency modulation, FM
调频加网/調頻加網　frequency modulated screening
调频网点/調頻網點　frequency modulated dot
调色板/彩色調色板　color palette
调试/除錯　debugging
调停/調解　mediation
调停者/調停者,仲介者　mediator
调优谱/蛻變頻譜　evolutionary spectrum
调优运算/蛻變作業　evolutionary operation, EVOP
调整成本/調整成本　adjustment cost

调整后托宾模型/調整後的杜賓模型　adjusted Tobit model
调整计划/補正計劃　rectification plan
调整问题/調整問題　adjustment problem
调整项目/調整專案　reconciliation item
调整型抽样/調整型抽樣　adjustable sampling
调整因素/調整因子　adjusting factor
调整账户/調整賬户　adjustment account
调整指数/補正指數　rectified index number
调整准备费用/準備成本　setup cost
调整准备时间/整備時間　setup time
4-6 调制/4-6 調制　four-six modulation
调制纹槽/調制紋槽　modulated groove
跳接/跳接　jump cut
跳栏/截面　cross section
跳批抽样方案/越批抽樣計劃　skip-lot sampling plan
跳跃矩阵/跳動矩陣　jump matrix
跳跃统计量/跳動統計量　jump statistic
AB 贴/AB 貼　front and back paste
贴版双面胶带/貼版雙面膠帶　double-side adhesive tape
贴标签/貼標簽　labelling
贴衬垫/貼襯墊　pasteup
贴花印刷/轉寫［印刷］　decalcomania
贴黄/貼黃　Tiehuang
贴码/背標　collating mark
贴片广告/電影院廣告　film advertisement, cinema advertising
贴书标量具/貼書標量具　labeling gauge
贴现/貼現,折現　discount for cash, discount
贴现窗口/貼現窗口　discount window
贴现贷款/貼現貸款　discount loan
贴现点/折現點　discount point
贴现额度/貼現額度　line of discount
贴现法/折現方法　discount method
贴现费用/貼現費用　discount charge
贴现经纪人/貼現經紀人　discount broker
贴现利息/貼現利息　discount interest
贴现率/貼現率,折現率　rate of discount, discount rate
贴现率政策/貼現率政策　discount rate policy
贴现票据/貼現票據　note on discount
贴现人/貼現申請人　applicant for discount
贴现市场/貼現市場　discount market
贴现收入/貼現收入　discount income
贴现损失/貼現損失　discount loss
贴现所/貼現商號　discount house
贴现信贷/貼現信貸　discounted credit
贴现银行/貼現銀行　bank of discount, discount bank
贴现政策/貼現率政策　discount rate policy
帖子/帖子　postings
铁饭碗/鐵飯碗　iron rice bowl
铁铬带/鐵鉻帶　Fe-Cr tape
铁路管理体系/鐵路管理體系　railway management system
铁路旁交货价/鐵路旁交貨價　ex rail
铁路统计/鐵路統計　railway statistics
铁券/鐵券　inscribed metal pledge of emperor
铁丝订/鐵絲訂　wire side-stitching
听证会/聽證會,公聽會　public hearing
听众热线/叩應　call-in
廷杖/廷杖　hit minister on the court
停泊费/港務費,入港税　harbor due
停订率/停訂率　suspended subscribing rate
停机时间/停機時間,待修時間　down time
停刊词/停刊詞　words for closure
停售报废/停售報廢　suspension and scrap
停售封存/停售封存　suspension and safekeeping
停业/關廠　shutdown
停用词/無用字　stop word, stop term
停用词表/虚字表,非用詞表　stop list
停战/停戰　armistice
停止规则/停止原規則,終止規則　stopping rule
停止美元与黄金兑换/停止美元與黄金兑換　suspension of convertibility of dollar into gold
停止时间/止步時間,終止時間　stopping time
停止损失委托/停損訂單　stop-loss order
停止销售条款/停止銷售條款　market out clause
停止营业点/停業點　shutdown point
停止域/終止域　stopping region
停止支付/止付　stop payment
停止支付通知/停止支付通知　notice to suspend payment
停止执行/停止執行　suspend execution
停滞/停滞　stagnation
停滞协议/停滞協議　standstill agreement
通版/通版　opened-up adjacent section
通报/通報　circular notice
通报批评/通報批評　notice of criticism
通常结算/通常結算　general closing
通道/管道　channel
通道定向/通道定向　channel orientation
通电/通電　Tongdian, publish a circular
通牒效应/截止日期效果　deadline effect

通读/通讀　full reading
通封/通封　Tongfeng
通告/通告　public notice
通过率/殖利率　yield ratio
通过时间/通過時間　passage time
通过投标的销售发盘/投標者的銷售報價,公開讓售　offer for sale by tender
通过投标发盘/投標者報價,標售法　offer by tender
通婚圈/通婚圈　intermarry circle
通货比率/通貨比率　currency ratio
通货贷款/通貨貸款　currency loan
通货的完全可兑换性/通貨的充分兌換性　full convertibility
通货紧缩/通貨緊縮　deflation
通货膨胀/通貨膨脹　inflation
通货膨胀的对冲工具/通貨膨脹的對沖工具,避險對抗通貨膨脹　inflation hedge
通货膨胀风险/通貨膨脹風險　inflation risk
通货膨胀理论/通貨膨脹論　inflation theory
通货膨胀输入/通貨膨脹輸入　import of inflation
通货膨胀税/通貨膨脹稅　inflation tax
通货膨胀影响声明/通貨膨脹影響評估報告　inflation impact statement
通货区理论/通貨區理論　theory of currency area
通货稳定/通貨穩定　stabilization of currency
通货性存款/通貨性存款　monetary deposit
通货再膨胀/再膨脹　reflation
通货债券/貨幣債券　currency bond
通缉/通緝　wanted for arrest
通缉令/通緝令　wanted order
通解/通解　general solution
通径分析/路徑分析,徑路分析　path analysis, PA
通栏/通欄　full measure
通栏标题/頭條標題　banner headline
通栏广告/通欄廣告　banner advertisement
通排法/通排法　letter-by-letter arrangement
通勤/通勤　commuting
通融票据经营/融資票據經營　financing of accommodation bill
通商条约/通商條約　treaty of commerce
通商协定/通商協定　agreement on commerce
通商许可证/通商許可證　license to trade
通商友好条约/通商友好條約　treaty of amity and commerce
通识教育/通才教育,普通教育　general education
通俗读物/通俗讀物　popular reading
通俗杂志/通俗雜誌,非學術性刊物　general interest magazine, popular magazine

通信/通信　correspondence
通信成本/通信成本　communication cost
Gtalk通信服务/Gtalk通訊服務　Google talk communication service
通信广告/通信廣告　communicated advertisement
通信基础设施/通訊基礎建設　communication infrastructure
通信秘密/通信秘密　confidential communication
通信统计/通信統計　communication statistics
通信卫星/通信衛星,通訊衛星　communication satellite, CS
通信自由/傳播自由　freedom of communication
通行价格/通行價格,現行價格　going price
通讯/新聞信　newsletter
通讯社/［新聞］通訊社　agency, news agency
通讯员/特派記者,駐外記者　correspondent
通讯者分类法/通訊者分類法　correspondent classification
通讯自由/傳播自由　freedom of communication
通洋运河/通洋運河　interoceanic canal
通用本体/常識本體　general ontology, common ontology
通用串行总线/通用序列匯流排　universal serial bus, USB
通用分面/通用分面　common facet
通用分组无线服务技术/通用封包無線服務　general packet radio service, GPRS
通用复分表/通用複分表　table of common subdivision, common subdivision
通用矩阵/GE矩陣　general electric matrix
通用款目/單元款目　unit entry, common entry
通用款目格式/通用款目格式　general entry format
通用名称/通用名稱　conventional name
通用文件处置期限表/通用檔辦理期限表　general record schedule
通用文种/通用文種　universal record type
通用职位分析法/通用工作分析法　generic job analysis method
通政使司/通政使司　Tongzhengshi Si
通知/通知　notification, notice
通知存款/通知存款　deposit at notice
通知单/通知單　letter of advice
通知放款/通知放款　call loan
通知付款/通知并付款　advice and pay
通知交货/通知交貨　delivery on call
通知银行/通知銀行　notifying bank
同伴压力/同儕壓力　peer pressure
同辈督导/同輩督導　peer supervision

同辈效应/年次效果 cohort effect
同步交流/同步通信, 同步通訊 synchronous communication
同步控制/同步控制 synchronous control
同步排程/同步排程 synchronous scheduling
同步生产/同步生產 synchronized production
同步式实习/同步式實習 synchronous field work
同步数字参考咨询/同步虛擬參考 synchronious virtual reference
同步信号/同步信號 sync signal
同步帧/同步幀 sync frame
同步作业分析图/同步作業分析圖 simultaneous motion chart, simo chart
同侪共同体/同儕共同體 community of peers
同侪文化/同儕文化 peer culture
同城票据/本地票據 local bill
同等和对等原则/同等和對等原則 principle of national treatment, principle of reciprocity
同等类/同等歸類 identical categorization
同等位次条款/平等受償 pari passu
同方差变异/均齊變異 homoscedastic variation
同方差模型/等變異數模型 homoscedastic model
同方差性/等變異性 homoscedasticity
同分布随机变量/相同分布隨機變數 identically distributed random variable
同峰度/等峰度 homokurtic
同工同酬/同工同酬 equal pay for equal work
同行间合作/同行間合作 intra-group cooperation
同行间交易/同行間交易 intra-group transaction
同行评议/同儕評閱, 同儕審查 peer review
同行评议期刊/同行評議期刊 peer-reviewed journal
同化/同化 assimilation
同化能力/吸收能力 assimilative capacity
同级/同級 homograde
同级类/同級類 same level class, collateral class
同级值/同級值 intergraduated value
同居/同居 cohabitation, live together
同居共财/同居共財 residence and wealth sharing
同居相隐不为罪/同居相隱不爲罪 an ancient Chinese legal principle of allowing cohabitation person to mutually conceal their offences
同类/同屬性 congeneric
同类婚/内婚 homogamy
同类机/同類機 uniform machine
同类客体/同類客體 category object
同龄群体/同儕團體, 同輩團體 peer group
同偏度/同偏態 homoclitic
同期聚合/同期總合 contemporaneous aggregation
同期相关干扰/同期相關干擾 contemporaneously correlated disturbance
同期相关性/同期相關 contemporaneous correlation
同期协方差/同期變異數 contemporaneous covariance
同情罢工/同情性的罷工 sympathy strike
同情效应/同情效應 sympathy effect
同生群分析/同齡族群分析, 世代分析 cohort analysis
同时博弈/同步賽局 simultaneous game
同时发生的/同時發生的 concurrent
同时抗辩权/同時抗辯權 right to defense of simultaneous performance
同时效度/同時效度 concurrent validity
同时行动博弈/同步行動賽局 simultaneous-move game
同时性/聯立性 simultaneity
同塑文化/同塑文化 cofigurative culture
同位穿孔检索系统/同位穿孔檢索系統 peek-a-boo system
同位类/同位類 coordinate class
同位叙词/同位敘詞 sibling
同乡会/同鄉會 association of fellows sharing native-place ties, townsmen association
同心多元化/集中式多角化 concentric diversification
同心圆理论/同心圓都市發展理論 concentric zone theory
同心圆模式/同心圓模式 concentric zone model
同形异义词/同形異義詞 homograph
同型法/同型法 isotype method
同型机/同型機 identical machine
同性恋/同性戀, 同性愛 homosexuality
同性恋家庭/同性戀家庭 homosexual family
同性恋恐惧症/恐同症 homophobia
同性恋文化/同性戀文化 homosexual culture
同业拆借/同業拆借 interbank loan
同业交易/同業交易 trader's transaction
同业透支/同業透支 overdraft on bank
同一控制下的企业合并/同一控制下的企業合併 business combination involving enterprises under common control
同义词/同義字 synonym
同义词环/同義字環 synonym ring
同义关系/同義關係 synonymous relationship
同源/親類 kindred
同质不完全竞争/同質不完全競爭 homogeneous imperfect competition
同质层/均齊層 homogeneous stratum

同质产品/同質產品　homogeneous product
同质货物/同質貨物　homogeneous cargo
同质竞争/同質競爭　homogeneous competition
同质商品/同質商品　homogeneous commodity
同质市场/同質市場　homogeneous market
同质性/同質性　homophily
同质预期/同質預期　homogeneous expectation
同质指数/和諧指數　index of homophily
同轴电缆/同軸電纜　coaxial cable
同族专利/專利家族　patent family
佟氏不等式/Tong 不等式　Tong's inequality
铜版/銅版　copper forme
铜版印本/銅版印本　copperplate edition
铜版纸/銅版紙　coated paper
童工/童工　child labor
统筹层次/統籌層次　pooling level
统筹城乡发展/統籌城鄉發展　urban-rural integrative development
统筹法/統籌法　overall planning method
统购包销/統購包銷　unified purchase and sale
统计变异/統計變異　statistical variation
统计标准/統計標準　statistical standard
统计标准分类/統計標準分類　standard classification of statistics
统计表/統計表　statistical table
统计测量/統計量測　statistical measurement
统计抽样表/統計抽樣表　statistical sampling table
统计单位/統計單位　statistical unit
统计单元/統計單位　statistical unit
统计档案/統計檔案　statistical file
统计地理[学]/統計地理[學]　statistical geography
统计地区/統計地區　statistical area
统计地图/統計地圖　statistical map
统计调查/統計調查　statistical survey, statistical investigation
统计独立[性]/統計獨立[性]　statistical independence
统计对策/統計賽局　statistical game
统计法/统计法规　statistics law
统计方法/統計方法　statistical method
统计分析/統計分析　statistical analysis
统计风险/統計上的風險　statistical risk
统计符号/統計符號　statistical symbol
统计关联/統計相聯　statistical association
统计归纳/統計歸納　statistical induction
统计规律性/統計規律性　statistical regularity
统计过程控制/統計製程控制　statistical process control, SPC
统计机构/統計機構　statistical agency
统计计划/統計計劃　statistical planning
统计计算/統計計算　statistical computing
统计假设/統計假設　statistical hypothesis
统计假设检验/統計假設檢定　statistical hypothesis testing
统计检验/統計檢定　statistical test
统计决策函数/統計決策函數　statistical decision function
统计决策理论/統計決策理論,统计判定理論　statistical decision theory
统计可靠性/統計可靠度　reliability of statistics
统计控制/統計管制　statistical control
统计控制状态/統計管制狀態　state in statistical control
统计库存控制/統計存貨控制　statistical inventory control
统计理论/統計理論　statistical theory
统计力学/統計力學　statistical mechanics
统计量/統計量　statistic
D统计量/D統計量　D-statistic
F统计量/F統計量　F-statistic
G统计量/G統計量　G-statistic
k统计量/k統計量　k-statistic
L统计量/L型統計量　L-statistic
M统计量/M統計量　M-statistic
O统计量/O統計量　O-statistic
P统计量/P統計量　P-statistic
Q统计量/Q統計量　Q-statistic
R统计量/R型統計量　R-statistic
U统计量/U統計量　U-statistic
W统计量/W統計量　W-statistic
Wn统计量/Wn統計量　Wn-statistic
Ψ^2统计量/Ψ^2統計量　psi-square statistic
统计量的期望值/統計量的期望值　expected value of statistic
统计量的效率/統計量的效率　efficiency of a statistic
统计描述/統計描述　statistical description
统计模式/統計型態　statistical pattern
统计模型/統計模型　statistical model
统计年鉴/統計年鑒　statistical yearbook
统计批/統計批　statistical lot
统计区域标准分类/統計地區標準分類　standard classification of statistical areas
统计曲率/統計曲率　statistical curvature
统计全域/統計全域　statistical universe
统计容忍分析/統計容許分析　statistical tolerance

analysis
统计容忍区间/統計容許區間 statistical tolerance interval
统计容忍限/統計容許界限 statistical tolerance limit
统计容忍域/統計容許域 statistical tolerance region
统计软件包/統計套裝軟體 statistical package
统计上的显著差异/統計上的顯著差異 statistical significant difference
统计设计/統計設計 statistical design
统计数据/統計數據,統計資料 statistical data
统计数据库/統計資料庫 statistical database
统计数字/統計圖表 statistical figure
统计数字汇集/統計資料收集 collection of statistical data
统计特征/統計特徵 statistical characteristic
统计图/統計圖 statistical diagram, statistical graph
统计图分析/統計圖分析 cartographic analysis
统计推断/統計推論 statistical inference
统计显著性/統計顯著性 statistical significance
统计相依[性]/統計相依[性] statistical dependence
统计信息系统/統計資訊系統 statistical information system
统计性歧视/統計歧視 statistical discrimination
统计序列/統計數列 statistical series
统计[学]/統計[學] statistics
统计学家/統計學家 statistician
统计验收抽样/統計允收抽樣 statistical acceptance sampling
统计遗传学/統計遺傳學 statistical genetics
统计质量控制/統計品質管制 statistical quality control, SQC
统计专家系统/統計專家系統 statistical expert system
统计资料库系统/統計資料庫系統 statistical database system
统计总体/統計母體 statistical population
统括价格/統括價格,一籃子價格,總價 lump price
统一标目/統一標目 uniform heading
统一偿债基金/統一償債基金 consolidated sinking fund
统一冲突规范/統一衝突規範 uniform conflict rules
统一公债/統一公債,不還本債券,無期債券 consolidated stock, consolidated bond, consol
统一惯用标目/統一慣用標目 uniform conventional heading
统一合伙企业法案/統一合夥條例 uniform partnership act
统一基金/統一基金 consolidated fund
统一价格/統一價格 flat price
统一建模语言/統一模組化語言 unified modeling language, UML
统一交货定价/統一交貨定價法,統一交運訂價法 uniform-delivered pricing
统一命令/指揮統一 unity of command
统一实体法规范/統一實體法規範 uniform substantive rules
统一书刊号/統一書刊號 Union Books and Serials Number, UBSN
统一税负/統一稅負 flat tax
统一税率/齊一稅率 uniform tax rate
统一诉讼程序规范/統一訴訟程式規範 uniform civil procedure rules
统一特许经营发行通告/統一特許經營要約公告 uniform franchise offering circular
统一题名/統一題名 uniform title
统一有限合伙企业法案/統一有限合夥法,统一有限公司法 uniform limited partnership act
统一指挥/統一指揮 unity of direction
统一资源标识符/通用資源識別符 universal resource identifier, URI
统一资源定位器/環球資源定位器 universal resource locator, URL
统一资源名称/一致資源名稱 uniform resource name, URN
统一资源属性/一致資源屬性 universal resource characteristic, URC
统账结合/統賬結合 combination of social pooling and individual account
统治阶级/統治階級 ruling class
偷税/偷稅 tax dodging
偷税罪/偷稅罪 crime of evading tax
头寸短缺/頭寸短缺 tight position
头寸限额/持倉限額 position limit
头脑风暴/腦力激盪[術] brainstorming
头脑风暴法/大腦風暴,腦力激盪術 brainstorm, brainstorming technique
头脑风暴预测法/頭腦風暴預測法 brainstorm forecasting approach
头条新闻/大新聞 big news
投保/投保 the process of entering into an insurance contract
投保单/投保單 insurance slip
投保货物/投保貨物 insured cargo
投保金额/保險金額 amount insured, amount covered

投保人/投保人,被保險人　insurance applicant, holder of policy
投保申请书/保險要保書　application for insurance
投币电唱机/光碟櫃　jukebox
投标/投標　bidding
投标保证金/投標保證金　tender bond
投标的有效性/投標的有效性　validity of bid
投标规则/投標規則　bidding rule
投标函/投標函　letter of tender
投标价格/投標價格,買價　bidding price, tender price, bid price
投标金额/投標價格　bidding price
投标买卖/投標買賣　bidding trade
投标人/投標人　bidder
投标人须知/投標人須知　instruction to bidder
投标-施工/投標-施工　bid-build
投标书/投標書　document bidder
投标书附录/投標函附錄　appendix to tender
投标书有效期/投標書有效期　bid validity
[投标]预备会/[投標]預備會議　preparatory meeting
投标债券/投標債券　tender bill
投产前资本输出/投產前資本支出　pre-production capital expenditure
投放危险物质罪/投放危險物質罪　crime of spreading hazardous material
投稿/投稿　contribution
投机/投機　speculation
投机动机/投機動機　speculative motive
投机进口/投機性輸入　speculative importation
投机买进/投機買進,看漲買進　speculative buying
投机市场/投機市場　speculation market
投机收益/投機收益　speculative gain
投机损失/投機損失　speculative loss
投机套利/投機套利　speculation arbitrage
投机投资/投機性投資　speculative investment
投机[性]泡沫/投機[性]泡沫　speculative bubble
投机性需求/投機性需求　speculative demand
投机者/投機者　speculator
投票悖论/投票矛盾,表决的矛盾性　paradox of voting, voting paradox
投票规则/投票法則　voting rule
投票理论/投票理論　ballot theory
投票制/投票制度　voting system
投入/投入　input
投入产出表/投入產出表　input-output table
投入产出分析/投入-產出分析　input-output analysis
投入产出过程/投入產出過程　input-output process
投入产出核算/投入產出賬　input-output account
投入产出模型/投入產出模型　input-output model
投入产出系数/投入產出係數　input-output coefficient
投入产出线性规划分析/投入產出線性規劃分析　input-output linear programming analysis
投入产出延长表/投入產出延長表　input-output prolong table
投入产出优化模型/投入產出優化模型,最適投入產出模型　optimal input-output model, input-output optimization model
投入产出预测模型/投入產出預測模型　input-output forecasting model
投入分布/投入分布　input distribution
投入税/投入稅　input tax
投入系数/投入係數　input coefficient
投入占用产出模型/投入占用產出模型　input-occupancy-output model
投入资本/投入資本　financing investment, vested proprietorship
投入资本收益率/投資資本回報,投入資本報酬率　return on invested capital, ROIC
投入资产/投入資產　investment asset
投射测验/投射測驗　projective test
投诉指数/抱怨指數　complaint index
投影/投影　projection
投影片/投影片　project film
投影图像/投影圖　overhead projection, projection figure
投影制版/投影製版　projection screen making
投影制品/投影製品　projection product
投影坐标系/投影坐標系統　projected coordinate system
投资/投資　investment
投资保险/投資保險　investment insurance
投资保证/投資保證,投資保障,投資承諾　investment guarantee, investment commitment
投资保证协定/投資保障協定　investment guarantee agreement
投资边际生产率/投資邊際生產力　marginal productivity of investment
投资标准/投資標準　investment criteria
投资补贴/投資抵減　investment allowance
投资补助金/投資補助金　investment grant
投资不足/投資不足,低度投資　under investment, underinvestment
投资场所/投資場所　outlet for investment

投资成本／投资费用　investment cost
投资承诺／投资承諾,投資保證　investment commitment
投资乘数／投資乘數　investment multiplier
投资额／投資金額　amount invested
投资方案比较法／投資方案比較法　investment project proposal comparison approach
投资分析／投資分析　investment analysis
投资风险／投資風險　investment risk
投资公司／投資公司　investment company, investment house
投资估算／投資估算　investment estimation
投资估算指标／投資估算指標　investment estimate index
投资股票／投資股票　investment stock
投资鼓励与投资保证制度／投資鼓勵與投資保證制度　encouragement and guarantee system of investment
投资顾问合同／投資顧問合約　investment advisory contract
投资过度学说／投資過度學說　overinvestment theory
投资函数／投資函數　investment function
投资合同／投資合約　investment contract
[投资]互补性效应／[投資]互補性效應　complementary effect
投资环境／投資環境　investment climate, investment environment
投资回报／投資報酬　investment return, return on investment
投资回收／投資回收　investment recovery, recovery of investment
投资回收期／回收期間,還本期間　payback period
投资回收期法／投資回收期法　term of investment return approach
投资活动／投資活動　investment activity, investing activity
投资货币市场／投資通貨市場　investment currency market
投资货物／投資貨物　investment goods
投资饥渴症／投資飢渴　investment hunger
投资机构／投資機構　investing institution
投资机会／投資機會　investment opportunity
投资基金／投資基金　investment fund
投资基金持有人／投資基金持有人　investment fund holder
投资基金管理人／投資基金管理人　investment fund manager

投资基金托管人／投資基金託管人　investment fund trustee
投资激励／獎勵投資,投資獎勵　encouragement of investment, investment incentive
投资计划／投資計劃　investment plan
投资技术／投資技術　investment technology
投资价值／投資價值　investment value
投资结构／投資結構　structure of investment
投资经纪人／投資經紀人　investment broker
投资景气／投資景氣　investment boom
投资决策／投資決策　investment decision
投资可行性研究／投資可行性研究　feasibility study of investment, investment feasibility study
投资控制／投資控制　investment control
投资扩张／擴大投資　investment expansion
投资利息／投資利息　interest on investment
投资率／投資率　investment rate, rate of investment
投资评价／投資評價　investment appraisal
投资期间／投資期間　investment period
投资前基金／投資前基金　pre-investment fund
投资倾向／投資傾向　propensity to invest
投资权益／投資權益　investment interest
投资融资／投資融資　financing of investment
投资市场／投資市場　investment market
投资收入附加税／投資收入附加稅　investment income surcharge
投资收益／投資收益　gain on investment, investment income, investment gain
投资收益率／投資收益率,投資所得率,投資報酬率　return on investment, investment income ratio, rate of return
投资损失／投資損失　investment loss
投资缩减／投資縮減,負投資　negative investment
投资限制／投資限制,投資管制　investment restriction
投资项目／投資專案　investment project
投资项目期限／投資專案期限　life of project
投资效率／投資效率　investment efficiency
投资信贷／投資信貸　investment credit
投资信托／投資信託　investment trust
投资信托公司／投資信託公司　investment trust company
投资性房地产／投資性房地産　investment real estate
投资需求／投資需求　investment demand
投资需求曲线／投資需求曲線　investment demand curve
投资意向／投資意向　investment intention
投资溢价／投資溢價　investment premium

投资银行/投資銀行　investment bank
投资银行业务/投資銀行業務　investment banking
投资优先权/投資優先權　priority of investment
投资诱导论/投資誘導理論　theory of inducement to invest
投资诱因/投資誘因　inducement to invest
投资余额/投資餘額　investment balance
投资与经营的分离/投資與經營的分離　separation of investment and management
投资预算/投資預算　investment budget
投资债券/投資債券　investment bond
投资账户/投資賬戶　investment account
投资者保护/保護投資人　investor protection
投资证券/投資證券　investment security
投资支出/投資支出　investment expenditure, investment outlay
投资中的分享外币期权/投資中的分享外幣期權　shared currency option under tender
投资中心/投資中心　investment center
投资周转/投資週轉　investment turnover
投资主体/投資主體　investment subject
投资准备金/投資準備金　investment reserve
投资咨询服务/投資諮詢服務　investment reference service
投资咨询账户/投資諮詢賬戶　investment advisory account
投资总收益/投資總收益　gross income yield
投资组合/投資組合,資產組合　investment portfolio
投资组合有效边界/資產組合效率前緣　portfolio efficiency frontier
投资组合在险价值/投資組合風險值　portfolio value-at-risk, portfolio VaR
透明片/透明片　transparency
透明性/透明性　transparency
透视分析/透視分析　transparency analysis
透印/透印　print through
透支/透支　overdraft
透支限度/透支限額　limit of overdraft
透支信用债券/透支信用債券　all money debenture
K 凸/K 凸　K-convex
凸版印刷/凸版印刷　relief printing
凸包/凸殼,線性殼　convex hull, linear hull
凸对策/凸對局　convex game
凸对称最大值检验/凸對稱最大值檢定　convex symmetric maximum, CSM test
凸多面体/凸多面體　convex polyhedron
凸二次规划/凸二次式規劃　convex quadratic programming
凸分布/凸分布,凸分配　convex distribution
凸规划/凸規劃　convex programming
凸函数/凸函數　convex function
凸集/凸集　convex set
凸技术/凸型生產技術　convex technology
凸偏好/凸性偏好　convex preference
凸性/凸性　convexity
凸印材料/凸印材料　relief printing material
凸印故障/凸印故障　relief printing defect
凸锥/凸錐　convex cone
凸组合/凸組合　convex combination
突变率/突變率　mutation rate
突变式变革/激進變革　radical change
突发故障/突發故障　sudden failure
突发事件/緊急事務,偶發　emergency, contingency
突发事件分级管理/災難分級處理　categorized emergency management
突发新闻/突發新聞,插播新聞　breaking news
突发性缺陷/突發性缺點　sporadic defect
突破性创新/激進創新　radical innovation
图/圖[式]　chart, diagram
np 图/np 管制圖　np chart
u 图/u 圖　u chart
x 图/x 圖　x chart
Z 图/Z 圖　Z-chart
图案/圖形,圖式　pattern
图标/圖標　icon
图标模型/圖示模型,圖形模型　graphical model
图柜/圖櫃,圖紙框　plan cabinet, plan case
图基表/Tukey 表　Tukey's table
图基检验/Tukey 檢定　Tukey's test
图基间隙检验/Tukey 間隙檢定　Tukey's gap test
图基快速检验/Tukey 簡易檢定　Tukey's quick test
图基模型/Tukey 模型　Tukey's model
图基统计量/Tukey 統計量　Tukey statistic
图集/圖集　collection of pictures, atlas
图记/圖記　Tuji, stamp
图解估计量/圖形估計量　graphical estimator
图解字典/圖解詞典　picture dictionary, visual dictionary
图库/圖庫　stock photography
图例/圖例　illustration
图录/圖譜　illustrative plates collection
图片/圖畫　picture
图片剪裁/圖片剪裁　crop image
图片文库/圖片庫　picture library
图片文字说明/圖片文字說明　picture writing explanation

图示/圖示　graphic representation
图示评审技术/圖解評審法　graphical evaluation and review technique, GERT
图书/[圖]書　book
图书报告会/圖書報告會　book talk
图书病害学/圖書病害學　pathology of books
图书博览会/書展　book fair
图书传送带/圖書傳送帶　book conveyor
图书磁条/磁條　magnetic strip
图书登记/圖書登記　book registration
图书典藏/典藏工作　book reservation, book collection
图书丢失率/圖書丟失率　book lose rate
图书防盗系统/圖書偵測系統　book detection system
图书分类法/圖書分類法　book classification
图书馆/圖書館　library
图书馆2.0/Library2.0　library 2.0
图书馆参考咨询服务/圖書館參考諮詢服務　library reference service
图书馆参与式管理/圖書館參與式管理　library participative management
图书馆成效评估/圖書館結果評價　library outcome assessment
图书馆导览/圖書館導覽　library tour
图书馆读者/圖書館讀者　library reader
图书馆罚款/圖書館罰款　library fine
图书馆法/圖書館法　library law
图书馆分馆/分館　branch library
图书馆服务/圖書館服務　library service
图书馆服务评估/圖書館服務評鑒　library service evaluation
图书馆功能/圖書館功能　library function
图书馆馆藏章/圖書館館藏章　property stamp
图书馆馆长/圖書館館長　library director, chief librarian
图书馆管理/圖書館管理　library management
图书馆管理规程/圖書館管理規則　library management regulation
图书馆管理学/圖書館管理　library management
图书馆规章制度/圖書館使用規則　library rules and regulations
图书馆合作/圖書館合作　library cooperation
图书馆核心价值/圖書館核心價值　library core value
图书馆基金/圖書館募款　library fund
图书馆计划管理/圖書館計劃管理　library plan management

图书馆绩效/圖書館績效　library performance
图书馆绩效评估/圖書館績效評估　library performance measurement, library performance appraisal
图书馆建筑/圖書館建築,圖書文獻大樓　library building
图书馆建筑学/圖書館建築學　library architecture
图书馆讲座/圖書館講座　library lecture
图书馆焦虑/圖書館焦慮　library anxiety
图书馆经费开支/圖書館支出　library expenditure
图书馆经济学/圖書館經營管理法　library economy
图书馆类型/圖書館類型　library type
图书馆理事会/圖書館託管者　library trustee
图书馆立法/圖書館立法　library legislation
图书馆联盟/圖書館聯盟,圖書館合作團體　library consortium, library consortia
图书馆伦理/圖書館倫理　library ethics
图书馆美学/圖書館美學　library aesthetics
图书馆门户网站/圖書館入口網站　library portal
图书馆目标管理/圖書館目標管理　library management by objectives
图书馆目录/圖書館目錄　library catalog
图书馆目录体系/圖書館目錄系統　library catalog system
图书馆目录组织/目錄組織　bibliographic organization
图书馆品牌/圖書館品牌　library brand
图书馆评估/圖書館評估　library assessment
图书馆权利/圖書館權利　library right
图书馆全面质量管理/圖書館全面品質管理　total quality management of library
图书馆设施/圖書館設施　library facility
图书馆社会学/圖書館社會學　library sociology
图书馆史/圖書館史　library history
图书馆使命/圖書館任務　library mission
图书馆事业/圖書館事業　librarianship
图书馆手册/圖書館手冊　library manual
图书馆术语/圖書館術語　library terminology
图书馆通讯/圖書館通訊　library bulletin
图书馆统计学/圖書館統計學　library statistics
图书馆网站/圖書館網站　library website
图书馆危机管理/圖書館危機管理　library crisis management
图书馆委员会/圖書館委員會　library commission
图书馆文化/圖書館文化　library culture
图书馆系统/圖書館系統　library system
图书馆协会/圖書館協會　library association
图书馆协作网络/圖書館合作系統　library

cooperative network
图书馆心理学/圖書館心理學　library psychology
图书馆行政管理/圖書館行政　library administration
图书馆宣传/圖書館推廣　library publicity
图书馆学/圖書館學　library science
图书馆学会/圖書館學會　library society
图书馆学家/圖書館科學家　library scientist
图书馆学教育/圖書館學教育　library science education
图书馆学情报学硕士/圖書館與資訊學碩士　master of library and information sciences, MLIS
图书馆学史/圖書館學史　history of library science
图书馆学硕士/圖書館學碩士　master of library science, MLS
图书馆学五定律/圖書館學五定律　the five laws of library science
图书馆学院/圖書館學校　library school
图书馆要素/圖書館要素　library element
图书馆要素说/圖書館要素说　theory of library element
图书馆业务辅导/圖書館專業輔導　professional work guidance in library
图书馆业务管理/圖書館服務管理　library service management
图书馆业务流程重组/圖書館業務流程重組　library sevice process reengineering
图书馆业务培训/圖書館專業訓練　professional training in library
图书馆业务外包/圖書館服務外包　library service outsourcing
图书馆印章/圖書館印章　library stamp
图书馆营销/圖書館服務行銷　library service marketing
图书馆用户/圖書館用户　library user
图书馆用品/圖書館用品　library supplies
图书馆预算/圖書館預算　library budget
图书馆员/圖書館管員，程式館管理員　library professional, librarian
图书馆员继续教育/館員繼續教育　librarian continuing education
图书馆员职业道德/圖書館員專業倫理，圖書館員職業道德規範　librarian professional ethics
图书馆员职业资格/圖書館員專業資格　librarian professional qualification
图书馆员职业资格认证制度/圖書館員專業資格認證系統　librarian professional qualification accreditation system
图书馆哲学/圖書館哲學　library philosophy

图书馆政策/圖書館政策　library policy
图书馆职业道德规范/圖書館職業道德規範　codes of library professional ethics
图书馆职业范式/圖書館職業範式　library professional paradigm
图书馆职业研究/圖書館職業研究　library profession study
图书馆职员/圖書館員，專業館員　library staff
图书馆志愿者/圖書館志願者　library volunteer
图书馆制度/圖書館制度　institution of library
图书馆治理/圖書館治理　library governance
图书馆咨询专家/圖書館諮詢顧問　library consultant
图书馆资源共享/圖書館資源共享　library resource sharing
图书馆自动化/圖書館自動化　library automation
图书馆自动化集成系统/整合性圖書館系統，整合式圖書館系統　integrated library system
图书馆自动化系统/圖書館自動化系統　library automation system
图书馆总馆/圖書館總館　central library
图书馆组织/圖書館組織　library organization
图书管理员/圖書館事務員　library clerk
图书加工/圖書加工　book processing
图书荐购/好書推薦，新書推薦，書籍推薦　book recommendation
图书俱乐部/讀書俱樂部　book club
图书流通/圖書流通　book circulation
图书贸易/圖書交易　book trade
图书目录/圖書目錄　book list
图书募捐/圖書捐贈　book drive
图书拍卖/圖書標售　book auction
图书漂流/圖書漂流　book crossing
图书评介/書評　book review, book report, book appraisal
图书评论/書評　book review, book report, book appraisal
图书破损率/圖書破損率　damage rate of books
图书情报工作/圖書館與資訊服務　library and information service
图书情报事业/圖書情報事業　library and information cause
图书情报一体化/圖書情報一體化　integration of library and information
图书史/圖書史　history of book
图书文化/圖書文化　book culture
图书消磁/圖書消磁　demagnetizing
图书消磁机/圖書消磁機　desensitizer

图书宣传/閱讀推廣 book publicity, reading promotion
图书学/圖書學 book study
图书验收/驗收 receipt and invoice-checking, receiving
图书运送升降机/圖書運送升降機 book hoist, book lift
图书在版编目/圖書在版編目 cataloguing in publication
图书征订代码/圖書徵訂代碼 book order number
图书征集/徵集 requisition
图书周转架/週轉架 turnover shelf
图书租借计划/圖書租借計劃 book rental plan
图腾崇拜/圖騰主義 totemism
图文处理制版/自動沖片機 image and text processing and platemaking
图文合一/圖文合一 text-image integration
图文信息处理/圖文資訊處理 graphic information processing
图像/圖像 image
图像采集/影像擷取 image capture
图像采样/影像取樣 image sampling
图像处理/影像處理 image processing
图像代换/圖像代換 image including
图像动画/圖像動畫 graphic animation
图像分辨率/影像解析度 image resolution
图像覆盖率/影像覆蓋率 image coverage rate
图像检索/影像檢索 image retrieval
图像校正/影像修正 image correction
图像滤镜/圖像濾鏡 image filter
图像锐化/影像鋭化 image sharpening
图像扫描/影像掃描 image scanning
图像扫描仪/掃描器 image scanner
图像输出机/底片輸出機 imagesetter
图像数据库/影像資料庫 image database
图像通道/影像通道 image channel
图像通信/影像通訊 image communication
图像文件/影像資料 iconographic record
图像文献/圖像文獻 iconic document
图像压缩/影像壓縮 image compression
图像元素/影像元件 image element
图像载体/圖像載體 image carrier, image store
图像噪声/圖像雜訊 image noise
图像制备/圖像製備 image preparation
图形/圖形 graphic
图形编排/圖形編排 graphic layout
图形处理/圖形處理 graphic processing
图形加速卡/圖形加速器卡 graphic accelerator card
图形评价法/圖形評等量尺 graphic rating scale
图形谱/圖形譜 graphic spectrum
图形文件/圖形檔案 graphic record
图形文献/圖形文獻 graphic document, iconic document
图域/圖域 chart field
图纸/圖紙 drawing
图纸会审/圖紙會審 blueprint review
图纸框/圖紙框,圖櫃 plan cabinet, plan case
途中报关进口/保稅運輸通關 immediate transportation entry
涂盖/遮去,塗去 blocking out
涂胶器/塗膠器 coating trough
涂料纸/塗布紙,銅版紙 coated paper, art paper
屠宰税/屠宰税 slaughter tax
土地/土地 land
土地产权/土地產權 land property right
土地承包期限/土地承包期限 land contract term
土地出让收入/土地出讓收入 revenues derived from transfer of right to use State-owned land
土地登记/土地登記 land registration
土地法/土地法 land law
土地改革/土地改革 land reform
土地规划/土地規劃 land planning
土地贵族/擁有土地的貴族階級 landed aristocracy
土地划拨/土地流轉 land assignment
土地利用/土地利用 land use
土地利用计划/土地利用計劃,土地使用計劃 land-use plan
土地伦理/土地倫理 land ethic
土地密集型产品/土地密集產品 land intensive product
土地密集型产业/土地密集產業 land intensive industry
土地密集型或资本密集型/土地或資本密集 land or capital intensive
土地使用权/土地使用權 land use right
土地使用权出让/土地使用權授 assignment of the right to land use
土地使用权有偿转让/土地使用權有償轉讓 compensated transfer of land use rights
土地税/土地税 land tax
土地所有者/地主 land owner
土地统计/土地統計 land statistics
土地投资/土地投資 investment in land
土地退耕/休耕 land retirement
土地退耕保护/保育休耕 conservation reserve
土地银行/土地銀行 land bank

土地用途分区/區域土地使用　land-use zoning
土地用途管制/土地使用管制,土地使用控制　land use control, land use regulation
土地用途控制/土地使用管制　land-use control
土地增值税/土地增值稅　land value increment tax
土地征收/土地的徵用　land expropriation
土地征用权/公用徵收　eminent domain
土地转让费/土地轉讓費　land transfer fee
土地租赁而非土地征收/以租代徵　land leasing instead of land expropriation
土木工程施工合同条件/土木工程施工合同條件　condition of contract for works of civil engineering construction
土壤流失/土壤流失　soil loss
土壤侵蚀/土壤侵蝕　soil erosion
土著/土著,本地人　aboriginal, native, local
吐鲁番文书/吐魯番文書　Turpan Instruments
团队/團隊　team
团队尺度/團隊尺度　team structuring dimension, TSD
团队多样性/團隊多樣性　team diversity
团队工作/團隊工作,團隊合作　teamwork
团队过程/團隊過程　team process
团队建设/團隊建立　team building
团队建设法/團隊建設　team-building method
团队奖励计划/團隊獎勵計劃,團隊誘因計劃　team incentive plan
团队精神/團隊精神　team spirit
团队凝聚力/團隊凝聚力　cohesive force within a team
团队式结构/團隊式結構　team-based structure
团队透镜模型/團隊透鏡模型,團隊透鏡模式　team lens model
团队销售/團隊銷售　team selling
团队型管理/團隊管理　team management
团队型研发组织/團隊型研發組織　team type research and development organization
团队学习/團隊學習　team learning
团购/團購　group purchase
团购网站/團購網站　group purchase website
团伙/團夥　gang
团结/團結　solidarity
团体成员/群體成員　group membership
团体订阅/團體訂閱　group subscription
团体督导/團體督導,團體視導　group supervision
团体访谈/團體訪談　group interview
团体供应/團體供應　group supply
团体著者/團體作者　corporate author

推定/推測　presumption
推定的法律选择/推定的法律選擇　implied choice of law
推定课税/推定課稅　presumptive taxation
推定全损/推定全損　constructive total loss, technical total loss
推定误差/推定誤差　putative error
推定责任者/推定責任者　supposed author
推动式供应链/推動式供應鏈　push supply chain
推断/推論,推測　inference
推荐/推薦,建议　recommendation
推荐读物/建議閱讀書目　recommended reading
推荐技术/推薦技術　recommendation technology
推荐目录/推薦目錄　recommendatory bibliography
推荐书目/推薦書目　recommended bibliography, list of best books, reading list
推荐性标准/建議標準　recommended standard
推荐意愿/推薦意願　willingness to recommend
推荐制/推薦制　recommendation system
推介服务/推介服務　recommendation service
推镜头/推鏡頭　track shot
推拉假说/推拉假說　push-pull hypothesis
推理机/推理機,推理引擎　inference engine
推理能力/推理能力　reasoning ability
推理片/推理片　reasoning film
推论性统计/推論統計　inferential statistics
推式策略/推式策略　push strategy
推式系统/推式[生產]系統　push system
推销观念/銷售觀念　selling concept
推销竞争/推銷競爭　sale contest
退出机制/退出機制,退場機制　withdrawal mechanism
退底/退底　cutout
退订/取消訂閱　cancel a subscription, unsubscribe, subscription cancelling
退稿/退稿　rejection
退股/退股　withdrawal share
退关/退關　shut out
退关货物/退關貨物　shut out cargo
退化/退化　degradation, degeneracy
退化分布/退化分布　degenerate distribution
退化区间/退化區間　degenerate interval
退化正态分布/退化常態分布,退化常態分配　degenerate normal distribution
退还/追繳　disgorgement
退回汇票/退回匯票　re-exchange bill
退回票据/退回票據　return bill

退回预付资金/退回預付款　restitution of advance payment
退伙/退夥　withdrawal from partnership enterprise
退货/退貨　return to vendor
退货单/退貨單　return document
退货率/退貨率　rate of return to vendor
退款保证/保證退款,現金買回保證,原價買回保證　money back guarantee
退票通知单/退票通知單　protest jacket
退书政策/退書策略　return policy
退税/退稅,税收回扣,出口税回扣　tax refund, drawback for duty paid, tax rebate
退税申请书/退稅申請書　application for drawback
退税制度/退稅制度　drawback system
退休/退休　retirement
退休福利/退休金福利,撫恤金福利　pension benefit
退休金计划/退休金計劃　pension plan
退休制度/退休制度　retirement system, system of retirement
退休综合征/退休症候群　retirement syndrome
退修/退修　returned for revision
退役安置/退役安置　veteran replacement
退褶/去摺　unfolding
托宾Q/杜賓Q值,杜賓Q比率　Tobin Q
托宾Q理论/Q投資論　Q theory of investment
托宾两阶段最小二乘法/杜賓二階段最小平方　Tobin two-stage least squares
托宾模型/杜賓模型　Tobin model
托宾效应/杜賓效果　Tobin effect
托存图书馆/寄存圖書館　depository library
托达罗模型/Todaro遷移模型　Todaro's migration model
托付信用证/託付信用狀　domicile credit
托管银行/保管銀行　custodian bank
托管账户/受益託管賬　custodian account
托管制度/託管制度,信託制　trusteeship, trusteeship system
托汇/託匯,匯款申請　apply for remittance
托基回合/托基回合　Torquay Round
托架书橱/托架書櫃　bracket shelf
托拉斯/托拉斯　trust
托马斯分布/Thomas分布　Thomas distribution
托盘/托盤　tray
托盘作业一贯化/托盤作業一貫化　consistency of the pallet transit
托收/託收申請　apply for collection
托收背书/託收背書,委任代收背書　endorsement for collection
托收成本/託收成本　collection cost
托收代理行/代收人,收款代理商　collection agency
托收费/託收費　collection charge
托收汇票/託收匯票　draft for collection
托收进口汇票/託收進口匯票　inward bill for collection
托收款项/應收託收款　due from collection
托收票据/託收票據　collection bill, bill for collection, bill sent for collection
托收期/託收期間　collection period
托收手续费/託收手續費　collection commission
托收委托书/託收委託書　advice for collection, collection order
托收项下的凭单付款/交單託收付款　payment against document through collection
托收银行/託收銀行　collection bank
托售成品/寄售成品　finished goods on consignment
托售发票/寄售發票　consignment invoice
托售账户/寄售賬戶　consignment account
托运/抵埠寄售　consignment
托运单/託運單　booking note
托运人/託運人　consigner
托运人出口报关清单/託運人出口報關清單　shipper's export declaration
拖欠订单/拖欠訂單　back order
拖欠关税/退稅　back duty
拖延/可避免延誤　avoidable delay
脱产培训/職外訓練　off-the-job training
脱机/離線　offline
脱机打印/離線列印　offline print
脱机检索/離線檢索　offline search
脱机模式/離線模式　offline mode
脱机下载/離線下載　offline download
脱机状态/離線狀態　offline state
脱离理论/脱離理論,減少參與理論　disengagement theory
脱墨/脱墨　roller stripping
脱贫致富/脱貧致富　alleviate poverty and become prosperous
脱嵌性/去鑲嵌　disembeddedness
脱酸/脱酸,去酸　deacidification
脱文/脱文　missing word
脱销/缺貨　stockout, out of stock
妥协成本/妥協成本　cost of compromise
椭圆对称分布/橢圓對稱分布,橢圓對稱分配　elliptically symmetric distribution
椭圆截面/橢圓截略　elliptical truncation

椭圆性/椭圆性　ellipticity
椭圆正态分布/椭圆常态分布,椭圆常態分配　elliptical normal distribution

拓展服务/外展服務,推廣服務　outreach service

W

挖掘性学习/挖掘性學習　exploitative learning
瓦尔德检验/渥得檢定　Wald test
瓦尔拉斯产量/瓦拉斯產出　Walrasian output
瓦尔拉斯定律/瓦拉氏定理　Walras' law
瓦尔拉斯-古诺均衡/瓦拉氏-庫諾均衡　Walras-Cournot equilibrium
瓦尔拉斯机制/瓦拉氏機制　Walrasian mechanism
瓦尔拉斯均衡/瓦拉氏均衡　Walrasian equilibrium
瓦克夫制度/瓦克夫制度　Waqf system
瓦楞纸板/瓦楞紙　corrugated board
瓦楞纸板柔版印刷/瓦楞紙板柔版印刷　corrugated flexographic printing
瓦楞纸板印刷开槽机/瓦楞紙板印刷開槽機　corrugated printing slotting machine
瓦楞纸箱预印工艺/瓦楞紙箱預印工藝　corrugated board pre-printing
瓦洛用人思想/瓦洛用人思想　personnel thought of Vallor
歪曲、篡改作品/歪曲、篡改作品　distortion of a work
外包/委外　outsourcing
外币/外幣　foreign currency
外币持有额/外幣持有額　foreign currency holding
外币存款/外幣存款　foreign currency deposit
外币兑换/外幣兌換　foreign currency exchange
外币兑换券/外幣兌換券　foreign currency conversion certificate
外币兑换损失/外幣兌換損失　loss on exchange
外币法定准备制度/外幣法定準備制度　reserve requirement system for foreign currency
外币公债/外幣公債　foreign currency bond
外币管制/外幣管制　foreign currency control
外币汇票/外幣匯票　bill in foreign currency, foreign currency bill
外币交易/外幣交易　foreign currency transaction
外币金融/外幣金融　foreign currency finance
外币信用证/外幣信用狀　foreign currency credit
外币业务/外幣業務　foreign currency operation
外币债权/外匯債權　claimable asset in foreign currency
外币债券利息/外幣債券利息　interest on foreign currency bond
外币账户/外幣賬戶　foreign currency account
外币折合率/外幣折合率　foreign currency conversion rate
外币折算/外幣折算　foreign currency translation
外币资金/外幣資金　foreign currency fund
外部变量/外擾變項　extraneous variables
外部不经济/外部不經濟　external diseconomy
外部成本/外部成本　external cost
外部筹资/外部籌資　outside finance
外部出版物/外部出版物　external publication
外部方差/外在變異數　external variance
外部公平/外部公平　external equity
外部规模经济/外部規模經濟, 外部經濟規模　economy of outside scale, external economics of scale
外部监督/外部監督　external supervision
外部经济/外部經濟　external economy
外部均衡/外部平衡　external balance
外部考订/外部考訂　external criticism
外部控制/外部控制　external control
外部链接/外部鏈接　external link
外部情报员/外源　external source
外部融资/外部融資, 向外籌措資金, 外部融通　external financing
外部审计/外部稽核　external audit
外部失效成本/外部失效成本　external failure cost
外部时间/外部時間　external time
外部实体/外部實體　external entity
外部收益/外部效益　external benefit
外部调整准备时间/外部整備時間　external setup time
外部效度/外部效度, 外在效度　external validity
外部效应/外部效果　external effect
外部信息源/外部資訊源　external information source
外部性/外部性　externality
外部选择权/外部選擇權　outside option
外部压力/外在壓力　outside pressure
外部因素评价矩阵/外部因素評估矩陣　external factor evaluation matrix

外部招聘/外部招募　external recruitment
外部资本/外部資本　outside capital
外部资金/外部資金　outside fund
外部资源/外來資源　external resources
外埠兑现支票/外埠兑現支票　domicile check
外埠付款票据/外埠付款票據,付款地匯票　domicile bill
外埠付款期票/外埠付款期票　domicile note
外埠贴现票据/外埠貼現票據　domicile discounted bill
外侧控制限/外側管制界限　outer control limit
外层空间/外太空　outer space
外层空间法/外太空法　law of outer space
外罚函数法/外部懲罰函數法　exterior penalty function method
外购件/外購零件　purchased part
外观标识/視力識別　visual identification
外滚筒型设备/外滾筒型設備　external drum device
外国法的错误适用/外國法的錯誤適用　misapplication of foreign law
外国法人/外國法人　foreign legal person
外国公司/外國公司,海外公司　foreign company, foreign corporation, overseas company
外国国家及其财产豁免原则/外國國家及其財產豁免原則　principle of immunity of foreign states and their property
外国汇票/外國匯票　foreign bill of exchange
外国货进口报单/外國貨進口申報單　application for import of foreign goods
外国货涌入/外國貨湧入　influx of foreign goods
外国借款/外國借款　foreign borrowing
外国进口订货单/外國代購訂單　inward indent
外国进口货物清单/外國進口艙單　inward foreign manifest
外国旅行信用证/國外旅行信用狀　foreign traveler letter of credit
外国企业/外國企業　foreign enterprise
外国人/外國人　foreigner
外国商品/外國貨　foreign goods
外国投资/外國投資　foreign investment
外国投资跨国公司/國外投資跨國公司　foreign investment transnational corporation
外国委托人/外國委託人　foreign principal
外国银行/外國銀行　overseas bank
外国银行欠款/應收國外銀行款項　due from foreign banks
外国债券/外國債券　foreign bond
外国证券/外國證券　foreign security

外国直接投资/外國直接投資　foreign direct investment
外国资本/外國資本,外資　foreign capital
外国资产/外國資產,國外資產　foreign asset
外国子公司/外國子公司　foreign affiliate, foreign subsidiary corporation
外化/外化　externalization
外汇/外匯　foreign exchange, forex
外汇保值协定/外匯保證協定　Agreement on Exchange Guarantees
外汇波动准备金/外匯波動準備金　reserve for foreign exchange fluctuation
外汇补进汇款/外匯補進匯款　covering remittance
外汇承兑行/外匯承兑行　foreign exchange acceptance house
外汇承兑率/承兑匯票外匯匯率　accepting rate of exchange
外汇持有额/外匯持有額,外匯頭寸　foreign exchange holding, foreign exchange position
外汇持有限额制/外匯持有限額制　foreign exchange holding restriction system
外汇储备/外匯儲備,外匯準備,外匯存底　foreign exchange reserve, reserve of foreign exchange
外汇储备规模/外匯存底規模　size of foreign exchange reserve
外汇储备耗尽/外匯儲備耗減　depletion of foreign exchange reserve
外汇储备条款/外匯儲備條款　foreign exchange reservation clause
外汇存款/外匯存款　foreign exchange deposit
外汇存款余额/外匯存款餘額　balance of foreign exchange deposit
外汇贷款/外匯貸款　loan for exchange
外汇贷款审计/外匯貸款審計　audit of foreign exchange loan
外汇短缺/外匯短缺　shortfall in foreign exchange
外汇兑换交易/外匯兑換交易　exchange transaction
外汇兑换券/外匯兑換券　foreign exchange certificate
外汇兑换水单/外匯兑換水單　exchange memo
外汇兑换损益/外匯兑換損益　profit and loss on foreign currency exchange
外汇额度审计/外匯額度審計　audit of foreign exchange quota
外汇分配制度/外匯分配制度　foreign exchange allocation system
外汇风险/外匯風險　exchange risk, foreign exchange risk

外汇风险管理/外匯風險管理　foreign exchange risk management
外汇风险升水/外匯風險升水　foreign exchange risk premia
外汇负债/外匯負債　foreign exchange liability
外汇附加税/外匯附加税　exchange supplementary duty
外汇购买力平价/外匯購買力平價　purchasing power parity of exchange
外汇管理/外匯管理　management of foreign exchange
外汇管理体制/外匯管制體制　foreign exchange management system
外汇管理条例/外匯管理條例　currency regulation
外汇管制/外匯管制　foreign exchange control, control of foreign exchange
外汇管制规定/外匯管制規定　exchange control regulation
外汇合同/外匯合約　exchange contract, foreign exchange contract
外汇互换/外匯交換,換匯　foreign exchange swap
外汇换算/外匯換算　foreign exchange conversion
外汇汇兑损失/外匯匯兑損失　loss on foreign exchange
外汇汇价波动损失/外匯匯率波動損失　loss from fluctuation of foreign exchange rate
外汇汇率/外匯匯率　foreign exchange rate
外汇汇率波动/匯率波動　exchange rate fluctuation, fluctuation in exchange
外汇汇率风险/匯率風險　exchange rate risk
外汇基金/外匯基金　exchange fund, foreign exchange fund
外汇集中/外匯集中　foreign exchange concentration
外汇集中制度/外匯集中制度　foreign exchange concentration system
外汇交易/外匯交易　foreign exchange transaction
外汇交易收益/外匯交易收益　profit on foreign exchange transaction
外汇交易损失/外匯交易損失　loss on foreign exchange transaction
外汇缴存凭证/外匯繳存憑證,外匯繳售憑證　exchange surrender certificate
外汇缴售凭证/外匯繳售憑證,外匯繳存憑證　exchange surrender certificate
外汇结存/外匯結存,國外餘額　foreign balance
外汇结算单/外匯結算單　clearing exchange slip
外汇经纪人/外匯經紀人　foreign exchange broker, foreign exchange dealer

外汇经营/外匯經營　exchange operation
外汇竞争/外匯競爭　exchange competition
外汇理论/外匯理論　theory of foreign exchange
外汇利润/外匯利潤　exchange profit
外汇留成/外匯留成　foreign exchange retention
外汇卖出价/外匯賣價　selling rate of foreign exchange
外汇逆差/外匯逆差　unfavourable exchange
外汇拍卖/外匯拍賣　exchange auction
外汇牌价/外匯牌價,外匯報價　exchange rate quotation, foreign exchange quotation, quotation of for foreign currency
外汇牌价表/外匯牌價表　list of exchange rate quotation
外汇配额/外匯配額,外匯限額　foreign exchange quota
外汇配额制度/外匯配額制度　exchange quota system
外汇配给/外匯配給　rationing of exchange
外汇票据/外匯票據　exchange bill
外汇平衡账户/外匯平衡賬户　foreign exchange equalization account
外汇平价/外匯平價,匯率平價　exchange rate parity, exchange parity
外汇平准基金/外匯平準基金　exchange stabilization fund
外汇平准账户/外匯均等賬户　equalization account
外汇期货/外匯期貨,遠期外匯,貨幣期貨　foreign exchange future
[外汇期货和现货]掉期交易/[外匯期貨和現貨]掉期交易　swap exchange transaction
[外汇]期货和现货间差价/外匯期貨和現貨間差價　forward margin
外汇期货市场/外匯期貨市場　foreign exchange futures market
外汇期权/外匯選擇權　foreign exchange option, foreign currency option
外汇期权市场/外匯期權市場　foreign exchange option market
外汇倾销/外匯傾銷　exchange dumping, foreign exchange dumping
外汇清算协定/外匯清算協定　exchange clearing agreement
外汇清算制/外匯清算制　exchange clearing system
外汇申请/外匯申請　application for exchange
外汇审计/外匯審計　audit of foreign exchange
外汇升水/外匯升水　exchange at premium, exchange premium

外汇市场/外匯市場　foreign exchange market
外汇市场的稳定性/外匯市場的穩定性　stability of foreign exchange market
外汇收入与支出/外匯收入與支出　foreign exchange receipt and disbursement
外汇收益/外匯收益　exchange earning, gain on foreign exchange
外汇收支/外匯收支　income and expense of foreign exchange
外汇税/外匯稅　exchange tax, foreign exchange tax
外汇损益/外匯損益　exchange gain and loss, foreign exchange gain or loss
外汇套汇汇率/外匯交叉匯率　exchange cross rate
外汇条款/外匯條款　foreign exchange clause, exchange clause
外汇调期保证/外匯調期保證　swap exchange guarantee
外汇贴水/外匯貼水　exchange discount
外汇头寸/外匯頭寸,外匯部位,外匯持有額　exchange position, foreign exchange position
外汇投机/外匯投機　speculation on foreign exchange, foreign exchange speculation, exchange speculation
外汇外流/外匯外流　outflow of foreign exchange
外汇危机/外匯危機　exchange crisis
外汇稳定/外匯穩定　stabilization of foreign exchange
外汇稳定基金/外匯穩定基金,外匯平準基金　foreign exchange stabilization fund
外汇稳定账户/外匯穩定賬戶　exchange stabilization account
外汇限制/外匯限制　exchange restriction
外汇信贷/外匯信貸　credit in foreign exchange
外汇许可证/外匯許可證　foreign exchange licence
外汇业务/外匯業務　foreign exchange business, foreign exchange operation
外汇银行/外匯銀行　foreign exchange bank
外汇预算/外匯預算　exchange budget, foreign currency budget, foreign exchange budget
[外汇]折扣/匯票貼現　discount on exchange
外汇支票/外匯支票　exchange check
外汇专业银行/外匯專業銀行　specialized foreign exchange bank
外汇转账/外匯轉移　foreign exchange transfer
外汇准备/外匯存底　reserve for foreign exchange
外汇准备耗竭/外匯準備消耗　drain on foreign exchange reserve
外汇资产/外匯資產　foreign exchange asset
外汇资金证券/外匯資金證券　foreign exchange fund bill
外汇资金自动分配制/外匯資金自動分配制　foreign exchange fund automatic allocation system
外汇自由兑换/外匯自由兌換　exchange freedom
外汇自由市场/外匯自由市場　foreign exchange free market
外汇总额/外匯總額　total foreign exchange
外纪档/外紀檔　Wai Jidang
外借/借閱　borrow file, library loan
外借登记卡/外借登記卡　transaction card, T-card
外借频率/外借頻率　loan frequency
外空物体的登记/外空物體的登記　registration of objects lauched into outer space
外来货币/外來貨幣,外國貨幣　exotic currency
外来基金/外來基金　external funding investment
外来投入/外來投入,外國資金　external input
外来文件/外來文件　document of external origin
外来暂住人口/外來暫住人口　migrant with temporary residence
外来资金/外來資金　capital foreign, external funding investment
外链/外鏈　external link
外贸出口退税审计/外銷退稅審計　audit of export trade duty refund
外贸单位价值/對外貿易單位價值　foreign trade unit value
外贸单位价值指数/對外貿易單位價值指數　foreign trade unit value index
外贸寄售/外銷寄售　foreign trade on consignment
外贸垄断/外貿壟斷　monopoly of foreign trade
外贸模式/外貿模式　pattern of foreign trade
外贸收益/外貿收益　gain from foreign trade
外贸物价指数/外貿物價指數　price index of foreign trade
外贸依存度/對外貿易依存度　degree of dependence on foreign trade
外贸依存率/外貿依存率　ratio of dependence on foreign trade
[外贸]最高限额/[外貿]最高限額　maximum amount limitation
外派经理人/外派經理人　expatriate manager
外派人员管理/外派管理　expatriate management
外群体/外團體　out-group
外商投资经济/外資經濟　foreign-funded economy
外设计/外設計　external design
外审/外審　external review
外生变量/外生變量,外生變數　exogenous variable

外生变迁/外生變遷 exogenous transition
外生货币/貨幣外生性 exogenous money
外生型现代化/外生型現代化 ectogenous modernization
外生性/外生性 exogeneity
外生性检验/外生性檢定 exogeneity test
外生因子/外生因素 exogenous factor
外推[法]/外插[法] extrapolation
外围设备/週邊設備 peripheral
外文出版物/外文出版物 foreign language publication
外文书店/外文書店 foreign language bookstore
外文图书/外文圖書 foreign language book
外系统/外系統 exosystem
外显领导理论/外顯領導理論 explicit leadership theory
外向/外向型 outward-looking
外向型经济/外向型經濟 external-oriented economy, outward-oriented economy
外销定单统计/外銷訂單統計 export order statistics
外延抽样/廣泛抽樣 extensive sampling
外源性/外生 exogenous
外运提单/外運提單 outward bill of lading
外在变异/外在變異 outward variation
外在货币/外存貨幣 outside money
外在奖励/外在報酬,外在酬賞 extrinsic reward
外在效度/外在效度,外部效度 external validity
外噪声/外干擾 external noise
外债/外債 external loan, external debt, foreign loan
外债偿还本息/外債償還本息 service payment of external debt
外债偿还期/外債償還期 period of paying foreign debt
外债利息/外債利息 interest on external bond
外装帧面/外裝幀面 printed cover
外装帧纸/外裝幀紙 surface printed cover
外资/外資 foreign capital
外资股/外資股 foreign share
外资管理/對外投資管理 management of foreign investment
外资管制/外資管制 control of foreign fund
外资流入/外資流入 foreign capital inflow
外资企业/外商投資企業 foreign-funded enterprise
外资企业业绩要求/外資企業業績要求 performance requirement for foreign enterprises
外资审查/審定外資 examination of foreign investment
外资涌进/外資湧進 influx of foreign capital
弯月面/彎月面 meniscus
完成到开始关系/完成到開始關係 finish to start
完成到完成关系/完成到完成關係 finish to finish
完工产品/製成品 finished goods
完工估算/完工估算 estimate at completion, EAC
完工检验/完工檢驗 completion inspection
完工尚需估算/完工尚需估算,竣工尚需估算 estimate to complete, ETC
完工预算/完工預算 budget at completion
完美信息/完備訊息 perfect information
完美资本市场假设/完美資本市場假說 perfect capital market hypothesis
完全背书/完全背書,記名背書 full endorsement
完全编目/完全編目 full level cataloging
完全差别定价/完全差別定價 perfectly discriminatory pricing
完全成本定价/完全成本定價 full-cost pricing
完全成本法/完全成本法 full costing
完全成本分摊/完全分攤成本 fully distributed cost
完全充分统计量/完備充分統計量 complete sufficient statistics
完全独立[性]/完全獨立[性] complete independence
完全多重共线性/完全線性重合 perfect multicollinearity
完全二阶模型/完全二階模型 full second-order model
完全方程组/完全方程組 complete system of equations
完全分类号/完全分類號 full class number
完全分散化资产组合/完全分散化資產組合 completely diversified portfolio
完全跟踪/完全跟蹤 full pegging
完全共线性/完全共線性 perfect collinearity
完全关联/完全相聯 complete association
完全关税同盟/完全關稅同盟 complete customs union
完全回归/完全回歸 complete regression
完全混杂/完全混同 complete confounding
完全积累制/完全積累制 full funding system
完全计数/完全計數 complete count
完全价格歧视/完全差別訂價,第一級差別訂價 perfect price discrimination
完全金本位制/完全金本位制 full gold standard
完全竞争/完全競爭,純粹競爭 complete competition, perfect competition, pure competition
完全竞争市场/完全競爭市場 perfect competitive

market, pure competition market
完全决策函数族/完備決策函數族　complete family of decision functions
完全均衡/完全均衡　perfect equilibrium
完全理性/完全理性　total rationality
完全垄断市场/完全壟斷市場　perfect monopoly market, pure monopoly market
完全密度函数族/完備密度函數族　complete family of densities
完全赔偿/完全賠償　perfect compensation
完全配置/完備配置　complete layout
完全平衡格[子]方阵/完全平衡格子方陣　completely balanced lattice square
完全歧视/完全差别待遇　perfect discrimination
完全契约/完全契約　complete contract
完全区组设计/完全區集設計　complete block design
完全生命表/完全生命表　completed life table
完全生育率/完全生育率　completed fertility rate
完全随机化/完備隨機化　complete randomization
完全随机化设计/完全隨機化設計　completely randomized design
完全随机缺失/完全隨機缺失　missing completely at random, MCAR
完全随机试验/完全隨機試驗　completely randomized experiment
完全统计量/完備統計量　complete statistic
NP完全问题/NP完全問題　NP-complete problem
完全消耗系数/完全消耗係數　total input coefficient
完全消耗系数矩阵/完全消耗係數矩陣　total input coefficient matrix
完全信息/完全訊息，完全資訊　complete information
完全信息博弈/完美訊息賽局　perfect information game
完全信息的预期价值/完全資訊的預期價值　expected value of perfect information
完全信息极大似然法/充分訊息最大概度法　full information maximum likelihood method
完全信息期望值/完全資訊期望值　expected value of complete information
完全性/完全性，完備性　completeness
完全修正最小二乘/完全修正最小平方法　fully modified least square
完全需要系数矩阵/完全需要係數矩陣　total requirement coefficient matrix
完全一体化/全部合一　full integration
完全应税等价收益率/完全應稅等價收益率　fully taxable equivalent yield, FTEY
完全正交的/完全正交的　completely orthogonal
完全著录/完全著錄　full description
完全专业化/完全專業化　complete specialization
完全资产组合/完全資產組合　complete portfolio
完全自由贸易区/完全自由貿易區　full free trade area
完全组合/完全組合　complete combination
完税后交货/税迄交貨　delivered duty paid, DDP
完税后买方关栈交货价格/買方保稅倉庫交貨價　ex buyer's bonded warehouse
完税价格/完稅價格　dutiable price, price at duty paid, price duty paid
完整服务批发商/提供充分服務的批發商　full-service wholesaler
完整基金/完整基金　completeness fund
完整提单/完整提單　complete bill of lading
完整性/完整性　completeness, integrity
玩忽职守罪/怠忽職守罪　crime of dereliction
玩具馆藏/玩具館藏　toy collection
玩具图书/玩具圖書　toy book
晚报/晚報　evening newspaper, evening paper
晚期成长阶段/後期成長階段　later growth stage
晚期重商主义/晚期重商主義　mercantilism of late time
万维网/環球資訊網　World Wide Web, Web
王权/王權　kingship
网版印刷/網板印刷　screen printing
网版印刷机/自動網版印花機　screen printing machine
网点/網點　dot
网点覆盖率/網點覆蓋率　dot area coverage
网点面积率/網點面積率　dot area percentage
网点形状/網點形狀　dot shape
网点阴图片/網陰片　half-tone negative
网点增大/網點擴大　dot gain
网格/網格　grid
网际协议版本4/網際網路協定第四版　internet protocol version 4, IPV4
网际协议版本6/網際網路協定第六版　internet protocol version 6, IPV6
网距/網距　off-contact distance
网孔宽度/網孔寬度　width of mesh opening
网框/網框　screen printing frame
网络/網路　network
网络安全/網路安全　network security, web security
网络百科全书/網路百科全書　network support encyclopedia

网络暴力/網路霸凌　cyberbully
网络本体语言/Web 本體語言　web ontology language, OWL
网络边界/網路邊界　network boundary
网络场/網路場　cyber Ba
网络抽样/網路抽樣　network sampling
网络出版技术/網路出版技術　web publishing technology
网络出版物/網路出版物　network publication
网络出版支撑系统/網路出版支撐系統　network publishing support system
网络传播/網路傳播　internet communication
网络传输/網路傳輸　network transmission
网络词典/網路詞典　online dictionary, internet dictionary
网络词汇/網路詞彙　network vocabulary
网络辞书/網路辭書　network dictionary
网络打印机/網路列印機　network printer
网络电视台/網路電視臺　internet TV station
网络电台/網路電臺　net radio
网络调查/網路調查　internet survey
网络动画/網路動畫　network animation
网络动力学/網路動力學　network dynamics
网络动漫/網路動漫　network cartoon
网络读者/網路讀者　network reader
网络对策/網形對策　network game
网络多媒体/網路多媒體　network multimedia
网络多媒体出版/網路多媒體出版　network multimedia publishing
网络法/網路法　internet law
网络分析/網路分析　network analysis
网络服务提供者/網路服務提供者　internet service provider, ISP
网络歌曲/網路歌曲　network song
网络广播/網路廣播　web broadcaster
网络广告/網路廣告　online advertisement, web advertising
网络互联/網間網路　internetworking
网络计量学/網路計量學　webometrics, cybermetrics
网络教学/網路教學　network teaching
网络结构/網路結構,網狀結構　network structure
网络竞争情报/網路競爭情報　network competitive intelligence
网络开发理论/網路開發理論　internet exploration theory
网络空间/網路空間,網際空間　cyberspace
网络会计/網路賬務　network accounting

网络联盟/網路合作戰略　network cooperative strategy
网络聊天/網路聊天　internet relay chat
网络聊天室/網路聊天室　internet relay chat room
网络浏览器/網頁瀏覽器　web browser
网络流行语/網路流行語　network buzzword
网络媒体/網路媒體　internet media, online media
网络媒体设计/網路媒體設計　media and web design
网络民主/網路民主　cyber democracy
网络匿名/網路匿名　anonymity on the internet
网络泡沫/網際網路泡沫　internet bubble
网络侵权/網路侵權　network infringement
网络清洁/網路清潔　network clean
网络日志/網頁日志　web log
网[络上]瘾/網路成瘾　internet addiction
网络社会/網路社會　network society
网络社区/網際網路社區,線上社群　internet community, online community
网络诗歌/網路詩歌　network poem
网络诗人/網路詩人　network poet
网络实名制/網路實名制　internet real-name system
网络市场/網路市場　network market
网络视频/網路視頻　online video
网络视频会议/網路視訊會議　network video conference
网络视频营销/網路視頻行銷　network video marketing
网络受众/網路受眾　internet audience
网络书店/網路書店　online bookstore
网络数据/網路資料　network data
网络数据分析/網路數據分析　web data analysis
网络数据库/線上資料庫,網路資料庫　online database, network database
网络水军/網[路水]軍　network navy, online water army, cyber army
网络素养/網路知識普及　network literacy
网络体/網路體　network body
网络通信/網路通訊　network communication
网络图/網路圖　network diagram
网络图书馆/網路圖書館　network library, net library
网络推手/網路推手　web backer
网络挖掘/網頁探勘,網路採礦　web mining
网络外部性/網路外部性　network externality
网络文化/網路文化　network culture
网络文学/網路文學　network literature
网络问政/網路問政　cyberpolitics

网络小区/網路社群，線上社群　online community
网络小说/網路小說　network novel
网络协议/網路協定　network protocol
网络新闻/網路新聞　network news
网络新闻学/網路新聞學　cyber journalism, online journalism
网络信息/網路資訊　network information
网络信息保存/網站典藏　web archiving
网络信息服务/網路資訊服務　network information service
网络信息检索/網路資訊檢索　web information retrieval, web information search, information retrieval on the Internet
网络信息检索工具/網路情報檢索工具　web-based information retrieval tool
网络信息资源/網路資訊資源　network information resource
网络信息组织/網路資訊組織　organization of network information
网络型组织结构/網路式組織　network organization
网络叙词表/網路敘詞表　web thesaurus
网络学术传播系统/網路學術傳播系統　network academic communication system
网络艺术/網路藝術　internet art
网络引文/網路引文　web citation
网络隐私权/網路隱私權　network privacy
网络营销/電子行銷，網路行銷　e-Marketing, internet marketing
网络影响因子/網路影響因子　web impact factor
网络用户/網路用戶　network user
网络游戏/網路遊戲，線上遊戲　network game, online game
网络游戏工作室/網路遊戲工作室　network game studio
网络游戏运营商/網路遊戲運營商　online game operator
网络舆论/網路輿論　network consensus
网络舆情/網路輿情　internet public opinion
网络舆情调查/線上民調　online poll
网络与实体混合公司/網路與實體混合公司　click-and-mortar company
网络语言/網路語言　internet language
网络远程教学/遠距教育　distance education
网络阅读/網路閱讀　network reading
网络杂志/網路雜誌，線上雜誌　webzine
网络招聘/網路招聘　e-recruitment
网络制式/網路系統　network system
网络治理理论/網路組織治理理論　network governance theory
网络著作权/網路版權　internet copyright
网络资源评价/網路資源評估　internet resource evaluation
网络作者/網路作者　network author
网民/網[路公]民　netizen, internet user
网目调/半色調　halftone
网目调凹印/半色調凹版印刷　halftone gravure
网目调值/網目調值　halftone value
网目角度/網屏角度　screen angle
网目频率/網目頻率　mesh frequency
网目线数/網目線數　screen ruling
网屏/網目屏　half-tone screen
网墙/網牆　cell wall
网上订购/網上訂購　online order
网上犯罪/網上犯罪　crime on internet
网上购物/網上購物　online shopping
网上交易/網路交易　online trading
网上拍卖/線上拍賣　online auction
网上视频广告/網上視頻廣告　online video advertisement
网上谈判/網上談判　internet negotiation
网上银行/網路銀行　e-bank, internet banking, online-banking
网上征订/網上徵訂　internet subscription
网上支付/線上支付　paying online, online payment
网纹辊/網紋輥　anilox roller
网线角度/網屏角度　screen angle
网穴/網穴　gravure cell
网页/網頁　web page
网页级别/網頁排名演算法　page rank
网页快照/網頁快照　web snapshot
网页浏览器/網頁瀏覽器　web browser
网页爬虫/網頁蜘蛛　web crawler, web spider
网页游戏/網頁遊戲　web game
网银账户/網銀賬戶　e-bank account
网印版/網印版　screen forme
网游防沉迷系统/網遊防沈迷系統　anti-addiction system for online game
网游实名制/網遊實名制　real online
网友/網友　net-user, online friend
网站/網站　website
网站代理出版/網站代理出版　website agent publishing
网站评价/網站評估　website evaluation
网址/網址，網站　website, internet protocol address, website address
网状创业团队/網狀創業團隊　net entrepreneurial

team
网状模型/網路模型　network model
网状数据库/網路資料庫　network database
网状职业路径/網狀職涯路徑　network career path
往来银行/往來銀行　bank with whom the credits are opened
忘却学习/忘卻學習　unlearning
危害公共安全罪/危害公共安全罪　crime of jeopardizing public security
危害公共卫生罪/危害公共衛生罪　crime of jeopardizing public health
危害人类罪/危害人類罪　crimes against humanity
危害行为/危害行爲　dangerous act
危机/危機　crisis
危机处置/危機處理　crisis handling
危机传播/危機傳播,危機溝通　crisis communication
危机沟通/危機溝通,危機傳播　crisis communication
危机管理/危機管理　crisis management
危机介入模式/危機介入模式　crisis-intervention model
危机决策/危機決策　crisis decision making
危机情报/危機情報　crisis intelligence
危机识别/危機識別　crisis identification
危险/危險　hazard
危险度/風險程度　degree of risk
危险犯/危險犯　potential damage offense
危险废物/有害廢棄物　hazardous waste
危险分析/危險分析　hazard analysis
危险函数/危險函數　hazard function
危险条款/危險條款　peril clause
危险源辨识/危害認定　hazard identification
威布尔分布/Weibull 分配,Weibull 分布　Weibull distribution
威布尔概率纸/Weibull 機率紙　Weibull probability paper
威布尔回归模型/Weibull 回歸模型　Weibull regression model
威尔科克森符号秩/Wilcoxon 符號秩　Wilcoxon signed rank
威尔科克森符号秩检验/威爾克森符號等級檢定,Wilcoxon 符號秩檢定　Wilcoxon signed rank test
威尔科克森检验/Wilcoxon 檢定　Wilcoxon test
威尔科克森-皮特曼有效性/Wilcoxon-Pitman 有效性　Wilcoxon-Pitman efficiency
威尔科克森统计量/Wilcoxon 統計量　Wilcoxon statistics

威尔科克森秩和检验/Wilcoxon 秩和檢定　Wilcoxon rank sum test
威尔科克森置信区间/Wilcoxon 信賴區間　Wilcoxon confidence interval
威尔科克森中秩/Wilcoxon 中秩　Wilcoxon midrank
威尔克斯空格检验/Wilks 空格檢定　Wilks empty cell test
威尔克斯-劳勒 U_1 统计量/Wilks-Lawley 的 U_1 統計量　Wilks-Lawley U_1 statistic
威尔克斯-罗森鲍姆检验/Wilks-Rosenbaum 檢定　Wilks-Rosenbaum test
威尔克斯内散布/Wilks 內散布　Wilks internal scatter
威尔克斯准则/Wilks 準則　Wilks criterion
威尔逊-希尔福特变换/Wilson-Hilferty 變換　Wilson-Hilferty transformation
威廉姆斯法案/威廉森法案　Williams Act
威尼斯兵工厂管理/威尼斯兵工廠管理　arsenal management of Venice
威尼斯商业管理/威尼斯商業管理　commercial management of Venice
威沙特分布/Wishart 分布,Wishart 分配　Wishart distribution
威慑效应/阻遏效果　deterrent effect
微变化研究法/微基因法　microgenetic method
微博/微網志　micro blog
微博实名制/微網志實名制　real-name microblogging registration
微出版/微出版　micropublishing
微处理机/微處理機　microprocessor
微电影/微膠片　microfilm
微动作分析/微動作分析　micro-action analysis, micro-motion study
微分对策/微分賽局　differential game
微分随机过程/微分隨機過程　differential stochastic process
微观分析/微觀分析　microanalysis
微观环境/微觀環境,個體環境　microenvironment
微观经济学/微觀經濟學,個體經濟學　microeconomics
微观理论/微觀理論,個體理論　microtheory
微观面板数据/微觀面板資料　micropanel data
微观模拟/微模擬　microsimulation
微观社会学/微觀社會學　microsociology
微观史/微觀史　microhistory, microstoria
微观营销/微觀行銷,小眾行銷　micromarketing
微级/個體層次　microlevel
微剧本/微劇本　microscript

微内容/微内容　microcontent
微泡胶片/微泡膠片　vesicular film
微群/微群　microgroup
微视频/微視頻　microvideo
微调/微調　fine tuning
微微理论/微觀的微觀理論　micromicro theory
微型词表/微型詞表　microthesaurus
微型计算机/微電腦　microcomputer
韦伯权威理论/韋伯權威理論　authority theory of Weber
韦伯组织理论/韋伯組織理論　organization theory of Weber
韦克斯勒成人智力量表/魏氏成人智力量表　Wechsler adult intelligence scale
韦林分布/Waring 分布, Waring 分配　Waring distribution
韦陀去酸法/韋陀去酸法　Weituo deacidification process
违背协议/違約　violation of agreement
违法发放贷款罪/違法發放貸款罪　crime of unlawfully granting loan
违反合同/違反合約, 違約　breach of contract
违反贸易保证/違反貿易保證　breach of trading warranty
违反授权保证/違反授權保證　breach of warranty of authority
违反危险物品管理规定肇事罪/違反危險物品管理規定肇事罪　crime of causing serious accident because of violating management regulations of hazardous substances
违反协议/違反協定, 違約　breach of agreement
违规排放检测/違規排放的偵測　detection of emissions violation
违禁出版物/違禁出版物　forbidden publication
违禁贸易/違禁貿易　contraband trade, illicit trade
违禁文献/違禁文獻　objectionable literature
违约/違約, 遲延履約　breach, default
违约风险/壞賬風險　default risk
违约金/違約金, 預先約定的賠償總額　default fine, liquidated damage
违约期权/違約選擇權　default option
违约索赔/違約索賠　claim arising from breach of contract
违约条款/不履約條款　default clause
违约溢价/違約溢價　default premium
违约责任/違約責任　liability for breach of contract
违约终止合同/違約合同終止　default to terminate contract

围产期死亡率/週產期死亡率　perinatal mortality rate
唯计划化/唯計劃論　planning fundamentalism
唯理智论/唯智論　intellectualism
唯名论/唯名論, 名義主義　nominalism, nominalist approach
唯社会学论/唯社會學主義　sociologism
唯物史观/唯物史觀　materialistic interpretation of history
唯物主义/唯物論　materialism
唯心史观/唯心史觀　idealistic interpretation of history
唯心主义/唯心論　idealism
唯一供源/唯一供應來源　sole source
唯一[性]/唯一[性]　uniqueness
唯一性变异数/獨特變異　unique variance
唯一性引用标准/獨特性引用標準　exclusive reference to standard
唯一因子/唯一因子　unique factor
唯一因子双线性法/唯一因子雙線性法　unique factor bilinear method
唯资本论/資本論　capital fundamentalism
维表/維度表　dimension table
维层次/維層次　dimension level
维成员/維成員　dimension member
维持保证金/維持保證金　maintenance margin
维持关税/維持關稅　preserving duty
维持汇价/維持匯價　support exchange rate
维持价格/維持價格　maintenance price
维持转售价格合同/維持轉售價格合約　resale price maintenance contract
维持转售价格制度/維持轉售價格制度　resale price maintenance system
维[度]/維[度]　dimension
维恩图/Venn 圖, 文氏圖　Venn diagram
n 维分布函数/n 維分布函數　n-dimensional distribution function
k 维分区组/k 維區集劃分　k-dimensional blocking
n 维概率空间/n 維機率空間　n-dimensional probability space
维护/維護　maintaining
维护费/維修成本, 保養成本　maintenance cost
维基/維基, 共筆　wiki
维基百科/維基百科[全書]　Wikipedia
维基经济学/維琪經濟學　wikinomics
维加风险/維珈風險　vega risk
维加值/維珈值　vega value
维克里拍卖/維克里競價　Vickery auction

维客/維基　wikis
维客模式/維客模式　witkey mode
维纳过程/威那過程,Wiener 過程　Wiener process
维纳-霍普夫技术/Wiener-Hopf 技術　Wiener-Hopf technique
维纳-辛钦定理/Wiener-Khintchine 定理　Wiener-Khintchine theorem
维数分析/維度分析　dimensional analysis
维斯比规则/威士比規則　Visby rules
维修时间限制/維護時間限制　time constraint for maintenance
维修性分析/維護度分析　maintainability analysis
维修预防/維修預防　maintenance prevention
维也纳学派/維也納學派　Vienna school
伪回归/虛擬回歸,虛假回歸　spurious regression
伪极大似然方程/擬的最大概方程式　pseudo maximum likelihood equation
伪逆/擬逆　pseudo-inverse
伪谱/擬頻譜　pseudo-spectrum
伪事件/僞事件,假事件　pseudo-event
伪书/僞書,僞經　pseudograph, pseudepigraph
伪似然/擬的概似　pseudo likelihood
伪随机数/擬隨機數　pseudo random number
伪凸函数/僞凸函數　pseudoconvex function
伪误档案/偽誤檔案　false archive
伪相关/僞相關,擬相關　pseudo-correlation
伪因子/擬因子　pseudo-factor
伪造/仿冒品　counterfeiting
伪造背书/偽造背書　forged endorsement
伪造单据/偽造單據　forged document
伪造货币罪/偽造貨幣罪　crime of forging money
伪造文件/偽造檔案　forgery document
伪造债券/偽造債券　forged bond
伪证罪/偽證罪　crime of perjury
尾部面积/尾部面積　tail area
尾部特性/尾部特性　tail behavior
尾端分布/尾端分布　tail distribution
尾注/尾注　endnote
委付人/委付者　abandoner
委付条款/委付條款　abandonment clause
委付通知/委付通知　notice of abandonment
委派/委派　delegate
委任取款背书/委任取款背書　endorsement by procuration
委任统治制度/委任統治制度　mandate system
委任制/聘用制,委任制度　appointment system
委托保管/委託保管,寄存　deposit
委托保险/委託保險　trust insurance
委托辩护/委託辯護　advocacy by mandate
委托采购/進貨約定付款額,採購承諾,預定進貨額　purchasing agency, commitment purchasing
委托代理/委託代理　agency by mandate, principal agency
委托代理关系/當事人-代理人關係　principal-agent relationship
委托代理理论/當事人-代理人理論　principal-agent theory
委托代理问题/委託人-代理人問題　principal-agent problem
委托代销商品/寄銷品　goods-out on consignment
委托发明/委託發明　commissioned invention
委托购买/委託購買　authority to purchase
委托购销/寄售與委託採購　consignment sale and purchase
委托合同/委託合同　contract of commission
委托加工物资/委託加工物資　materials for consigned processing
委托进口/委託進口　consignment import
委托开发/委託開發　commissioned development
委托贸易/委託貿易　commission trade
委托人/主理人　principal
委托人和代理人/委託人和代理人　principal and agent
委托任务范围/參考規約,權責範圍　term of reference
委托授权账户/授權賬戶　power-of-attorney account
委托书/委託書　letter of proxy, letter of abandonment, warrant of attorney
委托诉讼代理人/委託訴訟代理人　party-appointed representative
委托投资/委託投資　entrusted investment
委托销售/寄售,寄銷　sale on consignment
委托效用法/委託效用法　entrust utility method
委托信用证/條件交付信用狀　escrow credit
委托执行/委託執行　commitment of enforcement
委托作品/委託作品　commissioned work
委员会制/委員會制　committee system
委员制/委員制　commission-based system
卫生保健/健康照護　healthcare
卫生保健筹资/照護的財務融通,醫療財政學　healthcare financing
卫生统计/衛生統計　health statistics
卫生信息/健康資訊　health information
卫生需求/健康需求　health demand
卫星传版/衛星傳版　satellite transmission of layout
卫星词表/衛星詞表　satellite thesaurus

卫星广播电视/衛星廣播電視　satellite radio and television
卫星接收器/衛星接收器　satellite receiver
卫星墨滴/衛星墨滴　satellite drop
卫星新闻采集/衛星新聞採訪,衛星轉播　satellite news gathering, SNG
卫星遥感地球/衛星遥感地球　remote sensing of the globe from satellite
卫星直接电视广播/衛星直接電視廣播　satellite TV broadcasting
卫星转播/衛星轉播,衛星新聞採訪　satellite news gathering, SNG
为令饬事/爲令飭事　Wei Lingchi Shi
为咨行事/爲諮行事　Wei Zi Xingshi
未保险存款/未保險存款　uninsured deposit
未保险利率平价/未保險利率平價　uncovered interest parity
未编目资料/未編目資料　arrears
未偿本金/未償本金　principal outstanding
未偿付金额/未償還金額　amount outstanding
未偿付债券/未清償債券　outstanding bond
未偿还的发行额/未償還的發行額　outstanding issue
未偿债务/未還債務　outstanding debt
未成年工/未成年工　nonage worker
未成年人/未成年人　juvenile
未成年人保护法/未成年人保護法　law on the protection of juveniles
未成年人福利/未成年人福利　welfare for juvenile
未出版著作/未出版作品　unpublished work
未达账项/在途賬目　account in transit
未到期票据/未到期票據　bill undue
未登记股票/未登記股票　unregistered stock
未定价股票/未定價股票　unvalued stock
未兑现票据/未兌現票據　outstanding bill
未兑现支票/未兌現支票　outstanding cheque
未发行抵押债券/未發行抵押債券　unissued mortgage bond
未发行股票/未發行股票　unissued capital stock
未分配利润/未分配利潤　unappropriated profit
未分组频数分布/未分組次數分佈　ungrouped fruquency distribution
未分组数据/未分組數據　ungrouped data
未付的到期负债/未付的到期負債　matured liability unpaid
未付利息/未付利息　outstanding interest
未婚率/未婚率　unmarried rate
未加权平均/未加權平均數　unweighted average
未加权指数/未加權指數　unweighted index number
未交货订单/延期訂貨　back order
未结办案卷/未結案公文　file of indigenous
未结汇出口/未結匯出口　export without foreign exchange settlement
未结算汇票/未結算匯票　outstanding exchange
未截尾抽样检验/未截略抽樣檢驗　uncurtailed sampling inspection
未截尾的/未截略的　untruncated
未解释方差/未解釋變異數　unexplained variance
未经背书的支票/未經背書的支票　unendorsed cheque
未经申报的货物/未經申報的貨物　undeclared cargo
未控制变异/未管制變異　uncontrolled variability
未来现实树/未來現實樹　future reality tree, FRT
未来用户/未來用戶　expectant user
未列限额许可证/無限制許可證　open license
未履行分期付款义务/未履行分期付款義務　failure to pay installment
未平仓量/未平倉量　open interest
未[清]偿贷款/未清償貸款　loan outstanding, outstanding loan
未授权访问/未授權存取　unauthorized access
未完成犯罪/未完成犯罪　inchoate crime
未修正距/未修正動差　unadjusted moment
未修正数据/未修正數據　unadjusted data
未用书/未用書　snag
未折进的包边/突出書面　overhang
未注册商标/未註冊商標　unregistered trademark
未注明日期的背书/未註明日期的背書　undated endorsement
未注日期证券/未註明日期的證券　undated security
未装订期刊/未裝訂期刊　unbound periodical
未组织的/非結構　unstructured
位/位元　bit
位图/點陣圖　bitmap image, bitmap
位相函数/位相函數　phase function
位相混杂设计/位相混同設計　phase confounded design
位序-规模法则/位元序-規模律,順位規模法則　rank size rule
位移备择假设/位置移動對立假設　location shift alternative hypothesis
位移泊松分布/錯置卜瓦松過程　displaced Poisson distribution
位元组/位元組　byte
位置/位置　location
位置参数/位置參數　location parameter

位置测度/位置測度,位置量測　location measure
位置尺度参数/位置-尺度參數　location-scale parameter
位置尺度参数族/位置-尺度參數族　location-scale parameter family
位置等变异估计量/位置等變異估計[量]　location equivariant estimator
位置定价/位置定價　location pricing
位置检索/位置檢索　position search, proximity search
位置检验/位置檢定　location test
位置运算符/位置運算元　proximity operator, positional operator
位置中心/位置中心　center of location
魏玛宪法/魏瑪憲法　Weimarer Verfassung
魏新律/魏新律　New Law of Wei Dynasty
温和的通货膨胀/緩升性通貨膨脹　creeping inflation
温湿试验/溫濕試驗　dump heat test
温室效应/溫室效應　greenhouse effect
温州模式/溫州模型　Wenzhou model
文本/文本　text
文本表示/文本表達　text representation
文本分析/文本分析　textual analysis
文本话语分析/文本論述分析　textual discourse analysis
文本检索/正文檢索　text retrieval
文本聚类/文本聚類　text clustering
文本朗读引擎/文本朗讀引擎　text-to-speech, TTS
文本链接广告/文本連結廣告　text-link advertisement
文本挖掘/文本挖掘,文本探勘　text mining
文本文件/文字檔　text record, textual record, textual archives
文本项/文本項　text item
文本性/文本性　textuality
文本叙事分析/文本敘事分析　textual narrative analysis
文本资料/文本資料　textual material
文本自动分类/自動文件分類　automatic text classification, automatic text categorization
文档/文檔　document
文档[管理]一体化/文檔[管理]一體化　integration of document management, document integral management
文档类型定义/文檔類型定義　document type definition
文档一体化/文檔一體化　document integral management

文风/風格　style
文号档号对照表/文號檔號對照表　comparison table of document number and archive number
文号目录/文號目錄　document number catalog
文化/文化　culture
文化霸权/文化霸權　cultural hegemony
文化保守主义/文化保守主義　cultural conservatism
文化边界/文化邊界　cultural boundary
文化变迁/文化變遷　cultural change
文化层/文化層　cultural layer
文化差异/文化差異　cultural difference
文化产品/文化產品　cultural product, cultural production
文化产业/文化產業,文化工業　culture industry, cultural industry
文化产业投资/文化產業投資　culture industry investment
文化冲击/文化衝擊　cultural shock, culture shock
文化冲突理论/文化衝突理論　cultural conflict theory
文化传播/文化傳播　diffusion of culture
文化传播论/文化擴散論　diffusionism of culture
文化创意产业/文化創意產業　cultural and creative industry
文化丛/文化叢　cultural complex
文化大熔炉/文化大熔爐　melting pot
文化的制度化权力/文化的制度化權力　institutionalized power of culture
文化的自主生产/文化的自主生產　auto production cultural
文化帝国主义/文化帝國主義　cultural imperialism
文化多样性/文化多樣性,文化多元性　cultural diversity
文化多样性论/文化多樣性論　multi-culturalism
文化多元主义/文化多元主義,文化多元論,多元文化主義　cultural pluralism
文化反哺/文化反哺　cultural feedback
文化工业/文化工業,文化產業　culture industry, cultural industry
文化共生/文化共生　cultural symbiosis
文化涵化/文化涵化　cultural acculturation
文化环境/文化環境　cultural environment
文化价值/文化價值　cultural value
文化间传播/文化間傳播　intercultural communication
文化交流/文化交流　acculturation
文化交融/文化互融　melting pot of culture

文化接受/文化接受性　cultural acceptability
文化解释/文化解釋　interpretation of culture
文化进化论/文化演化論　cultural evolutionism
文化精英/文化菁英　cultural elite
文化景观/文化景觀，文化地景　cultural landscape
文化决定论/文化決定論　cultural determinism
文化科学/文化科學　cultural science
文化客体/文化客體　cultural object
文化类型/文化模式　culture pattern
文化连续性/文化連續性　cultural continuity
文化旅游/文化觀光業　cultural tourism
文化民族主义/文化民族主義　cultural nationalism
文化排斥/文化排斥　cultural exclusion
文化批评/文化批評　cultural critique
文化偏见/文化偏見　cultural bias
文化歧视/文化歧視　cultural discrimination
文化侵略/文化侵略　cultural aggression
文化区/文化區　culture area
文化趋同/文化趨同　cultural convergence
文化圈/文化圈　cultural area, kulurkreis
文化人类学/文化人類學　cultural anthropology
文化认同/文化認同　cultural identity
文化融合/文化融合　culture fusion
文化濡化/文化濡化　cultural enculturation
文化社会心理学/文化社會心理學　social psychology of culture
文化社会学/文化社會學　sociology of culture
文化审计/文化稽核　culture audit
文化渗透/文化滲透　cultural infiltration
文化生产/文化生產　cultural production
文化史/文化史　cultural history
文化适应/文化適應　acculturation
文化特质/文化特質　cultural trait
文化同化/文化同化　cultural assimilation
文化唯物论/文化唯物論　cultural materialism
文化习惯/文化習慣，文化習性　custom, habitus
文化系统/文化系統，文化體系　cultural system
文化现象/文化現象　cultural phenomenon
文化相对性/文化相對性　cultural relativity
文化相对主义/文化相對主義，文化相對論　cultural relativism
文化消费/文化消費　cultural consumption
文化效应/文化效應　cultural effects
文化行政管理/文化管理　cultural administration
文化型战略实施/文化型策略執行　culture-type strategy implementation
文化选择/文化選擇，文化篩選　cultural selection
文化学派/文化學派　cultural school

文化研究/文化研究　cultural study
文化遗产/文化遺產　cultural heritage
文化异质性/文化異質性　cultural heterogeneity
文化语境/文化情境，文化脈絡　cultural context
文化再生产/文化再生產　cultural reproduction
文化折扣/文化折扣　cultural discount
文化震惊/文化衝擊　culture shock
文化智力/文化智力　cultural intelligence
文化滞后/文化失調，文化落差　cultural lag
文化转向/文化轉向　cultural turn
文化资本/文化資本　cultural capital
文化资源/文化資源　cultural resources
文化自觉/文化自覺　cultural consciousness, cultural identity
文件/文件　document
文件保护盒/檔案保護盒　record box
文件保护技术学/檔案保護技術學　study of archival protection technology
文件编制/檔案編製　documentation
文件重整/重製作文件　redocumentation
文件处置/檔案處置　doucment disposal
文件处置办法/檔案處置辦法　record disposal method
文件处置期限表/檔案處置期限表　record schedule
文件传递/檔案傳遞　file transfer
文件的三要素/檔案的三要素　three elements of a record
文件调查/檔案調查　record survey
文件格式/檔[案]格式　file format
文件工作制度/檔案工作制度　institution of file work
文件管理元数据/檔案管理元資料　record-keeping metadata, record management metadata
文件管理员/檔案管理員　records manager
文件归档/歸檔　archive, filing
文件恢复/檔案恢復　file recovery
文件汇编/檔案匯編　collect and edit of document
文件级条目著录格式/檔級條目著錄格式　file level item description format
文件加工/檔案加工　file processing
文件夹/資料夾　portfolio
文件交换/檔案交換　file exchange
文件连续体理论/檔案連續體理論　theory of record continuum
文件清退/檔案清退　check and return file
文件全宗/檔案全宗　documentary fonds
文件生命周期理论/檔案生命週期理論　theory of document life cycle, theory of record life cycle

文件双重价值论/檔案雙重價值論　double value theory of document, doucment dual value theory
文件系列/檔案系列　record series, file series
文件系统/檔案系統　file system
文件匣/檔案匣　document case
文件信息检索/檔檢索　document retrieval, document information retrieval
文件验定书/檔案鑒定書　vidimus
文件暂存/檔案暫存　temporary storage of file
文件中心/文件中心,檔案中心,記錄中心　record center
文盲/文盲　illiteracy
文明/文明　civilization
文明冲突/文明衝突　clash of civilizations
文明分析/文明分析　analysis of civilization
文明间遭遇/文明間遭遇　inter-civilization encounter
文明进程/文明進程　civilizing process
文明性/禮貌　courtesy
文凭/文憑　diploma
文凭主义/文憑主義　credentialism
文书/文書　official correspondence, document
文书处理部门立卷制度/文書處理部門立卷制度　filing regulation of document processing department
文书档案/文書檔案　administrative archival document
文书档案改革运动/文書檔案改革運動　Reform Movement of Administrative Archival Document
文书档案连锁法/文書檔案連鎖法　chain method of documentary archive
文书档案室/文書檔案室　document record office
文书工作管理/文書管理　paperwork management
文书学/文書學　secretarial science
文体考订/文體考訂　style criticism
文献/文獻　literature
文献半衰期/文獻半衰期　half life of document
文献保护/文獻保護　document conservation and preservation
文献保障/文獻保障　guarantee of required document
文献保障率/文獻保證率　literature ensuring rate, literature guarantee rate
文献保障体系/文獻保障體系　guarantee system of required document
文献保证原则/文獻保證原則　principle of literary warrant
文献编号/文獻編號　literature number
文献编纂/文獻編纂　documentation compilation
文献标识/文件識別　document identification
文献标引/文件索引　document indexing

文献补充/文獻補充　collection supplement
文献采访/文獻採訪　selection and acquisition of literature
文献采访预算/文獻採訪預算　aquisition budget
文献采购招标/文獻招標採購　document procurement bidding
文献查询频率/文獻查詢頻率　document consultation frequency
文献出版物/文獻出版品　documentary publication
文献传递/文獻傳遞　document delivery
文献传递服务/文獻傳遞服務　document delivery service, DDS
文献传递服务体系/文獻傳遞服務系統　document delivery service system
文献传递时间/文獻傳遞時間　document delivery time
文献簇/文獻簇　document cluster
文献单元/文獻單元　literature unit
文献登记/文獻登記　literatrue registration
文献对/文獻對　pair of documents
文献分类/文獻分類　document classification
文献分类标准/文獻分類標準,文件分類標準　document classification criterion
文献分类基本规则/文獻分類基本規則　basic rule of document classification
文献分析/文獻分析　document analysis
文献服务/文件服務　document service
文献覆盖率/文獻覆蓋率　literature coverage ratio
文献改编/文獻改編　document adaption
文献工作/文獻工作　documentation
文献工作标准化/文檔格式規範　standardization of documentation
文献工作者/文獻資料工作者　documentalist
文献管理/文件管理　documentation, document management
文献计量学/書目計量法　bibliometrics
文献计量指标/計量指標　bibliometric indicator
文献检索/文件檢索　document retrieval
文献检索教育/書目性教學　bibliographical instruction
文献检索系统/文件檢索系統　document retrieval system
文献交流/文獻交流　document communication
文献交流说/文獻通信理論,文獻通訊理論　document communication theory
文献老化/文獻老化　document obsolescence, literature obsolescence
文献类别/文獻類別　material category

文献类型定义/文件類型定義　document type definition, DTD
文献利用率/文獻利用率　literature utilization rate, literature utilization ratio
文献流通率/文獻流通週轉率　rate of literature circulation
文献描述/文檔說明　document description
文献目录/文獻目錄　literature catalogue
文献清洁/文獻清潔　document cleaning
文献数据库/文件資料庫　document database
文献损坏/文獻損壞　document damage
文献特殊细节项/文獻特殊細節項　material specific details area, type of publication specific details area
文献提供/文獻供應　document supply
文献相似度/文件相似　document similarity
文献向量/文件向量　document vector
文献信息/文獻資訊　literature information
文献信息中心/資訊文獻中心　documentation and information center
文献信息资源/文獻資訊資源　document and information resources
文献修复/文獻修復　document restoration
文献修整/文獻修整　document repair
文献学/文獻學　documentation science, bibliography
文献学家/文獻學家　documentalist
文献研究/文獻研究，文件研究法　document studies, literature research
文献引用规律/文獻引用規律　law of literature citation
文献增长/文獻成長　growth of literature, literature growth
文献增长定律/文獻增長定律　growth law of literature
文献战略/文獻戰略　documental strategy
文献主题/文獻主題　document subject
文献资料类型/文獻資料類型　material type
文献资源/文獻資源　literature resources
文献资源布局/文獻資源布局　overall arrangement of document resources
文献资源共享/文獻資源共享　document resource sharing
文献资源建设/館藏發展　literature resource construction
文学档案/文學檔案　literary file
文学档案馆/文學檔案館　literary archive
文学社会学/文學社會學　sociology of literature
文学手稿/文學手稿　literary manuscript
文-语转换系统/文-語轉換系統　text-to-speech conversion system
文摘服务/摘要服務　abstracting service
文摘号/文摘號　abstract number
文摘期刊/文摘期刊　digest periodical
文摘数据库/文摘資料庫　abstract database
文摘页/文摘頁　abstract page
文摘员/摘錄者　abstractor
文摘杂志/文摘雜志　abstracting journal
文摘质量评价/文摘質量評價　evaluation of abstract
文章/文章　article
文章审读/文章審讀　re-reading the article
文种/文種　record type
文种复分号/文種複分號　language subdivision number
文种选用规则/文種選用規則　rule of file type selection
文字编辑/文字編輯　desk editor, copy editor
文字处理软件/文字處理軟體　word processing software
文字脚本/文字腳本　text script
文字排版/電腦排版　typesetting
文字商标/文字商標　word trademark
文字识别/文字辨識　character recognition
文字输入/正文輸入　text input
文字型档案/文字檔　textual record, textual archive
文字作品/文字作品　written works
纹槽间距/紋槽間距　pitch, groove spacing
纹槽角/槽角　groove angle
纹槽宽/環槽寬度　groove width
纹槽深/槽深　groove depth
纹章调查清册/紋章調查清冊　visitation book
纹章学/紋章學　heraldry
稳定币值/穩定幣值　monetary stability
稳定操作条件/穩定操作條件　stable operating condition
稳定存货/穩定存貨　stabilization stock
稳定的但可调整的平价/穩定的但可調整的賬面價值　stable but adjustable par value
稳定的汇率/穩定的匯率　stable exchange rate, steady exchange rate
稳定概率/平穩機率　stationary probability
稳定股利政策/穩定股利政策　stable dividend policy
稳定过程/穩定過程　stable process
稳定货币/穩定貨幣　stable money
稳定价格/穩定價格　stable price
稳定阶段/穩定階段　stabilization stage
稳定均衡/安定均衡　stable equilibrium
稳定 p 控制图/穩定 p 管制圖　stabilized p-chart

稳定律/穩定律　stable law
稳定帕累托分布/穩定 Pareto 分布，穩定 Pareto 分配　stable Pareto distribution
稳定人口/穩定人口　stable population
稳定随机变量/穩定隨機變數　stable random variable
稳定通货/穩定的通貨　stable currency
稳定性检验/穩定性檢定　stability test
稳定性条件/穩定條件　stability condition
稳定性政策/穩定政策　stabilization policy
稳定因素/穩定因子　stable factor
稳定增量过程/平穩性增量過程，恆定性增量過程　process with stationary increment
稳定债券/穩定的債券　stable bond
稳定战略/穩定策略　stability strategy
稳定[状]态/穩定狀態　stable state
稳定总体/穩定母體　stable population
稳健方法/穩健方法　robust method
稳健估计/穩健估計，穩定估計　robust estimation
稳健估计量/穩健估計量　robust estimator
稳健设计/穩健設計　robust design
稳健统计方法/穩健統計程序　robust statistical procedure
稳健型融资策略/穩妥型投資策略　conservative financing strategy
稳健性/穩健性　robustness
稳态/恆定狀態　stationary state
稳态磁带张力/穩態磁帶張力　steady-state tape tension
稳态均衡/穩態均衡　steady-state equilibrium
问答服务/問答服務　question-and-answer service, Q and A service
问答式检索系统/問答檢索系統　question answering retrieval system
问卷/問卷，調查表　questionnaire
问卷调查/問卷調查　questionnaire survey
问卷调查法/問卷調查法　questionnaire investigation approach
问卷调查研究/調查研究法　survey research
问卷法/問卷法　questionnaire method
问卷转换/調查表的轉移，問卷的轉移　translation of questionnaire
NP 问题/NP 問題　NP-problem
P 问题/P 問題　P-problem
问题分类法/問題分類法　classification scheme according to theme, question classification
问题界定与分析解释/問題界定與分析解釋　analysis and explanation, problem definition
问题-年度分类法/問題-年度分類法　question-year classification
问题识别/問題確認　problem recognition
问题业务/問題業務　question mark business
问题意识/問題意識　research question
问责制/問責制，責任追究制度　accountability system
窝藏、包庇罪/窩藏、包庇罪　crime of harboring and covering up a criminal
沃尔德分布/Wald 分布，Wald 分配　Wald distribution
沃尔德分解/Wold 分解　Wold decomposition
沃尔德分类统计量/Wald 分類統計量　Wald classification statistic
沃尔德基本恒等式/Wald 基本恆等式　Wald fundamental identity
沃尔德条件/Wald 條件　Wald condition
沃尔德-沃尔福威茨检验/Wald-Wolfowitz 檢定　Wald-Wolfowitz test
沃尔德-沃尔福威茨游程检验/Wald-Wolfowitz 連串檢定　Wald-Wolfowitz run test
沃尔福威茨最短距离法/Wolfowitz 最小間距法　Wolfowitz minimum distance method
沃克概率函数/Walker 機率函數　Walker probability function
沃森 U_n^2 检验/Watson 的 U_n^2 檢定　Watson's U_n^2 test
沃森 U 统计量/Watson 的 U 統計量　Watson's U-statistic
沃森-威廉斯检验/Watson-Williams 檢定　Watson-Williams' test
握持/握持　hold
斡旋/斡旋　mediate
乌斯潘斯基不等式/Uspensky 不等式　Uspensky inequality
乌托邦/烏托邦　utopia
乌托邦思想/烏托邦思想　utopianism
污秽/汙穢　filthy
污名/汙名　stigma
污名化/汙名化　stigmatization
污染/汙染　pollution
污染防治法/汙染防治法　law on pollution prevention and control
污染防治统计/汙染防治統計　pollution prevention statistics
污染分布/有瑕疵的分布　contaminated distribution
污染控制/汙染控制　pollution control
污染控制成本/汙染管制成本　pollution control cost

污染控制的经济激励/汙染管制之經濟誘因 pollution control economic incentive
污染控制政策/汙染管制政策 pollution control policy
污染许可证/汙染許可證 pollution license
污染许可证交易/汙染許可市場 pollution permit market
污染削减/汙染防治 pollution abatement
污染预防/預防汙染 prevention of pollution
污染源/汙染源 pollution source
污染者负担原则/汙染者付費原則 polluter-pays principle
污染正态分布/有瑕疵常態分布,有瑕疵常態分配 contaminated normal distribution
污水处理厂/家庭汙水處理廠 sewage treatment plant
巫/巫 witch
巫蛊/巫蠱 evil witch
巫术/巫術 witchcraft
诬告反坐/誣告反坐 impose fines on false charge
诬告陷害罪/誣告陷害罪 crime of malicious accusation
无版印刷/無版印刷 formless printing
无保额保险单/無保額保險單 no amount policy
无保留意见/無保留意見 unmodified opinion
无边界组织/無疆界組織,無國界組織 boundaryless organization, borderless organization
无差别定律/無差別定律 law of indifference
无差别区/無差異區間 zone of indifference
无差别原理/無差異原則 principle of indifference
无差别质量水平/無差別品質水準 indifference quality level
无差异区域/無差異區域 indifference region
无差异曲线/無[差]異曲線 indifference curve
无差异水平指数/無差異水準指數 indifference-level index number
无差异统计/無差異統計量 indifference statistics
无差异营销/無差異行銷 undifferentiated marketing
无产阶级/無產階級,普羅階級,普羅大眾 proletarian
无产阶级化/無產階級化,普羅化 proletarianization
无偿出口/無償出口 unrequited export
无偿付期政府金边债券/無償付期政府金邊債券 undated stock
无偿技术转让/無償技術轉讓 naked transfer of technology
无偿劳动/無酬勞工 unpaid labor
无偿契约/無償契約,無擔保契約 naked contract

无偿信托/無償信託,名義信託 naked trust
无船承运人/無船承運人 non-vessel operation carrier
无担保背书/無追索權的背書,無擔保的背書 indorsement without recourse
无担保公司债券/無擔保公司債[券] naked debenture
无担保股票/無擔保股票 unsecured stock
无担保合同/無保證合約,無條件契約 bare contract
无担保票据/無擔保票據 straight paper
无担保契约/無擔保契約,無償契約 naked contract
无担保信贷/無擔保信貸,無擔保貸款 unsecured credit, open credit
无担保信用债券/無擔保信用債券 simple debenture
无担保信用证/無擔保信用狀 unsecured letter of credit
无担保债权/無擔保債權 unwarranted claim
无担保债券/無擔保債券 bond plain, plain bond
无抵押贷款/無抵押貸款,無擔保放款 clean loan, unsecured loan
无抵押往来账透支/無抵押往來賬透支 overdraft on current account unsecured
无抵押债券/無抵押債券 unfunded debt
无发展增长/沒有發展的成長 growth without development
无法表示意见/無法表示意見 disclaimer of opinion
无法收回的票据/無法收回的票據 uncollectible note
无法收回的投资/無法回收的投資 non-recoverable outlay
无风险利率/無風險利率 risk-free interest rate
无风险套利/無風險套利 riskless arbitrage
无风险资产/無風險資產,安全資產 risk-free asset, safe asset
无股利支付股票/無紅利股票 non-dividend paying stock
无固定期限劳动合同/無固定期限勞動合同 unfixed-term labor contract
无关变量/不相關變數 irrelevant variable
无关方案独立性/無關選擇的獨立性 independence from irrelevant alternative
无关装置的色彩再现/設備獨立色彩 device independent color, DIC
无国籍货币/無國籍貨幣 stateless currency
无国籍人/無國籍人士 stateless person
无国籍状态/無國籍狀態 statelessness
无过错责任/無過錯責任 liability without fault

无过失保险／無過失保險　no-fault insurance
无过失责任原则／無過失責任原則　principle of liability non-fault
无害通过权／無害通過權　right of innocent passage
无后效性／無後效性　nonregular dependence of local characteristics
无回答／無回應　nonresponse
无回答层／無回應層　stratum of nonrespondent
无回答调整／無回應調整　nonresponse adjustment
无回答误差／無回應誤差　nonresponse error
无记名背书／空白背書　blank endorsement, open endorsement, endorsement in blank
无记名承兑／空白承兌　blank acceptance
无记名公司债券／不記名公司債　bearer debenture
无记名股票／無記名股票　stock certificate to bearer, unregistered share
无记名国债／無記名國債　unregistered government bond
无记名划线支票／無記名劃線支票　open crossed check
无记名汇票／無記名匯票，不記名匯票　bearer bill, bill drawn payable to bearer
无记名提单／不記名提單　unnamed bill of lading, blank bill of lading
无记名债券／不記名債券　unregistered bond, blank bond
无记名支票／不記名支票　bearer cheque, check payable to bearer
无记忆性／無記憶性　lack-of-memory property
无家可归／無家可歸　homeless
无结构问卷／無結構問卷　unstructured questionnaire
无结汇／不結匯　no exchange surrendered
无截断检索／無截斷檢索　identical search
无解雇政策／無解雇政策　no-layoff policy
无领导小组讨论／無領導者團體討論　leaderless group discussion
无免赔率／無自負額，無自付額　irrespective of percentage
无面值股票／無面額股　no-par stock
无名氏定理／俗定理，無名定理　folk theorem
无谬误差／無謬誤差　infallibility
无墨印刷／無墨印刷　inkless printing
无牌价证券市场／無牌價證券市場　unlisted security market
无抛补利率平价／未拋補利率平價　uncovered interest rate parity
无赔款退货／無賠款退貨　return for no claim
无偏的／不偏的　unbiased
无偏估计方程／不偏估計方程式　unbiased estimating equation
无偏估计[量]／不偏估計[量]　unbiased estimator
无偏检验／不偏檢定　unbiased test
无偏决策规则／不偏決策規則　unbiased decision rule
无偏临界域／不偏臨界域　unbiased critical region
无偏设计／不偏設計　unbiased design
无偏误差／不偏誤差　unbiased error
无偏性／不偏性　unbiasedness
无偏样本／不偏樣本　unbiased sample
无偏置信区间／不偏信賴區間　unbiased confidence interval
无偏最大功效检验／不偏最強力檢定　unbiased most powerful test
无品牌产品／無品牌產品　generics
无期徒刑／無期徒刑　life imprisonment
无其他原因／無它因　no alternative cause
无歧视待遇／無歧視　no discrimination
无穷可分分布／無限可分分布　infinitely divisible distribution
无穷可分律／無限可分定律　infinitely divisible law
无穷可分性／無限可分性　infinite divisibility
无穷马尔可夫链／無限馬可夫鏈　infinite Markov chain
无穷维概率空间／無限維機率空間　infinite dimensional probability space
无区别点／無差異點　point of indifference
无区别域／無差異[區]域　indifference zone
无权代理／無權代理　unauthorized agency, agency without right
无权占有／無權占有　unentitled possession
无缺点规划／無瑕疵計劃　zero defect program
无人销售／無人銷售　unmanned sales
无神论／無神論，反有神論　antitheism, atheism
无水胶印／無水膠印　waterless offset
无税货物／無稅貨物，免稅貨物　non-dutiable goods
无私性规范／無私性規範　norm of disinterestedness
无讼／無訟　no ligitation
无讼社会／無訟社會　no-litigation society
无酸纸／無酸紙，除酸紙　acid-free paper
无损检验／非破壞性檢驗　non-destructive inspection
无损压缩／無損壓縮　lossless compression
无弹性劳动需求曲线／無彈性的勞動需求曲線　inelastic labor demand curve
无弹性需求／需求不具彈性　inelastic demand
无套利均衡／無套利均衡　no-arbitrage equilibrium
无条件背书／無條件背書，單純背書　absolute endorsement, unconditional endorsement, unqualified endorsement

无条件承兑/無條件承兑，單純承兑　unconditional acceptance, unqualified acceptance, absolute acceptance
无条件担保/無條件擔保　unconditional guarantee
无条件概率/非條件機率　unconditional probability
无条件合同/無條件合約　unconditional contract
无条件极大似然估计量/非條件最大概似估計式　unconditional maximum likelihood estimator
无条件交货/無條件交貨　absolute delivery
无条件均方预测误差/非條件均方預測誤差　unconditional mean square prediction error
无条件支付令/純粹支付命令　absolute order to pay
无条件最惠国待遇/無條件最惠國待遇　unconditional most-favored-nation treatment
无条件最惠国条款/無條件最惠國條款　unrestricted most-favored nation clause
无条件最小平方估计量/非條件最小平方估計量　unconditional least square estimator
无跳跃过程/免跳過程　skip free process
无外汇进口/無外匯進口　import without foreign exchange, no draft import
无为而治/無爲而治　non-interference government
无谓损失/無謂損失　dead-weight loss
无文字社会/無文字社會　nonliterate society
无息公债/無息公債　non-interest-bearing bond
无息或低息贷款/無息或低利貸款　loan with no or low interest
无息票据/無息票據　non-interest-bearing note
无息债券/無息債券，零息債券　zero coupon bond
无息证券/無息證券　non-interest-bearing security
无瑕疵单据/無瑕疵單據　flawless document
无现金社会/無現鈔社會　cashless society
无限博弈/無限賽局　infinite horizon game
无限产能排程/無限產能排程　infinite scheduling
无限定条件信用证/無限制信用狀　open letter of credit
无限额抵押债券/無限額抵押債券　bond open-end
无限额支票/無限額支票　unlimited cheque
无限防卫/無限防衛　boundless defense
无限分布滞后/無限分配落遲　infinite distributed lag
无限公司/無限公司　unlimited company
无限截断检索/無限截斷檢索　unlimited truncation retrieval
无限期进口许可证/無限期輸入許可證　open-end import license
无限市场/無限市場　market without contraints
无限责任/無限責任　unlimited liability
无限制的法定货币/無限法償　unlimited legal tender
无限制的美元融通资金/無限制的美元融通資金　unlimited dollar financing
无限制进口/無管制進口　unrestricted import
无限总体/無限母體　infinite population
无线传输/無線傳輸　wireless transmission
无线电/無線電　radio
无线网络/無線網路　wireless fidelity, WiFi
无线相容性认证/無線相容性認證　wireless fidelity, Wi-Fi fidelity
无线移动载体/無線移動載體　wireless mobile carrier
无线应用[通信]协议/無線應用通訊協定　wireless application protocol, WAP
无响应/無回應　nonresponse
无效动素/無效動素　ineffective therblig
无效发行/無效發行　noneffective distribution
无效果无报酬/無效無償　no-cure no-pay
无效合同/無效合同，無效合約　contract void, invalid contract, void contract
无效劳动合同/無效勞動合同　invalid labor contract
无效支票/無效支票　dead cheque
无信息先验分布/無資訊事前分布　noninformative prior distribution
无形出口收入/無形出口收入　invisible export income
无形交易/無形交易　invisible transaction
无形进口支出/無形進口支出　invisible import expenditure
无形经常项目/無形經常專案　invisible current item
无形贸易/無形貿易　invisible trade
无形贸易赤字/無形貿易赤字　invisible trade deficit
无形贸易[收支]差额/無形貿易[收支]差額　balance of invisible trade, invisible trade balance
无形贸易收支项目/無形貿易收支項目　invisible item of trade
无形贸易盈余/無形貿易盈餘　invisible trade surplus
无形年金/無形年金　immaterial annuity
无形收入/無形收入　invisible receipt
无形输出/無形輸出　invisible export
无形输入/無形輸入　invisible import
无形效益/無形效益　intangible benefit
无形学院/無形學院　invisible college
无形之手/無形之手　intangible hand
无形支付/無形支付　invisible payment
无形资本/無形資本　immaterial capital, intangible capital
无形资产/無形資產　immaterial asset, intangible

asset
无形资源/無形資源　intangible resources
无形宗教/無形宗教, 看不見的宗教, 隱形宗教　invisible religion
无序系数/無序係數　coefficient of disarray
无益品/不名譽財　demerit goods
无因管理/無因管理　spontaneous agency
无因回避/無因迴避　peremptory challenge
无因行为/無因行爲　abstract act
无用信息/無用訊息　useless information
无约束非线性规划/無約束非線性規劃　unconstrained nonlinear programming
无约束随机样本/不限制隨機樣本　unrestricted random sample
无障碍服务/無障礙服務　barrier-free service, accessibility service
无证逮捕/無證逮捕　arrest without warrant
无证拘留/無證拘留　detention without warrant
无证搜查/無證搜查　search without warrant
无纸动画/無紙動畫　paperless animation
无纸化信息系统/無紙資訊系統　paperless information system
无著作权著作/無版權的作品　work in public domain
无追索权背书/無追索權[的]背書, 無擔保[的]背書　endorsement without recourse, indorsement without recourse
无追索权贷款/無追索權貸款　non-recourse loan, without-recourse financing
无追索权汇票/無追索權[的]匯票　draft without recourse, non-protestable bill
无追索权信用证/無追索權信用狀　without-recourse letter of credit
无追索权债务/無追索權債務　non-recourse debt
无总题名文献/無總題名文獻　items without a collective title
无罪辩护/無罪辯護　defense of not guilty
无罪判决/無罪裁決　verdict of not guilty
无罪推定/無罪推定　presumption of innocence
无罪证据/無罪證據　evidence of innocence
蜈蚣博弈/蜈蚣賽局　centipede game
五代刻本/五代刻本　Five Dynasties edition
五花判事/五花判事　Wuhua Panshi
五年计划/五年計劃　five-year plan
五年刊/五年刊　quinquennial issue
五史/五史　Wushi
伍德伯里分布/Woodbury 分布, Woodbury 分配　Woodbury distribution

伍德拉夫卷盒/伍德拉夫捲盒　Woodruff roll box
伍德沃德权变组织论/伍德沃德權變組織論　contingency organization theory of Woodward
仵作/仵作　Wuzuo
侮辱罪/侮辱罪　crime of insulting
舞弊审计/舞弊查核　fraud audit
舞蹈作品/舞蹈作品　choreographic works
物/物　thing
物的瑕疵担保/物的瑕疵擔保　warranty against defect of thing
物价调查/物價調查　price survey
物价冻结/物價凍結　price freeze
物价监测/價格監測　retail price survey
物价检查/價格調查　retail price inspection
物价水平/物價水準　price level
物价统计/物價統計　price statistics
物价与现金流动机制/物價與黃金流動機能　price specie flow mechanism
物价折算指数/物價平減指數　price deflator
物价指数/物價指數　price index
物理归档/物理歸檔　physical filing
物理接近/實體距離　physical proximity
物理卷/物理卷　physical file
物理模拟/物理模擬, 實體模擬　physical simulation
物理模型/實體模型　physical model
物理扇区/實體扇區　physical sector
物理性污染/物理汙染　physical pollution
物料搬运时间/物料搬運時間　material handling time
物料流/物料流　material flow
物料清单/物料表　bill of materials
物料需求计划/物料需求規劃　material requirement planning, MRP
物料主导排程/物料主導排程　material-dominated scheduling, MDS
物流/物流　logistics
物流标签/物流標籤　logistics label
物流成本/後勤成本　logistics cost
物流服务/後勤服務中心　logistics service
物流服务质量/物流服務品質　logistics service quality
物流公共信息平台/物流公共資訊平臺　logistics information platform
物流共同化/物流共同化　logistics commonization
物流管理/物流管理　logistics management
物流管理信息系统/物流管理資訊系統　logistics management information system
物流技术/物流技術　logistics technology

物流客户服务/物流客戶服務 logistics customer service
物流企业/物流企業,物流公司 logistics firm
物流外包/物流外包 logistics outsourcing
物流信息编码/物流資訊編碼 logistics information coding
物流信息技术/物流資訊技術 logistics information technology
物流信息系统/物流資訊系統 logistics information system
物流园区/物流園區 logistics park
物流中心/物流中心 logistics center
物流咨询服务/物流諮詢服務 logistics consulting service
物流作业/物流作業 logistics operation
物品记录/物品記錄 item record
物品留置权/物品留置權 lien on goods
物品主文档/物品主檔 item master file
物权/物權 real right
物权抽象原则/物權抽象原則 abstract principle of real right
物权法/物權法 law of property
物权法定原则/物權法定原則 statutory principle of real right
物权公示原则/物權公示原則 principle of summons in public for real right
物权绝对原则/物權絕對原則 absolute principle of real right
物权请求权/物權請求權 claim right of real right
物权行为/物權行爲 juristic act of real right
物物交换/以物易物 barter
物物交换经济/物物交易經濟 barter economy
物业/物業 property
物业管理/物業管理 property management
物业税/物業稅 property tax
物业委托管理/物業委託管理 property commission management
物业自管/物業自管 property self-management
物因分析/物因分析 matter factor analysis
物证/物證 material evidence
物之所在地法原则/物之所在地法原則 principle of lex rei situs
物质产品净值/淨物質產出 net material product
物质利益/物質利益 material interests
物质平衡法/物質平衡法 material balance approach
物质生活质量指数/生活品質指標 physical quality of life index
物质文化/物質文化 material culture
物种主义/物種主義 speciesism
物资管理/物料管理 material management
物资计划管理/物料計劃管理 material plan management
物资质量验收/材質驗收 material quality acceptance
误报/誤報,錯誤訊息 misinformation
误差/誤差 error
α误差/α誤差 α-error
误差带/誤差帶 error band
误差方差/誤差變異數 error variance
误差分析/誤差分析 error analysis
误差函数/誤差函數 error function
误差合并/誤差合并 pooling of errors
误差减缩力/誤差減縮力 error reducing power
误差均方/誤差均方 error mean square
误差空间/誤差空間 error space
误差率/誤差率 error rate
误差平方和/誤差平方和 error sum of squares
误差曲线/誤差曲線 error curve
误差图/誤差圖 error graph
误差向量/誤差向量 error vector
误差项/誤差項 error term
误差修正机制/誤差修正機能 error correction mechanism
误差修正模型/誤差修正模型 error correction model, ECM
误差因素/誤差因子 error factor
误差因子/誤差因子 error factor
误差原因消除/誤差原因消除 error cause removal, ECR
误检/誤檢 false combination, false drop
误检率/誤檢率,錯檢率 false retrieval ratio, noise ratio, fallout ratio
误字/誤字 wrong word

X

西部片／西部片　western movie
西多会／天主教隱修會，西都會　Cistercians
西尔不等式系数／Theil 不等式係數　Theil inequality coefficient
西尔混合回归估计[量]／Theil 混合回歸估計[量]　Theil mixed regression estimator
西方化／西方化　westernizaton
西方中心论／西方中心論　western-centrism
西方主义／西方主義　occidentalism
西非关税同盟／西非關稅同盟　West African Customs Union
西非货币联盟／西非貨幣聯盟　West African Monetary Union
西非经济共同体／西非經濟共同體　West African Economic Community, WAEC
西哥特罗马法典／西哥特羅馬法典　Lex Romana Visigothorum
西格尔-图基方差检验／Siegel-Tukey 變異數檢定　Siegel-Tukey test of variance
西格尔-图基检验／Siegel-Tukey 檢定　Siegel-Tukey test
西格玛水平／西格瑪水準　sigma level
西蒙论组织功能／西蒙論組織功能　Simon's view on organization function
西蒙论组织设计／西蒙論組織設計　Simon's view on organization design
西蒙权威理论／西蒙權威理論　authority theory of Simon
西蒙组织理论／西蒙組織理論　organization theory of Simon
西宁青海番夷成例／西寧青海番夷成例　Xining in Qinghai Fan Yi established practice
西塔风险／系塔風險　theta risk
西文编目／西文編目　western language cataloging
西文字母的上伸部分／西文上升部　ascender
西文字母的下伸部分／西文下降部　decender
西文字母紧排／西文字間縮排　kerning
西肖尔金字塔模型／西肖爾金字塔模型　pyramid model of Seashore
西周礼制思想／周禮思想　Zhou Li thought
吸收壁／吸收屏障，吸收界限　absorbing barrier

吸收犯／吸收犯　absorbable offense
吸收分布／吸收分布　absorption distribution
吸收分析法／支用學派　absorption approach
吸收律／吸收律　absorption law
吸收能力／吸收能力，吸收容量　absorptive capacity, assimilate capability
吸收外国技术／吸收外國技術　absorption of foreign technology
吸收外汇／吸引外匯，吸引外資　foreign exchange inducement
吸收外资／吸收外资　absorption of foreign fund
吸收系数／吸收係數　absorption coefficient
吸收性／吸收性　absorptivity
吸收原则／吸收原則　absorption principle
吸收状态／吸收狀態　absorbing state
吸引力／吸引力　attractiveness
吸引外资／吸引外资　inducement of foreign capital
吸引-选择-消退框架／吸才-選才-流才架構，吸才-選才-汰才架構　attraction-selection-attrition framework
吸引指数／吸引指數　index of attraction
吸脂效应／刮脂　cream skimming
析出文献／析出文獻　precipitation literature
析因设计／因子設計　factorial design
析因试验／[多]因子實驗　factorial experiment
析因试验设计／[多]因子實驗設計　factorial design of experiment
牺牲／犧牲　sacrifice
牺牲品定价／犧牲品訂價法　loss-leader pricing
牺牲-诱因／犧牲-誘因　sacrifice-inducement
息票／息票　dividend coupon, coupon
息票单／息票單　coupon sheet
息票到期日／息票到期日　due date of coupon
息票利率／息票利率　coupon rate
稀缺性／稀少性　scarcity
稀释每股收益／稀釋每股盈餘　diluted earnings per share
稀释效应／稀釋效果　dilution effect, stock watering
稀疏表／稀疏表　sparse table
稀疏矩阵／稀疏矩陣　sparse matrix
稀疏数据／稀疏資料　sparse data

嬉皮士文化/嬉皮士文化　hippie culture
习惯法/習慣法　customary law, common law
习惯国际法/習慣國際法　customary international law
习惯化范式/慣化法　habituation paradigm
习惯化研究/慣化法　habituation paradigm
习惯型购买行为/習慣性購買行爲　habitual buying behavior
习惯性防卫/習慣性防衛　defensive routine
习俗/習慣　custom
习俗水平/習俗水平　level of convention
习俗志/風俗志　custumal
洗钱/洗錢　money laundering, laundering
洗钱罪/洗錢罪　crime of laundering
洗冤集录/洗冤集録　Xiyuan Collection
铣背/銑背　milling
喜剧片/喜劇　comedy
系列/系列　series
系列出版物/系列出版物　series of publication
系列题目/系列題目　series of topics
系列债券/分次償還債券　serial bond
ISO 系列质量标准/ISO 系列品質標準　ISO series quality standards
系属公式/系屬公式　formula of attribution
系数/係數　coefficient
β系数/β係數　β coefficient, beta coefficient
φ系数/φ係數　φ coefficient, phi coefficient
系数的阶/係數階數　order of coefficient
系数矩阵/係數矩陣　coefficient matrix
系统/系統　system
系统变量/系統變數　systematic variable
系统变异/系統變異　systematic variation
系统部件/系統元件,系統零件　system component
系统测试/系統測試　system testing
系统抽样[法]/系統抽樣　systematic sampling
系统导入区/系統導入區　system lead-in area
系统的/系統的　systematic
系统调用/系統呼叫　system call
系统动力学/系統動力學　system dynamics
系统动力学分析/系統動力學分析　system dynamics analysis
系统动力学模型/系統動力[學]模型　system dynamics model
系统发行/分布系統　system distribution
系统方法/系統方法　system approach, system method
系统方法论/系統方法論,系統方法學　system methodology
系统仿真/系統模擬　system simulation
系统仿真模型/系統模擬模型　system simulation model
系统分析/系統分析　system analysis
系统分析法/系統分析法　system analysis method
系统风险/系統性風險,體系風險　systematic risk, systemic risk
系统工程/系統工程　system engineering
系统公开市场账户/公開市場操作部門　system open market account
系统功能/系統功能　system function
系统功能分析/系統功能分析　system function analysis
系统功能模型/系統功能模型　system function model
系统故障率/系統故障率　system failure rate
系统过敏/系統神經質　system nervousness
系统函数/系統函數　systematic function
系统化压力测试/系統化壓力測試　systematic stress testing
系统环境/系統環境　system environment
系统恢复程序/系統恢復程序　system recall procedure
系统集成/系統整合　system integration
系统接口/系統介面　system interface
系统结构/系統結構　system structure, system configuration
系统结构分析/系統結構分析　system structure analysis
系统结构模型/系統結構模型　system structure model
系统结构图/方塊圖　block diagram
系统开发/系統開發　system development
系统科学/系統科學　system science
系统可靠性/系統可靠性,系統可靠度　system reliability
系统累积误差/系統累積誤差　systematic cumulative error
系统模型/系統模型　system model
系统目标/系統目標　system objective
系统能力/系統能力,系統容量　system capacity, system capability
系统排列法/順序排列　systematic arrangement
系统偏倚/系統偏誤　systematic bias
系统评价/系統評價　system assessment
系统设计/系統設計　system design
系统生命周期/系統生命週期　system development life cycle, software development life cycle

系统思想/系統思考　system thinking
系统体系结构/系統架構　system architecture
系统图/系統圖　systematic diagram
系统误差/系統誤差　systematic error
系统销售/系統銷售　system selling
系统型培训模式/系統化培訓模式,系統化培訓模型　systematic training model
系统性风险/系統性風險　systematic risk
系统性原理/系統性原理　principle of system
系统学/系統分類學　systematics
系统学派/系統學派　system school
系统演化/系統演化　system evolution
系统演化分析/系統演化分析　system evolution analysis
系统演化模型/系統演化模型　system evolution model
系统样本/系統樣本　systematic sample
系统优化/系統優化　system optimization
系统优化模型/系統優化模型　system optimization model
系统有效性/系統有效度　system availability
系统元素/系統元素　system element
系统约束/系統限制　system constraint
系统征订/系統徵訂　system subscription
系统种类/系統變種　varieties of a system
系统状态/系統狀態　system state
系统综合/系統綜合　system synthesis
系统最小割集/系統最小割集　minimal cut set of system
系统最小路径集/系統最小路徑集　minimal path set of system
细分/細分　subclass, in-depth classification, close classification
细分定价/細分定價　segmented pricing
细分景框/細分景框　fractionized scene frame
细分市场/細分市場　segment market
细分市场整合/跨市場細分　intermarket segmentation
细分原理/細分原則　principle of subdivision
细节测试/細節測試　test of detail
狭义货币/狹義貨幣　narrow money
狭义货币供给/狹義貨幣供給　narrow money supply
狭义银行/窄義銀行業　narrow banking
狭窄汇率浮动幅度/狹窄匯率浮動幅度,小差距匯率幅度　narrow exchange rate margin
瑕疵履行/瑕疵履行　defective performance
辖区间外溢/區域間外溢效果　interregional spillover
下标/下標　suffix, subscript

下不保底/下不保底　setting no ceiling limit and giving no minimum guarantee
下侧风险/下方風險　downside risk
下层阶级/底層階級　underclass
下岗分流/下崗分流　leaving post and flowing respectively
下岗、失业人员/下崗、失業人員　laid-off and unemployed
下极限/下限　lower limit
下交叉/下交叉點　down-cross
下界/下[邊]界　lower boundary, lower bound
下四分位数/下四分位數　lower quartile
下位参照/向下引用,向下參照　downward reference
下位词/下位詞　narrower term
下位概念/從屬概念,下序概念　subordinate concept
下位功能/下位功能　lower order function
下位类/下位類　subordinate class
下行沟通/向下溝通　downward communication
下行文/下行文　downlink file
下有界/下有界　bounded from below
下载/下載　download
下置信区间/下信賴區間　lower confidence interval
下组配检索/下組配檢索　subordinate search
夏皮罗-威尔克检验/Shapiro-Wilk檢定　Shapiro-Wilk test
夏皮罗-威尔克统计量/薛卜若-維克統計量　Shapiro-Wilk statistics
夏普比率/夏普比率　Sharpe ratio
夏普假说/夏普假說　Sharpe hypothesis
夏普利值/夏普力值　Shapley value
先并后减/先并後減　reduction after combined sentence
先到先服务规则/先到先服務規則　first come first served, FCFS
先发优势/先動優勢　first-mover advantage
先赋角色/先賦角色　ascribed role
先赋性身份/先賦地位　ascribed status
先合同义务/先合同義務　obligation before contract
先核后签/先核後簽　sign after examination
先减后并/先減後并　combination of sentence after reduction
先进技术/先進技術,時尚科技　advanced technology, up-to-date technology
先进先出/先進先出,先入先出　first in first out
先进先出法/先進先出法,先進先出原則　first-in-first-out, FIFO
先决变数/先決變數　predetermined variable
先决论/預選說　predeterminism

先履行抗辩权/先履行抗辯權　right of plea against the advance performance
先买权利/優先購股權　pre-emptive right
先期承兑/提前承兑,預先承兑　anticipated acceptance
先期贷款/預先融資　pre-financing
先期付税票据/先期付稅票據　tax anticipation note
先期违约/先期違約　anticipatory breach of contract
先行工作/先行工序　preceding activity
先行者/先進者,首動者　first mover
先验参数/事前參數　prior parameter
先验法/先驗法　gestalt method, a prior method
先验分布/事前分布,事前分配　prior distribution
先验概率/事前機率,先驗機率,先天機率　prior probability
先验概率密度/事前機率密度,先驗機率密度　prior probability density
先验密度函数/先驗密度函數,事前密度函數　prior density function
先验信息/事前訊息,事前資訊　information prior, prior information
先用权/先用權　right of prior use
先予执行/先予執行　prior execution
先占/先占　occupation
先占原则/先占取得法則　rule of first possession
先组词/先組詞　pre-coordinated term
先组式标引/先組式標引,先組式索引　pre-coordinate indexing
先组式检索语言/先組式檢索語言　pre-coordination retrieval language
先组式索引/先組式索引,先組式標引　pre-coordinate index
先组式语言/先組式語言　pre-coordinate index language
先组式字顺主题索引/先組式字順主題索引　pre-coordinate subject index in alphabetical order
纤维素光解/纖維素光解　photo-degradation of cellulose
纤维素光氧化/纖維素光氧化　photo-oxidation of cellulose
纤维素降解/纖維素降解　degradation of cellulose
纤维素水解/纖維素水解　hydrolysis of cellulose
纤维素氧化/纖維素氧化　oxidization of cellulose
闲话/閒話,八卦　gossip
闲谈传递/閒談傳輸　confabulatory transmission
闲暇/休閒　leisure
闲置备用的活期存款/閒置備用的活期存款　idle demand deposit

闲置产能/閒置產能　idle capacity
闲置货币余额/閒置貨幣餘額　idle money balance
闲置库存/閒置存貨　idle inventory
闲置资本/閒置資金,游資　dormant capital
闲置资产/閒置資產　idle asset
闲置资金/閒置資金　laid up capital, idle fund
显德刑统类/顯德刑統類　XianDe Criminal Category
显名代理/顯名代理　named agency
显失公平/欺罔或顯失公平行爲,不正當　obviously unfair
显示存储器/光顯示記憶體　display memory
显示偏好强公理/強顯現偏好公設　strong axiom of revealed preference
显示偏好弱公理/弱性顯現偏好公設　weak axiom of revealed preference
显示屏/螢幕,顯示器　display unit
显示性比较优势指数/顯示性比較利益　revealed comparative advantage, RCA
显示性偏好/顯示偏好　revealed preference
显示性偏好理论/顯示偏好原理　principle of revealed preference
显示原理/揭示原理　revelation principle
显式权[重]/顯性權數　explicit weight
显微镜幻灯片/載玻片　microscope slide
显[性]成本/外顯成本　explicit cost
显性创新效益/顯性創新效益　explicit innovation benefit
显性低度就业/顯性低度就業　visible underemployment
显性效应/優勢效果　dominance effect
显性知识/外顯知識　explicit knowledge
显性知识管理/顯性知識管理　explicit knowledge management
显性主题/顯性主題　explicit subject
显影/顯影　development
显影印相纸/相紙　developing-out paper
显著差检验/顯著差檢定　test of significant difference
显著差异/顯著差異　significant discrepancy
显著点/顯著點　point of significance
显著概率/顯著機率　significance probability
显著性/顯著性　significance
显著性的星标/顯著性的星標　asterisk for significance
显著性检验/顯著性檢定　significance test, test of significance
显著性水平/顯著性水準　significant level, significance level

显著域/顯著域 significant zone, region of significance
现场/場,域 field
现场抱怨/現場抱怨 field complaint
现场表现/現場績效 field performance
现场采购/現場採購 on-the-spot acquisition
现场存货/店面存貨 floor stock
现场调查研究/田野研究,田野調查 field research
现场督导/現場督導 onsite supervision
现场服务/現場服務 field service
现场管理/現場管理 field management
现场技术/田間技術 field technique
现场检查/實地檢查 on-site examination
现场交货/現場交貨 delivery on spot
现场交货价/現場交貨價,當地交貨價 ex point of origin
现场勘查/現場勘查 crime scene investigation
现场勘验笔录/現場勘驗筆錄 record of inspecting the scene
现场可靠性试验/現場可靠度試驗 field reliability test
现场控制/現場控制 shop floor control
现场审核/現場稽核 field auditing
现场失效数据/現場故障數據 field failure data
现场试验/現場試驗,現場實驗,現場測試 field experiment, field test
现场数据/現場資料,實測值 field data
现场制度/現場制度 scene system
现场质量/現場品質 field quality
现存总体/實存母體 existent population
现代管理理论/現代管理理論 modern management theory
现代化/現代化 modernization
现代化理论/現代化理論 modernization theory
现代环境社会学理论/現代環境社會學理論 modern theory of environmental sociology
现代货币数量论/現代貨幣數量論 modern quantity theory
现代凯恩斯主义者/現代凱因斯主義 modern Keynesian
现代农业/現代農業 modern agriculture
现代排序/現代排序 modern scheduling
现代企业制度/現代企業制度 modern enterprise system
现代社会/現代社會 modern society
现代社会的实证法/現代社會的實證法 positive law in modern society
现代数字体/齊線數字 lining figure

现代性/現代性 modernity
现代主义/現代主義 modernism
现代资产组合理论/現代投資組合理論 modern portfolio theory, MPT
现代组织理论/現代組織理論 modern administrative organization theory
现购/現購 purchase with cash
现汇/現匯,即期外匯 spot exchange
现汇市场/現匯市場,即期外匯市場 spot exchange market
现货/現貨 actual goods
现货报价/現貨報價 spot price quotation
现货黄金市场/現貨黃金市場 spot gold market
现货汇率/現貨匯率 spot rate
现货价格/現貨價格,即期價格,付現價格 price on spot, spot price, cash price
现货交易/現貨交易 actual transaction, spot transaction
现货-期货平价定理/現貨-期貨平價定理 spot-futures parity theorem
现货契约/現貨契約 spot contract
现货市场/現貨市場,實體交易市場,即期市場 physical market, actual market, spot market
现价/市價,時價 present price, current price, going rate
现金/現金 cash
现金报价/現金募股 cash offer
现金比率/現金比率 cash ratio
现金储备/現金準備 cash reserves
现金等价物/約當現金 cash equivalent
现金订货/現金訂貨 cash order
现金股利/現金股利 cash dividend
现金管理服务/現金管理服務 cash management service
现金价格/現金價格,付現價格 cash price
现金交易/現金交易,當日交割 cash transaction, cash trade
现金结算/現金結算 cash settlement, settlement in cash
现金流动机制/物價與現金流量機能 price-specie-flow mechanism
现金流动债券/現金流動債券 bond cash flow
现金流分析/現金流分析 cash flow analysis
现金流量/現金流量 cash flow
现金流量表/現金流量表 statement of cash flow
现金流量折现法/淨現金量 discounted cash flow
现金流匹配/現金流匹配 cash flow matching
现金流折现模型/現金流量折現模型 discounted

cash flow model, DCF model
现金收付凭证/現金收付憑證　receipt and payment document
现金收支表/現金收支表　statement of cash, statement of cash receipt and disbursement, statement of receipt and disbursement of cash
现金通货/現金通貨　cash currency
现金头寸/現金頭寸　money position
现金投入/現金投入　input in cash
现金投资/現金投資　investment in money
现金外流/現金流失　cash drain
现金销售/現金銷售　cash sale, sale by real cash
现金预算/現金週轉預算　cash budgeting
现金账户/現金賬戶　cash account
现金折扣/現金折扣　cash discount
现金支出成本/私人成本,實際支付成本　out-of-pocket cost
现金支付/現金支付　payable in cash, spot cash payment
现金周转期/現金週轉週期　cash conversion cycle, cash cycle
现金资本/現金資本　capital in cash
现刊/現刊,當期刊物　current periodical
现刊陈列架/現刊陳列架　stack of current issue
现刊登记/當期刊物記到　registration of current issue, registration of current periodicals
现刊目次/當期刊物目次　current contents
现款交易/現款交易　for money
现期收入/經常收入　current income
现时购买力/現時購買力　current purchasing power
现时市价/現時市價　current market price
现时售价/現時售價　current selling price
现实读者/實際讀者　actual reader
现实工作预览/真實工作預覽,實際工作預覽　realistic job preview
现实价值/現實價值　realistic value
现实市场/現貨市場　actual market
现实性偏好/偏好顯現　preference revelation
现实用户/現實用戶　actual user
现收现付/隨收隨付　pay-as-you-go system
现收现付制/隨收隨付制,量入爲出法　pay-as-you-go
现象/現象　phenomenon
现象学/現象學　phenomenology
现行抵押/現行抵押　existing mortgage
现行价格/現行價格,時價,當期價格　going price, prevailing price, current price
现行人口调查/現時人口調查　current population survey
现行书目/現行書目　current bibliography
现行特惠关税/現行特惠關稅　existing preferential duty
现行文件/現行檔　current records
现行文件汇编/現行文件匯編　collection of current records
现行文件阅览中心/現行文件閱覽中心　current document reading center
现行效用/現行效用　current utility
现有技术/現有技術　technology known by the public before the application date
现有竞争者/現存競爭者　existing rivalry
现值/現值　present value
现值成本/現值成本　present value cost
现值美元/現值美元　current dollar
现值模型/現值模型　present value model
现值收益/現值收益　present value benefit
现状情报研究/現狀情報分析　current situation intelligence analysis
3σ限/三標準差界限　three-sigma limit
限产超雇/強迫雇用,插花　featherbedding
限定版/限定版　limited edition
限定订货单/限定訂貨單　closed indent
限定期限的担保/限定期限的擔保　limited duration guarantee
限定区域内的贸易/限定區域內的貿易　trade within area
限定用户群/閉路用戶組　closed user group, CUG
限定组配/限定組配　qualified coordination
限额出口/限額出口　rationed export
限额抵押/限額抵押,封閉式抵押　closed mortgage
限额基金/限額基金　closed fund
限额设计/限額設計　design of quota
限额支票/限額支票　limited check
限价/限價　limit price
限价定单/限價定單　limit price order
限价委托/限價單　limit order
限价止损指令/限價止損指令　stop-limit order
限价指令/限價訂單　limited price order
限量版/限定版　limited edition
限期淘汰落后生产工艺设备制度/限期淘汰落後生產工藝設備制度　institution on setting a deadline for phasing out backward industrial processes and equipments
限期治理制度/限期治理制度　system of treating environmental pollution within a prescribed time
限时使用资料/限時使用資料　reserved material

限阅图书/限閱圖書　restricted book
限制贝叶斯估计量/受制貝氏估計量　restricted Bayes estimator
限制发行的连续出版物/限量發行之連續出版品　controlled circulation serial, controlled release serial
限制符/限制符　limited operator
限制股/限制性股票　restricted stock
限制加重原则/限制加重原則　principle of limitative aggravation
限制交易/限制交易　tied transaction
限制进口商品货单/限制進口商品清單　negative list
限制竞争/限制競爭　limit competition
限制竞争行为/限制競爭行爲　restricted competitive behavior
限制贸易制度/限制貿易制度　restrictive trade system
限制声明/限制聲明　restriction declaration
限制误差/受制誤差　restriction error
限制信用证/限制信用狀　limited letter of credit, restricted credit
限制性背书/限制性背書　restrictive endorsement
限制性措施/限制性措施　restraint measure
限制性贷款/限制性貸款　tied loan
限制性定价/限制性定價　limit pricing
限制性关税/限制性關稅　restrictive tariff
限制性交易措施/限制交易行爲　restrictive trade practice
限制性契约条款/限制性契約條款　restrictive covenant
限制性商业惯例/限制性商業習慣　restrictive commercial practice
限制性投标/限制性投標　limited tender
限制性信贷政策/限制性信貸政策　restrictive credit policy
限制性许可证/限制性許可證　restrictive license
限制性援助/有條件援助　tied aid
限制序贯程序/受制逐次程序　restricted sequential procedure
限制原则/限制原則　principle of restriction
线抽样/線抽樣　line sampling
线雕凹印/凹紋印花　intaglio printing
线截距/線截距　intercept of a line
线频谱/線頻譜　line spectrum
线人/報導人,消息來源,線民　informant
线上对线下/線上對線下　online to offline, O2O
线图/線圖　line diagram, line chart
线性编辑/線性編輯　linear editing
线性变换/線性變換　linear transformation

线性不等式约束/線性不等式限制　linear inequality restriction
线性插值[法]/線性内插[法]　linear interpolation
线性充分性/線性充分性　linear sufficiency
线性的市场拉动模型/線性的市場拉動模型　linear market pull model
线性定价/線性定價　linear pricing
线性对照/線性對比　linear contrast
线性非时变滤波器/依時不變線性過濾器　time-invariant linear filter
线性分配法/線性分配法　linear assignment method
线性分式规划/線性分式規劃　linear-fractional programming
线性概率模型/線性機率模型　linear probability model
线性估计[量]/線性估計量　linear estimator
线性规划/線性規劃　linear programming
线性过程/線性過程　linear process
线性过滤器/線性過濾器　linear filter
线性函数关系/線性函數關係　linear functional relationship
线性化/線性化　linearization
线性化合同/線性契約　linear contract
线性回归/線性回歸　linear regression
线性回归分析/線性回歸分析　linear regression analysis
线性回归模型/線性回歸模型　linear regression model
线性回归预测/線性回歸預測　linear regression prediction
线性回归预测模型/線性回歸預測模型　linear regression forecasting model
线性极大似然法/線性最大概度法　linear maximum likelihood method
线性技术内生增长模型/線性技術内生增長模型　linear technology endogenous growth model
线性加权法/線性加權法　linear weighted method
线性假设/線性假設　linear hypothesis
线性假设检验/檢定線性假設　testing linear hypothesis
线性假设模型/線性假設模型　linear hypothesis model
线性结构关系/線性結構關係　linear structural relation
线性进步观/線性進步觀　unilinearity
线性近似/線性近似,線性逼近　linear approximation
线性联系/線性相聯　linear association
线性流形/線性流形　linear manifold

线性滤波器／線性過濾器　linear filter
线性模型／線性模型　linear model
线性判别函数／線性判別函數　linear discriminant function
线性齐次约束／線型均齊性限制條件式　linear homogeneous restriction
线性趋势／線性趨勢　linear trend
线性趋势模型／線性趨勢模型　linear trend model
线性生产模型／線性生産模型　linear production model
线性失效率分布／線性故障率分布　linear failure rate distribution
线性搜索／線性搜尋　linear search
线性算子／線性算子　linear operator
线性随机差分方程／線性隨機差分方程式　linear stochastic difference equation
线性随机过程／線性隨機過程　linear stochastic process
线性损失函数／線性損失函數　linear loss function
线性所得税／線性所得税　linear income tax
线性无关／線性獨立　linear independence
线性无偏估计[量]／線性不偏估計量　linear unbiased estimator
线性系统／線性系統　linear system
线性系统统计量／線性系統統計量　linear systematic statistic
线性相关／線性相關　linear correlation
线性响应／線性反應　linear response
线性循环相关／線性循環相關　linear-circular correlation
线性预测／線性預測　linear prediction, linear forecasting
线性约束／線性制限　linear restriction
线性约束方程／線性等式限制　linear equality restriction
线性支出系统／線性支出系統　linear expenditure system
线性秩检验／線性秩檢定　linear rank test
线性组合／線性組合　linear combination
线性最佳估计[量]／線性最適估計[量]　linear optimum estimator
线性最小二乘[平方]法／線性最小平方法　linear least squares method
线性最优／最適線性的　linear-optimal
线性最优设计／最適線性設計　linear-optimal design
线装／線裝　Chinese traditional thread sewing
线装书／線裝書　Chinese style book, thread-bound Chinese book, thread-bound book

宪法／憲法　constitution
宪法修正案／憲法修正案　constitutional amendments
宪章／憲章　charter
宪章派／憲章派　chartist
献祭／祭獻　sacrifice
乡财县管／鄉財縣管　finance of township supervised by the government of county
乡城迁移／城鄉遷移　rural-urban migration
乡村建设／鄉村重建，農村復興　rural reconstruction
乡村俱乐部型管理／鄉村俱樂部式管理　country-club management
乡绅／鄉紳　gentry
乡约／鄉約　rural convention
乡镇企业／鄉鎮企業　township and village enterprise, TVE
乡镇图书馆／農村圖書館　rural library, township and village library
乡族之制／鄉族之制　clan system, family lineage organization
相伴变量／伴隨變數　concomitant variable
相当因果关系说／相當因果關係說　theory of correspond casuality
相对剥夺感／相對剝奪[感]　relative deprivation
相对产出供给／相對産出供給　relative output supply
相对产出需求／相對産出需求　relative output demand
相对次数多边图／相對次數多邊形圖　relative frequency polygon
相对法／相對法　relative method
相对反差值／相對反差值　relative contrast value
相对方差／相對變異數　relative variance
相对风险／相對風險　relative risk
相对工资／相對工資　relative wage
相对供给／相對供給　relative supply
相对供给曲线／相對供給曲線　relative supply curve
相对购买力平价／相對購買力平價法則　relative purchasing power parity
相对过剩人口／相對過剩人口　relative surplus population
相对极差／相對全距　relative range
相对技术优势／相對技術優勢　relative technology advantage
相对价格／相對價格　relative price
相对价值法／相對價值法　relative value method
相对价值形式／相對價值形式　relative form of value
相对精[密]度／相對精確度　relative precision
相对[离]差／相對離差　relative deviation
相对离散／相對離勢　relative dispersion

相对离散度量／相對離勢量測　relative measure of dispersion
相对利益／相對利益　relative advantage
相对量／相對數量　relative quantity
相对灵敏度／相對靈敏度　relative sensitivity
相对密度／相對密度　relative density
相对贫困／相對貧窮　relative poverty
相对频率法／相對頻率法　relative frequency method
相对频率分布／相對次數分配　relative frequency distribution
相对频率直方图／相對次數直方圖　relative frequency histogram
相对剩余价值／相對剩餘價值　relative surplus-value
相对湿度／相對濕度　relative humidity
相对湿度控制／相對濕度控制　relative humidity controlling
相对市场份额／相對市占率　relative market share
相对数／相對數　relative number
相对条图／相對長條圖　relative bar chart
相对位势／相對效能　relative potency
相对位置估计法／相對位置估計法　estimate method of relative place
相对误差／相對誤差　relative error
相对效率／相對效率　relative efficiency
相对信息／相對資訊　relative information
相对性修改／相對變化　relative change
相对需求／相對需求　relative demand
相对需求曲线／相對需求曲線　relative demand curve
相对业绩评价／相對績效評估　relative performance evaluation
相对指数／相對指數　relative index
相对主义／相對主義　relativism
相对准确度／相對準確度　relative accuracy
相反组／反組　contrary class
相关／相關　correlation
相关表／相關表　correlation table
相关参照／相互參照，交互參照　see also reference, reciprocal reference
相关产业／關聯產業　relating industry
相关度量／相關測度　correlated measure
相关度排序／相關排序　relevance ranking
相关多元化／相關多角化　related diversification
相关反馈／相關回饋　relevance feedback
相关方／相關方　relevant side
相关分析／相關分析　correlation analysis, analysis of correlation
相关分析预测模型／相關分析預測模型　correlation analysis forecasting model
相关关系／聯想關聯，相關　associative relationship, correlation
相关观测［值］／相依觀測［值］　dependent observations
相关函数／相關函數　correlation function
相关回归／關係回歸　related regression
相关回馈／相關回饋　relevance feedback
相关技术／相關技術　related technology
相关［矩］阵／相關矩陣　correlation matrix
相关矩阵函数／相關矩陣函數　correlation matrix function
相关均衡／關聯性均衡　correlated equilibrium
相关排架法／相關排架法　relative location
相关曲面／相關曲面　correlation surface
相关散布图／相關散布圖　correlation scatter chart
相关市场／相關市場　relevant market
相关索引／相關索引　correlative index
相关题名／相關題名　related title
相关题名附注／相關題名附注　note pertaining to related title
相关图／相關圖　correlogram
相关团体著者／相關團體著者　related corporate body
相关系数／相關係數　correlation coefficient, coefficient of correlation
相关系数变换／相關係數的變換　transformation of correlation coefficient
相关性／攸關性　relevance
相关性原理／關聯原則，相關原理　relevance principle, principle of correlation
相关需求／相依需求，非獨立需求　dependent demand
相关需求库存／相依需求存貨　dependent demand inventory
相关叙词／相關項　related term
相关样本／相關樣本，相依樣本　correlated sample, dependent sample
相关原则／相關原則　principle of pertinence
相关指数／相關指數　correlation index
相关字段／相關字段　related field
相合估计／一致估計　consistent estimation
相合估计量／一致估計量　consistent estimator
相合估计［值］／一致估計［值］　consistent estimate
相合统计量／一致統計量　consistent statistic
相互保险／相互保險　mutual insurance
相互保险公司／相互保險公司　mutual insurance company
相互保险基金／相互保險基金　mutual insurance

fund
相互承兑/相互承兑　mutual acceptance
相互持股/相互持股,交叉持股　reciprocal shareholding
相互持有通货/相互持有通货　mutual currency holding
相互订货/相互訂貨　cross order
相互控股/交叉持股　mutual holding
相互通货账户/相互通貨賬戶　mutual currency account
相互往来账户/相互往來賬戶　reciprocal account
相互需求法则/相互需求法則　law of reciprocal demand
相互需求原理/需求互惠原則　principle of reciprocal demand
相互依赖/相互依賴性　interdependence
相互影响分析预测法/相互影響分析預測法　interactive effect forecasting method
相加干扰项/相加性干擾項　additive disturbance
相连的二值随机变量/相聯二元隨機變數　associated binary random variable
相连样本/連環樣本　linked samples
相联成对比较设计/連環配對比較設計　linked paired comparison designs
相联随机变量/相聯隨機變數　associated random variables
相联因变量/相聯因變數　associated dependent variable
相联因子组/相聯因子組　associated factor set
相联元件/相聯元件　associated component
相联组/相聯組　associate class
相邻权/鄰接權　neighboring right
相容度/相容度　compatibility degree
相容性/相容性,一致性　compatibility, consistency
相似/相似　resemblance
相似检验/相似檢定　similar test
相似矩阵/相似矩陣　similar matrix
相似系数/相似係數　similarity coefficient
相似行动/相似行動　similar action
相似性/相似度　similarity
相似性测度/相似性量測　similarity measure
相似性检索/相似性檢索　similarity retrieval
相似性系数/相似性係數　coefficient of likeness
相似性指数/相似性指數　similarity index
相似域/相似區域　similar region
相同商标/相同商標　identical trademark
相同专利/相同專利　equivalent patent
相依/相依　dependent
相依量/相依量　dependent quantity
相依事件/相依事件　dependent event
相依性/相依性　dependence
相依样本/相依樣本　dependent samples, correlated samples
相依因子/相依因子　dependent factors
相异度/相異度　dissimilarity
相异性指数/相異性指數　dissimilarity index, index of dissimilarity
相遇群体/會心團體　encounter group
香港股票交易所/香港股票交易所　Hong Kong Stock Exchange
香港恒生指数/香港恆生指數　Hong Kong Hang Seng index
香料贸易/香料貿易　spice trade
香烟卡模型分布/香菸卡模型分佈　cigarette card distribution
厢/厢　xiang
箱式价差期权/箱式價差期權　box straddle
详式提单/詳式提單　long form bill of lading
详析模式/詳析模式　elaboration method
详细规划设计/詳細規劃設計　detailed concept design
详细可行性研究/詳細可行性研究　detailed feasibility study
详细评审/詳細評估　detailed evaluation
详细书目记录/詳細書目記錄　full record
享乐主义/享樂主義　hedonism
响应/反應　response
响应方差/反應變異數　response variance
响应偏倚/反應偏差　response bias
响应曲面/反應曲面　response surface
响应曲面设计/反應曲面設計　response surface design
响应曲面实验/反應曲面實驗　response surface experiment
响应时间/響應時間,反應時間　response time
响应时间分布/反應時間分佈　response time distribution
响应误差/反應誤差　response error
响应指数/反應指數　index of response
响应转换值/反應轉換值　response metameter
想象/想像　imagine
想象的共同体/想像的共同體,想像社群　imagined community
想象竞合犯/想像競合犯　imaginative joinder of offences
向公众传播权/向公眾傳播權　right of

communication to the public
向后弯曲的劳动供给曲线/後彎的勞動供給曲線 backward bending labor supply curve
向后预测法/向後預測法 backcasting method
向量误差修正模型/向量誤差修正模型 vector error correction model, VECM
向量相关/向量相關 vector correlation
向量相关系数/向量相關係數 vector correlation coefficient
向量移动平均模型/向量移動平均模型 vector moving average model, vector MA model, VMA model
向量余相关系数/向量餘相關係數 vector alienation coefficient
向量值估计量/向量值估計量 vector-valued estimator
向量值位置参数/向量值位置參數 vector-valued location parameter
向量自回归移动平均模型/向量自回歸移動平均模型 vector ARMA model, VARMA model
向前选择法/前進選擇法 forward selection procedure
向上累积/向上累積 upward cumulation
向上累计次数/以上累加次數 decumulative frequency
向上链/向上連串 runs up
向上偏倚/[向]上偏誤 upward bias
向上调整/向上調整 upward adjustment
向上销售/向上銷售 up-selling
向下累加/向下累加 downward cumulation
向下链/向下連串 runs down
向下流动/向下流動 downward mobility
向下偏倚/[向]下偏誤 downward bias
向下型偏倚/向下型偏誤 downward type bias
向心性/居中程度 centrality
项目/①项目,②事案 ①item, ②project
项目编码/專案編碼 code of project
项目变更/專案變更 project change
项目变更控制/專案變更控制 project change control
项目筹资贷款/專案籌資貸款 project financing loan
项目贷款/專案貸款 project loan
项目得分的方差/項目分數變異量,題項分數變異量 item score variance
项目反应理论/項目反應理論,試題反應理論 item response theory
项目范围/項目範圍 project scope
项目分析/項目分析,題項分析 item analysis

项目风险/項目風險 project risk
项目风险管理/專案風險管理 project risk management
项目构思/專案構思 project conception
项目管理/專案管理 project management
项目管理办公室/專案管理辦公室 project management office
项目管理承包模式/專案管理承包模式 project management contract model, PMC model
项目管理后评价/專案管理後評價 post evaluation of project management
项目管理计划/項目管理計劃 project management plan
项目管理软件/專案管理軟體 project management software
项目管理系统/專案管理系統 project management system
项目管理信息系统/工程執行資訊系統 project management information system, PMIS
项目管理专业人员资质认证/專案管理專業人員資格認證 project management professional, PMP
项目合同/專案合同 project contract
项目后评价/專案後評價 post project evaluation
项目化管理/專案化管理 management by project
项目集/專案集 programme
项目集管理/專案集管理 programme management
项目计划/專案計劃 project plan
项目计划管理/項目計劃管理 project plan management
项目建议书/專案建議書 project proposal
项目鉴别指数/項目鑑別度指數,題項鑑別度指數 item discrimination index
项目交接/專案轉移,專案移轉 project transfer
项目经理/專案經理 project manager
项目决策/專案決策 project decision
项目开发因素/專案開發因素 development characteristics and factors, DCF
项目排序/專案進度安排 project scheduling
项目评估/專案評估 project evaluation
项目评价/專案評估 project appraisal
项目清算/專案清算 project liquidation
项目区分度/項目鑑別度,題項鑑別度 item discrimination
项目融资/專案融資,工程融資 financing of project, project financing
项目审计/專案審計 project audit
项目生命期/專案生命週期 project life cycle
项目式[项目管理]组织/專案式專案管理組織

projectized organization of project management
项目团队/專案團隊　project team
项目无回答/項目非反應　item non-response
项目效益后评价/專案效益後評價　post evaluation of project benefit
项目验收/專案驗收　project acceptance
项目章程/專案章程　project charter
项目质量/專案品質　project quality
项目质量管理/工程品質管制　project quality management
项目质量控制复核/專案品質控制覆核　engagement quality control review
项目质量验收/專案品質驗收　project quality acceptance
项目资金/專案資金　project fund
项目资金筹措/專案資金籌措　project financing
项目总承包招标/專案總承包招標　total contract tendering
项目总控模式/專案總控模式　project controlling model, PC model
项目组/專案團隊　project team
项目组合/專案組合　project portfolio
项目组织者/專案組織者　project organizer
相变喷墨/相變噴墨　phase change inkjet
相机决策/權衡性政策　discretionary policy
相［位］/位相　phase
相［位］图/位相圖　phase diagram
象鼻/象鼻　trunk
象限/象限　quadrant, quad
象限和检验/象限和檢定　quadrant sum test
象限相依/象限相依　quadrant dependence
象形图/象形圖　pictogram
象征/象徵,符號　symbol
象征性出口/象徵性出口　token export
象征性进口/象徵性進口　token import
象征性死亡/象徵性死亡　symbolic death
象征主义/象徵主義　symbolism
VHS像带/VHS像帶　VHS tape
像素/像素,畫素,像元　pixel
像素编辑/像素校訂　pixel editing
像素数/像元數　pixel count
橡皮布/橡皮布　blanket
橡皮布滚筒/橡皮筒　blanket cylinder
橡皮凸版/橡皮凸版　rubber relief plate
肖特分布/Short 分布　Short distribution
枭首/梟首　Xiaoshou
消除季节影响的时间序列/消除季節的時間數列　deseasonalized time series
消除危险请求权/消除危險請求權　claim for eliminating hazard
消磁器/消磁器　degaussing device
消磁头/消磁頭　degaussing head
消磁效果/消磁效果　degaussing effect
消防系统/消防系統　fire extinguishing system
消费/消費,開銷　consumption, spending
消费不足/消費不足　underconsumption
消费不足理论/消費不足論　underconsumptionism
消费差距/消費缺口　consumption gap
消费贷款/消費貸款　consumer loan
消费定价/消費定價　consumer goods pricing
消费函数/消費函數　consumption function
消费基金/消費基金　consumption fund
消费价格指数/消費者物價指數　consumer price index, CPI
消费结构/消費結構　consumption structure
消费可能线/消費可能線　consumption possibility line
消费理论/消費理論　consumption theory
消费扭曲损失/消費扭曲損失　consumption distortion loss
消费品/消費品,消費財　consumer goods, consumption goods
消费品进口报单/消費品進口報單　entry for consumption
消费社会/消費社會　consumer society
消费社会学/消費社會學　sociology of consumption
消费束/消費組合　consumption bundle
消费税/消費稅　consumption tax
消费外部性/消費外部性　consumption externality
消费文化/消費文化　culture of consumption
消费物价/消費者價格　consumer price
消费信贷/消費［者］信貸　consumer credit
消费账户/消費賬　consumption account
消费者/消費者　consumer
消费者保护主义/消費者主義　consumerism
消费者促销/消費者推廣　consumer promotion
消费者抵制/消費者需要的下降　consumer resistance
消费者动机/消費者動機　consumer motive
消费者动机研究/動機研究　motivation research
消费者对企业/消費者對企業　consumer to business, C2B
消费者风险/消費者風險　consumer risk
消费者概况/消費者輪廓　consumer profile
消费者感知/消費者知覺　consumer perception
消费者感知风险/顧客感知風險　consumer perceived

risk
消费者感知价值/消費者感知價值　consumer perceived value
消费者个性/消費者人格　consumer personality
消费者关系/顧客關係　customer relationship
消费者广告/消費者廣告　consumer advertising
消费者价格指数/消費者價格指數,消費者物價指數　consumer price index, CPI, index of consumer price
消费者接收规范/消費者允收規格　consumer acceptance specification
消费者卷入/消費者涉入　consumer involvement
消费者决策过程/消費者決策過程　consumer decision making process
消费者理论/消費者理論　consumer theory
消费者目标群体/消費者目標群體　target customer segment
消费者偏好/消費者偏好　consumer preference
消费者清单/消費者列單　consumer list
消费者驱动型哲学/顧客驅動型哲學　customer-driven philosophy
消费者权利/消費者權利　consumer's right
消费者剩余/消費者剩餘　consumer surplus
消费者剩余总额/毛消費者剩餘　gross consumer surplus
消费者市场/消費者市場　consumer market
消费者态度/消費者態度　consumer attitude
消费者效用/消費者效用　consumer utility
消费者协会/消費者協會,消費者聯合會　consumer association
消费者信念/消費者信念　consumer belief
消费者信用控制/消費者信用管制　consumer credit control
消费者行为/消費者行為　consumer behavior
消费者选择/消費者選擇　consumer choice
消费者学习/消費者學習　consumer learning
消费者研究/消費者研究　consumer research
消费者支出/消費者支出　consumer spending
消费者主权/消費者主權,消費者主義　consumer sovereignty
消费支出税/支出稅　expenditure tax
消费资本主义/消費資本主義　consumer capitalism
消费资本资产定价模型/消費資本資產定價模型　consumption-based capital assert pricing model, consumption-based CAPM, CCAPM
消费资料/消費財　consumption goods
消耗的等待时间/耗費等待時間　spent waiting time
消耗量定额/消耗定額　consumption quota

消极式函证/消極式函證　negative confirmation
消极信托/無利息信託　passive trust
消极信息/負面資訊　negative information
消极行政管理/消極行政　passive administration
消极修辞/消極修辭　negative rhetoric
消极债券管理/消極債券管理　passive bond management
消极资产组合/被動投資組合　passive portfolio
消遣读物/消遣性讀物　light reading, reading for pleasure
消息/消息,訊息,信息　message
消息来源/消息來源,新聞來源,出處　news source, attribution
萧条/蕭條　depression
销毁/銷毀　destruction
销货清单/銷貨清單　bill of sales
销货账/銷貨清單　account of goods sold
销货账户/銷貨賬戶　sales account
销售/銷售,出售　sale
销售百分比法/銷售百分比法　percentage-of-sale method
销售拜访/銷售拜訪　approach
销售包装/銷售包裝　sales package
销售成本/銷售成本　sales cost
销售促进/促銷　sales promotion
销售代理商/銷售代理商　sales agent
销售单价/銷售價格　selling price
销售导向/行銷導向　marketing orientation
销售定单/銷售定單　sales order
销售定额/銷售定額　sales quota
销售队伍管理/銷售人員管理　sales force management
销售队伍有效性比率/銷售隊伍效能比率　sales force effectiveness ratio
销售额/銷售額　sales amount
销售发票/銷售發票　sales invoice
销售访前准备/推銷之前導作業　preapproach
销售费用/行銷費用,推銷費用　marketing expense, selling expense
销售分析/銷售分析　analysis of sales
销售号/銷售號　sales number
销售合同/銷售合約　contract of sales, sales contract
销售合作/銷售合作　sales association
销售利润/銷售利潤　sales profit
销售利润率/純益率　profit margin
销售量市场份额/銷售量市場份額　unit market share
[销售]毛利/毛利　gross profit

销售潜力/銷售潛力　sales potential
销售侵犯注册商标专用权的商品/銷售侵犯註冊商標專用權的商品　selling counterfeited goods
销售侵权复制品/銷售侵權複製品　distributing infringing copies
销售驱动型哲学/銷售驅動型哲學　sales-driven philosophy
销售渠道/行銷管道　marketing channel
销售人员/銷售員　salesman
销售融资公司/銷售融資公司　sales finance company
销售融资机构/銷售融資機構　sales finance institution
销售商标/銷售商標　trademark of selling
销售时点系统/銷售時點系統　point of sales
销售收入/銷售收入　sales income
销售收入最大化理论/銷售收入最大化理論　theory of sales revenue maximization
销售损失/銷售損失　loss on sales
销售协议/行銷協議,銷售合約　marketing agreement, sales agreement
销售辛迪加/銷售辛迪加,銷售委員會　selling syndicate
销售要约/銷售要約　selling offer
销售佣金/銷售佣金　sales commission
销售预算/銷售預算,行銷預算　marketing budget, sales budget
销售增长/銷量增長　sales growth
销售折让/銷售折讓,銷貨折讓　sales allowance
销售最大化/追求銷售額之最大　sales maximization
销数/銷數　reader amount
小标题/小標題,副標題　subhead, sub-heading, minor heading
小册子/小冊子　booklet, brochure, pamphlet
小传统/小傳統　folk tradition
小岛模式/小島模式,國際投資比較利益理論　theory of comparative advantage of international investment
小道消息/小道消息,傳聞,謠傳　hearsay
小额贷款/小額貸款　small loan
小额贷款公司/小額貸款公司　small loan company
小额债券/小額債券　small bond
小而全/小而全　small and all-round
小国贸易条件/小國貿易條件　small country terms of trade
小集团控制/派系控制　clan control
小计/小計　sub-total
小金库/小金庫　small coffer

小康/小康　Xiaokang, well-off
小康社会/富裕社會,豐裕社會　affluent society, well-off society
小科学/小科學　folk science
小麦淀粉浆糊/小麥澱粉漿糊　wheat starch paste
小面额钞票/小鈔　small-denomination bill
小农农业/小農農業　peasant agriculture
小企业融资/小企業融資　small business financing
小区/社區　community
小区建设/社區營造　community building
小区论坛途径/社區論壇途徑　community forum approach
小区人口统计/社區人口統計　community demographics
小区中介组织/社區仲介組織　community intermediary organization
小区自治/社區自治　community autonomy, community self-governance
小区组织/社區組織　community organization
小全版广告/小全版廣告　junior full page
小群体/小團體　small group
小人书/小人書　children picture book
小世界/小世界　small-world
小世界现象/小世界現象　small-world phenomenon
小世界研究/小世界的研究　small-world study
小数标记制/十進[位]記法　decimal notation
小数[定]律/小數法則　law of small-numbers
小数条件/小數條件　small-numbers condition
小型光碟/光碟　compact disc, CD
小型计算机/迷你電腦　minicomputer
小型开放经济/小型開放經濟　small open economy
小型音频光盘/迷你磁碟,迷你唱片　minidisc
小型营利企业/小型營利企業　small profitable venture
小型影碟/影音光碟　video compact disc, VCD
小样/小樣　galley proof
小样本/小樣本　small sample
小样本检验/小樣本檢驗　small sample inspection
小样本理论/小樣本理論　theory of small sample
小样对红/小樣對紅　galley proof comparison
小页/小頁　shrunken page
小域抽样/小區域抽樣　small area sampling
小资产阶级/小資產階級,小布爾喬亞　petty bourgeoisie
小字本/小字本　small character edition
小组/小組　group
小组工作基本程序/小組工作基本程序　basic procedure of teamwork

小组计划书/小組計劃書　teamwork proposal
小组生命历程/團體過程　group process
小组座谈/焦點團體　focus group
孝[道]/孝[道]　filial piety
肖像权/肖像權　portraiture right
校报/校園報紙　college newspaper
校外教育机构/校外教育機構　extra-school educational institute
校园暴力/校園霸凌　school bullying
校园文化/校園文化　campus culture
效标关联效度/效標關聯效度　criterion-related validity
效度/[有]效度　validity
效果器类插件/效果器類外掛程式　effector mod
效果研究/效果研究　effect research
效果意思/效果意思　effective intention
效果指数/效度指標　effectiveness index
效力未定的法律行为/效力未定的法律行爲　legal act with open effect
效率/效率　efficiency
效率成本/效率成本　efficiency cost
效率等价/效率對等　efficiency equivalence
效率工资/效率工資　efficiency wage
效率工资假说/效率工資假説　efficiency wage hypothesis
效率工资理论/效率工資理論　efficiency wage theory
效率工资目标/效率工資目標　efficiency wage objective
效率工资制/效率工資制　efficiency wage system
效率损失/效率損失　efficiency loss
效率违约/有效率的違約　efficient breach
效率型企业/效率型企業　efficiency-type corporation
X效率一般理论/X效率理論　general X efficiency theory
效率因子/效率因子　efficiency factor
效率与公平/效率與公平　efficiency and equity
效益评价/效益評估　benefit evaluation
效益审计/效益審計　effectiveness audit
效应/效應　effect
效应变量/效應變數　effect variable
效应分析/效應分析　effect analysis
效应系数/效應係數　effect coefficient
效应消除/效應消減,效應遞減　effect elimination
效用/效用　utility
效用的不可分割/不可分散　non-divisibility
效用函数/效用函數　utility function
效用函数构造法/效用函數構造法　structure method of utility function
效用可能性边界/效用可能曲線　utility possibility frontier
效用可能性集/效用可能集合　utility possibilities set
效用贸易条件/效用貿易條件　utility terms of trade
效用曲线/效用曲線　utility curve
效用曲线拟合/效用曲線擬合　fitting of utility curve
效用无差别曲线/效用無異曲線　utility indifference curve
效用系数法/效用係數法　utility coefficient method
效用指数/效用指數　utility index
效用最大化/效用最大化,效用極大　utility maximization
楔形方案/楔形計劃　wedge plan
协变/共變異　covariation
协变量/共變量　covariate
协变量的乘法效应/共變量的乘積效果　multiplicative effect of covariate
协定/協定　agreement
协定缔约国/協定締約國　agreement country
协定关税/協定關稅,關稅協定　agreement tariff, conventional duty
协定价格/協定價格　stipulated price
协定贸易量/議定貿易量　agreed quantity of trade
协定税则/協定稅率　conventional tariff
协定税则制/協定稅則制　conventional tariff system
协方差/共變異數　covariance
协方差分析/共變數分析　analysis of covariance, covariance analysis, ANOCVA
协方差分析表/共變異分析表　analysis of covariance table, ANOCVA table
协方差分析模型/共變異分析模型　analysis of covariance model
协方差函数/共變異數函數　covariance function
协方差核/共變異數核　covariance kernel
协方差矩阵/共變異數矩陣　covariance matrix
协方差矩阵母函数/共變數矩陣母函數　covariance matrix generating function
协方差平稳过程/共變異數平穩過程　covariance stationary process
协方差平稳性/共變數平穩性　covariance stationarity
协会/行會　guild
协拍片/協拍片　association of film
协谱/餘譜　cospectrum
协商/協商,談判　consultation, negotiation
协商理论/協商理論　bargaining theory
协商式解读/協商解讀,協商閱讀　negotiated reading

协商式民主决策/商議式民主,審議式民主　deliberative democracy
协调标准/調和標準　harmonized standard
协调博弈/協調賽局,整合賽局　coordination game
协调发展原则/協調發展原則　principle of harmonious development
协调市场经济/協調市場經濟　coordinated market economy
协调系数/協和係數,協合係數　coefficient of concordance
协调型购买行为/和諧型購買行爲　dissonance-reducing buying behavior
协调性/協和性　concordance
协调样本/協調樣本　concordant sample
协同编辑/協同編輯　collaborative editing
协同出版/協同出版　collaborative publishing
协同创新/協同創新　synergy innovation
协同价值/綜效價值　synergy value
协同推荐/協同推薦　collaborative recommendation
协同效应/綜效　coordinated effect, synergy
协同效应战略联盟/綜效性策略聯盟　synergistic strategic alliance
IP 协议/網際網路協定　internet protocol
协议公司/協議公司　agreement corporation
协议管辖/協議管轄　agreement to jurisdiction
协议管辖原则/協議管轄原則　principle of agreement to jurisdiction
协议选择法院公约/協議選擇法院公約　Convention on Choice of Court Agreements
协整/共整合　cointegration
协整回归/共整合回歸　cointegrating regression
协整检验/共整合檢定　cointegration test
协作计划-预测和补货方法/協同規劃-預測與補貨　collaborative planning-forecasting and replenishment, CPFR
协作图/協作圖　collaboration diagram
协作系统/合作系統,合作制度　cooperative system
协作意愿/協作意願　cooperative willingness
协作营销/合作行銷　cooperative marketing
胁从犯/脅從犯　coerce accomplice
胁迫/脅迫　coerce
挟书律/挾書律　Xieshu Lyu, book possession prohibition
斜交极小法/互變異數最小法　oblimin
斜交因子/斜交因子　oblique factor
斜交转轴/斜交轉軸　oblique rotation
斜交转轴法/最小斜交法　oblimin roation
斜率比测定/斜率比分析　slope ratio assay
斜面报架/斜面報架　newspaper slope

斜面读书台/報告臺　lectern
斜向沟通/斜向溝通　diagonal communication
写本/手寫本　handwritten copy
卸岸日期/抵埠日期　date of landing
卸货港/卸貨港　port of discharge
卸货港费用变更/更改卸貨港費用　alteration of destination fee
卸货价格/到岸價格　landed price
卸货日期/卸貨日期　date of discharge
械斗/械鬥　armed confrontation
谢尔登管理哲学/謝爾登管理哲學　management philosophy of Sheldon
谢尔曼法案/反獨占法　Sherman act
谢尔曼反托拉斯法/休曼反托拉斯法案　Sherman anti-trust act
谢尔曼检验/Sherman 檢定　Sherman test
谢泼德校正/Sheppard 校正　Sheppard correction
谢泼德引理/薛福輔理　Shephard lemma
心境/心境,心情　mood
心理/心理　mentality
心理安全/心理安全感　psychological safety
心理测验/心理測驗,心理測試　psychological test
心理场理论/心理場説　psychological field theory
心理成本/心理成本　psychic cost
心理定价/心理定價[法]　psychological pricing
心理动力模式/心理動力模式　psychodynamic model
心理动力学/心理動力理論　psychodynamics
心理分析/心理分析　mental analysis
心理分析理论/心理分析理論,精神分析理論　psychoanalytic theory
心理份额/心占率　share of mind
心理概率/心理機率　psychological probability
心理计量向度/心理計量標準　psychometric dimension
心理健康/心理健康　mental health
心理健康风险/心理健康風險　psychic risk
心理健康服务/心理健康服務　mental health service
心理距离/心理距離　psychological distance
心理能力测验/心智能力測驗　mental ability test
心理年龄/心智年齡　psychological age
心理契约/心理契約　psychological contract
心理收入/精神收入　psychic income
心理授权/心理賦權,心理賦能　psychological empowerment
心理统计[学]/心理統計學　psychological statistics
心理卫生/心理衛生　mental hygiene
心理细分/心理區隔　psychological segmentation
心理学法学派/心理學法學派　psychological theory

of law
心理依恋/心理依戀　psychological attachment
心理账户/心理賬户　psychological account, mental account
心理资本/心理資本　psychological capital
心形分布/心形分布,心形分配　cardioid distribution
芯片/晶片　chip
辛迪加/辛迪加　syndicate
辛迪加贷款/銀行團聯合貸款　syndicate loan
辛迪加协议/團體協議,企業組合協議　syndicate agreement
辛钦定理/Khintchine 定理　Khintchine theorem
新巴塞尔协议/新巴塞爾協議　New Basel Agreement
新版/新版　new edition
新比旧佳/新比舊佳的　new-better-than-used, NBU
新比旧佳分布/新比舊佳分布　new-better-than-used distribution, NBU distribution
新产品/新產品　new product
新产品开发/新產品開發　new product development, NPD
新产品开发过程/新產品研發流程　new product development process
新产品开发时间/新產品開發時間　new product development time
新产品扩散/新產品擴散　diffusion of new product
新产品扩散曲线/新產品擴散曲線　diffusion curve new product
新产业经济学/新產業經濟學　new industrial economics
新城市主义/新城市主義　new urbanism
新储备资产/新儲備資產　new reserve asset
新达尔文学说/新達爾文主義　neo-Darwinism
新订率/新訂率　new subscribing rate
新分析实证主义法学/新分析實證主義法學　neo-analytical positilist jurisprudence
新工人阶级/新工人階級　new working class
新公共管理/新公共管理　new public management, NPM
新公共行政/新公共行政　new public administration
新古典方法论/新古典方法論　neoclassical methodology
新古典价格理论/新古典價格理論　neoclassical price theory
新古典经济学/新古典經濟學,新興古典總體經濟學　neoclassical economics, new classical economics
新古典理论/新[興]古典理論　new classical theory, neoclassic theory

新古典模型/新古典模型　neoclassical model
新古典契约/新古典契約　new classical contract
新古典行政组织理论/新古典行政組織理論　neoclassical administrative organization theory
新古典学派/新古典學派　neoclassical school
新古典依赖模型/新古典依賴模型　neoclassical dependence model
新古典主义/新古典主義　neoclassicism
新古典综合学派/新古典綜合派　neoclassical synthesis school
新股发行认购额/新股發行認購額　subscription to new share issue
新股认购权/新股認購權　pre-emption right
新股认购权证/新股認購權證　call warrant
新合同主义/新合同主義　new contratualism
新黑格尔主义法学派/新黑格爾主義法學派　neo-hegelian school of law
新华富时中国 A50 指数/新華富時中國 A50 指數　FTSE Xinhua China A50 index
新华书店/新華書店　Xinhua Bookstore
新技术/新技術　new technology
新技术革命/新技術革命　new technological revolution
新济贫法/新濟貧法案　new poor law
新剑桥经济增长模型/新劍橋增長模型　new Cambridge growth model
新剑桥学派/新劍橋學派　neo-Cambridge school
新教伦理/新教倫理　protestant ethic
新阶级/新階級　new class
新进入者/新進者　new entrant
新经济/新經濟　new economy
新经济社会学/新經濟社會學　new economic sociology
新经济史/新經濟史　new economic history
新经济学/新經濟學　new economics
新经济政策/新經濟政策　new economic policy
新凯恩斯主义经济学/新興凱因斯主義經濟學派　new-Keynesian economics
新康德主义法学派/新康得主義法學派　neo-kantian school of law
新拉纳克工业小区/新拉納克工業社區　industrial community of new Lanark factory
新来源观/新來源觀　new concept of provenance, new view of provenance
新李嘉图模型/新李嘉圖模型　neo-Ricardian model
新李嘉图学派/新李嘉圖學派　neo-Ricardian school
新历史学派/新歷史學派　neo-historical school
新联邦主义/新聯邦主義　new federalism

新贸易理论/新貿易理論　new trade theory
新媒体/新媒體,新媒介　new media
新媒体出版/新媒體出版　new media publishing
新媒体艺术/新媒體藝術　computer graph, CG
新媒体制作中心/新媒體製作中心　new media production center
新民族志/新民族志　new ethnography
新品牌策略/新品牌策略　new brand strategy
新设计控制/新設計管制　new design control
新社会史/新社會史　new social history
新社会运动/新社會運動　new social movement
新生儿死亡率/新生兒死亡率　neonatal mortality rate
新生态范式/新生態範式　new ecological paradigm
新世界信息与传播秩序/新世界資訊與傳播秩序　new world information and communication order, NWICO
新书简介/新書出版預告文宣,新書紹介　new book introduction, prospectus
新书书目/新書書目　current bibliography, frontlist
新书推荐/新書推薦　recommendation of new publication
新书预告/新書預告　announcement of forthcoming book
新思想新概念/新思想新概念　new thought and new concept
新泰勒管理/新泰勒管理　neo-Taylorian management
新韦伯主义阶级理论/新韋伯主義階級理論　neo-Weberian class theory
新文化史/新文化史　new cultural history
新闻/新聞　news
新闻版面/新聞版面　news hole
新闻报道/新聞報導　news reporting
新闻报料人/新聞報料人　news informer
新闻背景/新聞背景,背景剪報　background
新闻编辑/新聞編輯　news editor
新闻标准/新聞標準　news standard
新闻采访/新聞採訪　news interview
新闻从业人员/新聞從業人員　news professional
新闻单位/[新聞]通訊社　news agency
新闻电头/新聞電頭　dateline
新闻发言人/新聞發言人,新聞官,新聞秘書　press spokesman, press secretary
新闻法规/新聞法規　press law
新闻封锁/新聞封鎖　news blackout
新闻稿/新聞稿　news release, dispatch
新闻工作常规/新聞常規　news routine
新闻机构/新聞組織　news organization
新闻集团/新聞集團　news corporation
新闻记者/新聞記者　journalist
新闻价值/新聞價值　news value
新闻简报/新聞簡報　news briefing
新闻节目/新聞節目　news program
新闻客观性/新聞客觀性　news objectivity
新闻框架/新聞框架　news frame
新闻类型化/新聞類型化　typification of news
新闻流通/新聞流通,新聞流程,新聞流　news flow
新闻伦理/新聞倫理　journalism ethics
新闻漫画/[政治]新聞漫畫　political comics, news cartoon
新闻媒体/新聞媒體　news media
新闻美学/新聞美學　news aesthetics
新闻门户/新聞門戶　news portal
新闻偏差/新聞偏見　news bias
新闻片/新聞片　newsreel
新闻频道/新聞頻道　news channel
新闻评价/新聞評價　news evaluation
新闻评论/新聞評論　news comment, commentary
新闻评论家/新聞評論家　commentator
新闻期刊/新聞雜誌　news magazine
新闻侵权/新聞侵權　media tort
新闻侵权纠纷/新聞侵權糾紛　media tort dispute
新闻摄影/新聞攝影,新聞照片　news photography
新闻审查/新聞審查　news censor
新闻生产/新聞產製　news production
新闻史学/新聞史學　history of journalism
新闻事件/新聞事件　news event
新闻守则/新聞守則,新聞信條,報業信條　Canons of Journalism
新闻特写/新聞特寫,特寫新聞　news feature
新闻特写采访/新聞特寫採訪　news-feature interview
新闻图片/新聞圖片　news picture
新闻网/新聞網　news net
新闻网站/新聞網站　web news site
新闻文本/新聞文本　news text
新闻五要素/新聞五要素　five Ws of news
新闻线索/新聞線索,新聞素材,新聞題材　news clue, news peg
新闻消费/新聞消費　news consumption
新闻性专刊/新聞性專刊　news of special issue
新闻修辞/新聞修辭　news rhetoric
新闻选择/新聞選擇　news selection
新闻学/新聞學　journalism
新闻议题/新聞議題　news agenda

新闻杂志/新聞雜誌 news magazine
新闻摘要/新聞摘要 news digest
新闻照片/新聞照片,新聞攝影 news photography
新闻主播/新聞主播 news anchor
新闻专业主义/新聞專業主義 journalistic professionalism
新闻自律/新聞自律 press self-regulation
新闻自由/新聞自由 freedom of press
新闻组群/新聞群組 newsgroup
新西兰与澳大利亚自由贸易区/紐西蘭與澳洲自由貿易區 New Zealand and Australia Free Trade Area
新写实主义/新寫實主義 neorealism
新新人类/新新人類 X generation
新新闻学/新新聞學 new journalism
新兴工业化国家/新興工業化國家 newly industrialized country
新兴工业化经济体/新工業化經濟體 newly industrializing economics
新兴股票市场/新興股票市場 emerging stock market
新兴技术/新興技術 emerging technology
新兴宗教/新興宗教 new religion
新型工业化/新型工業化 new pattern industrialization
新型农村养老保险制度/新型農村養老保險制度 new rural pension system
新熊彼特学派/新熊彼特學派 neo-Schumpeterian school
新颖率/新穎率,出新率 novelty ratio
新颖性/新穎性 novelty
新造词/新創詞,應變詞 coined term
新增存货率/新增存貨率 rate of new stock
新增馆藏/新增館藏 acquisition
新增长理论/新成長理論 new growth theory
新政/新政 new deal
新制度主义/新制度主義,新制度經濟學派 neoinstitutionalism
新中产阶级/新中產階級,新中等階級 new middle class
新自然法学派/新自然法學派 neo-natural school of law
新自由主义/新自由主義 neo-liberalism
新左派/新左派 new left
薪酬/薪酬,薪資 earning, compensation
薪酬调查/工資調查 wage survey, salary survey
薪酬阶梯模型/臺階模式,臺階模型 stair-step model
薪酬水平/薪酬水準 compensation level
薪酬业绩敏感度/薪酬-績效敏感度 pay-performance sensitivity
薪金持续方案/續薪計劃 salary continuation plan
薪资/薪資 salary
薪资差别/差別薪酬 compensating differential
薪资奖金计划/薪資加獎金計劃 salary-plus-bonus plan
薪资均衡指标/薪資均衡指標 compa-ratio
薪资佣金计划/薪資加佣金計劃 salary-plus commission plan
信/信 letter
信贷担保债券/信用擔保債券 bond of credit
信贷额度/信貸額度 line of credit
信贷公司/信貸公司 financing corporation
信贷合同/信貸合約 credit contract, finance contract
信贷机构/信貸機構 credit institution
信贷机制/信貸機制 mechanism of credit
信贷交易/信貸交易 credit transaction
信贷结构/信貸結構 credit structure
信贷经纪人/信貸經紀人 credit broker
信贷可获得性/信用可獲性 credit availability
信贷控制/信用管制 credit control
信贷配给/信貸配給 credit rationing
信贷期限/信貸期限 period of credit
信贷渠道/信用傳遞管道 credit channel
信贷市场上的配给/信貸市場配給 rationing in credit market
信贷市场债务/信貸市場債務 credit market debt
信贷数量分析/信貸數量分析 quantitative credit control
信贷限额/信貸限額 limit of credit
信贷业务审计/信貸業務審計 audit for credit operation
信贷银行/信貸銀行 credit bank
信贷约束/信用限制 credit constraint
信贷政策/授信政策 credit policy
信贷资本/信貸資本 credit capital
信道/管道,頻道 channel
信道码元/通道碼元 channel symbol
信道容量/通道容量 channel capacity
信道位/通道位元 channel bit
信度/信度,可靠性 reliability
信访工作/信訪工作 work for handling petitions via letters and visits
信封/信封 envelope
信函管理/信件管理 correspondence management

信号博弈/傳訊賽局　signaling game
信号传递/發信號　signaling
信号传递模型/標簽模型　signaling model
信号因素/信號因素　signal factor
信汇/信匯　letter transfer, mail transfer
信汇汇率/信匯匯率　mail transfer rate
信件/信件　correspondence
信赖保护原则/信賴保護原則　principle of legitimate expectation
信赖利益/信賴利益　interest of trust
信赖损害/因信賴所受之損害　detrimental reliance
信赖域法/信賴域法　trust-region method
信念/信念　belief
信任/信任　trust
信任品/信譽財　credence goods
信宿/訊息收訊者　information receiver
信托/信託　trust, fiduciary
信托财产/信託財產　trust property, trust estate
信托存款/信託存款　trust deposit
信托贷款/信託貸款　trust loan
信托单位/信託單位　trust unit
信托法/信託法　trust law
信托费/信託費　trust charge
信托公司/信託公司　trust company
信托管理人/信託管理人　trust administrator
信托机构/信託機構　fiduciary institution, trust institution
信托基金/信託基金　fiduciary trust, trust fund
信托会计/信託會計　trust accounting
信托契据/信託契據　trust deed
信托契约/信託契約　deed of trust, trust indenture
信托受益人/信託受益人　beneficiary
信托书/信託書　letter of trust
信托投资/信託投資　fiduciary contribution, trust investment
信托投资公司/信託投資公司　trust and investment corporation
信托委托人/信託委託人　trust settlor
信托协议/信託協議　trust agreement
信托业审计/信託業審計　audit of trust service
信托业务/信託業務　trust business, fiduciary business
信托业协会/信託業協會　trustee association
信托银行/信託銀行　trust bank
信托银行业务/信託銀行業務　trust banking
信托有价证券/信託有價證券　securities in trust
信托账户/信託賬戶　trust account
信托资产/信託資產　trust asset

信托资金/信託資金　fiduciary fund
信息/資訊　information
信息安全/資訊安全　information safety, information security
信息安全道德/資訊安全道德　information security moral
信息把关人/守門人　gatekeeper
信息保护/資料保護　information protection
信息保真/資訊保真度　information fidelity
信息爆炸/資訊爆炸　information explosion
信息悖论/資訊佯謬　information paradox
信息标准/資訊標準　information standard
信息表示/資訊表示法　information representation
信息不等式/資訊不等式　information inequality
信息不对称/資訊不對稱　informational asymmetry, information asymmetry
信息不对称理论/資訊不對稱[理]論　asymmetric information theory
信息不对称模型/資訊不對稱模型　asymmetric information model
信息不对称条件下的拍卖/具有不對稱資訊的拍賣　auction with asymmetric information
信息不平等/資訊不平等　information inequity
信息采集/資訊採集，資訊獲取　information capture, information acquisition, information collection
信息产品/資訊產品　information product
信息产业/資訊工業　information industry
信息超载/資訊超載　information overload
信息成本/訊息成本　information cost
信息重获/資訊重現　recovery of information
信息抽取/資訊擷取　information extraction
信息处理/資訊處理　information processing
信息储存/資訊儲存　information storage
信息传播/資訊傳播　information communication
信息传播者/傳播者　disseminator
信息传播中心/資訊傳播中心　information dissemination center, IDC
信息传递/資訊傳送，資訊轉移　information dissemination, information transfer
信息传递角色/資訊傳遞角色　information role
信息存储与检索/資訊儲存與檢索　information storage and retrieval
信息单元/資訊單元　unit of information
信息导航/資訊導航　information navigation
信息道/資訊通道　information channel
信息定制/資訊定製　information customization
信息动机/資訊動機　information motivation

信息对抗/資訊對抗　information countermeasure
信息发布/資訊發布　information distribution
信息法/資訊法　information law
信息法规/資訊法律法規,資訊法律規章　information laws and regulations
信息法学/資訊法學　information legal studies
信息反馈/資訊回饋　information feedback
信息泛滥/資訊泛濫　information profusion
信息分析/資訊分析　information analysis
信息分析师/資訊分析員　information analyst
信息分析中心/資訊分析中心　information analysis center
信息否定/資訊否定　information denial
信息服务/資訊服務　information service
信息服务补救/資訊服務補救　information service recovery
信息服务策略/資訊服務策略　information service strategy
信息服务对象/資訊服務物件　information service object
信息服务环境/資訊服務環境　information service environment
信息服务机制/資訊服務機制　information service mechanism
信息服务集成/資訊服務集成　information service integration
信息服务绩效/資訊服務績效　information service performance
信息服务模式/資訊服務模式　information service mode
信息服务能力/資訊服務能力　information service ability
信息服务平台/資訊服務平臺　information service platform
信息服务体系/資訊服務系統　information service system
信息服务条款/資訊服務條款　information terms of service
信息服务网络/資訊服務網路　information service network
信息服务系统/資訊服務系統　information service system
信息服务限制/資訊服務限制　information service restrictions
信息服务业/資訊服務業　information service industry
信息服务质量/資訊服務品質　quality of information service

信息富有/資訊豐富　information rich
信息高速公路/資訊高速公路　information highway
信息革命/資訊革命　information revolution
信息工程/資訊工程　information engineering
信息公开/資訊披露,資訊揭露　information disclosure
信息公开法/資訊公開法　information freedom act
信息公平/資訊公平　information fairness
信息共享/資訊分享,資訊共享　information sharing
信息共享空间/資訊共用空間,資訊共享空間　information common, IC
信息沟/資訊差距,資訊溝　information gap
信息沟通/資訊溝通　information communication
信息构建/資訊架構　information architecture
信息构建理论/資訊構建理論　information architecture theory
信息管理/資訊管理　information management
信息管理师/資訊管理師　information manager
信息管理系统/資訊管理系統　information management system, IMS
信息管理学/資訊管理學　information management science, information management studies
信息管理与信息系统/資訊管理與資訊系統　information management and information system
信息广告/資訊性廣告　informative advertising
信息过滤/資訊過濾　information filtering, message filtering
信息过剩/資訊溢流　information overflow
信息含量效应/資訊含量效應　information content effect
信息化/資訊化　informationization, informatization
信息化测度/資訊化的測度　measurement of informatization
信息化指数/資訊化指數　informatization index
信息环境/資訊環境　information environment
信息回馈/資訊回饋　information feedback
信息获取/資訊獲取　information acquiring, information acquisition
信息获取权利/資訊取得權　right of access to information
信息机构/資訊機構　information institution
信息基础设施/資訊基礎建設　information infrastructure
信息集成/資訊統合　information integration
信息集成商/資訊集成商　information aggregator
信息计量学/計量情報學　informetrics
信息技术/資訊科技　information technology, IT
信息加工/資訊處理　information processing

信息价值/資訊價值　information value
信息检索/資訊檢索　information retrieval
信息检索模型/資訊檢索模型　information retrieval model
信息检索系统/資訊檢索系統　information search system, information retrieval system
信息检索行为/資訊檢索行爲　information search behavior
信息建构师/資訊架構師　information architect
信息交换/資訊交換　information exchange
信息交换格式/資訊交換格式　information exchange format, format for information exchange
信息交换中心/資訊交換中心　information clearing house, information exchange center
信息焦虑/資訊焦慮　information anxiety
信息阶段/資訊階段　information phase
信息接受者/資訊接受者　monitor
信息经纪人/資訊中介者，資訊掮客　information broker
信息经济/資訊經濟　information economy
信息经济学/資訊經濟學　information economics, economics of information
信息矩阵/資訊矩陣　information matrix
信息聚合/資訊加總，資訊收歛　information aggregation, information converge
信息聚合函数/資訊加總函數　information aggregation function
信息科学/資訊科學　information science
信息可视化/資訊視覺化　information visualization
信息可用性/資訊好用性，資訊優使性　information usability
信息空间/網路空間　infosphere, information space, cyberspace
信息控制/資訊控制　information control
信息匮乏/資訊匱乏，資訊貧窮　information poor
信息理论/資訊理論　information theory
信息联系七原则/資訊聯繫七原則　seven principles of information linkage
信息链/資訊鏈　information chain
信息量/資訊量，情報容量　information content, information volume, amount of information
信息流/資訊流　information flow
信息流程分析图/資訊流程分析圖　information process analysis chart
信息伦理/資訊倫理　information ethics
信息密度/資訊密度　information density
信息描述/資訊描述　information description
信息模式/資訊模型，資訊模式　information model

信息内涵效应/資訊內涵效應　information connotation effect
信息能力/資訊能力　information competency
信息披露制度/資訊披露要求　information disclosure requirement
信息贫乏/資訊匱乏，資訊貧窮　information poor
信息瀑布/資訊階流　information cascade
信息请求/資訊請求　request for information
信息区/資訊區　information area
信息取样模型/資訊抽樣模型　information sampling model
信息权利/資訊權利　information right
信息融合/資訊融合　information fusion
信息冗余/資訊冗餘［度］　information redundancy
信息商品/資訊商品　information commodity
信息熵/資訊熵　information entropy
信息社会/資訊社會　information society
信息生产/資訊生產　information production
信息生命周期/資訊生命週期　information life cycle
信息生态学/資訊生態學　information ecology
信息时代/資訊時代　information age
信息市场/情報市場　information market
信息收集/資訊蒐集　information gathering
信息收集技术/資訊蒐集技術　information gathering technology
信息衰减/資訊衰減　information decay
信息搜集/資訊搜尋　information search
信息素养/資訊素養　information literacy
信息素养教育/資訊素養教育　information literacy education
信息素养指标/資訊素養指標　information literacy indicator
信息宿/訊息收訊者　information receiver
信息损失/訊息損失　loss of information
信息提供者/資訊供應者　information provider
信息通信技术/資訊傳播科技　information and communication technology
信息挖掘/資訊挖掘　information mining
信息网关/資訊閘道　information gateway
信息网络/資訊網路　information network
信息网络传播权/資訊網路傳播權　right of communication through information network, right of information network dissemination, right to network dissemination of information
信息污染/資訊汙染　information pollution
信息无障碍/資訊無障礙　barrier-free of information transmission
信息系统/資訊系統　information system

信息系统安全/資訊系統安全性　information system security
信息系统模型/資訊系統模型　information system model
信息系统软件质量/資訊系統軟體品質　software quality of information system
信息系统外包/資訊系統外包　information system outsourcing
信息系统项目/資訊系統專案　information system project
信息先验/資訊先驗　informative prior
信息先验分布/資訊事前分布　informative prior distribution
信息消费/資訊消費　information consumption
信息效率/資訊效率性　information efficiency
信息行为/資訊行為　information behavior
信息需求/資訊需求　information demand, information need
信息选择/資訊選擇　information choosing
信息压缩/資訊壓縮　information impactedness
信息意识/資訊意識，資訊認知　information awareness
信息溢出/資訊噴溢　information extravasation
信息隐蔽/資訊隱藏　information hiding
信息隐藏/資訊隱藏　information hiding
信息隐私/信息隱私　information privacy
信息营销/資訊行銷　information marketing
信息映射/域間資訊映射　information mapping
信息用户/資訊利用者，資訊使用者　information user
信息有效性/資訊有效性　informational efficiency
信息元/資訊單位，資訊單元　information unit, information item
信息源/資訊[資]源　information source
信息再分组/資訊重新包裝　information repackaging
信息载体/資訊載體　information carrier
信息增值/資訊增量　information increment
信息增值服务/資訊增值服務　information increment service
信息战/資訊戰　information war
信息战略/資訊策略　information strategy
信息站/資訊站　information station
信息哲学/資訊哲學　information philosophy, philosophy of information
信息整序/資訊編排　information arrangement
信息政策/資訊政策　information policy
信息质量/資訊品質　information quality
信息中介/資訊中間商　information intermediary
信息主管/資訊長，信息長　chief information officer, CIO
信息主权/資訊主權　information sovereignty
信息主义/信息主義　informationalism
信息专家/資訊專家　information specialist
信息专业人员/資訊專業人員　information professional
信息准则/訊息準則　information criterion
信息咨询/資訊諮詢　information consulting
信息咨询机构/諮詢服務機構　advisory service agency
信息咨询业/資訊諮詢業　information consulting industry
信息资源/資訊資源　information resource
信息资源保障体系/資訊資源保障系統　information resource system
信息资源布局/資訊資源分布　distribution of information resources
信息资源分配/資訊資源配置　information resource allocation
信息资源共享机制/資訊資源分享服務機制　information resource sharing mechanism
信息资源管理/資訊資源管理　information resource management
信息资源规划/資訊資源規劃　information resource planning
信息资源建设/資訊資源發展　information resource development, collection development
信息资源建设政策/館藏發展政策　collection development policy
信息资源开发/資訊資源開發　information resource development
信息资源配置/資訊資源分配　information resource allocation
信息资源评价/資訊資源評估　information resource evaluation
信息资源整合/資訊資源整合　integration of information resources
信息自由/資訊公開，資訊自由　freedom of information
信息综合征/資訊綜合徵　information syndrome
信息组织/資訊組織　information organization, organization of information
信息组织方法/資訊組織方法　information organization method
信仰/信仰　belief
信用/信用　credit
信用保险/信用保險　credit insurance

信用保险单/信用保險單　honor policy
信用保证书/信用保證書　letter of guarantee
信用承兑人/信用参加承兑人　acceptor for honor
信用储备/信用儲備　fiduciary reserve
信用创造/信用創造　credit creation
信用创造功能/信用創造函數　credit creation function
信用贷款/信用貸款　fiduciary loan
信用担保贷款/信用擔保貸款　loan secured by credit
信用档案/信用記錄　credit record
信用发行/信用發行　fiduciary issue
信用分配/信用分配　credit allocation
信用风险/信用風險　credit risk
信用关系/信賴關係　fiduciary relationship
信用合作社/信用合作社　credit cooperative, credit union
信用汇票/信用匯票　credit bill
信用货币/信用貨幣　fiduciary currency, credit money
信用记录/信用記錄　credit record
信用价差/信用價差　credit spread
信用紧缩/信用緊縮　contraction of credit
信用卡/信用卡　credit card
信用卡业务/信用卡業務　credit card business
信用扩张/信用擴張　expansion of credit, credit expansion
信用联社/信用聯社　credit union
信用买卖/信用買賣　sale by credit
信用票据/信用券,信用借據　paper credit
信用评级/信用等级,信用評等　credit rating
信用评级机构/信用評比機構　credit rating agency
信用评价的5C标准/信用5C　Five Cs of credit
信用期限/信用期限　term of credit, credit period
信用认证网站/信用認證網站　credit certification website
信用受让人/信用[狀]受讓人　transferee of credit
信用体制/信用制度　credit system
信用条件/信用條件　credit term
信用违约互换/信用違約交換　credit default swap, CDS
信用衍生工具/信用衍生性商品　credit derivative
信用-引致型创新/信用增加式創新　credit-generating innovation
信用约束/信用限制　credit constraint
信用增级/信用增強　credit enhancement
信用债券/信用債券,信託債券,無抵押公司債　trust bond, bond debenture, debenture bond
信用证/信用狀　letter of credit
信用证持有人/信用狀持有人　holder of letter of credit
信用证当事人/信用狀當事人　party to letter of credit
信用证汇票/信用狀匯票　bill drawn on letter of credit
信用证结汇证明书/信用狀結匯證實書　exchange settlement certificate for letter of credit
信用证开立方/授信人,開狀銀行　accrediting party
信用证开立与收到的差额/信用狀開立與收到的差額　balance of letter of credit opened and received
信用证开证申请书/開發信用證申請書　application for letter of credit
信用证开证银行/[信用狀]開狀銀行　letter of credit issuing bank, issuing bank
信用证买方/受信人,開狀申請人　accredited party
信用证券/信用證券　instrument of credit
信用证确认手续费/信用狀確認手續費　letter of credit confirmation commission
信用证申请代理人/信用狀申請代理人　accredited agent
信用证申请人/開狀申請人,受信買方　accredited buyer
信用证通知书/信用狀通知書　advice of credit
信用证通知银行/信用狀通知銀行　letter of credit advising bank, letter of credit notifying bank
信用证转让/信用狀轉讓　transfer of credit
信用证转让申请书/信用狀轉讓申請書　application for transference of letter of credit
信用政策/授信政策　credit policy
信用制度/信用制度　credit system
信噪比/信噪比,訊息對干擾比,干擾對訊息比　signal-to-noise ratio
兴业银行/實業銀行　industrial bank
星火计划/星火計劃　Spark Program
星探/星探　talent scout
星形序/星形序　star-shaped ordering
星型模式/星型模式,星狀網目　star schema
星状创业团队/星狀創業團隊　star entrepreneurial team
星座模型/星座模型　constellation schema
刑案汇览/刑案匯覽　Compilation of Criminal Cases
刑部/刑部　criminal department in feudal China
刑鼎/刑鼎　Xingding
刑罚/刑罰　criminal punishment
刑罚个别化/刑罰個別化　individualization of criminal punishment
刑罚目的/刑罰目的　goal of punishment

刑罚权/刑罰權　power of punishment
刑罚体系/刑罰體系　system of punishment
刑罚消灭/刑罰消滅　annihilation of punishment
刑罚学/刑罰學　penology
刑罚种类/刑罰種類　classification of punishments
刑法/刑法　criminal law
刑法典/刑法典　criminal code
刑法分则/刑法分則　specific provision of criminal law
刑法基本原则/刑法基本原則　basic principle of criminal law
刑法空间效力/刑法空間效力　space effect of criminal law
刑法时间效力/刑法時間效力　time effect of criminal law
刑法溯及既往的效力/刑法溯及既往的效力　retroactivity of criminal law
刑法学/刑法學　criminal jurisprudence
刑法因果关系/刑法因果關係　causality in criminal law
刑法总则/刑法總則　general provision of criminal law
刑起于兵/刑起於兵　publishment from the war
刑事裁定/刑事裁定　criminal ruling
刑事裁定书/刑事裁定書　written criminal ruling
刑事简易程序/刑事簡易程式　criminal summary procedure
刑事抗诉/刑事抗訴　protest against criminal judgment
刑事抗诉书/刑事抗訴書　written protest against criminal judgment
刑事判决/刑事判決　criminal judgement
刑事判决书/刑事判決書　written criminal judgement
刑事上诉/刑事上訴　criminal appeal
刑事上诉权/刑事上訴權　right to appeal in criminal proceedings
刑事上诉人/刑事上訴人　criminal appellant
刑事审判/刑事審判　criminal adjudication
刑事司法/刑事司法　criminal justice
刑事司法协助/刑事司法協助　criminal judicial assistance
刑事诉讼/刑事訴訟　criminal proceedings
刑事诉讼程序/刑事訴訟程序　criminal litigation procedure
刑事诉讼法/刑事訴訟法　criminal procedure law
刑事诉讼阶段/刑事訴訟階段　stage of criminal proceedings
刑事诉讼结构/刑事訴訟結構　structure of criminal proceedings
刑事诉讼客体/刑事訴訟客體　object of criminal proceedings
刑事诉讼模式/刑事訴訟模式　model of criminal proceedings
刑事诉讼目的/刑事訴訟目的　aim of criminal proceedings
刑事诉讼职能/刑事訴訟職能　function of criminal proceedings
刑事诉讼主体/刑事訴訟主體　subject of criminal proceedings
刑事责任/刑事責任　criminal liability
刑事责任能力/刑事責任能力　capacity for criminal responsibility
刑事责任年龄/刑事責任年齡　age for criminal responsibility
刑讯逼供/刑求逼供　confession by torture
刑讯逼供罪/刑訊逼供罪　crime of extorting a confession by torture
行动/行動　action
行动法/行動法　law in action
行动科学/行動科學　action science
行动空间/行動空間　action space
行动理论/行動理論　action theory
行动时滞/行動遲延　action lag
行动系统/行動系統, 行動體系　action system
行动研究/行動研究　action research
行动者/行動者　actor
行动者网络理论/行動者網路理論　actor-network theory
行动者之间的关系网络/網路關係　network of relations among actors
行贿罪/行賄罪　crime of offering bribery
行为/行爲　behavior
行为不确定性/行爲不確定性　behavioral uncertainty
行为参数/行爲參數　behavioristic parameter
行为地法/行爲地法　lex loci actus
行为犯/行爲犯　behavioral offense
行为方程/行爲方程式　behavior equation
行为公司财务/行爲公司金融　behavioral corporate finance
行为关联分析法/行爲關聯分析法　behavioral linkage approach
行为观察量表/行爲觀察量表　behaviorally observation scale
行为假设/行爲假設　behavioral assumption

行为奖励计划/行爲獎勵計劃　behavior encouragement plan
行为矫正/行爲矯正　behavior modification
行为金融学/行爲金融學　behavioral finance
行为决策/行爲決策　behavioral decision
行为决策函数/行爲決策函數　behavioral decision function
行为科学/行爲科學　behavioral science
行为锚定法/行爲錨定評定量表　behaviorally anchored rating scale
行为描述面试/行爲描述面試　behavioral description interview
行为模式/行爲模式　behavior pattern
行为偏差/行爲偏差　behavioral bias
行为评价法/行爲評價法　behavioral evaluation method
行为识别/認同的行動　act of identity
行为事件访谈法/行爲事件面談法　behavior event interview
行为退化/行爲退化　physical withdrawal
行为细分/行爲區隔　behavioral segmentation
行为型风格/行爲型風格　behavioral style
行为障碍儿童/行爲障礙兒童　children with behavioral disorder
行为职业生涯路径/行爲職涯路徑　behavior career path
行为治疗模式/行爲治療模式　behavior modification model
行为主义/行爲主義　behaviorism
行为主义理论/行爲主義理論　behaviorism theory
行为准则/行爲準則,行動法則　action rule, code of conduct
行为资产定价模型/行爲資產定價模型　behavioral asset pricing model, BAP model
行为组合理论/行爲投資組合理論　behavioral portfolio theory, BPT
行文/行文　communicate officially
行文方向/行文方向　direction of sending an official doucment to other organizations
行文关系/行文關係　communicative relation
行文规则/行文規則　communicative regulation
行政编制/行政建制　administrative establishment
行政补偿/行政補償　administrative compensation
行政不作为/行政不作爲　administrative omission
行政裁决/行政裁決,行政裁定　administrative adjudication
行政程序/行政程序,行政程式　administrative procedure

行政程序瑕疵的补正/行政程式瑕疵的補正　healing of an administrative procedural flaw
行政处罚/行政處罰　administrative penalty
行政处理的撤销/行政處理的撤銷　revocation of an administrative decision
行政处理的废止/行政處理的廢止　abolishment of an administrative decision
行政处理的无效/行政處理的無效　voidness of an administrative decision
行政处理附款/行政處理附款　attached clause to an administrative decision
行政档案/行政檔案　administrative archive
行政惰性/行政惰性　administrative inertia
行政发展/行政發展　administrative development
行政服务/行政服務　administration service
行政复议/行政覆議　administrative reconsideration
行政复议被申请人/行政覆議被申請人　respondent of application to administrative reconsideration
行政复议的管辖/行政覆議的管轄　jurisdiction of administrative reconsideration
行政复议第三人/行政覆議第三人　third party to administrative reconsideration
行政复议范围/行政覆議範圍　scope of administrative reconsideration
行政复议机构/行政覆議機構　administrative reconsideration department
行政复议申请人/行政覆議申請人　applicant to administrative reconsideration
行政功能/行政職能　administrative function
行政沟通/行政溝通　administrative communication
行政关系/行政管理關係　administrative relationship
行政管理/行政管理　administrative management
行政管理层次/行政管理層次　administration hierarchy
行政管理相对人/行政相對人　administrative counterpart
行政管理支出/行政事業費　expenditure for government administration
行政规划/行政規劃　administrative planning
行政规章/行政規章　administrative rule
行政合理性原则/行政合理性原則　principle of administrative reasonableness
行政合同/行政契約　administrative contract
行政机构/行政機構　administrative department
行政给付/行政給付　administrative supply
行政计划/行政計劃　administrative plan
行政价值/行政價值　administrative value
行政监察/行政視導　administrative supervision

行政监督/行政監督　administrative supervision
行政检查/行政檢查　administrative inspection
行政奖励/行政獎勵　administrative encouragement, administrative award
行政解释/行政解釋　executive interpretation
行政救济/行政救濟　administrative remedy
行政拘留/行政拘留　administrative detention
行政距离/行政距離　administrative distance
行政决策/行政決策　administrative decision
行政决定/行政決定　administrative decision
行政决定的转换/行政決定的轉換　conversion of administrative decision
行政控制/科層控制, 官僚控制　bureaucratic control
行政立法/行政立法　administrative legislation
行政领导/行政領導　administrative leader, administrative leadership
行政垄断/行政壟斷　administrative monopoly
行政免除/行政免除　administrative immunity
行政命令/行政命令　administrative order, executive order
行政没收/行政沒收　administrative forfeiture
行政能力/行政能力　administrative capacity
行政赔偿/行政賠償　administrative compensation
行政赔偿请求人/行政賠償請求人　claimant for administrative compensation
行政赔偿义务机关/行政賠償義務機關　department for administrative compensation
行政契约/行政契約　administrative contract
行政强制/行政強制　administrative compulsion, administrative enforcement
行政区划/行政區分　administrative division
行政权力/行政權力　administrative power
行政确认/行政確認　administrative confirmation, administrative affirmation
行政人/行政人　administrative man
行政三分/行政三分制　trisection administration system
行政神话/行政神話, 行政迷思　administrative myth
行政审批/行政審批　administrative examination and approval
行政生态学/行政生態學　administrative ecology
行政事实行为/行政事實行爲　administrative factual action
行政授权/行政授權　administrative authorization
行政诉讼/行政訴訟　administrative litigation
行政诉讼当事人/行政訴訟當事人　litigant of administrative lawsuit
行政诉讼的被告/行政訴訟的被告　defendant of administrative lawsuit
行政诉讼的管辖/行政訴訟的管轄　jurisdiction of administrative litigation
行政诉讼的审查对象/行政訴訟的審查對象　object of administrative litigation review
行政诉讼的受案范围/行政訴訟的受案範圍　scope of accepting administrative litigation
行政诉讼的原告/行政訴訟的原告　plaintiff of administrative lawsuit
行政诉讼第三人/行政訴訟第三人　third party of administrative lawsuit
行政体制/管理體制　administrative system
行政听证/行政聽證　administrative hearing
行政文化/行政文化　administrative culture
行政效率/行政效率　administrative efficiency
行政效率原则/行政效率原則　principle of efficient administration
行政效能/行政績效　administrative performance
行政协调/行政協調　administrative coordination
行政行为/行政行爲　administrative behavior
行政性垄断/行政壟斷　administrative monopoly
行政性收费收入/行政規費　administrative charge
行政许可/行政許可　administrative permission, administrative license, administrative licensing
行政责任/行政責任　administration accountability
行政征购/行政徵購　administrative compulsory purchase
行政征收/行政徵收　administrative requisition, administrative taking
行政征用/行政徵用　administrative confiscation
行政执法/行政執法　enforcement of administrative law
行政执法监督/行政執法監督　oversight of law enforcement
行政执法责任制/行政執法責任制　executive responsibility system
行政执行/行政執行　administrative execution
行政职能/行政職能　administrative function
行政指导/行政指導　administrative guidance
行政指示/行政指令　administrative directive
行政主体/行政主體　administrative subject, administrative entity
行政资源/行政資源　administrative resource
行政自我约束原则/行政自我拘束原則　principle of self-constrained administration
行政自由裁量权/行政裁量　administrative discretion
行政组织/行政組織, 行政機關　administrative organization

行政组织法/行政組織法　administrative organization law
行政[组织]结构/行政[組織]結構　administrative structure
行政组织体制/行政組織系統　administrative organizational system
形成权/形成權　right of formation
形成系列型新产品/形成系列型新產品　new product of family line
J形分布/J形分布　J-shaped distribution
U形分布/U形分布, U形分配　U-shaped distribution
U形密度/U形密度　U-shaped density
S形曲线/S形曲線　S-shaped curve
U形曲线/U形曲線　U-shaped curve
形式/形式　form
形式标目/書型標題　form heading
形式独立/形式獨立　independence in appearance
形式非理性法/形式非理性法　formal unrational law
形式理性法/形式理性法　formal rational law
形式联系/形式聯繫　format relation
形式排架法/形式排架法　form arrangement
形式社会学/形式社會學　formal sociology
形式主义/形式主義　formalism
形态分析法/形態分析法　morphological analysis method
形态频数/型態次數　pattern frequency
形态效用/形式效用　form utility
U形危险函数/U形危險函數　U-shaped hazard function
形象/形象　image
形象差异化/形象差異化　image differentiation
形象管理/形象管理　image management
形象广告/形象廣告　image advertising
形象权/形象權　right of publicity
形象修复/公關形象修復　image restoration
形状参数/形狀參數　shape parameter
型/型　type
A型操作特性曲线/A型OC曲線　type A OC curve
B型操作特性曲线/B型OC曲線　type B OC curve
I型抽样/第一型抽樣　type I sampling
II型抽样/第二型抽樣　type II sampling
A型分布/A型分布, A型分配　type A distribution
B型分布/B型分布, B型分配　type B distribution
C型分布/C型分布, C型分配　type C distribution
型号分类法/型號分類法　type classification
型交叉/型交叉　type crossing
H型结构/H型結構　holding company, H-form structure
M型结构/部門式結構　multidivisional structure, divisional structure
U型结构/U型結構　united structure
A型流程/A型流程　A-type process flow
I型流程/I型流程　I-type process flow
T型流程/T型流程　T-type process flow
V型流程/V型流程　V-type process flow
型偏倚/型偏誤　type bias
M型企业/多部門型態廠商　multidivisonal-form firm, M-form firm
A型区域/A型區域　type A region
B型区域/B型區域　type B region
C型区域/C型區域　type C region
D型区域/D型區域　type D region
E型区域/E型區域　type E region
I型人才/I型人才　qualified personnel of I-type
T型人才/T型人才　qualified personnel of T-type
π型人才/π型人才　qualified personnel of π-type
A型人格/A型人格　type A personality
B型人格/B型人格　type B personality
M型社会/M型社會　multidivisional society
A型数列/A型級數　type A series
B型数列/B型級數　type B series
C型数列/C型級數　type C series
A型无偏临界域/A型不偏臨界域　unbiased critical region of type A
B型无偏临界域/B型不偏臨界域　unbiased critical region of type B
C型无偏临界域/C型不偏臨界域　unbiased critical region of type C
III型误差/第三型誤差　type III error
V型罩/V形罩　V-mask
A型组织/A型組織　A-type organization, American organization
J型组织/J型組織　J-type organization, Japanese organization
Z型组织/Z型組織　Z-type organization
兴趣/興趣　interest
幸存者综合征/幸存者病症　survivor's sickness
性/性　sex
性爱/性愛　sexual love
性暴力/性暴力　sexual violence
性别/性別　gender, sexuality, sex
性别暴力/性別暴力　gender violence
性别本质主义/性別本質主義　gender essentialism
性别比/性別比[例]　sex ratio
性别差距指数/性別差距指數　gender gap index

性别差异/性別差異　gender difference
性别等级制/性別等級制　gender hierarchy
性别二元论/性別二元論　dichotomy of gender, dualism of gender
性别发展指数/性別發展指數　gender-related development index
性别分布/性別分布　sex distribution
性别分层/性別分層　gender stratification
性别分化/性別分化　differentiation of gender
性别赋权指数/性別賦權測度　gender empowerment measure
性别概念/性別概念　concept of gender, concept of sex
性别构成/性別組成　sex composition
性别关系/性別關係　gender relationship
性别化访谈/性別化訪談　gendered interview
性别建构论/性別建構論　gender constructuralism
性别角色/性別角色　gender role
性别刻板印象/性別刻板印象　stereotype of gender
性别偏好/性別偏好　gender preference
性别偏见/性別偏見　gender bias
性别平等/性別平等,兩性平等　gender equality
性别平等指数/性別平等指數　gender parity index
性别歧视/性別歧視　gender discrimination
性别认同/性別認同,性別身份　gender identity
性别社会化/性別社會化　socialization of gender
性别社会学/性別社會學　sociology of gender
性别细分/性別細分　gender segmentation
性别研究/性別研究　gender studies
性别意识/性別意識　gender consciousness
性别意识形态/性別意識形態　gender ideology
性别与工作/性別與工作　gender and work
性别与家庭/性別與家庭　gender and family
性别主义/性[別]歧視　sexism
性的多元论/性的多元論　pluralism of sexuality
性度/性度　sex degree
性发展/性發展　development of sexuality
性法律/性法律　law of sex
性犯罪/性犯罪　sex crime
性规范/性規範　norm of sex
性教育/性教育　sex education
性伦理/性倫理　ethics of sex
性能测试/效能測試　performance testing
性能-功能矩阵/性能-功能矩陣　performance-function matrix
性能属性矩阵/性能屬性矩陣　performance attribute matrix
性能特性/性能特性　performance characteristic

性能质量/性能品質　performance quality
性取向/性取向,性傾向　sexual orientation
性权利/性權利　sexual right
性三品说/性三品説　Xing Sanpin theory
性骚扰/性騷擾　sexual harassment
性少数族群/性少數族群　sexual minority
性社会学/性社會學　sociology of sex
性意识发展/性意識發展　development of sexual consciousness
性欲/性欲　sexual desire
性征/性徵　sex character
姓名权/姓名權　right of name
姓氏标引/姓氏標引　surname indexing
熊彼特经济学/熊彼特經濟學　Schumpeterian economics
熊市/熊市,空頭市場　bear market
休哈特控制图/Shewhart 管制圖　Shewhart control chart
休假/研究休假　sabbatical
休假服务系统/休假服務系統　service system with vacation
休刊/休刊　suspend
休刊词/休刊詞　word for suspension
休克疗法/休克治療,震擊療法　shock therapy
休斯特周期图/Schuster 週期圖　Schuster periodogram
休息/休止　rest
休息时间/休息時間　break time
休闲/休閒　leisure
休战/休戰　truce
修版/修版　retouching
修补/修補　repairing of archive
修辞/修辭,語藝　rhetoric
修档制度/修檔制度　regulation of archive restoration in Qing
修订/修訂　revision
修订版/修訂版　revised edition
修订本/修訂本　revised document
修订法律馆/修訂法律館　amendment to the law department
修复/修復　restoration
修复率/修復率　repair rate
修复时间/修復時間,修理時間　time to repair, repair time
修复室/修復室　restoration laboratory
修复性维修/修復性維修　corrective maintenance
修复-运行-移交模式/ROT 模式　repair-operate transfer model, ROT model

修改稿本/修正草稿　revised draft, revised manuscript
修改权/修改權　right of alteration
修剪时间序列/修剪時間數列　clipped time series
修理物料清单/修理物料清單　repair bill of material
修饰词/资格符,限定詞　qualifier
修匀曲线/修匀曲線　graduation curve
修正的犯罪构成/修正的犯罪構成　amendatory constitution of a crime
修正的平均股票价格/修正的平均股票價格　revised average stock price
修正二项分布/修正二項分布,修正二項分配　modified binomial distribution
修正冯诺曼比率/修正 von Neumann 比　modified von Neumann ratio
修正概算造价/修正經費概算　modified budgetary estimation
修正后重购/修正再購　modified rebuy
修正混合模型/修正混合模型　modified mixed model
修正久期/修正久期　modified duration
修正均方连续差/修正均方接續差　modified mean square successive difference
修正均值/调整均值,修正平均數,調整平均數　modified mean, adjusted average, adjusted mean
修正控制限/修正管制界限　modified control limit
修正拉丁方/修正的拉丁方陣　modified Latin square
修正率/修正率　revised rate
修正确定系数/调整確定係數　adjusted coefficient of determination
修正设计概算/修正設計概算　modified design estimation
修正外汇汇率制/修正外匯匯率制　modified exchange rate system
修正系数/調整係數　adjustment factor
修正限/修正界限　modified limit
修正正态分布/修正常態分布,修正常態分配　modified normal distribution
修正值/調整值　adjusted value
修正指数曲线/修正指數曲線　modified exponential curve
修正主义/修正主義　revisionism
修正最小卡方法/修正最小卡方法　modified minimum chi-square method
袖珍本/袖珍本　pocket edition
袖珍词典/袖珍詞典　pocket dictionary
袖珍判决书/袖珍判決書　pocket judgement
须付关税/須付關稅　subject to customs duty

虚报注册资本罪/虛報註冊資本罪　crime of misstating registered capital
虚工作/虛設作業　dummy activity
虚构出版项/虛構出版項　false imprint, fictitious imprint
虚构性/虛構性　fictionality
虚假广告/騙人廣告,不實廣告　deceptive advertising, false advertising
虚假广告罪/虛假廣告罪　crime of false advertising
虚假示意/偽旗行動,虛旗,虛假事件　false flag
虚假相关/虛假相關　spurious correlation
虚假信息/不實訊息,不實資訊　disinformation, false information
虚卖/虛賣,沖銷交易　wash sale
虚拟变量/虛[擬]變數,虛擬變項　dummy variable
虚拟变数陷阱/虛擬變數陷阱　dummy variable trap
虚拟产业/虛擬產業　virtual industry
虚拟创新组织/虛擬創新組織　virtual innovation organization
虚拟工作团队/虛擬工作團隊　virtual work team
虚拟股票/虛擬股票　phantom stock
虚拟观测[值]/虛擬觀測[值]　dummy observation
虚拟广告/虛擬廣告　virtual advertisement
虚拟环境/虛擬環境　virtual environment, VE
虚拟技术创新联盟/虛擬技術創新聯盟　virtual technological innovation alliance
虚拟联合目录/虛擬聯合目錄　virtual union catalog
虚拟期刊/虛擬期刊　virtual journal
虚拟亲属/虛擬親屬　fictive kin
虚拟商务/虛擬商務　virtual commerce
虚拟社区/虛擬社群,網路社群,線上社群　bulletin board system, online community, virtual community
虚拟水平技术/虛擬水準技巧　dummy level technique
虚拟团队/虛擬團隊　virtual team
虚拟物料清单/虛擬物料清單　phantom bill of materials
虚拟系统/虛擬系統　virtual system
虚拟现实/虛擬實境　virtual reality, VR
虚拟星状创业团队/虛擬星狀創業團隊　virtual star team
虚拟学习/虛擬學習　virtual learning
虚拟研发联盟/虛擬研發聯盟　virtual research and development alliance
虚拟演播室/虛擬演播室　virtual studio
虚拟演播室技术/虛擬演播室技術　virtual studio technology

虚拟演播室系统/虛擬演播室系統　virtual studio system
虚拟银行/虛擬銀行　virtual bank
虚拟咨询台/虛擬參考諮詢檯　virtual reference desk
虚拟资本/虛擬資本　virtual capital
虚拟组织/虛擬組織　virtual organization
虚无主义/虛無主義　nihilism
虚值期权/價外期權,失值期權　out-of-the-money option
需付利息的债务/活動債券,活性債務　active debt
需求/需求　demand
需求变动/需求[的]變動　change in demand, demand change
需求表/需求表　demand schedule
需求导向定价/需求導向定價法　demand-oriented pricing
需求的收入弹性/需求的收入彈性　income elasticity of demand
需求调研/需求調研　requirement investigation
需求定律/需求法則　law of demand
需求方/需求面　demand side
需求分析/需求分析　requirement analysis
需求管理/需求管理　demand management
需求管理政策/需求管理政策　demand management policy
需求函数/需求函數　demand function
需求合同/強制契約　requirement contract
需求弧弹性/需求的弧彈性　arc elasticity of demand
需求价格/需求價格　demand price
需求价格弹性/需求-供給價格彈性　price elasticity of demand
需求建议书/需求建議書　request for proposal
需求交叉工资弹性/需求的交叉工資彈性　cross wage elasticity of demand
需求交叉价格弹性/需求的交叉價格彈性　cross price elasticity of demand
需求交叉弹性/需求的交叉彈性　cross elasticity of demand
需求拉动说/需求拉動學說　demand-pull theory
需求拉上型通货膨胀/需求推動型通貨膨脹　demand-pull inflation
需求理论/需求[理]論　demand theory, theory of demand
需求量变动/需求量的變動　change in the quantity demanded
需求曲线/需求曲線　demand curve
需求数量/需求量　quantity demanded
需求速率/需求速率　demand rate
需求弹性/需求彈性　demand elasticity, elasticity of demand
需求特征/需求特性　demand characteristics
需求同构性/需求同質性　homogeneity of demand
需求效应/需求效果　demand effect
需求展开/需求展開　requirement explosion
需要/需要,需求　need
需要层次理论/需求層次論,需求階層理論　need hierarchy theory
需要担保的贷款/抵押貸款　advance against collateral
需要评估/需求評估　needs assessment
需要确认/確認需要,需求認知　needs recognition
需用产能/需用產能　required capacity
许可/授權　license, licensing
许可打印/許可列印　license to print
许可复印/許可複印　license to copy
许可贸易模型/許可證貿易方式　license trade mode
许可证/許可證　license, letter of licence
许可证保险/許可證保險　license insurance
许可证费用/許可證費用　license fee
许可证合同/許可證合約　license contract
许可证价格/許可證價格　license price
许可证贸易/許可證貿易　licensing trade, license trade
许可证贸易制度/許可證制度　licensing system
许可证协议/許可證協議　licence agreement
许可证业务/許可證業務　licensing operation
许可证制度/許可證制[度]　license system, system of licensing
许诺销售/許諾銷售　offering for sell
序/序言　preface
序贯博弈/序列賽局,逐步賽局　sequential game
序贯抽样/逐次抽樣　sequential sampling
序贯抽样方案/逐次抽樣計劃　sequential sampling plan
序贯抽样检验方案/逐次抽樣檢驗計劃　sequential sampling inspection plan
序贯二项抽样/逐次二項抽樣　sequential binomial sampling
序贯法/逐次法　sequential method
序贯分析/逐次分析　sequential analysis
序贯符号检验/逐次符號檢定　sequential sign test
序贯概率比检验/逐次機率比檢定　sequential probability ratio test, SPRT
序贯概率模型/逐次常態機率模型　sequential probit model
序贯估计/逐次估計　sequential estimation

序贯回归/逐次回歸　sequential regression
序贯计数检验/逐次計數檢定　sequential count test
序贯检验/逐次檢定　sequential test
序贯 t 检验/逐次 t 檢定　sequential t test
序贯交易模型/序貫交易模型　sequential trade model
序贯决策/逐次決策　sequential decision
序贯均衡/序列性均衡　sequential equilibrium
序贯卡方检验/逐次卡方檢定　sequential chi-squared test
序贯理性/序列[性]理性　sequential rationality, sequentially rational
序贯容忍区域/逐次允差區域　sequential tolerance region
序贯实验/逐次檢定　sequential test
序贯试验法/序貫法　sequential experiment method
序贯寿命试验/逐次壽命試驗　sequential life test
序贯讨价还价/逐序談判　sequential bargaining
序贯讨价还价博弈/序列談判賽局　sequential bargaining game
序贯线性最优设计/逐次線性最適設計　sequential linear optimal design
序贯信息不等式/逐次資訊不等式　sequential information inequality
序号/序號　serial number
序列/序列　sequence
序列变异/序列變異　serial variation
序列波动/序列波動　sequence fluctuation
序列抽样检验方案/序列抽樣檢驗方案　serial sampling inspection scheme
序列的随机性/序列的隨機性　randomness of sequence
序列排队/序列等候　series queue
序列群/序列叢聚，序列群聚　serial cluster
序列设计/序列設計　serial design
序列图/序列圖　sequence chart
序列相关/序列相關　serial correlation
序列相关[性]检验/序列相關檢定　serial correlation test
序数效用论/序數效用論　theory of ordinal utility
序言/序言　preface
叙词/敘詞，描述符，記述子　descriptor
叙词标引法/敘詞標引法　thesauri indexing
叙词表/索引典　thesaurus
叙词表维护/敘詞表維護　thesaurus maintainance
叙词表显示/敘詞表顯示　thesaurus display
叙词法/敘詞法　method of descriptor, descriptor indexing, thesaurus method
叙词组配/敘詞組配　descriptor coordinating
叙录/敘錄　summary of a book
叙录体/敘錄體　summary style
叙明罪状/敘明罪狀　explain fact about a crime
叙事/敘事　narrative
叙事的理解/敘事的理解　narrative understanding
叙事的转向/敘事的轉向　narrative turn
叙事分析/敘事分析，敘說分析　narrative analysis
叙事建构/敘事建構　narrative construction
叙事结构/敘事結構　narrative structure
叙事史/敘事歷史　narrative history
叙事学/敘事學　narratology
叙事治疗模式/敘說法療，敘事治療　narrative therapy
叙述的犯罪构成/敘述的犯罪構成　explanatory constitution of a crime
叙述评价法/文字敘述評核法　essay method
叙述社会学/描述社會學　descriptive sociology
叙述式检索工具/敘述式檢索工具　narrative style
绪言/前言，緒論　introduction
续编/續編　sequel, continuation
续存效应/續存效應　carry-over effect
续订/續訂　subscription for late applicant, subscription renewal
续借/續借　renewal, renew
续借请求/續借請求　renewal request
宣称发行量/宣稱發行量　claimed circulation
宣传/宣傳　propaganda
宣传教育作用/宣傳教育作用　propaganda and education action
宣传图片/宣傳照片　publicity photo
宣传研究/宣傳研究，競選傳播研究　campaign study
宣告失踪/宣告失蹤　declare a citizen missing
宣告失踪程序/宣告失蹤程式　procedure of declaration of disappearance
宣告死亡/宣告死亡　declare a citizen death
宣告死亡程序/宣告死亡程式　procedure of declaration of death
宣告无罪/宣告無罪　pronouncement of not guilty
宣告刑/宣告刑　declaratory penalty
宣战/宣戰　declaration of war
宣纸/宣紙　Xuan paper
悬行式著录格式/懸行式著錄格式　suspended format
悬赏广告/懸賞廣告　advertisement to offer a reward
旋摆运动/旋擺運動　cranking motion
旋经/旋經　Xuan Jing
旋转/旋轉，輪動，回旋　rotation

旋转分析/旋轉分析　pivot analysis technique
旋转设计/可旋轉設計　rotatable design
旋转式卡片柜/旋轉式卡片櫃　revolving card filing cabinet
旋转式书架/轉動書架　revolving bookcase
选拔决策/甄選決策　selection decision
选拔率/選擇率,甄選率　selection ratio
选本/選本　selection of edition
选编/選編　selected works
选编书目/選編書目　partial bibliography
选材标准/選材標準　criterion of selecting archival data
选材方案/選材方案　scheme of selecting archival data
选材方法/選材方法　method of selecting archival data
选材卡/選材卡　card of selecting archival data
选材原则/選材原則　pricinple of selecting archival data
选词标引法/詞索引　term indexing
选点法/選點法　selected point method
选港费/選港費　optional charge
选购品/選購品　shopping product
选集/選集　anthology, selected works, analects
选举/選舉　election
选举保证金/選舉保證金　election margin
选举法/選舉法　election law
选举广告/選舉廣告　electoral advertising
选举监督/選舉監督　election monitoring
选举联盟/選舉聯盟　election union
选举权/選舉權　suffrage
选举人团/選舉人團　electoral college
选举日/選舉日　election day
选举诉讼/選舉訴訟　election litigation
选举委员会/選舉委員會　election committee
选举无效/選舉無效　election invalid
选举争议/選舉爭議　election dispute
选举制度/選舉制度　electoral system
选民/選民　voter
选民登记/選民登記　voter registration
选民证/選民證　voter ID card
选民资格/選民資格　voter eligibility
选区/選區　constituency
选取值/選取值　selective value
选任制/選任制　selection system
选书标准/圖書選擇準則　selection criteria
选题/選題　selected subject, selected topic
选题策划/選題策劃　topic planning

选题规划/選題規劃　project of selected topic
选择/選擇　select
选择成本/替代成本　alternative cost
选择反转/選擇反轉　choice reversal
选择关税/選擇[性]關稅　alternative duty, alternative tariff
选择机制/篩選機制　selection mechanism
选择理性/選擇理性　selective rationality
选择利息/選擇利息　selection interest
选择适用的冲突规范/選擇適用的衝突規範　choice rules for regulating the conflict of laws
选择数据/關係資料　choice data
选择提单/選擇卸貨港提單　optional bill of lading
选择系数/選中係數　coefficient of selection
选择型分销/選擇性配銷,選擇式分配　selective distribution
选择型福利/選擇型福利　selective welfare
选择性编目/選擇性編目　selective cataloging
选择性出口/選擇性出口　selective export
选择性贷款/選擇性貸款　selective lending
选择性繁殖家畜/家禽家畜選育法　selective breeding of livestock
选择性分类/選擇性分類　selective classification
选择性干预/選擇性干預　selective intervention
选择性激励/選擇性激勵　selective incentive
选择性记忆/選擇性記憶　selective memory
选择性进口/選擇性進口　selective import
选择性就业补贴/選擇性雇用補貼　selective employment subsidy
选择性理解/選擇性理解,選擇性感知　selective perception
选择性流产/選擇性流產　sex-selective abortion
选择性配额/選擇性配額　selective quota
选择性偏差/選擇偏誤　selection bias
选择性偏误/選擇偏誤　selection bias
选择性取用/選擇性的取用　selective appropriation
选择性套头交易/選擇性避險　selective hedging
选择性文摘/選擇摘要　selective abstract
选择性信用控制/選擇性信用管制　selective credit control
选择与排序问题/選擇與排序問題　selection and ranking problem
选择之债/選擇之債　obligation alternative
选择指标/選擇指標　choice indicator
选择置信区间/選擇信賴區間　selective confidence interval
选择住所/選擇住所　domicile of choice
选址策略/選址政策　location policy

选址问题/選址問題 facility location problem
选址因素评分法/選址因素評分法 location factor rating
旋风装/旋風裝 whirlwind binding
削减时间/削減時間 subtracted time
学报/學報 acta, journal, academic journal
学会/學會 academic society
学会会刊/學會會刊,學會出版物 society publication
学科/學科 discipline
学科百科全书/學科百科全書 subject encyclopedia
学科导航/學科導航 subject navigation
学科分类体系/學科分類體系 subject classification system
学科馆员/學科專家 subject librarian, subject specialist
学科化服务/學科服務 subject service
学科会聚/學科會聚 discipline convergence
学科群/學科群 discipline cluster
学科信息门户/學科資訊門戶 subject information portal, subject information gateway
学科影响因子/學科影響因子 subject impact factor
学科知识库/學科知識庫 disciplinary repository
学历/學歷 education
学前教养机构/學前教養機構 pre-school education institute
学生[氏]比率/Student 比例 student ratio
学生[氏]分布/Student 分布, Student 分配 student distribution
学生[氏]t 分布/Student t 分布, Student t 分配 student t-distribution
学生[氏]化极差/Student 化全距 studentized range
学生[氏]化极差分布/Student 化全距分布 studentized range distribution
学生[氏]化均值/Student 化平均數 studentized mean
学生[氏]化最大绝对差/Student 化最大絕對離差 studentized maximum absolute deviate
学生[氏]假设/Student 假設 student hypothesis
学生[氏]t 检验/Student t 檢定 student t-tests
学生[氏]配对法/Student 成對法 student pair method
学生运动/學生運動,學運 student movement
学生助理馆员/圖書館工讀生 student assistant
学术讲座专论丛书/專題講稿叢集 lecture series
学术利用/學術利用 academic use
学术论文/學術論文 academic paper, academic article

学术期刊/學術期刊 academic journal
学术通讯/學術通訊 scholarly communication
学术性图书/學術性圖書 scholarly book
学术影响力/學術影響力 academic influence
学术著作/專門著作 academic work
学术自由/學術自由 academic freedom
学说/學說 doctrine
学说汇纂/學說彙纂 pandect
学说汇纂学派/學說匯纂學派 pandectist
学徒工/學徒工 apprentice worker
学徒模式/學徒模式 apprenticeship model
学徒制/徒弟制度 apprenticeship
学位论文/學位論文 thesis, dissertation
学习/學習 learning
学习过程/學習過程 learning process
学习曲线/學習曲線 learning curve
学习效应/學習效果 learning effect
学习行为/學習行爲 learning behavior
学习型经济/學習型經濟 learning economy
学习型期权/學習型期權 learning option
学习型区域/學習型區域 learning region
学习型组织/學習型組織 learning organization
学习型组织理论/學習型組織理論 theory of learning organization
学习学派/學習學派 learning school
学习循环模型/學習循環模型 learning loop model
学习中心/學習中心 learning center
学校/學校 school
学校社会工作/學校社會工作 school social work
学校图书馆/學校圖書館 school library
学院/學院 college
学院督导/學院督導 school supervisor
学院科学/學術科學 academic science
学院为本的实习模式/學院爲本的實習模式 school-based internship model
雪花模式/雪花模式,雪花綱目 snowflake schema
血汗制度/血汗制度 sweating system
血亲/血親 blood relation, consanguinity
血亲复仇/血親復仇 feud
血统主义/血統主義 jus sanguinis
血缘婚/親族婚姻 consanguine marriage
血缘家庭/親族家庭 consanguine family
血缘群体/血緣群體 consanguinity group
熏蒸法/蒸熏法 fumigation
熏蒸室/蒸熏室 fumigation chamber
旬刊/旬刊 periodical issued once every ten days
寻呼机/無線電叫人收信器 pager
寻价者/尋價者 price searcher

寻找/搜尋　search
寻找潜在客户/尋找潛在客戶　prospecting
寻租/競租　rent seeking
寻租模型/競租模型　rent-seeking model
寻租行为/競租行爲　rent-seeking behavior
巡回辅导/巡迴輔導　mobile coaching
巡回检查/巡迴檢驗　roving inspection
巡回票据/循環票據　circular bill
巡回图书馆/巡迴圖書館　traveling library
巡回支票/循環支票　circular check
巡视/現場檢視　patrolling
询价/詢價　solicitation
询价单/詢價單　inquiry list
询价函件/詢價函件　letter of inquiry
询价计划编制/詢價計劃制定　solicitation planning
询问/詢問　question witnesses
荀子礼制思想/荀子的禮學思想　social institution thought of Xunzi
循环/循環　cycle
循环比较三元组/循環比對三元組　circular triads
循环波动/週期波動　periodical fluctuation
循环测时法/週期測時,週程測時　cycle timing
循环次序/循環次序　cyclic order, circular order
循环分布/循環分布,循環分配　cyclic distribution
循环公式/循環公式　circular formula
循环级数/循環數列　cyclic series
循环检验/循環檢定　circular test
循环经济/循環經濟　recycling economy
循环累积因果关系/累積因果理論　circular and cumulative causation
循环[离]差/循環離差　cyclical deviation
循环马尔可夫链/重現馬可夫鏈　recurrent Markov chain
[循]环排列/環狀排列　circular permutation
循环取货/循環取貨　milk run
循环设计/循環設計　cyclic design
循环时间/重現時間　recurrence time
循环事件/重現事件　recurrent event
循环效应/循環效應　cyclical effect
循环信贷/循環信貸　revolving credit
循环信贷额度/循環信用協議　revolving credit limit
循环信贷协议/循環信貸合約　revolving credit agreement
循坏信贷账户/循環信貸賬户　revolving credit account
循环信用证/循環信用狀,巡迴信用狀　circular letter of credit
循环序列相关系数/循環的序列相關係數　circular serial correlation coefficient
循环状态/重現狀態　recurrent state
训/訓　Xun
训诂/訓詁　interpretation of Chinese ancient text
训练/訓練　training
讯问笔录/訊問筆錄　record of interrogation
讯息策略/訊息策略　message strategy
徇私枉法罪/徇私枉法罪　crime of bending the law to serve one's personal considerations for favoritism

Y

压凹凸/壓凹凸,壓紋,壓花　embossing
压电喷墨/壓電噴墨　piezoelectric ink-jet
压电喷墨技术/壓電噴墨技術　piezoelectric ink-jet technology
压感式触摸屏/壓感式觸控式螢幕　pressure sensing type touch screen
压痕/折皺　creasing
压力/壓力　stress
压力测试/壓力測試　stress testing
压力管理/壓力管理　stress management
压力集团/壓力團體　pressure group
压力面试/壓力面談　stress interview
压力团体/壓力團體　pressure group
压力源/壓力源　stressor
压敏标签纸/壓敏標籤紙　pressure-sensitive label paper
压书架/壓書架　book cradle
压缩/壓縮　compression
压缩标准/嚴格標準　tight standard
压缩估计[量]/收縮估計[量]　shrinkage estimator
MP3 压缩技术/MP3 壓縮技術　moving picture experts group audio layer 3
压缩篇幅/壓縮[篇幅]　boil
压缩限/壓縮界限　compressed limit
压缩限规则/壓縮界限規測　compressed limit gauging
压抑/壓抑　suppression
压印滚筒/共用壓力圓筒式印刷機　impression cylinder
压制性法律/壓制型法律　repressive law
押船契约/押船契約,[船货]抵押契约　hypothecation agreement
押金/押金,保證金　marginal deposit, cash deposit as collateral, margin
押金返还制度/押金退費制度　deposit refund system
鸦片战争/鴉片戰爭　opium war
哑处理/虛擬處理　dummy treatment
轧平/軋平,餘額平衡　square off
亚非经济合作组织/亞非經濟合作組織　Afro-Asian Organization for Economic Cooperation
亚里士多德/亞里斯多德　Aristotle
亚里士多德论管理/亞里斯多德論管理　Aristotle's view on management
亚里士多德政体论/亞里斯多德政體論　Aristotle's view on government
亚实时模拟/亞即時模擬　sub-real-time simulation
亚式期权/亞式期權　Asian option
亚太经济合作组织/亞太經合會　Asia-Pacific Economic Cooperation, APEC
亚文化/次文化　subculture
亚音频/亞音訊　continuous tone controlled squelch system
亚洲开发银行/亞洲開發銀行　Asian Development Bank
亚洲美元市场/亞洲美元市場　Asian dollar market
砑光/砑光　calendering
砑平丝网/砑平絲網　calendared mesh
烟草托拉斯/菸草托拉斯　tobacco trust
烟叶税/菸稅　tobacco leaf tax
阉割/閹割　castration punishment
燕京学派/燕京學派　Yenching school
延长合同期限/延長合約期限　extend contract period
延迟/延遲,延誤　delay
延迟付款/延遲付款　delay in payment, delayed payment
延迟交货/延遲交貨　delay in delivery
延迟交货费用/延遲交貨費用　backorder cost
延迟接受报盘/遲延接受報價　late acceptance
延迟进入战略/延遲進入策略　delay entry strategy
延迟期权/延遲期權　delay option, option to postpone
延迟容差/延遲寬放,延誤寬放　delay allowance
延迟时间/延遲時間　delay time
延迟约价期权/延遲履約選擇權　deferred strike option
延付即期信用证/延付即期信用狀　deferred sight credit
延交订货/積欠訂單　back order
延期订单/積欠訂單　back order
延期付款/延期付款,延期支付　deferred payment

延期付款标准/遞延支付的標準　standard of deferred payment
延期付款方式出口/延期付款方式出口　export on deferred payment basis
延期互换/可展期交換　extendable swap
延期交货/延期交貨　deferred delivery, delayed delivery, late delivery
延期交货通知单/延期訂貨通知單　back order memo
延期纳税/遞延納稅　tax deferral
延期批准/延遲批準　delay approval
延期期限/延期期限,遞延期限　term of deferment
延期索偿同意书/延期索償同意書　letter of licence
延期薪酬计划/遞延薪酬計劃　deferred compensation program
延期装运/遲延裝運　late shipment
延时开放/延遲開放　delayed open
延误/延誤,延遲　delay
严格的模型确认/模式驗證　strict model confirmation
严格拟凸函数/嚴格準凸函數　strictly quasiconvex function
严格偏好/嚴格偏好　strict preference
严格平稳性/強平穩,強恆定　strict stationarity
严格平行/滿足強平行　strictly parallel
严格受控的/嚴格受制於　strictly dominated
严格凸函数/嚴格凸函數,狹義凸函數　strictly convex function
严格伪凸函数/嚴格偽凸函數　strictly pseudoconvex function
严格误差/嚴格誤差　strictness error
严格责任/嚴格責任　strict liability
严平稳过程/強平穩過程　strictly stationary process
严重缺陷/主要缺點,主要瑕疵　critical defect, major defect
言词证据/言詞證據　verbal evidence
言后行为/成事行爲　perlocutionary act
言论自由/言論自由　freedom of speech
言语交际民俗学/傳播民族志　ethnography of communication
言语能力/語文能力,語言能力　verbal ability
言语行为/斷言　assertive
沿革刑法学/沿革刑法學　science of evolution of criminal law
沿海开放城市/沿海開放城市　open coastal city
沿海贸易/沿海貿易　coastal trade
研发成本/研發成本　research and development cost
研发规模/研發規模　research and development scale

研发经费/研發經費　research and development expenditure
研发联合体/研發聯合體　research and development consortium
研发流程/研發流程　research and development process
研发密度/研發密度,研發銷售比　research and development sales ratio
研发评价/研發評價　research and development evaluation
研发强度/研發強度　research and development intensity
研发投入/研發投入　research and development input
研发团队/研發團隊　research and development team
研发外包/研發外包　research and development strategy outsourcing
研发网络/研發網路　research and development network
研发文化/研發文化　research and development culture
研发项目/研發專案　research and development project
研发项目风险管理/研發專案風險管理　research and development project risk management
研发项目规划/研發專案規劃　research and development project program
研发项目绩效评价/研發專案績效評價　research and development project performance evaluation
研发项目战略/研發專案戰略　research and development project strategy
研发预算/研發預算　research and development budget
研发战略/研究發展　research and development strategy
研发政策/研發政策　research and development policy, R and D policy
研发专属权/研發專屬權　research and development appropriability
研究/研究　research
研究报告/研究報告　research report
研究处理/研究處理　research treatment
研究单位/研究分析單位　unit of study
研究馆员/圖書館研究員　research librarian
研究前沿/研究前沿　research front
研究前沿分析/研究前沿分析法　research front analysis
研究设计/研究設計　research design
研究图书馆/研究圖書館　research library

研究小间/研究小間　study carrel
研究型大学/研究型大學　research university
研究用书/研究用書　research collection
研究与开发/研究發展　research and development
研究与开发战略/研究發展策略　research and development strategy
研究域/研究域　domain of study
研究指南/研究指南　research guide
研究质量/研究品質　research quality
盐雾试验/鹽霧試驗　salt-spray test
筵席税/筵席税　feast tax
颜色编码/顏色編碼　color encoding
颜色值/色值　color value
衍生产品/衍生性産品　derivative product
衍生类金融产品/衍生性金融商品　financial derivatives, derived class financial product
衍生需求/衍生性需求　derived demand
衍文/衍文　surplus word
衍字/衍字　superfluous word
演出经纪人/藝人經紀人　artist agent
演出者附注/演出者附注　performer note
演化/演化,進化　evolution
演化博弈/演化賽局　evolutionary game
演化规划/演化規劃　evolutionary programming
演化过程/蜕變過程　evolutionary process
演化经济学/演化經濟學　evolutionary economics
演化模型/進化模型　evolutionary model
演化预测方法/演化預測方法　evolutionary forecasting method
演讲法/講述法　lecture method
演练/訓練,練習　exercising
演示带/展示[版]　demo
演示阶段/演示階段　presentation phase
演替/演替　succession
演绎法/演繹法　deductive method
演绎作品/演繹作品　derivative work
厌恶品/負商品　bads
验单付款/驗單付款　payment against bill of lading
验关地点/驗關地點　place of customs inspection
验货/檢驗貨物　inspection of goods
验收/驗收,允收　checking and acceptance, examine and receive, acceptance
验收标准/驗收準則　acceptance criteria
验收抽样/允收抽樣　acceptance sampling
验收抽样方案/允收抽樣計劃　acceptance sampling plan
验收抽样计划/允收抽樣方案,允收抽樣計劃　acceptance sampling scheme

验收抽样检验/驗收抽樣檢驗　acceptable sampling inspection
验收检验/驗收檢驗,允收檢驗　acceptance inspection
验收控制图/允收管制圖　acceptance control chart
验收控制限/允收管制界限　acceptance control limit
验收试验/驗收試驗,允收試驗　acceptance testing
验收移交阶段/驗收移交階段　acceptance and transfer phase
验证/驗證,印證　authentication, verification
验证试验/驗證試驗　demonstration test
验证图/驗證圖　certified chart
验证性因素分析/驗證性因子分析　confirmatory factor analysis
验资/驗資　capital verification
雁行形态发展论/雁行形態發展論　catching-up product cycle theory
鞅/鞅,平賭　martingale
羊皮纸/羊皮紙　parchment, lambskin
羊皮纸档案/羊皮紙檔案　parchment archive
羊皮纸文件/羊皮紙文件　parchment file
羊皮纸页/羊皮紙頁　membrane
羊群效应/樂隊花車效果　bandwagon effect, herd behavior
羊群行为/羊群行爲　herd behavior
阳光地带/陽光帶　sunshine zone
阳图PS版/陽片PS版　positive-type PS plate
阳性选择假说/正向選擇假說　positive selection hypothesis
杨基债券/洋基債券,美元債券　Yankee bond
养成教育/養成教育　formative education
养老保险/生死合險,年金保險　endowment insurance, pension insurance
养老基金/退休基金　pension fund
养老金/老年年金,退休金　old age pension, pension
养老金法案/老年年金法案　old age pension act
养老金给付担保公司/退休金給付擔保公司　pension benefit guarantee corporation
养老金计划/退休金計劃　pension plan
养老金确定给付制/退休金確定給付制　defined benefit pension plan
养老金确定缴费制/退休金確定繳費制　defined contribution pension plan
养老金制度/退休金計劃,老年年金制　pension system
氧垂曲线/溶氧降低曲線　oxygen sag curve
氧化纤维素/氧化纖維素　oxidized cellulose
氧化有害气体/氧化有害氣體　oxidation harmful gas

样本/樣本　sample
样本比/樣本比　sample ratio
样本比例/樣本比例　sample proportion
样本变异性/樣本變異性　sample variability
样本标准差/樣本標準[離]差　sample standard deviation
样本不合格品/樣本不良品　sample defective
样本不合格品率/樣本不良率　sample fraction defective
样本乘积和/樣本乘積和　sample product sum
样本乘积矩/樣本乘積動差　sample product moment
样本抽选/樣本抽選　sample selection
样本大小/抽樣大小　sampling size
样本点/樣本點　sample point
样本店/樣本店　sample bookstore
样本调查/樣本調查，抽樣調查　sample survey, sampling survey
样本多元相关系数/樣本多元相關係數　sample coefficient of multiple correlation
样本方案/樣本計劃　sample plan
样本方差/樣本變異數　sample variance
样本分布/樣本分配　sample distribution
样本分布函数/樣本分布函数　sample distribution function
样本分位数/樣本分位數　sample quantile
样本构成/樣本形相　configuration of sample
样本回归线/樣本回歸線　sample regression line
样本极差/樣本全距　sample range
样本间变异/樣本間變異　between-sample variation
样本间方差/樣本間變異數　between-sample variance
样本矩/樣本動差　sample moment
样本均值/樣本平均數　sample mean, sample average
样本均值的标准误差/樣本平均數的標準誤　standard error of sample mean
样本均值分布/樣本平均數的分布　distribution of sample mean
样本可决系数/樣本判定係數　sample coefficient of determination
样本空间/樣本空間　sample space
样本累积量/樣本累積值　sample cumulant
样本量/樣本大小　sample size, size of sample
样本量分配/樣本規模分配　sample allocation
样本量为n的随机样本/大小爲n的隨機樣本　random sample of size n
样本量字码/樣本大小代碼　sample size code letter
样本内变异/樣本內變異　within sample variation, variation within samples
样本内估计/樣本內估計　in-sample estimation
样本配置/樣本配置　allocation of a sample
样本批/樣本批　sample batch
样本平均差/樣本平均差　sample mean deviation
样本平均方差/樣本平均差方　sample mean square deviation
样本平均值的抽样分布/樣本平均數的抽樣分配　sampling distribution of sample mean
样本谱/樣本譜　sample spectrum
样本设计/樣本設計　sample design
样本生存函数/樣本存活函數　sample survival function
样本时点/抽樣時點　sample time point
样本统计/樣本統計　sample statistic
样本外预测/樣本外預測　out-of-sample forecasting
样本网络/樣本網　network of samples
样本误差/樣本誤差　sample error
样本线/樣本線　sample line
样本相关系数/樣本相關係數　sample correlation coefficient
样本协方差/樣本協方差，樣本共變異數　sample covariance
样本选择模型/樣本選擇模型　sample selection model
样本选择性偏差/選擇性偏誤　sample selectivity bias
样本依赖/樣本依賴　sample dependent
样本中位数/樣本中位數　sample median
样本自相关/樣本自我相關　sample autocorrelation
样本自相关函数/樣本自我相關函數　sample autocorrelation function
样稿/樣稿　sample
样片/樣片　rush print
样品/樣品　specimen
样品出口/樣品出口　sample export
样品进口/樣品進口　sample import
样品赠送促销/樣品贈送推廣　sampling promotion
样书/樣書　sample copy, proof copy
样条函数/樣條函數，弧狀函數　spline function
样条近似/樣條逼近，弧線近似　spline approximation
样条平滑法/樣條平滑法，弧線平滑法　spline smoothing method
样条曲线/樣條曲線，雲規曲線　spline curve
要求/要求，需求　requirement
要求偿还款项/償還款項的請求　claim for reimbursement
要求赔偿/賠償請求　claim for compensation

要求赔偿损失/要求賠償損失　claim against damage
要求赔偿损失诉讼/要求損害賠償訴訟　action for compensation for loss
要求索赔/損失賠償請求　claim for indemnity
要求退回原物诉讼/要求回復原狀訴訟　action for restitution
要求退税/要求退稅　claim for tax refund
要求支付贷款诉讼/要求補償損失訴訟,要求代價訴訟　action to recover the price
要式合同/要式合同　formal contract
要约/要約　offer
要约撤回/要約撤回　withdrawal of offer
要约收购/公開出價收購,公開收購要約　tender offer
要约邀请/要約邀請　invitation to offer
腰封/腰封,紙帶　belt cover, paper tape
邀请招标/邀請招標　selective tendering, selected tendering
谣言/謠言　rumour
摇镜头/橫搖鏡頭　pan
摇篮本/搖籃本　incunabulum
摇钱树/金牛　cash cow
徭役劳动/強迫勞役勞工　corvee labor
遥距督导/遠距監督　long-distance supervision, remote supervision
药典/藥典　pharmacopoeia, codex
药品监督管理/藥品監督管理　drug administration
要辑/要輯　important album
要径法/要徑法　critical path method, CPM
要目/要目　essential content
要目索引/要目索引　main entry index
要素比例/[生产]要素比例　factor ratio, factor proportion
要素比例模型/要素比率模型　factor proportion model
要素禀赋/要素稟賦　factor endowment
要素禀赋理论/要素稟賦學說　factor endowment theory
要素价格/要素價格　factor price
要素价格均等化/生產要素價格均等化　factor price equalization, equalization of factor price
要素价格均等化定理/要素價格均等化定理　factor-price equalization theorem
要素价格扭曲/要素價格扭曲　factor-price distortion
要素价值/要素價值　factor value
要素可逆性/要素可逆性　factor reversibility
要素贸易条件/要素貿易條件,階乘貿易條件　factorial terms of trade
要素密集度/要素密集度　factor intensity
要素密集性逆转/要素密集度逆轉　factor intensity reversal
要素市场扭曲/要素市場扭曲　factor-market distortion
要素收入/要素所得,因素支付　factor income, factor payment
要素税/要素稅　factor tax
要素所得贸易条件/生産要素收入貿易條件　factor income terms of trade
要素替代性/要素代替性　factor substitutability
要素需求/要素需求　factor demand
要素资本比率/生産要素資本比率　factor capital ratio
要素资产组合/因素投資組合　factor portfolio
要闻/要聞　highlight
要闻版/要聞版　important news version
耶茨法/Yates 法　Yates method
耶茨-格伦迪估计量/Yates-Grundy 估計量　Yates-Grundy estimator
耶茨校正/Yates 校正　Yates correction,
耶林/耶林　Rudolf von Jhering
耶鲁学派/耶魯學派　Yale School
野蛮时期/野蠻狀態　barbarism
野生地域/原野地區　wilderness areas
野生动物保护法/野生動物保護法　law on protection of wild animal protection
野生植物保护法/野生植物保護法　law on protection of wild plants
野史/外史　unofficial history
野外考察/田野工作　field work
业务层的合作战略/業務層的合作戰略　business-level cooperative strategy
业务层战略/事業層級策略　business-level strategy
业务档案/業務檔案　archival operation
业务价值/業務價值　franchise value, business value
业务类公务员/永業文官　career civil servant
业务流程/事業營運流程　business process
业务流程管理/商業流程管理　business process management
业务流程图/業務流程圖　transaction flow diagram, TFD
业务流程再造/企業流程再造　enterprise process reengineering, business process reengineering, BPR
业务线/業務線　line of business
业务消息格式/業務消息格式　job messaging format, JMF
业务约定书/委任書　engagement letter

业务知识测试/工作知識測驗　job knowledge test
业务指导关系/業務指導關係　business guidance relationship
业务组合/業務組合　business portfolio
业余教育/業餘教育　sparetime education
业缘群体/職業團體,職業群體　occupational group
业主/業主　owner
业主单位/業主單位　owner unit
业主监督权/業主監督權　owner supervisory authority
业主收入/業主所得　proprietor income
业主违约/業主違約　default to employer
业主维权/業主維權　rights protection movement of urban property owners
业主委员会/業主委員會　owner committee
业主委员会监督权/業主委員會監督權　owner committee supervisory authority
页/頁　page
页边/頁邊　margin
页码/頁碼,頁數,頁號　page number
页码索引/頁碼索引　page reference
页面/頁面　page
页面功能部件/頁面功能部件　page functional unit
页面浏览量/網頁面讀取量　page view
页面描述语言/頁描述語言　page description language
页面描述语言解释器/解譯器　interpreter
页面元素/頁面元素　page element
页末注/頁末注　note located in the last part of a page
页头标题/頁頭標題　headline, page head
页头题名/頁頭題名　running title
夜间作业/夜工　night work
液相去酸法/液相去酸法　liquid-phase deacidification
一般保证/一般保證　general guaranty
一般背书/一般背書,無記名背書　general endorsement
一般参照/説明参照　explanatory reference
一般藏书/一般藏書　ordinary collection
一般代理/一般代理　general agency
一般等价物/一般等價物　universal equivalent
一般地域管辖/一般地域管轄　ordinary territorial jurisdiction
一般独立输入/一般獨立輸入　general independent input
一般法律原则/一般法律原則　general principle of law
一般更新过程/一般更新過程　general renewal process
一般购买条件/一般購買條件　general condition of purchase
一般管理理论/一般管理理論　general management theory
一般合伙人/一般合夥人,普通合夥人　general partner
一般机会研究/一般機會研究　general opportunity study
一般价值形式/一般價值形態　general form of value
一般减税/一般減稅　general tax reduction
一般交货条件/一般交貨條件　general conditions of delivery
一般交易条件/一般交易條件　general terms and conditions of trade
一般均衡/全面均衡　general equilibrium
一般均衡分析/一般均衡分析　general equilibrium analysis
一般均衡论/一般均衡理論　general equilibrium theory
一般客体/一般客體　general object
一般利率/一般利率　general rate of interest
一般利润率/一般利潤率　general rate of profit
一般侵权行为/一般侵權行爲　general tort act
一般生育率/一般生育率　general fertility rate
一般史事注释/一般史事注釋　event annotation
一般税率/一般税率,普遍税率　general tariff
一般司法协助/一般司法協助　general judicial assistance
一般图书/普通圖書　general book
一般误差法则/一般誤差法則　general law of error
一般系统论/一般系統理論　general system theory
一般线性假设/一般線性假設　generalized linear hypothesis
一般线性模型/一般線性模型　general linear model
一般行政法/一般行政法　general administrative law
一般性附注/一般注解　general note
一般性信用控制/一般性信用管制　general credit control
一般性转移支付/一般性轉移支付　general transfer payment
一般需要描述/一般需要描述　general need description
一般许可证/一般許可證,普通許可證　general licence
一般要素/一般要素　general element
一般依存系统/一般依存系統　general interdependent system

一般诱因/一般誘因　general inducement
一般资产货币/一般資産貨幣　general asset currency
一般资料标识/資料類型標示　general material designation, GMD
一笔过拨款/一筆過撥款　lump sum grant
一步转移概率/單步遞移機率　one step transition probability
一步转移矩阵/單步遞移矩陣　one step transition matrix
一触式换模/一觸式換模　one-touch exchange of die, OTED
一次抽样/一次抽樣,單次抽樣　single sampling
一次抽样方案/單次抽樣方案　single sampling plan
一次档案文献/一次檔案文獻　original archival documentation
一次付清/一次付清　pay in full
一次命中模型/一次命中模型　one-hit model
一次随机抽样/單次隨機抽樣　single random sampling
一次文献/一次文獻　primary literature, primary document
一次污染物/一次汙染物　primary pollutant
一次信息[源]/一次資訊[源]　primary information source
一次性博弈/單期賽局　one-shot game
一次性补贴/定額補貼　lump-sum subsidy
一次性偿还贷款/一次還本貸款　bullet loan
一次性付款/一次給付　lump sum payment
一次性计划/一次性計劃　single-used plan
一次性征税/定額稅　lump-sum tax
一次总付制度/一次總付制度　lump-sum system
X一代/X一代　generation X
Y一代/Y一代　generation Y
一读/第一[次]讀　first reading
一夫一妻制家庭/一夫一妻制家庭　monogamian family
一级价格歧视/第一級差別取價　first-degree price discrimination
一级批发/一級批發　exclusive wholesale
一级银行票据/一級銀行票據,主要銀行票據　prime bank bill
一级资本/一級資本　first tier capital
一价定律/單一價格法則　law of one price
一阶抽样/一段抽樣,單段抽樣　one stage sampling
一阶[抽样]单元/第一階段[抽樣]單位　first-stage sampling unit
一阶单整/一階單積　integrated of order 1

一阶辅助/一階補助　first order ancillary
一阶交互作用/一階交互作用　first order interaction
一阶矩/一級動差　first order moment
一阶决策/單段決策　single-stage decision
一阶模型/一階模型　first order model
一阶设计/一階設計　first order design
一阶随机占优/一階隨機占優　first order stochastic dominance
一阶自回归过程/一階自我回歸過程　first order autoregressive process
一阶自回归模型/一階自[身]回歸模型　first order autoregressive model
一阶自回归误差/一階自我回歸誤差　first order autoregressive errors
一阶自回归误差模型/一階自[身]回歸誤差模型　first order autoregressive error model
一篮子期权/一籃式選擇權　basket option
一览表/一覽表　list
一揽子保险/一攬子保險　package insurance
一揽子保险单/一籃子保險單　package insurance policy
一揽子贷款/一籃子貸款　credit package, package credit
一揽子合同/一籃子合約　blanket contract
一揽子货币/一籃子貨幣　currency basket
一揽子技术/一攬子技術　technology package
一揽子价格/一籃子價格,共同價格,統括價格　blanket price, package price, lump price
一揽子交易/一籃子交易　package deal
一揽子期权/组合式選擇權　basket option
一揽子投资/一籃子投資,總額權益　lump-sum interest, package investment
一揽子协议/集體協議,一籃子協定　bouquet arrangement, blanket agreement
一揽子协议发布书/開立綜合訂單　blanket release
一年期债券/一年期債券　yearling bond
一人公司/一人公司　one-person company
一事不再罚/一事不再罰　ne bis in indem
一事不再理/一事不再理　not twice for the same
一书目录/一書目錄　table of content
一套人马、两块牌子/一套人馬、兩塊牌子　one-team two-names
一体化集团/集團整合化　integration grouping
一体化区域合作/整體區域合作　integrated regional co-operation
一体化审核/整合性稽核　integrated audit
一体化物流服务/一體化物流服務　integrated logistics service

一体化信息服务/一體化資訊服務　universal information service, UIS
一体化战略/整合策略　integration strategy
一文一题标题法/一文一題標題法　method of one archive headlined one title
一线书库/一線書庫　first-tier stack
一型计数模型/第一型計數器模型　type one counter model, counter model, type I
一元概率单位模型/單元常態機率模型　univariate probit model
一元式中央银行制度/一元式中央銀行制度　unit central bank system
一元有序概率单位模型/單元排序性常態機率模型　univariate ordered probit model
一院制/一院制　unicameral parliament system
一站式服务/一站式服務　one-stop service
一整套技术/一整套技術　technological package
一致抽样比/均匀抽樣率　uniform sampling fraction
一致估计量/一致估計量　consistent estimator
一致较佳决策函数/均匀較佳決策函數　uniformly better decision function
一致收敛/一致收斂　uniform convergence
一致无偏渐近正态估计量/一致不偏漸近常態估計量　consistent unbiased asymptotic normal estimator
一致系数/一致性係數　coefficient of agreement
一致性/一致性　consistency, consistence
一致性比率/一致性比率　consistent ratio
一致性检验/一致性檢定　consistent test, consistence test
一致性离差/同向離差　concurrent deviation
一致性原则/一致性原則　consistency principle
一致性指数/一致性係數　consistency index
一致性质量/一致性品質　conformance quality
一致指数/諧和係數　agreement index
一致最大功效检验/均匀最强[檢定]力檢定　uniformly most powerful test, UMP test
一致最大功效检验的渐近功效/均匀最强力檢定的漸近檢力　asymptotic power of uniformly most powerful test
一致最大功效临界域/均匀最强[檢定]力臨界域　uniformly most powerful critical region
一致最大功效无偏检验/均匀最强[檢定]力不偏檢定　uniformly most powerful unbiased test, UMPU test
一致最佳不变风险估计量/均匀最佳常數風險估計量　uniformly best constant risk estimator, UBCR estimator
一致最佳估计量/均匀最佳估計量　uniformly best estimator
一致最佳检验/均匀最佳檢定　uniformly best test
一致最佳距离功效检验/均匀最佳差距檢力檢定　uniformly best distance power test, UBDP test
一致最小方差无偏估计不可容许性/均匀最小變異數不偏估計量不可容性　inadmissibility of UMVUE
一致最小方差无偏估计量的相合性/均匀最小變異數不偏估計量一致性　consistency of UMVUE
一致最小方差无偏估计值/均匀最小變異數不偏估計量　uniformly minimum variance unbiased estimator, UMVUE
一致最小风险/均匀最小風險　uniformly minimum risk
一致最准确/均匀最準確　uniformly most accurate
一致最准确置信界/均匀最準確信賴界　uniformly most accurate confidence bound, UMA confidence bound
一种方式分组/單因子分類,單向分類　one-way classification
一准乎礼/一準乎禮　Yi Zhunhu Li
伊壁鸠鲁学派/伊壁鳩魯學派　school of Epikouros
伊曼纽尔不平等交换理论/伊馬紐爾不平等交易論　Emmanuel unequal exchange theory
伊斯兰法系/伊斯蘭法系　Islamic law system
伊塔函数/Eta 函數, η 函數　Eta-function, η-function
伊藤定理/伊藤定理　Itô's lemma
医患关系/醫患關係　patient-doctor relationship, patient-physician relationship
医疗/醫療照護　medical care, medicare
医疗保险/醫療保險,健康保險　medical insurance, health insurance
医疗服务/醫療服務　medical service
医疗机构/醫療機構　health facility
医疗救助/醫療救助,醫療協助,醫療援助　medical relief, medical assistance
医疗事故/誤診　medical malpractice
医疗事故罪/醫療事故罪　crime of medical accident
医疗需求/醫療需求　demand for medical care
医疗营销/醫療保健行銷　health care marketing
医疗专业/健康專業　health profession
医务社会工作/醫務社會工作　medical social work
医务社会工作服务/醫務社會工作服務　medical social work service
医学化/醫療化　medicalization
医学情报学/醫學資訊科學　medical information science

医学社会学/醫學社會學,醫療社會學　medical sociology, medical sociology, sociology in medical practice
医学统计/醫學統計　medical statistics
医学图书馆/醫學圖書館　health science library, medical library
医学信息/醫學資訊　medical information
医药卫生统计/醫藥與公共衛生統計　medical and public health statistics
医药新闻/醫藥新聞　medical journalism
医院市场/醫院市場　hospital market
医院图书馆/醫院圖書館　hospital library
依测度收敛/測度收斂　convergence in measure
依γ次均值收敛/γ次均數收斂　convergence in γth mean
依从/順從　compliance
X依Y的回归线/X依Y的回歸線　line of regression of X on Y
Y依X的回归线/Y依X的回歸線　line of regression of Y on X
依法提请仲裁/依法提請仲裁　legally filing award
依法则收敛/法則收斂　convergence in law
依分布收敛/分配收斂,分布收斂　convergence in distribution
依附概率/附著機率　adherent probability
依附理论/依附理論,依賴理論　dependence theory, dependency theory
依附性/依賴性　dependence
依附性发展/依賴性發展,依賴性發展　dependent development
依概率收敛/機率收斂　convergence in probability
依据合同的诉讼/依據合約的訴訟　action ex contract
依赖/依賴[性]　dependency, dependence
依恋/依戀　attachment
依恋理论/依戀理論　attachment theory
依约照付/依約照付　pay as may be paid
仪式/儀式,禮儀　ritual
仪式化/儀式化　ritualization
移动本期权数量指数/移動本期權數量指數　quantum index with moving current weights
移动出版/移動出版　mobile publishing
移动出版行销/移動出版行銷　mobile publishing marketing
移动电话/手機,行動電話　cell phone, cellular telephone, mobile phone
移动电视/移動電視　mobile television
移动服务/移動業務　mobile service
移动观测者法/移動觀察法　moving observer technique
移动互联网/移動上網　mobile internet
移动极差/移動全距　moving range
移动极差法/移動全距法　moving range method
移动季节性方差/移動季節變異數　moving seasonal variance
移动客户端广告/移動用戶端廣告　mobile client advertisement
移动流媒体技术/移動流媒體技術　mobile streaming media technology
移动年总计/移動年總數　moving annual total
移动配合/移動配合　running fit
移动平均/移動平均　moving average
移动平均比率/移動平均比率　ratio of moving averages
移动平均比率法/比率移動平均　ratio-to-moving average
移动平均多项式/移動平均多項式　moving average polynomial
移动平均法/移動平均[數]法　moving average method
移动平均过程/移動平均[數]過程　moving average process
移动平均计划/移動平均[數]方案　moving average scheme
移动平均模型/移動平均[數]模型　moving average model
移动平均扰动/移動平均[數]干擾　moving average disturbance
移动平均数/移動平均[數]　moving average
移动平均算子/移動平均[數]算子　moving average operator
移动平均图/移動平均[數]圖　moving average chart
移动平均预测模型/滑動平均預測模型　moving average forecasting model
移动前期权数量指数/移動前期權數量指數　quantum index with moving anterior weights
移动权重/移動權數　moving weight
移动商务/移動商務　mobile commerce, mcommerce
移动视频监视/移動視頻監視　mobile video monitoring
移动视频消息/移動視頻消息　mobile video news
移动搜索/移動搜索　mobile search
移动信息助理/移動資訊助理　mobile information assistant
移动学习/行動學習　mobile learning
移动游戏/移動遊戲　mobile game

移动阅读/移動閱讀,手機閱讀　mobile reading
移动总和过程/移動總和過程　moving summation process
移动总量/移動總數　moving total
移交/移交　transfer
移交-经营-移交模式/轉移-操作-轉移模式,TOT 模式　transfer-operate-transfer model, TOT model
移交清册/移交清冊　transfer list
移交物/移交物　handoff
移民/移民　immigration
移情/同理心　empathy
移送管辖/移送管轄　transfer of case
移位模型/移位模型　shift model
移物/運貫　transport loaded
移植法/移植法　transplanting method
遗产/遺產　inheritance
遗产税/遺產稅,繼承稅,死亡稅　inheritance tax, death tax, estate duty
遗产与赠与税/遺產與贈與稅　estate and gift tax
遗传方差/遺傳變異數　genetic variance
遗传生态学/遺傳生態學　genecology
遗传算法/遺傳程式,基因演算法　genetic algorithm
遗传算法模型/遺傳演算法模型　genetic algorithm model
遗传随机模型/遺傳隨機模型　genetic stochastic model
遗传统计[学]/遺傳統計[學]　genetic statistics
遗传系数/遺傳係數　coefficient of heredity
遗憾理论/遺憾理論　regret theory
遗憾最少原则/遺憾最少決策原則　minimax regret rule
遗漏观察值/遺漏觀察值　missing observation
遗失汇票/遺失匯票　lost exchange bill
遗失流通票据/遺失流通票據　lost negotiable instrument
遗失票据/遺失票據　lost note
遗失图书/遺失圖書　missing copy, missing item
遗失支票/遺失支票　lost cheque
遗赠/遺贈　bequest, legacy
遗赠抚养协议/遺贈撫養協議　bequeathal-support agreement
遗嘱/遺囑　testament
遗著/遺著　literary remain, posthumous work
已保险的出口商/已保險出口商　insured exporter
已背书担保债券/已背書擔保債券　indorsed bond
已背书债券/已背書債券　bond endorsed
已承兑票据/已承兌票據　accepted bill, accepted draft
已承兑信用证/已承兌信用狀　accepted letter of credit
已订未交货物/已訂未交貨物　goods on order
已兑付支票/已兌現支票　canceled check
已兑回债券/已兌回債券　retired bond
已发出订单/已發出訂單　released order
已付保证金/已付保證金　guarantee deposit and margin paid
已付股利/支付股利　paid dividend
已付合同保证金/已付合約保證金,存出保證金　contract deposit paid
已付金额/已付金額　amount paid
已付款保险单/已付款保險單　paid-up policy
已付款账户/已付款賬戶　account settled
已付清信用证/已押匯信用狀,已補償信用狀　paid credit
已付税的货物/完税货物　duty-paid goods
已缴清股票/已繳清股本　paid-up share
已结账户/已結賬戶,結清賬戶　closed account
已借出/出借的,暂借　on loan
已开出汇票/已開出匯票　drawn bill
已履行合同/已履行合約　executed contract
已清偿的损失额/已清償的損失額　liquidated damage
已清偿债务/已清償債務　liquidated debt
已实现利润/已實現利潤　realized profit
已实现收益/已實現收益　realized income
已实现收益率/已實現收益率　realized yield, horizon yield
已实现投资/已實現投資　realized investment
已收合同保证金/已收合約保證金,存入保證金　contract deposit received
已赎回汇票/已贖回匯票　retired bill
已贴现汇票/已貼現匯票　discounted bill
已贴现票据/已貼現票據　bill discounted, discounted note
已贴现应收票据/已貼現應收票據　bill receivable discounted, note receivable discounted
已投入资本/已投入股本　invested capital
已修正的 R 方/已修正的 R 方　adjusted R-squared
已用提单/已用提單　spent bill of lading
已支付票据/付訖票據　paid bill
已知资料检索/已知資料檢索　known-item search
已转让信用证/已轉讓信用狀　transferred credit
已装船背书/已裝船背書　on board endorsement
已装船提单/已裝船提單,裝船載貨證券　on board bill of lading, shipped bill of lading
已作拒付证书的应收票据/已作拒絕付款的應收票

据 note receivable protested
以本国货币表示的汇率/以本國貨幣表示的匯率 rate in home currency, rate in home money
以不正当手段获取商业秘密/以不正當手段獲取商業秘密 obtain trade secret via unfair method
以产品支付/以産品支付 payment in product
以德去刑/以德去刑 returning punishment for kindness
以法为教、以吏为师/以法爲教、以吏爲師 taking the law as teaching content and taking officials as teachers
以概率1收敛/以機率1收斂,強機率收斂,幾乎到處收斂 convergence with probability one
以顾客为关注焦点/以顧客爲焦點 customer focus
以获得出口许可证为条件/以獲得輸出許可證爲條件 subject to export license being obtained
以获得进口许可证为条件/以獲得輸入許可證爲條件 subject to import license being obtained
以获取配额为条件/以獲得配額爲條件 subject to quota
以机遇为导向/以機遇爲導向 opportunity orientation
以记账支付的支票/以記賬支付的支票 check payable in account
以旧换新折让/抵換折讓,舊換新折讓 trade-in allowance
以礼入法/以禮入法 essentials of Confucianism into the law
以立即答复为有效的发盘/以即刻回覆爲條件的報價 offer subject to immediate reply
以立即回电为有效的发盘/以即刻回電爲條件的報價 offer subject to immediate acceptance by telegram
以邻为壑策略/以鄰爲壑策略 beggar-my-neighbor tactics
以领得出口许可证为准的发盘/以取得輸出許可證爲條件的報價 offer subject to export license
以领得进口许可证为准的发盘/以取得輸入許可證爲條件的報價 offer subject to import license
以买方检验或接受为准的发盘/買方看貨後報價 offer subject to buyer inspection or approval
以脉冲数码调制/博碼調變,脈衝調變 pulse code modulation
以前年度损益调整/調整前期損益 prior-period gains and losses adjustment
以取得出口许可证为条件/以取得輸出許可證爲條件 subject to approval of export license
以取得进口许可证为条件/以取得輸入許可證爲條件 subject to approval of import license
以人力资本投资/以人力資本投資 investment in human capital
以人为本/以人爲本 people-oriented
以特别提款权计值欧洲贷款/以特別提款權計值歐洲貸款 SDR-denominated Eurocredit
以特别提款权计值辛迪加贷款/以特別提款權計值辛迪加貸款 SDR-denominated syndicated credit
以未出售为有效发盘/以未出售爲條件報價 offer subject to being unsold
以物易物/以物易物,實物交易 barter
以刑去刑/以刑去刑 executing cruel torture to decrease crime
以牙还牙策略/以牙還牙策略 tit-for-tat strategy
以议付汇票方式使用信用证/簽發匯票請求讓購信用狀 credit available by negotiation of draft
以支票支付/以支票支付 payment by cheque
以组织为中心职业规划/組織本位職涯規劃 organizational-centered career planning
义绝/義絶 compulsory divorce in feudal China
义务/義務 duty
义务教育/義務教育 compulsory education
艺术档案/藝術檔案 artistic archive
艺术电影/藝術電影 art movie
艺术社会学/藝術社會學 sociology of art
艺术图书馆/藝術圖書館 art library
艺术印刷品/藝術印刷品 art print
艺术指导/藝術指導,美術指導 art director
艺术作品/工藝作品 artistic work
议案/議案 proposal, motion
议标/議[價投]標,協商性招標 negotiated bidding, negotiated tendering
议宾/議賓 Yi Bin
议程/議題 agenda
议程建构/議題建構 agenda building
议程建构过程/議題建構過程 agenda-building process
议程设定/議程設定,議題設定 agenda setting
议程设定功能/議題設定功能 agenda-setting function
议程设置假说/議題設定假說 agenda-setting hypothesis
议程设置理论/議題設定理論 agenda-setting theory
议程设置效应/議題設定效應 agenda-setting effect
议定关税/協定關税 agreed duty
议定黄金价格/議定黄金價格 gold fixing
议定价格/議定價格,談妥價錢 agreed price
议定支付额/約定支付額 agreed payment

议付行/議付行　negotiating bank
议付金额/議價金額　negotiated amount
议付手续费/押匯手續費　negotiation commission
议付外国票据/讓購外國票據　negotiation of foreign bill
议付信用证/押匯信用狀,讓購信用狀　negotiation credit
议复档/議復檔　reconsidered archive
议功/議功　Yee Gong
议购议销/議購議銷　negotiated purchasing and selling
议会/議會　congress
议会党团/議會黨團　parliamentary group
议会调查权/議會調查權　power of parliamentary investigation
议会历史/議會歷史　parliamentary history
议会图书馆/議會圖書館　parliamentary library
议会至上/議會至上　parliament supreme
议会制/議會制　parliamentary system
议价成本/協商成本　bargaining cost
议价能力/議價能力　ability to bargain
议论方式/議論方式　discussion way
议员/議員　congressman
议长/議長　speaker
异步交流/異步通信,非同步通訊　asynchronous communication
异步数字参考咨询/異步虛擬參考　asynchronous virtual reference
异常/異例　anomalies
异常波动/異常變異　special variation
异常原因/異常原因　special cause
异地存储/異地存儲　off-site storage
异方差/不等變異　heteroscedastic variation, heteroscedastic
异方差模型/不等變異數模型　heteroscedastic model
异方差性/異方差性,變異數不齊一性,不等變異性　heteroscedasticity
异峰度曲线/異峰度曲線　allokurtic curve
异构数据/異質資料　heterogeneous data
异构数据库/異質資料庫　heterogeneous database
异号/異號　contrary sign
异号相关/異號相關　unlike signed correlation
异化/疏離　alienation
异化劳动/異化勞動　alienated labor
异教/異教　heathenism
异类分布/異類分布　anisotropic distribution
异量/異量　heterograde
异时抗辩权/異時抗辯權　right to defense of later performance
异象/異常,反例　anomaly
异形光盘/異形光碟　abnormity optical disc
异型/異質型　heterotypic
异议登记/異議登記　registration of dissenting challenge
异议之诉/異議之訴　action regarding objection to enforcement of a judgment
异质层/異質層　heterogeneous strata
异质群体/異質群體,異質團體　heterogeneous group
异质性/異質性,非均齊性　heterogeneity
异质性产品/異質產品　heterogeneous product
异质总体/異質母體　heterogeneous population
异族结婚/外婚[制]　exogamy
抑制机制/抑制機制　suppressor mechanism
佚名文献/不具名資料　anonymous literature
佚名著作/不具名作品,匿名作品　anonymous work
译稿校订/譯稿校訂　revision of translation
译者/[翻]譯者　translator
译著/譯著　translation
易读性/易讀性　legibility
易腐产品库存管理/易腐產品庫存管理　perishable inventory management
易管理性/可管理性　manageability
易货贸易安排/以貨易貨安排　barter arrangement
易货贸易合同/以貨易貨合約　barter contract
易货贸易条件/以貨易貨貿易條件　barter terms of trade
易货贸易协议/以貨易貨協議　barter agreement
易货贸易制度/以貨易貨制度　barter system
易撕线/易撕線　tear line
易性癖/變性症　transsexualism
易装癖/易裝癖　transvestite
益智游戏/教育性遊戲　educational game
意大利科学管理协会/義大利科學管理協會　Scientific Management Society of Italy
意大利民法典/義大利民法典　Italian Civil Code
意见/意見　opinion
意见领袖/意見領袖　opinion leader
意见自由市场/意見自由市場　free market of ideas
意识觉醒小组/意識覺醒小組　consciousness-raising group
意识形态/意識[觀念]形態　ideology
意识形态叙事/意識形態敘事　ideological narrative
意思表示/意思表示　declaration of will
意思表示不自由/意思表示不自由　not-free declaration of will
意思能力/意思能力　capacity of intention

意思与表示不一致/意思與表示不一致　inconsistency of will and declaration
意思自治原则/意思自治原則　principle of party autonomy
意图/意圖　intention
意外变动/突出變動　episodic movement
意外[伤害]保险/意外[傷害]保險　accident insurance
意外事件/意外事件　fortuitous event
意外之财/意外之財　windfall income
意外准备金/危險準備金　contingent reserve
意向书/意向書　statement of intention, letter of intent
意向通知/交割意願通知書　notice of intention
意向性/意向性,意圖性　intentionality
意义/意義　meaning
意义阐释/意義詮釋　meaning interpretation
意义分类/意義分類　meaning categorization
意义凝结/意義濃縮　meaning condensation
意指/意指,表意　signifying
意志理论/意志理論　will theory
溢出/外溢　spillover
溢出效应/外溢效果　spillover effect
溢价/溢價,價格升水　price premium
溢价发行债券/溢價發行債券　bond issue at premium
溢价债券/溢價債券　premium bond
劓刑/劓刑　sentence cut off the nose in feudal China
因变量/因變數,依變數　dependent variable
因果/因果　cause and effect
因果报应/因果報應　karma
因果分析图/因果分析圖　causal analysis diagram
因果关系/因果關係,因果性　causation, causality, causal relationship
因果关系推定/因果關係推定　inference of causation
因果回归/因果回歸　causation regression
因果连锁模型/因果鏈模型　causal chain model
因果链/因果鏈　causal chain
因果律/因果律,因果法則　law of causality
因果模型/原因模型,因果關係模式法　causal model, causal modeling
因果图/因果圖　cause-and-effect diagram
因果系统/因果系統　causal system
因果因子/因果因子　causal factor
因果营销研究/因果行銷研究　causal marketing research
因[货币]贬值造成损失/貨幣貶值損失　loss from devaluation
因货物不符[合同]索赔权/因货物不符[合約]索賠權　claim based on lack of conformity of goods
因货物灭失或损失索赔/對貨物實際損失或破損索賠　claim based on physical loss or damage
因金钱损失产生债权/因金錢損失索賠　claim based on pecuniary loss
因欺诈而产生诉讼权/因詐欺舞弊索賠　claim based on fraud
因素贝塔/因素貝塔　factor beta
因素比较系统/因素比較系統,因素比較制度　factor comparison system
因素点分评价法/計點法　point method
因素负荷/因素負荷,因子負荷　factor loading
因素模型/要素模型,因子模型　factor model
因特网/網際網路　Internet
因特网报纸/網際網路報紙　Internet newspaper
因特网媒体/網際網路媒體　Internet media
因特网内容提供者/網際網路內容提供者　Internet content provider, ICP
因子/因素,要素　factor
因子成本/因子成本　factor cost
因子对偶/因子對偶　factor antithesis
因子分布/因子分布　factorial distribution
因子分解定理/分解定理　factorization theorem
因子分析/因子分析,因素分析　factor analysis
因子分析模型/因數分析模型　factor analysis model
因子风险/因子風險　factor risk
因子互换检验/因子互換測驗　factor reversal test
因子矩阵/因子矩陣　factor matrix
因子空间/因子空間　factor space
因子水平/因子水準　factor level, level of factor
因子效度/因素效度　factorial validity
因子效应/因子效應　factorial effect
因子旋转/因素旋轉　factor rotation
因子载荷/因子負載,因素負載　factor loading
阴图 PS 版/陰片 PS 版　negative-type PS plate
阴阳图/陰陽圖　silhouette chart
阴阳盈亏图/陰陽盈虧圖　silhouette excess and deficit chart
音轨/磁軌　track
音量/音量　volume
音频/音訊　audio
音频采集/音訊擷取　audio extraction
音频多用途数字光盘/音訊多用途數位光碟　digital versatile disc-audio
音频非线性编辑/音訊非線性編輯　audio nonlinear editing
音频技术/音訊技術　audio technology

音频检索/音頻檢索　audio retrieval
音频文件/聲音檔案　audio record
音响商标/音響商標　sound trademark
音像出版物/音像出版物　audio-video publication
音像档案/影音檔案　audio-visual archive
音像录制合同/音像錄製合同　audio-video reproducer contract
音像书店/音像書店　audio-visual bookstore
音像数据库/音像數據庫　audiovisual database
音像图书馆/視聽圖書館　audiovisual library
音像制品/音像製品　audiovisual product
音像制品许可制度/音像製品許可制度　licensing system for audio and video product
音效/音效,音響效果　sound effect, foley
音源插件/音源外掛程式　audio plug-in
音乐电视/音樂電視　music television, MTV
音乐动画/音樂動畫　musical animation
音乐节目主持人/音樂節目主持人,廣播節目主持人　disc jockey, DJ
音乐录音师/音樂錄音師　musical sound engineer
音乐录音资料/樂音資料　musical sound recording
音乐图书馆/音樂圖書館　music library
音乐作品/音樂作品　musical work
姻亲/姻親　affinity
姻亲关系/姻親關係　relationship by affinity
殷墟甲骨档案/殷墟甲骨檔案　oracle bones archive of Yin dynasty ruins
银本位/銀本位　silver standard
银本位集团/銀本位集團　silver bloc
银本位制/銀本位制　silver standard system
银根紧缩/銀根緊繃　credit squeeze
银根紧缩的金融市场/銀根緊繃的金融市場　tight money market
银行/銀行　bank
银行背书/銀行背書　bank endorsement
银行本票/[銀行]本票,銀行支票　bank check, officer cheque, treasurer cheque
银行产业化组织/銀行產業化組織　industrial organization of banking
银行厂商/銀行廠商　banking firm
银行承兑/銀行承兑　bank acceptance
银行承兑汇票/銀行承兑匯票　bank acceptance, banker acceptance bill
银行承兑票据/銀行承兑票據　banker acceptance
银行承兑限额/承兑限額　acceptance line
银行承兑信用证/銀行承兑信用狀　banker acceptance credit
银行存款/銀行存款　bank deposit
银行存款余额调节表/銀行調節表　bank reconciliation
银行贷款/銀行貸款　loan from bank, bank loan
银行贷款审计/銀行借款審計　audit of bank loan
银行担保/銀行擔保,銀行保證函　bank guarantee
银行担保书/銀行擔保書　banker letter of guarantee
银行电汇/銀行電匯　bank telegraphic transfer
[银行]电汇卖出价/電匯賣價　selling rate of telegraphic transfer
银行对账单/銀行對賬單　bank statement
银行管制/銀行管理條例　bank regulation
银行光票/銀行光票　banker clean bill
银行汇款/銀行匯款　bank remittance
银行汇票/銀行匯票,銀行券　bank draft, bank bill
银行混业经营制度/兼營銀行制度　mixed banking system
银行即期汇票/銀行即期匯票　bank demand draft, bank demand draft
银行即期支付/銀行見票即付　bank demand
[银行]挤兑/[銀行]擠兑　bank run
银行假日/銀行停付日　bank holiday
银行间浮存/銀行間浮存,銀行間浮動　inter-bank float
银行间交易/銀行間交易　inter-bank trading
银行间利率/銀行間利率　inter-bank rate
银行兼并/銀行兼并,銀行購并,銀行合并　banking acquisition, bank merger
银行检查/銀行金融檢查　bank examination
银行见票/銀行見票即付　bank demand
银行结汇/銀行結匯　bank's exchange settlement
[银行开立信用证所需]保证金/[銀行開立信用狀所需]保證金　margin money
银行可承兑资产/銀行可承兑資產,銀行可接受資產　bankable asset
银行可担保项目/銀行可擔保項目　bankable project
银行可接受资产/銀行可接受資產,銀行可承兑資產　bankable asset
银行控股公司/銀行控股公司　bank holding company
银行联机制度/銀行連線系統　on line banking system
银行卖出汇率/銀行賣出匯率　bank selling rate
银行批发和零售业务/銀行批發和零售業務　bank retail and wholesale
银行批发业务/批發銀行業務　wholesale banking
银行票据/銀行票據　bank paper
银行券/銀行鈔票　bank note
银行融通/銀行資金融通　bank accommodation

银行特许/銀行特許　bank charter
银行体系/銀行體系　banking system
银行贴现/銀行貼現　bank discount, banker discount
银行贴现率/銀行貼現率,銀行利率　bank discount rate, bank rate
银行通货/銀行通貨　bank currency
银行同业拆放贷款/銀行同業拆放貸款　inter-bank loan
银行同业拆借/銀行同業拆借　inter-bank lending
银行同业市场/銀行同業市場　inter-bank market
银行同业外汇交易/銀行同業外匯交易　inter-bank exchange dealing
银行团/銀行團　syndicate bank
银行信贷/銀行信貸,銀行信用狀　bank credit, banker's credit
银行信贷规则/銀行信貸規則　rule of bank credit
银行信贷资金/銀行信貸資金　bank credit capital
银行信托公司/銀行信託公司　banker trust company
银行信用/銀行信用　bank credit
银行信用卡/銀行信用卡　bank credit card
银行信用证/銀行信用狀　banker's letter of credit
银行学派/銀行學派　banking school
银行衍生存款理论/銀行衍生存款理論　derivative deposit theory of banking
银行业金融机构/銀行業金融機構　banking and financial institution
银行业竞争性/銀行業競爭　competitiveness in banking
银行业中非价格竞争/銀行業中非價格競爭　non-price competition in banking
[银行账号上]闲置余额/[銀行賬號上]閒置餘額　idle balance
银行支票/銀行支票,銀行本票　bank cheque
银行转账业务/銀行轉賬,銀行通匯　bank transfer
银行准备金/銀行準備金　bank reserves
银行资本/銀行資本,銀行資金　bank capital
银行资产业务/[銀行]資產業務　asset business of bank, asset business
银行资金头寸/銀行資金頭寸,銀行資金部位　fund position of bank
银汇兑/銀匯兌　silver exchange
银块本位制/銀塊本位制　silver bullion standard
银块市场/銀塊市場　silver bullion market
银团贷款/銀行團聯合貸款　syndicate loan
银团信贷/聯合信貸　syndicate credit
银盐胶片/銀鹽軟片　silverhalide film
银盐胶片档案/銀鹽膠片檔案　silver film archive
淫秽出版物/淫穢出版物　pornographic publication
淫秽物品/猥褻物品,淫穢性資料　obscene material
淫秽品法/淫穢品法　obscenity law
引渡/引渡　extradition
引进外资/引進外資　importation of foreign capital, introduction of foreign investment
引力模型/重力模型　gravity model
引题/引題　primer title
引文/引文　citation
引文动机/引用動機　citation motivation
引文分析/引用[文獻]分析　citation analysis
引文矩阵/引文矩陣　citing matrix
引文数据库/引文數據庫　citation database
引文索引/引文索引　citation index
引文索引语言/引文索引語言　citation index language
引文网络/引文網路　citation network
引叙用语/引敘用語　quoting term
引用/引用,引證　quote, citing
引用标准/引用標準　reference to standard
引用次序/圖書類目引用次序　citation order
引用认同/引用認同　citation identity
引用书目/引用書目　cited reference
引语词典/引文詞典　dictionary of quotations
引证参考书目/引證參考書目　supporting bibliography
引证文献/引用[參考]文獻　citing reference
引证罪状/引證罪狀　cite facts about a crime
引致投资/勸誘投資,誘發性投資　induced investment
隐蔽财产/隱蔽財產,賬外財產　hidden property
隐蔽成本/隱蔽成本　hidden cost
隐蔽的贸易壁垒/隱蔽的貿易壁壘,變相的貿易壁壘　covert trade barrier
隐蔽方法/隱藏研究　covert method
隐蔽工程/隱蔽工程　hidden project
隐蔽倾销/隱蔽傾銷,秘密傾銷　hidden dumping
隐蔽失业/隱藏性失業　disguised unemployment, hidden unemployment
隐蔽税/隱蔽稅　hidden tax
隐蔽信息/隱藏資訊　hidden information
隐蔽行为/隱藏行動　hidden action
隐藏单元/隱藏單元　hidden unit
隐藏确定性过程/隱藏確定性過程　crypto-deterministic process
隐藏式广告/置入行銷,產品置入　product placement
隐分层/隱分層　implicit stratification
隐含波动率/隱含波動率　implied volatility

隐含的协方差矩阵/共變數矩陣　implied covariance matrix
隐含期权/隱含期權　embedded option
隐含契约/隱含契約,默認契約　implied contract
隐名代理/隱名代理　undisclosed agency
隐名合伙/隱名合夥　dormant partnership
隐匿资产/隱匿資產　hidden asset
隐权数/隱含權數　implicit weight
隐私/隱私　privacy
隐私权/隱私[權]　privacy, right of privacy
隐性/隱性　invisibility
隐性补贴/價格暗補　hidden subsidy
隐性不充分就业/隱性低度就業　invisible underemployment
隐性成本/內含成本,隱含成本　implicit cost, shadow cost
隐性创新效益/隱性創新效益　tacit innovation benefit
隐性关税/隱藏性關稅　implicit tariff
隐性合谋/隱藏性勾結　implicit collusion
隐性合约/隱含性契約　implicit contract
隐性就业/隱藏性就業　unregistered employment
隐性就业合同/雇用默契　implicit employment contract
隐性薪酬/隱含工資　implicit wage
隐性知识/內隱知識,默會知識　tacit knowledge
隐性知识管理/隱性知識管理　implicit knowledge management, tacit knowledge management
隐性周期[性]/潛伏週期　hidden periodicity
隐性主题/隱性主題　implicit subject
印版/印版　printing plate, printing form
印版滚筒/版圓筒　plate cylinder
印版回弹/印版回彈　snap-off
印版制作/印版製作　forme making
印次/印次　impression
印度法系/印度法系　Hindu law system
印发机关和印发日期/印發機關和印發日期　issue government institution and issue date
印后/印後　postpress
印后加工设备/印後加工設備　postpress equipment
印花/印花　stamped paper
印花税/印花稅　stamp duty, stamp tax
印票/印花　stamped paper
印前/印前處理　prepress
印前设备/印前設備　prepress equipment
印数/印數　copy number, printing number
印刷/印刷　printing
印刷本目录/印刷本目錄　printed catalog
印刷材料/印刷材料　printed material
印刷厂/印刷廠　printing house
印刷方式/印刷方式　printing process method
印刷工程/印刷工程　printing engineering
印刷机/印刷機　printing machine
印刷技术/自動化圖形技術　graphic technology
印刷媒介/印刷媒體　print media
印刷媒体/印刷媒體　print media
印刷面/印刷面　printing side
印刷品档案/印刷品檔案　printed archives
印刷缺陷/印刷缺陷　printing trouble
印刷生产格式/印刷生產格式　print production format, PPF
印刷适性/印刷適性　printability
印刷速度/印刷速度　printing speed
印刷台/印刷檯　printing table
印刷型信息[源]/印刷型資訊[源]　printed information source
印刷压力/印刷壓力　printing pressure
印刷油墨/印刷油墨　printing ink
印刷原版/印刷原版　printing original plate
印刷原稿/印刷原稿　printing original
印刷原色/印刷原色　process color
印刷原色油墨/印刷原色油墨　process color ink
印刷乐谱/印刷樂譜　printed music publication
印刷者/印刷者　printer
印刷专色/印刷專色　special color
印象管理/印象管理　impression management
印象形成/印象形成　impression formation
印象主义/印象主義　impressionism
印张/印張　printing sheet, printing signature, sheet
印章/印章　seal
印章考订/印章考訂　seal criticism
印章学/印章學　sigillography
应得到补偿投资/應得到補償投資　investment worthy of compensation
应得支持/該當性　deservedness
应付本币外汇/應付本國貨幣外匯　home currency bill payable
应付承兑票据/應付承兑票據　acceptance payable
应付贷款/應付貸款　loan payable
应付电汇/應付電匯　telegraphic transfer payable
应付股利/應付股利　dividend payable
应付合伙人票据/應付合夥人票據　partner's note payable
应付金额/應付金額,應支出金額　amount payable
应付款凭单/應付賬款憑單　warrant payable
应付利息/應付利息　interest payable

应付贸易账款/應付貿易賬款　trade account payable
应付票据/應付票據　bill payable, note payable
应付凭单/應付傳票　voucher payable
应付税款/應付稅款　tax due, tax payable
应付外币汇票/應付外幣匯票　foreign currency bill payable
应付外国汇票/應付外國匯票　foreign bill payable
应付银行款/應付銀行款項　due to bank
应付债券/應付債券,應付公司債　bond payable
应付债券利息/應付債券利息　bond interest payable
应付[债券]息票/應付[債券]息票　coupon payable
应付账款/應付賬款　account payable
应付账款清单/應付賬款清單　statement from creditor
应付账款审计/應付賬款審計　audit of account payable
应付账款周转率/應付賬款週轉率　payables turnover ratio
应付账款周转天数/應付賬款週轉天數　days payables outstanding
应付职工薪酬/應付員工福利,應付員工給付　employee benefits payable
应付租金/應付租金　rent payable
应计项目/應計數　accrual
应计异象/應計異象　accrual anomaly
应纳税商品进口报单/應納稅商品進口報單　entry for dutiable goods
应纳税所得额/課稅所得　taxable income
应纳税暂时性差异/應納稅暫時性差異　taxable temporary difference
应收本币外汇/應收本國貨幣外匯　home currency bill receivable
应收承兑票据/應收承兑票據　acceptance receivable
应收出口汇票/應收出口匯票　export bill receivable
应收贷款/應收貸款　loan receivable
应收抵押票据/應收抵押票據　mortgage note receivable
应收电汇/應收電匯　telegraphic transfer receivable
应收股利/應收股利　dividend receivable
应收金额/應收[入]金額　amount receivable
应收利息/應收利息　interest receivable
应收贸易账款/應收貿易賬款　trade account receivable
应收票据/應收票據　bill receivable, note receivable
应收融资/應收融資　receivable from financing
应收外币汇票/應收外幣匯票　foreign currency bill receivable
应收外币外汇/應收外幣外匯　foreign exchange receivable in foreign currency
应收外国汇票/應收外國匯票　foreign bill receivable
应收银行本票款/應收銀行本票款　promissory bank note receivable
应收债券利息/應收債券利息　bond interest receivable
应收账款/應收賬款　account receivable
应收账款筹资/應收籌資賬款　account receivable financing
应收账款担保贷款/應收賬款擔保貸款　loan secured by account receivable
应收账款抵押/應收賬款質押　pledging of receivable
应收账款审计/應收賬款審計　audit of account receivable
应收账款周转率/應收賬款週轉率　receivables turnover ratio
应收账款周转天数/應收賬款週轉天數,銷貨懸賬天數　days sales outstanding
应收租费/應收租金　rent receivable
应受国际保护人员/應受國際保護人員　internationally protected person
应税货物/應稅貨物　dutiable goods
应索供应/應索供應　demanding supply
应一次总付/應一次付清　payable in lump sum
应以法币支付/應以法幣支付　payable in legal tender
应以黄金支付/應以黃金支付　payable in gold
应以期票支付/應以期票支付　payable in note
应优先偿还的债务/應優先償還的債務　privileged debt
应征关税的进口货/應稅進口貨　dutiable imported goods
英镑/英鎊　sterling
英镑存款单/英鎊存款單　sterling certificate of deposit
英镑公债/英鎊公債　sterling bond
英镑汇兑/英鎊匯兑　sterling exchange
英镑汇兑本位制/英鎊匯兑本位制　sterling exchange standard system
英镑汇率/英鎊匯率　sterling exchange rate
英镑汇票/英鎊匯票　sterling bill, sterling draft
英镑集团/英鎊集團　sterling bloc
英镑结存/英鎊結存　sterling balance
英镑利率/英鎊利率　sterling interest rate
英镑-美元交叉汇率/英鎊-美元交叉匯率　sterling-dollar cross rate
英镑平价/英鎊平價　sterling parity
英镑区/英鎊區　sterling area

英镑区国家/英鎊區國家　zone sterling
英镑融资/英鎊融資　sterling financing
英镑投资者/英鎊投資者　sterling investor
英镑危机/英鎊危機　sterling crisis
英镑信用证/英鎊信用狀　sterling letter of credit
英镑远期价格/英鎊遠期價格　sterling forward price
英镑证券/英鎊證券　sterling security
英镑证券市场/英鎊證券市場　security sterling market
英式拍卖/英式[最高價]拍賣　English auction, English and first-price auction
英雄崇拜/英雄崇拜　hero worship
婴儿潮/嬰兒潮,生育高峰　baby boom
婴儿潮一代/嬰兒潮一代　baby-boom generation, baby boomer
婴儿室/嬰兒室　baby room
婴儿死亡率/嬰兒死亡率　infant mortality rate
盈亏点分析/損益平衡點分析　break-even point analysis
盈亏分析图/收支平衡圖　break-even chart
盈亏平衡点/損益平衡點　break-even point
盈亏平衡定价/損益平衡訂價法　break-even pricing
盈亏平衡分析/損益平衡分析　break-even analysis
盈亏平衡销售水平/盈虧平衡銷售水準　break-even sales level
盈亏图/盈虧圖　excess and deficit chart
盈利标/盈利標　profit tender
盈利潜力/盈利潛力　earning potential
盈利性/獲利力　profitability
盈利性顾客/盈利性顧客　profitable customer
盈利指数/獲利力指標　profitability index, PI
盈利指数法/盈利指數法　profitability index method
盈利资产/收益性資產　earning asset
盈余持续性/盈餘持續性　earning persistence
盈余反应系数/盈餘反應係數　earning response coefficient, ERC
盈余分析表/盈餘分析表　statement of surplus analysis
盈余公积/盈餘準備,剩餘準備　surplus reserve
盈余管理/盈餘管理　earnings management
盈余品质/盈餘品質　earnings quality
营利/營利　profit-making, profit-seeking
营利冲动/貪求衝動　acquisitive impulse
营利法人/營利法人　profit-making corporation
营利性医院/營利醫院　for-profit hospital
营利组织/營利組織　for-profit organization
营销策略/外銷策略　marketing game
营销策略开发/行銷策略開發　marketing strategy development
营销成本/行銷成本　marketing cost
营销分类/行銷分類　sale classification
营销服务机构/行銷服務機構　marketing service agency
营销管理/行銷管理　marketing management
营销环境/行銷環境　marketing environment
营销机会/行銷機會　marketing opportunity
营销计划/行銷計劃　marketing plan
营销计量/行銷度量　marketing metrics
营销近视症/行銷近視病　marketing myopia
营销控制/行銷控制　marketing control
营销情报/行銷偵查　marketing intelligence
营销审计/行銷稽核　marketing audit
营销实施/行銷實施　marketing implementation
营销数据仓库/行銷資料倉儲　marketing data warehouse
营销数据挖掘/行銷資料採擷　marketing data mining
营销投资回报/行銷投資報酬　marketing return on investment, ROI
营销网站/行銷網站　marketing website
营销物流/運銷　marketing logistics
营销信息系统/行銷情報系統　marketing information system
营销研究/行銷研究　marketing research
营销样本/行銷樣本　marketing sample
营销战略/行銷策略　marketing strategy
营销中介/行銷中間機構　marketing intermediary
营销组合/行銷組合　marketing mix
营养统计/營養統計　nutrition statistics
营业/營業　business-running
营业保险/營業保險　proprietary insurance
营业表/營業報告書　statement of business operation
营业成本/營業成本　operating cost
营业利润/營業利潤　business profit
营业收入/營業收入　operating revenue
营业收益表/營業收益表　statement of operating earning
营业税/營業稅　business tax
营业税法/營業稅法　act of business tax
营业税金及附加/主營業務稅金及附加　tax and associate charge
营业外收入/營業外收入　non-operating income
营业外支出/營業外費用,營業外費損　non-operating expense
营业性发行/營業性發行　business distribution
营运能力/營運能力　operating ability

营运现金流/營運現金流量　operating cash flow
营运用基金/營運基金　working capital fund
营运资本/營運資金,流動資金　working capital, circulating estate
营运资金表/營運資金表　statement of working capital
赢者诅咒/贏家詛咒　winner curse
赢者诅咒假说/贏家詛咒假說　winner curse hypothesis
影抄/影抄　duplicating
影碟/影碟　video disc
影片档案/影片檔案,电影资料,電影檔案　film file
影片档案馆/影片檔案館　film archive
影片资料/電影片　motion picture, movie-related material
影宋抄本/影宋抄本　traced copies of Song edition
影响函数/影響函數　influence function
影响评价/影響評量,影響評估　impact assessment
影响曲线/影響曲線　influence curve
影响图/影響圖　influence diagram
影响因子/影響因子,影響因數　impact factor
影响者/影響者　influencer
影像/影像　image
影像传媒/影像傳媒　image media
影像分析/影像分析　photograph analysis
影像区/影像區　image area
影像阅读/視訊閱讀　video reading
影印/影印　photocopy
影印版/影印版　pirated edition
影印本/影印本　photocopy, photo lithographic edition
影子浮动汇率/影子浮動匯率　shadow floating exchange rate
影子公开市场委员会/影子公開市場委員會　shadow open market committee
影子汇率/影子匯率　shadow exchange rate
影子价格/影子價格　shadow price
影子经济/影子經濟　shadow economy
影子要素价格/影子要素價格　shadow factor price
应变关税/應變關稅　contingent duty
应答率/回覆率　response rate
应急保障/應急保障　emergency support
应急处理/突發事件應對　emergency handling
应急储备/應急儲備　contingency reserve
应急管理中的属地管理/應急管理中的屬地管理　jurisdiction-based emergency management
应急基金/應急基金　emergency fund
应急计划/應急計劃,緊急計劃　emergency plan

应急情报研究/應急情報分析　emergency intelligence analysis
应急预案/應急預案　emergency preplan
应力分布/應力分布　stress distribution
应试教育/應試教育　examination-oriented education
应用本体/應用本體　application ontology
应用程序/應用程式,應用軟體　application
应用档案学/應用檔案學　applied archival science, study of archival application
应用科学/應用科學　applied science
应用目录学/應用目錄學　applied bibliography
应用情报学/應用資訊科學　applied information science
应用社会学/應用社會學　applied sociology
应用统计学/應用統計學　applied statistics
应用图书馆学/應用圖書館學　applied librarianship
应用研究/應用研究　application research
硬币/硬幣　coin
硬币价格流通机制/硬幣價格流通機制　specie flow price mechanism
硬币流入/硬幣流入　inflow of specie
硬币流通机制/硬幣流通機制　specie flow mechanism
硬币流通价格调整机制/硬幣流通價格調整機制　specie flow price adjustment mechanism
硬币输出/硬幣輸出　specie export
硬币输入/硬幣輸入　specie import
硬币输送保险/硬幣運輸保險　specie insurance
硬币外流/硬幣外流　outflow of specie
硬币准备/硬幣準備　specie reserve
硬贷款/強勢貨幣貸款　hard loan
硬技术/硬技術　hard technology
硬件/硬體　hardware
硬拷贝/硬拷貝　hard copy
硬拷贝打样系统/硬拷貝打樣系統　hard copy proofing system
硬科学/硬科學　hard science
硬口/光環　halo
硬通货/高利率,銀根緊俏,硬幣　hard money
硬通货地区/硬通貨地區,強勢貨幣地區　hard currency area
硬新闻/硬性新聞　hard news
硬信息/硬訊息,可驗證訊息　hard information
硬行套利/硬行套利　hard arbitrage
硬质封面/硬質封面　hardbound hard cover
拥堵成本/擁擠成本　congestion cost
拥挤性公共物品/擁擠性公共財　congestible public goods

拥挤性物品/擁擠財　congested goods
永佃权/永佃權　emphyteusis
永恒法/永恆法　eternal law
永久功能/永久功能　all-the-time function
永久使用权/永久使用權　permanent access right
永久投资/永久投資　permanent investment
永久性归还/永久性歸還　permanent withdrawal
永久性融资/永久性融資　permanent financing
永久性授权/永久性授權　permanent authorization
永久性统一资源定位器/持久型環球資源定位器　persistent URL, PURL
永久性协定/永久性協議　permanent agreement
永久性账户/永久性賬戶,實賬戶　permanent account
永久性资本/永久性資本　permanent capital
永久性资产/永久性資産　permanent asset
永久债务/永久性債務　permanent debt
永久中立国/永久中立國　permanent neutral country
永续保险/永續保險　perpetual insurance
永续年金/永續年金　perpetuity, perpetual annuity
永续盘存/永續盤存　perpetual inventory
永续盘存制/永續盤存制　perpetual inventory system
涌现/苗生,湧生,突現　emergence
用户/用戶,客戶　user, client
用户帮助/用戶幫助　user aid
用户保证原则/用戶保證原則　principle of user warrant
用户创新/用戶創新　user innovation
用户创新工具箱/用戶創新工具箱　user toolkit of innovation
用户代理/用戶代理　user proxy
用户导向/使用者導向　user oriented
用户调查/使用者調查　user survey
用户反馈/用戶反饋　user feedback
用户分析/使用者分析　user analysis
用户管理/使用者管理　user management
用户互动/使用者交互作用　user interaction
用户教育/利用指導　user education
用户接口/使用者介面　user interface
用户满意度/用戶滿意度　user satisfaction
用户培训/使用者訓練　user training
用户偏好/用戶偏愛性,用戶優先權　user preference
用户期望/用戶期望　user expectation
用户情报行为/資訊使用者行爲　information user behavior
用户群/用戶群　user community, user group, patron community
用户身份识别码/使用者識別碼　user ID, patron ID
用户生成内容/使用者供應內容,使用者自創內容　user-generated content, user-created content, consumer generated media
用户特征/使用者特徵　user characteristics
用户体验/使用者經歷　user experience
用户相关性/相關資料　user relevance
用户信息行为/用戶資訊行爲　user information behavior
用户兴趣/用戶興趣　user interest
用户需求/使用者需求　user demand, user need
用户需求委托单/使用者興趣檔　user profile
用户研究/用戶研究　user study
用户友好/使用者親和性,用戶滿意介面　user-friendly
用户知情权/使用者知情權,使用者知的權利　user's right to know
用户指南/使用者指南　user guide
用户至上/用戶至上　user first
用脚投票/用腳投票　voting by feet
用尽当地救济/用盡當地救濟　exhaustion of local remedy
用例图/用例圖　use case diagram
用人单位/用人單位　employment unit
用益物权/用益物權　usufructuary right
用印/用印　affix official seal to document, seal a document
用中学/用中學　learning by using
佣金/[代理]佣金,代理手續費　agency commission, commission
佣金预支计划/生活費加佣金計劃　commission-plusdraw plan
优等汇票/優等匯票,初級票據　prime bill
优等商业票据/優等商業票據　prime commercial paper
优等信贷/優等信貸,主信用狀　prime credit
优等银行承兑/優等銀行承兑　prime banker acceptance
优抚安置/優撫安置　veteran benefit and placement
优化劳动组合/最適勞動組合　optimizing labor combination
优惠贷款/優惠貸款　concessional loan
优惠贷款净额/優惠貸款淨額　net concessional loan
优惠贷款利率/優惠貸款利率　prime interest
优惠待遇/優惠待遇　favourable treatment, preferential treatment
优惠放款利率/優惠放款利率　prime lending rate
优惠关税/優惠關税,特惠關税　beneficial tariff,

preferential tariff, preferential duty
优惠国/優惠國　favoured nation
优惠国待遇/優惠國待遇　favoured nation status
优惠价格/優惠價格　favourable price
优惠价零售店/平價零售商　off-price retailer
优惠减税额/優惠減稅額　preferential tariff cut
优惠利率/優惠利率　favorable interest rate
优惠率/優惠費率　rate of concession
优惠贸易条件/優惠貿易條件　favorable terms of trade
优惠票据/優惠票據,資金融通票據　preferential bill
优惠券/點券,折價券　coupon
优惠券促销/點券推廣　coupon promotion
优惠税/獎勵租稅　favorable tax
优惠税率/優惠[税]率　preferential rate
优惠税收待遇/優惠租稅待遇　favorable tax treatment
优惠条件/優惠條件,減讓性條件　preferential terms, concessional term, favorable condition
优良股票/優良股票　high grade stock
优批/良批　good lot
优生学/優生學　eugenics
优士丁尼法典/優士丁尼法典　Code Justinianius
优[势]比/勝算比,優劣比　odds ratio
优势规则/優勢規則　dominant rule
优势集/優勢集　dominant set
优势视角/優勢觀點　strength perspective
优势证据/證據確鑿　preponderance-of-the-evidence
优先出口/優先出口　preferential export
优先抵押/優先抵押　senior mortgage
优先购买权/優先購買權　priority of purchase
优先股发行/優先股發行　senior issue
优先规则/優先法則　priority rule
优先汇率/優先匯率　preferred rate
优先级控制/優先順序控制　priority control
优先检验/優先順序檢定　precedence test
优先接收区域/偏好允收域　zone of preference for acceptance
优先进口/優先進口　preferential import
优先拒绝区域/偏好棄却域　zone of preference for rejection
优先留置权/優先留置權　prior lien, senior lien
优先排队/優先排隊　priority queueing
优先权/優先權　right of priority, priority
优先权计划/優先規劃　priority planning
优先权益/優先權益　senior interest
优先认股权/優先認股權　preemptive right
优先索赔权/優先索賠權　prior claim

优先通货/優先通貨　preferred currency
优先投资项目/優先投資專案　high priority investment project
优先外币/優先外幣　preferred foreign currency
优先外币制度/優先外幣制度　preferred foreign currency system
优先债权/優先債權　prior charge
优先债权人/優先債權人　preferential creditor
优先债券/優先債券　bond preference, bond senior, preference bond
优先资本/優先資本,優先股本　capital preferred, preference capital
优心态管理/優心態管理　eupsychian management
优秀主厨战略/優秀主廚戰略　great chef strategy
优序融资理论/優序融資理論　pecking order theory
优选法/優選法　optimum seeking method
尤登方/Youden 方陣　Youden square
尤登矩形/Youden 矩形　Youden rectangle
尤登设计/Youden 設計　Youden design
尤尔方程/Yule 方程式　Yule equation
尤尔分布/Yule 分布,Yule 分配　Yule distribution
尤尔过程/Yule 過程　Yule process
尤尔双曲分布/Yule 雙曲分布,Yule 雙曲分配　Yule hyperbolic distribution
尤尔-沃克方程/Yule-Walker 方程式,于爾-華克方程式　Yule-Walker equation
尤尔-沃克估计量/Yule-Walker 估計式,于爾-華克估計式　Yule-Walker estimator
尤尔制造业哲学/尤爾製造業哲學　manufacture system of Ure
尤利西法典/尤利西法典　Codex Eurici
由常设仲裁机构处理仲裁/由常設仲裁機構處理仲裁　institutional arbitration
由于质量低劣索赔/對品質低劣索賠　claim for inferior quality
邮递调查/郵遞調查　mail survey
邮递拍卖/郵遞拍賣　mail auction
邮递问卷抽样/郵遞問卷抽樣　mail questionnaire sampling
邮发/郵發　postal distribution
邮发报刊/郵發報刊　post-distributed newspaper and periodical
邮发合一/郵發合一　mail-distribution unite, integration of post and distribution
邮购/郵購　mail order, purchase by mail
邮购[订单]/郵購[訂單]　mail order
邮购批发商/郵購批發商　mail-order wholesaler
邮购书店/郵購書店　mail-order bookstore

邮购销售/郵購銷售　mail-order sale
邮购信贷/郵購信貸　mail credit
邮寄日期利息/郵寄日期利息　mail day interest
邮寄问卷/郵寄問卷　mail questionnaire
邮件管理/郵件管理　mail management
邮件列表服务/郵寄清單服務　mailing list service
邮件列表广告/郵寄清單廣告　mailing list advertisement
邮件营销/郵件行銷　e-mail marketing
邮件杂志/電子雜志　e-zine
邮局发行/郵局發行　post office distribution
邮局发行网/郵局發行網　post office distribution net
邮政保险/郵政保險　postal insurance
邮政报刊门市部/郵政報刊門市部　sales department of newspaper and periodical
邮政报刊亭/郵政報刊亭　postal kiosk
邮政储金汇业局/郵政儲金制度　postal savings system
邮政贷款/郵政貸款　mail loan
邮政汇款/郵政匯款,郵局匯款　postal remittance, mail remittance
邮政汇票/郵政匯票　postal money order
邮政统计/郵政統計　postal service statistics
邮政银行/郵政銀行　postal bank
邮政转账存款/郵政劃撥存款　postal transfer deposit
邮政转账户头/郵政劃撥賬戶　postal transfer account
犹太政令集/猶太政令集　Capitula de Judaeis
犹豫-抉择模式/猶豫-抉擇模式　hesitation-choose model
油墨叠印/油墨疊印　ink trapping
油墨乳化/油墨乳化　ink emulsification
油墨消耗量/油墨消耗量　ink consumption
游程/[連]串　run
游程长度/連串長度　run length, length of run
游程长度分布/連串長度分布　distribution of run length
游程检验/連串檢定　run test
游程数/串數　number of run
游钓/遊憩或娛樂漁業　sport fishing
游猎民族/游獵民族　hunting people
游牧部落/游群,斡爾朵　horde
游牧民/游牧民　nomad
游士社会/遊士社會　society accomodating roaming scholar and recluse
游戏出版备案/遊戲出版備案　record system for online game publishing
游戏广告/遊戲廣告　game advertisement
游戏私服/遊戲私服　game private server
游戏外挂/遊戲外掛　cheating in online game
游戏玩家/競賽參加者　game player
游戏下载/遊戲下載　game download
游戏引擎/遊戲引擎　game engine
游戏运营商/遊戲運營商　game operator
游行自由/遊行自由　freedom of procession
游资/游資,閒置資金　dormant capital
游资移动/游資移動　hot money movement
友好解决/友好解決,和解　amicable settlement
友善访问员/友善訪問員　friendly interviewer
有版印刷/有版印刷　forme-based printing
有保证收益债券/有保證收益債券　guaranteed income bond
有偿借阅资料/有償借閱資料　leased material
有偿新闻/有償新聞　checkbook journalism
有偿信息服务/有償信息服務　information charge service
有担保贷款/有擔保貸款　guaranteed loan
有担保抵押债务/有擔保抵押債務　collateralized mortgage obligation
有担保公司债券信托/有擔保公司債券信託　mortgage debenture trust
有担保票据/有擔保票據　secured bill
有担保期票/有擔保期票　secured note
有担保信贷/有擔保信貸　guaranteed credit
有担保信用证/有擔保信用狀　secured letter of credit
有担保债权/有擔保債權　secured claim
有担保债券/有擔保債券　secured debenture, bond secured
有担保债务/有擔保債務　secured debt
有担护看跌期权/保護性賣權　protective put
有担值看涨期权/掩護性買權　covered call
有抵押往来账透支/有抵押往來賬透支　overdraft on current account secured
有第三人效力处理/有第三人效力處理　administrative decision with effect on a third party
有电汇条款信用证/有電匯條款信用狀　letter of credit with telegraphic transfer reimbursement clause
有毒垃圾/毒性廢棄物　toxic waste
有毒武器禁用/有毒武器禁用　prohibition on the use of poisonous weapon
有毒物质/毒性物質　toxic substance
有毒物质控制法/毒性物質管制法　toxic substances control act

有毒有害物质管理法/有毒有害物質管理法　law on management of poisonous and harmful material
有害变量/有害變數　detrimental variable
有害废物管理政策/有害廢棄物管制政策　hazardous waste control policy
有机垃圾/有機廢棄物　organic waste
有机式组织/有機式組織　organic organization
有机职能论/有機職能論　organic function theory
[有价]票据持有人/票據持有人　holder for value
有价证券/有價證券　valuable document, marketable securities
有价证券储蓄/有價證券儲蓄　saving by investing in securities
有价证券担保贷款/有價證券擔保貸款　loan secured by stock and bond
有价证券估价/有價證券估價　valuation of securities
有价证券管理信托/有價證券管理信託　securities administration trust
有价证券信托/有價證券信託　securities trust
有价证券账户/有價證券賬戶　securities account
有价证券准备金/有價證券準備金　securities reserve
有界损失函数/有界損失函數　bounded loss function
有界完备充分统计量/有界完備統計量　boundly complete sufficient statistic
有界完备性/有界完全性　bounded completeness
有理批/合理批　rational lot
有理趋势/合理趨勢　rational trend
有理样本/合理樣本　rational sample
有利产品/有利產品　salutary product
有连锁反应的价格/有連鎖反應的價格,觸發價格　trigger price
有名合同/有名合同　named contract
有扭曲作用的税收/具扭曲性的課稅　distortionary tax
有偏/有偏　biased
有偏估计[量]/有偏估計[量]　biased estimator
有偏检验/有偏檢定　biased test
有偏[离]差/有偏離差　biased deviation
有偏误差/有偏誤差　biased error
有偏样本/有偏樣本　biased sample
有期徒刑/有期徒刑　fixed-term imprisonment
有权代理/有權代理　authorized agency
有权先售的发盘/有權先售的報價　offer subject to prior sale
有权占有/有權占有　authorized possession
有缺陷单元/有缺陷單位　spotty unit
有伸缩性的加速数模型/弹性加速模型　flexible accelerator model
有神论/有神論　theism
有声报刊/有聲報刊　talking newspaper, audio newspaper
有声[图]书/有聲圖書　talking book, audiobook, book-on-tape
有损检验/破壞性檢驗　destructive inspection
有损压缩/有損壓縮　lossy compression
有弹性需求/需求具彈性　elastic demand
有体物/有體物　corporeal thing
有条件背书/附條件背書　qualified endorsement, conditional endorsement
有条件发货通知/附條件託運單　conditional shipping order
有条件合同转让/有條件轉讓　conditional assignment
有条件汇票/有條件匯票　draft payable with terms
有条件交货/附條件交貨　conditional delivery
有条件免税进口/附條件免稅進口　conditional duty-free importation
有条件认购/附條件認購　conditional subscription
有条件提单/附條件提單　conditional bill of lading
有条件提款权/附條件提款權　conditional drawing right
有条件支付/有條件支付　conditional payment
有条件转让/附條件轉讓　conditional transfer
有无比较/有無對比法　with and without comparison
有闲阶级/有閒階級　leisure class
σ有限/σ有限　σ-finite
有限编目/有限編目　limited cataloging
有限差分法/有限差分法　finite difference method
有限产能排程/有限順排計劃　finite forward scheduling
有限乘子/有限乘子　finite multiplier
有限兑换/有限兑换　limited convertibility
有限二项抽样方案/有限二項抽樣計劃　finite binomial sampling plan
有限反正弦分布/有限反正弦分布,有限反正弦分配　finite arc-sine distribution
有限分布滞后/有限的分配落差　finite distributed lags
有限服务批发商/有限服務批發商　limited-service wholesaler
有限浮动汇率/有限浮動匯率　limited floating rate
有限浮动汇率制/有限浮動匯率制　limited floating rate system
有限负荷/有限負荷　finite loading
有限概率空间/有限機率空間　finite probability

space
有限公司/有限公司　limited company
有限过程/有限過程　finite process
有限合法清偿/有限法幣　limited legal tender
有限合伙/有限合夥　limited partnership
有限合伙企业/有限合夥企業　limited partnership enterprise
有限合伙人/有限合夥人　limited partner
有限豁免主义/有限豁免主義　restrictive immunity doctrine
有限截断检索/有限截斷檢索　limited truncation retrieval
有限竞争性招标/有限競爭性招標　limited competitive bidding
有限理性/有限理性　bounded rationality
有限理性决策模型/有限理性決策模型,有限理性决策模式　bounded rationality decision model
有限利润/有限利潤　limited profit
有限马尔可夫链/有限馬可夫鏈　finite Markov chain
有限赔偿保险单/有限責任保單　limited policy
有限期的特许/有限期的特許　limited franchise
有限让与/有限讓與　limited concession
有限委托销售/有限委託銷售　limited consignment
有限效果[模式]论/有限效果[模式]理論　limited effect model, limited-effect theory
有限信息方法/有限訊息法　limite information method
有限信息极大似然估计量/受限訊息最大概似估計量　limited information maximum likelihood estimator
有限责任/有限責任　limited liability
有限责任公司/有限[責任]公司　limited liability company, limited liability corporation
有限责任股东/有限責任股東　limited liability shareholder
有限制进口/限制進口　limit entry
有限制随机化/受制隨機化　restricted randomization
有限追索权/有限追索權　limited recourse
有限追索权融资/有限追索權融資　limited recourse finance
有限追索权项目贷款/有限追索權專案貸款　limited recourse project financing
有限资源/時間、財力的限制　limited resource
有限总体/有限母體　finite population
有限总体修正[系数]/有限母體校正數　finite population correction, FPC
有限总体修正因子/有限母體校正因素　finite population correction factor
有线电视/有線電視　cable television
有线电视节目服务/有線電視節目服務　cable programming service, CPS
有线电视系统/有線電視系統　cable television system
有线广播/有線廣播電視　cable broadcast
有线广播电视管辖权/有線廣播電視管轄權　cable jurisdiction
有线广播电视规范/有線廣播電視規範　cable regulation
有效保护率/有效保護率　effective rate of protection
有效边界/效率前緣　efficient frontier
有效辩护/有效辯護　effective defence
有效成分定价规则/有效成分定價法　efficient component pricing rule
有效重复/有效重複　effective replicate
有效的授权/有效授權　effective delegation
有效等待时间过程/實質等候時間過程　virtual waiting time process
有效动素/有效動素　effective therblig
有效发行/有效發行　effective distribution, valid circulation
有效分辨率/有效解析度　effective resolution
有效缝隙长度/有效縫隙長度　effective gap length
有效工时/有效工時　effective working hour
有效估计/有效估計　efficient estimation
有效估计量/有效估計量　efficient estimator
有效顾客响应系统/有效客戶回應系統　efficient customer response system
有效关税/實際關稅稅率　effective tariff
有效汇率/有效匯率,實質匯率　effective exchange rate, real exchange rate
有效价差/有效價差　effective spread
有效价格/有效價格　effective price
有效检索/專利有效性檢索　validity search
有效竞争/可運作競爭　workable competition
有效票据/有效票據,有效文件　effective instrument
有效日期/有效日期　effective date
有效市场假说/效率市場假說　efficient market hypothesis
有效数字/有效數字　significant figure, significant digit
有效税率/有效稅率　effective tax rate
有效似然估计量/有效概度估計量　efficient likelihood estimator, ELE
有效统计量/有效統計量　efficient statistic
有效投资/有效投資　efficient portfolio

有效位数/有效位數　number of significant digit
有效信贷/有效信貸　effective credit
有效性/有效性　efficiency
有效需求/有效需求　effective demand
有效需求理论/有效需求理論　effective demand theory
有效预测/有效預測　valid prediction
有效资产组合管理/效率投資組合管理　efficient portfolio management
有效自由度/有效自由度　effective degree of freedom
有形出口/有形貿易出口　visible export
有形进口/有形貿易進口　visible import
有形利益/有形效益　tangible benefit
有形贸易/有形貿易　visible trade
有形贸易差额/有形貿易差額　visible balance
有形贸易赤字/有形貿易赤字　visible trade deficit
有形贸易收支差额/有形貿易收支差額　balance of visible trade
有形[贸易]项目/有形[貿易]項目　visible item
有形商品贸易/有形商品貿易　tangible goods trade
有形性/有形的　tangibility
有形之手/有形之手　tangible hand
有形资产/有形資產　tangible asset
有形资源/有形資源　tangible resources
有序备择假设/有序對立假設　ordered alternative hypothesis
有序尺度/順序尺度　ordinal scale
有序分类/有序分類　ordered categorization
有序概率单位模型/排序常態機率模型　ordered probit model
有序概率模型/排序機率模型　ordered probability model
有序观测值/有序觀測值,順序觀測值　ordered observations
有序平稳点过程/順序平穩點過程　orderly stationary point process
有序评定模型/階層羅吉特模型,有序勝算對數模型　ordered logit model
有序数据/順序數據　ordinal data
有序数列/有序數列,順序數列　ordered series
有序随机样本/有序隨機樣本,順序隨機樣本　ordered random sample
有序响应模型/排序性反應模型　ordered response model
有序性原理/有序性原理　order principle
有序总体/順序母體,有序母體　ordered population
有益品/優良財　merit goods
有意错误/有意錯誤　willful error
有因回避/有因迴避　challenge for cause
有因行为/有因行爲　causative juristic act
有约束力发盘/有約束力報價　offer with engagement
有责性/有責性　responsible
有执行力仲裁裁决/仲裁裁決執行　enforceable award
有追溯力保险/可追溯保險　retroactive insurance
有追索权汇票/有追索權匯票　draft with recourse
有追索权信用证/有追索權信用狀　with recourse letter of credit
有组织犯罪/組織性犯罪　organized crime
有组织怀疑/有組織懷疑　organized skepticism
有组织倾销/有組織傾銷　systematic dumping
有罪判决/有罪判決　verdict of guilty
有罪推定/有罪推定　presumption of guilt
有罪证据/有罪證據　accusing evidence, guilty evidence
右侧检验/右端檢定,右尾檢定　right-sided test, right-tailed test
右方截断指数模型/右方截斷指數模型　right-truncated exponential model
右偏/右偏　skewed to the right
右偏态/右偏度　right skewness
幼儿园/幼兒學校,幼稚園,託兒所　kindergarten, infant school, nursery school
幼稚产业/幼稚產業　infant industry
幼稚产业保护/幼稚產業保護　infant industry protection
幼稚产业保护论/幼稚產業保護說　infant industry argument for protection
幼稚产业理论/幼稚工業說　theory of infant industry
诱导性技术变迁/引發科技改變　induced technological change
诱发性出口/誘發性出口　induced export
诱发性进口/誘發性進口　induced import
诱供/誘供　inducement to confession
诱因经济/誘因經濟　inducement economy
诱致性制度变迁/誘導性制度變遷　induced institutional change
迂回生产理论/迂迴式生產　roundabout production
余额/餘額　balance
余额包销/餘額包銷　standby underwriting, standby underwrite
余额包销配股/餘額承銷購股權　right offering with standby underwriting

余额表/餘額表　list of balance
余额平衡/餘額平衡,軋平　square off
余额清单/餘額清單　statement of balance
余额受益人/剩餘受益人,剩餘遺產承受人　remainderman
余函数/餘函數　cofunction
余相关/餘相關　alienation
余相关系数/餘相關係數　coefficient of alienation
余因子/餘因式　cofactor
鱼背运输/舟車聯運　fishyback
鱼骨图分析法/原因及效應　cause and effect, fishbone diagram
鱼鳞图册/魚鱗圖冊　fish-scale inventory
鱼鳞装/魚鱗裝　fish scale binding
鱼尾/魚尾　fishtail, Yuwei
娱记/狗仔隊　paparazzi
娱乐/娛樂　entertainment
娱乐广告/娛樂廣告　advertisement
娱乐统计/娛樂統計　amusement statistics
娱乐新闻/娛樂新聞　entertainment news
娱乐指数/娛樂指數　amusement index
渔业法/與貿易相關漁業法　law on fishery
渔业普查/漁業普查　fishery census
渔业统计/漁業統計　fishery statistics
逾期/逾期　exceed time limit
逾期贷款/逾期貸款　overdue loan
逾期通知单/過期通知單　overdue notice, reminder, recall notice
逾期未分配的股利/逾期未分配的股利　passed dividend
愉悦产品/愉悅產品　pleasing product
舆论/輿論,民意　public opinion
舆论导向/輿論導向　public opinion direction
舆情监测/輿情監測　public opinion monitoring
舆图/輿圖　map, territorial map
舆图档案/輿圖檔案　ancient Chinese map
与版本有关责任说明/與版本有關責任說明　statement of responsibility relating to the edition
与大小成比例概率/依大小成比例機率　probability proportional to size
与供方互利关系/與供應商互利關係　mutually beneficial supplies relationship
与规模成比例的概率/依大小成比例機率　probability proportional to size
与贸易有关投资协议/貿易有關投資措施協定　agreement on trade-related investment measures
与贸易有关知识产权协定/與貿易有關智慧財產權協定　agreement on trade-related aspects of intellectual property rights
与贸易有关知识产权协议/智慧財產權協議　trade related intellectual property system
宇宙飞船经济/太空艙經濟　spaceship economy
宇宙观/宇宙學　value of universe
禹刑/禹刑　Yu Laws
语词索引/要詞索引,重要語彙索引　concordance
语调/語調　verbal intonation
语境分析/前後關係分析法　contextual analysi
语料库/語料庫,資料體,詞料庫　corpus
语言/語言　language
语言符号学/語義符號學　linguistic semiotics
语言复分表/語言複分　language subdivision
语言能力/語言能力　linguistic competence
语言排架法/語言排架法　shelving by language
语言学/語言學　linguistics
语言学转向/語言學轉向,語言轉向　linguistic turn
语义本体/語言本體論　semantic ontology
语义差异量表/語意辨別量表　semantic differential scale
语义出版/語義出版　semantic publishing
语义检索/語義檢索,語意檢索　semantic search, semantic retrieval
语义解释/語義解釋　literal interpretation
语义链接/語意鏈接　semantic linking
语义浓缩/意義濃縮　meaning condensation
语义三连体/語意三連式　semantic triplet
语义网/語意網　semantic web
语义网格/語意網格　semantic grid
语义网络分析/語義網路分析　semantic networks analysis
语义学/語意學　semantics
语音合成/語音合成　voice synthesis
语音旁白/語音旁白　speech narrator
语音识别/語音辨識　voice recognition
语用学/語用學　pragmatics
玉牒/玉牒　imperial genealogy
育龄妇女/育齡婦女　women at childbearing age
育种者权/育種者權　breeder right
狱掾/獄掾　Yuyuan
浴盆型曲线/浴缸型曲線,船型曲線　bathtub curve
浴盆型失效率/浴缸型故障率,船型故障率　bathtub shape failure rate
浴盆型失效曲线/浴缸型故障曲線,船型故障曲線　bathtub failure curve
预案/預案　preplan
预白[噪声]化/預先白訊化　prewhitening
预备中止/預備中止　preparation abandonment

预编目/預編目　pre-cataloging
预编书目/預編書目　pre-bibliography
预测/預測，预报，预估　predict, forecast, forecasting
预测变量/預測變數　predicted variable
预测的标准误差/預測值標準差　standard error of forecast
预测对象/預測對象　forecasting target
预测方法/預測方法　forecasting approach
预测公式/預測公式　forecasting formula
预测估计/預測估計　forecasting estimation
预测函数/預測函數　prediction function
预测精度/預測準確度　forecast accuracy
预测竞争情报/預測競爭情報　predictive competitive intelligence
预测空间/預測空間　predictor space
预测控制/預測控制　forecasting control
预测跨度/預測跨度　forecasting horizon
预测理论/預測理論　forecasting theory
预测密度函数/預測密度函數　predictive density function
预测模式/預測模式　forecasting mode
预测模型/預測模型　forecasting model
预测评价/預測評價　forecasting evaluation
预测情报研究/預報情報分析　forecast intelligence analysis
预测区间/預測區間　prediction interval
预测驱动式生产/預測驅動式生產　forecasting-driven production
预测识别/預測識別　forecasting identification
预测误差/預測誤差　forecasting error, prediction error
预测系统/預測系統　forecasting system
预测限/預測界限　prediction limit
预测效度/預測效度　predictive validity
预测效率指数/預測效率指數　efficiency index of forecasting
预测[性]分析/預測分析　forecasting analysis, predictive analysis
预测性评估/預想式回顧　prospective hindsight
预测研究/預測研究　forecasting research
预测样本/預測樣本　forecasting sample
预测有效性/預測有效性　effectiveness of forecasting
预测支持系统/預測支援系統　forecasting support system
预测值/預測值　predicted value
预测指标/預測指標　forecasting indicator
预测置信度/預測可信度　forecasting confidence
预测准确性/預測精度　forecasting accuracy
预测准则/預測準則　prediction criterion
预测资料/預測資料　forecasting data
预调查/預查　pre-survey
预订查重/預訂查重　duplicate checking, pre-order checking
预订单/預訂單　advance order
预订书价/認購價格　subscription price
预订图书/圖書徵訂　book subscription, subscribe for a book
预订信息/訂閱資訊　subscription information
预定标准/預定標準　predetermined criteria
预定到期日的票据/預定到期日的票據　instrument with fixed maturity date
预定动作时间/預定動作時間　predetermined motion time
预定动作时间标准/預定動作時間標準　predetermined time standard, PTS
预定动作时间系统/預定動作時間系統　predetermined motion time system, PMTS
预定日期付款汇票/指定日期付款匯票　bill payable at definite time
预定日期后若干日付款汇票/出票後若干日付款的匯票　bill payable at fixed period after date
预对/預對　pre-position
预防成本/預防成本　prevention cost
预防措施/預防措施　preventive measure
预防动机/預防性動機　precautionary motive
预防维护/預防維護，预防保养　preventive maintenance
预防行动/預防行動，预防措施　prevention action
预防性保护/預防性保護　preventive preservation
预防性抽样检验/預防性抽樣檢驗　preventive sampling inspection
预防性检验/預防檢驗　preventive inspection
预防性控制/預防性控制　preventive control
预防性维修时间/預防維護時間　preventive maintenance time
预防性支出/預防性支出　precautionary expenditure
预防性自卫/預防性自衛　anticipatory self-defence
预防原则/預防原則，预警原则　precautionary principle
预分奖金/預分紅利　predetermined allocation bonus
预付/預付　payment in advance
预付保险费/預付保險費　prepaid insurance
预付部分货款/預付部分貨款　partial cash advanced
预付费制度/前瞻性支付制度　prospective payment system
预付关税/預付關稅　duty forward

预付价格/預付價格　advance price
预付款/預付款,訂金　advance payment, money paid in advance
预付款经济/預付款經濟　cash in-advance economy
预付利息/預付利息　prepaid interest
预付年金/預付年金　prepaid annuity
预付票据/預付票據　advance draft, advance bill
预付现金/預付現金　cash advance
预付运费/預付運費　advance freight
预付账款/提前清償,預先付款　anticipated payment, prepayment
预付资本/預付資本,墊付資本　advanced capital
预付资产/預付資産,遞延資産　prepaid asset
预付资金/預付資金　advance fund
预稿库/預稿庫　pre-draft library
预告登记/預告登記　registries of advance notice
预告片/預告片　trailer, teaser
预告性裁员/預告性裁員　dismissal with notice
预购[买]/預購　forward buying, purchase in advance
预估/評估,評量　assessment
预估最高损失额/預估最高損失額　maximum loss expectancy
预后验分析/後驗分析　prediction posterior analysis
预计投资/預計投資　ex-ante investment
预加重/預强調　pre-emphasis
预检/預檢　pre-check
预交进口保证金/預繳進口保證金　prior import deposit
预交外汇证明书/預繳出口外匯證明書　certificate for advance surrender of export exchange
预交押金/預交押金,進口保證金　advance deposit
预缴出口外汇/預繳[出口]外匯　advance surrender of export exchange
预警/預警　early warning
预警研究/預警分析　early-warning analysis, prewarning analysis, precaution analysis
预扣所得税/預扣所得税　pay as you earn
预览/預覽　preview
预览图像/預覽圖像　preview image
预留金/準備金　reserve
预谋故意/預謀故意　premeditated intent
预期/期望　expectation
预期边际损失/預期邊際損失　expected marginal loss
预期概率/預視機率　foresight probability
预期货币价值/期望貨幣值　expected monetary value, EMV
预期货币价值分析/預期貨幣值分析　expected monetary value analysis, EMV analysis
预期价格/預期價格　anticipated price, expected price
预期库存/預期庫存,預期存貨　anticipation inventory
预期理论/預期理論　expectation theory, expectancy theory
预期利润/預期利潤　imaginary profit, anticipated profit, expected profit
预期票据/已設定還本財源債券　anticipation note
预期事件/符合預期事件　expected event
预期收入理论/預期收入理論　anticipated income theory
预期收益/預期收益　expected yield, expected profit
预期收益率/預期收益率　rate of prospective yield
预期寿命/預期壽命,期望壽命　expected life
预期损失/預期損失　expected shortfall
预期通货膨胀/可預期通貨膨脹　anticipated inflation
预期投资/既定目的投資,預定目的投資　intended investment
预期违约/預期違約　anticipatory breach
预勤/實質審查,盡職調查　due diligence
预收款/預收款　advance receipt
预收收入/預收收入　revenue received in advance
预收收益/預收收益　prepaid income
预收账款/其他預收款　receipt in advance
预售/預售　advance sale
预算/預算　budget
预算编制/預算編製,預算籌編　budget establishment, budget preparation
预算草案/預算草案　budget draft
预算赤字/預算赤字　budget deficit
预算定额/預算定額　budget quota
预算法/預演算法　budget law
预算管理/預算管理　budget management
预算监督/預算監督　budget supervision
预算监管/預算監督　budget intendance
预算结余审计/預算結餘審計　audit for balance of budget
预算年度/預算年度　budget year
预算批准/預算核準　budget approval
预算平衡/預算平衡　budget balance
预算审查/預算審查　budget audit
预算收入/預算收入　budget revenue
预算松弛/預算鬆弛　budget slack
预算体系/預算制度　budget system

预算调整/預算調整　budget adjustment
预算投资/預算內投資　budgetary investment
预算外投资/預算外投資　extra-budgetary investment
预算外资金/預算外基金　extra-budgetary fund
预算线/預算線　budget line
预算盈余/預算盈餘　budget surplus
预算约束/預算限制　budget constraint
预算造价/估計成本　estimated cost
预算支出/預算支出　budget expenditure
预算资金/預算內資金　budgetary fund
预算资金运用表/預算資金運用表　statement of estimated application of fund
预提费用/應計費用　accrued expense
预涂感光版/預塗感光版　presensitive plate
预先颁发许可证制度/預先許可制　prior licensing system
预先打包破产/事先整装倒闭　prepackaged bankruptcy
预先分解/預定分解　predictive decomposition
预先付款/預先付款　payable in advance
预先控制/預先管制　pre-control
预先支付/預付　payment in advance
预言书/預言書　sibylline book
预印本/預印本　preprint
预约/預約　reservation, reserve
预约保单/預約保險單　open policy
预约通知单/預約通知單　reserved notice
预约图书/預約圖書,指定參考書　reserved book, item on hold
预约销售/預約銷售　appointment sale, sale by subscription
预兆分析预测法/預兆分析預測法　portent analysis forecasting approach
预支票据/預支票據　advance note
预支信用证/預支信用狀　anticipated letter of credit
预知维护/預測性維修　predictive maintenance
σ域/σ體　sigma field, σ-field
域名/域名　domain name
域名系统/網域名稱服務　domain name service, DNS
域名争议/域名爭議　domain name dispute
域名注册/域名註冊　domain name registration
域名注册簿机构/域名註冊簿機構　domain name registry
阈值/門檻值　threshold value
阈值模型/門檻模型　threshold model
阈值效应/門檻效應　threshold effect

御史/御史　historiographer in feudal China
御史台/御史臺　Yushi Tai
鬻贩书目/鬻販書目　list of trading books
元本体/元本體　meta-ontology
元抄本/元抄本　Yuan handwritten edition
元词法/元詞法　uniterm indexing system
元典章/元典章　Collection of Laws of the Yuan Dynasty
元分析/元分析,統合分析,後設分析　meta analysis
元概念/元概念　meta-concept
元沟通/元傳播,後設傳播　meta communication
元广告/元廣告　meta advertisement
元律/元律　Laws of the Yuan Dynasty
元目录/元目錄　meta directory
元数据/元數據,解釋用資料,元資料　metadata
元数据编码语言/元資料編碼語言　metadata encoding language
元数据仓储/元資料庫　metadata repository
元数据登记/元資料登記　metadata registry
元数据方案/後設資料方案,元資料綱要　metadata schema
元数据复用/元資料複用　metadata reuse
元数据管理/元資料管理　metadata management
元数据规范/元資料標準　metadata standard
元数据集/元資料集　metadata set
元数据开放机制/元資料開放性　metadata opening mechanism
元数据框架/元資料框架　metadata framework
元数据命名域/元資料名稱空間　metadata namespace
元数据收割/元資料收割　metadata harvesting
元数据应用纲要/元資料應用設定檔　metadata application profile
元数据映射/元資料映射　metadata mapping, metadata crosswalk
元数据元素/元資料元素,後設資料　metadata element
元数据置标/元資料置標　metadata markup
元搜索/元搜索引擎,原搜索引擎　meta search
元搜索引擎/元搜尋引擎　meta search engine
元索引/元索引　meta-index
元语言/元語言,後設語言　meta language
员工安全措施/員工安全措施　employee security measure
员工补偿/勞工賠償　worker compensation
员工参与/員工參與　employee involvement
员工持股计划/員工持股計劃,員工認股制,員工認股計劃　employee stock ownership plan, ESOP

员工服务福利/員工服務福利　employee service benefit
员工福利/員工福利　employee benefit
员工过剩/員工過剩　employee surplus
员工激励/員工激勵　employee motivation
员工绩效考核/員工績效考核　employee performance assessment
员工健康计划/雇員健康修煉計劃　employee wellness program
员工教育投资/職工教育投資　investment of education for workers and staff
员工进入率/員工進入率　labor accession rate
员工开发/員工發展　employee development
员工离职率/人員流動　staff turnover
员工逻辑/員工邏輯　worker logic
员工赔偿/工業災害補償　workman compensation
员工手册/員工手冊　employee manual
员工态度调查/雇員態度調查　employee attitude survey
员工推荐/員工推薦　employee referral
员工退出率/員工退出率　labor separation rate
员工协助方案/員工協助方案　employee assistance program
员工援助计划/員工協助方案　employee assistance program
员工自助服务/員工自助服務　employee self-service
爱书/愛書　judicial document in feudal China
袁记约法/袁記約法　Yuan Law
原版部分/原版部分　original part
原版初印/原版初印　primary publication
原本/原本　original edition
原材料/原料　raw material
原材料检查/原料檢驗　raw material inspection
原产地/原產地　place of origin, area of origin
原产地标志/原產地標誌　mark of origin
原产地规则协议/原產地規則協定　agreement on rules of origin
原产地离岸价格定价/FOB 原產地定價　FOB-origin pricing
原产地申报/原產地聲明書　declaration of origin
原产地证书/原產地證明　certificate of origin
原产国标志/原產國標誌　country of origin mark
原点/零點　zero point
原点矩/對原點的動差　moment about origin
原稿/原稿　original manuscript
原稿剪辑/剪輯　clip, clipping
原告/原告　plaintiff
原假设/原始假設,虛無假設　null hypothesis
原件/原件　original
原教旨主义/原教義主義,基本教義派,基本教義主義　fundamentalism
原理知识/技術原理　know-why
原料指数/原料指數　index of material
原强/原強　An Inquiry to the Nature and Causes of the Power of Nations
原色/原色　primary color
原生数字资源/原生數位資源　born digital resources
原生性电子文件/原生性電子檔　born electronic record
原始编目/原始編目　original cataloging
原始编目机构/原始編目機構　original cataloging agency
原始创新/原始創新　original innovation
原始存款/原始存款,自發性存款　primary deposit
原始调查/原始調查　primary survey
原始定单/原始訂單　original order
原始对偶内点算法/原始對偶內點演算法　primal-dual interior-point algorithm
原始分布/起始分布　initial distribution
原始公社/原始公社　primitive commune
原始股/原始股　original issue stock
原始记分/原始計分　raw score
原始记录/原始記錄　original record, primary record
原始价值/初始價值　primary value
原始检验/原始檢驗　original inspection
原始矩/原始動差,概約動差　raw moment, crude moment
原始凭证/原始憑單　original voucher
原始区组/原始區集　initial block
原始取得/原始取得　original acquisition
原始群/原始群,原始組　primitive group, primitive horde, original group
原始群落/原始群落　primitive community
原始社会/原始社會　primitive society
原始书目/原始書目　primary bibliography
原始数据/原始資料,初級資料　raw data, original data
原始投资/原始投資　original investment
原始信息/原始資訊　original information
原[始]信用证/主信用狀,正本信用狀　master credit, original credit
原始样本/原始樣本　primary sample
原始营销资料/原始行銷資料　primary marketing data
原始证据/原始憑證　original evidence
原始周期/原始週期　primitive period

原始资料/原始文件　source document
原始宗教/原始宗教　primitive religion
原题名/原題名　original title
原型/原型,原器　prototype
原型法/原型設計　prototyping
原因/原因　cause
原因分析/原因分析　reason analysis
原因说/原因説　cause theory
原著/原著　original work
原子性/原子性　atomicity
原作版本附注/原作版本附注　original version note
原作者/原創者　originator
圆函数/圓函數　circular function
圆环/圓環　circular ring
圆网印版/圓網印版　cylinder screen forme
圆网印刷机/圓網印刷機　cylinder screen press
圆形分布/圓形分布,圓形分配　circular distribution
圆形概率误差/圓形機率誤差　circular probable error
圆形平均[离]差/環狀平均離差　circular mean deviation
圆形四分位数[离]差/環狀四分位數離差　circular quartile deviation
圆形图/圓形圖　circular chart
圆形直方图/環狀直方圖　circular histogram
缘坐/緣坐　Yuan Zuo
源代码/原始碼　source code
源数据自动管理/原始資料自動管理　source data automation
源头品质/源頭品質　quality at source
源叙词表/源敘詞表　source thesaurus
源字段/源欄位　source field
远程备份/遠程備份　remote backup
远程访问/遠端取用　remote access
远程服务/遠程服務,遠端服務　distance service, remote service
远程工作/遠距工作　teleworking
远程教育/遠距教育,電傳教學　teleeducation
远程培训/遠距培訓　remote training
远程数据库/場外資料庫　off-site database
远程数据库访问/遠程資料庫存取　remote database access, RDA
远程用户/遠端使用者　off-site user, remote user
远东国际军事法庭/遠東國際軍事法庭　International Military Tribunal for the Far East
远期报价/期貨報價　forward quotation
远期订货/遠期訂貨,期貨訂單　forward order
远期付款/遠期付款　payable at usance
远期付款交单/遠期付款交單　document against payment after sight
远期购买/期貨購買　forward purchase
远期合同/遠期合約　forward contract
远期合约/遠期契約　forwards
远期互换/遠期交換契約　forward swap
远期汇兑/遠期兑换　long exchange
远期汇兑合约/遠期外匯合約　forward exchange contract
远期汇率/遠期[外匯]匯率　forward exchange rate
远期汇票/遠期匯票,遠期票據　term draft, usance draft, date bill
远期汇票价/遠期匯票價　usance bill rate
远期汇票买入价/遠期匯票買入價　buying rate for usance bill
远期交货/遠期交貨　forward delivery
远期利率/遠期利率　forward interest rate
远期利率协议/遠期利率協議　forward rate agreement
远期票据/遠期票據　long dated bill
远期升水/遠期升水,期貨升水　forward premium
远期生效期权/遠期生效選擇權　forward start option
远期市场/遠期契約市場,期貨市場　forward market
远期套利/遠期套利　time arbitrage
远期套头交易/遠期避險交易,多頭避險　long hedge
远期外汇/遠期外匯　forward exchange
远期外汇操作/遠期外匯操作　forward exchange operation
远期外汇交易/遠期外匯交易　forward exchange transaction
远期外汇交易汇率/遠期外匯交易匯率　forward exchange dealing rate
远期外汇市场/遠期外匯市場　forward exchange market
远期销售/期貨銷售　executory sale
远期信贷/遠期信貸　time credit
远期信用证/遠期信用狀　time letter of credit, usance credit
远期证券/遠期證券　long security
远洋贸易/遠洋貿易　ocean trade
怨恨/憤恨　resentment
院线制/院線制　cinema line system
愿景/願景,遠見　vision
愿景型领导/願景型領導　visionary leadership
约当产量/約當產量　equivalent production unit
约当恒等式/Jordan 恆等式　Jordan's identity
约当年均成本/約當年均費用　equivalent annual

cost, EAC
约定价值/承諾價值　commitment value
约定利率/約定利率　contracted interest rate, contract interest rate
约定利息/約定利息　contract interest
约定损失价值/約定損失價值　stipulated loss value
约定信守/條約信守　pacta sunt servanda
约法省禁/約法省禁　a feudal Chinese idea of act to be simple-sparse wider criminal network
约稿/約稿　call for paper
约翰·穆勒国际价值理论/約翰密爾國際價值說　John Mill theory of international value
约翰循环不完全区组设计/John 循環不完全區集設計　John cyclic incomplete block designs
约翰逊法则/詹森法則　Johnson rule
约翰逊分布族/Johnson 分布系統　Johnson system of distribution
约化相关矩阵/縮減相關矩陣　reduced correlation matrix
约束/限制條件　constraint
约束抽样设计/受制抽樣設計　restricted sampling design
ε约束法/ε約束法　ε-constraint method
约束关心/約束關心　constraint concern
约束极大似然估计[量]/受制最大概度估計量　restricted maximum likelihood estimator
约束性固定成本/既定性固定成本　committed fixed cost
约束最小二乘估计/受限最小平方估計量　restricted least squares estimator
月刊/月刊　monthly
月平均/月平均　monthly average
月平均法/月平均法　method of monthly average
月折包/月折包　memoriala used to be made up into packet twice a month
乐谱/樂譜　music book, music score, notation
刖刑/刖刑　Yue penalty in feudal China
阅读/閱讀　reading
阅读放大器/讀[出]放大器　reading amplifier
阅读复印机/閱讀影印機　reader-printer
阅读计划/閱讀推薦計劃　reading plan
阅读架/閱讀架　book holder
阅读疗法/圖書醫療法,閱讀治療　bibliotherapy
阅读率/閱讀率　readership rate
阅读目的/閱讀目的　reading purpose
阅读能力/閱讀能力　reading ability
阅读器/閱讀機　reader
阅读倾向/閱讀傾向　reading trend

阅读软件/閱讀軟體　reading software
阅读设备/讀值裝置　reading device
阅读社会/閱讀社會　reading society
阅读社会学/閱讀社會學　reading sociology
阅读推广/閱讀植根推廣　reading promotion
阅读卫生/閱讀衛生　reading hygiene, hygiene of reading
阅读习惯/閱讀習慣　reading habit
阅读效果/閱讀效率　reading efficiency
阅读心理/閱讀心理　reading mentality
阅读心理学/閱讀心理學　reading psychology
阅读行为/閱讀行爲　reading behavior
阅读兴趣/閱讀興趣　reading interest
阅读需求/閱讀需求　reading need
阅读障碍/閱讀障礙,失讀症,閱讀失能症　dyslexia
阅读指导/閱讀指導　reading guidance, reading instruction
阅览服务/閱覽服務　reading service
阅览规则/閱覽規則　reading regulation, reading room regulation, reading room rule
阅览人数/閱覽人數　reading room attendance
阅览室/閱覽室　reading room
阅览证/讀者證　library card
越轨行为/越軌,逸脱　deviance
越级晋升制/加速晉升　accelerated promotion system
越级组配/越級組配　exceed level coordination
越权无效/越權無效　ultra vires doctrine
云出版/雲出版　cloud publishing
云计算/雲端運算　cloud computing
云梦秦简/雲夢秦簡　Qin dynasty bamboo slips in Yunmeng
云母剥离室实验/雲母剝離室實驗　mica stripping room experiment
匀墨辊/匀墨輥　distributing roller
允许变换/可容轉換　admissible transformation
孕产妇死亡率/孕産婦死亡率　maternal mortality ratio
运筹学/運籌學　operation research, operational research
运带机构/運輸機構　shipping agency
运动捕捉/動作擷取系統　motion capture
运动长镜头/運動長鏡頭　sport long len
运动神经能力测试/運動神經能力測試　psychomotor ability test
运费率/運費率　freight rate
运费吸收定价/免收運費定價法　freight-absorption pricing

运河时代/運河時代　canal age
运输/運輸　transportation
运输-仓储及通信业/運輸-倉儲及通信業　transportation-storage and communications
运输、仓储及通信业统计/運輸、倉儲及通信業統計　transportation, storage and communications statistics
运输成本/運輸成本　transport cost
运输费/運輸費　traffic expense
运输合同/運送合同　carriage contract
运输经济半径/運輸經濟半徑　economic radius of transportation
运输浪费/運輸浪費　transportation waste
运输区位论/運輸區位理論　transport location theory
运输时间/運輸時間　transportation time

运算符号/運算符號　sign of operation, operative symbol
运算规则/運算規則　operational rule
运算特征/操作特徵　operating characteristic
运行环境/運行環境　runtime environment
运行绩效/運行績效　operational performance
运行时间/工作時間,運轉時間　running time
运行维护阶段/操作與維護階段　operation and maintenance phase
运营创新/營運創新　operational innovation
运营计划/營運計劃　operational plan
运作/作業,操作　operation
运作策略/作業策略　operation strategy
运作型基金会/運作型基金會　operational foundation
晕轮误差/暈輪誤差,月暈誤差　halo error
晕轮效应/月暈效應　halo effect

Z

杂辑/雜輯　unimportant album
杂技艺术作品/雜技藝術作品　acrobatic art work
杂家/雜家　eclecticism
杂耍蒙太奇/雜耍蒙太奇　vaudeville montage
杂志/雜志　magazine
杂志扉页广告/雜志扉頁廣告　gatefold
杂志书/雜志書　mook
杂著/雜文集,综合性著作　miscellaneous work
灾害救助/災害救助　natural disaster emergency aid, natural disaster relief
灾害统计/災害統計,損害統計　disaster statistics, damage statistics
灾难恢复/災難復原　disaster recovery
灾难片/災難片　disaster film
灾难新闻/災難新聞　disaster news
载文量/載文量　number of articles published
再版/再版,翻印　republication
再参数化模型/重新参数化模型　reparameterized model
再抽样/重抽樣　resampling
再出口货/複運出口貨　goods reexported
再出口与对外交易保险/再出口與對外交易保險　cover for re-export and external transaction
再贷款/再貸款,轉融資　reloan, relending
再抵押/再抵押　remortgage
再订货点/再訂購點　reorder point
再定位/再定位,重新定位　repositioning
再分股票/再分股票　sub-divided share
再分配/再分配,重新分配　redistribution
再分配市场/再分配市場　market for redistribution
再分配政策/再分配政策　redistributive policy
再估计/再估計　reestimation
再回购协议/復買回協議　reverse repo
再婚/再婚　remarriage
再婚家庭/再婚家庭　remarried family
再婚率/再婚率　remarriage rate
再进口报关单/再進口報關單　reimport entry
再进口价格/再進口價格　reimport price
再进口手续/再進口手續　reimport procedure
再进口许可证/再進口許可證　reimport permit
再进入者/再進入者　reentrant

再就业/再就業　reemployment
再就业服务中心/再就業服務中心　service center of reemployment
再就业援助/再就業援助　outplacement assistance
再排程/再排程　rescheduling
再融资/重新借款　refinance
再融资信贷/再融資信貸　refinance credit
再社会化/再社會化　resocialization
再审程序/再審程式　retrial procedure
再生表/再生表　phoenix schedule
再生产/再生産　reproduction
再生产率/再生率　reproduction rate
再生产生存率/再生存活率,再生殘存率　reproduction survival rate
再生文献/再生文獻　regeneration document
再生信息[源]/再生資訊[源]　tertiary source
再生纸/再生紙　recycled paper
再贴现/重貼現　rediscount
再贴现率/重貼現率　rediscount rate
再投资/再投資　plow back
再投资风险/再投資風險　reinvestment risk
再现/再現　represent, representation
再现型人才/再現型人才　repeative talent
再现性/再現性　reproducibility
再循环/回收再利用　recycle
再制造件/再製造件　remanufactured part
再制造资源计划/再製造資源計劃　remanufacturing resource planning
再组织/改组,重组　reorganization
在版编目/出版品預行編目　cataloging in publication, pre-cataloging
在版书/現版圖書　book in print
在版书目/在版書目　books in print, BIP
在册员工辞职人数/受雇員工進退人數　number of labor turnover of employees on payroll
在朝党/在朝黨　ruling party
在订存货/在訂庫存　on-order stock
在公共部门投资/在公共部門投資　investment in public sector
在架生命期/儲架壽命　shelf life
在建工程/在建工程　construction-in-progress

在交易所出售/在交易所出售　sale at exchange
在途库存/在途庫存　in-transit inventory
在途时间/在途前置時間　in-transit lead time
在途物资/在途存貨　inventory in transit
在先权利/在先權利　prior right
在险价值压力测试/風險值壓力測試　value-at-risk stress testing, VaR stress testing
在险资本/風險資本　capital at risk
在线传播/線上傳播　online communication
在线词典/線上詞典　online dictionary
在线电影/線上電影　online film
在线订购/線上訂購　online ordering, teleordering
在线翻译/線上翻譯　online translation
在线访问/線上訪問　online access
在线服务/線上服務　online service
在线工具书/線上工具書　online reference book
在线公共查询目录/網頁爲基線上公用目錄　web-based OPAC, WebPAC
在线观看/線上觀看　online viewing
在线广告/線上廣告　online advertising
在线归档/線上歸檔　online filing
在线检测/線上檢測　inline inspection, online inspection
在线检查/線上檢驗　online inspection
在线教育/線上教育　online education
在线考试/線上考試　online examination
在线漫画/線上漫畫　online comic
在线排序/線上排序　online scheduling
在线社区/網路社群, 線上社群　online community
在线索引/線上索引　online index
在线音乐/線上音樂　online music
在线营销调研/線上行銷研究　online marketing research
在线营销数据库/線上行銷資料庫　online marketing database
在线载体/線上載體　online carrier
在信用证项下支取款项/在信用狀項下支款　drawing under credit
在原稿上标注排版要求/標注　mark-up
在职培训/在職訓練　on-the-job training
在制品/在製品, 在產品　work in process, WIP
载货率/載貨率　weight load factor
载客率/載客率　passenger load factor
载体/媒體　medium
载体标识面/載體標識面　media printed surface
载体表现/表現　manifestation
载体分类法/媒體分類法　medium classfication
载体货币/工具貨幣　vehicle currency
载体考订/媒體考訂　medium criticism
载体类型标识项/載體類型標識項　carrier type identification item
载体形态附注/載體形態附注　note pertaining to physical description
载体形态项/載體形態項　carrier form item, physical description area
暂定配额/暫定配額　provisional quota
暂缓执行/暫緩執行　probation of execution
暂扣或者吊销许可证、执照/暫扣或者吊銷許可證、執照　temporary suspension or rescission of permit or license
暂列金额/不可預見費用　provisional sum
暂时逆差/暫時逆差　temporary deficit
暂时停止交易/交易暫停　trading suspension
暂时相关/暫時相關　temporal correlation
暂时休养服务/喘息照顧　respite care
暂行本/暫行本　trial issue, trial edition, preliminary edition
暂行标准/暫行標準　temporary standard
暂准通关/暫準通關　admission temporary
赞助/贊助　patronage
赞助订阅/贊助訂閱　sponsored subscription
赞助商/贊助商　sponsor
赞助性流动/舉薦流動　sponsored mobility
早恋/早戀　puppy love
早期成长阶段/早期成長階段　early growth stage
早期公开延迟审查/早期公開延遲審查　early public delayed examination
早期故障/早期故障, 初期故障　initial failure
早期失效期间/早期故障期間　early failure period
早期预警系统/先期預警系統　early warning system
早期阅读/早期閱讀　early reading
早熟收敛/早熟收斂　premature convergence
造法性条约/造法性條約　law-making treaty
造林面积统计/造林面積統計　reforested area statistics
噪声/雜音, 雜訊, 噪音　noise
噪声交易者/擾嚷投資人　noise trader
噪声控制/噪音控制　noise control
噪声模型/雜訊模型　noise model
噪声谱/雜訊光譜　noise spectrum
噪声污染/噪音公害, 噪音汙染　noise pollution
噪声污染防治法/雜訊汙染防治法　law prevention and control of pollution from environmental noise
噪音交易者/擾嚷投資人　noise trader
噪音效应/雜訊效應, 噪音效應　noise effect
躁狂抑郁性精神病/躁鬱性精神病　manic-depressive

psychosis
躁狂症/躁狂症　mania
则例/則例　special regulations in feudal China
责令关闭/責令關閉　order issued to shut down an enterprise
责令停产停业/責令停產停業　ordering for suspension of production or business
责令停业/責令停業　order enforced to suspend operation
责任保险/責任保險　liability insurance
责任编辑/責任編輯　responsible editor
责任成本/責任成本　responsibility cost
责任方式/責任方式　function of responsibility
责任分析/責任分析　responsibility analysis
责任管理/課責管理　accountable management
责任规则/責任法則　liability rule
责任校对/責任校對　responsible proof-reader
责任竞合/責任競合　liability concurrence
责任扩散/責任擴散,責任分散　diffusion of responsibility
责任说明/責任說明　statement of responsibility
责任限制条款/責任限制條款　limitation clause
责任型营销/責任型行銷　accountable marketing
责任性/當責,課責　accountability
责任者/責任者　responsiblity
责任者参照/責任者參照　author reference
责任者分析款目/責任者分析款目　author analytic entry
责任者附加款目/責任者附加款目　author added entry
责任者款目/責任者款目　author entry
责任者项/責任者項　liability item
责任者主要款目/責任者主要款目　author main entry
责任中心/責任中心　responsibility center
择偶/擇偶　mate choice
择偶梯度理论/擇偶梯度理論　mate gradient theory
择式期权/決擇型選擇權　chooser option
泽伦不等式/Zelen不等式　Zelen inequality
贼盗/賊盜　stealing
增补版/增補版　augmented edition
增补关键词索引/增補關鍵詞索引　enriched keyword index
增词标引/增詞標引　adding words indexing
增大因子/擴大因子　raising factor
增订版/增訂版　revised and enlarged edition
增订本/增訂本　updated version
增发股息/增發股息,附加股息　supplementary dividend
增广迪基-富勒检验/擴大後的迪克-福勒檢定,增廣DF檢定　augmented Dickey-Fuller test
增加部下法则/增加部下法則　law of increasing staff
增刊/增刊,號外　supplement, supplementary issue
增量/增量　increment
增量成本/增支成本,增額成本　incremental cost
增量销售/新增銷售　incremental sale
增量预算/增量預算　incremental budget
增强清晰度电视/高解析[度]電視　high definition television, enhanced definition television, EDTV
增权理论/增權理論　empowerment theory
增湿/增濕　humidification
增意标引/增意標引　explicit indexing
增长壁垒/增長壁壘　growth wall
增长-份额矩阵/成長率-市占率矩陣,成長-占有率矩陣　growth-share matrix
增长核算/成長會計　growth accounting
增长机会现值/成長機會現值　present value of growth opportunity, PVGO
增长极/成長標竿　growth pole
增长极理论/成長極理論　growth pole theory
增长极限论/增長極限論　limits-to-growth theory
增长理论/增長理論　growth theory
增长率/增率　increment rate
增长期权/增長期權　growth option
增长曲线/增長曲線,成長曲線　growth curve
增长曲线模型/成長曲線模型　growth curve model
增长型战略实施/增長型策略執行　increasing-type strategy implementation
增长引擎/成長機器　growth engine
增长战略/成長策略　growth strategy
增值价值/附加價值　value added
增值税/增值稅,從價稅,加值稅　value added tax
增值税专用发票/增值稅專用發票　special invoice for value-added tax
增值物流服务/增值物流服務　value-added logistics service
增值债券/Z债券　accretion bond
增资/增資　capital increase
赠品/贈品　gift
赠品促销/贈品推廣　premium promotion
赠券抵用率/贈券抵用率　coupon redemption rate
赠券销售率/贈券銷售率　percentage sales with coupon
赠书者记录/贈書者記錄　donor file
赠与/贈與　donation

赠与税/贈與稅　gift tax
赠阅图书/寄贈書　gift book
扎根理论/扎根理論　grounded theory
扎普尔规则/扎普爾規則　Zapple rule
诈骗罪/詐騙罪　crime of swindling
摘录/摘錄　extract
摘要/摘要　abstract
摘译/摘譯　abridged translation
摘由/摘由　Zhaiyou
宅基地使用权/宅基地使用權　right of the use of curtilage
宅青/宅青　youth staying in the house and indulging in the Internet
窄限量规/窄限量規　narrow limit gage
债保全/债保全　preservation of obligation
债换股交易/債權換股　debt-equity swap
债权/債權　creditor right
债权抵押/契約質押　pledge of obligation
债权国/債權國　creditor nation
债权类金融产品/債權類金融產品　bonds financial product, debt securities
债权人/債權人　creditor
债权人撤销权/債權人撤銷權　creditor right to withdraw
债权人代位权/債權人代位權　creditor right of subrogation
债权人会议/債權人會議　creditor meeting
债权人委员会/債權人委員會　creditor committee
债权人住所地法/債權人住所地法　law of creditor domicile
债权申报/債權申報　declaration of claims
债权证券/債權證券　credit securities
债权转股权/以股换债　debt-for-equity swap
债券/債券　bond, debenture
债券保险/債券保險　bond insurance
债券偿还/債券償還　redemption of bond
债券持有人/債券持有人　bondholder
债券担保贷款/債券質押借款　bond collateral loan
债券等值收益率/債券等值收益率　bond equivalent yield
债券浮动市场/債券浮動市場　bond float market
债券购买者指数/債券購買者指數　bond buyer index
债券换新/債券更新　bond refunding
债券回购/債券贖回　bond buy-back
债券价格/債券價格　bond price, price of bond
债券经纪人/債券經紀人　bond broker
债券利息收益/債券利息收益　bond interest income
债券票据/債券票據　bond note
债券期权/債券期權　bond option
债券市场/債券市場　bond market
债券收益率/債券收益　bond yield
债券套利/債券套利　bond arbitrage
债券投资/債券投資　investment in bond
债券信托/債券信託　debenture trust
债券溢价/債券溢價　premium on bond
债券账户/債券賬户　bond account
债券指数/債券指數　bond index
债券中性/債務中立性　debt neutrality
债券转让/債券轉讓　debenture transfer
债券资本/借入資本　debenture capital
债务/債務,负债　liability, debt
债务承担/債務承擔　share of liability
债务承担并购/債務承擔并購　pay debt merger
债务重新安排/重訂還債安排　debt rearrangement, debt rescheduling
债务重组/債務重組,債務重整　debt restructuring
债务抵销/債務抵消　set-off of debt
债务回购/債務回購　debt buyback
债务履行到期日/債務到期日　date of eligibility of obligation
债务率/經濟債務率　debt-to-gdp ratio
债务免除/債務免除　waiver of obligation
债务奴隶/負債擔保　debt bondage
债务清偿/債務清償　debt service
债务人财产/債務人財產　debtor estate
债务融资/債務融資,舉債融資　debt financing
债务通货紧缩/債務緊縮　debt deflation
债务危机/債務危機　debt crisis
债务陷阱/以債養債　debt-trap
债务优先权/債務優先權　seniority of debt
债务证券/債務工具　debt instrument
债务资本/債務資本　debt capital
债务资本成本/債務成本　cost of debt
占卜/占卜　divination
詹姆斯-斯坦估计量/James-Stein估計量　James-Stein estimator
詹生不等式/Jensen不等式　Jensen's inequality
斩监候/斬監候　suspended the death penalty system in Qing dynasty
斩立决/斬立決　immediately put to death
展开式水平布局/展開式水平布局　open-type horizontal layout, horizontal layout in expanded form
展览/展覽,陳列　exhibition

展览合同/展覽合同　exhibition contract
展览权/展覽權　right of exhibition
展平/鋪平　flattening
展期贷款/展期貸款　rollover loan
展期票据/展期票據　renewed bill
展期信用/展期信用　rollover credit
展期信用证/展期信用狀，循環預支信用　extended credit
展示广告/完整呈現廣告　display advertising
展望理论/展望理論，前景理論　prospect theory
展销/展銷　publication exhibition and sale
展延有效期/展延有效日期　extend expiration date
占用问题/占有問題　occupancy problem
占优策略/優勢策略　dominant strategy
占优策略均衡/占優策略均衡，優勢策略均衡　dominant strategy equilibrium, equilibrium in dominant strategy
占优集/占優集　dominate set
占有/占有　possession
占有保护/占有保護　protection of possession
占有辅助/占有輔助　possession assistance
占有改定/占有改定　possession change
战略/策略　strategy
战略必要性假说/策略性必要假說　strategic necessity hypothesis
战略成本管理/策略成本管理　strategic cost management
战略承诺/策略承諾　strategic commitment
战略传播/策略性溝通　strategic communication
战略窗口/策略之窗　strategic window
战略创新/策略創新　strategic innovation
战略导向性竞争情报/策略性導向競爭情報　strategy-oriented competitive intelligence
战略地位和行动评估矩阵/策略地位和行動評估矩陣　strategic position and action evaluation matrix
战略方格分析/策略網格分析　strategic grid analysis
战略分析和选择/策略分析和選擇　strategy analysis and choice
战略规划/策略規劃　strategic planning
战略规划学派/策略制定學派　strategic formulation school
战略互动/策略性互動　strategic interaction
战略集群/策略群組　strategic group
战略集团分析/策略集團分析，策略群析　strategic group analysis
战略计划/策略計劃　strategic plan
战略经营单位/策略事業單位　strategic business unit, SBU
战略竞争力/策略競爭力　strategic competitiveness
战略决策/策略性決策　strategic decision making
战略控制/策略性控制　strategic control
战略联盟/策略聯盟　strategic alliance
战略灵活度透视/策略靈活度透視　strategic agility perspective
战略领导力/策略領導　strategic leadership
战略贸易政策/策略性貿易政策　strategic trade policy
战略情报/策略情報　strategic intelligence
战略情报研究/策略情報分析　strategic intelligence analysis
战略柔性/策略彈性　strategic flexibility
战略实施/策略執行　strategy implementation
战略使命/策略使命　strategic mission
战略手艺化/手藝式策略　crafting strategy
战略态势/策略態勢　strategic posture
战略替代/策略性替代　strategic substitute
战略投资/策略性投資　strategic investment
战略效应/策略性效果　strategic effect
战略薪酬计划/策略性薪酬計劃　strategic compensation plan
战略信息/策略資訊　strategic information
战略信息管理/策略資訊管理　strategic information management
战略信息系统/策略資訊系統　strategic information system
战略行动/策略行動　strategic move
战略行为/策略性行爲　strategic behavior
战略性复兴/策略更新　strategic renewal
战略性竞争情报/策略性競爭情報　strategic competitive intelligence
战略性贸易政策理论/策略性貿易政策論　theory of strategic trade policy
战略性人力资源管理/策略性人力資源管理　strategic human resource management
战略性社会性别需求/策略性社會性別需求　strategic gender need
战略性行为/策略性行爲　strategic action
战略性资产/策略性資產　strategic asset
战略选择/策略性選擇　strategic choice
战略意图/策略意圖　strategic intent
战略游戏/策略遊戲　strategy game
战略预警/策略預警　strategic early warning
战术导向性竞争情报/戰術性導向競爭情報　tactics-oriented competitive intelligence
战术决策/戰術性決策　tactical decision making
战术情报/戰術情報　tactic intelligence

战术情报研究/戰術情報分析　tactical intelligence analysis
战术性竞争情报/戰術性競爭情報　tactical competitive intelligence
战术性行为/戰術性行爲　tactical action
战争/戰爭　war
战争法/戰爭法　law of war
战争赔偿/戰爭賠償　compensation of war
战争片/戰爭片　war movie
战争受难者/戰爭受難者　victim of war
战争责任/戰爭責任　responsibility of war
战争债券/戰時公債　war bond
战争债务/戰債　war debt
战争状态/戰爭狀態　state of war
战争罪/戰爭罪　war crime
张/張,頁　leaf
张伯伦双寡头模型/張伯倫寡占模型　Chamberlian duopoly model
张贴式目录/張貼式目錄　poster catalog
章程/章程　constitution
长老统治/老人統治　gerontocracy
长老制/老人統治　gerontocracy
涨跌幅限制/漲跌停限制　price limit
涨价/漲價　advance price
涨停板/漲停　limit up
掌舵而非划船/掌舵而非劃船　steering not rowing
掌上电脑/個人數位助理　personal digital assistant
掌上阅读器/掌上閱讀器　palm-held reader, hand-held reader
账簿/賬簿　account, account book
账单/賬單　statement of account
账号/號碼賬戶,不具名賬戶　numbered account
账户/賬戶　account
账面成本/賬面成本　book cost
账面价值/賬面價值　book value, carrying value
账面库存/賬面盤存,賬面存貨　book inventory
账面利润/賬面利潤　paper profit
账面损失/賬面損失　paper loss
账目表/賬目表,會計科目表　chart of account
账期/賬期　days of payment
账外资产/賬外資產　asset out of account
账项基础审计/賬項基礎審計　account-based audit
障碍函数/障礙函數　barrier function
障碍期权/關卡選擇權,界限選擇權　barrier option
瘴气说/瘴氣説　miasmatic theories
招标/招標　invitation for bid, call for tender, tendering
招标代理/招標代理　tender agent

招标档描述现场条件失误/招標檔描述現場條件失誤　mispresentation of site condition
招标公告/招標公告　bidding announcement
招标期限/投標期　tender period
招标人/招標人　tenderee, bid-inviter
招标申请/招標申請　application for tendering
招标通知/招標通知　call for bid
招标文件/標單　tender document
招标文件补编/招標文件附錄　addendum to tender document
招股说明书/募股公開説明書　prospectus
招聘/招募　recruitment
招聘备择方案/招聘備擇方案　recruitment optional program
招聘广告/徵人廣告　recruitment advertising
招聘计划/招聘計劃　recruitment plan
招贴画/招貼,海報　poster, placard
招摇撞骗罪/招搖撞騙罪　crime of cheating and bluffing
招赘/招贅　uxorilocal marriage
召回/召回　recall
诏书/詔書　imperial edict
诏狱/詔獄　Zhao Yu
照度/照度,照明　illuminance
照会/照會　diplomatic note
照料者负担/照料者負擔　caregiver burden
照明实验/照明實驗　lighting test
照片/照片,像片,相片　photograph
照片档案/攝影類檔案　photographic archive
照片光盘/照片光碟　photo-compact disc
照片文件/照片檔案　photographic record, photographic archive
照相凹印/照相凹版　photogravure
照相成像/攝影,照相　photography
照相排版/照排　photocomposition
折半信度/折半信度　split-half reliability
折本/折本　pleated book
折标/背標　collating mark
折叠/折叠　folding
折叠层/折叠層　collapsed strata
折叠层法/折叠層法　collapsed stratum method
折叠分布/折叠分布　folded distribution
折叠列联表/折叠列聯表　folded contingency table
折叠式图书/折貼式圖書　folded book
折叠中位数/折叠中位數　folded median
折耗/折耗　depletion
折价发行债券/折價發行債券　bond issue at discount

折价债券/折價債券　discount bond
折价债务/貼現債務　discount liability
折校法/折校法　proofreading technique of comparing with original
折旧/折舊　depreciation
折旧率/折舊率,貶值率　ratio of depreciation, rate of depreciation
折旧税盾/折舊稅盾　depreciation tax shield
折扣/折扣　discount
折扣店/有折扣零售商,廉價商店　discount retailer, discount store
折扣价[格]/折扣價[格]　price at a discount, discount price
折扣率/貼現率　discount rate
折扣模型/折扣模型　discounted reward model
折扣偏好倾向性/折扣偏好傾向性　deal proneness
折扣偏好消费者/折扣偏好消費者　deal-prone consumer
折扣准则/折扣準則　discount criterion
折现回收期/折現回收期間,折現還本期間　discounted payback period
折现值/折現值　present discounted value, PDV
折页/折頁　paper folding
折页标记/折疊痕　fold mark
折页机/折頁機　paper folding machine
折狱龟鉴/折獄龜鑒　Zheyu Guijian
折杖/折杖　Zhe Zhang
折中家庭制/折中家庭制　reciprocal support in family
折中模式/折中模式　eclectic model
折中准则/折中準則　compromise criterion
哲理法学派/哲理法學派　philosophical school of law
谪/謫　Zhe
磔/磔　Zhe
褶皱/壓折痕,縐紋　crease
浙本/浙本　Zhejiang edition
贞操/貞操　chastity, virtue
贞观律/貞觀律　Zhenguan Law in Tang Dynasty
贞洁/貞節　chastity
针孔摄影/針孔攝影　pin-hole photography
针幕动画/針幕動畫　pinscreen animation
侦查/偵查　criminal investigation
侦查羁押/偵查羈押　custodial investigation
侦查监督/偵查監督　supervision of investigation
侦查权/偵查權　investigatory power
侦查实验/偵查實驗　investigative experiment
侦查终结/偵查終結　closure of investigation
侦探片/偵探片　detective movie

珍贵地图/珍貴地圖　rare map
珍贵文献/稀有文獻資料　rare material
帧率/每秒播放格數　frames per second, FPS
真标准差/真標準差　true standard deviation
真回归/真回歸　true regression
真空干燥法/真空乾燥法　vacuum drying
真实出售/真實出售　true sale
真实过程/正當過程　honest process
真实过程平均/真製程平均,真過程平均　true process average
真实合同/真實的合約　bona fide contract
真实汇率/真實匯率　true exchange rate
真实经济周期观点/實質景氣循環觀點　real business cycle view
真实经济周期学派/實質經濟週期學派　real business cycle school
真实票据/真實票據　bona fide bill
真实票据[理]论/實質票券說　real bill doctrine, real bill theory
真实商业周期理论/真實商業週期理論,實質商業週期理論　real-business-cycle theory
真实性/真實性,本真　authenticity
真误差/真誤差　true error
真相关/真相關　true correlation
真意保留/真意保留　real reservation
真正无面值的股票/真正無面額股票　true no-par value stock
真众数/真眾數　true mode
真组限/真組界　true class limit
甄别/鑒定　screening
诊断/診斷　diagnosis
诊断性评估/診斷式評量　diagnostic evaluation
诊断研究/診斷研究　diagnostic study
阵列/陣列　array
振荡过程/波動過程　oscillatory process
振荡指数/波動指數　index of oscillation
振动/振動,波動　oscillation
振动模型/震盪模型　shock model
振动试验/震動試驗　vibration test
振动污染/震動汙染　vibration pollution
赈灾/災害救濟　disaster relief
镇/集鎮,市鎮　town
争端裁决委员会/爭端裁決委員會　dispute adjudication board, DAB
争端解决/紛爭仲裁　dispute settlement
争端解决机构/爭端解決機構　dispute settlement body
争端解决谅解/爭端解決規則與程式瞭解書　dispute

settlement understanding
争端评审委员会/爭議評審委員會,爭議審議委員會　dispute review board, DRB
争论/論辯　argument
争议性档案要求/爭議性檔案要求　conflicting archival claim
征订/徵訂　solicit subscription
征订包销/徵訂包銷　solicit subscription and exclusive sales
征订代码/徵訂代碼　code of soliciting for subscription
征订经销/徵訂經銷　solicit subscription and distribution
征订目录/徵訂目錄,訂閱目錄　list of soliciting for subscription, subscription catalog
征服/征服　conquest
征稿/徵稿　solicit for articles
征求意见稿/徵求意見稿　paper of calling for comment
征税/徵稅　tax collection
征税标准/徵稅基礎　basis of assessment
征税单/稅單　tax bill
征税级距/課稅級距　taxable income bracket
征税价值/徵稅價值　rateable value
征文/徵文　call for paper
整版广告/整頁廣告　full-page advertisement
整版校对/整版校對　full-page proofreading
整笔付清费用/整筆[付清]費用　lump-sum fee
整车运输/整車運輸　truckload
整订/整訂　termed subscription
整合/整合　integration
整合方法/整合方法,整合取向　integrative approach
整合公关媒体模式/整合公關媒體模式　integrated public relations media model
整合实务/整合實務　comprehensive practice
整合实务中几种角色/整合實務中幾種角色　several roles in comprehensive practice
整合式谈判/整合性協商,整合性談判　integrative bargaining
整合数据/整合資料　integrated data
整合物流管理/物流集成管理　integrated logistics management
整合性资源/整合性資源,集成性資源　integrating resources
整合移动平均/整合移動平均　integrated moving average, IMA
整合营销传播/整合行銷傳播　integrated marketing communication

整合直接营销/整合直接行銷　integrated direct marketing
整理/整理　sort
整理原则/整理原則　principle of arrangement
整批采购/整批採購　bulk purchase, purchase in bulk
整批出售/整批出售　bulk sale
整批交易/整批交易,成批交易　round lot sale
整群抽样/叢聚抽樣,群聚抽樣,集群抽樣　cluster sampling
整饰工艺/加工製程　finishing process
整数变量/整數變量　integral variate
整数标记制/整數標記制　integer notation
整数规划/整數規劃　integer programming
0-1整数规划/0-1整數規劃　0-1 integer programming
整套提单/整套提單　set of bill of lading
整体标引/整體標引　integral indexing, summary indexing
整体补助款/整體補助款　block grant
整体-部分关系/整體-部分關係　whole-part relation
整体观/整體論　holism
整体管道观念/整體管道觀念　whole-channel view
整体管理计划/綜合管理規劃　integration management plan
整体解/大域解　global solution
整体网/整體網　whole network
整体消磁器/整體消磁器　overall degaussing device
整体性医疗范式/整體性醫療範式　holistic medical treatment
整体颜色变化/整體顏色變化　global color change
整箱/集装箱整箱货物　full container load
正本/正本　original of a document, original copy
正本信用证/正本信用狀　original credit
正本支票/正本支票　original cheque
正常报酬率/正常報酬率　normal rate of return
正常波动/正常變異　common variation
正常操作时间比/正常操作時間比　up-time ratio
正常产出/正常產出　modal output
正常产出率/正常產出率　normalized yield, NY
正常成本/正常成本　normal cost
正常储备/正常存量　normal stock
正常的生产条件/正常生產條件　normal plant condition
正常分布/適當分布　proper distribution
正常工作区域/正常工作區域　normal working area
正常汇率/正常匯率　normal rate of exchange
正常货物/正常貨物　normal goods

正常绩效/正常績效　normal performance
正常价格/正常價格　regular price
正常检验/正常檢驗　normal inspection
正常竞争/正常競爭　normal competition
正常离散/常態離勢　normal dispersion
正常利润/正常利潤　normal profit
正常贸易途径/正常貿易途徑　ordinary course of trade
正常时间/正常時間　normal time
正常收入/正常收入　normal income
正常税率/正常税率　normal tax rate
正常投资收益/正常投資收益　normal return
正常余额/正常餘額　normal balance
正常原因/共同原因　common cause
正常资产/正常資產　normal asset
正当成本抗辩/成本正當理由抗辯　cost justification defense
正当程序/正當程序　due process
正当程序原则/正當程式原則　principle of due process
正当持票人/善意持票人　holder in due course
正当防卫/正當防衛　justifiable defense
正当执票人/正當執票人,善意持票人　holder with good title
正当职务行为/正當職務行爲　due official act
正递归状态/正遞回狀態　positive recurrent state
正定/正定　positive definition
正二项分布/正二項分布,正二項分配　positive binomial distribution
正反馈/正反饋,正回饋　positive feedback
正规抵押/正規抵押　regular mortgage
正规方程/正規[化]方程式　normalized equation, normal equation
正规方程组/正規方程式組　system of normal equation
正规化 T 记分/正規化 T 計分　normalized T score
正规化 Z 记分/正規化 Z 計分　normalized Z score
正规化累积周期图/正規化累積週期圖　normalized cumulative periodogram
正规化设计/正規化設計　normalized design
正规化因子/正規化因子　normalized factor
正规化最优 D 设计/正規化 D 型最適設計　normalized D-optimal design
正规武装部队/正規武裝部隊　regular armed force
正辑/正輯　official album
正交变换/正交變換　orthogonal transformation
正交变量变换/正交變量變換　orthogonal variate transformation
正交对照/正交對比,直交對比　orthogonal contrast
正交多项式/正交多項式　orthogonal polynomial
正交方阵/正交方陣　orthogonal square
正交分割/正交分割　orthogonal partition
正交过程/正交過程　orthogonal process
正交函数/正交函數　orthogonal function
正交函数法/正交函數法　method of orthogonal function
正交化过程/正交化過程　orthogonalization process
正交回归/正交回歸　orthogonal regression
正交矩阵/正交矩陣　orthogonal matrix
正交拉丁方/正交拉丁方陣　orthogonal Latin square
正交排列/正交陣列,直交排列　orthogonal array
正交设计/正交設計　orthogonal design
正交实验设计/直交實驗設計　orthogonal experiment design
正交试验/正交實驗　orthogonal test
正交随机变量/正交隨機變數　orthogonal random variable
正交系/正交系統　orthonormal system
正交线性变换/正交線性變換　orthogonal linear transformation
正交向量/正交向量　orthogonal vector
正交性/正交性　orthogonality
正交旋转/直交轉軸　orthogonal rotation
正偏态/正偏態　positive skewness
正片/正片　positive copy, postive film
正签/正簽　Zhengqian, initialling
正确度/正確度　trueness
正确分类率/正確區別率　correct classification rate
正确选择/正確選擇　correct selection
正式部门/正式部門　formal sector
正式出版物/正式出版物　formal publication
正式订单/正式訂單　formal order, firm order
正式沟通/正式溝通　formal communication
正式规则/正式規則　formal rules
正式记录/正式記錄,官方檔　official record
正式交流/正式溝通　formal communication
正式解释/正式解釋　formal interpretation
正式控制/正式控制　formal social control
正式名称/正式名稱　official name
正式签字文件/正式檔　chirograph
正式群体/正式團體　formal group
正式收据/正式收據　formal receipt
正式通知/正式通知　formal notice
正式文本/正本檔　official document
正式信息交流网络/正式資訊交流網路　network of formal communication

正式债券/正式債券　definitive bond
正式制度/正式制度　formal institution
正式组织/正式組織,正规组织　formal organization
正似然比相依/正概度比相依　positively likelihood ratio dependence
正态变换/常態[化]變換　normalizing transform, normal transformation
正态变量和/常態變量和　sum of normal variates
正态二样本问题/常態雙樣本問題　normal two-sample problem
正态法则/常態法則　normal law
正态方差/常態變異數　normal variance
正态分布/常態分配,常態分布　normal distribution
正态-伽马先验/常態伽瑪事前機率　normal-gamma prior
正态概率/常態機率　normal probability
正态概率法则/常態機率法則　normal probability law
正态概率分布/常態機率分配　normal probability distribution
正态概率密度函数/常態機率密度函數　normal probability density function
正态概率图/常態機率圖　normal probability plot
正态概率纸/常態機率紙　normal probability paper
正态回归模型/常態回歸模型　normal regression model
正态混合/常態混合　normal mixture
正态记分/常態計分　normal score
正态记分估计量/常態計分估計量　normal score estimator
正态记分检验/常態計分檢定　normal score test
正态检验/常態[性]檢定　normality test
正态近似/常態逼近　normal approximation
正态均值/常態平均數　normal mean
正态离差/常態離差　normal deviate
正态频率分布/常態次數分布　normal frequency distribution
正态频率曲线/常態次數曲線　normal frequency curve
正态曲面/常態曲面　normal surface
正态曲线/常態曲線　normal curve
正态随机变量/常態隨機變數　normal random variable
正态随机过程/常態隨機過程　normal stochastic process
正态随机样本/常態隨機樣本　normal random sample
正态误差律/誤差常態法則　normal law of error

正态先验分布/常態事前分布　normal prior distribution
正态相关/常態相關　normal correlation
正态性/常態性　normality
正态性假定/常態性假設　assumption of normality, normality assumption
正态性检验/常態性檢定　test of normality, test for normality
正态众数/常態眾數　normal mode
正态自回归马尔夫序列/常態自[身]回歸馬可夫數列　normal autoregressive Markov series
正态总体/常態母體　normal population
正题名/正題名　title proper
正题名项/正題名項　plus title item
正文/正文　main textbody, main body
正文后的版面/書後附錄　end matter
正误个案法/正誤個案法　right and wrong cases method
正相关/正相關　positive correlation
正向工程/正向工程　forward engineering
正向市场/正向市場　contango
正象限相依/正象限相依　positively quadrant dependent
正像/正像　postive appearing image
正义/正義,公平　justice
正则估计量/正則估計量　regular estimator
正则化/正則化　regularization
正则假定/規律性假定　regularity assumption
正则可分组不完全区组设计/正則可分組不完全區集設計　regular group divisible incomplete block design
正则马尔可夫更新过程/正則馬可夫更新過程　regular Markov renewal process
正则马尔可夫链/正則馬可夫鏈　regular Markov chain
正则模型/正則模型　regular model
正则目标/正則目標　regular criteria
正则平稳点过程/正則平穩點過程　regular stationary point process
正则条件/正規條件　regularity condition
正则图形设计/正則圖形設計　regular graph design
正则形式的博弈/常態賽局　normal form of a game
正则性条件/正則條件,正常條件　regularity condition
正则状态/正則狀態　regular state
正则最佳渐近正态估计量/正則最佳漸近常態估計量　regular best asymptotically normal estimator
证据/證據　evidence

证据分类/證據分類　classification of evidence
证据关联性/證據關聯性　relevance of evidence
证据规则/證據法則　rule of evidence
证据合法性/證據合法性　legitimacy of evidence, legaility of evidence
证据价值/證據價值　evidential value
证据交换制度/證據交換制度　evidence exchange system
证据开示程序/證據開示程式　procedure of discovery, procedure of evidence discovery
证据可采性/證據可採性　admissibility of evidence, evidence admissibility
证据客观性/證據客觀性　objectivity of evidence
证据能力/證據能力　capacity of evidence
证据提供/證據提供　evidence of proof
证据种类/證據種類　kind of evidence
证据资料/證據資料　evidence material
证明/證明,驗證　certificate, proof, certification
证明标准/證明標準,舉證標準　standard of proof
证明对象/證明對象　object of proof
证明范围/證明範圍　scope of proof
证明妨害/證明妨害　obstruction of proof
证明力/證明力　probative force, weight of proof
证明商标/證明標章　certification mark
证明书/證明書　testimonial
证权证券/證權證券　certificate authority securities
证券/證券　securities
证券包销/證券包銷　underwriting
证券保证金交易/證券保證金交易　securities margin trading
[证券]偿还条款/[證券]償還條款　redemption provision
证券承销/證券承銷　securities underwriting
证券承销团/證券包銷集團　underwriting syndicate
证券承销协议/證券承銷協議　securities underwriting agreement
证券存款/證券存款　stock deposit
证券代销/證券代銷　commission underwriting
证券贷款/證券貸款　securities loan
证券担保贷款/有價證券抵押貸款　advance against securities
证券担保放款/證券擔保放款　securities collateral loan
证券担保汇票/證券擔保匯票　securities bill
证券登记结算机构/證券登記結算機構　securities registration and settlement organization
[证券等]发行公司/[證券等]發行公司　issuing company
证券二级市场/二級證券市場　secondary securities market
证券发行/證券發行　securities issue
证券发行登记制/證券發行註冊制　registration for issue of securities
证券发行核准制/證券發行核準制　approval for issue of securities
[证券]发行价格/[證券]發行價格　issue price
证券发行人/證券發行人　securities issuer
证券发行上市保荐制/證券發行上市保薦制　sponsor's system for issue of securities
证券发行审批制/證券發行審批制　examination and approval system for issue of securities
证券发行市场/證券發行市場　securities issue market
证券法/證券法　securities law
证券公司/證券公司　securities company, stock exchange firm
证券化/證券化　securitization
证券价格/證券價格　securities price
证券监督管理机构/證券監督管理機構　securities regulatory organization
证券交易/證券交易　securities exchange, dealing in securities, securities transaction
证券交易服务机构/證券交易服務機構　securities service institution
证券交易价格/證券交易價格　stock exchange price
证券交易清算/證券交易清算　stock exchange settlement
证券交易清算公司/證券交易清算公司　stock exchange clearing house
证券交易市场/證券交易市場　securities exchange market
证券交易税/證券交易稅　securities exchange tax, securities transaction tax, transfer tax on stock
证券交易所/證券交易所　securities exchange center
证券交易所报价单/證券交易所報價單　stock exchange quotation
证券交易所补偿基金/證券交易所補償基金　stock exchange compensation fund
证券交易所交易/證券交易所交易　stock exchange transaction
证券交易所每日牌价/證券交易所每日牌價　stock exchange daily official list
证券交易所牌价/證券交易所牌價　stock exchange list
证券交易委员会/證券交易委員會　securities and exchange commission

证券经纪公司/證券經紀公司　securities brokerage company
证券经纪人/證券經紀人,證券經紀商　securities broker, dealer in securities, stock broker
证券经纪业务/證券經紀業務　agiotage
[证券]票面价格/[證券]票面價格　face par
证券期货交易/證券期貨交易　securities futures transaction
证券期权交易/證券期權交易　securities option transaction
证券清算/證券清算　stock clearing
证券商/證券商　securities dealer
证券市场/證券市場　securities market
证券市场线/證券市場線　securities market line
证券市场指数/證券市場指數　stock market index
证券所有权/證券所有權　ownership of securities
证券特征线/證券特徵線　securities characteristic line, SCL
证券统计/證券統計　securities statistics
证券投机/證券投機　speculation in securities
证券投资/證券投資,債券投資,公司債投資　bond investment, investment in securities, portfolio investment
证券投资风险/證券投資風險　portfolio risk
证券投资基金/證券投資基金　securities investment fund
证券投资损益/證券投資損益　profit and loss on security and investment
证券投资信托/證券投資信託　securities investment trust
证券投资选择理论/證券投資組合理論　theory of portfolio selection
证券无纸化/證券無實體化　security dematerialization
证券信托银行/證券信託銀行　securities trust management bank
证券信用交易/證券信用交易　securities credit transaction
证券选择/證券選擇　security selection
证券业协会/證券協會　securities association
证券纸/證券紙　bond paper
证券指数基金/證券指數基金　securities index fund
证券转让/證券轉讓　transfer of security
证券组合/證券投資組合　securities portfolio
证人/證人　witness
证人证言/證人證言　testimony of witness
证人作证资格/證人作證資格　qualification of witness
证书/證書　certificate, credential
证书暂停/證書暫停　certification suspension
证伪/否證　falsification
证真偏差/驗證性偏誤,驗應性偏誤　confirmation bias
政策/政策　policy
政策本位主义/政策本位主義　policy parochialism
政策边界分析法/政策界限分析　policy boundary analysis
政策变量/政策變數　policy variable
政策采纳/政策採納　policy adoption
政策层级分析法/政策層級分析法　policy hierarchical analysis
政策倡导者/政策提倡者　policy advocator
政策倡议/政策倡議,政策倡導　policy advocacy
政策成本-收益率/政策本益比　cost-benefit ratio of policy
政策抵触/政策抵觸　policy contradiction
政策多角度分析法/政策多元觀點分析法　policy multiple perspective analysis
政策法律因素/政策法律因素　political and legal segment
政策法学派/政策法學派　school of policy-science of law
政策分类分析法/政策類別分析法　policy classification analysis
政策分析/政策分析　policy analysis
政策服务对象/政策服務對象　policy clientele
政策个案研究法/政策個案研究　policy case study
政策工具/政策工具　policy instrument
政策功能/政策功能　policy function
政策沟通/政策溝通　policy communication
政策构建/政策規劃　policy formulation
政策过程/政策過程　policy process
政策合法化/政策合法化　policy legitimization
政策合法性/政策合法性　policy legitimacy
政策环境/政策環境　policy environment
政策假设分析法/政策前提分析法　policy assumption analysis
政策监控/政策監控　policy supervision and control
政策精英/政策菁英　policy elite
政策科学/政策科學　science of policy
政策可信度/政策可信度　policy credibility
政策可行性分析/政策可行性分析　policy feasibility analysis
政策控制/政策控制　policy control
政策宽放/政策寬放　policy allowance
政策困境/政策困境　policy dilemma

政策立法/政策立法　law making from policy
政策利益相关者/政策利害關係者　policy stakeholder
政策论证/政策論證　policy argument
政策模拟分析法/政策模擬分析法　policy analogy analysis
政策目标/政策目標　policy goal
政策目标对象/政策目標物件　policy target
政策内容分析法/政策内容分析　policy content analysis
政策偏好函数/政策偏好函數　political preference function
政策评价/政策評價　policy assessment, policy evaluation
政策情报研究/政策情報分析　policy intelligence analysis
政策趋势外推法/政策趨勢外推法　policy trend extrapolation
政策权衡/政策權衡,政策取捨　policy trade-off
政策社群/政策社群　policy community
政策失灵/政策失靈　policy failure
政策受益者/政策受益者　policy beneficiary
政策条文/政策聲明　policy statement
政策调整/政策調整　policy adjustment
政策脱轨/政策脱軌　policy derailment
政策外部性/政策外溢　policy externality
政策维持/政策維持　policy maintenance
政策牺牲者/政策犧牲者　policy victim
政策系统/政策系統　policy system
政策协商/政策協商　policy deliberation
政策协商阶段/政策協商階段　policy deliberation phase
政策性补贴支出/政策性補貼支出　expenditure for price subsidy
政策性贷款/政策性貸款　policy loan
政策性价格/政策性價格　political price
政策性银行/政策性銀行,政策银行機構　policy bank, policy banking institution
政策性租赁住房/政策性租賃住房　policy-based rental housing
政策议程/政策議程　policy agenda
政策意识形态/政策思想　policy ideology
政策游说/政策遊説　policy lobbying
政策预测/政策預測　policy forecasting
政策执行/政策執行　policy implementation
政策执行连接/政策執行連接　policy implementation linkage
政策制定/政策制定　policy making

政策质询/政策探究　policy inquiry
政策终结/政策終結　policy termination
政策周期/政策循環　policy cycle
政党认同/政黨認同　party identification
政法体制/政法體制　political and legal system
政法院校/政法院校　political and legal school
政府/政府　government, administration
政府经济学/公共經濟學　public economics
政府在线/線上政府　government online, GO
政教分离/政教分離　separation of church and state, church-state separation
政教分离原则/政教分離原則　separation of church and state
政教合一/政教合一　caesaropapism
政论节目/政論節目　political discussion program
政略学派/政治學派　political school
政书/政書　book on government
政务信息/行政管理資訊　administrative information
政务信息发布/公共資訊傳播　public information release
政治管理/政治管理　political management
政治广告/政治廣告　political advertising, political advertisement
政治环境/政治環境　political environment
政治均衡/政治均衡　political equilibrium
政治可行性/政治可行性　political feasibility
政治权力/政治權力　political power
政治权利/政治權利　political rights
政治社会学/政治社會學　political sociology
政治市场/政治市場　political market
政治文化/政治文化　political culture
政治问题/政治問題　political questions
政治性经济周期/政治景氣循環　political business cycle
政治性移民/政治性移民　political immigrants
政治宣传/政治宣傳　political propaganda
政治压力/政治壓力　political pressures
政治营销/政治行銷　political marketing
政治与行政二分法/政治行政二分法　politics administration dichotomy
政治杂志/政治雜誌　political magazine
政治制度/政治制度　political institution
政治中立/政治中立　political neutrality
挣值/挣值　earned value, EV
挣值管理/挣值管理　earned value management, EVM
支撑/支集　support
支撑函数/支持函數　support function

支撑技术／支撐技術　backstop technology
支持公诉／支持公訴　support prosecution
支持功能／支持功能　supportive function
支持关系理论／支持關係理論　support relation theory, supportive relationship theory
支持向量回归预测法／支援向量回歸機預測方法　support vector regression forecasting
支出／支出，開銷　expenditure, spending
支出额／支出金額　volume of expenditure
支出法／支出法　expenditure method
支出转换效应／支出移轉效果　expenditure-switch effect
支出转换政策／支出移轉政策　expenditure-switch policy
支出最小化／支出極小化　expenditure minimization
支付／支付　effect a payment, payoff
支付安全／支付安全　payment security
支付差额／支付差額　payment balance
支付代理人／付款代理人　paying agent
支付风险／付款風險　payment risk
支付函数／支付函數　payoff function
支付合同／支付合約　contract of payment
支付货币／支付貨幣　currency of payment
支付矩阵／支付［矩］陣，償付矩陣，報價矩陣　payoff matrix
支付令／支付令　payment order
支付能力原则／量能課稅原則　ability to pay principle
支付票据／支付票據　bill of payment
支付凭证／支付憑證　payment instrument
支付期限／支付期限　term of payment
支付清算系统／交換清算系統　payment and clearing system
支付手段／償付工具　means of payment
支付授权书／付款授權書　authorization of payment
支付条件管制／支付條件管制　terms control
支付调整／收支調整　payment adjustment
支付系统／支付系統　payment system
支付协定／支付協定　payment agreement
支付意愿／支付意願　willingness to pay
支款凭证／付款憑證　pay order
支配／支配　domination
支配企业行为／優勢廠商行為　dominant firm behavior
支配权／支配權　right of control
支票／支票　check
［支票］承兑申明／［支票］承兑說明　statement of acceptance on cheque
支票持有人／支票持有人　holder of cheque
支票出票人／支票出票人　check drawer
支票存款／支票存款　check deposit, checkable deposit
支票汇款／支票匯款　remittance by cheque
支票汇率／支票利率　check rate
支票货币／支票貨幣　check book money
支票交易／支票交易　check trading
支票受票人／支票抬頭人，支票持有人　check drawee
支票贴现／支票貼現　discount on check
支票账户／支票賬戶　check account
［支票］止付通知书／［支票］止付通知書　stop payment note
芝加哥交易所／芝加哥交易所　Chicago Board of Trade, CBOT
芝加哥期权交易所／芝加哥選擇權外匯交易所　Chicago Board of Options Exchange, CBOE
芝加哥商业交易所／芝加哥商業交易所　Chicago Mercantile Exchange
芝加哥学派／芝加哥學派　Chicago school
知沟理论／知識［鴻溝］理論　knowledge gap
知觉／知覺　perception
知觉定势／知覺取向　perceptual set
知觉运动型职位设计／知覺運動工作設計　perceptual-motor job design
知名度／知名度　popularity
知名商品／知名商品　famous or noted commodity
知情交易概率／知情交易概率　probability of informed trading
知情交易者／知情交易者　informed trader
知情权／知情權，知的權利　right to know
知情同意／知情同意，告知同意　informed consent
知识／知識　knowledge
知识保护／知識保護　knowledge protection
知识本体／知識本體　knowledge ontology
知识表示／知識表示　knowledge representation
知识表示本体／知識表示本體論　knowledge representation ontology
知识表示系统／知識表示系統　knowledge representation system
知识采集／知識收集　knowledge gathering
知识仓库／知識倉庫　knowledge warehouse
知识产品／知識產品　knowledge product
知识产权／智慧財產權　intellectual property, intellectual property right
知识产权保护边境措施／智慧財產權保護邊境措施　border measure of IPR protection

知识产权地域性/智慧財產權地域性 regionality of intellectual property
知识产权法/智慧財產權法 intellectual property law
知识产权管理/智慧財產權管理 intellectual property management
知识产权管理机构/智慧財產權管理機構 institution of intellectual property management
知识产权国际贸易争端解决机制/智慧財產權國際貿易爭端解決機制 WTO mechanism of IP dispute settlement
知识产权互惠原则/智慧財產權互惠原則 principle of reciprocity
知识产权鉴定/智慧財產權鑑定 appraisal of intellectual property
知识产权客体/智慧財產權客體 subject-matter of intellectual property right
知识产权滥用/智慧財產權濫用 abuse of intellectual property right
知识产权民事救济/智慧財產權民事救濟 civil remedy for intellectual property right owner
知识产权侵权判定流程/智慧財產權侵權判定流程 judgment of intellectual property infringement
知识产权权利穷竭原则/智慧財產權權利窮竭原則 exhaustion doctrine of IPR
知识产权权利限制/智慧財產權權利限制 limitation on intellectual property right
知识产权确权程序/智慧財產權確權程式 approval procedure of intellectual property right
知识产权审判庭/智慧財產權審判庭 intellectual property tribunal
知识产权时间性/智慧財產權時間性 time limit of intellectual property right
知识产权司法保护/智慧財產權司法保護 judicial protection of IPR
知识产权无形性/智慧財產權無形性 immateriality of intellectual property right
知识产权刑事救济/智慧財產權刑事救濟 criminal remedy for intellectual property right
知识产权行政救济/智慧財產權行政救濟 administrative remedy for intellectual property right
知识产权战略/智慧財產權策略 intellectual property strategy
知识产权执法/智慧財產權執法 enforcement of intellectual property law
知识产权质押/智慧財產權質押 intellectual property mortgage
知识产权中介/智慧財產權仲介 intermediary agency intellectual property
知识产权主体/智慧財產權主體 intellectual property right owner
知识产权专门法院/智慧財產權專門法院 special court of intellectual property
知识产权资产/智慧財產權 intellectual property right
知识抽取/知識萃取 knowledge extraction
知识创新/知識創新 knowledge innovation
知识创新工程/知識創新工程 Knowledge Innovation Project
知识创新能力/知識創新能力 knowledge innovation capability
知识创造/知識創造 knowledge creation
知识存储/知識蓄積,知識儲存 knowledge storage
知识存量/知識存量 knowledge stock
知识导航/知識導航 knowledge navigation
知识地图/知識圖 knowledge map
知识度量/知識度量 measurement of knowledge
知识发现/知識發現,知識發掘 knowledge discovery
知识发现系统/知識發現體系 knowledge discovery system
知识分类/知識分類法 knowledge classification
知识分析师/知識分析師 knowledge analyst
知识服务/知識服務 knowledge service
知识服务平台/知識服務平臺 knowledge service platform
知识工资制度/知識論薪制度 knowledge pay system
知识工作者/知識工作者 knowledge worker
知识供应链/知識供應鏈 knowledge supply chain
知识供应者/知識提供方 knowledge provider
知识共享/知識共用 knowledge sharing
知识共享平台/知識共用平臺 knowledge sharing platform
知识共享协议/創用CC,版權宣告 creative commons, CC
知识构建/知識構建 knowledge architecture
知识管理/知識管理 knowledge management
知识管理策略/知識管理策略 knowledge management tactic
知识管理成熟度/知識管理成熟度 knowledge management maturity
知识管理体系/知識管理架構 knowledge management system
知识管理系统/知識管理系統 knowledge management system, KMS
知识管理学/知識管理學 knowledge management science, knowledge management studies

知识管理战略/知識管理策略　knowledge management strategy
知识鸿沟/知識缺口　knowledge divide, knowledge gap
知识获取/知識獲取，知識取得　knowledge acquisition
知识积累/知識積累　knowledge accumulation
知识集成平台/知識整合平臺　knowledge integration platform
知识架构/知識構建　knowledge architecture
知识检索/知識檢索　knowledge retrieval, knowledge search
知识交流/知識交流　knowledge communication
知识交流论/知識認識論　knowledge communication theory
知识交流平台/知識溝通平臺　knowledge communication platform
知识阶层/知識階級　knowledge class
知识经济/知識經濟　knowledge-based economy
知识经营/知識經營　knowledge operation
知识考古学/知識考古學　archaeology of knowledge
知识库/知識庫　knowledge base, stock of knowledge
知识扩散/知識擴散　knowledge diffusion
知识联盟/知識聯盟　knowledge alliance
知识链/知識鏈　knowledge chain
知识领域/知識領域　knowledge area
知识流/知識流　knowledge flow
知识流失/知識流失　loss of knowledge
知识门户/知識入口　knowledge portal
知识密集型产业/知識密集產業　knowledge intensive industry
知识密集型服务/知識密集型服務　knowledge intensive service
知识密集型服务业/知識密集服務業　knowledge intensive business service, KIBS
知识评价/知識評價　knowledge evaluation
知识社会/知識社會　knowledge society
知识社会学/知識社會學　sociology of knowledge
知识社群/知識社群　knowledge community
知识生态系统/知識生態系統　knowledge ecosystem
知识使用/知識使用，知識應用　knowledge use
知识体系/知識體系　body of knowledge
知识图谱/知識製圖　knowledge mapping
知识挖掘/知識挖掘　knowledge mining
知识外溢/知識外溢　knowledge spillover
知识网络/知識網路　knowledge network
知识吸收/知識吸收　knowledge absorption
知识系统/知識系統　knowledge system
知识系统工程/知識系統工程　knowledge system engineering
知识相关性/知識關聯性　knowledge relatedness
知识效应/知識效應　cognitive effect
知识型员工/知識工作者　knowledge worker
知识型组织/知識型組織　knowledge-based organization
知识性失业/教育性失業　educated unemployment
知识需求模型/知識需求模型　knowledge demand model
知识学派/知識學派　school of knowledge
知识循环/知識循環　knowledge cycle
知识元/知識元　knowledge element
知识责任附注/知識責任附注　note pertaining to intellectual responsibility
知识增值/增值增值　knowledge increment
知识重用/知識重用　knowledge reuse
知识转化/知識轉化　knowledge transformation
知识转化模型/知識轉化模型，SECI 模型　SECI model
知识转移/知識轉移　knowledge transfer
知识资本/知識資本　knowledge capital
知识资本化/知識資本化　knowledge capitalization
知识资本运营/知識資本運營　knowledge capital operation
知识资产/知識資產　knowledge asset
知识资产评估/知識資產評估　knowledge asset evaluation
知识资源/知識資源　knowledge resource
知识组织/知識組織　knowledge organization, knowledge construction
知识组织系统/知識組織系統　knowledge organization system, KOS
执笔人/執筆者　drafter, draftsman
执票人/執票人　person possession of instrument
执行标的/執行標的　object of enforcement
执行撤销/執行撤銷　reversal of enforcement
执行程序/執行程式　executive procedure
执行措施/執行措施　enforcement measure
执行担保/執行擔保　security provided for postponed enforcement
执行罚/執行罰　enforcement fine
执行费用/執行費用　cost of enforcement
执行根据/執行根據　basis of enforcement
执行和解/執行和解　settlement of enforcement
执行回转/執行回轉　revocation of enforcement based on an erroneous judgment

执行豁免/執行豁免 exemption from execution, immunity from execution
执行机构/執行機構 organization of executive
执行机关/執行機關 agency of executive, enforcement organization
执行价/執行價格,行使價格,履約價格 exercise price
执行进口限制许可/實行進口限制許可 licensing administer import restriction
执行救济/執行救濟 relief of enforcement
执行力/執行力 execution
执行领导/執行領導 executive
执行令/執行令 executive writ, warrant of execution
执行通知书/執行通知 notice of execution
执行刑/執行刑 executed punishment
执行异议/執行異議 execution objection
执行摘要/執行摘要 executive summary
执行中止/執行中止 suspension of enforcement
执行终结/執行終結 termination of enforcement
执行终了/執行終了 end of enforcement
执照/執照 licence
直播卫星/直播衛星 direct broadcast satellite, DBS
直达汇票/直達匯票 straight arrival bill
直达运输/聯運 through transportation
直方图/直方圖,矩形圖 histogram
直观订货系统/目視訂貨系統 visual review system
直观概率/直覺機率 intuitive probability
直和设计/直和設計 direct summing design
直角设计/直角設計 right angular design
直接背书/直接背書 direct endorsement
直接标价/直接報價 direct quotation
直接材料/直接材料 direct material
直接参与保证合同/直接參與保證合約 immediate participation guarantee contract
直接产品延伸/直接產品延伸 straight product extension
直接成本/直接成本 direct cost
直接成像/直接成像 direct imaging
直接重购/直接再購 straight rebuy
直接抽样/直接抽樣 direct sampling
直接筹融资/直接資金融通 direct finance
直接传播/直接傳播 direct communication
直接贷款/直接貸款 direct loan
直接档案类别/直接檔案類別 direct archival category
直接档案全宗/直接檔案全宗 direct fonds
直接读者/直接讀者 direct reader
直接对外投资/直接對外投資 direct foreign investment
直接发货/直接裝運 drop ship
直接发行/直接發行 direct issuing
直接法制版/直接法製版 direct screen making
直接费/直接成本 direct cost
直接费用/直接費用 direct out-of-pocket expense
直接服务/直接服務 direct service
直接付款/直接給付 direct payment
直接概率/直接機率 direct probability
直接故意/直接故意 actual intent
直接汇兑/直接匯兌 direct exchange
直接汇率/直接匯率 direct rate of exchange
直接汇票/直接匯票 direct bill, direct draft
直接检索/直接搜尋 direct search, direct retrieval
直接-间接法制版/直接-間接法製版 direct indirect screen making
直接鉴定法/直接鑒定法 direct appraisal
直接交付/直接交付 direct delivery
直接金融/直接金融 direct finance
直接进出口/直接進出口 direct export and import
直接纠正行动/立即改正行動 immediate corrective action
直接客体/直接客體 direct object
直接劳动/直接勞動 direct labor
直接劳动标准/直接勞工標準 direct labor standard
直接贸易/直接貿易 active commerce, direct trade
直接民主/直接民主 direct democracy
直接平版印刷/直接平版印刷 direct planographic printing
直接强制/直接強制 direct compulsion
直接侵权/直接侵權 direct infringement of intellectual property
直接渠道/直接管道 direct channel
直接热成像/直接熱成像 direct thermography
直接人工/直接人工 direct labor
直接入库/直接入庫,免驗入庫 dock-to-stock
直接受益人/直接受益人 immediate beneficiary
直接税/直接稅 direct tax
直接送达/直接送達 direct service
直接套利/直接套利 direct arbitrage, simple arbitrage
直接投资/直接投資 direct investment, straight investment
直接推算预测法/直接推算預測法 direct inference forecasting approach
直接显示偏好/直接顯示偏好 directly revealed preference
直接显示原理/直接顯示原理 direct revelation

principle
直接消耗系数/直接費用係數,直接產品消耗係數　direct expense coefficient, direct input coefficient
直接消耗系数矩阵/直接產品消耗係數矩陣　direct input coefficient matrix
直接效应/直接影響　direct effect
直接薪酬/直接薪酬　direct compensation
直接信贷/直接信貸　straight forward credit
直接信用控制/直接信用控制　direct credit control
直接信用证/直接信用狀　direct letter of credit, straight credit
直接印刷/直接列印　direct printing
直接营销/直接行銷　direct marketing
直接营销渠道/直接行銷管道　direct marketing channel
直接影印件/影遞檔　photostat
直接邮寄营销/郵遞行銷　direct-mail marketing
直接正犯/直接正犯　direct principal
直接证据/直接證據　direct evidence
直接制版机/直接製版機　platesetter
直接转运/直接轉運　cross docking
直接转账/直接轉賬,直接劃撥　giro
直接转账银行/直接轉賬銀行,劃撥銀行　giro bank
直接租赁/直接租賃　straight lease
直觉/直覺　intuition
直觉决策/直覺式決策　intuitive decision-making
直觉政策预测/直覺政策預測　intuitive policy forecasting
直丝绺/直絲流　grain direction
直系血亲/直系血親　lineal relative by blood
直线基准/直線基準　straight line basis
直线结构/直線結構　line structure
直线趋势/直線趨勢　straight line trend, rectilinear trend
直线相关/直線相關,線性相關　straight line correlation, rectilinear correlation
直线性/直線性　rectilinearity
直线折旧法/直線折舊法　straight line depreciation, depreciation straight-line method
直线职能结构/直線幕僚結構,直線-功能結構　line-staff structure, line-functional structure
直线职权/直線職權　line authority
直销/直接銷售　direct sale
直销网站/直銷網站　direct selling website
直效营销/直效行銷　direct marketing
直序名称/直序名稱　name in direct order
直营店/直營店　company-owned bookstore
直邮广告/直接郵件[廣告],直接信函廣告　direct mail advertising
直运商/承訂批發商　drop shipper
p值/p值　p-value
α值/α值　α value, alpha value
γ值/γ值　γ value, gamma value
δ值/δ值　δ value, delta value
θ值/θ值　θ value, theta value
值比指数/值比指數　value ratio index number
p值假设检验法/p值檢定法　p-value method of hypothesis testing
Z值模型/Z值公式　Z score formula
职场性骚扰/職場性騷擾　sexual harassment in workplace
职称/職稱　position title
职代会/職工代表大會,員工大會　workers' congress
职等/職等　grade level
职工/員工　workers and staff members
职工代表大会/職工代表大會,員工大會　workers' congress
职工股/職工股　staff stock
职工教育评价/職工教育評估　evaluation of education for workers and staff
职工教育形式/職工教育形態　form of education for workers and staff
职工满足度/員工滿意度　satisfaction degree of employee
职官注释/職官注釋　official post annotation
职号/職號　operator
职级/職級　rank
职门/職業階級　occupational class
职能部门/職能部門　functional department
职能部门化/功能部門化　functional departmentalization
职能[层]战略/功能層策略　functional-level strategy
职能分类法/職能分類法　function classification
职能工长制/職能工長制　functional foremanship
职能机关/職能機關　functional organ
职能鉴定论/職能鑒定論　functional approach to appraisal, function appraisal theory
职能结构/功能式結構　functional structure
职能经理/職能經理　functional manager
职能来源/職能來源　functional provenance
职能式[项目管理]组织/功能式專案管理組織　functional organization of project management
职能式职位分析法/功能性工作分析　functional job analysis
职能型团队/功能性團隊　functional team
职能战略制定/功能策略規劃　functional strategy

formulation
职能职权/功能性職權，功能性權威 functional authority
职能制/職能制 organizing system based on function
职权设计/職權設計 authority design
职位/職位 position, job
职位程序化/職位程式化 job routinization
职位等级/職位等級 job class
职位分类/職位分類，工作分類 job classification, position classification
职位分类系统/工作分類系統，工作分類制度 job classification system
职位分析/職位分析 job analysis
职位分析问卷/職位分析問卷 job analysis questionnaire
职位积分累计模型/工作積分累計模型，工作點增加模型 job-point accrual model
职位排序系统/工作排序系統 job ranking system
职位匹配/工作媒合 job matching
职位评价/職位評價 job evaluation
职位群/職位群 job cluster
职位设计/工作設計 job design
职位说明书/工作說明書 job description
职位要素/工作要素 job factor
职位诊断调查/工作診斷調查表 job diagnostic survey
职位族/工作群 job family
职务发明/職務發明 invention by employee
职务作品/職務作品 service work
职系/職系 occupational series
职业/職業 occupation
职业安全卫生培训/職業安全衛生訓練 occupational safety and health training
职业标准分类/職業標準分類 standard classification of occupations
职业病/職業病 occupational disease
职业病防治/職業病防治 prevention and cure of occupational disease
职业病防治法/職業病防治法 law on prevention and control of occupational diseases
职业代表制/職業代表制 professional representation
职业道德/專業倫理 professional ethics
职业的性别隔离/職業的性別隔離 gender segregation of occupation
职业发展计划/職涯發展計劃 career development program
职业分层/職業分層 occupational stratification
职业分类/職業分類 classification of occupations
职业分立/職業分立 division of occupation
职业风险/職業風險 career risk
职业辅导/職業輔導 vocational counselling
职业隔离/職業隔離 occupational segregation
职业环境/職業環境 occupational environment
职业健康安全/職業衛生安全 occupational health and safety, OHS
职业健康安全管理体系/職業衛生安全管理體系 occupational health and safety management system, OHSMS
职业教育/職業教育 vocational education
职业介绍/職業介紹 occupational introduction
职业介绍所/職業介紹所，就業中心 career service center
职业康复/職業復原輔導 vocational rehabilitation
职业流动/職業流動 occupational mobility
职业锚/生涯定向 career anchor
[职业]能力倾向测验/性向測驗 aptitude test
职业年金/職業年金 occupational pension
职业培训/職業訓練 career training
职业培训协作法案/工作訓練夥伴法案 job training partnership act
职业培训中心/職業訓練中心 career training center
职业期望/職業期望 occupational expectation
职业歧视/職業歧視 occupational discrimination
职业倾向测试/職業偏好測驗 vocational preference test
职业生涯/事業生涯，職涯 career
职业生涯发展/職涯發展 career development
职业生涯高原/職涯高原 career plateau
职业生涯管理/生涯管理，職涯管理 career management
职业生涯规划/職涯規劃 career planning
职业生涯路径/職涯路徑 career path
职业生涯培训/職涯訓練 career training
职业生涯曲线/職涯曲線 career curve
职业生涯-人匹配理论/職涯-個人適配理論 career-person matching theory
职业生涯选择/職業選擇，職涯選擇 career choice
职业生涯周期/職涯週期 career cycle
职业声望/職業聲望 occupational prestige
职业适应性/職業適應性 occupational adaptability
职业危害/職業危害 occupational harm
职业协会/專業協會 professional association
职业兴趣测验/職業興趣測驗 vocational interest test
职业选择/職業選擇 occupational choice
职业压力/職業壓力 occupational stress

职业责任保险/職業責任保險　professional liability insurance
职业指导/職業指引,職業輔導　vocational guidance, occupational guidance
职业转换培训/轉崗培訓　career shift training
职业资格证书/專業認證　professional certification
职业自由/職業自由　occupational freedom
职组/職業團體,職業群體　occupational group
植入[式]广告/置入行銷,產品置入　product placement
植物新品种/植物新品種　new breed of plant
殖民地/殖民地　colony
殖民地帝国主义/殖民帝國主義　colonial imperialism
殖民地化/殖民化　colonization
殖民地经济/殖民地經濟　colonial economy
殖民主义/殖民主義　colonialism
止付/止付　stop payment
止付命令或通知/止付命令或通知　stop payment order
止付通知/拒付通知　order not to pay
止损指令/停損訂單　stop-loss order
只读存储多用途数字光盘/唯讀存儲多用途數位光碟　digital versatile disc-read only memory
只读存储光盘/唯獨光碟　compact disc-read only memory
只读光盘/唯讀光碟　compact disc-read only memory, CD-ROM
只读型 DVD/唯讀式 DVD　versatile disc-recordable, DVD-R, DVD+R
纸本期刊/紙本期刊　print periodical, print journal
纸币/紙幣　bank paper, paper currency, soft money
纸币本位制/紙幣本位制　paper standard system
纸草档案/紙草檔案,莎草檔案　papyrus archive
纸草文件/紙草檔案　papyrus file
纸黄金/賬面黃金,紙金　paper gold
纸基底版/紙版　paper master
纸浆和纸制造业/紙漿與造紙工業　pulp and paper manufacturing
纸浆修补/紙漿修補　leafcasting
纸面规则/紙面規則　paper rule
纸墙/紙牆　paper wall
纸上封锁/紙上封鎖　paper blockade
纸样/紙樣　print pattern
纸张/紙張　paper
纸张白度/紙張白度　paper whiteness
纸张定量/紙張定量,紙張基本磅數　basis weight, paper weight
纸张厚度/紙張厚度　paper thickness
纸张加固/紙張加固　reinforcement
纸张紧度/紙張緊度　paper density
纸张抗张强度/紙張抗張強度　tensile strength of paper
纸张耐久性/紙張耐久性　paper permanence
纸张耐破度/紙張耐破度　bursting strength of paper
纸张耐折度/紙張耐折度　folding strength of paper
纸张起毛/紙張起毛　paper fluff
纸张施胶度/紙張施膠度　degree of sizing of paper
纸张水分/紙張水分　water content of paper
纸张撕裂度/紙張撕裂度　tearing strength of paper
纸张酸化/紙張酸化　acidification
纸张酸碱度/紙張酸鹼度　pH value of paper
纸张糟朽/紙張糟朽　paper rotting
纸张粘连/紙張粘連　conglutination
纸张纵向横向/紙張縱向橫向　vertical and horizon orientation of paper
纸制品加工/紙製品加工　converting
纸质档案/紙質類檔案　paper archive
纸质档案数字化/紙質檔案數位化　digitization of paper-based archive
纸质文件/紙質檔案　paper document, paper-based record
指标/指標　indicator, index
指标函数/示性函數,指示函數　indicator function
指导人/導師　mentor
指导人计划/師徒制,導師制　mentoring program
指导式咨询/指導式諮商　directive counseling
指导性计划/指導性計劃,導引性計劃　guidance plan
指定保税地区/指定保稅地區　designated bonded area
指定辩护/指定辯護　advocacy by designation
指定持牌银行/指定簽證銀行　appointed licensing bank
指定存款/指定存款　designated deposit
指定代理/指定代理　demonstrative agency, appointed agency
指定代理人/指定代理人　authorized agent
指定分包商/指定分包商　nominated subcontractor
指定概率抽选/暫定機率選取法　selection with arbitrary probability
指定管辖/指定管轄　designation of jurisdiction, designative jurisdiction
指定货币/指定貨幣　designated currency
指定监护/指定監護　named guardianship
指定教学参考书/指定教學參考書　required

teaching reference book
指定模型/指派模型　assignment model
指定目的港/指定目的港　named port of destination
指定式背书/指定式背書　endorsement to order
指定式汇票/指定式匯票,指示式匯票　bill drawn to order
指定通货/指定通貨　specified currency
指定统计/指定統計　designated statistics
指定[外汇交易]银行/指定[外匯交易]銀行　authorized bank for exchange operation
指定外汇银行/指定外匯銀行　appointed foreign exchange bank
指定信用证/特別通知信用狀　specially advised credit
指定银行/指定銀行　designated bank
指定灾害保险/指定災害保險,記名保險單　named-peril insurance
指定装运港/指定裝運港,指定裝貨港　named port of shipment
指挥链/指揮鏈　chain of command
指挥型战略实施/指揮型策略執行　conductor-type strategy implementation
指己汇票/指己匯票　self-ordered bill of exchange
指令/指令　instruction
指令回避/指令迴避　order to avoid
指令经济/指令經濟　command economy
指令驱动市场/指令驅動市場　order-driven market
指令性计划/指令性計劃　mandatory plan
指令性文件管理/指示性檔案管理　directives file management
指南/指南,導引　guide, directory encheiridion
指派问题/指派問題　assignment problem
指示性价格/參考報價　indicative price
指示性文摘/指示性摘要　indicative abstract
指示性引用标准/指示性引用標準　indicative reference to standard
指示因子/指示因子　indicative factor
指数/指數　index, index number
H 指数/H 指數　Hirsch index, H-index
δ 指数/δ 指數　δ-index, Gini
指数分布/指數分布,指數分配　exponential distribution
指数分布族/指數分布族　exponential distribution family
指数广义自回归条件异方差模型/指數廣義自回歸條件異方差模型　exponential generalized autoregressive conditional heteroskedasticity model, exponent

指数函数/指數函數　exponential function
指数化/指數連動　indexation
指数化证券/價格指數證券　indexed securities
指数回归模型/指數回歸模型　exponential regression model
指数基金/指數[型]基金　index fund
指数加权/指數加權　weighting of index number
指数加权移动模型/加權指數移動模型　exponentially-weighted moving model
指数加权移动平均模型/指數加權移動平均模型　exponentially weighted moving average model, EWMA model
指数偏倚/指數偏離　bias of index number
指数平滑法/指數平滑法　exponential smoothing
指数平滑控制图/指數平滑管制圖　exponential smoothing control chart
指数平滑预测法/指數平滑預測法　exponential smoothing forecasting approach
指数期货/指數期貨　index future
指数期权/股指選擇權　index option
指数曲线/指數曲線　exponential curve
指数死亡率/指數死亡率　index death rate
指数套利/指數套利　index arbitrage
指数线性模型/指數線性模型　exponential linear model
指数相关/指數相關　index correlation
指数影响因子/指數影響因素　factor of change to index
指数有序记分/指數有序計分　exponential ordered score
指数债券/指數連動債券　indexed bond
指数资产/指數資產　index asset
指数族/指數族　exponential family
指数族的完备性/指數族的完備性　completeness of exponential family
DNA 指纹/DNA 指紋　DNA fingerprint
指引卡/指引卡,引導片　guide card
指针函数/指標函數　index function
志愿部队/志願部隊　volunteer corps
志愿失灵/志願失靈　voluntary failure
志愿团体/志願團體,自願結社,志願結社　voluntary association, voluntary group
志愿者/志工　volunteer
志愿者管理/志工管理　volunteers' management
志愿组织/志工組織　voluntary organization
制版照相机/製版照相機　reproduction camera
制裁/制裁　sanction
制袋/製袋　bag-making

制定价格/制定價格　price making
制度安排/制度安排　institutional arrangement
制度变迁/制度變遷　institutional change
制度创新/制度創新　institutional innovation
制度法学/制度法學　institutional theories of law
制度方程/制度方程式　institutional equation
制度厚度/制度厚度　institution thickness
制度化/制度化　institutionalization
制度环境/制度環境　institutional environment
制度基础审计/制度基礎審計　system-based audit
制度均衡/制度均衡　institutional equilibrium
制度控制/系統控制　system control
制度史/制度史　institutional history
制度图书馆学/制度圖書館學　institutional librarianship, system library science
制度信任/制度信任　institutional trust
制度型福利/制度型福利　institutional welfare
制度性宗教/制度性宗教　institutional religion
制度学派/制度學派　institutional school
制度主义/制度論　institutionalism
制盒/製盒　box-making
制片人/製作經理　production manager
制图文件/製圖檔　cartographic record
制图资料/地圖資料　cartographic material
制箱/製箱　carton-making
制造/製造　manufacture, manufacturing
制造策略/製造策略　manufacturing strategy
制造单元/製造單元　manufacturing cell
制造、贩卖、传播淫秽物品罪/製造、販賣、傳播淫穢物品罪　crime of producing, selling and spreading obscene articles
制造费用/製造費用　manufacturing overhead
制造共识/製造共識　manufacturing consent
制造理念/製造理念　manufacturing philosophy
制造权/製造權　right of making
制造日历/製造日曆　manufacturing calendar
制造业/製造業　manufacturing industry
制造业普查/製造業普查　census of manufactures
制造业统计/製造業統計　manufacture statistics
制造执行系统/製造執行系統　manufacturing execution system, MES
制造资源计划/製造資源規劃　manufacturing resource planning, MRPII
制作人/製作人　producer
质量/品質　quality
质量保证/品質保證　quality assurance, QA
质量变异/品質的變異　variation of quality
质量标志/品質標誌　quality mark

质量标准/品質標準　quality standard
质量不确定性/品質不確定性　quality uncertainty
质量策划/品質規劃　quality planning
质量差别模型/品質差別模型　quality-differentiation model
质量差异/品質差異　quality differentiation
质量成本/品質成本　quality cost, cost of quality
质量成本特性曲线/品質成本特性曲線　quality cost characteristic curve
质量成熟度/品質成熟度　quality maturity
质量调查/品質調查　quality survey
质量方针/品質政策　quality policy
质量分等计划/品質分等計劃　quality rating plan
质量改进/品質改進　quality improvement
质量工程/品質工程　quality engineering
质量功能展开/品質機能展開　quality functional deployment, QFD
质量关键点/品質關鍵點　critical-to-quality, CTQ
质量关键树/品質關鍵樹　critical-to-quality tree
质量管理/品質管理　quality management
质量管理基本原则/品質管制基本原則　foundational principle of quality management
质量管理十四要点/品質管制14要點　14 key points of quality management
质量管理体系/品質管理系統　quality management system, QMS
质量管理体系认证/品質管理制度認證　certification of quality management system
质量管理体系文件/品質管制體系文件　document of quality management system
质量管理小组/品質管理圈,品管圈,品質管理小組　quality control circle, QCC, quality control group
质量规格/品質規格　quality specification
质量计划/品質計劃　quality plan
质量计量学/品質統計學　qualimetry
质量记录/品質記錄　quality record
质量监管/品質管制　quality regulation
质量鉴定/品質評估　appraisal of quality
质量经理/品質經理　quality manager
质量控制/品質管制,品質控制　quality control, QC
质量控制点/品質控制點　hold point in quality control
质量控制手册/品管手冊　quality control manual
质量控制图/品質管制圖　quality control chart
质量螺旋线/品質螺線　quality spiral
质量目标/品質目標　quality objective
质量期望值/品質期望值　quality expectancy
质量歧视/品質差別　quality discrimination

质量认证标志/品質認證標誌　quality certification mark
质量设计/品質設計　quality design
质量数据/品質資料　quality data
质量水平/品質水準　quality level
质量损失/品質損失　quality loss
质量损失函数/品質損失函數　quality loss function
质量特性/品質特性,品質特徵　quality characteristic
质量体系/品質系統　quality system
质量体系认证/品質制度認證　certification of quality system
质量型企业/品質型企業　quality-type corporation
质量选择模型/有無計數選擇模型　quality choice model
质量意识/品質意識　quality consciousness
质量责任/品質責任　quality responsibility
质量职能/品質功能　quality function
质量指数/品質指數　quality index
质权/質押　pledge
质押/質押　pledge
质押票据/質押票據　bill as security
质证/質證　cross-examine
治安管理/治安管理　public security administration
治理/治理　governance
治理理论/治理理論　governance theory
治理性保护/治理性保護　curative preservation
治疗模式/治療模式　remedial model
治乱说/治亂說　the theory of chaos and order
致命故障/致命性故障　catastrophic failure
致命缺陷/致命缺陷,致命缺點,嚴重缺陷　critical defect
致命失效/嚴重故障　critical failure
秩/秩　rank
秩变换/秩變換,等級變換　rankit
秩差/秩差,等級差　rank difference
秩分布/秩等級分布　rank distribution
秩和检验/秩和檢定,等級和檢定　rank sum tests
秩回归/回歸秩　rank in regression
秩检验/秩檢定,等級檢定　rank test
秩随机化检验/秩隨機化檢定　rank-randomization test
秩条件/秩條件　rank condition
秩统计量/秩統計量,等級統計量　rank statistic
秩相关/秩相關,等級相關　rank correlation
秩相关系数/[等]秩相關係數,等級相關係數　rank correlation coefficient, coefficient of rank correlation
秩序/秩序　order
秩序统计量/等級順序統計量　rank order statistics

秩序行政/秩序行政　order administration
掷骰子实验/擲骰試驗　dice experiment
智慧地球/智慧地球　smart planet
智慧决策/智慧決策　intelligent decision-making
智慧型规范/智慧型規範　intelligent regulation
智库/智庫　think tank
智力/智力　intelligence
智力测验/智力測驗　intelligence test
智力成果/智力成果　intellectual product
智力发展/智力發展　intellectual development
智力活动/心智工作,勞心工作　mental work
智力投资/智力投資　intellectual investment
智力转让/智慧財產轉讓　intellectual transfer
智力资本/智慧資本　intellectual capital
智力资本管理/智慧資本管理　intellectual capital management
智力资源/智力資源　intellectual resources
智囊团/智庫　think tank
智能城市/智慧城市　intelligent city
智能化电子数据流/智慧化電子資料流程　intelligent electronic data stream
智能化信息检索/智慧型資訊檢索　intelligent information retrieval
智能检索/智能檢索,智慧檢索　intelligent search, smart search, intelligent retrieval
智能检索系统/智慧檢索系統　intelligent retrieval system
智能决策支持系统/智慧決策支援系統　intelligent decision support system, IDSS
智能卡/智慧卡　smart card
智能模型/智慧模型　intelligence model
智能配送/智慧型配送　intelligent distribution
智能手机/智能手機,智慧型手機　smartphone
智能书架/智慧書架　smart bookshelf
智能体/智慧型代理　intelligent agent
智能维护/智慧型維修　intelligent maintenance
滞后变量/落遲變數　lagged variable
滞后变量模型/滯後變數模型　lagged variable model
滞后城市化/滯後城市化　under urbanization
滞后工资水平政策/滯後工資水準政策　lag pay level policy
滞后回归/落後回歸,落階回歸,落期回歸　lag regression
滞后内生变量/落遲內生變數,前期內生變數　lagged endogenous variable
滞后现象/滯後　hysteresis
滞后相关/落後相關,落階相關,落期相關　lag correlation

滞后效应/遲滯效果,磁滯效果　hysteresis effect
滞后协方差/落後共變異數,落階共變異數,落期共變異數　lag covariance
滞后异常现象/時差異常現象　lag hysteresis
滞后因变量/落遲因變數　lagged dependent variable
滞后准备金计算法/落後準備金提存制　lagged reserve accounting
滞架时间/滯架時間　shelf time
滞架书/滯架書　sleeping book
滞留时间/滯留時間　sojourn time
滞墨现象/滯墨　backing away
滞销利息/遲納利息　arrears of interest
滞销书/滯銷書　remaindered book, unsaleable book, remainder
滞胀/停滯性膨脹　stagflation
置标语言/標記語言,標志語言　markup language
置换变量强度/移轉變異強度　intensity of transvariation
置换学派/置換學派　displacement school
置墨区/置墨區　ink set
置信带/信任帶　confidence band, confidence belt
置信的/置信的　fiducial
置信度/信賴度　degree of confidence
置信分布/置信分布　fiducial distribution
置信概率/置信機率　fiducial probability
置信集/信賴集合　confidence set
置信区间/信賴區間　confidence interval
置信区间宽度/信任區間寬度　width of confidence interval
置信曲线/信賴曲線　confidence curve
置信上界/上信賴界　upper confidence bound
置信上限/上信賴限　upper confidence limit
置信水平/信賴水準　confidence level
置信推断/信賴推論　confidence inference
置信椭圆/信賴橢圓　confidence ellipsoid
置信系数/信賴度,信賴係數　confidence coefficient
置信下限/下信賴限　lower confidence limit
置信限/信賴界限　confidence limit
置信域/信賴[區]域　confidence region
中层管理者/中階管理者　middle manager
中插/中插　centerfold
中产阶级/中産階級,中等階級　middle class
中产阶级文化/中産階級文化　middle class culture
中程数/中程數　mid-range
中等收入国家/中所得國家　middle-income country
中点/中點　mid-point
中度读者/中度讀者　average reader
中断分布/中斷分布　cooked distribution

中断趋势/中斷趨勢　broken trend
中非关税经济同盟/中非關稅經濟同盟　Central African Customs and Economic Union
中缝/中縫　book groove, middle strip
n中k复系统/n中k複系統　k-out-of-n system
中国现代城市/中國現代城市　modern city in China
中华法系/中華法系　Chinese Legal Genealogy, Chinese Legal System
中华老字号/中華老字號　China's Time-Honored Brand
中华民族多元一体格局/中華民族多元一體格局　the pattern of diversity in unity of the Chinese nation
中间产品/中間產品,中間財　intermediate goods, intermediate product
中间产品市场/中間財貨市場　intermediate-goods market
中间代理商/中間代理商　intermediary agency
中间道路/中間道路　middle way
中间调/中間調　midtone
中间调平衡控制块/中間調平衡控制塊　midtone balance control patch
中间读者/中間讀者　medium reader
中间辊/中間墨輥　intermediate roller
中间画/中間畫　inbetween
中间汇率/中間匯率,中心匯率　intermediate rate, middle rate of exchange
中间技术/中間技術　intermediary technology, intermediate technology
中间贸易/中介貿易,轉口貿易,居間貿易　intermediate trade, intermediary commerce
中间片/中間片　intermediate
中间商/中間商　reseller, middleman
中间商市场/轉售市場　reseller market
中间税率/中間稅率　intermediate tariff
中间投票人定理/中位投票者定律　median voter theorem
中间投入/中間投入　intermediate input
中间系统/系統間系統　mesosystem
中间消费/中間消費　intermediate consumption
中间性/居间度　betweenness
中间性存贮/中間性存貯　intermediate storage
中间需求/中間需求　intermediate demand
中间业务/中間業務　intermediary business, intermediate business
中间一致检索/中間一致檢索　middle match retrieval
中间银行/中間銀行　intermediary bank

中间状态/居间态　intermediate state
中截断检索/中截斷檢索　middle truncation retrieval
中介/中介　intermediate, mediation
中介变量/仲介變項,仲介變數　mediating variable
中介机制/中介機制,中間機制　intervening mechanism, mediating mechanism
中介模式/中介模式　intermediary model
中介目标/中間目標　intermediate target
中介式互动/中介式互動　mediated interaction
中径/中徑　pitch diameter
中立/中立　neutrality
中立法/中立法　laws of neutrality
中美洲比索/中美洲披索　Central American Peso
中盘/中盤商　wholesaler
中频词/中頻詞　medium-frequency word
中期/中期　medium run
中期贷款/中期貸款　medium-term loan
中期负债/中期負債　medium-term liability
中期利率/中期利率　medium-term interest rate
中期投资/中期投資　medium-term investment
中期信贷/中期信貸　medium-term credit
中期债券/中期債券　medium-term bond
中期证券/中期證券　medium dated security
中期制作/中期製作　mid-production
中世纪法/中世紀法　mediaeval law
中世纪文件/中世紀檔　chrysographer
中书科/中書科　Zhongshu Ke
中四分位数/中四分位數　mid-quartile
中外合资企业/中外合資企業　Chinese-foreign joint venture
中外合作经营企业/中外合作經營企業　Chinese-foreign contractual joint venture, Chinese-foreign comanagement enterprise
中外合作企业/中外合作企業　Chinese-foreign cooperative enterprise
中位差/中位數離差　median deviation
中位检验/中位檢定　median test
中位时间/中位時間　median time
中位数/中位數　median
中位数方向/中位數方向　median direction
中位数回归曲线/中位數回歸曲線　median regression curve
中位数检验/中位數檢定　median test
中位数控制图/中位數管制圖　median control chart
中位数F统计量/中位數F統計量　median F-statistic
中位数无偏性/中位數不偏性　median unbiasedness
中位数无偏置信区间/中位數不偏信賴區間　median unbiased confidence interval

中位数误差/中位數誤差　median error
中位数线/中位數線　median line
中位数有效量/中位數有效劑量　median effective dose
中位数秩/中位數等級　median rank
中位数组/中位數組　median class
中位选民/中間選民　median voter
中位致死[剂]量/中位數致死劑量　median lethal dose
中文编目/中文編目　Chinese language cataloging
中文全文检索/中文全文檢索　Chinese full-text search, Chinese full-text retrieval
中文新闻技术标准/中文新聞技術標準　Chinese news technical standard
中文新闻信息分类/中文新聞資訊分類　Chinese news classification
中文新闻信息置标语言/中文新聞資訊標記語言　Chinese news markup language, CNML
中文信息处理/中文資訊處理　Chinese information processing
中文信息处理系统/中文資訊處理系統　Chinese information processing system
中文元数据/中文元數據　Chinese metadata
中项/中項　middle term
中小企业/中小企業　small and medium-sized enterprise
中小型公司/中小型公司　medium and small company
中心差分/中心差分　central difference
中心地理论/中地理論　central place theory
中心定位/定心　centering
中心度/鄰近度　closeness
中心对称/中心對稱　central symmetry
中心复合设计/中央合成設計　central composite design
中心汇率制度/中心匯率制度　pivotal rate system
中心极限定理/中央極限定理　central limit theorem
中心阶乘矩/中心階乘動差　central factorial moments
中心矩/中心動差,對平均數的動差　moment about mean, central moment
中心跨页广告/中心跨頁廣告　center spread
中心密度/中心密度　core density
中心外围理论/核心邊緣理論　theory of center-periphery
中心-外围模型/核心-邊陲理論　core-periphery model
中心位置系统抽样/中央位置系統抽樣　centrally

located systematic sampling
中心线/中[心]線　central line
中心页/中心頁　central spread, centerfold
中心置信区间/中心信賴區間　central confidence interval
中心纵坐标/中心縱坐標　central ordinate
中性财政政策/中性財政政策　neutral fiscal policy
中性技术进步/中性技術進步　neutral technology progress
中性曲线/中性曲線　neutral curve
中性物品/中性物品　neutral goods
中修/中級維修　intermediate maintenance
中央处理机/中央處理機　central processing unit, CPU
中央处理器/中央處理器　central processing unit, CPU
中央现货市场/中央現貨市場　central spot market
中庸型管理/中庸式管理　middle-of-the-road management
中值/中值　mid-value
中值引文年龄/中值引文年齡,中值引文年限　median citation age
中止协议/中止協議　suspension agreement
中秩法/中秩法　mid-rank method
中转仓库/中轉倉庫　pass-through warehouse
中转港/中轉港,轉運港　port of transshipment
中转运输/中轉運輸　transfer transportation
忠诚度计划/忠誠度計劃　loyalty program
忠实读者/忠實讀者　royal reader
终端/終端　terminal
终端节点/終端節點　terminal node
终混录音师/終混錄音師　final mixer
终极归因误差/終極歸因偏誤　ultimate attribution error
终极目标/最終目標　ultimate target
终局判决/終局判決,最終判決　final judgment
终刊/終刊　final issue
终身保险/終身保險　whole-life insurance
终身雇佣制/終身雇傭[制]　career-long employment, life-long employment
终身教育/終身教育　lifelong education
终身年金/終生年金　life annuity
终身生育率/終身生育率　life-time fertility rate
终身学习/終身學習,終生學習　life-long learning
终审/終審　final review
终值/終值　future value
终止/終止契約,解除契約　termination
终止要约/終止要約　termination of offer

钟-富克斯定理/Chung-Fuchs 定理　Chung-Fuchs theorem
钟形分布/鐘形分布,鐘形分配　bell-shaped distribution
钟形曲线/鐘形曲線　bell-shaped curve
种次号/種次號　title number
种概念/種概念　specific concept
16种个性因素问卷/[卡特爾]十六種人格因素測驗　16 personality factor questionnaire
A种股票/A種股票　A-share
B种股票/B種股票　B-share
7种浪费/7種浪費　the seven wastes
种类物/種類物　Indefinite Thing
种类之债/種類之債　obligation genera
种群年龄/種群年齡　age of population
种群调节/種群節制　population regulation
种姓制度/種姓制度　caste system
种族/種族　race
种族差异/種族差異　race difference
种族冲突/種族衝突　race conflict
种族隔离/種族隔離　apartheid
种族化/種族化　racialisation
种族混合/種族融合　a melt pot of different races
种族类似系数/種族類似係數　coefficient of racial likeness
种族偏见/種族偏見　racial prejudice
种族歧视/種族歧視　racial discrimination
种族优越感/種族優越感　racial superiority
种族中心主义/種族中心主義,民族中心主義　ethnocentrism
种族主义/種族主義　racism
中标/中標,得標　winning bid, successful bid, acceptance of bid
中标合同金额/中標合同金額　accepted contract amount
中标人/中標人,得標人　winning bidder, successful bidder
中标通知/中標通知　notice of award
中标通知书/中標通知書　letter of acceptance
仲裁/仲裁　arbitration
仲裁程序/仲裁程式　procedure of arbitration, arbitral procedure
仲裁程序中提出的索赔申请/仲裁程式中提出的索賠申請　statement of claim in arbitration proceeding
仲裁地点/仲裁地點　place of arbitration
仲裁法/仲裁法　arbitration law
仲裁费/仲裁費　arbitration fee

仲裁机构/仲裁機構　arbitral authority
仲裁举行地法/仲裁舉行地法　Lex Loci Arbitri
仲裁契约/仲裁合約　contract of arbitration
仲裁申请/仲裁申請　request for arbitration
仲裁条款/仲裁條款　arbitration clause
仲裁委员会/仲裁委員會　arbitration committee
仲裁协议/仲裁協定　arbitral agreement
仲裁员/仲裁人　arbitrator
众包/群眾外包　crowdsourcing
众数/眾數　mode
众数点/眾數點　modal point
众数组/眾數組　modal class
种植园/大型栽培農場　plantation
重大错报/重大誤述,重大不實表達　material misstatement
重大错报风险/重大錯報風險　risk of material misstatement
重大环境污染事故罪/重大環境汙染事故罪　crime of serious environment pollution accident
重大技术装备研制计划/重大技術裝備研製計劃　Major technical Equipment Development Program
重大缺陷/重大缺失　material weakness
重大误解/重大誤解　significant misconception
重大新闻/大新聞　big news
重大责任事故罪/重大責任事故罪　crime of negligently causing a serious accident
重典惩贪/重典懲貪　severely punish corrupt official
重点读者/重點讀者　key reader
重点发行/重點發行　intensive distribution
重点书/重點書　important book
重点投资/重點投資　key-point investment
重度读者/重度讀者　heavy reader
重度使用者/重度使用者　heavy user
重法地/重法地　the special region to impose heavy penalties
重金主义/金銀通貨主義,重金銀主義　bullionism
重量级团队/重量級團隊　heavy weight team
重量检验/重量檢驗　inspection of weight
重量检验证书/重量檢驗證書　inspection certificate of weight
重男轻女/重男偏好　son preference
重农学派/重農學派　physiocrats
重农主义/重農主義,農業爲本論　agricultural fundamentalism, physiocracy
重商主义/重商主義,重商制度　commercialism, mercantilism, mercantile system
重税/重税　heavy tax
重尾/厚尾　heavy-tailed

重尾分布/重尾分布　heavy tail distribution
重心/重心　centroid
重心法/重心法　center-of-gravity technique, centroid method
重刑轻罪/重刑輕罪　heavy sentence for minor crime
重要案例/關鍵個案　critical, crucial case
重要缺陷/重要缺陷　significant deficiency
重要商品交易/重要商品交易　staple merchandise trade
重要他人/重要他人,重要他者　significant other
重要他者/重要他者,重要他人　significant other
重要新闻/重要新聞　important news
重要性抽样技术/重要性抽樣　importance sampling
重要性-绩效分析/重要性-績效分析,重要性-表現分析　importance-performance analysis
重要性水平/重大性水準　materiality level
重罪十条/重罪十條　ten felony
周报/週報　weekly publication, weekly newspaper
周边绩效/脈絡績效,情境績效　contextual performance
周刊/週刊　weekly
周礼/周禮　Etiquette of Zhou Dynasty
周期/週期　period
周期变换/週期變換　periodic transformation
周期分析/週期分析　period analysis
周期减缩库存/週期減縮庫存　cycle reduction stock
周期盘点/定期盤點,定期審查　periodic review
周期图/週期圖　periodogram
周期图标法/週期圖示法　cycle graph technique
周期图法/週期圖　periodogram
周期图分析/週期圖分析　periodogram analysis
周期性/週期性　periodicity
周期性变动/循環變動　cyclical movement
周期性变异/循環變異　cyclical variation
周期性波动/循環變動,循環波動　cyclical fluctuation
周期性过程/週期過程　periodic process
周期性节律/週期性節律　cyclical rhythm
周期性趋势/循環趨勢　cyclical trend
周期性失业/循環性失業,景氣性失業　cyclical unemployment
周书/周書　document of Zhou dynasty
周转/週轉　turnover
周转基金/週轉基金　revolving fund
周转库存/週期存貨　cycle inventory
周转率/週轉率　turnover rate
周转箱/紙[板]箱　carton

轴测法/軸測法,軸量法　axonometry
轴承失效/軸承失效　ball bearing failure
轴向分布/軸分布　axial distribution
轴向量/軸向量　axial vector
轴心文明/軸心文明　axial civilization
朱墨套印本/朱墨套印本　red-and-black print
朱批奏折/朱批奏摺　annotate in red ink
朱印/朱印　red mark
朱印本/朱印本　red print
朱谕/朱諭　vermilion edict
猪背运输/背负法　piggyback
蛛网定理/蛛網定理　cobweb theorem
蛛网模型/蛛網理論　cobweb model
竹简/竹簡　bamboo slip
竹刑/竹刑　criminal law written on bamboo slips in feudal China
逐步二次规划方法/序列二次規劃法　sequential quadratic programming method
逐步法/逐步法,步進法　step-by-step method
逐步回归/逐步回歸　stepwise regression
逐步回归方法/逐步回歸程序　stepwise regression procedure
逐步回归分析/逐步回歸分析　stepwise regression analysis
逐步删失抽样/逐步設限抽樣　progressively censored sampling
逐步淘汰策略/按序排除式規則　elimination-byaspects strategy
逐步消除贸易壁垒/逐步消除貿易壁壘　phased removal of trade barrier
逐步应力试验/逐步應力試驗　step stress test
逐词排列法/逐詞排列法　word-by-word filing
逐次差分统计量/接續差統計量　successive difference statistic
逐段回归/逐段回歸　piecewise regression
逐段回归法/逐段回歸程序　stagewise regression procedure
逐级征订/逐級徵訂　stepwise subscription
逐件分析/逐件分析　piece-to-piece analysis
逐渐故障/逐漸故障　gradual failure
逐批/逐批　lot for lot
逐批订货/逐批訂購　lot-for-lot ordering
逐批检验/逐批檢驗　lot-by-lot inspection
逐批验收抽样/逐批允收抽樣　lot-by-lot acceptance sampling
逐日盯市/逐日結算　mark-to-market
逐日盯市制度/逐日結算制度　marked-to-market system

逐项序贯抽样检验/逐項逐次抽樣檢驗　item-by-item sequential sampling inspection
逐帧动画/逐幀動畫　frame-by-frame animation
主办单位/主辦單位　sponsor
主笔/總主筆　chief editorial writer
主编/主編　chief editor
主标目/主標頭　main heading
主标题/主標題　main title, major heading, main heading
主表/主表　main table
主播/主播　anchorperson
主簿/主簿　zhubu
主成分/主成分　principal component
主成分分析/主成分分析　principal component analysis
主成分分析法/主成分法　method of principal component analysis
主成分回归分析/主成分回歸　principal component regression analysis
主城市/主城市　primate city
主持人/主持人　host
主出借方/主出借方　main net lender
主从博弈/主從博弈　leader-follower game
主从模型/主從模型　leader-follower model, client-sever model
主丛编/主叢編　main series
主导部门/主導部門　leading sector
主导产业/主導產業　leading industry
主导技术/主導技術　dominant technology
主导企业/優勢廠商　dominant firm
主导设计/主導設計　dominant design
主导轴/主導軸　leading shaft
主导作用/主導作用　leading role
主动报价/主動報價　unsolicited offer
主动待机/主動備便　active standby
主动分配/主動分配　initiative subscription
主动服务/主動服務　active service
主动加工贸易/主動加工貿易,加工輸出貿易　active improvement trade
主动贸易/主動貿易　active trade
主动式竞争情报/主動競爭情報　active competitive intelligence
主动受众/主動受眾　active audience
主动信息服务/主動資訊服務　active information service
主动型客户驱动质量/主動式顧客驅動品質　proactive customer-driven quality
主动型营销/主動式行銷　proactive marketing

主动性虚假信息/主動不實訊息　active disinformation
主动赠送资料/主動贈送資料　unsolicited material
主发/主發　unsolicited delivery
主犯/主犯　prime culprit
主干家庭/主幹家庭　stem family
主观贝叶斯法/主觀貝氏法　subjective Bayes approach
主观抽样/立意抽樣,立意取樣　purposive sampling
主观概率/主觀機率　subjective probability
主观概率预测法/主觀機率預測法　subjective probability forecasting approach
主观期望效用/主觀預期效用　subjective expected utility
主观期望效用理论/主觀期望效用理論　subjective expected utility theory
主观权利/主觀權利　subjective right
主观修削平均值/主觀修飾平均數　subjectively trimmed mean
主观诱因/主觀誘因　subjective inducement
主观指数/主觀指標　subjective index
主观主义学派/主觀主義學派　school of subjectivity
主管单位/主管單位　responsible institution
主合同/主合同　master contract
主给付义务/主給付義務　primary obligation of performance
主矩/主動差　principal moment
主流经济学/正統經濟學　orthodox economics
主流媒体/主流媒體　mainstream media
主区集/主區集　principal block
主渠道/主管道　national distribution, public distribution channel
主权财富基金/主權財富基金　sovereign wealth fund, SWF
主时间数据法/主時間資料法　master stand data, MSD
主送机关/主送機關　main delivery government institution
主题/主題　subject
主题编目/主題編目　subject cataloging
主题标目系统/主題標目系統　subject heading system
主题标引/主題標引　subject indexing
主题参照/主題參照　subject reference
主题抽取/主題擷取　topic extraction
主题词/主題詞,關鍵字　keyword, subject term
主题词表/主題詞表,索引典　subject thesaurus, subject heading list, thesaurus
主题词组配标引/主題詞組配標引　subject words collocation indexing
主题词组配规则/主題詞組配規則　subject words collocation rule
主题地图/主題圖　topic map
主题发现/主題發現　topic discovery
主题法/主題標引方法　subject indexing system
主题范畴索引/主題範疇索引　subject category index
主题分布/主題分布　topic distribution
主题分析/主題分析　subject analysis
主题分析款目/主題分析款目　subject analytic entry
主题附加款目/主題附加款目　subject added entry
主题附注/主題附註　note pertaining to subject access
主题概念/主題概念　subject concept
主题概念阵/主題概念陣　thematic conceptual matrix
主题规范档/主題標準檔　subject authority file
主题检索/主題檢索　subject retrieval, subject search
主题结构/主題結構　subject structure
主题聚类/主題聚類　topic clustering
主题款目/主題款目　subject entry
主题类目/主題範疇　subject category
主题描述/主題描述　topic description
主题目录/主題目錄　subject catalog, subject directory
主题索引/主題索引　subject index, thematic index
主题统觉测验/主題統覺測驗　thematic apperception test
主题要素/主體要件　subject element
主题主要款目/主題主要款目　subject main entry
主题组织法/主題組織法　subject-based organization method
主体技术/主體技術　main technology
主体间性/主體間性　inter-subjectivity
主位/主位　emic
主位与客位区别/主位與客位區別　emic-etic distinction
主物/主物　principal thing
主误差/主誤差　primary error
主效应/主效應,主效果　main effect
主信用证/主信用狀　master letter of credit, prime letter of credit
主刑/主刑　principal punishment
主样本/主要樣本　master sample
主要变量/主要變數　dominant variable, primary

variable
主要材料/主要材料　major material
主要出口货物量值/主要出口貨物量值　quantity and value of principal export
主要分布族/受制分布族　dominated family of distribution
主要分类号/主要分類號　main classification number
主要货币/主要貨幣　principal currency
主要进口货物量值/主要進口貨物量值　quantity and value of principal import
主要经济指标/主要經濟指標　main economic indicator
主要款目/主要款目　main entry
主要款目格式/主要款目格式　main entry format
主要类目/主要類目　main class
主要贸易伙伴/主要貿易夥伴　principal trade partner
主要缺陷/主要缺點　major defect
主要题名页/主要題名頁　main title page
主要信息源/主要著錄來源,主要資訊來源　chief source of information
主要叙述/主述敘事　primary narrative
主要银行票据/主要銀行票據,一級銀行票據　prime bank bill
主要营业项目/主要營業專案　main business line
主要责任者/主要責任者　primary author
主要著录单元/主要著錄單元　main element
主页/主頁　home page
主页面设计/主頁面設計　general page design
主因子/主因子　primary factor
主营业所所在地法/主營業所所在地法　law of principal place of business
主营业务成本/主營業務成本　prime operating cost
主营业务收入/主營業務收入　prime operating revenue
主元素/主元素　principal element
主宰/主宰　dominance
主轴/主軸　principal axis
主轴编码/主軸編碼　axial coding
主轴定理/主軸定理　principal-axis theorem
主租约/主租約　master lease
助理编辑/助理編輯　assistant editor
助理导演/助理導演　assistant director
助理馆员/助理圖書館員　assistant librarian
助理技术编辑/助理技術編輯　assistant technical editor
助人行为/助人行爲　altruistic behavior
助人自助/助人自助　help people to help themselves

助他型组织/助他型組織　altruistic organization
住房保障制度/住房保障制度　housing security system
住房贷款/住宅貸款　housing loan
住房单位/住宅單位　housing unit
住房抵押贷款支持证券/住宅房貸擔保證券　residential mortgage-backed securities, RMBS
住房公积金/住房公積金　public accumulation fund for housing saving, housing provident fund
住房救助/住房救助　housing assistance, housing security
住房问题/住宅問題　housing problem
住房政策/住宅政策　housing policy
住户/住户　household
住宿式服务机构/住宿式服務機構　accommodation-service agency, residential care agency
住所/住所　domicile
住所冲突/住所衝突　conflict of domicile
住所地法/住所地法　Lex Domicilii
住所地法主义/住所地法主義　doctrine of domicile
住友铜矿管理/住友銅業管理　management of Sumitomo copper industries
住院病人/住院病人　in-patient
住院人数/住院人數　number of admission
住宅贷款/住宅貸款,房屋貸款　home loan, housing loan
住宅贷款保险/住宅貸款保險　housing loan insurance
住宅贷款公司/住宅貸款公司　housing loan corporation
住宅抵押贷款/住宅抵押貸款　residential mortgage
住宅金融/住宅金融,住宅融資　housing finance
住宅投资/住宅投資　housing investment
住宅信贷/住宅信貸　housing credit
住宅用地/居住地土地使用　residential land use
贮藏黄金/貯藏黄金,囤積黄金　hoarded gold
贮藏货币/貯藏貨幣,囤積貨幣　hoarded currency
贮藏手段/存储手段　means of storage
贮藏现金/貯藏現金,囤積現金　hoarded cash
贮存书库/典藏庫　repository
贮存图书馆/寄存圖書館　depository library
注册/註冊　enrollment
注册读者/註冊讀者　registered reader
注册股东/註冊股東,登記股東　holder of record
注册会计师/註冊會計師　certified public accountant, CPA
注册会计师审计/執行會計師稽核　CPA audit
注册商标/註冊商標　registered trademark

注册商标条约/商標註冊條約 trademark registration treaty, TRT
注册商标移转/註冊商標移轉 transfer of registered trademark
注册税务师/註冊稅務師 certified tax agent
注册用户/註冊用戶 registered user
注册资本/登記資本額 registered capital
注明付款地点的汇票/註明付款地點的匯票 domicile bill of exchange
注释/註釋 annotation
注释法学家/註釋法學家 glossator
注释书目/註釋書目 annotated bibliography
注释刑法学/註釋刑法學 explanatory criminology
注释性文摘/註釋牲文摘 annotated abstract
注疏/注疏 notes and commentaries
注塑/注塑 injection
注销书/註銷書 discard
注销支票/註銷支票 cancelled cheque
驻点/平穩點 stationary point
驻点记者/駐點記者 stagnation point reporter
柱面旋转设计/圓柱形可旋轉設計 cylindrically rotatable design
[著录]标目/著錄標目 heading
著录标识符号/著錄標識符號 description mark symbol
著录单元/著錄單元 element
著录格式/著錄格式 description format, entry format
著录规则/説明目錄規則 descriptive cataloging rule
著录详简级次/著錄層次 level of description
著录项目/著錄項目 description item, data element
著录信息附注/著錄信息附注 note pertaining to descriptive information
著录信息源/著錄來源 source of descriptive information
著录用标识符/著錄用標識符 punctuation for description
著者/著者,作者 author
著者标目/著者標目 author heading
著者号/作者號 author number
著者目录/作者目録 author catalog
著者索引/作者索引 author index
著者文摘/作者文摘 author abstract
著作/著作 authoring, works
著作财产权/著作財產權 property right of works
著作区分号/著作區分號 work mark, work number
著作权/著作權,版權 copyright
著作权保护/著作權保護,版權保護 copyright protection
著作权保护期/著作權保護期,版權保護期 term of copyright protection
著作权标记/版權標記 copyright notice
著作权的限制/著作權的限制 limitations on copyright
著作权登记/著作權登記,版權登記 registration of copyright
著作权法/著作權法,版權法 copyright law
著作权法定许可制度/著作權法定許可制度 statutory license of copyright
著作权管理/著作權管理 copyright management
著作权集体管理/著作權集體管理 collective management of copyright
著作权交易/版權交易 copyright trading
著作权纠纷/著作權糾紛,版權糾紛 dispute of copyright
著作权开放/無版權 copyleft
著作权强制许可/著作權強制許可 compulsory license of copyright
著作权穷竭/著作權窮竭 exhaustion of copyright
著作权人/著作權人 copyright owner
著作权许可使用合同/著作權許可使用合同 contract of copyright licensing
著作权页/版權頁 colophon
著作权增值/版權增值 copyright increment
著作权主管机关/著作權主管機關 department in charge of copyright
著作权专有使用许可/著作權專有使用許可 exclusive licence of copyright
著作权转让/著作權轉讓,版權轉讓 assignment of copyright
著作权自动产生原则/著作權自動產生原則 principle of automatic produce in copyright
著作人身权/著作人身權 personal right of copyright owner
著作者简介/著作者簡介 author introduction
铸币/鑄幣 coinage
铸币价格/鑄幣價格 mint price
铸币平价/鑄幣平價 specie par, mint parity
铸币税/鑄幣收益權 seigniorage
抓大放小/抓大放小 invigorate large enterprises while relaxing control over small ones
抓拍/抓拍 snapshot, snapshooting
抓取/抓取,捕獲 capture, grasp
专函征订/專函徵訂 special mailing subscription
专集/專集 special works
专家/專家 specialist

专家检索系统/專家檢索系統　expert retrieval system
专家判断/專家判斷　expert judgment
专家权力/專家權[力]　expert power
专家系统/專家系統　expert system
专家用户/專家用戶,有經驗用戶　expert user
专家预测法/專家預測法　expert forecasting approach
专家责任/專家責任　liability of expert
专家咨询法/專家諮詢法　expert consultation method
专刊/特刊　special issue
专科词典/專科詞典　specialized dictionary, subject dictionary
专科目录学/專科目錄學　subject bibliographic science
专科情报学/學科資訊科學　subject information science
专科书目/專科書目　special bibliography, subject bibliography
专栏/專欄　special column
专栏记者/專欄記者　columnist
专栏作家/專欄作家　columnist
专利/專利　patent
专利标的物/專利標的物　patent subject matter
专利查新/專利查新　patent novelty searching
专利池/專利池　patent pool
专利代理人/專利代理人　patent agent
专利档案/專利檔案　patent archive
专利的单一性/專利的單一性　principle of single patent application
专利抵触申请/專利抵觸申請　conflicting application of patent
专利地图/專利地圖　patent map
专利对比文件/專利對比檔　comparative document of patent
专利发明在先原则/專利發明在先原則　first-to-invention principle
专利法/專利法　patent law
专利费/專利費　patent fee
专利分析/專利分析　patent analysis
专利复审委员会/專利復審委員會　patent reexamination board
专利公报/專利公報　patent gazette, patent bulletin
专利馆藏/專利館藏　patent stock
专利国别代码/專利國別代碼　patent national name code
专利国际申请/專利國際申請　international patent application
专利号索引/專利號索引　patent number index
专利合作条约/專利[權]合作條約　treaty of patent cooperation, patent cooperation treaty
专利技术/專利技術　proprietary technology
专利检索/專利檢索　patent retrieval
专利检索报告/專利檢索報告　retrieval report on patent
专利竞赛/專利競賽　patent race
专利控制信息/專利控制資訊　patent control information
专利垄断/專利壟斷　patent monopoly
专利目录/專利目錄　patent list
专利强制许可/專利強制許可　compulsory license of patent
专利情报研究/專利情報研究　patent information research
专利[权]/專利[權]　patent, patent right, right of patent
专利权范围界定折中原则/專利權範圍界定折衷原則　subject-matter claiming principle
专利权范围界定中心限定原则/專利權範圍界定中心限定原則　central claiming principle
专利权范围界定周边限定原则/專利權範圍界定週邊限定原則　peripheral claiming principle
专利权合作条约/專利權合作條約　Patent Cooperation Treaty
专利权获得要件/專利權獲得要件　requirement for granting patent right
专利权交换/專利權交換　patent exchange
专利权客体/專利權客體　subject-matter of patent
专利权立法/專利權立法　patent legislation
专利权利穷竭/專利權利窮竭　exhaustion of patent right
专利权利要求书/申請專利要求書　patent claim
专利权期限/專利權期限　term of patent
专利权人/專利權人　patent owner
专利权人索引/專利權人索引　patentee index
专利权使用费/專利權使用費　patent royalty, royalty
专利权所有人/專利權所有人　patentee, patent holder
专利权无效/專利權無效　invalidation of patent
专利权限制/專利權限制　limit of patent
专利权许可/專利權許可　license of patent
专利权账户/專利權賬戶　patent account
专利权终止/專利權終止　cessation of patent
专利权转让/專利權轉讓　assignment of patent,

patent assignment
专利申请/專利申請　application for patent
专利申请权/專利申請權　right of filing patent application
专利申请日/專利申報日　date of filing
专利申请书/專利申請書　patent application
专利申请在先原则/先申請主義　first-to-file principle
专利审查/專利審查　examination of patent
专利实施权/專利實施權　right of patent exploitation
专利实质审查/專利實質審查　substantive examination for patent
专利使用权/專利使用權　right of using patent
专利税/專利稅　patent tax
专利税率/專利稅率　royalty rate
专利说明书/專利說明書　description of patent, patent specification
专利索引/專利索引　patent index
专利图书馆/專利圖書館　patent library
专利委托人/專利委託人　patent attorney
专利文献/專利文獻,專利文件　patent document
专利文摘/專利文摘　patent abstract, patent abridgement
专利协议/專利協定　patent agreement
专利信息/專利資訊　patent information
专利形式审查/專利形式審查　formal examination of patent
专利许可/專利許可　patent grant
专利许可贸易/專利授權貿易　patent licensing trade
专利许可证/專利許可證　patent licence
专利引文分析/專利引文分析　patent citation analysis
专利优先权/專利優先權　patent priority date
专利在先使用/專利在先使用　using prior to the date of filing
专利战略/專利策略　patent strategy
专利证书/專利證[書],特許證　certificate of patent, letter of patent, patent certificate
专利制度/專利制度　patent system
专利主管机关/專利主管機關　department in charge of patent
专卖/專賣　monopoly of sale
专卖店/專門店　specialty store
专门档案/專門檔案　special file, special archive
专门档案馆/專門檔案館　special archives
专门化/專門化　specialization
专门基金/專門基金　specialty fund
专门技术使用费/專門技術使用費　royalty as to know-how
专门技术市场/專門技術市場　know-how market
专门贸易/專門貿易　special trade
专门书库/專門書庫　special stack room
专门图书馆学/專門圖書館學　special librarianship
专门训练/專用訓練　specific training
专门元数据/專門性元數據　special metadata
专色/專色　spot color
专属管辖/專屬管轄　exclusive jurisdiction
专属金融公司/專屬金融公司　captive finance company
专属经济区/專屬經濟區　exclusive economic zone
专题/專題　topic, specialized topic
专题案卷/專題案卷,專案檔　case papers, case file
专题报道/專題報導　editorial coverage
专题报告/專題報告　monograph report, report on a special topic
专题出版物/專題出版品　monographic publication
专题丛书/專題叢書　subject series
专题分类法/專題分類法　topic classification
专题复分法/專題複分法　subject device
专题概要/專題概要　thematic summary, sepcial subject summary
专题检索/專題檢索　special subject search, special subject retrieval
专题卷/專題檔　subject title file
专题目录/專題目錄　special subject bibliography, special list
专题排架法/專題排架法　arrangement in special theme
专题情报研究/主題情報分析　subject intelligence analysis
专题书目/專題書目　bibliography on specific topic, subject bibliography
专题数据库/主題資料庫　subject database
专题图书馆/專業圖書館　subject library
专题文摘/專題文摘　subject abstract
专题选目/專題選目　selective bibliography
专题指南/專題指南　special subject guide
专题制作/綜合報告　monograph
专题咨询/專題諮詢　subject enquiry
专题综述/專題綜述　monograph review
专题组合法/專題組合法　topic combination method
专项补助/類別補助款　categorical grant
专项工程承包招标/專項工程承包招標　special project contract tendering
专项基金/專項基金　special fund
专项集体合同/專項集體合同　specific collective

contract
专项投资组合/專屬投資組合　declicated portfolio
专项转移支付/專項轉移支付　special transfer payment
专销市场/專銷市場　market exclusivity
专业报/專業報　professional newspaper
专业参考书/專業參考書　subject reference book
专业出版社/專業出版社　professional publishing house
专业档案/專業檔案　professional file
专业档案馆/專業檔案館　professional archives
专业分类表/專業分類表　special classification, professional classification
专业分类法/專業分類法　specialty classification
专业馆员/專業圖書館員　professional librarian
专业合作组织/專業合作組織　specialized cooperative organization
专业户/專業戶　specialized household
专业化/專業化,專門化　specialization, professionalization
专业化服务/專業化服務　professional service
专业化服务模式/專業化服務模式　specialized service model
专业价值/專業價值　professional value
专业监理工程师/專業監理工程師　professional surveillance engineer
专业类图书/專業類圖書　professional book
专业人员管理/專業人員管理　professionals' management
专业施工队/專業施工隊　specialized team
专业书店/專業書店　professional bookstore
专业特质/專業特質　trait of profession
专业图书馆/專門圖書館　special library
专业网点/專業網點　professional outlet
专业信息中心/專業資訊中心　specialized information center
专业[性]/專業[性]　professionalism
专业性刊物/專業性刊物　technological journal
专业性组织/專業組織　professional organization
专业叙词表/專題級詞表　micro-thesaurus
专业银行制度/專門銀行制度　specialized banking
专业整合服务/專業整合服務　disciplinary integrated service
专业组合法/專業組合法　specialty combination method
专用/可分撥　appropriablity
专用贷款/專用貸款　earmarked loan
专用复分表/專用複分表　specific subdivisions

专用情报简报/特種情報簡報　special intelligence briefing
专用索引/專用索引　special index
专用文种/專用文種　special record type
专用信贷/專用信貸　earmarked credit
专用性投资/特定投資　specific investment
专用资本/專用資本　specialized capital
专有技术档案/專有技術檔案　know-how archive
专有技术合同/專門技術合約　know-how contract
专有技术使用权/專有技術使用權　right to use technical know-how
专有技术许可贸易/專有技術許可證貿易　proprietary technology permits trade
专有技术许可证/專門技術執照　know-how license
专有信息/專有資料　proprietary information
专有叙词/專有敘詞　specific descriptor
专指原则/專項原則　principle of specificity
专著/專著　monograph, monography
专著丛编/專著叢編　monographic series
转包合同/分包　subcontract
转播/轉播,中繼　relay
转承履约/轉承履約　vicarious performance
转递银行/轉遞銀行　transmitting bank
转分保合同/轉分保合同　retrocession treaty
转化型电子文件/轉化型電子檔　converted electronic record
转换/轉換　conversion
转换成本/轉換成本　switching cost
转换函数/轉換函數　transfer function
转换回归模型/轉換回歸模型　switching regression model
转换价格/轉換價格　conversion price
转换价值/轉換價值　conversion value
转换率/轉換比率,轉化比　conversion ratio
转换期权/轉換期權　switch option
转换期限/期限轉換　maturity transformation
转换曲线/轉換曲線　transformation curve
转换树/轉換樹[狀圖]　transition tree, TRT
转换溢价/轉換溢價　conversion premium
转换因子/轉化因子,换算因子　conversion factor
转换值/轉換值　metameter
转嫁危机/轉嫁危機　crisis export
转交送达/轉交送達　service through transfer
转介/轉介　case referral
转开信用证/轉開信用狀　overriding credit
转口港/過境港　port of transit
转口海关手续/過境海關手續　transit entry
转口货物/轉口貨物,過境貨物　transit cargo,

transit goods
转口贸易/轉口貿易,過境貿易,再出口貿易　intermediary trade, transit trade, re-export trade
转口税/過境稅　transit duty
转口信用证/過境信用狀　transit letter of credit
转录/轉錄　transcription
转让/轉讓　transfer
转让背书/轉讓背書　endorsement to transfer
转让成本/移轉成本　transfer cost
转让汇票/轉讓匯票,押匯匯票　bill for negotiation
转让交易/轉讓交易　transfer transaction
转让扩散模式/轉讓擴散模式　transformation diffusion model
转让契据/轉讓契據　instrument of transfer
转让契约/轉讓契約　deed of transfer
转让证书/讓與證書　deed of conveyance
转手交易/轉手交易　switch operation
转手贸易/轉手貿易　switch trade
转售合同/轉售合約　resale contract
转售价格/轉售價格　resale price
转税制/兩税合一　imputation tax system
转贴现票据/再貼現票據　bill rediscount
转为非上市/轉爲非上市　going-private transaction
转委托/轉委託　remandate
转型变革/轉型變革　transformational change
转型经济学/轉型經濟,過渡經濟　transformation economics, transition economics
转型式领导/轉換型領導　transformational leadership
转移/移轉,轉嫁　transfer, shifting
转移变换群/遞移變換群　transitive transformation group
转移变异/轉移變異　transvariation
转移变异相对区域/移轉變異相對面積　relative area of transvariation
转移程序/轉移程序　switching procedure
转移定价/轉移定價,移轉訂價　transfer pricing
转移概率/傳遞機率,遞移機率　transition probability
转移概率矩阵/轉移機率矩陣　transition probability matrix
转移贸易关税/轉移貿易關稅　trade diverting tariff
转移收入/移轉所得　transfer income
转移问题/移轉支付問題　transfer problem
转移性决策制定/遞移性決策製訂　transitivity decision-making
转移性支出/移轉[性]支出　transfer expenditure
转移印刷/轉移印刷,轉印　transfer printing

转移账户/轉移賬户　transferred account
转移支付/移轉性支付　transfer payment
转译/轉譯　transfer translation
转印/轉印,轉移印刷　transfer printing
转运港/轉運港,中轉港　port of transshipment
转运批量/轉運批量,轉送批量　transfer batch
转运许可证/轉運許可證　reshipment permit
转账卢布/轉賬盧布　transferable rouble
转账凭证/支出傳票　transfer voucher
转账支付/轉賬支付　payment through transfer account
转账支票/轉賬支票　cheque only for account, cheque for transfer, transfer cheque
转折点/轉向點　turning point
转质/轉質　sub-pledge
转置矩阵/轉置矩陣　transposed matrix
传录体/傳錄體　biography style
庄园制[度]/莊園制[度],采邑制　manorialism, manorial system
装版设施/器材安装裝置　mounting device
装裱/裱貼　mounting
装订/裝訂　binding
装订工艺/裝訂過程　binding process
装订及获得方式附注/裝訂及獲得方式附注　note pertaining to binding and availability
装盒/裝盒　boxing
装货费/裝貨費,裝船費　loading charge
[装货港]船上交货价/船上交貨價格　freight on board, FOB
装配/裝配　assembly
装配订单/裝配訂單　assembly order
装配检验/裝配檢驗　assembly inspection
装配模型/裝配模型　assembly model
装配图/裝配圖,組合圖　assembly drawing
装配线/裝配線　assembly line
装配线平衡/裝配線平衡　assembly line balancing
装箱/裝箱　packing
装箱单/裝箱單　pack list
装卸/裝卸　loading and unloading
装卸费用/裝卸費用,裝卸成本,搬運成本　loading and unloading expense, handling cost
装卸货口岸/裝卸貨口岸　loading port and destination
装卸证明书/裝卸證明書　loading certificate
装运港船上交货价/裝運港船上交貨價　free on board port of shipment
装帧设计/圖書設計　book design
装置定格/設備依賴　device depend

状/狀 Zhuang
状态/狀態 state
状态变量/狀態變數 state variable
状态点/狀態點 state point
状态方程/狀態方程式 state equation
状态价格/狀態價格 state price
状态空间模型/狀態空間模型 state space model
状态图/狀態圖 state diagram
状态向量/狀態向量 state vector
状态周期/狀態週期 period of a state
状态转移概率/狀態轉移機率 state transition probability
追加保险费/加保費,額外保險費 additional premium
追加保证金通知/追加保證金 margin call
追加订单/追加訂單 additional order
追加订货/追加訂貨 reorder
追加订数/追加訂數 reordered quantity
追加关税税率表/追加關稅稅率表 supplemental tariff
追加融资/追加融資 supplementary financing
追加投标/追加投標 supplementary bid
追加投入/追加投入 supplementary input
追加信贷/追加信貸 supplemental credit
追诉时效/追訴時效 limitation of prosecution
追溯检索/追溯檢索 tracing retrieval
追索权/追索權 recourse
追星族/星迷 fan
追续权/追續權 droit de suite
追踪证券组合/追蹤投資組合 tracking portfolio
准备阶段/準備階段 preparation phase
准备金/準備金,準備貨幣 reserve money, reserve fund
准备金集中化/準備金集中化 centralization of reserve
准备金投资/準備金投資 investment of reserve
准备状态评估/準備狀態評估 readiness assessment for concurrent engineering, RACE
准充分性/準充分性 quasi-sufficiency
准固定成本/準固定成本 quasi-fixed cost
准固定劳动成本/準固定勞動成本 quasi-fixed labor cost
准固定要素/準固定要素 quasi-fixed factor
准国际私法/準國際私法 quasi-private international law
准合同/準合約 quasi-contract
准货币/準貨幣 quasi-money, near money
准极大似然估计/準最大概似估計式 quasi-maximum likelihood estimator
准静态过程/準靜態過程 quasi-static process
准据法/準據法 applicable law, Lex Causae
准逆矩阵系数/準逆矩陣係數 quasi-inverse matrix coefficients
准确度/準確度 accuracy
准入成本/參進成本 entry cost
准入条件/參進條件 entry condition
准时排序/及時排序 just-in-time scheduling
准时生产/及時生產 just-in-time, JIT
准实验/準實驗 quasi-experiment
准实验研究/準實驗研究 quasi-experimental study
准市场/準市場 quasi-market
准市场机制/準市場機制 quasi-market mechanism
准随机抽样/準隨機抽樣 quasi-random sampling
准同义词/準同義詞 quasi-synonym
准稳定分布法则/準穩定律 quasi-stable law
准线性效用函数/準線性效用函數 quasi-linear utility function
准许进口的货单/正面表列清單 positive list
准许免税输入商品/準許免稅輸入商品 admission of goods free of duty
准则/準則 criteria, criterion
D准则/D型準則 D-criteria
L准则/L型準則 L-criteria
准中位数/準中位數 quasi-median
准租金/準租 quasi-rent
桌面出版/桌上出版 desktop publishing, DTP
桌面出版系统/桌上出版系統 desktop publishing system, DTP system
桌面类游戏/桌上類遊戲 table game
卓越公关理论/卓越理論 excellence theory
卓越公司八大质量/卓越公司八大品質 eight qualities of excellent company
酌定情节/酌定情節 circumstance for discretion
酌量性固定成本/裁決性固定成本 discretionary fixed cost
啄食顺序/融資順位 pecking order
啄序模型/融資順位模型,融資順位模型 pecking order model
着墨孔/墨坑 ink hole
咨商地位/諮商地位 consultative status
咨询/諮詢,顧問 consult
咨询服务/諮詢服務 reference service, consulting service, counseling
咨询服务性缩微摄影/諮詢性微縮攝影 reference microfilming
咨询面谈/諮詢晤談 reference interview

咨询文档/諮詢文件　reference file
咨询问题/諮詢問題　reference question
咨询协议书/諮詢協定　consultancy agreement
咨询者/諮詢者　consultant
咨询中心/諮詢服務中心　consulting center
咨询终端/諮詢終端　teller terminal
咨议局/諮議局　conference board
资本/資本　capital
资本边际生产率/資本邊際生產力　marginal productivity of capital
资本边际效率/資本邊際效率,投資邊際效率　marginal efficiency of capital
资本不变原则/資本不變原則　principle of capital constancy, principle of unchanging capital
资本不流动性/資本不流動性　immobility of capital
资本-产出比率/資本產出比　capital-output ratio
资本-产出系数/資本產出係數　capital-output coefficients
资本产值比率/資本產值比率,資本產出比率　capital output ratio
资本偿还准备基金/資本償還準備金　capital redemption reserve fund
资本成本/資本成本,資金成本　capital cost, cost of capital
资本充足率/資本適足率,資本充足比率　capital adequacy ratio
资本充足性/資本適足性　capital adequacy
资本存量/資本存量　capital stock
[资本的]盈利能力/[資本的]盈利能力　earning power
资本多数决原则/資本多數決原則　principle of majority decision
资本二次循环/資本二次循環　two circuits of capital
资本负债/資本負債　capital liability
资本负债比率/資本負債比率　capital and liability ratio
资本公积/資本公積　capital reserve
资本管制/資本管制　capital control
资本国际化/資本國際化　internationalization of capital, capital internationalization
资本过剩/資金過剩　excess of capital
资本化/資本化　capitalization
资本化方法/資本化方法　capitalization method
资本化收益法/資本化收益法　capitalize proceeds method
资本回报率/資本回報率　rate of capital return
资本回流/資金回流　reflow of capital
资本积累/資本積累,資本累積　capital accumulation, accumulation of capital
资本积累率/資本積累率　rate of capital accumulation
资本基金/資本基金　capital fund
资本集中/資本集中　centralization of capital
资本技术构成/資本技術構成　technical composition of capital
资本家/資本家　capitalist
资本价值/資本價值　value of capital
资本价值构成/資本價值構成　value-composition of capital
资本建设投资/資本建設投資　investment in capital construction
资本交易/資本交易　capital transaction
资本交易账户/資本交易賬戶　capital transaction account
资本交易自由化/資本交易自由化　liberalization of capital transaction
资本接受国/資本接受國　capital recipient country
资本节约/節省資本　capital-saving
资本节约型技术进步/節省資本或勞動使用型技術進步　capital-saving or labor-using technology progress
资本结构/資本結構　capital structure
资本结构决策/資本結構決策　capital structure decision
资本结构权重/資本結構權重　capital structure weight
资本解构/資本解構　decomposition of capital
资本净额/資本淨額　net capital
资本净收益额/資本利得淨收益　capital gain net income
资本净值/淨值　net worth
资本净值表/資本淨值表　statement of net worth
资本宽化/資本廣化　capital widening
资本来源/資本來源　source of capital
资本-劳动比率/勞動資本率　capital-labor ratio
资本利息/資本利息　capital interest
资本流出/資本流出　capital outflow
资本流动/資本流動　capital flow, capital movement
资本流动性/資本流動性　mobility of capital, capital mobility
资本流入/資本流入,資金流入　capital inflow, inflow of capital, influx of capital
资本密集度/資本密集度　capital intensity
资本密集型产业/資本密集[型]產業　capital intensive industry
资本密集型技术/資本密集[型]技術　capital

intensive technique
资本密集型经济/資本密集型經濟　capital intensive economy
资本密集型商品/資本密集型商品　capital intensive goods
资本明细表/資本明細表　schedule of capital
资本配置决策/資本配置決策　capital allocation decision
资本品/資本財　capital goods
资本品目/資本項　capital item
资本融通/資本融通，籌集資本　capital financing
资本深化/資本深化　capital deepening
资本生产力指数/資本生產力指數　capital productivity index
资本市场/資本市場　capital market
资本市场工具/資本市場工具　capital market instrument
资本市场利率/資本市場利率　capital market rate
资本市场容量/資本市場胃納量　volume in capital market
资本市场线/資本市場線　capital market line
资本收回/資本收回，收回資本　capital recovery
资本收入/資本收入　capital receipt
资本收益/資本收益，資本利得　capital gain, capital revenue
资本收益净额/資本利得淨額　net capital gain
资本收益率/資本收益率　return on capital
资本收益税/資本增值稅　capital gains tax
资本输出/資本輸出　capital export, export of capital
资本输出国/資本輸出國　capital exporting country
资本输出净额/資本輸出淨額　net capital export
资本输入/資本輸入　capital import
资本输入国/資本輸入國　capital importing country
资本税/資本稅　tax on capital
资本损失/資本損失　capital loss
资本损益/資本損益　capital gain and loss
资本所得/資本所得　capital income
资本所得比率/資本所得比率　capital income ratio
资本调整帐户/資本調整賬　capital reconciliation account
资本投入/資本投入　capital input
资本投入额/資本投入額　input capital
资本投资/資本投資　capital investment
资本投资计划/規劃資本投資　planning for capital investment
资本外流/資金外流　flight of capital
资本外逃/資金外逃，資本逃竄　capital flight

资本维持原则/資本維持原則　principle of capital maintenance
资本项目/資本賬　capital account
资本项目可兑换/資本賬可兑换　capital account convertibility
资本项目收支差额/資本賬戶結餘　capital account balance
资本消耗补偿/資本消耗補償　capital consumption allowance
资本信贷和货币市场/資本信貸和貨幣市場　capital credit and money market
资本形成/資本形成　capital formation
资本形成总额/資本形成毛額　gross capital formation
资本性贷款/資本性貸款　capital loan
资本[性]支出/資本支出　capital expenditure
资本性资产/資本資產　capital asset
资本需求/資本需求　capital requirement
资本循环/資本循環　circular of capital
资本业务/資本業務　capital business, property business
资本溢价/股本溢價　premium on capital stock
资本盈余/資本盈餘，資本公積　capital surplus
资本有机构成/資本有機構成　organic composition of capital
资本预算/資本預算　capital budgeting
资本原始积累/資本原始積累　primitive accumulation of capital
资本增值/資本增值　capital appreciation, self-expansion of capital
资本帐户/資本賬[戶]　capital account
资本周转/資本週轉　capital turnover, turnover of capital
资本主义/資本主義　capitalism
资本主义地租/資本主義地租　capitalist land rent
资本主义精神/資本主義精神　spirit of capitalism
资本主义社会/資本主義社會　capitalist society
资本主义文化矛盾/資本主義文化矛盾　cultural contradiction of capitalism
资本转让税/資本轉讓稅　capital transfer tax
资本转移/資本轉移，資本移轉　capital transfer
资本转移手段/資本轉移手段　medium of capital transfer
资本-资产比率/資本-資產比率　capital asset ratio
资本资产定价理论/資本資產定價理論　capital asset pricing theory
资本资产定价模型/資本資產定價模型　capital asset pricing model, CAPM

资本自由化/資本自由化　liberalization of capital
资本总公式/資本總公式　general formula of capital
资本总公式矛盾/資本總公式的矛盾　contradiction in the general formula of capital
资本租约/資本租約,融資租賃　capital lease
资不抵债/支付不能　insolvency
资产/資產　asset
资产报酬率/資產報酬率　return on asset
资产重估/資產重估　asset revaluation
资产重组/資產重組　asset reorganization, portfolio restructuring
资产抵押/資產抵押　pledge of asset
资产定价/資產定價　asset pricing
资产定价理论/資產定價理論　asset pricing theory
资产负债表/資產負債[平衡]表　balance sheet, list of ledger balance, statement of asset and liability
资产负债表日/資產負債表日　date of balance sheet
资产负债表日后非调整事项/資本負債表日後非調整事項　nonadjusting event after the balance sheet date
资产负债表日后事项/資產負債表日後事項　event after the balance sheet date
资产负债表日后调整事项/資本負債表日後調整事項　adjusting event after the balance sheet date
资产负债表外融资/資產負債表外融資　off-balance-sheet financing
资产负债观/資產負債觀　asset-liability view
资产负债管理/資產負債管理　asset-liability management
资产购置/購置資產　acquisition of asset
[资产]估价利润/[資產]估價利潤　valuation profit
资产管理/資產管理　asset management
资产管理理论/資產管理理論　asset management theory
资产互换/資產交換　asset swap
资产回报/資產報酬　asset return
资产价格/資產價格　asset price
资产价格膨胀/資產價格膨脹　asset price inflation
资产减值/資產減損　impairment of asset
资产阶级/資產階級,布爾喬亞　bourgeois
资产阶级化/資產階級化　embourgeoisement
资产阶级形式法范式/資產階級形式法範式　bourgeois formal law
资产结构/資產結構　asset structure
资产流动性/資產流動性　asset liquidity
资产配置/資產配置　asset allocation
资产品质监管/資產品質監管　supervision on assets quality

资产升值/重估增值　write-up
资产市场/資產市場　asset markets
资产市场分析方法/資產市場學派　asset-market approach
资产市场实验/資產市場實驗　asset market experiment
资产市场一体化/資產市場整合　asset-market integration
资产市场中总体不确定性/資產市場中加總不確定性　aggregate uncertainty in asset market
资产收益/資產收益　asset income
资产收益率/資產收益率,資產報酬率　return on asset, ROA
资产收益税/資產報酬稅　tax on asset returns
资产替代/資產替代　asset substitution
资产替代性/資產替代性　asset substitutability
资产证券化/資產證券化　asset securitization
资产支持证券/資產擔保證券　asset-backed securities, ABS
资产置存损益/持有資產損益　holding gain or loss
资产专用性/資產專用性,資產特性　asset specificity
资产组合保险/資產組合保險　portfolio insurance
资产组合平衡分析法/資產平衡分析法　portfolio-balance approach
资格后审/資格後審　post-qualification
资格审查/任職資格　qualification
资格刑/資格刑　punishment against competence
资格预审/預審資格　prequalification
资格证券/資格證券　qualifying securities
资金/資金　financial resource
资金表/資金表　statement of fund
资金成本/資本成本　cost of capital
资金分配/資金分配　distribution of capital
资金过剩与不足/資金過剩與不足　financial surplus and deficit
资金控制/資金控管　fund control
资金匮乏/資金匱乏　lack of fund
资金来源和运用表/資金來源和運用表　statement of source and application of fund
资金流量/資金流量　flow of fund
资金流量统计/資金流量統計　flow of fund statistic
资金缺口/資金缺口　financing gap
资金吸收/資金吸收　fund collection
资金运用表/資金運用表　statement of application of fund
资金转移/資金轉移　transfer of financial resource
资历/年資　seniority, qualification
资历工资/年資薪　seniority pay

资历晋升制/依據資歷提升　seniority-based promotion system
资历组表/資格資料庫　seniority grouptable
资料/資料　data
资料存储/數據儲存　data storage
资料分析/資料分析　data analysis
资料盒/資料盒　pamphlet file
资料获得率/資料使用率　document availability ratio, material availability ratio
资料室/參考室　reference room
资料收集方式及类型/資料收集方式及類型　data collection method and type
资料特殊细节附注/資料特殊細節附注　note pertaining to material specific information
资料性要素/資料性要素　informative element
资料验收/資料驗收　material acceptance
资深馆员/圖書館高級管理員　senior librarian
资源/資源　resource
资源禀赋/資源稟賦　resource endowment
资源重组/自願性重整　voluntary restructuring
资源储备/資源存量　resource stock
资源导航/資源導航　resource navigation
资源调配/資源指派　resource assignment
资源动因/資源動因　resource driver
资源发现/資源發現　resource discovery
资源分配者/資源分配者　resource allocator
资源负荷表/資源負荷表　resource profile
资源共建/資源共建　resource co-construction
资源共享/資源分享　resource sharing
资源购置经费/資源購置經費　acquisition fund
资源管理/資源管理　resource management
资源规划/資源規劃　resource planning
资源和能力评估/資源和能力評估　evaluation of resources and capabilities
资源活力/資源活化　activation
资源获取模式/資源獲取模式　resource acquisition model
资源集合/資源合集　resource collection
资源集合元数据/資源集合元數據　collection metadata
资源库/資源庫　resource library
资源密集型技术/資源密集技術　resource intensive technology
资源描述框架/資源描述框架,資源描述架構　resource description framework, RDF
资源描述与检索/資源描述與檢索　resource description and access, RDA
资源配置/資源配置,資源分配　allocation of resources, resource allocation
资源使用型技术/資源利用技術　resource using technology
资源受限排程/資源受限排程　resource-limited scheduling
资源税/資源税　resource tax
资源特征/資源特徵　characteristic of resources
资源相似性/資源相似性　resource similarity
资源依附理论/資源依賴理論　resource dependence theory
资源有限-工期最短/資源有限-工期最短　limited resources and minimum project duration
资源最优配置/最適資源分配　optimal resource allocation
资助型基金会/資助型基金會　grant making foundation
子泊松分布/子卜瓦松分布,子卜瓦松分配　sub-Poisson distribution
子博弈/子賽局　subgame
子博弈精炼/子賽局完全性　subgame perfection
子博弈精炼纳什均衡/子賽局精煉那許均衡　subgame perfect nash equilibrium
子博弈完美均衡/子賽局均衡　subgame perfect equilibrium
子层控制/副層管制　control of substrata
子抽样/子抽樣　subsampling
子公司/子公司,附屬事業　subsidiary company, constituent company
子行列式/子行列式　minor of a determinant
子类/子類　sub-class
子系统/子系統,次系統　subsystem
子系统测试/子系統測試　subsystem testing
子项组合法/子項組合法　subitem combination method
子序列/子數列　seriola
子鞅/次鞅,下鞅　submartingale
子样本/子樣本　subsample
子银行/子銀行　subsidiary bank
子指数分布/次指數分布,次指數分配　subexponential distribution
子字段/子域,分區　subfield
子字段代码/子欄位代碼　subfield code
紫外灯/紫外燈　ultraviolet lamp
紫印/紫印　purple mark
自白/自白　confession
自办发行/自辦發行　publisher self-distribution, self-management distribution
自备箱/自備箱　shipper's own container

自被引率/自被引率　self-cited rate
自绷式网框/自繃式網框　self-stretching screen frame
自变量/自變數　independent variable
自偿性理论/自償性理論　self-liquidating theory
自偿性融资/自償性融資，自动清償性融資　self-liquidating financing
自筹资金公司/自籌資金公司　self-financing company
自筹资金项目/自籌資金專案　self-financing project
自出版/自出版　self-publishing
自创生法/自創生法　autopoiesis law
自催化曲线/自觸曲線，自身成長曲線　autocatalytic curve
自大假说/自大假說　hubris hypothesis
自动标引/自動索引法　automatic indexing
自动仓储系统/自動倉儲存取系統　automated storage retrieval system
自动抽词标引/自動抽詞標引　automatic derived indexing
自动出口配额/自動出口配額　voluntary export quota
自动出口限制/自動出口限制　voluntary restraint of export
自动存取/自動存提　automatic deposit and withdraws
自动分词/自動分詞　automatic segmentation
自动分类/自動分類　automatic classification
自动分类标引/自動分類標引　automatic classification indexing
自动赋词标引/自動賦詞標引　automatic assignment indexing
自动规定最高利息/自動規定最高利息　voluntary maximum limit of money
自动化仓库/自動化倉庫　automatic warehouse
自动化立体仓库/自動化立體倉庫　automatic storage and retrieval system
自动检索/自動檢索　automatic retrieval, automatic search
自动交互检测/自動交互作用偵測　automatic interaction detection
自动校对/自動校對　automatic proofreading
自动进口配额制[度]/自動進口配額制[度]　automatic import quota system, AIQ
自动聚类/自動聚類　automatic clustering
自动均衡/自動均衡　automatic equalization
自动利率调整机制/費率自動調整機能　automatic rate adjustment mechanism

自动平衡分类账/自動平衡分類賬　self-balancing ledger
自动切换复联/自動切換複聯　automatic switch-over redundancy
自动清偿性贷款/自動清償性貸款　self-liquidating loan
自动清偿性票据/自動清償性票據　self-liquidating paper
自动清偿性融资/自動清償性融資，自償性融資　self-liquidating financing
自动清偿性证券/自動清償性證券　self-liquidating security
自动清算/自動清算　voluntary liquidation
自动清算所/自動清算系統　automated clearing house
自动取款机/自動櫃員機　automated teller machine
自动数据处理/自動化資料處理　automatic data processing, ADP
自动数据处理文件管理/自動化資料處理檔管理　ADP records management
自动谈判/自動協商　automatic negotiation
自动谈判系统/自動協商系統　automatic negotiation system
自动调整机制/自動調整機制　automatic adjustment mechanism
自动调整条款/伸縮條款　escalator clause
自动停工/自動停工　autonomation
自动外汇分配/自動外匯分配　automatic foreign exchange allocation
自动文献请求服务/自動文件請求服務　automatic document request service
自动文摘/自動文摘，自動摘錄　automatic text summarization, automatic abstraction
自动稳定器/自動穩定器　automatic stabilizers
自动误差控制/自動錯誤控制　automatic error control
自动限制措施/自動限制措施　voluntary restrictive measure
自动许可证/自動許可證　automatic licensing
自动续订/自動續訂　automatic renewal
自动续借/自動續借　automatic renewal
自动转账服务/自動轉賬服務　automatic transfer service
自发罢工/野貓罷工　wildcat strike
自发性存款/自發性存款　autonomous deposit
自发性秩序/自發的秩序　spontaneous order
自反性现代化/反身現代化，反思型現代化　reflexive modernization

自方差/自動方差　autovariance
自费出版/自費出版　publishing at the author's expense
自负盈亏/自負盈虧　taking full responsibility for profits and losses
自更新总量/自身更新總合　self-renewing aggregate
自共轭拉丁方/自身共軛拉丁方陣　self-conjugate Latin square
自回避随机游动/自[身]迴避隨機漫步　self-avoiding random walk
自回归/自[身]回歸　autoregression
自回归变换/自[身]回歸變換　autoregressive transformation
自回归多项式/自我回歸多項式　autoregressive polynomial
自回归分布滞后模型/自回歸分布滯後模型　autoregressive distributed lag model, ADL model
自回归过程/自我回歸過程,自身回歸過程　autoregressive process
自回归计划/自[身]回歸方案　autoregressive scheme
自回归模型/自[我]回歸模型,自身回歸模型,AR模型　autoregressive model, AR model
自回归谱估计/自我回歸譜相估計值　autoregressive spectral estimation
自回归求积移动平均/整合型自我回歸移動平均模型　autoregressive integrated moving average
自回归数列/自[身]回歸數列　autoregressive series
自回归条件持续期模型/自我回歸條件久期模型　autoregressive conditional duration model, ACD model
自回归条件异方差模型/自我回歸條件異質變異數模型　autoregressive conditional heteroscedastic model
自回归移动平均/自我回歸移動平均　autoregressive moving average
自回归移动平均过程/自我回歸移動平均過程　autoregressive moving average process
自回归移动平均模型/自[身]回歸移動平均模型,ARMA模型,自我回歸移動平均模型　autoregressive moving average model, ARMA model
自回归移动平均预测模型/自回歸滑動平均預測模型　autoregressive moving average forecasting model
自回归预测模型/自回歸預測模型　autoregressive forecasting model
自己代理/自己代理　agency by self

自己占有/自己占有　possession by self
自给农业/自給自足式農業　subsistence agriculture
自给自足/自給自足　autarky
自给自足的经济/基本生活維持經濟　subsistence economy
自加权半样本/自[身]加權半樣本　self-weighting semi-sample
自加权设计/自[身]加權設計　self-weighting design
自加权样本/自[身]加權樣本　self-weighting sample
自检轭标准方/自身共軛標準方陣　self-conjugate standard square
自建数据库/自建資料庫　self-built database
自校正样本/自身校正樣本　self-correcting sample
自净能力/自淨能力　self-cleansing power
自决权/自決權　right to self-determination
自决专业关系/自決專業關係　self-determined professional relationship
自刊本/自刊本　privately printed edition
自来水哲学/自來水哲學　tap water philosophy
自理能力/自理能力　self-care ability
自力救济/自力救濟　act of helping oneself
自利/自利　self-interest
自链/自[身]鏈,内鏈　self-link
自留额比率/自留額比率,留存比率　retirement
自媒体/自媒體　we media
自媒体时代/自媒體時代　self-media age
自谱/自我頻譜　auto spectrum
自然保护/自然保護　natural conservation
自然保护法/自然保護法　law of natural protection
自然保护区/天然保存區　nature reserve
自然参数空间/自然參數空間　natural parameter space
自然尺度/自然尺度　natural scale
自然充分统计量/自然充分統計量　natural sufficient statistic
自然崇拜/自然崇拜　nature worship
自然单位/自然單位　natural unit
自然法/自然法,自然律　natural law
自然犯/自然犯　natural crime
自然肥力/自然肥力　natural fertility
自然更新/自然更新　natural regeneration
自然公正/自然公正　natural justice
自然共轭先验/自然共軛先驗　natural conjugate prior
自然观察法/自然觀察法　natural observation
自然化/自然化　naturalization
自然环境/自然環境　natural environment, physical environment

自然价格/自然價格　natural price
自然经济/自然經濟　natural economy
自然利率/自然利率　natural rate of interest
自然垄断/自然獨占　natural monopoly
自然权利/自然權利　natural right
自然人/自然人　natural person
自然人犯罪/自然人犯罪　crime by a natural person
自然人化/自然人化　humanization of nature
自然容限/自然允差界限　natural tolerance limit
自然-社会环境/自然-社會環境　physico-social environment
自然神论/自然神論　deism
自然失业率/自然失業率　natural rate of unemployment
自然死亡率/純自然死亡率　bereinigte Sterbeziffer
自然系统/自然系統　natural system
自然选择/天擇,自然淘汰　natural selection
自然语言/自然語言　natural language
自然语言标引/自然語言標引　free language indexing, natural language indexing
自然语言处理/自然語言處理　natural language processing
自然语言检索/自然語言查詢　natural language retrieval, natural language search
自然灾害/自然災害　natural disaster
自然灾害救助/自然災害救助　natural disaster relief
自然增长率/自然增加率,自然成長率　natural increase rate, natural growth rate
自然债务/自然債務　natural debt
自然指数族/自然指數族　natural exponential family
自然主义/自然主義　naturalism
自然状况/自然狀況　state of nature
自然资源/自然資源　natural resources
自然资源经济学/自然資源經濟學　natural resource economic
自然资源使用权/自然資源使用權　right to use natural resources
自融资/自籌資金　self-financing
自杀率/自殺率　suicide rate
自上而下原则/自上而下原則　top-down principle
自适应估计/適應估計　adaptive estimation
自适应估计量/適應估計量　adaptive estimator
自适应R估计量/適應R型估計量　adaptive R-estimator
自适应控制/[自]適應控制　adaptive control, self-adapting control
自适应滤波方法/適應性濾波器法　adaptive filter method
自适应模型/適應性模型　adaptive models
自适应推断/適應推論　adaptive inference
自适应系统/[自]適應系統　adaptive system
自适应预期模型/自適應預期模型　adaptive expectation model
自适应质量控制/適應品質管制　adaptive quality control
自适应最优化/適應最適性　adaptive optimization
自收自支管理/自收自支管理　management of self-controlled revenue and expenditure
自守等价/同型同位　automorphic equivalence
自首/自首　confession of one's offense
自诉/自訴　private prosecution
自诉案件/自訴案件　case of private prosecution
自诉人/自訴人　private prosecutor
自提/自提　take by self
自填式问卷/自填問卷　self-administered questionnaire
自卫/自衛　self-defense
自卫本能/自衛本能　self-preservation
自卫权/自衛權　right to self-defense
自我参照效应/自我參照效果　self-reference effect
自我呈现/自我呈現　presentation of self
自我存档/自我典藏　self-archiving
自我导向搜寻量表/自我導向搜尋量表,職業自我探索量表　self-directed search
自我服务偏差/自利偏差　self-serving bias
自我概念/自我概念　self-concept
自我沟通/自身傳播,內在傳播　intrapersonal communication
自我构念/自我構念　self-construal
自我管理团队/自我管理團隊　self-managed team
自我归因/自我歸因　self-attribution
自我监控/自行監測,自我監測　self-monitoring
自我决定/自決　self-determination
自我觉察/自覺,自我覺察　self-awareness
自我控制/自我控制　self-control
自我类别化/自我類別化　self-categorization
自我披露/自我揭露,自我坦露　self-disclosure
自我评价/自我評價　self-evaluation
自我认同/自我認同,自我認定　self-identity
自我审查/自我審查　self-censorship
自我实施/自我執行　self-enforcing
自我实施雇用契约/自我執行雇用契約　self-enforcing employment contract
自我实现/自我實現　self-realization
自我实现人假设/自我實現人假設　self-realization person assumption

自我实现预期/自我實現預期　self-fullfiling expectation
自我实现预言/自我實現預言,自我應驗預言　self-fulfilling prophecy
自我提升/自我提升,自我彰顯　self-enhancement
自我调节/自[我]調節　self-regulation
自我调整过滤预测法/自我調整過濾預測法　adaptive filtering forecasting approach
自我调整性/自體適應　self-adaptation
自我图式/自我基模　self-schema
自我效能[感]/自我效能　self-efficacy
自我形象/自我形象　self-image
自我选择/自我選擇,自我功能　self-select, self-selection, self-selectivity
自我意识/自我意識　self-consciousness
自我意象/自我形象　self-image
自我知觉/自我知覺　self-perception
自我中心主义/自我中心主義　egocentrism
自物权/自物權　Jus in re Propria
自下而上估算/自下而上估算　bottom-up estimating
自相关/自[身]相關　autocorrelation
自相关函数/自[身]相關函數　autocorrelation function
自相关矩阵函数/自我相關矩陣函數　autocorrelation matrix function
自相关生成[母]函数/自我相關母函數　autocorrelation generating function
自相关系数/自[身]相關係數　autocorrelation coefficient
自相关总体/自身相關母體　autocorrelated population
自协方差/自協方差　autocovariance
自协方差函数/自協方差函數　autocovariance function
自协方差矩阵函数/自協方差矩陣函數　autocovariance matrix function
自协方差母函数/自協方差母函數,自協方差生成函數　autocovariance generating function
自协方差生成函数/自協方差生成函數,自協方差母函數　autocovariance generating function
自行保险准备金/自行保險準備金　self-insurance reserve
自行估税制/自行估税制　self-assessment system
自行回避/自行迴避　self-withdrawal
自学考试/自學考試　examination of self-study
自益信托/自益信託　self-benefit trust
自引/自我引用　self-citation
自引率/自引率　self-citing rate

自营仓库/自營倉庫　private warehouse
自营银行/自營商銀行　dealer bank
自由/自由　freedom, liberty
自由本位制/自由本位制　free standard
自由变动汇率/自由彈性匯率　freely flexible exchange rate
自由变数/自由變數　freedom variable
自由标引/自由標引　free indexing
自由波动汇率/自由波動匯率　freely fluctuating exchange rate
自由参数/自由參數　free parameter
自由出口/自由輸出,免税出口　free export
自由处置/自由處置　free disposal
自由词/自由詞　free term
自由词标引/自由詞標引　free word indexing
自由的多边贸易/自由的多邊貿易　free multilateral foreign trade
自由度/自由度　degree of freedom
自由兑换货币/自由兑換貨幣　freely convertible currency, free convertibility currency
自由法学派/自由法學派　free-law school of law
自由法运动/自由法運動　free-law movement
自由放任/自由放任,放任主義　laissez faire
自由浮动汇率/自由浮動匯率　freely floating exchange rate
自由浮动汇率制[度]/自由浮動匯率制[度]　system of freely fluctuating exchange rate, variable exchange rate system, free floating exchange rate system
自由港/自由港,免税港　free port, free dock
自由港区/自由港區　free port area
自由公债/自行交易債券　free bond
自由关税区/自由關税區　tariff-free zone
自由和特权宪章/自由與特權憲章　Charter of Liberties and Privileges
自由回忆/自由回憶　free recall
自由汇率/自由匯率,不固定匯率　free exchange rate
自由汇率制/自由匯率制　free exchange rate system
自由货币政策/自由貨幣政策　discretionary monetary policy
自由货单/自由貨單,[海關]免税貨單　free list
自由价格/自由價格　free price
自由结算贸易/自由結算貿易　free liquidation trade
自由进口/自由進口,免税進口　free import
自由进入和退出/自由進出　free entry and exit
自由进入市场/自由進入市場　free entry
自由经济/自由經濟　free economy, liberal market

economy
自由经济区/自由經濟區 free economic zone
自由竞争/自由競爭 free competition
自由竞争原则/自由競爭原則 principle of free competition
自由来源原则/自由來源原則 free principle of provenance
自由流动/自由流動 free mobility
自由贸易/自由貿易 free trade
自由贸易港/自由貿易港 free trade port
自由贸易关税/自由貿易關稅 free trade tariff
自由贸易码头/自由貿易碼頭 free trade wharf
自由[贸易]区/自由[貿易]區,免税區 free trade area, free zone, free district
自由贸易协定/自由貿易協定 free trade agreement
自由贸易政策/自由貿易政策 free trade policy
自由贸易制度/自由貿易制度 free trade system
自由女性主义/自由主義女性主義 liberal feminism
自由时差/自由浮時 free float
自由世界贸易/自由世界貿易 free world trade
自由市场/自由市場 free market
自由市场汇率/自由市場匯率 free market exchange rate
自由市场价/自由市場價 free market price
自由市场经济/自由市場經濟 free market economy, liberal market economy
自由市场理论/自由市場論 free market theory
自由特许状/自由特許狀 charter of liberties
自由外汇/自由外匯 free exchange, free foreign exchange
自由外汇市场/自由外匯市場 free exchange market
自由文本检索/自由正文搜尋 free-text search, free-text retrieval
自由现金流/自由現金流量 free cash flow
自由刑/自由刑 punishment against freedom
自由许可制/自由許可制 liberal licensing
自由意志/自由意志 free will
自由银行体制/無中央銀行制度 free banking system
自由银行业务区/自由銀行業務區 free banking zone
自由主义/自由主義 liberalism
自由主义理论/自由放任主義理論 libertarian theory
自由铸币/自由鑄幣 free coinage
自由转口区/自由轉口區 free transit zone
自由撰稿人/自由撰稿人,自由作家 freelance writer, freelancer

自由准备金/自由準備金 free reserve
自有资金/自有資金,股東權益資金 equity fund, owing fund
自愿出口限制/自願出口限制,出口自我設限 voluntary export restriction, voluntary export restraint
自愿兑换/自願償還,自願贖回 voluntary redemption
自愿服务/自願服務 voluntary service
自愿服务机构/自願服務機構 voluntary service agency
自愿交易学说/自願交易説 voluntary exchange approach
自愿连锁店/自願連鎖店 voluntary chain bookstore, voluntary chain store
自愿拍卖/自願拍賣 voluntary auction
自愿失业/自願失業 voluntary unemployment
自愿限制协定/自我限制條款 voluntary restraint agreement
自愿性标准/自願性標準 voluntary standard
自愿性认证/自願性認證 voluntary certification
自愿支付/自願支付 voluntary payment
自愿仲裁/自願仲裁,任意仲裁制 voluntary arbitration
自制短片/自製短片 homemade video clip
自制股利政策/自製股利政策 homemade dividend policy
自制-外购决策/自製-外購決策 make-or-buy decision
自治/自治 autonomy
自治机关/自治機關 organ of self-government
自治旗/自治旗 autonomous banner
自治区/自治區 autonomous region
自治条例/自治條例 autonomic regulation
自治县/自治縣 autonomous county
自治州/自治州 autonomous prefecture
自治组织/自治組織 self-government organization
自致角色/獲得角色 achieved role
自致性身份/獲得地位 achieved status
自主/自主 autonomous, autonomy
自主创新/自主創新 indigenous innovation, home grow
自主创新能力/自主創新能力 indigenous innovation capability
自主创新战略/自主創新策略 indigenous innovation strategy
自主方程式/自主方程式 autonomous equation
自主化管理/獨立管理 independent management

自主经营/自負盈虧　taking full responsibility for profits and losses
自主开发/獨立開發　independent development
自主品牌/自主品牌　self-owned brand
自主权/自主權　autonomy
自主税则/自主關稅　autonomous tariff
自主阅读/獨立閱讀　independent reading
自主占有/自主占有　possession of one's own
自主知识产权/自主智慧財產權　indigenous intellectual property right
自助抽样/自舉採樣　bootstrap sampling
自助法/自助法,靴環法,自我重複抽樣法　bootstrap, bootstrap method
自助服务/自助服務　self-service
自助-互助型组织/自助-互助型組織　self-help and mutual aid organization
自助借还/自助借還　self-loan
自助群体/自助團體　self-help group
自助图书馆/自助圖書館　self-service library
自传/自傳　autobiography
自组织/自組織　self-organization
自组织理论/自組織理論　self-organization theory
自组织系统/自組織系統　self-organizing system
自尊/自尊　self-esteem
字典/字典　dictionary, character dictionary
字典式目录/字典目錄　dictionary catalog
字典序法/字典序法　dictionary ordered method
字段分隔符/欄間分隔符號　field separator
字段后缀符/尾綴運算子　suffix operator
字段间连接数据/字段間連接數據　interfield linking data
字段检索/字段檢索　field search, field retrieval
字段前缀符/前置運算子　prefix operator
字段指示符/欄位指示符　field indicator
字段终止符/欄位終止符　field terminator
字符/字[元]　character
字符串检索/字串檢索　string search, string retrieval
字符轮廓/字元輪廓　glyph
字符轮廓的度量规格/字元輪廓的度量規格　glyph metric
字符字形库/中文字元字型館　character font library
字迹加固/字跡加固　stabilization for ink
字迹扩散/字跡擴散　diffusing
字迹耐久性/字跡耐久性　ink permanence
字迹褪色/字跡褪色　ink fading
字迹洇化/字跡洇化　ink spreading
字间/字間　letter space

字间隔空/字間調整　letter spacing
字节/位元組　byte
字库/字庫　character library
字面侵权/文義侵權　literal infringement
字面组配/文字協調　literal coordination
字母次序模型/詞典編纂模型　lexicographic model
字顺分类目录/字順分類目錄　alphabetical and classified catalog
字顺目录/字眼目錄　alphabetical catalog
字顺排架法/字順排架法　alphabetical arrangement
字顺排序法/字順排序法　alphabetization
字体/字體　typefont
字体考订/字體考訂　font criticism
字帖/字帖　copybook
Z字形/鋸齒形,折形　zigzag form
字形轮廓/字元輪廓　glyph
字形提示/字元提示　font hint
宗/氏族　clan
宗法继承/宗法繼承　patriarchal inheritance
宗教/宗教　religion
宗教剥夺理论/宗教剝奪理論　religion deprivation theory
宗教补偿/宗教補償　religion compensation theory
宗教出版物/宗教出版物　religious publication
宗教档案/宗教檔案　religious archive
宗教多元论/宗教多元論　religious pluralism
宗教法/宗教法　religious law
宗教符号/宗教符號　religious symbol
宗教改革/宗教改革　Reformation
宗教个人主义/宗教個人主義　religious individualism
宗教共同体/宗教共同體　religious community
宗教管制/宗教管制　religious regulation
宗教激动/宗教激動　religious thrill
宗教经济/宗教經濟　religious economy
宗教拒世/宗教拒世　religious rejection
宗教立法/宗教立法　religious legislation
宗教膜拜/宗教膜拜　religious cult
宗教人类学/宗教人類學　anthropology of religion
宗教认同/宗教認同　religious identity
宗教社会学/宗教社會學　sociology of religion
宗教身份/宗教身份　religious identity
宗教体验/宗教體驗　religious experience
宗教团体/宗教團體　religious order
宗教心理学/宗教心理學　psychology of religion
宗教信仰自由/宗教信仰自由　freedom of belief and religion, freedom of religion
宗教性/宗教性　religiosity

宗教仪式/宗教儀式　religious rite, ritual
宗教组织/宗教組織　religious organization
宗派/教派　sect
宗派主义/教派主義　sectarianism
宗桃/宗桃　Zongtiao
宗主国/宗主國　sovereign state
宗族/宗族,氏族　clan, patriarchal clan
综合/合成　synthesis
综合报道/綜合報導　wrapup
综合避险/整體避險　macro hedge
综合标准化/綜合標準化　integrated standardization
综合财务报表/聯合財務報表　conglomerate financial statement
综合抽样/綜合抽樣　synthetic sampling
综合出版社/綜合出版社　comprehensive publishing house
综合单价/綜合單價　comprehensive unit price
综合档案馆/綜合檔案館　general archives
综合档案室/綜合檔案室　general record office
综合法学/綜合法學　integrative jurisprudence
综合服务模式/綜合服務模式　integrated service model
综合服务数字网络/整體服務數位網路　integrated service digital network, ISDN
综合估计值/綜合估計值　pooled estimate
综合管理/集成管理　integration management
综合计划/整體規劃,總體規劃,總合規劃　aggregate planning
综合价格/綜合價格　composite price
综合价格指数/總合價格指數　aggregate price index
综合奖/綜合獎　comprehensive award
综合介入/綜合介入　comprehensive intervention
综合经济指标/綜合經濟指標　composite economic indicator
综合可行性方法/綜合可行性方法　comprehensive feasibility approach
综合库存/總存貨　aggregate inventory
综合款目/綜合款目　integrated entry
综合类/綜合類　general class
综合模型/總合模型　aggregative model
综合平衡/綜合平衡　overall balancing
综合评估/綜合評估,綜合評價　comprehensive assessment
综合评价/綜合評價　integrated evaluation
综合评价决策支持系统/綜合評價決策支援系統　comprehensive evaluation decision support system
综合情报研究/綜合情報分析　comprehensive intelligence analysis
综合社会调查/綜合社會調查,社會基本調查　general social survey, GSS
综合收益/綜合損益　comprehensive income
综合书店/綜合書店　comprehensive bookstore
综合书目/綜合書目　comprehensive bibliography
综合税率/綜合稅率　composite rate of tax
综合提货单/綜合提貨單,合并提單　omnibus bill of lading
综合网点/綜合網點　comprehensive outlet
综合文件全宗/綜合檔全宗　general record fond
综合文件组合/綜合檔組合　general record group
综合险保单/全險保單　all risks policy
综合信息中心/綜合資訊中心　general information center
综合性百科全书/綜合性百科全書　general encyclopedia
综合性报纸/綜合性報紙　general newspaper
综合性出版物/綜合性出版物　compatibility issue
综合性词典/綜合詞典　comprehensive dictionary
综合性分类表/普通分類　general classification
综合性检索工具/綜合性檢索工具　general retrieval device
综合性图书馆/綜合圖書館　comprehensive library
综合叙词表/大敘詞表　macrothesaurus
综合银行/綜合銀行　universal bank
综合造价指数/綜合造價指數　composite index of construction cost
TQCS综合指标/TQCS綜合指標　time-quality-cost-service indicator, TQCS indicator
综合指数/綜合指數,複合指數　aggregative index, comprehensive index
综合住户统计调查/一般家户調查　general household survey
综合著录/集中著錄　integrated description
综论本/綜論本　commented text
综述/綜述　review
综述性文摘/綜述性文摘　survey abstract
棕榈叶档案/棕櫚葉檔案　palm leaves archive
总罢工/總罷工　general strike
总包合同/統包合同　package contract
总保险单/主保險單　master policy
总编办/總編辦　bureau chief department
总编辑/總編輯　editor-in-chief
总编室/總編室　editorial office
总变动成本/總變動成本　total variable cost
总变异/總變異　total variation, over-all variation
总表/總表　general table
总操作时间/總操作時間　total operating time

总差分/總差異　total difference
总产量曲线/總產量曲線　total product curve
总产品/總產量　total product
总成本/總成本　total cost
总承包服务费/總承包服務費　general-contract service charge
总[承包]合同/統包合約　general contract
总抽样比/總抽樣率　over-all sampling fraction
总代理/總代理,總經銷　general agency
总导演/總導演　chief director
总[的]/總的　gross
总额清算/總額結算　lump-sum settlement
总额预算/總額預算　global budget
总发行/總發行　general distribution
总发行单位/總發行單位　general distribution agency
总方差/總方差　total variance, over-all variance
总分馆制/總分館制　central-branch library system
总分行制度/分支銀行制度　branch banking system
总分类账/總分類賬　general ledger
总福利/總福利　aggregate welfare
总抚养比/總撫養比　general dependency ratio
总概算/總概算　general cost estimation
总公司/總公司　head office
总公司管理费/總公司管理費　head office expense
总公司控制账户/總公司控制賬戶　head office control account
总公司账户/總公司賬戶　head office account
总供给/總合供給　aggregate supply
总供给冲击/總合供給衝擊　aggregate supply shock
总供给函数/總供給函數　aggregate supply function
总供给曲线/總合供給曲線　aggregate supply curve
总供求模型/AS-AD模型　AS-AD model
总估计值/總估計值　over-all estimate
总固定成本/總固定成本　total fixed cost
总顾客成本/顧客總成本　total customer cost
总顾客价值/顧客總價值　total customer value
总和/總合　aggregation
总和的或扩大的价值形式/總和的或擴大的價值形式　total or expanded form of value
总和法/總和法　method of summation
总回归/總回歸　total regression
总回归系数/總回歸係數　total regression coefficient
总汇编目/合集層次編目　collection level cataloging
总稽核负责制/總稽核負責制　chief auditor's responsibility system
总集/總集　total collection, general collection
总计/總計　grand total
总价合同/總價契約　lump sum contract

总监理工程师/總監理工程師　chief surveillance engineer
总监理工程师代表/總監理工程師代表　delegate of the chief surveillance engineer
总检验量曲线/總檢驗數曲線　total inspection curve
总交易/總交易　general trading
总接触人次/總接觸人次　coverage
总结性评估/總結性評量,總結性評鑒　conclusive evaluation
总会计师/總會計師　general accountant
总括/總括　blanket
总括保险/總括保險　blanket insurance
总括保险单/總括保險單　blanket insurance policy
总括出入港许可证/總括出入港許可證　blanket clearance
总括登记/總括登記　union accession
总括登记簿/總括登記簿　union accession list
总括订货单/總括訂貨單　blanket order
总括信贷/統括貸款　omnibus credit
总括许可证/總括許可證　blanket licence
总累积/總累積　total cumulation
总离差/總差值　total deviations
总利润/總利潤　total profit, aggregate profit
总量管理/總量管理　quantity management
总量控制/總量控制　total quantity control
总论复分表/標準複分表　standard subdivisions
总贸易/總貿易　general trade
总面值/總面值　aggregate par value
总目录/總目錄　general catalog, central catalog
总频数/總次數　total frequency
总平方和/總平方和　sum of squares total, total sum of squares
总平均数/總平均數　grand mean, grand average, general mean
总谱/樂曲,樂譜　score
总期号/總期號　whole number
总清单/總清單　master list
总人口增加率/總人口增加率　total population increase rate
总社会产品/社會總產品　total social product
总社会成本/社會總成本　total social cost
总生育率/總生育率,一般生育率　general fertility rate, total fertility rate
总生殖率/總生殖率　gross reproductive rate
总时差/總浮時　total float
总市值/總市值　aggregate market value
总试验时间/總試驗時間　total time on test
总收入/總和收入,所得總額　aggregate income,

gross income
总收益/總收益　total revenue
总收益互换/總報酬交換契約　total return swap
总收益率/總收益率　overall yield
总索引/總索引　general index
总题名/總題名　collective title
总体/全體,母體　population
总体百分数/母體百分位數　population percentile
总体比例/母體比例　population proportion
总体标准差/母體標準差　population standard deviation
总体布局/總體布局　general layout
总体参数/母體參數　population parameter
总体多重判定系数/母體多元判定係數　population coefficient of multiple determination
总体方差/母體變異數　population variance
总体方差估计/母體變異數的估計　estimation of population variance
总体分布/母體分布　population distribution
总体估计值/母體估計值　population estimate
总体环境/一般環境　general environment
总体回归模型/母體回歸模型　population regression model
总体回归系数/母體回歸係數　population regression coefficient
总体回归直线/母體回歸線　population regression line
总体矩/母體動差　population moment
总体均值/母體平均數　population mean
总体均值估计/母體均值估計　estimation of population mean
总体均值与方差联合置信域/母體平均數及變異數聯合信賴區域　joint confidence region for population mean and variance
总体类型/母體類型　type of population
总体量估计/母體大小估計　estimation of population size
总体平均/整體平均,實現體平均　ensemble average
总体史/總體史　total history
总体薪酬/總報酬　total compensation
总体中位数/母體中位數　median point of population
总替代品/毛替代品　gross substitute
总统/總統　president
总统制/總統制　presidential system
总投资/總投資,投資總額　gross investment, total investment
总投资率/總投資率　gross investment rate
总相联/總相聯　total association

总效应/總影響　total effect
总效用/總效用　total utility
总需求/毛需求,總合需求　aggregate demand, gross demand, gross requirement
总需求曲线/總合需求曲線　aggregate demand curve
总需要量/毛需求,總合需求　aggregate demand, gross demand, gross requirement
总悬浮颗粒物/總懸浮微粒,總懸浮粒狀物　total suspended particulate
总要素生产力指数/總要素生產力指數　total factor productivity index
总移动率/總移動率　total movement rate
总易货贸易条件/以貨易貨貿易條件毛額　gross barter terms of trade
总预算/總預算　main budget
总占地面积/總樓地板面積　total floor area
总政策/總方針　general policy
总值/總值,綜合值　aggregate
总值加权法/綜合值加權法　aggregate-value method of weighting
总指数/總指數　total index number, general index number
总主笔/總主筆,總編輯　editor-in-chief, chief editor
总装配计划/總裝配計劃　final assembly schedule
总资产周转率/總資產週轉率　total asset turnover ratio
总资源供需预测/總資源供需預測　forecasting of aggregate supply and demand
纵长页/直式　lengthwise page
纵剖面/縱剖面　longitudinal section
纵条图/縱條圖　vertical bar chart
纵向/縱向,追蹤　logituidinality
纵向并购/垂直購并,垂直并購　vertical acquisition
纵向磁化/縱向磁化　longitudinal magnetization
纵向地域限制/垂直地域限制　vertical territorial restriction
纵向调查/追蹤調查　longitudinal survey
纵向公平/縱的公平　vertical equity
纵向国际专业化分工/垂直性國際分工　vertical international specification
纵向合并/垂直整合　vertical integration
纵向价格固定/垂直統一定價　vertical price fixing
纵向兼并/垂直合并　vertical merger
纵向交易/垂直交易　vertical transaction
纵向景框/縱向景框　vertical scene frame
纵向贸易/垂直貿易　vertical trade
纵向排队/縱等待線排陣　tandem queue
纵向数据分析/縱向數據分析　longitudinal data

analysis
纵向限制/垂直性的限制競爭行爲　vertical restraint
纵向研究/縱向研究　longitudinal study
纵向一体化/垂直整合　vertical integration
纵向约束/垂直性限制競爭行爲　vertical restraint
纵向约束指导原则/垂直限制指導方針　vertical restraint guideline
纵向转让/垂直轉讓　vertical transfer
纵轴/縱軸　axis of ordinate
邹氏检验/鄒氏檢定　Chow test
邹至庄检验/鄒氏檢定　Chow test
走动管理/走動式管理　management by walking around
走廊原则/通道原則　corridor principle
走势预测/趨勢預測　tendency forecasting
走私、贩卖、运输、制造毒品罪/走私、販賣、運輸、製造毒品罪　crime of smuggling, trafficking in, transporting or producing drugs
走私普通货物、物品罪/走私普通貨物、物品罪　crime of smuggling ordinary goods or articles
走私武器、弹药罪/走私武器、彈藥罪　crime of smuggling weapons or ammunition
走私罪/走私罪　crime of smuggling
奏折/奏摺　palace memorial
租船合同/備船契約　charter party
租购价格/分期付款價格　hire-purchase price
租购融资/分期付款融資　hire-purchase finance
租借订购/租借訂購　rental plan
租借法案/租借法案　lend lease act
租金/租金　rent
租金控制/租金管制　rent control
租赁/租賃　leasing
租赁保险/租賃保險　lease insurance
租赁财务公司/租賃財務公司　lease finance company
租赁筹资/租賃籌資　lease financing
租赁费/租賃費　lease expense
租赁费用/租賃費用，租賃成本　rental expense, rental cost
租赁公司/租賃公司　leasing company
租赁购买合同/租賃購買合約　lease-purchase agreement
租赁合同/租賃合同，租賃契約　contract for lease, lease contract
租赁经纪人/租賃經紀人　lease broker
租赁贸易/租賃貿易　lease trade
租赁贸易方式/租賃貿易方式　leasing trade method
租赁权益保险/租賃權益保險　leasehold interest insurance
租赁市场/租賃市場　leasing market
租赁协议/租賃合約　tenancy agreement
租赁信贷/租賃信貸　leasing credit
租赁业/租賃業　leasing industry
租赁业务/租賃業務　leasing business
租赁制/租賃制度　rental system
租赁资产/租賃資產　leasing asset
租让制/特許制度　concession system
租用线路/租用專線　leased line
足本/足本　unabridged edition
足本词典/足本詞典　unabridged dictionary
足价/完整價格　full price
族/族首詞　top term
族规/族規　regulations of the clan
族刻本/族刻本　family-printed edition
族谱/族譜　genealogy
族群/族群，族裔［團體］　ethnic group, ethnic
族群类聚/族群類聚　ethnic homophily
族群性/族群特性　ethnicity
族首词/族首詞　top term
族刑/族刑　family penalty
族性检索/家族搜索　family search
阻断/阻斷　block
阻断因子/區段因子　blocking factors
阻尼因子/減幅因子　damping factor
阻尼震荡/減幅振盪　damped oscillation
阻塞作业/阻隔作業　blocked operation
组/組　class
组版/組版　image assembly, workgroup edition
组标/組標　class mark
组别生育率/年次別生育率　cohort fertility
组代关系/組代關係　compound equivalence
组稿/組稿　solicit contributions
组稿编辑/組稿編輯　commission editor
组号/組別記號　class symbol
组合/組成　composition, combination
组合安排/組合配置　combinatorial arrangement
组合并/類合并　pooling of class
组合创新/組合創新　portfolio innovation
组合动作/合并動作　combined motion
组合分析/組合分析　combinatorial analysis
组合检索/組合檢索　combinatorial searches
组合检验/組合檢定　combinatorial test
组合幂均值/組合冪平均數　combinatorial power mean
组合模型/組合模型　combinatorial model
组合商标/組合商標　composed trademark

组合试验/組合試驗　combined experiment
组合文件/組合紀錄　combined record
组合优化/組合最優化　combinatorial optimization
组合预测/組合預測　ensemble forecasting
组间变异/組間變異　variation between classes, among class variation
组间方差/組間變異數,組間方差　interclass variance, between-class variance
组间估计量/群組間估計量　between estimator
组间平方和/組間平方和　sum square between groups
组间设计/族群中設計　between-group design
组间相关/組間相關,內相關　interclass correlation, intercorrelation
组间相关系数/組間相關係數　interclass correlation coefficient
组件/組件,組成部分　component
组件图/構件圖　component diagram
组界/組界　class interval boundary
组距/組[間]距　class width, class interval
组均值/組平均數　class mean
组控制/區段管制　block control
组内比率/組內比率　intraclass ratio
组内变异/組內變異　variation within class
组内方差/組內變異數,組內方差　within class variance, intraclass variance
组内估计量/跨群組估計量　within estimator
组内平方和/平方誤差總和　sum of squared error
组内相关/組內相關　intraclass correlation
组内相关系数/組內相關係數　coefficient of interclass correlation, intraclass correlation coefficient
组配/協調　coordination
组配标引/組合索引法　coordinate indexing
组配方式/協調型[式]　mode of coordination
组配分类法/組配分類法,分面[式]分類法　synthetic classification
组配符号/組配符號　facet indicator
组配关系/協調關係　synthetic relation
组配规则/協調規則　rule for coordination
组配货/組配貨　assembly goods
组配权限/組配權限　permission of coordination
组频数/組次數　class frequency
组群/組群　class group
组上限/組上限　class upper limit
组数/組數　number of class, class number
组下限/組下限　class lower limit
组限/組[界]限,組界　class boundary, true class limit, class limit
组形/組形　class form
组织/組織　organization
组织边界/組織邊界　organizational boundary
组织扁平化/扁平化組織　flattening organization
组织变革/組織變革　organizational change
组织承诺/組織承諾　organizational commitment
组织冲突/組織衝突　organizational conflict
组织重组/組織重組　organizational restructuring
组织创新/組織創新　organization innovation
组织发展/組織發展　organizational development
组织发展理论/組織發展理論　organizational development theory
组织犯/組織犯　organizing offender
组织防卫/組織防衛　organization routine
组织分解结构/組織分解結構　organizational breakdown structure, OBS
组织分析/組織分析　organizational analysis
组织复杂性/組織複雜性　organizational complexity
组织公民行为/組織公民行爲　organizational citizenship behavior
组织沟通/組織溝通　organizational communication
组织关系/組織關係　organization relationship, organizational relationship
组织管理/組織管理　organization management, organizational management
组织惯例/組織例規　organizational routine
组织规范/組織規範　organizational rule
组织规模/組織規模　organizational size
组织过程/組織程序,組織流程　organizational process
组织过程资产/組織過程資產　organizational process assets
组织化/組織化　organizationalization
组织化群体/組織化群體　organized group
组织环境/組織環境　organizational environment, organization environment
组织机构分类法/組織機構分類法　frame classification, organization classification
组织机构-年度分类法/組織機構-年度分類法　organization-year classification
组织基本制度/組織基本制度　basic organizational institution
组织记忆/組織記憶　organizational memory
组织绩效/組織績效,組織效益　organization performance, organizational performance
组织价值观/組織價值觀　organization value
组织架构/組織架構　organizational structure

组织奖励/組織獎勵　organization reward
组织结构/組織結構　organization structure, organizational structure
组织结构权变分类法/組織結構權變分類法　contingency classification method of organization structure
组织[结构]图/組織圖　organizational chart, organization chart
组织决策/組織決策　organizational decision-making
组织控制/組織控制　organization control, organizational control
组织类型/組織類型　organizational type
组织理论/組織理論　organization theory
组织隶属/組織隸屬　organizational affiliation
组织伦理/組織倫理　organizational ethics
组织卖淫罪/組織賣淫罪　crime of organizing others to engage in prostitution
组织目标/組織目標　organization objective, organizational goal, organizational target
组织内谈判/組織內談判　intraorganizational bargaining
组织能力/組織能力　organizational capacity
组织凝聚力/組織凝聚力　organization cohesion
组织平衡论/組織平衡理論　organizational equilibrium theory
组织气氛/組織氣候　organizational climate
组织趋同/組織趨同　organizational convergence, organizational isomorphism
组织认同/組織認同　organizational identity
组织冗余/組織鬆散　organizational slack
组织三要素/組織三要素　three elements of organization
组织设计/組織設計　organizational design
组织社会化/組織社會化　organization socialization, organizational socialization
组织社会学/組織社會學　organizational sociology
组织生命周期/組織生命週期　organizational life cycle
组织生态/組織生態　organizational ecology
组织声誉/組織聲譽　organizational reputation
组织胜任力/組織能力,組織能耐　organizational competency
组织调节/組織調節　organization balance
组织网络/組織網路　organizational network
组织文化/組織文化　organizational culture, organization culture
组织吸引/組織吸引力　organizational inducement
组织系统/組織系統　organization system

组织效率/組織效率　organization efficiency
组织效率三原则/組織效率三原則　three principles of organization efficiency
组织效能/組織效能　organizational effectiveness
组织协调/組織協調　organization coordination
组织行动/組織行動　organizational action
组织行动者/組織行動者　organizational actor
组织行为[学]/組織行爲　organizational behavior
组织形态/組織形態　organizational form
组织学习/組織學習　organizational learning
组织沿革/組織沿革　historical evolution of organization, evolutionistic development of organization
组织仪式/組織儀式　organizational ritual
组织遗忘/組織遺忘　organizational unlearn
组织营销/組織行銷　organization marketing
组织再造理论/組織再造理論　strategic reconstruction theory
组织诊断/組織診斷　organizational diagnosis
组织政治行为/組織政治行爲　organizational political behavior
组织支持感/知覺組織支援　perceived organizational support
组织知识/組織知識　organizational knowledge
组织知识管理/組織知識管理　organizational knowledge management
组织制度/組織制度　organization institution, organizational institution
组织秩序/組織秩序　organizational order
组织忠诚/組織忠誠　organizational loyalty
组值/組值　class value
组中点/組中點　class mid-point
组中值/組中值　class mid-value
祖本/祖本　parent edition
祖先崇拜/祖先崇拜　ancestor worship
钻取分析/鑽取分析　drill analysis
钻石模型/鑽石模型　diamond model
最不发达国家/最低度開發國家　least less developed country, LLDC
最不利分布/最不利分布　least favorable distribution
最不利先验分布/最不利事前分布　least favorable prior distribution
最不喜欢同事问卷/最不喜歡同事問卷　least-preferred co-worker questionnaire
最长加工时间法则/最長處理時間　longest processing time, LPT
最迟开始时间/最遲開始時間　latest start time, LST

最迟完成时间/最晚完成時間　latest completion time, LCT
最初的编码/初步編碼　initial coding
最初投入/原始投入　primary input
最大 F 比/最大 F 比　maximum F-ratio
最大变异抽样/最大變異抽樣　varimax sampling
最大标准差/最大標準差　maximum standard deviation, MSD
最大不变函数/最大不變函數　maximal invariant function
最大持续产量/最大永續生產量　maximun sustainable yield
最大反差/最大反差　max contrast
最大方差膨胀因子/最大變異膨脹因子　maximum variance inflation factor
最大工作区域/最大工作區域　maximum working area
最大功效检验/最强力檢定　most powerful test
最大功效临界区域/最強[檢]力棄却域　most powerful critical region
最大功效秩检验/最強力秩檢定　most powerful rank test
最大共享性/最大共用性　maximum sharing
最大经济产量/最大利潤之產量　maximun economic yield
最大可能准则/最大容許準則　maximum permissible criterion
最大库存量/最大庫存量　maximum inventory
最大库存水平策略/最大庫存水準策略　order-up-to policy
最大流最小割定理/最大流量最小切點定理　max-flow min-cut theorem
最大期望利润/最大期望收益　maximum expected profit
最大期望收益准则/貨幣期望值　expected monetary value
最大期望算法/EM 演算法　expectation maximization algorithm, EM algorithm
最大熵原理/最大熵原則　maximum entropy principle
最大输出电平/最大輸出電平　maximum output level
最大似然法/最大概似法　maximum likelihood method
最大似然估计/最大概度估計,最大概似估計　maximum likelihood estimate, maximum likelihood estimation
最大似然估计量的渐近分布/最大概度估計量漸近分布,最大概度估計量漸近分配　asymptotic distribution of maximum likelihood estimator
最大似然估计量的渐近最优性/最大概度估計量的漸近最適性　asymptotic optimality of maximum likelihood estimator
最大似然估计量的相合性/最大概度估計量的一致性　consistency of MLE
最大效用原则/最大效用原則　maximum utility principle
最大斜交法/最大斜交法　oblimax rotation
最大最小准则/最大化低所得判準,小中取大準則　maxmin criterion, maxmini criterion
最低保留额/最低保留額　minimum retention
最低保险费/最低保險費　minimum premium
最低报盘/最低報價　minimum quotation
最低成本/最低成本　minimum cost
最低筹资额/最低認購額,最低認購股　minimum subscription
最低储备率/最低儲備率　minimum reserve ratio
最低递盘价/最低投標價　lowest bid
最低费用/最低費用　minimum charge
最低风险/最低風險　minimum risk
最低工资/最低工資　minimum wage
最低工资法/最低工資法　minimum wage law
最低工资制度/最低工資制度　minimum wage system
最低关税[率]/最低關稅[率]　minimum tariff
最低汇率/最低匯率　floor rate, lowest exchange rate
最低价差/最低價差　minimum margin
最低价格/最低價格　minimum price, lowest price
最低价评标法/最低投標價法　lowest bidding price method
最低可持续失业率/最低可持續失業率　lowest sustainable rate of unemployment
最低利率/最低利率　lowest interest rate
最低利润/最低利潤　minimum profit
最低利润率/最低利潤率　minimum rate of profit
最低免税收入/最低免税收入　minimum exempt income
最低生活保障制度/最低生活保障制度　minimum living standard security system
最低生活费/最低生活費　minimum living expenditure
最低适合状态/最小有利狀態　least favorable configuration
最低收益率/最低報酬率　minimum rate of return
最低税额/最低税負　minimum tax

最低限价/最低限價,價格下限　lowest price limit, price limit, price floor
最低应税收入/最低應稅收入　minimum taxable income
最低余额/最低餘額　minimum balance
最低预付保险费/最低預付保險費　minimum deposit premium
最低运费/最低運費　minimum freight
最低征税限额/最低課稅限度　lowest taxable limit
最短加工时间规则/最短處理時間法則　shortest processing time, SPT
最短路径/最短路徑　shortest path, minimal path
最短置信区间/最短信賴區間　shortest confidence interval
最高保险费/最高保險費　maximum premium
最高额抵押权/最高額抵押權　mortgage of maximum amount
最高额质权/最高額質權　pledge of maximum amount
最高法院/最高法院　supreme court
最高法院指导性案例/最高法院指導性案例　supreme people's court instructs cases
最高后验密度/最高的事後機率密度　highest posterior density
最高价格/最高價格　maximum price
最高检察院/最高檢察院　supreme prosecutor's office
最高利率/最高利率　maximum interest rate
最高利润率/最高利潤率　maximum rate of profit
最高录音磁平/最高録音磁平　maximum recording magnetic flat
最高税率/最高稅率　maximum tariff
最高所得/最高所得　highest income
最高限度/最高限度　maximum limit
最高限额制度/最高限額制度　maximum limit system
最高限价/最高限價,價格上限　maximum price fixing, price ceiling
最高效设计/最有效設計　most efficient design
最高最低关税[率]制度/最高最低[關]稅率制度　minimum and maximum tariff system
最高最低税则制/最高最低稅則制　maximum and minimum tariff system
最后背书人/最後背書人　last endorser
最后贷款人/最後貸款人,最後貸款者　lender of last resort
最后交货日期/最後交貨日期　deadline delivery date, DDD
最后交易日/最後交易日　last trading day
最后结余/最後結餘　final balance
最后清偿率/最後清償率　final repayment ratio
最后确定的保险金额/最後確定的保險金額　closed line
最后确认/最終確認　final confirmation
最后通牒/最後通牒　ultimatum
最后通牒博弈/最後通牒遊戲,承讓賽局　ultimatum game
最后要价仲裁/最終[提案]仲裁　final-offer arbitration
最后页/最後頁面　final page
最坏情景分析/最壞情境分析　worst-case analysis
最惠国/最惠國　most favored nation, MFN
最惠国待遇/最惠國待遇,最惠國資格　most favored national treatment, most favored nation status
最惠国待遇原则/最惠國待遇原則　principle of most favored nation treatment
最惠国关税率/最惠國關稅率　most-favored nation tariff rate
最惠客户条款/最惠待遇消費者條款　most-favored-customer clause
最佳不变决策规则/最佳不變決策規則　best invariant decision rule
最佳测度/最佳測度　optimal scaling
最佳城市规模/最適城市規模　optimal city size
最佳城市人口规模/最適城市人口　optimal urban population
最佳估计量/最佳估計量,最適估計量　optimum estimator, best estimator
最佳估计值/最佳估計值　best estimate, optimum estimate
最佳检验/最佳檢定　best test
最佳检验统计量/最適檢定統計量　optimal test statistic
最佳渐近正态估计[量]/最佳漸近常態估計[量]　best asymptotically normal estimator, BAN estimator
最佳决策法则/最佳決策規則　best decision rule
最佳绝对无偏估计[量]/最佳絕對不偏估計[量]　best absolutely unbiased estimator
最佳可持续产量/最適永續生產量　optimal sustainable yield
最佳临界[区]域/最佳棄却域　best critical region
最佳贸易/最佳貿易　optimum trade
最佳偏磁/最佳偏磁　optimum magnetic bias
最佳妊娠期/最適生產期　optimal gestation period
最佳生产期/最適生產期　optimal gestation period

最佳投资/最適宜投資　optimum investment
最佳图书/最佳圖書　best book
最佳威慑/最適嚇阻手段　optimal deterrence
最佳无偏估计[量]/最佳不偏估計[量]　best unbiased estimator
最佳无偏临界域/最佳不偏棄却域　best unbiased critical region
最佳现金持有量/最佳現金持有量　target cash balance
最佳线性不变估计[量]/最佳線性不變估計[量]　best linear invariant estimator
最佳线性不变估计[值]/最佳線性不變估計[值]　best linear invariant estimate
最佳线性无偏估计/最適線性不偏估計　best linear unbiased estimator
最佳线性无偏估计[量]/最佳線性不偏估計[量]　best linear unbiased estimator, BLUE
最佳线性无偏估计[值]/最佳線性不偏估計[值]　best linear unbiased estimate
最佳线性指数/最佳線性指數　best linear index
最佳样本容量/最適樣本數　optimal sample size
最佳置信区间/最佳信賴區間　best confidence interval
最佳准线性估计量/最佳準線性估計量　best quasi-linear estimator
最佳最终决策/最適終結決策　optimal terminal decision
最简单流/最簡單流　simplest flow
最简级编目/最簡級編目　minimal level cataloging
最紧迫检验/逼近最強力檢定　most stringent test
最经济法则/簡約原則　law of parsimony
最可能估计时间/最可能時間估計　most likely time estimate
最可能值/最可能值　most probable value
最密切联系说/最密切聯繫説　doctrine of the most significant relationship
最密切联系原则/最密切聯繫原則　principle of the most significant relationship
最难共事者问卷/最難共事者問卷　least-preferred co-worker questionnaire
最弱环节模型/最弱環節模型　weakest-link model
最少信息分布/最少訊息分布　least informative distribution
最适保留工资/最適保留工資　optimal reservation wage
最适产量/最適產量　optimal yield
最适利率/最適當利率　optimum rate of interest
最速上升法/最陡上升法　steepest ascent method
最速下降法/最陡下降法，最陡坡度法　steepest descent method
最小安全过程平均/最小安全製程平均　minimum safe process average
最小报价单位/最小升降單位　tick size
最小贝叶斯风险/最小貝氏風險　minimum Bayes risk
最小变动价位/漲跌一碼，最小變動點數　minimum fluctuation, tick
最小差异化原则/最小差異原則　principle of minimum differentiation
最小充分分割/最小充分分割　minimal sufficient partition
最小充分统计量/最小充分統計量　minimal sufficient statistic
最小充分统计量的维数/最小充分統計量的維度　dimensionality of minimal sufficient statistic
最小订货量/最小訂貨量　minimum order quantity
最小二乘残差/最小平方殘差　least squares residuals
最小二乘法/最小平方[法]　least squares method, method of least squares, ordinary least squares
最小二乘法原理/最小平方原則　principle of least squares
最小二乘方/最小二乘方，最小平方　least square
最小二乘估计[量]/最小平方估計[量]　least squares estimator, LSE
最小二乘拟合/最小平方[法]配適　fitting by least squares method
最小二乘误差准则函数/最小平方準則函數　least square criterion function
最小二乘预测函数/最小平方預測函數　least square prediction function
最小二乘原理/最小平方原理，最小平方定律　least squares principle
最小二乘准则/最小平方評估準則　least square criterion
最小范数二次无偏估计/二次最小距離不偏估計式　minimum norm quadratic unbiased estimator
最小范数二次无偏估计量/最小範數二次不偏估計量　minimum norm quadratic unbiased estimator, MINQUE
最小方差/最小方差，最小變異數　minimum variance
最小方差比/最小方差比，最小變異比　least variance ratio
最小方差比估计量/最小變異數比例估計量　least variance ratio estimator

最小方差差分法/最小變異數差異法　least variance difference method
最小方差估计量/最小方差估計量,極小變異估計量　minimum-variance estimator
最小方差无偏估计量/最小變異數不偏估計量　minimum variance unbiased estimator
最小方差资产组合/最低變異數資產組合　minimum variance portfolio
最小风险不变估计[量]/最小風險不變估計[量]　minimum risk invariant estimator
最小公倍数/最小公倍數　least common multiplier
最小机会损失准则/預期機會損失　expected opportunity loss
最小基本完备性/最小本質完備性　minimal essential completeness
最小检验量/最低檢驗數量　minimum amount inspection
最小交易原理/最小交易原則　principle of minimum transaction
最小距离估计法/最小距離估計式　minimum distance estimator
最小绝对残差估计量/最小絕對殘差估計式　least absolute residual estimator, LAR estimator
最小绝对差估计量/最小絕對差估計量　least absolute deviation estimator
最小绝对偏差估计量/最小絕對差估計式　minimum absolute deviation estimator
最小绝对误差估计量/最小絕對誤差估計式　least absolute error estimator
最小绝对值估计量/最小絕對值估計量　least absolute value estimator, LAV estimator
最小绝对值估计[值]/最小絕對值估計[值]　least absolute value estimate
最小均方误差估计值/最小均方差估計值　minimum mean square error estimator
最小均方误差预测/最小均方差預測　minimum mean square error forecast
最小卡方方法/最小卡方方法　minimum chi-square method
最小卡方估计/最小卡方估計式　minimum chi-square estimator, minimum χ^2 estimator
最小描述长度原则/最短描述法則　minimum description length principle
最小努力原则/最小努力原則　principle of least effort
最小判别信息统计量/最小判別資訊統計量　minimum discrimination information statistic
最小期望损失/最小預期損失　minimum expected loss
最小冗余度/最小冗餘,最少多餘,最少重複　minimum redundancy
最小时间/最小時間　minimum time
最小顺序统计量/最小順序統計量　smallest order statistic
最小完备性/最小完備性　minimum completeness
最小完全类/最小完備類　minimal complete class
最小稳定分布/最小穩定分布　minimum stable distribution
最小显著差数/最低顯著差異值　least significant difference, LSD
最小斜交法/最小斜交法　oblimin roation
最小有效规模/最小有效規模　minimum efficient scale
最小预期风险/最小預期風險　minimum expected risk
最小-最大系统/最小-最大系統　min-max system
最小最大遗憾原则/大中取小悔憾原則　minimax regret principle
最新技术水准/最新技術,目前最佳技術,技術現況　state of the art
最新款目/最新款目　latest entry
最优保险/最適保險　optimal insurance
最优不变估计量/最佳不變估計量　best invariant estimator
最优策略/最適策略,最佳策略　optimal strategy
最优产量/最適產出　optimum output
最优抽样方案/最適抽樣計劃　optimal sampling plan
最优纯策略/最優純策略　optimal pure strategy
最优定价/最適當定價　optimal pricing
最优二次型无偏估计/最佳二次式不偏估計量　best quadratic unbiased estimator
最优二次型无偏预测量/最佳二次式不偏預測量　best quadratic unbiased predictor
最优反应/最適反應　best response
最优方案/優化方案　optimal scheme
最优非线性两阶最小二乘估计量/最佳非線性二階段最小平方估計量　best nonlinear two-stage least squares estimator
最优分层/最適分層　optimum stratification
最优关税/最適[當]關稅　optimum tariff
最优关税论/最適當關稅理論　optimum tariff theory
最优化/最優化,最佳化　optimization
最优化程序/最適化程式　optimization procedure
最优混合战略/最適混合策略　optimal mixed strategy

最优货币量/最適貨幣數量　optional quantity of money
最优货币区/最適通貨區,最理想貨幣區域　optimum currency area
最优价格/最優價格　best price
最优检验/最適檢定　optimum test
最优渐近检验/最適漸近檢定　optimal asymptotic test
最优解/最佳解　optimal solution
最优决策/最適決策　optimal decision
最优决策规则/最適決策規則　optimum decision rule
最优均方预测量/最佳均方預測量　best mean square predictor
最优可行解/最適可行解　optimum feasible solution
最优控制/最適控制　optimal control
最优控制理论/最適控制理論　optimal control theory
最优控制模型/最適控制模型　optimal control model
A最优离散设计/A型最適離散設計　A-optimal discrete design
Q最优离散设计/Q型最適離散設計　Q-optimal discrete design
最优贸易政策/最適貿易政策　optimal trade policy
最优拟合/最佳配適　best fit
最优拟合曲线/最佳配適曲線　best fitting curve
最优拟合线/最佳配適線　best fitting line, line of best fit
最优配置/最適配置　optimum allocation
最优权函数/最適權函數　optimum weight function
最优人口规模/最適人口　optimum population, optimum population size
最优设计/最適設計　optimal design
A最优设计/A型最適設計　A-optimal design
D最优设计/D型最適設計　D-optimal design
E最优设计/E型最適設計　E-optimal design
G最优设计/G型最適設計　G-optimal design
L最优设计/L型最適設計　L-optimal design
S最优设计/S型最適設計　S-optimal design
A最优设计迭代过程/A型最適設計迭代過程　iterative process of A-optimal design
最优生产技术/最佳化生產技術　optimized production technology, OPT
最优水平/最適水準　optimum level
最优税收/最適稅收,最適租稅　optimal taxation
最优税制/最適租稅體制　optimal tax system
最优调和解/最佳調和解　best compromise solution

最优停止规则/最適止步規則　optimal stopping rule
最优通行税率/最好的现行税率　best prevailing tariff rate
最优统计量/最適統計量　optimum statistic
最优投资行为/最適宜的投資行爲　optimal investment behaviour
最优无偏性/最小變異不偏性　best unbiasedness
最优线性无偏性/最佳線性不偏誤性　best linear unbiasedness
最优线性无偏预测量/最佳線性不偏預測量　best linear unbiased predictor
最优线性预测[量]/最佳線性預測量,最適線性預測量　best linear predictor, optimum linear predictor
最优行动/最適行動　optimum action
最优型决策/最優型決策　optimization type decision
最优性能/最適履行　optimal performance
最优性准则/最優性判據　optimality criteria
最优序贯抽样方案/最適逐次抽樣計劃　optimal sequential-sampling plan
最优样本量/最適樣本大小　optimum sample size
最优原则/最適性原則　principle of optimality
最优终止时间/最適止步時間　optimal stopping time
最优专利保护期限/最適專利期間　optimal patent life
最优资本结构/最優資本結構　optimal capital structure
最优资产组合/最適投資組合　optimal portfolio
最有效估计[量]/最有效估計[量]　most efficient estimator
最有效规模/最大效率規模　most efficient scale
最有效线性系统/最有效線性系統　most efficient linear system
最早开始时间/最早開始時間　earliest start time, EST
最早完成时间/最早完成時間　earliest completion time, ECT
最早完工期限规则/最短交貨期優先規則　earliest due date, EDD
最终报表/最終報表　final report form
最终裁决/最終仲裁判決　final award
最终产出率/最終產出率　final yield, FY
最终产品/最終產品　final product, final good
最终单位/最終單位　ultimate unit
最终价格/最終價格　final price
最终价格法/最終價格法　last price method
最终检验/最後檢驗　final inspection
最终决策/最終決策　terminal decision
最终可交付成果/最終可遞交成果　final deliverable

最终需求/最終需求　final demand
最终因子相关法/最終因子相關法　ultimate factor correlation method
最终用户/最終用戶,終端用戶　end user
最终预测函数/最終預測函數　eventual forecasting function
最终组/最終組　ultimate class
罪名/罪名　charge
罪数论/罪數論　theory of crime quantity
罪刑法定原则/罪刑法定原則　principle of a legally prescribed punishment for a specified crime
罪责刑相适应原则/罪責刑相適應原則　principle of suiting punishment to crime
罪状/罪狀　fact about a crime
尊重/尊重　respect
尊重档案结权原则/尊重檔案結權原則　principle of respect for archival structure
尊重全宗原则/尊重全宗原則　principle of respect for the fonds
遵从成本/遵循成本　compliance cost
左侧检验/左端檢定　left-sided test
左截取/左方受限　left-censored
左偏/左偏［態］　left skewness, skewed to the left
左尾递减/左尾遞減的　left tail decreasing
左尾检验/左尾檢定　left-tailed test
左-右拓扑/左-右位向　left-right topology
作出仲裁裁决/作出仲裁裁決　render award
作品/作品　works
作品标题/作品標題　heading of works
作品表现形式/作品表現形式　form of expression concerning works
作品复制品/作品複製品　copy of work
作品号/作品號,作品編號,作品序號　opus number
作品内容/作品內容　contents of works
作品使用许可合同/作品使用許可合同　exploitation of work contract
作品收回权/作品收回權　author's right of retraction
作品素材/作品素材　material of works
作品完整权/作品完整權　right to the integrity of work
作品修改权/作品修改權　right of modification

作为共同海损得到补偿/作爲共同海損補償　loss allowed as general average
作物复种指数/作物複種指數　multiple cropping index
作业/作業　activity
作业成本法/作業基礎成本法　activity-based costing, ABC
作业成本库/作業成本集　activity cost pool
作业传票/派工單,工作通知單　job ticket
作业定义格式/作業定義格式　job definition format, JDF
作业动因/作業動因　activity driver
作业分解/作業分解　activity decomposing
作业分析/作業分析　operation analysis
作业管理/作業管理　activity-based management, ABM
作业计划图/作業計劃圖　schedule chart
作业绩效评定/績效評定　performance rating
作业决策/作業決策　operating decision-making
作业相关图法/作業相關圖法　relationship diagram method
作业信息/作業資訊　operational information
作业优先权/作業優先權　operation priority
作业转换时间/換線時間,換規格時間,更迭時間　changeover time
作业组合/作業組合　job mix
作战条令/作戰條令　mandatory regulation on combat
作者/作者　author
作者分类法/作者分類法　author classification
作者考订/作者考訂　writer criticism
作者权利/作者權利　right of author
作者身份不明/作者身份不明　unidentified authorship
作者影响因子/作者影響因子　author impact factor
作者著作目录/作者著作目錄　author bibliography
作者组合法/作者組合法　author combination method
坐标系/坐標系統　coordinate system
做市商/造市者　market maker

附录

中国历代纪元表

1. 本表从"五帝"开始,到1949年中华人民共和国成立为止。
2. "五帝"以后,西周共和元年(公元前841年)以前,参考2000年公布的《夏商周年表》进行了调整。
3. 较小的王朝如"十六国"、"十国"等不列表。
4. 各个时代或王朝,详列帝王名号("帝号"或"庙号",以习惯上常用者为据),年号,元年的干支和公元纪年,以资对照。(年号后用括号附列使用年数,年中改元时在干支后用数字注出改元的月份。)

干支次序表

1.甲子	13.丙子	25.戊子	37.庚子	49.壬子
2.乙丑	14.丁丑	26.己丑	38.辛丑	50.癸丑
3.丙寅	15.戊寅	27.庚寅	39.壬寅	51.甲寅
4.丁卯	16.己卯	28.辛卯	40.癸卯	52.乙卯
5.戊辰	17.庚辰	29.壬辰	41.甲辰	53.丙辰
6.己巳	18.辛巳	30.癸巳	42.乙巳	54.丁巳
7.庚午	19.壬午	31.甲午	43.丙午	55.戊午
8.辛未	20.癸未	32.乙未	44.丁未	56.己未
9.壬申	21.甲申	33.丙申	45.戊申	57.庚申
10.癸酉	22.乙酉	34.丁酉	46.己酉	58.辛酉
11.甲戌	23.丙戌	35.戊戌	47.庚戌	59.壬戌
12.乙亥	24.丁亥	36.己亥	48.辛亥	60.癸亥

五帝
(约前 30 世纪初—约前 21 世纪初)

| 黄 帝 | 颛顼 [zhuānxū] | 帝喾 [kù] | 尧 [yáo] | 舜 [shùn] |

夏
(约前 2070—前 1600)

禹 [yǔ]
启
太康
仲康
相
少康
予
槐
芒
泄
不降
扃 [jiōng]
廑 [jǐn]
孔甲
皋 [gāo]
发
癸 [guǐ]
(桀 [jié])

商
(前 1600—前 1046)

商前期 (前 1600—前 1300)

汤
太丁
外丙
中壬
太甲
沃丁
太庚
小甲
雍己
太戊
中丁
外壬
河亶 [dǎn] 甲
祖乙
祖辛
沃甲
祖丁
南庚
阳甲
盘庚(迁殷前)

商后期 (前1300—前1046)

盘庚(迁殷后)*			
小辛	(50)		前1300
小乙			
武丁	(59)		前1250
祖庚			
祖甲			
廪辛	(44)		前1191
康丁			
武乙	(35)	甲寅	前1147
文丁	(11)	己丑	前1112
帝乙	(26)	庚子	前1101
帝辛(纣)	(30)	丙寅	前1075

* 盘庚迁都于殷后，商也称殷。

周
(前1046—前256)

西周 (前1046—前771)

武王(姬[jī]发)	(4)	乙未	前1046
成王(～诵)	(22)	己亥	前1042
康王(～钊[zhāo])	(25)	辛酉	前1020
昭王(～瑕[xiá])	(19)	丙戌	前995
穆王(～满)	(55)共王当年改元	乙巳	前976
共[gōng]王(～繄[yī]扈)	(23)	己亥	前922
懿[yì]王(～囏[jiān])	(8)	壬戌	前899
孝王(～辟方)	(6)	庚午	前891
夷王(～燮[xiè])	(8)	丙子	前885
厉王(～胡)	(37)共和当年改元	甲申	前877
共和	(14)	庚申	前841
宣王(～静)	(46)	甲戌	前827
幽王(～宫涅[shēng])	(11)	庚申	前781

东周 (前770—前256)

公元前770年至公元前476年,为春秋时代;公元前475年至公元前221年,为战国时代,主要有秦、魏、韩、赵、楚、燕、齐等国。

平王(姬宜臼)	(51)	辛未	前770	悼王(～猛)	(1)	辛巳	前520
桓王(～林)	(23)	壬戌	前719	敬王(～匄[gài])	(44)	壬午	前519
庄王(～佗[tuó])	(15)	乙酉	前696	元王(～仁)	(7)	丙寅	前475
釐[xī]王(～胡齐)	(5)	庚子	前681	贞定王(～介)	(28)	癸酉	前468
惠王(～阆[làng])	(25)	乙巳	前676	哀王(～去疾)	(1)	庚子	前441
				思王(～叔)	(1)	庚子	前441
襄[xiāng]王(～郑)	(33)	庚午	前651	考王(～嵬[wéi])	(15)	辛丑	前440
顷王(～壬臣)	(6)	癸卯	前618	威烈王(～午)	(24)	丙辰	前425
匡王(～班)	(6)	己酉	前612	安王(～骄)	(26)	庚辰	前401
定王(～瑜[yú])	(21)	乙卯	前606	烈王(～喜)	(7)	丙午	前375
				显王(～扁)	(48)	癸丑	前368
简王(～夷)	(14)	丙子	前585	慎靓[jìng]王(～定)	(6)	辛丑	前320
灵王(～泄心)	(27)	庚寅	前571	赧[nǎn]王(～延)	(59)	丁未	前314
景王(～贵)	(25)	丁巳	前544				

秦 [秦帝国]
(前221—前206)

周赧王59年乙巳(前256),秦灭周。自次年(秦昭襄王52年丙午,前255)起至秦王政25年己卯(前222),史家以秦王纪年。秦王政26年庚辰(前221)完成统一,称始皇帝。

昭襄王(嬴则,又名稷)	(56)	乙卯	前306	始皇帝(～政)	(37)	乙卯	前246
孝文王(～柱)	(1)	辛亥	前250	二世皇帝(～胡亥)	(3)	壬辰	前209
庄襄王(～子楚)	(3)	壬子	前249				

汉

(前206—公元220)

西汉 (前206—公元25)

包括王莽（公元9—23）和更始帝（23—25）。

高帝（刘邦）		（12）	乙未	前206		五凤（4）	甲子	前57
惠帝（～盈）		（7）	丁未	前194		甘露（4）	戊辰	前53
高后（吕雉）		（8）	甲寅	前187		黄龙（1）	壬申	前49
文帝（刘恒）		（16）	壬戌	前179	元帝（～奭[shì]）	初元（5）	癸酉	前48
		（后元）（7）	戊寅	前163		永光（5）	戊寅	前43
景帝（～启）		（7）	乙酉	前156		建昭（5）	癸未	前38
		（中元）（6）	壬辰	前149		竟宁（1）	戊子	前33
		（后元）（3）	戊戌	前143	成帝（～骜[ào]）	建始（4）	己丑	前32
武帝（～彻）		建元（6）	辛丑	前140		河平（4）	癸巳三	前28
		元光（6）	丁未	前134		阳朔（4）	丁酉	前24
		元朔（6）	癸丑	前128		鸿嘉（4）	辛丑	前20
		元狩（6）	己未	前122		永始（4）	乙巳	前16
		元鼎（6）	乙丑	前116		元延（4）	己酉	前12
		元封（6）	辛未	前110		绥和（2）	癸丑	前8
		太初（4）	丁丑	前104	哀帝（～欣）	建平（4）	乙卯	前6
		天汉（4）	辛巳	前100		元寿（2）	己未	前2
		太始（4）	乙酉	前96	平帝（～衎[kàn]）	元始（5）	辛酉	公元1
		征和（4）	己丑	前92				
		后元（2）	癸巳	前88	孺子婴（王莽摄政）	居摄（3）	丙寅	6
昭帝（～弗陵）		始元（7）	乙未	前86		初始（1）	戊辰十一	8
		元凤（6）	辛丑八	前80	[新]王莽	始建国（5）	己巳	9
		元平（1）	丁未	前74		天凤（6）	甲戌	14
宣帝（～询）		本始（4）	戊申	前73		地皇（4）	庚辰	20
		地节（4）	壬子	前69	更始帝（刘玄）	更始（3）	癸未二	23
		元康（5）	丙辰	前65				
		神爵（4）	庚申三	前61				

东汉 (25—220)

光武帝(刘秀)	建武(32)	乙酉六	25	冲帝(~炳[bǐng])	永憙[xī](嘉)(1)	乙酉	145
	建武中元(2)	丙辰四	56	质帝(~缵[zuǎn])	本初(1)	丙戌	146
明帝(~庄)	永平(18)	戊午	58	桓帝(~志)	建和(3)	丁亥	147
章帝(~炟[dá])	建初(9)	丙子	76		和平(1)	庚寅	150
	元和(4)	甲申八	84		元嘉(3)	辛卯	151
	章和(2)	丁亥七	87		永兴(2)	癸巳五	153
和帝(~肇[zhào])	永元(17)	己丑	89		永寿(4)	乙未	155
	元兴(1)	乙巳四	105		延熹[xī](10)	戊戌六	158
殇[shāng]帝(~隆)	延平(1)	丙午	106		永康(1)	丁未六	167
安帝(~祜[hù])	永初(7)	丁未	107	灵帝(~宏)	建宁(5)	戊申	168
	元初(7)	甲寅	114		熹[xī]平(7)	壬子五	172
	永宁(2)	庚申四	120		光和(7)	戊午三	178
	建光(2)	辛酉七	121		中平(6)	甲子十二	184
	延光(4)	壬戌三	122	献帝(~协)	初平(4)	庚午	190
顺帝(~保)	永建(7)	丙寅	126		兴平(2)	甲戌	194
	阳嘉(4)	壬申三	132		建安(25)	丙子	196
	永和(6)	丙子	136		延康(1)	庚子三	220
	汉安(3)	壬午	142				
	建康(1)	甲申四	144				

三国
(220—280)

魏 (220—265)

文帝(曹丕[pī])	黄初(7)	庚子十	220		嘉平(6)	己巳四	249
明帝(~叡[ruì])	太和(7)	丁未	227	高贵乡公(~髦[máo])	正元(3)	甲戌十	254
	青龙(5)	癸丑二	233		甘露(5)	丙子六	256
	景初(3)	丁巳三	237	元帝(~奂[huàn])(陈留王)	景元(5)	庚辰六	260
齐王(~芳)	正始(10)	庚申	240		咸熙(2)	甲申五	264

蜀汉 (221—263)

昭烈帝(刘备)	章武(3)	辛丑四	221		景耀(6)	戊寅	258
后主(～禅[shàn])	建兴(15)	癸卯五	223		炎兴(1)	癸未八	263
	延熙(20)	戊午	238				

吴 (222—280)

大帝(孙权)	黄武(8)	壬寅十	222	景帝(～休)	永安(7)	戊寅十	258
	黄龙(3)	己酉四	229	乌程侯(～皓[hào])	元兴(2)	甲申七	264
	嘉禾(7)	壬子	232		甘露(2)	乙酉四	265
	赤乌(14)	戊午九	238		宝鼎(4)	丙戌八	266
	太元(2)	辛未五	251		建衡(3)	己丑十	269
	神凤(1)	壬申二	252		凤凰(3)	壬辰	272
会稽王(～亮)	建兴(2)	壬申四	252		天册(2)	乙未	275
	五凤(3)	甲戌	254		天玺(1)	丙申七	276
	太平(3)	丙子十	256		天纪(4)	丁酉	277

晋
(265—420)

西晋 (265—317)

武帝(司马炎)	泰始(10)	乙酉十二	265		太安(2)	壬戌十二	302
	咸宁(6)	乙未	275		永安(1)	甲子	304
	太康(10)	庚子四	280		建武(1)	甲子七	304
	太熙(1)	庚戌	290		永安(1)	甲子十一	304
惠帝(～衷)	永熙(1)	庚戌四	290		永兴(3)	甲子十二	304
	永平(1)	辛亥	291		光熙(1)	丙寅六	306
	元康(9)	辛亥三	291	怀帝(～炽[chì])	永嘉(7)	丁卯	307
	永康(2)	庚申	300				
	永宁(2)	辛酉四	301	愍[mǐn]帝(～邺[yè])	建兴(5)	癸酉四	313

东晋 (317—420)

东晋时期，在我国北方和巴蜀，先后存在过一些封建割据政权，其中有：汉（前赵）、成（成汉）、前凉、后赵（魏）、前燕、前秦、后燕、后秦、西秦、后凉、南凉、南燕、西凉、北凉、北燕、夏等国，历史上叫作"十六国"。

元帝（司马睿[ruì]）	建 武（2）	丁 丑 三	317	哀帝（～丕[pī]）	隆 和（2）	壬 戌	362
	大 兴（4）	戊 寅 三	318		兴 宁（3）	癸 亥 二	363
	永 昌（2）	壬 午	322	海西公（～奕[yì]）	太 和（6）	丙 寅	366
明帝（～绍）	永 昌	壬 午 闰十一	322				
	太 宁（4）	癸 未 三	323	简文帝（～昱[yù]）	咸 安（2）	辛 未 十一	371
成帝（～衍[yǎn]）	太 宁	乙 酉 闰八	325	孝武帝（～曜[yào]）	宁 康（3）	癸 酉	373
	咸 和（9）	丙 戌 二	326		太 元（21）	丙 子	376
	咸 康（8）	乙 未	335	安帝（～德宗）	隆 安（5）	丁 酉	397
康帝（～岳）	建 元（2）	癸 卯	343		元 兴（3）	壬 寅	402
穆帝（～聃[dān]）	永 和（12）	乙 巳	345		义 熙（14）	乙 巳	405
	升 平（5）	丁 巳	357	恭帝（～德文）	元 熙（2）	己 未	419

南北朝
(420—589)

南朝

宋 (420—479)

武帝（刘裕）	永 初（3）	庚 申 六	420		景 和（1）	乙 巳 八	465
少帝（～义符）	景 平（2）	癸 亥	423	明帝（～彧[yù]）	泰 始（7）	乙 巳 十二	465
文帝（～义隆）	元 嘉（30）	甲 子 八	424		泰 豫（1）	壬 子	472
孝武帝（～骏[jùn]）	孝 建（3）	甲 午	454	后废帝（～昱[yù]）（苍梧王）	元 徽（5）	癸 丑	473
	大 明（8）	丁 酉	457				
前废帝（～子业）	永 光（1）	乙 巳	465	顺帝（～准）	昇 明（3）	丁 巳 七	477

齐 (479—502)

高帝（萧道成）	建 元（4）	己 未 四	479	明帝（～鸾）	建 武（5）	甲 戌 十	494
武帝（～赜[zé]）	永 明（11）	癸 亥	483		永 泰（1）	戊 寅 四	498
郁林王（～昭业）	隆 昌（1）	甲 戌	494	东昏侯（～宝卷）	永 元（3）	己 卯	499
海陵王（～昭文）	延 兴（1）	甲 戌 七	494	和帝（～宝融）	中 兴（2）	辛 巳 三	501

梁 (502—557)

武帝(萧衍[yǎn])	天监(18)	壬午四	502		太清(3)*	丁卯四	547
	普通(8)	庚子	520	简文帝(～纲)	大宝(2)**	庚午	550
	大通(3)	丁未三	527	元帝(～绎[yì])	承圣(4)	壬申十一	552
	中大通(6)	己酉十	529				
	大同(12)	乙卯	535	敬帝(～方智)	绍泰(2)	乙亥十	555
	中大同(2)	丙寅四	546		太平(2)	丙子九	556

* 有的地区用至 6 年。
** 有的地区用至 3 年。

陈 (557—589)

武帝(陈霸先)	永定(3)	丁丑十	557	宣帝(～顼[xū])	太建(14)	己丑	569
文帝(～蒨[qiàn])	天嘉(7)	庚辰	560				
	天康(1)	丙戌二	566	后主(～叔宝)	至德(4)	癸卯	583
废帝(～伯宗)(临海王)	光大(2)	丁亥	567		祯明(3)	丁未	587

北朝

北魏 [拓跋氏,后改元氏]
(386—534)

北魏建国于丙戌(386年)正月,初称代国,至同年四月始改国号为魏,439年灭北凉,统一北方。

道武帝(拓跋珪[guī])	登国(11)	丙戌	386		延和(3)	壬申	432
	皇始(3)	丙申七	396		太延(6)	乙亥	435
	天兴(7)	戊戌十二	398		太平真君(12)	庚辰六	440
	天赐(6)	甲辰十	404				
明元帝(～嗣[sì])	永兴(5)	己酉十	409		正平(2)	辛卯六	451
	神瑞(3)	甲寅	414	南安王(～余)	永(承)平(1)	壬辰三	452
	泰常(8)	丙辰四	416				
太武帝(～焘[tāo])	始光(5)	甲子	424	文成帝(～濬[jùn])	兴安(3)	壬辰十	452
	神䴥[jiā](4)	戊辰二	428		兴光(2)	甲午七	454
					太安(5)	乙未六	455

		和平（6）	庚子	460	孝昌（3）	乙巳六	525
献文帝（～弘）		天安（2）	丙午	466	武泰（1）	戊申	528
		皇兴（5）	丁未八	467	建义（1）	戊申四	528
孝文帝（元宏）		延兴（6）	辛亥八	471	孝庄帝（～子攸[yōu]）		
		承明（1）	丙辰六	476	永安（3）	戊申九	528
		太和（23）	丁巳	477	长广王（～晔[yè]）	建明（2）	庚戌十	530
宣武帝（～恪[kè]）		景明（4）	庚辰	500	节闵[mǐn]帝（～恭）	普泰（2）	辛亥二	531
		正始（5）	甲申	504			
		永平（5）	戊子八	508	安定王（～朗）	中兴（2）	辛亥十	531
		延昌（4）	壬辰四	512	孝武帝（～脩）	太昌（1）	壬子四	532
孝明帝（～诩[xǔ]）		熙平（3）	丙申	516		永兴（1）	壬子十二	532
		神龟（3）	戊戌二	518		永熙（3）	壬子十二	532
		正光（6）	庚子七	520			

东魏 (534—550)

孝静帝（元善见）	天平（4）	甲寅十	534	兴和（4）	己未十一	539
	元象（2）	戊午	538	武定（8）	癸亥	543

北齐 (550—577)

文宣帝（高洋）	天保（10）	庚午五	550	后主（～纬）	天统（5）	乙酉四	565
废帝（～殷）	乾明（1）	庚辰	560		武平（7）	庚寅	570
孝昭帝（～演）	皇建（2）	庚辰八	560		隆化（1）	丙申十二	576
武成帝（～湛）	太宁（2）	辛巳十一	561	幼主（～恒）	承光（1）	丁酉	577
	河清（4）	壬午四	562			

西魏 (535—556)

文帝（元宝炬）	大统（17）	乙卯	535	恭帝（～廓）	—（3）	甲戌一	554
废帝（～钦）	—（3）	壬申	552			

北周 (557—581)

孝闵[mǐn]帝 （宇文觉）	一	(1)	丁丑	557	建 德(7)	壬辰三	572
					宣 政(1)	戊戌三	578
明帝(～毓 [yù])	一 武 成	(3) (2)	丁丑九 己卯八	557 559	宣帝(～赟 [yūn])	大 成(1)	己亥	579
武帝(～邕 [yōng])	保 定 天 和	(5) (7)	辛巳 丙戌	561 566	静帝(～阐 [chǎn])	大 象(3) 大 定(1)	己亥二 辛丑二	579 581

隋
(581—618)

隋建国于581年，589年灭陈，完成统一。

文帝(杨坚)	开 皇(20) 仁 寿(4)	辛丑二 辛酉	581 601	恭帝(～侑 [yòu])	义 宁(2)	丁丑十一	617
炀[yáng]帝 (～广)	大 业(14)	乙丑	605				

唐
(618—907)

高祖(李渊)	武 德(9)	戊寅五	618		永 隆(2)	庚辰八	680
太宗(～世民)	贞 观(23)	丁亥	627		开 耀(2)	辛巳九	681
高宗(～治)	永 徽(6)	庚戌	650		永 淳(2)	壬午二	682
	显 庆(6)	丙辰	656		弘 道(1)	癸未十二	683
	龙 朔(3)	辛酉三*	661	中宗(～显又 名哲)	嗣 圣(1)	甲申	684
	麟 德(2)	甲子	664				
	乾 封(3)	丙寅	666	睿[ruì]宗(～ 旦)	文 明(1)	甲申二	684
	总 章(3)	戊辰三	668				
	咸 亨(5)	庚午三	670	武后(武曌 [zhào])	光 宅(1)	甲申九	684
	上 元(3)	甲戌八	674		垂 拱(4)	乙酉	685
	仪 凤(4)	丙子十一	676		永 昌(1)	己丑	689
	调 露(2)	己卯六	679		载 初**(1)	庚寅正	690

武后称帝,改国号为周	天授(3)	庚寅九	690	德宗(～适[kuò])	建中(4)	庚申	780
	如意(1)	壬辰四	692		兴元(1)	甲子	784
	长寿(3)	壬辰九	692		贞元(21)	乙丑	785
	延载(1)	甲午五	694	顺宗(～诵)	永贞(1)	乙酉八	805
	证圣(1)	乙未	695	宪宗(～纯)	元和(15)	丙戌	806
	天册万岁(2)	乙未九	695	穆宗(～恒)	长庆(4)	辛丑	821
	万岁登封(1)	丙申腊	696	敬宗(～湛)	宝历(3)	乙巳	825
	万岁通天(2)	丙申三	696	文宗(～昂)	宝历	丙午十二	826
					大(太)和(9)	丁未二	827
	神功(1)	丁酉九	697		开成(5)	丙辰	836
	圣历(3)	戊戌	698	武宗(～炎)	会昌(6)	辛酉	841
	久视(1)	庚子五	700	宣宗(～忱[chén])	大中(14)	丁卯	847
	大足(1)	辛丑	701				
	长安(4)	辛丑十	701	懿[yì]宗(～漼[cuǐ])	大中	己卯八	859
中宗(李显又名哲),复唐国号	神龙(3)	乙巳	705		咸通(15)	庚辰十一	860
	景龙(4)	丁未九	707	僖[xī]宗(～儇[xuān])	咸通	癸巳七	873
睿[ruì]宗(～旦)	景云(2)	庚戌七	710		乾符(6)	甲午十一	874
	太极(1)	壬子	712		广明(2)	庚子	880
	延和(1)	壬子五	712		中和(5)	辛丑七	881
玄宗(～隆基)	先天(2)	壬子八	712		光启(4)	乙巳三	885
	开元(29)	癸丑十二	713		文德(1)	戊申二	888
	天宝(15)	壬午	742	昭宗(～晔[yè])	龙纪(1)	己酉	889
肃宗(～亨)	至德(3)	丙申七	756		大顺(2)	庚戌	890
	乾元(3)	戊戌二	758		景福(2)	壬子	892
	上元(2)	庚子闰四	760		乾宁(5)	甲寅	894
	-(1)***	辛丑九	761		光化(4)	戊午八	898
代宗(～豫)	宝应(2)	壬寅四	762		天复(4)	辛酉	901
	广德(2)	癸卯七	763		天祐(4)	甲子闰四	904
	永泰(2)	乙巳	765	哀帝(～柷[chù])	天祐****	甲子八	904
	大历(14)	丙午十一	766				

* 辛酉三月丙申朔改元,一作辛酉二月乙未晦改元。
** 始用周正,改永昌元年十一月为载初元年正月,以十二月为腊月,夏正月为一月。久视元年十月复用夏正,以正月为十一月,腊月为十二月,一月为正月。本表在这段期间内干支后面所注的改元月份都是周历,各年号的使用年数也是按照周历的计算方法。
*** 此年九月以后去年号,但称元年。
**** 哀帝即位未改元。

五代
(907—960)

五代时期,除后梁、后唐、后晋、后汉、后周外,还先后存在过一些封建割据政权,其中有:吴、前蜀、吴越、楚、闽、南汉、荆南(南平)、后蜀、南唐、北汉等国,历史上叫作"十国"。

后梁 (907—923)

太祖(朱晃,又名温、全忠)	开 平(5)	丁卯四	907		贞 明(7)	乙亥十一	915
	乾 化(5)	辛未五	911		龙 德(3)	辛巳五	921
末帝(~瑱[zhèn])	乾 化	癸酉二	913				

后唐 (923—936)

庄宗(李存勖[xù])	同 光(4)	癸未四	923	闵[mǐn]帝(~从厚)	应 顺(1)	甲午	934
明宗(~亶[dǎn])	天 成(5)	丙戌四	926	末帝(~从珂[kē])	清 泰(3)	甲午四	934
	长 兴(4)	庚寅二	930				

后晋 (936—947)

高祖(石敬瑭[táng])	天 福(9)	丙申十一	936		开 运(4)	甲辰七	944
出帝(~重贵)	天 福*	壬寅六	942				

* 出帝即位未改元。

后汉 (947—950)

高祖(刘暠[gǎo],本名知远)	天 福*	丁未二	947	隐帝(~承祐)	乾 祐**	戊申二	948
	乾 祐(3)	戊申	948				

* 后汉高祖即位,仍用后晋高祖年号,称天福十二年。
** 隐帝即位未改元。

后周 (951—960)

太祖(郭威)	广 顺(3)	辛亥	951	世宗(柴荣)	显 德*	甲寅一	954
	显 德(7)	甲寅一	954	恭帝(~宗训)	显 德	己未六	959

* 世宗、恭帝都未改元。

宋
(960—1279)

北宋 (960—1127)

太祖(赵匡胤[yìn])	建 隆(4)	庚申	960		庆 历(8)	辛巳十一	1041
	乾 德(6)	癸亥十一	963		皇 祐(6)	己丑	1049
	开 宝(9)	戊辰十一	968		至 和(3)	甲午三	1054
太宗(～炅[jiǒng],本名匡义,又名光义)	太平兴国(9)	丙子十二	976		嘉 祐(8)	丙申九	1056
				英宗(～曙)	治 平(4)	甲辰	1064
	雍 熙(4)	甲申十一	984	神宗(～顼[xū])	熙 宁(10)	戊申	1068
	端 拱(2)	戊子	988		元 丰(8)	戊午	1078
	淳 化(5)	庚寅	990	哲宗(～煦[xù])	元 祐(9)	丙寅	1086
	至 道(3)	乙未	995		绍 圣(5)	甲戌四	1094
真宗(～恒)	咸 平(6)	戊戌	998		元 符(3)	戊寅六	1098
	景 德(4)	甲辰	1004	徽宗(～佶[jí])	建中靖国(1)	辛巳	1101
	大中祥符(9)	戊申	1008		崇 宁(5)	壬午	1102
	天禧[xī](5)	丁巳	1017		大 观(4)	丁亥	1107
	乾 兴(1)	壬戌	1022		政 和(8)	辛卯	1111
仁宗(～祯)	天 圣(10)	癸亥	1023		重 和(2)	戊戌十一	1118
	明 道(2)	壬申十一	1032		宣 和(2)	己亥二	1119
	景 祐(5)	甲戌	1034	钦宗(～桓[huán])	靖 康(2)	丙午	1126
	宝 元(3)	戊寅十一	1038				
	康 定(2)	庚辰二	1040				

南宋 (1127—1279)

高宗(赵构)	建 炎(4)	丁未五	1127		嘉 熙(4)	丁酉	1237
	绍 兴(32)	辛亥	1131		淳 祐(12)	辛丑	1241
孝宗(～昚[shèn])	隆 兴(2)	癸未	1163		宝 祐(6)	癸丑	1253
	乾 道(9)	乙酉	1165		开 庆(1)	己未	1259
	淳 熙(16)	甲午	1174		景 定(5)	庚申	1260
光宗(～惇[dūn])	绍 熙(5)	庚戌	1190	度宗(～禥[qí])	咸 淳(10)	乙丑	1265
宁宗(～扩)	庆 元(6)	乙卯	1195	恭帝(～㬎[xiǎn])	德 祐(2)	乙亥	1275
	嘉 泰(4)	辛酉	1201				
	开 禧(3)	乙丑	1205	端宗(～昰[shì])	景 炎(3)	丙子五	1276
	嘉 定(17)	戊辰	1208				
理宗(～昀[yún])	宝 庆(3)	乙酉	1225	帝昺(～昺[bǐng])	祥 兴(2)	戊寅五	1278
	绍 定(6)	戊子	1228				
	端 平(3)	甲午	1234				

辽 [耶律氏]
(907—1125)

辽建国于907年,国号契丹,916年始建年号,938年(一说947年)改国号为辽,983年复称契丹,1066年仍称辽。

太祖(耶律阿保机)	—(10)	丁卯	907		统和(30)	癸未 六	983
	神册(7)	丙子 十二	916		开泰(10)	壬子 十一	1012
	天赞(5)	壬午 二	922		太平(11)	辛酉 十一	1021
	天显(13)	丙戌 二	926	兴宗(～宗真)	景福(2)	辛未 六	1031
太宗(～德光)	天显*	丁亥 十一	927		重熙(24)	壬申 十一	1032
	会同(10)	戊戌 十一	938	道宗(～洪基)	清宁(10)	乙未 八	1055
	大同(1)	丁未 二	947		咸雍(10)	乙巳	1065
世宗(～阮[ruǎn])	天禄(5)	丁未 九	947		大(太)康(10)	乙卯	1075
穆宗(～璟[jǐng])	应历(19)	辛亥 九	951		大安(10)	乙丑	1085
					寿昌(隆)(7)	乙亥	1095
景宗(～贤)	保宁(11)	己巳 二	969	天祚[zuò]帝(～延禧[xī])	乾统(10)	辛巳	1101
	乾亨(5)	己卯 十一	979		天庆(10)	辛卯	1111
圣宗(～隆绪)	乾亨	壬午 九	982		保大(5)	辛丑	1121

* 太宗即位未改元。

西夏
(1038—1227)

1032年(北宋明道元年)元昊嗣夏王位,1034年始建年号,1038年称帝,国名大夏。在汉籍中习称西夏。1227年为蒙古所灭。

景宗(嵬名元昊)	广运(2)	甲戌 十	1034		天祐民安(8)	庚午	1090
	大庆(2)	丙子 十二	1036		永安(3)	戊寅	1098
	天授礼法延祚(11)	戊寅 十	1038		贞观(13)	辛巳	1101
毅宗(～谅祚)	延嗣宁国(1)	己丑	1049		雍宁(5)	甲午	1114
					元德(8)	己亥	1119
	天祐垂圣(3)	庚寅	1050		正德(8)	丁未	1127
					大德(5)	乙卯	1135
	福圣承道(4)	癸巳	1053	仁宗(～仁孝)	大庆(4)	庚申	1140
					人庆(5)	甲子	1144
	奲[duǒ]都(6)	丁酉	1057		天盛(21)	己巳	1149
					乾祐(24)	庚寅	1170
	拱化(5)	癸卯	1063	桓宗(～纯祐)	天庆(12)	甲寅	1194
惠宗(～秉常)	乾道(1)	戊申	1068	襄宗(～安全)	应天(4)	丙寅 一	1206
	天赐礼盛国庆(5)	己酉	1069		皇建(1)	庚午	1210
				神宗(～遵顼[xū])	光定(13)	辛未 八	1211
	大安(11)	甲寅	1074				
	天安礼定(2)	乙丑	1085	献宗(～德旺)	乾定(3)	甲申 十二	1224
				末帝(～睍[xiàn])	宝义(1)	丁亥	1227
崇宗(～乾顺)	天仪治平(3)	丁卯	1087				

金 [完颜氏]
(1115—1234)

太祖(完颜旻[mín],本名阿骨打)	收国(2)	乙未	1115	章宗(~璟[jǐng])	明昌(7)	庚戌	1190
	天辅(7)	丁酉	1117		承安(5)	丙辰十一	1196
					泰和(8)	辛酉	1201
太宗(~晟[shèng])	天会(15)	癸卯九	1123	卫绍王(~永济)	大安(3)	己巳	1209
					崇庆(2)	壬申	1212
熙宗(~亶[dǎn])	天会*	乙卯一	1135		至宁(1)	癸酉五	1213
	天眷(3)	戊午	1138	宣宗(~珣[xún])	贞祐(5)	癸酉九	1213
	皇统(9)	辛酉	1141		兴定(6)	丁丑九	1217
海陵王(~亮)	天德(5)	己巳十二	1149		元光(2)	壬午八	1222
	贞元(4)	癸酉三	1153	哀宗(~守绪)	正大(9)	甲申	1224
	正隆(6)	丙子二	1156		开兴(1)	壬辰一	1232
世宗(~雍)	大定(29)	辛巳十	1161		天兴(3)	壬辰四	1232

* 熙宗即位未改元。

元 [孛儿只斤氏]
(1206—1368)

蒙古孛儿只斤·铁木真于1206年建国。1271年忽必烈定国号为元，1279年灭南宋。

太祖(孛儿只斤·铁木真)(成吉思汗)	—(22)	丙寅	1206	英宗(~硕[shuò]德八剌)	至治(3)	辛酉	1321
拖雷(监国)	—(1)	戊子	1228	泰定帝(~也孙铁木儿)	泰定(5)	甲子	1324
太宗(~窝阔台)	—(13)	己丑	1229		致和(1)	戊辰二	1328
				天顺帝(~阿速吉八)	天顺(1)	戊辰九	1328
乃马真后(称制)	—(5)	壬寅	1242	文宗(~图帖睦尔)	天历(3)	戊辰九	1328
定宗(~贵由)	—(3)	丙午七	1246	明宗(~和世瓎[là])*		己巳	1329
海迷失后(称制)	—(3)	己酉三	1249		至顺(4)	庚午五	1330
宪宗(~蒙哥)	—(9)	辛亥六	1251	宁宗(~懿[yì]璘[lín]质班)	至顺	壬申十	1332
世祖(~忽必烈)	中统(5)	庚申五	1260	顺帝(~妥懽帖睦尔)	至顺	癸酉六	1333
	至元(31)	甲子八	1264		元统(3)	癸酉十	1333
成宗(~铁穆耳)	元贞(3)	乙未	1295		(后)至元(6)	乙亥十一	1335
	大德(11)	丁酉二	1297		至正(28)	辛巳	1341
武宗(~海山)	至大(4)	戊申	1308				
仁宗(~爱育黎拔力八达)	皇庆(2)	壬子	1312				
	延祐(7)	甲寅	1314				

* 明宗于己巳(1329)正月即位，以文宗为皇太子。八月明宗暴死，文宗复位。

明
(1368—1644)

太祖(朱元璋)	洪 武(31)	戊申	1368	孝宗(～祐樘[chēng])	弘 治(18)	戊申	1488
惠帝(～允炆[wén])	建文(4)*	己卯	1399	武宗(～厚照)	正 德(16)	丙寅	1506
成祖(～棣[dì])	永 乐(22)	癸未	1403	世宗(～厚熜[cōng])	嘉 靖(45)	壬午	1522
仁宗(～高炽[chì])	洪 熙(1)	乙巳	1425	穆宗(～载垕[hòu])	隆 庆(6)	丁卯	1567
宣宗(～瞻[zhān]基)	宣 德(10)	丙午	1426	神宗(～翊[yì]钧)	万 历(48)	癸酉	1573
英宗(～祁镇)	正 统(14)	丙辰	1436	光宗(～常洛)	泰 昌(1)	庚申	1620
代宗(～祁钰[yù])(景帝)	景 泰(8)	庚午	1450	熹[xī]宗(～由校)	天 启(7)	辛酉	1621
英宗(～祁镇)	天 顺(8)	丁丑	1457	思宗(～由检)	崇 祯(17)	戊辰	1628
宪宗(～见深)	成 化(23)	乙酉	1465				

* 建文四年时成祖废除建文年号，改为洪武三十五年。

清 [爱新觉罗氏]
(1616—1911)

清建国于1616年，初称后金，1636年始改国号为清，1644年入关。

太祖(爱新觉罗·努尔哈赤)	天 命(11)	丙辰	1616	仁宗(～颙[yóng]琰[yǎn])	嘉 庆(25)	丙辰	1796
太宗(～皇太极)	天 聪(10) 崇 德(8)	丁卯 丙子	1627 1636	宣宗(～旻[mín]宁)	道 光(30)	辛巳	1821
世祖(～福临)	顺 治(18)	甲申	1644	文宗(～奕[yì]詝[zhǔ])	咸 丰(11)	辛亥	1851
圣祖(～玄烨[yè])	康 熙(61)	壬寅	1662	穆宗(～载淳)	同 治(13)	壬戌	1862
世宗(～胤[yìn]禛[zhēn])	雍 正(13)	癸卯	1723	德宗(～载湉[tián])	光 绪(34)	乙亥	1875
高宗(～弘历)	乾 隆(60)	丙辰	1736	～溥[pǔ]仪	宣 统(3)	己酉	1909

中华民国
(1912—1949)

中华民国(38)	壬子	1912

中华人民共和国
1949年10月1日成立

国际单位制

1. 国际单位制(Le Système International d'Unités)及其国际简称 SI 是在 1960 年第 11 届国际计量大会上通过的。国际单位制单位由基本单位、导出单位(包括辅助单位在内的具有专门名称的导出单位和组合形式的导出单位,组合形式的导出单位本附录不予收录)及其倍数单位构成。

2. 圆括号中的名称,是它前面的名称的同义词。

3. 无方括号的量的名称与单位名称均为全称。方括号中的字,在不致引起混淆、误解的情况下,可以省略。去掉方括号中的字即为其名称的简称。

表1　基本单位

量的名称	单位名称	单位符号
大陆名/台湾名	大陆名/台湾名	
长度/長度	米/公尺	m
质量/質量	千克(公斤)/公斤	kg
时间/時間	秒/秒	s
电流/電流	安[培]/安培	A
热力学温度/熱力學溫度	开[尔文]/克耳文	K
物质的量/物[質]量	摩[尔]/莫耳	mol
发光强度/發光強度	坎[德拉]/燭光	cd

表2　包括辅助单位在内的具有专门名称的导出单位

量的名称	导出单位		
	单位名称	单位符号	换算关系
大陆名/台湾名	大陆名/台湾名		
[平面]角/[平面]角	弧度/弧度,弳度	rad	$1\ \text{rad}=1\ \text{m}/\text{m}=1$
立体角/立體角	球面度/立弳	sr	$1\ \text{sr}=1\ \text{m}^2/\text{m}^2=1$
频率/頻率	赫[兹]/赫	Hz	$1\ \text{Hz}=1\ \text{s}^{-1}$
力/力	牛[顿]/牛頓	N	$1\ \text{N}=1\ \text{kg}\cdot\text{m}/\text{s}^2$
压力,压强,应力/壓力,壓強,應力	帕[斯卡]/帕斯卡	Pa	$1\ \text{Pa}=1\ \text{N}/\text{m}^2$
能[量],功,热量/能[量],功,熱[量]	焦[耳]/焦耳	J	$1\ \text{J}=1\ \text{N}\cdot\text{m}$
功率,辐[射能]通量/功率,輻射能通量	瓦[特]/瓦特	W	$1\ \text{W}=1\ \text{J}/\text{s}$
电荷[量]/電荷量	库[仑]/庫侖	C	$1\ \text{C}=1\ \text{A}\cdot\text{s}$
电压,电动势,电位,(电势)/電壓,電動勢,電位,(電勢)	伏[特]/伏特	V	$1\ \text{V}=1\ \text{W}/\text{A}$
电容/電容	法[拉]/法拉	F	$1\ \text{F}=1\ \text{C}/\text{V}$
电阻/電阻	欧[姆]/歐姆	Ω	$1\ \Omega=1\ \text{V}/\text{A}$
电导/電導	西[门子]/西門	S	$1\ \text{S}=1\ \Omega^{-1}$

(续表)

量的名称	导出单位		
	单位名称	单位符号	换算关系
大陆名/台湾名	大陆名/台湾名		
磁通[量]/磁通量	韦[伯]/韋伯	Wb	1 Wb=1 V·s
磁通[量]密度,磁感应强度/磁通[量]密度,磁感應強度	特[斯拉]/特士拉	T	1 T=1 Wb/m^2
电感/電感	亨[利]/亨利	H	1 H=1 Wb/A
摄氏温度/攝氏溫度	摄氏度/攝[氏溫]度	℃	1 ℃=1 K
光通量/光通量	流[明]/流明	lm	1 lm=1 cd·sr
[光]照度/照度	勒[克斯]/勒克斯	lx	1 lx=1 lm/m^2

表3 由于人类健康安全防护需要而确定的具有专门名称的导出单位

量的名称	导出单位		
	单位名称	单位符号	换算关系
大陆名/台湾名	大陆名/台湾名		
[放射性]活度/放射活性	贝可[勒尔]/贝克	Bq	1 Bq=1 s^{-1}
吸收剂量/吸收劑量 比授[予]能/比授能 比释动能/比釋動能	戈[瑞]/戈雷	Gy	1 Gy=1 J/kg
剂量当量/等價劑量,當量劑量	希[沃特]/西弗	Sv	1 Sv=1 J/kg

表4 国际单位制词头

因数	词头名称	词头符号
	大陆名/台湾名	
10^{24}	尧[它]/佑	Y
10^{21}	泽[它]/皆	Z
10^{18}	艾[可萨]/艾	E
10^{15}	拍[它]/拍	P
10^{12}	太[拉]/太,兆	T
10^{9}	吉[咖]/吉,十億	G
10^{6}	兆/百萬	M
10^{3}	千/千	k
10^{2}	百/百	h
10^{1}	十/十	da
10^{-1}	分/分	d
10^{-2}	厘/厘	c

(续表)

因数	词头名称 大陆名/台湾名	词头符号
10^{-3}	毫/毫	m
10^{-6}	微/微	μ
10^{-9}	纳[诺]/奈	n
10^{-12}	皮[可]/披,微微	p
10^{-15}	飞[母托]/飞,毫微微	f
10^{-18}	阿[托]/阿,微微微	a
10^{-21}	仄[普托]/介	z
10^{-24}	幺[科托]/攸	y

注：词头与基本单位、导出单位共同组成一个新单位，即构成倍数单位。词头只用于构成倍数单位，不单独使用。

表5 可与国际单位制单位并用的计量单位

量的名称 大陆名/台湾名	单位名称 大陆名/台湾名	单位符号	换算关系
时间/時間	分/分	min	1 min＝60 s
	[小]时/[小]時	h	1 h＝60 min＝3 600 s
	日,(天)/日,天	d	1 d＝24 h＝86 400 s
[平面]角/[平面]角	度/度	°	$1°=(π/180)$ rad
	[角]分/[角]分	′	$1′=(1/60)°=(π/10\ 800)$ rad
	[角]秒/[角]秒	″	$1″=(1/60)′=(π/648\ 000)$ rad
体积/體積	升/公升	L,(l)	$1\ L=1\ dm^3=10^{-3}\ m^3$
质量/質量	吨/公噸	t	$1\ t=10^3$ kg
	原子质量单位/原子質量單位	u	$1\ u≈1.660\ 540×10^{-27}$ kg
旋转速度/轉速	转每分/每分鐘轉速	r/min	$1\ r/min=(1/60)\ s^{-1}$
长度/長度	海里/海里,浬	n mile	1 n mile＝1 852 m(只用于航行)
速度/速度	节/節	kn	1 kn＝1 n mile/h＝(1 852/3 600) m/s (只用于航行)
能/能	电子伏/電子伏[特]	eV	$1\ eV≈1.602\ 177×10^{-19}$ J
级差/位準差	分贝/分貝	dB	
线密度/線密度	特[克斯]/德士	tex	$1\ tex=10^{-6}$ kg/m
面积/面積	公顷/公頃	hm^2	$1\ hm^2=10^4\ m^2$

注：1. 平面角单位度、分、秒的符号，在组合单位中采用(°)、(′)、(″)的形式。例如，不用°/s，而用(°)/s。
    2. 升的符号中，小写字母 l 为备用符号。
    3. 公顷的国际通用符号为 ha。